Empires at War

Francis Pike studied history at Cambridge and is an historian and journalist. He lived and worked for 20 years in Japan, China and India as an economic and political strategist and in this capacity, he advised a number of financial institutions as well as governments.

Empires at War

A SHORT HISTORY OF
MODERN ASIA SINCE WORLD WAR II

Francis Pike

I.B. TAURIS
LONDON · NEW YORK

Published in 2010 by I.B.Tauris & Co Ltd
6 Salem Road, London W2 4BU
175 Fifth Avenue, New York NY 10010
www.ibtauris.com

Distributed in the United States and Canada Exclusively by Palgrave Macmillan
175 Fifth Avenue,
New York NY 10010

ISBN: 978 1 84885 079 8

A full CIP record for this book is available from the British Library
A full CIP record is available from the Library of Congress

Library of Congress Catalog Card Number: available

Typeset in Perpetua by Macmillan Publishing Solutions
Printed and bound in Great Britain by CPI Antony Rowe, Chippenham

FSC
Mixed Sources
Product group from well-managed
forests and other controlled sources
Cert no. SGS-COC-2953
www.fsc.org
© 1996 Forest Stewardship Council

To India Jane and Eben
and
Nina, my Bombay pie-dog

Contents

Acknowledgements

Though I had been writing all my professional business life and occasionally for *The Spectator* and other newspapers and journals, it was a significant leap to write my first book, particularly one with the ambitious scale of *Empires at War*. I am particularly indebted to the people who advised and guided my first nervous footsteps. The historian Andrew Roberts was as prolific in his encouragement and advice as he is in his output of wonderful books. In addition, he introduced me to the equally eminent Paul Johnson whose broad-scope histories were a model for my own work; he gave me particularly useful advice on planning and notation. Additionally, the support and hard work of my agent Georgina Capel and her staff at Capel & Land was essential whenever my spirits or resolve needed bracing. My editor at I.B.Tauris, Lester Crook, provided wise counsel and guidance.

Historians who have been particularly helpful to my cause include Professor John Whitehead, who taught me at Cambridge University, and, as a frontier historian and formerly professor of history at Alaska University, was a particularly helpful commentator on American expansionism. Professor Norman Stone has long been a friend since we worked together on the launch of a private equity company in Eastern Europe in 1989–90 and he kindly reviewed my draft manuscript.

Other historians and writers who were generous with acts of kindness or words of encouragement include Professor John Morrill of Selwyn College, Cambridge (my alma mater) and the following: Albert Aletzhauser, Conrad Black (Lord Black of Crossharbour), Michael Dobbs-Higginson, Flora Fraser, Leonie Frieda, Harriet Sergeant, William Shawcross, Rupert Thomson, Julian West and Daniella Zimmerman. Historians who taught me, gave me tutorials and read my essays, thus inspiring my passion for history at Cambridge University, include Professor Christopher Andrew, Professor Vic Gatrell, Professor Richard Overy and Dr Clive Trebilcock. Also at Selwyn College, the master, the Reverend Owen Chadwick, Regius Professor of Modern History at Cambridge and Professor Blair Worden were unfailingly supportive. Gordon Johnson, president of Wolfson College, Cambridge, under whose guidance I studied the Maharata Empire, inspired my interest in the sub-continent. Basil Morgan, who taught me history at Uppingham School, was both an outstanding teacher and a formative influence. So too was David Gaine who encouraged me, then a somewhat diffident student, to apply to Cambridge University. I am also greatly indebted to Bruce Anderson and the late Frank Johnson, the former editor of *The Spectator*, who encouraged me to write about Asia.

Many readers gave helpful comments and advice; foremost amongst them was the philosopher and international political advisor, Dr Simon May. The prodigiously well-read and well-informed Grant Manheim, with whom I worked at N.M. Rothschild & Co., was also an invaluable reader. Julian West, a novelist, journalist and war correspondent based in New Delhi, also commented on the entire manuscript and was most helpful on the subject of her native Sri Lanka. India Jane Birley was also an eager recipient of my early drafts. My thanks also go to various helpers who either did research or fact checking for *Empires at War*; these include Jordan Nassar, my nieces Helen and Rebecca Pike, and Katharina Rietzler.

Other people who kindly read parts of my manuscript include the following: Steven Barber, Conrad Black (Lord Black of Crossharbour), Mark Birley, Robin Birley, John Everett, Sir David Frost, Lady Annabel Goldsmith, Maureen Jeram, Elaine Moore, Susanne Moser, George Ortiz, John Pike, Andrew Roberts, Patrick Robertson, Victoria de Rothschild, John Studd, Sarah Studd, Meri Tessari, Rupert Thomson, Emilie Trice and Patrick Ward.

To Stephen Barber, a former colleague and brilliant crafter of language, I am also indebted for his careful attention to what I wrote in my early career. Similarly I owe a great deal to David Stevens (Lord Stevens of Ludgate) and Nicholas Johnson, who not only sent me to live in Japan in 1983, and were thus instrumental in fulfilling a long-held desire to explore the Far East, but whose unflagging intellectual rigour and attention to detail were models from which I greatly benefitted in writing *Empires at War*.

In Asia, friends, colleagues and advisors from whom I learnt a great deal include Christopher Wood, formerly head of the *The Economist*'s Japanese desk in Tokyo, who is now the author of the Asian strategy newsletter *Greed & Fear*; Andrew Smithers and Ken Courtis have been authoritative and invaluable commentators on the Japanese economy; about China and the Far East generally I was greatly helped by the Hong Kong-based financier Philip Tose; in South Korea, Paul Pheby gave me unique insights into Korean life and organised our visit to North Korea to meet senior party members; in India, I was most indebted to K.R. Bharat, Shankar Dey, Suhel Seth and above all to Bakul Jain; I was introduced to the Philippines by Roberto Delgado shortly after Ferdinand Marcos's hasty departure from Manila; Runa Alam, with whom I set up an investment bank in Dhaka, was a source of great knowledge about Bangladesh's politics and history; her false arrest by the Bangladeshi government in 1996 and my attempts to rescue her were a source of both comedy and insight; Imran and Jemima Khan gave me a unique view of Pakistan; William Daniel, a friend from school and university, was an invaluable guide to Thailand and Indonesia; In Singapore, I was indebted to Soon Mee Sam, her mother and her husband.

Thanks also for various reasons to the following people: Assamiri Abderrahim, Mala Banarji, Kimiko Barber, Mark and Michiko Bedingham, Robin Birley, Nina Campbell, Gail and Caesar Bryan, Miranda Brooks, Mark and Suzie Bullough, Maria Caridia, Nick and Yoko Colfer, Guy Cubitt, Caroline Curtius, Sarah Daniel, Marie-Christine Dokhélar, Jo Elford, Kate and Ratan Engineer, Louise and Eric

Franck, Virginia Fraser, David Frum, Nicholas George, Joanna Hicks, Petra Hubertus, Peter and Gemma Johnson, Paul Kirkby, Joachim and Marie-Elisabeth Köhler, Manjeet Kripalani, Francis Leung, Katinka Langloh, Livi Mai, Lady Claire Mackintosh, Saya Mizuno, Mary McBain, Jasper Morris, Simon Murray, Dr Nakamae, Nigel and Joanna Newton, Raphaëlle Neyton, David Ogilvy (Lord Ogilvy), Hugh O'Neill (Lord Rathcavan), Father Terry Phipps, Elisabetta Pilia, Paul Pheby, Sir Evelyn de Rothschild, Johannes and Xiaoyang Schoeter, Henny Sender, Franco Sersale, Mia Spence, Hilary Stephenson, Tim Stephenson, Tarun Tahiliani, Sir David Tang, Dr Sir Richard Temple, Angelica Von Hase, Bettina Von Hase, Claus Von Bülow, Karin Von Joest, Robert White, Sylvia Wolf and Yat Su.

I was able to work in a number of university libraries and am grateful for their help; the British Library, the School of Oriental and African Studies (SOAS) and Humboldt University. I am also grateful to the following people for allowing me to work while staying in their homes in various locations around the world: Albert Aletzhauser and Anne Cabot, Harley Baldwin and Richard Edwards, Annabel Goldsmith, Francois and Jacqueline Granier, Lynn Guinness, Mark Lloyd, Peter Munster, Paul Pheby, Pierre Sapin and Charlotte Scott.

Heywood Hill was an ever-dependable provider of books, and their shop in Curzon Street was a constant joy to visit; John Saumarez-Smith, the best book-seller ever, was enormously helpful as was Heywood Hill's brilliant staff including Anthony Smith, Venetia Vyvyan and Amy Engineer.

I would like to thank my mother Elizabeth Pike for her help in organisational aspects of *Empires at War*, and my sister Jane Bracher, who taught me the importance of perseverance. My brother John Pike was a true enthusiast for my project and, as an eye witness to events in Manila in the aftermath of the murder of Benigno Aquino, was an important contributor to this story. Lastly, I would like to thank India Jane Birley who was the inspiration for my writing this book, and her son Eben who was a constant source of delight and diversion.

A Reader's Guide to *Empires at War*

While *Empires at War* covers Asia from Pakistan in the West to Japan in the East, there has nevertheless been a particular focus on the 'big three' countries in the region: Japan, China and India. These countries account for 17 of the 62 chapters. In all, there are chapters devoted to 14 Asian countries plus 3 chapters on Taiwan and 2 on Hong Kong. There is also extensive coverage of the wars in Indochina and Korea, which provided the defining conflicts of the Cold War epoch. In all, *Empires at War* comprises 62 chapters divided into *five parts*.

Part I **American Empire and Its Competitors 1621–1945: Chapter 1** explores the dynamism, growth and ideological development of the American Empire since its inception. This section also traces the development of its competitor Asian empires.

Part II **Asia's Post-War Settlement: Chapters 2–19** covers the immediate aftermath of the Second World War and the political agreements, forced or voluntary, that were arrived at around the Asian region.

Part III **Cold War in the Balance: Chapters 20–42** roughly covers the period 1960–85 when it was still unclear to contemporaries who would win the Cold War, and with it the control of Asia.

Part IV **Communism in Retreat: Chapters 43–60** covers the period from the early 1980s to the end of the millennium when communism suffered reverses, retreat and collapse throughout Asia.

Part V **End of America's Asian Empire: Chapters 61 and 62** comprises two parts: *Asia Redux*, which is a summary of the most recent developments in Asian countries, and *From Cold War to End of Empire*, which explores the nature of America's Asian Empire and explains the beginnings of its dissolution in the post-communist era.

Apart from **Chapter 1**, *America 1621–1945: American Empire and Its Competitors*, which serves as a prologue, **Chapter 61**, *Asia 1997–2009: Asia Redux*, and **Chapter 62**, *America–Asia 1945–2009: From Cold War to End of Empire*, which serve as an epilogue to *Empires at War*, every chapter is between 7 and 15 pages long.

Each chapter is a self-contained narrative about a single country or group of countries covering a defined time line or event, for example **Chapter 21** *The Great Leap Forward: China 1949–61* and **Chapter 36** *Tết Offensive: Lost Victories: America-Vietnam 1968–75*.

Readers can either read through the chapters in chronological order, or follow the chapters dedicated to a single country, for example **Chapter 12** *From*

An Explanation of the Maps in Empires at War

Eight maps have been prepared to show the ebb and flow of the battle for control of Asia in the 45 year period after 1945.

Map I shows the many western Empires which controlled Asia in 1941; the respective colonial possessions of Great Britain, France, Holland, and America are all shown. In addition Japan's control of Korea and most of North Eastern China is also illustrated.

The remaining seven maps take 'snap-shots' of the conflict starting in 1945 (**Map II**) when America and Great Britain by dint of their defeat of Japan, controlled almost all of Asia. **Map III** – **Map VIII** show maps of Asia in 1949, 1961, 1966, 1972, 1984 and 1991. These dates have been chosen to show key inflection points in the battle between the USA and the Soviet Union for the control of Asia.

The maps cannot be simply 'black and white'; there were many shades of grey in the calculus of cold war strategy. Importantly China moved out of the Soviet camp in 1961 but remained hostile to the USA until the famous Nixon-Kissinger rapprochement in 1972. India too is difficult to judge, just as it would have been for the policy advisors sitting in the White House and the Kremlin; after independence Nehru took a vehemently anti-American stance while still receiving her financial handouts. While Indira Gandhi moved India, both economically and diplomatically, even further into the Soviet Block, the country remained broadly democratic except for the period of the 'Emergency'.

Over certain periods the relationship of Burma, Cambodia and Laos to the superpowers was also difficult to call. Both North Vietnam and North Korea flip-flopped in their relationship with China and the Soviet Union, often playing one off against the other. Meanwhile Malaysia, after the rise to power of Dr Mahathir, remained anti-communist but became vocally anti-American under his leadership although her economy prospered with large amounts of western investment and easy access to America's consumer markets. In Indonesia, the country's founding father, President Sukarno, was strongly supported by the USA in his bid for freedom from the Dutch; however, by the early 1960s Indonesia had moved almost entirely into the communist camp. Like Sri Lanka, after 1961 Indonesia also increasingly looked to China rather than the Soviet Union for anti-American communist support. Even staunch allies of the West such as Pakistan, had their periods of 'falling-out' with the USA.

In conclusion the maps should only be used as a guide to the shifts in the balance of power; in truth there are not enough shades of grey to illustrate the extreme complexity of the state of the respective hegemonies of the Soviet Union and the United States over the period covered by *Empires at War*.

Introduction and Background

The idea of writing *Empires at War* first occurred to me in 1984 on a small car ferry taking me from Matsuyama, one of the larger cities on the Japanese island of Shikoku, to Hiroshima, situated on the main Japanese island of Honshu.

Inside, the main saloon of the ferry was crowded with about 50 Japanese passengers, who were watching the film *Tora! Tora! Tora!* (1970), a joint American–Japanese directed portrayal of the Japanese attack on Pearl Harbor, with an American and Japanese all-star cast, which won seven Oscar nominations. I had watched astounded as the Japanese audience had screamed their delight and cheered when the American ships were sunk by Japanese Mitsubishi 'Zero' planes launched from Admiral Yamamoto's carrier fleet. Particularly, appreciation was given to the scenes showing the blowing up and sinking of *USS Arizona*, in which 1,102 Americans died. I had to leave.

Later as I stood alone on deck, it struck me as incongruous that firstly this film should have elicited a reaction which would not have been possible in the similarly defeated Germany after World War II, and that secondly this film was playing as we were steaming towards Hiroshima, where the dropping of the atom bomb had heralded Japanese defeat. It was a calm, warm summer's evening; the sun was setting over Japan's magical Inland Sea with its myriad islands silhouetted against the horizon. Perhaps shocked by this strange episode, it occurred to me that I should write a history of modern Asia, though it would take some years before I would get around to starting this work.

The writing of *Empires at War* came about after a period of 20 years in which I had the rare experience of living in the three major countries of Asia (Japan, China and India), had studied and written about the region as a specialist Asian economic and political strategist, started numerous financial businesses and had advised Asian governments in various capacities. Over time I had become increasingly frustrated in the search for a book that adequately explained how modern Asia had come into being. *Empires at War* is an attempt to fill this gap in the written history of the region.

Given that Asia comprises some 4 billion people, almost two-thirds of the global population, about 30 per cent of its land mass and also in aggregate the world's largest economic block, and in addition contains its fastest growing economies, the writing of *Empires at War* appears to be a timely introduction to the region's modern origins. In recent years there has been increasing focus on the economic challenge provided to the West by the growth of India and China. Their competition for natural resources, particularly energy, has also drawn attention.

The rising geopolitical power of the Asian region is evident, and events such as the Beijing Olympics in 2008 have focused attention on this shift in the global balance. *Empires at War* is written both for historians and the broad market of interested readers for whom 'Modern Asia' is of increasing interest, but for whom its recent history is still a mystery.

Empires at War (subtitled *A Short History of Modern Asia since World War II*) is a narrative work that attempts to explain the key events that have shaped the countries of Asia, defined for the purposes of this book as the region stretching from Pakistan in the west to Japan in the east and from China in the north to Indonesia in the south. The main countries covered in this history include Bangladesh, Burma, Cambodia, China, India, Indonesia, Japan, North Korea, South Korea, Malaysia, Pakistan, Singapore, Sri Lanka and Vietnam. There are also chapters on Taiwan, and on Hong Kong covering the period up to its handing-back to China.

In the history of post-war Asia, there is an extraordinary story to tell. When juxtaposed against the concurrent history of Europe with its emphasis on constitutional development and the relatively grey bureaucrats who built it, Asia's recent past has a much greater dramatic and indeed gothic character. Larger-than-life figures dominated the Asian stage: Mao Zedong, Emperor Hirohito, Mahatma Gandhi, Chiang Kai Shek, Jawaharlal Nehru, Muhammad Ali Jinnah, Sukarno, Suharto, Kim Il Sung, Indira Gandhi, Lee Kuan Yew, Dr Mahathir, Zhou Enlai, Ferdinand Marcos, King Bhumibol, Zulfikar Ali Bhutto, Benazir Bhutto, Sheikh Mujib, Hô Chí Minh, Aung San and Deng Xiaoping. In addition to these indigenous figures, Asia's modern history is not complete without reference to global giants such as Soviet First Secretaries Joseph Stalin, Nikita Krushchev and Leonid Brezhnev; Presidents Franklin D. Roosevelt, John F. Kennedy, Lyndon B. Johnson, Richard Nixon and Ronald Reagan; and powerful leaders such as Earl Mountbatten of Burma, General MacArthur, and Henry Kissinger. These are figures of history to match the great and infamous individuals who helped form the nation states of Europe and America.

Additionally, Asia experienced some of the most dramatic events of the post-war world; revolutions, battles, coups d'état, genocides, massacres and assassinations proliferated in the whirlpool of events that reformulated Asia after the Second World War; the most famous battles of the post-war period were Inchon, Diên Biên Phu and the Tết Offensive; Japan experienced the greatest boom and bust of any country since the 'Great Depression'; the twentieth century's bloodiest religious conflict took place during the 'Partition' of India and Pakistan; the greatest man-made catastrophe in human history was Mao's *Great Leap Forward*; the most infamous genocide of the second half of the twentieth century was committed by the *Khmer Rouge* in Cambodia and the least known was *The night of the intellectuals* that took place in Dhaka, Bangladesh. Meanwhile the savage massacre of communists throughout Indonesia in that country's *Year of living dangerously* is now a barely remembered event.

The greatest turnaround in fortunes was achieved by the National Socialist dictator Chiang Kai Shek, who, having been defeated by Mao's Red Army, fled to Taiwan and, in spite of a ruthless suppression of its indigenous population by his *Kuomintang* forces, initiated a remarkable recovery of her economy. The most miraculous escape of the epoch was achieved by Emperor Hirohito, who not only managed to avoid prosecution and execution as a war criminal but also went on to be the longest serving monarch in the twentieth century. Typically, his role in the genocide carried out in Northern China, famously in Nanking, was not covered in Christiane Amanpour's recent CNN documentary on the history of genocide, *Scream Bloody Murder* (2008). Hirohito's reputation, along with those of other seminal figures in post-war Asian history including Lord Mountbatten, Mao Zedong, Aung Sang, Nehru, Indira Gandhi and J.F. Kennedy, have defied critical judgement for too long. At the other end of the scale, the achievements of Harry Truman, Shigeru Yoshida, General Park Chung-hee, Narasimha Rao and above all Deng Xiaoping have been undervalued. *Empires at War* aims to be both an explanation as to how 'Modern Asia' has come into being and a narrative that describes the great dramas of the epoch.

Empires at War is set in the background of the superpower conflict between the USA and the Soviet Union. Political nature abhors a vacuum; the implosion of the Asian Empires after the Second World War, both Japanese and European, and the power vacuum it created is perhaps the obvious interpretation of how America came to dominate the post-war history of Asia. This is only a partially accurate explanation of post-war Asian history; it ignores the rapid expansion of the US power and influence in the region from the beginning of the nineteenth century. By 1918, the USA was already the dominant imperial power in Asia. Without attaching any of the pejorative connotations that the word 'Empire' often brings with it, it is evident that USA, through the dynamism of its social and economic systems, was in every sense an imperial power from its earliest inception as an independent nation situated on a sliver of coastline along the American continent's eastern shore.

Empires at War argues that America's post-war domination of Asia was a part of a continuum of long-term growth of the US global power and influence. Westward commercial and territorial expansionism has been the defining characteristic of its 388-year history (from the landing of the Pilgrim Fathers aboard the *Mayflower*); it is a history which saw the USA conquer America, in the process forcing Britain, Spain, Mexico, France and Russia to give up their claims. In the early nineteenth century, the USA barely drew breath on arriving at North America's West Coast before moving inexorably into the Pacific Ocean.

The structure of modern Asian history can be understood only against the background of America's pre-war expansion into Asia and its logical continuation thereafter. America's overwhelming presence in Asia after the Second World War was neither sudden nor a break with the past but a continuation of the competition for power in the region in which it had been engaged for over 100 years. After 1945, the contest to dominate Asia would pitch the USA against its post-war rival, the Soviet Union, and at least in the early years, their communist confederate, the People's Republic of China.

Some might argue that the word 'hegemony' rather than Empire best describes America's post-war role in Asia. Neither *de jure* nor *de facto* did America rule its Asian allies. However, just as the Delian League of the fifth century BC, an association of Greek city states led by Athens to fight Persia is called by historians 'The Athenian Empire' without it ever having been formally constructed as such, so it seems reasonable, by the same criteria, to describe the post-war Asian alliances with the USA to fight communism as being in the nature of an 'American Empire'. Also we tend to refer to 'Imperial Russia' because of the expansion of the Muscovite Kingdom from the sixteenth century, which, as this book argues, bears comparison with the expansion of the former 13 colonies of the USA after the War of Independence. However, the issue of whether it is correct to describe America as an 'Empire' is a largely semantic discussion best put to one side. For the purposes of this book I have chosen to describe America as an Empire, a description which renowned historians, such as Niall Ferguson, happily endorse (*Colossus: The Rise and Fall of the American Empire*; 2005). More importantly, *Empires at War* argues that however imperfect the creation and operation of America's 'Asian Empire' after the Second World War, it was an entirely preferable model to Asia's indigenous inhabitants than the alternatives on offer from the USA's communist competitors.

Although by the outbreak of the Second World War in 1939, the USA had already rejected the traditional notion of imperial territorial conquest, it nevertheless continued to propose the expansion of American commerce, culture and political ideals. The astonishing rise of the USA served to bolster Americans' fervent belief in their moral values, their economic and political system and indeed their 'manifest destiny'. This had inevitably brought the USA into conflict with the emerging Asian Empire of Japan before the Second World War and would bring it into conflict with the Soviet Union afterwards. That the concept of 'self-determination' of nations had, by the 1920s, already become a core moral cause espoused by the Anglo-Saxon Empires of America and Great Britain, who were by then readying themselves to divest their Asian conquests, did not mean that they were prepared to see emerging Asian nations fall to the expansion of the Japanese or Soviet Empires and their ideologies. Both before and after the Second World War, the Anglo-Saxon model of autonomous liberal political and economic development in Asia was engaged in a battle for supremacy with competing autarkic systems.

While this is the geopolitical context in which *Empires at War* is set, exploration of this superpower conflict is not the only objective of this book. Too often, Asia is written about from a Euro-centric or an America-centric viewpoint. Asian nations were not simply the biddable entities of the American and Soviet superpowers which backed them. As Sophie Quinn-Judge concludes in *Hô Chí Minh: The Missing Years* (2003), '... the Comintern was far from being the efficient tool for spreading communist power which Cold War political science and history would have had us believe'. Similarly Tim Weiner, in his *Legacy of Ashes: The History of the CIA* (2007), believes that the CIA mythologised the importance of its role in post-war history. While the structural security and balance of power in the region may have been defined by superpower politics, in the large part the intricacies of national political development in Asia were not.

The other main and equally important theme of *Empires at War* is therefore the exploration of the peculiarly indigenous national economic, social and political developments as they affected the emerging Asian nations in the post-war era. *Empires at War* demonstrates in its narrative account that the development of political and economic culture in Asia's post-war nation states, particularly but not exclusively within the American Bloc, was *sui generis*, with a dynamic that was largely independent of the structure of the superpower conflict within which emerging Asian countries operated.

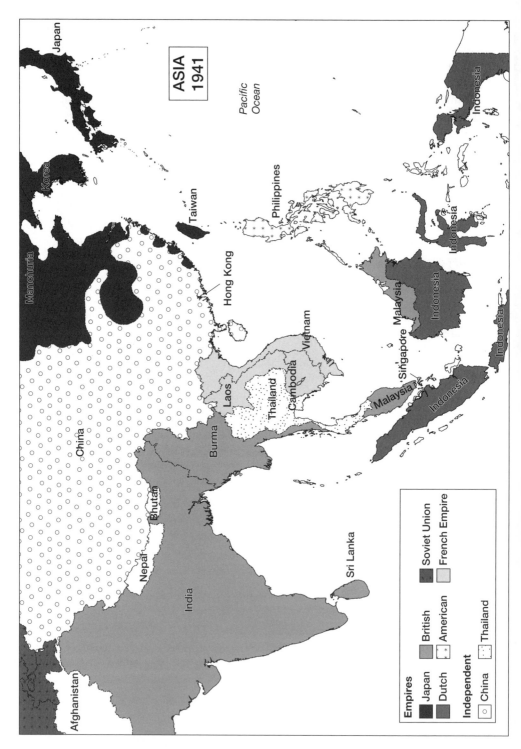

MAP 1: It is sometimes forgotten that Japan had already been at war with China for 10 years before the attack on Pearl Harbor in 1941. Having established a 'protectorate' over Korea in 1910, the Japanese Army with the backing of Emperor Hirohito used the fabricated 18 September 1931 Mukden Incident (the blowing up of a section of railway) as an excuse to annexe Manchuria and expand Japan's 'co-prosperity sphere'. However a full scale war against China did not develop until 1937; arguably World War II started in Asia in this year rather than the normally stated 1939.

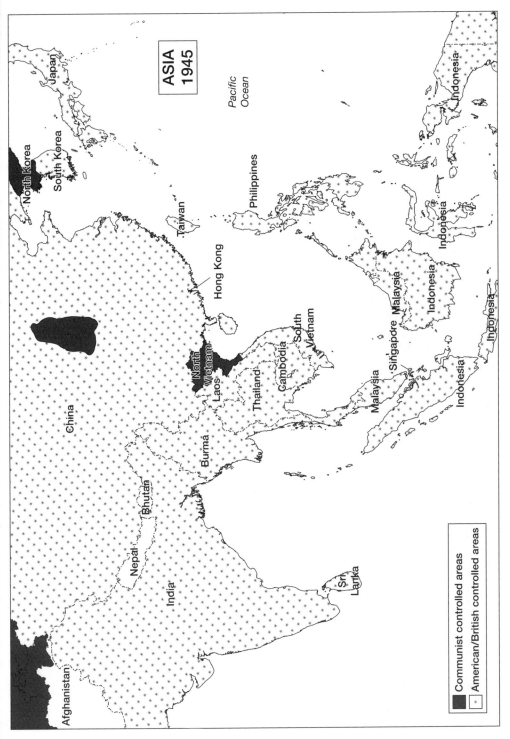

MAP II: The Allied Powers were not as sanguine about post-war Asia as this map might suggest. There were powerful communist insurrections in Malaysia, Burma, Vietnam and the Philippines. In Manchuria Mao's communists and Stalin moved rapidly to fill the vaacuum left by the defeat of the Japanese. Furthermore there were strong communist parties or underground movements in Japan, Indonesia, Singapore, Laos, Cambodia, and Thailand. Nevertheless in 1945, the USA could have had no reason to believe that her domination of Asia would be seriously challenged in the post-war world.

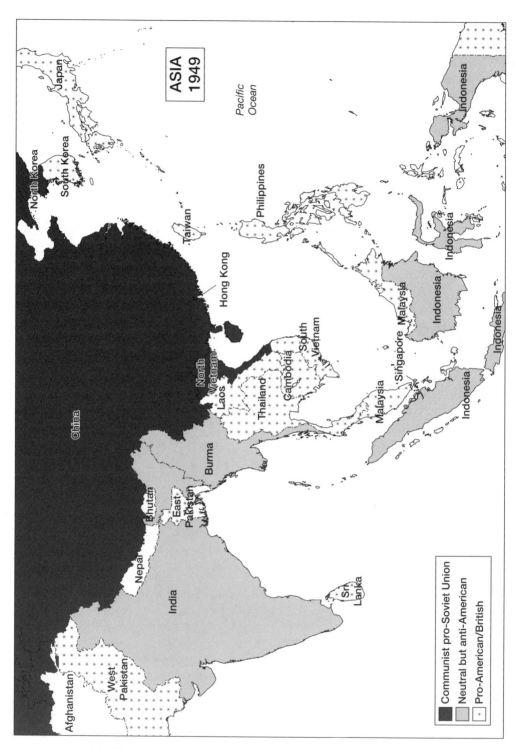

MAP III: The loss of China to communism shows what a traumatic event this would have been to President Truman and Congress as they poured over their geopolitical maps in Washington. At this stage China was very much in the Soviet camp and a junior partner in seeking a world communist revolution. Amost as worryingly India and Indonesia, Asia's second and third most populous countries, turned anti-American almost as soon as independence was achieved, albeit at this stage they remained nominally neutral.

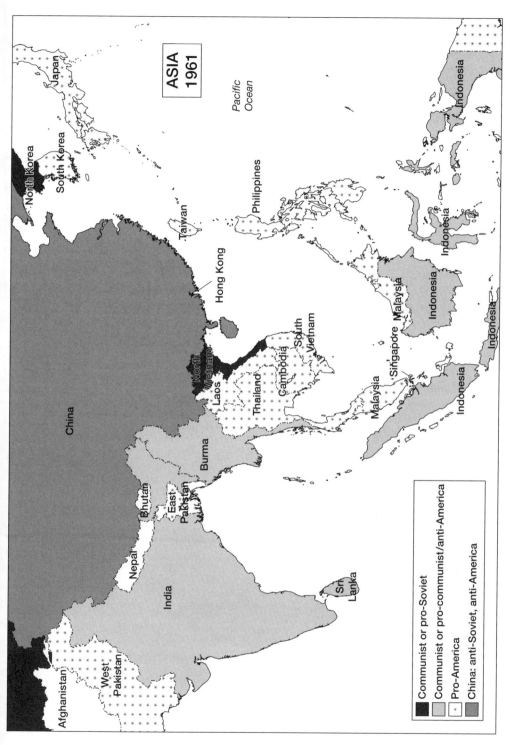

MAP IV: The Sino-Soviet split in 1961 fundamentally altered the geopolitical map of Asia. Unfortunately neither President Kennedy nor President Johnson fully understood the importance of this event; both men viewed China through the prism of the Korean War in which the Chinese army fought the US led United Nations forces to a standstill. The geopolitical shift indicated by this map was not begun to be exploited until Richard Nixon won the Presidency in 1968.

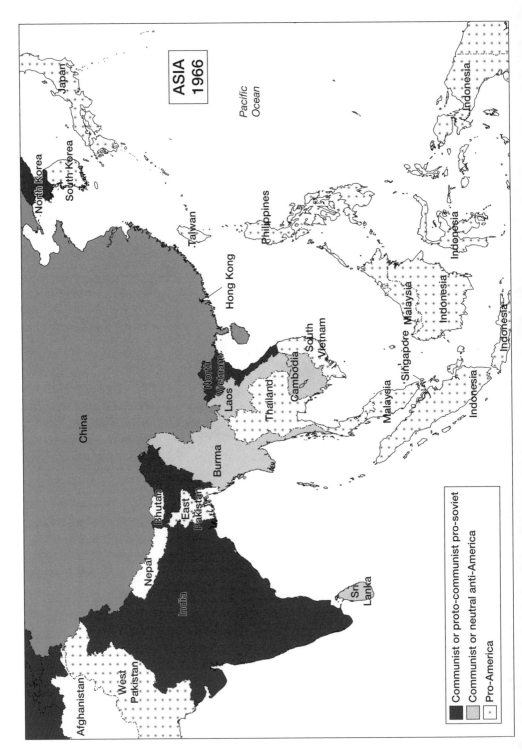

MAP V: The fall of Sukarno and the slaughter of an estimated one million communists in 1966 was one of the more unexpected victories for the USA in their battle for control of Asia. Set against this Indira Gandhi was planting India ever more firmly in the Soviet block through her autarkic, Sovietic economic policies and her diplomatic alliance with the Soviet Union which was formalised in 1972.

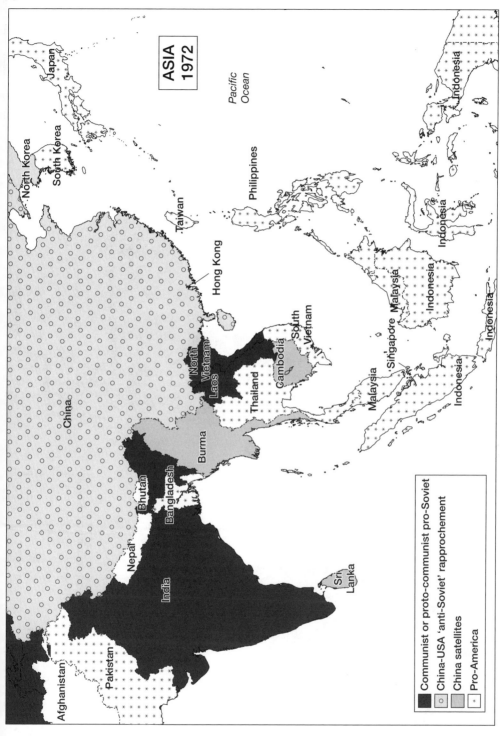

MAP VI: The major diplomatic coup of the 20th Century was the Nixon-Kissinger inspired rapprochement with China. It is interesting to note that at this time Mao and his foreign minister Zhou Enlai believed that the Soviet Union was winning the 'Cold War' in Asia and wished to encourage the Americans to continue the battle for Indochina. For America and the West, the change to the geopolitical map was immensely important for the future security and stability of the region while opening the path for the eventual incorporation of China into the global free market economic system.

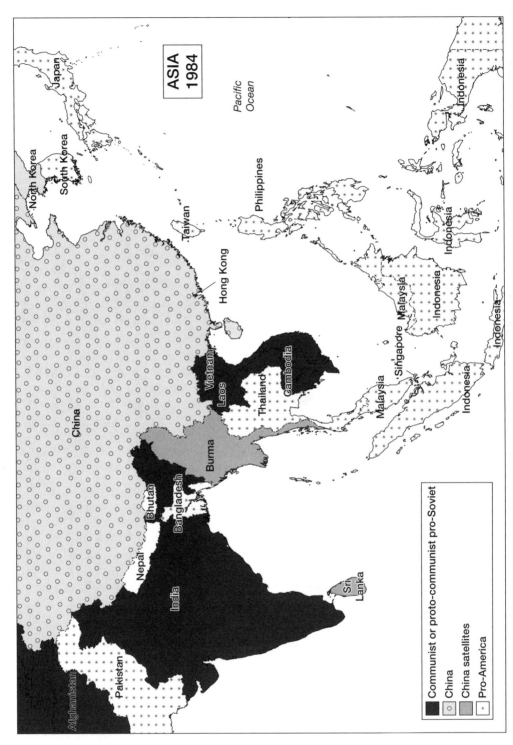

MAP VII: The 1970s saw the fall of Vietnam to the Soviet Union to be followed shortly afterwards by Cambodia. Curiously China and the West ended up supporting the genocidal Khmer Rouge regime because it was hostile to the Soviet supporting Vietnamese; Ronald Reagan and Mrs. Thatcher thus became unlikely allies with Pol Pot's Khmer Rouge. The loss too of Afghanistan to the Soviet Union showed that the Soviet threat to Asia was very real well into the 1980s; a fact which in hindsight has sometimes been overlooked.

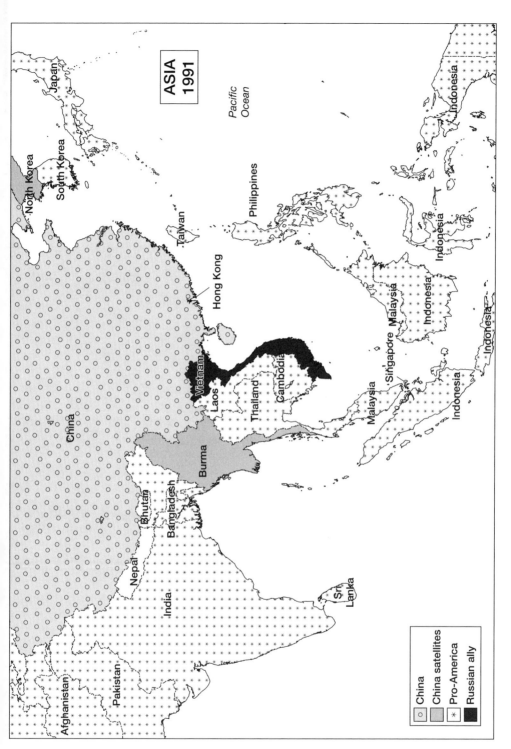

MAP VIII: America had clearly emerged as the complete 'Cold War' victor by 1991. Ground down by the Mujahideen guerilla fighters financed by Saudia Arabia and the USA, the Soviet Union was forced to flee Afghanistan. Subsequently the Soviet Union was itself broken up though Russian remained a nominal ally of Vietnam. Until it gave up its Pacific Ocean naval base at Cam Ranh Bay in 2002, the Soviet presence was eradicated in both countries. Also in 1991 Cambodia effectively surrendered when the ruling Communist Party abolished itself and rang up the United Nations to ask for its help in setting up western style governmental institutions. China ceased to support the Burma Communist Party in 1988 which opened up the way for that country to enter the Chinese orbit of influence along with North Korea; the map thus illustrates the new battle for hegemony in Asia though one which may be muted by the symbiotic trading relationship between China and the US.

PART I

American Empire and Its Competitors
1621–1945

1

American Empire and Its Competitors

America: 1621—1945

*Ancestors give them the love of equality and of freedom; but God Himself gave them
the means of remaining equal and free by placing them upon a boundless continent.*

Alexis de Tocqueville, 'Democracy in America' (1835)[1]

The USA has been the most expansionist and successful empire of the modern
age. The early American settlers proved to be hardy adventurers; a spirit of
enterprise and taste for commercial venture ran through their veins, and above everything, they possessed an all-consuming appetite for land. The achievements of
these early pioneers and their successors were truly astonishing. From their tenuous foothold on the eastern seaboard of America, the colonists survived their early
hardships, to win independence, establish nationhood and then conquer the North
American continent.

Old empires were challenged. Both Spain and France were overwhelmed by
the newcomers. Great Britain was forced to agree to American suzerainty over
the Oregon territories. The independent kingdom of Hawaii was colonised and its
people subjugated. Having become a major participant in the Chinese opium trade,
American forces landed in Guangzhou and defeated a Chinese army in pitched
battle. Also, Commander Mathew Perry's black-hulled gunboats forced Japan to
open its markets.

By the end of the nineteenth century, Imperial Russia, aware that it could no
longer defend Alaska and Oregon from the pioneer onslaught, sold Alaska and all
its claims and was pushed off the American continent. In a dispute over Cuba, the
American fleet stationed in Hong Kong sailed to the Philippines, sank the Spanish
fleet in Manila Bay and took its colonial possessions in Asia. The USA had become
the emerging new power in Asia; the formerly dominant position of Great Britain
was now challenged. Towards the end of the nineteenth century, Admiral Shufeldt
wrote that the Pacific was the ocean bride of America and that Japan and China
were the bridesmaids.

By the end of the First World War, the USA, under President Woodrow Wilson, had victoriously sent an army to Europe, and then dominated the protracted

peace negotiations at Versailles. America subsequently dictated the size of British and Japanese navies at the Washington Naval Treaty (1922) and the subsequent London Treaties (1930 and 1936). The Great Depression notwithstanding, by the end of the Second World War, the USA accounted for more than half of global economic output. By 1945, in just 324 years after the arrival of the Pilgrim Fathers, the USA had become an economically prolific and populous nation and the great arbiter of world power. As the historian Paul Johnson has concluded, the Americans had achieved 'the transformation of a mostly uninhabited wilderness. . . .'[2]

In Asia, moreover, in the vacuum created by the defeat of Japan, the collapse of the European Empires and the economic exhaustion of Great Britain, America was left standing at the head of a vast Asian hegemony. Also, as the world's only nuclear power, not just Asia but the world lay at its feet. In explaining the origins of this great surge of humanity across the American continent and Asia beyond, which catapulted America to the head of the world's nations, it is necessary to look at the origins and character of the mass migration which made it possible. This had its beginnings in Europe in the seventeenth and eighteenth centuries with the emergence of modern nation states which had intellectually revolutionary concepts of government, technological advances, rapidly growing economies and burgeoning populations.

The Rise of European Nations and Migration to America

Arriving some 28 years after the Pilgrim Fathers committed themselves to set up a colony in newly discovered America, the 1648 Treaty of Westphalia, which settled the Thirty Years War, proved a defining moment in the development of the modern nation state. Before 1648, 'Europe was thought of as a collection of communities arranged vertically in a hierarchy, at the head of which reigned the temporal power of the Emperor and the spiritual power of the Pope.'[3] Writing in 1677, the German philosopher Leibniz, seeking an answer to the establishment of perpetual peace, was looking back to history when he suggested that 'All Christian Kings and princes are subject to the orders of the Universal Church, of which the Emperor is the Director and temporal head.'[4]

In truth, after Westphalia, the teetering remnants of the Holy Roman Empire were finally shattered; Rome's claims to European suzerainty were effectively ended. The drawing to a close of one empire in Europe was to have a profound effect on the emergence of a new nation on the other side of the Atlantic, a country that would achieve nationhood and become the world's dominant hegemonic power.

Even before the Thirty Years War, the power of Rome had been under threat from the rise of the secular 'nation states'. More than a century earlier, Henry VIII had severed the English church from Rome, and in spite of his autocratic qualities, best displayed in the despatch of successive queens, he had overseen significant advances in the development of constitutional government and the development of legal process; furthermore, 'enclosures' – the process by which feudal strip farming was replaced by more efficient agricultural practice – proceeded rapidly during this period and, by its liberation of capital and labour from the land, laid the preconditions of an industrial economy. The organs of a modern state had been formed. Nevertheless, his daughter, Queen Elizabeth I, had had to battle a Spanish armada and the constant threat of a European alliance which aimed to bring England and the United Provinces (the Netherlands) back to Rome.

It was not only in England that the Reformation transformed the relationship between the state and its people. Before Protestantism, the European monarchies could appeal above the heads of national interest groups to the Roman Church and to God. The severance of the Roman link forced the northern protestant monarchies, in addition to the Republic of the United Provinces, to increasingly focus attention on cultivating support and validation from temporal interest groups, not only the nobility but more importantly the rising commercial class.

In effect, the Treaty of Westphalia accepted the separation of the protestant nations and 'defined the modern idea of sovereignty of the nation which declared that a state's domestic conduct and institutions were beyond the reach of the other states'.[5] Henceforth, a state's accumulation of power would be independent of international religious bonds but increasingly beholden to domestic institutional structures. In international politics, until the arrival of Napoleon, an uneasy recognition of the new nations was accepted as the norm. Writing in 1751, Voltaire noted that the European states were 'at one in the wise policy of maintaining among themselves as far as possible an equal balance of power'.[6]

France, which had consolidated its own borders and effectively ended English claims to the throne by the mid-fifteenth century, emerged as the greatest of the new nation states after the *Thirty Years War*. French power and culture reached its apogee in the glittering reign of Louis XIV, 'the Sun King'. France was only briefly diminished by the collapse of the Bourbon monarchy. Following the French Revolution, Napoleon would threaten to unite Europe under French power. England, perhaps 'constitutionally' and 'institutionally' the most sophisticated of Europe's new nations, battled France, not with the aim of creating a European Empire but with the objective, achieved by British Foreign Minister Castlereagh at the 1815 Congress of Vienna, of creating a balance of power between independent nation states.

Meanwhile, the Hapsburg Empire, the great fourteenth-century power centred on Austria, was much diminished in the aftermath of Westphalia, but would stagger along in increasing decrepitude. Just over a century later, the empire, centred in Vienna, would lose its dominant position in Germany to Frederick the Great of Prussia, the last of Europe's warrior kings. A final 'coup de grâce' was not given until 1919, when, after the First World War, President Wilson's utopian vision of 'self-determining nation states' gave independence to the Eastern European states such as Hungary and Czechoslovakia at the Treaty of Versailles.

Spain, the strongest of European countries in the late-fifteenth and sixteenth centuries, had been in steady decline after the great gold-induced inflation and subsequent depression of the sixteenth century. Population continued to fall in the seventeenth century, and the loss of vitality and declining birth rate seriously compromised Spain's ability to sustain it's New World Empire in the face of the rapid expansion of the Anglo-Saxon colonies in North America. A British traveller contemptuously observed of Spain's American Empire that

> The sole purpose for which the Americas existed was held to be that of collecting together the precious metals for the Spaniards; and if the wild horses and cattle which overrun the country could have been trained to perform this office the inhabitants might have been altogether dispensed with, and the colonial system would then have been perfect.[7]

Indeed, gold and silver accounted for 90 per cent of South America's exports to Spain, and in aggregate, bullion from this source amounted to more than 50 per cent of global coinage.

Within the space of a little over 20 years, Spain's 300-year-old American Empire, which comprised the Audiencias of Mexico (extending into New Mexico, California, Texas and Florida) and Santo Domingo; the captaincy- generalships of Guatemala and Cuba and of Santiago de Chile (modern Chile); the presidency of Quito (approximately modern Ecuador); the Audiencias of Santa Fé de Bogotá (modern Columbia), of Caracas (modern Venezuala), of Buenos Aires (modern Argentina) and of Cuzco (modern Peru); and the presidencies of Asunción (modern Paraguay), Charcas (modern Bolivia) and Banda Oriental (modern Uruguay), was destroyed. The trigger to this collapse was the forced abdication by Napoleon of Charles IV of Spain and his son Ferdinand VII in 1808, and their replacement on the Spanish throne by Napoleon's elder brother Joseph Bonaparte.

However, with the example of the USA to the north, combined with the promptings of General Miranda – a freebooting soldier with epicurean taste, a former lover of Catherine the Great of Russia and the father of revolutionary thought in South America – the seeds of revolt had already been sown. England also participated, only too keen to revenge itself for the loss of its own colonies; the Pan-American Centennial Congress of 1926 noted that 'there was no battlefield in the war of Independence on which British blood was not shed'.[8]

Yet the leaders of the revolts were a rag-tag bunch of romantic visionaries such as the aristocratic playboy Simon Bolivar, San Martin (an Argentine general), Bernardo O'Higgins (a viceroy's illegitimate son), Iturbide (a soldier who went from military obscurity to become Emperor of Mexico) and Crown Prince Pedro of Portugal (who overthrew his father to make Brazil independent). The political instability in South America, which these revolutionaries brought in their wake, in no small measure contributed to the ease and speed with which the USA became the dominant power in the Americas.

England was not the only protestant nation to emerge from the Reformation and the Thirty Years War with new vitality. Smaller protestant nations such as Sweden and Denmark also emerged with clearer identities during the Thirty Years War. After a long-drawn-out revolt, the Republic of the United Provinces (the Netherlands) secured its formal independence from Spain in 1648; the celebrated American historian, Barbara Tuchman, would later claim that the winning of its own sovereignty 'vindicated the struggle for political liberty that was to pass in the next century to Amsterdam'.[9]

The United Provinces continued to achieve a trading and mercantile success that was built on innovative boat-building technology. The Dutch developed a shallow-bottomed 250-ton cargo ship called a 'flute', which was quick and in-expensive to build and, with its simplified rigging, could be sailed by a crew of just ten. In 1697 Peter the Great came to reside at Zaandam to learn the secrets of Dutch naval technology.

The Dutch drove to the forefront of European exploration and established set-tlements in South Africa and the East Indies, bringing back exotic oriental spices. In the west, the coast of America was surveyed and a colony founded at New Amster-dam. The Hudson River was exploited for furs, and in South America, a sugar trade was developed. In 1626 the island of Manhattan was purchased from the Indians. The Dutch East Company was founded in 1602, and was followed by the develop-ment of innovative financing techniques. The Bank of Amsterdam was founded in 1609, and a stock market developed with the bank printing regular lists of prices: a world first.

After Westphalia, Prussia – a small agricultural state pressed against the Baltic – would develop a unique military culture, almost Spartan in the centrality of sol-diering to its social and political system; Frederick the Great in the eighteenth century significantly enhanced Prussian power and prestige but realised the limits to his expansionist tendencies. The equalising trend in national power since West-phalia was noted by Frederick the Great, who observed that

> Arms and military discipline being much the same throughout Europe and the alliances as a rule producing an equality of force between the belligerent parties, all that princes can expect from the greatest advantages at present is to acquire, by accumulation of successes, either some small cities on the frontier or some territory which will not pay the expenses of war.[10]

It was not until the age of steel in the nineteenth century that Chancellor Bis-marck would finally overawe the independent German states into a free trade and currency union as a precursor to sovereignty for a united German nation. Sense of nationhood was finally conferred to Germany after the Franco-Prussian War of 1870 when Prussian forces, under the brilliant generalship of Von Moltke, de-feated Napoleon III in successive battles and captured Paris itself. The war de-stroyed French claims to be the most powerful nation of Europe. Germany's rapid industrialisation and the concomitant growth of its population in the nineteenth century would provide a major component of America's immigration in this period. Between 1820 and 1920, Germany provided America with 5.5 million immigrants, the largest of any country; by comparison, over the same period, there were 2.5 million migrants from Great Britain.

In spite of the constant warring and vying for power of the European powers after Westphalia, because of the competition it engendered, the embryonic nation states of Europe enjoyed constant technological and economic advance. Developments in land management and animal husbandry improved agricultural output and, by generating product beyond the need for nutritional survival, enabled the accumulation of capital for investment in trade and industry; also in Italy in the sixteenth century, Florence had developed an international textile trade and innovative banking techniques.

England's industrial revolution grew from these origins and from the development of property rights enshrined in law, which had their origins in Magna Carta, the treaty between King John and his barons in 1215 which curtailed his powers. Without the transparency given to the legal right to own land under the law, and hence outside the purview of government, modern lending techniques and industrial investment would not have been possible.

It was not coincidental that the seventeenth century's two fastest growing economies, Britain and Holland, were the earliest European nations to adopt recognisably modern institutions and to develop sophisticated 'property rights' that dispensed with the Royal Prerogative to grant monopolies, thus creating competitive commercial conditions. By contrast, the more backward continental European states clung to a more outdated view of monarchical government; this was neatly summed up by Prince Kaunitz, first minister to Maria Theresa and Joseph II of Austria, when he concluded that 'politics is the art of sheltering the rights of the crown from the incursions of the Estates. . . .'[11]

That the USA was to inherit the Anglo-Dutch model of government, based on property rights and commerce, rather than the monarchic 'Ancien Regime' model transferred to South America, does much to explain the discrepancies in success of their respective revolutionary movements.

Throughout Europe, the breakdown of feudal systems of land tenure increased agricultural productivity and liberated capital and labour. As agricultural technology, communications and finance developed, European population grew explosively. Starting in the seventeenth century in Holland and England, European populations were launched on a broadly based and sustained acceleration by the mid-eighteenth century. An estimated European population of 100 million in 1650 grew to 140 million by 1750, and 266 million by 1850; moreover, the population growth rate accelerated from just 0.3 per cent in the seventeenth century to 0.6 per cent by the eighteenth century. (In Asia a similar expansion was taking place, with populations in the region rising from 330 million in 1650 to 749 million in 1850).

Liberated from feudalism, labour became mobile as well as more productive. Development of naval technology, for reasons of national security, promoted exploration and trade, particularly by Dutch and British merchants. Perfection of navigational technologies also enabled the development of commerce in far-flung regions of the world including the opening up of the Indian and Pacific oceans. By some estimates, there were as many as 10,000 Dutch ships at sea by 1648. It is noticeable that the 'Separatists', who formed the backbone of the *Mayflower* venture, had originally sought refuge for 12 years in Leiden, Holland. The Pilgrim Fathers may have been impoverished farmers, but they showed a surprising degree of mobility – a trend that was to multiply with population growth in Europe over the succeeding century.

The voyage of the Pilgrim Fathers to the 'New World' on 16 September 1620 was a product of Europe's religious, social, political and technological developments. The *Mayflower* pilgrims sought the religious freedoms enabled by the Reformation; however, it was the possibility of acquiring land 'for free' which was probably the greater driver of migration. Indeed, about half of the *Mayflower*'s passenger did not belong to the 'pilgrim' party and could be better described as 'economic migrants'.

Though the early American colonists adopted the unconventional and anti-authoritarian spirit of the non-conformist, as the seventeenth and eighteenth centuries progressed, and with it religious tolerance in Europe increased, it was the draw of land, economic adventurism and speculation which drove people to the American colonies. Notably, the pioneers took with them ideals strongly rooted in the new concepts of law, land and the political responsibility of government towards the 'people', rather than the divine rights of kings.

In spite of the rigors of passage (even into the mid-nineteenth century, until after the development of larger steel hulls, up to 10 per cent of passengers could die on the three- to six-month journey), America proved attractive to the liberated but growing landless populations of England and Holland and later Germany. Ultimately, American land would provide the 'escape valve' for the rising populations of Europe in the eighteenth and nineteenth centuries.

On arrival, conditions were harsh, and disease, famine and sometimes hostile Indians made life difficult for the settlers. This remained true well into the nineteenth century, as Charles Dickens's description of the hardships of settler life in his novel *Martin Chuzzlewit* (1844) clearly demonstrates. Nevertheless, the success of American agricultural ventures stimulated new waves of emigration, such that by the 1770s the 13 colonies had established themselves in the new world of 'America' with a sizeable population of about 3 million people, plus about 700,000 African slaves. Given that the population of England at this time was just 10 million, having grown from about 5.5 million at the time of the *Mayflower* voyage, the sustained economic success and population advance of the American colonies was no mean achievement.

The Land Motive for Independence

The economic benefits of land acquisition were soon apparent. Some of the *Mayflower* pilgrims may have sought in America a land of religious freedom, but from the beginning, economic opportunism dominated. The *Mayflower* pilgrims started by buying land from the *Pokanokets*, but within 50 years they had destroyed this indigenous tribe in a bloody war, killed its king and sold his family and remaining tribespeople into slavery. It was a pattern that was to be constantly repeated.

Indeed, it was an attempt by the British Crown to limit the colonist's ever more extensive land grabs that first brought serious conflict between Great Britain and the 13 American colonies. By the Royal Proclamation of 7 October 1763, all land claims of the colonies beyond the Appalachian Mountains that ran parallel to the East Coast of America, some 100–300 miles inland, were swept away. The crest of the Appalachians now defined the colonial perimeter.

The colonies were soon speculating illegally to acquire land to the west of the 'Proclamation line'. Indian Superintendent Sir William Johnson negotiated a treaty with the Iroquois whereby for the sum of £10,000 they relinquished their rights to a large part of central New York, Pennsylvania and land south of the Ohio River. Some of the New World adventurers aimed to buy up land without Indian consent; the Vandalia Company, which boasted Benjamin Franklin of Philadelphia as one of the promoters, sought 10 million acres in the Ohio Valley at £1 for every 1,000 acres.

In another scheme promoted by Franklin, Sir William Johnson pressed for the Crown to grant them land to be called *Charlotiana*. In 1751, Benjamin Franklin, an autodidact and polymath, predicted, in *'Observations Concerning the Increase of Mankind'*, that the rapidly growing American population would exceed that of Great Britain and that territorial expansion would lie at the heart of economic growth.

> So vast is the territory of North America that it will require many ages to settle it fully; and till it is settled, labor will never be cheap here, where no man continues long a laborer for others but gets a plantation of his own, no man continues long a journeyman to trade, but goes among those new settlers and sets up for himself.[12]

At heart Franklin was an imperialist who, like George Washington, believed in a vast Anglo-American Empire stretching to the Pacific.

Not surprisingly, these vested interests were infuriated by the Royal Proclamation of 1774 which sought to protect the property rights of native Indians. It is unlikely that the British government's motives were high-minded in their protection of the 'Indian Race'. Trouble with the Indians would have to be dealt with at British military and taxpayers' expense. It seems very likely that the British government's efforts to restrain the land-grabbing tendencies of the American colonists were every bit as significant in creating the ground swell of discontent against Britain as the raising of taxes, the granting of a tea monopoly to the East India Company or the lack of American political representation back in London. Also it could not have gone unnoticed that independence would liberate southern estate owners from the obligation of loan repayments to London's financiers; plantation owners became staunch supporters of the revolution.

The so-called Boston Tea Party, where a young group known as the Sons of Liberty dressed themselves up as Mohawks and tipped a cargo of 342 tea chests belonging to the East India Company into the sea, was followed by the Coercive Acts in June 1774 which closed the port of Boston and changed the government of Massachusetts. What may have horrified the other colonies more, however, was the 1774 Quebec Act whereby the British government extended the boundaries of that province to cover all the territories to the west of the Appalachians and north of the Ohio River. The First Continental Congress subsequently met at the Carpenter's Hall in Philadelphia on 5 September 1774 and passed a declaration of rights and grievances which preceded the formal military hostilities, which began in 1775.

The War of Independence which followed was in effect as much a civil war as a war against the English where vested interest in the outcome was finely balanced. The surrender of General Burgoyne to the rebel forces at Saratoga in October 1777 was a key factor in bringing the French on board in formal alliance against the British, and it was the victory of American and French forces under Lafayette at Yorktown in October 1781 which proved decisive to the outcome of the war.

Notably, however, the last action of the war was against a raiding party of pro-British Shawnee Indians at Chillicothe in Ohio in 1782. The British continued to hold New York, Charleston, Savannah and Detroit, and the British fleet, following the 1782 defeat of the French fleet by Admiral Rodney at the Battle of the Saints (near Guadaloupe), continued to command America's long East Coast; however, British political will to maintain their incipient American Empire was broken. At home many Englishmen would have agreed with Richard Hayes, a yeoman farmer from Kent, that the conflict in America was an 'unnatural war against our best allies or friends the Americans'.[13]

With victory assured, George Washington, in his last Circular to the States issued in June 1783, launched a long history of American utopianism when, ignoring the land and commercial motives for independence, he declared that the creation of America 'seemed to be peculiarly designated by Providence for the display of human greatness and felicity. Heaven has crowned its other blessings by giving the fairest opportunity for political happiness than any other nation which would have a meliorating influence on all mankind'.[14]

Yet the reality of the American Revolution was more accurately noted by Washington's contemporary and military accomplice the South American revolutionary General Francisco de Miranda, who was appalled by what he considered to be the low level of debate in the new American Congress with its obsession with land and trade: 'Why, in a democracy whose basis is Virtue, is there no place assigned to it? On the contrary all the dignity and powers are given to Property, which is the blight of such a democracy.'[15]

Miranda was wrong; far from being a 'blight on democracy', it was the American obsession with property which gave the new country and democracy its strength. Despite the grandiloquent utopian rhetoric of the US's early leaders, in the outcome of the American Revolution and, clearly reflecting the causes of the conflict, it was conservative middle-class values such as order and property which won out against radical men and their ideas.

Property was a theme which was to have enduring resonance in American history and culture. The Hollywood 'western' as a genre is largely built on protecting the rights of the homesteader or rancher. Also it is not coincidental that the most popular film in American history, *Gone with the Wind* (1939), based on Margaret Mitchell's civil war novel of the same name, starts with the heroine, Scarlett O'Hara, being scolded by her father, 'Why, land's the only thing in the world worth working for, worth fighting for, worth dying for, because it is the only thing that lasts.'[16]

The recurring theme of the book and film is the need to find money to fight for survival and to secure land – namely O'Hara's cotton plantation, Tara. After countless misfortunes including murder, rape, pillage, the death of children and broken marriages, the film ends, not with a reflection on these tragedies, but with more 'materialistic' sentiments being reprised by a ghostly voice speaking to the film's heroine: 'Land's the only thing that matters, it's the only thing that lasts.'[17]

Westward Expansion and the Louisiana Purchase

If the British will to conquer had been temporarily halted, the newly victorious 13 colonies, which with some difficulty cobbled together a federal constitution, embarked almost immediately on an energetic land grab with a rapaciousness that would alarm even the empire-building Europeans. In defiance of the Royal Proclamation, entrepreneurs had crossed the Appalachians to settle at Watauga in 1769; with the war over, American settlers poured into the fertile and abundant lands of Kentucky and Tennessee. They duly became the 15th and 16th states of the union (after Vermont, the 14th state, which, under their property-dealing leader, Ethan Allen, had split away from New York).

This was not a land grab ordered by America's new federal government. Although Articles of Confederation had been adopted by the Congress on 15 November 1777, the limits of the federal powers were such that in 1781 Rhode Island was able to defeat a proposal for a 5 per cent customs duty which would have provided the federal government with income. The desire for land came from the pioneering individuals' quest for adventure and financial reward. Nevertheless, this 'bottom-up' approach was no less effective and perhaps more so than the continental European style of state-sponsored empire building.

'Go West young man' may well have become the familiar mantra to the fortune seeker, but it soon became a fiscal necessity for the union's financially hard-pressed government. Secession by the USA of all land south of Canada, north of Ohio, west of the Alleghenies and east of the Mississippi enabled Congress to finance its operations by selling land; thus, sales of 1.5 million acres to the Ohio Company of Associates were done at nine cents per acre. A perfect symbiosis thus developed that nurtured in America's fledgling state a genus of expansionary zeal. 'For a century to come, the subduing of the temperate regions of North America was to be the main business of the United States.'[18] Indeed, ownership of property under law stood at the heart of the new nation; as John Adams, America's second president wrote, 'Property must be secured, or liberty cannot exist.'[19] It cannot be overestimated how the simple free market model, whereby the General Land Office in Washington and its 40 district offices sold off land at low prices to first comers, served to build a vibrant and populous nation.

By the time that the state government (bar Rhode Island) had accepted Alexander Hamilton's written invitation to meet for a Federal Convention in Philadelphia, from which the American Constitution emerged in September 1787, the empire established by the American colonies had expanded beyond the Appalachian boundaries of the 13 colonies and had advanced as far as the Mississippi. The attempt by Spain to introduce a buffer state between the Appalachians and the Mississippi failed to thwart the onward rush of the New World pioneers.

The Philadelphia Convention reflected the youthful spirit and energy of the USA. Most of the participants (including Hamilton aged 32 and Madison aged 36) were in their 30s or younger. Within less than five years of defeating Britain, one of Europe's greatest powers, America, with a population of just 4 million people (including some 70,000 slaves), controlled an area equal to Britain, Germany, Spain and France combined. It was a largely rural community with an urban population of just 3 per cent and only six cities with a population exceeding 8,000.

But the young nation already had enemies. Britain to the north controlled the Canadian provinces and insisted on its rights over Oregon; France, whose pro-independence leaders such as Lafayette were now either in exile or dead, was in trade dispute with America, while Spain, which, since the peace with England in 1763, had controlled the Mississippi and its port head at New Orleans, watched anxiously as American entrepreneurs cast covetous eyes over the Louisiana territories which extended all the way from the Mississippi to the Rocky Mountains and from Canada to the Mexican border.

A Spanish Empire in decline may not have been the most formidable of America's first continental enemies, but Spain soon paled into insignificance when the victories won by Napoleon Bonaparte in Spain for the 'Directory' precipitated the transfer of Louisiana to France. The move created near panic in Washington; President Jefferson wrote in April 1802: 'Nothing since the Revolutionary War has produced such uneasy sensations through the body of the nation.'[20] The young

American nation now faced an army sent by Napoleon to secure France's New World possessions; conflict must have appeared inevitable when, in a classic display of Colbertist protectionism, American merchants were denied access to the strategically crucial port of New Orleans. Fortunately for the USA, on their way to America via Guadaloupe, 30,000 of Napoleon's most experienced troops and his brother-in-law commander, General Leclerc, were lost to the ravages of yellow fever; Napoleon, in desperate need of funds to renew hostilities with Britain, instructed Talleyrand to negotiate a sale of the Louisiana territories.

In probably the greatest property deal ever recorded, 'The Louisiana Purchase', America snapped up an area much larger than the modern state of the same name, comprising some 530 million acres of mainly excellent farming land stretching in the north as far as the Canadian border, for US$ 15 million (including US$ 3.75 million of French debts to American citizens) on 30 April 1803. The purchase merely whetted the American government's appetite for further expansion. Just a year later in May 1804, President Jefferson persuaded Congress to authorise and finance a secret expedition from the New Territories to explore the best routes as far as the Pacific Ocean. The expedition initiated the famous 'Oregon Trail', stretching from Missouri to Oregon, down which the early pioneers would venture to settle the West.

American Setback in Canada

Having completed so easy an acquisition of a country the size of Europe, America's next target appeared to be Canada. When President Madison took the country into a war with England in 1812, it was with the full expectation that the English would finally be driven out of North America. This was the sincere wish of Madison's long-time mentor Thomas Jefferson; he wrote to Madison predicting that

> The acquisition of Canada this year as far as the neighborhood of Quebec, will be a mere matter of marching, and will give us experience for the attack on Halifax next, and the final expulsion of England from the American continent.[21]

However, bad generalship and the reluctance of the New England states to engage in military adventurism undermined the whole campaign; the hubris of the Washington establishment was devastatingly exposed when a British expeditionary force under Sir George Cockburn marched into Washington with 1,200 troops; the 8,000 American troops supposedly guarding the capitol simply evaporated. Defeat brought to the fore the remarkable backwoodsman Andrew Jackson, who routed the British forces at New Orleans and thereby secured America's ability to exploit the Louisiana Purchase.

Both sides now wanted peace, and the Treaty of Ghent secured the long-term status quo and basis for future friendship between England and America. Castlereagh, Britain's foreign minister, was the first British statesman to accept the existence of the USA and its place in the international political order; it was a strategy which enabled both countries to further the expansion of the Anglo-Saxon Empires. Emperor Joseph II of Austria could not have been more wrong when he concluded after the loss of the American colonies that Britain was 'fallen entirely and forever . . . descended to the status of a second-rank power, like Sweden or Denmark'.[22] On the contrary, the respective Anglo-Saxon Empires now went from strength to strength.

The Alamo and the Annexation of Texas and Florida

America's next land grab required some tidying up of its East Coast. Florida had remained under the Spanish flag, but by 1817 its loosely governed cities did not have the administrative or military strength to control its own native populations, the *Seminole* (part of the *Creek* nation), who had taken to committing atrocities against American settlements. President Monroe ordered General Andrew Jackson, later president and founder of the Democratic Party, to deal with the situation. This he easily accomplished by ejecting the Spanish administrations of St. Marks and Pensacola. Florida was theirs for the taking. In a pattern that was to become familiar over the course of the next century and a half, America planted a fig leaf over its naked territorial ambitions by concluding a purchase of the state for US$ 5 million; essentially it was an offer the Spanish could not refuse. The 1819 Treaty of Florida (or Adams–Onis Treaty) also provided an added bonus with the transfer to America of the Spanish claim to the Oregon territories, though it should be added that in the previous year the USA and Britain had signed a 'convention' whereby Oregon would be treated as jointly owned.

The conquest of Florida illustrated the growing importance of both the Caribbean and South America. The immediate linkages were trade, but from 1815 the rapid spread of revolutionary movements produced a domino effect as seven new republics in as many years overthrew their European rulers. President Monroe recognised the new South American states in 1822 and, in a speech on 2 December 1823, set what would later be regarded as the framework for America's future foreign policy when he claimed for his country the right to protect all the Americas from foreign interference.

> . . . the occasion has been judged proper for asserting as a principle in which the rights and interests of the United States are involved, that the American continents, by the free and independent condition which they have assumed and maintained, are henceforth not to be considered as subject for future colonization by any European powers. . . . We owe it, therefore, to candor and the amicable relations existing between the United States and those powers, to declare that we should consider any attempt on their part to extend their system to any portion of this hemisphere as dangerous to our peace and safety.[23]

That statement, which after the American civil war came to be known as the Monroe Doctrine, remains the single most important canon of American foreign policy.

Monroe's 1823 speech also rejected the notion that America would necessarily support the liberation movements of other countries. 'With the existing colonies or dependencies of any European power we have not interfered and shall not interfere.' Monroe goes to assert that 'In the wars of the European powers in matters relating to themselves we have never taken part, nor does it comport with our policy so to do.'[24] As we shall see, these aspects of the Monroe Doctrine were soon challenged by international events and later by the start of the First and Second World Wars; in the latter, President Roosevelt would openly challenge the right of the European nations to have their own empires. Roosevelt's successor, Harry Truman, would later expand the Monroe Doctrine to cover Western Europe, the Middle East and Asia.

The broad expulsion of Spain and Portugal from their colonial conquests did not necessarily make the new South American Republics happy bedfellows with their northern counterparts. Mexico had superseded Spain in its claims to Texas. Although the USA had relinquished any claim to Texas at the Treaty of Florida, President John Quincy Adams and his successor Andrew Jackson continued to press the Mexican government for the sale of the territory. Again the work of territorial expansion was done by pioneers on the ground. Ignoring territorial claims, American settlers pushed forward into the huge expanse of Texas.

By 1830, Austin, a colony based on land granted by Moses Austin to his son Stephen, had grown to 5,000 Americans plus slaves; these slaves were illegally held since Mexico, unlike the US, had, by decree of President Guerrero, abolished slavery in 1829. Surprisingly, the Mexican government seemed happy to attract American pioneers to fill their sparsely populated territory and by 1830 Americans outnumbered Mexicans by three to one; it was a strategy that could work for the Mexican government only as long as the new settlers remained content with Mexican suzerainty.

That uneasy balance was broken in 1835 when Mexican President Antonio de Padua Maria Saverino López de *Santa Anna* y Pérez de Lebron abolished Texan state rights as part of a constitutional unification. Mexico's unruly American immigrants proceeded to revolt. There followed the legendary siege of the Alamo by *Santa Anna*'s Mexican Army, in which the iconic frontier characters, David Crockett and Jim Bowie, and the other American rebels, laid down their lives fighting to the last man. The heroic defence of the Alamo did for Texas what the Battle of Thermopylae did for the Greeks; it created an enduring legend of a heroic defence of the homeland against an overwhelming force of foreign invaders. 'Remember the Alamo' was a legend which completely obscured the reality of a land grab by American settlers, which enabled America to take Texas by force from Mexico.

The Texans were revenged at the Battle of Jacinto, an ambush which succeeded in capturing President *Santa Anna* himself. Having thus won their rebellion, the Texans proceeded to pass a constitution and elect Sam Houston to the presidency. On his last day in office, 3 March 1837, President Jackson recognised Texas as an independent country. It remained an independent nation for barely eight years before President Tyler annexed Texas for the USA.

The Mexican War and the Seizure of California and Oregon

If the expansion of the original 13 states of the union had proceeded at a breathless pace with little articulation of its aims, from the 1840s the American expansion was about to enter its most vociferously imperialistic phase. As with most empires, the excuse for the next stage of America's land grab was defence of the realm; however, a deterministic historical and moral case for empire found its most articulate proponent in the form of President James Knox Polk in 1845.

The 'roaring 40s', as they came to be called, saw the idea of American imperialism become rampant. In 1845 a Congressman affirmed that 'This continent was intended by Providence as a vast theater on which to work out the grand experiment of Republican government, under the auspices of the Anglo-Saxon race.'[25] The term 'manifest destiny', which came to define the logic of American imperialism, was also coined in the same year. John L. O'Sullivan complained in the *Democratic Review* that foreign powers might limit 'the fulfillment of our *manifest destiny* to overspread the continent allotted by Providence for the free development of our yearly multiplying millions'.[26]

Washington politicians were also alerted to the possibilities of California by the travel book entitled *Two Years before the Mast* in 1840. The writer Richard Dana travelled aboard the Pilgrim out of Boston in 1834 and, arriving in California, became captivated by its charms, if not by its people:

> The men are thriftless, proud, extravagant, and very much given to gaming; and the women have but little education, and a good deal of beauty, and their morality, of course, is none the best.... Such are the people who inhabit a country embracing four or five hundred miles sea-coast, with several good harbors; with fine forests in the North; the waters filled with fish, and the plains covered with thousands of herds of cattle; blessed with a climate than which there can be no better in the world; free from all manner of diseases, whether epidemic or endemic; and with a soil in which corn yields from seventy to eighty fold. In the hands of an enterprising people, what a country this might be![27]

The workaholic Polk, who had read *Two Years before the Mast*, arrived in office with a determination to resolve the Oregon issue in America's favour and also to conclude the acquisition of California, another Mexican territory. His fear was that England or France would claim them first. It was a breathtaking assumption on the part of Polk. As an area, California, apart from Richard Dana's book, was little known to the American government in spite of the hide and tallow trade which had started there in 1821. It was only in 1843 that Polk organised an exploration of the area under the command of the 28-year-old Second Lt John Frémont, who discovered California's fertile lands and reached the Pacific coast with the help of the legendary guide Kit Carson. Frémont – soldier, explorer, adventurer and politician – would eventually join the California Gold Rush and become in 1856 the first Republican presidential candidate.

In 1846, Polk provoked a war with Mexico when he sent troops to occupy disputed border areas. When a mission by Congressman John Slidell to purchase these territories failed, Polk used a border clash in Texas over the disputed Rio Grande, in which a small number of American troops were killed, as an excuse for the USA to mobilise for war. No doubt, Polk's ardour for war to avenge the supposed slights on America's Texan border would have been resolved if Mexico had not rejected an offer of US$ 5 million for its territories. In July 1846, Commodore Sloat raised the American flag at Monterey, and California was declared a territory of the USA.

Over the next two years, Captain Robert E. Lee established his reputation as a great commander, in a brilliant campaign culminating in the defeat of the Mexican army at Churubusco; further battle victories followed in early 1847 and finally at Molino del Rey on 8 September. With the impending arrival of American armies in front of Mexico City, the Mexican government surrendered. In California meanwhile, the Spanish population was soon overwhelmed and ruthlessly suppressed.

At the Peace Treaty of Guadalupe-Hidalgo on 2 February 1848, Mexico gave up its rights to Texas, the Rio Grande boundaries and Upper California, amounting to some 55 per cent of its country; the lands included in this latter parcel would later constitute the states of California, Utah, Nevada, New Mexico and Arizona as well as parts of Colorado and Wyoming. For America a modicum of respectability was applied to this annexation of a neighbour's territories by the granting to Mexico of US$ 15 million in compensation.

By the time Polk had concluded the Treaty of Guadalupe-Hidalgo, he had already secured Oregon for the USA. This territory, which had been subjected to the past claims of France, Spain, Russia and Great Britain, was effectively conquered by the American pioneers of the Oregon Trail. In 1831 Hall J. Kelley had founded 'The American Society for Encouraging Settlement of the Oregon Territory', and this provided the launch pad for expeditions in 1832 and 1834. In spite of the perilous conditions endured by the early trailblazers, including starvation, Indian attacks or simply getting lost, some 4,000–5,000 people had settled in Oregon by 1845. As had been seen previously in Texas and elsewhere, physical possession of the land proved the key determinant of ultimate sovereignty.

With Spain and France out of the picture, Great Britain was now the main stumbling block to a final resolution of the Oregon issue. The 1814 Treaty of Ghent had left the Oregon issue unresolved with both parties agreeing to disagree. However, when Polk finally opened negotiations with a claim to Oregon up to latitude 54°, Britain responded with a proposal for latitude 49°, which took the Canadian

border as far as the Puget Sound. The Oregon Treaty of 15 June 1846 was a compromise agreement which both parties could live with. Whatever his expansionist
instincts, Polk did not intend to add a war with Great Britain to his agenda.

The final piece of the expansion to make up what now consists of America's
southern border was the purchase of another slice of Northeastern Mexico, an
area to the east of the Rio Grande and incorporating such towns as Tucson and
Tombstone in what is now Southern Arizona and part of New Mexico. The so-
called 1853 Gadsden Purchase for US$ 10 million was done principally to aid the
construction of a railroad to link the East Coast with Southern California; (the
Gadsden Purchase, named after the US ambassador to Mexico who negotiated the
treaty, eventually proved its worth but, as a result of the interruption of the civil
war, the South Pacific Railroad project did not get off the ground until 1865).
Indeed, now that America's continental acquisitions were completed, the next half
century was given over to filling out the infrastructure and population of their vast
new empire.

Railroads and Territorial Consolidation

Less well known than other aspects of the 1787 American Constitution, the banning of interstate tariffs formed a backbone to the economic advance of the fledgling
nation. As the nation advanced its empire westward, the business and economic
attractions to the building of transport and communications structure were self-
evident.

At first the Pony Express and subsequently Wells Fargo provided the key communication linkages with the new territories, but the invention of an electric telegraph by Samuel Morse in 1837 and subsequent chartering of the Western Union
Telegraph Company in 1856 transformed the technology of communication. Even
more significant was the rapid improvement being made in railway technology.
Rivers and canals, such as the Erie, which linked the Atlantic Ocean with the Great
Lakes of Illinois, had provided the earliest transportation links ferrying homesteaders to the virgin lands of the Midwest, but it was only the railroad that could overcome the mountain barriers that stood in the way of linking the markets of east
and west.

However, while railroads linking the East Coast to the Mississippi River were
largely completed by the 1840s, it was not until 1869 that the first transcontinental
railway was completed in Utah at the juncture of the Union Pacific coming from
Omaha, Nebraska, and the Central Pacific Railroad coming from Sacramento, California. The railway brought people as well as trade to America's continental empire. The building of up to eight miles of track per day needed as many as 20,000
labourers (many of them Chinese); it was a vast logistical task which brought infrastructure and habitation in its wake.

The importance of the railroad was foretold by Leland Stanford, the founder of Central Pacific, who envisaged,

> railroads bearing to and fro the produce and merchandise of each extreme. I shall look out through the Golden Gate and I shall see there fleets of ocean steamers bearing the trade of India, the commerce of Asia, the traffic of the islands of the ocean. . . .[28]

Stanford's vision, however, did not extend to regulating the near-monopolistic position enjoyed by his railroad. In one recorded instance, a Central Pacific official, having doubled the transport costs of sending ore from a prospering mine, suggested that the mining company submit its account books for inspection so that they could determine what the company could afford.

However, Central Pacific's monopoly was short-lived; four more transcontinental routes soon followed: the Southern Pacific (enabled by the Gadsden Purchase), the Northern Pacific, the Santa Fe and the Great Northern. Before 1865 America had built 35,000 miles of railroad; eight years later that mileage had more than doubled, and by 1900 there were some 200,000 miles of track, more than the whole of Europe combined. The results were dramatic; the journey from east to west now took just one week compared to four months previously.

Genocide: The Destruction of the American Indian

In the course of America's headlong rush for empire at the expense of its European competitors, the rights of the indigenous tribes, the American Indians, were barely considered by any of the incomers. Although land purchase was favoured by the earlier settlers, force of arms soon became an expedient alternative. However, the extermination of the Indians began in earnest after the 1812–14 war against Britain, in which many of the tribes were armed by the British to fight America. The lead was taken by then Major General Jackson, who revenged an Indian massacre by surrounding and destroying the *Creek* settlement at Talushatchee; Davie Crockett, the noted Tennessee sharpshooter, later recorded that 'We shot them like dogs.'[29]

The subsequent 'burnt earth policy', whereby all villages and crops were destroyed and the Indian tribes massacred, brought about the capitulation of the main *Creek* chief, Red Eagle, on 14 April 1814. Jackson, the land speculator, was delighted with a deal which ceded to America half of the *Creek* lands. To a business partner Jackson wrote, 'I finished the convention with the *Creeks* . . . [which] cedes to the United States 20 million acres of the cream of the *Creek* Country, opening a communication from Georgia to Mobile.'[30]

Jackson embarked on Indian policies, which by today's standards would be considered genocidal; between 1816 and 1850 the Indian tribes located between the original 13 colonies and the Mississippi were effectively wiped out or removed. In some 40 treaties the *Cherokees*, *Chickasaws*, *Choctaws*, *Creeks* and *Seminoles* were forced to sign away their lands to the American government. Becoming president in 1829, Andrew Jackson outlined a policy that would relocate all of the Indian nations from the east. The 1830 Indian Removal Act sanctioned the transfer of 100,000 Indians to the west; in theory the removals were voluntary, but in practice enormous pressure was put on Indian tribes to get out.

Notwithstanding ineffectual federal laws on Indian policy passed in the 1790s, the US actions towards its indigenous population, which would have been considered barbaric in the latter twentieth century, were completely normal in a society which had come into existence through territorial conquest and subjugation; for Americans the destruction of the Indians, while never a conscious policy, was the natural outcome of economic and military superiority. Nevertheless, it caused one of the earliest recorded genocides by a modern nation state, a genocide for which many American presidents have subsequently apologised.

The *Cherokee* tribes of Georgia were particularly harshly treated. Although the *Cherokees* had increasingly adopted western ways of agriculture and settlement, even intermarrying with Scottish traders to create an 'intellectual' subset of the *Cherokee* nation, they had by 1819 lost 90 per cent of their tribal lands. The finding of gold in Georgia in 1828, followed two years later by President Jackson's signing of the Indian Removal Act, sealed their fate. Lotteries were held to offer *Cherokee* land and its gold rights to American pioneers; meanwhile, Georgian state laws were passed to prevent *Cherokees* from entering business contracts, from testifying in court and from mining gold even on their own land.

When these laws were successfully challenged in the Supreme Court, President Jackson reportedly declared that '[Chief Justice] John Marshall has made his decision; let him enforce it now if he can.'[31] The *Cherokee* nation was finally coerced into ceding their lands at the Treaty of New Echota in 1835. In 1838 the *Cherokee* tribes were rounded up in stockades and families separated while their farmsteads were looted. Some were transported by boat, rail or wagon, but 12,000 *Cherokees* were split into groups of 1,000 and were forced to march westward on what became known as the 'Trail of Tears'. The poorly provisioned Indians died from lack of water and food. The dire conditions also brought fatal diseases. Some simply died from cold in the harsh winter conditions. By the time the bedraggled groups arrived in the west by spring of 1839, one-third, accounting for about 20 per cent of the *Cherokee* nation, had died.

California's Indians were next to be decimated. Prior to the 1849 California Gold Rush, the number of Indians in the territory was estimated at over 100,000; within a decade that number was reduced to just 35,000. Diseases, particularly smallpox, cholera and venereal ailments, wiped out swathes of the native population; conditions and life expectancy may have been harsh for the American settlers but, unlike the Indians, their replacements were pouring into the port of New York.

The treatment of the Eastern Indians and the collapse of California's Indian population provided a foretaste of what was to come in the newly acquired western territories. In the Great Plains and Rocky Mountains the pioneering settlers were confronted by *Sioux, Blackfeet, Crow, Cheyenne* and *Arapahoe* in the north and by the *Comanche, Kiowa, Ute, Apache* and *Southern Arapahoe* in the south. The unending oncoming rush of the settlers could not be halted. Within a generation the buffalo herds, on which the tribes of the Great Plains had fed, were exterminated and with it an ancient way of life. The structure of Indian life was destroyed; the ancient no-madic, hunter-gatherer societies could not survive the population onslaught from the east. New technologies including railways, farming and ranching with fences, property rights, the Colt repeater pistol and the Winchester rifle overwhelmed the indigenous populations of the west.

The era was marked by notable atrocities. In 1864 the *Cheyenne* confined to an 'Indian post' at *Sand Creek* were murdered en masse by Colonel Chivington. A former Methodist preacher, Chivington, and his militiamen were recruited by Governor John Evans of Colorado to eradicate the *Cheyenne* and *Arapahoe* tribes after they refused to either sell their land or agree to settlement on Indian reserva-tions. On the pretext of a few violent incidents, Chivington attacked Indian villages and raised them to the ground.

At Sand Creek, a peaceable tribal chieftain called *Black Kettle* and his encamp-ment were attacked with canon and rifles. Fleeing men, women and children were butchered. Robert Bent witnessed the slaughter; he later recounted that

> they sent out a little girl about six years old with a white flag on a stick; she had not proceeded but a few steps when she was shot and killed. . . . The squaws offered no resistance. Every one I saw dead was scalped. I saw one squaw cut open with an unborn child. . . . I saw the body of White Antelope with the privates cut off, and I heard a soldier say he was going to make a tobacco pouch out of them. . . .'[32]

Given these events, Black Kettle was remarkably restrained when he complained that 'I once thought that I was the only man that persevered to be the friend of the White man, but since they came and cleaned out our lodges, horses and everything else, it is hard for me to believe white men any more.'[33]

The unrelenting march of the Westerners may have suffered a famed reverse when General Custer and his troop of 264 men were killed by the *Sioux* at Little Big Horn in 1876, but by this date the end game of Indian extermination was already in sight. Gold had been found in the Black Hills belonging to the *Sioux*, and the miners could pay for protection whatever the niceties of law. The *Sioux* warrior Crazy Horse was captured and then murdered, while Chief Sitting Bull was put into an Indian reservation before being 'rescued' to appear in Buffalo Bill's 'Wild West Show' in Europe.

With the removal of the Indian threat, commercial development of the Great Plains could begin. Between 1866 and 1888, cowboys drove some 6 million head of cattle from Texas for wintering on the high plains of Colorado. Competition came from sheep farmers and settlers, who under the 1862 Homesteader Act were granted 160 acres of land as long as it was farmed for five years. Competition for land and water resources spurred numbers of range wars and became the bedrock of the Hollywood 'Western'. The Lincoln County War of 1878 spawned the career of legendary gunfighter William Bonney, alias Billy the Kid, while competition between cattle barons and homesteaders resulted in the 1892 Johnson County War, sometimes known as the Wyoming Civil War; this episode was reprised in Michael Cimino's epic 'western' *Heaven's Gate* (1980). The short-lived life of the open range came to an end after a series of harsh winters in the late 1880s and was gradually replaced by fenced-in ranches.

It was only with the completion of the destruction of the American Indian, involving, over the course of a century, more than 1,250 military engagements with the indigenous tribes, that the government in Washington was spurred into action to define an Indian policy. Although the East Coast establishment may frequently have been appalled by the numerous atrocities committed against the Indians, it was unlikely that the animal spirits of the frontiersmen could have been restrained even if they had tried.

When the 1887 Dawes Act arrived, it was designed more to civilise and incorporate the Indians into American life than to defend their ancient rights. It took another 14 years before the five so-called civilised tribes of Oklahoma were offered American citizenship. Remarkably, it was only in 1924 that citizenship of America was granted to all Indians; there can be no more telling indication that the Indian natives were a conquered and largely eradicated race and victims of the astonishing advance of the American Empire. Even after the Dawes Act, Indian land holdings declined from 138 million acres in 1887 to 48 million acres in 1937.

Population, Gold and the Pioneer Spirit

The American Empire, which so imbuded, was made possible, not so much by the grand designs of government but by the pioneering spirit which so imbucd America's early inhabitants. De facto, those who were prepared to uproot themselves from their European abodes to make the hazardous journey to the New World were inevitably pioneers by nature. A British observer noted that Americans venture

> as their avidity and restlessness incite them. They acquire no attachment to place; but wandering about seems engrafted in their nature; and it is weakness incident to it that they should forever imagine the land further off, are still better than those upon which they are already settled.[34]

Nothing typified this spirit more than the 1849 California Gold Rush; the gold-hunter and writer James Hutchings wrote,

> Never, since the Roman legionary shadowed the earth with their eagles, in search of spoil_ not even when Spain ravished the wealth of a world, or England devastated the Indies for its treasures_ never has such a gorgeous treasury been opened to the astonished world.[35]

Another speculator succumbing to the lure of gold wrote,

> Piles of Gold rose up before me at every step; castles of marble, dazzling the eye with
> their rich appliances; thousands of slaves bowing to my beck and call; myriads of fair
> virgins contending with each other for my love_ were among the fancies of my fevered
> imagination. The Rothschilds, Girards, and Astors appeared to me but poor people.
> In short, I had a violent attack of gold fever.[36]

The California Gold Fever initiated one of the greatest human transmigrations. Few were made wealthy, but the Gold Rush enabled the rapid population of the states of the Western seaboard; the potato famine in Ireland contributed a sizeable contingent, but in truth, gold fever spread the globe over. From South America, Australia, Europe and China, the speculators endured the hardships of passage and poured into San Francisco. By 1853 California's gold-hunters numbered more than 250,000; indeed, immigration into America as a whole reached a peak of 427,833 in 1854.

California was not the only new state to be populated by gold and mining generally. George Hearst, the most successful of the miners, went to the Black Hills of Dakota where he found ore which could be quarried rather than mined; he bought some 250 claims covering 2,600 acres. Albeit relatively low grade, the 'Homestake' mine became profitable in 1879 and in the next 20 years yielded profits of US$ 80 million. The Hearst fortune would later be turned into a vast media empire by William Randolph Hearst. Another great gold fortune was made by Leland Stanford, a New Yorker, who became a lawyer in Wisconsin before being lured to California to start a grocery and general store business; by taking shares in exchange for provisions, he became a prodigiously rich citizen of Sacramento which would lead to his chartering of the Leland Stanford Junior University in 1885 and its construction at a horse farm that he owned at Palo Alto.

Gold discovered in the Rocky Mountains near *Pike's Peak*, named after the military explorer Montgomery Zuberon Pike, brought thousands to Colorado and populated the cities of Denver and Boulder. The discovery of telluride (a compound of gold with the very rare metallic element tellurium: Te) provided the name of a booming Colorado mining town, spawning a wealthy bank which provided the first target for 'The Hole in the Wall Gang', whose leaders were immortalised in *Butch Cassidy and the Sundance Kid* (the 1969 film starring Robert Redford and Paul Newman). By 1880, however, it was Leadville which had become Colorado's second largest city. In Montana and Arizona it was the discovery of copper which provided the initial lure for pioneers. In Arizona the discovery of the famed Anaconda Mine allowed its owner Phelps-Dodge to dominate the economy and politics of the entire state. In 1896 the discovery of gold along the River Klondike brought an estimated 30,000 fortune hunters to Alaska.

America could not have expanded without people; perversely its growth was enabled by the industrialisation of Europe, which saw the continent's population rise from 150 million in 1750 to over 400 million by 1900. Emigration to America proved a natural outlet for this flow of humanity. When famine intermittently struck Europe, America with its vast and inexpensive stock of land now beckoned. From 1815 onwards, what had been a trickle of settlers turned into a flood, and some 100,000 people a year landed in America, without having to show any identification papers. Land was sold cheaply to the new setters in Georgia and Ohio. The 'American dream' was made possible by acquisition of land, and many of its leaders were prime beneficiaries. Both President Jackson and his Secretary of State Martin Van Buren became multi-millionaires on the back of land speculation.

Legends of the Conquest of America

The conquest of America was patriotically recalled in *How the West Was won*, a 1962 Hollywood epic; the movie traces the story of a single family, over four generations, who, starting in New York state, make their way westward to find land and fortune, ending up at the Pacific Ocean. This collaborative epic, directed by John Ford and other Hollywood titans, had a Hollywood ensemble star cast which included Spencer Tracy, Gregory Peck, James Stewart, Debbie Reynolds, John Wayne, Richard Widmark, George Peppard, Henry Fonda, Van Heflin, Lee Van Cleef and many others; it was a sentimental and unabashed glorification of American expansionism.

If the film glossed over some of the rougher and more unsavoury aspects of the great settler expansion across the American continent, the breadth of its story and thrust of its narrative truly reflected the extraordinary transformation wrought by the pioneering American families. Wyatt Earp, the US Marshall who became most famous for a gunfight at the O.K. Corral in Tombstone, Arizona, was a typical product of this generation of Americans. Ultimately, Earp's legendary career merged with the fictional world of Hollywood. He ended his life working as a consultant on 'Western' movies in Hollywood, sometimes appearing in them as an 'extra'. He befriended Hollywood actors. John Wayne recalled that his famed portrayals of cowboys were imbued with knowledge gleaned from meeting Wyatt Earp. The veteran gunslinger died at the age of 81 in Los Angeles and was buried in his wife's family's plot at the Little Hills of Eternity, a Jewish cemetery in Colma.

Earp's family history can be traced to the East Coast in 1787 when his paternal grandfather, later a school teacher and Methodist preacher, was born in Montgomery County, Maryland. They are thought to have been of Irish decent possibly arriving as indentured servants in the seventeenth century from Ireland with the name, Harp. They moved to North Carolina where Wyatt Earp's father, Nicholas Earp, was born, and later to Kentucky. Nicholas Earp served in the American army and named his son Wyatt after his commanding officer in the Illinois Mounted Volunteers with whom he fought in the Mexican–American War, which secured California and other territories for the rapidly expanding USA.

Wyatt Earp, born in Monmouth, Illinois, was soon moved by his father to a 160-acre farm in Pella, Iowa. Nicholas sold the farm six years later in 1856 and moved back to Monmouth, where he became a municipal constable. However, he returned to farming in Iowa, during which time Wyatt's elder brothers James, Virgil and Newton joined the Union Army to fight in the American Civil War. Afterwards the entire family joined a wagon train headed for California, and Wyatt gained his first employment as a stagecoach driver in Southern California. Wyatt then became a teamster, taking cargoes between Wilmington, California, and Prescott, Arizona, and subsequently took a job as a haulage supplier for the construction of the Union Pacific Railroad.

The Earps moved back east to Missouri in 1868, where Wyatt became the local constable. His first wife, Urilla, from New York City, died in childbirth. Subsequently, Wyatt Earp ran into difficulties over charges of fraud as well as horse thieving. He reappeared in Wichita, Kansas, in 1874 after several years spent, by some accounts, as the operator of a bordello in Peoria, Illinois, or, by other accounts, as a buffalo hunter. In Wichita he became a 'deputy' officer and, in this role, moved to Dodge City, Kansas, which had become a booming cattle town on the Santa Fe Trail. Here Wyatt became a deputy Marshall and befriended the legendary lawman, gunman and gambler Bat Masterson. Bat Masterson would eventually move back to New York where he became a close friend of President Roosevelt and ended his career as a highly successful sports writer and editor on the *New York Morning Telegraph*. His character was reprised as 'Sky Masterson' in the classic Broadway musical *Guys and Dolls* (1950).

Other friends included Shanghai Pierce, a legendary wild Texas cattleman, who made great fortunes driving his cattle from his coastal ranch on the Gulf of Mexico up to the Great Plains. Pierce would later travel the Orient and inspired the development of the famous American 'Brahman' breed of cattle, which mixed American and Indian cattle stock. Most famously, Wyatt Earp befriended Doc Holiday, a graduate of the College of Dental Surgery in Philadelphia, who, after contracting tuberculosis, headed for the drier climes of the Midwest and became a legendary gambler and gunfighter. With him came his girlfriend, 'Big Nose Kate', the Hungarian daughter of the physician to Emperor Maximillian of Mexico, who became a famous prostitute and constant consort to Doc Holiday.

In Dodge City, Wyatt made his mark. *The Dodge City Times* noted in July 1877 that 'He had a quiet way of taking the most desperate characters into custody. . . . It wasn't considered policy to draw a gun on Wyatt, unless you got the drop and meant to burn powder without any preliminary talk.'[37] Having made his reputation as a deputy Marshall on the wild 'Front Street' of Dodge City, where its patrons frequently ended by being carted up to be buried in Boot Hill, the Earps moved on to Tombstone, where Wyatt drove shotgun for Wells Fargo and invested in mining claims and also a gambling concession at the Oriental Saloon. After the O.K. Corral, a series of vendettas were played out in which Wyatt's brother Morgan was gunned down while they were playing pool, and Wyatt himself killed numbers of other cowboys in revenge. Earp headed for New Mexico and then Colorado, where he played faro at a local saloon in Gunnison.

Wyatt spent the last 46 years of his life with his third wife, 'Josie' Marcus. She was brought up in Brooklyn, New York, before being taken to San Francisco by her parents. At the age of 18, she was taken to see a production of Gilbert and Sullivan's *HMS Pinnafore* and immediately ran off with the theatre troupe. She became a dance hall girl and ended up fiancéed to the corrupt sheriff of Tombstone before switching her affections to Wyatt Earp.

In the mid-1880s Wyatt owned or leased four saloons in San Diego, the most famous of which was the Oyster Bar, located in the Louis Bank Building at 837 5th Avenue. He spent the next decade running gambling concessions and investing in mines in Colorado and Idaho. In 1896, having moved to Santa Rosa to become manager of a horse stable, Wyatt Earp officiated as referee in the Heavyweight World Boxing Championship between Bob Fitzsimmons (the heavyweight world champion from Cornwall) and Tom Starkey. (Earp disqualified Fitzsimmons on a technicality when Starkey was all but knocked out; it was often alleged that Earp was the beneficiary of a side bet.)

In the autumn of 1897 Wyatt and Josie moved again to follow the Alaska Gold Rush and ran saloons in Nome. Here Wyatt befriended Jack London, the renowned early-twentieth-century American writer. Eventually he returned to Los Angeles where he mixed with his Hollywood friends between working mining claims in the Mojave Desert.

The life of Wyatt Earp and his friends neatly encapsulates the animal spirits and peripatetic nature of the American settlers who made the conquest of the west possible and gave character to the relentless energy and bravado of the American nation. Even today the typical American has a far greater propensity to move from city to city than his European counterpart. It was an energy which could not be contained by the boundaries established at the Pacific Ocean. By the time that Doc Holiday, Wyatt Earp and his brothers were facing down the Clanton Gang at the O.K. Corral, other members of this aggressive American pioneer tribe were already bearing down on Asia.

Hawaii, Cuba and the Philippines: Empire Beyond the American Continent

With the completion of the conquest of the American continent by the middle of the nineteenth century (with only the acquisition of Alaska remaining), after a breathless expansion which had lasted barely more than 60 years since the 13 colonies had declared independence, the new nation could now turn its attention to international conquest. The independent monarchic nation of Hawaii, a third of the way across the Pacific, had only been discovered by Captain Cook's first expedition in 1776, when he happened upon Sandwich Island. The exotic islands became a convenient staging post for China traders and whaling ships; by the 1850s some 500 whaling ships a year were stopping for provisions in Hawaii.

Merchants were followed by American missionaries. In the early nineteenth century a largely congregational group of religious leaders set up a Board of Commissioners for Foreign Missions. In October 1819 a mission led by Hiram Bingham and Asa Thurton plus two teachers, a doctor, a printer and a mechanic set out from Boston for Hawaii aboard the *Thaddeus*. Some four years later the spread of Christianity made a momentous breakthrough among the chiefs and general population when Kaahumanu, the queen regent, was cured by Dr Holman.

Thereafter, American influence spread rapidly, and by 1848 some 184 missionaries had arrived in the islands. In a pattern that was to be repeated throughout Asia, American missionaries sought to instill Western mores even if this meant the destruction of traditional cultures and religions. In Hawaii the notoriously licentious behaviour of its people, integral to what was a communal tribal culture, was a particular object of attack. One American missionary complained that

> Hawaiians had about twenty forms of what he considered illicit intercourse, with as many different names in the language; so that if any one term were selected to translate the Seventh Commandment, it was bound to leave the impression that the other nineteen activities were still permitted.[38]

In spite of the difficulties, austere congregationalism prevailed. Writing of a visit in 1849, Henry Martin, a captain in the Royal Navy, no doubt brought up on the 'Paradise Island' legends of Captain Cook, complained that 'Sunday is kept strictly here as in Glasgow.'[39]

In the American tradition, missionaries were also alive to the possibilities of acquiring land. At first this was achieved through leasehold grants, but after sweeping American-inspired legal reforms in 1844, private ownership became the norm and many of the early missionary families became sugar plantation owners. In his history of the *Pacific Paradises* (1999), Trevor Lumis recalls the saying that 'the Hawaiians were taught to close their eyes in prayer, and when they opened them the land was gone'.[40] By the end of the century, Hawaiian ownership of their land was about 1 per cent of total acreage. Perhaps more remarkably, within 100 years of its discovery by Captain Cook, the good intentions of the missionaries managed to reduce the native population of the country from over 200,000 to less than 50,000.

Expansion of commercial and missionary control of the islands enabled the USA to beat off French and British efforts to secure Hawaii when the administration of President Ulysses S. Grant in 1875 concluded a treaty with Queen Liliuokalani, which guaranteed the country's independence in return for the granting of exclusive trading privileges for American companies. American global commercial expansionism had begun. In a renewal of the treaty 12 years later, the port of Pearl Harbor on the island of Oahu was ceded to the USA.

The 'protectorate' of Hawaii thus secured saw an influx of American capital for the development of the sugarcane industry. By 1890, American enterprises accounted for almost a 100 per cent of Hawaiian exports. However, the rising prosperity of Hawaii was dealt a fatal blow when President McKinley, seeking to protect American sugar plantations in the southern states from competition, granted them a two cents per pound bounty. In Hawaii land prices collapsed, leading to demands for annexation by American plantation owners. Meanwhile, Queen Liliuokalani, realising the dangers inherent in her country's over-reliance on American trade, sought both to restore her power and to reduce American influence. However, on 17 January 1893, she was deposed by a group of missionaries who masqueraded their coup d'état as a 'Committee of Safety'. Chief Justice Sanford B. Dole was subsequently appointed head of government, and he proceeded to negotiate with the USA for the annexation of Hawaii.

Although President Harrison was sympathetic to the idea of annexation, he left it to his successor to make a decision. Queen Liliuokalani appealed to President Grover Cleveland's sense of decency and justice when she said that 'I mistake the Americans if they favor the odious doctrine that there is no such thing as international morality; there is one law for a strong nation and another for a weak one.'[41] Yielding to her pleas, Cleveland sent a commission to Hawaii, which reported back negatively on the action and motives of the missionary plotters. However, the coup leaders refused to yield office, and Grover, using the argument that Hawaii was too weak to stand by itself and fearing the effect of Japanese immigration in particular, ultimately both declined to restore Hawaiian independence and agreed to annexation.

The last twist in this unsavoury episode was the refusal of the Senate to ratify the annexation of Hawaii by a formal treaty. Instead, the annexation was effected by a joint resolution by both governments on 7 July 1898. Two years later, citizenship was conferred on all Hawaii's inhabitants. However, it was only in 1959, when Hawaii's strategic value was recognised in the battle to control Asia after the Second World War, that America's colony was granted statehood. Colonial depredations committed by America were only finally recognised on 23 November 1993, when President Clinton signed an 'Apology Resolution' passed by Congress. The resolution recognised that prior to Western incursions, 'Hawaiian people lived in a highly organised, self-sufficient, subsistent, social system based on communal land tenure with a sophisticated language, culture and religion....'[42]

After Hawaii, America's acquisition of small countries advanced apace both in the Caribbean and in the Pacific. Puerto Rico was ceded to America by Spain in 1898. Two years later the USA and Germany agreed to divide up the Samoan Islands. Also protectorates were established for Cuba in 1901, the Dominican Republic in 1905, Nicaragua in 1911 and Haiti and Panama in 1915. In the following year, America purchased the Virgin Islands from Denmark.

America's rapid international advance was made possible by its increasing sea power. In 1880 America's naval fleet ranked just 12th in the world, but within a decade it advanced to third. With 17 battleships and 6 cruisers, America had become a great naval power by the end of the century. It enabled America's government to strut purposefully on the world stage. Cleveland's Secretary of State Olney now reinterpreted the meaning of the Monroe Doctrine: 'Today the United States is practically sovereign on this continent, and its fiat is law upon the subjects to which it confines its interposition. . . .'[43] If this statement alarmed the Latin American states, Olney also offended both Great Britain and Canada when he went on to say that 'Distance and three thousand miles of intervening ocean make any permanent political union between a European and American state unnatural and inexpedient.'[44]

American interest in the Caribbean and Cuba in particular was long standing. As early as 1848, President Buchanan had affirmed that 'We must have Cuba. We can't do without Cuba. . . . We shall acquire it by a coup d'état at some propitious moment.'[45] America would have to wait 50 years for the propitious moment, by which time acceptable political language had already toned down the idea of conquest for one of 'liberation'. The Cuban Revolution in 1898 brought American antipathy towards the European Empires to a head. Spurred by the social misery caused by falling sugar and tobacco prices, insurgents sought to liberate Cuba from Spain.

The Spanish colony had already fallen under American influence with some US$ 50 million of investment and a trade with America worth US$ 100 million per annum. American sympathies were with the rebels. When the battleship *USS Maine*, anchored in Havana Harbor, exploded and killed 260 American sailors, the USA launched into a frenzy of pro-Cuban support. In a letter, Theodore Roosevelt echoed the sentiments of many Americans when he said that 'The blood of the murdered men of the Maine calls not for indemnity but for the full measure of atonement, which can only come by driving the Spaniard from the New World.'[46] On the unproven assumption that the *USS Maine* had been attacked by the Spanish, President McKinley demanded Cuban independence. When Madrid refused, McKinley declared war. It was a victory easily won by the US navy.

Trade and the Expansion of America's Asian Interest

Even before the conquest of California and Oregon and the establishment of the Pacific seaboard, American traders were active in Hong Kong and other Asian ports. The right to trade, embedded in America's own revolution, lay at the heart of American support for its merchants. Thus, President Adams denounced the Chinese refusal to accept British opium 'as an enormous outrage upon the rights of human nature, and upon the first principles of the rights of nations'.[47] It was axiomatic that American traders, who became almost as complicit in the opium trade as the British, were owed military protection. As early as 1843, American marines had landed at Guangzhou (Canton) to protect Americans from Chinese mobs.

The completion of the US continental expansion gave a further boost to America's trading and commercial interests. In 1856 Andrew Hull Foote, commander of *USS Portsmouth*, after coming under attack from shore batteries, landed in Guangzhou (Canton) and defeated a 5,000-strong Chinese army. American interests were such as to justify the permanent stationing of a marine force for the protection of their diplomats, traders and missionaries, who flocked with increasing numbers into the Chinese mainland. After the Boxer Rebellion erupted in Shantung in 1900, American forces were despatched under European command to suppress the uprising.

Americans held firmly to the view that freedom to trade and exploit economic opportunities lay at the heart of foreign policy; it was the culture and the very blood of their revolution. The kernel of this truth lay in the origins of the 13 colonies' dispute with England. Alexander Hamilton, who set the financial and economic path for the newly independent colonies, went as far as to describe foreign policy as

> the freedom of American citizens, American goods, and American ships to travel wherever they wish in the world in the interests of peaceful trade. No sea, no ocean, no strait should be closed to American ships. Piracy must be suppressed, and foreign nations must abide by international law in their treatment of shipping . . . '.[48]

There is no better example of the building of America's development of its commercial empire than the opening of Japan to trade. This most famous example of gunboat diplomacy was carried out by the determined Commodore Perry. Born into a seafaring family in Newport, Rhode Island, Perry's life defined the growth of America's international power. As an aide to Commodore John Rogers, aboard the *USS President*, Perry participated in a successful engagement against the British shortly before the declaration of war in 1812. Between 1819 and 1820 he served on *USS Cyane* while it was patrolling the coast of Africa to suppress piracy and the slave trade. Later, while stopping in a Russian port, he was offered, but declined, a commission in the Russian navy; in a world of expanding global empires, good naval officers were in short supply.

Perry was a farsighted officer and an enthusiastic supporter of new technologies and the training they required. He helped develop the curriculum for the US Naval Academy and became a leading spokesman for naval modernisation. He oversaw the construction of the navy's second steamship, *USS Fulton*, and organised the first dedicated corps of naval engineers. In command of the *USS Fulton*, he conducted the first US naval gunnery school in 1839 before becoming the chief of the New York Navy Yard two years later. However, he was transferred to the command of the Africa Squadron in 1843 but was hastily brought back to command the Gulf of Mexico fleet in the Mexican–American War; in this capacity he captured Frontera, Tabasco and Laguna in 1846 and in 1847 supported the siege of Vera Cruz.

In 1852 Perry, with the urging of President Millard Fillmore, whose letter he carried, embarked from Norfolk, Virginia, determined to open up Japan for trade with America. A former venture had met with singular failure. In 1837, Charles King, an American businessman, had determined to open trade with Japan by the return of three shipwrecked Japanese seamen, but had been fired upon when he approached the Japanese coast. In 1846 Commander James Biddle, sent by the US government to demand a trade agreement, was also rebuffed.

Commodore Perry, however, was determined not to be denied. With *USS Mississippi*, *USS Plymouth*, *USS Saratoga* and *USS Susquehanna*, Perry dropped anchor in Uraga Harbor near Tokyo in July 1853. His black hulled steamships with their huge guns were terrifying to the Japanese, who immediately called them *Kurofune* (black ships of evil appearance). Bowing to this show of force, in spite of its forbidden and illegal entry into Japanese coastal waters, Perry was met by the Shogun's representatives who directed him to Nagasaki, the Dutch freeport, which was the only allowed entrance for foreigners into Japan. Perry refused and threatened to bombard Japan unless he was allowed to present President Fillmore's letter. The Japanese caved in and the Shogun's delegates duly received this letter near Yokosuka. This task accomplished, Perry then sailed to China and promised to return in expectation of a favourable reply. When he returned with double the number of warships in February 1854, America's demands for access were granted. On his return to China, Perry stopped at *Formosa* (later Taiwan), which he unsuccessfully tried to persuade the American government to annexe.

Inevitably, as American commercial and economic power grew, there developed the need to conduct an ever-increasing range of foreign policy and if necessary the international use of force. Even President Jefferson, who loathed international entanglements, was prepared to send naval expeditions to fight the Barbary pirates who were interfering with American trade. Indeed, 'freedom to trade' became an integral and unwavering part of all subsequent American foreign policy.

America's pursuit of 'freedom to trade', however, did not come with a belief in 'free trade'. British belief in 'free trade' did not carry to the USA, which continued to operate high-tariff policies until the Second World War. By contrast, Britain believed that it could benefit from free trade even when countries like America did not reciprocate. In 1790 Great Britain accounted for a sizeable 35 per cent of American exports, but a 100 years later this figure had expanded to 52.2 per cent. In effect, America enjoyed a free ride on the coat-tails of the British Empire. This even extended to Hong Kong and the opium trade in which American traders were major participants. Also, 'American businessmen . . . benefited enormously from sharing the language and the legal system of the world's hegemonic power.'[49]

The Philippines: Conquest and Suppression

In the late nineteenth century, Brooks Adams had declared that 'Our geographical position, our wealth, and our energy pre-eminently fit us to enter upon the development of South East Asia and to reduce it to part of our economic system.'[50] Curiously, it was America's Caribbean War with the Spanish that led to American domination of Asia. At the outbreak of war with Spain in 1898, the US fleet sailed from its base in Hong Kong to Manila Bay where they sought out and sank the Spanish fleet. At a stroke, the Philippines were conquered. The subsequent pacification took longer and cost an estimated 100,000 Filipino lives. Siding with the Philippines' establishment forces, the American army took several years to quell the *insurectos* led by Aguinaldo, American forces took several years to quell the Philippines establishment forces. However, the Philippines was considered too weak to risk it falling into the hands of stronger emerging empires than Spain; Germany and also Japan were particularly feared. Conveniently, the Filipinos were not deemed fit for government and President McKinley observed that '... there was nothing left for us to do but take them all, and to educate the Filipinos, and uplift and Christianize them'.[51]

The irony of the fact that America, in setting out to liberate Cuba, had ended by conquering the Philippines was not left unnoticed by many observers. Indeed, the inherent contradictions of America's 'pro-liberty' foreign policy towards Spain started a backlash against international adventurism and inspired a new morality in the conduct of foreign affairs. In concluding the Treaty of Paris on 10 December 1898, the American negotiators attempted to salve their consciences by forcing Spain to accept US$ 20 million in compensation for the Philippines.

However, in view of the Filipino insurrection which ended by killing more American troops than the Spanish War, McKinley decided not to buy Cuba on the basis that he did not want to buy into a conflict. Indeed, the 1898 Teller Amendment disclaimed any American rights for the annexation of Cuba. Nevertheless, fearing foreign interference, under the 1901 Platt Amendments, the USA gained a veto over Cuba's diplomatic and economic relations with other nations. Additionally in February 1903, America acquired a perpetual lease for a military base at Guantànamo Bay on the coast of Cuba. For the first time America declined an outright territorial expansion in return for a looser hegemonic interest; it was a turning point in America's approach to empire.

The Treaty of Paris marked the high-water mark of American Empire in the Pacific. For the 'imperialists' in Congress, the conquest of the Philippines was just the beginning of America's economic domination of Asia. Senator Albert Beveridge of Indiana declared that 'The Philippines are ours forever' and that

> just beyond the Philippines are China's illimitable markets. We will not retreat from either.... We will not renounce our part in the mission of our race, trustees of God, of the civilization of the world.... God has marked us as his chosen people, henceforth to lead in the regeneration of the world.... He has made us adept in government that we administer government among savages and senile people.[52]

In more moderate tone, Henry Cabot Lodge averred that 'the Philippines mean a vast future trade and wealth and power'.[53]

American Empire historian Professor John Whitehead has argued, however, that after the 1880s, the Imperial expansionists in Washington represented a limited factional interest rather than a broad political consensus. The post-civil war opening of the south and continental expansion within America provided more than enough economic opportunities for expansion without foreign adventure. Opposition to empire within the political system was significant. Apart from economic priorities, many, particularly on the East Coast, viewed the conquest of the Philippines as a violation of the spirit of the American Revolution, a view that would soon gain traction as the majority view with America's political leaders. George Hoare of Massachusetts believed that the USA was 'trampling on our own great Charter'.[54] In the end the Senate only ratified the assumption of the Philippines by 57 to 27, a bare one vote more than the statutory requirement for a two-thirds majority.

From the start, however, it was recognised that the Philippines would not be fully incorporated into the American political system. The 1902 Organic Act was passed to recognise the Philippine Islands as an 'unincorporated territory of the United States'. The act also created a legislature for the Philippines. American diplomatic pressure at the Vatican secured lands from the religious orders for distribution to the peasant classes. It was a start, albeit modest, on the land reform which continued to be one of the main political issues in the Philippines well after the Second World War. However, rapid advance was achieved in education where school attendance rose from 5,000 to over 1 million by 1920. Health also improved rapidly with death rate falling from 80 per thousand to 20 per thousand. Nevertheless, American interest was not altruistic. Exclusive access to the Philippines was provided for American businessmen. Pride in American expansionism was clearly displayed at the St. Louis World's Fair in 1904 when the organisers also turned it into a celebration, not only of the Louisiana Purchase, but also of global expansion. Notably the organisers revelled in the newly acquired colonies of the Philippines and imported six villages as a centrepiece to the trade fair.

Theodore Roosevelt, the Panama Canal and Economic Imperialism

In 1788 a French demographer, Messance, wrote that 'The people that last will be able to keep its forges going will perforce be the master; for it alone will have arms.'[55] The prophetic truth of this statement became apparent in the American Civil War where the north's superior industrial output eventually overwhelmed the south.

From the inception of the USA, its leaders, such as Benjamin Franklin, had been interested in technological advance and industry. Writing back to America, Thomas Jefferson had noted that 'I could write you volumes on the improvements which I find made ... one deserves particular notice ... the application of steam as an agent for working grist mills.'[56] While land and agriculture drove the early American economy, from the mid-nineteenth century, America enjoyed an industrial expansion matched only by Germany. At the international level, underpinning the rise of American power, industrialisation and its commitment to commerce was the engine that drove America's international expansion.

Although expansion of US interest into the Caribbean and South America is often associated with Theodore Roosevelt, the area had been considered the American 'back yard' since the Monroe Doctrine had warned off European interest. As American economic and political power grew, so did its proprietary relationship with South America. In 1895 when a border dispute erupted between British Guiana and Venezuela, President Grover threatened Britain with war unless the dispute was arbitrated.

Under Theodore Roosevelt, the arch exponent of 'Realpolitik', American interests continued to be advanced in South America. In 1901 the Hay–Paunceforte Treaty allowed for US construction and control of the Panama Canal (Panama being part of the territory of Colombia); the key condition was that it should be open to all nations on an equal basis. Originally the concession to build a canal had been owned by the French; however, the engineer, De Lesseps, who had succeeded in building the Suez Canal, failed in his attempt to repeat the success in Colombia. Congressional approval for the Panama Canal came with the passing of the 1902 Spooner Act, which authorised the purchase of the French concession for US$ 40 million; in addition, a 100-year lease with the Colombian government was negotiated for a 10-mile-wide canal zone for US$ 10 million plus US$ 250,000 per annum. However, the refusal of the Columbian legislature to ratify the agreements threatened to scupper the deal.

Faced by the delay or possible collapse of the canal project, Roosevelt was ruthless in the pursuit of American commercial interests. The secession of Panama from the Republic of Colombia was encouraged, and when Panama declared independence in 1903, it was done with the full support of the US navy. Over the next decade, US Army Corps of Engineers constructed a canal whose economic benefit to the USA was paramount. Roosevelt later candidly admitted that 'I took Panama.'[57] It was a measure of American guilt that in 1921 Colombia was paid off with US$ 25 million.

Although the Roosevelt era displayed both a pragmatic and an aggressive approach to dealing with America's colonies and protectorates, its international actions could nevertheless be interpreted as largely benign. In 1905 the USA effectively took over the management of the Dominican Republic when it was put in control of customs. Revenue was split between debt repayment (55 per cent) and current expenditure (45 per cent); outsourcing of governance achieved a remarkable transformation of Santo Domingo and the Dominican Republic economy. Roosevelt has often been portrayed as an 'Imperialist', but his approach to international expansion was solely calculated on pragmatic economic advantage; he had no ideology of empire. Other presidents might have absorbed the Dominican Republic, but Roosevelt stated that 'I have about the same desire to annex [the Dominican Republic] as a gorged boa constrictor might have to swallow a porcupine wrong-end-to.'[58]

America's increasing international power was also reflected in her ability to arbitrate settlements between other countries. In the aftermath of the Russo-Japanese War, which ended with the destruction of the Russian fleet at the Battle of Tsushima (the straits between Japan and Korea), Roosevelt brokered the Treaty of Portsmouth, a service whose reward was the embitterment of both sides. Later he would also intervene between France and Germany in the Moroccan Crisis of 1905 and urge France to participate at the Algeciras Convention to promote a North African settlement.

Theodore Roosevelt had been perhaps the first American president to espouse the Hamiltonian idea that active intervention to maintain the balance of power should be the guiding principle of international relations. In what became known as the Roosevelt Corollary to the Monroe Doctrine 1904, he proclaimed that

> Chronic wrongdoing, or an impotence which results in a general loosening of the ties of civilized society, may in America, as elsewhere, ultimately require intervention by some civilized society, and in the Western hemisphere may force the United States, however reluctantly, in flagrant cases of such wrong doing or impotence, to the exercise of an international police power.[59]

He profoundly distrusted the utopianism, not to say evangelism that had often characterised American foreign policy. He proclaimed that 'A milk-and-water righteousness unbacked by force is to the full as wicked and even more mischievous than force divorced from righteousness.'[60] Roosevelt was an aberration, however. After his presidency, American foreign policy returned to its more moralistic and utopian course.

The Growth of 'Moralism' in American Politics and Foreign Policy

With the increasing wealth of the American economy came the desire to improve the lot of the poor. The philanthropic movement was exemplified by Andrew Carnegie, who having built up *Pittsburgh's Carnegie Steel Company* and a host of other investments in railways and oil, sold out to JP Morgan who merged it with *Federal Steel* to create *US Steel* in 1901, and devoted the rest of his life to giving away his fortune, particularly for the endowment of educational institutions.

At the start of the century, even the American Socialist Party enjoyed a brief flourish with congressmen elected in New York and Milwaukee in addition to some 70 mayors. Although socialism as a political movement barely survived the First World War, nevertheless, the wish to 'equal up' opportunities for advancement became broadly accepted. Politicians such as President Wilson advanced on the back of a progressive movement which felt that the power and influence of the great financial and industrial barons had grown excessively. Support grew for welfare legislation and workers' rights. The creation of a Federal Reserve Bank (following the Federal Reserve Act of December 1913), to which member banks were forced to subscribe 6 per cent of their capital, sought to protect depositors from the ruthless forces of the market.

Changing attitudes filtered into a new view of foreign policy. Half a century earlier, American politicians had been keen to scoop up new territories, but the assumption of a quasi-protectorate in Cuba brought Woodrow Wilson's response that 'We had gone to war with Spain not for annexation but to provide the helpless colony with the opportunity of freedom.'[61] The Cuban War with Spain and its Philippine Islands aftermath brought an increasing perception that unfettered acquisition of overseas domains was inimical to the instincts and culture of the USA, which itself had thrown off the yoke of foreign control just over a hundred years previously.

Even that arch exponent of 'realpolitik', Theodore Roosevelt, was not as cold blooded, illiberal and nationalist as he is sometimes portrayed; in 1902 he became the first user of the International Court of Arbitration at The Hague. Moreover, through his work in interceding in international disputes, Roosevelt was awarded the Nobel Peace Prize in 1906.

Concepts of 'fairness', 'rightness', 'justice' and 'self-determination' now entered the political debate on foreign affairs. The new liberalism was barely passive, however; indeed, American politicians increasingly saw their role as an Olympian one above the fray of warring nations. At the turn of the twentieth century, William Jennings Bryan saw the USA as 'a republic gradually but surely becoming the supreme moral factor in the world's progress and the accepted arbiter of the world's disputes'.[62]

Although President Wilson declared neutrality at the outset of the First World War, favouritism towards England and France was evident from the start. Apart from sentimental attachments to both of these countries, American popular opinion was genuinely horrified by the German invasion of Belgium and the violation of this neutral state. The Allied powers were able to float some US\$ 2 billion of debt on Wall Street versus just US\$ 27 million for the Central Powers. There was a financial interest in an allied victory, but the push to American participation in the war came from fury at the loss of American lives from the German U-boat campaign. This reached a peak with the horrific sinking of the passenger liner RMS, *the Lusitania*, off the coast of Ireland, in which 128 of the 1,100 who died were American.

Curiously, in view of its longer term ramifications, the overthrow of the Russian Tsar on 17 March 1917, by removing an 'autocracy' from the Allied cause, eased the American dilemma about participation in the war. America's entry into the war on 2 April 1917 was momentous not only for the decision itself, but also

for the reasons President Wilson gave for going to war. Wilson expounded a political philosophy that embraced the application of a 'moral' line in the conduct of
a vigorous American foreign policy; he also justified intervention on grounds that
were not related to national self-interest. '...right is more precious than peace',
he declared,

> and we shall fight for the things which we have always carried nearest our hearts, _ for
> democracy, for the right of those who submit to authority to have a voice in their own
> government, for the rights and liberties of small nations, for a universal dominion of
> right by such a concert of free peoples as shall bring peace and safety to all nations and
> make the world itself at last free'.[63]

Wilson's view of American impartiality was based on a certainty of moral and
Christian superiority:

> We have no selfish end to serve. We desire no conquest, no dominion. We seek no
> indemnities for ourselves, no material compensation for the sacrifices we shall freely
> make. We are but one of the Champions of the rights of mankind.[64]

For the post-war world, President Wilson envisaged an 'age ... which demands a new order of things in which the only question will be: Is it right? Is
it just? Is it in the interest of mankind?'[65] For him the 'realpolitik' of Theodore
Roosevelt was the outmoded politics of the autocratic European nations. Wilson
firmly believed that Europeans did not understand democracy and that 'the men
whom we are about to deal with did not represent their own people'.[66] When
he addressed the Senate on 12 January 1917, he demanded that 'There must be,
not a balance of power, but a community of power; not organized rivalries, but an
organized common peace.'[67] Wilson was not just seeking American support for
his international utopian vision. In preparing his famous 14 points outlined in January 1918, President Wilson was appealing to a global audience above the heads
of national politicians.

President Wilson was convinced of America's impartial status and seemed
oblivious to the idea that the creation of a peaceful global order could in any way be
of benefit to American commercial interests; he went as far as to assert that the US
delegation would be 'the only disinterested people at the Peace Conference'.[68] To
help the poor, desperate citizens of Europe, Wilson also launched a concept that
was to become a backbone of twentieth-century American foreign policy: 'self-
determination'; he wished for a world made safe 'for every peace-loving nation
which, like our own, wishes to live its own life, determine its own institutions'.[69]

His utopianism won him the Nobel Peace Prize but not the peace he craved.
The extent to which Woodrow Wilson had overreached himself vis-à-vis the
American electorate in his interventionist and 'universal' moral approach to foreign policy was displayed when ratification of the Treaty of Versailles was voted
down by the Senate. Wilson and the progressives may have curtailed American
territorial expansion, but their entry into the Great War as part of a global moral

crusade merely served to launch an isolationist reaction that was to last for over two decades.

Emergence of America as 'the' Global Superpower

According to Sir Richard Borden, a Canadian MP, the end of the Great War and the defeat of Germany brought a world in which there were 'only three major powers left in the world; the United States, Britain and Japan'.[70] The reality was simpler. America had become the world's dominant superpower. In truth, America had already overtaken the European nations decades previously. It was a measure of American economic supremacy that by 1910 it was already producing more steel than both Germany and the United Kingdom combined. The First World War, in bringing the European economies to their knees, merely clarified what was already fact.

With Congressional rejection of Versailles, American foreign policy turned to the balancing of power between the three remaining naval powers. It was a balance of weaponry largely dictated by America. The 1922 Treaty of Washington was notable for President Warren Harding's forcing of Great Britain to scrap 23 ships so that it could meet the agreed ratios for warships of America, five; Great Britain, five; and Japan, three. (The treaty covered ships over 10,000 tons not including submarines, cruisers and destroyers.) Admiral Beattie reacted with predictable fury, but Lloyd George was correct in his assessment that Great Britain could not afford an arms race with America.

America not only dictated the scope of international arms limitation but also redirected Britain away from its historic relationship with Japan. The Anglo-Japanese alliance was replaced by the Four Power Pacific Treaty, which was a consultative agreement between America, Britain, Japan and France. Furthermore, a Nine Power Treaty orchestrated by America sought to underline America's attachment to 'open door' trade policy throughout Asia and for the same commercial reasons guaranteed China its independence.

If it was not clear beforehand, the balance of global power had clearly shifted during the Great War from Great Britain to America. 'Pax Britannica' had now been replaced by the 'Washington System'. The cost of the Second World War had shattered British finances. Having started the war as a net creditor, Britain had been forced to borrow US$ 4 billion from the USA and had in turn lent US$ 11 billion to their European allies. By contrast, America, which had started the war as a net debtor, was now a significant creditor nation. President Calvin Coolidge refused to accept any debt cancellation, and the result was that Britain was forced to accept a 62-year schedule of repayment. Britain's trophy assets also had to be sold; this included the whole of New York.

Further naval conferences were called by President Coolidge in 1927 and by the British government in 1930. Here the main issue now turned to numbers of cruisers allowed to the naval powers. The British claimed that their extended empire required at least 70 cruisers for protection of trade. However, Britain's first socialist Prime Minister MacDonald was forced to accept just 50. Again the agreement avoided an un-winnable arms race with the USA. For the Japanese, the Treaty of London, which increased their ratio of capital ships to its competitors from 60 per cent to 65 per cent, was still considered a failure by many back in Japan. Admiral Kato resigned after declaring that 'It's as if we had been roped up and cast into prison by Britain and America.'[71] A Japanese politician confided to a German friend that 'Of course, what is really wrong with us is that we have yellow skins. If our skins were as white as yours, the whole world would rejoice at our calling a halt to Russia's inexorable aggression.'[72]

About America's strategy to contain a global arms race, Sir Warren Fisher, head of the British Civil Service, noted that '...in any collaboration with the United States in regard to a naval agreement the difficulty was that on the one hand Great Britain antagonized Japan while on the other she could not be absolutely certain of United States assistance'.[73] It would be hard to argue that America did not act responsibly as the superpower of the post-war world in trying to prevent an arms race. However, as Sir Warren Fisher alluded, the USA could not be counted on to stave off the aggression of the rising nations such as Japan, or indeed Germany. The problem in brief was that just at the moment that America assumed global economic and military leadership, it also embraced 'isolationism' as the mantra of its foreign policy.

American Isolationism after the First World War

Jan Smuts, at a speech to the Royal Institute of International Affairs in November 1934, described 'The Washington treaties of 1922 as probably the greatest step forward yet taken since the peace on the road to a stable future world order.'[74] However, having set the framework for a post-war balance of power, Americans promptly turned their back on the world. That America turned inward to an isolationist stance on foreign policy, just as it emerged as undisputedly the world's most powerful nation, is one of the great ironies of post-First World War history. Wilsonian idealism had not died with his failure to carry through Congress the Treaty of Versailles and the League of Nations; however, the idea had taken hold that the European powers were fatally decadent and that the horrors of the Great War, into which America had become embroiled, should not be repeated. The Monroe Doctrine, eschewing American interference in Europe, had been ignored in the Great War; America would now maintain its high ideals in splendid isolation, unsoiled by contamination from Europe.

International isolationism was further enhanced by the 1929 Wall Street Crash and the ensuing Great Depression. The depression provided the first major setback to America's seemingly linear political and economic advance and forced it to focus attention on its own institutions. In 1934 the Tydings–McDuffie Act set a timetable for Philippines independence; the Platt Amendment, giving America intervention rights in Cuba, was abrogated; Haiti was abandoned and economic control of the Dominican Republic was yielded. President Franklin Roosevelt seemed to sum up the new philosophy when he stated in 1936 that 'We shun political commitments which might entangle us in foreign wars; we avoid connection with the political activities of the League of Nations.'[75]

With the rise of European fascism, America's move to isolation became even more extreme. Roosevelt banned the sale of arms to either side in the Spanish Civil War. Believing it was a foretaste of what was to come in Europe, Congress took the precautionary move of passing a Neutrality Act in 1937; Roosevelt signed it into law.

The Russian Empire: A Competitor to US Hegemony

The growth of the Russian Empire was a continental expansion not dissimilar to America's own history. However, it started somewhat earlier. The importance of Moscow had grown from the thirteenth century, and in 1328 this was recognised by the Orthodox Metropolitanate which moved its principal seat there from Kiev. Indeed, when Byzantium (Constantinople) fell to the Ottomans in 1453, the movement of scholars and clerics to 'Rus' fostered the legend that Moscow was now the 'third Rome'.[76] As the Ottoman Empire was growing, the Moguls were in retreat. In the fifteenth century, Russia overthrew the 200-year yoke of Mogul rule; their rule was formally repudiated in 1480. Tsar Ivan III then created a strong Russian state around Moscow in the 1480s. To the north the independent state of Novgorod, which had long resisted Mogul rule, had already capitulated to Moscow in 1478.

By the early sixteenth century, however, both Europe and Russia were being pressed by the new Muslim threat, this time in the form of the Ottomans who took Belgrade in 1521 and Rhodes in 1522 and destroyed Hungary's Jagiellonian Kingdom at the Battle of Mohacs in August 1526. In 1529 Suleiman the Magnificent laid siege to Vienna. Of more concern to Russia was the overthrow of the *Voevoda* of Moldavia in 1538. For the emerging European nations, Russia was now becoming a key ally in the fight to halt the Ottoman's Islamic Empire.

Driven by the search for security, Ivan the Terrible significantly expanded the Russian Empire by conquering the Mogul Khanate of Kazan in 1552, which took it to the Volga River. In the manner of the Roman Empire, Kazan lands were widely distributed to the 'officer' classes. In spite of this example of military conquest, a great deal of Russian territorial advance was not so different from the 'bottom-up' approach of America where free-wheeling pioneers and settlers drove the expansion process. However, the growth of Russia was not without its setbacks, and fear of invasion was more than imaginary; in 1571, the tartars led by the Khan of

Crimea briefly occupied Moscow, and the Khan himself occupied Ivan's Palace of Kolomenskoe.

At the same time that Ivan the Terrible was seeking to combat external threats old and new, like the Western European nations he was also aiming to centralise a Russian state in which significant power had been held by the Riurikid feudal princedoms. However, the post-Westphalian ideas of statehood, the republican concepts of antiquity that the Renaissance brought to Europe and the revolutionary thinking inspired by the Reformation and counter-Reformation were excluded by Ivan's fearsome rule. Unlike the more advanced European states, such as England and Holland, Ivan and his successors failed to develop sophisticated state institutions independent of the person of the ruler. Beside the Orthodox Metropolitanate from which the *Tsars* (Caesar) derived most of their ideas of sovereignty, independent social or government institutions were virtually non-existent; it was an authoritarian style that was to continue into the late twentieth century and arguably beyond.

Naturally the expansion of Russia was driven by a different ideology from the USA; it was the autocratic granting of licences rather than America's market-driven, 'free-for-all' model which drove expansion. The Stroganov family, who were granted fur and salt mining monopolies in Siberia, hired a private Cossack army to fight the Khan of Siberia. After capturing the Khan capital on the River Irtysh, the whole of Siberia was opened to invasion. In 1639 Cossack pioneers reached the Pacific and later founded the port of Okhotsk. However, the vast expanses of Siberia, lacking the legal and financial structures as well as the immigration flows available to America, were not rapidly filled out by land settlers. For a long period, control was nominally held by the linkage of fortresses (*ostrogi*) strategically placed at river crossings.

Also for Russia the conquest of Siberia and Kazakhstan was slowed by hostile climactic conditions, size and topographical problems such as un-navigable rivers and vast mountain ranges. As in America, indigenous inhabitants suffered. The nomadic Kazakhs were forced into cantonments and their way of life destroyed. It is estimated that their population fell by half when Russian colonists began to barrel their way into the region in the mid-nineteenth century. In the long-drawn-out conquest of Siberia and the Central Asian states of Kazakhstan, Uzbekistan, Kyrgyzstan, Turkmenistan, Azerbaijan, Georgia and the Caucasus, the farmer-settler Russians proved far more durable than the largely nomadic groups that they faced. In this respect the displacement of indigenous peoples of Russia closely resembled the conquest of America.

In Russia, expansion leapt forward under the drive of strong Tsars. In the eighteenth century, Catherine the Great consolidated much of Poland and the Caucasus in spite of fierce resistance from Chechen tribesmen; it was a brutal contest in which much of the Chechen population was wiped out. Nevertheless, the autocratic Russian model was much more painstaking than America's spectacularly rapid land grab. As Lobanov-Rostovsky has pointed out,

> It took the Russians six centuries to reach the Ural Mountains and then a century
> more to reach the Pacific. The reason for this was the onrush of counter-invasions. . . .
> while in the westward drive in America the greatest resistance came from local Indian
> tribes.[77]

Russian expansion was only halted when it started to abut other stable countries. Borders with China were established at the Treaty of Nerchinsk in 1689 and formed the basis of their relationship for the next 200 years. In the east however, the Russians crossed unopposed into Alaska and the West Coast of America; tribute in the form of furs and other commodities was extracted from the native populations. In September 1821, Emperor Alexander I issued a *ukase* (edict) which extended their province of Alaska to latitude 51° north, which grabbed a large slice of the Oregon Territory; Russia also claimed sole control of the Bering Straits.

However, in the face of determined American expansion, Alexander II agreed to relinquish control of Alaska, a territory deemed to be of little economic value and impossible to defend. For the sum of just US$ 7.2 million, America completed the purchase of Alaska in October 1867. 'Seward's Icebox', as Alaska was called in honour of the secretary of state who signed the agreement, took almost a century to become a state; only after the Second World War and the start of the 'Cold War' with Russia did Alaska, still with a population of just 250,000, become a full state of the union in 1959.

As for Europe, it was only at the beginning of the eighteenth century that Russia took a decisive step towards becoming a major European power under Tsar Peter the Great. He looked to the West for technology to transform the backward Russian economy and secure it from the incursions of Northern European competitors such as Sweden. He also sought an outlet to the Baltic to provide him with a 'window' on the West. The opportunity came with Charles XII of Sweden's foolhardy invasion of the Ukraine, which was repelled by a crushing defeat at Peter's hands at the Battle of Poltava in 1708 and forever destroyed Swedish pretensions to being a great power. Peter now established the city of St. Petersburg on the Baltic and confirmed Russia as a major European power. Even for Peter, however, the West was not the future of empire. As the Tsar remarked to a friend, 'We shall need Europe for a few decades, and then we can turn our backside to her.'[78]

Although the Russian Tsars sought to exploit the economic potential of their expanding empires, this was largely an afterthought to what was in essence a territorial expansion driven by fears for national security. By contrast the balance of interest in the American quest for empire was the other way around: commerce before security. History had taught the Russians the dangers of neighbouring hordes. As former Soviet leader Gorbachev observed,

> Two centuries of domination by the Mogul Khans inclined the Russian leaders and
> the Russian people to deep suspicion of predatory powers on its borders, or rather to

the suspicion that any powers on its borders must be predatory which posed potential threats. Extending the frontiers of the nation was, from this point of view, a defensive necessity rather than an act of aggression. The wider the circle of Russian power, the wider the circle of powers which posed potential threats.'[79]

Perhaps not surprisingly the Russian Revolution proved only a minor jolt to the nation's expansionary tendencies. Indeed, now added to Russia's traditional security fears was the paranoia often faced by successful revolutionaries, who fear that what can be easily won can just as easily be taken away. Stalin, a ruthless political operator, who succeeded the sickly Lenin, was riven by paranoid fears of rivals both internal and external. In 1931 Stalin noted that

> One feature of the history of old Russia was the continual beatings she suffered because of her backwardness. She was beaten by the Mogul Khans. She was beaten by the Turkish Beys. She was beaten by the Swedish feudal Lords. She was beaten by the Polish and Lithuanian gentry. She was beaten by the British and French capitalists. She was beaten by the Japanese barons. All beat her_ because of her backwardness, military backwardness, cultural backwardness, political backwardness, industrial backwardness, agricultural backwardness. . . . That is why we must no longer lag behind.[80]

However, the fact that the Soviet Empire would prove to be a formidable enemy and rival to the USA's Asian and indeed global hegemony was probably not clear until after the Second World War. Yet the concept of fomenting a campaign to expand the revolution globally took root almost as soon as Imperial Russia was overthrown in 1918. Indeed, Marxist ideology added an aggressive 'universality' to a Russian expansionism which had previously been seen as largely defensive. As E.H. Carr, the doyen of Soviet historians, pointed out in 1942, 'The Soviet Union was the first national unit to preach an international doctrine and to maintain an effective world-propaganda organisation.'[81]

Just as America was coming to terms with its own territorial restraint, while beginning to lecture European states on the immorality of their Asian Empires and seeking to limit the aggressive Imperial ambitions of Japan, the Soviet Union was busy planting the seeds of revolutionary and nationalist movements in Asia. In the 1920s and 1930s the Comintern, the international revolutionary arm of the Soviet Union designed to destabilise countries and to prepare them for revolution, was an aggravation to the European powers in Asia and elsewhere. However, they failed to gain much traction until the Second World War, when the enfeebled European nations and their Asian colonies were much more susceptible to communist ideology that seemed to fit with the new nationalism that filled the vacuum left by the departing Europeans.

Manchuria and the Rise of Japan

Less spectacular perhaps than the rise of the American Empire, Japan had nevertheless accomplished the remarkable feat of turning itself from an isolated, feudal, decadent and defenceless country in the mid-nineteenth century into one of the world's emerging powers. After almost two and half centuries of isolationism introduced by the Tokugawa Shogunate at the beginning of the seventeenth century, Japan started to look outwards.

In 1855 at the Treaty of Amity, Russia recognised the Island of Hokkaido and the northern chain of Kuril Islands as being sovereign Japanese territory. After the civil war and revolution which overthrew the Shogunate, the so-called Meiji Restoration, the new government established the Hokkaido Colonization Office. Northern migration was encouraged by the appeal of cheap land paid for by government loans. By 1889 some 2,000 Samurai families had been thus enticed to the north.

In 1876, an agricultural college was founded in Sapporo, and William Smith Clark, an American agriculturist, earned lasting fame in the region by bringing modern American farming techniques. As with the American Indians, Hokkaido's indigenous nomadic 'hunter-gatherer' tribal population – the 'Ainu' – were suppressed, and their culture destroyed as they were driven into reservations. Conversion to Shinto religion was enforced as was the use of Japanese language names. By 1908, the Ainu population had dwindled to 18,000, just 1.25 per cent of an island population that had risen to 1.45 million as a result of the Japanese settler onslaught.

As the revolutionary Meiji government looked outwards, it was soon apparent to them that the successful European states were empire builders. As Japanese trade expanded, the preferential trading terms enjoyed by the European Empires and the USA were also noted. Not surprisingly a resurgent Japan started to cast its eyes northwards to its historic client state Korea. After the Meiji Restoration, the Japanese government 'requested' Korea to recognise Imperial rule. Commodore Perry's gunboat diplomacy, which had forced the opening up of Japan, inevitably became a model. The failure of the Korean government to respond led to Saigo Takamori's proposal to send a punitive expedition to Korea in 1873. (Saigo Takamori was the great Samurai general who led the Imperial forces in the Boshin War, which enabled the restoration of the Meiji Emperor to power.)

After years of pressure, Japan established a protectorate in Korea in 1910 and a decade later abolished the Korean monarchy and turned the country into what was effectively a slave colony. The Japanese thinking on foreign policy was defined by its need for security against what it saw as the growing Asian incursions of the European nations. The main exponent of Japanese 'Realpolitik', Yamagata Aritomo, was a veteran oligarch from the Meiji Restoration, who became prime minister in December 1889. He tapped into a national mood of increasing bellicosity bolstered by Japan's rapidly developing economy. In 1887 the political writer Tokutomi Soho founded a fiercely nationalist and successful journal, *Kokumin No Tomo* (the nation's friend), which strongly advocated the creation of a Japanese Empire. Tokutomi wrote of his 'scorn of the white peoples'.[82] Overseas influence on foreign policy was also apparent. In 1885, the Japanese government brought a Major Klemens Meckel from the German army to teach at the Army War College; he famously advised that Korea was 'a dagger pointed at the heart of Japan'.[83]

Fearing that Russia was about to build the Trans-Siberian Railway, Yamagata advocated the need for an aggressive policy 'to preserve our independence and enhance our national position' and that 'If we wish to maintain the nation's independence among the powers of the world at the present time it is not enough to guard only the line of sovereignty, we must also defend the line of advantage.'[84] In the ensuing clash with Imperial Russia, the Japanese navy, under Admiral Togo Heihachiro, destroyed the Russian fleet at the Battle of Tsushima in 1905. By the outbreak of the Second World War, Japan's ambitions to become an Imperial power on the European model were clearly established. An alliance concluded with Great Britain in 1902 was a match with the strongest of the European Empires and a marriage of convenience with another power which also feared Russian expansionism.

During the Great War, Japan's elder statesman had noted that it was 'extremely important . . . to take steps to prevent the establishment of a white alliance against the yellow people'.[85] Already by 1916, Japan's feelings were being ruffled by the treatment of its nationals in Asia's British colonies. A message was sent to the British government complaining that 'a general feeling of regret is prevalent in the Imperial Diet that anti-Japanese feeling is strong in British colonies.'[86]

In 1918 Billy Hughes, prime minister of Australia, told Balfour, the British prime minister, that the industrious Japanese were moving in everywhere and that 'We too must work in like fashion or retire like my ancestors from the fat plains to the lean and rugged hills.'[87] Lord Curzon, British foreign secretary in 1921, also warned that Japan was a 'restless and aggressive power, full of energy, and somewhat like the Germans in mentality'.[88]

Their warnings were prescient. Japan's acquisition of Korea left Japan with a border to the north where it faced a disintegrating China. The First World War gave Japan the opportunity to extend its holdings in the region with the usurpation of Germany's possessions in the Northern Chinese province of Shantung, including railroads, factories and coalmines. Russia, Japan's natural competitor in the region, having undergone a revolution, re-emerged from the Great War as the United Soviet Socialist Republic with a new revolutionary energy. To begin with, however, the Soviet Union's main concerns were internal. Also in 1916 Japan had signed a treaty with Russia recognising Japan's special position in Southern Manchuria and Eastern Mongolia. For Japan, the Chinese province of Manchuria lay open to the north.

Although China was a subsidiary issue at the peace conference at Versailles, attended by 32 leaders, representing 75 per cent of the world's population, the fault lines created here set the course for future conflict in Asia. While Maynard Keynes famously pointed out the mistakes of Versailles in *The Economic Consequences of Peace* (1920) with regard to Europe, the consequences of the treaty in Asia were equally deleterious.

At Versailles, US President Woodrow Wilson's instincts were wholly support-ive of China. He was convinced of the need to foment the moral regeneration of that poor country. Indeed, Wilson's cousin edited a Presbyterian weekly paper in Shanghai. Wilson stated that he wanted the USA to stand by China as a 'friend and exemplar'.[89] In Peking, Wilson's ambassador gave stern warnings against Japan's activities in bribing officials and stirring civil unrest; with remarkable foresight he also warned that

> Should Japan be given a freer hand and should anything be done which could be inter-preted as a recognition of a special position of Japan, either in the form of a so-called Monroe Doctrine or in any other way, forces will be set in action which make a huge armed conflict absolutely inevitable within one generation. There is no single problem in Europe which equals in its importance to the future peace of the world, the need of a just settlement of Chinese affairs.[90]

Whatever his own preferences, with regard to China, Wilson was wholly out-manoeuvered at Versailles. China clamoured against the Japanese usurpation of Shantung and was supported by the US delegation, which supported the Chi-nese with information. To allow continued Japanese control would leave a 'dagger pointed at the heart of China'.[91] However, Lloyd George supported Britain's old ally, Japan; the French Prime Minister Clemenceau also sided with the Japanese position. Wilson was hard pressed given that of the five main powers (America, Britain, France, Italy and Japan), Italy had already walked out of the conference over the issue of Fiume (now the Croatian port city of Rijeka). Having been given private verbal assurances that Japan would in the future give Shantung back to China, Wilson reluctantly agreed to the Japanese position.

Nevertheless, it was a mark of American suspicion of Japan that in 1921 Lord Curzon was warned by the US government that they viewed 'the renewal of the Anglo-Japanese Alliance in any form with disquietude'.[92] The alliance, which had been signed in 1902 to protect their mutual interests in China and Korea, was allowed to lapse in 1923. In some quarters the Asian foreign policy being forced on them by America was counter to Britain's long-term Imperial interests. At the Imperial Conference of 1921, former Prime Minister Arthur Balfour had asserted:

> . . . it is a fact that if we had not Japan on our side we should be second or third power in the Pacific after a considerable number of years . . . it is, from a strategic point of view, of very great importance that the Japanese Alliance should be maintained.[93]

Versailles satisfied none of the parties. Japan continued to view America and Europe as hypocritical and, without the British alliance, was now friendless in the West, leaving it open to German diplomatic overtures. Having built up their em-pires by force of arms, it now seemed that the Anglo-Saxon powers were now trying to deny Japan the same opportunity. It is hard not to disagree with Noam Chomsky when he writes that in building its empire, Japan 'was simply following precedent established by Great Britain and the United States; it was establishing its own Monroe Doctrine and realizing its manifest destiny'.[94]

However, Chomsky completely overlooks the fundamental differences between American concepts of free trade and political self-determination on the one hand and Japanese autarkic despotism on the other. On the ground, the differences experienced by the colonised were significant. In the case of America, self-interest was increasingly generously sprinkled with altruism; the same could not be said of Japan's territorial expansion in North East Asia which followed an altogether more rapacious and exploitative model.

The arrival of economic depression in Japan also hastened the country down the path of autarkic development. One of the more dire consequences of the depression was America's reversion to a narrow economic isolationism. The passing of the Smoot–Hawley Tariff Act by the US Congress raised duties on Japanese goods by 23 per cent at a time when their exports to America, their main market, had already collapsed. The historian R. Hofstadter went as far as to describe the Smoot–Hawley Tariffs as 'a virtual declaration of economic war on the rest of the world'.[95]

Japan began to see in empire and the theory of a co-prosperity sphere a logical solution to its own economic problems. Increasingly also the expansion of empire was dressed into a fatalistic nationalist rhetoric which saw the Western Empires as their natural foe. General Araki, a leader of the right-wing nationalist camp, declared that

> We are the leading Asiatic power and we should now take matters into our own hands. We must be active, ever expanding the last portion of our national strength. We must be prepared to wage a desperate struggle. The Whites have made the countries of Asia mere objects of oppression and Imperial Japan should no longer let their impudence go unpunished.[96]

While Japanese leaders saw the advance into Manchuria as a solution to its problems, the US pro-China lobby continued to be alarmed by the carve-up of a country for which Americans, in the political, social and religious elite, had developed a fond regard. As for the Chinese, Versailles was a sell-out of the moral and utopian ideals proclaimed by Wilson. Tiananmen Square erupted with popular demonstrations, and one student recalled, '. . . we could no longer depend upon the principles of any so-called great leader like Woodrow Wilson'.[97] Not surprisingly many student leaders in China, and elsewhere in Asia, would now turn to the Soviet model for inspiration in their national liberation movements.

As the 1930s progressed, the main alternative to the Soviet revolutionary model, and sometimes a partner with it in seeking to undermine the Western Empires, was Japan and its alliances of convenience with radical Asian nationalist groups. After leaving the League of Nations in February 1933, in the following month Japan founded the Great Asia Association; the aims were clearly to expel Western influence from Asia. Although intellectuals preoccupied themselves with *wangtao* (principle of benevolent rule), the realities in Korea and Manchuria were starkly totalitarian.

What is now evident is that Japanese leaders had not understood that Asia's leading empires in the 1930s, England and America, were already moving along a path towards independence in their main colonies, India and the Philippines, respectively. This liberation was not being done out of weakness, but through intellectual and moral conversion to the concept of 'self-determinism'. That the Anglo-Saxon powers were beginning to loosen their grip on colonial rule, however, did not mean they would surrender their position to a new Asian invader. Given Japan's military trajectory, it was only a matter of time before it would clash with the western empires.

Isolationism Abandoned

Within months of signing the Neutrality Act, Roosevelt was beginning to have regrets. He was already fearful about the rise of fascism in Europe. Roosevelt was clear that the regimes of Hitler and Mussolini posed a threat not only to liberal democracy in Europe, but also to the USA. In October 1937 a Chicago audience was warned, 'let no one imagine that America will escape, that America may expect mercy, that this Western hemisphere will not be attacked'.[98] He went on to suggest that America might not be able to stand by and watch; 'When an epidemic of physical disease starts to spread, the community approves and joins in a quarantine of the patients in order to protect the health of the community against the spread of the disease.'[99]

The Chicago statement marked a revival of the Wilsonian belief in 'moral' interventionism. In viewing the ideological battles unfolding in Europe, Roosevelt now believed that the USA had a moral responsibility to help further the philosophies which underpinned its own republic. On 14 April Roosevelt requested Hitler and Mussolini not to violate smaller nations; Hitler did not reply to the message. Although isolationist sentiment among the American political elite was already beginning to crumble, Roosevelt's attempt to repeal the Neutrality Act fell by one vote in the Senate Foreign Relations Committee.

In spite of his increasing doubts, particularly after Hitler's invasion of France, Roosevelt sustained the isolationist stance throughout his 1940 presidential re-election campaign, in which he pledged that he would never send Americans to fight in Europe; in a debate with Republican opponent Wendell Willkie, Roosevelt declared that 'I have said this before, but I shall say it again and again and again. Your boys are not going to be sent into any foreign wars.'[100] Nevertheless, fearing that Great Britain would lose the war with Germany, leaving America open to invasion, Congress had already passed a record US$ 37 billion defence appropriation. After the election Roosevelt went further and agreed a 'lend-lease' deal with Britain to fortify her defences with American military equipment, including oil tankers, destroyers and access to American shipyards. Throughout America the popularity of isolationist policies was crumbling. When Japanese forces invaded Indochina, Admiral Harold Stark, chief of naval operations, advised the president to do nothing, though opinion polls indicated that 70 per cent of Americans would rather risk war than allow unchecked Japanese expansion.

When the Japanese threw in their lot with Germany against the allies, they calculated that they could only gain and declared that 'Japan must take the chance of a millennium to establish rights and interests in Asia.'[101] The defeat of France and the Netherlands had opened up the opportunity to acquire their Asian Imperial assets in Indochina and Indonesia, respectively. A Britain under siege also offered the possibilities of Malaya, Burma and India. When Japan announced a 'protectorate' of Indochina on 25 July 1941, Roosevelt responded by freezing Japanese financial assets in the USA and cutting off supply of essential raw materials including oil and rubber. Japanese withdrawal from China was also demanded.

In their 14 August 1941 Atlantic Charter, F.D. Roosevelt and Winston Churchill agreed to adhere to a set of principles to guide their conduct and motive for the war ahead; there would be no warring for self-aggrandisement; territorial changes would be made only in the interests of the people; self-determination would be the guiding principle of constitutional development, and the allies would be committed to the concept of free trade. They also announced their commitment to establish a global 'permanent security system'.

The forced entry of the Soviet Union into the war after Hitler's surprise attack on his former ally muddied the clear waters of the Atlantic Charter. The American and British alliance with Soviets was a pact of convenience with an ideological foe, albeit Stalin gave his nominal consent to the Atlantic Charter and later to the declaration on liberated Europe. The allies were probably unaware of the depths of Stalin's suspicions and paranoia. As early as July 1942, after Churchill's departure from Moscow, Stalin ruminated,

> All is clear. A campaign in Africa and Italy. They simply want to be the first in reaching the Balkans. They want us to bleed white in order to dictate to us the terms later on.... Nothing will come of this! The slavs will be with us.... They hope that we shall lose Stalingrad and lose the springboard for offensive.[102]

In the cynical world inhabited by Stalin, it was perhaps not surprising that the utopian goals of the Atlantic Charter did not long survive the end of the war.

Events moved now rapidly towards bringing America into the war. In October the sinking of an American destroyer, the USS Reuben James, with the loss of 96 men enabled the president to repeal the Neutrality Act with little difficulty. Then on 7 December, the Japanese, thwarted in their Imperial ambitions by the American trade embargo, sought to break out of the apparent American containment of their 'Co-Prosperity Sphere' by launching the surprise attack on Pearl Harbor.

The cream of America's capital ships was destroyed, and 2,403 Americans were killed. The manner of Japan's attack on America may have been a surprise, but there is little doubt that Roosevelt, by his economic embargo and the scale of his demands on Japan to roll back their newly acquired Asian Empire, was far from reluctant to engage in a war which would enable him to break out of America's isolationist straight-jacket and defend his country's Asian interests.

In the 14th part of the encrypted Japanese message, which was meant to be delivered to the American government as a declaration of war prior to the attack on Pearl Harbor (but was in fact delivered after the event), the Japanese government averred that 'Obviously it is the intention of the American government to conspire with Great Britain and other countries to obstruct Japan's efforts toward the establishment of peace through the creation of a New World Order in Asia.'[103]

From the first 13 parts of the war declaration which Washington's 'Magic' decrypting room had already deciphered, it must have been clear to Roosevelt that war was coming, but according to Conrad Black, in his definitive biography, Roosevelt 'was insistent on allowing them the first blow, however destructive'.[104] Indeed, he concludes that

> Roosevelt's achievement in bringing the United States out of isolation, invaluably sup-
> porting the Allies, and engineering entry into the war by becoming a target of Axis
> aggression, was the greatest feat of any American statesman in the country's history. . . .
> He and his country were about to assume a primary role as the principal savior of West-
> ern civilization and builder of a new world.[105]

Roosevelt himself told Churchill and Stalin at Yalta in 1945 that without an attack on US territory, it would have been almost impossible to get the American people into the war.

Later in analysing the causes of the war, Roosevelt and the 'New Deal' administration came to the conclusion that economic nationalism, and the rise of extremist parties in Europe, was the root cause of the political instability. Harry Dexter White, deputy treasury secretary, forewarned that 'the absence of a high degree of economic collaboration among the leading nations, will, during the coming decade, inevitably result in economic warfare that will be the prelude and instigator of military warfare on an even vaster scale'.[106] He suggested that the world needed a Stabilization Fund and International Bank. His was not a lone voice in the Washington establishment. In 1943 Henry Wallace (later secretary of commerce) also insisted that the USA must collaborate 'with the rest of the world to put resources fully to work'.[107]

In England similar sentiments were also emerging. Dexter White's analysis fitted perfectly with that of Keynes who, in *The Economic Consequences of the Peace* (1919), had castigated the Treaty of Versailles for its failure to put in place an economic and financial framework for post-war recovery. Keynes was particularly concerned that in the post-Second World War period, Britain and other countries would suffer balance of payments difficulties which could threaten a repeat of the economic catastrophes, hyper-inflation followed by depression which characterised the 1920s.

The outcome was a conference at *Bretton Woods* in 1944 at which Maynard Keynes and Dexter White forwarded a proposal for the post-war creation of stabilising institutions, the International Monetary Fund and the World Bank. They would not only provide the financial wherewithal for international currency stabilisation, but would also arrange loans to countries. The result would be the maintenance of a stable world trading system.

An important part of this stable currency system required from America that it offered a fixed parity to gold for its currency. It was a role for which America, emerging as it did from the Second World War with an economy accounting for over half of global GDP, was uniquely qualified. It also set the structure for the post-war trading system. Currencies would be freely convertible into US dollars at a fixed parity, while America would open its commercial markets to all comers; in effect *Bretton Woods* created a global financial system managed by the US Treasury and Federal Reserve Board.

The global trading system was later solidified in 1948 by the setting up of the General Agreement on Tariffs and Trade (GATT). It was a system guaranteed to benefit both the USA and the nations which were gathered into America's geopolitical net. Thus, *Bretton Woods* prescribed the post-war hegemonic structure that formed the basis of America's post-war empire in Asia; this would not be an empire of territorial acquisition, but an empire of influence based on the defence of Asian nations free to follow a path of self-determination and a free trading system with America at its heart.

A New Clash of Empires

In the 166 years between 1779 and 1945 the USA grew into one of the most successful empires in world history. Yet few issues arouse more partisan debate than the subject of the American Empire's existence, let alone its purpose. Except on the extreme left, American political opinion is peculiarly coy on the subject. William Appleman Williams in an article for the *Pacific Historical Review* in November 1955, entitled *The Frontier Thesis and American Foreign Policy*, commented that 'One of the central themes of American historiography is that there is no American Empire. Most historians will admit, if pressed that the United States once had an empire. They then promptly insist that it was given away.'[108]

For the most part, international commentators have accepted the myth that America's remarkable expansion was 'empire-less'. For instance former British Prime Minister Margaret Thatcher refused to acknowledge that America had ever had an Empire. She would no doubt have agreed with 'Sandy' Berger, President Clinton's national security advisor, who affirmed that America was the first global power in history that was not an imperial power. As eminent 'empire' historian Niall Ferguson has concluded, America 'is an empire, in short, that dare not speak its name. It is an empire in denial.'[109]

Even where the American Empire was admitted, American voices have been quick to distance themselves from the usual unflattering connotations; Ronald

Steel, in *Pax Americana* (1977), noted that '. . . the American Empire came into being by accident and has been maintained from a sense of benevolence . . . we have
not exploited our Empire'.[110] This view is delusional. From inception, the growth
of America was entirely based on the possibility of individual advancement through
the acquisition of land and the economic opportunities that it brings. One does
not have to be an opponent of US foreign policy or a hater of America, like Noam
Chomsky, author of his vitriolic *American Power and the New Mandarins* (1969), to accept that the USA has been the most successful expansionist nation of the Industrial
Age.

It needs to be asked why it is that America remains in denial of its Imperial
past, particularly since in the latter part of its history the USA has operated a benign, if not entirely selfless, form of economic and security hegemony, which has
often benefited its client states as much as if not more than itself. The reason seems
to lie both in America's religious and moral determinism and in the mythologies
of its own fight for independence. As the classical historian Bryan Ward-Perkins
points out in explaining the historiography of empire in *The Fall of Rome, and the
End of Civilization* (2005), 'In Europe, empires and imperialism went firmly out of
fashion in the decades following the Second World War, while in the United States,
which traces its origins to a struggle for freedom from British control, they have
seldom enjoyed explicit favor.'[111]

The conquest of what is now the USA beyond the East Coast sliver of territory
occupied by European colonists was never viewed by Americans as imperialism
though in practice it is difficult to see how their migratory, economic and ultimately
military expansion was any different in nature from any other expanding power
throughout the ages. That North America was sparsely populated, though no less
so than the barren wastes of Eastern Russia, does not mean that the American
colonists were any less 'Imperial' in their conquests.

While western historians frequently describe the expansion of Russia from its
Moscow base as empire, hence 'Imperial Russia', the same standards are never
applied to the expansion of the USA. In the post-war world, the ability of America
to rationalise its own past in these terms has been even further disabled by the
increasingly prejudicial moral connotations that the word 'Empire' now delivers.
It is no coincidence that 'The "Empire" in Hollywood's *Star Wars* (1977) is the force
of evil, its storm troopers modeled partly on Roman praetorian guards.'[112]

Equally important in America's denial of its 'Imperial' past was its view of
itself as a peculiarly moral entity. In his book *Farewell Address: Ideas of Early American Foreign Policy*, Felix Gilbert notes that George Washington's famed farewell
address, scripted by Alexander Hamilton, 'reveals the basic issue of American attitude toward Foreign Policy; the tension between Idealism and Realism'.[113] Just
as America was about to embark on one of the fastest territorial expansions of
any nation in history, James Madison typified the peculiar mix of aggression and
missionary zeal, which characterised the growth of American Empire, when he

stated in 1804 that 'The United States owe to the world as well as to themselves to let the example of one government at least protest against the corruption which prevails.'[114]

America was founded on the ideals of low taxes, the right to own property under law and freedom from central government. Yet it is interesting to note that by many measures, England – the country that the 13 colonies had defeated in the name of 'liberty' – was more democratic in terms of suffrage than America. It is a mark of the importance of land in the American Revolution that as late as 1820 the USA had higher property qualifications for the right to vote than Great Britain. It was only with the first Democratic Party presidencies of Andrew Jackson (1829–1837), and his successor Martin Van Buren (1837–1841), that America moved towards a broad male suffrage and with it the creation of modern political organisation; however, African Americans and other races would have to wait for their right to vote until the 15th Amendment to the constitution in 1870 and women would have to wait a further 50 years for the 19th Amendment. Strangely the indigenous Native American Indians only acquired the right to become citizens, and with it the right to vote, after the passing of the Indian Citizen Act in 1924.

However, in the process of gaining independence, America's founders promoted the myth that the revolution was pure and utopian and above the grubby venality of a 'corrupt' Europe. The harsh realities of the economic motivations for independence, particularly with regard to property speculation, have been gradually obliterated from the independence story. The absence of historic self-analysis meant that the more successful America's economic and political model grew, the more Americans became convinced of their moral rightness and indeed their 'manifest destiny'.

Thus the 13 colonies managed to conquer the American continent and then to advance into South America and the Pacific, an extraordinarily brutal exposition of military and economic power, while maintaining a myth of a moral and utopian nation. Yet even George Washington, an integral part of the 'legend' of American virtue, predicted that America would become an empire. Similarly a contemporary Bostonian wrote in 1789 that America would become 'the largest Empire that ever existed'.[115]

The extraordinary success of the American Empire created an unwavering faith in progress and the belief that American values were universally applicable. For the American people history had demonstrated 'a steady march toward greater prosperity, freedom, and justice, of which American experience was the defining symbol....'[116]

For the most part, American politicians acknowledged limits to intervention in world politics in order to advance their own ideologies. Secretary of State John Quincy Adams, the intellectual progenitor of the Monroe Doctrine, argued in relation to the decision not to throw its weight behind the Greek Independence

Movement in 1821 that 'Wherever the standard of freedom and independence has been or shall be unfurled, there will be America's heart, her benedictions, and her prayers. But she goes not abroad in search of monsters to destroy. . . .'[117]

Adams feared that foreign adventurism to support America's own ideals might end by destroying them; if America pursued every righteous cause, 'She might become the dictatress of the world; She would no longer be the ruler of her own spirit.'[118] Yet in dealing with the world during its global expansion, American political leaders nearly always called upon its nation's utopian mythology to justify their actions. Before the Second World War, only America's first Secretary of State, Alexander Hamilton, and later Theodore Roosevelt fully divorced utopian rhetoric from the realities of the exercise of power. However, most American politicians confused the two concepts, nobody more so than President Wilson in his utopian approach to American entry into the First World War.

American utopianism created an extreme disconnection between how American leaders saw the USA and how the rest of the world viewed America. The resentment of American power was already well established by the Second World War. Europeans feared US expansion and its apparent mission to proselytise the world with its democratic and egalitarian ideals. Jules Cambon, the French ambassador to the USA from 1897 to 1902, complained that 'These people [the Americans] are ignorant and brutal and if they stick their hand in the complicated and patient game that the old world is playing it will little trouble them to set fire to the four corners of the Empire.'[119] Figures as diverse as the Austrian Foreign Minister Count Agenor von Goluchowski and the historian Ugo Ojetti were also calling for a united Europe to guard against the American advance.

Nevertheless, there was a real change in the expression of America's foreign power at the beginning of the twentieth century. After the appropriation and suppression of the Philippines, it began to dawn on American consciousness that the colonial expansion of empire by conquest was neither moral, compatible with the ideals of America's own battle for independence, nor politically practical. Increasingly, America turned to the ideal of 'self-determination' as the framework through which international interventions would be justified.

This change may have denoted a softer approach to international expansion, but it did not change the realities of the growth of American power and the US desire to expand its commercial empire or affect the need to exercise power when required. The whole process of naval limitation treaties during the interwar period was predicated on the understanding by Britain and Japan that America could, if it chose, win any arms race.

Also, in spite of the avowed 'isolationism' of American foreign policy in this period, itself an expression of moral superiority, American presidents took pains to warn off Japan from further encroachment in Asia, particularly Manchuria. These warnings were backed up with severe economic sanctions. American 'Isolationism' and the Neutrality Act that it inspired merely served to confuse Germany and Japan and those international leaders who considered the exercise of international power, commensurate with domestic economic and military strength, to be a normal function of government. Doubts that America would defend the vested interests of its empire were clearly an invitation to aggressive action by the Axis powers.

The reality, which President Franklin D. Roosevelt and others largely overlooked before 1939, was that America was competing with three largely autarkic economic systems, German, Japanese and Soviet. 'In the interwar years the decisive factors in international relations were the effort of Germany and Japan to re-order the balance of power in their favor within their respective spheres.'[120] In spite of these realities, Roosevelt, seemingly oblivious to America's own Imperial past, entered the war in Asia determined that the European Empires, even those of his allies such as Britain, would be dismantled as thoroughly as that of Japan.

Roosevelt affirmed that 'When we've won the war, I will work with all my might and main to see to it that the United States is not wheedled into the position of accepting any plan that will ... abet the British Empire in its Imperial ambitions.'[121]

Roosevelt failed to realise that by 1939 Britain had already abandoned Imperial ambitions. Neither did he understand that in looking to dismantle Europe's far eastern empires, America would be left standing as Asia's only Imperial nation. In the last of his volumes on Keynes, *Fighting for Britain 1936–1947* (2000), the historian Robert Skidelsky went as far as to observe that in the Second World War, the USA's three principal war aims were the 'defeat of Japan, the defeat of Germany and the defeat of Great Britain'.[122]

American hegemony in post-war Asia cannot be seen in isolation from the development of American foreign policy in the pre-war era. American expansion in Asia in the post-war period was not simply the result of filling a power vacuum left by the European nations; it must be seen as part of a continuum with the expansion of American global power since the early nineteenth century. By 1939 America was already the major military power in Asia; the huge American fleet based at Pearl Harbor, and the American army stationed in the Philippines, were ample testaments to that fact.

American pre-war expansion in Asia was a corollary of its economic and financial success. Even without the specific 'German' causes of the Second World War, America would, in any case, have had cause to bump up against the Asian economic and political ambitions of both Imperial Japan and the Soviet Union. The ideals of economic liberalism and free trade, in an Asia economically and militarily dominated by the USA and its Anglo-Saxon 'blood-brothers' – the British – would inevitably have clashed with the autarkic economic philosophies of *Marxist–Leninism* on the one hand and Japan's *Co-Prosperity Sphere* on the other.

Whereas before the Second World War, America was the strongest among many competing Imperial powers in Asia, afterwards, with the destruction of

Japan's Imperial ambitions and the collapse of the European Empires, the path was opened to the USA's apparently unassailable domination of the region. That this did not happen was because the Soviets were able to co-opt communist China and other successful socialist revolutionary movements in Asia (see Maps I, II & III). The result was a bi-polar battle for control of the region, between America's 'free trade' hegemony and the Soviet Union's alliance of socialist autarkies. As the nuclear bombing of Hiroshima and Nagasaki brought the Second World War to a close, the world was unaware that a new clash of empires in Asia was about to begin.

PART II

Asia's Post-War Settlement

2

Potsdam, Hiroshima and the Atom Bomb

Japan: August 1945

At 8.15 am on 6 August 1945, a lone B-29 bomber, which had hastily been named the *Enola Gay* after it's commander's mother, dropped a single bomb over Hiroshima and headed out to sea. The bomb, 10.5 feet long, 29 inches in diameter, weighing 9,700 pounds and, according to one of its crew, looking like 'an elongated trash can with fins', fell towards its target, the Aioi Bridge, in the heart of Hiroshima. The city was just awakening to a warm and sunny morning. The temperature was already 80°C; the trams just north of Aioi Bridge at the Fukuya department store were packed; the streets were full of cyclists on their way to work; at the parade grounds to the west of Aioi Bridge, bare-chested soldiers, some of the 43,000 stationed in the city, were doing morning exercises. Further from the centre, school children were being coaxed into classrooms. A junior college student recalled looking up at the sky after hearing her teacher exclaim, 'Oh there's a B . . !'[1] At that moment, the bomb, inappropriately named 'Little Boy', which had drifted to a point some 550 feet southeast of its target to 1,900 feet above the Shima Hospital, exploded in 'a tremendous flash of lightning'. The same college student recalled, 'In an instant we were blinded and everything was just a frenzy of delirium.'[2]

At the explosion site, the temperature reached 5,400°C. Even metal was vaporised at proximity to the blast. People simply disappeared, sometimes leaving just their shadows imprinted on stone or tarmac. Those Japanese within half a kilometer of the explosion had their internal organs melted within a millisecond; over 90 per cent of them died. Birds ignited in mid-air. At 4,000 yards away wooden poles burst into flames. At 1 km over 70 per cent of people were killed; at 1.5 km 30 per cent were killed. Some 62,000 buildings, two out of three in the city, were destroyed. Within an instant 'Little Boy' had killed some 50,000 of the 340,000 civilians and soldiers who resided in Hiroshima. By the end of the year this figure had risen to 70,000 and eventually rose to 140,000 as radiation sickness took its toll. The suffering did not end there. The *hibakusha* (explosion-affected people as they came to be known) experienced large number of deaths by cancer and other illnesses, and to this day they and their progeny suffer from social discrimination, alienation and exclusion.

On the *Enola Gay*, tail gunner Robert Carron remembered, 'the mushroom itself was a spectacular sight, a bubbling mass of purple-grey smoke and you could see it had a red core in it and everything was burning inside'.[3] Two hours later, a message from Washington was decoded on board the battle cruiser *USS Augusta* wherein President Truman was returning from the three-week Potsdam Summit with Stalin, Churchill and, following Churchill's election defeat, Clement Attlee. Truman immediately set about informing the crew. He said that he had never been happier about any announcement he had ever made. Major Donald Regan, a veteran of five campaigns from Guadalcanal to Okinawa, who was later to become President Ronald Reagan's treasury secretary, recalled that he 'understood the horror of the bombing. Nevertheless, these events filled me with joy when they were announced, and I will not pretend otherwise today'.[4] In France, the news was heard by Paul Fussell, a 21-year-old officer, who was due to be part of the invasion force on Honshu, the main island of Japan; he recalled, 'we cried with relief and joy. We were going to live. We were going to grow up to adulthood after all'.[5]

The dropping of the atom bomb may have been the dramatic 'finale' to the ending of the Second World War in Asia, but the Japanese defeat had been inevitable from June 1942, when the Japanese fleet was engaged by American aircraft carriers as it approached Midway Island. Four Japanese aircraft carriers were torpedoed and sunk; loss of control of the Pacific ripped the heart out of Japan's strategic plan to crush the American will to fight.

From the start, the Japanese navy, particularly its great Admiral Isoroku Yamamoto, who had lived in America, had realised that, faced by the overwhelming industrial might of their opponents, their only hope of winning was to deal successions of stunning blows to the US forces in the Pacific. By this strategy, they would force America to allow Japanese control of Indochina and access to petroleum products on which Japan was dependent. However, within six months of Japan's destruction of the US Pacific fleet by its sneak attack on Pearl Harbour, the Emperor's ambitions of an Asian Empire, built over 12 years of constant warfare, were effectively ended. From Midway onwards, the Emperor and his generals, whom Hirohito increasingly criticised for their poor performance, could only fight to stem the American tide.

As General MacArthur jumped from one Pacific island to another, building landing strips for the air force as he went, the US army advanced bit by bit across the Pacific – first Guadalcanal, then the Solomons and New Guinea, followed by the Marshall and Gilbert Islands. The island of Truk followed in February 1944, thereby breaking through Tojo's absolute defensive perimeter and ending his political and military leadership of Japan as the Emperor's first minister. Meanwhile in Burma, in the greatest land defeat ever suffered by Japan, the Japanese 15th army was routed by the British army under General Slim at the Irrawaddy River; the

Imperial army had 30,000 soldiers dead and 42,000 sick and wounded. While the remnants of Japan's shattered Burma army retreated towards Rangoon, the USA launched decisive offensives against Saipan, Guam and Tinian, from where bombing of the Japanese mainland would start. It was also from here that the *Enola Gay* began its fateful flight. On 18 July 1944, Tojo and his war cabinet resigned.

Some eight months later, while working on his papers in 'The Little White House' in Warm Springs, Georgia, the sickly President Roosevelt suffered a cerebral haemorrhage and crashed to the floor, dead. The same evening, 12 April 1945, Vice President Harry Truman, the obscure and plain ordinary former senator from Kansas, Missouri was sworn into office in the cabinet room in the west wing of the White House. After a cabinet meeting 11 days later, Secretary of War Henry Stimson lingered and begged a confidential word; he informed Truman that the US Army Corps of Engineers was in advance stages of developing a bomb of immense power. Indeed Admiral Yamamoto's doom-laden prophesies of American industrial might were about to be realised. The US military had spent nearly US$2 billion on the Manhattan Project which employed 150,000 people in developing the atom bomb. By contrast, Japan's effort to develop a nuclear weapon at the Japanese Nuclear Research Laboratory, established at Riken in 1935, employed just 110 scientists.

Just 12 weeks after becoming president, Truman headed off with some trepidation to Potsdam, the elegant town 20 miles from Berlin, where Frederick the Great had built his exquisite rococo palace, *Sans Souci*, and where also, on the adjacent Lake Wannsee, Nazi officers and clerks had planned in great detail the liquidation of the Jews. This was to be the last of the major wartime conferences, and was to have a dramatic impact on the shape of post-war Asia. Truman knew neither Churchill nor Stalin. Churchill, he came to like and respect, in spite of his verbosity and grandiloquence, which was absolutely not the style of the farmer's son from Independence, Missouri. For his part, Churchill immediately took to Truman declaring, '. . . he is a man of immense determination. He takes no notice of delicate ground, he just plants his foot firmly upon it'.[6] As for 'Uncle Joe' Stalin, Truman, like most other international statesmen before him, was soon charmed in spite of his pallid 'Kremlin' complexion and runt like stature. The same warm feelings did not flow for Prime Minister Clement Attlee, accompanied by Foreign Minister Ernest Bevan, who replaced Churchill mid-conference, when much to Stalin's shock, he lost the General Election to the Labour Party; these two Labour politicians Truman described as 'sourpusses'.[7]

This was not the grand triumphal conference that had been expected. Churchill appeared tired. The exertions of war had depleted his energies. No doubt also the death of his close friend Roosevelt affected him deeply. Moreover the British Empire was close to bankruptcy. The war in Europe may have been won but the cost was 25 per cent of Britain's Gross Domestic Product. Britain was a spent force and both Stalin and Truman knew it. The future of Asia would not be decided by

Britain. As for Stalin, he deliberately arrived late at the conference as a tactic to magnify his importance; he felt that, through the loss of more dead than all the other combatant nations put together, it was his country that had done the 'heavy lifting' in defeating the German armies.

However, it was Truman, conscious of his 'new boy' status, who became the decisive figure at Potsdam. In part this was due to meticulous preparation of his briefs and his direct no-nonsense approach to negotiation. However, his confidence must, in part, have come from the trump card delivered to him on the afternoon of the second day of the conference. At the New Mexico air base of Alamogordo, at 5.29 am (US time), the American army successfully detonated the first atomic bomb.

Churchill welcomed the news as a 'miracle of deliverance'.[8] As for Stalin, to whom Truman gave the 'nuclear bomb' news at the end of meetings on 24 July, he urged that the weapon should be used against the Japanese. In truth there had never been any doubt that the bomb would be used; it was a 'war-ending' weapon. Subsequently the decision was much criticised. In 1957, the Oxford philosopher Elizabeth Anscombe opposed the award of an honorary degree to Truman on the grounds that 'For men to choose to kill the innocent as a means to their ends is always murder, and murder is one of the worst of human actions . . . in the bombing of (Japanese cities) it was certainly decided to kill the innocent as a means to an end.'[9]

Some also argued that the 'atom bomb' was used as a cynical ploy to prevent Soviet military occupation of more territory, after Stalin's Potsdam assertion that he would open hostilities on the Asian front in mid-August. British physicist P.M.S. Blackett concluded that the dropping of the bomb was 'the first major operation of the cold diplomatic war with Russia'.[10] The charge is without foundation. No conversations or memoranda have ever been recovered which indicate that the decision to drop the bomb was made for any other reason than to end the war and save the lives of allied troops. Truman and Churchill may have been suspicious of Stalin but he was an ally nonetheless; indeed, America's sponsoring of the United Nations in the spring of 1945, as an organisation that would embrace the Soviet Union in a federated global protectorate, was clear evidence of their expectation of a positive post-war relationship with their wartime allies.

Furthermore, Secretary of State Byrnes and some of Truman's advisors felt that knowledge of the atom bomb would need to be shared with the rest of the world. Dean Acheson, then under secretary of state, was instructed to come up with a proposal for the United Nations Atomic Energy Commission of which the Soviets would be a part. Acheson himself affirmed that 'what we know is not a se-cret which we can keep to ourselves. . .'.[11] That there were strategic geo-political benefits of dropping the atom bomb and ending the war rapidly only became evi-dent later as the Cold War chill spread into the relationship between Stalin and the West. As it turned out, the biggest winner of this post-hoc benefit was Japan itself that avoided the trauma of division and communist occupation suffered by Germany.

That Truman and his cabinet were aware of the special horrific nature of the weapon that they had created was clear from the outset. On 25 July Truman wrote in his diary 'We have discovered the most terrible bomb in the history of the world.'[12] However, there were overwhelming political, military and humanitarian reasons why the bomb had to be used. By 1945, American leaders were being increasingly apprised of the horrors of war. Stories of Japanese atrocities were circulating throughout America. At sea, *Kamikaze* (divine wind) attacks and the hazards of submarines were also taking their toll on Washington's patience.

At midnight of 29 July the American heavy cruiser *USS Indianapolis*, having just delivered nuclear material for 'Little Boy' on Tinian Island, was sunk by a Japanese submarine torpedo attack; of the full complement of 1,196 some 300 crew were killed; the remainder survived in the warm waters of the Philippine Sea, only to be picked off by sharks. Drowning and madness did for others. After three days and nights in the water only 318 were picked up. This episode was fresh in the minds of Truman's advisors as they planned the dropping of the bomb. As Charles Bohlen, the State Department's Russian expert, succinctly put it, 'the spirit of mercy was not throbbing in the breast of any Allied official'.[13]

Truman could never have faced an electorate with the knowledge that he had failed to use a weapon that could almost instantly have relieved the sufferings of American GIs and their families. This was not an imagined fear. In spite of the inevitability of Japanese defeat, the cost in human terms was rising as the US forces neared the Japanese home islands. In the three months between becoming president and visiting Potsdam, the American army's casualties were as high as for the previous three years. A foretaste of the human cost of forcing Japan into submission came with the operation to take the island of Okinawa, Japan's southernmost province. Using civilians as a shield the Japanese army were prepared to sacrifice a third of the population of the island in a bloody battle of attrition. With some 2.5 million soldiers on the four main islands of Japan, the piecemeal conquest of that country would have been a daunting task.

It is clear with hindsight that the American forebodings were not illusory. Civilians of all ages were being taught to fight with bamboo spears if necessary. Women were instructed how to wrap themselves in explosives before throwing themselves under tanks as human mines. Even after the dropping of the second nuclear bomb on Nagasaki on 9 August, at the Imperial Conference that night, Baron Kiichiro Hiranuma argued that 'Even if the entire nation is sacrificed to war, we must preserve the *Kokutai* [National Essence] and the security of the Imperial household.'[14] Four days after this conference, the vice chief of the Japanese navy general staff, who had conceived and planned the *Kamikaze* suicide attacks on American ships, barged into a government meeting to offer a plan for certain victory which would sacrifice 20 million Japanese lives in a special attack.

The degree to which the ultranationalists were prepared to continue the fight even after the dropping of nuclear weapons shows how impossible it would have been for the Japanese leadership to surrender to the conventional force of arms. Fortunately, some Japanese leaders had a clearer foresight. For Navy Minister Mitsumasa Yonai, the nuclear bombs were a blessing in disguise; he told Admiral Takagi that 'the atomic bombs and the Soviet entry into the war are, in a sense, gifts from God'[15] because they gave Japan an excuse to surrender. Clearly the dropping of the atom bombs saved millions of Japanese civilian lives in the slaughter that would inevitably have ensued from a land war in Japan.

Saving Japanese lives, however, was not in the forefront of the US military thinking. General Marshall gave Truman an estimate that the possession of the Japanese mainland by force would cost 250,000 American lives. This overwhelming reason for using the atom bomb was summed up by Stimson, secretary of war, in *Harper's* in 1947, 'My chief purpose was to end the war in victory with the least possible cost in the lives of the men in the armies which I had helped to raise. I believe that no man . . . could have failed to use it and afterwards looked his countrymen in the face.'[16]

With the utter conviction that they now had the means to impose a crushing and immediate defeat on the Japanese, Truman's administration drew up the terms to be offered to the Japanese. Under Secretary of State Joseph Grew, formerly the US ambassador to Japan, scripted what came to be known as the Potsdam Declaration. With some confidence the declaration promised the 'prompt and utter destruction'[17] of Japan. Most importantly, the declaration demanded Japan's unconditional surrender. In an argument that came to dominate thinking about the future of Japan both in Tokyo and Washington, Grew argued that the declaration should guarantee the future of the Imperial system. However, Byrnes fought for this issue to be left open.

Truman, whose first speech to Congress as president had endorsed the Roosevelt line on demanding unconditional surrender from Japan, had little room for manoeuvre on this issue. This fact was clearly understood by those Japanese who stood at a certain distance from Tokyo. Ambassador Sato in Moscow, who was being used as the main conduit for dialogue with the Western powers, pleaded with Tokyo, 'In the final analysis if our country truly desires to terminate the war, we have no alternative but to accept unconditional surrender or something very close to it.'[18] However, Emperor Hirohito, and the military cabal that surrounded him, were locked in a fanatical embrace that precluded them from facing the stark realities of defeat and its consequences.

Perhaps the most remarkable aspect of the dropping of an atom bomb on Hiroshima was that Japan did not surrender immediately. The incendiary bombing of Tokyo on 8 March that year had killed over 100,000 people as great fireballs swept through the city. This attack had comprised some 1,000 B-29s. Massive conventional bombing had failed to bring Japanese surrender. Hiroshima's destruction was the result of a single bomb and a single plane. Although communication in the city was paralysed, it was clear to the Japanese military command and to the government that a terrible new weapon had been deployed against them. A nuclear device was certainly suspected and Japan's own nuclear physicists were sent to Hiroshima for confirmation. Within days, all of Japan knew of the catastrophe not only because of fast-spreading war rumours, but because the Americans themselves informed the Japanese of the Hiroshima event by dropping over 6 million leaflets over 47 cities. General Marshall was probably not alone in being shocked that the government in Tokyo had not immediately sued for peace.

Indeed, even the Emperor, locked in his war-room bunker, had become resigned to defeat by early 1945. Prince Konoye, a former prime minister and one of Hirohito's closest confidantes, was already urging peace on almost any terms. To Konoye, surrender was a preferable alternative to the looming threat of communism. However, Hirohito was concerned above all about what the enemy would do to him, suspecting as General Umezu had told him that the Americans would massacre his entire family. In addition to worrying about a bloody end to his own life, Hirohito must also have reckoned it likely that the Japanese Imperial system would be abolished. This indeed was the sticking point on which so many American and Japanese lives were lost in the final months of the war.

Some 48 hours after the dropping of a bomb on Hiroshima, Tojo urged the Emperor to surrender. At last, the hitherto paralysed Hirohito reacted and informed his Lord Chamberlain Kido that the war must be brought to an end. Yet the Supreme War Council, at which Hirohito urged surrender, was not convened until 9 August, some three days after the nuclear devastation of Hiroshima. However, at this meeting, while Prime Minister Suzuki urged acceptance of the Potsdam Declaration, most of the military members of the council led by General Anami, minister of war, believed that better terms could be negotiated. Alternatively, Anami suggested, 'Would not it be wondrous for this whole nation to be destroyed like a beautiful flower?'[19] The meeting dragged on into the evening, with Hirohito appearing in person to persuade a divided council to accept the Potsdam Declaration. To add to the surreal drama of these discussions, it should be remembered that a plutonium bomb 'Fat Man' (named after Sydney Greenstreet's character in the film *The Maltese Falcon* (1941)) had been dropped on Nagasaki that morning killing 25,000 people outright and, on the same day, Soviet troops had poured across the border into Manchuria. Still the council dithered.

Eventually, a cable was transmitted to the Japanese embassies in neutral Bern and Stockholm to the effect that the Potsdam ultimatum would be accepted, but with the proviso that 'the said declaration does not compromise any demand which prejudices the prerogatives of his Majesty as a Sovereign Ruler'.[20] In Washington, Secretary of War Stimson wanted to accept the Japanese offer, although Secretary of State Byrnes argued vehemently against it.

Everywhere opinion was finely divided. In the House of Commons the newly elected member of parliament, James Callaghan, later to become British prime minister, devoted his maiden speech to arguing the need to 'get rid of him [Hirohito]',[21] although Clement Attlee fell into line behind Stimson and Grew. After the arguments were made, Truman sided with Stimson on the grounds that the institution of Imperial household could be moulded as America saw fit. However, in drafting a reply Byrnes merely referred to a future government as 'by the freely expressed will of the Japanese people'.[22] Also Truman gave orders to halt the atomic bombing; according to his secretary of commerce, Henry Wallace, the president was appalled at the thought of killing another 100,000 at a stroke, particularly 'all those kids'.[23]

Byrnes's message was received in Tokyo after midnight on 12 August. Hirohito now accepted surrender though the military remained horrified at the threat to their *Kokutai*, implicit in the American response, and the War Council remained deadlocked throughout 13 August. In Tokyo, novelist Yukio Mishima noted that in expectation of surrender, 'everywhere there was an air of cheerful excitement'. However, by this stage, even Stimson was tired of the Japanese prevarication and his thoughts turned to the possibility of getting the next atom bomb delivered to a Japanese target by 17 August. Also impatient, Truman ordered the restart of conventional bombing and authorised raids on Kumagaya and Isezaki. Finally on 14 August, the Emperor again appeared before the War Council, and eventually won over even General Anami, who argued to the end that the war was not lost. After a day of wrangling over the nature of the script, the Emperor recorded a message to be delivered by radio; it was the first time an Emperor had ever been heard by the Japanese people.

The drama continued to the last. A group of four fanatical young officers killed the commander of the First Guards division in order to hijack the Emperor's recording; when they failed to find it, the conspirators committed suicide. Finally the Emperor's broadcast was heard at noon on 15 August.

> After pondering deeply the general trends of the world, and the actual conditions obtaining to our Empire today, we have decided to effect a settlement of the present situation by resorting to an extraordinary measure. We have ordered our government to communicate to the governments of the United States, Great Britain, China and the Soviet Union that our Empire accepts the provisions of their Joint Declaration ... Despite the best that has been done by everyone ... the war situation has developed not necessarily to Japan's advantage, while the general trends of the world have turned against her interest ... The Enemy has begun to employ a new and most cruel bomb, the power of which to do damage is indeed incalculable, taking the toll of many innocent lives. Should we continue to fight, it would result in an ultimate collapse and obliteration of the Japanese nation, but it also would lead to the total extinction of human civilization.[24]

In spite of the curmudgeonly acceptance of defeat and the peculiarities of the Emperor's court language, the Japanese, huddled in groups over their radios in every village and town in Japan, understood the enormity of the message. Some wept, others collapsed to the ground, but film director Akira Kurosawa noted that in the streets of Tokyo, 'The people in the shopping streets were bustling about with cheerful faces as if preparing for a festival the next day.'[25]

The Japanese military was less happy. Several factions within the army, anticipating the end of the Imperial system, started to plan the rearing of a young Emperor who could be brought back at some future date. As for General Anami, he wrote a *tanka* (short poem) on a scroll and, facing the Imperial Palace, committed *seppuku* (ritual suicide by sword pressed into the abdomen followed by slashing of the throat).

3

Mao and the Chinese Revolution

China: 1945—54

When the Emperor announced Japan's surrender on 15 August 1945, the relief in China must have been palpable. Few countries had suffered more than China, which had been at war with Japan for eight years following the Japanese invasion in 1938 from its Chinese base in Manchuria, a province that they had sequestered from China in the early 1930s. They were not pleasant visitors. Just as the Japanese had brutalised and enslaved the people of Korea earlier in the century, so the Chinese suffered ruthless suppression; in some areas a deliberate policy of genocide was pursued.

The worst episode came in December 1937, as the reinforced Japanese armies in Manchuria advanced down into the Tientsin—Peking region of Northern China. The now infamous *Rape of Nanking*, with its estimated 150,000 victims, may have been the apogee of Japanese brutality in urban China, but the slaughter of Chinese peasants was equally robust. At Ten Mile Inn, a village in the foothills of the Taihang Mountains, a passing Japanese unit killed ten villagers for doing nothing more than hiding. For good measure houses in the village were also burnt to the ground. Ten Mile Inn was lucky; in many villages entire populations were massacred. Across Northern China, Japanese aviators sprayed bubonic plague–carrying fleas; flasks of deadly bacteria including cholera, dysentery and anthrax were tossed into rivers; 'cakes laced with typhoid were scattered around bivouac sites to entice hungry peasants'.[1]

In aggregate, the slaughter in the countryside far exceeded the Japanese army's urban atrocities. Some estimates suggest that over 40 per cent of North China's population of 44 million people were eradicated. Iris Chang in her stomach churning account of *The Rape of Nanking* suggests that the total military and civilian death toll of the Chinese population during the eight-year war with China may have been as high as 19 million. Whatever else was produced by the *Chinese Holocaust*, it is clear that fertile conditions were created for a new Chinese power structure that could show itself capable of defending China from foreign barbarians.

Although the depredations of Generalissimo Chiang Kai Shek's forces were on a different scale to the Japanese, nevertheless the *Kuomintang*'s (Nationalist Party) conduct did little to alleviate the sufferings of the Chinese peasant. In the four years preceding the arrival of the Japanese, Huang, a *Kuomintang* officer of the 53rd Army, had installed himself in the best house in Ten Mile Inn and had co-opted the village's clan leaders to extort taxes and procure peasant girls. When Chiang Kai Shek decamped from the capital of 'Free China' from Nanking to Wuhan in 1938, and subsequently to Chungking, in Szechwan province, for the duration of the Second World War, his *Kuomintang* forces behaved and were treated like an invading army. For a country that had already suffered from the collapse of the *Qing* Dynasty in 1911, and the breakdown of the Confucian social order and its replacement by a system of 'Warlord-ism' and banditry, the ravages of foreign invasion, combined with an oppressive *Kuomintang* government, had inevitably left a deep sense of exhaustion.

Not surprisingly, therefore, the two former combatants, the *Kuomintang* led by Chiang Kai Shek and the communists led by Mao Zedong, were both anxious to avoid a resumption of the civil war that had been patched up in 1937 in order to fight the Japanese. The fragility of this relationship reflected its shallow roots. The United Front itself had developed out of a curious episode where Chiang had been captured and taken prisoner by one of his own commanders at Xian in 1936. He was only released, on condition that he cease his campaigns against the communists so that the country could unite to defend itself against the Japanese. In reality the United Front was little more than a truce; the communist government in Yanan even refused to have nationalist officers in its area. What little trust there may have been between the two sides was comprehensively shattered in January 1941, when a unit of several thousand communists troops was ambushed and wiped out by the *Kuomintang*.

Nevertheless when a war-weary Mao went to Chiang's temporary capital at Chungking in August 1945, it may well have been with a genuine intention to come to terms. However, while Mao was prepared to cede nine of his base areas to the *Kuomintang*, he rejected the integration of the remaining ten communist bases and insisted on keeping communist forces under his control. Meanwhile, communist and nationalist forces raced each other to take control of the formerly Japanese-controlled areas of Northern China and Manchuria. By October 1945 the talks were deadlocked and Mao left Chungking never to return. Sporadic hostilities inevitably broke out between the two sides and, although General George Marshall, sent by President Truman, arranged a truce in January 1946, tensions continued to increase. When communist troops moved into the parts of Manchuria, garrisoned and then vacated by the Russian army, Chiang sent nationalist troops to evict them. A breakdown in the ceasefire ensued, and Marshall gave up his doomed mission in June with the complete knowledge that any compromise between the two sides was impossible. War fatigue notwithstanding, civil war would not be avoided.

During the year of negotiations following the end of the war with Japan, both sides had continued to build their strength. Mao's army had grown rapidly to 910,000 soldiers in 1945 compared to 92,000 soldiers in 1937; still Chiang had more than twice that number, backed up by American tanks and aeroplanes. In July 1946, Chiang launched a full-scale offensive against the communists in the North China Plain. Avoiding major engagements, Mao beat a tactical retreat and even evacuated Yanan, his base since 1935, to set up a new headquarters at Shanxi. By the end of 1946 most of the North China Plain was in *Kuomintang* hands. Even though the nationalists suffered much higher casualties than the communists, to the outside world a complete victory for Chiang must have seemed inevitable.

However, in July 1947, Mao counter-attacked. In an audacious gambit General Liu Bocheng, supported by his Military Commissar, Deng Xiaoping, lead the People's Liberation Army's (PLA) 129th Division across the Yangtze River and surprised the nationalist forces in southwestern Shandong. After inflicting 50,000 casualties and capturing four nationalist headquarters, Liu and Deng then set off on a 300-mile march in 20 days as they sought refuge in the Dabie Mountains from the pursuing nationalist forces. For the remainder of the autumn and winter, the communists were pursued by Bai Chongxi, Chiang's best general. However, in the best traditions of guerrilla warfare, the communists eluded and harassed the *Kuomintang* forces in the mountains.

Liu and Deng were reinforced in spring 1948 and, by the autumn, Mao was confident enough of victory against the increasingly demoralised nationalist forces that he launched the first of three offensives in Manchuria and Central China that were to secure him ultimate victory. Again the 129th Division with a force of 300,000 communist soldiers took a leading role in what became known as the Huai-Hai campaign; after the Battle of Huai-Hai and the ensuing surrender of the nationalist forces, Mao set out exacting peace terms. Although Chiang rejected the terms, he nevertheless resigned as president of the Republic. From this point the communists were faced with little more than 'mopping up' operations. Only Bai Chongxi in Hunan held up Lin Biao's advance. By the spring of 1949, the communists were triumphant. Beijing had surrendered on 22 January and the Victory March was celebrated on 2 February, with a PLA resplendent in their captured American tanks and uniforms. Mao, who had chosen Beijing, the traditional capital of the emperors, as his own, slipped unnoticed into the city on 25 March.

In little more than three years after the cessation of hostilities with Japan, the 55-year-old Mao had overcome seemingly insurmountable odds to achieve victory in a revolution for which he had struggled for 28 years. On paper Chiang should have been invincible. At the end of the Second World War, Chiang controlled three quarters of China, its cities, its ports and its tax revenues; he was also financed by the Americans, who had poured money and weapons into the *Kuomintang* since the beginning of the Pacific War. He had American aeroplanes and tanks; his soldiers were trained and advised by the US military. Chiang also had the tacit support of the Soviet Union. As Mao was later to tell the French novelist Andre Malraux, 'The Russians' feelings were for Chiang Kai Shek. When Chiang escaped from China, the Soviet Ambassador was the last person to wish him goodbye.'[2] How had Mao achieved such a crushing victory in so short a space of time? After all, Mao himself had predicted in 1947, that it would take five years to defeat the nationalists; yet he had achieved victory in less than two years.

To a large degree, the military success of the Chinese Communist Party must be attributed to the extraordinary character and talents of its first Chairman, Mao Zedong. Mao, the eldest of three brothers and a sister, was born at Shaoshan in Hunan Province on 26 December 1893. His home was a hillside farmhouse over-looking a lotus pond and close to the three acres that his soldier father had managed to acquire after leaving military service. Mao's father was a brutal, taciturn man who showed and received little affection from his son. However, Mao seems to have had a deep affection for his Buddhist mother. His father prospered by farming and added to his wealth by trading grain and lending money. By the categorisations which the Communist Party would later assess the peasantry he would probably have been described as a middle peasant and possibly even a rich one. Nevertheless Mao, who worked in the rice fields from the age of five, was and remained in every sense a typical peasant. In later life he would boast, 'I am the son of peasants and I have peasants' living habits.'[3]

However, by dint of his father's wealth, Mao benefited from a primary educa-tion from the age of eight. Here, Mao was fortunate in being born in a province, his-torically a corridor for the Imperial armies, that brought with them new ideas and intellectual exchange. The Hunanese were also renowned as forward thinkers, and had in the past produced famous Confucian philosophers such as the seventeenth-century Wang Fuzhi. Hunan produced the first girls' school in China in 1903, and when Yale came to sponsor an education programme, Changsha, the capital of Hunan, was chosen. It was there, following a food riot by hungry peasants, that a formative event took place in Mao's adolescence. The peasant protestors were de-capitated and poled. Mao would subsequently tell the American journalist Edgar Snow, 'I felt that there with the rebels were ordinary people like my family, and I deeply resented the injustice of the treatment given to them.'[4]

At age 13 Mao's father curtailed his education and brought him home to work in the fields, and manage the family ledgers. Mao, however, had already become a 'book worm' and in spite of his workload on the family farm continued to read voraciously. Eventually, he ran away to Dongshan Primary School that was located in his mother's home district of Xiangxiang. Here he befriended a teacher who had been overseas and started to become interested in modern technology and Western institutions. Perversely, one of his earliest heroes was George Washington and he developed an abiding interest in the history of warfare, martial strength and military courage. In an early article he was to write that 'the principal aim of physical education is military heroism'.[5]

His chance for military activity soon arrived. In the autumn of 1911, at the time that Sun Yat Sen was in the process of ending the *Qing* Dynasty, and bringing

Republican government to China, Mao had set off on foot to Changsha to enrol in a secondary school. In a symbolic act of anti-feudal feeling, Mao cut off his pigtail, the sort of rebellious action that he had typically displayed since childhood. Then he joined the revolutionary army for six months; it was during this period that he became acquainted with socialism for the first time. He later enrolled at the Hunan First Normal School where he developed his taste for scholarship and poetry. More importantly for the future, he made his first contacts with the intellectual 'avant garde' in Beijing. In 1917, Mao wrote his first article for Chen Duxiu's *New Youth* magazine. Chen, professor of literature at Beijing University, was later to become first secretary of the Chinese Communist Party. A year later, Mao initiated his first political organisation when he set up the New People's Study Society, whose aim was to denounce the 'Four Demons': foreign imperialism, capitalism, religion and Confucianism.

The timing of Mao's first foray was impeccable. It was the year of the Russian Revolution: an event which had a profound effect on the intellectual elite in China. Chen Duxiu reacted by setting up the *Society for the Study of Marxism*, which later became the Chinese Communist Party. Before the Russian Revolution there had been almost no interest in Marxism; it was only in 1920 that *The Communist Manifesto* by Marx and Engels was translated into Chinese. By 1920, Mao too had become a Marxist and began to organise communist activity in Hunan. Personal tragedy soon followed. Having rejected the arranged marriage organised by his parents at the age of 14, Mao fell in love and married Yang Kaihui, daughter of a professor at the Hunan First Normal School. The following year, Yang Kaihui and Mao's sister were arrested and executed in 1930 for their political activities.

It was in the next ten years of revolutionary activity that Mao was to develop his distinctive revolutionary philosophy. In the classic interpretation of Marxist–Leninist philosophy, revolution would first be led by the urban proletariat. Yet China was above all a peasant economy. Moreover, it was an agrarian economy that did not conform to the patterns of the vast German 'Junker' estates with which Marx was familiar. In 1918, China was a nation of small landowners with a higher ratio of farmer proprietors than in the USA, Japan or Germany; 51.6 per cent were owner-occupiers, while a further 22.8 per cent of the population owned part of their land while renting the rest. Landless peasants were a minority. The main agrarian problem was not so much equitable distribution of property but productivity and, worst of all, famine. Nevertheless, there were inequalities to be exhibited and unlike the urban intellectuals, Mao, with his peasant background, understood the revolutionary potential of the Chinese peasantry. He once explained to Edgar Snow, in one of those aphorisms that were to become his trademark, that 'Whoever wins the peasants will win China. Whoever solves the land question will win the peasants.'[6]

As early as 1928, when Zhu De joined the now renegade Mao in the mountains of Hunan to form the first Soviet and the Red Army, his followers were taught to help and respect the peasantry. Mao was following a different path from the sophisticated urban intellectuals, who had dominated the Chinese Communist Party since its inception and who were to orchestrate Mao's expulsion from the Politburo. These urban rivals, General Secretary Chen Duxiu and Li Lisan both led failed communists' uprisings respectively in Nanchung and Changsha.

The failure of the Russian model for urban revolution increasingly began to focus communist activity on Mao's unorthodox agrarian revolutionary approach that combined an understanding of both peasant motivations and guerrilla warfare. Mao himself explained, 'because warfare basically derives from the masses and is supported by them, it can neither exist nor flourish if it separates itself from their sympathies and co-operation'.[7] Mao's genius was to discover ways in which peasants, previously an ultra-conservative lumpen agricultural class, could be moulded into the backbone of a revolutionary movement.

Chiang Kai Shek, who had replaced Sun Yat Sen as head of the *Kuomintang* after the latter's death in 1925, began to recognise the threat posed by Mao's Red Army, which by the early 1930s had set up a Soviet in Jiangxi Province. In the fifth campaign to eradicate Mao's so-called bandits, Chiang is estimated to have killed over 2 million people by slaughter and starvation. Mao and Zhu De finally broke out of the *Kuomintang* encirclement and created the legend of the Long March that entailed a 14-month running battle with the nationalist forces. By the time Mao arrived in Shanxi in 1935, with just 8,000 of the 90,000 strong force with which he had started, he was the undisputed head of the Chinese Communist Party, having been elected to chairmanship of the Politburo during the Long March. The benefits of this epic battle were incalculable. Mao possessed a hardened core of battle-tested soldiers. Also the lessons of mobile guerrilla warfare were fully absorbed. Young revolutionaries flocked from all over China to the now famous communist leader installed at Yanan. The strategy for a long drawn-out struggle with the *Kuomintang* had fallen into place. In 1937, with brilliant clarity, Mao summed up his campaign plan, 'Our *strategy* is to pit one against ten, and our *tactics* are to pit ten against one.'[8] It is not surprising to learn that as a young man Mao had been an enthusiastic admirer of *The Water Margin*, a classical Chinese novel about banditry; guerrilla tactics were part of China's cultural tradition.

However, Mao absorbed the lessons of guerrilla tactics, which were to a large extent forced on the communists by their relative poverty vis-à-vis the *Kuomintang*; it was Mao's mobilisation of the villages which would win him the war. Unlike the *Kuomintang* who lived off the land, Communist Party officials, or soldiers under the direction of the military commissar, actively engaged in winning over the peasant communities. The hallmark of this communist activity, somewhat astonishing given later atrocities, was its moderation towards the rich peasants. Perhaps this was even more surprising, given Mao's uncompromising views as expressed in his 1927 report on the peasants of Hunan, 'We must create a short reign of terror in all parts of the countryside. A revolution is not like a dinner party, or composing an article, or doing embroidery.'[9]

However, for the time being, Mao's intellectual brutality took a back seat to pragmatism. While they may have been subject to a progressive increase in taxation, the wealthier peasants continued to farm their land privately and collect rents and interest from their tenants, albeit at reduced rates. Even when mutual aid groups were introduced in the villages that fell within the communist base areas, they were not harshly administered or repressive against the better-off peasants. Rewards from the group were shared out relative to what each had put in. Even mutual aid itself was not a system foreign to the Chinese peasants. As David and Isabel Crook pointed out in their pioneering sociological analysis of Ten Mile Inn, 'a certain amount of mutual aid had long been practiced in Chinese villages.'[10]

What is also clear is that the brutality with which the landlords and richer peasants were treated in the communist-controlled areas varied enormously from village to village and region to region. The hard-line Lin Biao, head of the army in Central China, apparently set off waves of slaughter in these regions, whereas others espoused a much more moderate line. The pragmatic Deng Xiaoping stated that 'our policy towards the rich peasants is to reduce their feudal aspects, but encourage their capitalistic aspects'.[11] In many cases, therefore, the communists were able to co-opt even the richer peasants to their first stabs at restructuring rural life, and in some cases the leading family clans retained their pre-eminent positions in village life.

It was only as the revolution was nearly won that repression of this class became more widespread. The 'Divide the Family Campaign', aimed at examining the 'rich peasant' background of those in positions of power, eventually yielded up its first anti-communist martyrs in Ten Mile Inn. At the end of this campaign, four men, against whom there were historic village grievances, were tried, found guilty and taken down to the river bed where they were stoned to death.

For the poor and middle peasants who constituted the vast bulk of the population on the land, the arrival of the communists was a godsend, at least to begin with. The poorest peasants were relieved of taxation and they naturally benefited from any redistribution of land from dispossessed landowners. In the restructuring of village governance, the middle peasants gained political position from the leaders of village clans, who either fled to join the *Kuomintang* or hung on precariously in the new environment. These middle peasants were often put in charge of the mutual aid groups and increasingly manoeuvred themselves into positions of power, as functionaries within the emerging communist state.

After the Japanese and *Kuomintang*, the communists proved benevolent rulers. In return the communists could count on the logistical support of the peasantry in the war against the *Kuomintang*. Through the organisation and indoctrination of Mao's military commissars, attached to every communist army unit, the peasantry were organised to perform 'rear services'; villages carried munitions and supplies, stretchered the wounded, made uniforms and importantly provided intelligence. As both the Americans and their military allies would find out in Vietnam, a politically motivated and logistically organised agricultural population massively reduced the odds in a battle between two armies so apparently mismatched in terms of equipment. Thus, John King Fairbank has noted:

> in the climactic battle of Huai-Hai region north of Nanking, the Nationalist armoured corps, which had been held in reserve as a final arbiter of warfare, found itself encircled by tank traps dug by millions of peasants mobilized by party leaders like Deng Xiaoping.[12]

The civil war between the communists and the *Kuomintang* is one which Chiang Kai Shek, with every advantage, should not have lost. However, unlike Mao, Chiang baulked at agrarian reforms that might have crossed the local warlords and their vassal landowners, to whom he was ultimately beholden. As the historian Richard Evans has commented:

> In the myriad villages of China, the administration of justice, the maintenance of law and order, the upkeep of roads, canals and irrigation, and the handling of representations to the county magistrate and his staff had all been in his [landowner] hands.[13]

Under the *Kuomintang* the power vested in the landlords had remained, but the social functions as required in the Confucian order of things had been undermined by the unrestrained corruption of Chiang's minions. Long before the end of the war, Chiang's government became little more than a self-serving military bureaucracy, whose main interests lay in carpetbagging rather than fighting. It is a notable fact that for all the US$ 2 billion that was poured into Chiang's regime by the USA, his army failed to launch a single significant offensive against the Japanese during the Second World War. Nevertheless, the war against Japan did assist in the depletion of Chiang's strength; the final Japanese offensive in 1944 cost the *Kuomintang* 700,000 troops.

That the supposedly devout Methodist, teetotal, prudish Chiang should have presided over a government of such legendary corruption is a curious paradox. That he should also combine this with an astonishing managerial and military incompetence was a misfortune for which the Chinese and the Western world would pay dearly. Spurning the advice of his American military advisors, Chiang hoarded his tanks and planes and refused to deploy them where it counted. After the initial successes of 1946, his army thus became marooned in their urban stockades by an increasingly communist indoctrinated and mobilised peasantry. Even in the cities, Chiang failed to garner support. Hyperinflation, nationalisation of industry, violent suppression of students, forced conversion of all foreign exchange and gold holdings into Yuan in 1948 and vexatious taxation of the professional bourgeoisie left Chiang virtually friendless outside his own cliques. In addition, constant micro-intervention in military operations added to failures in logistics that compounded his underlying failures of governance. It is hard not to agree with President Truman's succinct explanation, 'We picked a bad horse.'[14]

In combining guerrilla tactics with mass mobilisation of the Chinese peasants in the Northern Chinese borderland, and then later in the northern plains and Manchuria, Mao transmuted Marxist–Leninism into a revolutionary formula which proved staggeringly successful. Apart from amazing Stalin and the US State Department amongst others with the speed at which they destroyed the *Kuomintang* forces, Mao had developed a system of revolutionary organisation that was to spawn imitators throughout the underdeveloped countries of Asia, Africa and South America. Marxist–Leninism may have remained the dominant doctrine of post-war revolutionary activity, but it was Maoist strategies that were to dominate the global battlefields of communist insurrection in the post-war era.

The moderate policies that had wooed the Chinese peasantry in the communist-held territories before and during the civil war with the *Kuomintang* continued to be sustained thereafter. In part, there had to be a period of catch-up. Some two-thirds of the country, the South, South West and East that fell to the communists in 1949, had had almost no contact with the Communist Party. Nevertheless, throughout China, between 1947 and 1952, some 40 per cent of China's arable land was confiscated from just 4 per cent of the population and distributed to an estimated 300 million peasants. It is reckoned that these policies led to the execution of between 800,000 and 2 million 'landlords'; this was a mere foretaste of the horrors of communist rule to come.

However, for the vast bulk of the peasants, the immediate post-war, post-revolution period would come to be seen as a golden period. In the village Ten Mile Inn, villagers poetically described the arrival of the communists as 'the time when the sun rose in the West'.[15] By 1952, agricultural output had been restored or bettered pre-war levels. In large part, peace was the major cause of this prosperity. Also the mutual aid groups and later the agricultural producers' co-operatives were modest structural agrarian reforms, in sharp contrast with the later co-operative policy, which did little harm to output and may indeed have been beneficial in the early stages. Although the Land Reform Law of 28 June 1950 formally abolished the landlord class, wealthy peasants were often given active encouragement to maintain their food production.

Industry too benefited from peace. In 1949, industrial production had sunk to just half pre-war levels, but three years later pre-war output had been restored. This was due only in small part to private enterprise that for a time continued to be allowed by the communists. The *Kuomintang* had itself nationalised some 90 per cent of iron and steel production, 73 per cent of machine tools and 75 per cent of the chemical industry. Political stability, combined with reintegration of communications, and rebuilding of the railways that had been largely destroyed during the long years of war, produced a dramatic economic recovery.

Effective law and order added to the impression of a renewed society; prostitution, gambling and opium were outlawed, while mafias such as the Green Gang were destroyed. The introduction of social legislation also swept away much that was repugnant about pre-war China. Polygamy, concubinage and child marriage were outlawed; women were given equal rights to initiate divorce proceedings and to inherit property. While former nationalist administrators were allowed to retain office, official corruption, which had been the bane of *Kuomintang* rule, was also heavily punished in a series of purges from 1951. The mass executions of landlords apart, the early impact of communist rule therefore was relatively benign compared with what was to follow, and it is interesting to note how few of the intellectual or professional classes fled to Taiwan along with Chiang Kai Shek.

In part the modest pace of revolutionary rule may be explained by the fact that in 1947, there were only 4 million party members out of a Chinese population of 540 million. At this stage, Mao did not possess the trained manpower to implement the revolutionary concoctions that his intellect would ultimately demand. Until 1954, therefore, when a full constitution was implemented, China was ruled largely on the basis of six large geographical areas, closely correspondent to the divisions of the *Qing* Dynasty, with primacy given to the army. The four main posts in each of the regions (North East, North West, North, East, Central South and South West) consisted of first party Secretary, chairman of the military political council, military commander and army military commissar. In addition to Zhou Enlai, elected prime minister in 1949, Liu Shiaoqui, Mao's deputy and putative successor, and Zhu De, head of the PLA, the men who controlled these regional posts, were the dominant figures of the tightly knit cabal of communist leaders who, with Mao, were to rule China for the next 15 years.

The 24 regional posts were held by just 13 men including Gao Gang, (four posts in the North East, i.e. Manchuria), Rao Shushi (three posts in the East), Lin Biao (three posts in Central South), Deng Xiaoping (two posts in the South West) and Peng Dehuai (two posts in the North West). What is now quite clear is that Mao did not command the same supreme authority as, for example, Stalin in Russia. In part, this was because of the extraordinary comradery enjoyed by the Chinese communist leaders in Yanan; 'The *Yanan Spirit* became famous for hard work, discipline, frugality, altruism, self sacrifice and self reliance.'[16]

Indeed part of the success of the communists in the civil war can be traced to the commonality of purpose displayed by their leaders. With the exception of Gao Gang and Rao Shushi, who were purged in 1953, there were few changes in the pecking order in the first decade of communist rule. It is notable here too that Gao and Rao were purged, not for some ideological impurity, but for plotting to replace Liu Shaoqi and Zhou Enlai as numbers two and three in the Politburo.

While Mao had been given greater powers as chairman of the Central Committee and Political Bureau, in a new constitution adopted by the Communist Party at the seventh Party Congress in April 1945, he used his authority sparingly. Surprisingly too at this stage he was quite happy to tolerate and indeed encourage ideological debate even when it did not accord with his own views. Neither does it seem that this was merely political pragmatism. For example, Liu Shaoqi, who had been trained in Russia, was much more Leninist in his belief in the primacy of power of the revolutionary vanguard than Mao, who emphasised the mass line. Unlike Mao who believed in a rapid move to collectivisation, both Liu and Zhou Enlai were of the opinion that collectivisation was a 'long-term' goal, which could be achieved only when China had been industrialised to produce enough tractors and fertilisers.

Apart from Mao's relatively minor 'rectification' campaign against unsound ideology at Yanan in 1942, there was no other hint in his behaviour of the purges to come. While Mao's tolerance may in part have been political pragmatism, there seems enough evidence to suggest that Mao himself had not yet developed the tyrannical qualities that would later manifest themselves with such alarming brutality towards his former colleagues in arms. On Mao's role, we may concur with Professor Frederick Teiwes, who states that 'Mao served as the final arbiter of policy disputes when his associates were unable to reach a consensus.'[17]

In conclusion, therefore, it may be said that if Mao had died in the early 1950s he might well have been remembered benignly, save for his savagery against the landlord class. He had proved himself a revolutionary of genius; he was the saviour of China's unity, and also the man who restored order to the ravages of a Chinese century that had hitherto seen the decay and collapse of the *Qing* Dynasty, the splintering of China into warlord fiefdoms, the incompetent government of Chiang Kai Shek's *Kuomintang* and a savage foreign war with Japan and its accompanying 'holocaust'. Few could have guessed that Mao would visit far greater tragedies than these on the Chinese people in the second half of the twentieth century.

4

Emperor Hirohito and the Tokyo War Crimes Trial

Japan: 1945—8

If the history of post-war Asia begins with Emperor Hirohito's surrender to the Allied forces on 15 August 1945, it could not have done so with a more disingenuous speech. Delivered in Hirohito's characteristic high-pitched squeak and in the language peculiar to the Emperor, the surrender speech was an artfully constructed tissue of lies which sought to deflect personal responsibility of the war from its true architect. The implicit reasoning for the surrender was to prevent the 'toll of many innocent lives' and 'the collapse and obliteration of the Japanese nation'.[1] If that had been the truth, Hirohito would have acceded to the unconditional surrender terms of the Potsdam Declaration months before the dropping of the atom bomb on Hiroshima at the cost of 140,000 lives.

Emperor Hirohito was fully aware that the war was lost at the beginning of 1945. An early surrender could have prevented the loss of some 150,000 Okinawan civilians, about 30 per cent of the population of the southernmost Japanese island, who were killed when used as a human shield for the Japanese army. In addition, had the loss of Japanese life been important to Hirohito, he would not have waited 11 days and the death of 70,000 more Japanese in Nagasaki before surrendering. The delay in surrendering, which so frustrated President Harry Truman and his Secretary of War Henry Stimson that the latter was considering dropping 50 more nuclear bombs on a target list of Japanese cities (excepting Kyoto, where Stimson had spent his honeymoon), was not caused by a fanatical military, but by an Emperor who wanted assurances as to his own personal survival.

Indeed, in order to make Secretary of State James Byrnes's reply of 11 August palatable, the army leaders — Hiranuma, head of the Emperor's Privy Council; Vice Foreign Minister Shinichi, after discussions with Foreign Minister Togo; and Chief Cabinet Secretary Sakomizu — resorted to mistranslation of the English text. The phrase 'shall be *subject to* the Supreme Commander of the Allied powers' was mistranslated to 'shall be *circumscribed by*'.[2] With this simple deceit, Hirohito was finally made to accept American terms. Indeed, he told Prince Asaka, the army commander directly responsible for the Rape of Nanking, that the war would have continued if the surrender terms had not allowed the continuation of the *kokutai* (the spirit of Imperial rule).

Even the sentiment expressed in the Emperor's speech that 'Despite the best that has been done by everyone . . . the war situation has developed not necessarily to Japan's advantage. . . .'[3] was a lie. Hirohito was vehement that he had been failed by his generals and soldiers. In a letter to Akihito – Japan's current Emperor – on 9 September 1945, Hirohito blamed this defeat on the incompetence of his generals. In fact, in the early years of the war, the Japanese army generals executed aggressive and imaginative battle plans with sheer brilliance. As for their soldiers, Japanese army units took higher percentage losses in battle than any other army engaged in the Second World War. Yet in his own diary, the young Akihito wrote, 'It was impossible for the Japanese to win this total war because from Taisho (Emperor Yoshihito) to early Showa (Emperor Hirohito), they thought only of their interests rather than the country, and behaved selfishly.'[4] These views clearly emanated from the Emperor and his court circle.

Most importantly, the surrender speech propagated the post-war myth that Hirohito had been a British-type constitutional monarch and a prisoner of the military faction, which had gained control of the government in the 1930s. Moreover, Hirohito set himself up as a 'saviour', not only of Japan by supposedly intervening to overrule the army's desire to continue to fight after the atom bomb, but also of the world. This is implicit in the statement 'Should we continue to fight, it would result in an ultimate collapse and obliteration of the Japanese nation, but it also would lead to the total extinction of human civilization.'[5] Remarkably, General MacArthur and SCAP (the office of the Supreme Commander of the Allied Powers), fully aware of the deceptions implicit in Hirohito's surrender, not only accepted the court version of Hirohito's wartime role, but also actively participated in creating the myth of his innocence.

Hirohito was born on 29 April 1901 at Aoyama Palace in Tokyo. His father, Yoshihito, was a sickly, indolent hunchback, whose life was blighted by meningitis caught soon after his birth. The dominant figure in Hirohito's early life was the transcending figure of Emperor Mutsuhito (Meiji), who gave his name to the Meiji Restoration that brought to an end the Shogunate system of government in 1869. As a cloak of respectability for the leading clans of the insurgency, the *Satsuma* (from the southern Kyushu island) and the *Choshu* (from southern Honshu), their rebellion was portrayed as a 'restoration' of the Emperor. The Meiji Constitution defined him as 'sacred and inviolable';[6] his role was defined as that of *genshu*, head of the empire, and *daigensui*, supreme commander.

Furthermore, the Emperor was given the power to summon the Imperial *Diet* (parliament), issue laws by diktat and appoint or dismiss the prime minister and his cabinet. He also controlled the pay and appointment of generals and civil servants.

The greatest of the nineteenth-century *genro* (senior advisors), Ito, produced *Commentaries on the Constitution* in 1889, which stated that 'The sacred throne was established at the time when the heavens and the earth became separated' (*Kojiki*). The Emperor is heaven descended, divine and sacred. He is pre-eminent above all his subjects. He must be reverenced and is inviolable.'[7] In practice, the young Meiji Emperor took the advice of his cabinet and counsellors, but nevertheless grew in stature and authority as his reign progressed. Hirohito gloried in the defeats of China in 1894–5 and Russia in 1904–5, with which his grandfather became closely associated.

With the death of Mutsuhito (Meiji) in 1912, Yoshihito (Taisho) ascended the Chrysanthemum Throne. The physically weak and inept new Emperor's arrival coincided with increasing calls for 'democratisation', particularly within the junior officer ranks of the army. In 1918 Yoshihito, who had become almost totally beholden to the *genro* (senior advisors), now became unable to carry out even the ceremonial civil, military and religious duties required of him. The future of the Imperial family was at crisis point. With the ending of the Great War in Europe, and the abolition of many of the great European monarchies, the very future of a Japanese Imperial system was called into question.

The ideas of industrialism, modernism and above all socialism, which swept the globe after the Great War, infiltrated the army and threatened the construct of the Meiji Constitution and the role assigned to the Emperor. The army, whose duty, after the Meiji Restoration, was seen as partly the defence of the empire and partly the defence of the state, also left ambiguous their attitude to the Meiji Constitution. Indeed, articles began to appear in the *Kaikosha Kiji* (the army journal), which implied a need to re-evaluate the role of the Emperor in binding the military with civil society. Added to these difficulties, the economy, which had prospered at the expense of the European powers during the Second World War, suffered a postwar downturn. The country was rocked by violent strikes at the Tokyo Artillery Arsenal (1919 and 1921), Kamaishi Iron Mine (1919), Yawata Steel (1920) and Kawasaki–Mitsubishi Shipyards (1921).

As a result of the threats to the Imperial system, the focus of the court elite now turned to re-energising a Japanese nationalism to counter the threat of foreign ideologies. This drive to define a uniquely Japanese system free from 'foreign contamination' centred on the concept of *Kodo*, literally the Imperial way. Fortune now favoured the reformers. The death of Emperor Yoshihito (Taisho) and the enthronement of Hirohito provided an important centrepiece for the revival of Imperial legitimacy.

As 'Emperor material', Hirohito was somewhat of an improvement on his degenerate father, but not a natural born leader. The 25-year-old Emperor, socially ill at ease, with a stooping gait and nervous mannerisms, was neither charismatic nor very articulate. Also, in spite of his interest in science, he was not regarded as academically gifted. After the war, Russell Brines, an Associated Press journalist, noted Hirohito's physical attributes: 'He was short, short sighted, round-shouldered . . . was weak chinned. His conversation consisted of inanities in a high pitched voice.'[8]

Nevertheless, for the court bureaucrats, Hirohito was all they had; they would have to make do. Fortunately, in elaborating on the nineteenth-century myth of the Emperor's descent from the God of the Earth and Sun Goddess, *Amaterasu Omikami*, the mystery was best built by keeping Hirohito out of sight and ear. The only photographs that the press was allowed to publish of the Emperor were carefully staged, showed him from the waist upward and never with another person. In schools, the nineteenth-century Rescript on Education was used to install a mass programme of Emperor worship.

Hirohito, a seemingly inconsequential individual of modest ability, did not, however, lack ambition. He longed to soar in the public esteem in the manner of his grandfather and to match his exploits with which he had grown up as a child. A tour of Western Europe, which helped to build up the image of the Crown Prince after his seven years of military training, also introduced him to a different picture of the world. He would later acknowledge how George V had shown him that his life had been like that of a 'bird in a cage'. He came back to Japan determined to engage in the real world of action; for him this meant politics and the army. He was determined to recapture the power and glory won by his grandfather.

Hirohito's first tentative political interventions came with his strong objection to Giichi Tanaka's cabinet formed in April 1927; no doubt, prompted by his advisors he objected to Tanaka's distributing ministries to members of his *Seiyaku* Party. A party-parliamentary system on the European model did not appeal to Hirohito, who did not want a rival institution to the authority of the Emperor and his inner circle. He therefore insisted on a cabinet chosen irrespective of 'ability', in other words, individuals who followed the Emperor's own policy line. By aiding the decline of 'government by cabinet', Hirohito helped usher in a government system which favoured the increasingly expansionist-minded army.

Emperor Hirohito did little to hold the army back even when confronted by evidence that they had exceeded their authority. Although he became aware within weeks that the Manchurian Incident of 18 September 1931, a supposed Chinese-organised explosion near the South Manchuria Railway, was in fact carried out by his own senior army officers as an excuse to launch an offensive in Northern China, Hirohito nevertheless supported the army's territorial aggression, which led to the creation of Japanese-controlled *Manchukuo* (Manchuria). In respect of these conquests, the Emperor was happy to attend parades, drills and march-pasts and granted some 3,000 military and civil awards. When the League of Nations voted by 41 to 1 against Japan's wanton aggression in February 1933, Hirohito supported the withdrawal of Japan from that organisation, beating even Adolf Hitler to that particular honour.

In 1933, Prince Konoe Fumimaro, an aristocrat who had increasing influence within Hirohito's court, published *Sekai no genjo o kaizo seyo* (reform the world's status quo), in which he stated:

> Unequal distribution of land and natural resources cause war. We cannot achieve real peace until we change the presently irrational state of affairs. In order to do that, we must . . . recognize two great principles. The first is freedom of economic exchange – that is to say, abolition of tariff barriers and the emancipation of raw materials. The other is freedom of immigration. Few possibilities exist for implementing these principles in the near future, however . . . as a result of our one million annual population increase, our national economic life is extremely burdened. We cannot wait for a rationalising adjustment of the world economic system. Therefore we have chosen to advance into Manchuria and Mongolia as our only means of survival.[9]

In the period up to 1941, Konoe would become Hirohito's favoured prime minister and a close confidante thereafter.

Hirohito also showed his steel when, on 26 February 1936, a revolt of 22 junior officers and 1,400 troops took control of the army headquarters and assassinated numbers of leading statesmen, including Finance Minister Takahashi and Saito Makato, the Lord Keeper of the Privy Seal; it was not coincidental that this attack came just a week after the pro-parliamentary and anti-fascist *Minseitō* (Constitutional Democratic Party) had won Lower House elections.

Hirohito ordered the ruthless suppression of the rebellion and the trial and execution of 17 of its ringleaders. Their demands were for faster rearmament, even though defence spending had risen from 3.47 per cent of GDP at the time of the Manchurian Incident to 5.63 per cent in 1936. The rebellion was put down, not because Hirohito did not, in fact, approve of the more aggressive inclinations of his junior officers, but because it was a perceived threat to his own position. Rather than reduce the military role of his government, Hirohito used the rebellion as an excuse to increase the military make-up of his subsequent cabinets. After the failed uprising, the power of the army was increased with the requirement that all ministerial defence posts be filled with serving officers. The '26th February' incident, as it became known, thus ended by fulfilling the objectives of its progenitors.

Using 'mass' techniques every bit as totalitarian as the Nazis in Germany, the Ministry of Education mobilised the populace with the publication in 1937 of an aggressively nationalist pamphlet, *Kokutai no hongi* (the fundamentals of the national polity). The pamphlet, which eventually sold 3 million copies, described the Japanese Emperor as a living God and attacked western individualism comparing it unfavourably with the selfless qualities of the Japanese. The people were also reminded of how the *kamikaze* (divine winds) had saved Japan from a Mongol invasion at the end of the thirteenth century.

As the ideological campaigns for war were geared up towards the end of the decade, the Emperor's active participation in war planning increased. After 1936, Hirohito set aside full cabinet meetings and instead caballed with a core of four or five ministers to set foreign policy. Foreign policy documents, *Criteria for National Policy* and *Foreign Policy of Empire*, preceded a build-up of forces in Manchukuo to prepare for a possible war with the Soviets, while increased spending was authorised for the Japanese navy so as to match the strength of the USA. Also between January 1938 and December 1941, Hirohito convened eight military conferences with senior ministers and generals to coordinate the policy. As military activity in Northern China became ever more extensive, the Emperor not only became involved in strategy but also made decisions on the planning and timing of campaigns; he even intervened in ongoing field operations. With ministers, Hirohito held audiences at which *naiso* (briefings) were given, and policies thus formulated were rubber stamped by the cabinet.

Although Hirohito did not order the infamous *Rape of Nanking* – where an estimated 150,000 Chinese men, women and children were butchered after the Emperor's uncle, Prince Asaka, lost control of his troops – the overall commander of the Japanese army in Northern China, General Matsui, was honoured for his achievements in February 1938; these awards were given in spite of the fact that Hirohito was fully aware of the massacres two months earlier. Neither did Prince Asaka go unrewarded; in April 1940 he was given the Order of the Golden Eagle. More importantly, it seems highly unlikely that Hirohito, a keen amateur scientist, did not know of, or indeed approve, the directives for Unit 731, which carried out hideous chemical, bacterial and neurological experiments on Chinese and other prisoners. The Emperor must also have had authorised the planned genocide of civilians in Northern China. These policies, known as *sanko sakusen* (burn all, kill all, steal all), were estimated to have killed some 2.7 million Chinese.

As for prisoners of war, Japanese breaches of the Geneva Convention were standard practice. Well-known atrocities included the 'Bataan Death March' and the infamous slaughter of captured troops in the construction of the Burma Railway. Even in prison camps, such as the one in Nagasaki, the mortality rate of youthful soldiers held in captivity was astonishingly high, some 25 per cent over three years. The full horror of prisoner treatment is shown by the fact that whereas 4 per cent of prisoners died in German captivity, the equivalent rate in Japan was 27 per cent.

Even Hirohito was subject to pangs of conscience. According to Kido, he vacillated over the conquest of South East Asia; Hirohito suggested that

> these were actions such as those taken by Frederick and Napoleon . . . [but] our country does not want to act in such Machiavellian ways. Shouldn't we always try to bear in mind the true spirit of *hakkōichi'u* [benevolent rule] which has been our policy since the age of the Gods.[10]

His high-minded sentiments did not bring him to overrule the quest for empire.

Another of Hirohito's teachers at court in the early 1930s, Matsuoka Yosuke, a former executive of the South Manchuria Railway Company, was chosen by

Konoe to become the foreign minister in his cabinet of July 1940. Before taking office, he gave a 'supposedly' off-the-record interview, which was promptly filed with the *New York Herald Tribune*. 'In the battle between democracy and totalitarianism,' Matsuoka opined, 'the latter adversary will without question win and control the world. The era of democracy is finished and the democratic system bankrupt ... Fascism will develop in Japan through the people's will. It will come out of love for the Emperor.'[11]

Not only was Hirohito intimate with the most fervent advocates of war with America, but he was also deeply involved with the planning process for the surprise attack on Pearl Harbor. He received the plans for the attack as early as 8 November and went over them in detail with the chiefs of staff on at least two occasions. In the week prior to the Pearl Harbor attack of 8 December, Hirohito had military meetings almost every day, and on the day of the attack, he listened to every available radio frequency for news of the outcome from his specially constructed 'war bunker': '... when I heard the good news of the surprise attack, I felt the goodwill of the Gods.'[12]

Given the overwhelming evidence of Hirohito's complete complicity in the ideology, strategy, planning and execution of Japan's war effort, his survival as Emperor to the ripe old age of 88 is one of the great paradoxes of post-war history. In large part, the decision lay with General MacArthur, the Supreme Allied Commander in Japan who was given virtually dictatorial powers in the execution of his task of ruling Japan after their unconditional surrender. Backed up by an army of 400,000 troops, the Supreme Commander's will was law.

MacArthur's leniency in dealing with Hirohito is even more peculiar, when set against the swift trial and execution of Japanese army leaders that he orchestrated after the liberation of the Philippines. Even the Japanese expected retribution. Plans were made for taking and nurturing a youthful new Emperor to take the place of Hirohito. The Emperor's youngest brother, the 31-year-old Prince Mikasa, urged that an abdication was necessary for the survival of the institution. However, when the Imperial household raised the issue of abdication with SCAP, it was emphatically rejected.

It seems likely that MacArthur arrived in Japan with an *idée fixe*: the Emperor must survive. Although senior officials in the Truman administration had favoured the removal of the Emperor, the 'New Dealers' at the State Department's 'Postwar Programmes Committee' concluded a report in favour of retention of the Emperor. At a conference in Manila at the beginning of 1945, Colonel Sidney Mashbir, the head of the Allied Translator and Interpreter Section, stated that 'It would be folly to kill the Emperor ... you cannot remove worship from these people by killing the Emperor.'[13]

Also the fanatical resistance of the Japanese army in Okinawa and elsewhere, even when defeat was inevitable, may have convinced MacArthur that an occupation of Japan, with a hostile population, would cost American lives and resources.

Retention of the Emperor, it was reasoned, could help mollify the populace and ease the governance of Japan. MacArthur would later write that

> Hanging of the Emperor to them would be comparable to the crucifixion of Christ to us. All would fight to die like ants. The position of the gangster militarist would be strengthened immeasurably. The war would be unduly prolonged; our losses heavier than otherwise would be necessary . . . the mystic hold the Emperor has on his people and the spiritual strength of the Shinto faith properly directed need not be dangerous. The Emperor can be made a force for good. . . .[14]

For his guidance, MacArthur also relied heavily on the advice of Brigadier General Fellers. Fellers, a member of the Office of Strategic Services (OSS; a forerunner of the CIA) and a former head of psychological warfare operations, became MacArthur's military secretary in the early years of occupation. He rated himself a 'Japan expert' and, indeed, in a paper entitled 'The Psychology of the Japanese Soldier' had correctly predicted the emergence of *kamikaze* (literally 'divine wind') pilots, who had been used as a last ditch attempt to save Japan. Fellers argued that 'The people of Japan, who believe themselves to be gods, are unaware of and absolutely cannot understand either democracy or American political idealism. . . .'[15]

As a student at Earlham College, Richmond, Indiana, Fellers had befriended Isshiki Yuri, a Japanese Quaker, and later Kawai Michi, a founder of the Keisen Girls School in Tokyo, whom he had met on his first visit to Japan in 1920. Also, his cousin Gwen was married to diplomat Terasaki Hidenari, who later worked at the Imperial court as a liaison to Fellers. From these disparate contacts in which he reengaged when he arrived in Japan, Fellers made it clear that he needed an introduction to the Palace so that he could assemble proof that Hirohito had no connection to Pearl Harbor. Throughout, Fellers appears to have been motivated principally by a desire to prove the correctness of his analysis. Privately, he admitted that 'as Emperor and acknowledged head of state, Hirohito cannot sidestep war guilt. He is a part of, and must be considered an instigator of, the Pacific War.'[16]

In addition to the 'pacification' rationale for the retention of Hirohito, MacArthur and the Republican right wing were in political conflict with the liberal 'New Dealers' in the Truman's administration. Fellers, at a meeting with Mizota, commented that 'The most influential advocate of un-American thought in the United States is Cohen [sic] [a Jew and a Communist], the top advisor to Secretary of State Byrnes.'[17]

For Fellers and MacArthur, the real enemy was communism. For them, Hirohito was potentially a bulwark against the left-wing influences which, in Japan, had been set free by the occupation. Indeed, Chiang Kai Shek, who might have had most reason to demand Hirohito's head for war crimes in China, backed off because he saw the Imperial system as a better bet to head off communism in Japan. For similar reasons, MacArthur, after the liberation of the Philippines, quickly sought to eradicate the communist insurgents who had fought the Japanese during the war, while rehabilitating right-wing politicians who had collaborated with the Japanese military regime. For MacArthur, the Emperor represented a conservative order with which he could naturally identify.

The fact that some 70 per cent of the American public wanted Emperor Hirohito to be harshly punished was irrelevant to MacArthur's larger aims. When on behalf of Truman, Eisenhower sought clarification as to Hirohito's responsibility for Pearl Harbor, MacArthur returned a telegram on 25 January 1946. Basing his reply on Feller's 'expert' advice, MacArthur asserted that 'No specific and tangible evidence has been uncovered with regard to [the Emperor's] exact activities which might connect him in varying degree with the political decisions of the Japanese Empire during the last decade.'[18] However, it seems inconceivable that MacArthur was not fully aware of the Emperor's real guilt.

In seeking to exonerate Hirohito from any war blame, MacArthur found a willing elite prepared to cover up for the Emperor. After the Emperor's surrender, Prime Minister Suzuki Kantaro immediately endorsed the myth of his beneficence by publicly claiming that 'His majesty gave the sacred decision to end the war in order to save the people and contribute to the welfare and peace of mankind.'[19] Similarly, Foreign Minister Shigemitsu Mamoru, a signatory to the surrender, who was later imprisoned as a Class A war criminal, assured the Americans of the Emperor's innocence. MacArthur was told the brazen lie that 'our Emperors always have been thoroughly pacifist.'[20] The Emperor's close advisor, Kido Koichi, also affirmed that Hirohito knew nothing about the attack on Pearl Harbor, until he chanced to hear it on the radio.

The Emperor also worked hard to obscure his culpability. The charge that if Hirohito could overrule the army to surrender, he could equally have done so to prevent the war and its concomitant atrocities was not easy to dismiss. On Sunday 5 March 1946, Hirohito called five trusted aides to his bunker to confide his version of the war. In a bizarre scene, the Emperor had a single bed set up in which he lay in pure white pyjamas on the finest soft cotton pillows. As Inada later recorded,

> people might ask why at such a moment we were hastily requested to listen to the Emperor's account. Around that time, however, people were questioning his responsibility in connection with the war crimes trials, and there was a need to record the Emperor's candid feelings quickly.[21]

In five meetings with aides over three weeks, Hirohito fabricated a self-serving story which fully distanced him from any responsibility for the war. He claimed to have always stood aloof from politics and said, 'as a constitutional monarch under a constitutional government, I could not avoid approving the decision of the Tojo cabinet at the time of the opening of the hostilities.'[22] In an English summary of Hirohito's testimony, which along with the full Japanese text was deposited with MacArthur's secretary, the Emperor essentially concluded that 'actually I was a virtual prisoner and powerless.'[23] The infamy of Hirohito's lies and his abandonment of former political and military friends and supporters were not discovered until the publication of the 'summary' in Japan in 1997. By this time, the contemporaries on whom Hirohito had pinned his own war crimes were long dead.

The Imperial household also played a critical role in developing friendly relations between the court and senior American officers within SCAP. Diversions included cherry blossom viewing within the Imperial Palace grounds, sword fight exhibitions and wild boar hunts. More importantly, they guarded the Emperor's diary, royal correspondence and any other material that might have incriminated the Emperor. This material is still inaccessible today. In addition, courtiers played a key role in persuading the senior military officers, who were committed at the Tokyo War Crimes Trial, to deflect criticism of the Emperor and to deny his involvement in the war.

The Tokyo War Crimes Trial itself was flawed from the start by the fact that the chief suspect, and by any observation the major criminal, Emperor Hirohito, was not only excused committal for trial, but was not even allowed to take the witness stand on behalf of the defendants. This would have been like conducting the Nuremburg War Crimes Trials without Hitler, supposing of course that he had still been alive. The decision not to bring Hirohito to trial was purely political. As Brigadier General Fellers told Mizota and Admiral Yonai, '... it is extremely disadvantageous to MacArthur's standing in the United States to put on trial the very Emperor who is co-operating with and facilitating the smooth administration of the occupation.'[24]

Indeed, SCAP engaged in priming the defendants' answers at their trial. According to the notes that Yonai kept of his meeting with Fellers, MacArthur's military secretary told him that

> it would be most convenient if the Japanese side could prove to us that the Emperor is completely blameless ... I want you to have Tojo [General and Prime Minister at the time of Pearl Harbor] say as follows; 'at the Imperial Conference prior to the start of the war, I had already decided to push for war even if His Majesty the Emperor was against going to war with the United States.[25]

MacArthur may well have believed that there would be civil difficulties without the Emperor, but it may also have been in the back of his mind that the perception of difficulties or failure in the post-war occupation of Japan could jeopardise his presidential ambitions. The result was an American political 'show trial'. This was a curiously paradoxical outcome for MacArthur, a general for whom the fight against Stalinist Russia was to become the centrepiece of his political and military strategies.

The Chief Prosecutor Joseph Keenan, sent from America to indict the Japanese war criminals, had had every intention of aiming his energies at the Emperor but, just before leaving America, was instructed by President Truman that on no account was Hirohito to be charged. Robert Dohini, a prosecution team member, would later recall that

> as we boarded the plane we learnt, from a letter delivered to Keenan by President Truman practically at the airport, that we should lay off Hirohito and . . . the whole Imperial Household . . . I was told personally: do not attempt to interrogate any of them.[26]

Whether it was the dubious validity of the whole exercise or whether it was Keenan, an inveterate lecher and alcoholic famed for helping bring to trial the famous 'bootlegger' and gangster Al Capone, that caused him to appear often inebriated and disinterested in court is open to question. Seven Class A criminals were duly executed by hanging, and others were given prison sentences. Those executed included General Tojo, prime minister and hero of the early war years, who won lasting infamy in Japan, not for his war crimes but for botching his suicide when the American soldiers came to arrest him. By comparison, the Emperor's aristocratic favourite, Prince Konoe Fumimaro, committed *seppuku* (ritual suicide) in exemplary style as soon as he was put on the list of those to be committed. This may have been a side deal with the Emperor, which went wrong; supposedly Konoe was being put on the list just for the sake of appearance, rather than any real intention to find him guilty of any crimes.

Prince Asaka, the local commander of Japanese forces at Nanking, also escaped trial and spent the occupation in discreet retirement; his immediate superior General Matsui, who was notably less responsible for Nanking, was not so lucky and was hanged. Perhaps most shockingly, General Ishii, the commander in charge of Unit 731, secured his survival; in the days before the Japanese surrender, Ishii injected his last 40 prisoners with prussic acid, cremated the bodies and dumped their ashes along with other 'specimens' into the Sungari River. Ishii then went into hiding and bartered his freedom, in exchange for the information he had gleaned from torturing and murdering prisoners in the process of biological and chemical experimentation. All charges against him were dropped. Prosecutor Colonel Sanders recalled that 'MacArthur agreed to immunity in return for all the information. I had MacArthur's word we would not prosecute.'[27] General MacArthur shamefully passed on this gruesome research information to US military scientists.

Three other men linked to Unit 731 and the chemical and biological war carried out against Chinese civilians, Hideo Futaki, Masaji Kitano and Ryoichi Naito, went on to found Green Cross, a Japanese pharmaceutical company specialising in blood products that later listed on the Tokyo Stock Exchange. By a quirk of fate, executives of this company were later found guilty of knowingly selling HIV-tainted blood products, and Green Cross was merged into the Mitsubishi Group in 2001.

The Tokyo War Crimes Trial did not go entirely to plan. On 31 December 1947, General Tojo went briefly 'off-message' regarding the pre-arranged farrago of a story that had been concocted prior to the trial. The degree to which the trial was a charade was clearly displayed by a prosecutor, who had not only been warned by Keenan that the Emperor was 'off limits', but also helpfully coached Tojo in secret so that he could go back into court and recant previous testimony that was damaging to Hirohito.

The flawed character of the trial was not lost on all the 11 judges. Some of the accused, such as Hirota with a 6–5 decision in favour of hanging, lost their cases by narrow margins. Incongruously, the Indian judge sent from Calcutta to sit on the tribunal, Radhabinod Pal, was a supporter of the Nazi sympathiser Subhas Chandra Bose, the Indian nationalist extremist, whose Indian forces had fought for the Japanese; Pal even supported the objectives of the Japanese 'Greater East Asia Co-Prosperity Sphere' and voted against every conviction on the grounds that the launching and waging of war by a sovereign state could not be considered a crime.

The president of the tribunal, Sir William Webb, perhaps unaware of the murky details of Japan's genocidal campaigns in Northern China, considered the Japanese defendants worthy of lighter sentences than the Germans, whose crimes had been greater. However, about the Emperor he noted that 'No ruler can commit the crime of launching aggressive war and then validly claim to be excused for so doing because his life would otherwise have been in danger.'[28] Judge Henri Bernard of France wrote possibly the most discerning dissenting opinion when he observed that the declaration of war by Japan 'had a principal author who escaped all prosecution and of whom in any case the present Defendants could only be considered accomplices'.[29]

Even members of SCAP were horrified at the poverty of American justice on display. Brigadier General Thorpe, one of the officers responsible for selecting the criminal candidates from the Japanese war elite, described the trials as 'mumbo jumbo'; he described the execution of Class A war criminals as simply an act of revenge. General Willoughby, MacArthur's head of intelligence, also panned the trial process as 'the worst hypocrisy in recorded history'.[30] Emperor Hirohito sailed blithely through the whole process. There is no record as to the Emperor's appetite, when he incongruously dined with the chief prosecutor on the day the death sentences were confirmed on his former subordinates.

At the Potsdam Conference, President Truman had described the Japanese as savage, merciless and fanatical. Days before the Japanese surrender, in response to a clergyman's protest about the use of the nuclear bomb, Truman had stated that 'The only language [the Japanese] seem to understand is the one we have been using to bombard them. When you have to deal with a beast you have to treat him as a beast.'[31] Yet at the conclusion of the war, Truman allowed the Japanese Emperor, the main perpetrator of the attack on Pearl Harbor and of atrocities throughout Asia, to escape unpunished; meanwhile, in a clearly flawed trial, lesser subordinates were condemned to death. The blame for this miscarriage of justice falls squarely on General MacArthur and his advisers, in particular Brigadier General Fellers. In their defence, it could be argued that throughout the Cold War period Japan proved to be a steady bulwark against communism and that in the broader geopolitical context, it could be argued the protection of the Emperor was fully justified.

However, would Japan have proved less malleable without their Emperor? This now seems unlikely. After 15 years of war, the Japanese people were exhausted, their economy in tatters. American troops arriving in Japan were simply amazed at the wholesale destruction of a city which had been burnt to the ground by fire-bombs; in spite of the devastation, Japanese troops had fought with fanatical bravery to the end. Yet beneath the surface, civil disobedience and opposition to the Emperor and the government were rife. In 1944 an officer of the *kempetei* (Japanese secret police) reported that the populace was febrile to the point of insurrection. Field intelligence confirmed that 'many people have reached a state where it is almost immaterial to them whether the Emperor is retained or not'.[32]

In spite of the war and the Emperor's nationalistic propaganda campaigns, there were 417 labour disputes in 1943. The left posed a not unreal threat to the Hirohito regime. Indeed, on the eve of Pearl Harbor, a Soviet spy network was uncovered with roots as far as Ozaki Hotsumi, an advisor to Prince Konoe. In fact, incidents of anti-government actions and prosecutions of public attacks on the Emperor increased rapidly after 1941. By 1945 the Home Ministry, whose *tokkotai* (special higher police) acted as a kind of 'thought police', reported that 'Antiwar thoughts and feelings finally have come to the point where they even curse and bear resentment against his majesty. . . .'[33]

At the very least, it seems likely that MacArthur could have forced the Emperor's abdication without risking social conflagration. That fact that he did not choose to do so was largely the result of a faulty analysis of the importance of the Imperial system in Japanese society, particularly the degree to which it had been tarnished by the end of the war. In part too, MacArthur's eyes were fixed on the bigger picture of the coming fight against communism. Lastly, MacArthur and the Truman administration may have fallen into the 'patronising' and demonstrably erroneous view that, whereas Nazism in Germany was a cancerous aberration, Japan's pre-war aggression was a result of primitive societal values.

The end result was a remarkable escape for the Japanese Emperor from punishment for the heinous crimes for which he was responsible. As the historian John Dower has concluded in his epic account of post-war Japan, *Embracing Defeat* (1999), America, by choosing to ignore Hirohito's guilt and by participating in the cover-up of this fact, 'came close to turning the whole issue of "war responsibility" into a joke.'[34] The outcome was hardly a matter for laughter. The fact that Hirohito, a cruel monster who matched Hitler for overwhelming ambition, for territorial conquest and for personal aggrandisement, and who was responsible for genocide in China and the incidental deaths of millions of civilians during his Asian wars, should live out his life as the constitutional monarch and head of state of Japan was surely the greatest miscarriage of justice of the Second World War.

5

Mahatma Gandhi: Passive Aggression

India: 1945–7

At midnight on 15 August 1947, Lord Louis Mountbatten, the last British Viceroy of India, passed the reins of power to the Congress party and its prime minister, Jawaharlal Nehru. Accompanied by rich pageants, grand ceremonies and popular demonstrations of rejoicing, 182 years of British rule in India was thus brought to an end. Yet Gandhi, the man who had brought about Britain's capitulation of its greatest Imperial territory, chose not to celebrate. Instead he remained in the Haoakali area of Bengal, where he had committed himself to the easing of communal tensions between Hindus and Muslims.

The perversity of this decision was consistent with the career of a revolutionary whose methods were entirely *Sui generis*. Unlike Mao, Gandhi did not borrow from Lenin and Marx; indeed he despised the violence implicit in Marxist–Leninism and fought to prevent it from polluting the spirit of the Congress-led fight for independence. Gandhi achieved his revolutionary goals by adopting 'non-violence' as his creed. At a personal level, while briefly accepting the presidency of the Congress, Gandhi renounced any personal ambition with regard to holding office. Neither was he a great orator, nor a writer of revolutionary literature. Apart from newspaper articles and interviews, Gandhi left little by way of books apart from his enigmatically titled autobiography, *The Story of My Experiments with Truth* (1927).

Moreover, for the last 25 years of his life, during the period in which he galvanised the move towards Indian independence, Gandhi spent most of his time teaching at the *ashram* he founded in Gujarat and spinning cotton on a primitive handloom. Yet, by the 1930s Mahatma Gandhi had achieved worldwide fame, and in 1944, with Indian independence now accepted as inevitable, Albert Einstein was to observe, 'In generations to come, it may be, will scarce believe that such a one as this ever in flesh and blood walked upon this earth.'[1] Mountbatten went even further, 'Mahatma Gandhi will go down in history on a par with Jesus Christ.'[2]

Gandhi was born on 2 October 1869 in Porbander, where his father was chief minister to the maharaja. He was the favourite youngest child, with three sisters and two brothers. The family later moved to the larger state of Rajkot, and at the age of 11 Gandhi was betrothed to Kasturba, the daughter of a wealthy Porbander merchant. His long-suffering wife, forced to follow the eccentricities of her husband's lifestyle, eventually died in the Aga Khan's Poona Palace where she and Gandhi were held under arrest for much of the Second World War.

After graduating from high school in 1887, Gandhi was persuaded by his eldest brother to pursue law rather than medicine. He broke Hindu strictures that forbade crossing of the 'dark waters' to London, and joined the Inner Temple. The stay in London was more remarkable for the people he met outside of his legal studies. Vegetarianism forced him away from normal society and into the arms of an avant-garde, liberal elite. The Vegetarian Society became his main entree to Victorian London. It also brought him into contact with the Theosophical Society's leading figures, Madame Blavatsky, and Annie Besant, a heroine of the Indian home rule movement who eventually became the only English woman elected to the Indian National Congress.

Another famous acquaintance of Gandhi's was Cardinal Henry Manning, whom he met after Manning's successful intervention on behalf of the dockers in their strike of 1889. He was to tell Manning, 'I had heard a lot about you and I felt I should come and thank you for the good work you have done for the strikers.'[3] Indeed, Manning may have been an inspiration for Gandhi's famed work as a negotiator and problem solver. Gandhi was certainly more adept in this area than as a litigator for which he lacked both temperament and intellectual rigour.

Notably at the legal bar back in Bombay, Gandhi was a comparative failure, while his future adversary and leader of the Muslim League, Jinnah, rose rapidly to the top of the profession. While Gandhi duly passed his bar exams to be admitted on 12 June 1891, his spiritual development during his time in London may well have had a deeper and more lasting impact than his legal training. With his introduction to Theosophist thinking, with its pantheistic universality and emphasis on spiritual experience, Gandhi's new friends shamed him into a much deeper inquiry into the *Bhagavad Gita*. In addition to developing his thoughts with regard to his own culture, Gandhi also studied the early Christian church and its communities, and benefited from the study of works by the great Catholic theologian and philosopher Henry Newman.

Gandhi was to develop a spiritual philosophy that saw all religions as different paths to the same goal. His belief in the need to unite Hindus and Muslims stemmed from his belief that there were no essential differences confronting the Indian people, either by race or by intrinsic belief. Gandhi later affirmed, 'I believe with my whole soul that the God of the *Koran* is also the God of the *Gita*. . . .'[4] At the heart of Gandhi's belief system was reverence for the ancient Hindu concept of *ahimsa* (divine love), by which society could be transformed by the power of love and gentle persuasion.

By dissolving the jagged edges that divided both religion and ideas, Gandhi believed that change could be effected without violence. The philosophy of non-violence that Gandhi evolved to undermine the British Empire in India was not simply a tactic to defeat the British, but was based on a deeply felt and practiced personal creed. 'My love for non-violence', Gandhi declared, 'is superior to every other thing mundane or supramundane. It is equalled only by my love for truth which is to me synonymous with the non-violence through which . . . alone I can see the Truth.'[5]

Not surprisingly, his esoteric views held little appeal or understanding to men of a more practical disposition. Winston Churchill dismissed him as a 'half-naked fakir', while Viceroy Linlithgow described him as 'the world's most successful humbug'.[6] Perhaps only in India could a revolution have been led by a non-violent spiritualist. As Michael Dobbs-Higginson has commented in his book, *Asia Pacific* (1994), 'Indians, be they rich or poor, literate or illiterate, are generally spiritually minded . . . few, if any, other countries have this constant and palpable presence of God in all his various forms.'[7]

If Gandhi's religious philosophy was highly individualistic, his attitude to family life became increasing eccentric. While he was in London, he was too ashamed by his youthful 'arranged' marriage to admit his marital status, a problem that caused him some embarrassing episodes with young women. Later his views caused him to renounce carnal lust completely, even within his marriage. The causes of this development are somewhat unclear although he apparently never fully forgave himself for leaving the bedside of his dying father, whom he tended during his last illness, in order to slake his lust for his then pregnant wife. Taking Catholic doctrines on sex to extremes in the traditions of Hindu asceticism, Gandhi propounded the view that sex should only have the function of procreation. He believed that, 'very few Indians need marry . . . a person who marries in order to satisfy his carnal desires is lower even than the beast'.[8]

This did not stop Gandhi from surrounding himself with attractive young women. He fell in love with many of them including Danish beauty Esther Faering, admiral's daughter Madeline Slade, Princess Amrit Kaur of Kapurthala, his physician Sushila and his granddaughter Manu. In later life, Gandhi would sleep naked next to his women admirers, and bathe with them; they would also massage him, and lie on top of him. There is no evidence that he ever broke his vows of celibacy. However, his long-serving secretary resigned when she found the 77-year-old Gandhi naked in bed with Manu. Nevertheless Gandhi was never furtive about his practices and beliefs, and spoke freely on the subject of sex. To the great industrialist G.D. Birla, he once wrote:

> If you give up salt and ghee it will certainly help you in cooling down your passions. It is essential to give up spices as well as *pan* and the like. One cannot subdue one's sex life and allied passions merely with a restricted diet . . . absolute cessation comes only after revelation of the supreme.'[9]

On returning to India in 1891, Gandhi did not immediately take up the life of a holy man or indeed a politician. He attempted to make his mark at the bar in Bombay, but when he failed to shine in his barrister's career, he accepted an offer to sort out a legal dispute for an Indian commercial family based in South Africa. He soon had his first experience of racial prejudice. A white conductor threw him out of his first class compartment for being 'coloured', and ordered him to join the van with the 'blacks'; when Gandhi refused he was thrown off the train. Thus began his first campaign against injustice.

It is perhaps curious to note that for a man who later went to extraordinary lengths to protect and advance the oppressed 'untouchables' of India, Gandhi made no attempt to advance the cause of South African blacks. He gradually established a legal practice with his Indian clients, but it was in his developing role as spokesman for the Indian merchant class and their grievances that he came to prominence. Back in India, Gandhi lectured on the problems facing Indians in Natal.

In 1902, he returned to South Africa and set up a law firm in Johannesburg, where most of his clients were Muslim businessmen. His first campaign of passive resistance came with his refusal to register for fingerprinting and ID cards, required by the Asiatic Ordinance Bill passed by the Legislative Council of the Transvaal. Eventually, he succeeded in forcing a compromise from General Smuts. The lessons of his success were valuable for the battle ahead. Gandhi commented that 'if we learn the use of the weapon *Satyagraha* (non-violent resistance), we can employ it to overcome all hardships originating from injustice . . . not here alone . . . more so in our home country'.[10]

In South Africa, Gandhi also distinguished himself by organising the Indian Ambulance Corps. Ever the enthusiastic nurse, Gandhi served as a sergeant major in his own corps for six weeks. While trying to set up a permanent corps, Gandhi went on a deputation to London where he clashed for the first time with Winston Churchill, who suggested that 'coloured people' could not be responsible rulers. Later, finding himself in London on the outbreak of the Second World War, Gandhi again raised an Indian Ambulance Corps to fight on the Western front. This time illness prevented him from serving, although he made up for it by tending to the dying Congress luminary Gokhale, who occupied the important post of the head of the Servants of India Society. In addition to nursing, Gandhi displayed other 'Florence Nightingale' tendencies; he developed a lifelong, almost obsessive interest in the cleanliness of public latrines. (He would often clean toilets himself as a means of highlighting one of the issues most associated with the 'low caste' problem.)

Although Gandhi had achieved a considerable reputation both inside and outside South Africa, the 46-year-old lawyer was now to embark on a radical transformation of both his lifestyle and his political career. On 20 May 1915, Gandhi established the *Satyagraha Ashram* near Ahmedabad; by the end of the year, his ascetic community comprised 33 residents. In a move that nearly caused his wife to leave him and which appalled the Hindu elite, three of Gandhi's invitees to join his commune were *Dheds* (untouchables).

At the same time, Gandhi abandoned western dress to adopt the *dhoti* (a primitive peasant garment folded to resemble an oversized nappy); even that was later abandoned for the loincloth, the clothing of the destitute. Increasingly Gandhi would dedicate his lifestyle and identify his political cause with the poorest classes. Travelling to political meetings on foot or, if necessary, in the teeming third class carriages of Indian trains, Gandhi developed a unique brand of political credibility. Virtually single handedly, Gandhi transformed the Congress movement from its middle-class roots. By adopting the lifestyle of a poor *sadhu*, Gandhi engaged with the vast Indian masses and became the focal point of the move to expel the British from India.

As well as taking on a more radical stance towards colonial rule, Gandhi also called for an anti-materialist way of life. His ideas were embodied in the simple commune at his ashram. Over time he became increasingly public about his beliefs. At the opening of the Banaras Hindu University, Gandhi, addressing a student audience in front of a committee of wealthy dignitaries and maharajahs, angered his hosts when he said, 'I feel like saying to these gentlemen, "There is no salvation for India unless you strip yourselves of this jewelry and hold it in trust for your countrymen.[11]"' This calculated insult forced the maharajahs, and even Annie Besant, from the stage. The students however were rapturous.

Gandhi now started to intervene actively in social affairs. He launched his first *Satyagraha* campaign in India on behalf of exploited Bihari peasants growing the Indigo plant. In the important commercial city of Ahmedabad, he persuaded Ambalal Sarabhai to cave in to his textile workers' demands. In spite of his antipathy to wealth, he nevertheless spent his life living from the copious handouts of rich patrons. As the Indian poet Sarojini Naidu joked, it cost a fortune to keep Gandhi in poverty.

However, Gandhi was not a socialist in the Marxist–Leninist mould. He believed in a voluntary form of socialism encompassing 'truth' and *ahimsa*. He asserted that 'Complete renunciation of one's possessions is a thing which very few even among ordinary folk are capable of. All that can legitimately be expected of the wealthy class is that they should hold their riches and talents in trust and use them for the service of the society.'[12] Unlike Nehru, a classic English-style socialist politician, Gandhi did not believe that India could be advanced materially through industrial development. While he rejected capitalism as exploitative, Gandhi also refused to allow the possibility that mechanisation of any kind could improve the living conditions of India's hundreds of millions of peasants. 'Heavy industry', he asserted, 'needs be centralized and nationalized. But they will occupy the least part of the vast national activity which will mainly be in the villages.'[13]

Gandhi believed that mass production was one of the means by which Britain was exploiting India. While his economic views would later bring him into conflict with Nehru and the socialist wing of the party led by Bose, in the 1920s Gandhi's populist views nevertheless struck a cord with the Indian masses. At Gandhi's prompting, Congress dropped its fees in May 1929 and a membership drive rapidly increased the numbers from 56,000 to 500,000. The sophisticated urban bias of Congress disappeared. In 1935, the Uttar Pradesh Congress had 62,703 members, of whom 62.2 per cent were rural, whereas the province's membership had swelled to 1.47 million members by 1938, of which 91.4 per cent were rural. Virtually single handedly Gandhi raised the political consciousness of the Indian masses.

There was also an increasing radical approach for dealing with the British. At the Nagpur Congress of 1920, Gandhi called for a move towards non-cooperation with India's colonial rulers. The 14,500 delegates resolutely affirmed his policies to the disgust of the Muslim Congress leader, Jinnah, who tried to amend Gandhi's radical stance. Shouted down and forced from the stage, the humiliated Jinnah left the Congress never to return. For the new Indian returnees from post-war London, the political excitement was immense. In his autobiography Nehru describes, 'a kind of intoxication. We sensed the happiness of a person crusading for a cause ... the thrill of mass feeling, the power of influencing the mass.'[14]

However, when Gandhi moved his new *satyagraha* campaign to a pledge to refuse tax payments to the British, disaster struck. At Chauri Chaura, a peasant demonstration turned violent after taunts from police. After the burning down of the police station, the hacking to death of policemen, and the resulting 21 deaths in all, Gandhi was so appalled that he suspended all civil action. Gandhi fasted for five days. On 22 March, he was sent to prison with a six-year jail sentence for his part in the incitement. Although Gandhi was soon released from prison after another fast that reduced his weight to just 99 pounds, he did not seek to re-ignite the contest with the British. To the fury of Nehru and the other young Congress leaders, Gandhi simply abandoned the field. In 1925 Gandhi resigned the presidency of the Congress.

It was now that Gandhi turned to spinning both in prison and in his ashram. The working of the *charkha* (primitive spinning wheel) became for Gandhi a devotional and spiritual exercise. Often taking vows of silence, he would spin cotton for 10 hours every day, sometimes for weeks on end. 'Hindu–Moslem unity is not less important than the spinning-wheel. It is the breath of life.'[15] The spinning wheel was also an important component of his economic philosophy. He loathed the squalor of urban slums that resulted from mass industrialisation and wanted to keep people on the land by employing them in spinning. Gandhi believed that machinery 'must not be allowed to displace the necessary human labour ... '.[16] Writing in the *Harijan* journal, Gandhi also noted that 'Mechanisation is good when hands are too few for the work intended to be accomplished. It is evil when there are more hands than required for the work. ... '[17] The importance of *charkha* movement became such that the wearing of traditional clothes made of *khadi* (home-spun cotton), became de rigueur for Congress politicians. Even today, the only wealthy people in India who wear *khadi* are politicians. Gandhian economics did not allow for changes in fashion.

Gandhi did not discard politics permanently however. Perhaps fearful that Jawaharlal Nehru, radicalised by his recent visit to Moscow, would seek to leave Congress and create a Marxist–Leninist party, Gandhi endorsed the radical proposals of Motilal Nehru that a campaign of nationwide non-cooperation would begin on 31 December 1931. In the meantime, Gandhi made specific demands including total prohibition of alcohol, reduction of land revenue demands and military expenditure by 50 per cent and an abolition of the salt tax. In the magazine *Young India*, Gandhi wrote, 'Next to air and water, salt is perhaps the greatest necessity of life. . . . It is the only condiment of the poor.'[18]

Gandhi's widely publicised 'salt' marches attracted huge popular attention and when he threatened to march on the salt beds of Dharasana, an alarmed Viceroy ordered his arrest. Nehru was also arrested, and he enthused that 'it is full-blooded war to the bitter end. Good'.[19] It was an epic encounter that captured the imagination of Indians and the world press. At Dharasana when the pacifist demonstrations were brutally broken up, Congress leader Patel commented, 'All hope of reconciling India with the British Empire is lost for ever.'[20] By the end of the year, 60,000 salt *satygrahis* were choking Indian prisons. The fact that salt only accounted for 2 per cent of revenues, the equivalent to one quarter of one rupee per head of population mattered little to Gandhi. Like 'tea' for the American colonies, Gandhi had turned salt into an emotive issue and a symbol of struggle against India's colonial rulers.

While to a Western eye, Gandhi's lifestyle and political methods may have seemed perverse and eccentric, he struck a deep cultural resonance with the Indian masses. Neither was Gandhi unaware of the international media and propaganda potential of his way of life. After release from prison, Gandhi went to London where he addressed bishops, MPs, unions and Lancashire mill workers. He met the King and Queen and was courted by celebrities such as Aga Khan and Charlie Chaplin. On his way back to India via Italy, he was given an audience by Mussolini. Dressed throughout in his *khadi* loincloth, the spindle-legged Gandhi, juxtaposed with his famous Western admirers, was a delight for the *paparazzi*.

In spite of the setbacks, Gandhi's methods were working. The Government Act of India in 1921 provided for a bicameral parliament. The Central Legislative Council comprised 140 members of whom 100 were elected; the Council of State provided 40 elected members out of 60. An Indian franchise of 5 million landowners and tax payers was constructed. The Viceroy's executive council was also provided with three Indian members. In 1927, Conservative Prime Minister Stanley Baldwin appointed a seven-man commission under Sir John Simon, and including Clement Attlee, to investigate and recommend further constitutional changes.

On 30 October 1929, Baldwin agreed to support dominion status for India combined with Indian all-elected legislative assemblies at provincial and national levels. Further advances were assured by the election victory of Ramsey

Macdonald's Labour Party in 1931. The tortuous process of reform thus took another leap forward with the 1935 Government of India Act that widened the Indian franchise to 35 million voters (including women and a 10 per cent allocation to untouchables) and provided for the creation of provincial legislatures in 11 provinces. In the ensuing elections, Congress won 716 out of 1,585 seats and took control of seven of the provincial assemblies.

Through such incremental gains, Congress, inspired if not led by Gandhi's charismatic presence, was well on its way towards achieving independence. Even the diehard supporters of empire such as Churchill framed their opposition to Indian independence in terms of the problems of religious antagonisms and the unacceptability of allowing Hindu governments while the caste system persisted. In May 1931, Churchill told the Indian Empire Society, 'Democracy is totally unsuited to India. Instead of conflicting opinions you have bitter ideological hatred.'[21]

Even Gandhi might have agreed on the latter point. Indeed there was always a tinge of hypocrisy in the attack on British rule while the 'untouchables' problem remained. Gandhi alone among the leadership fought the 'untouchable' cause. In March 1925, he battled with the maharaja of Travancore, who, siding with his Brahman elite, decided not to allow the *Dheds* to walk along a road in front of the holy temple at Vykom. Without the support of the *harijans* (children of God), as he renamed the untouchables, Gandhi believed that a bourgeois Congress elite would simply replicate the *Raj*.

While Gandhi became a masterly revolutionary, his views and method of combating the British conspired perfectly with the weaknesses of his enemy. Gandhi noted that the most effective way of combating British Imperial power was 'by turning the values of British Society in the twentieth century against it'.[22] These values were wholly liberal, even in the nineteenth century. Contrary to Congress's post-war rewriting of history, British rule in India was never characterised simply by an exploitative philosophy. The conquest of India had taken place largely by the ad hoc military adventures of the East India Company, a British commercial enterprise which sought to defend its commercial interests in a sub-continent riven by competing war lords and princely states. Only after the Great Mutiny in 1857 did the British government take direct responsibility for India and abolish the anachronistic position of the company.

Over the next century, British liberalism evolved. The era of competing empire-building between America and the European nations ended with the First World War. The electoral franchise had been widened and after 1918 included women. The whole apparatus of the now familiar 'liberal' state had started to come into being. Asquith and Churchill (then with the Liberal Party) had introduced the first tentative welfare acts in 1910. By the 1930s, the idea of empire no longer sat squarely with the feelings of a British electorate of liberal sentiment, which was now prepared to elect to office a Labour Party imbued with the fervour of utopian egalitarianism.

Even as early as 1917, the British government announced policies calling for 'the gradual development of self governing institutions with a view to the progressive realisation of responsible government in India as an integral part of the British Empire'.[23] After the ravages of life and spirit in the First World War, doubts about the durability of Indian Empire increasingly seeped into the India office. Sir John Seeley questioned whether control of India could be viable on economic grounds. 'It may be fairly questioned', he asked 'whether the possession of India does not or ever can increase our power and security, while there is no doubt that it vastly increases our dangers and responsibilities.'[24]

From a practical viewpoint too, the ravages of manpower in the First World War and the General Strike of 1927, followed by the onset of a worldwide depression, undermined the historic certainties of British mercantile strength. The industrial strength of America and Germany was beginning to impinge on the 'Greatness' of Britain. In 1943, Viceroy Linlithgow wrote that he was loath to 'lie back and let ourselves be pushed off the map by the Americans.'[25] The British establishment sensed that Britain was in relative decline; astute Indian politicians such as Nehru knew it.

Although British companies continued to dominate India, their position was being increasingly challenged by newly emerged Indian industrialists such as the Birla family, Marwari traders who developed vast enterprises around jute and cotton, or Dalmia Jain, who built a business empire on sugar, paper and cement. Increasingly India was self-sufficient in basic industrial commodities. Stock markets, which had been established in the nineteenth century, were also developing and showed a high degree of activity and sophistication compared to many parts of Europe.

Also, contrary to the myths propagated by Congress during their campaign for independence and later years, Britain did not monopolise trade or seek to isolate India from the rest of the world. It was a frequent complaint in London that despite the expenditures on Indian rule, Britain had failed to exploit and capitalise on the country's economic potential. This was the conclusion of the 1918 Report on Indian Constitutional Reforms. By 1939, the share of British imports to India had fallen to just over 30 per cent.

On the other hand, the Second World War brought further advantage to India's economy as its industrial base was built up to supply its armies in Burma. New industries included motor manufacture, chemicals, pharmaceuticals and light engineering. With an annual output of 1.5 million tons, the Tata family, *parsi* from Bombay, became the largest producer of iron and steel in the British Empire. Electric power production grew by 45 per cent during the course of the war.

The realisation in Britain that the era of empire was drawing to a close was also indicated by a sharp fall off in applications to join the Indian Civil Service (ICS). Whatever the feelings of the British establishment in London, it was not advising its sons to bet on a career in India. From the 1920s, new recruits from the ICS were increasingly drawn from the ranks of native Indians. While the British view of their Indian Empire was increasingly undermined at home, in India increased urbanisation, education, industrialisation and political representation, combined with decades of Congress propaganda, was naturally conspiring to bring about a sense of Indian national identity.

In the end, Britain did not lose its empire in India because it was undone by a World War that caused a 25 per cent fall in its GDP. Neither did Britain abandon its empire at the behest of a liberal American president. In fact, Roosevelt refused all overtures from the Congress leaders that could have been seen as dividing him from his British allies. Britain's Empire in India was lost well before 1939, and it is debatable as to whether the formalities were hastened or slowed by the onset of the World War.

Hitler may have believed that Britain should maintain its Indian Empire, but most British believed it was a losing cause; indeed many increasingly believed on moral grounds that India should be independent. Britain's weakness was that it was not a tyranny. It may have been fair political game for Gandhi and Nehru to describe it as such, but the truth was quite the opposite. If Gandhi had practiced civil disobedience under a Japanese regime, an event that Gandhi fully expected at the beginning of the war, there is little doubt that he would have been summarily executed. As Dr Kenneth Kaunda, president of Zambia, pointed out:

> In one way, the Mahatma Gandhi and I were equally fortunate in facing a colonial power which fell far short of being a ruthless tyranny. Britain has always been very sensitive to public opinion _ that is one of her glories. So the Viceroy who allowed reporters and even film cameramen into Gandhi's cell was inadvertently contributing to the effectiveness of the Mahatma's campaign of passive resistance.[26]

This is not to deny Gandhi's credentials as a revolutionary. His economic views may have been arcane, his religious life and practice eccentric, but he proved himself masterful at arousing the national consciousness of the mass of Indians and at exploiting the weaknesses of British rule. As Indian independence became inevitable, Gandhi's relevance declined.

By 1947, Mountbatten, influenced by the more traditional power brokers Nehru and Patel, whom Gandhi had aided in unseating the radical socialist Bose, judged their mentor to be a spent force. This little diminishes Gandhi's role. As a young man, the leading Indian national Bal Gangadhar Tilak had warned Gandhi that 'Politics is a game of worldly people, and not of *sadhus* [holy men].'[27] Gandhi was both *sadhu* and revolutionary genius who, in undermining the credibility of Britain's role in India, proved his many doubters wrong.

6

'An Iron Curtain Has Descended'

America—Soviet Union: 1945—61

In 1940, John Buchan noted with more than a little foresight that '. . . If the world is ever to have prosperity and peace, there must be some kind of federation— I will not say democracies, but of States which accept the reign of law. In such a task she [America] seems to me to be predestined leader.'[1] It was not a role for which the USA was psychologically prepared. Franklin Roosevelt had entered the war with the express purpose of defeating fascism and ending the European Empires, including those of its allies; the thought of creating a quasi-Empire or global American hegemony was a long way from his mind.

Neither did his successor, President Truman, a parochial mid-Westerner, step into Roosevelt's shoes with global domination in mind. As a senator, Harry Truman had been ferociously anti-totalitarian. Above all he was a pragmatist. Asked what he thought of Germany's invasion of Russia in 1941, Truman answered, 'If we see that Germany is winning, we should help Russia and if Russia is winning we ought to help Germany. . . .'[2] In spite of this stance, when Truman succeeded the deceased President Roosevelt, he found in Potsdam an opponent in Stalin who quickly disarmed him with his blunt, peasant manner and rough humour. 'I like Stalin,' Truman declared, 'He is straightforward. Knows what he wants and will compromise when he can't get it.'[3]

Like Roosevelt before him, there were grains of distrust towards their wartime ally, but on the whole Truman accepted the relationship at face value. We now know that from Stalin's side the relationship was purely one of convenience, and that the ending of the war against the axis powers merged seamlessly with the renewal of conflict against capitalist Western countries. To some observers this was soon self-evident. In November 1945, when Moscow Ambassador Averell Harriman asked Soviet Deputy Foreign Minister Maxim Litvinov what the West could do to satisfy Stalin, his reply was a blunt 'Nothing'.[4]

America's leaders were far more ambivalent, believing that a spirit of cooperation could continue long after the conflict. It was even anticipated that the experience of dealing with the West would open up trade with the Soviets; American industrialists waited eagerly in anticipation. The United States Bureau of Foreign and Domestic Commerce estimated that the Soviets would account for over 30 per cent of American exports after the war; this figure turned out to be less than 1 per cent.

Such was the genuine spirit of co-operation that both Truman and Acheson, on hearing of the first successful tests of the atom bomb, believed that America should share its technology with others including the putative United Nations. By contrast, when Stalin was told about the 'bomb' by Truman at the Potsdam conference, he immediately ordered Russian scientists to redouble their efforts and spurred on his armies to reach Berlin, where one of the prizes on offer was German industrial and scientific technology which would enable them to catch up with America.

As the only country with a nuclear weapon, America had the opportunity to win the Cold War before it had started. World domination was an open goal. Had the situations been reversed, it is inconceivable that the Soviets would have spurned the chance of global conquest. Stalin realised that the ending of the war would leave America as the sole world superpower; however, it was not a role for which the Americans themselves were preparing. In Congress the main concern of the dominant Democrats was troop reductions and cuts to military budgets.

There was a year of gestation before it fully dawned on the American political consciousness that having defeated two formidable enemies, Germany and the Japanese Empire, an even more formidable adversary had emerged in their wake. Churchill, relieved of his prime ministership by defeat in the general elections of 1945, had more time than most to ponder the future and, as during his 'wilderness years' of the 1930s, when he forecast the rise of an expansionist Germany, Churchill now predicted a new threat to the Western world.

Speaking at Westminster College in Fulton, Missouri on 5 March 1946, Churchill gave a speech that was prescient as it was alarming. Firstly he acknowledged America's overwhelming position of global power as a result of both its military and economic strength; this he believed made America accountable to the future. Also, as well as fully comprehending America's overwhelmingly dominant position, Churchill, understanding all too well the economic bankruptcy that war had wrought on Great Britain, realised that only America now could stand the strain of the battle ahead.

The nature of this battle was outlined with Churchill's usual clarity:

> From Stettin in the Baltic to Trieste in the Adriatic *an iron curtain has descended* across the Continent. Behind that line lie all the capitals of the ancient states of Central and Eastern Europe. Warsaw, Berlin, Prague, Vienna, Budapest, Belgrade, Bucharest and Sofia; all these famous cities and the populations around them lie in what I must call the Soviet Sphere, and all are subject, in one form or another, not only to Soviet influence but to a very high and in some cases increasing measure of control from Moscow. . . . In a great number of countries, far from the Russian frontiers and throughout the world, Communist fifth columns are established and work in complete unity and absolute

obedience to the directions they receive from the Communist centre. Except in the
British Commonwealth and in the United States where Communism is in its infancy,
the Communist parties or fifth columns constitute a growing challenge and peril to
Christian civilization ... what they desire is the fruits of and the indefinite expansion
of their power and doctrines.[5]

Churchill saw in America's post-war equivocation in taking up the position of
global guardian of the free world, that it had won by force of arms during the
Second World War, a possible repeat of the dithering by European powers in the
face of Germany's re-armament and expansionism under Hitler. Churchill's Fulton
speech was a clear call to President Truman and America to stand up to the Soviet
threat. America needed to demonstrate strength.

From what I have seen of our Russian friends and allies during the war, I am convinced
that there is nothing they admire so much as strength, and there is nothing for which
they have less respect than for weakness, especially military weakness'.[6]

Truman was never altogether convinced by the flamboyant Churchill and would
not have accepted it at face value. However, Churchill's speech added confirmation
to alarming reports of Soviet activity throughout Europe which were now reaching the State Department. Truman had seen free elections in Poland as a test case
of the Yalta agreements and told Soviet Foreign Minister Molotov that it would
be 'the symbol of the future development of our international relations'.[7] Already
General Marshall had bluntly warned Truman and Acheson at the end of February
1946 that 'It is not alarmist to say that we are faced with the first crisis of a series
of which might extend Soviet domination to Europe, the Middle East and Asia.'[8]

This view was most coherently argued by George Kennan, who served as
Averell Harriman's deputy head of mission in Moscow from May 1944 to April
1946. In his famous 'long telegram' of 8,000 words sent to Washington on 22
February 1946, Kennan argued that at the 'bottom of the Kremlin's neurotic view
of world affairs is the traditional and instinctive Russian sense of insecurity. Originally, this was insecurity of a peaceful agricultural people trying to live on vast
exposed plain in neighbourhood of fierce nomadic peoples'.[9] This sense of insecurity had now allied itself with a Marxist–Leninist ideology of world revolution
and global conquest. Soviet communism embraced a deterministic philosophy of
eventual global domination; Mao, not mentioned in the 'long telegram', also embraced this world view, though, in his mind, it would be China rather than Russia
which would eventually sit at the centre of this revolution.

The accuracy of Kennan's analysis of the Soviet Union's global ambitions is now
clear from the abundance of material available from the Kremlin archives; even
with this benefit of hindsight, Kennan himself quoted Stalin's words to a group of
American workers in 1927:

In the course of further development of international revolution, there will emerge
two centres of world significance: a socialist centre, drawing to itself the countries

which tend toward socialism, and a capitalist centre, drawing to itself the countries that incline toward capitalism. Battle between these two centres for command of world economy will decide the fate of capitalism and of communism in the entire world.[10]

As Kennan himself concluded, 'In summary, we have here a political force committed fanatically to the belief that with the US there can be no permanent modus vivendi. . . .'[11] If at the denouement of the Second World War, the Truman administration was unclear as to the future course of American relations with the Soviets, Stalin by contrast had no doubts whatsoever.

Also, according to Kennan, Stalin needed to demonstrate that the world was Russia's enemy as a legitimisation of his own rule. Marxist–Leninism provided a 'justification for their instinctive fear of outside world, for the dictatorship without which they did not know how to rule. . . . In the name of Marxism they sacrificed every single ethical value in their methods, tactics. . . . It is a fig leaf for their moral and intellectual respectability'.[12] In order to combat the innate expansionism of Marxist–Leninism, Kennan advocated a policy of resistance; strong diplomatic, institutional and propaganda action to stem the tide of communism, until such time that a melioration in Russian attitudes or more likely a collapse of their system allowed a more constructive dialogue. The long telegram became the intellectual progenitor of America's post-war policy of 'containment'.

The 'long telegram' led to Kennan being brought back to Washington by Truman's hard-line 'anti-communist' advisor, Secretary of the Navy James Forrestal. Under the latter's influence, Kennan also published, under the pseudonym 'X', an article which appeared in the July 1947 issue of *Foreign Affairs*, entitled 'The sources of Soviet conduct.' Here Kennan refined his arguments to conclude that

> the main element of any United States policy toward the Soviet Union must be a long-term, patient but firm vigilant containment of Russian expansive tendencies. . . . Soviet pressure against the free institutions of the Western World is something that can be constrained by the adroit and vigilant application of counterforce at a series of constantly shifting geographical and political points, corresponding to the shifts and manoeuvres of Soviet policy.[13]

Kennan also surmised that America would largely have to undertake this global exercise unilaterally and hope that over time the strain on the resources of the Soviet Union would force the 'gradual mellowing of Soviet power'.[14]

A mere seven weeks after Kennan's long telegram and a week after Churchill's 'Iron Curtain' speech at Fulton, Truman gave a speech to a joint session of Congress, specifically in relation to providing economic aid to Greece and Turkey, but in broad terms enunciating the strategy that would become 'containment'. While nodding politely in the direction of the United Nation's important role, Truman argued vigorously for independent American action to ensure America's prime foreign policy objective, 'the peaceful development of nations, free from coercion'.[15]

He argued that

> We will not achieve our objectives, however, unless we are willing to help free peoples to maintain their free institutions and their national integrity against aggressive movements that seek to impose upon them totalitarian regimes . . . [which] undermine the foundations of international peace and hence the security of the United States.'[16]

It was a speech which defined the thrust of American foreign policy to the present day.

For Truman, his policies were less swayed by the analyses of Kennan and Churchill than by the observation of Soviet actions in the post-war period. He observed:

> The peoples of a number of countries of the world have recently had totalitarian regimes forced upon them against their will. The government of the United States has made frequent protests against coercion and intimidation, in violation of the Yalta agreement, in Poland, Rumania, and Bulgaria. I must also state that in a number of other countries there have been similar developments'.[17]

Truman's speech, which went on to advocate a package of economic measures to alleviate the plight of Greece and Turkey, in effect foreshadowed 'domino' theory by which America needed to intervene to prevent the spreading contagion of communism.

It was not an easy sell to Congress. As with the end of the First World War, many American politicians wished to draw in budgets and turn their backs on the world. In February 1946, Great Britain, through its own economic difficulties, had been forced to end their financial support for Greece. Acheson told a journalist:

> There are only two powers left. The British are finished, they are through. And the trouble is that this hits us too soon, before we are ready for it. We are having a lot of trouble getting money out of Congress.[18]

As Truman pointed out, the benefit of economic assistance to stave off communism would come at a fraction of the price of the Second World War, which had cost America some US$ 341 billion. It was an economic and financial logic which was most famously pursued with the Marshall plan in Europe, but was carried out with an equally vigorous dispersal of funds throughout Asia in the post-war period. Financial assistance was increasingly accepted after China had been lost to communism; in America the 'China lobby' attributed the loss to the stinginess of American aid to Chiang Kai-shek. Later even quasi-ideological enemies such as India were awarded copious handouts by American tax payers in the hope of staying a complete switch to the communist cause.

It was not a strategy that was one-sided. By the mid-1950s Russia itself responded to America's economic onslaught by entering into foreign-aid agreements with some 20 countries including India and Indonesia. Mao would later follow with his economic diplomacy in Indonesia, Sri Lanka and particularly in Africa.

Nevertheless, in foreign-aid strategy, America could always outbid the Soviets and the Chinese. Economic diplomacy, both through financial support and by opening American markets to global exporters, remained the backbone of American hegemony in both Europe and Asia. Truman concluded his speech to Congress by telling them that,

> The free peoples of the world look to us for support in maintaining their freedoms. If we falter in our leadership, we may endanger the peace of the world—and we shall surely endanger the welfare of our own nation.'[19]

The 'Truman Doctrine' was a remarkably consistent extension of early American foreign policy; just as the Monroe Doctrine in the early nineteenth century had thrown the blanket of American protection over South America in the face of European Imperial domination, Truman now declared that the USA would protect the rights of all nations to self-determination in the face of the encroachments of the Soviet Empire. America's 'sphere of interest' was now global.

It was a statement of policy which resolutely rejected the isolationist stance that America had adopted after it had emerged as the world's major economic and military power after the First World War; Truman declared an intent that remained a fixed point of reference in the foreign policy of all American presidents up until the defeat and collapse of the Soviet Empire in 1991.

Any action taken by the USA in Asia throughout the post-war period can only be seen through the prism of the Truman Doctrine. Although Truman's Congressional speech only made reference to determined 'economic' action to support 'free' countries, it can be assumed that all who heard the speech would come to the conclusion that defence of the 'free world' could not preclude military possibilities.

Defence of the 'free world' would not be unilateral however. In Europe a military defence alliance against the Soviets would ultimately take form in the North Atlantic Treaty (NATO), which was signed on 4 April 1949. In December 1950, Eisenhower would be appointed as supreme commander of NATO; America's power and prestige was such that Eisenhower could insist on direct access to NATO heads of government. Although it was dressed as an alliance, the bankrupt European nations' contribution towards their own defence was largely window dressing for American military hegemony. Far from regaining their ability to defend themselves, over time, the European nations, except Great Britain and occasionally France, slipped into passivity under the defence umbrella provided by the Americans.

Henry Kissinger would later complain that Wilsonian idealism had triumphed in Europe, '. . . war is no longer accepted as an instrument of policy'.[20] Even Britain, America's staunchest post-war ally in the battle to defeat communism, was often ambivalent about the nature of the conflict. The socialist Prime Minister Clement Attlee asked Truman, 'Am I to plan for a peaceful or a warlike world? If the latter I ought to direct all people to live like troglodytes underground as being the only hope of survival, and that by no means certain.'[21]

British leaders were not universally enamoured of America's 'big brother' role, although Prime Minister Edward Heath's leading of Britain into the European Union should not be seen as the creation of an alternative to American hegemony; Heath, like Kennedy before him and most American politicians since, saw a European political structure as complementary to and not an alternative to American hegemony.

If the development of the Truman Doctrine showed America a clear path to its global hegemonic responsibilities in 1946, it was not until 1949 that the scale of the task ahead became clear; enlightenment as to the danger came with the loss of China to Mao's communists in 1949, and the explosion of a nuclear bomb in Soviet-controlled Kazakhstan on 23 September of the same year.

Post-war, Stalin, with a sparsely populated Siberia on his Eastern flank, realised that Asia could not be his immediate priority; although he had Asian allies, Kim II Sung in North Korea and Mao in China, he expected little of them. The defeat of Chiang Kai Shek, as much as it was a shock to Washington, was an unexpected bonus in Stalin's plans for global domination. Asia was now in play. For the Americans, the development of a Soviet nuclear threat also robbed them of their ultimate trump card in dealing with communist aggression. Truman now decided, with the encouragement of General Omar Bradley, to press ahead with the development of a thermonuclear fusion device. The nuclear arms race had begun in earnest.

On 30 January 1950 Truman called for the State Department 'to make an over all review and assessment of American foreign policy in the light of the loss of China, the Soviet mastery of atomic energy and the prospect of the fusion bomb'.[22] The resulting paper, along with the 'long telegram', became one of the two key documents of the Cold War; National Security Council paper *NSC no. 68*, as it became known, was authored by Paul Nitze, Paul Lovett and others, and concluded that America needed 'an immediate and large-scale build-up in our military and general strength and that of our allies with the intention of righting the power balance and in the hope that through means other than all out war we could induce a change in the nature of the Soviet system'.[23] The paper argued that given the known build-up of Soviet military capability the Russians would be able to destroy the USA within four years.

In the same year, John Foster Dulles, who was to become the most vigorous post-war anti-communist to head the State Department, published a book entitled *War or Peace* (1950). Dulles expounded a vigorous anti-communist crusade. 'There is no illusion greater or more dangerous than that Soviet intentions can be deflected by persuasion ... ', he concluded, 'Power is the key to success in dealing with the Soviet leadership. Power, of course, includes not merely military power, but economic power and the intangibles, such as moral judgement and world opinion. ...'[24]

Dulles's response to the global communist threat was rational and coherent. However, moral judgement soon deserted America, as Senator Joseph McCarthy, a junior senator from Wisconsin, whipped up a storm of populist terror at the possibility that the USA was already undermined by communists. In this respect, the grotesque McCarthyite communist witch-hunt, which began early in 1950, proved that excessive zeal could be almost as damaging to the anti-communist cause as complacency.

In January 1950, Alger Hiss, a former State Department employee who had been a member of the American delegation at Yalta, was found guilty of perjury after purportedly passing information to the Russians, a charge that was never proved. Nevertheless, the possibility of communists operating within government agencies created a media storm. In February 1950, Joseph McCarthy told a women's club in Wheeling, West Virginia, that 'I have here in my hand a list of 205 State Department employees who have been named as members of the Communist Party ... and who nevertheless are still working and shaping the policy of the State Department.'[25] Starting with this infamous speech, McCarthy, a drunken fantasist, whipped up a storm of popular alarm and became the most celebrated demagogue in American history.

Lyndon B. Johnson (LBJ) was dismissive of McCarthy while acknowledging his short-term impact:

> Joe McCarthy's just a loudmouth drunk. Hell, he's the sorriest senator up here. Can't tie his goddamn shoes. But he's riding high now, he's got people scared to death some Communist will strangle 'em in their sleep, and anybody who takes him on before the fevers cool—well, you don't get in a pissin' competition with a polecat.[26]

As LBJ predicted, the paranoia whipped up by McCarthy and his attempted purge of government institutions did not last. In trying to investigate the army, McCarthy overplayed his hand and was eventually censored by the senate by 67 votes to 22 for behaviour which brought the senate into disrepute. His career effectively ended, McCarthy sank into obscurity. The long-term effect of his ill-judged campaign rebounded against America's fight against communism because some liberal political groups later used 'McCarthyism' to scaremonger and to undermine the mainstream political effort to combat the very real threat posed by the Soviet Union. Given the state of fear about the communist threat, it is perhaps not surprising that in 1952 the American people voted their greatest military figure, General Eisenhower, into the presidential office. Although he doubted that America could afford to spend up to 20 per cent of its GDP on defence as advocated by *NSC no. 68*, Dwight Eisenhower fully endorsed the policy of containment and in a foreign policy, which he titled 'New Look', promoted a massive build-up of thermonuclear weapons.

The arms race that ensued became the leitmotif of the Cold War conflict and was to dominate relations between the two countries for the next 30 years even when the tide turned towards Strategic Arms Limitation (SALT I and SALT II) and later Strategic Arms Reduction under Ronald Reagan (START). In fact the SALT I treaty signed in 1972 simply increased, rather than decreased, the arms race. Inter-Continental Ballistic Missile (ICBM) deployment may have been frozen, but multiple independently targeted re-entry vehicles (MIRVs) which could deploy up to 10 nuclear heads in a single missile were not included in SALT I. In the four years from 1973 to 1977, American nuclear warheads increased from 6,000 to 10,000 while those of Russia increased from 2,500 to 4,000. Given that each device was now 20 times the power of the Hiroshima device, the possibility of total global destruction seemed very real. The ghoulish construct of 'mutually assured destruction' (MAD) and its global ramifications gave the dinner party doomsters their major topic for a generation; it was a subject which made Stanley Kubrik's *Dr. Strangelove* (1964) one of the seminal films of the period.

Given the lack of enthusiasm on the part of Europeans to defend themselves with conventional forces, it was that deterrent provided by America's nuclear cover which provided the basis of European security. It was only in Asia however that the possible use of nuclear weapons was seriously discussed and then only when communist forces threatened to overrun Korea and later South East Asia. The only exception to this rule was with regard to the development of nuclear capability in China. In 1963, William Foster, President Kennedy's director of Arms Control and Disarmament Agency told the Kennedy Library:

> it wouldn't be too hard if we could somehow get an anonymous airplane to go over there, take out the Chinese facilities—they've only got a couple and maybe we could do it, or maybe the Soviet Union could do it, rather than face the threat of nuclear weapons.[27]

The development of ICBMs gave the USA unprecedented hegemonic power over its allies. Eisenhower for one was wise enough to realise that power would need to be carefully husbanded. As early as 1953, in a speech to the Society of Newspaper Editors, Eisenhower noted that 'Every gun that is made, every warship launched, every rocket fired signifies, in the final sense, a theft from those who hunger and are not fed, those who are cold and are not clothed.'[28]

Eisenhower may have been the architect of the greatest arms race ever witnessed, but he cautioned against the expansion of American power for its own sake. In his valedictory address, President Eisenhower emphasised the dangers of American power to its own core values; he noted the 'conjunction of an immense military establishment and large arms industry' and suggested that 'In the councils of government, we must guard against the acquisition of unwarranted influence, whether sought or unsought, by the military–industrial complex.'[29]

In addition to the rapid development of nuclear deterrent, the Eisenhower administration also supported a burgeoning global intelligence operation; developing out of the wartime Office of Strategic Services (OSS), the Central Intelligence

Agency (CIA) was established by Truman's National Security Act of 1947, and further refined by a Central Intelligence Agency Act in 1949. In a report by the Doolittle Committee to Eisenhower in 1955, it was made clear that a more aggressive role for the CIA was essential:

> It is now clear that we are facing an implacable enemy whose avowed objective is world domination by whatever means and at whatever cost. There are no rules in such a game. Hitherto acceptable norms of human conduct do not apply. We must develop effective espionage and counterespionage services and must learn to subvert, sabotage and destroy our enemies by more clever, more sophisticated, and more effective methods than those used against us.[30]

The operations of the CIA, albeit frequently overstated in importance, were to become synonymous with the Cold War struggle. In Asia, where institutions in the post-war period were either new or poorly formed and their economies weak, CIA money could, on occasions, go a long way in shaping policy. In the Philippines, Vietnam, Thailand and South Korea in the post-war period, the CIA would play critical roles at certain junctures, while it would later play a dramatic role in Pakistan and the attempt to throw back Soviet power in Afghanistan.

Contrary to early expectations, the Cold War erupted into real conflict in Asia rather than Europe. Stalin's main interest in terms of expansion and concern about the Soviet Union's own security lay in the future of Europe. By the early 1950s however, Europe had largely been carved up, and America, with the help of the Marshall Plan, was shoring up the institutional resistance to the communist political groupings which were strongly represented in France and Italy. In hindsight, Asia, with weaker economies, nascent institutional structures and emergent nationalist movements, was always more likely to be more fertile ground for communist expansion.

Most importantly, the fall of China to the Maoists opened Asia to the possibility of the Soviet Union making significant inroads into America's regional hegemony. Korea was the first test. Charles Bohlen, another Kremlinologist and former Moscow colleague of George Kennan, telegraphed the State Department to suggest that Kim Il Sung's invasion of South Korea appeared to be 'a very clear case of typical Stalin methods whereby he initiates action not formally and directly involving the Soviet Union which he can and will press to the full only if weakness is encountered . . . you may be sure that all Europeans to say nothing of the Asiatics are watching to see what the United States will do'.[31] It was the biggest test of Truman's resolve. He did not fail. 'Korea is the Greece of the Far East', he told George Elsey, 'If we just stand by. . . . There's no telling what they'll do, if we don't put up a fight now.'[32]

Mao had shown that, with his brand of peasant-based guerrilla warfare, Asian government could be toppled. Furthermore, not wishing to yield global communist leadership to the Chinese, Stalin and his successors became increasingly committed to competing with their ideological allies. Although Acheson had nurtured the possibility of splitting Mao from Stalin, and even when he failed, cherished long-term hopes of success, it would be over 20 years before America would make a start to accommodation with China. In the meantime, as the Chinese army was to demonstrate in Korea, a formidable new threat to American defence of free Asia had emerged. Until the presidency of Richard Nixon, American foreign policy was posited on the belief that the Soviet Union and China were coterminous.

In looking for the causes of America's aggressive defence of its post-war Asian hegemony, it must be concluded that the USA sought to preserve the global trading system which had propelled its original revolutionary 13 colonies in the late eighteenth century to become the dominant global power by the beginning of the twentieth century. The Soviet Union with its closed autarkic economic system posed a drastic threat to America's very existence and to the moral and cultural values on which its society was based. Furthermore, the Soviet Union did not simply wish to exist within its post-war boundaries, but sought through dissemination of revolutionary propaganda and judicious use of military support to undermine democratic constitutional systems with the aim of expanding its autarkic Leninist–Marxist world. As the Cold War historian Robert Conquest has concluded, 'The Soviet assumption that all other political life forms and beliefs were inherently and immutably hostile was the simple and central cause of the Cold War.'[33]

It was not a challenge that America could afford to ignore. The Soviet quest for global domination initiated a response which called for not only the defeat of what President Ronald Reagan would call 'the Evil Empire', but also victory for America's free trade and liberal democratic system. Albeit with a moral, political and social construct altogether different from the Soviet Union, America, in trying to achieve its geopolitical objectives in Asia, established what was in effect a quasi-Empire or hegemony, which was not lessened by the fact that the political development of Asian countries in the post-war period, notwithstanding the interventions of the CIA and other American agencies, was largely self-determined.

7

Stalin, Mao and Truman: Post-War Alliances

China: 1945–50

Geopolitical stress often manifests itself in pressure points. In the post-war era in Asia, there was no relationship more critical than that between America and China, and there was no pressure point more sensitive than the independent existence of Taiwan, or the Republic of China as it became after Chiang Kai Shek's occupation of the island in 1949. Although for most of the post-war period it was the 'Cold War' between America and the Soviet Union that caught the limelight, it was the geopolitical relationship between the USA and China that has been arguably of greater historic significance. The modern relationship between these three nations has its origins in the immediate aftermath of the Second World War; at this time the fulcrum around which these relationships balanced was the future of Taiwan.

While it seems obvious that the youthful communist revolution in China should have allied itself to the Soviet Union, this was not an inevitable outcome. At the birth of Communist China, the American government pondered the possibility of detaching Communist China from the Soviet Union. Mao also considered the course that China should pursue in foreign affairs. In large part, the ambiguity of the situation related closely to the unease of the relationship between Stalin and Mao.

The blunt but affable 'Uncle Joe' image that Stalin projected in his meetings with Roosevelt and Churchill did not carry over in his relationship with Mao Zedong or the Chinese Communist Party. Whereas Mao, despite his peasant background, imagined himself a poet and classical scholar, Stalin was an uncultured man with little or no knowledge of Chinese history. Mao, the aesthete, may have played to the earthiness that was rooted in his upbringing, but Stalin more naturally fitted the role of the country bumpkin. In international relations Stalin always groped forward cautiously, and, indeed, his early relations with China were characterised by incomprehension, surprise and vacillation. Perhaps this is not surprising, given the confused ideological relationships between the two countries since their respective revolutions earlier in the century.

In 1923, Sun Yat Sen, having failed to garner support in the West, formed a United Front with the Chinese Communist Party as a means of accessing Soviet aid. From the late 1920s, Soviet Comintern agents were active in China. Their first impressions could not have been very encouraging in terms of the potential for revolution. Agent Maring, having been sent to China to co-ordinate the disparate communist groups into a functioning Congress and having authorised their assimilation into the Republican *Kuomintang* (Nationalist Party), had much of his work undone when Chiang Kai Shek murdered his left-wing allies in 1927.

The attitude of the Soviet Union to this setback was equivocal. Overall it seems that Comintern agents advocated policies that supported the nationalists and the retention of political gains brought by the *Kuomintang* alliance; Mao could not have been unaware that Soviet agents could in part have been responsible for many of the setbacks in the early years of the Communist Party's existence in China. Clearly the agrarian-based 'bandit' tactics increasingly favoured by Mao were contrary to any experience or Marxist–Leninist ideological understanding of the Comintern agents sent by Moscow.

In spite of this pro-*Kuomintang* stance, the Soviets also received and trained Chinese Communist Party officials of whom Liu Shaoqi and Lin Biao, consecutively the putative successors to Mao, were to become the most prominent. In spite of this no doubt useful service, the presence of the Chinese Communist Party in Moscow tended to skew Soviet views of the Chinese revolution. The Moscow-based leadership of the Chinese Communist Party was given greater weight than the fighters on the ground in China. Much to Mao's annoyance, Stalin supported the Moscow-based Wang Ming as the head of the Chinese Communist Party until as late as 1942.

Even after Stalin recognised Mao's position, he refused to abandon Chiang Kai Shek with whom he continued friendly relations after the Second World War. In 1945 Stalin, wanting to secure his eastern borders so as to concentrate on the Soviet's main arena in Eastern Europe, signed a treaty of friendship with the *Kuomintang*. Mao was ordered to make peace with Chiang. While Stalin may have supported international revolution, the practicalities of geopolitics clearly took precedence. Also given that Sun Yat Sen had structured the *Kuomintang* on the model of the Russian Communist Party, it may have been difficult for Stalin to fully understand how far the *Kuomintang*, which also believed in state control of the economy, really differed from the Chinese Communist Party.

Indeed Stalin's biographer, Dimitri Volkogonov, suggests that Stalin was incapable of understanding the nature of the conflict between Mao and Chiang. From an ideological viewpoint too, Stalin found the Chinese revolution incomprehensible. 'Stalin once declared that a rising of millions of starving peasants had nothing in common with a socialist or democratic movement.'[1]

A clue as to the ideological divide in the early post-war years is the curious episode of the American communist Anna Louise Strong; born in 1885 in Friend, Nebraska, Strong, a daughter of missionaries, who, after staying with Mao, produced a book on *The Thought of Mao Tse-Tung*. A book lauding such an independent line of revolutionary thought was most unwelcome to Stalin, particularly when it was published in Eastern Europe. For her pains Strong, on her next visit to Moscow, was accused of being a CIA spy and locked up in Lubyanka Prison. Her Russian friends were executed.

Even when the Chinese communists started to perform above Stalin's expectations from 1947 onwards, he was circumspect in his support. In 1948 Stalin sent an emissary, Anastas Mikoyan, with a message to persuade Mao from crossing the Yangtze. In part, Stalin was not only compromised by his earlier treaty with Chiang Kai Shek but Stalin also feared that a crushing defeat for the *Kuomintang* would draw America into the civil war in China, an event that might destabilise the Soviet Union's eastern borders.

With regard to where the Soviets stood to their supposed ideological Chinese brothers, it is interesting to note that the Soviet ambassador fled from Nanking along with Chiang Kai Shek. Having disobeyed Stalin's directions not to cross the Yangtze, Mao despatched his deputy Liu Shaoqi to his former training ground, Moscow, to attempt to restore relations. In part he seems to have succeeded; untypically, Stalin conceded his error in underestimating Mao.

Even then however, Mao's own visit to Moscow was not without its upsets. A difficult journey during which Mao's train's heating failed did little to assuage an ego already bruised at the prospect of being seen to pay homage to Stalin on his 70th birthday. Mao too was furious to be largely ignored on his visit to Moscow. Even *Pravda* barely acknowledged his arrival. There was no grand schedule of meetings arranged. When Mao was finally allowed to meet Stalin, the latter was left in some incomprehension by Mao speaking in the riddles of Chinese folklore. According to translator N.T. Fedorenko and Andrei Gromyko who was also present, Mao recounted a story of two high mountains, which the peasant Yui-gun and his two sons decide to remove with their hoes. This allegorical tale, in which the two mountains represented imperialism and feudalism, seems to have done little to stir the warmth of the straight-talking Stalin.

Also it is not recorded how Stalin reacted to Mao's birthday gift. After much debate within the Chinese communist leadership, it had been decided to give Stalin a wagonload of vegetables, including onions, turnips, cabbage and garlic, from the province of Shandong.

In light of Stalin's behaviour to China throughout the early post-war period, it is perhaps not surprising that Mao had serious early doubts about the future relationship with the Soviet Union. Zhou Enlai, who Henry Kissinger described as 'the elegant, charming, brilliant administrator',[2] was elected premier in 1949 and put out feelers to the West in May of 1949. Reputedly an oral message was received by both the American consul and an Australian journalist, to the effect that the party leadership was split between the pro-Soviet camp, led by Liu Shaoqi, and the pro-USA camp, led by Zhou Enlai.

When the same message reached the desk of the Foreign Office in London, the recipient was none other than the Soviet mole, Guy Burgess. He opined that the message was a trick. Even though Mao announced a 'lean to one side' policy favouring the Soviets on 30 May 1949, it seems clear that Mao was not entirely en-amoured with the Soviets; indeed the Soviets, by their behaviour, had given Mao considerable scope for disenchantment. What is not clear is whether Mao's approaches to the West were a genuine countenance of a bipolar international strategy or a means of upping the support, financial and otherwise, that he could get from Stalin.

Whatever Mao's real inclinations towards the West, however, the Americans were deeply divided on what strategy to follow with regard to the ascension to power of the Chinese Communist Party. While some American liberals such as Edgar Snow and Anna Strong were clearly pro-Mao, in general, the 'China Lobby' was god fearing, staunchly anti-communist and pro-*Kuomintang*. In addition to powerful Congressional support for the 'China lobby', influential journalists such as Henry Luce and Walter Lippman were numbered in its ranks. (Luce had been born in Dengzhou in China where his parents were missionaries; after returning to America, Luce went on to found the iconic and influential *Time* magazine in 1922.) America's post-war ambassador to China, Major General Patrick Hurley, also joined the broadly right-wing Republican alliance.

The eccentric Hurley, who hollered 'Yahoo!' when he first met Mao, was to become a passionate supporter of Chiang, and a fierce critic of Truman's post-war Democrat administration. Such was the level of support for the *Kuomintang* that Acheson took the extraordinary step of publishing a voluminous *White Paper* (August 1949) to explain the history of America's relations with China. In the letter of transmittal that Acheson wrote as an introduction to the *White Paper* he suggested, in relation to the failure of Chiang Kai Shek's nationalist regime, that 'History has proved again and again that a regime without faith in itself and an army without morale cannot survive the test of battle.'[3]

Indeed the regard of the Truman administration for Chiang Kai Shek's nationalist government, and its record in war and peace, could barely have been lower. At this point Acheson, in pursuit of an American rapprochement with Mao, would probably have been only too happy to see Mao invade and conquer Taiwan. He even persuaded the Joint Chiefs of Staff to reject military action to protect Taiwan at the end of 1949. Acheson's Head of Policy Planning Staff George Kennan went even further and recorded in his memoirs, '. . . it was a great mistake on our part to permit the Chiang regime to establish itself on Formosa'.[4]

However, with the *Kuomintang* in control of the island, there was little that Acheson could do, bar usurping Chiang's rule and replacing him with an American administration, a course of action advocated by Kennan. In practice, the horse-trading of Washington politics precluded such robust action. For Truman as well as for Stalin, the centre of gravity for post-war geopolitics was Eastern Europe, not Asia.

Both President Truman and General Marshall, Acheson's predecessor as secretary of state, had only reluctantly supported the China Aid Act of April 1948; in large measure this was a sop to assuage Senator Vandenberg and the Republican 'China' lobby, so that they could ensure the European Recovery Programme. The 'Marshall Plan', as it famously became known, was seen as essential for shoring up the economies of Europe against the possibility of communist insurgence. Although before Chiang's flight to Taiwan, Acheson managed to resist a further US$ 1.5 billion requested for the *Kuomintang*, he was forced to allow an extension of the funding provided by the China Aid Acts beyond the cut-off date of 2 April 1949.

In relation to wooing Mao, matters were further complicated by the detention of the American consul, Angus Ward, by the communist government on charges of spying in Mukden, Manchuria, until late 1949, and by the increasing hostility of General MacArthur to the communists. Also, Truman's international actions were compromised by a Republican Congress in which Senator McCarthy, with his House Un-American Activities Committee, was in the full swing of his anti-communist 'witch-hunt'.

As George Kennan tellingly observed:

> McCarthy and ... many reputable publicists, political figures and prominent citizens across the county, (think) that our greatest post-war problems, including outstandingly the falling to the Communists of Eastern Europe and China, were the result not primarily of the outcome of the military operations against Germany and Japan, and not of the serious ... human errors by which that outcome had been determined, but rather of the fact that the United States government had been insidiously infiltrated.[5]

For drawing attention to the grievous weakness of the *Kuomintang* and the improbability of its success in any prolonged further conflict with the communists, Kennan's colleague, John Paton Davies, was dismissed from the State Department and his pension withheld. For his support for Alger Hiss, a state department official and the secretary general of the Charter organisation of the United Nations, who was accused though never found guilty of being a Soviet spy, Acheson also came under personal attack from McCarthy and Richard Nixon. It is interesting to note that even some Democrats, including John F. Kennedy, senator for Massachusetts, blamed Truman for the loss of China. In conclusion therefore, with regard to the preferred policy of recognising China and using Sino–American trade as a bait to tempt Mao away from the Soviets, Acheson was constantly thwarted by the staunch domestic American political support for Chiang.

By the end of 1949, Acheson's delicate balancing act of managing Congressional Republicans and keeping Mao warm was running out of time. Whatever

Mao's grievances against Stalin, the Soviets were the natural allies of the Chinese revolution. Many of Mao's colleagues had been trained in the Soviet Union; the links between the respective *nomenklatura* were established and at this point Mao was not the all-powerful dictator who would emerge later. At the time, the American State Department may have seen no way back to power for the *Kuomintang* in China, but we now know that Mao and the Chinese communist leaders were anything but sanguine about their own chances of survival, particularly as they assumed, with no formal signal to think otherwise, that American policy in Asia would primarily be geared to the overthrow of the newly installed communist regime in Beijing. On their part neither Truman nor Acheson could, for valid domestic political considerations, give any overt indication that they could live with the status quo of a Communist China. With these uncertainties in mind, a decision by Mao to throw over the Soviet connection for the uncertainty of an alliance with the capitalist West was always going to be an unlikely outcome. Truman and Acheson were deluding themselves if they thought otherwise.

After the unpromising 'birthday' meeting with Stalin, Mao was packed off to Leningrad to go sightseeing, where he displayed complete disinterest in Peter the Great's Winter Palace and its art collection. Meanwhile a treaty was drawn up and readied for Mao's return to Moscow. The *Treaty of Friendship, Alliance and Mutual Assistance* was signed on 14 February 1950 and convinced most Western observers including the CIA that Mao had yielded sovereign supremacy to the Soviets.

For Acheson the treaty was a disaster; as George Kennan observes in his memoirs, '. . . we were wholly unprepared. This was at the height of the McCarthyite Hysteria. The China lobby, in particular, was in full cry. There were violent differences in Congress over Far Eastern policy . . . .'[6] Interestingly, Article I of the Treaty, in requiring China and the Soviets to prevent 'aggressive action on the part of Japan or any other State which should unite with Japan, directly or indirectly, in acts of aggression',[7] seemed to anticipate the coming change in America's Japan policy, from one of occupation to one of alliance. Acheson's stratagem with regard to Mao was in ruins. Although he told the Senate Foreign Relations Committee on 29 March 1950 that 'the Chinese, inevitably, we believe, will come into conflict with Moscow',[8] suggesting that he had not given up hope entirely, for the short run at least Acheson's game was up. In hindsight it is clear that the weight of anti-communist sentiment in America and the fierce pro-Chiang lobby limited the Truman administration's scope for manoeuvre as much as Mao was constrained by the pro-Soviet ideologues within the Chinese Communist Party.

Following the Sino–Soviet Treaty, with China now seen as Stalin's puppet, America needed to rethink its strategy of containing the Soviet communist threat in Asia. The focus of attention inevitably moved to Taiwan. Albeit reluctantly, Truman and Acheson were no longer able to use their distaste for Chiang Kai Shek as an excuse to distance themselves from the defence of Taiwan. Given that post-revolution Mao's overriding goal in foreign policy was the restoration of China's historic borders, America's move to reconcile itself with Chiang would inevitably ratchet the coolness between China and the USA. Truman announced that 'The occupation of Formosa (Taiwan) by the Communist forces would be a direct threat to the security of the Pacific area and to United States forces performing their lawful and necessary functions in the area.'[9]

As Dr Henry Kissinger concluded in his book *Diplomacy*, Mao construed Truman's words 'as the opening move in an American attempt to reverse the communist's victory in the Chinese civil war'.[10] On Mao's part it was an understandable mistake. On the 27 June Truman committed the Seventh Fleet to the defence of Taiwan. For Mao, this was tantamount to a declaration of war; perversely, however, it was Korea not Taiwan that was to provide the opportunity for Mao to initiate real hostilities with his new enemy.

8

Chiang Kai Shek and the Flight to Taiwan

Taiwan: 1945–9

C hiang Kai Shek was a curious choice as 'pin-up' hero for the Republican and religious right wing in post-war American politics. In the 1920s, Chiang had worked closely with Stalin's Soviet Comintern agent, Borodin; indeed, after the reorganisation of the *Kuomintang* by Borodin in January 1924, when communists were invited to take up ten of the Central Executive Committee's 41 seats, Chiang set up a military academy at Whampoa with Soviet help. His then wife, Jenny Chen (formerly Ah Feng), recalled Chiang saying that 'If I control the army, I will have power to control the country . . . it is my road to leadership.'[1]

After the death of Sun Yat Sen on 12 March 1925, Chiang effectively inherited the leadership of the *Kuomintang* (KMT) in triumvirate with Borodin and Wang Jingwei (a left-winger who, after going into exile following an abortive coup against Chiang, later became Japan's puppet ruler of China in 1940 after the Japanese occupation). Such was Chiang's association with the left that Reuters reported that 'Canton is under the absolute control of Chiang Kai Shek, a General in the employ of the Soviet High Command.'[2]

The uneasy alliance lasted only until March 1927, when Chiang countered Wang Jingwei's attempt to impose powerful military commissars within the structures of the army. Wang Jingwei's political bastion in Shanghai was targeted through Chiang's alliance with underworld leader 'Big eared' Du. On the evening before a planned mass rally of workers, 'Big eared' Du invited union leader Wang Shouhua to dinner at his home, where he had him throttled. Finding that Wang Shouhua was still alive, Du ordered the trade union boss to be taken away and buried alive. Subsequently some 10,000 leftists were purged. Additionally some 6,000 of their wives and daughters were sold by Chiang as prostitutes and indentured factory workers. Twenty-five thousand others were arrested. Displaying no ideological bias to his depredations, Chiang also held businessmen to ransom to exhort funds.

In spite of this setback to Soviet influence, Stalin remained predisposed to support Chiang throughout the 1930s, even after the *Kuomintang* leader's capture in 1936. Zhang Xueliang, a 34-year-old warlord and a former playboy drug addict, turned on his leader Chiang Kai Shek and surrounded his quarters in Xian. Chiang, dressed only in his nightshirt, jumped out of a back window leaving behind his uniform, shoes and false teeth; scrambling barefoot up a brambled hill, some of his bodyguards were shot dead while he was fortunate enough to make it to the safety of a cave. Chiang was forced to give himself up to Zhang's troops at daybreak; his captor now declared that he had wanted Chiang to back an alliance with the Communists to better fight against the Japanese.

On hearing the news of Chiang's capture, Stalin informed a no doubt exasperated Mao Zedong that this was a setback to the anti-Japanese cause. Subsequently, meetings of the captive Chiang, which Zhang set up with Mao's loyal henchman, Zhou Enlai, took place in the unlikely setting of a Catholic Church. Zhou, who had trained at military college together with Chiang some 12 years earlier, told Chiang that 'All the time we have been fighting, I have often thought of you. I hope we can work together.'[3]

In spite of overtures from the communists, Chiang remained stubbornly resistant to changing his position. Although popular pressure eventually forced Chiang into an uneasy accommodation with the Communists, which lasted for the duration of the war, he was never in any doubt that the rivalry between the *Kuomintang* and Mao's communists would be a fight to the death. Meanwhile Zhang, never again trusted or forgiven by Chiang, was rewarded for his efforts at reconciliation with the communists by imprisonment until 1991 though he did have the honour of becoming a communist icon described by President Jiang Zemin as being a 'hero for eternity'.[4]

Aside from his proto-communist background, Chiang Kai Shek's private life also made him an unlikely candidate as hero for America's religious right wing. As a young revolutionary, Chiang abandoned his first wife and became renowned for his drunkenness and debauchery. His second wife, Jenny Chen, recalled in her memoirs that at the age of 13, she was lured under false pretences to the 32-year-old Chiang's room where he attempted to rape her. Though she made her escape, Chiang continued to pursue her, and at the age of 15 she agreed to marry him. Upon marriage, Jenny immediately contracted *gonorrhoea* from her husband, thus making her infertile. In a mood of sombre penitence, Chiang henceforth forswore alcohol and remained a teetotaller for the rest of his life.

Though it seems likely that Jenny was the love of his life, when the opportunity came for a dynastic marriage, the ambitious Chiang shooed her off to America. Meanwhile on 27 December 1927, he concluded an alliance with aristocratic Meiling Soong, who had described Jenny as 'a very good housewife . . . for a Ningbo peasant'.[5] Her sister Ailing Soong was married to the wealthy industrialist HH Kung, while her brother, T.V. Soong, was Sun Yat Sen's brother-in-law and financial comptroller of the *Kuomintang*.

Meiling Chiang became one of the most famous female figures in the twentieth century, as she used her considerable feminine and intellectual charms to bedazzle elite society, political circles and media barons of Europe and America. Her father was the wealthy Shanghai tycoon, Charlie Soong, who converted to Methodism and sent his daughter to Wellesley College near Boston, where the academically gifted Meiling graduated with distinction with a major in literature. She proved a tireless ambassador for her husband. General Stilwell, no friend of Chiang, described his wife as

> Quick, intelligent. Wants to get things done. Wishes she was a man.... Very frank and open.... Direct, forceful, energetic, loves power, eats up publicity and flattery, pretty weak on history. No concession to the Western viewpoint in all China's foreign relations.[6]

Chiang converted to Methodism and, with his wife's tireless promotion, he developed a wholly undeserved reputation for moral rectitude. Meiling Chiang or Madame Chiang, as she became known, amazed Gardner Cowles of *Look* magazine when she told him that her husband only believed in sex to produce children, 'and since he already had a son by a previous marriage and was not interested in having any more children, there would be no sex between them.'[7] In fact while she was away in America, Chiang happily took a mistress. On one occasion, after returning from America, Meiling found a pair of high-healed shoes, which she threw out of a window, inadvertently hitting a guard. It would be difficult to explain their relationship as anything other than a political marriage of convenience.

As for Meiling, British press baron Lord Beaverbrook averred to Joseph Kennedy that she was a lesbian. Whatever her charms, it worked with the press and politicians. Henry Luce, the editor and owner of *Time* magazine, was one of the many children of American missionaries to China and was naturally empathetic to the Methodist Meiling. She won the rare honour of featuring on the front cover of *Time* magazine for a story on the Chinese fight for democracy versus fascism.

Given that Chiang, a totalitarian dictator who, in his views and actions, virtually defined the description 'National Socialist' (or Nazi), *Time* magazine's article was a curious perversion of the truth. American politicians were also converted to the *Kuomintang* cause. In one of his famous 'fireside chats', President Roosevelt referred to Chiang as 'an unconquerable man ... of great vision and courage'.[8] More importantly, he promoted Chiang as the leader of one of four great powers that would dominate the post-war world. This was not a scenario which convinced Churchill, who dismissively described China as 'four hundred and twenty million pigtails'.[9] It should be noted that Chiang was equally dismissive of British military prowess after the fall of Singapore and Malaya.

Clearly, Chinese power was considerably less than the sum of its armed forces. In 1929 Chiang had launched a northern expedition against Mao's forces with 290,000 troops in alliance with Feng's 310,000 troops, the Guangxi Clique's 240,000 and the governor of Shanxi's 150,000. Over the next four years, not only were the Communists pushed back to the mountains, surviving the rigours of the Long March, but Chiang also came to dominate his allied commanders. Perversely

Japan's invasion of Northern China in 1938 probably saved Mao, when it forced Chiang to retreat from Nanking, which had been his capital since 1 January 1928. A new headquarters was set up on the sacred mountain of Nanyue, near Chungking, where he stayed for the duration of the Second World War.

In fighting the Japanese, however, Chiang was fatally compromised. He refused to expend all his energies on fighting the Japanese, in the fear that success in this effort might so thoroughly exhaust his forces that he would lay himself open to destruction by the Communists. Understandable though this stance might have been, Chiang's anaemic conduct of the war undermined much of the international credibility and support that he had formerly enjoyed.

T.V. Soong negotiated US loans to Chungking of some US$ 245 million by 1940, and in return, Chiang agreed to the acceptance of Lt General 'Vinegar' Joe Stilwell as his chief of staff. However, Stilwell was constantly thwarted by Chiang's generals and warlord allies, whose order of priority was advancement of personal wealth, loyalty to Chiang and fighting the communists; the fight against Japan and the importance of the chain of command brought up last places in the pecking order.

On one occasion, a Chinese commander refused an order to move his division into battle because he needed his trucks to transport his American-financed supplies for sale on the black market. In his diary, Stilwell contrasted Chiang's rule unfavourably with the Communists'; the *Kuomintang* government was a 'cesspool [of] . . . corruption, neglect, chaos . . . hoarding, black market, [and] trading with the enemy'.[10] Such was the corruption and inefficiency of Chiang's government that even in Chungking his people starved. At the height of the famine, women were known to exchange babies on the basis of 'You eat mine. I'll eat yours.'[11]

Stilwell called Chiang a 'crazy little bastard with that hickory nut he uses for a head. . . .'; as for his military prowess, Stilwell denounced his '. . . Usual cockeyed reasons and idiotic tactical and strategic conceptions. He is impossible.'[12] Such were the reports coming back to Washington that Stilwell is reported to have told his deputy that Roosevelt had insisted that 'If you can't get along with Chiang and can't replace him, get rid of him once and for all. You know what I mean. . . .'[13] Vice President Henry Wallace described Chiang as 'a short term investment' and concluded that the Chinese leader did not have 'the intelligence or political strength to run post-war China'.[14]

However, in a move that would later come back to haunt the Democrats, Roosevelt sent Patrick Hurley, a former Republican minister of war, as an emissary to China. Hurley, a somewhat ageing and eccentric senator from Oklahoma, revelled in referring to Mao Zedong as 'Moose Dung' and amazed diplomats by his habit of yelping 'Yahoo!' at the top of his voice when meeting senior Chinese politicians, Mao included. Hurley, the former coalminer-turned-cowboy, wrongly believed that Chiang could be persuaded to follow a democratic path, and also sided with the nationalist dictator in his dispute with General Stilwell.

Stilwell was duly recalled. However, by the time of the 'great power' summit at Yalta in February 1945, Chiang had become so thoroughly discredited with the Democrat administration that he was now not only excluded from the conference, but was also not informed of its conclusions for a further four months. A furious Chiang, notwithstanding the American financial and military support that had sustained his regime throughout the war, prepared to play off the post-war superpowers. In June 1945 a pact was concluded with Stalin, which recognised Chinese sovereignty in Manchuria, in return for allowing the Soviets to use Port Arthur as a naval base. Most importantly, as Chiang prepared to battle Mao, the *Kuomintang* had achieved Soviet recognition of their government in China.

While the surrender of the Japanese led to a grab for ports and cities by the Americans, Nationalists and Communists, all sides recognised China's complete war exhaustion. Under pressure from the allies, both Chiang and Mao agreed to talks. Mao agreed to fly to Chungking for talks, taking with him the 'cowboy' Hurley for insurance. Mao described this first flight of his life on 28 August 1945 as 'very efficient'.[15]

On arrival, Mao, in a prepared statement, 'resolved in accordance with justice and reason, as well as on the basis of peace, democracy and unity to build a unified, independent, prosperous and strong new China'.[16] Initial meetings were friendly. At the first formal dinner, Chiang called for a return to the relationship of the two sides in 1924; at a later tea party, Mao proposed a toast of 'Long live President Chiang Kai Shek.'[17]

Predictably, the bonhomie did not last. An agreement between the two sides to produce a temporary announcement of plans for an all-party government was little more than a sham. Moreover, during the talks held under the good offices of the US military acting as neutrals, General Wedemeyer was forced to protest to Mao about the communists, who bayoneted to death an OSS officer, Captain John Birch; in death he gave his name to the eponymous anti-communist lobby group, the John Birch Society.

If Chiang was resistant to reaching a meaningful agreement with the Communists, he was no less resistant to moving towards a more liberal regime. General Marshall, despatched by President Truman to bring resolution to the unstable Chinese situation, tried to broker a peace. He pressed Chiang for a broad political spectrum to be represented on a state council and urged a disbandment of the Nationalist's notorious secret police.

This was contrary to Chiang's authoritarian instincts; as a Nationalist police colonel commented, 'The Chinese masses are used to what you might call cruelty, they understand it.'[18] Unfortunately this attitude even pertained within Chiang's own army. Army commanders treated their troops as slave labour for the implementation of carpetbagging operations in areas of China newly liberated from the Japanese. In effect, the Chinese military high command had institutionalised government by kleptocracy.

In spite of the corruption and ineptitude of his government, Chiang continued to garner international acclaim. General De Gaulle awarded Chiang the Grand Cross of the Legion of Honour in recognition of his fight for democracy. More importantly, in America, Hurley, who had resigned his post at the end of 1945, citing his constant battles with Truman's State Department officials, became a cheerleader for Chiang in his fight against communism. The bipartisan conduct of American post-war foreign policy now broke decisively over the issue of Truman's Democrat administration's perceived lack of support for Chiang and the *Kuomintang* against the rising threat of Mao's communists.

By the first quarter of 1946, Chiang's tactic of playing off America and the Soviets was wearing thin. In Russian-occupied Manchuria, the Soviets stripped former Japanese industrial assets worth an estimated US$ 2 million; whole factories were dismantled and taken to Siberia. Stalin was also increasingly wary of the presence of large numbers of American soldiers holding key Chinese ports.

Nevertheless, Stalin was unwilling to risk a conflict with America, and when Chiang complained about Soviet behaviour in Manchuria and demanded an immediate withdrawal from the area, the Soviet leader complied on 1 March 1946. This did not work necessarily to Chiang's advantage. A Japanese arsenal amounting to some 700,000 rifles, 14,000 machine guns, 700 vehicles and artillery fell into the hands of the Chinese Communists. Marshall warned Chiang that the Communists were too strong to be easily defeated. The American general was clearly aware of the fighting deficiency of Chiang's impressively large but militarily inept forces. In effect, apart from 11,000 crack troops, Chiang's army consisted of little more than bandit commanders and troops that were better trained at civilian oppression and criminal extortion in an urban setting than fighting Mao's agrarian-based guerrilla forces.

As well as military incompetence, corruption and economic mismanagement in the Nationalist areas brought any semblance of orderly government to an end. Of some 10,250 miles of railway track destroyed by the Communists, the *Kuomintang* were able to repair less than a third. In urban China the Nationalist's strongholds were being strangled. Shortages of all commodities caused chronic privation.

Even nationalist troops died of starvation. Printing of money to finance military operations brought hyperinflation, hoarding and, with it, civil unrest. In Shanghai between 1946 and 1947, there were reported 4,200 labour strikes. There the French photographer Henri Cartier-Bresson took remarkable photographs of the queues, reportedly 200,000 long, caused by the government's decision to issue certificates, which could later be redeemed for gold. Seven Chinese were trampled to death in the stampedes.

Meanwhile, Chiang had already been in control of Taiwan since October 1945, when *Kuomintang* troops entered Taipei to take control of the city from the surrendering Japanese. The sizeable military and civilian population was put into camps prior to repatriation. While an estimated 300,000 Taiwanese civilians had

welcomed the arriving mainlanders, there was an almost instant mismatch of expectations. The Taiwanese had expected to be liberated but instead found that
the mainlanders were suspicious of people who they believed had been tainted
by their association with the Japanese. An article in the *Kuomintang* magazine *New
Taiwan Monthly* in September 1946 noted the need to re-educate the Taiwanese
because they had been 'poisoned intellectually and were forced to accept twisted
notions'.[19]

Within a year, 48,000 *Kuomintang* troops were relocated to Taiwan, where the
poorly paid troops scrounged and plundered a living. Buildings and not just the
Japanese residences occupied by the troops were routinely looted and this contributed to a dramatic collapse in the relationship of the indigenous population
with the mainlanders. Rather than making Taiwan a province of China, Chiang put
it under military government which suggested that the island was a conquest. A
long-time Chiang protégé, Chen Yi was made governor general and Taiwan garrison commander.

Chen Yi promoted state-run socialism with administrators brought from the
mainland. Forty thousand Japanese administrators were replaced by mainland bureaucrats. Over 90 per cent of the economy was brought under government control, which was even more draconian than under the Japanese. The system gave
ample opportunity for corruption, for which the Chen regime became notorious;
officials would frequently operate black markets from which they made huge fortunes. Official positions were also used in more sinister ways; a Taiwanese activist
complained that 'When a Chinese with some influence wanted a particular property, he had only to accuse a Formosan of being a collaborationist during the past
50 years of Japanese sovereignty.'[20] Rigged auctions of Japanese property invariably ended up in mainlander hands. Many Taiwanese came to regret the departure
of the Japanese, and the aphorism 'Dogs go and pigs come'[21] became well known
during this period.

Predictably the economy suffered. Lacking fertiliser from Japan, and by allowing irrigation systems to fall into disrepair, the *Kuomintang*'s first harvest produced
a crop of just 640,000 metric tons of rice compared to the 1.4 million tons produced in 1938. Moreover, farmers were forced to sell their rice at low fixed prices,
which allowed for *Kuomintang* profiteering when it arrived on the mainland. Also
American officials reported that 'economic paralysis has set in, attributed primarily
to the policy of creating semi-official companies against which private enterprise
cannot successfully compete'.[22]

In view of the rapaciousness of Chen Yi's government, it is surprising that
Taiwanese rebellion was so slow to emerge. The spark that lit the conflagration
had its origins in the granting of state monopolies to the *Kuomintang*, including
salt, opium, tobacco and alcohol. When an aged grandmother, Lin Chiang Mai,
was arrested for illegally selling cigarettes and was beaten over the head with a

pistol by an agent for the Monopoly Bureau, who then shot dead a bystander in the angry crowd that had assembled, the popular mood turned ugly.

The incident was followed by a demonstration by several thousand protestors at the headquarters of the Monopolies Bureau. They were fired on by guards, and the result was a popular uprising throughout the island, which saw thousands killed in the brutal *Kuomintang* suppression that followed. Known dissidents were hunted down and killed and their properties looted. The wife of one victim recalled,

> After we took the bloody bodies of my husband and my brother-in-law home, we found that our possessions were ransacked. We did not have anything for the bodies to wear for the burial. The Chinese soldiers took everything.[23]

By some estimates, in the suppression that followed, in what became known as the 'two-two-eight Incident', up to 20,000 civilians were killed. Brutal military actions were organised under campaigns entitled 'exterminate traitors' and 'clearing of the villages'.[24] That the two populations were eventually able to co-exist, albeit in muted hostility rather than mutual harmony, owed mostly to their common fear and loathing of the communists; as one islander is reported to have said of the mainlanders, 'The Red pigs are worse than the white ones—we hate them all, but if we can't get independence we'd rather have the present ones.'[25]

In the event, Chen Yi was reprimanded by the *Kuomintang* Central Executive Committee, and in April he returned to the mainland where Chiang made him governor of Zhejiang Province. Chen Yi was later caught parleying with the Communists with a view to switching sides, and Chiang had him arrested, imprisoned and sent to Taiwan, where he was shot in June 1950.

When Chiang realised that Taiwan would become the last redoubt of the *Kuomintang* cause against the gathering Communist advance on the mainland, he appointed a close ally, General Chen Cheng, as governor general on 29 December 1948. Also his son, Chiang Ching Kuo, was sent to supervise internal security, and the following year saw a crackdown on dissidents who faced arrest and summary execution. Unsurprisingly there was a constant hunt for Communist 'moles'. Chiang Kai Shek was not long in following his advance guard across the water. In face of the dramatic collapse of civil government in the Nationalist strongholds, Chiang, by the beginning of 1949, realised that defeat was inevitable, and he departed for the island sanctuary of Taiwan on 21 January. Chiang and his mainlanders would find a sullen, oppressed and largely hostile population.

9

MacArthur, Yoshida and the American Occupation of Japan

Japan: 1945–54

In August 1941, the US army, caught humiliatingly unprepared by the Japanese in the Philippines, had surrendered and then suffered the horrors of the infamous 'Bataan Death March'. Their commander General MacArthur, the supreme commander of American forces in the Pacific, fled to Australia. He was fortunate to survive this early debacle, and had it not been for an iron will, a towering self-belief and an ability to blame all failures on others, it is unlikely that he would have survived as Pacific commander. He was also a master manipulator of the press. As a deliverer of memorable, understated sound-bites, he was without peer; on landing in Japan after their eventual defeat, he declared with well-prepared irony, 'Melbourne to Tokyo; it was a long way.'[1]

As Supreme Commander of the Allied Powers (SCAP) in Japan, an appointment which MacArthur pompously called 'Mars last gift to a warrior',[2] he landed at Atsugi air base and made his way to Tokyo. Between Victory Japan (VJ) day and the Korean War, he left Japan on only two occasions including a reluctant trip to meet President Truman at Wake Island after the Battle of Inchon during the Korean War. A prolific reader, he immersed himself in the history and culture of Japan, concluding that the Japanese were cultured people with the fierce traditions of islanders.

This was not a judgement based on personal observation as he refused to tour the country or make public appearances. It can be assumed that MacArthur's personal nostrums of Japan's true nature were entirely a figment of his own intellectual musings, particular as he was known to prefer his own discourse to listening to others. He commuted daily between his home and the sixth floor of the *Dai-ichi Seimei* Building (Dai-ichi Mutual Life Insurance) where he set up his GHQ (general headquarters). (The Dai-ichi Building, overlooking the Imperial Palace, was one of the few structures in central Tokyo to survive the American fire-bombing of the city.) He lived and worked seven days a week including Christmas day and his own birthday. As if cultivating the mystery of divine leadership himself, he ruled invisibly in the manner of the emperors and shoguns before him.

Indeed MacArthur saw a messianic mission for himself. Aboard the *USS Missouri*, where the Japanese surrender was formally signed on 2 September, he declaimed that a 'holy mission had been accomplished'.[3] Like an evangelical preacher, he thundered that the Japanese 'are thoroughly beaten and cowed and tremble before the terrible retribution the surrender terms impose upon their country in punishment for its great sins'.[4] His place in history he asserted was 'to carry to the land of our vanquished foe the solace and hope and faith of Christian morals'.[5]

In this role, he was prepared neither to share responsibility with nor brook any interference from the US government. When it was mooted in Washington that it might be wise to share power with Britain and the Soviets, MacArthur threatened to resign. When the Truman administration baulked at the cost of his demand for food requisitions to feed the Japanese, he cabled them to say 'give me bread or give me bullets'.[6] Although he supposedly reported to an Allied Council for Japan (AJC), he increasingly ignored this group. Written memos of initiatives soon petered out. An official remembered that 'SCAP Directives came in writing in the early days; then they began to come verbally, and later not at all.'[7] Within Japan itself, his rule was just as dictatorial; America's own ambassador Sebald was forbidden by MacArthur from accepting invitations to the Imperial Palace without his approval.

Neither did the vainglorious MacArthur bother to hide the extent of his power; in 1951, he told a US Senate Committee that 'I had not only the normal executive authorities such as our president has in this country, but I had legislative authority. I could by fiat issue directives.'[8] Paradoxically, while describing the job as 'the world's greatest laboratory for an experiment in the liberation of a people from a totalitarian military rule',[9] for the duration of his role as supreme commander in Japan, MacArthur conducted a totalitarian military rule of his own.

For some, MacArthur was brilliant in conversation, even hypnotic; others however found his monologues pedagogic. George Kennan, the noted Soviet expert, recounted being called to lunch by MacArthur after a 48-hour journey to Tokyo with his two advisers, Brigadier General Shuyler and a foreign service officer. At the end of the meal, Kennan was far from impressed when MacArthur, who hero-worshipped Napoleon Bonaparte, turned his back towards him as he addressed a two-hour lecture to Schuyler on military history. He later remembered that 'Caesar's experience in the military occupation of Gaul was cited . . . as the only other example of a productive military occupation.'[10] Keenan, a man not averse himself to his own opinions, sat 'motionless in my humble corner'.[11] Throughout his time in Japan, MacArthur gave the strong impression that he was the colonial ruler sent by a great Imperial power, which indeed he was.

The scene that greeted arriving US troops, some 400,000 in the early stages of occupation, was one of utter devastation. In Tokyo, 65 per cent of all residences were destroyed. The population was starving. In July 1945, factory worker absentee rates rose to 45 per cent as employees spent their time scavenging for food. In the August–September issue of *Shojo Kurabu* (Girl's Club), there were articles on 'How to eat acorns' and 'Let's catch grasshoppers'. In December 1945, rations supplied half of the required daily intake of calories required to support a working man. To add to the privations of war, 1945 produced the worst harvest in Japan for a generation. In spite of the American government's efforts to meet MacArthur's desperate pleas for more food shipments, the feeding of a nation was beyond even SCAP's logistical capabilities.

The system broke down mid-year in both 1946 and 1947; in June 1946, the black market price of rice rose to 30 times the official ration price. Restoration of the pre-war food chain depended on more than American imports; before 1942, Korea, Taiwan and China had provided some 31 per cent of rice imports, 92 per cent of sugar and 45 per cent of salt, but during the war some 80 per cent of Japan's merchant fleet was destroyed. One Japanese businessman recalled his youthful, post-war years in Tokyo, where '. . . for five years I was hungry every single day'.[12] In 1947, tuberculosis killed 150,000 people; for the next three years, some 100,000 per year were killed by this disease. Between 1945 and 1948, there were 650,000 cases of cholera, dysentery, typhoid fever, diphtheria, epidemic meningitis and polio.

The population of Japan was literally demoralised. A Japanese military comprising some 7.2 million combatants had to be absorbed by a devastated economy. Soldiers, now despised by the populace, slung away their military uniforms and slunk back to their families, defeated and humiliated. These were the lucky ones; in China, some 60,000 Japanese soldiers were kept captive until 1949. Civic values collapsed. Senior officers stole from military stores and made money on the black market; politicians joined them in the profiteering. It was every man for himself. Some 1.22 million Japanese citizens were arrested for dealing illegally in the black market.

Recorded crime soared. Between 1946 and 1949, there were 1,177,184 thefts per annum compared to 724,000 in 1934, when Japan was suffering the indignities of the Great Depression. Gangs of prostitutes flourished; one famously called itself the 'Blood Cherry Gang'. Many were pressed into destitution by abject poverty and hunger. A young war widow living in the depths of Ueno railway station, even today a favourite haunt of the homeless, recorded in a letter to the *Mainichi* newspaper on 29 September that 'a man I did not know gave me two rice balls. I devoured them. The following night he again brought me two rice balls. He then asked me to come to the park because he wanted to talk with me. I followed him. That is when I sank into the despised profession of being 'a woman of the dark'.[13] As well as prostitution, drug addiction and alcoholism increased, many even resorting to drinking methylated spirits.

The arrival of 400,000 randy, young American soldiers did little to stabilise Japan's social structure. The worried Home Ministry, clearly not unaware of the

proclivities of its own soldiers in conquered Asia over the previous 15 years, immediately took on the job of organising 'comfort' woman for the American invaders.
'Please defend [from rape] the young women of Japan',[14] pleaded Vice Prime Minister Konoe, as he asked the national commissioner of police to take charge of the
Home Office's sex service. Later, he set up a financing arrangement with the heads
of Japan's *Yakuza* (gangsters) so that the puritan MacArthur could avoid direct accountability for these operations. At first, recruits proved difficult to find; Japanese
women feared they would suffer appalling internal injuries if penetrated by the reputedly massive American penises.

However, by 27 August, some 1,360 women had been recruited for the *Tokushu
Ian Shisetsu Kyodai* (the Recreation and Amusement Association; RAA); the RAA
employees serviced 15–60 GIs per day at 15 yen each. Strict racial segregation was
observed, which was just as well for the civilian Japanese population as venereal
infection within the US army threatened to get out of control. By the time that the
RAA had been abolished, some units of the 8th Army were suffering syphilis rates
as high as 70 per cent.

With the collapse of Hirohito's Imperial ideology, a moral vacuum destroyed
old codes of conduct. Apart from the professional comfort women, many young
Japanese women, dazzled by the wealth and glamour of the American soldiers,
became concubines to their conquerors; they were so numerous that mistresses
of foreigners became known in Japan by the ironic generic name of *onrii wan*
(only one).

American consumer culture soon found a rapt following with many young
Japanese women who adopted a materialistic lifestyle. Abandoning traditional cultural values, young people indulged in hedonistic pursuits. There was an explosion
in the publication of sex magazines and *manga* (erotic cartoon magazines). Tamura
Taijiro's *Nikutai no Mon* (Gate of Flesh) (1947) precipitated an explosion of 'flesh'
novels. The Japanese writer Sakaguchi wrote a damning essay 'On decadence', in
which he noted that 'The look of the nation since defeat is one of pure and simple decadence.'[15] He wailed that even former pilots trained as *kamikaze* were now
working the black market. Far from ennobling the Japanese spirit of selfless devotion as planned, the Emperor's war had led to the complete demoralisation of
Japanese society.

For MacArthur however, his immediate priority was to establish American
control and dismantle the apparatus of Japanese society which Truman's administration believed had created the appetite for military expansionism. 'The present
economic and social system in Japan which makes for a will to war will be changed',
asserted Secretary of State Dean Acheson, 'so that the will to war will not
continue'.[16] Perversely, this was not to include the Emperor whose ambitions had
been at the heart of all Japanese pre-war stratagems. Although the Americans had
agreed to operate through a Japanese administration, it soon became clear that this
was no more than a veneer on direct rule. The Japanese government was required

to carry out SCAP directives issued by the GHQ; these orders had to be carried out with immediate effect and came initially in the form of 'emergency orders' and later, when the new constitution was formulated, as government ordinances. Japanese government officials gave them the nickname of 'Potsdam Orders'.

MacArthur's first task was to re-order the constitution. On 4 October 1945, MacArthur intimated to Konoe, now the minister of state in the Higashikuni government, that the constitution needed revision. A shocked Japanese government resigned. The revision was again suggested to the new government of Prime Minister Shidehara Kijuro on 11 October. Two months later, SCAP took the symbolically important step of abolishing the role reserved for Shinto as the state religion. MacArthur's decree on 15 December 1945 ordered that 'Shinto theory and beliefs turned into militaristic and ultra-nationalistic propaganda designed to delude the Japanese people and lead them into wars of aggression.'[17]

This was a logical prelude to the Emperor's New Year announcement in 1946, at which he was forced to publicly deny his divine status, a myth which he himself had propagated in the pre-war period. On 4 January, all 'militarists' were purged from public office; this included some 200,000 politicians and bureaucrats. The selection and its results were often arbitrary. American journalist Mark Gayn noted that a senior officer in the *Kempeitai* (Thought Police) was purged one day, and the next day appointed as a liaison officer to the US military. George Kennan was appalled at MacArthur's disbandment of the Japanese army and the *Kempetai* as it left the government no means of policing domestic security, let alone the security threats posed by communist elements; it was a criticism that would be reprised when similar actions were taken by the American administration after the invasion of Iraq in 2003. The spiralling crime wave in post-war Japan was ample testament to the absence of those institutions which had kept Japan's darker forces in check.

In spite of the Emperor's public acceptance of being a human being, not a God, the setting up of a new committee, under the new Minister of State Matsumoto Joji, failed to move forward the issue of a new constitution; the committee came to the conclusion that the role of the Emperor should not be changed. Resistance to change, an endemic problem of Japanese institutions, was finally broken by a frustrated MacArthur, who ordered GHQ to draft a constitution on 3 February 1946.

This duly shocked the Japanese cabinet when it was presented to them by General George Whitney on 13 February; apart from GHQ's desire for a unicameral system, which the Japanese government managed to change, the dramatic increase of the electoral franchise proposed by SCAP and the reduced role of the Emperor were accepted virtually unchanged.

The new constitution insisted upon by MacArthur was pushed through the amendment procedures written in Article 73 of the Meiji Constitution of 29 November 1890. Whereas the earlier Japanese constitution embedded the person of the Emperor with the rights of sovereignty as immutable fundamental law, the MacArthur constitution for Japan emphasised that sovereignty lay with the people. Nevertheless, MacArthur had insisted 'to keep the Emperor at all costs'.[18] The Emperor was now reduced to a symbolic status. Article 1 went to the heart of the matter: 'The Emperor is head of state . . . his duties and powers will be exercised in accordance with the constitution and responsible to the basic will of the people.'[19]

Also of importance for the future as a major bone of contention between left and right was the commitment to pacifism within the constitution. Article 9 asserted that 'the Japanese people forever renounce war as a sovereign right of the nation and the threat or use of force as a means of settling international disputes'.[20]

In general, the constitutional changes and the move towards democracy was readily accepted by the Japanese, and proved the most successful and enduring of MacArthur's post-war achievements in Japan. Cartoonist Kato Eturo, who had spent the war years doing cartoons against the enemy, became overnight an ardent supporter of the USA. In a cartoon depicting canisters of democracy being parachuted into Japan, the caption reads, 'Chains were cut_ but we must not forget that we did not shed a drop of blood, or raise a sweat, to cut these chains.'[21] The establishment was easily won over to the concept of Western democracy, though the President of Tokyo University noted on a visit to Washington in 1949 that the Meiji Restoration had only modernised Japan by 'external appearance'. As Milo Rowell, a member of the judicial drafting committee, noted in a different context, 'You cannot impose a new mode of social thought on a country by law.'[22]

As well as constitutional changes, MacArthur, in spite of his right wing leanings, also introduced a broad range of policies promoting a liberal American agenda. Mark Gayn recalled in his diary of 7 December 1945:

> 'This is an exciting place at an exciting time in history. . . . Headquarters is full of 'reformers'. Lights burn late in buildings where these young men work on a blueprint for a new Japanese democracy. . . . There is wrecking a plenty, but this is a feudal land, and no democracy can rise here until the old structure is demolished'.[23]

A revised civil code promoted sexual equality. The result was an explosion in the divorce rate. In 1943, there had been 49,705 divorces, while in 1950 this rose to 83,869; significantly, the great majority of these were initiated by women. In 1948, SCAP also legalised abortion. Perhaps most importantly, women were included on the electoral franchise for the first time in 1949.

Also, in order to promote a more egalitarian society less likely to be suborned by militarism, the SCAP reformers also set about a wide-ranging land reform programme. Farmers in Japan who cultivated more than 3 *cho* of land (1 *cho* being approximately 2.45 acres) or 12 *cho* in less populated northern island of Hokkaido were forced to sell their land to the government, which re-sold it to tenant farmers. In addition, owners of tenanted land had to sell all but 1 *cho* (4 *cho* in Hokkaido).

Land under tenancy agreements fell from 40 per cent of the total to just 10 per cent. The result was an increase of 4.75 million farmers who owned their own land by 1950. For the long term, this group, who were prime beneficiaries of the post-war settlement, became a powerful conservative political electoral force for the soon to be entrenched Liberal Democratic Party (LDP).

Trade union membership was also encouraged by deregulation. In 1945, there were just two trade unions; by 1948, the number of unions had increased to over 34,000. Membership moreover grew from just 1,000 to 7 million. The release of communist agitators from prison after the war was a further invitation to worker militancy. Unleashing the suppressed frustrations of more than a decade of totalitarian rule, labour deregulation produced a seemingly irrepressible wave of labour militancy which damaged an already wounded Japanese economy. A concerned MacArthur, fearful of the social unrest that his policies had wrought, condemned a 250,000 strong workers' demonstration in May 1946. When the *Sanbetsu* (Confederation of Unions) called for a general strike on 1 February 1947, MacArthur pre-empted the event by prohibiting it.

Japan's first election by universal suffrage was held on 10 April 1946 and a new constitutional revision bill was outlined just a week later. Although the Liberal Party won most seats and formed the government, its leader Hatoyama was purged by SCAP for war crimes, and he was obliged to yield leadership to Shigeru Yoshida.

However, at the insistence of MacArthur, Yoshida was forced to call another general election to be held under the revised House of Representatives Election Law, which also included elections for a revised upper chamber, the House of Councillors. With the Japan Socialist Party emerging as the largest party, its leader Katayama now became prime minister after forging a coalition alliance with the *Minshuto* (Democratic Party) and the *Kokumin Kyodoto* (the National Co-operative Party).

Katayama's government was short-lived. The left wing of the socialist party split with the moderates and forced Katayama's resignation after eight months. A weak Democrat administration under Ashida lasted one month less; he was forced to resign after his arrest and indictment along with his deputy prime minister and 60 others for receiving bribes from Showa Denko K.K., a chemical company, in exchange for access to loans.

Yoshida now stepped forward again, and in January 1949 after winning a majority for the *Minshu Jiyuto* (LDP) in the Lower House, formed the first stable government of Japan's post-war era. Backed by big business, the *Minshu-Jiyuto* had filled its candidate list with former bureaucrats and increased its seats from 152 to 264. Yoshida now had a platform to reverse the disastrous 'liberal' policies forced on him by the young 'New Deal' ideologues at SCAP.

Shigeru Yoshida, the son of a samurai, was brought up in Yokosuka, a port city located on Tokyo Bay, by a wealthy merchant. Educated at the prestigious Tokyo University, his career in the diplomatic service was dramatically advanced by his marriage to the daughter of Makino Nobuaki, an eminent pre-war political figure and diplomat. Yoshida was an arrogant autocratic figure who tolerated no opposition within his party. With expensive aristocratic tastes and a caustic wit, he was the charismatic figure needed by Japan to lead it out of its post-war despond.

More importantly, his policies promoted a simple message. If Japan was to re-cover its prestige in the world, it must do so through economic growth, and the government could only achieve that by fiscal prudence combined with a commit-ment to capitalism and free trade. A staunch conservative, Yoshida had opposed the pre-war drift of the Japanese government's quasi-socialistic co-option of the busi-ness sector for realisation of the co-prosperity sphere. He was even more appalled by what he considered the American New Dealers left wing agenda to disman-tle Japan's industrial structure, and the encouragement of the political participa-tion of left wing Japanese politicians. From the beginning of 1948, Yoshida and the American administration began a ruthless purge of 'Reds' from the bureau-cracy, schools and universities. It was a policy which received the full support of MacArthur, who, in June 1949, went as far as to demand the removal and exclu-sion of 'the full membership of the Central Party of the Japan Communist Party from public service . . . '.[24] It is estimated that some 20,000 leftists were purged from office.

In foreign policy, Yoshida recognised that the main threat to Asia came from the left and that Japan must accept its position as a subordinated ally and junior partner to the USA. Under America's protective umbrella, Japan might regain some of its former pre-eminence. If these policies brought him under attack from both the left and the far right, including former Liberal leader Hatoyama who criticised Yoshida for being too close to the USA, the future was to prove the wisdom of his policies; the path which he delineated became the foreign policy roadmap for Japan over the next 40 years.

Perhaps the most pressing task facing SCAP was how to rebuild the Japanese economy so that it could feed itself. By the end of the war, in addition to some 80.6 per cent of shipping which had been destroyed, Japan had lost 34.2 per cent of machine tools and 21.9 per cent of all vehicles, including rolling stock. Although Japan had lost almost 3.5 per cent of its population versus 8.5 per cent in Germany, more than 7 million former soldiers needed employment. Needless to add that trade with America, which had accounted for 18.4 per cent of exports and 38.4 per cent of imports in 1939, was now zero.

Faced with these challenges, the New Dealers in MacArthur's GHQ staff, in-stead of seeking to rebuild Japanese capacity, embarked on a disastrous path of in-dustrial deconstruction. The pre-war *zaibatsu*, ten vertically integrated industrial conglomerates, had controlled some 4,000 operating companies and accounted for more than three quarters of all Japan's economic activity. Seeing in Japan's military–industrial complex one of the root causes of the war, the dismantling of Japan's *zaibatsu* structure was imposed through a Holding Company Liquidation Commission, which organised the sale of family businesses and the dissolution of major holding companies.

Taking the advice of Liberal economist Corwin Edwards, MacArthur also forced the Japanese Diet to accept an anti-monopoly law which prohibited trusts, interlocking corporate controls and established a Fair Trade Commission. MacArthur's anti-business policies not only attracted the opprobrium of Japanese businessmen; in America, *Newsweek* protested that the new laws threatened to 'atomize the Japanese business base as effectively as the famous bomb destroyed Hiroshima'.[25]

The aim to defenestrate Japan's *zaibatsu* inevitably distracted the country's main generators of wealth from setting about the economic reconstruction that the populace craved. In addition, the New Dealers, misapplying Keynesian remedies, supported an expansionary fiscal policy. Expansion of government demand, pump-priming, which had worked so well in America in the 1930s when the economy was operating hugely below capacity, was clearly inappropriate in post-war Japan where demand massively exceeded industrial capacity. The result was relentless inflation. Between the surrender in 1945 and August 1948, prices rose by 700 per cent. In short, MacArthur's economic policies were catastrophic in the early years of occupation.

Combined with growing awareness of the deficiencies in SCAP's economic policies in Japan, the priorities of the Truman administration in Washington were also beginning to shift. By 1948, it was apparent that the new enemy was communism. A sharp deterioration of relations with the Soviet Union was matched in seriousness by Chiang Kai Shek's losing ground to the Chinese Communists led by Mao. Reviewing Asian policy, Secretary of State Dean Acheson realised that if America was to have an Asian-based industrial 'powerhouse' as an ally to counter the Soviet threat, projected at this point through Mao, it would have to be Japan rather than China, as had reasonably been predicted in the immediate aftermath of the war.

With this aim, Joseph Dodge, a former Chairman of the Detroit Bank, was despatched to Tokyo by Dean Acheson in December 1948. He now threw the liberal economic programme of the New Dealers into reverse. Dodge successfully persuaded MacArthur to undo the *zaibatsu* dissolution programme. He then packed the De-concentration Review Board with his supporters, and they proceeded to overturn the more than 300 'reorganisation directives' issued by the Holding Company Liquidation Commission. With Yoshida of the Liberal Party sweeping into office within a month of Dodge's arrival, he had an ally in his pursuit of a return to conservative economics. 'Keynesian' stimulation was abandoned in favour of a period of staunch fiscal rectitude, which soon brought to a halt what had been runaway inflation.

In addition to the implementation of disciplined fiscal policy, Yoshida and SCAP also sought to rein back the unions which had so damaged the economy since their post-war deregulation. In the spring of 1949, Yoshida stood up to the Railways Unions by dismissing 126,000 employees in spite of incidents of sabotage, one of which caused a fatality when a train derailed at Matsukawa. The power of management–labour councils within corporations was reduced to an advisory role, while *mindo* (literally 'democratised leagues') were set up for breakaway groups from the unions, which had become infiltrated by Communists. In 1950, a rival federation of trade unions was set up to counter the influence of *Sanbetsu*. The results were dramatic. By 1951, the membership of *Sanbetsu* had fallen to 50,000 from its peak of 1.5 million; just seven years later it was abolished altogether.

With the understanding that trade was the key to economic recovery, Dodge boosted US-funded trade credits. These were particularly focused on the textile sector. To aid the export economy, the yen was fixed at an advantageous level of 360 to the US dollar, which combined with America's commitment to free trade (i.e. open accessibility to US markets), formed the basic building block to Japan's post-war recovery. Also, the establishment of the Ministry of International Trade and Industry (MITI) in 1949 gave the Japanese government power to prohibit or restrict imports of any product or commodity. In real terms however, the major turning point for the Japanese economy, whose output did not return to pre-war levels until 1952, was the Korean War, which boosted demand for Japanese products. Between 1951 and 1960, it is estimated that US procurements put US$ 5.5 billion into the Japanese economy.

The power of the left within government was also attacked. In December 1948, civil servants were denied the right to strike by the National Public Service Law; in 1952, this law was extended to regional government. Yoshida also purged the bureaucracy of communist sympathisers. With the dramatic shift in US perceptions, Yoshida took the opportunity to rehabilitate bureaucrats and politicians purged by MacArthur. Indeed, Shigemitsu Mamoru, a convicted war criminal, was released from prison in November 1950 and three years later went on to become Japan's minister of foreign affairs.

Negotiations for a peace treaty with the USA began in 1951 and were concluded in September of that year. Yoshida took the pragmatic view that Japan needed to be a long-term subordinate ally and at the Treaty of San Francisco he agreed to the provision of naval, military and air bases on the mainland of Japan and Okinawa. Such was the changing climate in Asia with the Soviet–Chinese alliance becoming the major regional threat that the USA now demanded that Japan re-arm itself. Curiously, Japan was reluctant to do so; a reflection of the swing of popular emotion away from extreme militarism to extreme pacifism.

The creation of a paramilitary National Police Reserve of 75,000 in Japan was less than half of that demanded by Truman. Noticeably, the word 'army' was carefully avoided. In 1952, the National Police Reserve was changed in name to the National Safety Force, and two years later to its current incarnation of *Jiei-tai* (the National Self Defence Force); administration of the Japanese 'Army' was carried out by the *Boei-cho* (Defence Agency) under a cabinet ministry. In 1954, Japan signed a Mutual Security Agreement with the USA by which Japan was provided with US$ 150 million in military equipment.

Yoshida recalled in his memoirs that the American occupation of Japan before 1951 was badly thought out and destructive to economic prosperity:

> ...the financial concerns were disintegrated through the complete break-up of the *zaibatsu* and by the institution of anti-monopoly measures, gravely retarding our economic recovery.... Communist leaders were released from prison and praised for their fanatical agitation, causing untold injury to our body politic ... organised labour was encouraged in radical actions, thus endangering law and order.[26]

With the benefit of hindsight, it is clear that in the initial stages the US occupation and administration of Japan was disastrously flawed in concept and execution. MacArthur's peremptory disbandment of the army and security forces before order had been fully established in Japan led to an explosion of crime and lawlessness as well as infiltration of communists into the institutions of state.

MacArthur's administration was not all bad. Arguably, at the end of the Second World War, Japan needed a 'larger than life' pro-consul to make the American occupation, if not palatable, at least acceptable. General MacArthur fitted this role perfectly. With the Japanese he was courteous, aloof and mysterious; not unlike the Emperor. General Eisenhower described him as having 'a reserved dignity_but he is most animated in conversation on subjects that interest him.... He is impulsive_able, even brilliant_quick_tenacious of his views and extremely confident'.[27] Many others saw this as a combination of arrogance and pomposity.

To his credit, his implementation of constitutional reform proved a success in providing Japan with stable government. This was a notable achievement. On balance however, MacArthur's role as supreme commander in Japan would have to be deemed a failure. His muddled understanding of Japanese culture and history caused him to support Emperor Hirohito, clearly the key Japanese war criminal, in his efforts to remain as Japan's figurehead leader, and made a charade of the Tokyo War Crimes trial, which left a legacy of deceit which still hampers Japan's relationships in Asia.

As for Japan's economic mismanagement in the immediate post-war period, the blame was MacArthur's and his alone; he boasted of his dictatorial powers and he would write later, 'I had to be an economist, a political scientist, an engineer, a manufacturing executive, a teacher, even a theologian of sorts.'[28] In the economic sphere, the best that could be said of him is that he changed course before it was too late; the abandonment of left wing economic policies did indeed set the platform for Japan's post-war economic prosperity. For this, Japan was largely indebted to the change of heart towards Japan by the Truman administration, the sending of new economic advisors to Tokyo and the conservative probity of Prime Minister Yoshida. As for MacArthur, it is perhaps fortunate for his enduring reputation as the 'great' rebuilder of post-war Japan, that of all his talents, the one in which he most excelled was self-publicity.

10

Hồ Chí Minh and the Battle of Diên Biên Phu

Vietnam: 1945—54

On 30 August 1945, Hồ Chí Minh arrived in Hanoi to establish independence for the Democratic Republic of Vietnam. Swapping the simple tunic that became his hallmark, for a borrowed khaki linen suit, Hồ stood in front of some 500,000 cheering Vietnamese in Ba Dinh Square and, mimicking America's own masterly Declaration of Independence, announced that 'All men are created equal. They are endowed by their creator with certain inalienable rights, among these are life, liberty and the pursuit of happiness.'[1]

Reflecting Hồ's appeal to a broad front of nationalist support, Sunday 2 September was chosen as Independence Day to coincide with the feast of Vietnamese Martyrs. Celebrations followed with ceremonies both at the main Buddhist temples and at the Catholic Cathedral. More importantly, by lifting phrases from Jefferson's *Declaration of American Independence*, Hồ did more than appeal to American support for a Vietnam independent from France; he recognised America as Asia's new superpower and its likely role as arbiter of Vietnam's future.

During the Second World War, the French Vichy government in Vietnam had collaborated with the Japanese to ensure its survival. Governor Admiral Jean Decoux with some 90,000 troops under his command never wavered in his support for the Axis powers. The result was that French Indochina was the only colonial power in Asia to survive Japanese occupation. This fact somewhat belied the post-war Japanese justification of military adventurism on the grounds that they had set about the liberation of Asia from European colonial rule.

It was a convenient alliance for both sides. In return for allowing colonial rule to continue, the Vichy French government in Indochina allowed the Japanese to use Vietnamese ports as a staging post for the war effort against the British in Malaysia and then Burma. Thanks to French compliance, there were never more than 60,000 Japanese soldiers stationed in Vietnam. It was from here that the Japanese launched the air attacks that famously sank the British battleship *HMS Prince of Wales* and the battle cruiser *HMS Repulse*.

However, Vichy Vietnam's quiet war did not survive to the end. In March 1945, the Japanese recognised that the 'liberation' of France now changed the situation in Vietnam. Admiral Decoux was removed from power in Saigon, and Vietnam's Vichy rulers incarcerated. In place of a 'puppet' Vichy government, the Japanese determined that their interests would be best served by fostering Vietnamese independence.

Emperor Bảo Dại was restored as a puppet ruler based in the traditional Imperial capital at Hué, with a cabinet government in Hanoi under Tran Trong Kim that consisted of four medical doctors, one professor and a lawyer. In a message to de Gaulle and world leaders, Bảo Dại prophetically declared that

> the Vietnamese people who have a history of twenty centuries and an often glorious past, no longer wish, no longer can support any foreign domination or foreign administration ... Even if you were to arrive to re-establish a French administration here, it would no longer be obeyed; each village would be a nest of resistance, every former friend an enemy.[2]

However, by handing power to a group of Vietnamese Francophile scholars and bureaucrats from central Vietnam, the Japanese increased rather than decreased domestic insurgency as the *Việt Minh* (league for the independence of Vietnam), who had gradually developed their strength in the rural areas during the Second World War, were now supplied by the allies. A French–American advisory group parachuted into Vietnam to meet with *Việt Minh* leaders in July 1945, and organised airdrops supplying about 5,000 weapons during the summer. As Jean Santenay, Commissioner for North Vietnam after the war would complain to *The New York Times* in January 1947, the allies 'supplied them [the *Việt Minh*] with arms, including the Sten guns that are now being used against the French. . . .'[3]

Bảo Dại was forced to abdicate on 25 August 1945. Whereas Hồ's forces in the North had gained control of Hanoi with just 1,000 troops, in the South, attempts by the communists to take control met with much greater difficulty. It had been decided at the Potsdam Conference that Chiang Kai Shek's Chinese forces would supervise the surrender of the Japanese North of the 16th parallel; in the South, the British army was allocated responsibility.

However, the Southern-based communists were much weaker than their Northern brethren. Riven by splits between Trotskyites and Stalinists, who themselves were split between rival factions, the Communist Front was disunited within itself, let alone with other nationalist elements, which it had not brought into a broad 'liberation' alliance. Above all, the South lacked a figure of Hồ Chí Minh's overriding genius and unifying charisma.

A small British force led by General Gracey arrived in Saigon on 22 August 1945 to find the southern capital in chaos, with open clashes between Vietnamese and French forces. He attempted to calm the situation by letting Japanese prisoners of war out of prison and rearmed them to police the city. They proved ineffective.

Gracey gave in to rearming 1,400 men of the 9th and 11th French colonial infantry; they evicted the *Việt Minh* and reoccupied all key buildings and strategic points. A French campaign of terror and mass arrest then ensued.

The macabre pantomime continued when, observing the French lust for revenge, Gracey confined the French colonial infantry to barracks and rearmed the Japanese. Vietnamese revenge on the French community was equally savage. In the Cité Herault, the *Việt Minh* massacred 216 mainly French citizens. However, the unlikely combination of English and Japanese soldiers fighting on the same side succeeded in thwarting a *Việt Minh* takeover.

The *Việt Minh* had finally succeeded in unifying all parties against them. General Leclerc's arrival with 1,000 troops enabled a clearing of the *Việt Minh* forces from Saigon, and when an additional French armoured division entered Saigon on 22 October, total French forces in the region outnumbered the *Việt Minh* by 25,000 to 15,000.

However, for the *Việt Minh* this was an opportunity lost. After March 1945 when the French were ejected from power by the Japanese, the *Việt Minh* had largely replaced French power in the villages. A well-orchestrated co-ordination of their forces, and a judicious assemblage of alliances with other groups, might well have pre-empted a return of French power in Saigon. As North Vietnam's Communist Party General-Secretary Trường Chinh recalled in his memoir *The August Revolution (1958)*, failure was the result of, 'the weakness of the *Việt Minh* organization in Nam Bo before Zero hour of the insurrection and to the lack of homogeneity in the ranks of the United National Front'.[4] In the event, the *Việt Minh* would have to wait another 30 years before they entered the city in triumph. However, it was to be the armies of North Vietnam that would carry them there.

The relative success of the Northern revolt against French power was in large part due to the strategies of one of the most remarkable revolutionary figures of the twentieth century. Born with the name Nguyễn Sinh Cung on 19 May 1890, Hồ's parents were genteel poor. His father was a Confucian scholar, the first person from his area of Central Vietnam to win a doctorate. In celebration, Hồ's name was changed to Nguyễn Tat Thanh ('he who will succeed').

From an early age, Hồ possessed the capacious intellectual curiosity that would characterise his life. As a young student he supposedly walked to the provincial capital to buy books on Vietnamese history. His country's decline into French servitude in the twentieth century was an abiding preoccupation. For Hồ, this decline was also relevant to his father's reluctant acceptance of minor bureaucratic posts at the Imperial Court, and later as a regional administrator. His father's clear preference was to teach the Confucian classics rather than work for a corrupt bureaucracy that had been humiliated by the French colonists. Hồ grew up sharing his father's distaste for French rule and the humiliations suffered by his country.

Although he learnt French and in 1907 enrolled at the leading Franco-Vietnamese school *Quốc Học*, the National Academy, Hồ chose to forego the advantages that he could have derived by working within the French colonial system. Hồ subsequently participated in an attempted coup in 1925 by the nationalist groups headed by Phan Bôi Châu's Reformation Society (*Duy Tân Hội*), founded in 1903. Phan Bôi Châu was arrested and spent the remainder of his life under house arrest in Hué. Hồ fled Hué and became a Chinese teacher in the remote coastal village of Phan Thiết where he introduced his students to Voltaire, Montesquieu and Rousseau. Hồ then followed his father to Saigon, where he did odd jobs before getting a job as a kitchen hand on the liner *Admiral Latouche-Treville* that was bound for Marseilles.

Thus began a life of astonishing global peripatetic activity. He may simply have left Vietnam because he was a wanted man, or because his career opportunities were thwarted, but Hồ would later explain to the American journalist Anna Louise Strong:

> The people of Vietnam, including my own father, often wondered who would help them to remove the yoke of French control. Some said Japan, others Great Britain, and some said the United States. I saw that I must go abroad to see for myself. After I had found out how they lived, I would return to help my countrymen.[5]

Arriving in Marseilles on 6 July 1911, Hồ was amazed to find poverty and prostitution. America also surprised him in this respect. Here he worked as a labourer and then as a domestic servant. It was also claimed that he worked at the Parker House Hotel in Boston. Whatever his employment, Hồ continued his international political education. He attended black activist meetings of the Universal Negro Improvement Trust, and went to the southern states of America where Hồ observed a Ku Klux Klan lynching. As for languages, these were picked up with ease. Hồ was a brilliant linguist. During his life, he mastered English, French, German, Russian, Czech, Japanese, three Chinese languages as well as numbers of Annamite dialects.

From America, he worked his passage again to London where he found employment as a snow sweeper. He then worked as a stoker and dishwasher at the Carlton Hotel. Here he came under the patronage of the great French chef, Auguste Escoffier, who spotted his rare intelligence and ability. 'Leave your revolutionary ideas for a moment', he told Hồ, 'and I will teach you the art of cooking, which will bring you a lot of money'.[6]

Apart from becoming a skilled confectioner under Escoffier's guidance, Hồ is also thought to have consumed Marx during his time in London. Moving back to France during the First World War, Hồ became a photographer in Montmartre, joined the French Socialist Party and became acquainted with Leon Blum, a future prime minister. Hồ also wrote for *Le Populaire*, discussed dreams, the soul and death in philosophical clubs and attempted a career as a playwright with *The Bamboo Dragon* (1922).

A fellow member at the Club du Faubourg described him as 'sympathetic but not at all fanatic, and very witty. He seemed to be mocking the world and at the same time to be mocking himself'.[7] By all accounts Hồ was a man of few vices, though he liked American cigarettes and in later life developed a partiality for stewed tiger's livers.

Hồ now changed his name again from Thanh to *Nguyễn Ái Quốc* (Nguyễn the Patriot), which was to become his best-known revolutionary alias. In 1919, sensing the new possibilities of a post-war world, he penned an appeal for Vietnamese independence which, to the anger of the French government, the uninvited Hồ delivered to the Versailles Peace Conference. Wearing a borrowed tailcoat, petition in hand, he made a highly theatrical appearance.

While he was denied a hearing here and at the National Assembly, Hồ's daring exploit made his name. *L'Humanité* published his petition, and 6,000 copies were also printed and distributed around Paris. Back in Hanoi, the article produced a sensation. From now on, Hồ would be tracked by the French authorities. His reputation as a revolutionary leader was assured. Tours of Europe followed. A German Communist commented on Hồ that it is his 'nationalism which impressed us European Communists born and bred in a rather grey kind of abstract internationalism'.[8]

At what point Hồ fully embraced the Leninist path is unclear, but in December 1923 he made his way to Moscow and enrolled at the Communist University of the Toilers of the East. He would later tell French journalists:

> I studied and chose Marx. Jesus said two thousand years ago that one should love one's enemies. That dogma has not been realized. When will Marxism be realized? I cannot answer . . . To achieve a Communist society, industrial and agricultural production is necessary . . . I do not know when that will be realized in Vietnam, where production is low.[9]

The intent of his visit to Russia was clear; his training included courses on military strategy, worker organisation and propaganda. During a wartime meeting with American intelligence officer Charles Fenn, Hồ told him:

> One doesn't in fact gain independence by throwing bombs and such. That was the mistake the early revolutionaries all too often made. One must gain it through organization, propaganda, training and discipline . . . a set of beliefs, a gospel, a practical analysis, you might even say a bible. Marxism–Leninism gave me that framework.[10]

During his time in Moscow, he also met Sun Yat Sen's senior advisor, Chiang Kai Shek, and Zhou Enlai, whom he had already met in Paris. Then at the Fourth Comintern (Communist International) Congress in Moscow, Hồ met Lenin, Trotsky and Bukharin. He was mixing in elevated circles and was marked as a key man to foment revolution in Asia. The famous Russian Comintern agent Borodin took him to Canton via Vladivostok as an assistant, and here he quickly established an expatriate Vietnamese communist group.

In Canton he also found time to marry Tăng Tuyết Minh, daughter of a wealthy merchant's concubine. It was a truncated marriage, an institution that was barely compatible with the life of an international revolutionary. Returning alone to Moscow, Hồ was employed as a government advisor but found time to publish *A Revolutionary Path* in 1926, and travelled extensively again in Europe before returning to Asia in 1928, where, disguising himself as a Buddhist monk, he organised Vietnamese communists based in Thailand.

In 1930, Hồ returned to China, where he reorganised a fractured Vietnamese Communist Party in Hong Kong. Here at a party conference he met Nguyễn Thi Minh Kai, who he is thought to have married before his arrest by British police in 1931. In prison, Hồ contracted tuberculosis and nearly died. By the time he was released, his wife had moved on to another man.

There followed the most mysterious period in Hồ's already extraordinary, peripatetic life. He simply vanished for almost a decade. He was variously reported as being in Spain, Java, Shanghai and Portuguese East Africa. By some reports, he settled down with a concubine. Another story has him fathering a daughter in the Soviet Union. Tracking a man with so many names and disguises was never easy; indeed, apart from the pseudonyms already mentioned, Hồ would also go under the names of Ly Thúy, Song Man Tcho, Nguyễn O Phap and Nguyễn Sinh Chin. Hồ never dispelled the air of mystery that was so much part of his revolutionary aura.

After the establishment of the puppet Vichy regime in Vietnam in May 1941, Hồ, wearing jungle clothing, consisting of rubber sandals, brown shorts and a khaki sun helmet, suddenly appeared at a meeting of communists and nationalists at Tsin-Li. Hồ, an almost mythological figure, long thought to have died, was elected to the post of general secretary, and set about burying ideological disputes in order to bring all the nationalist anti-French and anti-Japanese factions together.

At Liu Chou in China and Bac Bo in Vietnam, Hồ united the nationalist and communist groups into the *Dộc Lập Dồng Minh Hội* (League for the Independence of Vietnam). This above all was his revolutionary genius. Ignoring the claims of purist Marxist ideology and Comintern internationalism, Hồ focused all energies on the pragmatic creation of alliances that would bring about an independent Vietnam. Some historians have questioned his revolutionary communist credentials. Whilst these were never in doubt, Hồ nevertheless realised that to create a socialist state one first needed to seize power.

At first, the building of an effective revolutionary movement was fraught with the difficulty of operating from Southern China, where the *Kuomintang* warlords were naturally hostile to communist groups. Hồ himself was arrested in 1941 by the *Kuomintang* secret police, and now changed his name so as not to be identified with the famous revolutionary Nguyễn Ai Quốc.

However, as the war progressed, the *Kuomintang* attitude to the Vietnamese revolutionaries changed. Combating the Japanese threat increased in importance. In 1943, Hồ was released by southern warlord Chang Fa Kwei, who gave him 100,000 *Kuomintang* dollars per month to carry out sabotage in Indochina. From this point, Hồ was able to start the process of building a true revolutionary guerrilla organisation.

At this point, Võ Nguyên Giáp emerged as the military genius who, over the next 35 years, would successfully take on the armies of France, America, the Khmer Rouge and China. The foundations of Vietnam's revolutionary army, which was to grow into one of the world's most effective fighting forces, were 31 men and 3 women who lined up in a jungle clearing on 22 December 1944. The First Armed Propaganda Brigade could muster 1 machine gun, 17 modern rifles and 2 revolvers. Giáp, a former lawyer and teacher with a passion for military history, wearing his favoured white linen suit and Homburg hat, presided over this motley group, which was the foundation of a Vietnamese People Liberation Army (VPLA) that would eventually number over a million men under arms.

Giáp was perhaps the greatest exponent of Maoist guerrilla stratagem. Dictums found in captured diaries revealed Giáp's military philosophy, 'The most appropriate guiding principle for our early activities was armed propaganda. . . . Political activities were more important than military activities. Fighting was less important than agit-prop work. Armed activities were used to safeguard, consolidate and develop political bases', and, 'maintain and gradually augment our forces. Nibble at and progressively destroy those of the enemy. Accumulate a thousand small victories to turn into one success'.[11]

Recruits were made to learn the Mao–Giáp revolutionary philosophy by heart. By co-opting the village communities in rural Vietnam, the PLA built a base in the countryside with astonishing rapidity. Slogans proclaimed, 'The whole people in arms _ each person a fighter, each village a fortress, each Party cell and resistance committee a general staff.'[12] Within a year, the PLA had grown to 10,000 men and was increasingly coming to the attention of American military intelligence. Four times, between 1944 and early 1945, Hồ visited American Strategic Services in Kunming looking for arms and money in return for sabotage operations against the Japanese.

However US policy was clear. Paul Helliwell, OSS intelligence chief later confirmed that 'OSS China was at all times consistent in its policy of giving no help to individuals such as Ho, who were known Communists and therefore obvious postwar sources of trouble.'[13] Nevertheless, relations remained cordial, and when American pilots were safely returned through the PLA network, Hồ was given six 0.38 calibre pistols and 20,000 rounds of ammunition.

Could Hồ have been turned towards a pro-Western stance at this point? The possibility is hinted at by an American report from Hồ's base in early 1945:

> You've got to judge someone on the basis of what he wants. . . . He was afraid of the Chinese, and he couldn't deal with them because they'd always demand their pound of flesh. . . . I think he was ready to remain pro-West.[14]

The report from Hồ's jungle hideout, where he occupied a 12-foot square hut, was typical of America's ambiguous attitude to Vietnam's post-war future. As

Edwin Reischauer, Asian expert and future US Ambassador to Japan, would observe, because of 'concern over the sensitivities and political problems of the colonial powers in Europe, we chose to ignore Asian nationalism, except in our own domain of the Philippines'.[15]

For Franklin Roosevelt, the moral point was clear. In 1944, he pronounced, 'France has milked Indo-China for a hundred years. The people of Indo-China deserve better than that.'[16] The fact that President Franklin D. Roosevelt considered France to be a completely worthless country must have been hard for the French to bear. However, in spite of these views, he ordered Cordell Hull to 'do nothing in regard to resistance groups in Indochina'.[17] At one point, trusteeship was considered and Chiang Kai Shek was asked whether China would like Vietnam. 'It's no help to us,' he replied, 'We don't want it. They are not Chinese. They would not assimilate with the Chinese people.'[18] In the end, America took no decision. In refusing to intervene either to court the nationalist groups resistant to the Japanese or to firmly oppose the build up of communist guerrilla groups, America allowed a conflict to develop in Indochina, over which they exercised no control. In hindsight, it was an abdication of responsibility, which was to cost them dear. As Asia's only post-war superpower, it was almost inevitable that they would be drawn into the mêlée.

In the vacuum left by American vacillation, the drive for the post-war settlement of Indochina came from France. For the post-war French government, the path was clear; they would reclaim their rightful empire. In the mid-nineteenth century, Vietnamese execution of French missionaries had provided the excuse for Napoleon III to begin the co-option of Vietnam. In a Treaty of 1862, the Vietnamese Emperor ceded control of the Southern Mekong Delta (Cochin) to France. Central Vietnam (Anam) and the North (Tonkin) followed in 1884–5.

China, which as late as the 1880s was receiving tribute from Vietnam, was also a party to the treaty. The name Vietnam was then outlawed by the French who sought to divide and rule by playing on the traditional regional divisions of the country. Accordingly, separate administrative regimes were set up in Cochin (capital; Saigon), Anam (capital; Hué) and Tonkin (capital; Hanoi). The area known as 'Indochina', consisting of Vietnam, Cambodia and Laos, was formed as a political entity in 1897. To a large extent, the area was second prize to losing out to Britain in the scramble for empire in the East. As the American historian John McAlister has pointed out, Indochina was a 'Semantic compensation for French colonial failures in India and China at the hands of the British.'[19]

France did not rule with a light touch. In 1910, there were more French administrators in Vietnam than Britain employed in the entire British Empire. Unlike the British in India, the French rulers did not come to regard Indochina as a country held in trust as many in the British colonial services felt about India; to a much greater extent, Indochina, as with other French colonies, was increasingly integrated into a centralised government system run from Paris.

Whereas a large degree of electoral and governmental autonomy had been granted India prior to the Second World War, there were no such concessions in French-ruled Indochina. Even after the crushing defeat of the French army by Hitler's Panzer divisions in 1939, there was little acknowledgement that the world had changed. At the French colonial conference at Brazzaville in Congo, at the beginning of 1944, the final communiqué declared that

> the aims of the work of civilization which France is accomplishing in her possessions exclude any idea of autonomy and any possibility of development outside the French Empire bloc. The attainment of 'self-government' in the colonies, even in the most distant future, must be excluded.[20]

Yet in August 1945, it soon became clear that re-establishing French power in the region would not be easy. General Leclerc, with British help, may have retaken Saigon, but the countryside was still full of *Việt Minh* forces. Furthermore, with just 20,000 available troops, Leclerc did not have the forces to retake Hanoi. In the North, meanwhile, the PLA was rapidly augmenting its strength by buying weapons and munitions from Chinese officers.

With the ending of the war, there were plentiful stocks of Japanese and American weapons. The *Việt Minh* harvested opium to pay for them. Between March 1945 and December 1946, the *Việt Minh* increased their stock of machine guns from 600 to 4,500 out of a total weapons stock of 40,000. In spite of these realities, many in France could not stomach the idea of negotiations favoured by Leclerc. De Gaulle's appointee, the High Commissioner for Indochina, a former Carmelite monk turned Admiral, Georges D'Argenlieu, fulminated against a strategy that he regarded as capitulation.

In spite of the hardline favoured by D'Argenlieu, negotiations did indeed proceed. The *Việt Minh*, according to Trường Chinh in his account of *The August Revolution*, sought 'Independence . . . to be given to this country in a minimum of five years and a maximum of ten.'[21] Hồ, stalling for time in his wish to avoid a military conflict with France, adopted a moderate stance at odds with the 'Independence or death' posters that covered Hanoi. Hồ told French negotiator Jean Sainteny, 'Even though we want to administer ourselves and though I ask you to withdraw your administrators, I still need your professors, your engineers, and your capital in order to build a strong and independent Vietnam.'[22]

Even the new socialist government in France, however, could not accept the idea of independence, and at the beginning of 1946 a landing of French troops at Haiphong was prepared. On 6 March, Hồ caved in to a compromise solution that gave the North Vietnam administration autonomy within the French Union. In Hanoi, Giáp was appalled. The hardliners in France were equally unhappy; D'Argenlieu wrote, '. . . I am amazed that France has in Indochina such a fine expeditionary force, and that its chiefs prefer to negotiate rather than to fight. . . .'[23]

On balance the advantage was to Hồ Chí Minh. He had won a legally recognised government; also by binding the French government to the outcome of a referendum on unification, Hồ destroyed the historic French fiction that Vietnam was not a single country. Future negotiations on diplomatic relations and economic matters were also agreed.

More importantly, for Hồ, the accord with France on 16 March 1946 bought time for Giáp to increase the military strength of the PLA in the North and the *Việt Minh* in the South. In May 1946, Hồ went to France to continue negotiations and scored a remarkable propaganda success with the French media. Dressed in his simple linen Chinese-style tunic, the softly spoken yet charismatic Hồ wooed the press and was widely compared to Confucius, Buddha, John the Baptist and Gandhi.

Even his adversaries were charmed; Sainteny in *The Story of a lost Peace, 1945–7* described him as an 'ascetic man, whose face revealed at once intelligence, energy, cleverness, and finesse . . .'.[24] Meanwhile, in Vietnam, notwithstanding the March accord, guerrilla attacks on French posts continued. Also, assassination of village heads and other terror tactics enabled a rapid expansion of village control and recruitment in the South. Schools were set up by Giáp to train officers for his burgeoning forces. By mid-1947, the *Việt Minh* had some 100,000 troops in the South and, in the North, where the accord restricted France to some 15,000 men, there were now some 75,000 troops in the PLA.

The spark that ignited the full-scale conflict came with a customs dispute involving the confiscation of motor oil brought into Haiphong. In the fighting that followed an oil trader's arrest, some 20 French soldiers were killed on 20 November. On the following day, 18 French soldiers, on their way to find war graves of troops killed by the Japanese, were ambushed and massacred by *Việt Minh* forces.

The French response was brutal. The Naval bombardment of Haiphong and subsequent assault killed 6,000 Vietnamese, mainly civilians. The French army now landed a Foreign Legion battalion at Da Nang, north of the 16th parallel. Hopes of peace were renewed when the socialist Leon Blum, who had spoken of an Independence solution for Indochina, was elected to office on 11 December 1946.

Optimism was short-lived. On 19 December, General Morlière presented Hồ with an ultimatum demanding the disarmament of his forces in Hanoi. Hồ, however, had returned from France in disgrace with his fellow revolutionaries. Giáp and Dang Xuan Khu strongly disapproved of his moderate tactics and for a while it seems that Hồ was put under house arrest. Although he was restored to office in 1947, Hồ's political power, other than as a figurehead, was now on the wane, although he would not be completely marginalised until the fall of Truờng Chinh and emergence of Lê Duẩn in 1956.

With the *Việt Minh*'s refusal of Morlière's ultimatum, fighting started in earnest. Within two months, Hanoi was taken at a cost of some 1,855 French troops killed or wounded. However, the *Việt Minh* now retreated to the countryside to fight the classic guerrilla war to which they were best suited and the French least able to cope.

The pattern of war mirrored that fought by the *Kuomintang* against Mao. While the French army controlled the cities and towns, the *Việt Minh* controlled the countryside. Even in the cities, infiltrators committed assassinations and bombings. Journalist Robert Shaplen noted that at the Red Mill, a popular restaurant on the outskirts of Saigon, people ate outside on a terrace covered in a grill to ward off grenades. Graham Greene would describe the same experience in his novel *The Quiet American* (1955). There was no music except the accompaniment of distant artillery and rifle fire. In effect, the French were besieged.

France now set about building a political construct for Vietnam. Emperor Bảo Dại was once again recalled. In July 1949, Bảo Dại decreed the establishment of the State of Vietnam. The political construction now envisaged was that Vietnam would join the two other supposedly independent states within the French Union.

However, the fiction fooled no one. Separate legal status for the French community was proposed, while the French government envisaged that the army would remain firmly under France's control. Even moderate nationalist opinion failed to be assuaged. As a former advisor to Bảo Dại explained:

> The Vietnamese people considered Bảo Dại's regime as a puppet regime, created and supported by the French for the sole purpose of endorsing French colonial policy and lending it an appearance of legality . . . consequently the Communists not only enjoyed the neutrality of the great majority of the Vietnamese population, but had also the active support of many sincere nationalists, who fought along with the *Việt Minh* against French colonialism.[25]

The war took a familiar course with isolated small-scale French victories countered by the constant wearing down of guerrilla attacks and terrorist activity. For France, the sudden collapse of Chiang Kai Shek and the Communist victory in China in 1949 was also ominous. Now the PLA would have the contiguous support of China, a vast communist power. On 18 January 1950, Mao Zedong's new government in China formally recognised the new government in North Vietnam. More importantly, after Hồ's visit to Beijing in April 1950, China opened her arsenals to her new allies; mortars, field guns and anti-aircraft guns flowed and for the first time enabled Giáp to professionally equip his forces. Ground down, the French once more opened negotiations on independence.

At Pau in the south of France, talks continued from June to November 1950. Plans were mooted to transfer administrative powers for immigration, communications, foreign trade, customs and finances. However, sovereignty and independence remained sticking points that the French were still reluctant to come to term with. As the American Charge D'Affaires in Saigon pointed out, 'The French were still unable to state unequivocally that Indochina states would be completely independent.'[26]

In Vietnam, war continued apace. Giáp had taken important French outposts at Dong Khe and Cao Bang, and by October a retreating French army had been pushed out of the northern border. With the failure of the Pau talks, General Jean de Lattre de Tassigny was appointed high commissioner and commander in chief of the French expeditionary forces. Although he lost his son in battle soon after arriving in Vietnam, de Lattre temporarily managed to restore French morale; so did the supply of American planes, the Grunman F-8F Bearcat and the Douglas B-26 Invader that for the first time used napalm bombs.

However, up until 1951, the French expeditionary force was handicapped by lack of basic equipment. They had to make do with a bewildering array of French, British, American and Chinese weapons supplemented in some cases by captured Japanese and German small arms. 'All required different ammunition, which made logistics a nightmare.'[27] It was only after 1953 that American equipment, including modern weaponry, trucks and armoured vehicles, arrived in bulk. There was also a shortage of well-trained troops; even the French Legion's training in North Africa had to be curtailed. Half of the Legionnaires were German, but by 1950 they were not the battle-trained Waffen-SS veterans of the Second World War, but 20–23-year-old recruits. They fared better though than the Tirailleurs Senegalais, who, mainly from the Savannah tribes of West Africa, were culturally and topographically unsuited to the war in Indochina.

In spite of his army's deficiencies, on 16–17 January 1950, de Lattre decisively defeated Giáp at Vinhyen. Although the Việt Minh lost 6,000 men, the road-bound French forces, supplied with new American M-26 tanks, were unable to pursue an enemy that retreated to its jungle lairs. However, such was the scale of the victory that Giáp did not attempt battle again in the Mekong Delta until the end of the war. However, de Lattre, France's apparent saviour, was dead from cancer within a year.

Political instability in France did not help smooth conduct of the war. In 1953, Jean Letourneau, minister of overseas France and also high commissioner for Indochina, was sacked by the new French Prime Minister, Joseph Laniel. His new choice of commander in chief, Henri Navarre, was informed that no more troops would be sent and that preparations for peace should be made. After seven years of conflict, France was war weary; by 1954, a Le Monde poll showed that only 15 per cent of voters supported continued vigorous conduct of the war. French Prime Minister Rene Mayer told Navarre that his objective should be to conduct the war so as to achieve an 'honourable way out'.[28]

The Mayer government fell three days after Navarre arrived in Saigon and his successor, Prime Minister Joseph Laniel, belatedly announced implementation of the Pau agreements. Bảo Dại complained, 'What's the matter with the French_they're always giving us our independence. Can't they give it to us once and for all?'[29] Navarre, ignoring the cautious advice of his prime minister, set out to engage Giáp in a decisive battle in early 1954.

Choosing the village of Diên Biên Phu, which stood at the junction of three roads, ten miles from Laos, Navarre's 16,000 troops dug a series of fortified entrenchments. Around the stronghold of Elaine, which included the village, were three main bastions Huguette, Claudine and Dominique, and four smaller fortifications. Navarre's plan was to draw out Giáp's army, into a pitched battle on terrain of Navarre's choosing. Thus far he succeeded.

Colonel Charles Piroth advised Navarre that it would be impossible for Giáp to manoeuvre heavy artillery through the Northern Highlands, let alone supply them with shells. Even if they could deploy their 105-mm guns, Piroth promised, 'General, no Viet cannon will be able to fire three rounds before being destroyed by my artillery.'[30] Navarre believed that his forces were impervious to bombardment. This fatal underestimation of the PLA's ability to manhandle artillery pieces through hostile terrain undermined the entire plan. Not only were the entrenchments subject to massive bombardment, but also planes were not able to use the airfield to bring in reinforcements. Even the Red Cross Dakotas were fired on when they attempted to evacuate the wounded. Neither could C-47s fly low enough to supply French forces with any accuracy; often the air force simply succeeded in supplying the enemy.

Blaming himself for the debacle, a depressed Piroth committed suicide with a hand grenade pulled to his chest. Suffering appalling losses, Giáp's troops dug trenches at night and inched forward, tightening the noose around the besieged French army. One Vietnamese officer of 312th Division recalled:

> The orders were given: 'No trenches, no battle_Diên Biên Phu is trench warfare'.
> They worked without ever complaining. The timetable was unchanging: return to unit
> area at 7 am or 8 am, eat, attend a work review meeting, then sleep from 9 am to noon;
> cut and carry timber from noon until 3 pm; another meal; then head for the trenches
> with picks and shovels, and work until long after sunrise.[31]

From 30 March, hand-to-hand fighting became commonplace. The French army was not without its heroes. In one of the legendary engagements of the month-long battle, German Legionnaires sang their battalion marching song as they mounted an uphill counter-attack to recapture Eliane 1.

Throughout the summer, the drama of French encirclement and impending defeat traumatised both France and America. The Americans, wanting to help on the one hand, were fearful on the other hand, that being too closely associated with a French defeat would do damage to their global war against communism. From 1950, the French war in Vietnam had been increasingly financed by America, in spite of President Truman's doubts about France's colonial ambitions. However, America held back from committing its own Air Force in the battle for Diên Biên Phu.

The policy of using France as a counterweight to communist expansion was not without its critics. George Kennan, a State Department expert on Asia protested to Dean Acheson on 21 August 1950 that

> In Indochina we are getting ourselves into a position of guaranteeing the French in an undertaking which neither they nor we, nor both of us together, can win . . . the closer view we have had of the problems of the area, in the course of efforts of the past few months to support the French position there, has convinced us that the position is basically hopeless. [32]

However, with the loss of China to communism, and the impending battle to save Korea from the same fate, the idea of abandoning Indochina to the 'Red tide' was not appealing.

For Dwight Eisenhower, who was sworn in as president in January 1953, the fate of Asia was of paramount importance. He thought that losing South East Asia would be, 'a calamity of the most terrible immediate and eventual consequences'. [33] Also in a memorandum to the operations coordinating he insisted that the struggle against communistic dictatorship should be global. As he famously observed:

> You have the broader considerations that might follow what you would call the falling domino principle . . . . So you could have a beginning of a disintegration that would have the most profound influences. [34]

However, American support for Indochina was compromised. US policy remained committed to independence for Vietnam, Cambodia and Laos. Eisenhower told the French government that they could not get the full backing of America unless they unequivocally pledged independence to all the countries of Indochina. He also had doubts about the weak French leadership. 'The only hope, 'he complained, 'is to produce a new and inspirational leader' and with a sharp-elbowed dig at de Gaulle, '. . . I do not mean one that is 6 feet 5 and who considers himself to be, by some miraculous biological and transmigrative process, the offspring of Clemenceau and Jeanne D'Arc.' [35]

Although the chairman of the Joint Chief of Staff urged the dropping of a tactical nuclear weapon on Giáp's forces at Diên Biên Phu, Eisenhower was unable to get either Congressional or allied support for even conventional bomber strikes. As for using nuclear weapons, Eisenhower told a gung-ho National Security Council, 'You boys must be crazy. We can't use those awful things against the Asians for the second time in less than ten years.' [36]

Although the Americans continued to support France to the extent of underwriting 80 per cent of their expenditure by the end of the war, there was no reprieve for Navarre's army. In spite of a delay caused by mutiny in Giáp's army as a result of the appalling casualties suffered in suicidal attacks on the remaining French fortresses, Elaine's defences were breached by the Việt Minh 308th Division on 7 May. General de Castries surrendered in his bunker. Nine thousand surviving

French troops, out of an original force of 15,000, surrendered to an enemy force that numbered over 50,000.

During their four months of captivity, half of the French prisoners would die or disappear; malaria, amoebic dysentery, beri beri and leptospirosis took their deadly toll on the already enfeebled troops. The remainder suffered torture and ideological brainwashing. In some cases it worked. Some Diên Biên Phu veterans, including officers, ended up being recruited by the Algerian National Liberation Army.

In Paris, the news was treated with shocked despair. Radio programmes were cancelled and replaced by sombre music such as Berlioz's *Requiem*. In one of the post-war's most decisive battles, French pretensions to an empire in the East were extinguished. The eight-year war had cost 92,797 French lives, in addition to 76,369 wounded and 48,673 evacuated sick. By comparison, *Việt Minh* and civilian lives lost have been estimated as high as one million.

While Navarre's army was fighting for survival at Diên Biên Phu on 9 March, Laniel indicated that France would negotiate independence for Vietnam. The Geneva Conference that started on 26 April 1954, debated Korea, Cambodia and Laos, but it was Vietnam that would provide the negotiating drama. Negotiating points including the truce lines and details of the enforcement commission appeared intractable for months, even after the French surrender at Diên Biên Phu. However on the 4 June, Prime Minister Laniel signed accords with Bảo Đại providing full independence for South Vietnam, and the right to 'free association' with France. However, the tempo of negotiation changed with the fall of Joseph Laniel's cabinet on 12 June. The new French Prime Minister Pierre Mendès-France pledged a rapid ceasefire or his resignation and, after a meeting with China's Foreign Minister Zhou Enlai on 23 June, the outline of a settlement was agreed. With peace now being pushed by its neighbour and major backer, the North Vietnamese government agreed to an armistice that divided the country at the 17th parallel.

Parties to the agreement included Britain, Russia and China, with only the USA refusing to sign the accord. Eisenhower and his Secretary of State, John Foster Dulles, were determined to meet the threat of communism, which they now saw sweeping Asia, and sought an active military alliance. On 7 April 1954, Eisenhower warned, 'You have a row of dominoes set up, and you knocked over the first one, and what would happen to the last one was the certainty that it would go over very quickly.'[37]

However, at Geneva, the fiercely anti-communist Dulles was completely out-manoeuvred by the Chinese and Indian delegations; the latter's foreign minister, Krishna Menon, lobbied fiercely against American policy. Dulles refused even to shake Zhou Enlai's hand, having announced before the conference that the only way that they might meet would be if their cars collided. Without allies, Eisenhower refused to contemplate unilateral action.

Whatever the agreement reached at Geneva, Hồ Chí Minh immediately made clear that the accord was just a temporary standstill. He pledged that

> We must devote all possible efforts during the peace to obtain the unification, independence and democratization of the entire nation. . . . The struggle will be long and difficult; all the peoples and soldiers of the North and South must unite to conquer victory.[38]

Although the accord provided for elections in two years, neither side realistically expected them to take place; the State of Vietnam (the South) had agreed to elections on condition that the country was not partitioned and that the elections were supervised by the United Nations. As part of the partition agreement, free movement of people between the North and South was allowed until 25 July.

Somewhat undermining the claims made by Hồ's apologists in the West, some 861,000 people fled from communist North Vietnam. Only 5,000 made the reverse journey. A greater number would have left the North without the use of summary arrests and show trials. Ninety-five thousand petitions of complaint were made to an International Control and Supervision Committee (ICC), made up of Poland and Canada with supposedly 'neutral' India acting as chairman. Predictably, not a single petition is known to have been resolved.

For both sides, the Geneva Conference was a holding agreement. Hồ Chí Minh and the Vietnamese leadership had expelled the French from Indochina and established a viable independent state in the North. They could now afford a breathing space while building resources for conquest of the South, a foothold in which was already held by *Việt Minh*-controlled villages.

For America, the loss of China and the fierce war fought against North Korea and China for control of the Korean peninsula had woken them to the threat global communism posed to their Asian hegemony. Immediately after Geneva, with the active support of Winston Churchill, Eisenhower sought a protective alliance to thwart further communist advances. The Manila Pact between America, Britain, France, Australia, New Zealand, Pakistan, the Philippines and Thailand created the South East Asia Treaty Organisation (SEATO), Asia's equivalent of NATO. While it was clear that America would have to provide the military backbone for such an organisation, Eisenhower was determined that in international affairs America should not be seen as a lone wolf. Eisenhower was fond of saying that 'without allies or associates the leader is just an adventurer like Genghis Khan'.[39]

Although America's tardy support for France certainly contributed to the failure to secure North Vietnam for the free world, it would be unreasonable to lay undue blame at her door. In the post-war period, it was from Eastern Europe, not Asia, that America expected the greatest threat. This, after all, was Stalin's main preoccupation too. With the fall of China to Mao in 1949, followed by the start of the Korean War in 1950, it was not surprising that American priorities would change. (See Map III)

Also, America was put in an impossible position by French reluctance to yield their empire to nationalist demands; a stance America could not support. Britain had yielded to the desire for Indian independence in 1948; so too had America in the Philippines. As George Kennan surmised in a lecture in Milwaukee in 1950:

> I can conceive of no more ghastly and fateful mistake . . . than for us to go into another great country and try to uphold by force of our own blood and treasures a regime which had clearly lost the confidence of its own people.[40]

In his *Mémoires de Guerres* (1954–9), General de Gaulle recalled that

> Indochina was like a great disabled ship that I could help only after a long process of gathering the rescue apparatus. Seeing her moving farther away in the mists, I swore to myself that one day I should bring her back.[41]

De Gaulle's insistence on the right to empire was typical of the French political caste. It was France's post-war reluctance to grant independence to the countries of Indochina that was a major determinant in driving the populace into the arms of the communists.

Unfortunately for France, Hồ Chí Minh's great contribution to the communist revolution in Vietnam was his ability to co-opt nationalist support from a broad political coalition in the drive to expel the French colonists. It was only in 1951 that the *Việt Minh* purged its ranks of non-communists. By then, it was too late to rescue the North from communism. As the mass exodus of people to the South after Geneva clearly demonstrated, it was not the experience of communism that was attractive to the Vietnamese people. Indeed, it is quite plausible that had France demonstrated a post-war inclination towards Vietnamese independence, as Britain had done in Malaysia, that communism could similarly have been beaten off. The tragedy for Vietnam was that by the time Laniel, and then Mendès-France, conceded independence for Indochina, a strong totalitarian state with a powerful army supported by both the Soviets and China had been established in the North.

11

General Phibun: National Socialist Dictator

Thailand: 1945—58

On the night of the great Thai festival of *Loy Krathong*, in November 1938, General Phibun (Luang **Phibun**songkhram), Thailand's prime minister, was changing for dinner. A bullet ripped through his arm. The would-be assassin, Phibun's trusted valet Aree, evidently a poor shot, had been hiding under his master's bed. Phibun immediately turned and fled his bedroom wearing just his underpants, and was pursued by his pistol-toting valet. Happily for the Thai prime minister, the pursuit around his house ended without fatal consequences.

A month later, an attempt to assassinate Phibun by poisoning the food at a dinner party in his house led to 38 guests being rushed to hospital to have their stomachs pumped. Earlier in his career, Phibun, when he was minister of defence, had survived being shot in the neck at a soccer match. Curiously, Phibun's poor choice of servants did little to damage his political credibility. Apart from creating a scarcity of willing dinner guests at his house, Phibun was little inconvenienced; his barely credible ability to survive assassination merely added mystique to his rise to power.

General Phibun (original name Plaek Khittasangkha), the son of a well-off fruit farmer, was born near Bangkok on 14 July 1897. He entered the Thai Military Academy at the age of 12, and later joined the Thai Artillery, historically the military branch that has often attracted the brightest of soldiers because of the need to master mathematics (viz. Napoleon). He received further military training for three years in France where, imbued by the revolutionary ideological fervour of the Parisian intellectual elite, he became an active supporter of the movement to remove the Thai monarchy.

This did not impede his military progress. Phibun returned to Bangkok in 1927 and was promoted to the rank of major and served on the Army General Staff. In recognition of his new rank, he changed his name to Luang **Phibun**songkhram. Phibun's wife noted that he had a 'scholarly disposition'[1]; he was apparently an able writer and teacher. Thawat observed that Phibun 'was extremely handsome and had a very polite and modest manner that won men . . .'.[2]

Phibun's career is unique in the history of post-war Asia, in that he managed to be the country's dominant leader, albeit with a short hiatus, both before and after the Second World War. In the 'constitutional' period from June 1932 to September 1957, there were 11 prime ministers; yet Phibun occupied this position for 15 years out of 25. This owed less to his own character and abilities than to the peculiarities of the history of Siam, as the country was called, until Phibun changed its name to Thailand in 1939.

By skillfully playing off the European powers, the Kings of Siam had contrived to remain an independent state during the nineteenth-century Asian land grab. Therefore, unlike its neighbours, Siam did not go through a pre-war struggle for independence; neither did it suffer a Japanese government during the war nor afterwards a struggle for independence from the Asian empires of Great Britain, France, Holland, Portugal or America.

Nevertheless, Siam was not impervious to the global revolutionary stirrings that had their origins in neighbouring China, where Sun Yat Sen overthrew the Emperor in 1912. Unlike China, however, Siam had the peculiar advantage of having had a dynamic monarch who had transformed his country. King Chulalongkorn the Great, who had come to the throne in 1868, abolished slavery and created an infrastructure of railways, canals and roads. The country also became renowned in Asia for the high standard of its medical facilities. By 1910, when Chulalongkorn died, Siam had a well-developed centralised administration making it one of Asia's more advanced societies.

However, in the 1920s, Paris, the ever present cauldron of political utopianism, played host to Asia's students, including those from Thailand. Not surprisingly, French utopian philosophies percolated back to Thailand. By 1932, a cabal of middle-ranking officers, including Colonel Phraya **Song**suradct, who held an influential post at the Military Academy in Bangkok from where he disseminated his ideas, had come to the conclusion that unfettered monarchic rule should end. An alliance was also formed with modernisers within the Siamese Civil Service. Civil servants and soldiers formed the backbone of the 20 or more secret associations known as *Kokan Kanpokkrong* (promoters of political change). In June 1932, 114 so-called 'promoters' overthrew the government. Reflecting the gentle manners of Siam, King Prajadhipok was informed of the coup on the eighth hole of the Hua Hin golf course.

Faced with an ultimatum that he must accede to the demand for a constitutional monarchy, Prajadhipok happily obliged. Typically for Thailand, the coup was bloodless. It was reported that 'Bangkok awaked this morning to find that the greatest political sensation in its 150 years of existence had taken place quietly and without forewarning in the early hours before dawn . . . Except for the scattering crowds in the neighbourhood of the Throne Hall and the Grand Palace, there was not the slightest sign of excitement . . . Police were on duty as usual. Courts functioned. Mail collections and deliveries were as usual.'[3]

He was a reluctant monarch but a man acutely aware of the need to press forward with constitutional reform. As early as 1910, King Chulalongkorn had declared that '. . . I will have my son, Vachiravudh, give the Thai people a present upon his ascending the throne. That is, I will have him grant a parliament and a constitution.'[4] (It was Chulalongkorn's father, King Rama IV, who had famously hired Anna T. Leonowens to teach him English, thereby providing the story line for the Rodgers and Hammerstein musical, The King and I (1951)). The irony is that Prajadhipok, Chulalongkorn's grandson, was himself developing plans to implement a democratic system of government with the monarchy maintained at its apex. The current monarch, King Bhumibol, would later say of his uncle that 'He would have set up a real democracy in a few years instead of the [Promoter's] government that was not well devised. . . .'[5] Unsurprisingly, the coup was not resisted.

A provisional constitution was validated by Prajadhipok on 27 June 1932, and consisted of 70 members appointed to an assembly by the 114 promoters; from this assembly was taken a smaller People's Committee, which acted in the capacity of the executive arm of government. It was planned that this assembly would at a later stage move to being half appointed and half indirectly elected. Finally, it was planned that a fully elected government would come into being when 50 per cent of the Thai population had received primary education. It was expected that this would take ten years. On this basis, the constitution was promulgated on a permanent basis on 10 December 1932.

Thailand's constitutional experiment lasted barely six months. The intrinsic problem with the constitution was that the promoter group was fatally divided between the conservative elements within the army, and a civilian group led by Pridi Phanomyong, who was mandated to develop a plan for Thailand's economic development. Pridi had been a child prodigy; he entered law school at 17 and was a barrister by 19. It was said that 'people liked Pridi because they respected his noble principles'.[6]

Like many precocious intellectuals however, Pridi's youthful views veered towards ultra-rational systems. Pridi had studied in Paris and had adopted the by now conventional Utopian philosophies of the liberal elite. Land and labour were to be nationalised in a centrally-driven plan to industrialise the economy. Also the Siamese aristocracy was to be incorporated into the bureaucracy.

Uproar followed. King Prajadhipok responded by saying:

> I do not know whether Stalin copied Luang Pradit [Pridi] or whether Luang Pradit copied Stalin. . . . This is the same programme that has been used in Russia. If our government adopted it, we would be assisting the Third International to achieve the aim of world communism. . . . Siam would become the second Communist state after Russia.[7]

Denunciations from the King and from within the army provided the spur to force Pridi into exile. More importantly, the National Assembly passed draconian anti-communist laws, which determined Thailand's political orientation for a generation. Simply writing about communist ideology could now bring a ten-year jail sentence.

On 20 June 1933, young army officers forced the removal of Praha Mano and the installation of Phraya **Phahon**phonphayuhasena as prime minister, along with seven 'promoters' in the cabinet. Siam was further rocked by a rebellion in the north by the monarchists led by Prince Boworadet, who was the grandson of King Chulalongkorn. A short but closely fought war ended with the flight of Boworadet, and brought the elevation of the military hero of the hour, Lt. Colonel Phibun, to national prominence; it was enough to launch his meteoric political career.

Meanwhile, a frightened King Prajadhipok took himself off to England for medical treatment, from where he demanded the right to nominate to the National Assembly and to give pardons. Failing to receive a satisfactory response, on 2 March 1935 Prajadhipok abdicated, and in a frank and pointed rebuke to the legitimate credentials of the military oligarchs told them:

> I am willing to surrender the powers I formerly exercised to the people as a whole, but I am not willing to turn them over to any individual or any group to use in an autocratic manner without heeding the voice of the people.[8]

In the absence of a Royal lead, the National Assembly chose the route of least trouble by appointing the ten-year-old Prince Ananda Mahidol as their new monarch. The reality of Siamese politics was now set for the next 70 years; a military oligarchy riven by factions whose power struggles were solved by innumerable but usually bloodless coups d'état. The election of representatives by popular mandate to the National Assembly remained a democratic fig-leaf for the self-serving power plays of the military elite.

With the effective advancement of the military to the political centre of power, Phibun, whose reward for military success was the post of minister of defence, now found himself well placed to advance his political career. The opportunity arose after the electoral rout of the veteran 'promoter' representatives in the November 1937 elections. Twenty-six per cent of the population could now vote for half of the 182 National Assembly representatives. On the back of disillusionment with a government which had been exposed as selling crown properties to favoured officials at knock-down prices, opposition candidates dominated the electoral list. The popular Phibun was now promoted to prime minister.

During the 1930s, Phibun increasing looked to Europe's new political leaders, Hitler and Mussolini, for his role models. Both the Munich crisis and the Japanese capture of Canton provided examples of what could be achieved by force of arms. In a society as dominated by the military as Siam, with an economy still largely feudal and without a strong commercial class except for the despised Chinese, it was perhaps natural that modernisation should ape Europe's national socialist parties. Phibun controlled the use of newspapers and the recently developed media of radio to promote the new nationalism, and with it a personality cult which saw his portrait widely displayed on billboards.

Phibun also sought to change Siam's social conventions and traditional dress, insisting on the wearing of trousers. Kukrit Pramoj, a minor member of the Royal family, complained that

> The Field Marshal [Phibun] started a cultural revolution long before Mao ever thought of one. People in Phibun's era were ordered to wear hats and shoes. . . . Betel chewing, ruled uncultural at that time, became a night time vice. But to crown it all every man was required to kiss his wife before departing to work in the morning.[9]

The name of Siam was dropped in 1939 and replaced by Thailand. This formed part of Phibun's attempt to forge a new 'modern' nationalism. A call to race hatred was another strand of this strategy. Relations between the Thai and Chinese communities descended to their lowest levels when it was implied by Phibun's ally, Lung Wichit, that Thais should treat the Chinese in the manner in which Germany was treating the Jews.

Thus, the successful Chinese business community was increasingly targeted in order to whip up popular support for Thailand's 'modern' national socialist state. Chinese Thais were forced to pay registration fees, and the teaching of the Chinese language was limited to just two hours a week. Young Thais were corralled into nationalist 'youth' organisations. Also, like Germany and Italy in the 1930s, the nationalists followed an intrinsically socialist economic policy. Business taxes were hiked; trade in salt, tobacco, pork and petroleum was effectively nationalised.

Internationally Phibun also realigned Thailand's foreign policy against the Western imperialists. In practice however, his foreign policies were much more directed by pragmatism than ideology. Colonel Net Khemayothin reported Phibun as saying that whichever side one thinks is going to lose the war 'that side is our enemy'.[10] When Phibun promised guaranteed supplies of rubber and tin to Japan, the USA held up the supply of petroleum to Thailand. The American government also halted the supply of military aircraft to the Thai Air force. Germany's invasion of France, and its subsequent capitulation to Germany, also provided Phibun with the opportunity to take revenge on Siamese loss of control of Laos and Cambodia to the French in 1893. Laos and Western Cambodia were invaded by land, although the military victory was somewhat tarnished by the sinking of several Thai boats in the Gulf of Siam, thus providing France with its only naval victory of the twentieth century.

About the conflict, a French officer observed:

> . . . it was soon over. . . but no one seemed to know what it was all about. . . . the Japanese, who had been pulling strings since the start of the incident, had found the moment favourable to appear in the light of mediators, and were seizing the opportunity to establish themselves in strength in Cochin-China.[11]

For Thailand the main purpose of the war was to puff Phibun's own military credentials and burnish his reputation as a 'strong man' in the mode of the European
dictators. A victory monument was built in Bangkok, and Phibun promoted himself to Field Marshal. A peace was subsequently brokered by the Japanese who, in
the vacuum left by the increasingly beleaguered European empires, were rapidly
expanding their military and diplomatic influence in Asia.

In spite of his international political realignments, Phibun remained fearful that
Japan would add Thailand to its conquests. In anticipation, the National Assembly
resolution on 28 August called for mass popular resistance. The critical moment
arrived on 7 December 1941, when Ambassador Tsubokami arrived at Phibun's
residence to demand rights of passage to Japanese troops being deployed for the
conquest of British-controlled Malaysia. To the fury of the Japanese Ambassador,
Phibun was out of town on a tour of the newly conquered Cambodian provinces.
The absence may well have been planned as a delaying tactic by Phibun. Disre-
garding the Thai foreign minister's protests, Japanese forces invaded the border
at Battambang. In addition, there were seven amphibious landings, and paratroops
took Don Muang airfield outside Bangkok.

Having seen that resistance was pointless, Phibun, on his return to Bangkok,
immediately agreed to Japanese demands. To ingratiate himself with his unwanted
guests, Phibun concluded a military alliance with Japan on 12 December, and in
a flourish of obsequiousness, on 25 January 1942, he declared war on America
and Great Britain. However, the nature of the relationship was evident from the
requirement for Thailand to pay ¥13 million per month to cover Japanese local
military expenditures.

Nevertheless, for Thailand there followed a brief 'golden' period as Phibun
was able to bask in his leadership of Asia's only independent nation, and he further
added to his stature by invading Burma. New territories were also added through
a treaty with Japan, by which Phibun reclaimed control of the four provinces of
Malaysia (Kelantan, Trengganu, Perlis and Kedah), which King Chulalongkorn had
ceded to Britain in 1909.

Any euphoria created by these events was soon dispelled. Rampant inflation
was exacerbated by disruption to trade with the West and also by the scale of losses
incurred by Japan's merchant fleet. Thailand may have had essential raw materials,
but Japan was decreasingly able to transport them. Phibun's decline mirrored that
of the Japanese war effort. When Tojo was forced to resign on 18 July 1944, Phibun
followed a week later.

By this time, the Thai resistance movement was in full flow. The Thai establishment was intrinsically anglophile. In 1941, former King Prajadhipok had written
that

> Siam does not want to be under the direction of any nation.... It has been the tra-
> ditional policy of all the kings of Siam to be friendly with Great Britain...to me it
> would seem that Siam would be behaving almost suicidally if she were to make herself
> Britain's enemy.[12]

However, the Thai Royal family had yet to wake to the reality that it would be America, rather than England, which would be the leading promoter of Anglo-Saxon values in post-war Asia.

In Washington, the Thai Ambassador Seni Pramoj had never accepted the legality of Thailand's alliance with Japan, and immediately launched a Free Thai movement, which took active form in Thailand with the American Office of Strategic Services (OSS). In Thailand, a covert pro-allied group within government was led by Pridi who, returned from exile, had by now perversely, given his former utopian anti-monarchic beliefs, become the king's regent; he immediately started to organise resistance to the Japanese.

The OSS organised parachute drops into the Thai hill territories occupied by the resistance. In a foretaste of the cultural clumsiness that would characterise much of America's post-war relationship with Asia, the Thais were shocked by the casual manners of the parachuted US officers. One of them told a formal Thai reception committee that 'American officers hate Japs, love Thai people. Otherwise no good. All the time drink whisky, shoot crap, fornicate and masturbate.'[13]

Within Thailand, the resistance movement grew rapidly and included much of the government leadership including Pridi, who headed the Regency Council. As General Slim began to push back the Japanese armies in Burma, there was increasing concern at the revenge that might be exacted against Thailand in an allied invasion. Even Phibun had considered when it might be safe to ditch the Japanese alliance. More importantly, Pridi offered to turn a 50,000 strong guerrilla force against the Japanese.

With the Japanese surrender on 15 August, the National Assembly grovelled before the new power in Asia by announcing that Thailand's pre-war ambassador to Washington and perceived friend of America, Seni Pramoj, would be invited to head the new post-war government. Pramoj had used his time in Washington wisely. When the British issued a list of demands for restitution from Thailand, including the gift of 1.5 million tons of rice, the State Department mobilised presidential support to quash a British government that had been infuriated by the atrocious treatment of British prisoners used as slave labour on the Siam–Burma railway. Pridi emerged as a key arbiter; he cleverly managed an almost seamless switch of sides after the war, when he ingratiated himself with his fellow socialist Lord Mountbatten, who commanded the occupying Allied troops.

Thailand did not get to keep its wartime gains. The captured provinces of Indochina voted in the Thai elections of 1946, but were given back the following year. In a classic piece of Machiavellian diplomacy, France, whose behaviour during the war had been no less craven than that of Thailand, threatened to veto Thailand's admission to the United Nations unless they gave back their Cambodian and Laotian territories. Thailand yielded.

After elections in January 1946, the two parties that supported Pridi won a majority of seats, but perversely elected Khuang Aphaiwond as prime minister. However, within months he was forced to resign in favour of Pridi who now organised a new constitution based on America's bicameral model. In April 1946, Thailand seemed to have buried its duplicitous wartime past when the prosecution of Phibun and his colleagues was halted and declared to be unconstitutional. With the end of war, the support of the USA, and the return of King Ananda Mahidol from Europe in December 1945, the path to constitutional stability now seemed clear.

However, on 9 June, King Ananda Mahidol was found dead from a wound to the head from a Colt 45 Automatic. Ananda was apparently a 'reluctant monarch who found his greatest pleasure in playing the saxophone and driving his American jeep about the Palace'.[14] Although a government commission including British and American doctors found that Ananda had been murdered and swiftly tried three accused officials who were eventually executed in 1954, suspicions remained that the anti-monarchist Pridi was responsible.

Perhaps in consequence of the king's murder, the parties supporting Pridi fared badly in the August elections held for the new bicameral constitution. In addition, the army, remembering Pridi's hard left stance of the early 1930s, suspected him of communist sympathies. In Bangkok, rumours swirled around the capital that agents had been sent to Switzerland to murder Ananda's successor, King Bhumibol.

After little more than a year in power, on 8 November 1947, a military-backed 'Coup Group' seized power. Pridi went into hiding before being spirited out of Thailand with British and American help aboard a Shell oil tanker. Khuang was again installed in power, and oversaw a purge of Pridi's followers. Khuang won only a small majority in the January 1948 elections, and perhaps foolishly began to draft a constitution that would have led to the marginalisation of the military. This was unacceptable to the army. In spite of the poor showing of Phibun's party in the 1948 elections, he was brought back to power on 8 April 1948.

The first major challenge to Phibun's return to power came from within the army. In October 1948, a military plot led by Major General Net Khemayothin was thwarted. Phao Sriyanon, a close aid to Phibun, used the rebellion to rid himself of a rival, Police Colonel Banchongsak; he was shot while allegedly resisting arrest.

A more credible coup attempt followed in February 1949. The navy attempted to restore Pridi to power and, unusually for a Thai coup, heavy fighting followed in Bangkok. After three days, forces loyal to Phibun restored order and instituted a harsh crackdown of the rebels, who were tortured and executed. After one of the bloodiest coup attempts in Thai history, Pridi fled to China before moving to Paris in 1970. In 1979, he admitted the causes of his political failures:

> All my knowledge was book knowledge. I did not take into account human elements as much as I should have. In 1932 I was 32 years of age.... When I had power, I had no experience, and when I had experience, I had no power....'[15]

Phibun immediately returned to the anti-Chinese policies which had characterised his pre-war rule. Again non-Chinese businesses were favoured. The new twist however was that Phibun's policies were driven less by the Chinese commercial threat than the emerging communist threat in China. Phibun at last found favour with Britain by his enthusiastic support for the anti-communist operations on the Malay border. Phibun also rounded up Pridi's supporters who were supposedly communist sympathisers. In the north, Thong-in Phuripat and others were arrested and shot for attempting to create a communist state linked to Indochina.

In March 1949, yet another constitution was introduced, which allowed for Royal nominations to a Senate that would now have the power to delay legislation. The army was apparently to be stripped of influence. However, in the June 1949 elections, Phibun won a convincing majority in the House of Representatives. Control was further enhanced by the buying over of opposition representatives.

With King Bhumibol now on his way back to Bangkok by boat via Singapore, Phibun announced yet another turn in Thailand's constitutional history. The 1932 constitution was to be restored because of 'the present worldwide situation and because of communist aggression and widespread corruption. . . '.[16] With Phibun and his deputies mainly responsible for the large-scale graft within the Thai government, this was a pathetic excuse to consolidate power and defenestrate the returning monarch. The legislature now consisted of 123 appointed representatives of mainly military background; in addition, a further 123 elected members joined after elections held in February 1952. After 20 years of experimentation after the overthrow of monarchic rule in 1932, the constitution had come full circle.

However, the real struggles for power were taking place within the armed forces. On 29 June 1951, Phibun went to inspect the dredger *Manhattan*, which had been presented to the Thai government as a gift from America; he was apprehended by navy officers and taken aboard the Thai fleet's sole cruiser, *Sri Ayudhya*, a 2,200-ton ship built by the Japanese in 1936. Air Chief Marshal Fuen Ronnaphakat, probably with the connivance of General Sarit, and head of police Phao Sriyanon, showed scant regard for the safety of their leader and ordered the air force to bomb the *Sri Ayudhya*, possibly with the hope of killing him. If that was their intention, they almost succeeded.

Even by Phibun's legendary standards, his narrow escape from both his captors and his supposed friends in the air force was extraordinary. While answering a call of nature in his bathroom, a shell scored a direct hit on the cabin in which he was being held. Miraculously it did not explode until it had penetrated further decks below. From the wreck of his cabin, Phibun was able to make his escape, threw himself overboard from the sinking *Sri Ayudhya*, and swam ashore.

Now followed a period of uneasy stability under Phibun, to whom the main threat was his own deputies. On the international front, the support of the USA became an increasingly important prop to Thailand's military rule. The country was now pivotal in the battle against communism in South East Asia. Predictably, Phibun kowtowed to America by becoming the first Asian ruler to send troops to help the United Nations forces in the Korean War.

As a reward, between 1951 and 1957, the USA gave Thailand some US$ 149 million in military aid and US$ 222 million in economic aid, which helped finance the expansion of Bangkok's port facilities as well as rail and road infrastructure. These improvements were essential, as Thai raw material exports were increasingly needed as the American army engaged first North Korea, and then China on the Korean peninsula. Money was also invested in the training of a 43,000 strong police force, which developed as a powerful paramilitary force and guarantor of internal security, and indeed political suppression. Nevertheless, the combined impact of political stability and international events helped produce healthy economic growth, which averaged almost 5 per cent per annum in the eight years to 1958.

Much of the economic growth was generated by drug trafficking and other illicit activity. While Phibun was primarily concerned with the exercise of power, his two key deputies, General Sarit and Chief of Police, Phao, who effectively formed a triumvirate with him, sought wealth through illicit commercial activities. Through use of patronage and political influence, Phao created a commercial empire with the *Soi Rajakru* clan, including insurance, gold trading, fishing, sugar and timber. Phao also controlled gambling and prostitution, which grew rapidly as Bangkok enjoyed explosive growth in the 1950s. Most importantly, Phao used his control of the police to exploit the growing international market for drugs. By 1958, it was estimated that Phao controlled half of the world supply of narcotics. According to C.L. Sulzberger of *The New York Times*, Phao was a 'superlative crook'.[17]

General Sarit, who would be appointed field marshal at the beginning of 1956, was the son of an army officer. His mother was Laotian. Having entered Military College at the age of 11, Sarit progressed to being made military commander of Lampang Province. After the war, he was largely responsible for the modernisation of the army and its reorganisation along American lines, and in 1954 he succeeded Phao's father-in-law, Field Marshal Phin, as commander-in-chief of the army. Like Phao, Sarit built up a large drug business using his troops to protect the vast opium caravans that travelled down the mountainous jungle tracks from the Shan states and other drug-producing areas within the so-called 'Golden Triangle'.

The semi-processed opium was then taken to refineries in Bangkok, from where it was shipped around the world. Sarit later switched to a business model in which production, manufacture and distribution were sub-contracted to Chinese businessmen in return for protection fees. Such was the wealth generated by this business, largely un-captured by the official economic statistics, that it was estimated that drugs financed over half of new construction in Bangkok. In addition to these activities, Sarit also became a controlling influence behind Thai Farmers Bank, one of the country's largest financial institutions.

In a deal to allow CIA access to the borderlands of Shan, Laos, Vietnam and Cambodia, Sea Supply (the CIA-established *Overseas Southeast Asia Supply* Company) founded a police parachute training school for the Thai police. Increasingly the police came to be armed by the CIA to the level of a paramilitary force, and were often better equipped than the army. Indeed on occasions, the police fought military engagements with General Sarit's armed forces for control of the drugs industry. In Lampang in 1950, the police captured an army opium convoy after a fire fight. A full military engagement was only prevented by the personal intervention of Sarit and Phao who jointly took charge of the disputed opium.

The CIA, probably not unwittingly, became one of the main contributors to the development of Thailand's drug industry. Understandably, their main concern in the 1950s was the growing threat posed by communism in China. Reflecting this shift of priorities, William 'Wild Bill' Donovan, a former General and founder of the OSS, was appointed Ambassador to Thailand in 1951.

Donovan was a close friend of Madame Chiang Kai Shek's brother, T.V. Soong, and was a leading member of America's 'China lobby' and fierce opponent of communism. For Donovan, Thailand was a key battleground:

> To Red China it is a tempting prize, for China needs rice, and Thailand's rice fields are among the most fertile in Asia. Moreover the conquest of Thailand, whether by invasion or subversion, would so expose neutralist Burma as to make its capitulation to communism almost inevitable. It would enable the communists to give direct support to their guerrilla forces in British Malaya. If Thailand should fall, in short, South East Asia might be lost. . . .[18]

Thailand, standing at the heart of South Asia, was seen as strategically critical to the battle against communism. Donovan's predecessor also observed that 'If Thailand's freedom and independence can be preserved, the heart and much of the body of South East Asia will have been saved.[19]

For Eisenhower's Secretary of State, John Foster Dulles, faced by what he considered to be the disaster of the Geneva Conference giving legitimacy to North Vietnam, the fight for Thailand and Indochina was now critical. The CIA-trained Thai Police Aerial Reconnaissance Unit was parachuted into remote areas to collect intelligence and to conduct sabotage operations. The border police were also armed to provide security against communist insurgents.

In effect, Thailand became the new line of defence in the war against communism. For President Eisenhower, the cold war had not been prosecuted with sufficient vigour; Truman, in his view, has been too 'soft on communism'.[20] John Foster Dulles was even more hawkish in his views, and told the Overseas Press Club on 29 March 1954 that the threat to South East Asia 'should not be passively accepted but should be met by action.'[21] The existence of an active ally like Thailand was far more important in Eisenhower's greater scheme than the wretchedness of its constitutional or its democratic performance, let alone the Thai military's development of the international drug trade.

The next shift in political direction came in 1955 after Phibun toured the USA and Britain. Phibun, the man who had previously adored Hitler and Mussolini, now underwent a damascene conversion to the benefits of liberal democracy. 'In a democracy', Phibun now declared, 'soldiers should not interfere in politics. . . . I feel we should promote the democracy of this country . . . by elections to Parliament and without having to use military or police force'.[22]

Restrictions on registration of political parties were lifted. Free speech and a liberal press were now allowed in anticipation of the 1957 elections. Phibun's understanding of democracy did not however extend to abandoning bribery and vote rigging. This ensured that his Manangkhasila Party won 85 of the 162 seats available.

The violent popular unrest that followed forced Phibun to declare a state of emergency and Sarit was made responsible for public order. For the ambitious Sarit, public order was the last thing he wanted, and instead, he proceeded to stir public discontent. Further setbacks for Phibun took place in August and September 1957 when severe droughts and the government's inept relief effort added to his unpopularity. The regime was further debilitated when Phao's corrupt involvement in the timber trade came to light. Astutely Sarit and his deputies made dramatic cabinet resignations. Their popularity soared when, backed by the officer elite of the army, they publicly called for the resignation of Phibun and his government.

It was an all or nothing throw of the dice by Sarit to secure power. Phibun had already reserved space for Sarit's incarceration on the fourth floor of the Erawan Hotel. However, when Phibun tried and failed to get legal support for Sarit's arrest, Phibun's long career in Thai politics was over. Huge public rallies indicated that Phibun's store of political credit had run bare. The army orchestrated a bloodless and popular coup; both Phibun and Phao fled Thailand. Phao went to Switzerland and lived in luxury from his ill-gotten gains but, bored by his life in exile, drank himself to death in 1961. Phibun, in keeping with his exotic past, managed to escape his captors by boat and then by car to Cambodia. It was a suitable end to a career that was as corrupt as it was ineffectual. Eventually, he died of a heart attack in Japan in 1964.

12

From Independence to Dependency

Philippines: 1945–60

By the 1930s the Philippines had achieved independence in all but name. While the Republican President Hoover, who was elected to office in 1928, had wanted, with the urging of his Secretary of State Stimson and Army Chief of Staff Douglas MacArthur, to increase American presence in the Philippines in order to deter Japanese expansionism, the onset of the Great Depression brought new priorities to the fore. By 1932 a wearied electorate threw Hoover out of office after one term and voted in Franklin D. Roosevelt, an avowed isolationist.

The new Democrat President, Franklin D. Roosevelt, with his attention focused on domestic economic issues, viewed America's Asian colony as a drain on resources rather than a geopolitical asset. The move towards independence was thus encouraged. Manuel Quezón, the leader of the Nationalist Party for over a decade, negotiated trade issues and the return of US property, resulting in the 1934 Tydings–McDuffie Act. The act allowed for a full transfer of independence to the Philippines after a ten-year period of Commonwealth. In anticipation of this event, the Philippine legislature agreed in 1936 to develop a national language. Quezón himself was elected to the presidency of the Philippines in 1936. 'I prefer a country run like hell by Filipinos to a country run like heaven by Americans', he declared, 'because however bad the Filipino government might be, we can always change it.'[1]

By 1938 however, Quezón became fearful that the Philippines, lying as it did in the path of Japanese expansion, would be swallowed by Japan's 'Asia Co-Prosperity Sphere'. After a visit to Japan to seek an alliance was rebuffed, Quezón sought an early accession to independence, so as to disassociate the Philippines from the USA. This too was denied by President Roosevelt, who was now coming to question the isolationist platform on which he had come to office. Ultimately, if Japan was to go to war with the USA, it was fanciful of Quezón to believe that the Philippines, so long a dependency of America, could have stayed neutral.

The conquest of the Philippines matched the unpreparedness of the American fleet at Pearl Harbor. General MacArthur, governor general of the Philippines, who was woken up to the news of Pearl Harbor while staying at the presidential suite of the luxurious Manila Hotel, failed to put his forces on a war footing even though he was warned of a likely attack. Through MacArthur's negligence, American forces were again caught cold by the Japanese air onslaught from their bases in Formosa.

Most of the US Air Force in the Philippines, which had thirty-six P-40s and seventeen B-17s, was destroyed as its planes stood neatly aligned on their runways. Although MacArthur used his excellent press contacts to proclaim victories against the Japanese, the truth of the situation was soon revealed when 43,000 Japanese landed in Lingayen Gulf in North West Luzon. Quezón and his Vice President Osmena fled to America and set up a government in exile.

Meanwhile, MacArthur evacuated Manila and, with 20,000 American troops, embedded his forces in strong defensive positions at Bataan and Corregidor. However, poor tactical deployment and a collapse in morale in the face of a much more adept and powerful enemy led to the largest ever surrender by an American force on 9 April 1942. In the ensuing 'Bataan Death March' to Japanese prison camps, some 10,000 men died. An additional 2,000 American and 25,000 Filipino troops died of hunger and disease in the following three months. Meanwhile, MacArthur had flown out of the Philippines; in a speech especially crafted by the propagandist Carlos Romulo, MacArthur famously proclaimed 'I shall return.'[2]

Japan established a puppet regime under the leadership of José Laurel, who was made president. Collaborators were plentiful. General Wachi called on the population to recognise that 'regardless of whether you like it or not, you are Filipinos and belong to the Oriental Race. No matter how hard you try, you cannot become white people'.[3] In a rallying call to pan-Asian nationalism, even the distinguished nationalist Aguinaldo was persuaded to support the new Philippines government. Elite Filipino families, with whom America had forged such a close nexus, also defected en masse to save their lives and their businesses. The Manila Falange, which had a membership of some 10,000 citizens, included the Sorianos, the Ayalas, the Zobels and the Elizaldes.

Domestic opposition to the Japanese was limited to the *Hukbong Bayan Laban* (commonly known as the Huks). The Huks were an assembly of former radical agrarian revolutionary and nationalist groups that had existed in pre-war incarnation as the *Katipunan, Colorum* and *Sakdalista* movements. Although largely an agrarian movement, the Huks were led by urban intellectuals who were mainly members of the Socialist Party and the PKP (the Philippine Communist Party); this was a classic Soviet-affiliated group, though it had received little financial or political support from the Comintern. When the Huks met Major Claude Thorpe, who was the American soldier in charge of anti-Japanese guerrilla activity on the Philippines, he refused to provide them with any assistance; his rebuttal of the Huks was undoubtedly consistent with the virulent anti-communist sentiments of MacArthur.

Ignoring the US slight, the Huks nevertheless continued to fight the American cause in the hope of participating in the post-war political settlement. So successful were the Huks' guerrilla campaigns that by 1945 they controlled large segments of the Philippines with some 70,000 irregular troops. Meanwhile the Filipino leadership railed at the American conduct of the war. Quezón, conveniently forgetting his pre-war attempts to woo Japan, complained to Mountbatten's chief of staff that 'America writhes in anguish at the fate of a distant cousin, Europe, while a daughter, the Philippines, is being raped in the back room.'[4]

However, MacArthur had his sights set on an early liberation. Ignoring the pleas of strategists to bypass the Philippines, thereby leaving the Japanese army stranded, and to head for Formosa from where aerial bombardments of Japan could be launched, MacArthur chose instead to liberate America's former colony. The Philippines, he claimed, was a strategic location 'unexcelled by that of any in the globe'.[5]

It was perhaps not surprising that America's vainglorious general refused to pass up the opportunity to liberate the country with which he had such close personal relations, not to mention business investments, and from which he had been so humiliatingly ejected. In characteristic fashion, MacArthur waded onto the beach at Leyte and, with the cameras whirring, told the waiting American television audience that 'I have returned. By the grace of Almighty God, our forces stand again on Philippine soil.'[6]

Having landed at Leyte at the end of 1944, MacArthur began the battle for Manila at the start of February. At the cost of 1,000 American and 16,000 Japanese lives, the Philippine capital was recaptured in a two-week battle. It is arguable whether the complete destruction of Manila at the cost of some 100,000 civilian lives was militarily justifiable when the re-taking of Formosa would have represented a lower cost target.

Having retaken Manila, MacArthur moved swiftly to restore American hegemony by promoting the political interests of the business and landed elite with whom the USA had ruled the Philippines since its forced acquisition from Spain in 1900. MacArthur himself was fully integrated into that elite, being a friend of leading businessmen such as mine owner Andres Soriano and the influential editor Carlos Romulo. As a director and shareholder in the Manila Hotel and an investor in other commercial concerns in the Philippines, MacArthur also had a vested interest in promoting leaders friendly to business.

MacArthur restored the 1941 legislature, of which eight out of the 14 senators and 19 out of the 67 representatives had worked with the Japanese. As for the government overseas, Quezón had died of tuberculosis in 1944. His successor Osmena, favoured by Secretary of the Interior Harold Ickes, was soon sidelined by MacArthur. On 29 June 1944 Franklin D. Roosevelt had asserted that 'Those who have collaborated with the enemy must be removed from authority and influence over the political and economic life of the country. . . .'[7] It was a sentiment blatantly ignored by MacArthur. His espousal of collaborators was in marked contrast to his later behaviour in Japan (the Emperor excepted).

The US military administration organised the selection of Roxas, who had served in the Japanese wartime puppet government, as the Liberal candidate for the Philippines presidential elections. Roxas was a close personal friend of MacArthur. In spite of earlier promises to 'run to earth every disloyal Filipino',[8] MacArthur freed some 5,000 collaborators. Neither was any action taken by MacArthur to purge the Philippine army of collaborators, although it was estimated that some 80 per cent of officers had worked with the Japanese occupiers. By contrast, General Tomoyuki Yamashita, head of the Japanese army in the Philippines, and other senior commanders were speedily tried and hanged.

By deferring to MacArthur's experience of the Philippines, President Truman allowed his most famous and popular general to determine the future course of political events in America's most important colony. As historian Amy Blitz has pointed out, MacArthur was 'heir to his father's rivalry with Taft decades before' and 'revived the long standing competition between the US military and political colonialist'.[9]

MacArthur went as far as to threaten to send home any civilian high commissioner. For the time being, Ickes, a liberal 'New Deal' Democrat, was stymied in his attempts to regain civilian control of the Philippines. When Ickes's high commissioner appointee Paul McNutt, a former Democrat governor of Indiana, did eventually arrive in Manila in September of 1945, he found that the key post-war decisions had already been made. He was appalled at the easy treatment of collaborators and the return to political power of the *falangista*, who had fallen in line behind Japanese rule. McNutt pressed for delays in granting independence and for a broader spread of war crimes trials. When he doubted whether it was possible to hold fair elections in the Philippines, MacArthur witheringly replied that 'the Filipinos will hold as honest an election as you ever had in the State of Indiana'.[10]

However, McNutt's observations were fully justified. Roxas, in a pattern that was to become familiar in post-war Philippines, effectively bought the election. The fact that he controlled a newspaper empire was also not un-useful. Roxas's Liberal Party won 54 per cent of the vote. Opposition to Roxas was now ruthlessly suppressed, and cabinet ministers of the outgoing Osmena administration, who raised the subject of the new president's collaborationist past, were expelled.

Meanwhile the communist *Huks*, who, after the liberation of Manila, had joined the opposition with the socialists and peasant unions to form the Democratic Alliance, won six seats in the legislature. In a monstrous abrogation of democratic procedure, Roxas charged the Huk representatives and five other opponents with electoral fraud, removed them from the legislature and replaced them with his own supporters, some of whom had been indicted for collaboration. The expulsion of the *Huks* led to a nationwide purge of their representatives. Arrests and murders followed. Those who survived fled to the jungle and formed the *Hukbong Magpagpalaya ng Bayan* (the People's Revolutionary Army).

Roxas pushed through the controversial Bell Trade Act, which the Huks and their supporters had opposed. The act legislated for unrestricted access of Philippine goods to the USA and for the pegging of the peso to the US dollar; by quid pro quo, American corporations were granted parity in gaining rights to exploit mining and forestry in the Philippines. In spite of opposition from sugar- and dairy-producing American states, the Bell Trade Act was passed by the US Congress in April 1946 and then by the Philippine Legislature on 2 July 1946. As for the US$ 2 billion in American aid, most of it went to Roxas's cronies who were able to rebuild their shattered companies. Journalist Robert Shaplen noted of Manila that 'It may well be that in no other city in the world was there as much graft and conniving after the war.'[11]

On 4 July America fulfilled the obligations of Roosevelt's 1934 Tydings–McDuffie Act by seeing in full independence for the Philippines. High Commissioner Paul McNutt stood before the assembled crowds in Luneta Park to lower the Stars and Stripes. MacArthur, who had flown from Japan where he was now governor, proclaimed, 'America buried imperialism here today.'[12] Ironically it was MacArthur's father who had suppressed the Philippine nationalist movement 40 years earlier.

If MacArthur had enabled the Philippines establishment right wing to run roughshod over democratic norms, it soon became apparent that he had good reason to fear Asian communism. The Soviet annexation of Eastern Europe presented a very real threat to America's free-market values. Also, in February 1946, George Kennan had sent his famous telegram from Moscow to the State Department explaining the Soviet's increasing hostility to the West, concluding that 'A hostile environment is the breath of life for [the] prevailing internal system in this country (Soviet Union).'[13]

Increasingly, the aggressive American approach to communism that MacArthur had pioneered in the Philippines would become commonplace throughout the American hegemony. On 12 March 1947 President Truman announced that henceforth 'it must be the policy of the United States to support free peoples who are resisting attempted subjugation by armed minorities or outside pressure'.[14] Two days later, 99-year leases were signed on Clark Air Base and the naval port of Subic Bay. Indeed, with the onset of the Korean War, staffing at Clark Air Base alone increased from 5,445 in 1949 to 15,830 in 1953. For the next half century these bases would be the fulcrum of American power in its Cold War battle for supremacy in Asia.

While Guam, Korea and Okinawa were also considered, America's longstanding relationship with the Philippines made this country the natural base for the projection of American power in Asia. America paid handsomely for the privilege. On 21 March, Roxas received US$ 19.7 million in military assistance plus a US$ 25 million emergency loan advance for economic reconstruction. This was a small downpayment on what was to become one of the country's major revenue earners in the early years of independence. By 1948, America had committed US$ 329.3 million to the Philippines.

Given the presence of the American forces at Clark Air Base and Subic Bay, the Philippines had little requirement for international defence. However, the need for counter-insurgency forces was critical. After the elections the security situation deteriorated rapidly as the Huks expanded their grip on Luzon. At first, Roxas had attempted negotiations with Huk leaders including Juan Feleo but, in what was probably a trap designed by Roxas's allies, Feleo and his colleagues were ambushed and captured by uniformed men while returning to Manila from a peace-keeping mission in the countryside. Feleo's decapitated body was found floating in the Pampanga River. A year and a half later, on 6 March 1948, the Huks and the PKP were banned, while all those accused of collaborating with the Japanese were pardoned in the following week. Effectively, Luzon, the main island of the Philippines, descended into a state of civil war.

The death of Roxas from a heart attack brought little relief to the Huks. He was succeeded by an even more right-wing successor, Elpidio Quirino, who embarked on a brutal suppression of the leftist opposition. More troubling to US Secretary of State Dean Acheson was Quirino's siphoning off American aid into his own account; even by the standards of the Philippines, Quirino was unacceptably corrupt.

The CIA complained of 'an irresponsible ruling class which exercises economic and political power almost exclusively in its own interests'.[15] The post-war economy was in desperate condition. In 1946 gross domestic product was just 38.7 per cent of 1937 levels. The Japanese army of 'liberation' had smashed industrial buildings, banks, government offices and hotels. Infrastructure including ports had been sabotaged or destroyed in the heavy fighting for Manila. In spite of the US\$ 1 billion, which America had poured into the Philippines, its economy had shown little sign of recovery; with masterly understatement, Acheson commented that 'much of the aid to the Philippines has not been used as wisely as we wish it had'.[16] However, Acheson's wish to withdraw aid was deflected by the intervention of John Melby, the head of the Philippine desk at the State Department.

In 1949, Quirino was nominated to run as Liberal presidential candidate versus the former wartime leader José Laurel, who ran for the Nationalists. The Huks abstained from voting. Quirino won in an election in which both sides spent lavishly to buy votes. Apart from vote buying, it was estimated that at least 20 per cent of votes cast were fraudulent. One observer noted that 'even the birds and the bees voted.'[17]

For Quirino, the military defeat of the communists remained a priority. This was a strategy wholly endorsed by the US military advisor to the Philippines, General Leland Hobbs, who advocated a much more vigorous campaign against the Huks. President Truman too, facing the consequences of the loss of China and their aggression in Korea, saw the defeat of communism within the Philippines as a priority, and he authorised an increase in resources.

As part of this stepped-up campaign, Air Force Colonel Edward Lansdale was sent to Manila to give specialist help and advice. Lansdale, who was the model for Graham Greene's character Alden Pye in *The Quiet American* (1955), was an expert in counter-insurgency. A former advertising executive, Lansdale was an employee of the Office of Policy Coordination; in spite of its anodyne title, this group specialised in 'covert operations' and was eventually absorbed within the CIA. Lansdale proved a master at developing elaborately constructed stratagems to the extent that Sterling Seagrave dubbed him the 'Walt Disney of covert action'.[18] The Philippines was to be the setting for many of his early career spectaculars.

Learning from the gross inadequacies of Chiang Kai Shek, Acheson told Truman that 'If there is one lesson to be learned from the China debacle it is that if we are confronted with an inadequate vehicle it should be discarded or immobilized in favour of a more propitious approach.'[19] Faced with numerous 'inadequate vehicles' in the Philippines, Lansdale set about the task of 'regime change'. Earlier in the year in Washington he had met Magsaysay, a guerrilla fighter who had fought against the Japanese. US government officials were impressed with his determined manner, apparent integrity and proven loyalty to the USA.

While Magsaysay was in Washington negotiating for aid for Filipino war veterans, he negotiated a political alliance with Lansdale. In essence, in return for American financial support, he would be their man. Lansdale persuaded his immediate superior to get Assistant Secretary of State Livingstone Merchant to go to Quirino and offer him financial support in return for the promotion of Magsaysay to secretary of defence. Agreement was followed by US$ 584 million of American aid.

Thus promoted, Magsaysay set to work on destroying communism. In *Foreign Affairs*, Magsaysay wrote that

> We learned from our own Communist *Hukbalahp* revolution that Communism is not just some distorted nationalist ambition, like Hitler's, to be satisfied with land or riches, but an unremitting universal campaign to rule the earth, to eradicate individual liberty, to destroy God and the souls of men.[20]

His pledge to eradicate communism could have been written from a CIA textbook.

In practice Magsaysay used a 'carrot and stick' approach; on the one hand he aggressively hunted down terrorist groups while on the other hand seeking to undermine their basis of popular support. Magsaysay set up agricultural banks to ease credit to farmers, opened medical clinics and local courts and financed new infrastructure. Even the Huks were enticed with land on the southern island of Mindanao.

Magsaysay also reorganised the notoriously corrupt police force and purged it of 10,000 of its 17,000 employees. The police were also subsumed into the Department of National Defence, which was similarly purged of corrupt officers, while total army numbers were doubled to 56,000. Training, including anti-communist propaganda, was also stepped up. Between 1950 and 1971, 8,729 officers were trained in the USA. Over the same period, 17,500 were trained at centres whose instructors had graduated from the International Police Academy in Washington D.C. Meanwhile, Lansdale conducted psychological warfare against the communists by organising macabre assassinations of its leaders.

In the face of a well-organised campaign, the Huks mistakenly concentrated their forces on Luzon, where they could be more easily targeted by the Philippine army. In October 1950, the Huks' poorly defended Manila headquarters was stormed; 111 *Huks* were arrested including six of their leaders; and the raid also yielded weapons and money. The following year, a series of military operations killed 2,000 *Huks* and captured a further 2,500. By the end of 1951, most of the surviving *Huk* groups had surrendered. The following year, William J. Pomeroy, that rare creature – an American communist terrorist – joined the *Huks*, but was captured and deported back to the USA, where he was jailed for 10 years.

With the election of Dwight Eisenhower to the presidency in 1953, America's anti-Soviet rhetoric was raised another notch. His secretary of state and key foreign policy advisor, John Foster Dulles, proposed a virulent anti-communist policy in Asia. As a State Department advisor, Dulles had previously advised Truman to pay greater attention to Asia, and in Eisenhower he found a sympathetic ear. Eisenhower had served under MacArthur in the Philippines and had a more confident approach to Asia than Truman, the parochial mid-Westerner who had taken time to get the measure of Asia and MacArthur, who dominated the region's post-war history.

In addition to his greater emphasis on the pursuit of anti-communist policies in Asia, Eisenhower gave free rein to the CIA and ushered in perhaps the most active period of covert 'regime change' in American history. In 1953, the CIA had ousted Iranian Prime Minister Mohammed Mossadegh, while the following year the elected leader of Guatemala was also removed from power.

In the Philippines, the CIA took it in hand to secure the election of Magsaysay as president. They secured him the Coca Cola franchise to provide him with funds, wrote his speeches, influenced the press and promoted a political jingle called the 'Magsaysay Mambo'.[21] Although Magsaysay's parents were landowners and not poor by the definitions of the time, much was made of his humble birth in a bamboo hut. Naturally, Quirino's reputation was besmirched in a vigorous smear campaign. To co-opt the media, the CIA set up the National Press Club. Lansdale also worked with a CIA associate George Kaplan, under the umbrella of the Committee for Free Asia, later renamed the Asia Foundation, to monitor the Filipino elections.

The CIA's contingency plan for a coup d'état against Quirino was never required. Magsaysay won the presidency for the Nationalists in a landslide. As president, Magsaysay's most controversial policy was the renegotiation of the Bell Trade Act, which was due to expire in 1954. Against fierce opposition, the Philippine economy was further opened to American investment. Though the Philippines suffered the Asia-wide economic downturn that followed the ending of the Korean

War, nevertheless Magsaysay appeared to have brought stability to post-war government. It was perhaps the greatest tragedy of post-war Philippine history that Magsaysay was killed in a plane crash in 1957.

His successor, Vice President Carlos Garcia, won the Nationalist presidential ticket and defeated the Liberal challenge, though in the electoral contest for vice president, Garcia's candidate, Diodado Macapagal, was defeated by Laurel. However, when the corruption practices of the new president became apparent, CIA agent Joseph Burkholder Smith was instructed to find a suitable replacement. In the meantime Burkholder Smith sought to control the 1959 elections by putting together a grand alliance of candidates. The CIA plan failed completely. In spite of American financial backing, the alliance lost legislative control to a new political grouping led by Ferdinand Marcos; Filipino politics were about to change for a generation.

In studying America's post-war relationship with the Philippines, it is difficult to avoid the conclusion that it was 'neo-colonial' in nature; although Roosevelt had clearly set America's former colony on the path towards independence in the pre-war period, in practice it was difficult for America to let go. Most American politicians would probably have agreed with Senator Robert Taft when he affirmed that

> ... the Philippines should always be an American outpost in the Pacific. The fact that they have a completely independent, autonomous government is, I think, a good thing. . . . But certainly we shall always be a big brother, if you please, to the Philippine Islands.[22]

Much as successive American administrations genuinely believed in Asian 'self-determinism', the Philippines, with its constant post-war battle against communism and its strategically essential military and naval bases, was too important a part of America's Asian hegemony, in its fight against communism, to leave to its own political devices. The net result of American political intervention was rarely successful. However, whether the Philippines, given its corrupt political and social elite, would have fared any better if left to its own devices is open to question. Indeed, with the arrival of the populist pro-American Ferdinand Marcos, America gave up on political tinkering and accepted the flawed dictator. It was a Filipino political solution but not one that augured well for the country.

13

Lord Mountbatten and the Partition of India

India–Pakistan: 1945–7

'I have not become the King's First Minister in order to preside over the liquidation of the British Empire,'[1] declared Prime Minister Winston Churchill. Whatever Churchill's bluster, he was too late. The tide of empire had already ebbed. When Churchill and Roosevelt met on the presidential flagship, the heavy cruiser *USS Augusta*, they agreed an Atlantic Charter that accorded 'the right of all peoples to choose the form of government under which they will live'.[2] They also expressed 'the wish to see sovereign rights and self government restored to those who have been forcibly deprived of them'.[3] If this was the requisite propaganda pitch with which to tie in the third-world countries to the allied cause, it also behoved real action when the war was ended.

Like America, Britain was already in the process of dismantling its empire. In India, the institutions of constitutional democracy had been clearly laid out in the 1930s. The British were already well under way to handing over full powers to the Indian people. In India, what was still to be decided were the mechanical issues: the what, when and how of independence. First and foremost of these issues was whether India would remain a unitary state, or whether a separate Muslim entity would be called into being. The issue of partition came to dominate Indian politics during and immediately after the Second World War. That an independence movement, which had been fought in such a remarkably non-violent way by Gandhi over the previous quarter of a century, should end in bloody massacres in Bengal and Punjab was a tragedy that blackened the early days of both India and Pakistan, and coloured the history of their future relationship in the sub-continent.

The Second World War started badly for Anglo–Indian relations. Under the 1935 Government of India Act, which devolved considerable power to the elected Indian assemblies, the defence of India and the running of the army remained firmly in control of the Viceroy. On the outbreak of the Second World War, Lord Linlithgow, without consulting the Congress Party, which dominated the legislative assemblies, declared war on Germany on India's behalf. Notwithstanding the provisions of the new Indian constitution, this unilateral act was understandably bound to cause friction.

If the British Viceroy behaved foolishly however, Congress managed to behave worse. Nehru, travelling overseas, returned to find Gandhi determined to prevent India becoming embroiled in war. Although Gandhi's sentiments were squarely behind Britain, he believed passionately in the pacifist approach. He wrote personally to Hitler to try to restrain him, and at home he suggested that it would be better to let Hitler and Mussolini occupy India rather than engage in fighting. Gandhi, who had started the war by telling the Viceroy that he was in favour of unconditional support, would later suggest that 'Roosevelt and Churchill are no less war criminals than Hitler or Mussolini.'[4]

Nehru too was pro-British, but in spite of assurances that he would not take advantage of the situation to leverage concessions from Britain, this is exactly what he set out to do. Congress declared that it could not support a government that had not consulted them, and its working committee issued a resolution declaring that 'A free democratic India will gladly associate with other free nations for mutual defence against aggression and for economic co-operation.'[5] The resolution of 15 September 1939 also asked the British government 'to declare in unequivocal terms what their war aims are in regard to democracy and imperialism and . . . how those aims are to apply to India and to be given effect to in the present'.[6] A few weeks later Congress let it be known that the price of support was 'an independent nation, and present application must be given to this status to the largest extent possible'.[7]

When Linlithgow failed to respond, Nehru ordered all the Congress-led state administrations to resign. Nehru and Congress had massively overplayed their hand however. Even Arthur Lall, later an envoy to the United Nations, conceded that if Nehru had fully backed the British war effort, this 'would have speeded assumption of government'.[8] Both Gandhi and Nehru, who had successfully used the weaknesses of British liberal democracy in gaining traction for their independence movement in the inter-war period, failed to understand that the necessities of war changed the British approach to government. Peacetime British democracy became a different animal in times of war. Fighting the enemy would take precedence over Congress's 'schoolboy' debating tactics which ignored the largely supportive Indian sentiment towards the English in their war effort.

Indeed it was notable that when an Indian division performed with distinction under General Wavell in defeating an Italian army in Cyrenaica, it was not just the British military that shared their pride back in India; there was also a broad-based popular rejoicing at the prowess of Indian arms. However, Congress' hostility to the British war effort persuaded Churchill that no political risks could be taken which might undermine the war effort. In a memorandum sent from Washington in January 1942, Churchill noted:

> Bringing hostile political elements into the defence machine will paralyse action. . . .
> The Indian troops are fighting splendidly, but it must be remembered that their

allegiance is to the King Emperor, and that the role of Congress and the Hindu priest-hood machine would never be tolerated by a fighting race.'[9]

In this, Churchill was referring to the Sikhs who comprised 20 per cent of the Indian army and were generally regarded as its best fighters.

If Gandhi and Nehru mishandled the situation however, their behaviour was a long way from some of their colleagues who came out in open support for the Axis powers. Subhas Chandra Bose who, like Nehru, stood on the left wing of Congress, resigned and formed the Forward Bloc Party in Bengal. The proto national socialist style organisation was swiftly banned, and Bose was arrested. After an escape to Kabul, his subsequent career took him to Moscow and Berlin (where he did daily broadcasts inciting an Indian uprising).

Finally, he reached Singapore by a submarine that travelled three months underwater to get there. From there he was sent to the Andaman Islands, where the British had paradoxically been intending to send him. Only now the islands were occupied by the Japanese. '...a Japanese army which caught Britain's command with their gin and tonics half down'[10] had forced a surrender of 60,000 Indian troops without a shot fired. Remarkably, only 20,000 of these foreswore their allegiance to the crown, thereby securing a much safer berth than that suffered by the remaining 40,000, who were interned in prison camps.

The renegade Indian troops thus turned, formed the backbone of the Indian National Army (INA) which served under Bose. He later moved to Rangoon to declare a provisional capital of *azad* (free) India, and the INA subsequently took part in the advance on Imphal (the capital of Manipur State in North East India). With the surrender of the INA in May 1945, Bose took the last plane out of Rangoon but was later killed in a crash landing in Formosa.

Meanwhile in India in October 1940, Gandhi launched a *satyagraha* campaign against the war. His disciple Vinoba Bhave, later to win fame as a wandering hermit, was arrested; Nehru's arrest followed soon afterwards. By the middle of the following year, some 14,000 *satyagrahis* had been imprisoned. Realising that something needed to be done to shore up India, Churchill despatched Sir Stafford Cripps, a man fully sympathetic to independence and an old friend of Gandhi and Nehru, with a view to settling full dominion status after the war; any Indian State or province would be able to opt out of British rule.

Gandhi capped what turned out to be a war of miserable misjudgements, by forecasting that Japan would vanquish the British. Thus, Gandhi, with a nasty jibe, declined to accept, 'a post dated cheque on a bank that was failing'[11] and, in a moment of supreme condescension, told Cripps, 'No thank you, Sir Stafford, I would not be able to get even a child to accept this kind of offer.'[12] Nehru and the Congress Working Committee followed suit. Jinnah who was personally in favour of the Cripps proposal also declined, so as not to be outflanked as a 'nationalist' by Congress.

The subsequent 'Quit India' campaign, which was to be his last such *Satya-graha* action, brought unprecedented civil disturbance with the arrest of 60,000

Congress supporters. Jinnah was appalled by the irresponsibility of the Congress-incited uprising. With some 57 divisions taken up with quelling an Indian uprising, Japan, if so inclined, would have faced little credible opposition if they had invaded the sub-continent. Gandhi, Nehru and all the Working Committee members were arrested again and imprisoned in Aga Khan's Palace in Poona. Gandhi himself came close to death in February 1943, when he embarked on a protest fast. However, Wavell, the new Viceroy and Governor-General who replaced Linlithgow in 1943, remained firm, and Congress leaders were locked up until Wavell felt confident to release them after General Slim's decisive defeat of the Japanese army at Imphal.

In Jinnah's presidential address to the Muslim League in 1937, he had savaged Congress's refusal to form joint administrations with the Muslim League, and he declared that '. . . the majority community have clearly shown their hand that Hindustan is for the Hindus'.[13] Jinnah was furious that Congress refused to accept that the Muslim League was the sole representative of Indian Muslims and fiercely contested Congress's claim that they too represented Muslim India.

From this point, the divisions between the two sides became an increasingly bitter war of words. Nehru went as far as to describe the Muslim League's actions as being 'reminiscent of Nazis methods'.[14] When Nehru made the tactical mistake of ordering all provincial administrations to resign in October 1939, Jinnah pronounced it a day of deliverance 'from tyranny, oppression and injustice during the last two and a half years'.[15] The opportunistic political games being played by Congress neither advanced the cause of independence that Gandhi had virtually won by the outset of war, nor promoted the possibility of rapprochement between Congress and the Muslim League.

Jinnah, already disillusioned by the corrupt and venal Congress provincial governments that had come to power after the 1937 elections, was further alienated by what he saw as the juvenile behaviour of Nehru and Gandhi; though he also feared that the 'Quit India' campaign might be 'the culminating point in the policy and programme of Mr. Gandhi and his Hindu Congress of blackmailing the British and coercing them to concede a system of government . . . which would establish a Hindu Raj immediately under the aegis of the British bayonet'.[16] However, while they remained incarcerated, Jinnah used the opportunity to further strengthen the organisation of the Muslim League. Nehru in turn distrusted the easy relations which Jinnah established with Viceroy Wavell. From the latter, he had extracted the valuable promise that no future constitutional scheme would be considered without approval from Indian Muslims.

In the 1930s, the revered poet Sir Muhammad Iqbal had proposed a Muslim homeland in the North West. Radical Islamic students took up this suggestion. Choudhary Rahmat Ali, a Cambridge law student, initiated the movement for an independent Pakistan from his rooms at 3 Humberstone Road, Cambridge, by writing a pamphlet entitled 'Now or never for the Pakistan Declaration' (1933). Three other Pakistan students co-signed the document. The idea of 'Pakistan' remained dormant with the Muslim League's leaders until Jinnah took up the theme once more in 1940, when he published an article stating that there should be a constitution 'that recognises that there are in India two nations who both must share the governance of their common motherland'.[17] It is quite possible that at first, Jinnah's call for a Muslim state was no more than a bargaining position. Certainly, most Indian Muslims at this point were not calling for an independent Pakistan, but simply for protection from the overwhelming Hindu majority.

However, positions hardened over the next seven years. Having floated the idea of a completely independent state, increasing numbers of Muslims warmed to this possibility. Furthermore, Sir Sikander Hyat Khan, the powerful Muslim head of the Unionist Party, who controlled the Punjab and fiercely opposed the idea of Pakistan, died in December 1942, and removed the main internal obstacle to Muslim advocacy of home rule.

Finally, fresh elections called by Wavell in August 1945 at Stafford Cripps' suggestion proved the extent of Jinnah's organisational work during the years that the Congress leaders had been incarcerated. The Muslim League made a virtual clean sweep of the Muslim vote and fully established their hitherto tenuous claim to represent all Muslims. Congress's claim to represent both the Hindu and Muslim franchise was dealt a fatal blow.

The Congress leaders, released from prison, therefore found in Jinnah, a hardened and an even more formidable political rival. Yet Gandhi and Nehru both failed to fully recognise the changed political landscape. Gandhi at first resisted all possibility of 'partition', and tried to fob Jinnah off with the promise of 'partition' after independence; a blatant ploy that the wily Jinnah was not inclined to swallow. As late as March 1947, Gandhi asserted that 'If Congress wishes to accept partition, it will be over my dead body. So long as I am alive I will never agree to the partition of India'.[18] After the failure of the first Simla Conference, presided over by Wavell, a further attempt at reconciliation between the two sides was attempted by the Cabinet Commission, headed by Sir Stafford Cripps, that Churchill had despatched to India to try to solve the Hindu–Muslim problem and thereby preserve Indian unity.

The new Cripps Plan envisaged a unified Indian state that would limit federal power to foreign affairs, defence and communication. This federal state would have an executive and legislative arm whose power over issues affecting the different religious communities would have to be agreed by a majority of each religious community. Nehru hardly helped build trust when he argued that it was inevitable that the power of central government would grow after the establishment of an independent India; Nehru's forecast was probably correct, but his forthright statement did little to engage the Muslim League's support. Jinnah interpreted these comments as 'a complete repudiation of the basic form upon which the long term scheme rests and all of its fundamentals'.[19]

Congress too rejected the plans, fearing that India would be denuded of strong government. Meanwhile, Nehru firmly rejected Partition, 'Congress is not going to agree to Pakistan under any circumstances.... Nothing on Earth is going to bring about Pakistan which Jinnah wants to create.'[20] Arthur Lall later accused Cripps of being biaseds toward Jinnah, believing that the Cabinet Commission plan for an Indian state 'was a cynical move in keeping with the whole divide and rule philosophy of the British.... by weakening India to the maximum extent possible, they hoped to induce it to become independent, and even subservient'.[21]

Perhaps it is not surprising that after a 25-year campaign for home rule Indian activists should have taken a cynical view of the motives of Englishmen; however, there is no evidence that the British government wanted to do anything more than unburden themselves of the Indian problem as quickly and as honourably as possible. What Congress almost certainly failed to realise was that post-war Britain, virtually bankrupt from its efforts to defeat Nazi Germany, was more preoccupied by the pressing domestic concerns of jobs, housing and welfare. In foreign policy, it was the stabilisation of Europe and specifically its concerns over the Soviet Union that dominated their agenda. India ranked relatively low down on Britain's 'to do' list.

With the failure of the Cabinet Mission, events moved on again with the shock election defeat of Winston Churchill and his replacement with a Labour government headed by Clement Attlee. The new prime minister was ideologically close to Congress, which greeted him with 'Hearty congratulations to the people of Great Britain on the results of the election which demonstrate their abandonment of the old ideas and acceptance of a new world.'[22]

Attlee, long sympathetic to the cause of Indian independence, now wanted to complete the process as quickly as possible; he announced that a British withdrawal would be made by June 1948. In view of the new Labour government's pressing domestic issues, Attlee's decision was understandable but as the Conservative opposition pointed out, it inevitably led to a loss of bargaining power in seeking out a Hindu–Muslim settlement. However, it is notable that by 1945 there was barely a murmur of opposition to Indian independence from the British establishment, Winston Churchill included. However, while the Attlee fiat on withdrawal was a debatable decision, his replacement of Wavell as viceroy with Louis Mountbatten was unambiguously catastrophic.

Born Prince Louis Battenberg, son of a minor branch of the Hesse family and the granddaughter of Queen Victoria, he could claim relationship with the Romanoffs, Hapsburgs and Hohenzollerns. His name was later changed to Mountbatten because of the First World War anti-German sentiment. Perhaps aware of the doubts about his royal lineage, Mountbatten craved Royal society, and throughout his life played on his connections to remarkable effect.

As a naval commander, albeit apparently popular with officers and ratings, Mountbatten became a legend for his scrapes and was nicknamed the 'Master of

Disaster' within the admiralty. Men of lesser birth would have been cashiered for his disregard of orders and regulations, which led to a serious naval accident at the start of the war. His career was a classic case of promotion being given to get rid of an incompetent but un-sackable naval officer. When Mountbatten objected to being moved from his command of the aircraft carrier *HMS Illustrious* to take up a post as advisor on Combined Operations, Churchill countered, 'What could you hope to achieve except to be sunk in a bigger and more expensive ship this time?'[23]

Military men were even less flattering about Mountbatten. Field Marshall Montgomery went as far as to suggest that Mountbatten's, 'knowledge of how to make war is NIL.'[24] General 'Vinegar Joe' Stilwell was ruder still about Mountbatten's military capabilities; 'The Glamour Boy is just that. Enormous staff, endless walla-walla, but damned little fighting.'[25] In his insatiable pomp and ambition, Mountbatten proved himself a callous leader, careless of other men's lives, whose main motive was self-glorification. These were hardly the attributes required to handle the delicate process of political, geographic and religious separation of tens of millions of Hindus and Muslims.

Yet Mountbatten did possess remarkable talents. For a man whose favourite books were low-brow novels by Agatha Christie, Barbara Cartland and anything on his own genealogy, he passed himself off as an all-round expert and man of brilliance; he was a fluent and articulate speaker and a brilliant flatterer of the rich and influential. A contemporary described him as a consummate 'actor'. His arrogance and conceit were breathtaking in their expansiveness. Looking back on his life, Mountbatten once reflected, 'It is a curious thing, but a fact, that I have been right in everything I have done and said in my life.'[26]

He was also a master politician, taking credit for other men's success while skillfully passing the blame for his copious mistakes to others. Mountbatten could also be relied upon to use and abandon friends and colleagues. Mountbatten ditched the hapless Duke of Windsor and Mrs Simpson, to whom he had been the fawning courtier and effortlessly switched sides to his brother George, after his unexpected accession to the throne.

Mountbatten took care that he always landed on the winning side. No more so than with the money that he acquired when he married the fabulously wealthy daughter of Sir Ernest Cassel. Although debates rage as to whether Mountbatten had homosexual preferences, there is no doubting the debauchery of his wife Edwina, who was adulterous, a nymphomaniac and allegedly a bisexual. They did at least match in their ambitions. In middle age, the ardour of her passions moved from sex to socialism, and her courting of Clement Attlee and the Labour Party was the prime reason for Mountbatten's appointment to the post. Attlee said of him that 'he had an extraordinary ability for getting on with all kinds of people . . . he was blessed with a very unusual wife'.[27]

Politically Mountbatten swung both ways; on the one hand, using his quasi-Royal status with the Conservatives, while on the other hand espousing the ideals of socialism to court the Labour Party. Needless to add, his socialism did not prevent him from being a crashing snob. On taking over the Indian viceroyalty from Wavell, the sturdy English soldier, a decorated veteran of the Boer War who had lost an eye at Ypres in the First World War, Mountbatten commented, 'Lady Wavell looked entirely like my wife's maid. She was very, sort of, mundane. And people out there were enormously struck by the difference . . . we went in with a panache which was entirely lacking before.'[28]

In spite of the career success that owed much to his wife's fortune, when Edwina died, Mountbatten cut his connections with the Cassel family. Prime Minister Antony Eden described him as a 'congenital liar', but his character was best summed up by Sir Gerald Templer when he famously addressed Mountbatten with the words, 'you are so crooked, Dickie, if you swallowed a nail you'd shit a corkscrew'.[29]

Gandhi immediately succumbed to Mountbatten's charms, and Nehru went one better by falling for both Mountbatten and his wife. He is generally thought to have seduced Edwina, and there was widespread gossip about the closeness of the relationship. The private secretary to the head of the Indian army, Sir Claude Auchinleck, complained that 'Nehru's relationship with Lady Mountbatten is sufficiently close to have raised eyebrows.'[30] Perversely Mountbatten not only seems to have known about his wife's affair, but was even happy to be entrusted with Nehru's love letters to her.

By contrast, Jinnah immediately saw through Mountbatten's veneer of flattery and bonhomie. The dislike was mutual. Mountbatten concluded that Jinnah was 'a psychopathic case; in fact, until I met him I would not have thought it possible that a person with such a complete lack of administrative knowledge or sense of responsibility could achieve or hold . . . so powerful a position.'[31] The partiality of Mountbatten to the Congress leaders was soon apparent to the Muslim League and did little to help heal the divisions between Hindus and Muslims. While V.P. Menon, a Hindu and friend of Patel, the deputy leader of Congress, was allowed to attend meetings to discuss action plans regarding communal clashes, there were no Muslim representatives. Mountbatten generally had a poor opinion of Muslims and even wondered, with breathtaking Islamophobia, 'whether there were likely to be sufficient intelligent Muslim officials to administer Pakistan'.[32]

Although Mountbatten arrived with instructions to try to avert a Partition of India, it was already too late. Jinnah was adamant in sticking to his demands for a nation based around the six provinces, including the Punjab and Bengal, while Nehru and his deputy Patel had come to the conclusion that division was inevitable; they wanted power sooner rather than later, and feared that any unitary arrangement with a decentralised federal structure might diminish the central government powers that they craved.

Mountbatten quickly ditched Attlee's 'unitary' government ambitions for India and proposed a system whereby each province might opt by election, whether to remain independent or join India or Pakistan. Nehru raged at this proposal because he feared that his plans for centralised government in India might slip from his grasp. Elections were still held, but the choice of 'destination' was severely circumscribed, and in the case of the Punjab and Bengal, given the evenness of the population split between India and Pakistan, it was decided to partition them rather than allow control to pass to the Muslims, who had small majorities in each of these states. With the agreement of Winston Churchill, head of the now opposition Conservatives, Attlee proceeded to pass an uncontested Indian Independence Bill through parliament.

There remained two key problems. There were some 562 states, ranging in size from provinces the size of Kashmir and Hyderabad to tiny impoverished principalities. The relationship of these states to the Crown was governed by individual treaties dating back to the nineteenth century. Given the size of these states, their autonomy was somewhat idiosyncratic in the context of changes taking place within India. However the British were protective of these relationships and most would have preferred the treaties to continue unless they opted out to join India. Wavell went as far as to assure them that their relationship with the Crown would not be transferred without their consent.

However, Nehru was openly hostile to the continuation of the princely states, and in bullying manner decreed that any prince who chose not to join the constituent assembly would be treated as an enemy. On 15 June 1947, Nehru warned foreign governments that recognition of any princely state would 'be considered an unfriendly act'.[33] Set against this harsh language, his deputy Patel, who was appointed to head the States Department, played soft cop to Nehru's hard cop with careful cajoling, using vague threats and vacuous promises of sovereignty, such as 'My scheme leaves you with all practical independence you can probably use.'[34]

Also Mountbatten reneged on the obligations of the historic princely treaties and promises of Wavell; the Indian princes were informed that they would either have to join India or Pakistan. Patel, for the Hindus, and Jinnah, for the Muslims, wooed them with promises to maintain the same support that they had been given by the Crown. Ultimately, all but three of the independent Raj states signed up to the two new states. Of these, Kashmir, a Muslim province ruled by a Hindu, would later sign up to India and precipitate a conflict which lasts to this day, while Junagadh and Hyderabad were later subsumed by Indian military actions of dubious legality.

By far the most contentious problem however was that of the Sikhs who were minorities divided more or less equally between Muslim and Hindu states. Weakened by a divided leadership, their demands for a united India were ignored; similarly with their later request for the establishment of a Sikhistan. Instead, a Boundary Commission was appointed under the auspices of the prominent English lawyer Sir Cyril Radcliffe, aided by eight high court judges from Punjab and Bengal. Difficult decisions were impossible to avoid. Using population as the basic common denominator, the Punjab and Bengal were divided up. Inevitably important religious sites belonging to the Sikhs, particularly in Lahore, would be lost to

Pakistan. With Sikhs, equally distributed either side of the border, and a religious minority in both areas, their community faced division or annihilation.

With the final haggling over, Mountbatten announced that independence for India and Pakistan would begin at midnight on 14 August 1947. Why did Mountbatten impose an independence date some nine months shorter than the deadline insisted upon by Attlee? Mountbatten's justification was plausibly predicated on the deteriorating relationship between the Hindu and Muslim communities. Better to force a rapid separation of the two sides than allow the situation to fester.

However, there are problems with this interpretation. First, while relations between the two communities were certainly bad, there is no reason to suggest that they were deteriorating. The situation had been much more threatening some nine months before Mountbatten's arrival in India, when Jinnah's call for a day of Direct Action led to sectarian massacres of both Hindus and Muslims in Calcutta. When the new interim government was then sworn in by Wavell on 1 September 1946, there was also widespread communal violence in Bihar and Bengal. So bad was the situation at this stage, with communal violence and the failure of the cabinet mission, that Wavell had contemplated a unilateral British withdrawal from India province by province.

Furthermore, with regard to Mountbatten's reasoning, if the threat of religious violence was so bad, why did he take such paltry precautions to avoid a Hindu–Muslim–Sikh conflict, which more experienced men advised him would lead to a bloodbath? Another possible explanation is that Mountbatten's vainglorious ego led him to bask in the possibility of resolving in six months a problem which had seemed intractable in the previous year to men he regarded as lesser mortals; or perhaps he simply wanted to solve the problem quickly so as to return speedily to London's social life.

In the report that he wrote covering his viceroyalty, Mountbatten claimed that 'not one of us . . . anticipated the exact form or magnitude of what was to follow'.[35] Yet Major Patrick Massey, who commanded a Sikh unit, reported on a number of occasions that his Sikh officers were warning him of plans by that community to attack the Muslims in the Punjab. Massey was ordered to desist from his 'alarmist' reports. Also Jenkins, the governor of the Punjab, warned on 27 April 1947 that 'there was a real peril we would be handing over to chaos . . . there is a grave danger of civil war'.[36] A.A. Williams, the district commissioner, warned that 'the precipitate departure of August 1947 made communal civil war almost inevitable'.[37] Even Lord Ismay, Mountbatten's chief of staff, wrote about Independence Day that 'I was in no mood for unrestrained rejoicing. . . . I had deep forebodings about the immediate future . . . many of my Indian friends were likely to lose their lives, and many more were certain to lose their homes.'[38]

In spite of the fears of his own staff, Mountbatten failed to attend adequately to the possibilities of the mass violence that would arise from partition. Jenkins estimated that the Punjab Boundary Force (PBF) would need at least 60,000 troops.

Only 15,000 were provided to protect 50 million people and 18,000 villages. Moreover, Mountbatten would not allow British troops to take part in this operation; this was a curious decision in view of the fact that they were the only available non-partisan force capable of preventing carnage.

The commanding officer of the 2nd Battalion of the Black Watch based in Lahore, Neville Blair, having been expressly instructed not 'to intervene in any outbreak that might occur between Muslim and Hindus'[39], had to stand idly by as appalling atrocities were committed. In the event, the PBF which was 75% comprised of Muslims gave way itself to communal violence. Mountbatten's complacency was remarkable. Even the religious press, which continued to exhort their religious followers to violence, was allowed to continue unimpeded throughout the catastrophe.

Though Mountbatten claimed to be overworked, this did not prevent him lavishing an inordinate amount of time on the planning and designing of flags, uniforms, medals and pageants; in addition to his other talents he was an inveterate 'popinjay'. When he was openly warned that the Sikhs would fight, Mountbatten blustered, 'If they start a war, Maharajah Sahib, it be against the entire might of India and will be ruthlessly put down.'[40] This was an entirely hollow threat.

Partition lived up to the disaster that had been widely predicted. Immediately after independence, Sikhs, who had been organising for this eventuality under the leadership of Master Tara Singh, started to drive out their Muslim neighbours from East Punjab. A sorry trek of homeless dispossessed began their cruel journey towards newly formed Muslim Pakistan. In a familiar pattern of savage mob behaviour, Muslim villages were burnt down; women were paraded naked, tortured and raped. Babies were ripped from wombs. Whole trains of refugees from East to West and West to East were boarded by Hindus and Muslims respectively, and their occupants hacked to pieces. Ghost trains would arrive at their destinations, filled with dead.

On foot, many refugees simply died of hunger and dehydration. Jenkins, the British governor of the Punjab, reported that 'Of one convoy that recently arrived over one thousand who had struggled on till they reached the frontier-post just laid down and died. They could go no further. The road was littered with corpses for miles.'[41] In Lahore, one of the great centres of Sikh culture, shrines were desecrated after whole communities were massacred. While the Punjab and Bengal represented the extremes of violence perpetrated by both sides, violence and atrocities were widespread across India, albeit stemmed in part by Gandhi's heroic efforts.

Delhi too was destabilised as Muslims also fled south to find refuge. In the capital city, Muslims comprised over half of the police force and many opted to move to Pakistan. Bomb explosions in Delhi caused a heightened tension as rumours circulated of a Muslim plot to overthrow the government. Only the Hindu migrations from the Sindh and Baluchistan, that took place later, remained relatively free of violence on a mass scale. From August until the end of the year, a seething mass of humanity was uprooted from their communities, and flung into the abyss of the unknown. Up to 10 million people were made homeless, and it is estimated that 1 million people were killed.

In the aftermath of the great catastrophe of Partition, Mountbatten worked overtime to blame others for the disaster, claiming that his actions had prevented worse, while at the same time claiming credit for his work in bringing about a political settlement. There was no substance in the assertion that the charms of Mountbatten and his wife had produced a solution to the Indian problem. Some form of Partition settlement had been accepted as inevitable before his arrival. As Sarvepalli Gopal asserts, 'even before Mountbatten came to India, both the British government and the Congress Party had come to the view that there was no alternative to accepting Jinnah's demand in some form or another'.[42] Gopal goes further in castigating Mountbatten for 'ambiguity on most of the vital issues'.[43]

Naturally, Mountbatten placed much of the blame on Jinnah, who had not only refused all of Mountbatten's political blandishments, but had also refused him the post-independence governor generalship of Pakistan that he coveted. In his recollections of the 1947 negotiations, he was to write, 'I could never have believed that an intelligent man, well educated, trained in the Inns of Court, was capable of simply closing his mind as Jinnah did. . . . He was an evil genius in the whole thing. The others could be persuaded but not Jinnah.'[44] V.P. Menon, Mountbatten's close associate and constitutional advisor, also sought to exonerate Mountbatten's responsibility for the disaster of Partition. 'It is easy to be wise after the event', he states, 'When in July 1947 the communal situation looked like getting out of hand, Lord Mountbatten took the precaution of getting assurances from the Congress, as well as from the Muslim League, that the minorities would be protected in their respective Dominions.'[45] However, in view of their non-existent record in being able to control the extremist elements within their parties and communities, Mountbatten's so-called 'precautions' were barely credible.

Neither did the Labour government of Prime Minister Clement Attlee want to rock the boat of Mountbatten's post hoc interpretation of Partition. Attlee noted that 'Broadly speaking the thing went off well.'[46] This was an outright lie. Khizr Hyat Khan Tiwana, Muslim chief minister of Punjab before Partition, asked Attlee why he had gone back on his promise not to divide the Punjab. Attlee's response was that 'we agreed to partition because we had come to the conclusion that without it there would be a civil war'. Khizr replied, 'But it didn't save us from civil war. There was a civil war.'[47]

In tracing the causes of 'Partition' and it consequences, there is no single answer. The nepotism, corruption and Hindu bias of the Congress-led administrations after the 1937 elections certainly brought Jinnah to the point where he felt at least capable of raising the prospect of 'Partition'. After 1939, Congress-led opposition to the British war effort also strengthened Jinnah's hand in consolidating the

Muslim League's dominance of the Muslim vote. Having in effect won the struggle for independence by 1939, Congress managed to throw away tactical advantages that could well have prevented the division of India, which they so vehemently opposed.

By 1945, the long-drawn-out bitterness between Jinnah, Nehru and their respective communities had become too entrenched to be resolved, even by a British government that clearly acted in good faith to find a happy political solution to the Hindu–Muslim problem. Britain's political establishment, drained by war, had no energy left to do anything more than try to unload this former trophy of empire as quickly as possible. Ultimately, the disaster of Partition must be laid at the door of individuals, whose acts of sectarian violence led, in aggregate, to the one of the great tragedies of the post-war period; quite possibly the massacres initiated by Partition would have happened, whatever schemes had been dreamt up by a British colonial administration. The Partition of India, which, perhaps masked by the preceding horrors of the Second World War, the economic hardships faced by Britain thereafter, and then by the cover-up orchestrated by Attlee and Mountbatten, has never been given the place of prominence it deserves in post-war history.

Overall, however, given the wealth of advice given to him by British officers and administrators with much greater experience of the sub-continent, Mountbatten's spurning of wise counsel makes him seriously culpable for the blunders, which enabled endemic religious hatred to spiral so badly out of control. Having by and large served India well for some 182 years, at the moment of leaving the sub-continent, the British government, in sending Mountbatten to oversee the independence process, served her very badly indeed.

14

Origins of the Korean War

Korea: 1945–50

Korea is made for trouble. Just 450 miles long and 150 miles wide, the country looks like an innocuous peninsula at the eastern end of the Asian continent. However, the straits of Tsushima separate the country from Japan by just 120 km. Korea was frequently described by Japanese politicians as a dagger aimed at the heart of Japan. To the north, Korea borders both China and Russia. From the end of the nineteenth century, and throughout the twentieth century, Korea was a pawn in the power struggles of its much larger neighbours.

After the Chinese Tang Dynasty unified Korea in the seventh century, the country became a vassal state to China for the best part of 1,200 years, albeit punctured by the interruptions of invasions by the Mongols, the Japanese and the Manchus. For a brief moment in the nineteenth century, with China in decline, Korea appeared to have the opportunity for true independence. However, with Japan in the ascendant after the economic and military reforms produced by the Meiji Restoration in 1869, Korea once again became the focus of rivalry between Japan and China. In the Sino-Japanese War of 1894, the Chinese were crushed in battle outside Pyongyang, and the Japanese won both Formosa (Taiwan) and the right to 'protect' Korea. However, Russia had not been party to the 'carve-up' between China and Japan at the 1995 Treaty of Shimonoseki. Following the Sino-Japanese War, Russia sent troops into the northern part of the country, while Japanese companies began their ritual exploitation of the South; an unseemly new squabble for control of Korea had begun. Conflict was inevitable. In 1904 the Japanese attacked Russian forces at Port Arthur and Inchon. Famously, the Russian fleet was destroyed at the Battle of Tsushima by a Japanese fleet that had been modelled on the British navy in every detail down to the issuance of tots of rum.

At the subsequent Treaty of New Hampshire, America's arch exponent of 'realpolitik', Theodore Roosevelt, acting as mediator, guaranteed the freedom of Korea but recognised Japan's 'paramount political, military and economic interests in Korea'.[1] Inserted into the treaty was also a clause requiring that the Russian government 'not interfere or place obstacles in the way of any measure of direction, protection, and supervision which the Imperial government of Japan may deem necessary to adopt in Korea'.[2] At the follow-up meeting in Japan, William Taft, later president but now secretary of war, signed another agreement with Katura, the Japanese foreign minister, whereby the USA recognised Japan's rights to Korea in return for Japanese disavowal of aggressive designs on the Philippines, which America had recently acquired from Spain.

The following autumn, Marquis Ito was despatched by the Japanese Emperor to Korea, where the cabinet was bullied into signing a protectorate agreement, which gave Japan effective control of Korea. This offer was made difficult to refuse after Prime Minister Han Kyu Sul was lured out of a cabinet meeting and shot dead. The king, whose wife had also been murdered by Japanese army officers ten years previously, demurely acquiesced. All pretence of a protectorate was abolished in 1910, and there began perhaps the most brutal enslavement of people witnessed in the twentieth century. Only Japanese language was taught in schools. Education for Koreans above basic literacy was abolished. Korean archives and treasures were burnt by the Japanese military occupiers in an attempt to erase Korea's culture. In 1919 the Democracy and Self-determination Movement appealed in vain for help from President Woodrow Wilson.

In revenge for their appeal to America for help, the Japanese slaughtered 50,000 Korean civilians, with Christians and those who had adopted Western culture being particularly targeted. Young Christian girls were stripped and strung up by their hair and put on public view. Over 1.5 million people went into exile. For the remainder, life was reduced to economic serfdom by the 750,000 Japanese who colonised Korea and turned it into the 'sweatshop' of their growing empire.

Of those who escaped, some like Dr Syngman Rhee, a politician related by blood to the Yi Dynasty, set up nationalist movements in exile, while others crossed into Manchuria and formed guerrilla units often with Chinese encouragement. It was from these respective backgrounds that the future leaders of Korea would emerge: Syngman Rhee in the South and Kim Il Sung in the North.

Even now little is known about Kim Il Sung. For one who spent so long developing the cult of the 'Great Leader', it is perhaps not surprising that separation of fact from fiction is difficult. However, it is known that between 1937 and 1940, Kim successfully commanded a 300-strong unit of Korean freedom fighters. In 1937 he attacked government offices and a police station at Pochonbo, and, in later skirmishing, Kim also managed to kill the local police chief. Kim repeated this success by killing Takashi Maeda and 58 out of 150 Japanese officers who had been trying to track him down. Eventually however, Kim was forced to flee to Russia where he joined the Soviet army.

By the end of the Second World War, therefore, Korea was a country hollowed out of all leadership. The entire administration was Japanese. Who would fill the void now that Japan was defeated? Although not a major item on the agendas of the war leaders, the issue of Korea was discussed. At the Cairo Conference in 1943, attended by Roosevelt, Churchill and Chiang Kai Shek, it was agreed that Japan would be expelled from all of its accumulated empire.

At Tehran later in the year, Roosevelt, Churchill and Stalin met again, this time without Chiang; Stalin confirmed that he would go to war against Japan three months after the European war had been won. Furthermore at their next meeting at Yalta, with Roosevelt dying, it was agreed that Russia would get the Kuril Islands and Sakhalin. However, the issue of Korea was left deliberately vague.

Roosevelt wanted an international trusteeship, with the USA, China and Russia acting as custodians, as an interim stage towards full Korean independence. However, it is probable that Stalin, whose army invaded North Eastern Korea six days before the surrender of Japan, had more extensive ambitions. Unlike the Russian port of Vladivostok that lay icebound for four months of the year, Korea possessed desirable warm weather ports that could be used for the Soviet Pacific fleet.

Having said at Potsdam that he would be ready for war in mid-August, Stalin's war declaration on 8 August came as a shock to Truman, who was alive to the danger that the Russians might occupy all of Korea. To head off this possibility, in mid-August, Truman suggested that the country be split between Soviet and American zones at the 38th parallel. The circumstances in which this line was drawn reveal much about the ad hoc decisions on the fate of nations in the chaotic close to the war. Lewis Haskins, executive secretary of the American Friends Service Committee, related that 'just before the surrender of Japan several one star generals hurried into an office in the Pentagon with the statement, "we have got to divide Korea. Where can we divide it?"'[3] A colonel with experience of the far east protested to his superiors, 'you can't do that. Korea is a social and economic unit. There is no place to divide it'.[4] The generals insisted that it had to be done. Their answer was, 'we have got to divide Korea and it has to be done by four o'clock this afternoon'.[5]

The division so rapidly drawn that afternoon survives to this day. However, there were hopes on both sides that the country would be united. Although the southern division below the 38th parallel had less area, most of it was fertile and the countryside supplied the bulk of the Korea's rice and agricultural products. Most importantly, the South had 20 million people, which was double the population of the North. If there was to be a plebiscite to unite the nation, it was clear which side would be dominant. By comparison the North was mountainous and held most of the country's industrial and mining assets which had been well developed during the Japanese 'protectorate'. Indeed Japanese investment in Korea was four times greater than Taiwan mainly because North of Korea was the conduit to Manchuria that Japan had gone on to conquer in the 1930s.

Contrary to the claims of Kim Il Sung, who boasted of defeating a fleeing Japanese army, it was Major General Lebedev who headed the Soviet invasion of Korea. Kim arrived in Korea with the 88th Division at Wonsan Harbour only on 19 September. By that time General Chistiakov had already entered the Capital Pyongyang with the main force of 40,000 troops. Such was Kim's obscurity at the time of this military operation that Lebedev did not meet him until much later.

At the age of 33, Kim was a barely known figure, and many people assumed that he was an impostor trained by the Soviets, an idea that may have been further encouraged by the fact that he changed his name to Kim Il Sung, who was a famed resistance leader in Korean history. Albeit unknown, he was not without influential supporters, which suggests that his years in Russia were usefully spent.

On a model that had already been established in Eastern Europe, a senior soldier, Major General Romanenko, was appointed chief civilian administrator. He and his right hand 'éminence grise', Colonel Ignatiev, who was responsible for handling local political relationships, orchestrated Kim's ascent to power. 'Conveniently' for Kim, the communist official, who was despatched to the North to organise the bureau in Pyongyang, was gunned down in the driver's seat of a truck as he was returning from a meeting with Romanenko. It is generally assumed, in the light of subsequent behaviour, that Kim and his Soviet backers were the perpetrators of the murder.

Far from being happy to remain the northern regional head of a Korean Communist Party which was headquartered with its leaders in the South, Kim immediately set out to build an independent communist group in the North. With the support of Kim's 'Soviet handler', Colonel Ignatiev, who attended every plenum meeting, the name of the branch was changed to the North Korean Communist Party in June 1946. By this time a radical communist agenda had already been implemented. Within six months of the North Korean provisional committee being established on 8 February 1946, a programme of six 'democratic' reforms had been implemented: nationalisation of all heavy industry, land reform with redistribution, working hours directives, agricultural tax in kind, equality of the sexes and a new election code.

Also Kim, who was to remain an ardent enthusiast for the populist mobilisation tactics employed by Mao, turned his hand to the creation of a mass party, a party in his own image. Ballads were written for school children about Kim's heroism in Manchuria. Writers and poets were activated. Legends were created. On becoming chairman of the party, Kim expelled 1,400 members of the 4,530 in the party, but by the time of the founding Congress of the North Korean Communist Party in August, a total of 335,000 new members had been recruited.

Although Kim faced some resistance from factions who heavily outnumbered him in the early days, in particular the Yunan guerrilla exiles, he ruthlessly played opposing factions against each other. While he may have been impressed by the cult of Mao, it is clear that Kim also absorbed the Stalinist art of brutal political infighting during his time in Moscow. However, with Ignatiev and the Soviet army behind him, there was a degree of inevitability about Kim's rise to power.

In the South, meanwhile, the 70-year-old Dr Syngman Rhee was making his more gradual bid for power. The occupying American forces under General Hodge had a deep distrust of the nationalists who emerged to claim power, to the extent that, at first, the occupying forces preferred to operate through Japanese bureaucrats than through the Korean returnees. General Hodge displayed the cultural flexibility that one might expect of a soldier from the American mid-west; when he arrived in Korea he claimed that people like the Japanese were 'all the same breed of cats'.[6] Encouraged by Hodge, Korea produced a litter of new parties. By November 1945, these numbered 205.

In May 1946, Rhee had gone on a tour of Korea to promote independence through the *National Society for the Rapid Realisation of Korean Independence*, and as one of the few known political leaders, it was not surprising that his right-wing party won the elections in October of that year. Although Hodge was fiercely anti-communist, he came into increasing conflict with the arrogant and duplicitous Rhee, who was described as a megalomaniac with dictatorial intentions by D.W. Kermode, the British consul general.

While there was a joint commission with the North to discuss the possibility of unification, these negotiations had fizzled out by 1947. Even without Kim and the Russians, the diffusion of power in the South became even more confused when, against Soviet opposition, the United Nations established the UN Commission on Korea (UNCOK). This came hard on the heels of the establishment in the South of the constitution of the Republic of Korea on 12 July 1948, followed shortly thereafter by the election of Rhee as president; meanwhile in the North, in the same month, the Democratic People's Republic of Korea People's Council approved their own constitution, and Kong Yong Wook, chief secretary, broadcast on Pyongyang radio that the Korean people would never recognise the South's National Assembly.

Within three years of Korea's liberation from the Japanese, therefore, the Cold War battle lines were clearly drawn along the 38th parallel. Both sides it seemed could live with a tied match. For the Americans, containment came with little cost. Truman provided funds and military support to train up a 60,000-strong South Korean army, and by 1948 Washington felt confident enough to withdraw General Hodge and the two remaining American divisions. That year, the Republican Congress's 25 per cent cut in the military budget had clearly focussed the Pentagon on their priorities; these did not include Korea. Berlin and Czechoslovakia were much more central to America's geopolitical concerns. In spite of these reductions, Rhee, champing for war, was 'sure that . . . [they] could take Pyongyang . . . in three days. An all-Korean border with Manchuria would be easier to defend than the 38th parallel'.[7]

It is unlikely that the US military withdrawal or Rhee's unpopularity within the Truman administration went unnoticed in Moscow. In July 1949, the CIA reported that the inefficiency, corruption and resulting unpopularity of the South Korean regime was such that it was likely to produce 'a public reaction favouring communism'.[8] Stalin must have calculated that America would not be prepared to lose soldiers on Korean soil. China had fallen to Mao without America lifting a finger to help.

Furthermore, stated American policy, as outlined by Secretary of State Dean Acheson, at the National Press Club in Washington on 12 January, suggested quite categorically that neither Korea nor Formosa were within the American security cordon. General MacArthur was similarly quoted in the press. Given that Stalin himself viewed the capitalist nations as in a state of imminent collapse right up to the time of his death, it would not be difficult to agree with Truman's view that the North Korean invasion, in the early hours of Sunday 25 June 1950, was a case of the reds probing 'for weaknesses in our armour'.[9]

For historians who view the world as a game of geopolitical chess, this has largely become the accepted view. Eric Hobsbawm argues in the *Age of Extremes* (1994) that the Cold War struggle for supremacy 'kept the Third World a zone of war, when the first and second worlds settled down to the longest era of peace since the 19th Century'[10], the implication being that third-world countries were simply pawns in a greater game. Similarly in his book *Diplomacy* (1994), Henry Kissinger criticises American post-war leaders who 'failed to consider that the communists might seek to break out at some point, choosing as their target an area of maximum political or strategic complexity for the United States'.[11]

Indeed it is inconceivable that Kim would have orchestrated an invasion without the knowledge of his Soviet minder, Colonel Ignatiev, or indeed the authority of his paymasters in Moscow. According to Soviet leader Khrushchev, Kim Il Sung raised the plan with Stalin in the winter of 1949; apparently, Stalin later authorised the North Korean's invasion at a vodka party at his dacha in March 1950. In spite of this evidence, there are problems with the view that the Koreans were merely puppets of the Cold War superpowers.

When Kim Il Sung visited Moscow in March–April 1949, he did so with a delegation of Korean trade and industry ministers. The main aim of the trip was evidently to beg for funds rather than to plot invasion. Indeed the economic difficulties of Korea may give a clue as to the real reason for the invasion of the South. By the beginning of 1950, it must have been clear to Kim Il Sung that his two-year socialist economic programme had failed. Any perceived advantage over the South was seeping away. It is estimated that by June 1950, over 1 million people had fled from the communists in the North to settle in the American-protected South. The flow of people the other way was negligible. For Kim, the situation must have seemed desperate.

Also, the fierce nationalism of the Koreans should not be underestimated. Kim played off his larger communist neighbours against each other; it is unlikely that he would have wanted to remain forever a puppet. A volatile, emotional people, sometimes called the 'Latins' of Asia, Koreans were used to steering an independent course by subterfuge if required, even while nominally a vassal state. Just as a Korean king had invented and replaced the Chinese Mandarin language with a new script and language to mark out Korea's linguistic and cultural independence, so Kim was to develop an independent national philosophy, 'Juche', which owed little to Marxist–Leninism.

In the South too Dr Rhee was far from being a passive client to American geopolitical ambitions. On the eve of the war, George Kennan, at the US State Department, was reassured by General MacArthur that the main problem in Korea 'was to restrain the South Koreans from resorting to arms to settle their differences with the North'.[12] In fact, Rhee was champing-at-the bit for war with the communists. A few months before the invasion, he was quoted in the *New York Herald Tribune* as saying that he 'would not much longer tolerate a divided Korea. . . . South Korea was strong enough to take Pyongyang in a few days'.[13]

As for the respective military strengths of the North and South, the US government was living under the delusion that they had military superiority. Brigadier William Roberts, commander of the Korean Military advisory group, went as far as to tell *Time* magazine that 'the South Koreans have the best damn army outside of the United States'.[14] Their 60,000 troops may indeed have been better trained than the 120,000 troops that Kim had over the border, but the South completely lacked tanks, artillery and planes. With porous borders between the two states it is unlikely that Kim would not have known this.

Faced with a failed economy, surrounded by hostile factions within his party and with a rapidly dwindling population, war may have been the only strategy that could have kept Kim in power. By June 1950, Kim probably had everything to gain and little to lose by going to war. While it is clear that Kim must have sought Stalin's approval for his ambitious venture to unite Korea by force, it is almost certain that the main push for this strategy did not come from Moscow.

Stalin may have persuaded himself that America was in terminal decline and that the USA showed insufficient strategic interest in Korea to draw themselves into a full-scale engagement, but he took extraordinary care not to appear aggressive; indeed, on the eve of the invasion he withdrew his military advisors for fear that their capture might give away his government's involvement. Dmitri Volkogonov, a colonel in the Soviet military academy, claimed that

> from indirect sources, I have been able to establish that Stalin took an extremely cautious view of events in Korea and from the outset made every attempt to avoid direct confrontation between the USSR and the USA. Mao was more decisive.[15]

While Stalin and the USA may have set the framework for the Cold War within months of the ending of the Second World War, it seems likely that Kim alone was responsible for initiating the first major engagement of the Cold War era.

15

Aung San: Revolutionary and Turncoat

Burma: 1945–9

Both topographically and racially Burma looks ungovernable. The country is flanked on the west by India and Bangladesh, in the north by China and in the east by Thailand and Laos. Natural boundaries are provided by a horseshoe of mountains and jungle terrain, which are inhabited by ancient tribal peoples hostile to the Burmese majority, who occupy the coastal plains and valleys that intersperse the three great north-to-south rivers of the Irrawaddy, Chindwin and Salween. The tribal peoples use thousands of different languages and dialects: the Mon-Khmers include Mons, Was, Palaungs and Padaungs; Tibeto-Burmans include Burmans, Rakhines, Chins and Kachins; T'ai-Chinese include the Karens, Paus and the Shans; and on the eastern borders are the Nagas of Nagaland.

Burma started to come into conflict with the British Empire in India at the beginning of the nineteenth century, as the expanding kingdom of the Konbaung Dynasty started to encroach on Assam and lay claims to parts of Bengal. The First Anglo-Burmese War ensued. Meanwhile Christian missionaries started the conversion of the oppressed Karen peoples. By the end of the century the Kachins too had largely converted to Christianity. The Second Anglo-Burmese War followed in 1852–3. Divisions within the monarchy were now apparent, and in 1878, King Thibaw murdered 80 of his half brothers and sisters to prevent their plotting to overthrow him. British observers were appalled by Thibaw's barbarity, but full annexation of Burma into Britain's Indian Empire did not take place until 1885–6 after the Third Anglo-Burmese War.

In the next 54 years of Imperial rule, there developed a particularly close relationship with the tribal peoples, many of whom were now Christian, and the British rulers who saw in the Karens, Kachins and Chins exemplary soldier material. The 'tribals' were naturally not averse to overthrowing the natural order of a world which had been dominated by the lowland Burmans. By 1938, the Burmese army consisted of 1,587 British, 1,423 Indians and 3,040 local troops of which just 1 in 39 were Burman. As for officers, the ratio of Burman to 'tribals' was even less. Similar dominance by the 'tribals' was achieved in the police force and in commerce. Moreover, whereas the British exercised direct rule over 'Ministerial

Burma', the tribal hill states were largely left to rule themselves through their traditional chieftains and kings.

Unsurprisingly the Burmans, finding themselves excluded from the institutions of power, started the first organisations aimed at invigorating Burmese society, with the ultimate objective of restoring independence to a Burma dominated by the Burman. In 1906, an English-trained barrister, U May Oung, started the 'Young Men's Buddhist Association'; a decade later a number of nationalist societies were founded along with the General Council of Burmese Associations. Pressure for change brought a separately designated governor for Burma in 1923 and an elected assembly, albeit largely ornamental, in the same year. Technically Burma remained part of British India. However, the establishment of the Home Rule Party by U Pu started to put pressure on the British, and in 1932, the Simon Commission advocated a formal split of Burma's government from the administration of India. The Government of Burma Act was passed in 1935, and the constitutional separation from India duly took place in 1937. It was now apparent that the demand for independent constitutional rule would mirror the progress being made in India.

As in many Asian countries, the ferment for independence in Burma came from the universities. In 1936 two students, Aung San and U Nu (also known as *Thakin Nu*), who would have a profound impact on their country's future, leapt to fame. Having gained control of Rangoon University Students Union, Nu as president and Aung as editor of the union magazine set a radical nationalist agenda and, in 1936, were duly expelled from the university. A student revolt forced the university authorities to reverse their decision.

Aung San was born in central Burma on 13 February 1915. Although from well-off farming stock, Aung's father, U Pha, became a barrister, though his career did not prosper; he then joined the communist resistance to British rule, for which he was duly captured and executed. Aung San, an able student who won a scholarship after coming first in national examinations, went to Rangoon University in 1933. A year earlier the Hsaya San uprising in Burma had ended with the execution of its ringleaders. Aung San's daughter would later describe Aung San as 'a raw country lad, dour of expression and untidy of dress ... '.[1]

Noted for his moral rectitude, Aung presented an aloof public face. Perhaps in conscious imitation of Mahatma Gandhi, Aung and his associates spurned Western dress in favour of homespun cotton *longyis* (sarongs). His reputation for eccentricity was further burnished by his insistence on participating in debates in poor English, although his persistence would eventually lead to a rare proficiency for someone from his country background. While he had had a youthful desire to become a monk, a profession not unsuited to his solitary nature, he believed that there was no room for religion in politics. Nevertheless he would later complain that there was a, 'spiritual vacuum ... among our youth ... unless we brace ourselves to withstand the tide ... we will soon be spiritual bankrupts par excellence'.[2]

However, it was Marxism that became the focus of Aung's religious fervour. He founded a Marxist study group which was in effect Burma's first communist cell. Never a believer in liberal democracy, Aung also admired Europe's totalitarian *Nazi* leaders, and in 1938, he abandoned his law degree to join a fascist-style paramilitary group called *Dobama Ye Tat* (our brave Burma army). The outbreak of war in 1939 presented him with the chance to rapidly promote nationalist aims. 'Colonialism's difficulty' he observed 'is Freedom's opportunity.'[3]

Aung became a founding member of 'Freedom Bloc', an alliance of Ba Maw's Sinyeth Party, *Dohbama Asi-ayone*, and other groups and individuals. Freedom Bloc offered their support to the British conditional on the promise of independence at the end of the war. Britain's refusal to buckle to blackmail led Aung to call for 'mass demonstrations and people's marches leading finally to mass civil disobedience'.[4] Freedom Bloc soon sought weapons for guerrilla activity and sent Aung overseas to look for arms and financial backing. Aung himself observed, '. . . as I was the only one leading an underground existence I was chosen for the task'.[5]

Aung set out for China on 8 August 1940 to seek help from Mao's communists but was intercepted by Japanese agents of the *Kempetai* (Japanese secret police), who persuaded him to fly with them to Tokyo. While the Freedom Bloc members, particularly the communists, including Than Tun, Aung's brother-in-law, were mainly against taking help from Japan, Aung was above all an opportunist. In Tokyo, Aung negotiated support for the Freedom Bloc with Colonel Keiji Suzuki. (Suzuki would later achieve fame and acclaim by Burmese nationalists as head of the *Minami Organ*, a special army unit charged with closing the Burma Road, the supply route between Mandalay to Kunming that had been completed in March 1940).

Aung attempted to curry favour with the Japanese military government by writing a *Blueprint for a Free Burma*, which optimistically assumed that Burma would be an independent entity within the Japanese Co-prosperity Sphere. His motives were plain: 'I went to Japan to save my people who were struggling like Bullocks under the British.'[6] Whatever the Japanese thought of Aung's aspirations, they did enough to convince him of their support. In the guise of a Japanese sailor, he was smuggled back into Burma, where he set about recruitment for a newly formed Burmese Independence Army (BIA). The recruits, later mythologised as the 'Thirty Comrades', were taken for training by the Japanese to Heinan Island off Southern China. In the last batch of recruits was Shu Maung, who later renamed himself Ne Win.

By the time of Japan's invasion of Burma, the BIA comprised just 300 troops who marched back to their own country behind the 55th Division of Lt General Iida Shojiro's 15th Imperial Army. They collected recruits along the way; given the small number of organised supporters, the majority of the new troops were thugs and petty criminals. Aung's BIA soon descended into little more than a criminal rabble that raised money by operating protection rackets.

Former soldiers from the British-run Burmese army were rounded up. The Karen and the Shan were particularly victimised. In some cases they were hacked to pieces; in one such episode 47 Karen were jailed and then taken out and publicly bayoneted. BIA units also burnt Karen villages and raped and murdered their inhabitants. Aung San's 'liberation' of Burma from British rule soon turned into an excuse for ethnic revenge and communal violence. The 'Tribals', favoured by the British, were purged. Their religion, Christianity, was also attacked. At the Catholic mission at Myaunagaya, the BIA shot Father Pascal in the stomach and proceeded to kill the women. Father Gaspar was burnt to death while another priest was axed in the back and murdered along with four lay sisters. The march of the BIA into Burma was hardly the occasion of great pride and joy to the Burmese,[6] which Aung San Suu Kyi describes in her biography of her father.

Indeed, Aung San himself indulged in the orgy of killing. In 1942 a Muslim village headman of Byugaone village in Thaton district, who was accused of helping the British, was taken by the BIA and locked up for eight days without food. His execution was publicly announced, and on the appointed day, Aung had the victim taken out to the village football pitch where he was strapped to a goal post. With his own hands, Aung San disemboweled the prisoner with a bayonet. Aung's casual explanation of his actions in the *Thadisone Journal* of 12 April 1946 suggests that this was not an exceptional incident. 'All that I remember is that the headman was a wicked person who ill treated his villagers . . . it was also reported to me that the offences he committed merit no less a punishment than death.'[7]

Such was the brutality and administrative chaos caused by the BIA that even the Japanese were appalled. In July 1942, the Japanese government disbanded Aung's army and proceeded to organise the Burma Defence Army with Japanese officers and NCOs. Predictably Japan also ignored the nationalists' demand for independent government and established a Japanese military regime that was a standard model for the Co-Prosperity Sphere. Meanwhile the 'tribals' who had formed the backbone of the British Burmese army slipped back to the hills with their weapons and started to form the backbone of the resistance to the Japanese. For the retreating tribesmen, however, their hatred of the Japanese was only exceeded by their distrust of the Burmese nationalists. The BIA's indiscriminate slaughter of the 'tribals', after their triumphant entry into Burma behind the Japanese army, created an atmosphere of revenge and distrust, which coloured all attempts at post-war settlement of the Burmese constitution.

During the course of the war, the relationship between the 'tribals' and the West was further burnished by the daring exploits of two groups who provided the first victories over the Japanese army in the Second World War. American–Chinese forces, trained in India, attacked and defeated the Japanese divisions sent to impede the building of the new India-to-China supply road; Merrill's Marauders, as this force became known, relied heavily on the local knowledge of Kachin Rangers. They were ferocious fighters. When General Stilwell asked a Kachin

Ranger to justify his Japanese kill claims after a raid, 'The Kachin opened a bamboo tube and dumped a pile of dry ears on the table. "Divide by two," he told Stilwell.'[8] The Kachin fighters also prevented the stationing of Japanese Zero fighter aircraft at air bases in the north.

Meanwhile the Karens were organised for guerrilla warfare by the special operations executive (SOE). The SOE 136 Unit, based in the jungle uplands above Sinlum Kaba, proved a constant thorn in the rear of the Japanese army and held down a 30,000 strong enemy force. Similarly, Brigadier Orde Wingate's Chindits, supplied from the air, wrought havoc behind the Japanese army and successfully captured the Japanese air base at Myitkyina. (The Chindits, named after the Burmese mythical beast *Chinthé*, were a special guerrilla force organised from the 77th Indian Infantry Brigade, which then became a model for Merril's Marauders.) Although the war in Burma was eventually won by regular forces, the 'tribals' wartime efforts, rightly lauded by allied officers, were due some political reward. Indeed in the final 'Battle of the Break', the Karen forces alone killed 12,000 Japanese troops. General Slim, who commanded the Anglo-Indian forces that inflicted the most crushing military defeats in Japanese history at the battles of Kohima and Imphal, described the Karens as a, 'race which had remained staunchly loyal to us even in the blackest days of Japanese occupation, and had suffered accordingly ...'.[9]

While the Karens and Kachins were fighting the Japanese, Aung San, who had been promoted to the rank of major general in the Burma National Army (BNA, changed from Burma Defence Army by the Japanese), was personally decorated by Emperor Hirohito in Tokyo. In January of that year, Tojo had promised Burmese independence; however, Aung San who, according to his daughter, 'did not take it [the promise of independence] terribly seriously'[10] nevertheless bided his time until March of 1945 to bring the Burma Defence Army into open conflict with the losing Japanese. On 17 March 1945, Aung San had led the BNA out of Rangoon under the salute of Japan's senior officer in Burma, Lt General Kimura Heitaro; Aung then proceeded to attack Japanese positions.

Although it was later suggested that Aung San had backed anti-Japanese guerrilla forces after 1943, there seems little evidence other than his daughter's assertions to support this claim. In spite of his last-minute conversion to the allied cause at a moment when Japanese defeat appeared inevitable, Aung did not lack for chutzpah when it came to dealing with the allied commanders. In spite of not knowing the whereabouts of his supposed forces, on meeting General Slim in May 1945, Aung 'was, he said, the representative of the Provisional Government of Burma, which had been set up by the people of Burma through the Anti-Fascist People's Freedom League [AFPFL] ... he was an Allied commander who was prepared to co-operate ...'.[11]

While informing Aung that his military help was not required and reminding him that he was a traitor and an accused murderer, General Slim was nevertheless

impressed by the man before him. 'He was not the ambitious, unscrupulous guerrilla leader I had expected. He was certainly ambitious and meant to secure for
himself a dominant position in post-war Burma.'[12] Aung's determination to learn
English and his quiet unassuming manner certainly enabled him to win over key
people. Most importantly, he won over Admiral Mountbatten, then Supreme Allied
Commander in South East Asia, and a man easily impressed by Asians with urbane
manners and socialist leanings.

By contrast both the Civil Affairs Service in Burma and General Leese, Commander in Chief of South East Asian Forces, believed that the BNA should not be
allowed a position of power in the reconstruction of Burma. For them Aung and
his troops were Japanese collaborators and any attempt to integrate them into the
government of post-war Burma would inevitably lead to rancour. Also, Aung was
no constitutional democrat. In 1941 he had written that 'What we want is a strong
state administration as exemplified in Germany and Italy. There shall be only one
nation, one state, one party, one leader. There shall be no parliamentary opposition, no nonsense of individualism.'[13] Not surprisingly, the Burmese authorities
knew that Aung and the BNA leadership presented an obstacle to the creation of
a stable post-war constitutional settlement; their prosecution was recommended
to Mountbatten. In a foretaste of his catastrophic rule in India, Mountbatten overruled his experts and also ignored the contrary opinions of Winston Churchill.

The English-speaking and smooth-talking Aung San had quickly seduced
Mountbatten. 'I am completely on their side',[14] he said of Aung and the BNA.
At a dinner given in Rangoon, Mountbatten refused to speak unless Aung was also
invited to do so. The left-wing journalist and MP Tom Driberg subsequently noted
that 'Aung San's was the speech of the evening.'[15]

From this point Aung's Burmese nationalists would always be in the driving
seat of Burma's constitutional future. The 27th March, the day when Aung turned
the BNA against the Japanese, was henceforth celebrated as Resistance Day; the
wartime contribution of the 'tribals' in the defeat of Japan was conveniently overlooked. On the retaking of Rangoon, Ne Win took the opportunity to broadcast
to the nation that the BNA was, 'not only the hope of the country but its real life
and soul ...'.[16]

The rewriting of history was completed when Dr Maung Maung, Ne Win's
biographer, wrote in 1969 that '... we won the war, and allied effort was of small
significance'.[17] In a memo to Prime Minister Attlee, Major the Reverend James
Baldwin, who had fought with the Karens of Unit 136, reported that after the war,

> people are forced to recognise the AFPFL in district areas where Military CAS (B)
> Government delayed to enter. No jubilation or rejoicing permitted at entry of
> Allies (14th Army) into Burma. Sympathetic allegiance to the returning British by
> village headmen and others was severely crushed. Strong propaganda directed to be-
> littling liberation of Burma by 14th Army_ all made to believe AFPFL ... routed
> Japanese'.[18]

Aung and his colleagues in the AFPFL deliberately set out to pervert the history of Burma's liberation and embed themselves as the only party of government. Through negligence and weakness, Mountbatten and Attlee simply helped Burma on its way towards the Nazi-style government favoured by Aung.

In the post-war chaos, Britain had set up a temporary military administration to rule Burma for a maximum three-year period. Power was vested in a governor working with the Civil Affairs Service (Burma). As for the future of the tribal minorities, it was decided that they would be 'subject to a special regime under the governor until such time as the inhabitants signify their desire for some suitable form of an amalgamation of their territories with Burma Proper'.[19] While the priority for the British authorities was a period of stability to help Burma recover from the ravages of a war which had decimated rice production, Aung and the nationalists sought an immediate grasp of power.

Within a week of the Japanese surrender, Aung was elected president of the AFPFL; ignoring his many years of service in the invading Japanese Imperial Army, in his election speech Aung had the chutzpah to boast of the achievements of the anti-Japanese resistance and called for the military administration to be replaced immediately by a provisional government provided by the AFPFL. Even an offer by Governor Dorman-Smith to give the AFPFL seven out of 11 seats on an executive council did not satisfy Aung. Faced by his refusal to co-operate, Dorman-Smith appointed loyalist politicians led by Sir Paw Tun and three minority members. Ominously Aung San warned that Paw Tun did not know where the dumps of arms were hidden.

However silver tongued and plausible as a politician, Aung understood the power of the gun. Critically he outmanoeuvred Mountbatten over the issue of Burma's reconstructed army. New divisions were created in the Burmese army to accommodate 5,200 BNA soldiers and 200 of their officers. At the same time Aung brought 3,500 former Japanese-trained colleagues into a paramilitary force, the *Pyithu Yebaw Ahphwe* (PVO: People's Volunteer Organisation), which remained directly under his command. With an impoverished Britain increasingly withdrawing resources from the region, Aung and his PVO were able to impose their military power on Burma's political settlement. Lord Wavell, the experienced army general and colonialist, commented that Aung 'struck me as a suspicious, ignorant but determined little tough';[20] it was an accurate assessment.

In effect Aung bypassed Britain's interim arrangements. At the first League Congress in January 1946, he attracted some 100,000 supporters and used the occasion to denounce Governor Dorman-Smith. Although Sir Paw Tun wanted Aung arrested for sedition and another member of the executive council, Tun Ok, called for the new Burmese leader to be tried for a murder, which he himself had witnessed, the British now judged it was too late and probably too dangerous to halt Aung's bandwagon. Mountbatten meekly submitted to the situation; regarding the murder he merely commented that 'In the unsettled conditions which must have existed, it was only to be expected, I suppose, that summary justice would rule, and that old scores would be paid off.'[21]

A sick and disillusioned Dorman-Smith returned to England to be replaced by Sir Hubert Rance in August 1946. The demoralised British administration, disastrously undermined by Mountbatten and the withdrawal of resources by Attlee's Labour government, could do little more than organise a handover of power as best as they could. When the Rangoon police went on strike soon after Rance's arrival, Aung's PVO took over the policing of Rangoon. In effect, he forced his way onto Rance's new executive council which now gave him six out of nine seats. Just one seat was allocated to the Karen. With his position strengthened, Aung also sought to purge the League of his enemies. The communists, who had turned against the Japanese as early as 1942, almost a year before Aung's BNA, were now outmanoeuvred by their erstwhile supporter and expelled from the League on 20 October.

With Aung now demanding independence within the year and hinting at open rebellion if he did not get it, Attlee called a delegation of Burmese for talks in London. Reneging on pledges made by Mountbatten and British officers that the tribal areas would not be handed over to the Burmans, Attlee concluded an agreement with Aung on 27 January 1947, stating that the 'objective of both His Majesty's government and the Burmese Delegates [was] to achieve the early unification of the Frontier Areas and Ministerial Burma ... '.[22]

Although this was to be achieved 'with the free consent of the inhabitants of these areas',[23] nobody was in any doubt as to who had gained the upper hand. Attlee, eager to wash his hands off this bothersome problem, simply ignored Noel Stevenson, the director of the Frontier Areas administration, who warned, 'I have come to the regrettable conclusion that the present Karen quiescence means simply that they refuse to quarrel with us. But if we go ... the war for the Karen State will start.'[24] As a face-saving excuse to cover Clement Attlee's 'sell out' of the 'tribals', the agreement with Aung provided for a Frontier Areas Committee of Enquiry (appropriately abbreviated to FACE) to determine the wishes of the minorities. It was a sham. A disillusioned Stevenson duly resigned.

Reaction from the 'tribals' was swift. A week after the Aung–Attlee agreement the Karens announced their intention to be an independent state. On 6 February the Shans, Kachins and Chins, who had not been represented in London, also refused to accept the agreement. Aung sought to smooth the fears of the tribal minorities by holding a meeting between a League delegation and the 'tribals' in the market town of Panglong on 12 February.

An agreement was drawn up with the 'tribals' whose meaning has been a subject of hot dispute ever since. Clause 5 stated that

> Through the Governor's Executive Council will be augmented as agreed above [by the appointment of hill peoples representatives to advise it on matters pertaining to the Frontier Areas] it will not operate in respect of the Frontier Area in any manner

which would deprive any portion of these areas of the autonomy which it now enjoys in internal administration. Full autonomy in internal administration for the Frontier Area is accepted in principle.[25]

Aung also guaranteed equal government expenditure on the Frontier Areas: 'If Burma [proper] receives one kyat, you will also get one kyat.'[26] It was a promise not kept. More importantly, Aung and the League interpreted the meeting as the 'tribals' having agreed to the union; even now 12 February is celebrated as Union Day. For the 'tribals', however, the agreement was supposedly a guarantee of autonomy.

To add further to the confusion, the Karen delegation arrived too late to participate. Neither were the Chins, Was, Nagas, Lushais, Palaungs, Paos, Akhas, Lahus and many others represented at the talks. While the minorities were frequently divided and in conflict, the one thing on which they all agreed was their preference for tribal autonomy. As the Karen leader Saw Po Chit said during a delegation to London in 1946, 'Karens are a nation according to any definition. We are a nation with our own distinctive culture and civilisation, language, literature, names, nomenclature, sense of value and proportion, customary laws and moral codes, aptitudes and ambitions; . . . By all canons of international law we are a nation.'[27]

When elections were held for the Constituent Assembly on 7 April 1947, the tribal minorities refused to participate while Burmans were forced to the polling station under Aung's PVO supervision. Those opposition candidates, who did put themselves forward, were intimidated into withdrawal; in the end only 28 opposition candidates stood for election. A former Burmese civil servant Mr Maybury wrote to the New Statesmen in 1949 and recalled that, prior to the elections, '. . . the semblance of unity between the Burmese and the Minority races were obtained by methods with which Hitler and Stalin have made familiar'.[28] Taking their orders from the top, the British troops stood back and watched pantomime democracy in action. An officer of the Welsh Regiment wrote, '. . . we were amazed at the flagrant intimidation and even more so when we spotted the British commander of the force, Captain Jimmy Battle, standing in the crowd and doing absolutely nothing'.[29] The 255 members of the Constituent Assembly met on 9 June and elected Nu as their president. Immediately, Aung carried a resolution that would take an independent Burma out of the Commonwealth.

Having achieved absolute power, jockeying for position within the League began in earnest. The League itself had been a marriage of convenience for different nationalist groups and these now began to splinter. Ba Pa, long considered the father of Burmese nationalism, was removed from the National Council. Aung was now intent on a Stalinist-style purge of his party. In May 1947 he suggested that the 'AFPFL and affiliated people's organisations should carry out a thorough cleansing process right through in order to be purged of rottenness in the blood.'[30] Kyaw

Nyein, co-head of the Socialist Party within the League with Ba, was also accused of theft of excise tax. Kyaw Nyein clearly feared that he would be next to be purged by his ruthless leader; working with Nyein, Ne Win started to build a private army to rival the staunchly pro-Aung PVO. Ne Win himself doubted his future under Aung, who had always disliked his drinking and womanising.

The struggle for power within the League came to its bloody resolution on Saturday, 19 July 1947. At 10.30 am four men wearing the uniforms of the 14th Army, but who were actually soldiers from Ne Win's 4th Burma Rifles, burst into a meeting of the Executive Council of the interim Burmese government. Aung San, who was chairing the meeting, stood up and was immediately gunned down by the intruders' 'Tommy' guns along with eight colleagues. ('Tommy' subma-chine guns with their drum cartridge magazine, which became notorious during the 'prohibition era', were inspired by General John Thompson and made by the Auto Ordnance Corporation). Conveniently, Kyaw Nyein was in Yugoslavia. The supposed killers were apprehended and one of them apparently turned king's evi-dence to implicate the nationalist politician U Saw, who, as leader of the Myochit Party, might well have been called by Governor Rance to replace Aung. On flimsy evidence, U Saw was found guilty and hanged.

Serious doubts about the trial and verdict persisted however, and the episode became murkier still when a senior police officer, Colin Tooke, who was investi-gating the case, was found murdered by a poisonous toxin. The real hands behind the assassins may never be known for sure. However, the Reverend James Baldwin surmised that the biggest winners from Aung's death were Kyaw Nyein, Ne Win and U Nu. U Nu was prime minister for the next 13 years, while Ne Win was given a double promotion to brigadier and, on 1 February 1949, became Supreme Com-mander of the Armed Forces. Most likely these men were his killers. For Aung, his own untimely death was not altogether unexpected. Before Dorman-Smith left Burma, Aung apparently told him, 'how long do national heroes last? Not long in this country; they have too many enemies. Three years is the most they can hope to survive. I do not give myself more than another eighteen months of life'.[31]

In one sense Aung was wrong. His early death guaranteed his fame as a nation-alist and martyr. His reputation was fortunate not to have been tarnished by the realities of rule. Had he succeeded in purging his enemies and establishing what would, in effect, have been a Nazi style dictatorship, Aung's reputation as a free-dom fighter and democrat, albeit fake, would inevitably have been sullied.

That he had managed to get his position of power was itself a stroke of for-tune, largely dependent as it was on Edwina Mountbatten's persuasion of her hus-band that all nationalist movements were desirable and should be supported. As Mountbatten later admitted, 'Nobody gave me an idea of the strength of the na-tionalist movements. Edwina was the first person to give me an inkling of what was going on.'[32] As Tom Driberg was to comment in a laudatory and wholly inaccurate assessment, 'She showed an instant sympathy with any Asian nationalist who was being oppressed by some American-backed regime.'[33] Thus he chose to ignore the fact that Aung had been a staunch ally of the Japanese and had subsequently sub-jugated the Burmese tribals with terror tactics where necessary. Nationalism for Burma was not to mean independence for the tribals upon whom the British had relied so heavily during the war.

Neither would Aung San's national-socialist, command economy leanings have produced a vibrant economy; in an address on 23 May 1947 Aung Sang re-vealed that 'Only by building our economic system in such a way as to enable our country to get over capitalism in the quickest possible time can we attain a true democracy.'[34] Like all the other Asian countries that marched down the totalitar-ian socialist path, it is certain that the experiment would have ended in failure.

Moreover, Aung Sang's Nazi sentiments, and belief in a centrally unified Burma, would hardly have solved the intractable problem presented by the tribal minori-ties. However, Aung's greatest stroke of fortune, in relation to his reputation, has been the daughter he never knew, Aung San Suu Kyi. She was just two years old when he died, and her saintly life and courageous fight to overthrow Burma's mili-tary rulers have thrown a golden light over her father's name. It is not deserved.

16

Sukarno: The Founding Father

Indonesia: 1945—50

Sukarno, an engineering student, started an incipient nationalist movement in 1928 called the *Partai Nasional Indonesia* aimed at the overthrow of Dutch colonial rule in Indonesia. Sukarno was a typical product of the emerging urban intelligentsia. A student at Technische Hoogeschool, he founded the *Algemene Studieclub* (general study club) in 1924 and became an early leader of a proto-independence movement. Over time he became a mesmeric speaker who, in classic demagogue style, was able to draw his audiences into moods of reverential ecstasy. Contemporary journalist John Hughes described him as 'the superb entertainer, performer, manipulator'.[1] Like many revolutionary communist leaders before and after, Sukarno would find no discrepancy in his attacks on imperialism and capitalism with his own penchant for limousines, glamorous consorts and grandiose palaces.

In part, Sukarno, like most of Asia's proto-nationalists, was influenced by Marxist–Leninism as well as nationalist movements in India and more significantly China. However, the defining problem for him was how to identify Indonesia (etymologically a pseudo-Hellenic name) as a nation, when it consisted of an archipelago of some 10,000 islands and at least 200 separate cultures. Never before in its history had the archipelago been federated into anything that could be described as a 'nation'. Sukarno's answer, and perhaps his greatest contribution to the creation of the state of Indonesia, similar to the strategy adopted by Nehru and Gandhi in India, was to create a mythology of nationhood out of Java's 'medieval' past.

The first major power to emerge was the seventh-century Buddhist kingdom of Srivajaya from Southern Sumatra, whose maritime prowess enabled it to dominate the archipelago. By contrast, the eighth-century kingdom of Mataram, based in Java, was a largely introspective rice-growing culture. Not until the thirteenth-century did Java become regionally expansive, as the Srivajaya kingdom fell into permanent decline. According to the court poet Mpu Prapanca in his epic fourteenth-century poem *Nagarakertagama* (Depiction of Districts), Gadja Mada of the Madjapahit Dynasty subjugated not only the modern-day Indonesian archipelago, but also Malaya, Borneo, Sumatra and parts of the Philippines. It seems likely that Mpu Prapanca's poem was largely fictional. Nevertheless, it was propaganda that would serve a convenient purpose for Sukarno.

Standing trial in a Bandung court for public disorder charges in 1930, Sukarno would assert that

> Even a child if he looks at a map of the world, can point out that the Indonesian archipelago forms one unity. On the map there can be shown a unity for the group of islands between two great oceans, the Pacific and the Indian Ocean, and between the two continents, the continent of Asia and the continent of Australia.[2]

Historically and geographically, this was pure invention.

Yet Sukarno was quite content to harness invention to turn the nationalist wheel. Again at his trial he declaimed:

> We had a glorious past; we had a period of brilliance! Your honours, can there be one Indonesian whose heart does not sigh as he hears the story of those beautiful times?. . . . Where is the Indonesian who does not sigh as he remembers the flag of bygone days, seen and honoured as far a field as Madagascar, Persia, and China.[3]

After independence, Indonesian academics would buff up the myth of Indonesia's historic nationhood. Published in 1959, Mohammad Yamin's *A Legal and Historical Review of Indonesia's Sovereignty over the Ages* concluded that historic Indonesia comprised 'the Malay peninsula, the islands of Sumatra, of Kalimantan, of Java . . . the islands of Sulawesi, the group of the Moluccas and the territory of West Irian'.[4]

Whatever the reality of Java's overseas kingdom, it could only have been short-lived. In 1414 the port city of Malacca on the Malay Peninsula adopted Islam and set out on a century of mercantile expansion, which took the religion throughout the Indonesian archipelago. Though Catholic Portugal conquered Malacca in 1511, Islam became increasingly embedded in Java, where the Mataram Empire became dominant in the sixteenth and seventeenth centuries. By the early seventeenth century, the Portuguese had been displaced by the Dutch as the main mercantile power of the region. The year 1619 saw incorporation of the *Verenigde Oost-Indische Compagnie* (VOC; better known as the Dutch United India Company). Although the VOC's monopoly charter eventually collapsed, leading to the charter not being renewed in 1799, the Dutch military and commercial presence continued. Their control of Java and Sumatra was formalised in an Anglo-Dutch Treaty of 1824 which also ceded control of the Malay Peninsula to Britain.

The treaty was followed by a war of liberation against the Dutch waged by Prince Diponegoro from 1825 to 1830. Thereafter, the Dutch operated very much as a 'protection racket' by taking 20 per cent levies of all produce, and it was not until the 1870s that the beginnings of a colonial administration were formed. In a pattern similar to apartheid as applied by the Dutch Boers in South Africa after the Second World War, they also introduced a caste system, which bestowed separate legal status on Dutch, racially mixed and indigenous races.

By the 1920s, Dutch rule in Indonesia had hardened into a harsh authoritarian regime bent on mercantilist exploitation. Governor General De Jonge proclaimed, 'We have ruled here for 300 years with the whip and club and we shall still be doing it in another 300 years.'[5] Even now there was no attempt to create a united state of Indonesia. Jakarta, rather like New Delhi to the British in India, became an administrative centre for the governance of numbers of sub-colonies, which were treated as independent states, rather than part of some greater identifiable nation.

In fact it was the defeat of the Dutch by Japan in 1941, and the subsequent Japanese rule of Indonesia, which significantly propelled the cause of national unity. By 1943 the Japanese had trained young Javanese Muslims into a 35,000 strong Auxiliary Army, which came to be known as the *Peta*, a Volunteer Army of Defenders of the Fatherland (*Tentuara Sukarela Pembela Tanah Air*); this force would ultimately become Indonesia's liberating army, the so-called ABRI (*Angkatan Bersenjata Indonesia*), in the post-war conflict with the Dutch.

While the Japanese ruled with their customary brutality, indeed few of the 300,000 Indonesians transported to labour camps survived, Indonesia is probably the best support, albeit tenuous, of Japan's spurious post-war claim that their Asian war liberated Asia. By necessity, Japanese rulers promoted Indonesians to senior roles in government administration and also encouraged the use of *Market Malay* as the national language. *Market Malay*, also *Bahasa Indonesia*, was a language of traders and merchants from the fourteenth century, which had begun to be more broadly adopted in the region at the beginning of the twentieth century.

Without question, the overrunning of the Dutch by Japan was a considerable boon to a nationalist movement, which in the 1920s was largely the plaything of the educated urban elite. Although Sukarno founded the Partai Nationalist Indonesia (PNI) in 1928, the nationalist movement remained shallow rooted. Indeed, by far the largest organisation in the region was the *Muhammadiyah*, founded in 1912, that was a largely social and educational organisation, whose defining principle was Islam, not Indonesia.

Not surprisingly perhaps, Sukarno came to view the supra-national philosophy of Islam as almost as much a threat to Indonesian nationalism as foreign imperialism. Though some 80 per cent of the population of Indonesia was Muslim, the followers of Islam split quite evenly between devout followers, known as the *santri* and the *abangan* who loosely followed a Muslim faith, intertwined with ancient Javanese religions based on 'Animism'; the *abangan* synthesised Islam with stories from both the Hindu *Ramayana* and *Mahabarata*.

Hinduism had become the dominant religion of Java in the eighth century, before it was succeeded by Buddhism in the tenth century, producing at Borabadur, near Jogyajakarta, the largest Buddhist temple in the world. Except on the island of Bali, where Hinduism remained the dominant religion, most of the archipelago was later converted again from Buddhism to Islam. In his famous *Birth of Pancasila* speech of 1 June 1945, Sukarno, while doffing his cap at Islam, made it clear that Indonesia would not be an exclusively Islamic state: 'The Prophet Mohammed gave sufficient proofs of tolerance, of respect for other religions; Jesus Christ also showed tolerance.'[6]

Faced by Indonesia's topographical diverse archipelago and its many races, cultures and religions, in addition to the dubious historiography of the region, it is perhaps not surprising that Sukarno sought a syncretic political philosophy to bridge the seemingly irreconcilable differences in indigenous beliefs. Thus, *Pancasila* (meaning five principles) was developed as the national ideology. The five principles identified included social justice, a just and civilised humanity, belief in one god, Indonesian unity and government by deliberation and consent. These homogenised, bland and somewhat vague principles became the bedrock of Indonesian political thought. By themselves they were not strong enough meat to grip the masses. Sukarno, a skilled populist, had other messages to stir the people.

While some early nationalists sought inspiration from President Wilson's plea for self-determination in the 14 points issued prior to the Versailles Peace Conference, Sukarno soon adopted socialism as the unifying ideology for Indonesian nationalism. In addition to anti-colonialism, socialism would remain a constant article of faith. Western imperialism was an issue not just for Indonesia but for all of Asia; as early as 1927, Sukarno questioned, 'how Asia could shake off the yoke of England and America'.[7]

In spite of his anti-Americanism, Sukarno nevertheless used the example of American independence as a paradigm of the anti-colonialist struggle. At the Asia–Africa conference hosted by Sukarno at Bandung in April 1955, a conference which became synonymous with the Nehru-inspired 'non-aligned' movement, Sukarno, displaying a chronic ignorance of European history, cited the example of the American Revolution as the earliest exponent of colonial resistance:

> On the 18th day of April 1775, just one hundred and eighty years ago, Paul Revere rode at midnight through the New England countryside, warning of the approach of British troops and of the opening of the American War of Independence, the first successful anti-colonial war in history.[8]

Sukarno saw no contradiction between this belief and his utter distaste for the USA.

Sukarno's hatred of America was poor reward for the helping hand proffered by the US government in the immediate post-war period. General MacArthur's order to Mountbatten, to delay an invasion of Indonesia until after the Japanese had signed the Instrument of Surrender on 2 September 1945, gave Sukarno time to organise the new republic. More importantly, neither Mountbatten nor MacArthur pressed for action against the nationalist leaders, including Sukarno and Dr Hatta, who had conspired so vigorously with the Japanese against the Allies.

Mountbatten's forces, under the South East Asia Command (SEAC) to whom responsibility had been passed from MacArthur's South West Pacific Area (SWPA), simply occupied the main ports and their periphery, and waited for the political situation to sort itself out; however, both the Americans and the British displayed a strong bias against the permanent return of the Dutch. This was in spite of frequent atrocities against the occupying British forces. Captain Telfer Smollett, aide-de-camp to Lieutenant General Christison in Batavia, recalled that they viewed Sukarno and his forces as little better than terrorists; in one appalling incident retold by Telfer Smollet, after a British Dakota from India crash landed, the Indian troops aboard were taken down to a river and hacked to pieces.

That British politicians were fighting their cause was not immediately apparent to the Indonesian nationalists. Indonesians would later celebrate the military clashes against the British in the city of Surabaya as 'Heroes Day' on 10 November; in reality these military actions were never more than minor skirmishes with the occupying British forces.

If the Indonesians thought that Britain and America were paving the way for a resumption of Dutch rule, they proved to be wildly mistaken. While a government spokesman stated on 20 October 1945 that the USA 'would be prepared to lend assistance, if requested to do so, in efforts to reach peaceful agreements in these disturbed areas',[9] in practice, Washington and London worked unceasingly to prevent the return of Dutch colonial rule. Sukarno's post-independence mythmaking has tended to further obscure the central role played by the Allied powers in securing an independent Indonesia.

When the battalion of Seaforth Highlanders landed in Java on the 28 November as an advance party of a 12,000-strong British force, Dutch personnel were excluded. In November 1945, Washington prohibited shipment of Dutch arms to Java. The Dutch government was further incensed when Secretary of State Dean Acheson instructed the American consul general to inform Van Mook, the Dutch consul, that '. . . the United States recognises de facto jurisdiction of the Republic of Indonesia in Sumatra, Java and Madura'.[10]

However, the USA could not prevent Holland, as a sovereign state, from pouring troops back into Indonesia at the earliest opportunity. The Dutch government, like France, failed to come to grips with the post-war reality of European power in Asia. The Japanese army's rapid sweep through Europe's Asian Empires had called the pre-war bluff of European government's military and financial muscle; once Europe's flabby underbelly was exposed, there was no turning back the nationalist tide. Van Mook, who had spent the war in Brisbane, was guilty of grossly underestimating the nationalist sway in Indonesia, although it is doubtful that even a realistic analysis of the situation would have brought the Dutch government to yield independence.

On 22 August 1946, the USA tabled a resolution at the United Nations Security Council, which provided for the setting up of a Committee of Good Offices (CGO) in Indonesia. Representatives of Australia, Belgium and the USA were selected, and the group arrived in Indonesia on 27 October with the aim of reconciling the Dutch government to an independence solution.

However, the American push for a peaceful settlement was not entirely driven by a benign interest in Indonesian self-determination. Already by 1948, America's interest in Indonesia increasingly focused on the threat of a Communist takeover. The pre-war communist leader Musso returned from the Soviet Union in August 1948 and installed a new leadership in the PKI (Indonesian Communist Party), which rejected the interim Linggadjati Agreement between Holland and the Republic of Indonesia. (Linggadjati is a small village in Central Java where the agreement was signed.) Musso demanded an uprising against 'Sukarno-Hatta, the slaves of the Japanese and America'.[11]

The American State Department reacted with alarm; a memo of 3 September 1948 concluded that 'The fall of the Hatta government, which is almost certain within a short time unless rapid progress is made in the settlement of this dispute, will inevitably result in a left wing government and in increasing disturbances.'[12] This led Secretary of State Marshall to instruct Bernard Baruch, the US ambassador at The Hague, that pressure should be brought to bear on the Dutch government to reach a final settlement with Sukarno and his Prime Minister Dr Hatta. As the historian Theodore Friend has pointed out, 'the Indonesian nationalists could be seen as allies in the Cold War _ a transfiguration never possible for the Vietnamese nationalist government, which was always led by communists'.[13]

The Dutch were furious. Foreign Minister Stikker stormed at Marshall and his advisors: 'Do you really believe that the advice of a handful of people who have been in Indonesia during three months is more worth than the experience which we have won there in more than three centuries?'[14]

In Indonesia, events now unfolded rapidly. In the autumn, Hatta's Republican government crushed a Stalinist uprising at Madiun. In November the PKI leaders were arrested and executed. At the same time the Dutch launched a military offensive against Indonesian forces and ordered the arrest of Hatta, Sukarno and the Indonesian leadership. America reacted by suspension of Marshall aid to Holland worth US\$ 72.7 million. The Dutch meanwhile ignored United Nations Security Council resolutions. They probably hoped that Indonesian Nationalism, stirred by the Japanese, would quietly fade away.

Pressure from the USA and the United Nations was unyielding, however. In November the Dutch agreed to acknowledge a federated union of 15 states, known as the Republic of the United States of Indonesia. The province of West Irian, a future bone of contention, was to remain under Dutch control. The new republic was forced to assume Netherlands East Indies debts of US\$ 339 million, which, from the outset, burdened Indonesia's primitive economy. Truman sent a strong message of support to Sukarno on 16 December:

> I have followed the course of events in your country very closely for the past several years. I have greatly admired the high statesmanship with which you, Dr. Hatta and your colleagues contributed with such distinction to the splendid settlements at The Hague which have provided independence and sovereignty to your country.... The

US welcomes Indonesia into the family of independent peace-loving nations. May God grant you and your people peace and prosperity in the years to come.[15]

On 27 December, Sukarno was sworn into office as president, with Hatta as his first prime minister. Sukarno, like Nehru in India, immediately sought a centralisation of his country that the Western colonists had never attempted. On 17 August 1950, Sukarno unilaterally abolished the Republic of the United States of Indonesia and introduced a centralised unitary state.

17

Independence and the Racial Contract

Malaysia: 1945–57

In addition to the Malay Peninsula, the Malay language is common to Indonesia, Sarawak, Borneo and Singapore; regional variations take Malay further to the Philippines, the Japanese island of Okinawa, the Ryukyu Islands, the Cape, Surinam and Madagascar. Like the Philippines and Indonesia however, the Malay Peninsular was never a unified country, let alone a nation state in any modern sense, until the arrival of Europeans set the preconditions to the development of a national entity. The Sultanate of Johor was the most powerful state in the region, but was always one of many. For the most part, the Malay Peninsula comprised a primitive feudal structure consisting of *Kampungs* (clusters of villages) which were largely self-sufficient in rice and fish, the staple diets.

For the most part, the interior of the country was impenetrable jungle. The first European traders were mainly Dutch and Portuguese; the latter establishing a thriving port at Malacca after its capture in 1511. The Straits of Malacca, which divide the modern-day Singapore from the Indonesian island of Sumatra, became recognised as being of significant strategic importance after the growth of trade between India and China.

British interest first settled on Penang which, reflecting British ascendancy in the region, soon outstripped Malacca in importance. By 1826, Britain was powerful enough to establish a 'Straits Settlement' on Penang, Singapore and Malacca; however, there was little interest in the Malay interior, and the British pursued a policy of studied non-intervention.

Even when the status of the British ports was formalised by the Treaty of Pangkor with the Malay Sultans in 1874, it was evident that British policy was to maintain a light touch; The secretary of state confirmed that Britain had 'no desire to interfere in the internal affairs of the Malay State'.[1] Nevertheless, the treaty did give Britain a mandate to mediate disputes between the Malay states. The development of a 'Resident' system, which placed a British representative at the courts of the various principalities, also lead to effective 'protection' of the Malay Peninsula and developed the origins of a federated political structure that exists to the current day.

If Britain had little political interest in imposing itself on the development of the Malay states, economic pressures would soon bring about radical developments in the makeup of Malay society. There had been tin mining in Malaysia for some time, but the economic boom, which followed the American Civil War, accompanied by the invention of the tin can, brought rapid growth in demand for tinned meat, fish, milk and vegetables. The development of new industrial processes also brought demand for rubber, which plantations in Malaysia could supply. British traders and entrepreneurs were quick to seize the opportunity, but needing skilled labour, which was only reluctantly offered by indigenous Malays, they had to look elsewhere for workers.

The result was the first great wave of Chinese immigration, which would lead to the Malay population being reduced to a minority by 1934. In that year, the Malay population amounted to just 34.7 per cent compared to a Chinese population of 41.5 per cent and an Indian population of 22.2 per cent. Even more remarkably, the Malay population of the rapidly expanding urban centres was just 10 per cent. Rapid changes taking place in Malaysian society seemed to have little impact on the social order. The sultans and the Malay elite, secure in their power through British protection, had no wish to change the status quo. With freedom to trade and prosper, neither was there much complaint from the Malay states' new Chinese immigrants.

As the Malaysian economy developed into an exporter of tin and rubber, mainly to the USA, which by 1929 accounted for 42 per cent of Malay exports compared to 14 per cent to the United Kingdom, British companies such as London Tin, Sime Derby, Dunlop and Guthrie became increasingly successful. Through the influence of their lobbyists, British rule inevitably began to encroach on the political structures of the Malay Peninsula.

As with commerce, much of the new administration ended up in the hands of the Chinese. There was a dearth of English-speaking Malays, and the Malay Administrative Service (MAS) was set up to attract members of the aristocracy and elite families. As W.H. Treacher, resident general of the Federated Malay States, commented in 1904, in the typical patronising manner reserved for native Malays, 'I do not despair of Malays eventually becoming valuable public servants in the higher grades of the civil service.'[2] However, training the Malays proved an intractable problem, and the MAS, in large part, proved a failure.

Nevertheless, the British ruled with a relatively light hand. Compared to other South East Asian countries, colonial resentment, nationalist movements and communism found less fertile roots in pre-war Malaysia than elsewhere. Although anti-colonial philosophies were imported from Egyptian Islamic reform groups of the 1920s, and caused the setting up of some radical groups, their influence remained marginal. In Malaya, political apathy ruled supreme.

Nevertheless, in line with administrative changes being introduced throughout the Indian sub-continent, Britain moved to modernise the government of Malaya

and introduced measures of self-rule. This took the form of increased power devolved to the individual Malay states. The various ethnic groups were added to state
councils, and in 1935 the post of chief secretaryship was abolished. In 1939, some
two years before the Japanese invasion, the departments of agriculture, education,
health, forestry, mining and public works were transferred to the Malay state level,
while legislative power was divided between the federal and state councils. By the
time of Japan's attack on Pearl Harbor, Malaya was clearly on the path of 'self-
determinism' and independence.

If there was any resentment, this soon disappeared under the yoke of the
Japanese invaders, whose dictatorial style stood in very sharp contrast to the British.
As Chin Kee Onn noted in *Malaysia Upside Down* (1946), 'Japanese savagery ...
proved the shallowness of Japanese understanding. They lacked the genius for compromise and adjustment of the British whom they supplanted.'[3] The sultans, who
along with the whole economy were soon impoverished by the hostilities, continued to support the British, albeit passively, throughout the war. Churchill assured them that 'we shall see them righted in victory'.[4] Nevertheless, the Malay
Peninsula had to endure a period of chaos in the immediate aftermath of war.

Resistance to the Japanese had been waged largely by a 6,000-strong guerrilla army led by the Malayan Communist Party (MCP), and also by the Malayan
People's Anti-Japanese Army (MPAJA). In the August and September period following the Japanese surrender, these rival forces launched a grab for power which
included a large dose of 'paying-off old scores'.

The post-war period was also marked by economic hardship. As early as
22 June 1945, the State Department reported concern about rice shortages: 'At
the end of the war, if they have not been able to bring in adequate food and other
necessaries, the British will probably face considerable unrest in Malaya.'[5] Industry
was destroyed and took several years to recover; in 1946, production of tin was just
8,500 tons, a fraction of pre-war production. John Edington of the Tebrau Rubber Estates complained that 'It wasn't until the Korean War [1950–53] had started
... that funds from profits made became available to pay shareholders a dividend
and acquire funds for replanting.'[6] However, the root cause of the political strife
may well have been economic disparities between the communities which were
exacerbated during a period of economic hardship. During the British Military
Administration (BMA) phase, which lasted to April 1946, some 1,000 Chinese
were killed.

The British army restored order and for the time being neutralised the communist threat by allowing MCP into the political processes. In the background, arguments raged towards the end of the war between the British and the Americans
as to what to do with Malaya.

Roosevelt and the State Department thought that a joint Anglo-American-
Chinese trusteeship might be an appropriate vehicle for post-war Malaya. That
America would not trust Britain alone sparked bitter resentment at the implied

criticism of pre-war rule. Lord Cranborne made a vigorous response:

> Our record of administration is not one of which we need to be ashamed. We created
> Singapore and Hong Kong, two of the greatest ports of the Pacific, out of nothing.
> We made Malaya one of the richest and most vital producing areas of the world. We
> brought to her peoples law and order, happiness and prosperity.[7]

Even more strongly, Leo Amery, secretary of state for India stated that '. . . as
for joint trusteeship, we might consider that when the United States is prepared
to concede to us a joint trusteeship'.[8] While Britain had no post-war aims to sustain Malaya as a long-term colony, nevertheless, British governments deemed it
appropriate that it would be up to Britain to establish the new political settlement.

Britain's first constitutional attempt was not a success. In December 1945, a
Malay Union came into being after the sultans agreed to pool their sovereignty.
The union proved deeply unpopular because of its guarantee of automatic Chinese
citizenship; a racial problem that had been largely submerged during the British
period, now became a critical factor as Malaya edged towards self-rule. Ishak Haji
Muhammed, who would later become chairman of the Labour Party of Malaya,
spoke for the indigenous races when he demanded that the British 'stop the Malays
being exploited by other races'.[9] It did not help that the post-war BMA had none of
the touch of the pre-war colonial service. J.S. Potter of Guthrie & Co. complained
that 'The British Military Administration was in power and it was a great shock to
find corruption rife at all levels. . . . I supposed British morals had declined in the
long war years of restrictions and shortages.'[10]

All parties demanded the abolition of the union, including the United Malays
National Organisation (UMNO) which was formed in reaction to the constitutional plan. As Virginia Thompson, a contemporary academic, noted, the Malaya
Union, 'awakened in the indigenous Malay population fears lest their Sultans lose
even their nominal sovereignty and they themselves be deprived of their former
privileged position vis-à-vis the Chinese and Indians.'[11] Neither were the fortunes
of the union helped by the cack-handed BMA. The secretary to the sultan of Penang
complained that:

> The people the BMA sent out here, having been clerks in a railway station or some-
> thing, and suddenly they were colonels, thought they were important. It was one of
> the problems of the BMA that the Sultans did not like them.[12]

Under the leadership of Tunku Abdul Rahman, UMNO, which was formed
with a core leadership of aristocracy, Malay Civil Service and leading clerics, now
claimed the sole right to negotiate the future constitution of the country with the
British. Tunku, a minor aristocrat, who had spent his childhood with his Siamese
mother in Bangkok, was a graduate of Cambridge. A lover of cricket and English
customs, he was possessed of an easy charm which made him comfortable whether
dealing with the English or Chinese.

Indeed he shared the Chinese love of horseracing and was on good terms with the Chinese business community. He also had impeccable claims to early participation in Malay nationalism by dint of his involvement with *Seberkas* (a Malay national group) in 1935, though he later left that organisation when they refused dialogue with the British.

Although Tunku claimed inspiration from Nehru, his methods were far less confrontational. Neither did he display any of the underlying bitterness towards the white man displayed by Nehru; indeed he generously admitted that Britain's post-war Governor General Malcolm Macdonald 'was really the man who gave the people of this country a sense of Malaysian consciousness; and it was he who taught the people to look ahead, with ultimate independence as a goal'.[13] In return, the British were equally complementary. Legal Administrator Colonel Massie described Tunku as 'A wonderful human being . . . one of the most charming men I have ever worked with _ a delight.'[14]

In February 1948, the hugely unpopular union was revoked and replaced by a Federation of Malaya, which guaranteed to uphold the sovereignty of the sultans and their principalities. The governorship was abolished and replaced with a high commissioner. In this role, General Macdonald oversaw a gradual move towards a democratic constitution.

Firstly he upgraded the Malay-Chinese Goodwill Committee to the Communities Liaison Committee which comprised six Malays, six Chinese and one each for India, Ceylon, Eurasia and Europe. From 1949 to1950, meetings would take place at the governor general's house in Johor Baru. The preparatory approach was further enhanced by the creation of a cabinet in 1951, in which appointees were drawn from, and made accountable to the Federal Legislative Council.

Increasingly the powers of government were passed from the British-controlled Executive Council to the cabinet. According to Fan Yew Teng in his account of *The UMNO Drama: Power Struggles in Malaysia* (1989), Tunku presided over cabinet meetings 'with the aplomb of an English vicar at a parish tea party'.[15] The way forward to democracy then started with local elections involving municipal councils and village committees.

In spite of the move towards democratic structures, the basic compromise established by the Federation of Malaya was that voting would be weighted in favour of the indigenous race at the expense of the majority Chinese population of whom only 10 per cent would qualify to vote. To register as voters, Chinese Malaysians had to prove residence for 15 of the last 25 years. In effect, the Chinese elites accepted under-representation in government as a trade-off for assurances that their economic interests would not be threatened.

In February 1949, a group of Western-educated Chinese, led by millionaires Tan Cheng Lock and H.S. Lee, set up the Malayan Chinese Association (MCA). While formally a party to rival UMNO, from an early stage the MCA sought to gain advantage by working with UMNO rather than against it; in the first national elections of 1952, a pact was agreed with UMNO based on MCA acceptance that special economic assistance would be directed towards the indigenous Malay population. A full communal spectrum was achieved by UMNO, when the Malayan Indian Congress (MIC) decided to join its 'umbrella' in 1954.

A pattern was set whereby, in return for supporting UMNO, cabinet posts would be shared out among the communities. Reflecting the commercial and financial acumen of the Chinese community, it was allocated the post of finance minister. Tan Siew Sin, the son of the MCA president, Tan Cheng Lock, who was a close friend of Tunku, became minister for commerce and industry and later minister of finance. The political balancing act required moderation and compromise on all sides. As Tunku explained, 'when one party asks for concessions, that party always tries to bear in mind the difficulties of the other party or parties, so that a final solution does not bear too harshly on any one community'.[16]

The sense of communal unity which characterised the early period of Malaya's democracy was heightened by the threat faced by the Communist Party's decision to abandon the democratic process. In March 1947, Communist leader Chin Peng, perhaps encouraged by the wave of strikes which followed a fall in rubber prices and wages, decided to embark on an armed insurrection to gain political control of Malaya. No doubt, Peng was also encouraged by the imminent fall of China to communism.

From the American point of view, Malaya was a prime enemy target. In a Joint Chief of Staff report of 9 June titled 'United States Policy towards China', it was warned that if China fell to the Communists, 'conditions would be such as to facilitate the eventual continued expansion of Soviet power in Asia southward through China and towards Indonesia, Malaysia and India'.[17] (See Map III)

After the murder of a number of European plantation managers on 16 June 1947, a state of emergency was declared throughout Malaya, and the Malay Communist Party (MCP) was outlawed. In July, Tam Kam, president of the All-Johor Labour Union, was killed in a gun battle with government forces. The emergency, as the war against Communist insurgents in Malaya became known, saw determined action to detain or expel 1,779 known communists; having been cleaned out of the urban centres, the MCP retreated to the jungles, covering 80 per cent of the peninsular, with a force estimated to be 12,000 strong. In 1949, there was a marked increase in communist guerrilla activity as the MCP took control of the Chinese squatter settlements, which were situated deep in the remote jungle areas.

American analysts, increasingly concerned by the global phenomenon of communist expansion, were also alarmed by the turn of events in Malaya. In August 1950, Charles J. Shohan, at the Office of Philippine and Southeast Asian Affairs, warned that:

> Judged on the basis of what is now being invested unsuccessfully to stem present hostilities, British suppression would have to be on an extremely large scale. The nearby spectacle of approximately one third of the Army of the French Republic fighting an

extensive and precarious holding action, in limited areas of Indochina, leaves nothing for the Westerner to be smug about in Malaya.[18]

In spite of these warnings and the increased insurgent activity at the start of the decade, in 1950, the American Melby Mission ranked Malaya last in priority for military assistance, behind Indochina, Thailand, the Philippines and Indonesia.

In part, this may have been because the Truman administration had finally acknowledged that Malaya was within the 'British' sphere. In March 1950, Lt. General Sir Harold Briggs was appointed to head the 35,000 British soldiers now stationed in Malaya. He put the country on a full war footing with conscription for both the army and the police force. The Briggs Plan, as it became known, built a Malay security force that at its peak consisted of 67,000 police, 300,000 home guards and 23 infantry battalions. It was a substantial force to combat just 8,000 guerrillas but, unlike other countries in the region, the British war against communism was won.

Briggs's main innovation however, and one whose success was later to attract the attention of the US army in Vietnam, was to resettle the Chinese villagers to 'protected' cantons. By 1953, he had moved some 400,000 people to new villages and thereby deprived the MCP of their agricultural logistical support. Cutting off the enemy's food supply was one of the keys to Britain's eventual defeat of the Communists. Guy Madoc, British director of intelligence in Malaya revealed that:

> We were able quite deliberately to enforce food control all round the perimeter of the Communist districts, but we would choose one or two places, and weaken the controls accidentally on purpose. . . . we allowed a certain amount of food to trickle out on the fringe. We called that the honey pot. And then when the Communists had really begun to get a bit careless, we put in ambushes.[19]

Also, between 1948 and 1951, the British covertly shipped back to their home country some 35,000 Chinese Malays suspected of being in collusion with the enemy.

Although in October 1951, British High Commissioner Sir Henry Gurney was assassinated by MCP guerrillas, who attacked his Rolls-Royce on the road to Fraser's Hill, 105 km from Kuala Lumpur, insurgent activity peaked shortly after. By 1954, terrorist incidents had fallen to 25 a week. Nevertheless, the emergency continued for another five years. Over that time, a further 10,000 Chinese were deported back to communist China. John Foster Dulles, impressed by the collapse of the communist threat in Malaysia, noted with approval in 1954 that 'the United Kingdom and Malayan effort against communism is often ignored in favour of more dramatic anti-communist effort elsewhere'.[20]

In spite of the communist insurrection, Tunku was confident enough to push for full independence when he visited London in January 1956. The request brooked no objections from a country that was now only too eager to dispense with its colonial responsibilities. The Rendel Commission in 1954 had already recommended the move towards self-government and independence, and the British held elections to a Legislative Assembly in 1955. It was a model transition from a colony to an independent state. In a low-key ceremony at the Selangor Club, the Union Jack was lowered after British legislation was passed for the creation of Malaya as an independent constitutional monarchy on 5 August 1957. A month later, the Duke of Gloucester handed independence to Tunku Abdul Rahman, who could henceforth claim the title *Bapa Malaya* (Father of Malaya).

With the effective defeat of communism by the early 1960s, the way was clear for an ambitious project to unify Malaya and Singapore. A union, the idea of which Tunku would have baulked at in the immediate post-war period, was favoured because of the fear that Singapore with its Chinese population would 'go' communist; it was now proposed by Tunku to Lee Kuan Yew on 2 March 1961. Since 1954 this had also been one of Lee's most cherished aims.

In addition to the expansion of Malaya to encompass Singapore, the 1962 Cobbold Commission came to the conclusion that Sabah and Sarawak should be folded into the newly independent Malaysia. For Tunku these were welcome additions. The inclusion of these two provinces along with North Borneo provided the attraction of bulking up the Malay population of the new Malaysia versus the Chinese. At independence, Tunku had brushed off overseas criticism, particularly from President Sukarno of Indonesia, that British troops remained on Malaysian soil; being called a 'colonial lackey' was a more than a fair price to pay for a continued guarantee of security.

However, the apparently impeccable expansion of Malaya into a larger more viable state was spoilt by an almost immediate falling out with Lee Kuan Yew and Singaporean interests. While Lee was passionate about Singapore being part of Malaysia, he was equally clear that this could not be done in the context of a constitutional framework which gave special rights to Malays. From the beginning, Lee campaigned vigorously for their abolition. After race riots marked a public procession for Prophet Muhammad's birthday on 21 July 1964, Tunku blamed Lee's treatment of the Malays; in return, the Singaporean government opined that the 'riots were willed by ... UMNO to re-establish its political influence among the Malays in Singapore'.[21]

For Tunku, the threat of Lee's political brilliance to the communal balance, which had been achieved through trade-offs with UMNO's partner, the MCA, was a terrifying prospect. While Tunku was in London for medical treatment, the acrimony between his party and that of Lee increased. After bitter exchanges in parliament in December, Deputy Prime Minister Tun Abdul Razak Hussein concluded that '... the only solution is a breakaway ...'.[22] In June 1965, fearing an inability to face Lee down politically, Tunku, from his hospital bed at the London Clinic, reached a decision that separation was the only alternative. A gloomy Lee reluctantly agreed and the separation was announced four days after Tunku's return from London on 5 August 1965.

After this failure, Tunku gave consideration to a federation to include the other major Malay countries, Indonesia and the Philippines to be called Maphilindo. Sukarno who had long cherished the vision of Indonesia at the heart of a Malay Empire was enthusiastic, and the idea was also supported by President Macapagal of the Philippines. Fortunately for Malaysia, Tunku soon changed his mind. A war of skirmishes, which ensued with Sukarno's Indonesia after the latter's declaration of *Konfrontasi*, was a small price to pay for avoiding the disasters that would soon befall Indonesia and the Philippines.

Although Tunku subscribed to American fears of the 'domino' spread of communism and agreed that the conflict in South Vietnam was a result of communist aggression, he decided to put Malaya on a 'neutral' footing. He therefore declined to sign up to the South East Asian Treaty Organisation (SEATO), which America envisaged as the Asian equivalent of NATO and a partner in the Cold War battle against Communism.

Nevertheless, he sought to develop regional relationships through the creation of the Association of South East Asia (ASA) in 1961. This organisation would later change its name to the Association of South East Asian Nations (ASEAN) after the inclusion of Indonesia and the Philippines in 1967. Ultimately, it would be ASEAN, rather than SEATO, which would become the more important regional forum.

In spite of communist insurrection, the divorce from Singapore and a conflict and trade war with Indonesia, the 1960s proved successful economically for Malaysia with real GDP growth of 5 per cent per annum. Moreover, private capital formation over the decade grew at an average 7.3 per cent per annum, and by 1970, manufacturing as a proportion of GDP had risen to 13 per cent, from just 8.5 per cent in 1960. Tunku's government did not make the mistake of so many of the post-war Asian economies of presuming that economic growth could only be achieved through government-controlled investment.

In the first Malay budget, industrial investment took just 1.3 per cent; while this increased to 2.5 per cent in the Second Malaya Plan from 1961 and to 3.3 per cent in the First Malaysia Plan 1966–70, government-directed industrial investment remained minimal. More importantly, the Malaysian government offered political stability. Tunku's government also created a favourable tax environment for private investment; a Pioneer Industries Ordinance in 1958 granted a 40 per cent tax exemption for new industries. Also in 1960, the government established the Malayan Industrial Development Finance Corporation (MIDF) to help finance industrial ventures. In line with common Asian practice, domestic industry was also given tariff protection. In such favourable conditions, Chinese businessmen needed little invitation to exercise their entrepreneurial talents.

When favouritism was given to Malay application for licenses, Chinese businessmen often stood behind them. Also in the early 1960s, when an agricultural minister bowed to pressure from Malay interest groups to affect the transfer of Chinese-owned rice mills to Malay co-operatives, the policies were declared unconstitutional. Aziz, the minister, was forced to resign and the policy was rescinded.

Whatever the 'Malay special rights' bias that Tunku had cemented as part of the 'political' settlement with the MCA, the first decade of Malay self-rule saw no forced transfer of wealth to the indigenous *bumi* (the indigenous Malay people; literally 'sons of the soil'). Although in 1964, Finance Minister Tan Siew Sin had introduced business taxes to finance the setting up of Bank Bumiputra and an agricultural bank, Bank Pertanian, in order to direct credit to the *bumi* population, these policies had little effect on the distribution of wealth between the communities. By 1969, 62 per cent shares in publicly traded Malay companies were owned by foreigners (non-Malaysians), 23.7 per cent by Chinese Malaysians and just 1.5 per cent by *Bumis*. In terms of wealth distribution, it was shown that 74 per cent of Malays earned less than US$ 200 per annum; this compared with 33 per cent of Chinese.

It was perhaps complacency on the part of Tunku, after a long period as both head of the Federation of Malaya and Malaysia's first prime minister that he failed to note the general dissatisfaction with UMNO's performance. The electoral setbacks to the ruling coalition in 1969 came as a significant shock; though UMNO retained working control of the Federal Parliament as the largest electoral grouping, the Pan-Malaysian Islamic Party (PAS), the Chinese-based Democratic Action Party (the DAP was based on Lee Kuan Yew's People's Action Party), Gerakan and other opposition parties now controlled 41 out of 93 seats. All these parties gained from the broad dissatisfaction with the ruling UMNO grouping.

The resulting celebratory processions by DAP and Gerakan in Kuala Lumpur on 13 May led to counter demonstrations by UMNO supporters and violent racial riots which lasted for four days in the capital city. In the weeks that followed, there were sporadic flare-ups as fears emerged that up to three state governments would be led by non-Malays. Tunku would later claim '[my] greatest regret is that I allowed the election to proceed. I was too proud, I felt so sure that I was going to win easily. . . . What I should have done [in the light of the reports I was receiving] was to suspend that election, declare a State of Emergency and allow time for everyone to cool off'.[23]

In this statement, Tunku revealed the peculiar essence of Malaysia's democracy; it was stable only as long as UMNO and its Communal political allies accepted the status quo of permanent Malay rule. Malaysia's unstated constitutional settlement was consensual, one-party rule; it worked as long as the Chinese were prepared to accept permanent racial discrimination against their community.

Instead of accepting the possibility of political setbacks, the UMNO establishment set out to entrench the racially lopsided post-war settlement ever more firmly. Tunku, who had largely blamed the ethnic Chinese for the riots and failed to address the deeper underlying issues to the 1969 riots, would not be a party to the revision of Malaysia's post-war settlement. He effectively stepped back from the exercise of power and remained prime minister in name only.

The National Operations Council (NOC), set up to deal with the crisis, was run by his deputy, Razak Hussein. Although Tunku announced in August 1970 that the 'deferred' Federal Parliament would reconvene on 1 February 1971, he resigned a month later. It was a sad departure for one of the rare post-war Asian politicians who managed to lead his country to independence without being corrupted by either power or money.

Compared to his predecessor, Razak was a dour, plain-speaking, hard-working bureaucrat. Like Tunku, Razak had been educated in England and on his return had immediately pursued a political career. He became head of UMNO youth, and in 1951, when Tunku became the leader of his party, Razak was promoted to vice president. After independence, he was promoted again to be deputy prime minister and also took on the defence portfolio. Proving to be the indispensable administrator to the newly independent country, he also initiated and managed the Federal Land Development Authority in 1956. The 'workaholic' Razak added the Ministry of National and Rural Development to his portfolio in 1959.

After the disappointment of the 1969 elections, Razak sought to win back overall control of parliament and the three states, Penang, Perak and Kelantan, which had elected non-UMNO governments; this was achieved by expansion of the UMNO umbrella into a new Barisan Nasional (United Front). The Ipoh-based People Progressive Party (PPP), the Gerakan Party, and smaller parties from Sabah and Sarawak were brought into Barisan, which was formally registered in 1974 to become an organ for UMNO control; UMNO officials assumed all major posts, and all important decisions were vetted by the cabinet before their submission to Barisan.

At the same time, UMNO sought new legislation to quell racial tensions. Sedition laws would now ban any criticism of Malay rulers and Malay special rights. Also the Constitution (Amendment) Act removed the right of discussion, public and private, of Malay special rights; this even applied to parliament. Remarkably perhaps, the Chinese communities not only accepted their political emasculation, but some six of their communal parties were absorbed into Barisan including the MCA, Gerakan, PPP, Sabah Chinese Association, SUPP (Sarawak) and the Sarawak Association. In addition, the Malay Indian Congress (MIC) was also incorporated into Barisan.

The increasingly nationalist tone of Malay politics was underlined by the recall of more radical Malay politicians Mahathir and Musa Hitam, who had initially been purged from UMNO after the 1969 race riots. By contrast, Tunku's supporters were removed from the higher offices of government.

Newly promoted figures also included Tengku Razaleigh Hamzah, who became UMNO treasurer and vice president and was promoted to finance minister in 1976. He would later become a director of both of the major state trading companies, Petronas and Pernas. Razak's brother-in-law became deputy prime minister and UMNO deputy president. Meanwhile, in 1973, Mahathir was given the important post of education minister. The tradition of giving the Finance Ministry to a Chinese figure from the MCA was quietly dropped; from now on, Chinese government representation would increasingly be relegated to the deputy level. The new political system and its dominant political figures had been put in place for the next 30 years.

An inquiry set up to investigate the 1969 race riots produced a government white paper entitled 'Toward National Harmony'. The paper vaguely concluded that the causes were political. By his actions however, Razak clearly decided that the real causes of the unrest were the economic disparities between the communities. Under the slogan *Masyarakat Adil* (Just Society), Razak launched the New Economic Policy (NEP).

The NEP, which would become the guiding light for all Malaysian economic policy over the next generation, aimed to transfer 30 per cent of the country's corporate wealth into Malay hands by 1990. In a radical corporatist style, which was in sharp contrast to the 'laissez faire' approach of his predecessor, Razak sought government intervention to achieve the targets; government acquisitions would be made by government-funded bodies such as Pernas, the Urban Development Authority (UDA) and the State Economic Development Corporations (SEDCs). London Tin and conglomerate Sime Darby were early acquisitions.

In addition, Razak pushed through a wide-ranging expansion of Malay special rights; these included land rights, subsidies for education and quotas for employment in government services. *Bumi* employment quotas were also demanded of private companies which were forced to agree *bumi* advancement plans to government agencies. Additionally, foreign companies were forced to submit to a rigorous licensing system.

The NEP rapidly proved successful in its redistribution aims. By 1975, Malay ownership of corporate assets had risen from 2.4 to 7.8 per cent. Also within three years the government moved to 98 per cent recruitment of Malay applicants versus an original target of just 75 per cent. Whereas Malays accounted for 49.7 per cent of students at the University of Malaya in 1970, their representation rose to 66.4 per cent in 1979.

NEP had its downside. Foreign investment was discouraged. Business costs rose as Chinese companies were often forced to employ extra managers to compensate for ill-qualified *bumi* executives. With monopolistic political and economic power, financial corruption also became a feature of everyday corporate life; although the figures for wealth transfer looked impressive, the beneficiaries were usually the UMNO political and bureaucratic elites. The traditional aristocratic and social elites also benefited from the gifting of free shares and positions as 'token' *bumi* directors on company boards. Nevertheless, the reforms took place against the background of an economy recovering rapidly from the First Oil Crisis. The Second Malaysia Plan achieved an annual real GDP growth rate of 7.1 per cent versus the target of just 6.8 per cent.

In foreign affairs, Malaysia pursued a policy of non-alignment. Through ASEAN Razak adopted ZOPFAN, an ungainly acronym for an equally ungainly policy, the Zone of Peace, Freedom and Neutrality. Predictably, Lee Kuan Yew ridiculed ZOP-FAN and preferred to place his defence needs on the broad shoulders of the USA.

In a more practical vein, Malaysia replaced the Anglo-Malaysian Defence Agreement with the Five Power Defence Agreement, which included Australia, New Zealand, Singapore and the USA. Razak also became the first ASEAN leader to restore relations with China after Kissinger's ground-breaking detente. Mao allayed fears by assuring Razak that he believed that Chinese citizens of Malaysia should be loyal to the country of their adoption. However, Razak was less successful in seeking the neutrality assurances of the communist regime in Vietnam after the fall of Saigon.

After Razak's death from leukaemia on 14 January 1976, there was a seamless transition of power and policies to his brother-in-law, Tun Hussein Onn, the deputy prime minister. Given the tradition of succession to the deputy prime minister, there was now an unseemly scramble to fill this post. The three presidents of UMNO demanded that one of them be chosen to become Onn's deputy; this strategy excluded the popular Tan Sri Ghazali Shafie, but in choosing Dr Mahathir over Ghafar Baba and Finance Minister Tengku Razaleigh, Onn released a wave of faction fighting within the party.

The lack of real political opposition and the creation of 'in effect' a one-party state made the development of factional politics almost inevitable. Where opposition did raise its head outside of UMNO's Barisan Nasional (National Front) umbrella, it was quickly stamped on. After regional elections in Kelantan brought a 22 to 14 seats victory for PAS over Barisan, the new Kelantan ruling party passed a motion of no confidence in the UMNO-appointed State Governor Mohammad Nasir. Hussein Onn responded to this threat to UMNO power by declaring a state of emergency and imposing direct federal rule.

The increasingly statist and Islamic bias of Malaysia's economic policy also brought squabbles with Barisan's Chinese partners. Discrimination against Chinese Malaysians, implicit in the 1975 Industrial relations Act, was seen as a break in the unwritten agreement for MCA support within Barisan. In the typical style of Malaysian political compromise, the legislation was enacted but the government was relaxed in its implementation.

Similar disputes also arose over the extension of Islamic education. In dealing with rising Islamic evangelism, the government took a moderate path by encouraging groups such as PERKIM, founded by Tunku in 1970, and *Darul Arquam* founded in 1971, while banning more extremist Islamic groups, which usually had their origins in India or Pakistan.

Athough Hussein Onn was on the liberal economic wing of his party, Finance Minister Razaleigh and pressure from UMNO forced a more interventionist path. Malay corporations were increasingly bought and fed into the Bumiputra

Investment Fund. In a major development of government participation in the economy, Petronas was established by the Petroleum Development Act of 1974; development of new oil fields in partnership with the oil majors produced a rapid growth in exports. By 1976, oil accounted for 18 per cent of all commodity exports.

A major push for acquisition of high-profile foreign corporations took place in September 1981 when the National Equity Corporation acquired Guthrie Corporation, Dunlop and Barlow Holdings. In spite of the interventionist stance of the government however, the overriding benefits of political stability showed in an economic performance that was consistently better than the other 'Malay' states of South East Asia. Endemic corruption may have become a feature of the Malay political system, but it was on a minor scale by comparison with Indonesia and the Philippines. In the Third Malaysia Plan ending in 1980, real GDP growth per annum averaged 8.6 per cent.

In spite of membership of ASEAN, the Five Power Defence Agreement and the idealist policies of ZOPFAN, Hussein Onn was alarmed by the Vietnamese push into Cambodia in 1979, and the defeat of the Chinese Army after it had attacked Vietnam's Northern border.

Hussein's attempts at diplomacy with Saigon were rebuffed. Also the post-Mao government in Beijing refused to renounce their ideological support for the remaining MCP guerrillas operating along the Thai borders. Fearful of the potential expansion of Vietnam's regional power, Hussein nevertheless managed to extract a pledge from Soviet First Secretary Leonid Brezhnev that he would persuade Vietnam to guarantee non-aggression towards Malaysia.

Not being entirely convinced of the surety of this pledge, Hussein persuaded ASEAN to give support to the Khmer Rouge, and to recognise Pol Pot as the head of the Khmer government in exile. Hussein also sponsored a United Nations seat for Pol Pot's government. For further security, military help was offered to Thailand if Vietnamese forces breached their borders. Reflecting their increased security fears, defence expenditures were increased by 150 per cent in the 1980 budget. In the event, the most alarming invasion threat came from Vietnamese refugees, the so-called boat people. Eventually, some 75,000 were allowed to settle in Malaysia. At the sudden death of Dato Hussein Onn, the Malay political succession moved smoothly into place with the elevation of his deputy, Dr Mahathir.

Therein lay the key to Malaysia's relative economic success in the post-war era. Claims to power lay within the political system. Unlike most Asian countries in the post-war era, there was no revolutionary army to pay off or military tradition which laid claim to a role in government. Malaysia's military culture, like that of the occupying British army, was non-interventionist in the political sphere. The British defeat of the Chinese communist insurgents left no debts to be repaid to Malaysian soldiers. As for the British, exhausted by the efforts of the Second World War, they had long ceased to harbour any desire for empire or continued influence.

It was to Tunku's credit too, that he acquiesced to a process whereby power would be gradually accreted until full independence was granted in 1957. The net result was the development of a civilian political process and institutions which offered a level of good governance not seen in the rest of South East Asia.

Yet the newly emerging state of Malaysia was not without its problems. The almost equal split between the indigenous Malay or *bumi* population and its nineteenth and early twentieth century imported Chinese workforce could well have caused disastrous political instability. The solution lay with a trade-off between allowing Chinese commercial life to flourish in exchange for their yielding political power and special 'economic' rights for the *bumis*.

Although Malaysia suffered from the level of corruption that inevitably came to haunt a de facto 'one party' system of government, this was a small price to pay for stability. With the exception of the 1969 riots, the relationship between the communities was a model of racial harmony. The reward for all communities from Malaysia's unique racial trade-off was peace, the rule of law and a level of economic prosperity far in excess of the comparable 'Malay' countries of South East Asia.

Although Malaysia maintained a 'neutral' approach with regard to the superpowers, its largely free market economy and 'nominally' democratic process put it clearly in the American camp. For the USA, the independent Federation of Malaya presented the opportunity for a 'wait and see approach'. Eric Kocher, the American consul in Kuala Lumpur, observed in the *New York Times* on 9 September 1955 that:

> As Malaya progresses towards self government, the US must see that any existing vacuum caused by the possible weakening of British Malayan ties either voluntarily by the British or by action of the Malayans, is filled with pro-democratic influences directly by Malayans themselves or indirectly by the US or some friendly third power.[24]

The fall-back plan was not required. In view of the vast political and financial capital that America had to expend elsewhere in the region, the fact that it was never necessary for America to extend its defence umbrella to Malaysia must have been a welcome relief.

18

Lee Kuan Yew: Pocket Giant

Singapore: 1945–64

Lee Kuan Yew was born in Singapore on 16 September 1923. He was a 'Han' who could trace his origins to the northern plains of China; his ancestors had moved south to Fujian and Guangdong. It was here that Lee's great grandfather was born in the village of Tangxi in 1846. He migrated to Singapore, whose Chinese population had already overtaken the indigenous Malays, and found a Singaporean Chinese bride. This was not wholly successful. When Lee's great-grandfather returned to China in 1882, his wife refused to go and went into hiding.

Lee's grandfather meanwhile typified the peripatetic nature of the Chinese diaspora by becoming a purser on a steamer that plied between Singapore and the Dutch East Indies (now Indonesia); he married in Central Java, and gave birth to Lee's father in Semarang in 1903. The family had prospered on the back of a trading business built on rubber, but when prices collapsed from US$ 0.8 per pound to just US$ 0.2 per pound the Lee family fortune was wiped out. Subsequently, Lee's father was forced to get employment as a storekeeper with Shell Oil Company.

Nevertheless, Lee's mother's family, Chuas from Malacca and the Dutch East Indies, remained wealthy, and Lee's holidays were spent at their rubber estate in Malaya. Lee's father, a weak man, who gambled away his wife's jewellery, was usurped by the teenage Lee Kuan Yew who, as de facto head of the family, was increasingly consulted by his mother on the direction of household affairs.

Lee, who grew up speaking English at home, proved to be an exceptional student. He went to Telok Kurau English School in 1930 and graduated top to win a place at the elite Raffles Institution for Secondary Education. Lee continued to prosper and placed first in Junior Cambridge exams and won two scholarships. He was also active as a scout and played cricket and tennis. Not surprisingly, he excelled in debating. In spite of his academic achievements, he was considered too mischievous to be made a prefect.

Lee was prevented by war in Europe in 1940 from pursuing his plan to read law in London. Instead, he won the top scholarship to Raffles College, an Oxbridge-style institution founded in 1928; in his first year, Lee, with typical brilliance, placed first in Mathematics, but the presumptuous and competitive student was shocked to be beaten into second place in English and Economics. His vanquisher, Kwa Geok Choo, would later become his wife. It was at Raffles College that Lee also came to know his future political collaborator, Goh Keng Swee, who was an economics tutor.

However, war now intervened to bring Lee's education to a halt. Lectures were abandoned when Japanese bombing of Singapore started on 8 December 1941. The capitulation of 130,000 British, Indian and Australian troops to a force of just 110,000 Japanese, who had literally bicycled their way down the Malay Peninsula, came as a profound shock.

> The superior status of the British in government and society was simply a fact of life. After all, they were the greatest people in the world. They had the biggest empire that history had ever known, stretching over all time zones, across all four oceans and five continents. We learnt that in history lessons at school. . . . I was brought up by my parents and grandparents to accept that this was the natural order of things.[1]

Whatever the eventual outcome of the war, the myth of British supremacy was destroyed forever. 'In 70 days of surprises, upsets and stupidities, British colonial society was shattered, and with it all the assumptions of the Englishman's superiority.'[2]

Any contempt for British rule was short-lived, as the 'liberating' Japanese soon proved 'more cruel, more brutal, more unjust and more vicious than the British'.[3] In his autobiography, Lee recalled that when he picked up an Australian hat and wore it, a Japanese soldier spotted him and 'thrust the bayonet of his rifle through the brim of my hat, knocking it off, slapped me roundly, motioned me to kneel. He then shoved his right boot against my chest and sent me sprawling on the road'.[4]

More importantly, he was lucky to survive the random cull of young Chinese men who were picked up at checkpoints and taken to Tanah Merah Bear Beach, where they were tied up and walked towards the sea. About 6,000 of them were machine-gunned and bayoneted, with only a handful surviving to tell the tale. In all, some 50,000–100,000 Singaporean Chinese were thought to have been murdered by the Japanese 'liberation' army commanded by Colonel Tsuji.

Political prisoners were tortured and killed in the 'airplane' position, where they were strung up with hands tied behind their back until they could only stand on tiptoe; death came in excruciating agony. Others were pumped full of water, and then had their stomachs jumped on by their torturers. Along with some Dutch, Koreans and Filipinos, Chinese women were forced into providing 'comfort' for Japanese troops. While appreciating the past benefits of British rule versus that of their Japanese 'liberators', Lee did note that crime disappeared; 'As a result I have never believed those who advocate a soft approach to crime and punishment.'[5]

Lee survived the war on his wits. He found work as a clerk working at the Japanese military department dealing with oil supplies, and then for the guild (*Kumiai*) that controlled essential food supplies including rice, oil, sugar and tobacco. Later, he was employed as an English language editor of Japanese propaganda. With access to news agency cables, he was able to glean information about the progress of the war though he had to be careful because he was often followed by the *Kempeitai* (Japanese secret police).

Lee also displayed an entrepreneurial streak; he traded jewellery with the Japanese invaders, and then bought and restored a full-size billiard table. After the Japanese surrender, further opportunity came with the British reoccupation. Needing labour to rebuild Singapore, Lee organised a business providing construction labour and made enough money to buy himself a Ford V8.

With the ending of the war, the opportunity now came for Lee to go to England to study law. However, his first view of English society was not reassuring. On the boat to England, he was appalled by the promiscuity of English women and noted with horror the proliferation of used condoms, which littered the decks of the ship. London itself he found cold, dirty and exhausting, and he was fortunate to transfer to Cambridge through the good offices of a friend from Raffles College, who secured him a place at Fitzwilliam House. After winning a double first in Law (his wife also collected a first class degree), Lee studied to become a barrister at the Middle Temple, while basing himself at Tintagel, a village on the Atlantic Cornish Coast. Not surprisingly, the gifted academic passed his bar exams with distinction.

Politically he attached himself to the left, whose egalitarian ideology attracted him. Ironically, a man who would later become a bastion of American support in South East Asia was considered to be proto-Communist by the authorities. Indeed, he would later discover from Singapore government files that Nigel Morris, director of Special Branch, had recommended that, on his return to Singapore, he should be detained; he was not and, covered in glory from press reports of his academic achievements in Britain, Lee accepted a pupillage at lawyers Laycock & Ong.

Nevertheless, Lee was soon attracted by the political opportunities that presented themselves in Singapore. After the war, British rule had resumed with a governor who operated through a Legislative Council on which there was a minority of six elected representatives. The political scene was dominated by an older cadre of Chinese lawyers, still somewhat in awe of colonial rule. Mass politics was still in its infancy. In the 1948 Legislative elections, only 23,000 votes were cast out of a total eligible electorate of 200,000.

Lee's political activity started with support for a post office workers strike in 1952. Importantly, this introduced him to mass politics, and gave him a first political profile. Ahead of the new elections for the Legislative Council planned for April 1955, Lee, with friends including Goh Keng Swee, who had achieved a first degree in science at the London School of Economics, started to form a political party.

In the same year, the Rendel Commission had approved a new Singaporean constitution under which there would be a council of nine ministers of which six would be appointed by the majority leader of the Legislative Council. However, the key portfolios of chief secretary, financial secretary and attorney general would remain in the hands of British appointees; nevertheless, the government was bound to accept council legislation, except for foreign affairs, defence and security.

In spite of the reforms, the Chinese-educated elite remained dissatisfied. As Lee pointed out the Chinese had no role to play in the official life of the colony, which employed only English-educated locals as subordinates. These disaffected middle-class Chinese became an ideal recruiting ground for the communists. Even Goh Keng Swee, who would later become Singapore's long-serving finance minister and later prime minister, noted, 'In those days I was mixed up with Marxists.'[6]

In light of their leading role in the resistance to the Japanese in Malaysia during the war, the Communists had been awarded a place in the post-war settlement. Indeed, Chin Peng (head of the MPAJA, Malaysian People's Anti-Japanese Army) and 16 other resistance leaders were awarded the Burma Star by Mountbatten for their wartime roles. It was with the help of the two proto-communist members of the Singapore Bus Workers Union that Lee set up the People's Action Party (PAP). It was a Faustian pact. Lee knew that allies such as Lim Chin Siong were communists who were using the PAP as a respectable front for their political ambitions. On the other hand, Lee too needed their ability to pull out the mass vote; 'He [Lim] knew I was not a communist and I knew that he was one. And we accepted each other as such. He needed me; I needed him.'[7]

In the April 1955 elections won by the Labour Front, the PAP won four seats including the two won by its communist leaders. Having proven its popular support, the PAP turned to industrial action to promote its cause. Popular agitation through the unions brought some 260 work stoppages between April and December 1955. The unions had in effect been completely infiltrated and taken over by the communists.

In the meantime, the pressure for an independence settlement was led by the Chief Minister David Marshall, a socialist of Iraqi-Jewish extraction who was leader of the majority Labour Front Government. In 1956, Marshall brought a delegation to London to negotiate terms for Singaporean independence with Secretary of State Alan Lennox-Boyd; however, Marshall, having won almost all his demands, finally overplayed his hand and the negotiations ended in a humiliating failure which forced his resignation.

Lim Yew Hock succeeded him as chief minister on 8 June 1956, and took on the 'poisoned chalice' by being made responsible for the autumn crackdown on communist sympathisers, during which over 1,000 arrests were made; this included Lee's PAP ally Lim Chin Siong. Lim Yew Hock may have won praise from the Americans, but he severely compromised his electoral position by being seen as a colonial lackey. Nevertheless, as a reward for his efforts, Lim Yew Hock successfully concluded an independence agreement with Lennox-Boyd in London in April 1957.

Lee was the PAP representative on the five-man delegation that visited London. Lee's main concern on returning to Singapore was that independence was doomed to failure unless it was preceded by merger with Malaya. However, it was his own political survival that was to dominate his year. Indeed, his enthusiastic support for merger with Malaya may well have been influenced by his desire to dilute the communist threat to which he was now subject. By the classic tactic of 'packing' meetings, the communist elements sought to infiltrate the PAP and take control of the party Lee had founded.

In spite of the PAP's internal difficulties, Lim Yew Hock's governmental problems were worse. The Labour Front was increasingly seen as out of touch with the people, too close to the colonial powers, and was also tainted by corruption. In the Legislative elections on 30 May 1959, the 35-year-old Lee used classic Communist methodology to win popular support including the Work Brigades; he also co-ordinated drives against gambling, opium and pornography.

Honest government and an end to nepotism were promised. The result was a landslide victory for the PAP, with 53.4 per cent of the popular vote and 43 out of 51 seats. Though daunted by the responsibilities of government, Lee set out to rapidly solve the country's economic problems. Setting a standard for probity and integrity, unique in post-war Asian history, Lee slashed ministerial salaries including his own and also those of 6,000 civil servants. Government expenditure was also cut to balance receipts. Lee realised better than anyone that his honeymoon period would be brief, and that the Communists would soon agitate the Chinese population. In his first speech to the Legislative Assembly, Lee warned, 'If the PAP government fails, it will not be the opposition that will be returned to power. They will be fleeing for their lives . . . in the last analysis, if we fail, brute force returns.'[8] By 'brute force', nobody could be in any doubt that he meant the Communists.

For the time being, he took a moderate approach to the Communist threat. Communist prisoners were released, and, within the PAP, Lee gave known communists government posts, albeit the less powerful positions. However, Lee also set up a political study centre to teach civil servants about the Marxist–Leninist threat and the realities of economic management including the importance of the free market. In cleaning up the city of rubbish and debris, Lee set a personal example by leading his ministers and civil servants in Sunday work gangs.

Meanwhile, the unemployed were co-opted into brigades to perform public works. People's associations were required to organise local activities. To resolve long-running labour disputes, Lee required that union disputes be settled in special arbitration courts. A rapid expansion of teacher numbers also enabled every child to be guaranteed a place in school, and helped force the pace of female emancipation. Most importantly, he refused to make martyrs of the disruptive Communist elements within the unions.

The prime minister's hard work, in the cause of rebuilding Singapore, was unstinting; in spite of his political commitments, Lee set himself the task of learning

Hokkien with its seven-tone spoken language (versus four tones for Mandarin) so as to be a more effective campaigner on the stump. In spite of Lee's reforms, the fear in London and Washington was that Lee was a communist sympathiser. British experts on the ground knew better. Sir William Goode, in his last report as governor, concluded that 'I remain convinced that to regard the present PAP leaders as crypto-communists would be an entire mistake. To describe them as crypto-anti-communists would be much nearer the mark.'[9]

To Lee's surprise, Tunku Abdul Rahman, Malaya's first prime minister, intimated in a speech at the Singapore Foreign Correspondents Association that sooner or later Malaya should have an understanding with Britain and the peoples of Singapore, North Borneo, Brunei and Sarawak. It was a clear call for confederation. Lee's greatest political wish had been answered. However, the possibility of a merger with Malaya precipitated a crisis within the PAP. The Communist element within the PAP, alarmed at the prospect of a Malaya merger which would scupper their plans to subvert Singapore, split the party, leaving Lee with a slim majority of 26 out of 51 members. Lee barely won a vote of confidence in July, and was then subjected to 153 union strikes between then and September. Fong Swee Suan and Lim Chin Siong were now openly hostile to Lee.

In response, Lee turned to the attack using all his legendary powers of persuasion. In the autumn of 1961, he gave a series of 12 radio talks recorded in three different languages; the lectures which were all crafted by Lee, explained the history and nature of the communist infiltration and attack on the PAP, as well as the background to the struggle for independence. Cheong Yip Seng, Editor in Chief of *The Straits Times*, would later write that Lee's performance was that of 'A master storyteller at work'.[10] Gradually Lee won over his audience. By the time of the merger referendum on 1 September 1962, Lee won with an overwhelming 71 per cent vote in favour.

However the communist threat was not finally defeated until February 1963, when, following Communist unrest in Brunei, Lim Chin Siong and his followers were imprisoned by an order of the Internal Security Council. 'Operation Cold Store', as it was called, marked an end to Lee's communist problems; he had out-manoeuvred and outlasted them, and when he finally crushed them their popular support had by then evaporated.

Having rid himself of the communist menace, Lee now had to face up to the difficult issues presented by the merger with Malaya. His first challenge was to fend off the acquisitive embrace of the Malay China Association (MCA) leadership, who saw Lee as a rival and Singapore as an opportunity to take control of their taxes. Tunku resisted Tan Siew Sin's demands for financial control of Singapore, and Lee was able to negotiate a duty-free entrepôt status and a contribution of 40 per cent of its taxes to Kuala Lumpur. The merger finally took place on 16 September 1963.

In the elections that followed, the seeds of trouble with the union were already evident. Tunku was shocked by the failure of United Malays National Organisation

(UMNO) in the Singaporean elections. Even seats with a majority Malay population voted for Lee's PAP in preference to UMNO; this was deeply alarming to Tunku who naturally began to fear that Lee might begin to encroach on UMNO support within Malaya.

Ominously Tunku's deputy, Syed Jaafar Albar, warned that the Malays in Singapore's election must have been misled, and that this would not be allowed again. By breaching a verbal understanding not to participate in Singapore's elections, Tunku had irritated Lee who in turn annoyed Tan Siew Sin's MCA by running PAP candidates in Malaya and threatening the long-term lock that they had on Malaya's Chinese vote. Above all, Lee, a fierce advocate of noncommunal politics, threatened the 'communal' basis of Malayan politics. Tunku and his colleagues above all felt threatened by a Singapore-based party, which wanted to represent both Chinese and Malays. Although in the final reckoning they won only one seat in Malaya, the PAP nevertheless refused to accept that Malaya's voters were 'off-limits'; this in essence was the nature of the deal that Tunku had locked up with the Malay Chinese political parties.

Lee would later reflect that Tunku 'was a nice man', but nevertheless cautioned that

> he was a Prince who understood power and knew how to use it. He did not carry a big stick, but he had many hatchet-bearers who would do the job for him while he looked the other way and appeared as benign as ever.[11]

Syed Jaafar Albar, born in Indonesia of Arab descent, was happy to take on the task of hatchet man. As deputy prime minister and secretary general of UMNO, he stoked Malay passions through the press and whipped up fury at supposed state-sponsored Chinese discrimination against the Malays in Singapore. On the 12 June 1964, the *Ultasan Malayu* newspaper reported that 'Malays in Singapore today face threats, pressure and oppression by government,' and it warned, 'Do not treat the sons of the soil [*bumi*] as stepchildren.'[12]

When Lee planned a meeting to allay Malay fears, UMNO pre-empted it on 30 June with a convention of Malay parties, where Albar orchestrated a hate campaign against the Singapore leader. Hecklers within the crowd chanted, 'Kill him [Lee] ...kill him....'[13] Meanwhile Lee's meeting, which passed calmly, was ignored by the Kuala Lumpur-controlled radio and TV media. In spite of Lee's efforts, the troublemaking of the Malay extremists did not go unrewarded. On the Prophet Mohammed's birthday on 21 July, riots broke out in Singapore killing 23 and leaving 454 people injured.

Predictably Albar poured petrol on the fire. On 26 July he declared 'There is a devil in Singapore who set the Malays and the Chinese against each other.... It is because Lee Kuan Yew has been trying to challenge and chaff at our spirit of nationalism.'[14] Atrocities were now reported on both sides. A Malay woman was supposedly raped by a Chinese man, and it was reported that a Chinese man arrested by Malay police was humiliated and forced to masturbate in front of his captors.

Anthony Head, the British high commissioner in Kuala Lumpur, reported back to London that there was 'no doubt that this extreme element of UMNO played a considerable part in stirring up the first communal riots which took place in Singapore'.[15] Similarly, Arthur Rosen, the American consul general in Singapore, told the State Department that the riots were 'politically inspired', and the 'logical outcome' of a 'long period of anti-PAP political agitation, with strong communal overtones, by UMNO leaders'.[16]

Political unanimity from impartial observers was confirmed by the New Zealand Department of External Affairs, which concluded that 'It appears that Razak and other UMNO leaders did not act soon enough to curb the excesses of extremists like Jaafar Albar . . . .'[17] Albar naturally denied all suggestions of his role in stirring communal strife. In response to an article in *The Observer* in England, Albar replied in a letter in *Utusan* in April 1965 that '. . . it was not the Malays who started the 1964 riots. The riots were started by agent provocateurs, who may even be in the pay of Lee Kuan Yew'.[18] In typically robust fashion, Lee proceeded to issue a writ for libel.

If the pressure from the Malay extremists against Lee was not enough, Singaporean Chinese were also being exhorted by the Indonesian President Sukarno to oppose the creation of an independent Malaysia, which he claimed was being set up to oppress them. On 17 August, 30 Indonesian troops were landed on the coast of Johor with the aim of stirring trouble, and a further 30 were parachuted into the country. Although Indonesia's so-called *confrontasi* never escalated into full-scale war with Malaysia, it was a distraction that the newly merged Singapore could well have done without.

By mid 1964, it was becoming clear that the UMNO leadership was manoeuvring to depose Lee. Razak went behind Lee's back to offer Goh Keng Swee a deal in July 1964, whereby the PAP would be brought into the federal government of Malaysia as long as Lee was removed; it was suggested that he be posted out of harm's way to an unimportant post, such as ambassador to the United Nations. Goh Keng Swee would later record that '. . . the riots took place, Razak was involved in it and it was clearly his intention to remove Mr. Lee from office. That was the purpose of Albar's campaign'.[19]

The pressure on Lee was not just from the Malays. Tan Siew Sin, in a move aimed to extract more money from Singapore, imposed a turnover tax and introduced a 2 per cent tax on total payrolls. Lee's Finance Minister Goh Keng Swee estimated that Singapore alone would provide more than 25 per cent of the turnover tax, and 40 per cent of payroll taxes. Tan quite openly declared that he wanted Singapore to contribute 60 per cent of its revenue to central government.

In a further effort to destabilise the Singaporean economy, applications for investment made to the Singapore Economic Development Board to qualify for tax breaks on 'Pioneer Investment', which had to be sent to Kuala Lumpur, were held up in the Malaysian bureaucracy. In two years, only 2 out of 69 applications were approved, and even those were hedged round with restrictions which made them useless. Tan advised industrialists to go directly to Kuala Lumpur. In another clear attempt to siphon jobs and investment to Malaya, Tan also proposed the takeover of Singaporean textile quotas.

Attacks on Lee Kuan Yew finally came to a head. In a rabid denunciation of Lee in the federal parliament, the extremist Malay politician Dr Mahathir bin Mohamad denounced the PAP as 'pro-Chinese, communist-oriented and positively anti-Malay'[20] and compared it unfavourably to the MCA by saying that the PAP Chinese were of 'the insular, selfish and arrogant type of which Mr. Lee is a good example . . . . They are in fact Chinese first, seeing China as the centre of the world and Malaysia as a very poor second'.[21]

In the Federal Malay Parliament, Lee returned Mahathir's invective with a brilliantly argued riposte in fluent Malay. Lee's Malay Cabinet colleague Othman Wok, who was present, recorded the event as one of paramount significance:

> The chamber was very quiet and nobody stirred. The Ministers of Central Government sunk down so low in their seats that only their foreheads could be seen over the desks in front of them. The backbenchers were spellbound. They could understand every word. That was the turning point. They perceived Lee as a dangerous man who could one day be the Prime Minister of Malaysia.[22]

Even Tunku, in his autobiography *Looking Back* (1977), acknowledged that this speech was a turning point, the 'straw that broke the camel's back'.[23]

The divide was both ideological and personal. Tunku and the UMNO leadership were committed to a form of political 'apartheid' in which political parties could only represent their racial communities. UMNO was in the process of constructing a political and economic system which was to be skewed in perpetuity in favour of the '*bumi*' Malays, against the significant Chinese and Indian minorities. For the Chinese community, the trade-off would be political stability and the liberty to engage in entrepreneurial activity albeit at a cost in terms of Malay 'special rights'.

This was not a political structure that Lee could tolerate. He had seen the break-up of multi-racial parties in Sabah and Sarawak, and was not prepared to allow the same thing to happen to the PAP in Singapore. Moreover, he insisted on competing on equal terms within Malaysia, thus threatening to break up the cosy arrangements that UMNO had made with the MCA. Lee warned Tan Siew Sin, the MCA leader, that over time this communal arrangement would become more and more one sided. In his autobiography, Lee notes that in 1974 when Tan realised that as a Chinese he could never be deputy prime minister, he resigned, overcome with shame and disappointment. An augury of what was to come was the ultra-nationalist election campaigning of the emerging Dr Mahathir in 1965 who, in addition to bizarrely attacking Lee Kuan Yew's 'socialist doctrines', also hypocritically accused him of 'Chinese chauvinism'.[24]

Also on a personal level, Lee found himself at odds with the leadership of UMNO. Abdul Razak bin Hussein had been in the same year as Lee at Raffles College, but they had not been friends. Lee explained that 'He was a member of the Malay aristocracy of Penang.'[25] Though Lee was a Malay speaker, as a Chinese man of relatively humble origins, he was more comfortable in the company of commoners. The discomfort was probably felt on both sides. A Malay friend from Kedah confided to Lee that 'You Chinese are too energetic and clever for us . . . we cannot stand the pressure.'[26] In a bizarre piece of self-deprecation and logic, Tunku would argue in the 1960s that '. . . because they, the Malays, are not very clever and not good at business, they must be in charge of government departments, the police and the army'.[27]

Intellectually, Lee was in a different league to his Malay political adversaries. By his own admission, Tunku, who was also at Cambridge reading law, spent his time in England on 'slow' horses and 'fast' women. He got on well with the high Tories such as the aristocratic Douglas Home and Prime Minister Macmillan, who described him as 'like a Spanish grandee. That's his world'.[28] Lee noted with some amusement that Tunku was practically given a degree at Cambridge because he was so lazy and intellectually ill-adept; Tunku also spent six years trying to pass his bar exams. Lee was simply too smart for his Malay political opponents; this alone might not have mattered had Lee not also possessed a public charisma and above all an iron will.

In the end, Tunku and the UMNO leadership simply could not cope with Lee. Not only was it looking increasingly unlikely that they could bend Singapore to their 'communal' system, but it also seemed very possible that the PAP could undermine Malaysia's racial settlement, which they saw as the guarantor of political stability. In his memoir, *The Labour Government 1964–1970*, former Prime Minister Harold Wilson noted that Tunku '. . . was losing patience with his parliamentary colleague, Lee Kuan Yew [Harry Lee], the Singaporean leader, to the point where Lee was in danger of being arrested and imprisoned . . .'.[29]

Leaders such as Syed Jaafar Albar, who, in the event, resigned as secretary general of UMNO in protest at the proposed separation of Singapore and Malaya, were almost certainly pushing for a coup against Lee; the aim of the extremists was to dominate Singapore, not just eliminate Lee. Tunku, a more easy-going and calmer head, resolved that separation was the preferable path; Wilson may also have warned him off a coup attempt. High Commissioner Anthony Head told Tunku that 'if Lee Kuan Yew were put inside for any reason other than for treasonable activities, it would shock and embarrass the British government and would undoubtedly have far reaching effects among world opinion'.[30]

Lee had much to be thankful for in Wilson's defeat of the Conservative patrician Douglas Home in the 1964 British elections, as the latter might well have been much more favourably disposed towards his old friend Tunku. Lee would always claim a debt to Wilson's Labour government, no matter how far his own economic and political programme came to be seen as antipathetic to socialism. While recuperating from an operation in London, Tunku came to the firm conclusion that separation was the only way forward. With a heavy heart, Lee reluctantly agreed.

The failure of the merger did not deflect Lee from his greater purpose, the development of the prosperity of Singapore. In his book *Leaders* (1990), former President Richard Nixon described Lee as 'above all a practical man, indifferent toward political theory and contemptuous of anything that did not contribute directly to his goal of strengthening and enriching Singapore'.[31]

The accolade probably underestimates the magnitude of the task that Lee undertook in resurrecting post-war Singapore, while at the same time preventing the communists from taking control of the city. For many observers, this fate was a racing certainty. Lee, by cloaking himself in the rhetoric and methods of the far left, managed to deflect the communist onslaught, while at the same time reviving the economic fortunes of his country.

Lee not only brought his country to the safe harbour of independence under a democratic constitution, but also proved himself a brilliant prime minister who ran his country much in the way that a chief executive runs a large corporation. From inception, Lee Kuan Yew set out a clear strategy for growth. In January 1996, he explained that soon after independence it was decided

> to link Singapore up with advanced countries and make ourselves a hub or nodal point for the expansion and extension of their activities. To attract such capital and human resources, Singapore set out to promote conditions and facilities better than those found elsewhere in the region.[32]

It was a corporate strategy that Lee would carry out with characteristic efficiency. Over the next two decades, Lee would indeed become recognised as a statesman of genius, and Singapore, with just 2 million citizens, would develop a global significance far above its pocket size. As a CEO, he had no rivals. As John Connally, Nixon's treasury secretary, would state after a world tour, 'Singapore is the best run country in the world.'[33]

19

Capitalist Redoubt

Hong Kong: 1945–97

Once Japan began its full-scale invasion of China with a deployment near Beijing on 7 July 1937, and a parallel attack on Shanghai, the future of Hong Kong must have seemed perilous indeed. Although Chiang Kai Shek's 700,000-strong army put up a better than expected defence against the smaller but better equipped and trained forces of the Japanese Emperor, within a year the Generalissimo was forced to withdraw to Chongqing in Sichuan Province. A total of 600,000 refugees flooded into Hong Kong, increasing the size of the population by 63 per cent. Only the sudden and enormous growth of Hong Kong as the main industrial centre and supply route for the Kuomintang army enabled the city to absorb this rapid increase in humanity.

Nevertheless support for Chiang had to be covert. Britain refused requests to send pilots to train the *Kuomintang* air force and also forbade a secret airplane assembly plant to be located within the colony. In spite of acquiescing to Japan's demand that Britain should not support China, a position taken out of military weakness in the region, most local Hong Kong Chinese continued to believe in the power of Pax Britannica. The reputation of British power far outlived the reality.

Though the new population logistics were a problem for the governor and his colonial administration, for the British government the main conundrum was how to defend Hong Kong itself. On being called into office, Churchill, constrained by his primary goal of defending Britain against Nazi expansion in Europe, could not reasonably have reinforced Hong Kong's defences or committed significant military resources to the region. With just 10,000 troops comprising six regular infantry battalions, (two English, two Indian and two Canadian), the Hong Kong garrison could do no more than hold up an invading army. Indeed Churchill even considered whether it was advisable to withdraw the troops altogether but decided that this would be a dishonourable course that would utterly undermine Britain's prestige in the region.

Four hours after the Japanese bombing of Pearl Harbor, the attack on Hong Kong was underway. In just one bombing mission the Hong Kong air force was annihilated. Then Lt General Takashi of the 23rd Corp led a 20,000-strong invasion force. Hong Kong's defenders put up a valiant resistance which lasted for 17 days; this was no foretaste of Britain's later abject military humiliation at Japan's hands in Malaya and Singapore. British casualties in Hong Kong numbered 2,232 killed and a further 2,300 injured; the garrison fought till all meaningful resistance was expended. Governor Sir Mark Young became the first British administrator to surrender a colonial possession since America had been yielded in 1782.

In this historic context it is perhaps not surprising that, in spite of the inevitability of the outcome, the loss of Hong Kong created a profound shock within Asia. Britain could never be looked at in the same light again. Leo Amery mused that '. . . we are on the eve of very great changes in the relation of Asia to Europe', and he doubted the possible existence, '. . . in the future empires like our Asiatic Empire'.[1] For Chinese *Kuomintang* officials watching events unfold from their defensive hideout in Sichuan, the assumption was that, in the event of a successful conclusion of the war, Hong Kong would be returned to China. Even the Colonial Office presented a defeatist scenario when it accepted that 'arrangements existing before the Japanese occupation would not be restored'.[2]

For the Chinese residents of Hong Kong, the fall of the city, in which thousands of civilians perished, was only a foretaste of what was to come. Lt General Isogai Rensuke took over from Sakai and became the city's new governor in February 1942. It was clear from the outset that, in spite of Japan's lofty rhetoric declaring its intention to liberate Asia from colonial oppression, its military commanders simply replaced a benevolent dictatorship with a despotic one. As Steve Tsang concluded in *Hong Kong, A Modern History* (2004), 'The Japanese never intended to treat other Asians as equals or genuine partners.'[3]

During the battle for Hong Kong itself the Japanese army gave a foretaste of what was to come when, at a medical station in St Stephen's College in Stanley, 56 British wounded patients, seven nurses and two doctors were murdered. Under the Japanese military police, the *Kempeitai*, a reign of terror was implemented. Failure to bow correctly to sentries could result in Chinese civilians being shot or decapitated on the spot. Homes were raided and their valuable possessions looted. Civilians were randomly chosen for target practice or to be used in bayonet training. Suspected resistors were rounded up and tortured, usually by extracting fingernails or being pumped so full of water that it would leach from other parts of the body. Resistance was futile though the British Army Aid Group did manage to smuggle several thousand people out of Hong Kong and back to allied lines. As in most of Asia the only effective military action was taken by communist guerrillas.

As the war in the Pacific drew to a close, the politics of post-war settlement began to heat up. Hong Kong was more complicated than most. One of Roosevelt's war aims had been to see the end of the European empires in Asia, not least that of his British allies. However, in April 1945, when America's ambassador to China suggested to Winston Churchill that at the end of the war Britain should return Hong Kong to China, he responded by saying that it would happen 'over my dead body'.[4] Nevertheless, the tug-of-war between the two allies continued. The British were not informed that the American Lt General Albert Wedemeyer was intending to liberate the Canton–Hong Kong region; when this aim was discovered at Potsdam, planning for restoration of British rule went into overdrive. On the day of the surrender, a naval taskforce comprising two carriers, a battleship, three cruisers and a flotilla of smaller vessels was despatched to Hong Kong.

In so doing, the British completely ignored the Allied protocol whereby Hong Kong fell into Chiang Kai Shek's theatre of operation. He naturally wanted to accept the Japanese surrender in Hong Kong for China. However, Chiang decided that the Hong Kong question could wait. Though his land-based forces could have arrived in Hong Kong first, he decided, not for the first or last time, that his priority was to deal with the communists. He did not want troops tied down in Hong Kong, and eventually it was agreed that the British Admiral Harcourt would accept the Japanese surrender equally for Britain and on behalf of Chiang's China. How different Hong Kong's future would have been if Chiang had pressed rapidly for liberation of the city by the *Kuomintang* army; in these circumstances it seems unlikely that Britain would have been able to prise Hong Kong away from China.

In Hong Kong itself, when news of the Japanese surrender spread, the senior British officer in the colony, Franklin Gimson, fearlessly demanded to see the Japanese commandant at the Stanley Prisoner of War Camp and informed him that he was taking over its administration. Gimson, by now a frail and undernourished figure, immediately gave orders for the Japanese garrison to maintain civil order. Harcourt arrived on 30 August and established a British administration; recognising Gimson's bravery, Harcourt appointed him Lt governor though he was soon repatriated for 'recuperation' from his long internment.

On 7 September, Brigadier MacDougall took over civilian administration in what was to become the model of government efficiency in liberated Asia. He set about dealing with the crucial problems of currency, labour, health, food and fuel. The yen was replaced by a new Hong Kong dollar, and over 30,000 labourers were employed to clean up the city. The city's utilities were rapidly restored, and by the end of the year, even the banks were open for business. Within months the population, which had fallen to 600,000 under the Japanese, had risen to 1 million. With characteristic British modesty, MacDougall was prepared to accept little of the credit. He told the Colonial Office that he 'would like still more to be able to assure you that our efforts are solely responsible for the gratifying transformation . . . the truth is a good deal simpler: if you give them half a chance, you cannot keep the Chinese down'.[5] It was an observation that was to characterise the peculiar symbiotic relationship between British colonial administrators and the Hong Kong Chinese in the post-war period.

To demonstrate that the Japanese rule of Hong Kong was a mere interlude in the British rule of its colony, the Colonial Office decided that Sir Mark Young should resume his governorship after a suitable period of recuperation in England.

Civilian rule and a Crown Colony system of government were thus restored on
1 May 1946. Young recognised immediately that psychologically the Chinese attitude to Europeans had now changed. They were no longer invincible masters;
Asiatic races were not necessarily subservient. This much at least had been gleaned
from the short-lived Japanese triumph. On restoration of civilian rule, the forward-
looking Young now declared that it was 'under consideration the means by which
in Hong Kong, as elsewhere in the Colonial Empire, the inhabitants of the Territory can be given a fuller and more responsible share in the management of their
own affairs'.[6] The British now had to do more than simply rule; they had to explain
the benefits of continued British administration.

Young repealed the prohibition that prevented Chinese living on Hong Kong's
'Peak' residential area, an important symbolic gesture. He also appointed the first
Chinese cadet officer. Proposals were announced for domestic political reform
with suggestions for an elected Chinese municipal council. However, these proposals, in a manner which was to become characteristic of Hong Kong's Chinese
population, were greeted with blank apathy. The lack of response may well have
reflected the effective job of administration being done by the British; as Young
pointed out to the Colonial Office, apathy 'may be flattering to the system ... and
to the government itself'.[7]

More likely the Chinese population of Hong Kong, the flotsam of people that
had washed up in the city after the depredations of the *Kuomintang*, the Japanese and
later the communists, were far more interested in survival and making money than
in politics. The economy recovered rapidly. Already by 1946, trade had regained
pre-war levels and the introduction of an income tax, combined with economic
growth, would enable the colony to cut all financial links with London and control
by its treasury as early as 1948. As Nigel Fisher, under secretary of state at the
Colonial Office, would later confide, 'I find that even Treasury Ministers smile
when I mention Hong Kong, because it is one of the few colonies that does not
make large demands on the British taxpayer.'[8]

Although Young's successor, Sir Alexander Grantham, started his job in the
belief that Young's planned democratic reforms had been pushed by the clamour
from Hong Kong's people, he was soon persuaded otherwise by a delegation of
prominent citizens who persuaded him to stop a madness which would ruin Hong
Kong. The prominent Chinese lawyer and legislator Sir Man Kam Lo argued that
'To suggest that members elected by a fractional electorate can and will more adequately represent the Colony as a whole than nominated members is a proposition with which I profoundly disagree.'[9] The Young Plan was buried and all talk
of democratic reform shelved for a generation. Grantham was nevertheless committed to a progressive dialogue with the Chinese people whom he regarded as
partners in the development of the city. He well understood Hong Kong's Chinese
priorities: '...provided that the government maintains law and order, does not
tax the people too much and that they can obtain justice in the courts, they are

satisfied and well content to devote their time to making more money in one way or another'.[10] Above all Hong Kong provided a safe haven from the chaos that was taking place in China itself.

As Chiang had predicted, he did indeed have his hands full in trying to deal with the communists. With regard to the future of Hong Kong he stayed consistent with the line he had espoused in August 1945, 'I wish to state here that the present status of Hong Kong is regulated by a treaty signed by China and Great Britain. Changes in the future will be introduced only through friendly negotiations between the countries.'[11] As for Mao, he first made his views on Hong Kong known in an interview with Western journalists at the end of 1946. Gordon Harmon recorded that Mao had stated that 'China has enough trouble in her hands to try to clean up the mess in her own country, leave alone trying to rule Formosa, or for us to clamour for the return of Hong Kong. I am not interested in Hong Kong; the communist party is not interested in Hong Kong; it has never been the subject of discussion amongst us . . . will certainly not allow it to be the bone of contention between your country and mine.'[12]

Although the Chinese Communist Party set up an office in Hong Kong, it refrained from stirring up local agitation which it expressly forbade. For the People's Republic of China (PRC), Hong Kong rapidly became important as a conduit point for information and international activity. In turn the Hong Kong administration was happy to turn a blind eye to their presence and activities as long as communist activity within the colony and its trade unions remained quiescent. The same rules applied to the CIA which operated one of its largest offices in the world from the British colony. In his autobiography, former Governor Sir Alexander Grantham complained that the CIA was 'extremely ham-handed at one time until we had to take a very strong line to stop them being so stupid'.[13] Rather like post-war Berlin, Hong Kong became a sort of free city in which all parties could operate within limits. It was a tacit understanding which suited all sides and one which worked with remarkable success in Hong Kong's post-war history.

Although the Hong Kong garrison comprised 30,000 troops plus tanks, heavy guns and a fleet equipped with an aircraft carrier, Hong Kong's governors always knew that they ruled with the acquiescence of the government of the mainland. This did not prevent conflict outside Hong Kong itself. In a famous incident, later portrayed in the 1957 film *Yangtse Incident* starring Richard Todd, the frigate, *HMS Amethyst*, was attacked while on a routine mission to Nanking. Caught in the crossfire of the communist artillery which held the north bank of the *Yangtse* River versus the Kuomintang on the south, the ship was badly damaged and effectively held hostage to the Chinese guns. Negotiations lasted for 101 gruelling days aboard the *Amethyst*, with the Chinese only too happy to humiliate the British before the ship was able to make good its escape.

To bolster the perceived vulnerability of Hong Kong, the British government sought the support of the USA. However, there was a natural American political ambivalence towards a British Crown colony. During the Quemoy crisis in 1955, Eisenhower wrote to Churchill, and in saying that it would not go down well with Americans if the USA was seen to be giving support to British Imperial conquests such as Malaya and Hong Kong, he implied that military assistance would not be forthcoming in case of attack by the Red Army. Nevertheless, while in the immediate aftermath of the post-war period, America was ambivalent about the defence of Hong Kong and indeed questioned whether this was beyond even its military reach, after the fall of China to communism and the Korean War, Eisenhower made it clear to Churchill that in spite of the domestic political difficulties, the USA would be at Britain's side.

Nevertheless, America's position on Hong Kong flip-flopped depending on the current state of its relationship with Britain. After British Labour Prime Minister Harold Wilson refused to send troops to Vietnam in the early 1960s, a piqued Dean Rusk bluntly warned them, '. . . don't expect us to save you again. They [the Red Army] can invade Sussex and we wouldn't do a damn thing about it'.[14]

Whether America would have risked military support for Hong Kong and a possible embroilment in a 'Third World War' is open to question. However, it must also have been a question that Mao and Zhou Enlai would have asked themselves, particularly after they had so badly misjudged America's aggressive response to Kim Il Sung's invasion of South Korea. On occasions, Hong Kong's position was made seemingly precarious by international events. In 1965, Chinese Foreign Minister Chen Yi feared that the British were using Hong Kong 'as a base for aggression against Vietnam', and warned that 'This action is most stupid. We hope it will choose a wiser course in its own interests.'[15] In spite of these spats, the balance of risks worked; Hong Kong's anomalous position remained intact throughout the Cold War, even when fears of the communist 'domino' were at their highest during the wars in Korea and Vietnam or indeed when the communists challenged the authority of Hong Kong's government during the Cultural Revolution.

Although international pressure forced Hong Kong to impose a trade embargo on the People's Republic of China (PRC) in December 1950, Hong Kong still proved a valuable conduit for the Chinese in terms of smuggled goods. The Hong Kong government was probably compliant in this respect and its notorious corrupt police force even more so. The truth was that the status of Hong Kong suited all parties. Nobody wanted to risk an East–West showdown. Hong Kong sat quietly in the middle as a sort of no-man's land. Governor Grantham observed that the strength of Hong Kong depended largely upon non-involvement in political issues. Neutrality was strictly applied. In the House of Commons, Labour Defence Minister A.V. Alexander stated that 'Hong Kong has long had a tradition of neutrality and non-interference with the politics of China . . . steps have been taken . . . to deal with any breach of the conditions under which Chinese nationals, either Kuomintang or communist, are allowed to reside there.'[16] In fact, the balance of power always lay with the PRC; if they wanted Hong Kong they could take it. Sir Robert Black, Grantham's successor, commented bluntly that 'we hold our position in Hong Kong at China's sufferance'.[17]

The British mandarins on Hong Kong need not have feared. Unbeknownst to them, during the Cultural Revolution, Zhou Enlai was told by Mao that 'Hong Kong remains the same'; too much violence he feared 'might lead to us having to take Hong Kong back ahead of time.'[18] Zhou Enlai had warned that this would have disastrous consequences. Apart from the calamitous social consequences of a communist Chinese takeover in Hong Kong and the likely damage to international prestige, the city-state was the main source for China of that precious commodity, 'hard currency'.

If Britain ruled Hong Kong by dint of its good administration and the preference of its people for British rather than communist rule, there was one major exception to this rosy picture. The corruption in the city's police force, which had been well known in the pre-war days, had, by the early 1960s, become endemic. It was generally estimated that a high proportion of the colony's police had been or were involved with organised crime. In effect the Chinese 'triads' operated their drug, prostitution and smuggling businesses with the connivance of the police authorities. The scandal reached its height with the investigation of Chief Superintendent Peter Godber and finally forced the governor to take vigorous action with the setting up of an 'Independent Commission against Corruption' in February 1974.

Whatever the apparent geographical complications, Hong Kong worked. The number of registered industrial establishments rose from 972 in 1947 to 1,522 in 1950. Over the same period the value of trade rose from HK$ 2.7 billion to HK$ 7.5 billion. The fall of Shanghai to Mao's People's Liberation Army proved a boon of sorts to Hong Kong. The Shanghaiese cotton magnates relocated to Hong Kong, injecting capital, technology and better management. They also brought production scale. Dick Wilson, editor of *The Far East Economic Review*, concluded that 'the economic impact of the Shanghai industrialists was decisive'.[19] Although with the arrival of the communists and the imposition of trade embargoes, Hong Kong's share of China trade fell from 32 per cent in 1951 to 5 per cent in 1959, the long-term impact was muted; with burgeoning international economies and consumer markets, the Hong Kong entrepreneurs could look elsewhere for sales.

Manufacturing boomed. Already in 1961 the administration of President John F. Kennedy was forced to open discussions with Hong Kong on textile export restraint to the USA. Employment in industry rose from 5 per cent in 1950 to 40 per cent in 1980. This was no centrally planned economic strategy, however. As Steve Tsang concludes in *Hong Kong, A Modern History*:

> The greatest contribution by the government to Hong Kong's economic transformation in the 1950s lay in providing the conditions for industries to develop and grow. It maintained political and social stability at a time when neither could be taken for granted in East Asia.'[20]

The British colonial administrators merely set the preconditions for growth with low taxes, minimal government interference, rights to ownership of property under law and political stability, and let the animal spirits of Chinese capitalists do the rest. As Hong Kong's last governor, Christopher Patten, pointed out in *East and West* (1998), 'Both Adam Smith and Milton Friedman would find much to celebrate in Hong Kong's record.'[21]

Insecurity about the future, given the history of China and the proximity of its Communist neighbour, may also have played a part in promoting Hong Kong's extraordinary work ethic. In the late 1950s, a British labour advisor noted that 'Capitalists ... want quick returns money back in five years not 20 for fear something happens before. No one knows how long Hong Kong will exist, or how long it will prosper.'[22] Five years was probably too long for most Hong Kong industrialists. Most of them developed copycat products with little or no capital investment or research and development content, simply using Hong Kong's cheap labour and its flexibility as a tool for profit. On a visit to the factory of a Hong Kong listed company in the early days of personal computers in the 1980s, Stephen Barber, a British investment manager, noted that the assembly line consisted of a small room full of trestle tables and benches with workers equipped with nothing more than soldering irons; in the room next door women were stitching garments and further on electric fans were being made. Unlike 'Made in Japan', the logo 'Made in Hong Kong' came to represent cheap and shoddy.

By the 1960s, American industrial investors were swarming to Hong Kong to re-establish their country's strong historic links with the colony. By mid-decade, America had become Hong Kong's main trading partner, and over 400 American companies were located there including 150 regional head offices. It was not all low-tech investment as shown by Fairchild's decision to establish a semi-conductor plant in 1965. Nevertheless, high returns enabled Hong Kong's industrialists to fund their own growth.

Although Hong Kong began to attract some foreign direct investment from America and Japan, by the late 1970s some 94 per cent of industrial establishments had been locally funded. Hong Kong companies provided 87 per cent of manufacturing employment and over 80 per cent of output. The success of the city was also evident in a population boom which saw the number of inhabitants rise from 2.5 million in 1955 to 4 million in 1970 and 6 million in 1990.

The origins of Hong Kong's laissez-faire approach to economic management can be traced to the immediate post-war period, but it was Financial Secretary John Cowperthwaite (1961–72) who put intellectual bones on the strategy. Professor Alvin Rabushka, an expert on the Hong Kong economy, described Cowperthwaite as 'brilliant, well-trained in economics, suffered no fools, and was highly principled. He wouldn't last five minutes in a similar post in Britain ...'.[23] In Hong Kong, he found more fertile ground for his 'libertarian' economic views than in socialist Britain of the late 1950s and 1960s where even the Conservative Party accepted the nationalisation of large parts of the economy. Cowperthwaite affirmed that the private sector was always a better alternative to the public and that the latter must be restrained at all costs and do only what is necessary and productive. He also averred 'a keen realisation of the importance of not withdrawing capital from the private sector of the economy'.[24] Cowperthwaite's successor Philip Haddon-Cave would describe this as the 'positive non-intervention policy'.[25] The results were spectacular. Defying the first and second oil crises which so crippled the economies of Europe and America, Hong Kong's GDP grew by five times between 1971 and 1981; this compared with a not insubstantial growth of 2.8 times in the preceding decade.

While the British provided the infrastructure and exacted modest financial demands on its citizens, it was the Hong Kong people themselves who added the dynamism peculiar to the city. Professor Rabushka, a specialist commentator on the Hong Kong economy, would joke that the Hong Kong entrepreneurs represented 'The pure form of homo economicus. His given name is Homo Hongkongus . . . '; Rabushka also pointed out the strange polarity between Britain's relative economic decline and the rising fortunes of Hong Kong claiming that 'Hong Kong = Happy Kingdom, while UK = Unhappy Kingdom'.[26]

A laissez-faire approach to public spending did not mean that there was no spending on social or physical infrastructure. Taxes may have been low, with income tax less than 20 per cent, but rapid economic growth boosted government revenue and filled its coffers for current expenditure while at the same time building a handsome reserve. Cowperthwaite was able to introduce mandatory free education and a rudimentary health service, and embarked on the construction of the first cross-harbour tunnel. The government also took upon itself the role of providing housing for the city's burgeoning population and became the city's biggest real estate developer.

The even more rapid expansion of Hong Kong's economy in the 1970s enabled Governor MacLehose, a career diplomat, to engage in an extensive welfare programme and a ten-year housing scheme which 'would lead to the virtual disappearance of squatter areas, eliminate overcrowding and sharing in both private and public housing . . . and keep pace with the natural expansion of the population'.[27] MacLehose also oversaw the construction of the Mass Transit Railway (MTR), which provided a means to handle the requirements of the city's rapidly growing population while establishing one of the essential infrastructures for a continued expansion of the city.

If property development was to become the key preoccupation of government, it was also the sector which was to provide Hong Kong with its most powerful business magnates. After a run on banks in 1965, the government had placed a ban on the creation of new banking licences, which was only lifted in 1978; this initiated a boom in the arrival of foreign banks from Europe and America, which sought to capitalise on Hong Kong and the region's rapid growth. Whereas previously manufacturing had been the city's engine of growth, increasingly it was services and particularly financial services which drove Hong Kong forward. Li Ka Shing, who had made his first fortune as owner of the Artificial Flower Works, made a series of bold acquisitions which catapulted him to top place among the city's property magnates.

The Cheung Kong Group became his flagship though he also orchestrated a bold stock market takeover of the venerable 'hong' company, Hutchison Whampoa, which he transformed into the world's largest private operator of container ports. Another 'hong' to fall was the Hong Kong and Kowloon Wharf and Godown Co., which had been founded by William Keswick in 1889 and controlled ever since by Jardine Matheson. Much to the chagrin of the Keswick family and 'hong' interests, this takeover by Sir Y.K. Pao was also backed by British financiers at the Hong Kong and Shanghai Bank among others. Other notable Chinese-owned property companies to emerge included New World, Henderson, Hang Lung, Hysan and Sun Hung Kai. Although the famous British 'hong' companies, Swire and Hong Kong Land (sister company of the historic trading house of Jardine Matheson), also prospered, they were gradually eclipsed by the Chinese upstarts in the 1980s.

Hong Kong's position as a regional financial centre was also bolstered by the merger of four stock exchanges into The Stock Exchange of Hong Kong in 1986. Most importantly perhaps, Deng Xiaoping's deregulation of the mainland Chinese economy served to provide remarkable opportunities for Hong Kong to prosper as the financial capital of China's emerging capitalist economy.

Early on in his leadership Deng had begun the process of property deregulation, creating the first wave of Chinese millionaires in the farming sector, but it was the creation of special economic zones which allowed private companies to compete with state-owned enterprises, which really spurred the growth of Hong Kong as a source of foreign direct investment. Across the border Hong Kong's textile manufacturers and others soon found they could employ labour at a fraction of the cost of Hong Kong; increasingly marketing, design and management infrastructure was provided in Hong Kong while manufacture and assembly was carried out in China. The number of workers employed by Hong Kong companies in the PRC increased to 2 million in 1988 and to 5 million in 1997.

By 1997, Hong Kong had become not only the financial powerhouse for the region but the gateway through which the virgin markets of China could be tapped. Globally, entrepreneurs greedily eyed the potential of selling consumer products to over 300 million households. Contrary to the expectations of Western media organisations, the Tiananmen Square episode proved a tiny glitch in the rapid liberalisation of China, and Hong Kong took full advantage of its booming economy.

It is perhaps the greatest of ironies that a city perched, seemingly precariously, on the borders of one of the world's most radical experiments in socialist organisation should have become an icon of all that was most vigorous and creative in the capitalist system. Peculiarly Hong Kong had been turned into a model of capitalist endeavour over exactly the same period that British politicians had taken the United Kingdom down the socialist 'mixed-economy' path. By contrast, in Hong Kong, Britain had achieved, through a paternalistic, indeed Confucian ethic, a 'mandarin' system of government renowned for a laissez-faire approach to enterprise, efficiency and fairness. By the 1980s Hong Kong had become a model for Britain's own economic reinvention under Mrs Thatcher. An even greater irony was that in having achieved all this, Britain would have to hand back this colonial gem to China whose communist political culture was inimical to everything that Britain had stood for.

PART III

Cold War in the Balance

20

The Korean War

Korea: 1950—3

W hen North Korea's (Democratic People's Republic of Korea: DPRK) Soviet-
supplied T-34 tanks rumbled past the 38th parallel on the morning of 25 June
1950, they met a Republic of Korea (ROK) army completely unprepared for combat. Poorly trained and equipped, the ROK forces crumbled against the communist onslaught; it was to be a pattern that would be repeated throughout the
Korean War. Brigadier General Roberts of the American Assistance Group had
reported on North Korean preparedness that sources indicated that the North
Koreans had up to 100 Russian planes and a training programme for pilots. However, Roberts's conclusions about the state of South Korea's defences were hugely
over optimistic; he enthused that the ROK 'had the best doggoned shooting army
outside the United States'.[1] Also American intelligence grossly underestimated
North Korean strength. In reality Kim Il Sung had a 135,000-strong army supported by Soviet tanks and a 200-strong air force comprising Yak-9 fighters and
Il-10 fighter bombers. By comparison Syngman Rhee in the South had just 90,000
troops which, because of American aversion and suspicion of the ROK president,
had been denied tanks, anti-tank weapons and any artillery bigger than 105 mm.

It was not just the ROK forces that were unprepared. In another repetition of
history, General MacArthur, ensconced in his headquarters at the Daiichi Insurance Building in Tokyo, failed to anticipate North Korea's invasion, just as he had
been unprepared for the Japanese invasion of the Philippines (this in spite of CIA
warnings that the North Koreans would attack in June). Conflict could not have
come as a surprise. Kim Il Sung had been sponsoring insurrection in the South,
and his army had already been engaged in a sporadic border war with the ROK for
over a year.

In truth the North Korean invasion of the South reflected a misunderstand-
ing on all sides. Mao had assumed that the USA would not intervene, 'since the
war would be an internal matter which the Korean people would decide for themselves'.[2] Stalin, a cautious leader who was careful to camouflage Soviet involvement in the attack, must also have assumed that America, which had stood by and
watched a Soviet-inspired coup d'état in Czechoslovakia in 1948, would not stir

itself to action. During Mao's visit to Moscow in December 1949, Stalin told him that Americans were too afraid to fight another war. Viewing events in Eastern Europe, Kim Il Sung would have made the same calculation. Given American apparent uncertainty as to the strategic importance of defending Korea and Taiwan, countries omitted by Acheson in a speech to the American Press Club in which he laid out America's 'line-in-the-sand' in Asia, it is perhaps not surprising that the Communist powers misunderstood the signals.

By contrast the American response to North Korea's invasion was almost instantaneous. 'By God I'm going to let them have it,'[3] Truman stormed at his advisors when he arrived in Washington on the evening of the attack; he even made plans to drop an atom bomb on Russia if their armies joined the invasion. On 27 June, President Truman committed American air and naval support to the ROK cause without consulting Congress, (a decision which would later come back to haunt him politically). Ground troops were authorised three days later. It was a decision Truman had to make. After losing China in 1949, a failure for which he was being blamed by the Republican Congress, the president had no option but to act aggressively to halt what was seen to be part of a global Soviet-backed advance. In hindsight, an earlier and clearer American position on the importance attached to Korea would have been helpful. The result reported by the British ambassador in Peking was that for the Chinese: 'The strength and extent of American reaction has been a shocking surprise. . . .'[4]

In addition to pledging military support, Truman called a meeting of the United Nations (UN) Security Council, which, at 10.45 pm on 27 June, passed a resolution calling for UN members to 'render such assistance to the Republic of Korea as may be necessary to repel the armed attack and to restore international peace and security to the area'.[5] The resolution was passed by a seven-to-one majority; by a quirk of history, the Soviets, who on 13 January 1950 had walked out of the UN because America blocked the People's Republic of China (PRC) from taking up the *Kuomintang's* seat on the National Security Council, were not present to veto action against the North Korean invasion. It remained the only UN resolution calling for war against another country, until the UN vote calling for the ejection of Saddam Hussein's Iraqi army from Kuwait in November 1990.

In America, popular reaction to the war was wholly positive. A nation traumatised by the fear of communism after the loss of China and the development of a Soviet atom bomb in 1949, followed by fears of infiltration heightened by the Alger Hiss espionage case, was psychologically prepared for war against Communist aggressors. In the press, only the strange alliance of the *Daily Worker*, the *Wall Street Journal* and the *Chicago Tribune* criticised American involvement in another foreign war.

In England reaction was similarly largely robust in favour of a vigorous stance against communism; even the far left was split, with Tom Driberg against the UN vote for war and Michael Foot, later a left-wing leader of the Labour Party,

aggressively in favour. Labour Prime Minister Clement Attlee told the British people that 'The fire that has started in distant Korea might burn down your own
house.'[6] There was also a fear that the action in Korea was merely a decoy for a
planned Soviet attack in Europe.

For British diplomat Oliver Franks, the US reaction merely confirmed the
resolve and talent of the president and a State Department which included such
brilliant intellects as Acheson, Kennan, Bohlen and Dean Rusk.

> Their thinking moved from the Czech coup in February 1948 to the Berlin Airlift,
> to Korea. These were stages in Soviet risk-taking that would culminate in their armed
> forces crossing boundaries ... the presence of that extraordinary group in the
> Administration_ made a difference to history.[7]

In hindsight, the decision to fight to save Korea was a critical moment which defined
America's hegemony over 'free' Asia in the post-war period.

With the collapse of the ROK army, which lost 40 per cent of its troops to
capture or desertion within the first week, it soon became apparent that, if the Korean Peninsula was to be saved, American troops would be needed on the ground.
Truman authorised this on 30 June, and the 24th Division was hastily despatched
from Japan. Within days, the troops, who had been cosily nestled in peace-keeping
activities in Japan, were dug in around Osan. Between 7.00 am and 9.30 am on
5 July, the American advance positions were overrun by T-34 tanks and the 24th
Infantry Division was thoroughly routed. The Second World War anti-tank shells
simply bounced off the Russian-made armour. After this defeat there followed a
desperate defence of the city of Taejon during which General Dean was humiliatingly captured.

American troops, untrained in the difficult art of fighting an orderly retreat,
fled southwards in disarray. Reinforcements in the form of the 25th Infantry Division and 1st Cavalry were hurriedly despatched. After relieving the 24th Infantry
Division, which had lost 30 per cent of its force, the 25th Infantry Division were
themselves flung back after a mere couple of hours of fighting at Yechon. The perceived cowardly flight of an all-black regiment within two hours of the opening
engagement at Yechon would contribute to the abandonment of racially segregated
units in the American army though Truman had initiated an integration policy in
July 1948. (It was seven years later that Rosa Parks would be arrested for refusing
to give up her seat to a white person on a segregated bus in Montgomery, Alabama,
an event that would spark the American Civil Rights Movement.)

The human wave tactics of the North Korean army, who attacked with bugles
and banshee cries, was no doubt a terrifying experience for poorly trained and led
American troops, but the bad performance of the US army was a serious indictment of how standards had lapsed since the end of the Second World War. General
McArthur, sitting in Tokyo, was quick to deflect criticism of his army's performance and informed Washington that 'The South Korea forces are in confusion,

have not seriously fought, and lack leadership.'[8] American soldiers on the ground knew that they were equally at fault. Colonel Paul Freeman described their performance as that of a completely 'defeated rag-tag that had lost all will'.[9] Another experienced soldier, Colonel John Michaelis, told the *Saturday Evening Post* that American recruits had spent 'a lot time listening to lectures on the differences between communism and Americanism and not enough time crawling on their bellies on manoeuvres with live ammunition zinging over them'.[10] It was all a far cry from the opinion of Clyde Alton, an Indiana veteran, who had predicted, 'This is going to be no war, cos these people are natives.'[11]

By August, the bedraggled 8th Army under General Walker was dug in at the South Eastern corner of the Korean Peninsula at Pusan, the major port of South Korea. Now there was nowhere to run. For the 7th Cavalry, whose most famous former commander was General Custer, it was another last stand. Surrender was not an option. The discovery of 26 American troops, hands bound with wire and bullets to the back of the head, stiffened the American infantry's resolve. If they did but know it, the 95,000 American troops and their 45,000 remaining ROK allies strung in a defensive perimeter around Pusan now outnumbered Kim's Il Sung's army. Though the human wave tactics had been successful, it was estimated that the North Koreans had taken 58,000 casualties in the first six weeks of the engagement. Appalling losses were suffered as they flung themselves at Walker's entrenched defences, and by 20 August the battle appeared to have been won by the defenders. A final North Korean attack on 31 August was easily repulsed and the fighting became stalemated.

Meanwhile in Tokyo, on 23 August, MacArthur took the critical decision (approved by Truman) on which much of his military reputation has since rested. Rather than reinforce Pusan, MacArthur decided to outflank the North Korean Army by landing the 7th Division and the 7th Marines under the command of his Chief of Staff General Almond at Inchon, a coastal city of 250,000 people, from where they could strike towards the capital, Seoul, and cut off supply lines to Kim's army in the South.

It was a bold decision. Inchon sits on a dreary tidal plain which for most of the day oozes waist-deep grey mud; the tides which, at 10 m, rank as some of the most extreme in the world meant that water only reached the high sea walls of the city for three hours a day. These high tides were needed to enable the Second World War vintage landing craft to unload their troops onto land. Only the 15 and 27 September and 11 October were suitable, with the added complication that the landing would have to be made at night. Furthermore the Americans' intent would have to be signalled by the capture of Wolmi-do Island, which overlooked the channels to the landing areas.

It was a brilliantly conceived strategy, though for many officers it was an unnecessarily risky, indeed foolhardy, operation. Rear Admiral James Doyle would only comment that 'The best I can say is that Inchon is not impossible.'[12] Objections were swept aside. MacArthur, who saw himself as a latter-day Caesar, seized the opportunity for an epic military venture which would confirm the greatness he craved.

In a typically grandiloquent speech in his Daiichi headquarters, MacArthur compared his decision to Quebec, where General Wolfe's audacious turning of the French lines by scaling the cliffs of the city brought a stunning victory. 'I can almost hear the ticking of destiny,' MacArthur told his assembled officers, 'We must act now or we will die . . . . We shall land at Inchon, and I shall crush them.'[13] It was a curious comparison. General Wolfe had died at Quebec, becoming the last British head of an army to be killed while leading his troops in battle; MacArthur would remain safely ensconced in Tokyo until Seoul had been taken.

In spite of having to sail through Typhoon Kezia, which had most of the troops retching throughout their sea journey, MacArthur's plan worked perfectly. On 15 September the wall front at Inchon was taken with just 21 casualties, and American forces advanced rapidly on Seoul, taking Kimpo Airport on 17 September. The 5th Marines reached the Capitol Buildings 10 days later on 27 September; MacArthur, who had wanted to retake Seoul exactly three months after its fall on 25 June, went ahead and announced the capture of the city two days before it happened. Not for the first time, MacArthur's personal propaganda agenda took precedence over military matters.

Meanwhile on 16 August, General Walker started the breakout from the Pusan Perimeter. The North Koreans, who had been reduced to just 70,000 troops, were now unhinged with their routes to the north cut off. The action also resulted in one of the most tragic-heroic episodes of the war. Having taken Hill 282 at great cost, the British Argyll and Sutherland Highlanders were driven from their prize after they were mistakenly strafed by American Mustang fighter planes; nevertheless, the hill was retaken in a heroic charge by Major Kenneth Muir, who lost 16 of his 30 troops. He declared that 'The gooks will never drive the Argylls off this hill.'[14] Muir, killed by machine gun fire, was awarded a posthumous Victory Cross for his bravery.

After Inchon, an alarmed Soviet Union, which had returned to the UN Security Council on 3 August 1950, called for the UN forces to halt at the 38th parallel and argued that the conquest of the North was not allowable under the UN resolution. President Truman had different priorities; conquest of the North and reunification of Korea was now considered a legitimate prize. However, whereas Washington was primarily concerned with not bringing China into the war, and thus instructed MacArthur not to use American troops close to the Chinese border on the Yalu River, MacArthur by contrast dismissed such concerns. Without authority, MacArthur infuriated Truman by unilaterally calling on the North to surrender. MacArthur, the hero of Inchon and lionised in the American press, was now out of control.

Truman's meeting with MacArthur at Wake Island, midway across the Pacific, failed to resolve the situation. The day before his meeting, Truman wrote to a cousin, 'I have a whale of a job before me. I have to talk to God's right hand man tomorrow.'[15] On 15 October, he greeted Truman with a handshake rather than the salute that protocol demanded; he was clearly telling the president that he was an equal not a minion. MacArthur was cynical about a meeting which he rightly saw as a photo opportunity for Truman, who sought to gain kudos from the success at Inchon and thus deflect his Republican critics back home. MacArthur, the lofty ruler of Japan, was also furious at having to deal with young policy wonks such as Dean Rusk, (an assistant Secretary of State for Far Eastern Affairs and later Secretary of State under Kennedy) who he described as a 'whippersnapper'.

However, he did assure Truman that the Chinese would not attack. Meanwhile the president passed up the opportunity to rein in his supreme commander in Asia. On returning to Tokyo, MacArthur, in direct contravention of his orders, removed all restrictions on US troops approaching the Chinese border at the Yalu River. In all probability, Truman, like many others before him, was intimidated by MacArthur and his ability to wield his public relations machine in the American media.

On 1 November 1950, a patrol of F Company of the 8th Cavalry reported that it was under attack from 'unidentified troops'.[16] Seemingly without notice, waves of Chinese troops in their padded cotton tunics had appeared out of the mists and charged in the now familiar human wave. Equally mysteriously the Chinese troops then disappeared. MacArthur either ignored this warning shot or decided that the Chinese retreat signified weakness, despite the CIA warning on 8 November that there were up to 40,000 Chinese troops already in North Korea. Early in October, the Indian ambassador in Beijing, Pannikkar, was warned by Zhou Enlai that if the UN crossed the 38th parallel, the Chinese would attack.

Washington, reassured by MacArthur, did not take the threat seriously. Walker's 8th Army pressed onward towards the Yalu River along Korea's western flank, while the Marines and X Army, divided from their comrades by mountains, advanced along the East Coast. MacArthur would later be correctly criticised for maintaining a divided command; hubris allowed him to spread his forces too thinly in the approach to the Yalu. Only later, after his sacking, would MacArthur's veil of media spin be lifted and his complacency and mismanagement be fully exposed by Congressional inquiries.

General Peng, who was directed by Mao to conduct the invasion of North Korea, had a formidable force at his command. The 13th Army group comprised four armies; each consisted of three divisions of 10,000 men. In addition there were cavalry and artillery regiments. Not wanting to openly bridge the Yalu while the Americans were occupying the southern bank, Peng secretly redeployed the entire army group, 130,000 soldiers in total, across the river which formed the border between China and North Korea.

It was a formidable feat. The fact that the American army were not aware of them was in part due to the lack of radio traffic – they had few radios – and the absence of significant mechanical support. Primitive technology had its advantages. The lightly equipped Chinese infantryman in his padded cotton jacket walked with his daily rations and was cheap to supply; whereas the American infantryman needed 60 pounds of supply per day, the Chinese fighter needed 10 pounds. This was brought by porters on foot in a vast human chain of logistical support. A People's Liberation Army (PLA) had a popular saying that the Red Army's two legs were better than the enemy's four wheels. Apart from the hardiness of his troops, Peng's other advantage was simply numbers; at one point the Chinese had more than a million men in Korea.

Peng's human wave tactics may have been basic, but they swept away the American forces that suffered both from complacency and stretched supply lines. For the second time in six months, General Walker's 8th Army was routed; it was only saved from annihilation by the fact that the Chinese troops could only march as fast as their feet could carry them. American air cover also slowed the Chinese advance. The US forces retreated in their trucks and troop carriers. It did not always save them. At Kunu-ri, where Chinese forces cut off the retreating 2nd Infantry Division and commanded the heights through which their retreat had to pass, the American forces were massacred. Immobilised vehicles backed up the retreating convoy, leaving them as sitting targets. The slaughter was prolific; as night fell, the Chinese infantry closed in for the kill. In just one afternoon the 2nd Division lost over 3,000 men.

The retreat to Pyongyang was chaotic. Colonel Freeman of the 23rd Infantry commented, 'Look around here. This is a sight that hasn't been seen for hundreds of years; the men of a whole United States Army fleeing from a battlefield, abandoning their wounded, running for their lives.'[17] The retreat was so rapid that the army's entire supply base at Pyongyang had to be torched.

On the East Coast, defeat was equally decisive, albeit the retreat was brilliantly conducted by the First Marine Division led by the tall, fair-haired Texan O.P. Smith. The Marines commander, much to the chagrin of the reckless Major General Almond, head of X Corps, refused to be rushed to the Yalu and planned his supply lines with traditional thoroughness. Nevertheless, at the Battle of Chosin Reservoir, where the Chinese had attacked in overwhelming numbers, Smith found his forces cut off from their line of retreat. He had not been helped by the fact that cut off by the mountains from the 8th Army, with whom Smith had no contact, MacArthur only chose to inform the Marines commander of the 8th Army's crushing defeat two days after the event. Smith remained phlegmatic. When a reporter described the Marines forthcoming action as a retreat, Smith contradicted this fact by pointing out that the enemy had them surrounded; 'Retreat, Hell,' he is reported to have said, 'we're just attacking in another direction'.[18]

With superb professionalism, in what turned out to be the highlight of the American army's war, Smith's Marines conducted a fighting withdrawal which allowed X corps to board ships at Hungnam with their equipment intact. Nevertheless, it was a brutal engagement conducted in sub-freezing temperatures. At $-40°C$, with a wind chill factor of $-70°C$, fuel froze and guns jammed. One soldier complained that between the field kitchen and his fox hole 40 yards away, gravy froze solid.

The Marines suffered 4,418 casualties with a further 7,313 non-battle casualties mainly caused by frostbite. The Chinese are thought to have suffered 37,500 casualties and, as an army not equipped with sleeping bags, it is thought that most of their troops must have suffered from frostbite. Unlike their troops in the West, where the Chinese infantry survived on abandoned American equipment, sleeping bags included, this was not a luxury that the Chinese foot soldier was afforded in the eastern Chosin campaign.

In spite of the heroics of O.P. Smith's Marines, the overall performance of the American army was not that expected of a force that had fought its way across the Pacific a little over five years earlier. Moreover, the lack of competence of the American forces had not improved since the start of the war. Sir Robert Mansergh, commander in chief of British forces in Hong Kong, noted that the American army's 'rations, supplies, and welfare stores are on such a scale as to be comical if they were not such a serious handicap to battle'.[19] This was not merely the stuff of jealousy and national rivalry. When American General Walker's jeep careered into an ROK truck and killed him, his replacement, a Second World War paratrooper, Lieutenant General Ridgway, a veteran of the 1945 Normandy landings and the Battle of the Bulge (the bloodiest battle in US history in which the American army repulsed a surprise German attack in the French Ardennes in December 1944), was equally dismissive of the 8th Army's performance. He was shocked by their poor training, pampered behaviour and above all their defeatist mentality. Within weeks Ridgway instilled a dramatic transformation in both morale and performance; most importantly, (like General Eisenhower and his field commanders Bradley, Patton and Montgomery at the Battle of the Bulge), Ridgway turned to the offensive.

Now it was the Chinese turn to suffer from over-ambition. Just as American supply lines and hubris had grown after Inchon, the Chinese army too became over-extended. The losses incurred by the human wave tactics mounted as American air power increased and as General Ridgway turned around the morale and performance of the 8th Army's troops. Although the Chinese army passed the 38th parallel on 27 March, their rate of progress began to slow. The American air force came to the rescue of the troops on the ground. The Chinese Mig-15s, which had so alarmed the Americans when they first appeared, were now being outperformed by the UN's 'Sabres', which proved to be the best fighter planes of the war. They accounted for 742 Migs shot down. For the American soldiers on the ground, the inability of the Chinese army to move by day, because of UN air superiority, eventually proved a decisive advantage.

Meanwhile Truman's dispute with MacArthur was coming to a head. While Truman and the State Department were determined at all costs to avoid bringing the Soviets into the conflict, to prevent turning the war into a global conflict, MacArthur was lobbying vigorously for a fully fledged bombing attack on mainland

China combined with a naval bombardment. For MacArthur, humiliated militarily so soon after his great military triumph at Inchon, the thought of fighting for a 'draw' at the 38th parallel was too much to bear. This is now what the Truman administration was determined to achieve. With some 66 per cent of the American population calling for withdrawal from the peninsula and waning support from its allies, Truman realised that a division at the 38th parallel was the most that could be gained from the Korean War. A letter from MacArthur to Joseph Martin, minority Republican leader in the House of Representatives, which called for the abandonment of the administration's 'Europe First' strategy, was made public. MacArthur's lobbying for war objectives diametrically opposed to the Truman administration amounted to gross insubordination; he had to go. On 11 April, at 1.00 am, the Washington Press Corp was called and the announcement of MacArthur's summary dismissal was made to a stunned world.

The method of dismissal appalled his fellow officers (although it is difficult to see how else it could have been done), but within a short while few disagreed with the decision. General Ridgway had quickly tired of the monster ego of his commanding officer. After launching Operation Ripper, a counterattack on the Chinese forces, he was amazed to find MacArthur flying to Korea to take command of a press conference, where he took all the credit for the attack. Ridgway would later write that MacArthur took the very real risk of igniting the Third World War. Similarly, General Bradley concluded that MacArthur's bid to widen the war with China would 'involve . . . [them] in the wrong war, at the wrong place, at the wrong time, and with the wrong enemy'. [20]

It was an argument that, overtime, has found few naysayers. MacArthur rapidly disappeared from public view, and his attempt to run for leadership of the Republican Party in 1953 was a humiliating failure. Colonel Ellis Williamson described him as 'a pompous old bastard; but a great soldier'. [21] Although Inchon was a military manoeuvre of real genius, perfectly executed, the overall assessment of MacArthur as a military commander is much less favourable. However, there is no disputing his brilliance as a propagandist, self-promoter and iconic leader.

In Korea, Peng was preparing for a final assault to take Seoul. The Battle of Imjin River saw some of the heaviest fighting of the campaign as Peng threw his raw recruits at the UN's defensive lines, in the hope that they would create breaches for his more experienced troops to exploit. In one of the most hard-fought actions of the war, the British 29th Brigade crucially held up the advance of Peng's 63rd Army. Facing overwhelming odds, the 'Gloucesters' fought one of the British army's most famous 'last stands'. Just 169 out of its 850 troops survived death or capture, while the British 29th Infantry Brigade lost 25 per cent of its front-line strength. Chinese losses were estimated at 10,000, but more importantly the enemy charge towards Seoul was halted on 25 April.

Although a new attack by Peng in mid-May saw a familiar collapse in ROK III Corps, Ridgway plugged the gap with the 3rd Division and 187th Airborne. It was the last major offensive of the war. Just as the American army had overextended itself as it approached the Yalu River, the Chinese army, having crossed the 38th Parallel, overreached its supply lines. Their infantry had suffered massive casualties, and the Chinese army was now a spent force.

Initial peace talks took place on 10 July when a UN delegation agreed to fly to Kaesong. It was a propaganda set up. Chinese propagandists used the UN flying of a white flag to claim victory, while at the meeting itself the UN were given lower chairs and bombarded with anti-imperialist speeches. China suspended talks on 22 August, after accusing the UN of attempting to murder their delegation in an air attack. China had won a propaganda victory, but when General Ridgway forced back the Chinese front in an October counterattack, the Communists again called for talks, this time held in neutral territory in no man's land at Punmunjom.

In the drawn-out talks, China now adopted a new strategy. They dug their 750,000 troops into an impregnable defensive line and prolonged the talks in the full knowledge that the western democracies would face increasing public pressure to end the war. In the five months of stalemate from July to November 1951, the UN forces suffered 60,000 casualties of which Americans accounted for more than a third.

Peace talks were to drag on for another 20 months. It was a period of immense frustration for the UN army, only occasionally leavened by the United Services Organisation, which arranged visits by Hollywood stars such as Bob Hope, Jack Benny and Danny Kay. Marilyn Monroe, who performed ten shows in February 1954, was later to claim that the experience was 'the best thing that ever happened to me .... I never felt like a star before in my heart ....'[22]

With the line of defence virtually established at the 38th Parallel, thus nominally achieving UN war aims, the main sticking point now remained the treatment of prisoners. The Communist negotiators wanted the return of all prisoners, while the UN was aware that a large number wanted to remain in the South. When Syngman Rhee defied Washington and simply opened the prison gates, some 16,000 of the 25,000 North Korean prisoners filtered into the South. Only 9,000 remained to be transported back to the North.

When an armistice was finally signed on 27 July 1953, a further 22,604 prisoners from the South were sent to neutral countries; meanwhile 12,773 prisoners were returned from the North. Embarrassingly, 21 Americans and one Englishman chose to stay in the North. Most of these Americans eventually filtered back to the West; the lone Englishman, Andrew Condron, returned to Britain in 1970 and sent his son by a Chinese wife to an English private school. Nevertheless, it should be noted that the prisoner exchanges demonstrated once again that given the choice, the vast majority of Koreans chose to live under American hegemony rather than communist rule.

The UN prisoners arrived back in skeletal condition, having suffered treatment compared unfavourably with that meted out by the Japanese in the Second World War; the degree of ideological brainwashing and psychological torture of the captured was also unique in modern warfare. Indeed George Blake, the British vice consul in Seoul, was turned into a communist stooge during his three years of captivity. American fears of communist infiltrators abounded, particularly in the midst of the McCarthyite hysteria of 1953. These fears formed the basis of John Frankenheimer's 1962 film *The Manchurian Candidate,* in which an American Korean War veteran is brainwashed into being a 'sleeper' for an assassination attempt on the president.

General Marshall described the Korean conflict as 'the century's nastiest little war'.[23] Alexander Haig, a staffer in Tokyo to General MacArthur and later secretary of state to Ronald Reagan, thought it was the most difficult conflict in American history. In essence the conflict was only nominally a UN war; in effect the USA, in support of South Korea, went to war against North Korea, the Soviet Union and China. The USA had lost 33,629 dead and over 100,000 wounded. This paled in comparison with the ROK, which lost 415,000 dead and 429,000 wounded. Combined British, Canadian, Australian and New Zealand losses amounted to 1,263 dead. Meanwhile Turkey, Belgium, Columbia, Ethiopia, France, Greece, Holland, the Philippines and Thailand lost 1,800 dead, of which Turkey accounted for half. An estimated 1.5 million Chinese and North Koreans lost their lives.

As ever, the civilian population suffered untold hardship. Families were forced to flee for their lives in circumstances of extreme hardship. Many perished of starvation, sickness or simply exhaustion. In 1953 an American economic survey mission estimated that the population's daily calorie intake was just 1,500 per day, some 30 per cent lower than normal survival rations. Witnesses recounted stories of mothers, too weak to carry their children, having to choose which ones to leave by the roadside to die. Often the elderly simply had to be abandoned. Many were never seen by their families again.

The war produced a number of important outcomes for the future conduct of the Cold War in Asia. Any complacency that America may have experienced following the Second World War was cut short. The USA now understood the scale of the challenge presented by the Soviet Union and China. The latter's armies had humiliated America on the battlefield and shown that the world's wealthiest and technologically most sophisticated power was not invincible.

America responded by an unprecedented build-up in military resources and technology over the succeeding decade; as a result of the Korean War, John Foster Dulles would develop the concept of 'massive retaliation' which dominated the next decade. Arguably however, the American military never fully absorbed the lessons of training, discipline and leadership failures, which characterised their army's performance during the Korean War; the USA never learnt the old military maxim that it is foot soldiers who win wars. Over-reliance on technology would reoccur in Vietnam and later in Iraq.

Mao, by his decision to invade Korea, won a psychological battle for leadership within the communist world but lost the opportunity to reclaim Taiwan. Deng

Xiaoping would later characterise Chinese participation in the war as a mistake. On balance, the outcome of the Korean War was advantageous to America. The USA was awakened to the very real threat posed by the Soviet Union and China to its Asian hegemony. South Korea was saved and went on to become one of the most remarkable economic success stories of the post-war period; perhaps most importantly, the Korean War turned American attention towards Asia as the main theatre in which the Cold War would be fought. Today, the Korean War is usually decried by American liberals as a futile episode in American history, a view propagated by Robert Altman's 1970 satirical film *MASH* (Mobile Army Surgical Hospital) and the popular long-running TV series of the same name.

Perhaps this viewpoint was not surprising given the Korean War's ebb and flow and its punctuation by long periods of stalemate, combined with its backdrop of a Korean climate which offers greater extremes of heat and cold than any other country. In many respects, particularly in its later stages, the Korean War shared the characteristics of the interminable and immobile conflict of the First World War. Also the Korean War did not end in complete victory for the USA. However, although it was a vicious war, costly in human life, military and civilian, in the fighting of it, America saved not only two-thirds of the Korean population from the woeful communist rule of North Korea's Kim Il Sung but probably saved Taiwan and much of Asia as well. President Truman had now drawn America's 'line-in-the-sand' and shown its Communist foes, the Soviet Union and China, that their expansionist policies in Asia would be resisted by aggressive military action where necessary.

21

The Great Leap Forward

China: 1949—61

In October 1958, Mao and his entourage set out on a tour of Southern China. Whether he noticed, along the route, the fields full of crops and the throngs of workers in brightly coloured clothing, is not recorded. The horizon was filled with squirts of black cloud from the newly built 'backyard' steel furnaces. The scene out of Mao's carriage window was a glowing testament to the twin pillars, grain and steel, that stood at the heart of Mao's Great Leap Forward. Other passengers on the train, however, were less impressed; some of them were aware that these idyllic views were a carefully managed stage-set, organised by the local party chiefs, whose fiefdoms abutted the railway. The party secretary of Hubei, Wang Renzhong, went as far as to order rice plants to be removed and replanted adjacent to the railway.

The reality of China's agricultural health was the opposite of the 'Potemkin' pantomime being elegantly portrayed along the route of Mao's imperial procession. The catastrophe of the Great Leap Forward, initiated at a politburo meeting in August 1958 with a decision to transform agricultural productivity by the introduction of collective communes, was already in progress. By the time the policies of the Great Leap Forward were put into reverse in 1962, it is estimated that some 40 million Chinese had died of starvation.

The economy was decimated. In 1981, figures were belatedly released showing that agricultural production fell 25 per cent between 1958 and 1960; grain output in that year was just 143 million tons, which was the lowest figure since 1950. Meanwhile, heavy industry, in 1961 alone, fell by 48.6 per cent over the previous year. The impact on the population was dramatic. The number of births in China fell from 21.1 million in 1957 to 12.5 million in 1960. Deaths per 1,000 people rose from 12.5 in 1958 to 29 in 1960.

The statistics themselves barely do justice to the scale or horror of the disaster. In the worst hit provinces of Hunan, Anhui, Shandong and Gansu, whole villages were wiped out. Families died by the wayside as they left their villages to seek food. Refugees poured across borders. In Anhui province, where the number of dead was estimated at five million, only 20 per cent of families survived. In Pingyuan, where party officials overstated their grain stores by a factor of five, the population was rationed to 100 g of food per day. This starvation diet offered a fast track to death.

While mass starvation had happened throughout Chinese history as a result of drought and other natural phenomena, the Great Leap Forward dealt death from famine on a spectacular scale. Even in the richest provinces, death from starvation became commonplace. In Sichuan, 'Heaven's granary', one in four people are estimated to have died. Forests were destroyed as trees were stripped of their bark. Children were sent out to pick wild grasses. Peasants attacked those who tried to steal vegetables from the fields. Pilfering from state granaries drew 10-year prison sentences.

Some survived through cannibalism. Chinese writer Hong Ying, born in the winter of famine of 1961, noted in her autobiography *Daughter of the River* (1997) that 'Only the thin layer of skin of my mother's belly separated me from hunger. She starved herself for the two years leading up to my birth in order to feed her five children'.[1] Hong Ying was fortunate. In Anhui province, the youngest children were eaten; parents, who could not stomach the eating of their own kith and kin, would swop their young children with other families. It was easier to butcher someone else's child to supply the dinner table.

Mao was not unaware of the sufferings of his people. Ever distrustful of official reports, he had sent his own people into the countryside to find out what was going on. His trusted guard, Ma Wei, brought back a loaf of bread made of sorghum and husk to demonstrate the appalling conditions. Mao cried. He gave up eating pork to show solidarity with the peasants. It was a brief interlude in the tricky task of satisfying Mao's epicurean palate. During the great famine his private secretary noted that meals, with unheard-of delicacies such as bear's paws, would be served on the huge bed where he entertained his mistresses.

If Mao cried for his people, they were crocodile tears. He had long prepared for the sacrifice of the Chinese people for the aims of global revolution. In Moscow in 1957, Mao boasted that China was prepared to sacrifice 300 million people for the victory of the world revolution. 'Even if China lost half its population', Mao said, 'the country would suffer no great loss. We could produce more people'.[2] As for death at a personal level, Mao was entirely indifferent. Displaying the cruelty of utopian logic, he believed that an individual's death in the cause of revolution was a cause for celebration and should be rejoiced over as death was a natural product of 'dialectics'.

China's ruler, a self-proclaimed peasant and expert on the countryside, came up with innovative solutions for the famine. Sparrows pilfered grain and reduced yields. Therefore at weekends, families were ordered to take tin mugs and spoons into the countryside; whenever a bird flew across there would be a din of banging and shouting. Birds fell to the ground dead or exhausted. In an episode which presaged the frenzies of the Cultural Revolution, a Sechuan artist, who specialised in painting birds, recalled a crowd chasing an exhausted bird shouting, 'Don't let the little bastard get away ...Kill it! Kill it!'[3] This led to a mass extinction of birds in China. Without birds, the following year's crops were ruined by plagues of insects.

Assuming that Mao did not plan to annihilate tens of millions of his fellow countrymen, what was the purpose of the Great Leap Forward? Ostensibly Mao set out to overtake the steel output of the United Kingdom in 15 years. This was a clear competitive reference to Khrushchev, who had earlier proclaimed that the Soviet Union would overhaul the USA in 20 years. Mao, an inept economist, who baulked at the technical papers sent by his officials, saw, in the massive population of China, a means to leapfrog the Western nations.

What China lacked in capital resources would be made up by its abundant man-power. Instead of growing output by centralised investment, rural so-called 'back-yard' furnaces would be built to produce iron. At the same time, Mao called for a massive effort to increase the production of grain using the methods of close crop-ping and deep ploughing. The Second Five Year Plan, beginning in 1958, would produce The Great Leap.

Party apparatchiks were never slow to follow Mao's cue. Encouraged by signs of a bumper harvest in the summer of 1958, bureaucrats colluded in the faked out-put figures from fearful local cadres. Then, fawning government officials increased the targets for grain output in rapid steps, from 200 million tons at the beginning of the year to 375 million tons by December. A similar frenzy of escalation engulfed Mao's steel strategy. The 15-year plan to overhaul the UK's production in steel was chalked up in school classrooms and relayed over the radio. Huge billboards were placed by the roadsides declaring, *'Catch up with Britain within 15 years.'* As optimism boomed, the government reduced the catch-up period to five years, and then to three. From the Olympian heights of Mao's court, the Great Leap rapidly took shape. According to Mao's personal physician, Zhisui Li, 'Everyone was caught in the grip of this utopian hysteria.'[4]

On the ground peasants were coerced into construction of primitive backyard furnaces. The unforeseen consequences of this strategy were that only women and children were left to reap the harvests. While 1958 was an exceptional year for the grain crop, it is now clear that the dissipation of manpower for Mao's steel project robbed the countryside of the labour needed to bring the harvest home. Also the Chinese government, lacking the wherewithal to distribute coal, created a rapacious need for charcoal to fire the furnaces and produced an environmental disaster as whole forests were cut down.

Moreover, a high proportion of the amateurishly produced steel was unusable. Very often, the search for raw materials was destructive of productivity. In areas lacking iron ore, party cadres rounded up pots, pans and agricultural tools and turned them into rough ingots. After 1958, there was a constant shortage of agri-cultural equipment. Rarely can the banality of socialist central planning have been more poignantly exposed. As Anhua Gao noted in her autobiography *To the Edge of the Sky* (2000), 'We had to catch up with Britain in 15 years. Britain was the reason I could not enjoy my grandmother's wonderful cooking and had to eat the not-so-good food from the canteen. Where I wondered, was Britain?'[5]

Yet it is too simplistic to see the Great Leap as just a misguided attempt by Mao to launch a rapid catch-up of the Western economies. The implication of this approach is to imply that Mao derailed a stable path of development in the decade following the revolution. The truth is much more complex. The causes of the Great Leap Forward lie in the political and economic policies adopted after 1949.

Like most revolutionaries Mao and his fellow long marchers suddenly found themselves faced with the unfamiliar task of governing rather than fighting. How was the country to be managed? Unlike revolutionary Russia, where 70 per cent of the Communist Party had been urbanites, in 1950, 80 per cent of the Chinese Communist Party (CCP) members were of peasant origin. In the early years of power, the CCP relied heavily on the 400,000 government workers of the old regime. In 1950, the 'co-management' system was explained by Zhou Enlai in the following way:

> Due to the long term war conditions of the past, we have developed a habit of often issuing orders in the name of the Party. It was especially so in the army. Now that we have entered a peaceful period and established our national regime, we should change this habit ... the party must exercise its leadership over the organs of the state power, but does not mean that party should directly manage state affairs.[6]

Although the 1954 Constitution acknowledged that the State Council, under its Chairman Zhou Enlai, was the highest organ of the state, its authority was already under attack. As early as November 1949, the CCP had decided to establish 'party core groups' (PCGs) in the newly established state institutions, in order to ensure that decisions by the CCP Central Committee would be carried out. A dual government structure may have been envisaged whereby bureaucrats would report horizontally to the party cadres, at the same time reporting vertically to their superiors. However, the net result was identical to the Soviet Union where a similar government system operated; the party cadres increasingly overwhelmed the non-party power structures.

In 1953, the CCP Central Committee decided, 'from now on major and important principles, policies, plans and matters of government work must be discussed, decided or approved by the Party Central Committee'.[7] By the mid-1950s, the balance of power in government had swung decisively towards the party. Whereas in 1950, there had been 14 directives from the government versus 10 from the party, in 1955, there were only 5 directives from the government compared to 12 from the party. By the end of the decade, the government had entirely ceased to issue directives in its own name.

Just as it took time for the authoritarian instincts of the party to assert themselves over the government structures, so the economy also developed with fits and starts towards the communist model. By 1953 agricultural output had recovered from the ravages of civil war. However, the requirements of the First Five Year Plan, where 48 per cent of state expenditures were to be allocated to heavy industry, meant that agricultural procurement would need to be increased. In 1953, the government established a unified purchase and supply system for cereals. The creation of a monopolistic buyer both handed more power to the party cadres and dealt a blow to the wealthier peasants who had prospered in the post-war recovery. In an ominous replay of Soviet collectivisation, China also embarked on a process of creating agricultural co-operatives. Like Russia, the process of collectivisation in China began slowly before launching into a hectic frenzy of transformation.

In Hunan, the home province of Mao and many of the CCP leaders, there were 54,000 co-operatives by October 1955, representing some 20 per cent of agricultural households. By spring the following year this increased rapidly to 45 per cent of the population, and some two months later by June 1956, it was reported that 95.7 per cent of households had been put into co-operatives. These consisted of an average of 358 households, although larger so-called 'higher' co-operatives, which increasingly became the norm, could consist of up to 1,000 families.

The disruption, cruelty and inefficiency of these operations can be too easily imagined. Party cadres, often de-mobbed red army soldiers, were recruited to fill the 80,000 positions needed to manage the new co-operatives. Helping themselves to the perks of office, the cadres awarded themselves the highest allocation of points in the new food distribution systems, commandeered the best hospital beds and medicines, and awarded themselves the luxury of evening classes to reinforce their bureaucratic advancements.

A microcosm of the failure of the co-operative movements can be seen in Jean-Luc Domenach's study of the small town of Xuliang. With 923 households, the town's 1,600 bamboo workers, out of a town population of 3,500, cultivated 67 hectares of land that produced 70 per cent of their income. But the planners, wanting cereals to meet central government targets, reduced the 1,600 bamboo workers to just 300. Not surprisingly, bamboo production fell by 75 per cent and the income of Xuliang collapsed.

What became clear is that in Hunan and other provinces, the Chinese economy was already facing its first setbacks in 1956–7, some two years before the disaster of the Great Leap. Also, the agricultural problems caused by the implementation of the co-operative system brought serious repercussions for the towns and cities. In Luoyang, the Sangoda cement works was able to meet only 47.5 per cent of the monthly plan in January 1957. After months of unavailability, bricks were suddenly surplus everywhere. Kaifung's engineering factories laid off 400 workers. The economic dislocation caused by centralised party control became increasingly apparent. The result was political unrest. Popular agitation was reported in the cities of Hunan in spring 1957, while in the countryside, there were cases of party cadres and their families being murdered and some examples of co-operatives breaking down under the resistance of co-opted rural households.

At the political level, the failings of the economy were also beginning to translate into rapid mood swings and U-turns in policy by Mao and the ruling elite. The failure of macro-economic management precipitated increasingly desperate plans from the leadership. Perhaps aware of the managerial failings of the new party cadres, in the spring of 1956, Mao launched the idiosyncratic, 'Let a 100 Flowers bloom, let a 100 schools of thought contend', campaign. As ever, the new policies, intended as a peace offering to the remaining intellectuals and educated middle classes, the *nomenklatura* of the former *Kuomintang* (nationalist) regime, were wrapped in slogans, jargon and platitudes, which obscured their true purpose and meaning: 'Now that we are undertaking technical revolutions and cultural revolutions in order to do away with ignorance. It won't do not to have (intellectuals) and only rely on us old rustic types.'[8]

Also, at the 8th Party Congress in September 1956, there seemed to be a drawing back from the follies of co-operatisation as the outlines for the Second Five Year Plan, to begin in 1958, suggested that there would be incentives for private plots and a return to limited free markets. At the same time, Deng Xiaoping, in a report on the *Revision of the Constitution of the Communist Party*, attacked officials who set targets too high for fear of being accused of rightist conservatism.

However, any hopes harboured by the intellectuals of an impending liberal dawn were soon dashed. In spite of a relatively cautious take-up of the offer to criticise the party, largely focusing on the dismissal and exile of the popular poet Hu Feng, this was enough to provoke rethinking of the '100 Flowers' campaign. Within five weeks, Mao inserted the words 'poisonous weeds' into a speech on 8 June; 'poisonous weeds' was a code to suggest that criticism had gone too far. Mao's intellectual construct for '100 Flowers' had put forward the idea that a *non-antagonistic contradiction* could exist between different socialistic forces in society. It was argued that this was entirely different from the *truly antagonistic contradiction* between the people and their enemies. However, distinguishing between good and bad 'contradictions', obtuse Marxist–Leninist mumbo jumbo, must have been difficult for a young revolutionary movement fearful of being overthrown. With uprisings in Hungary and Poland that summer Mao may have dithered between deciding to mollify or to crush potential enemies of his regime.

In spite of Mao's belief that even non-party citizens were in basic sympathy with the CCP aims, his '100 Flowers' policies never found favour with the party cadres. Mao was too shrewd to cut himself off from his power base. By June 1957, he had clearly ceased to push his '100 Flowers' philosophy. Typically, the ending of the campaign came without explanation; Mao simply launched a new campaign against 'rightists'. Those who had taken up the '100 Flowers' offer to criticise had been caught in a vicious trap and were summarily punished.

Wang Meng, a young writer, who was later made minister of culture by Deng Xiaoping, had written a critique of local government and was exiled to Sinkiang for 20 years. Government workers of the old regime were specifically targeted as rightists, and, in some areas, up to 99 per cent of these people were formally investigated. In all over half a million intellectuals, professionals and government workers were purged. Their places were filled with poorly qualified party activists.

While current Chinese revisionism, pandering to the requirement that the communist party not be entirely discredited, likes to portray the Maoist revolution in glowing terms up to the Great Leap Forward, the reality was that the party and country were already in crisis. The centralised investment planning of the First Five Year Plan had yet to yield significant increases in industrial output, while collectivisation had only succeeded in producing a disaffected peasantry. Between 1952 and 1957, the urban population of China increased by 30 per cent and yet food output rose by only 1.3 per cent. How could China fund industrial development, while at the same time increasing agricultural productivity? This was the classic dilemma that had also faced the Soviets in 1928. Yet China's per capita agricultural output of 290 kg in 1957 was almost half the Soviet Union's per capita output in 1928. Requisition of grain for export to fund industrialisation barely seemed feasible.

In the debates that raged at the Third Plenum of the 8th Congress in October 1957, Chen Yun, minister of state for commerce, supported by Zhou Enlai, pushed for material incentives to be introduced as a means of increasing agricultural output. Market incentives would thereby improve the funding and supply of the light industrial products that China sorely needed.

For Mao, however, who despised both the centralised Soviet model as well as the pragmatist model with its 'rightist' concessions, such as 'material incentives', there was the third way of mass political mobilisation. Harking back to his successful war strategy, Mao believed that mass mobilisation could serve the economy as successfully as it had served the overthrow of the *Kuomintang*. Chen Yun, like the Russian pragmatist Bukharin in the Soviet Union in 1928, was moved sideways; he was given the title of head of the State Capital Construction Commission, which never in fact became active. From December 1957, provincial leaders were purged as power was decentralised to new administrative units answerable to Deng Xiaoping at the party secretariat.

In place of centralised economic management with 'market aspects', Mao wished to mobilise the economy through revolutionary fervour. Displaying an ideological purity that was later taken to even more absurd extremes by the Gang of Four, Mao believed that economic growth achieved with market concessions was barely worth having. Harking back to the Yunan era, Mao would exhort the Chinese people to sacrifice themselves through work. China might be devoid of capital, but it had a vast population, and, by using that advantage, Mao believed it was possible to leapfrog the West in production of steel and output of grain. In the People's Liberation Army, Mao had the perfect role model for rebuilding the Chinese economy. Chen Hang Seng, reminiscing in 1987 at the age of 91, believed that Mao had even introduced the commune's collective kitchen system because he believed that people who ate together would work together like an army.

The Great Leap Forward should be viewed in its context. It was not simply another move forward in the implementation of Maoist ideology. The Great Leap Forward was a response to the failed centralisation of the economy in the years after 1949. As Jean-Luc Domenach has concluded in *The Origins of The Great Leap Forward* (1995), 'The launch of the Great Leap Forward must above all be understood as the brutal reaction of a young political organisation that had just suffered its first serious wound.'[9]

Not able to accept that a socialist command economy structure did not work, Mao refused to allow the pragmatic market solutions that, after his death, Deng Xiaoping would ultimately drive through. For Mao prosperity was not worth having if it had to be achieved through market solutions. Rather than admit the failings of socialist economics, Mao, with great resolve and ruthlessness, dragged the party forward along an even more revolutionary path of mass economic mobilisation. The Great Leap Forward was a desperate gambit for survival by a young and paranoid revolutionary government and leader that dared not go backwards. The result was a humanitarian catastrophe, which, in the sheer scale of suffering and the number of deaths it produced, dwarfed anything offered up by Stalin's purges or the Holocaust.

22

Dictatorship and Prosperity

Taiwan: 1947–75

Portuguese merchantmen named Taiwan *Ilha Formosa* (beautiful island). Situated some 144 km from the Chinese mainland, the status of Taiwan had long been the subject of dispute. Even the racial origins of the island's people are uncertain. DNA analysis would suggest that the indigenous inhabitants of the island were closer to the Malay races than the Chinese Han; however, the nine original aboriginal tribes, which came to be known as *Shanbao*, were gradually displaced by a Chinese migration, which started in the ninth century but accelerated after the sixteenth century as Asia's population underwent a rapid and sustained growth. By 1929, the aboriginals in Taiwan had been reduced to just 2 per cent of the population.

Change was also brought about by the increasing financial and trading importance of the island after the arrival of the Europeans. Spanish settlers were first to arrive but they were expelled by the Dutch East India Company in 1642. Within 20 years they in turn were defeated by Zheng Chenggong, a warlord loyal to the recently toppled Ming dynasty; not for the last time Taiwan would become a refuge for an overthrown government.

Although control of the island was eventually ceded to the Qing dynasty, Formosa only became a province of China in 1887. This lasted for a mere eight years; indeed the brevity of official Chinese rule, compared to the 60 years of Japanese rule that followed the Treaty of Shimonoseki (17 April 1895), where Taiwan and the Pescadores were ceded after China's defeat in the Sino-Japanese war, led many to conclude that they were not part of China's integral borders, as claimed by the People's Republic of China.

With the move of 1.2 million mainland Chinese to Taiwan in 1949, of whom about half were soldiers, the balance of the population changed once again. The mainlanders represented some 15 per cent of the population; they were 85 per cent Fukienese, with the remainder speaking the Hakka dialect. Given the scale of the influx and the fact that the incomers held all the political power, indeed behaved more like a conquering army than refugees from another part of the country, it was not surprising that relations with the islanders were strained. Hatred of the incomers was to last for a generation. In 1951, Professor Russell Fifield, formerly an American vice consul in Hankow in 1947, concluded that 'If the Taiwanese had any choice today they would probably opt for United Nations control first, if they couldn't get independence, then perhaps American or Japanese rule.'[1] Fortunately for Taiwan, the very existence of Mao and a virulent Communist government across the water meant that both islanders and mainlanders had a common enemy. This binding interest was just strong enough to keep communal passions at bay.

In effect, the opponents to the incoming Nationalists (*Kuomintang*) were themselves split between pro-communists and liberals who ultimately sided with the Nationalists. While this outcome may have expressed the reality of popular sentiment, the political realities were that the *Kuomintang's* military-backed authoritarian government dispensed with the niceties of popular will. Informal political criticism was allowable, but only within the fixed parameters of a constitution which only recognised a single party, the *Kuomintang*.

The Nationalist Legislative elected in mainland China in 1947, under the constitution promulgated in that year, simply transferred to Taiwan. When representatives failed to make it across from the mainland, the runners-up in their seats were nominated in their place; in some cases, the third-placed candidate was appointed. While the system of 'filling in' (*dibu*) was ridiculed by the islanders, they possessed no voice for change. Indeed no new parliamentary elections were held in Taiwan until 1969. Even then the elections were only 'filling in' to replace eight vacancies in the National Assembly and 11 members in the Legislative *Yuan*. Further liberalisation had to wait until 1972, when the ailing Chiang Kai Shek's son, Chiang Ching Kuo, allowed elections for 119 candidates for the three branches of parliament.

The 1947 Constitution had been drawn up on the template of Sun Yat Sen's three principles of Nationalism, Democracy and People's Livelihood. However, the democracy envisaged by Sun Yat Sen's revolutionary overthrow of the Qing dynasty in 1911, and which became central to the 1919 May 4th Movement for cultural and intellectual reform of Chinese society, was far removed from the Western model; in short, the aim was to overthrow Confucianism rather than introduce liberal Western democracy.

As the French historian Lucien Bianco concluded rather admiringly:

> The May 4th Movement was a kind of Chinese enlightenment, a movement that advanced such eminently reasonable ideals as science and democracy . . . it foreshadowed and paved the way for 1949 [the Maoist Revolution] just as Voltaire had for 1789 [The French Revolution].[2]

In common with most twentieth-century government constructs other than 'Anglo-Saxon' democracy, Sun's beliefs had their origins in French political philosophy; in this case, Montesquieu's system of checks and balances was taken as the model for China. As with the other utopian systems developed by the French intelligentsia, the three principles became a chimera to cloak the reality of authoritarian rule.

On paper, the legislative *Yuan* was controlled by an executive that reported to the president. In theory, the National Assembly was empowered to elect and recall the president and vice president, initiate and veto legislation; meanwhile, further 'Montesquieu' checks were meant to be provided by a judicial *Yuan* and an examination *Yuan*. Chiang Kai Shek, a democratic Asian hero for right wing Republicans, naturally ran roughshod over the constitution when it suited him. His presidency, won by election in Nanking in 1948, should have come to an end in 1954; however, Chiang's tenure was extended by the simple expedient of emergency decree. He remained president until his death in 1975. Indeed from 1960, presidential and vice presidential elections were contested by only one candidate for each post.

Aside from the construction of a constitutional charade, Chiang used the generic methods of totalitarian states. The two most widely circulated daily newspapers were firmly under *Kuomintang* control with their proprietors both represented on the Central Committee. A government critic Chen Yanghao complained:

> The KMT's censorship policy was everywhere in society and for no explicable reason the KMT prohibited every kind of behaviour: it forbade any revision of the constitution before recovering the mainland; it forbade any new party from forming; it forbade the registration of any new newspaper; it forbade strikes, demonstrations, and criticisms of national policy; . . . it forbade students to have long hair and to help politicians in elections. Most of these kinds of activities do not violate the constitution.[3]

In his three principles, Sun Yat Sen had articulated that

> The Chinese people have only family and clan groups; there is no national spirit. Consequently, in spite of four hundred million people gathered together in one China, we are in fact a sheet of loose sand. We are the poorest and weakest state in the world, occupying the lowest position in international affairs; . . . we must espouse Nationalism and employ the national spirit to save the country.[4]

Accordingly, the answers, which Sun and later Chiang demanded for the resuscitation of their country, lay with a centralised prescriptive ideology in which the views of the people were barely consulted. For example, Article 158 of the 1945 Constitution demanded that 'Education and culture shall aim at the development among the citizens of the national spirit, the spirit of self government, national morality, good physique, scientific knowledge, and the ability to earn a living.'[5] Civil Defence Training was established in 1950 to enable the annual military and ideological training of every citizen. From 1956, a two-year period of national service was required of 150,000 Taiwanese every year. This training would include citizenship training and anti-communist indoctrination.

At its lowest level, soldiers were forced to learn simplistic propaganda by rote. In *The Soldier's Chant*

> If someone defects and becomes a traitor he shames his ancestors and hurts his parents. The whole mainland soaked with blood. The red bandits are crazy and violent. So poor are our fellow countrymen. They are like sheep and oxen on a chopping block waiting to be slaughtered.[6]

Furthermore, in imitation of the Communist use of political commissars stationed alongside officers, the Nationalists appointed political officers at company level to monitor political views and to keep dossiers on all soldiers. The Nationalists established a General Political Warfare Department to manage political ideology, and in 1952 it set up a Political Warfare College.

The military also took it upon itself to organise political youth groups. In effect, the entire population was put on a semi-war footing as the likelihood of a communist Chinese invasion edged closer after their invasion of Korea to throw back the occupying United Nations forces. In 1952, the Ministry of Education produced a paper announcing an 'Outline for Military Spirit and Physical Skill Training for High Schools and Above During the Period of Mobilization and Rebellion Suppression'.[7] In this document it was noted that 'High school and above male students should undergo military training and military management. Female students should undergo military training and nursing training.'[8] Chiang, who appointed his son as the first director of the Youth Corps founded in 1952, emphasised the importance of indoctrination from an early age; he asserted that 'We must unite with youths of any organization, group, factory or farm to participate in this great time of fighting communists and resisting Russia.'[9]

The Kuomintang's military bureaucracy, like the National Socialists in pre-war Europe, set up a parallel civilian universe consisting of print works, arts groups, radio stations, magazines and book publications. The Nationalists 'Psywar Group' even lobbed shells onto the mainland with anti-communist propaganda. If Chiang's authoritarian political programme in Taiwan mirrored the type of government which the Nationalists had formerly conducted on the mainland, the same was also true of economic policy in the early stages of occupation. To begin with, Chiang introduced the same socialistic, command economy model, which he had operated throughout his years as China's leader.

In spite of these policies, Taiwan possessed a number of advantages; in addition to bringing 100 cases of art treasures to Taipei, Chiang also brought all of China's gold reserves. Sophisticated infrastructure assets left from 60 years of Japanese rule, albeit much damaged by the war, were usurped by the Nationalists and they provided a platform for the rapid post-war development of the Taiwanese economy. American aid was also pivotal. A China Aid Act was passed in 1948, and the onset of the Korean War brought a further attempt by the American government to shore up Taiwan as a bulwark to communism. Apart from weapons and military aid, America provided US$1.5 billion in civilian aid for the ten years after the end of the Korean War. Between 1950 and 1965, when US civilian aid came to an end, some 74 per cent of investment in Taiwanese infrastructure was provided by America.

However, the most important boost to growth came with Chiang's abandonment of socialist economic policies under pressure from the USA to open up Taiwan's economy, which, in 1953, had 80 per cent of industrial capacity owned by the state. After 1954, the economy was thrown open to private enterprise and foreign investment. A notable leader in the successful privatisation of the economy was Y.C. Wang's Formosa Plastics, part financed by America which, by the 1980s, had become the country's leading conglomerate. A willing partner was found in Premier Chen Cheng, who passed legal reforms and enforced bureaucratic changes. The Taiwan dollar was devalued, import tariffs and other restrictions were lifted, the process of credit supply to private businesses was streamlined, and foreign investment was encouraged by allowing repatriation of profits.

Chen Cheng also implemented a land reform programme including extensive redistribution. Learning from his experience on the mainland, Chen Cheng recognised that capturing the hearts of the peasantry was a key to political control and national security; he had noted the ease with which the Communists in mainland China had infiltrated the villages and determined not to repeat the mistakes of the past. Land reform was pivotal to his survival strategy. Between 1949 and 1953, the percentage of land cultivated by owners rose from 51 to 79 per cent; over 2 million Taiwanese were given property rights. Furthermore, land productivity increased by 50 per cent during the next decade. However, for the *Kuomintang*, land reform had the major benefit of embedding political support amongst a large swathe of the agrarian population.

Chen Cheng's cabal of reformers moved rapidly to foster a private sector ethos within the government bureaucracies. Notably, over a third of Taipei's cabinet ministers between 1952 and 1957 were educated in the USA. Reformers used a visit from American Under Secretary of State Douglas Dillon, and a proposal for change by the American Agency for International Development (AID), as a cover for a much more radical 19 Point Program of Economic and Financial Reform.

In 1963, a further successful experiment, later copied by Deng Xiaoping in mainland China in the 1980s, was to establish special export processing zones, where standard tariffs and taxes were suspended. The success of the Free Economic Zone at Kaohsiung was followed by new zones set up at Nantze and Taichung in 1970. The results of the new private sector orientation of Chiang's economic policies were spectacular. Between 1952 and 1959, trade had grown at a modest 4 per cent per annum; in the seven years thereafter it grew by 22 per cent per annum. Success bred success. More importantly, economic growth brought foreign direct investment; the relocation of Singer sewing machines to Taiwan was at first met with fierce local resistance, but later provided the model for streams of American companies.

Growth produced a dramatic shift in the structure of the economy. Agriculture as a percentage of GDP fell from 36 per cent in 1952 to just 7 per cent in 1985. More importantly, the role of public sector enterprises in economic activity fell precipitously; from 80 per cent in 1953, to just 46 per cent of GDP in 1962 and 19 per cent a decade later. Underlying all the structural changes wrought by Chen

Cheng and his reformist team was the fact that under the American umbrella, its vast consumer markets were made freely accessible to Taiwanese products.

That a free Taiwan was able to exist at all was the result of geopolitical events elsewhere. Dean Acheson, President Truman's powerful secretary of state had toyed with the idea that Taiwan would be yielded to the Communists if Mao could be persuaded to overthrow his alliance with Stalin. This idea was not unlinked to the visceral detestation of Chiang by most senior officials in the State Department, who correctly saw the Nationalist leader as a corrupt and incompetent ruler. For several years, the future of Taiwan hung in the balance; after securing the Chinese mainland, People's Republic of China (PRC) generals Chen I and Su Yu plotted an invasion of Taiwan with 300,000 troops.

However, before an invasion could be launched, events threw the USA and Taiwan together. Mao could not be dislodged from his Communist allegiances by Dean Acheson's diplomacy. Moreover, Mao gave tacit support for Kim Il Sung's invasion of South Korea, and the American response that it inevitably provoked. Hitherto excluded from the defence ring enunciated by the State Department, Truman immediately threw America's protective cloak over Taiwan, by ordering the 7th Fleet to patrol the channel separating it from the mainland. China later retaliated with artillery bombardment of the islands of Quemoy and Matsu, sited between Taiwan and the mainland, which were also occupied by the *Kuomintang* during their retreat.

In the Mutual Defence Treaty of 23 November 1954, the Americans insisted that the smaller islands of Tachen and Nanchi be abandoned to the PLA, but supported the joint defence of Quemoy and Matsu, where some 60,000 and 15,000 troops respectively were stationed. Intermittent hostilities ended in August 1958, when a breakdown in Chinese talks with Washington led to a sustained bombardment of Quemoy.

On the first day, an estimated 57,000 shells landed on the island. For reasons best known to the PRC, bombardment of the island continued every other day, for the next 20 years. In spite of this bellicose ritual, in 1955 Mao asserted that 'The Chinese people are willing to strive for the liberation of Taiwan by peaceful means so far as this is possible.'[10] In this respect at least, Mao's approach was realistic. Shielded by the overwhelming military might of the USA, it was clear that China had no immediate prospects of regaining Taiwan.

Nevertheless, the issue remained a major bone of contention in the Cold War struggle. In the three years after 1949, the Soviet Union supported China's demands for United Nations recognition with 100 motions brought for the removal of the Republic of China (ROC) from the United Nations and its replacement with the PRC. From America's tepid early endorsement of Chiang's control of Taiwan, defence of his totalitarian dictatorship became a leitmotif for both Democrats and Republicans.

A Congressional Republican told a Committee of International Relations in 1949 that Taiwan was a key strategic position that needed to be defended; 'The battle line was drawn all around the world between the democratic forces and Communism. It stands to reason that we cannot finance that battle everywhere; you have to take strategic points to do it and be successful.'[11] Democrats were equally committed. In a communiqué issued after a meeting with Chiang Kai Shek in May 1961, Vice President Lyndon Johnson stated that

> The United States means to stand with her allies in the Asian area; the United States has no intention of recognizing the Peking regime; the United States opposes seating the Peking regime at the United Nations and regards it as important that the position of the Republic of China in the United States should be maintained. The United States will continue to work with the Republic of China on its accelerated growth program.'[12]

Other countries were equally wary of giving encouragement to the PRC's ambitions to take control of Taiwan. Although in January 1964, France recognised the PRC, not for the last time invoking the fury of her supposed American allies, President Pompidou nevertheless equivocated on the issue of Taiwan, stating that the country's future 'must be decided one of these days, taking the wishes of the Formosa population into account'.[13]

Yet any illusions that Chiang Kai Shek may have harbored that he could now relax in a comfort zone of security provided by the USA was laid bare by the volte-face in American foreign policy provided by Kissinger's secret mission to the PRC, and the subsequent Shanghai communiqué. Geopolitics now determined that America's greater interest lay in courting Chinese friendship; for communist China, America's retreat from South Vietnam in the face of the Soviet-backed Northern regime suggested that Soviet power was a greater threat to China than the USA. As Nixon later recorded in 1982, 'The key factor that brought us together ten years ago was our common concern with the Soviet threat, and our recognition that we had a better chance of containing that threat if we replaced hostility with co-operation between Peking and Washington.'[14]

The key point of difficulty in the negotiations lay with America's relationship with Taiwan. In a passage of the famous Shanghai Communiqué of 28 February, which defined the new relationship of America with its erstwhile enemy, the USA was forced to acknowledge that

> all Chinese on either side of the Taiwan Strait maintain there is but one China and that Taiwan is a part of China. The United States government does not challenge that position. It reaffirms its interest in a peaceful settlement of the Taiwan question by the Chinese themselves.[15]

Chiang and the Nationalist elite were devastated. Whatever the careful wording of the communiqué, it was now clear that the PRC had opened a chink in the relationship between Taiwan and its protector of last resort. The fall of Nixon to the Watergate scandal may have delayed the further development of America's relationship with the PRC, but Nationalists could not have been left in any doubt that a new and less certain era of political relations lay ahead.

Appropriately perhaps, the now ailing dictator had already handed day-to-day control of Taiwan to his son; the era of Generalissimo Chiang Kai Shek was drawing to a close, and in 1975 he passed away. He left a mixed legacy. As a national Socialist dictator in the mould of Mussolini and Hitler, Chiang had been out-manoeuvred politically, economically and militarily by Mao; his credibility with the American political elite, a die-hard Republican right notwithstanding, was all but lost as he retreated ignominiously to Taiwan.

However, in spite of an inauspicious start to his rule of Taiwan, Chiang had, by the time of his death, developed one of the region's most prosperous economies. In this respect he was fortunate. The Korean War made the defence of Taiwan from Communism a priority of American foreign policy; also, it was an advantage that Chiang's ministers did not spurn free market economic policies that, in pursuit of free market development, were diametrically opposed to Chiang's own socialistic instincts.

By the time of his death, Chiang had laid the groundwork for peace and prosperity based on America's own formula for success. With a rapidly growing economy and a stable constitutional framework in place, it could also be argued that Chiang paved the way for the development of Western democracy, an ideal with which the Generalissimo had long been mistakenly associated by America's Republican 'China Lobby'. Ironically, Taiwan would eventually come to resemble the democratic, capitalist, anti-communist bastion that Chiang Kai Shek's Republican supporters had believed in, long before it became a political reality.

23

Nehru: The Fashioning of a Legend

India: 1945–65

That they were 'Kashmiris' was a legend that both Nehru and his daughter, Indira Gandhi, were keen to promote throughout their respective careers. Their ancestors were *Pandits*, the famous Hindu Brahmins from whose ranks the Kashmiri maharajas traditionally chose their advisors. However, that was generations in the past. Nehru's great grandfather was an East India Company lawyer, his grandfather a police officer and his father, Motilal Nehru, a spectacularly successful lawyer, who built his practice and fortune in Allahabad, the nineteenth-century capital of Uttar Pradesh, one of India's most populous states, wedged into the heart of northern India.

Nehru was brought up as the son of a wealthy lawyer with aristocratic pretensions. These were honed first at Harrow, an English private school that also educated Winston Churchill, and later at Oxford. Of average height, and slight of frame, Nehru was finely featured, aquiline nosed and handsome; he was a 'royal figure and matinee idol'.[1] In 1937 he was described by Beatrice Webb, the famous English Fabian, as 'the last word in aristocratic refinement and culture. . .'.[2]

He was always the spoilt favourite son. Even after his expensive education in England, Nehru relied on the financial support of his father. When Nehru returned to Allahabad, he dabbled in law, but soon gave this up to pursue politics on a full-time basis; in this respect he followed in the footsteps of both his father, Motilal, and his adopted mentor Mahatma Gandhi. Intellectually able and a tireless public speaker, Nehru, throughout his life, displayed the impatience of a man for whom everything had been delivered on a platter. For social snobs like Louis Mountbatten and his wife, Edwina, he was an intriguingly charming, cultured individual, whom they considered 'one of them', in spite of his race.

For others, he 'was brilliant, aristocratic, a man of quick temper and enormous ego'.[3] Richard Nixon was not alone in finding Nehru a difficult man to deal with. Both aloof and quixotic, Nehru, as a decision-maker, was a master extemporiser, and when he finally achieved power as India's first prime minister in 1947, he found it easier to manage policy through a coterie of sycophants than through his Congress Party politicians.

A disdain for opposition was perhaps not surprising for a man whose career had appeared to glide so effortlessly into place. In 1929, after his reign as president of Congress drew to an end, Motilal promoted Nehru's candidacy for leadership, notwithstanding his son's frequent attacks on his own lack of left-wing radicalism. When Gandhi refused the crown himself and also supported the claims of his young protégé above Sardar Patel who was the overwhelming choice of Congress officials, Nehru was catapulted to a position that secured his future claims to become the first prime minister of an independent India. As Nehru himself confessed in his youthful autobiography in 1936, he arrived 'not . . . by the main entrance or even a side entrance; I appeared suddenly by a trap door. . . . '[4] He became an instantly charismatic figure as he was led off through the cheering streets of Lahore on a white charger.

His popular charisma was conferred on him by dint of tireless campaigning. In the lead-up to the 1937 elections, he travelled 110,000 miles in 22 months and made up to 150 speeches per week. While it was the overwhelmingly popular support for Mahatma Gandhi that elevated the Congress Party to its dominant political position, Gandhi nevertheless recognised in Nehru a charismatic leader who could succeed him and hold India together as a nation.

First however, he would have to control Congress. As a party of opposition to British rule, the issue of independence was the unifying fact of Congress's existence. With Congress's key job done in 1947, where would Nehru lead the party? Before the war, Gandhi, with Nehru's help, had seen off the extreme national-socialist faction of Subhas Chandra Bose, who then left to set up a quasi-Nazi organisation that allied itself to Japan during the course of the war. This left three main wings to the party. The first of these was Gandhi and his followers, such as Vinoba Bhave; they sought a return to a romantic concept of a rural idyll combining agriculture with cottage industry. This movement lost sway after Gandhi's assassination.

Second, big business, in the form of the great industrial groups, such as the Birla family, who had been major contributors to Congress, was broadly represented by Sardar Patel. As deputy prime minister under Nehru, to whom he was 14 years senior, Patel wielded significant power. Unlike Nehru, he was a brilliant administrator and his power within the party organisation was unequalled. While he never saw himself as a rival for Nehru's position as prime minister, Patel was powerful enough to cramp Nehru's authoritarian style. In 1950, against Nehru's wishes, Patel even succeeded in getting his own candidate, C. Rajagopalachari, elected as India's first president under the new constitution.

Patel's untimely death on 15 December 1950 deprived India of a leader who might have seen off the implementation of Nehru's increasingly Marxist agenda. Thereafter Congress's business supporters traded free market economics for privileged oligopoly. Eventually protectionist-supporting businessmen would coalesce in an informal grouping known as the 'Bombay Club', which cloaked its self-interest behind arguments for Indian economic nationalism and calls for a 'level playing field' against international competition.

Although Nehru's wing of the party was temporarily weakened by the break-away from Congress of a socialist party in 1948, the ultimate power of Nehru lay in his unique ability to pull in votes. After Patel's death, Nehru would never again ap-point a deputy and, by making himself president of Congress, prevented potential rivals from building up a power base within the party. For the remainder of his life, Nehru remained unchallenged. Increasingly, the independent powers of ministers in a cabinet form of government diminished, as Nehru centralised government around a 'kitchen cabinet' comprised of Westernised intellectual friends.

Among these were Professor P.C. Mahalanobis, a physician and statistician, who was the prime mover behind the National Planning Commission. Also Krishna Menon, a Theosophist and Bloomsbury Socialist and acolyte of Harold Laski, a socialist economist at the London School of Economics (and later a model for Ellsworth Toohey, the socialist protagonist in Ayn Rand's novel *The Fountainhead* (1943)), was to become Nehru's minister of defence and closest confidante.

Menon's vitriolic hatred of America and 'Western Imperialism' undoubtedly contributed to Nehru's caustic relations with the West. While eschewing the temp-tations to overthrow democratic government that his overwhelming fame and popularity might have led him to, Nehru nevertheless introduced a highly per-sonalised and individualistic approach to democracy, whose functioning he once described as 'largely the sensation you create in the public mind. . . . Whenever I feel stale and tired, I go among the people and I come back refreshed'.[5] Albeit allowing for the rhetorical flourish of this statement, it was nevertheless the case that for Nehru and his family, identification of their egos with the health of the state often fused into a single entity.

Compared to gaining absolute control of his party, the unification of India as a country was to prove a much thornier task. Whereas Jinnah's argument for the creation of Pakistan was partly grounded on the view that India had never been a country, Nehru and Gandhi opposed 'Partition' on the basis that India was an indi-visible nation. Yet the logic of this assertion is difficult to sustain. Until 1947 India had never been ruled as a single political and administrative entity. The history of India had been characterised by successive invasions beginning with the 'Paleo-Mediterranean' people who brought Dravidian speech to an aboriginal tribal peo-ple who spoke *Santali*.

A later Aryan conquest brought Indo-European language in the form of *Sanskrit*. Yet the first language with a formed literary tradition was *Tamil* in south-ern India. *Sanskrit* developed into *Hindi* and the linked languages of *Rajasthani* and *Gujarati*. Another branch developed: *Marathi, Bihari, Bengali, Assamese* and *Oriya*. The twelfth-century conquest of much of India by the Moghuls brought *Pashto, Baluchi, Persian, Arabic Hindustani* and also *Urdu*. In the eighteenth century the East India Company brought the English language, and basing themselves principally in

Calcutta, their most profitable enclave, it was not surprising that *Bengali* flourished as the tongue of the educated middle classes.

Only later in the nineteenth century did *Hindi* start to gain an upper hand when it began to be adopted by Delhi newspapers. However, in 1947 there was no such thing as a common language, a feature that normally defines a nation. Unlike China, the other mega-populous state, which had more than a thousand years of coherent centralised government (indeed the Chinese invented the concept of the professional administrator, *mandarin*), which had racial homogeneity and an accepted language of government (*mandarin*) and religion (*Confucianism*), India was a mishmash of race, language, religion and administration.

While Gandhi had derived his Romantic, pastoral economic ideas from nineteenth century English liberal thinkers such as Ruskin and William Morris, his concept of the Indian nation seemed to derive mostly from the thinking of German philosophers. The great nineteenth-century philosopher Arthur Schopenhauer commented that

> The fanatical crimes perpetuated in the name of religion are in reality attributable only to the adherents of monotheistic religions, that is to say, Judaism and its two branches, Christianity and Islam. There is no question of anything resembling it among the Hindus and Buddhists.[6]

In the same tradition, Max Muller in a recent work *India, What Can It Teach Us?* (2003) has defined India in terms of being a spiritual entity; this indeed was exactly how Gandhi viewed his country's role in the world. Both Gandhi and Nehru brought into being the myth of Indian exceptionalism. In *Independence and After* (1950), Nehru, with typical grandiloquent flourish, wrote that 'At the dawn of history India started on her unending quest, and the trackless centuries are filled with her striving and the grandeur of her success and her failures.'[7]

The creation of an imaginary past for India was a useful device for feeding the propaganda of the independence movement, even if it was largely divorced from reality. Also, not all Indians were blinkered as to the positive role played by Britain. As V.P. Menon, a friend of Patel and constitutional advisor to the governor general, asserted in *The Transfer of Power in India* (1957), it was the British who

> had gradually built in India an administrative and political system hitherto unknown. They brought about the consolidation and unity of the country; they created an efficient administrative organisation on an all-India basis; it was they who, for the first time, introduced the rule of law; and they left India that most precious heritage of all, a democratic form of government. As long as there is an India, Britain's outstanding contributions to this country will continue to abide.[8]

However, the supposedly anglophile Nehru saw a more prosaic reason for unity that lay in the 'appalling poverty, superstition, and the crushing Burden of British rule'.[9] Not surprisingly perhaps, in seeking to establish India's new identity, Nehru drew on an imaginary ancient past, while denigrating the British rulers, who had in fact partially created an administrative Indian state, albeit somewhat loosely, for the first time.

The brutal reality of 1947 was that India's cornucopia of languages, combined with the diversity of religious communities, created potential for conflict, which lay becalmed during the period of loosely federated British rule, but increased in tension as the prospect of independence and centralised political power beckoned. It is to Nehru's credit that he resisted Patel's inclination to deny jobs to Muslims in the aftermath of the depravities exacted on the Hindu communities in the bitter slaughters that followed Partition. Yet how could Nehru bridge the communal divide?

The 'multi-cultural' experiment tried by the great Moghul emperor Akbar in the sixteenth century had failed to break down India's deeply entrenched communal beliefs. By contrast the British had merely accepted the divisions and worked within the limitations of a system of government in India that was completely fragmented. Management of India and Burma, which was only severed from India in 1937, was conducted through a patchwork quilt of negotiated arrangements with some 562 principalities, in addition to the highly decentralised management of Indian states through governors and the officials of the Indian Civil Service (ICS). Not surprisingly many English 'India-hands' thought that India would be ungovernable as a single country.

Whatever the emotional and intellectual reasons for Nehru's belief in the historical nationhood of India, the harrowing experience of Partition gave notice that the unity of India could not be taken for granted. The indivisibility of the Indian territory became one of the key tenets of the constitution drawn up by the brilliant outcaste lawyer Dr Ambedkar. Nehru soon showed that he would create a united Indian state the old-fashioned way, by brute force, if necessary.

The princely states were the first test of Nehru's approach. The Nawab of Junagadh was the Muslim head of a 4,000 square mile coastal principality in the northeast of India. Waiting until after independence, the Nawab declared for Pakistan on 15 September 1947, and Nehru, using as a pretext appeals from two subsidiary Hindu territories of Junagadh, authorised an invasion to 'restore order' until a plebiscite could be held. Liaquat Ali, Pakistan's deputy prime minister, was informed that the measures were temporary. However, with 80 per cent of the Junagadh's population being Hindu, the result of the plebiscite in February 1948 was a forgone conclusion. Junagadh was appropriated for India.

The Muslim Nizam of Hyderabad was similarly inclined, to declare independence, maintain dominion status links with Britain or associate with Pakistan. Like Junagadh, Hyderabad had an overwhelming 80 per cent plus Hindu majority. However, in contrast to Junagadh, Hyderabad was a medium-size country with 16 million people covering 82,000 square miles. The country was also landlocked.

Nehru's intentions were not simply to blockade Hyderabad. Again using the euphemism of 'restoring order', Hyderabad was invaded, and the Nizam was forced to accede to India. As Nehru wrote to Mountbatten just before the invasion in August 1948, 'I am quite convinced now that there can be no solution of the Hyderabad problem unless some effective punitive measures are taken.'[10] The Hyderabad problem was simply that its monarch wanted to be independent from India. The supposed crime, for which the Nizam was to be punished, was the escalation of communal acts of violence against Hindus. Given the far greater levels of communal crime in other parts of India, this was a self-serving moral justification for Nehru's invasion of a sovereign state.

However, by far the most aggressive, controversial and historically significant of Nehru's acts of territorial consolidation lay with his invasion of the state of Jammu and Kashmir (usually referred to just as Kashmir). Like Junagadh and Hyderabad, Hari Singh, the Maharaja of Kashmir failed to declare for either Pakistan or India before Independence. However, in a reversal of the position of the other two states, Kashmir was overwhelmingly Muslim in population but was headed by Hari Singh, a Hindu maharaja, who feared that joining Pakistan might compromise his own position.

The situation was also complicated by a chief minister, Sheik Muhammad Abdullah, whose party, the All-Jammu and Kashmir Muslim Conference, was later to become the National Conference (NC); Sheik Abdullah, the 'Lion of Kashmir', was a formidably independent politician, but as a friend of Nehru, he, unlike Kashmir's hereditary ruler, also favoured accession to India. Further tensions in the region were added by the flight of persecuted Sikhs and Hindus from Pakistani Punjab to Jammu; that province of Kashmir had a Hindu majority, and serious communal tensions now developed, as Hindu refugees began to take revenge on their new minority Muslim neighbours.

Meanwhile in the Muslim district of Poonch, an area whose martial people had been a significant contributor to the British army in India, old soldiers demonstrated for accession to Pakistan and opened fire on Kashmir's Hindu troops. Muslim tribes took control of the border regions, and Muslim forces, no doubt encouraged by elements in Pakistan, seized areas to within 25 miles of Srinagar. On 24 October 1947, the frightened maharaja acceded to India and appealed to Delhi for troops.

The line of control between the opposing Muslim and Hindu forces now divided Kashmir along a temporary frontier that remains to this day. The legitimacy of India's role was further called into question in 1953, when the popular Chief Minister Sheik Muhammad Abdullah began to call openly for Kashmir's independence, only to be overthrown and imprisoned by his supposed friend Nehru. The plebiscite on the future of Kashmir promised by Nehru, and long endorsed by United Nations Security Council resolutions, has never materialised in spite of the fact that it was Nehru who had first appealed to the United Nations.

The reasons for Nehru's failure to implement a plebiscite for Kashmir are worth analysing. Nehru's insistence that the popular will should be exercised in

Junagadh and Hyderabad, and his failure to implement this solution in Jammu and Kashmir, was obviously grossly hypocritical. Quite simply, his fear of losing a plebiscite, and with it Kashmir, was not something he was prepared to concede. Nehru's 'fig leaf' rationale for not allowing a plebiscite was that it was conditional on Pakistan's withdrawal of its forces. Nehru, throughout his prime ministership, remained obsessed by the dangers of a militaristic Pakistan; indeed at a meeting with Richard Nixon in 1953, Nehru spent most of the time haranguing him on the subject. However, both Britain and America, having concluded that it was the state-sponsored slaughter of Muslims that had initiated hostilities, sided heavily with Pakistan and saw Nehru's position for what it was, a blatant land grab.

This position was reinforced by Nehru's refusal to sanction a United Nations Commission, under Admiral Nimitz, to arbitrate a staged withdrawal of the armed forces of both sides. A further attempt to mediate a Kashmir solution saw the United Nations appoint an Australian lawyer, Sir Owen Dixon, to report on the problem. He also concluded that a fair plebiscite could not be held as long as Indian troops occupied Kashmir. By now it was clear to most observers that Nehru was filibustering for time, in the knowledge that the longer India occupied Kashmir, the more unlikely it was that the status quo would ever be changed. Nehru himself observed in August 1952 that 'Our general outlook should be such as to make people think that the association of Kashmir state with India is an accomplished fact and nothing is going to undo it.'[11]

Apart from his commandeering of the recalcitrant princely states, Nehru also broke his pre-independence promise of 'partnership' with the Raj Princes. Although for the time being the princes were generously pensioned off, their states, with some 90 million people, were reorganised by Patel into some 12 units and fully integrated into India. Nehru did not confine himself to trampling the constitutional rights and liberties of the princely states. He also demanded the transfer of other European colonies to Indian rule. While Mendes-France, the French prime minister, duly handed over the French enclave at Pondicherry in 1954, the Portuguese infuriated Nehru by their insistence on retaining the west coast state of Goa. Regardless of the fact that the vast majority of Goans were quite content with their status, Nehru attempted to agitate a popular campaign, and when this failed he authorised the invasion and annexation of the Portuguese colony in December 1961.

While conducting an aggressive military expansionist policy within the subcontinent as the means of securing the unity of India, Nehru incongruously sought to develop a 'Pacifist' international policy through the concept of an alliance of the 'non-aligned' nations. 'Peaceful coexistence is not a new idea to India . . . ,' Nehru asserted, '. . . about 2,000 years ago, a great son of India, Asoka, proclaimed it on rock and stone which exist today. . . .'.[12] On the one hand, this policy developed out of the Gandhian philosophy of *Ahimsa* (divine love), and on the other hand, this was a response to a world order that was beginning to divide neatly between America and the Soviet Bloc including the Chinese.

The five principles of Nehru's strategy, referred to as *Panchsheel* (The five principles of peaceful coexistence), first mentioned in a joint communiqué with the People's Republic of China in 1954, were respect for territorial integrity and sovereignty, non-aggression, non-interference in internal affairs, equality and mutual benefit and coexistence. Although Nehru had displayed none of these qualities, either in the run-up to Partition or in his dealings with the independent Indian states thereafter, this did not deflect him from the zealous espousal of *Panchsheel*. The great fruition of his 'non-alignment' movement was the conference of unaligned nations at Bandung (Indonesia) in 1955. This meeting, overblown in its self-importance, featured appearances by Nehru, his daughter Indira, Zhou Enlai, Jomo Kenyatta and Albert Einstein.

It was 'the de facto assertion by the Bandung participants of being a distinct political group constituted the first public statement of the creation of an independent transcontinental political consciousness in Africa and Asia'.[13] Nehru himself pompously declared to the Indian parliament that 'Bandung proclaimed the political emergence in world affairs of over half the world's population. . .'.[14] Although the supposedly unaligned nations met again in Belgrade in 1961, Nehru's fantasy of a global community of anti-colonial powers, with him standing at its head, was doomed to failure. At the end of his life, Nehru would learn belatedly that just as India's unity was established at the point of a gun, so power in the international arena resided with those countries that had the power to enforce their will. In the meantime, however, Nehru roamed the globe, preaching a high moral vision of a new world order.

In promoting his views, Nehru vastly overestimated India's importance to the Great Powers. In October 1949 he affirmed that 'It is well recognised today all over the world that the future of Asia will be powerfully determined by the future of India.'[15] In this Nehru was utterly self-deluded. In the post-war period the great geopolitical issues of the day involved Eastern Europe and then China, Korea and Vietnam. A brief scan of the autobiographies of the great statesmen of the period is enough to show that India was of infinitesimal importance to them. Henry Kissinger would later observe that India virtually 'disappeared' from the global scene.[16] While Britain and America undoubtedly felt strong good will to the world's largest democracy, Nehru did everything in his power to strain relations with his natural allies. Paradoxically, India would only begin to achieve the international importance that Nehru predicted when his own socialist edifice was overthrown.

President Truman and his Secretary of State Dean Acheson detested Nehru's high-handed moralising on his visit to Washington in October 1949. Acheson complained that 'He talked to me, as Queen Victoria said of Mr. Gladstone, as though I were a public meeting.'[17] Indeed, years on the stump had given Nehru a preachy manner which was almost universally offensive to foreign politicians. President

Eisenhower was equally offended by Nehru's long harangues, followed by the pregnant silences for which he was famous. He concluded that Nehru suffered from 'terrible resentment . . . to the domination of the white man'.[18] Not surprisingly, Eisenhower's secretary of state, the fiercely anti-Soviet John Foster Dulles, loathed Nehru, whom he saw as a closet communist. Contrary to the expectations of the then American ambassador in Delhi, J.K. Galbraith, on his visit to the USA in 1961, Nehru also failed to hit it off with John F. Kennedy, who was puzzled by his uncommunicative monosyllabic responses to questions. Kennedy claimed that it was 'the worst head of state visit I have had'.[19]

Only Vice President Lyndon Johnson deigned to visit to India, where he acted the tourist by riding a bullock, visiting villages and issuing a Texan cowboy cattle yell in the Taj Mahal. This seemed a better use of his time than talks with Nehru, which were largely insubstantive. Galbraith, with characteristic irony, reported that 'Both Nehru and Johnson spoke rather formally on education, which they favoured; poverty, which they opposed; freedom, which they endorsed; [and] peace, which they wanted.'[20] In desperation to find fruitful conversation, Johnson talked about the success of rural electrification in America.

Apart from a desire to see a negotiated settlement of the Kashmir issue, India remained the lowest of priorities to American eyes throughout the Nehru era. As for Britain, Nehru gave his former Imperial masters short shrift particularly over their concern for Kashmir: 'it is very good of the British government to take such deep interest in our affairs and be so lavish with their advice to us that we should behave. I fear I am a little tired of their good intentions and good offices.'[21] It was the issue of Kashmir, combined with Nehru's antipathy to America and the former colonial masters, that prevented India from taking up its natural position of the free world's bulwark to communism in Asia.

Also, in spite of his protestations of 'non-alignment', Nehru clearly displayed a loathing for America and a strong preference for the Soviet Union. In dealing with the USA, Nehru's aims were to secure wheat and cheap loans to fund his centrally planned economy. Indeed, America provided some US$ 9 billion in foreign aid in the 30 years after independence; however, the taking of money from America did nothing to diminish Nehru's visceral hatred of America's free market culture and her Asian 'imperialism'. His prejudices notwithstanding, he was wily enough to understand that it was in America's interest to subsidise and support the world's largest democracy.

By contrast Nehru's dealings with the Russians displayed a natural empathy that extended from his early years of political activity. In 1927 Nehru had visited Brussels to attend an anti-colonial conference, organised by the 'League against Imperialism' to which he was elected honorary president. The delegates included such notables as Mohammad Hatta of Indonesia and Albert Einstein. Subsequently he made the first of his visits to the Soviet Union and came away impressed with their apparent industrial advances. While he disappointed some of his radical friends by clinging to the Western model of 'bourgeois democracy', his preferences with regard to economics were conventionally Marxist–Leninist. As early as 1931, Nehru was urging industrial nationalisation.

In power however, Nehru moved slowly to implement a socialist economic agenda. At first, Patel, the Congress businessman's friend, held sway over domestic affairs, while the death of Gandhi and the split of the socialists from Congress in 1950 also inhibited his freedom of action. Nehru's first government restricted itself to public ownership of rail, munitions and atomic facilities, and an attempt at redistributive land reform. These restraints vanished after Patel's death. As chairman of both the Planning Commission and later of the National Development Council, Nehru gradually increased the tempo of socialist advance. Whereas India's First Five Year Plan, from 1951 to 1956, was largely a programme of public works investment in agriculture and transport, the Second Five Year Plan (1956–61), guided by Nehru's economic advisor, P.C. Mahalanobis, was altogether more radical.

The new programme doubled the investment budget and, in imitation of the industrialisations in Russia and China, emphasised government investment and ownership of heavy industry including steel, railways and power. However, Mahalanobis's plans to introduce higher taxes were resisted by Nehru's wealthy and middle class backers. Unlike Stalin and Mao, Nehru could not resort to forced agricultural procurements to fund investments, and relied heavily on the ability to tap the World Bank, the Western powers and the Soviet Union for funds.

In the event, poor monsoons and low agricultural productivity meant that India also needed to import grain to feed its burgeoning population. Indeed India, which had to import 4 million tons of grain from the USA in 1951, remained a net importer of food for two decades. The inevitable exchange crisis that followed in 1958 forced some pruning of the Second Five Year Plan. The Third Five Year Plan followed the same formula, but was also disrupted by the need to increase military expenditure. While the creation of state-run industries did not augur well for the future performance of the Indian economy, it was Nehru's isolationist policies that probably did most long-term damage. By banning foreign capital investment in Indian companies and restricting access to foreign-manufactured goods, Nehru created a closed economy, in which India's private sector companies would become almost as lacking in international competitiveness as India's state-owned enterprises.

In areas of social policy, Nehru attacked sensitive issues of sex, religion and gender. In 1949 legal barriers to inter-caste marriage were removed; in 1955 Hindu women were given the right to initiate divorce; the minimum age of marriage was raised to 15, and female right to equal inheritance was guaranteed by the 1956 Hindu Succession Act. By imposing these sweeping reforms across the new nation, Nehru imposed a centralised government authority to a degree that the British Raj had never dared to do. The Raj bureaucracy, the ICS, was taken over as it stood, with its name simply changed to the Indian Administrative Service (IAS).

However, its functions, powers and numbers began to expand rapidly under first Patel and then Nehru. This was the opposite of Gandhi's vision of a decentralised agrarian economy based on village *Panchayats* (councils) and local production of *Khadi* (loom-spun cotton).

Furthermore, Nehru used the powers of the centre that were embedded in the executive powers allocated to the president in the new constitution to act ruthlessly against states that threatened the unity of India. Particularly notorious was the suppression of the democratically elected Communists in the southern state of Kerala, after the defeat of the Congress Party in the 1957 state elections. In July 1959 Nehru coerced India's president to dismiss the state government. Nehru may have been a proto-communist, but this empathy did not extend to a party which threatened his Congress Party's monopoly of power. Also at this point, Nehru had somewhat fallen out of love with his Russian friends after the Soviet invasion of Hungary.

However in one area, notably language, the Hindi-dominated Congress Party failed to impose itself. Nehru had wanted Hindi to be India's official language, while 14 other major languages were also to be recognised; it was conceded that English should remain the 'principal' language of India for 15 years after independence. In fact when the time came, the opposition of the Dravidian south was such that the imposition of Hindi had to be abandoned. The 1963 Official Languages Act confirmed Hindi as the sole official language, but guaranteed the indefinite use of English as the 'de facto' language of government.

Nehru's belief that linguistic claims were not a justification for regional political boundaries was overpowered by the depth of popular sentiment. The importance of language in driving the local political processes was illustrated throughout the Nehru era by the constant adjustment of state boundaries or their bifurcation in order to make electoral areas conform to language.

However, the rise of powerful language-based regional parties, such as the DMK in the southern state of Tamil Nadu, showed that the centrifugal forces of regionalism were far from dead. Nehru's increased centralisation of government may have forced through the creation of an Indian nation, but in a democratic system this process inevitably produced a counter-reaction. Although Congress continued its spectacular electoral success under Nehru, it is noticeable that the party, even in this period, never won an overall majority of the national vote.

While it was left to future generations to deal with the consequences of Nehru's socialist economics, his non-aligned movement was shown up to be a hollow vessel while he was still prime minister. Soon after independence, India's relations with China became strained. Showing neither strength nor guile, Nehru took four years to acknowledge China's annexation of Tibet. He annoyed Peking further by agreeing to host the exiled Dalai Lama.

However, the Sino-Indian Agreement on Tibet of April 1954, which included an enunciation of the principles of *Panchsheel*, seemed to pave the way for a new era of cooperation between the two emerging regional powers. Indeed, Nehru took great pleasure in escorting Zhou Enlai, in the following year, to the Third World 'love-fest', at Bandung. Within three years, India and China were at logger-heads again over borders known as the McMahon Line after the nineteenth-century British soldier who surveyed it. China, never having accepted this line, began construction of a road through the Aksai Chin, a region located next to Jammu and Kashmir in remote northern India, in order to link the province of Sinkiang with Tibet. Such was the remoteness of the region that India only discovered the Chinese road's existence after 18 months of construction; even then they were only alerted through an announcement in the Beijing press.

Such was Nehru's embarrassment that he hid the facts not only from the Indian public, but also from the cabinet. Nehru then highhandedly provoked the Chinese by sending border patrols and refusing all China's overtures for talks, including an offer from Zhou to visit Delhi. Nehru and his favourite Defence Minister Krishna Menon compounded the diplomatic errors through lack of military preparation.

A sickly staff officer, Lieutenant General Kaul, a distant relative of Nehru and a favourite of Menon, was despatched to command the Indian troops at the disputed front, in spite of the fact that he had never held a field command. On the night of 19 October 1962, the Chinese army launched an attack. Outnumbering the Indians by five to one, better armed and with shorter lines of supply, the Chinese simply overwhelmed the Indian North-East Frontier Army, which could not even muster enough winter clothing for its troops.

Having given India a beating and shown the world who was 'top dog' in the region, the Chinese army withdrew. Indeed Liu Shaoqi, then Mao's putative successor, said to Felix Bandarnaike, nephew and foreign policy advisor to Sri Lankan Prime Minister, Sirima Bandaranaike, that China had taught India a lesson and if necessary would do so again and again. Nehru was devastated. He confided to an old friend Padmaja Naidu, 'We are passing through not only a national crisis, but a personal one also for many of us.'[22] Although Nehru survived as prime minister, his tarnished performance in the war with China fatally diminished his hold over his party. Increasingly, Congress's power brokers, who came to be known as 'The Syndicate', circled the broken leader with an eye to his successor.

On the inauguration of India's independence on 14 August 1947, Nehru had declared,

> It is fitting that at this solemn moment we take the pledge of dedication to the service of India and her people and to the still larger cause of humanity. . . . The service of India . . . means the ending of poverty and ignorance and disease and equality of opportunity.[23]

Unfortunately for India the man chosen by Gandhi to lead India into the new age of Indian independence, with all of its challenges so grandiloquently identified in his inauguration speech, was wholly unfit for the task.

Nehru was a good talker on both the public and the private stage. When it came to getting himself elected, he was an effective and hard-working campaigner. However, like Mao, he was bored by and felt himself above the rigours of administration. As a legendary prevaricator and extemporiser, a man almost incapable of making a decision, Nehru was unsuited for the role of prime minister. This might have mattered less if his instincts had been sound or he had been good at choosing capable ministers.

Unfortunately his view of the world – sometimes pacifist, sometimes socialist, always utopian – was out of tune with a post-war era, when the great statesmen and leaders such as Truman, Acheson, Churchill, Adenauer, Stalin, Mao and Zhou Enlai were actively reshaping the globe. By comparison with these men, Nehru was a lightweight who, outside of India, left little mark on his epoch. By comparison, within India, Nehru pursued a policy of brutal and opportunist expansion of power, which showed up his international moral posturing as both hypocritical and foolish. In particular, in Kashmir, he left a legacy of deceit that later generations have come to rue. Also his attachment to command socialism, adopted without any rigorous work on the subject of economics, doomed his country to under-perform relative to its potential, a fact that has come into stark contrast with India's current free market boom.

As for his ministers, after the challenge to his authority from the much more effective Patel, Nehru undermined the Congress hierarchy and surrounded himself with compliant ciphers. The idea of cabinet government was effectively ditched as he moved decision-making to a small cabal around his own household. Furthermore, in politicising the civil service and introducing the 'License Raj', Nehru was responsible for leading India down the path of energy-sapping bureaucratic sloth, for which it was to become so famous.

More dangerous for the future, however, was the creeping nepotism that Nehru allowed to develop. While destroying the vestiges of Indian princely power, Nehru in effect recreated a regal form of government around his own person. The best that could be said for him in government is that he succeeded in creating a centralised Indian state which sustained the country's unity after independence. This was no mean achievement in a country of such bewilderingly diverse languages, cultures and religions. Also India did not descend into communal violence as many had predicted; it is to his great credit that in spite of his creation of a centralised Hindu state, Nehru preached racial and communal tolerance. He also did much to further the rights of women and lower castes.

Finally, it must also be admitted that Nehru, in spite of his ruthless military suppression of the princely states, did not allow himself to succumb completely to the allures of tyranny; an intrinsic belief in democracy did not allow him to go down the path of totalitarian Marxism – Leninism. To his lasting credit, Nehru, gifted the chance to run India by Mahatma Gandhi, was a brilliant political operator who moulded a unified Indian nation. However, in his calls for international harmony and non-aggression around the agenda of the 'non-aligned' nations, he became little more than a pious humbug; in the subcontinent, Nehru was always prepared to use military force to crush opposition to a centralised Hindu state. However, his greatest failure was to hold back the advance of material comforts for his countrymen by his adoption of a socialist command economy model, which held back India's remarkable potential for half a century.

24

Jinnah and Pakistan's Failed Constitution

Pakistan: 1945–65

Quaid-i-Azam Muhammad Ali Jinnah's career virtually defined the struggle for Indian independence and the creation of a separate Pakistan state. Born in Karachi
on Christmas day 1876, Jinnah was the son of an Ismaili Khoja of Kathiawar.
(Ismailis, though they only accept 7 out of the 12 Imams of the Shia sect, are
nevertheless considered by the Pakistan Sunni majority to be Shiites.) The curiosity regarding Jinnah's background is that 'This community is now hated in Pakistan
as they are considered Shias.'[1] Being a successful business family, Jinnah's parents
could afford to educate him at the Sindh Madrasa and then the Mission School in
Karachi, and from the age of 16 in England where he studied law before being
called to the bar in 1897.

Before going to England, Jinnah told his cousin Fatima Ganji Valji, 'I will return a great man from England . . . the whole country will be proud of me.'[2] Unlike Gandhi and Nehru, he established a very successful legal practice when he
returned to India. Dressed in expensive western suits, with a taste for cars, good
food, whisky and cigarettes, he could not have been more different from Gandhi.
According to Naval Chief, Syed Ahsan, Jinnah had '200 hand tailored suits in his
wardrobe'[3] and never wore a silk tie twice. Usually he changed his clothes two or
three times a day.

Albeit a brilliant lawyer, Jinnah began a political career when he attended the
Calcutta session of the All India Congress in 1906. Four year later he was elected to
the Imperial Legislative Council. In 1913 he formed the All India Muslim League,
and in 1917 he united Hindus and Muslims in common cause at joint sessions of
the Congress and the Muslim League at Lucknow. The so-called Lucknow Pact
remained intact until Nehru's inflammatory speech in 1928 forced out both Jinnah
and the Muslims.

After a sojourn in England, Jinnah returned to reorganise the Muslim League,
and in 1934 was appointed its permanent president. In 1940, Jinnah chaired the

League session in Lahore at which the demand for an independent Pakistan was first seriously aired. It was an idea that had long been in gestation; in the *Spirit of Islam* published in 1891, Ameer Ali, had affirmed that the 'real history of India commences with the history of Musalmans'.[4] Also Maulana Obaidullah had told Gandhi that 'India should not be considered as one country, but like Europe it should be divided on linguistic and cultural lines.'[5] However, it was Jinnah who virtually single-handedly brought the idea of an Islamic state into fruition. Finally at the age of 71, Jinnah lived to see his ambitions fulfilled when he became governor general of an independent Pakistan on 14 August 1947. It had been a long battle, and Jinnah confided to Syed Ahsan on Independence Day, 'Do you know I never expected to see Pakistan in my lifetime.'[6]

As governor general, Jinnah succeeded in stabilising a remarkably chaotic situation in the early days of Pakistan's independence. Partition brought 7.2 million Muslim refugees from India, while 7.3 million indigenous Hindus had moved the other way. Herculean logistical tasks were demanded of an administration bereft of funds. The Pakistan treasury inherited enough to pay government salaries for one month only. Having lost a high proportion of its civil servants in the Partition process, institutions of government had to be rebuilt from the ground up. For a time, British civil servants were contracted on a stop-gap basis. Apart from the unfair division of civil spoils, the Pakistan army was also starved of an equal allocation of military resources.

For the US government, the precariousness of Pakistan's early existence posed a serious dilemma. Warren Phillips, an American diplomat, had warned that '. . . to break India into two separate nations would weaken both and might open Pakistan, at least, to the designs of ambitious neighbours.'[7] Ominously Russia, alone of the major countries, failed to congratulate Pakistan on its independence. Indeed America now took on Britain's role in the nineteenth-century 'Great Game', the name given to the geopolitical rivalry between Great Britain and Russia for control of Central Asia and the Middle East. For post-war America, the rapid rise in domestic oil and gasoline consumption had significantly increased the geopolitical importance of the region. Pakistan was seen as a potential guarantor of regional stability and an ally against the advance of Soviet interests.

For Jinnah the importance of aid from Washington was paramount, and one of his first international acts was to call for a US$ 2 billion loan from the US government. Unlike Nehru, who constantly called for American aid, while at the same time pursuing a pro-Soviet internationalist socialist agenda, Jinnah was a fervent supporter of the West. Jinnah made it clear to the first American ambassador to Pakistan, Paul Alling, that he would like Pakistan to have the same closeness to the USA as its neighbour Canada.

At a cabinet meeting on 7 September, Jinnah asserted that:

> Pakistan is a democracy and communism does not flourish in the soil of Islam. It is clear therefore that our interests lie more with the two great democratic countries, namely, the UK and the USA, rather than with Russia.[8]

As for Islam, it would be a guide rather than a ruler of the constitution. Iskander Mirza, later president of Pakistan, summed up the establishment attitude when he told *The New York Times* in February 1955, 'We can't run wild on Islam; it is Pakistan first and last.'[9]

While Pakistan initially avoided the disastrous foray into command socialism, which stymied India's development in its first half century of development, Jinnah, in his albeit brief tenure as governor general, did little to advance a permanent democratic constitution. While Jinnah was a keen advocate of democracy, he believed that the British parliamentary system was unsuitable for the sub-continent. As early as 1947, Jinnah advocated a 'Presidential form of government more suited for Pakistan'.[10] At independence, powers were invested in the governor general to 'adopt' laws up to 31 March 1948. The Constituent Assembly had to extend the time limit of the special powers for a further year. (By contrast, in India, before the deadline was originally set for the Adaption of Central Acts and Ordinances Order, the whole Indian statute book was adapted.) Delay in finalising Pakistan's constitutional settlement would prove costly.

In Pakistan, as an interim solution, distribution of power was allocated between the centre and the provinces on a decentralised model, as before independence, provincial areas of authority included administration of justice, police, prisons, local government, education, railways, public health, agriculture, and mineral rights. A concurrent list of areas for federal or local laws included criminal law, marriage, divorce, wills, property, contracts, trade unions and electricity. Federal areas of control included national finances, taxation, defence and foreign policy.

However, as governor general, Jinnah failed to set an appropriate example for the future by trampling over the existing institutional arrangements. Having appointed Liaquat as prime minister, Jinnah nevertheless accepted the invitation to chair the government's cabinet meetings. As he was already governor general, president of the Muslim League and head of the Constituent Assembly, it would be fair to describe Jinnah's powers as overreaching. Indeed, he had told Lord Mountbatten, 'I will be the governor general, and the Prime Minister will do what I tell him.'[11]

No matter how high his reputation for integrity it was difficult for Jinnah, for so long the figurehead of Muslim independence, to relinquish the powers that were not so much sought as thrown upon him. Also Jinnah, prior to Partition, never clearly defined what the Islamic state would be like. The vagueness was deliberate. At a meeting in Bombay in 1944 he explained, 'We shall have time to quarrel among ourselves, we shall have time when these differences will have to be settled, . . . we shall have time for domestic programmes and policies, but first get the government.'[12]

Disastrously for the new country, within nine months of taking office, Jinnah was too ill to be able to work. His health had long been suspect; at a reception in Delhi on 13 August 1947, Jinnah was described as 'like a walking, talking corpse'.[13] By spring, he needed to leave Karachi for the cool airs of Ziarat in

Baluchistan; he was flown back to Karachi on 11 September 1948 where he died at Government House.

If his death was a blow to Pakistan, his succession also left much to be desired. His long-serving deputy and Pakistan's first prime minister post-independence, Liaquat Ali Khan, a skilled administrator and politician of the highest standing, inherited just one of Jinnah's titles, the presidency of the Muslim League. Khwaja Nazimuddin from East Pakistan became governor general, while Maulvi Tamiz ud Din, also from East Pakistan, was elected president of the Constituent Assembly.

Apart from being shorn of many of his predecessor's powers, Liaquat, originally from the Indian province of Uttar Pradesh, was also hampered by a noted prejudice against Muslims not born within Pakistan's borders. Without a strong leadership, Constituent Assembly talks drifted, and on 18 October 1951, when Liaquat was killed by a lone assassin, Pakistan lost its second notable leader while still remaining bereft of a permanent constitution, some four years after being granted independence.

The failure to develop a constitution and a political leadership to succeed Jinnah and Liaquat led to a succession of short-lived governments, which lacked popular support or electoral mandates. There were seven prime ministers in the first ten years of Pakistan independence; apart from Liaquat Ali Khan, who was prime minister for four years, the other six, Khwaja Nazimuddin, Mohammad Ali Bogra, Chaudri Mohammad, Shaheed Suhrawardy, I.I. Chundrigar and Feroz Khan Noon shared less than six years between them. In all cases, it could be argued that the governor generals, Ghulam Mohammad and then Iskander Mirza, like Jinnah a Shia Muslim, both former bureaucrats, over-used their powers to dismiss prime ministers.

Attempts to curb the power of the governor general met with little success. On 21 October, Prime Minister Bogra, while on an overseas trip, was ordered to return to Karachi by Governor General Ghulam Mohammad, for trying to form a political alliance to curb the governor general's power. Bogra was driven to the governor general's bedside where he was threatened with the sack and then forced to replace his cabinet.

In 1955, Ghulam, who was becoming increasing mentally unstable, was replaced by Mirza who became acting governor general. He too exercised the power of the office. Prior to the election of a 'New' Constituent Assembly, Mirza forced through the merger of Pakistan's four western provinces into a single electoral unit in order to counter-balance the significantly more populous province of East Bengal, which was now named East Pakistan. In spite of this reorganisation, the western based Muslim League saw a collapse of its vote in East Pakistan, with the result that it now commanded a mere 25 seats of the 80 seats provided by the Constituent Assembly.

Although Eastern members now sat in the majority, their votes were split between Hussein Shaheed Suhrawardy's Awami (People's) League and the United

Front. Out of personal dislike of Suhrawardy, Mirza ignored his claim to form a government from the Constituent Assembly and chose Chaudri Mohammad Ali as prime minister. Nevertheless, it was his government, almost seven years after independence, which managed to promulgate Pakistan's first constitution. It was in essence a tutelary democracy, with a strong elective president, and a legislature which acted largely as a rubber stamp. With the abolition of the post of governor general, Mirza became the first president of the Islamic Republic of Pakistan on 23 March 1956.

The Republic's first government was short-lived. In September, Prime Minister Chaudri Mohammad Ali resigned following internecine manoeuvrings, and Mirza reluctantly replaced him with Suhrawardy. In a particularly illuminating episode, the limits of Pakistan's pro-western policies were exposed when mobs in Karachi attacked the British High Commission following the Suez crisis. Also in Lahore, a crowd of some 300,000 demonstrators railed against the Franco-British invasion of Egypt. Both president and prime minister stood firm against the popular sentiment, however; Suharwardy pronounced, 'I refuse to be isolated. We must have friends.'[14]

Indeed, Suhrawardy agreed to allow CIA flights by U-2 planes to be launched from Pakistan. (On 1 May 1960 Captain Gary Powers, whose U-2 was famously shot down over the Soviet Union and who was subsequently tried and imprisoned for espionage, thus intensifying further the Cold War, set off on his mission from Pakistan with the intention of landing in Norway.) The new Republic benefited significantly from the American relationship. Between 1954 and 1957, the value of arms and aid to Pakistan rose from US\$ 171 million per annum to US\$ 505 million per annum; the staunchly anti-communist administration of Eisenhower, led in its foreign policy by John Foster Dulles, saw in Pakistan an important ally in the policy of Soviet containment. Apart from securing a fighter squadron of F-86 fighter jets, the Pakistanis also received B-57 bombers and later on F-104s.

That there was a mismatch in the strategic objectives of the two allies was quietly ignored by both. America wanted to arm Pakistan as a potent bulwark to Soviet power in the region, while Pakistan wanted to protect itself from India. As the *Pakistan Review* pointed out as early as 1954:

> We have sold our souls without caring to obtain any precise idea of price we are to get for it . . . . For those who range themselves behind this pact as a matter of conviction, it is not entirely easy to refute the view that it has managed to get Pakistan to underwrite United States' interests in these regions for all this country is worth in terms of manpower and strategic geographic position, but enabled the USA to steer clear of reciprocal assurance against certain dangers to the very existence of Pakistan as an independent entity.[15]

In spite of the evident differences in objectives, Pakistan actively responded to the creation of an Asian equivalent of the North Atlantic Treaty Organisation

(NATO); in 1956 Pakistan joined the USA and Thailand in forming the South East
Asia Treaty Organisation (SEATO).

Prime Minister Suhrawardy lasted a little over a year before he too resigned in
October 1957 after losing his majority in the National Assembly. His dismissal
owed in part to the connivance of President Mirza. Suhrawardy's replacement
I.I.Chundrigar survived just a few weeks before being replaced by the lightweight
gentleman farmer Feroz Khan Noon. In March 1958, elections slated for that year
were postponed. Throughout the summer, popular unrest mounted. Under the
leadership of Khan Abdul Qayyum Khan, a former chief minister of the North
West Frontier Province, with a deep dislike of Mirza, the Muslim League had undergone a revival, and was now pressing for an unbundling of the former western
provinces. In addition, the League planned a buildup of its own paramilitary force.

Disharmony was also mounting in the provincial assembly of East Pakistan
in Dacca. Matters developed into a crisis when on 21 September 1958, during a
melee in the assembly, an inkwell thrown at the Deputy Speaker Shahed Ali struck
him on the head and killed him. With increasing political paralysis it was perhaps
not surprising that the army, the Pakistan institution held broadly in highest regard
for its integrity, would eventually be drawn into the problems of government.

With the full support of the head of the army General Ayub Khan, but against
the wishes of the US government, Mirza imposed martial law on 7 October 1958.
The relief was audible. Opposition to the abrogation of the Constitution was mute.
As the British High Commission reported, 'If this morning's newspapers did not all
of them carry the president's proclamation under very large headlines one would
hardly realise that anything had happened.'[16]

The outcome was not one which Mirza anticipated. Without the constitution,
Mirza was now redundant. The envisaged duumvirate lasted barely a month. Mirza
was unwilling to confine himself to the role of 'elder statesman' envisaged by Ayub
Khan, and when Mirza pressed for more he was visited by three generals during the
night of 27 October 1958, who persuaded him that resignation would be a good
idea. Apparently Mirza appeared in his bathrobe surprised to find troops brandish-
ing automatic weapons in every corner of his house; he was probably even more
surprised that one of the generals, when he at first resisted their demands to resign,
drew his pistol. Mirza was held briefly in Quetta, the capital of Baluchistan, before
being bundled off to exile in London. Having failed to avail himself of overseas
bank accounts when he was in office, Mirza was reduced to living on the charity
of friends. It was a lesson, particularly for his protégé, Zulfikar Ali Bhutto, which
would be taken to heart.

Ayub Khan, who 'was temperamentally allergic to the very sight of politicians'.[17] now assumed the full reins of power and confirmed his already excellent
relations with Eisenhower by signing a bilateral security treaty with the USA on
5 March 1959. However, the agreement was not all embracing, allowing for the
USA to come to Pakistan's aid only in the event of Communist aggression.

Ayub Khan, a Punjabi-born Pashtun, did not envisage himself as a long-term dictator; as a graduate of Sandhurst, followed by distinguished service in the Indian Army during the Second World War, Ayub was fully imbued with an Anglo-Saxon preference for democratic modes and set about planning a more stable democratic future for his country. Eisenhower himself described him as 'pleasant and modest, but with incisive characteristics that gave an aura of credibility to his avowed purpose of steadily developing healthy democratic institutions in his country'.[18]

By introducing universal suffrage for election to a system of local councils, Ayub hoped to engender a tradition of democratic responsibility. He also appointed 80,000 so-called 'basic democrats' later increased to 120,000, who would in turn elect a national assembly in 1962, with full presidential elections to be held in 1965. In addition, Ayub sought to purge the political system of the politicians who had failed so miserably to establish a stable democracy in the post-independence period; Ayub issued an Elective Bodies [disqualification] Order (EBDO) as a pretext to exclude from office many former ministers and politicians.

Political parties were temporarily suspended, and at the same time Ayub sought to distance government from Pakistan's religious leadership. The mode of the constitution was proposed by a commission appointed by Ayub with Justice Shahab-ud-din as its head. The drafters of the new constitution continued to refute those who argued for incorporation of Islamic Sharia Law, though they doffed their hats to religious leaders by declaring that no law should be repugnant to Islam. Predictably Pakistan's Mullahs remained dissatisfied.

Ayub enhanced his popularity by proving to be a rare honest politician who cracked down on corruption. Under his presidency, the economy also prospered. Benign global conditions, an economy free of socialist prescriptions, continued high levels of American aid and political stability combined to allow the Pakistan economy to record an average annual growth rate of 5.2 per cent per annum between 1960 and 1965. In 1962, Ayub established the Pakistan Industrial Development Corporation, which financed 25 major private sector projects up until 1969. Internationally, observers now started to talk of the Pakistan miracle, and South Koreans visited Karachi to learn how economic growth should be done. As historian Ian Talbot has observed, 'The emphasis on a private sector-led development stood in stark contrast with that of many other "third world" countries.'[19] However, the imbalance in growth and prosperity between West Pakistan and East Pakistan, which had some 53 per cent of the population, would contribute to the latter's increasing dissatisfaction with the post-Partition political settlement.

Although in the 1965 presidential campaign, Ayub's opponent Fatima Jinnah, sister of Pakistan's great founder, ran a strong campaign on a united opposition platform and spoke effectively against the government's pro-American bias, Ayub won a convincing 64 per cent of the 'basic democrat' vote. In spite of Fatima Jinnah's opportunistic attacks on Pakistan's special relationship with the USA, the reality of this relationship was less stable than it appeared on the surface.

When President Kennedy came to power in 1961, after Eisenhower's eight years, he brought with him an administration which leant heavily towards India. Deputy Secretary of State Chester Bowles, who had been ambassador to New Delhi, was a liberal friend of the new president. Former CIA analyst Robert Komer, who covered South East Asia for Kennedy's National Security Advisor George Bundy, also favoured strategic closeness with India. Kennedy made an early pledge of US$ 1 billion to India and brought near panic to Pakistan by offering them a mere US$ 150 million.

Fortunately for Pakistan, Nehru's foreign minister, the crypto-communist Krishna Menon, so alienated the Kennedy administration, as did Nehru himself by a display of superior disdain on a visit to Washington, that relations with Pakistan were soon rebalanced. By contrast Ayub endeared himself to Washington during his visit when he presented Jacqueline Kennedy with a fine stallion called Sardar. Nevertheless, the fault lines in the USA–Pakistan relations still continued. After the Chinese People's Liberation Army trounced the Indian army in a brief border conflict in 1962, Ayub saw China as a natural ally versus India, while President Kennedy preferred to see Pakistan as a bulwark to communism, whether Soviet or Chinese.

Indeed Kennedy earned Ayub's undying enmity when he offered India military assistance against China and thereby broke a promise to discuss this matter with Ayub before taking such action. Kennedy justified himself by saying, 'I can also understand Ayub's feeling that what is happening to India is [the] result of its own foolish policies. On the other hand, [the] US cannot stand idly while China tries to expand its power in Asia.'[20]

By contrast, for Ayub the greater threat, as he informed parliament in November 1963, was Hindu imperialism rather than international communism. In reality, the USA, even under Kennedy, was far more determined to defend Pakistan from India than the Pakistan government might have realised. Secretary of State Dean Rusk even suggested to Kennedy that the USA might use a nuclear weapon against India if it invaded Pakistan; Kennedy's response was that this option should be reserved for a Soviet crisis.

Pakistan's relations with Lyndon Johnson also ran into difficulties in spite of the new president's admiration for Ayub. During a vice presidential trip with Robert Komer, Johnson asked, 'Why is it that Jack Kennedy and you India lovers in the State Department are so Godamned ornery to my friend Ayub?'[21] Nevertheless, LBJ dealt a shattering blow to Ayub's global diplomatic trip taking in Beijing, Moscow and Washington, when the State Department cancelled his visit some four days before he was due to arrive. It was put to him, 'Your visit at this time would focus public attention on the differences between Pakistan and the United States policy toward Communist China.'[22] Although aid to Pakistan continued unaltered, Ayub's confidence in the USA never recovered. In a speech on 14 June 1965, he went as far as to tell the Muslim League that 'The US has always acted in a manner that [is] prejudicial to Pakistan's interests in the context of Indo-Pakistan relations.'[23]

Increasingly, Pakistan's relations with India, particularly over the fraught issue of Kashmir, were becoming central to Pakistan's conduct of international relations. While most international observers reckoned that Pakistan had been cheated out of Kashmir as part of the Partition settlement, Nehru remained intractable on the subject. Kennedy was soundly rebuffed when he requested that India make some adjustment to their position. In essence, after independence, neither Britain nor America retained any purchase on Nehru. Meanwhile for India, the retention of Kashmir, in opposition to the wishes of its largely Muslim population, became not only an issue of national virility but also a measure of the Indian government's own insecurity about the centrifugal forces of regionalism, that some observers feared would split the country asunder.

In May 1963, the sixth and final round of talks on Kashmir, which took place in New Delhi, ended when Nehru rejected the proposal for internationalisation of the valley, to be followed by a plebiscite. By contrast, India merely wanted an agreement with Pakistan that force would not be used to change the status quo in Kashmir. The unsatisfactory deadlock gnawed at the minds of Ayub and his government. In particular, Ayub's Foreign Minister Zulfikar Ali Bhutto led a group of hawkish politicians and generals who were keen to seek an opportunity to resolve the Kashmir issue by force if necessary. Bhutto referred to Kashmir as the 'handsome head of the body of Pakistan', and described India's hold on the province as 'against all norms of morality'.[24]

By 1965 many leading Pakistanis had deluded themselves into believing that a military solution to the Kashmir problem was practicable. The generous military aid provided to Pakistan by the USA to enable them to counter a Soviet threat had created an armed force which, if less than half the size of India's military, was probably better equipped and trained.

Also the crushing defeat inflicted on India by the Chinese People's Liberation Army (PLA) on the borders of North East India had exaggerated the perceived weakness of the Indian Army. In reality the PLA's surprise attack on an ill-prepared and poorly equipped border force was not a true reflection of India's overall military preparedness; in addition, the inhospitable terrain of the North Eastern borders with China had made the logistics of supply to India's forces in that region virtually impossible.

The overriding impression of India's military weakness was further increased by the ease with which the Pakistan army drove back the Indian Army's infiltration of the Rann of Kutch. The Rann of Kutch, an area in the far north-western corner of Gujarat, bordering the Pakistan province of Sindh, is a marshland wilderness famous for its exotic wildlife, particularly its pink flamingoes. In February 1965, Indian soldiers had occupied disputed border areas in the Rann of Kutch; in April, Ayub mobilised the Pakistan Army and the 8th Division, commanded by Major

General Tikka Khan, defeated the Indian forces at Biar Bet and reoccupied the disputed territories of Kutch. (Curiously, the heads of both air forces came to a mutual agreement not to engage in the conflict.)

The engagement further encouraged the hawks to believe in Pakistan's military superiority. Finally, Ayub was convinced by his Foreign Minister Bhutto that in any engagement with India, the allied western powers would be forced to intervene and bring their weight to bear on a Kashmir settlement more in Pakistan's favour than the current status quo. As Altaf Gauhar would later testify, 'The whole foreign office strategy was designed as a quick fix to force the Indians to the negotiating table.'[25] Convinced by these arguments, Ayub threw his energies behind Operation Gibraltar, which began on 5–6 August 1965. Pakistani infiltrators were poured into Kashmir with the task of stirring an uprising to draw in the Indian army. In the event, the rebels were quickly rounded up having failed to ignite a revolt.

Instead of stepping back from Stage two, in which the Pakistani army would move to cut off and encircle the Indian forces 'supposedly' drawn into Kashmir, Ayub pressed forward with an armoured force cutting across the borders into Southern Kashmir, and towards Akhnur, which controlled the only route to Srinagar and the Kashmir valley from India. Contrary to the original plan, the Indian army was not inside this loop.

For reasons difficult to fathom, but possibly believing that America would come to their aid in spite of the explicit limitations of their mutual security pact, Ayub believed that the Indian army would never invade Pakistan. In this he was wholly mistaken. Ignoring the UN Secretary General U Thant, who urged a halt to further military action, the Indian army invaded the Pakistan Punjab and pressed towards Lahore. Pakistan soldiers, taken by surprise by the night attack, rushed to their defences wearing their pyjamas. Perversely the Pakistan government claimed that the Indian invasion was 'naked aggression'.

Although the remainder of the Pakistan army was now brought to bear in a counter offensive, this attack came to a halt on 11 September to the south of Lahore. President Johnson would do no more than back the UN call for a cease-fire, leading to charges of treachery within Pakistan. A desperate Ayub flew to Beijing with Bhutto. Unhelpfully, Zhou Enlai advised that Ayub should flee to the mountains, in the manner of Mao's Long March, and then fight a guerrilla war; hardly an attractive proposition for the Sandhurst-trained Ayub.

Bhutto, the consummate duplicitous politician, despite being the architect of Pakistan's predicament, now sought to gain domestic political capital from Pakistan's disastrous military foray. At the National Security Council debate in New York, Bhutto gave a passionate and uncompromising speech about Pakistan's determination to fight on to claim their rights over Kashmir; all the while he had a cable accepting a UN ceasefire sitting in his pocket. The speech, widely reported in the Pakistan press, burnished his populist image in Pakistan.

For Ayub, the war had been a disaster, setting back the economy and passing the moral 'high ground' regarding Kashmir to India, and possibly sinking forever the possibility of regaining that province. On meeting him, President Johnson now observed that Ayub was 'much chastened . . . subdued, pathetic and sad . . . he had gone on an adventure and been licked'.[26]

The USA supported a Soviet call for peace negotiations to take place at Tashkent, the capital of Uzbekistan; perhaps fortunately for Ayub, the Indian prime minister, Lal Bahadur Shastri, dropped dead immediately after the Tashkent Declaration on 10 January 1966, leaving Indira Gandhi to conclude arrangements. The Declaration, in agreeing to a territorial standstill, was the most favourable outcome that Pakistan could have hoped for though it left them with no mechanism let alone moral standing for negotiation of the Kashmir issue. Ayub's reputation would never recover.

Ever the opportunist, Bhutto railed publicly against the Tashkent agreement; though in 1966 he was dropped from the cabinet, Bhutto emerged a hero from a disastrous war of which he had been the main instigator, while Ayub took the full opprobrium of the popular feeling for the military disaster.

Bhutto took the summer in Europe to attend to his health but returned in the autumn to launch the Pakistan People's Party (PPP). The programme he set out was staunchly Islamic, socialist and pitched internationally against the USA; in its 'Founding Documents', the PPP affirmed that 'Islam is our faith; Democracy is our polity; Socialism is our economy; all Power to the people.'[27]

Up to this point, Pakistan, in spite of its constitutional failings, had at least avoided the socialist, command economy policies that had blighted post-independence India. Now even that advantage was about to be dissipated. Pakistan's military failure also encouraged the revitalisation of the Awami League in East Pakistan under its new leader Sheikh Mujibur Rahman; a politicised Bengal, the heart of East Pakistan, would start to unravel the inherent flaws in Pakistan's constitutional structure. Whatever stability Pakistan had hitherto enjoyed was about to come to an end.

25

Fall of Rhee and Park's 'Economic Miracle'

South Korea: 1954—79

Albeit relieved by the end of the Korean War, the problems of reconstruction in the South loomed large. Even with American aid, the prospects were daunting. What little infrastructure and wealth that existed had been destroyed during the course of the bloody war with Kim Il Sung's North Korean armies abetted by the vast troop resources of China's People's Liberation Army. The supporting American army too, in effect masquerading as a United Nations force, had poured huge military resources into the conflict to the extent that its demands had kick-started the recovering post-war economies of Asia. Armies and military operations on this scale had not been seen since the Second World War, and the devastation they left in South Korea in their wake was immense.

Not surprisingly, Rhee's political fortunes were little damaged by the war. No political rivals had emerged to steal his position during a period when party politics inevitably took a back seat to the fight for national survival. Moreover land reform, on the eve of National Assembly elections in May 1954, brought millions of tenant farmers and their dependents into the government fold. Property formerly controlled by Korea's Japanese colonial rulers was redistributed. This alone represented some 13 per cent of farmland. A further 29 per cent of farmland, which had become available after the 1949 Land Reform Act, was also distributed after the end of the Korean War.

The reforms provided the governing establishment with a solid phalanx of conservative supporters for Rhee's Liberal Party. Control of media, slanted electoral laws and even police coercion skewed Rhee's already abundant advantages. In South Korea's third National Assembly elections, the Liberal Party won a clear majority by winning 114 out of 203 seats, compared to just 57 seats previously. The main opposition party, the Democratic Nationalists, won just 15 seats compared to 40 in the previous assembly.

Rhee immediately used his new political strength in the assembly for personal advantage. In seeking a third term as president, Rhee needed a two-thirds majority of the National Assembly to change the constitution, which limited the presidency to two terms. In a vote in November 1954, Rhee, with not a little financial inducement, mustered 135 votes out of 203 members; technically he had fallen short of the target by 0.5 votes. The vice speaker ignored the mathematical logic, which should have demanded 136 votes, to carry the amendment and declared that the resolution for an increase in the term limits had been carried.

However, in the presidential race that followed, Rhee, in spite of all his incumbent advantages, won just 56 per cent of the popular vote compared with 72 per cent in 1952. This was hardly a strong endorsement given that his opponent Shin Ik Hui had a heart attack and died during the campaign. Moreover, Rhee's putative successor and vice presidential candidate Yi Ki-bung, Rhee's adopted son, lost his electoral race to Chang Myon.

Rhee's position had deteriorated further by 1958, when May elections to the fourth National Assembly produced just 38.7 per cent poll for the Liberal Party. Rhee responded by introducing such repressive internal security laws in December 1958 that democracy was all but suspended. Rhee had no intention of yielding power. Vote rigging produced an implausible 88.7 per cent tally for Rhee in the 1960 presidential contest.

University students, in a role which became a pattern for the future, led a popular uprising. Even after police gunned down Koryo University students on 19 April, protests continued. In the following month there were some 170 student demonstrations and a further 35 organised by trade unions. Even Rhee's professorial appointees joined the ranks of the rebels. Finally the army took a decisive stance; by refusing to fire on the demonstrators, they effectively signed the death knell of Rhee's authoritarian regime. On 26 April Rhee resigned and fled to Hawaii where he died in 1965. His adopted son, Yi Ki-bung, committed suicide with his family. The next months ushered in the most liberal period of political freedom that Korea had enjoyed since the founding of the country by Tan-gun in 2333 BC.

It was a tawdry end for Rhee, whose early liberal democratic political beliefs had turned to authoritarian corruption as an old man. While it could be said that Rhee had established a stable platform which had, with American help, seen off the threat of communism, there was little to show for his 15 years of political dominance. Although there was reasonable economic growth following the Korean War, by 1960 Korea was economically little better off than in 1940.

Ho Chong, appointed as prime minister and acting president by the departing Rhee, pushed through a new constitution on 15 June 1960. The new bicameral National Assembly was designed to increase the power of the legislative institutions vis-à-vis the executive branch of government. A cabinet system which drew its president from the National Assembly rather from direct popular vote was designed to diminish the presidential system with its authoritarian potential.

Elections conducted in July 1960 predictably produced an overwhelming Democrat majority of 175 out of 233 seats. However, politics was more dominated by the individual quest for power than by policy differences. When former Vice President Chang Myon secured the prime ministership, his former colleague and rival within the Democrat Party, Yun Posun, simply took his 86 supporters into opposition.

The new constitution did little to prevent the corruption of political patronage and the fight for lucrative government sinecures. Korea had simply exchanged corrupt authoritarian government for a weaker democratic version. Some seven months after the election of the New Assembly, no budget or economic plan had been delivered. In this atmosphere of increasing paralysis, a military coup was welcomed by many and protested by few.

In a pattern familiar throughout Asia, the coup in May 1961 was led by junior generals and colonels. The coup leader, Park Chung-hee, ushered in the Third Republic by dissolving the National Assembly and replacing it with a Junta of 30 army officers. Park and his clique of generals had uncomplicated motives: to eliminate corruption, grow the economy and achieve political and social stability. The new Military Revolutionary Council dropped some 350,000 leaflets containing six pledges; the first of these was that 'Anti-communism will be the cardinal point of national policy and the nation's anti-communist alignment, which has thus far been no more than a matter of convention and a mere slogan, will be rearranged and strengthened.'[1] The leaflet also promised that 'All corruption and past evil practice in this country will be wiped out and fresh and clean morality will be pursued in order to redress the degenerated national morality and spirit.'[2]

Park, from a poor peasant background in North Kyongsang Province, did not come from the educated and aristocratic elite which had so far dominated post-war Korean politics; he was antipathetic to what he saw as the rotten corruption of the cities and their urban elites. Indeed most of the 3,500 troops provided for the coup came from Marine Major General Kim Dong-ha, from the rural north-east, who resented the political dominance of Seoul located in the north-west of the country.

Park's rise was based on academic and military ability. He entered Taegu Normal School in 1932 and became a teacher after graduation. He later joined the Manchuko Military Academy run by the Japanese occupying army in China and in 1944 became a commissioned officer in the Imperial Japanese army. This became no hindrance to his returning to Korea and becoming a captain in the newly formed army of South Korea. Secondments included the US Army Artillery School at Fort Sill in Oklahoma.

His career now entered a rocky patch. In 1948, Park was implicated in an attempted coup known as the Yeosu rebellion. In April of that year a rebellion on the island of Cheju, situated in the Sea of Japan, was ruthlessly put down with the loss of some 60,000 lives; the communist-backed insurgency spread to the south-west tip of the mainland. The truth of Park's involvement seems somewhat murky, but he was arrested, interrogated and sentenced to death; the punishment was commuted only when he exposed communists within the police force.

Subsequently he was forced to resign from the army, and his fortunes revived only with the onset of the Korean War. As an experienced officer, Park was, by necessity, reinstated. Nevertheless, his lowly birth and besmirched record reduced any prospects of higher promotion. Park may well have calculated that he had little to lose from leading a military rebellion. Cynical ambition, however, was not his only motive. Noted for his frugal habits and personal integrity, he was genuinely appalled by the venal politicians and bureaucrats who had run Korea since the Second World War.

The diminutive Park, a quiet, hardworking and capable administrator, was perhaps the perfect man to lead Korea out of its post-war slough. The turnaround in Korea's fortunes was both effective and achieved with remarkable speed. The former administrative bureaucracy was purged, and some 38 per cent of jobs in the government were given to military appointees. In August 1961, Park established the Federation of Korean Industries and started building up Korea as an industrial exporter through the provision of cheap loans and tax credits.

Historian Gary Saxonhouse has estimated that from the mid-1960s, South Korea's government subsidies on exports amount to as much as 20 per cent compared to 10 per cent in Taiwan. Park himself would attend monthly export promotion meetings, and his weekly routine included a constant round of opening highways, bridges and new industrial plants. The dirigiste approach to export-led growth was highly effective. Real GNP growth responded dramatically with 9.3 per cent achieved in 1963, compared to 4.1 per cent a year earlier. As with Taiwan, America's protective umbrella and the unfettered access proffered to its domestic markets provided a simple route to rapid economic acceleration. In this model of export-led growth, Japan had already shown the way.

The increasing American embroilment in Vietnam also helped boost demand for Korean products. Also in spite of student unrest, the pragmatic Park normalised relations with Japan to take advantage of economic possibilities notwithstanding Japan's enslavement of the Korean people in the 35 years prior to 1945. Park's attitude to Japan contrasted strongly with his predecessor Syngman Rhee, who had asserted to John Foster Dulles that the 'Korean people are worried more about Japan than the Soviet Union. . . . Japan is aiming at its old colonial ideas.'[3] As President Nixon and Prime Minister Sato of Japan noted in a joint communiqué in November 1969, 'The security of the Republic of Korea is essential to Japan's own security.'[4]

International relations remained closely bound to the USA, whose government was little embarrassed by the coup which ended Korea's bicameral experiment. After consolidating power, President Park travelled to Washington to 'confer' with the American president; the granting of this meeting was seen as an official endorsement by President Kennedy of Park's military regime. Not for

the last time in its conduct of Asian policy, an American administration would conclude that a well-managed free market economy, under a military dictatorship, was
preferable to the chaos of a corrupt democracy. W.W. Rostow, professor of economics at the Massachusetts Institute of Technology, forecast as early as 1962 that
'South Korea is going to get up and go.'[5]

American aid continued until 1971, by which time an aggregate US$ 3.8 bil-
lion, representing some 4 per cent of GNP, had been received by Korea. Although
Nixon's withdrawal of a single division from Korea in July 1970 sent shocks through
the Korean political system, a feeling that recurred when Carter threatened to
withdraw all US forces in 1977, these were budgetary and tactical moves; in every
strategic and geopolitical sense, US and South Korean relations remained umbil-
ically linked. A curious sideshow to the increasing cultural integration of South
Korea with American values came with the explosive growth of Christian con-
verts; between 1945 and 1974 the number of Christians in South Korea grew from
300,000 to 4.3 million. Also, an increasing proportion of the country's elite began
to go to the USA for their university education.

Although China treated Korea's rapprochement with Japan with suspicion,
and declared the 1974 Continental Shelf Agreements, signed between Japan and
Korea, as null and void, Park authorised the opening of secret political and trade
links with China. As *The Economist* noted in February 1981, 'For the last several
years Seoul and Peking have been building up a covert two way trade.'[6]

Park also moved to normalise relations with the Soviet Union by passing re-
visions to trade laws to allow commerce with 'non-hostile' communist countries.
His philosophy was clearly enunciated in June 1973, when he asserted that 'the
Republic of Korea will open its doors to all nations of the world on the basis of
principles of reciprocity and equality'.[7] Unsurprisingly, Park's view of the need for
social cohesion, to combat the lingering fear of Communism, did not endear him
to social liberals. Park's approach to homeland security, law and order, and monitoring of possibly dangerous 'elements' was unswervingly robust. In *Our Nation's
Path: Ideology of Social Reconstruction* (1962), President Park declared that

> Compromise with the Communist Party is the beginning of defeat. It must be remem-
> bered that the advocacy of territorial unification with the society in a state of chaos, as
> it was under the Chang regime, is the way to national suicide. Theories about unifying
> the country under neutralism, such as those loudly proposed by the students, provide
> opportunity for a bloodless Communist coup d'état. We must defend to the last the
> democracy and freedom we now enjoy.[8]

In 1963, Park felt confident enough of the new regime both to retire from the
military and put himself up for election to the presidency. Announcing his retirement on 30 August, Park declared that '. . . I will end this message of retirement
with the hope that never again will any soldier be forced along such an unfortunate
pathway as the one I have trod.'[9] In the event, Park's victory in the presidential

elections, with a majority of just 181,126 out of 11 million votes cast, was much closer than he had expected. It was a measure of the economic success and stability that Park had brought to Korea that in the next presidential elections in 1967, Park increased his share of the vote to 51.4 per cent versus his leading opponent Yun Posun's 41 per cent.

Such was his popularity that Park won a 65.1 per cent vote when he sought a plebiscite for constitutional change to allow him to run for a third term in 1969. In 1971 Park again won election with 51.2 per cent of the vote. His opponent this time, Kim Dae Jung, won 43.6 per cent of the popular vote. However, the propitious circumstances which had favoured Korea during the 1960s had almost run their course.

The end of the Vietnam War resulted in a sharp downturn in demand; an exhausted American economy went into recession. The economic stresses of America's Asian allies were further exacerbated by Nixon's forced abandonment of the currency parities set by Bretton Woods. The ensuing cost pressures of the First Oil Crisis, and the slump in world demand, also added to Korea's problems. Furthermore to face down America's ballooning trade deficit, the Nixon administration imposed quotas on Asian textile imports. In addition to these problems, the rapid urbanisation of South Korea, particularly its capital, Seoul, whose population had more than doubled to 5.5 million in the 1960s, was leading to increasing strains on infrastructure. Student unrest also reflected grievances in a Korean workforce which had not experienced an improvement in living standards commensurate with the growth of the economy.

In the face of increasing social instability, and aware that students had brought down his predecessors, Park declared a state of national emergency in December 1971, and in the following year, the so-called *Shiwol Yushin* constitutional coup orchestrated by the president brought an end to South Korea's Third Republic. (The word *Yushin* was borrowed from the Japanese Meiji Restoration.) On 17 October 1972, martial law was established and the Republic of Korea's National Assembly was dismissed. The following month a national referendum was won, which authorised Park to appoint one-third of the National Assembly. The Fourth Republic, normally known as the *Yushin* period, was launched.

Like President Rhee before him, Park's rule was increasingly characterised by repressive authoritarian control. Pivotal to the rule of the Fourth Republic was the growing role played by the president's own secretariat and the Korean Central Intelligence Agency (KCIA). Under Park, this organisation, whose primary function had been to collect intelligence relating to North Korea and its sympathisers in the South, moved to suppress domestic political opposition to the regime.

In a bizarre episode in 1973, opposition leader Kim Dae Jung, while living in exile in Japan, was drugged in his hotel room and bundled into a vehicle by his KCIA kidnappers. Only a hasty intervention at the Blue House, the Korean president's residency, by the US ambassador Philip Habib prevented Kim from being dumped overboard in the Sea of Japan. A beaten and bedraggled but very fortunate Kim Dae Jung was unceremoniously pushed out onto the streets of Seoul.

Meanwhile the formal opposition to Park's government was riven by personal rivalries. After the *Yushin* coup and the arrest of Kim Dae Jung, Kim Young Sam had become the leader of the New Democratic Party (NDP) in August 1974. He in turn was ousted by Lee Chul Seung in 1976. However, Kim Young Sam turned the tables on his rival when he regained the party leadership in 1979.

Following the economic downturn accompanying the start of the Second Oil Crisis, strident opposition to the regime again resurfaced, and on 4 October 1979, President Park had Kim expelled from the National Assembly. Demonstrations, reminiscent of the downfall of Rhee, now spread to all parts of South Korea; on 18 October, martial law was declared in Pusan, while uncontrollable street rioting took place in nearby Masan.

At this point an extraordinary episode intervened to bring President Park's long and largely successful domination of government to an end. On 26 October at a dinner with senior colleagues, at which a clutch of models and dancers acted as hostesses, KCIA Director Kim Chae-gyu pulled out a revolver and shot Park dead. The motive was apparently Park's admonitions to his KCIA head for failing to deal adequately with South Korea's security situation. As part of the pre-arranged plan, KCIA officers also murdered four presidential guards. This episode not only brought the *Yushin* system of government to an end, but would also mark the denouement of the military's domination of post-war Korean politics.

Although he had ruled largely as an autocrat, President Park's skillful management of his country had ensured political stability, while his economic policies had set the stage and indeed the conditions for democracy to take root. In stark contrast to Kim Il-Sung in the North, Park was self-effacing and disinclined to pursue aggrandisement, let alone a personality cult. In the South, there were no great monuments for their country's great post-war leader.

Between 1960 and 1975, the Korean economy expanded in real terms by 9.5 per cent per annum; in the three years thereafter, growth averaged a staggering 12.3 per cent per annum. When Park died, South Korea's GDP per capita had increased to US\$ 1,644, a figure which was four or five times higher than that achieved by the Communists in the North. Although by 1980, North Korea had increased its armed forces to 1.11 million (47.8 persons per 1,000) compared to 750,000 in the South (16.9 persons per 1,000), the South Korean government's defence expenditure of US\$ 5.1 billion dwarfed the US\$ 1.34 billion spent by Kim Il-Sung in the North.

By 1980, Seoul, a provincial backwater in pre-war Korea, had become a sprawling metropolis of 10.3 million people, out of a total population of 40 million, making it one of the world's largest and fastest growing cities; South Korea had become one of the world's most dynamic economies, though this did not become widely perceived until the 1988 Seoul Olympics. This was a colossal achievement. Japan is usually spoken of as the great post-war 'economic miracle'; yet Japan, unlike Korea, was a great industrial economy before the Second World War. South Korea, an agrarian backwater, was transformed in the Park era into one of the emerging industrial powerhouses not only of South East Asia but also of the World. This was a record of accomplishment, for which Park's role has rarely been given prominence or credit outside of South Korea.

26

Kim Il Sung: The 'Great Leader'

North Korea: 1945—50

If Kim Il Sung's invasion of the South, in the opening gambit of what was to become known as the Korean War, can be seen partly as a means of securing his own position of power, the post-war period saw a continuation of his attempts to stay atop the North Korean totalitarian bureaucracy. Though with hindsight Kim Il Sung's long rule of North Korea is sometimes seen as an immutable state of affairs in the post-war history of the country, the unchanging face of the leadership should not obscure the fact that the first 20 years of his rule was a personal fight for survival. Also, like many dictators before him, Kim Il Sung was paranoid about his personal security. Modest men vaulted to vast power tend to doubt their ascent and believe that around every corner lies an equally rapid fall from grace; Kim was no exception.

At first divisions within North Korea, the Democratic People's Republic of Korea, centred around differences in economic policy. The ex-Manchurian communist guerrillas had adopted an aggressive Stalinist stance towards socialist development through forced investment in heavy industry. By contrast, the communists, formerly from the South, wanted to temper this approach with a more modest development of light industry and agriculture. However, Kim Il Sung was intent on the Stalinist approach, which more closely turned with his militant ideological beliefs and authoritarian instincts.

In December 1955, Kim launched a startling verbal attack on the leading economic planner Pak Chang Ok and the Soviet-backed Korean cadre who, subsequent to the death of Stalin, now favoured the gradualist approach of his successor Nikita Khrushchev. In the following month, Pak was removed as chairman of the State Economic Planning Commission. Internal dissension continued, however; following Khrushchev's denunciation of Stalin, Kim's opponents were bolstered in their courage to air dislike of their leader's dictatorial ways and hardline economic policies. Conveniently Kim was overseas. However, his opponents were not ruthless enough in their scheming. Kim hurried home and quickly purged his enemies.

By the time of the Korean Worker's Party Third Congress in April 1956, Kim had virtually eliminated the Southerners from the politburo; when Leonid

Brezhnev suggested in his address that there were 'errors connected with the cult of personality',[1] a clear call for the WKP leadership to control Kim, it was already too late. Purges among the broader party continued for several years; by 1960 some 70 per cent of the members of the Korean Worker's Party Central Committee had been removed from office.

Unsurprisingly, Kim also manoeuvred a rapid de-linkage of North Korea from the Soviet track. Though Stalin remained a revered figure, the 1950's slogan *'Learn from the Soviet Union'* was quietly shelved. Increasingly, Kim began to move his political propaganda towards a more domestically oriented agenda. *'Learn from the glorious revolutionary tradition founded by Kim II Sung and his anti-Japanese partisans'*[2] became the new battle cry. In imitation of Mao, Kim orchestrated belief in the infallibility of his own sayings. Increasingly too, Kim became referred to as the 'Fatherly Leader'.

Having expunged the southern element, Kim was free to implement his more radical economical agenda. In 1958, Kim II Sung launched the *Chollima* (flying horse) movement which was aimed at a rapid economic advance to catch up with the West; *Chollima* mirrored China's 'Great Leap Forward', which itself was a copy of Stalin's agricultural 'collectivisation' of the 1930s. By contrast with the vast collective farms created by the Soviets, North Korea's collectives averaged just 2,500 hectares in size. Despite this more human scale, Kim II Sung's economic policies were no more successful than those of Stalin or Mao.

However, whereas Mao was forced to abandon the 'Great Leap Forward' after the catastrophic famine which it engendered, Kim persevered and later followed up with the so-called 'speed' campaigns which aped Mao's desire for rapid industrialisation; the last of these was launched by Kim's son Kim Jong II. As with Mao's China, economic failure, which followed every incompetent North Korean government plan, had to be dealt with by identification of new enemies and regurgitation of revolutionary initiatives. Kim II Sung thus noted that '. . . revolution demands uninterrupted advance. We cannot be content with the fulfillment of one revolutionary task. We must set forth and accomplish one new task after another.'[3]

Meanwhile, disillusionment with the Soviet Union continued. Their incipient rapprochement with the USA, combined with perceived Soviet humiliation after they backed down to President Kennedy over the sending of nuclear missiles to Cuba, left Kim II Sung even more disgusted with the leadership of his erstwhile Communist sponsors.

Indeed the constant flux of Kim's relationship with his fellow communists, in China and the Soviet Union, was a feature of his rule; just as in domestic politics, he played one side off against the other. This was not difficult after the Sino-Soviet split in 1960. Kim's good relations with the Soviet Union plummeted in 1961, only to be revived again between 1967 and 1970. Meanwhile the People's Republic of China (PRC), in close rapport with Kim between 1960 and 1964, fell out of favour for three years after 1967; during the Cultural Revolution, Kim was depicted in the Chinese media as a 'fat revisionist' and a disciple of Khrushchev. However, relations with China improved again towards the end of the 1970s after the death of Mao, as those with the Soviet Union went into reverse.

Far from removing Kim Il Sung's fear of internal coups, the 1960s saw the 'Fatherly Leader' maintain an atmosphere of imminent attack so as to deflect from the continuing failures of economic policy. Typical of his railings against the USA was a speech reported by the *Minju Choson* on 24 July 1962, in which Kim described 'The American way of life' as

> the most shameless and degenerate way of life of the ugliest, most barefaced and bestial cannibals, with no precedent in the East and West, and it is an ideological-moral weapon to ensure the exploitation and plunder by the monopoly capitalists and the annihilation of the working people and small nations which are weak politically and economically.[4]

At the party plenum in December 1962, Kim launched a new slogan *'Arms in one hand and a hammer and sickle in the other'*.[5] The North Korean economy was now put on a permanent war stance. In the next three years Kim directed a rapid rearmament which took military spending from 6 per cent to 30 per cent of GDP. As the military build-up coincided with a period of 'coolness' with the Soviets, leading Khrushchev to stop military aid and reduce economic support, the results for North Korea's non-military economy were predictably dire. Unfortunately for Kim, the militarisation of the North Korean economy, and the economic stagnation which it instigated, produced further splits within the party.

In preparation for another internal challenge, Kim, in a speech in Indonesia in 1965, referred to 'anti-Party elements within the Party and their supporters abroad, revisionists, big-power chauvinists [who] . . . resorted to subversive activities in an attempt to overthrow the leadership of our party and government'.[6] Divisions within the party came to a head at a special conference called by Kim in October 1966; again Kim took the initiative by purging 9 out 16 politburo members, including all 6 responsible for economic management. From now on, the government ceased to publish economic statistics.

As Kim increased his grip on the party, he also began the development of an all-embracing personality cult, which was lavish even by the standards of Stalin and Mao. Every office carried his portrait, the state media slavishly followed the 'Fatherly Leader's' every move, and statues to Korea's corpulent ruler became ever larger. Meanwhile, Kim Il Sung's birthplace at Mangyongdae was turned into a tourist shrine and a mandatory place of homage for all school children, whose every school day consisted of learning by rote homilies to the 'Great Leader'. The Worker's Party of Korea (WPK) bylaws of 1980 spelled out that the first of their ten duties was to 'be boundlessly loyal to the Great Leader Comrade Kim Il Sung'.[7]

Particularly diligent members of the WPK were given watches and TV sets whose 'Made in Japan' labels were replaced by plaques announcing 'Gift of the

Great Leader Kim II Sung', or the even more bountiful epithet 'Benevolent Great Leader'. Unlike other communist leaders, Kim nevertheless showed himself to be a devout family man by lavishing epithets on his relations; his father was the 'devout communist', his mother became 'mother of Korea,' while his brother who died while fighting the Communist cause was the 'revolutionary fighter'.

Workers in North Korea were regimented into just 8 salary grades compared to 24 in Chinese urban areas. The allocation of grades was supposedly based on merit, but as with all institutional monopolies, promotion through the grades inevitably depended on kowtowing to authority. Access to information was also carefully tuned to a worker's grade. At the bottom levels, worker's homes were fitted with loud speakers, through which the local party apparatchiks fed propaganda. From cradle to grave, the entire population was 'institutionalised'.

By the mid 1970s even shops had largely ceased to exist, as communal canteens in factories and places of education replaced home eating. With the market in domestic merchandise effectively ended, having been replaced by a process of allocation according to rank, Kim took the next logical step of abolishing tax altogether. This achievement was much trumpeted. However, Kim II Sung did not point out that with no income in North Korea's all-embracing socialist accountancy systems, there was nothing to tax.

Following the last major purge of his regime, Kim increasingly promoted a policy of military aggression against the South. In 1967 a dramatic 11-fold increase in military incidents was registered along the Demilitarised Zone (DMZ) between North and South. Armed incidents between the two countries numbered 829 in 1967 and 761 in 1968. In 1968, an especially trained unit of commandos from the Korean People's Army was infiltrated into Seoul, where they launched an attack on the Blue House, South Korea's presidential compound.

Also in the international waters off its East Coast, the North Korean navy seized the *USS Pueblo*, an American surveillance ship. On South Korea's sparsely populated East Coast, North Korean trained insurgents were landed with instructions to organise revolt among a population which they had wrongly been told were sympathetic to the communist cause. The guerrillas were quickly tracked down and killed. After the failure of these military excursions, attempts to destabilise the South were scaled back after 1969. Armed incidents fell to 106 in 1970 and just 1 in 1972.

In addition to insurgency action against the South, Kim II Sung set up global terrorist facilities. From 1966, Kim authorised the organisation of a dozen training camps for terrorists from 25 countries. The North Korean foreign ministry was also instructed to use its foreign embassies to support and finance terrorist activity in countries such as Tanzania, Mexico, and the Palestine.

After the fall of Prince Sihanouk in Cambodia in 1970, North Korea offered 'volunteer' fighters. In April 1971, the Sri Lankan government was forced to evict North Korean diplomats, and in May of the same year, warnings were given to

North Korean officials by India. The aim of these policies reflected the fanatical anti-American policies of Kim II Sung; in 1968, Kim declared that it was his intention 'to tear off the left and right arms of US imperialism, tear off its left and right legs, and behead it . . . .'.[8]

The 1960s also saw a degree of social engineering in North Korean society, which even Mao had not attempted in China. The entire education system was militarised. Schools were made responsible for providing marchers and performers at synchronised public spectacles; mass ensembles of choristers amazed foreign visitors, but beneath the public performances, scholarly endeavour virtually ceased to exist. In its place students were taught Kim's own home-grown philosophy 'Juche'; this vacuous ideology dedicated to the principles of self-reliance filled the intellectual void of real scholarship and the emotional void left by the abandonment of Soviet Marxist–Leninism.

By 1972, the constitution of the Democratic People's Republic of Korea stated that 'Juche' was a creative application of Marxist–Leninism to the conditions of the country. Instructed to portray only the joys of revolutionary life, Kim II Sung co-opted the artistic establishment as he embarked on a mass brainwashing of his own people. By the end of the decade individual intellectual or artistic effort had all but ceased.

Kim II Sung described Juche as philosophy of independence derived from the masses: 'In a nutshell, the idea of Juche means that the masters of the revolution and the work of construction are the masses of the people and that they are also the motive force of the revolution and the forces of construction. In other words, one is responsible for one's own destiny and one has also the capacity for hewing out one's own destiny.'[9]

By the 5th Korean Workers Party Congress in Pyongyang on 2 November 1970, 12 of 16 members of the 1961 politburo had been purged and replaced by loyal cronies, ensuring that Kim II Sung was unassailable within the Korean political system; over the next 23 years there were only two new politburo appointees. The central committee was also purged of 133 members, who were replaced with Kim's own 'Manchurian Campaign' acolytes. Kim's now unquestioned authority also revealed itself in the increasing advancement of his son, Kim Jong II; the 'Dear Leader', as Kim's son became known, was appointed to direct the Three Revolutions Team Movement in 1974, in a programme which sent youthful 'Red Guards' to factories to help increase output. Though this was an apparent imitation of Mao's 'Cultural Revolution', Kim II Sung, the strict authoritarian, did not court the anarchy which had characterised the Red Guard Movement in China.

The radical social programme coincided with another attempt by North Korea to catch up with the industrial West. Using international credits, the communist regime implemented a hastily conceived plan to acquire Western industrial plant, mainly from compliant Scandinavian countries; much of this was eventually found rotting and unused in Korean warehouses. Displaying all the farcical ineptitude of centrally planned socialist economies, the North Korean bureaucrats failed to match available engineers and factories with the imported technologies. The 'love affair' between North Korea and the socialist countries of Scandinavia was short-lived.

Throughout the 1970s, raw and semi-processed materials continued to account for 80 per cent of exports. Though any usable figures for the North Korean economy are lacking, it seems likely that the whole economy was by now contracting. Whatever the fiasco of the Three-Revolution economic campaign, no opprobrium fell on the 'Dear Leader'; at the 6th KWP Congress in 1980, Kim Jong Il was put forward as his father's successor. Given the abject failure of his government, surrounding himself with diehard loyalists and family became ever more important for Kim Il Sung's survival.

Elsewhere in the communist world, relations with the West were beginning to thaw. In the Soviet Union, First Secretary Brezhnev had commenced talks on strategic arms limitation, while Mao and his foreign minister Zhou Enlai were receptive to the feelers being put out by the Nixon administration for the first serious diplomatic engagement since the Korean War. Kim Il Sung's instinct was to turn his back on these trends. He viewed Nixon's visit to Beijing as a humiliation for America. Kim described it as 'a trip of the defeated, fully reflecting the destiny of US imperialism which is like a sun sinking in the Western sky'.[10]

However, in spite of his unyielding words, Kim was forced, by the new relationship between America and China that followed the Shanghai Communiqué, to bow to the pressure for reconciliation negotiations with the South; no better example exists of the historic client–state relationship which Mao had reestablished with Kim's North Korea.

First contacts were made through the offices of the Red Cross in both countries, before meetings between high-level envoys took place in March 1972. A joint communiqué followed, which proclaimed a 'great national unity, as a homogeneous people, transcending differences in ideas, ideologies and systems'.[11] Though there was some progress with the humanitarian issue of contact between families, any advance towards a political settlement predictably arrived at a dead end. Talks effectively ended with Kim's demand for political and constitutional change in the South.

For over a decade, there was practically no further contact between North and South. In the intervening period, Kim pursued a steady military build-up. Armed forces totaling 400,000 troops in 1970, which already absorbed 31.3 per cent of the national budget, increased to over 1 million by the end of the decade. There was a concomitant accumulation of weaponry including tanks and artillery. Kim's vision of a military solution to reunification was still alive as evidenced by the discovery of a network of tunnels discovered in the DMZ.

Undoubtedly, Kim was encouraged by the fall of South Vietnam to communism, and what he saw as the denouement of American military and diplomatic vibrancy after Watergate. On 1 August 1975, *The New York Times* reported Kim as saying that

> The US imperialists are now talking a lot of nonsense in an attempt to cover up their shameful plight after their miserable setback in Indochina. . . . But the Asian people will not tolerate imperialist aggression. The US has long been going downhill. Nowadays it is undergoing a serious economic crisis, and militarily speaking, though we cannot say it has gone totally bankrupt, it has stretched its tentacles to so many places that it has not enough strength to stretch them any further.[12]

In 1973, Kim Il Sung had asserted that

> The reunification issue of the fatherland can never be resolved by any outside force; it can only be resolved successfully by the *Juche's* might of our people alone, comprising the revolutionary forces of the Republic's northern half and southern half'.[13]

However, Kim's 'go-it-alone' views were entirely bogus. In reality, Kim realised that North Korea was too weak to take on the South alone.

After the fall of Saigon in 1976, Kim travelled to Beijing to call on the Chinese government to support another military adventure against South Korea; however, with Deng Xiaoping now in the ascendant, Kim's aggressive intentions towards the South were restrained. Nevertheless, the objective of Korean unification remained a priority for Kim Il Sung. In December 1977, when the East German leader of the German Democratic Republic (GDR), Erich Honecker, visited North Korea, Kim Il Sung took the opportunity to admonish his guest by pointing out that while the 'people of the GDR want Germany to exist as two states . . . the Korean people call for the unification of their country'.[14]

However, after the 1970s, China gave no backing for reunification. Having seen what happened in Vietnam, where a victorious North Vietnam formed a military alliance with the Soviet Union and turned against its former ally, China, it is perhaps not surprising that Chinese leaders were less than enthusiastic about the unification of Korea. China's main concern was not to allow Korea to threaten her own attempts at reconciliation with America and Japan. When he visited Japan in 1978, Deng Xiaoping commented that the unification of Korea might take 1,000 years; even for a man famous for his long-term vision, this comment came close to saying 'never' to the reunification of the two Koreas.

In a rare moment of honesty, Kim Il Sung admitted to Harrison Salisbury in 1972, 'Frankly speaking we had to divert large sums of funds to defense construction, we ran into difficulties _to an extent_ in raising the people's living standards.'[15] In reality, the rapid forced march towards a planned socialist economy based on heavy industry, combined with unrestrained military expansion, had already led to a decade of declining living standards. Even the per capital GDP levels released by the government have to be treated with utter skepticism.

It is clear that by the early 1970s Kim had turned North Korea, a relatively prosperous and industrialised pre-war (the Second World War) economy, into one of the world's poorest places. Though in one sense, the relative economic outperformance of South Korea might have appeared to diminish the threat of war with the North, the failed North Korean state, led by a tyrant determined to cling to power, was rightly perceived as a source of global instability.

In the face of the structural collapse of his economy would Kim II Sung seek desperate remedies? In July 1980, Stephen Solarz, the chairman of the Asian and Pacific Subcommittee of the House of Representatives Foreign Relations Committee, visited North Korea and concluded that 'the Korean peninsula is a danger area where the potential for explosive crisis is higher than the Middle East.'[16] It was an observation that was to become an increasing fear for the West; while the 'Madman', or 'Rogue State' analysis of North Korea was seen as a containable threat in the era of conventional weapons, the possibility of a 'nuclear' North Korea would escalate that state's perceived threat to America, and its Asian hegemony, to new dimensions.

27

The Todai Oligarchs

Japan: 1955–92

As late as 1957, the highly respected American Ambassador to Tokyo Edwin O Reischauer observed that 'The economic situation in Japan may be so fundamentally unsound that no policies, no matter how wise, can save her from slow economic starvation and all the concomitant political and social ills that situation would produce.'[1] Within 30 years of this doom-laden statement, Japan's economy would emerge as the acknowledged miracle of the post-war period.

It was to become an economy feared as much as admired for its dynamism; by the late 1980s, American commentators were almost defeatist in their view of the US competitiveness against Japan. Clyde Prestowitz in his book *Trading Places* (1988) noticed that 'Few, if any, American companies can compete with the Japanese in areas the latter deem important.'[2] At the base of this transformation lay a single pro-business party, the Liberal Democratic Party (LDP), which from 1955 dominated the political landscape in a manner unique among the post-war democracies. The stability provided by the Japanese political system, combined with the US security guarantees and its open consumer markets, the preconditions of their anti-communist alliance, formed the bedrocks of Japan's shift from recovery to global economic power.

The political system in Japan formed a remarkable nexus between politicians and bureaucrats. It had been a pre-war practice to appoint bureaucrats to high political office and this continued afterwards. Japan's post-war saviour, Prime Minister Yoshida, had been a diplomat, while his successor Kishi Nobusuke, who had played a key role in bringing the Liberals and Democrats together, had been a vice minister in the Department of Commerce, Industry and Munitions under Tojo. In the 25 years after 1955, a fifth of cabinet ministers were former retired bureaucrats; over the same period, career politicians would hold the post of prime minister for just five years.

The tightness of political–bureaucratic connection reflected some of the peculiarities of the Japanese system of government. For the post-war Japanese politician, the main order of the day was not the deliberation of policy, but the process of fundraising and distribution of patronage; lacking support staff and analysts normal in the USA, Japanese politicians and ministers became increasingly reliant on bureaucrats with specialist expertise who acted more in the capacity of political assistants. The concept of bureaucratic political impartiality, so central historically to the British democratic system, was wholly lacking in the Japanese government structure. The power of the bureaucracy was further enhanced by the widespread use of 'Administrative Guidelines' (*Kanryo*), which were in effect legislative orders.

Much to the bafflement of visiting foreign political leaders, their Japanese counterparts were usually found to be bereft of policy ideas or even the ability to discuss them. This was largely the role of the bureaucrat. As Chalmers Johnson has concluded in his study of the Japanese bureaucracy, they 'make most major decisions, draft virtually all legislation, control the national budget, [are the] source of all major policy innovations in the system'.[3] Inevitably, the bureaucrats were drawn into political life, and became a major source of recruitment for the LDP. In the post-war period, the Japanese bureaucracy became in effect an extension of the ruling party.

Bureaucrats were required to produce policies pleasing to the LDP. Bizarrely, top bureaucrats would have to register their post-ministerial salaries as bonds, which they would forfeit if they failed to implement LDP preferences. The institution of *amakudari* (literally 'descent from heaven'), whereby senior bureaucrats would finally achieve financial reward by being posted to the directorships of major corporates or financial institutions, became an essential part of the glue which bound politicians, bureaucrats and industry in a self-serving oligarchy of power.

The collegiality of the governing system was further enhanced by recruitment to the echelons of the top ministries from Tokyo University (commonly referred to as *Todai*), and particularly its law department. In the 1980s, it was estimated that *Todai* graduates occupied over 80 per cent of the top administration posts in the Japanese government. It was an educational oligarchy only matched in the major democracies by the stranglehold of the *Enarques* (graduates of the École Normale) in France.

In addition to the politicisation of the bureaucracy, the judiciary too was suspect. With no tradition of an independent judiciary, the government directly controlled appointments; judgements of which it did not approve would quickly lead to a truncated career. When, in 1968, a district judge, a brilliant *Todai* graduate (Tokyo University law graduate), Haruhiko Abe, ruled that the LDP's ban on door-to-door canvassing was unconstitutional, he soon found himself banished to a lowly court in the boondocks to look after 'family affairs'.

Another potent power broker emerged in the post-war era in the form of the *Keidanren* (the Federation of Economic Organisations). Founded in 1946 to represent the major business groups of Japan, the *Keidanren* was originally suppressed by the post-war American administration in its bid to stamp out monopolistic practice; however, the *Keidanren* came back to prominence after 1952, and went on to become one of the country's key power brokers. Its main function was to provide the LDP with political funding, the source of all power in the Japanese political system. The *Keidanren* financed the merger of the Liberals and Democrats and became thereafter the main funding organ.

Nihachiro Hanamura, who became the vice chairman and managing director of the *Keidanren*, developed a system whereby letters would be sent annually to corporate presidents, in which their expected political contributions to the LDP would be detailed, based on the company's capital base and profitability. The so-called Hanamura Memos became one of the mainstays of LDP funding. In return, a favourable business environment was demanded; inevitably, this was one of the root causes of the protectionist nature of the post-war Japanese economy.

The Diet member was a prisoner of the drip feed of funding. A member of the Japanese Diet was forced into a regime of overt expenditure on local weddings and funerals; handsome sums in cloth-wrapped packages were traditionally presented on these occasions. A funeral gift would typically require a gift of US$ 75 (¥10,000) while a wedding might be US$ 225 (¥30,000). Attendance at between 25 and 35 funerals per month was considered normal.

Entertainment had to be provided to constituents; in essence, the Diet member had to show he was an influential local figure. A Diet member might also be required to sponsor baseball, sumo, marathons, chess, fishing, tea ceremonies and any number of cultural activities. 'A typical LDP Diet member has 50 to 80 constituency organizations, ranging from current-events discussion groups to hobby and sports clubs, women's activity circles, and social groups for the elderly.'[4] Such was the extent of the investment in a Diet member's good name and connections that it usually paid for his successor to be his son or daughter; in essence, LDP politics in Japan became a family business.

It is estimated that a typical Diet member's direct costs on office expenses were typically just 15 per cent of total expenditures. According to the *Asahi Shimbun* (*Asahi Daily*), in 1989 the average Diet member spent US$ 770,000 per annum of which US$ 140,000 was salary. Effectively being elected to the Diet was like running a small business. In a breakdown of a typical Diet member's funding, the *Asahi Shimbun* estimated that 39 per cent came from corporates, 17 per cent from fundraising, 15 per cent from individual contributions, 12 per cent from government, 9 per cent from faction leaders and 8 per cent from loans. The exhausting nature of running a Diet constituency, conducting factional politics and fundraising, meant that political life left little time for the study of policy, let alone seeing to the mechanics of its implementation.

Perhaps the most important part of the Diet member's role was in providing 'pork barrel' contracts for major public works programmes in his area. Public works expenditure also had the other welcome advantage of producing 'political contributions' from the construction companies who were the lucky recipients of these contracts. A brief driving tour of Japan, with its concreted riverbanks, immaculate rural roads, tunnels and bridges provides a clear demonstration of the power of 'pork'. This system of 'pork barrel' politics reached its apogee in the prime ministership of Tanaka, who is said to have read the obituaries before he did anything else in the morning. Tanaka, who built a fortune as a building contractor in the post-war period, became a skilled fundraiser, assembled the LDP's largest faction, and after a stint as finance minister and trade minister became prime minister in 1972.

Although his prime ministership was effectively scuppered by the First Oil Crisis, when his popularity rating fell to an all-time low of 12 per cent, he remained the head of the LDP's largest faction and 'Kingmaker' for his party until suffering a cerebral haemorrhage in February 1985. He achieved this in spite of being arrested for accepting bribes from the Lockheed Corporation in 1976 for which he was eventually found guilty in 1983. Tanaka continued to serve in the Diet while on bail and, even when he left the LDP to run as an independent, still managed to retain his seat and run his faction within the ruling party.

The role of factions within the LDP is possibly unique in the structure of a party system in a major democratic country. From its origins, the LDP was a cobbled-together grouping formed to combat socialism; it was never a coherent political structure. In 1955, there were 11 factional groupings, and although this number had reduced to 5 by the early 1980s, their role remained the same.

Factional strength was largely driven by the ability of the faction leader to generate funding; this was the root of Tanaka's success and that of all good faction leaders. The strongest faction would then stand in the strongest position to elect a party president. The allocation of cabinet posts by the LDP involved a ritual passing out of jobs based on factional strengths. In essence, a Japanese prime minister's power was severely constrained; he could do little more than speak on behalf of his government. It was a situation which drove foreign leaders, particularly American presidents, to distraction.

However, given the lack of policy-making role allocated to political leaders within the system, and the constant pressing need for funds, the factional structure was indeed logical. Far from weakening the LDP, inter-factional competition enhanced the chances of maintaining a legislative majority in Japan's multi-member district electoral system. This was effective in the same way that internal competition and pricing is usually encouraged within large corporations.

The LDP, using the nexus of bureaucracy, big industry and a conservative rural electorate which it protected through agricultural subsidies, proved itself a phenomenal electoral machine, winning every election between 1955 and 1992. It survived the opprobrium of both oil crises with a diminished vote in the 1970s, but bounced back with thumping electoral victories in 1980, 1986 and 1990, respectively. A *Yomiuri Shimbun* poll in 1982 questioned why a voter would support a cabinet led by Prime Minister Suzuki; 44 per cent of respondents agreed with the statement, 'because it was an LDP cabinet'.[5]

The monopoly of power even began to worry some LDP members. In 1982, former Prime Minister Miki concluded that '. . . if one party holds on to power too long, it becomes corrupt. I would therefore like to propose to the members of the opposition that they form a new party capable of taking upon itself the government of Japan . . .'.[6] Indeed, the strength of the LDP was mirrored by the weakness of the opposition parties. The Japan Socialist Party (JSP), a hard-left party, would not only not work alongside the Japanese Communist Party (JCP) but was also splintered in 1960 with the formation of the Democratic Socialist Party (DSP).

The DSP was a breakaway from the JSP by a group which believed that the JSP had moved too far to the left. Over time it came to be seen as the political arm of *Domei* (All Japan Labour Federation) which was formed as a right-wing splinter from the JSP supporting *Sohyo* (General Council of Trade Unions of Japan). In effect, it was a moderate centrist party, and a DSP member of the House of Councillors questioned whether it '. . . would be a bad idea if we changed the party's name.'[7] Placed at the centre of Japanese politics, the DSP might have been thought a natural alternative party of government, but it was held back by its *Domei* affiliation and an inability to raise funds which would have enabled it to finance a nationwide candidature.

The JCP had been formed in 1922 in the middle-class suburb of Shibuya and had steadily grown its membership, albeit suppressed during the Second World War. Afterwards, Nosaka Sanzo, who had been the Japanese Comintern delegate during the 1930s, decided to advance the party along a parliamentary route. The party had emerged from the war as one of the few relatively untainted political groupings, and in 1949 it reaped its reward with 3 million votes (10 per cent) and 35 elected members. However, after Stalin ordered the party to adopt extra-parliamentary revolutionary activity, JCP support collapsed and they lost all their seats in 1952. It took 20 years to recover to 3 million votes, though by that stage it accounted for just 6.8 per cent of the poll.

By 1976, it was also clear that the JCP had become fully 'Japonised'. At the 13th Extraordinary Party Congress, a revised manifesto made approving reference to the American Declaration of Independence and concluded that

> The Communist Party of Japan reiterates that it will make no model of the experi-
> ences of any foreign countries, such as the Soviet Union and the People's Republic of
> China . . . it will continue to pursue a unique way to an independent democratic Japan
> and a socialist Japan, hand in hand with the people.[8]

However, by the 1980s, with Japan's evident economic success, the JCP appeared irrelevant and increasingly appealed only to an ageing voter profile.

The left vote was also split by the *Komeito* founded in 1964, a left leaning but socially conservative party with links to the *Soka Gakkai* (Value Creating Academic Society). *Soka Gakkai* was founded by schoolteacher Makiguchi Tsunesaburo in November 1930 with the aim of improving Japanese society by restructuring its education system; it became the fastest growing of the post-war 'new' Buddhist religions, which filled the void created by the country's post-war economic and moral bankruptcy and collapse of its 'Emperor' personality cult.

Like the Communist Party, *Soka Gakkai* emerged strongly from Japan's wartime defeat after its founder Tsunesaburo was jailed for opposing the war and later died in prison. By 1979, *Soka Gakkai* had attracted 10 million members. *Newsweek* would note that 'the *Soka Gakkai* looks like an Oriental blend of Christian Science and the John Birch Society.'[9] The cult was loosely affiliated to the traditional nationalist Buddhist sect of *Nichiren Shoshu* which traced its roots back to Nichiren, a monk born in the early thirteenth century. The *Komeito*, with its appeal to a largely working-class audience unimpressed by socialist secularism, denuded the left of much of its natural support.

As effective one-party rule continued, corruption and appetite for funds within the political system became endemic. With the unprecedented stock market boom of the 1980s, the increasingly powerful brokerage companies, Nomura, Daiwa, Nikko and Yamaichi, were increasingly tapped for funds. On the pre-listing of shares or share warrants, politicians were favoured with allocations on secret accounts where profits were guaranteed. Corruption was institutionalised. Yamaichi Securities ran a covert department of over 30 employees whose full-time job was the organisation of political funding through the stock market.

The scam was finally blown at the end of 1988 with the listing of Recruit Cosmos; former Prime Minister Nakasone was implicated along with Prime Minister Takeshita. Miyazawa was forced to resign. When Takeshita was found to have received Cosmos money, he too was forced to resign in April 1989. His successor, former Foreign Minister Uno Sosuke, was forced from office after a sex scandal.

The Ministry of Trade and Industry (MITI) has normally taken the lion's share of credit for Japan's post-war economic miracle which saw the industrial index rise from 55 in 1948 (versus the 1936 base of 100) to 181 in 1955 and 410 in 1960. Indeed, the prestige of MITI rose rapidly after it successfully persuaded the Diet to amend the law to authorise government-sponsored cartels in industries that were depressed or undergoing reconstruction.

In the 30 years that followed, seven out of ten prime ministers were at one time in their careers ministers of trade and industry. In reality, MITI played a much lesser role than many foreigners have usually imagined. Essentially, Japanese companies were able to invest heavily in research and plant and equipment because of the generally compliant labour force and pro-business laws. Labour conflicts were largely eradicated after the draconian actions of Yoshida, and although large-scale conflict would break out at Nissan Motor in the late 1950s, this proved to be the exception rather than the norm.

The Zaibatsu structure was largely reformulated with a close nexus built between banking groups and their related industrial concerns, which held bank shares in return for guaranteed access to capital; the largest pre-war groupings included Mitsubishi, Mitsui and Sumitomo. In spite of this typical structure, the post-war period saw burgeoning growth in new technology industries and the start-up companies that developed them; the explosive growth of consumer electronics saw the emergence of Sony, Matsushita and Hitachi.

Matsushita, which had started as a manufacturer of bicycle lamps in 1918, took off in the post-war period when it gained access to the technology of the Dutch company NV Philips. Sony, founded by Morita Akio and Ibuka Masaru, started by manufacturing Japan's first tape recorders but achieved its greatest breakthrough after licensing transistor technology from Western Electric in 1953, from which it developed the first transistor radios.

Japan proved to be a voracious assimilator of foreign technology, some purchased and much developed by reverse technology or industrial espionage. The appetite for international knowledge is best expressed by the fact that in 1995 there were 2,466 translations of books from English into Japanese, whereas only 32 Japanese books were translated into English. The asymmetry was similarly apparent in news and television coverage. Just as the pioneers of the Meiji Restoration in 1869 scoured the world for technology to bring back to Japan, so too did Japanese industrialists after the Second World War, as they sought foreign help in rebuilding their businesses and the economy. In particular, Japanese engineers developed an appetite for American management techniques.

Peter Drucker, the father of 'time management' became an early hero, but even he was eclipsed by William Edward Deming. Born in Sioux City, Iowa, in October 1900, Deming was a classic product of the Westward migration of Americans seeking land. Brought up in Wyoming where his father had been granted land, Deming graduated in Electrical Engineering from the University of Wyoming at Laramie before doing a PhD in Mathematics at Yale. He developed statistical sampling techniques for helping American wartime production and became an early pioneer of Statistical Process Control (SPC).

After the Second World War, Deming went to Japan to help plan the 1951 Japan census; his stay in Japan ended with an invitation by the Japanese Union of Scientists and Engineers (JUSE) to teach statistical control. The series of lectures he delivered to JUSE became the bedrock of Japanese post-war management techniques with their emphasis on Total Quality Management (TQM). It was a revolutionary approach to improving product quality, increasing productivity and raising market share. Even today JUSE gives an annual TQM award called the Deming Prize. For his work in revitalising the Japanese economy, Prime Minister Kishi, in 1960, gave Deming the *Second Order of the Sacred Treasures*; he was the first American recipient of the award. Remarkably, Deming received recognition in America only after an NBC documentary entitled *If Japan can . . . Why can't we?* (1980) began to focus on his pioneering work.

Toyota and Nissan emerged as car giants domestically and internationally, frequently taking their post-war models from British manufacturers, but making them better. Honda, originally a manufacturer of motorcycles, defied MITI to enter the automobile sector and it too became an international brand name. Indeed, Honda would become the first Japanese auto manufacturer to open a plant in the USA. Similarly, MITI opposed the entry of Toyota into the market for diesel-powered trucks, which had hitherto been dominated by Isuzu, on the grounds that Japan did not need two such manufacturers. The response of the chairman of Toyota was quite blunt, 'government has no right to tell us to stop. Toyota will continue selling diesel trucks even if the ministry is against it.'[10] Indeed, the roots of the global competitiveness of Japanese manufacturers did not lie in the direction of MITI, a relatively weak ministry, but in the animal spirit of competition within Japan itself.

In the 1950s, domestic consumer demand was driven by what became known as the three 'S's: *senpuku* (electric fans), *sentaku* (washing machines) and *suihanki* (rice cookers). The 1960s were characterised as the decade of the three 'K's: *ka* (motor car), *kura* (air conditioner) and *kara terebi* (colour television). In the following decade, this was followed by the three 'J's: jewels, jet vacations and *jutaku* (modern houses). This somewhat simplistic analogy nevertheless characterised the rapid wealth progression within the economy.

By contrast, the textile industry, which had powered the pre-war Japanese economy, was already in decline by the beginning of the 1960s. American political resistance to Japanese textile imports led to a 'voluntary' restraint agreement in 1971. MITI saw its role in industry partly as a manager of decline, always with LDP votes in mind. With regard to textiles, a MITI bureaucrat admitted that 'We know the industry won't last. We've known that for years. But in the meantime these textile firms use people who vote LDP. The party's got to be able to show that it cares.'[11] Voluntary restraint proved to be a model for future problems over semi-conductors in the mid-1980s, which led to similar export restraint programmes. Although much play was made on America's lack of competitiveness, it was largely forgotten that by and large the USA operated an open door policy on imports from countries granted 'Most Favoured Nation' (MFN) status.

Only with Japan's burgeoning trade surplus in the 1980s did America start to put pressure on Japan to open its own markets to foreign liquor, motor cars, rice, oranges, beef and financial services. Reform was pushed by Prime Minister Nakasone who seized enthusiastically on the Maekawa Report by a former Bank of Japan governor, who advocated the opening of Japanese markets for consumer and capital goods. However, not only formal protectionist measures but also non-formal blockages to importation remained an unbalancing factor in the Japanese economy well into the 1990s. However, there is little doubt that Japan's advantageously lopsided trade bargain with America was a major contributing factor to its post-war economic performance.

Although the high Japanese savings rate and rapid rate of growth of private fixed capital formation were frequently cited as overriding causes of Japanese economic success, it was the availability of open markets in the USA and access to its technology and capital, combined with the stability provided by Bretton Woods, which was the main contributor to Japan's industrial success. Contrary to the immediate post-war expectations of American economic planners that Japan would revive by export of manufactured goods to the primary commodities producing countries of Asia, the same assumption that largely underlay the ideology of the 'co-prosperity sphere', the USA became the main driver of demand for Japanese output. By 1970, 30 per cent of Japanese exports were to the USA versus 15 per cent to Europe and 15 per cent to Asia.

The result was export-led growth. In the 1960s, Japan achieved a remarkable average of 10 per cent per annum GDP growth during the decade. Trade finally came into balance in 1965 and a surplus grew explosively thereafter. By 1972, Japan's trade surplus rose to US$ 9 billion and, although this was sharply eroded during the First Oil Crisis (1972–4), by 1978 the Japanese annual surplus had again climbed to US$ 24 billion. Similarly, after the Second Oil Crisis in 1979, the Japanese trade surplus surged again to US$ 90 billion in the year ending March 1987. By contrast, American exports to Japan fell sharply from 29 per cent of the total in 1970 to just 17 per cent in 1980.

The structure of the Japanese manufacturing economy was also transformed. In 1955, textiles accounted for 50 per cent of exports; two decades later this proportion had fallen to just 5 per cent. Meanwhile, manufactured goods as a percentage of total exports rose from 80 per cent to 95 per cent over the same period. In this epoch of high growth, companies also sought to increase the leverage of their balance sheets; this resulted in an increase in average corporate borrowing from 40 per cent of gross capital to 75 per cent within 30 years of the war's ending.

Leverage enabled high growth if somewhat volatile stock market performance during economic downturns. High rates of investment were enabled by a savings rate (as a percentage of disposable income) of 44.9 per cent in Japan by comparison with just 7.9 per cent in the USA. A high rate of private fixed capital formation was also matched by a similar startling increase in public investment. Taking the highway system as an example, tarmac road increased from 14,000 km to 674,000 km.

Even the de-linkage of the yen from the dollar with the collapse of Bretton Woods, which saw a 16 per cent rise of the yen against the dollar in 1972, and a consistent appreciation thereafter, could not halt the dynamism of Japanese industry. Japan's post-war rise was driven by a cadre of remarkable industrial leaders. Akio Morita, co-founder of Sony, was a case in point. Morita would come into a meeting room wearing his workers' overalls and cap, dressed like any other production line worker. In spite of their apparently egalitarian apparel, the industrialists who rebuilt Japan were ruthless autocrats who defied the consensual approach with which Japan is often mistakenly identified. In the harsh post-war conditions, it was only the strongest of characters who survived.

Japan's rapid economic growth was accompanied by a concomitant change in the structure of the population. Although the birth rate fell from 33 for every 10,000 people in 1948 to 14 in 1966, the Japanese population rose rapidly from

83 million in 1950 to 120 million by 1985 as life expectancy rose to 74 for men and 80 for women. Population growth was accompanied by rapid urbanisation. Farmers fell from 27 per cent of the population in 1960 to just 9 per cent two decades later. Family life was also transformed. In 1920, 30 per cent of Japanese households comprised three generations compared to just 15 per cent by 1985.

Having been rabidly militaristic in the pre-war period, the post-war era was marked by a popular backlash against active foreign policy engagement. As an international power, Japan, its economic 'miracle' notwithstanding, became a nonentity. There developed a virulent anti-nuclear peace movement. In part, the failure of MacArthur to make the Emperor accountable for wartime atrocities created a culture of cover-up with regard to Japan's conduct of the war and imbued its people with a sense that they were victims rather than perpetrators.

It was commonly taught that Japan's conquest of Korea, Manchuria and South East Asia was a war of 'liberation' from the Western empires. Japanese atrocities in Nanking and elsewhere were generally ignored in school textbooks – an issue which still resonates strongly in China and Korea. In 1982, an international storm of protest was provoked when a high school history textbook, under pressure from the Ministry of Education replaced the word 'invasion' (of Manchuria) with the word 'advance'. In 1994, a minister in the Hatta government, Nagano Shigeto, opined, with regard to the Second World War, that

> ... Japan was in danger of being crushed, the country rose up to ensure its survival. We also sincerely believed in liberating Asia's colonies and establishing the Greater East Asia Prosperity Sphere.... The objective of the war was a justifiable one.... I think the Rape of Nanking is a fabrication.[12]

Similarly, Sakurai Shin of the LDP, a director general of the Environmental Agency, was forced out of his job for saying:

> I do not think that Japan intended to wage a war of aggression.... It was thanks to Japan that most nations in Asia were able to throw off the shackles of colonial rule under European domination and to win independence. As a result education also spread substantially ... and Asia as a whole was energized for dramatic economic reconstruction.[13]

It was a line of argument first proposed by the Emperor himself in his Second World War surrender speech.

In another example of breathtaking ignorance, if not perverse disinformation about Japan's Imperial past, Watanabe Michio, former minister of foreign affairs and deputy prime minister, affirmed that

> ... Japan governed Korea for 36 years, but you would look in vain for any reference in print to colonial rule. Both sides have now recognized the legitimacy of the annexation treaty ... annexation was completely peaceful [*ignoring the murder of Korea's Queen and Prime Minister amongst many others*] ... a different matter from colonization by the use of force.[14]

Not surprisingly, this statement in 1995 caused riots in Korea where the Japanese Culture Centre in Seoul was firebombed with Molotov cocktails.

In 1995, Hashimoto Ryutaro, chairman of the Association of Bereaved Families, who was about to become prime minister, deplored, 'how those who live today and cherish the memory of their deceased kinsfolk would feel if they were told, "that was a war [The Second World War] of aggression after all." '[15] The durability of Japanese post-war myths about their recent past can be traced in a direct line to the obfuscation organised by General MacArthur after 1945, in order to protect the Emperor Hirohito, Japan's main war criminal.

The problems of 'truth' created by MacArthur and the farcical 'show trial' he organised for the Tokyo War Crimes Trial left a lasting legacy in Japan's inability to deal with its Asian neighbours. As Lee Kuan Yew pointed out, Japan, unlike Germany, failed to assuage the fears of Asian countries because of wildly inflammatory statements of right-wing Japanese politicians. From a political viewpoint, the problem was that Japan's perverse historicity of the Second World War was not so much right wing as mainstream.

Inevitably, the 'un-purging' process which rehabilitated many of the senior participants in Japan's rapacious rule of its Korean colonies was a direct cause of much of the Asian discomfort. Prime Minister Kishi, for example, having studied at Tokyo University, under the ultra-nationalist Professor Uesugi Shinkichi, was formerly the senior bureaucrat responsible for the economic exploitation of Manchuria.

War myths abounded at all levels of post-war Japanese society. Students were taught that Japan may have been defeated by America but had nevertheless defeated Great Britain; their history books did not record that the Japanese army's biggest defeats in its history were at the hands of the British Army at the battles of Imphal and the Irrawaddy River. Irie Akira noted in *Shin-Nihon no Gaiko* (new Japan diplomacy) that 'Leaders in Japan . . . apparently clung to the last image of Japan as the, "Champion of Asian Liberation" presumably because they had no other ideological support to fall back on.'[16]

By contrast with Germany, which has adopted a rigorous, indeed over-rigorous policy of mea culpa with regard to the Second World War, Japan has largely shrugged off personal responsibility. It would be inconceivable that Germany's political leaders would annually honour their fallen wartime generals, let alone their war criminals, as the Japanese prime minister does at Yasukuni Shrine, which commemorates numbers of those executed after the Tokyo War Crimes Trial; this pre-war tradition was restarted by Prime Minister Miki. Later, the LDP passed a bill to make the government responsible for the upkeep of the shrine.

It is notable that the introduction to the Hiroshima Peace Museum describes the dropping of an atom bomb as an atrocity, with no reference to the role it played in saving millions of lives by ending the war quickly or the role that Hiroshima itself played as a major logistical centre for the Japanese war effort, making it an important and justifiable military target. Neither does the museum put into context the scale of atrocities committed by Japan's armies nor the fact that Japan was also developing a nuclear weapon to use against the USA.

The peace movement became the dominant subtext of all Japanese international activity. Prime Minister Miki summed up the post-war pacifist mood of Japan when, in 1976, he affirmed his 'belief that precisely because the Japanese people have themselves resolved to renounce nuclear weapons, even while possessing the technology and economic power to acquire them if desired, a moral persuasiveness for peace that can appeal to the world will be born'.[17] Ritual pacifist platitudes became the norm in post-war foreign policy statements by Japanese prime ministers, where real responsibility was abdicated to the USA. As Prime Minister Kaifu acknowledged in 1991, 'The Japanese–United States relationship is the axis of our country's diplomacy.'[18]

Nevertheless, defence issues proved fatal to three prime ministerial incumbents. Though Kishi had been indicted as a 'war criminal', he was subsequently 'un-purged' and moved to implement a more nationalist policy. In 1960, when Kishi renegotiated a treaty with the USA giving Japan a greater say in the use of American military bases, violent demonstrations by communists, trade unions and students followed. A young girl died in a student demonstration on 26 May and this was followed by a railway strike.

The new treaty was ratified on 18 June after Kishi ordered police in the Diet building to remove opposition members who were blockading the speaker in his office. Nevertheless, Kishi, who survived being stabbed by a right-wing fanatic, resigned soon afterwards. The chairman of the JSP was less fortunate and was killed by a similar attack. Kishi's successor, Ikeda, sought a conciliatory approach:

> The government party and the party not in power must come together in both foreign
> and domestic affairs. It is necessary therefore for us in the majority party to extend
> our hand in a humble spirit and treat the other side with forbearance.[19]

Foreign policy retreated to a standpoint of what Japan would not do, rather than what it could do. Defence, as implied by the name given to the Japanese army, The Self-Defence Force, was the only function of the military. In July 1961, the government cautiously expanded the capability of the defence forces to be able to hold off an attack pending American reinforcements and accordingly expanded its manpower to 235,000 from the limit of 165,000 in 1954. Nevertheless, defence policies remained cautious. In 1967, Prime Minister Sato announced the three nuclear principles: no manufacture of nuclear weapons, no possession of nuclear weapons and no nuclear weapons allowed to be brought into Japan (i.e. by American warships). However, Sato himself fell over foreign policy.

In 1976, it became a formal requirement of government to restrain military expenditure to less than 1 per cent of GDP. In addition to the trade advantages accorded to Japan by America in the post-war period, the Japanese economy was also awarded a peace dividend in the relinquishment of having to provide for its own defence. By contrast, the USA has spent between 3 per cent and 5 per cent of its annual GDP on global defence in the post-war period.

Japan's relations with China and Korea were slow to be restored. Only in December 1962 was Prime Minister Ikeda able to make a first exchange of trade missions with China, but it was only after the Cultural Revolution that relations began to thaw. Prime Minister Tanaka visited Beijing in September 1972 and met Mao and Zhou Enlai to formally restore relations between the two countries. When the Korean president visited Tokyo in 1974, a post-war first, some 20,000 troops were stationed on the streets and the Emperor made the first of what was to become a litany of expressions of regrets. However, in the absence of changes to school textbooks, these apologies were never taken at face value.

In May 1981, Prime Minister Suzuki was roundly condemned by the mainstream *Asahi Shimbun* for referring to the American–Japanese relationship as an alliance after talks with President Reagan. Only with the rising value of the yen and with a sense of Japan's economic superiority did Japanese politicians start to exude more international self-confidence. Nakasone, who developed a close relationship with Ronald Reagan, endeared himself to America when he declared in Washington that Japan was like an 'unsinkable' aircraft carrier.[20] Nakasone also sought to abolish the 1 per cent limit on Japanese defence expenditure.

Nevertheless, during the First Gulf Crisis in 1990, under pressure from President Bush, Prime Minister Kaifu called for members of the Defence Corps to be seconded to a new Peace Co-operation Corps to be sent overseas, not in a fighting role but merely for logistical support; even this largely inert measure was supported by a mere 30 per cent of the population. A Peace Keeping Operation bill was eventually passed, but only because Japan coveted a permanent seat on the UN Security Council. Kaifu funded the American operations in the gulf to the tune of ¥13 billion, which was a sizeable jump on the initial offer of just ¥1.0 billion; all round it was a somewhat shameful episode in Japan's less than distinguished post-war foreign policy.

For 40 years after the Second World War, Japan enjoyed a virtuous circle of success based on the simple formula of political stability and a pro-business economic policy. Having taken the decision that fighting communism was a more important priority than denuding Japan of its industrial strength, America became a powerful ally in the reconstruction process. Apart from the boosts to demand that Japan enjoyed as a result of US military expenditure during the Korean and Vietnam wars, Japan was given virtually unrestricted access to America's vast consumer markets.

In addition, the post-war financial stabilisation of Japan, combined with the Bretton Woods stable currency model, with the dollar acting as supplier of global liquidity of last resort, enabled Japanese manufacturers to plan long-term investment in an export-growth strategy. The remarkable stability of the *Todai* oligarchic

political structure, which the LDP managed to put in place, simply aided the process of economic advance. Without the burden of a foreign policy, abandoned in all
but name, and with only a minor outlay for defence, Japan was unencumbered with
problems that could have deflected it from its economic mission. In their hubris,
many Japanese now believed in the supremacy of the Japanese economic model;
many foreigners were equally convinced of the need to copy Japan. By 1990, Japan
had all the appearance of economic invincibility.

28

The Cultural Revolution

China: 1961–70

On 23 August 1966, the 16- and 17-year-old Red Guards of the Academy of Fine Arts of Middle School Numbers 2, 12, 23 and 63 rampaged through Beijing's capital library, ripped out ancient manuscripts, books and cultural heirlooms, heaped them in front of the Gate of Highest Scholarship and lit a bonfire. The same gangs of youths apprehended writers, academics and officials at the Bureau of Culture. Among them was the 67-year-old Lao She, a Chinese writer who, having written the global best seller, *Rickshaw Boy* (1936), was personally invited by Zhou Enlai to return to China from the US in 1949. Using the dollar profits of his best seller, Lao She bought a lavish old courtyard house in Beijing and settled down as a devout supporter of Mao and the revolution. Mao's regime was happy to wheel him out to meet foreign dignitaries.

To the Red Guards however, his famous career simply marked him as a 'bourgeois' to be punished. Punched, kicked and beaten with sticks and whipped with straps, Lao She was dragged to the bonfire and his head pushed into the black smoke. He was ritually draped with a placard scribbled with juvenile slogans and dragged by the mob to the local police station, where his wife later found him badly bloodied and semiconscious. The following day, his chauffeur did not arrive to take him to his office. Instead, he took a bus and went to Taiping Pond where, in imitation of the revered ancient poet Qu Yuan, he committed suicide by drowning himself.

Lao She may have been the most 'cultured' victim of the Cultural Revolution, but he was not the most famous or the most powerful. Just a month earlier, Liu Shaoqi, second only to Mao in the ranks of the politburo's Standing Committee, had been 'struggled against' by the junior staff of the Bureau of Secretaries. Mao's own doctor, Zhisui Li, witnessed the scene outside the State Council Auditorium; 'Liu's shirt had already been torn open, and a couple of buttons were missing, and people were jerking him around by the hair . . . others tried to force him . . . in the position known as the airplane . . . pushed his face toward the ground until it was nearly touching the dirt, kicking and slapping his face.'[1]

Liu's wife Guang Mei was also 'struggled against'; brought before a crowd of 300,000 people to be bated, she was forced to wear high-heeled shoes, a potent symbol of western bourgeois decadence. Mao's dislike of Liu and Guang Mei was such that he ordered that their six-year-old daughter should watch them being tortured. One of Liu's sons from a previous marriage committed suicide. Remarkably, the nearly 70-year-old Liu and his wife survived. Only later in October 1968 was he removed from the politburo, and the following year, deprived of food and medicine, 'Capitalist Roader No. 1' died on the squalid floor of a remote provincial prison.

Deng Xiaoping, 'Capitalist Roader No. 2', and general secretary of the Chinese Communist Party fared somewhat better. Deng was sent to Jiangxi Province, where he was provided with a modest house. He chopped wood, grew vegetables and did housework. He and his wife were sent to work part-time in a tractor repair factory. After 1971, this aged couple had the arduous task of looking after their paralysed son who had been thrown off the top of a building by the Red Guard. Foreign Minister Zhou Enlai had secretly improved Deng's lot by the provision of a small library. However, Deng was later to claim that Lin Biao and Jiang Qing would have had him killed had it not been for Mao's protection. Deng had always been one of Mao's favourites.

The cull carried out by the Red Guard was prolific. In scenes reminiscent of the butchery of the Commune in the French revolution, suspected bourgeois cadres were dragged out onto the stage of Beijing Stadium, where they were tortured and beaten. One woman who screamed incessantly had her throat cut. Women were paraded in western clothes, plastered with lipstick and make-up, and were publicly bated. Others were murdered off-stage. The houses of suspected bourgeois were marked and doors had to be kept unlocked. Homes were ransacked in the search for foreign goods. In Shanghai, people, in an attempt to rid themselves of belongings that could be deemed bourgeois, queued with gold and jewellery to sell them to the state bank. Neither were the streets safe; long hair was frowned upon and students held down their victims to shave their heads. Women's trousers were subject to the ink-bottle test. If the bottle could not pass down the trousers without being forced, they were deemed too tight and western. A group of Red Guards from a Beijing middle school drew up a list of 100 banned activities including drinking, smoking, keeping fish, cats and dogs, visiting bath houses, and massage parlours and employing people to do laundry. Puerile dogmas such as 'smashing the old and establishing the new' were propagated through posters and pamphlets.

As if to prove Lenin's description of ultra-left-wing behaviour as 'infantile disorder', Red Guards suggested that in future red stop signs at traffic lights should mean 'go' rather than 'stop'. In schools and universities, classes and admission exams were suspended; millions of students were allowed free passes on railways and buses and crisscrossed the country to attend mass rallies. Under the stress of urban turmoil, people hoarded food, banks were forced to close, and transport and power broke down.

The urban economy collapsed. Throughout China, the cities showed all the signs of anarchy as the Red Guards formed different power blocks and in many cases fought each other. Against the radical guards were many groups, sons and daughters of party cadres, who defended party order. In Shanghai, up to 700 revolutionary groups were reported to control the city after the woman who initiated the poster campaign in Beijing, junior philosophy lecturer Nie Yuanzi, arrived in the city to expose the head of the Shanghai Education Department. Mayor Cao Diqiu was rapidly deposed. In Shanghai and elsewhere in China, radical groups took over factories, docks and newspapers.

Throughout China, the governmental institutions were rendered powerless as the senior cadres faced 'struggles' with students and disaffected junior staff who opportunistically jumped on the radical bandwagon. Only Mao's governmental compound, Zhongnanhai, remained inviolate. To protect the state of which he was premier, Zhou Enlai invited 20–30 cabinet ministers to take turns living in the guarded compound. All regional first secretaries were also moved to Beijing. Not all could be protected. Zhang Linzhi, the minister in charge of the coal industry was beaten to death; the first secretary of Tianjin municipality died as a result of his 'struggle' with radical students; another, Pan Fusheng of Heilongjiang, was held captive and starved for four days before being admitted to hospital. A young diplomat, formerly in Indonesia, led a group of Red Guards to take control of the Foreign Office and issued communiqués. Even Zhou Enlai was held captive in his office for two days. The Cultural Revolution also gave cover for purges of colleagues. Kang Sheng, Mao's notorious minister of state security, allegedly compiled a list of 100 Central Committee members that he wanted expelled.

In some areas of China, heavy fighting broke out. Weapons on their way to Vietnam were hijacked in Guangxi and were used in what was effectively a civil war. In the slaughter that ensued, bodies were thrown into the Pearl River and embarrassed the Chinese government by turning up in their hundreds floating in Hong Kong waters.

While the Cultural Revolution was above all an urban phenomenon, the countryside did not escape entirely. In his biographic account, *Colours of the Mountain* (2000), Da Chen recalls the hardships visited on the remaining landlord class:

> Since the beginning of the cultural revolution, the commune cadre in charge of landlord reform had set the following rules: Grandpa could not visit his friends, he could not leave town without advance permission, and he was to write a detailed diary of his life every day . . . he wasn't welcome in any public places, could not engage in any political discussions, and should look away if someone spat in his face. If they missed, he was to wipe the spit off the ground.[2]

The degree to which petty bureaucrats used the excuse of the chaos of the Cultural Revolution to score humiliations on their enemies can easily be imagined.

For Mao meanwhile, impervious to the maelstrom outside and protected by his security police in his Imperial residence in the government compound at Zongnanhai, life was not unbearable. The upheavals of the Cultural Revolution produced a succession of Mao's former girlfriends, who sought out his protection from the excesses of the Red Guards. He was reported as saying, 'If they don't want you, you can stay with me. They say you are protecting the Emperor? Well, I am the Emperor.'[3] During the Cultural Revolution, the 'Emperor' moved from his lavishly appointed palace to the swimming pool complex at Zhongnanhai. Here he was able to entertain women in and out of the water. At the peak of the Cultural Revolution, Mao would have as many as five women in his bed at any time. (Curiously Chairman Mao's predilection for group sex and sexual foreplay in swimming pools was shared by his contemporary American counterpart, President John F Kennedy.)

The death toll of the terror inspired by the Cultural Revolution has been estimated by Roderick Macfarquhar at some half a million, although some historians put the figure far higher. By comparison with the Great Leap Forward, the numbers killed were miniscule. However, in its use of naïve schoolchildren and students, there is something particularly chilling about the barbarities of the Cultural Revolution and the 'Great Terror' it produced in urban China. In part, much of the litany of savagery of the Cultural Revolution can be described as one of those strange passages of blood lust that traumatise nations at moments of change; in this case though, the hand of a puppeteer was evident. Mao was the puppet master.

Why did Mao unleash the Cultural Revolution? To fully understand the reasons for the Cultural Revolution, it is necessary to recall the denouement of the Great Leap Forward and its aftermath. By the time of the Lushan Conference in 1959, it was already clear that a disaster was emerging in the Chinese countryside. Although much was covered up on his official tours of the country, Mao's spies kept him fully informed of the agrarian disaster caused by the Great Leap Forward.

No doubt all the party leadership was equally well informed of the disaster, but only Peng Dehuai, head of the army and hero of the Korean War, refused to stay silent and openly voiced his dissent at the policies pursued in the Great Leap Forward. In blunt terms he castigated the absurdity of the 'backyard furnaces' that were iconic symbols of a leap to catch up with the industrial West. Mao, steeped in the knowledge of Chinese history and well aware of the dangers of a disgruntled military, saw this as the first major threat to his leadership. A sign of the danger was Jiang Qing's early reading of the signals. She decamped from Mao's beach house, where she had been effectively ostracised, and rushed to his side. For the rest of Mao's life, she sustained her marriage in a non-conjugal political partnership of ultra-left radical intent.

At the critical meeting in Lushan on 23 July, Peng obstinately refused to sit with the other politburo members at the front of the hall, in spite of Mao's request for him to do so. In a speech that electrified his audience, Mao challenged Peng and the leadership to stand against him: 'If Peng's army won't follow me then I will go down to the countryside, reorganize the guerrillas and reorganize my army.'[4] Peng left the hall alone and defeated. The leadership, whatever their personal thoughts about Mao's responsibility for the disaster of the Great Leap Forward, were too cowed to react to the possibilities of change. Mao had brazened his way through the crisis. In the aftermath, Peng was publicly denounced by Mao's toadies, Zhou Enlai and Kang Sheng, and also by the notoriously sycophantic Lin Biao, who took Peng's job as head of the People's Liberation Army. Peng was purged and banished. A mass purge of supposed Peng sympathisers numbering many millions soon followed.

Although Mao's victory ensured another year of ruinous Great Leap policies, there was a personal cost to his victory against Peng. Up until the Great Leap, Mao had been the all-conquering hero of the revolution; he was its foremost intellectual, the proselytiser of the guerrilla military strategy and the country's leader during the post-war years of economic recovery. Mao's aura of infallibility among the 'Long March' leadership now lay in tatters. Although nothing was said, he must have known that they held him responsible for the Great Leap Forward catastrophe, even if they did so only in private. Before Lushan, Mao's position of power existed by dint of awe and reverence for his achievements; afterwards it was coloured by sycophancy and fear. Previously Mao was confident enough of his position to welcome open criticism and debate, but increasingly he brooked no dissent and like the Emperors before him increasingly turned to intrigues and political manoeuvres to maintain his power base.

While Mao was still the supreme leader in China, he had already stepped back from the 'first line' in 1958, when he arranged for Liu Shaoqi to become head of state. In his role in the 'second line', as Mao liked to describe it, he moved into the background of day-to-day government. However, this was a retreat from work rather than power. Mao hated bureaucratic routine and the study of technical papers and briefings. He became an amateur philosopher and historian whose intellectual energies were absorbed by Chinese history and classical literature. As for dispensing judgements and decisions, his methods were deliberately obscure. Normally the leadership would have to make do with vague and cryptic comments written on the margins of reports.

For Mao, the business of government was not the slow accretion of progress through orderly administration. The painstaking accumulation of national advance was for beings and countries of a lower order. The post-war history of China was marked by Mao's sponsorship of dramatic initiatives with brilliantly turned 'sound-bites'; simplistic catch phrases to engage and motivate the masses. While Mao spouted forth on mass engagement in government by the peasant classes, he looked disdainfully at the impotence of the leaders of the Western democracies. Like Hitler, Mao believed in the primacy of will. 'If one has an unbreakable will, there is nothing that cannot be accomplished,'[5] he wrote in his early essay on the role of physical education. Also, in an annotation of Friedrich Paulsen's *System of Ethics* (1899), written by the young Mao, he noted that '... force is like that of a powerful wind arising from a deep gorge, like the irresistible sexual desire for one's lover, a force that will not stop, that cannot be stopped. All obstacles dissolve before him.'[6]

His dalliances were not only cerebral. A constant stream of young girls was needed to sustain his demands for dancing, swimming and sex. Kang, as head of security, used that office in time-honoured fashion to become Mao's main procurer of girls. He also acquired a library of thousands of volumes of pornographic literature for the chairman's use. In the post Great Leap period therefore, Mao grew increasing distant from colleagues whose work on the daily administration of government naturally made them pragmatic, and therefore appear increasingly revisionist.

By comparison, Mao in his chosen 'second line', continued to indulge in the romance of ideological purity. In a private comment, Mao was reported as saying that the leadership 'complain all day and get to watch plays at night. They eat three meals a day and fart. That's what Marxism–Leninism means to them'.[7] For Mao, the stultification and comforts of bureaucracy were not qualities to be commended. '. . . the party was not above the revolution or its ideology,' he argued, 'In this conception, the central party apparatus is not sacred nor does it possess immunity from the challenge of reform, as it does in the Lenin–Stalin tradition.'[8]

By 1962, both agricultural and industrial output had largely recovered from the ravages of the Great Leap Forward, and the leadership had felt confident enough to hold an unusually populous convention that became known as the Seven Thousand Cadres Conference. Here, the leadership indulged in self-criticism albeit of a ritualistic and clichéd variety. In a hall in which everyone present must have known Mao's ultimate responsibility for the catastrophe in the countryside, Mao himself offered his own self-criticism; 'Any mistakes that the Centre has made ought to be my direct responsibility . . . there are some other comrades who also bear responsibility, but the person primarily responsible should be me.'[9]

There was an air of a new beginning at the conference, and many of those purged in the wake of Peng were now rehabilitated, including some 5 million party members and citizens who were judged to have been wronged during the Great Leap Forward period. Noticeably, Peng was not among them, in spite of his having penned an 80,000-character statement to the Central Committee in which he requested an end to his rustification, on the not unreasonable grounds that his criticisms at Lushan had proved correct. In spite of the tactical retreat that Mao was prepared to make at this juncture, the rehabilitation of Peng would have cut too close to the bone for his comfort. Whatever their private feelings, none of the leadership was prepared to voice support for Peng. Their craven behaviour was certainly not lost on Mao, and in due course he would use it to devastating effect.

In the aftermath of the Seven Thousand Cadres Conference, the leadership began to behave as if a new era had dawned. While acknowledging Mao's leadership, they must have felt that the path was clear for them to steer a pragmatic course towards economic restoration. In July 1962, Deng circulated a document asking for answers to 41 problems. For agriculture, the underlying suggestion was that the re-division of land back to households should be considered.

Wedded to the ideology of collectives, Mao viewed Deng's paper as revisionist. Liu also came into conflict with Mao's proposed Socialist Education Movement, and there was further conflict over Mao's 23 Articles in January 1965 that suggested an alliance of peasants, cadres and work teams to attack individual enterprise and corruption. In a foretaste of what was to come, Mao wanted these criticisms from below to go all the way to Central Committee level. Meanwhile, in Mao's absence, Liu's profile was being increasingly raised in the press; also Liu's short book on *How to be a Good Communist*, first published in 1939, was revised and reissued.

On the eve of the Cultural Revolution therefore, Mao was feeling increasingly isolated from his senior colleagues. Mao, who unlike Liu was uninterested in the process of government or the primacy of the party, lived for revolution. His greatest fear was that revisionism would sideline the revolution and therefore his own relevance. He complained that he was being treated like a dead ancestor. Furthermore, Mao had the example of the Soviet Union before him. Khrushchev had attacked Stalin at the 20th Soviet Congress in 1956; in 1959 the Soviet leader visited the American presidential retreat at Camp David; then in 1960 he lambasted the Great Leap Forward and withdrew technical support from China.

In Mao's eyes, Khrushchev had been faced down in Cuba in 1962, and had subsequently signed a partial nuclear Test Ban Treaty in 1963. Also, Khrushchev had attacked fellow Albanian communists in 1961, and in the Sino-Indian border clashes of 1959 and 1962 the Soviets had declared themselves neutral. As Mao himself observed, '. . . the capitalist class can be reborn; that's how it is in the Soviet Union.'[10]

In the autumn of 1965 Mao's plan to recapture the commanding heights of the revolution began to uncoil. The deputy mayor of Beijing was playwright Wu Han whose play *Hai Rui*, about a Ming Emperor who cruelly and unfairly destroys his faithful and able official, was construed by Mao to be an allegory on his treatment of Peng Dehui. It now seems likely that Mao had sprung a trap by prompting Wu to write this play; indeed Mao's doctor, Zhisui Li, records, 'Mao himself had promoted the traditional opera of Hai Rui.'[11]

At a politburo meeting in September, Mao criticised Wu and requested the Mayor of Beijing Peng Zhen to head a cultural reform group to investigate. Peng Zhen, a close ally of Liu Shaoqi, could do little but accept the poisoned chalice. At first, he took no action, hoping that the issue would blow over. However, on 10 November, an article criticising Wu was published in Shanghai. Mao's wife, Jiang Qing, was the sponsor. A shift in the political wind was not lost on the leadership. Deng Xiaoping immediately gave up his regular bridge games with Wu. Peng Zhen's five-man committee cautiously drew up an outline report in which he advocated reasoning with Wu rather than a policy of suppression. When Peng Zhen travelled to Wuhan to seek Mao's imprimatur, Mao refused to read the report or comment. Then, when Lin Biao asked Jiang Qing to set up a forum on culture in the armed forces, she rejected Peng Zhen's report and called for a *Great Socialist Cultural Revolution*; the defining phrase of the epoch had been coined.

By 1966, when the Standing Committee of the politburo met from 17 to 20 March, Peng Zhen was now abandoned by his erstwhile friends; Zhou, Liu and Deng all called for his dismissal. In typical fashion, Lin Biao went even further and suggested that Peng Zhen had been plotting a coup. Meanwhile, his report group was replaced by a new body, the Cultural Revolution Group, including Jiang Qing and Chen Boda, a senior party member in the Chinese Academy of Sciences, and a former secretary to Mao. This group was to be the kernel of Cultural Revolution-ary activity.

The climate of fear now engulfing the leadership was further heightened by a 16 May circular, which emphasised the threat of counter-revolutionary elements. In the new climate of encouragement to the young, Nie Yuanzi, a female lecturer in philosophy, posted a 'wall newspaper' criticising the head of the party at the Beijing University. Mao organised its publication in the People's Daily. In addition to Peng Zhen, who commanded the capital, other leaders swept up in the May purge were Lu Dingyi, head of propaganda, Luo Ruiqing, chief of staff of the army, and Yang Shangkun who, as director of the Chinese Communist Party's General Office, directed the flow of reports to the Central Committee. The removal of party leaders all in key areas of responsibility looked far from coincidental.

In response to the mounting crisis, and in the absence of Mao who had left for an extended stay in Central China, Liu tried to restore the authority of the party by sending work teams to universities. Mao however started to send strong signals in favour of youth. On 16 July, Mao went for a widely reported 'photo opportunity' swim in the fast-flowing Yangtze River with 5,000 young people. The symbolic intent of this event was manifest to all. Such were the Chinese press eulogies to Mao's swimming prowess that the president of the World Professional Marathon Swimming Federation invited Mao to race competitively on the grounds that his reported speed was four times faster than the world record.

For the first time since 1962, Mao then called for a meeting of the Central Committee Plenum, at which members found Mao's own wall poster stuck to the door with the proclamation 'Bombard the Headquarters', which was a thinly veiled attack on Liu and the leadership. At this point, Mao sent Wu Faxian to Dalian to bring an ailing Lin Biao back to the capital on 5 August to inform the reluctant head of the PLA that he was to be Mao's deputy and successor. At this moment of crisis, Mao wanted his chief sycophant at the centre.

On 8 August 1966 the Central Committee adopted a 16-point resolution; it argued that

> large numbers of revolutionary young people . . . have become courageous and daring path breakers. . . . Through the media of big-character posters and great debates, they

argue things out, expose and criticize thoroughly and launch resolute attacks on the open and hidden representatives of the bourgeoisie. . . . The Cultural Revolutionary groups are an excellent bridge to keep our Party in close contact with the masses.[12]

On 18 August, Mao put a final stamp of approval on the Red Guards when he addressed a mass rally of 1 million young students in Tiananmen Square. Never a man to miss a symbolic gesture, Mao sported a Red armband. The Red Guards of the Cultural Revolution were now launched in full flow.

Was the orchestration of the Cultural Revolution by Mao an absurdly elaborate scheme to destroy a communist party leadership that threatened his own position? In fact, Mao's own position was never threatened; there is certainly no evidence of real plots to overthrow Mao, even from Liu and Deng once they knew themselves to be under attack. However, the threats may have been real enough in Mao's own mind. By 1965, Mao was a man in sharp physical and mental decline.

In a characteristic manifestation of opium addiction, Mao suffered through his life from appalling constipation. When he squatted in the fields, he would call his guards to remove rock-like turds from his anus with their hands. To help him sleep, he took copious quantities of sodium barbiturate, but counteracted that with the consumption of massive amounts of stimulant in the form of tea. Mao's developing neurasthenia produced insomnia, dizziness, itchiness, impotence and anxiety attacks.

Also, Mao's refusal to clean his teeth produced a coating of heavy green plaque and severe dental problems including gum disease. His rampant satyriasis was an invitation to frequent bouts of venereal disease. After transmitting *trichomonas vaginalis* to most of the young dancers in a cultural troupe, Mao refused to take medicine on the grounds that 'if its not hurting me then it doesn't matter'.[13] It didn't help that he never washed his genitals.

Mao's doctor also noted that in the autumn of 1965, 'The paranoia I had first sensed in Chengdu in 1958, when Mao suspected that his swimming pool was poisoned, was tightening its grip.'[14] At Wuhan, as Mao sat contemplating his attack on Peng Zhen, he complained of noises in the attic. The change in his personality was also noted by Ji Dengkui, who observed that Mao 'often contradicted himself with his thinking. In later years almost nobody trusted him. We very seldom saw him . . . we were afraid of what we said for fear of committing an error'.[15]

Like paranoid dictators before him, he increasingly surrounded himself with sycophantic security men. The Public Security Bureau (PSB) in Beijing became a vital force in the faction battles within Beijing, and acted as a career launch pad after 1966 for Kang Sheng, Hua Guofeng and Wang Dongxing. Less famous perhaps than its Soviet equivalent, the KGB, the PSB took the lead role for arrests and the terror instilled in the urban party elite during the Cultural Revolution. Mao also increasingly used Unit 8341, a form of Praetorian Guard, originally formed to provide security to the Central Committee, to carry out investigations and arrests.

Lastly, Mao took care to co-opt the military to his cause. After Mao's removal of Peng Dehuai at Lushan, his successor as head of the PLA, Lin Biao, proved himself a slavish devotee to Mao. Lin's promotion of the little Red Book, which was a breviary of Mao's writings, was a brilliantly successful tool of indoctrination, and convinced Mao that he was a loyal and useful acolyte. The slavish complements that he used to pay to Mao were cringingly embarrassing. At the enlarged politburo meeting in May 1966, Lin's speech claimed that

> Chairman Mao has experienced more than Marx, Engels and Lenin . . . he is unparalled in the present world . . . Chairman Mao's sayings, work, and revolutionary practice have shown that he is a great proletarian genius . . . every sentence of Chairman Mao's works is a truth: one single sentence of his surpasses ten thousand of ours . . . whoever is against him shall be punished by the entire party and the whole country.[16]

In addition, unlike Liu Shaoqi, Lin Biao had little interest in politics or civil administration, and no inconvenient views on contentious issues such as collectivisation; he was a compliant cipher.

Yet in spite of the increasing signs of megalomania displayed by Mao, it would be absurd to believe that Mao created the whirlwind of street revolution simply to rid himself of the Communist Party leadership. For a dictator with his autocratic powers, there would have been simpler methods of disposing of potential rivals, real or perceived. Mao too would have been fully aware of the history of the French Revolution and the fate of Robespierre and Danton, who perished at the hands of a 'commune' terror of which they had been the chief authors.

When the February 1967 edition of the revolutionary journal *Hongqi*, edited by Chen Boda,recounted and praised the history of the French Commune, and thereby endorsed the implementation of a Commune form of government in Shanghai led by Zhang Chunqiao, Mao pulled back and banned the use of the term 'people's commune'. At every point where the Cultural Revolution appeared to be getting out of hand, when the ultra-leftists led by his wife pushed too far, Mao would use Lin Biao and the threat of the People's Liberation Army (PLA) to whip them back into order.

In particular, Mao would not allow the guards to adopt their 'struggle' tactics within the ranks of the PLA itself. In effect, the PLA was his backstop to make sure the Cultural Revolution did not get out of hand. After the seizure of the Ministry of Foreign Affairs in August 1967, and the destruction of the British diplomatic mission, Mao reacted swiftly to rein in the ultra-leftists. The Cultural Revolutionary Group was reorganised with the removal of four radicals. The ultra-leftist 516 Group was accused of attempting to overthrow Zhou Enlai, and Jiang, sensing another shift in the wind, began to distance herself from this and other more radical groups. A final flare up of violence at Qinghua University brought swift retribution, as Mao ordered in troops from Unit 8341 to restore order. By September 1967, Mao was advocating that 'The party organization must be restored.'[17] In a final crackdown on anarchy in 1968, some 18 million Red Guards were expelled from the cities and posted to the countryside. For a generation of young urbanites, it was a cruel and traumatising experience. Resented by the primitive peasant societies on which they were foisted, the young Red Guards were often bullied, beaten and starved. Girls were frequently raped, and suicide became commonplace.

In the lexicon of Chinese ideology, the Cultural Revolution remained, for a decade or more, a movement of great achievement in its restoration of the purity of the Chinese revolution. By means of whipped up urban terror, the increasingly paranoid and egomaniacal Chairman Mao had rid himself of his co-leaders who, in their attempt to manage China in a more pragmatic manner, and in particular to solve the economic catastrophes of Mao's 'Great Leap Forward', had erred towards a revisionist course.

However, the Cultural Revolution was not a design simply to enhance Mao's own power or to destroy the party; above all, it was a master plan to sustain the purity of a revolution that was an ageing dictator's monument to himself. With intimations of mortality now haunting him, Mao's Cultural Revolution was his last hurrah. In June 1966, as the Cultural Revolution was entering its most virulent phases, he confided to Hô Chí Minh, 'We are both more than seventy, and will be called by Marx someday. Who our successors will be, Bernstein, Kautsky or Khrushchev we can't know. But there's still time to prepare.'[18]

29

Indira Gandhi: A Study in Nepotism

India: 1966–84

Indira Gandhi's childhood set the pattern of loneliness and misery that was to become the hallmark of her life. The frequent incarcerations of Nehru, her father, combined with the tubercular illness of her mother, Kamala, robbed her childhood of the normal parental relationships. Even when Nehru was at liberty, his all-consuming political schedule meant that he rarely had time for his daughter. It is perhaps symptomatic of the relationship that it is best known through Nehru's correspondence with his daughter, started in prison in 1922 and later published in 1930 as *Letter from a Father to His Daughter*.

Without the company of siblings, and often alone at home with a sickly mother, Indira Gandhi's childhood was both melancholy and lacking in love and affection. Brought up as a wealthy upper class Indian on her grandfather's legal earnings, Indira was also isolated at school; at St. Cecilia's she was the only child to wear *khadi*, the politically correct, homespun, cotton clothing worn by the Congress Party elite. Schooling was frequently interrupted, however, both at St. Mary's Convent in Allahabad and later at the *Santiniketan* (abode of peace) School that had been founded by the Bengali Nobel Prize-winning poet Rabindranath Tagore.

Although it was here that she developed a taste for Indian classical dance, it was on her extensive tours to Europe, accompanying Nehru and Kamala to the finest sanitaria in Germany and Switzerland, that Indira acquired her most useful accomplishments. Learning to speak fluently in English, German and French, she acquired language skills that would help burnish her reputation in European eyes. However, much to Nehru's disappointment, she was academically a mediocre student who managed, with some difficulty and not a little influence, to get into Somerville College, Oxford. Though she failed to match her father's intellectual skills, Indira shared her father's agnosticism. When asked about the afterlife, she told Dom Moraes, 'I don't think about an afterlife. I have too little time in this one.'[1]

Although she became acquainted with Iris Murdoch among others while being 'crammed' for exams at Badminton, she had few friends. This cannot simply be put down to her peripatetic life. Throughout her life, Indira Gandhi exceeded even her father for aloofness and indifference. Curiously, given her strong emotional and intellectual preference for the Soviet Union over the USA, her closest friendship developed with a pseudo-intellectual American socialite, Dorothy Norman, who introduced her to such contemporary luminaries as W.H. Auden, Lewis Mumford and Anais Nin. Her attachments were not necessarily driven by politics, however. While she disliked Jackie Kennedy, she was to develop a warm mutual relationship with her ideological opposite Margaret Thatcher.

Her relationships with men were also few and never satisfactory. In spite of her dutiful obeisance to her father's needs at Nehru's residency throughout his time as prime minister, there is every reason to believe that this was in large part motivated by her desire to escape from her philandering husband, Feroze Gandhi (no relation to Mahatma Gandhi). Feroze, a Parsi by religion, had been a political devotee and reputed lover of Indira's mother, Kamala, and had gradually transferred his affections to Indira, who he followed to Europe. Here he studied at, but failed to graduate from, the London School of Economics. Indira Gandhi, at 5 feet 2 inches, sickly and tubercular like her mother, with hawk-like nose, hooded eyes and sharp features much coarser than her father's, was no beauty. While withdrawn in character, Indira also possessed her father's arrogance and sense of *lese-majesté*. She once commented, 'We didn't deserve a normal, bland boring life.'[2]

Predictably, marriage with Feroze proved a volatile relationship, and no sooner had she married, under Nehru's reluctant auspices, than he used Indira's family connections, while actively pursuing other women. Such was the breakdown in the relationship that he was soon forced into a tent outside their Delhi home. Feroze, an ebullient and bombastic chancer, who sponged jobs and money, ended as a radical politician, who set up in quasi-opposition to his own father-in-law. Effective separation from Indira was only broken when one or the other was ill or the needs of their two sons pulled them together.

Thereafter, Indira was widely publicised to have had an affair with Nehru's loyal, albeit corrupt and drunken, private secretary, Mathai, who scandalously proclaimed her sexual appetites in memoirs published by Indira's subsequently estranged daughter-in-law, Maneka (Sanjay Gandhi's widow). Other liaisons were frequently assumed, although without clear evidence, with close confidantes such as her cabinet secretary, Haksar, and her yoga guru, Dhirendra Brahmachari, who arrived penniless in Delhi from Kashmir, where he was reported to have seduced his young charges to become one of the most politically influential men in the land.

It could be argued that the emotional void experienced in her parental relations brought about a pattern of emotional dependency that blinded her to the character of the men to whom she became devoted. As *The New York Times'* foreign correspondent Anthony Lukas observed, Indira was a 'profoundly lonely person . . . by upbringing and circumstances she stands remarkably_almost frighteningly_alone'.[3] This dark void in her life was ultimately to lead to disastrous consequences with regard to the over indulgence of her dissolute son, Sanjay, on whom she doted.

From an early age, Indira was drawn into the political world of her parents. In 1930 at her mother's suggestion, Indira was put in charge of the 'Monkey Brigade' of young Congress supporters. (The name referred to a Hindu legend recorded in the *Ramayana* of a bridge built by monkeys to enable Lord Rama to rescue his wife Sita from Sri Lanka.) From this point she was never to disengage from politics, although, like her father, she assumed the air of one for whom it was her unhappy lot to carry the burdens of the Indian people. Nevertheless, like Nehru, when threatened with being unburdened of power, she fought tenaciously to keep it.

As she developed in confidence, Indira also fell out with her father's politics just as Nehru had fallen out with the political views of his father, Motilal. Indira expressed her displeasure at her father's British political friends, particularly the Marquis of Lothian, who was one of the Cliveden set of supporters of Chamberlain's German appeasement policy. When war arrived, however, she displayed her unalterably pro-Soviet stance by blaming their axis alliance with Nazi Germany on British foreign policy. Like Nehru, Indira displayed a schizophrenic attitude to the West; her enjoyment of the cultural perquisites of Britain and America was combined with a hostile critique of its capitalistic underpinnings.

After independence, Indira moved into her father's Delhi residence and performed all the duties of a social hostess. This role naturally enhanced her political education and more importantly put her into a position which allowed her to exercise influence. She was courted by ambitious Congress politicians, and although Nehru seems to have been sensitive to the accusation of nepotism, he did nothing to prevent it. Indira soon became vice chairman of the Social Welfare Board, president of the Indian Council of Child Welfare and vice chairman of the International Council for Child Welfare. She was also a leading figure in the women's section of Congress.

More importantly, Nehru thrust her onto the important Congress Working Committee in 1951. Over time she became more independent and outspoken. In 1959 she petitioned the Congress Party against an apparent move away from the 'socialist line'. Yet when the far left threatened Congress, as it did with the Communist elected government of Kerala in July 1959, Indira Gandhi sided with right-wing Hindu forces. She is also widely believed to have been the hand behind Nehru in the ruthless dismissal of Kerala's Communist government.

In later years, Nixon would complain that 'Mrs. Gandhi expected to be treated as a woman and acted with the ruthlessness of a man.'[4] Her political position was by now consolidated by the fact of her election to the presidency of the Congress Party. Contrary to the suppositions of many 'women's lib' supporters in the West, for whom Indira Gandhi became something of a totem, Mrs Gandhi's gender was never a major political issue or barrier to her career. Indeed, she was only the fourth woman president of Congress, the first being Annie Besant, the redoubtable English theosophist and early independence activist.

On the death of Nehru, the Congress political leaders, known as 'The Syndicate', successfully manoeuvred to block the ambitions of the pro-business Desai and enabled the election of Lal Bahadur Shastri as prime minister. Indira Gandhi, at this point not considered a realistic contender for the top job, was offered the sop of a cabinet post, as minister for information and broadcasting.

However, she soon proved her manliness for the task of high office; when the Pakistan President Ayub Khan, who had boasted that 'After Nehru's death we will have no difficulty in taking Kashmir and whatever else we want to take,'[5] attacked India, Indira Gandhi, who was vacationing in Kashmir at the time, won plaudits by refusing to quit the state and by going in person to the front line. The better armed Pakistanis, albeit equipped with the American Patton tank, failed to win the hoped-for decisive encounter and readily agreed to the United Nations Security Council's call for a ceasefire. At the invitation of the Soviet Foreign Minister Kosygin, Shastri went to Tashkent, where he successfully negotiated a favourable treaty to end the war. However, before he could get on the plane to return in triumph to Delhi, Shastri had a heart attack and died.

This was a fortunately timed development in Indira's career. Having shown some mettle during the conflict with Pakistan, and being younger than her 70-year-old rival Desai, and therefore less prone to sudden death, she was preferred to her more experienced rival. To prevent a party rift, the thwarted Desai nevertheless accepted the post of deputy prime minister and finance minister. However, if 'The Syndicate' had expected Indira to be little more than a compliant cipher, they were soon relieved of their delusions.

The exigencies of war had brought rampant inflation in addition to rice riots in Kerala, communal conflict in the Punjab and secessionist demonstrations in Nagaland. In defiance of the Congress 'kingmaker' Kamaraj and 'The Syndicate', Mrs Gandhi drove through a 57.5 per cent devaluation of the rupee against the dollar. She also defied the left of her party by seeking aid from President Johnson in Washington in 1966 and, accordingly, toned down her criticism of the US war in Vietnam and mouthed the platitude that 'India understood America's agony over Vietnam.'[6] Having pocketed American aid, she would later make more public her condemnation of the bombing of Hanoi. When Chester Bowles, America's ambassador to Delhi, pointed out to President Johnson that U Thant, UN secretary general, and the Pope had also condemned US policy in Indochina, the president wryly observed that neither of these two wanted American wheat. Like her father, Indira Gandhi played America for what she could receive by way of aid, all the while cosying up to the Soviet Union. Morarji Desai was far from inaccurate in his knowledge of her instinctive political leanings, when he bitterly complained that 'that woman will sell the country to the communists'.[7]

Indira could afford to alienate her own party leaders. They needed the vote-pulling power of the Nehru – Gandhi dynasty, and she could appeal to the Indian voters without the intermediation of Congress or its leaders. Her family inheritance should not belittle her skills as a political campaigner. Like her father, Indira was indefatigable on the stump. With her use of colloquial language, and adaptation of dress by adopting the local style of *sari* (Indian female garment), she always managed to identify with the poor voter and engage them with populist rhetoric.

She was also aggressive in putting down her enemies. When the Maharani of Jaipur (once described by Cecil Beaton as one of the most beautiful people in the world) tried to disrupt Indira's political rallies in that state, Mrs Gandhi countered that: 'If you look at the account of their [the maharajas] achievements before Independence, it is a big zero.'[8] Neither was she above petty vengeance. The exquisitely elegant Maharani of Jaipur was later incarcerated in prison at Indira Gandhi's instigation.

Indira Gandhi's first electoral campaign took in 15,000 miles, and like Nehru she spoke dozens of times every day. In a phenomenon not unique to her, political power despite its physical demands evidently improved her health. Standing for the first time for the lower house, Indira won her deceased husband's seat at Rae Bareilly, and Congress, notwithstanding the loss of 95 seats, retained a majority of 282 seats out of 520.

With her majority secure, Indira Gandhi immediately embarked on a radical left-wing programme that travelled further down the path of Marxist-socialism initiated by her father. The nationalisation of 14 major commercial banks in July 1969 was followed by a state takeover of the insurance industry. Also curbs on landlord rights were initiated, which were eventually to rob owners of the freeholds of their properties. In a final insult to the princely states and in continuation of the 'bad faith' of her father, Indira Gandhi now reneged on the privy purses that had been granted to the maharajas in return for the usurpation of their countries.

As her father did before her, Indira Gandhi undermined the constitutional role of ministers in cabinet through a clique of advisors that became known as the 'Kashmiri mafia' and included her yoga teacher and two Kashmiri *Pandits*, Arun Nehru and Makhan Lal Fotedar. Her key policy advisor, however, was Narain Haksar. While studying at the London School of Economics, Haksar had cooked Kashmiri food for Indira during the Blitz. Nehru had brought him into government to work under Foreign Minister Menon, and he subsequently became head of Indira's prime minister's secretariat. Like Nehru, Haksar was both a model of English urbanity and a vigorous critic of the capitalism that had built Britain into a great empire. In isolating herself and her cabal of personal advisors from Congress and its power structures, Indira inevitably antagonised elements within her own party that objected both to the further move to the left and to their own exclusion from power.

As well as undermining the power structures of her party, Indira also continued the trend towards removing the civil service's spirit of independence and impartiality. A former Foreign Secretary J.N. Dixit, who served under Indira Gandhi, noted in his memoir *My South Block Years* (1996) that there was increasing politicisation of the foreign service after 1969; 'This pressure was applicable not only to the Foreign Service but also to all branches of the Indian Civil Service. The pressure was the new requirement of "commitment to the ideologies and policies of the ruling party". '⁹

The constitution was also increasingly undermined by a prime minister who resented having to articulate a defence of her policies and, outside of the populist stump, was such a poor performer on her feet in parliament that she became known as *Goongi Gudiya* (the dumb doll). She was much more comfortable holding *darshans* (audiences), where upwards of 100 people a day would bring their petty grievances to her in the style of a Moghul emperor's court.

Her attitudes to government were regal rather than constitutional. Indira once commented, 'In many parts of the country I am called mother, and I regard India as my family.'[10] In 1982 she asked newspaper editors not to call her empress; however, it is clear they were accurately expressing the manner of her governmental style and the way it struck India's simplistic rural population. Poet and journalist Dom Moraes recalled how village peasants would ask, 'How is the health of our Empress?'[11]

In 1969 Desai was sacked over his opposition to bank nationalisation. Meanwhile 'The Syndicate's' plan to back Sanjiva Reddy as president, possibly as a means to control or even remove Indira Gandhi, was thwarted, and former Vice President V.V. Giri was promoted to the role of state president. The internal Congress war came to a head in November 1969 with a 'Syndicate' inquiry finding Indira guilty of being in defiance of party wishes. The political farce ended with the expulsion of Indira Gandhi. Of the elected Congress members, some 220 out of 297, now broke with Congress to form a pro-Indira Congress R (R for requisitionist), while the remaining 77 Congress MPs stayed with Congress, which now became known as Congress O (O for organisation).

Although Indira had succeeded in breaking the opposition within her own party and she could now rely on the Communist Party to support her radical left-wing programme, she was now thwarted by the Supreme Court, which invalidated bank nationalisation as being unconstitutional. Furthermore, when the bill to abolish the privy purses was defeated by one vote in the *Rajya Sabha* (the upper house of parliament), Indira pressured the new President V.V. Giri to override this by proclamation. This action too was declared to be unconstitutional. Indira now decided to take her agenda to the people. While the opposition launched *Indira Hatao* (remove Indira) campaign, Indira deftly responded with a *Garibi Hatao* (remove poverty) campaign to bolster her populist left-wing agenda.

Surpassing even her 1967 electioneering performance, she travelled 30,000 miles and addressed 20 million voters. The vote produced a landslide victory for Indira and Congress R, which was returned with 325 seats. Apart from allowing Indira to pass bills for the nationalisaton of banks and the coal industry, and her abolition of the privy purses, Mrs Gandhi now passed legislation aimed at undermining both the 1947 constitution and the judiciary.

In July and August 1971, the 24th and 25th amendments allowed government legislation to alter the 'inalienable' rights that had been embedded in the constitution. Furthermore, legislative changes were exempted from judicial review. Checks were also imposed on the media through the Press Objectionable Matter Act. For Indira the inconveniences of the constitution, with its appropriate checks and balances, were dispensable for a person who felt herself uniquely capable of running India. When in 1973 the Supreme Court ruled against the government's constitutional amendments, she went even further in her ruthless disregard for constitutional niceties by forcing the president to appoint A.N. Ray as chief justice of the Supreme Court. In protest at this flagrant abuse of the legal system, three Supreme Court justices resigned.

Aside from her constitutional depredations, Indira also showed scant regard for government propriety by the licence given to her son Sanjay, a man who alarmed even Indira's most fervent supporters. Vain and pigheaded like his father, Sanjay appears to have inherited a double dose of his parents' intellectual mediocrity. Apart from car magazines and other technical journals, for which he and his elder brother Rajiv had an obsession, Sanjay almost never read a book. This did not prevent him from being a driven, opinionated brat. Having failed to complete an apprenticeship at Rolls Royce in Britain, where he was most noted for speeding in his Jaguar sports car, Sanjay returned to Delhi as a fully fledged playboy, who stole cars in Delhi for joy rides.

Feeding his obsession for cars, he opened a garage business and eventually parlayed this into a licence from the Ministry of Industry in 1971 to produce 50,000 low-cost city cars per annum. The imbued corruption of the system, which would in the 1990s become known throughout Asia as 'crony capitalism', was apparent in the government's overlooking of the superior competitive bids of Renault, Morris and Toyota. Sanjay's company Maruti Udyog (*Maruti: son of the wind*) became the leitmotif of the corruption and nepotism of Indira's prime ministership. By some accounts Sanjay also fraudulently acquired land from his friend Bansi Lal, the chief minister of Haryana, and used his influence to raise sums from the Central Bank of India and the Punjab National Bank.

Those who stood in his way such as D.V. Taneja, chairman of the Central Bank, were sacked. Critics were silenced. In spite of taking deposit advances from would-be dealers, the Maruti car never arrived, although a decrepit truck produced by the offshoot, Maruti Heavy Vehicles, was sold at inflated prices to state governments. Meanwhile, Sanjay established Maruti Technical Services to skim fees, salaries and expenses from the moribund Maruti project. Through Maruti and other scams, it was generally understood that Sanjay built up considerable sums in overseas bank accounts that helped feed his passion for expensive toys, most notably foreign imported aeroplanes. (Only after his death in 1980 was Sanjay's Maruti revived in joint venture with the Japanese company Suzuki, Maruti Suzuki India Ltd., to become the major motor manufacturer in India.)

It could be argued that in undermining the key props of the 1947 constitutional settlement, Indira Gandhi merely continued down the path initiated by her father. The same could be said of her approach to foreign policy. Although Nehru had espoused a non-aligned path, while in reality loathing the USA and leaning heavily towards the Soviet camp, Indira followed this path to its logical conclusion by negotiating a pact with the Soviet Union.

In part this was driven by reaction to America's support for Pakistan, which President Nixon and his Security Advisor Henry Kissinger saw as a key regional ally and most importantly as an intermediary with China. Although during a trip to the sub-continent in July 1971, Kissinger made it clear that American arms supplied to Pakistan would not be used to attack India, Indira was nevertheless furious at the continued American support for a Kashmir settlement.

Also, she could not have been delighted to learn that Kissinger's visit was largely designed as camouflage for his famous secret visit to see Mao and Zhou Enlai in Beijing. However, for a woman who often found more support for her policies from the Bengali Communists than from her own party, the Soviet 'peace and friendship' pact was also a logical fulfilment of an ideological preference. Then there was also a matter of personal vitriol between Nixon and Mrs Gandhi, who, according to the mannered understatement of Kissinger, 'were not intended by fate to be personally congenial'.[12]

Indira Gandhi, like her father a pompous moraliser and lecturer, who also overrated India's importance to the world, irritated Nixon to the extent that at a meeting at the White House on the second day of her visit to Washington, he kept her waiting in an anteroom for 45 minutes. Their advisors were no friendlier. Haksar thought the president 'lacked moral principles' and Kissinger was 'an egomaniac who fancied himself another Metternich'.[13]

The conflict came to a head with a Pakistan civil war precipitated by the arrest of the Bangladeshi leader Sheikh Mujibur Rahman. The close relationship between America and the Pakistan government of Yahya Khan, who had helped intermediate the rapprochement with China, was such that it precluded intervention on behalf of the Bengalis when the Pakistan army started a reign of terror in East Pakistan. On her part, Indira Gandhi's intervention in the civil war was not driven by a sense of moral justice, however. Ten million Bangladeshi refugees had flooded into India and threatened political and economic stability. Indira confided to a cabinet colleague that 'if the refugees do not go back soon they will never go'.[14]

More importantly, with the Kashmir dispute in mind, the opportunity to embarrass Pakistan was too good to miss. In this context her plea in *Foreign Affairs*, 'How could we ignore a conflict which took place on our very border and overflowed into our territory?'[15], was not wholly convincing. As well as massing its troops on the borders of East Pakistan, Indira also authorised the covert training and equipping of the Bangladeshi independence forces. While fearful of the possibility of Chinese involvement, an outcome that Kissinger dreaded, Indira was nevertheless planning an assault on Dhaka when Pakistan, aware that India was about to strike, precipitated hostilities by bombing Indian air bases in December 1971.

A relieved Mrs Gandhi commented, 'thank God, they've attacked us'.[16] Her evident glee at the opportunity to attack East Pakistan did not prevent Indira sending a letter to Nixon, in which she accused him of responsibility for the war. Noticeably she also questioned whether Pakistan would give up 'its ceaseless and yet pointless agitation of the last 24 years over Kashmir?'[17] Fortunately, although the American and Soviet fleets were both despatched to the Bay of Bengal, the Pakistan army surrendered before they could arrive. China's reticence in becoming involved also prevented Indira's aggressive foreign policy from developing into a global conflict of much greater consequence.

Mrs Gandhi's victory fed her soaring ego. She was lauded in parliament as *Durga* (the Hindu goddess of war). Even her critics changed their tune. She was acknowledged as 'the greatest leader India had ever had'[18] Overseas, the *Sunday Times* described her as 'The most powerful woman in the world',[19] while Aubrey Menen in *The New York Times* called her a 'sort of De Gaulle of India'.[20]

The last restraints on her autocratic rule now began to disappear. Unfriendly state legislatures were dissolved and presidential rule imposed. In 1975 the Indian army invaded the autonomous 'protectorate' of Sikkim and abolished the ruling monarchy. Indira Gandhi perversely hailed the incorporation of Sikkim as India's 22nd state, as a great democratic victory. The entire Congress Working Committee was now hand-picked by Mrs Gandhi. Corruption within Congress, influenced by the methods of Sanjay, now became endemic. Fundraising, often through cash donations, was moved by Sanjay to Indira's offices at No. 1 Akbar Road, then to her own home at No. 1 Safdarjung Road. Party rallies, rent-a-crowd events, were increasingly motivated by money rather than belief.

More long-term damage to the vitality of the economy was inflicted by the passing of the Monopolies and Restrictive Trade Practices Act in 1970 and the Foreign Exchange Regulations Act of 1973; these socialist economic policies further extended the 'licence raj' and created a culture of permits and graft in the increasingly politicised and corrupt civil service. In the short term however, it was the monsoon or lack of it which was the larger determinant of the Indian people's experience of relative poverty. A series of poor monsoons in 1972, 1973 and 1974 were a catalyst for rising inflation, which began to create pockets of discontent, and in some places food riots became widespread.

Against this background of economic discontent and nepotistic misrule, a politician of the Mahatma Gandhi school of self-restraint and moral righteousness, Jayaprakash Narayan, emerged to lead a campaign to purge India of its spiralling corruption. Narayan, who had walked the country with Vinoba Bhave, Mahatma Gandhi's loyal acolyte, to encourage the voluntary land transfer movement, had also succeeded in persuading marauding *dacoits* (bandits), who had grown in number since independence, to surrender.

Objecting to the corruption of government in Bihar, Narayan set up village committees on a Gandhian model. They rejected the authority of the state government, which he called upon to resign. Meanwhile in Gujarat, Morarji Desai was rehabilitating his political career by calling for an end to corrupt government in Gujarat. Eventually, Indira called for fresh elections after a fast by Desai forced her hand. Sensing blood however, Narayan now called for all-out revolution. On 16 February 1975, Narayan was reported as saying to the Indian people,

> Your loyalty is to the national flag and the Constitution, not to the Prime Minister or the Government of the day. If an order appears to your conscience as something against the popular will and the national interest, then it is your duty not to obey such an order.[21]

On 6 March Narayan led a march of 500,000 demonstrators in Delhi.

Dramatic events now unfolded in June, as the Gujarati elections provided a stunning victory for the four opposition parties running against Congress. Even more alarmingly for Indira, a defeated opponent of the 1971 elections, Raj Narain, petitioned the court in Allahabad to have her election in Uttar Pradesh declared void. Found guilty on two charges, Indira appealed to the Supreme Court, and while the case and its punishments (including barring from elected office for six years) were left suspended, she found herself politically hobbled.

Narayan and Desai now launched a national campaign of civil disobedience with which they confidently expected to topple the Congress government; 'We intend to overthrow her, to force her to resign. . .'.[22] This they achieved but not before they had both spent several years in prison. On the night of 25 June, Indira Gandhi persuaded the president, on dubious interpretation of Article 74 of the constitution, to declare a state of emergency. Minutes after the presidential proclamation, Indira authorised the arrest of Narayan and Desai and a long list of now proscribed political opponents. To the nation she declared, 'I am sure that internal conditions will speedily improve to enable us to dispense with this proclamation as soon as possible.'[23]

Characteristically, the decision to declare 'emergency' and round up opponents was taken outside of cabinet, by Indira alone, with the promptings of Sanjay and her cabal of cronies. The cabinet meeting called to rubber stamp the 'emergency' decision was somewhat frosty, with the minister of defence asking, 'under what law were the arrests made?'[24] However, cabinet independence, long since lobotomised by Nehru, provided a mere ripple of dissent; as had become the custom under her father, Indira declined to take a vote. Repressive rule soon followed. The arrest of Mark Tully of the BBC was ordered with the instruction, 'pull down his trousers, give him a few lashes and send him to jail'.[25]

More importantly, 26 Communist organisations were banned, and the 'emergency' was exempted from judicial review by the passing of constitutional amendments within parliament. Non-Congress governments were replaced by 'presidential rule' in the states of Gujarat and Tamil Nadu. Within six months of the 'emergency', 25 ordinances were issued to enact extraordinary laws. Hundreds of journalists were arrested and 40 foreign correspondents expelled. More than matching the British imprisonment of those who followed Mahatma Gandhi and Nehru's 'civil disobedience' movement during the Second World War, Indira Gandhi's proscribed list put 110,000 people in jail.

Even more alarmingly, Sanjay, who had increasingly taken to the issuance of orders directly to Indian ministers, now promoted a plan for the modernisation of India. The two most controversial policies were slum clearance and a forced vasectomy programme. In Delhi over 100,000 people were displaced by the precipitate clearance of slums, while in the ancient city of Varanasi, seventeenth-century houses were bulldozed. Meanwhile heavy-handed family-planning programmes also brought corruption in its wake, with forged or fraudulently purchased certificates of sterilisation. Nevertheless, in the first five months of the emergency, some 3.7 million people were sterilised.

Against this background, the press merely grovelled in their support for the new regime. As the current BJP home minister said at the time, journalists 'crawled when they were merely asked to bend'.[26] As a self-appointed crown prince, Sanjay now developed his own political power base through Congress Youth, which hand in hand with a corrupt police force rapidly degenerated into a mafia-style protection racket. Sanjay's criminal gangster activities allegedly went as far as the organisation of 'hits' on underworld rivals and even reputedly on the love rival of his mistress. Enamoured of absolute power, Indira Gandhi heeded Sanjay's calls to postpone elections on two occasions. Finally yielding to a spasm of conscience, or perhaps realising the changing popular mood, and for once rejecting her son's pleadings, she announced elections for March 1977.

Sensing the popular mood, Agriculture Minister Jagjivan Ram resigned from the Gandhi cabinet and joined the 'Janata block' opposing Congress in the elections. In calling for an end to 'totalitarian and authoritarian trends . . . in the nation's politics',[27] he correctly judged the national mood. The Congress Party was annihilated, and Indira Gandhi even lost her own seat of Rae Bareilly. The incoming Prime Minister Morarji Desai exacted his due revenge by kicking her out of her home and moving in himself. Desai, a moral disciplinarian, had finally brought himself to power, a position which he had long believed to be his by right.

A bitter opponent of Indira Gandhi, Desai could not have come from a more different background. His father, a Brahmin schoolteacher, had committed suicide by jumping down a well when he was 15. Married three days later, Desai then took it upon himself to support all his siblings. His own family followed when he took up conjugal rights with his wife some seven years after his marriage. In the next 11 years he produced five children until he took on a vow of *brahmacharya* (the foregoing of sensual pleasures, i.e. celibacy). He famously ascribed his robust constitution to the daily consumption of a glass of his own urine. Tragically for Desai, two of his sons died young, while one of his daughters committed suicide after a broken romance with a Muslim.

Pious, arrogant and obstinate, Desai was hardly the man to manage a fractured coalition. Apart from his vindictive pursuit of Indira Gandhi, a tactical error which turned her into a martyred victim, Desai achieved little in the way of rolling back Indira's Marxist – Leninist economic edifice. While the Janata government pursued

Sanjay and Indira through the courts, it was Desai's own son who was found guilty of fraudulent business transactions. Also, photographs of the son of Deputy Prime Minister Jagjivan Ram having sex with an underage girl were published in Maneka Gandhi's gossip magazine *Surya*. In a flurry of personal discord, the Janata block fell apart and new elections were called for in January 1980.

By their clumsy vendetta against Indira, the Janata government played to her greatest strength, which was her ability to woo the public. She began to stump the country, even touring southern India in the unlikely company of socialite travel writer Bruce Chatwin. Her speeches were sprinkled with small doses of 'mea culpa' with regard to the 'emergency', combined with large helpings of self-justification and gloss. A visit to London and meetings with her old friend Margaret Thatcher also helped refurbish her international image. Later, Lady Thatcher, on being asked why she liked someone so diametrically opposite in political belief, simply responded, 'Because she was a strong woman.'[28]

Meanwhile Indira split the Congress Party again. The leadership, who considered her dead meat, had studiously ignored her after her election defeat two years earlier, but on 1 January 1980, Indira displayed her considerable following by taking 70 of the Congress Party's 146 MPs to form Congress (I). The remaining 76 members, led by Swaran Singh, became known as Congress (S).

With the catastrophe of the emergency forgotten in little over two and a half years, Mrs Gandhi swept back to power. It was a remarkable comeback. In the national broadsheet *Times of India*, India's best loved cartoonist R.K. Laxman portrayed Indira as a hypnotist casting her spell on the audience, 'You can't remember a thing! There was no emergency! Nobody suffered! Nobody was hurt! Everybody was free and happy.'[29] There was certainly a large element of self-hypnosis; displaying little humility from her previous reverse, when asked about her return to power, she answered, 'I have always been India's leader.'[30]

Once back in power, the judiciary soon relieved Sanjay of the legal charges against him; with the following of 150 new MPs, largely a lumpen mass of money grubbers, Sanjay also returned with more power than ever. By remarkable good fortune for India, Sanjay, who did not possess an aerobatics licence, was killed while flying his new Pitts-2A plane over New Delhi on 23 June 1980. Few would dissent from the view expressed by his uncle that it was 'the best thing that could happen to India'.[31]

Neither the death of Sanjay nor the experience of opposition changed Mrs Gandhi's ill-considered political opportunism, both at home or overseas. In Sri Lanka, Indira offered support for the Tamil Tigers, the Hindu separatist terrorists in the north of the island, so as to curry political favour with the Tamil-speaking voters of the southeastern state of Tamil Nadu. As for Kashmir, Indira's invasion and defeat of the Pakistan army in East Pakistan did not bring a settlement of the key issue that had divided the countries since independence. At the Simla Agreement talks, Zulfikar Ali Bhutto had convinced Indira that he would not survive if he returned to Pakistan having ceded Kashmir. In this analysis he was almost certainly correct. To finalise a settlement,

> both Governments agree that their respective Heads will meet again at a mutually convenient time in the future and that, in the meanwhile, the representatives of the two sides will meet to discuss further the modalities and arrangements for the establishment of durable peace and normalisation of relations, including . . . a final settlement of Jammu and Kashmir. . .'.[32]

Indira could do little to persuade Pakistan to yield their claims, but by her interventionist follies in her last administration, she ensured that the Kashmiris themselves became the most formidable proponents for Kashmir's secession. With the death of Sheikh Abdullah on 8 September 1982, his son, Farooq, inherited his father's position as both chief minister and leader of the National Conference Party, which he led to victory in the June 1983 state elections. The defeat was a humiliation for Indira Gandhi, who campaigned vigorously for Congress in Kashmir.

Speaking in *Urdu* rather than native Kashmiri, her claim '*Main Kashmir ki ladki hun*'[33] (I am a daughter of Kashmir) failed to play to the electorate. For once her campaigning skills failed her. Ending her rallies at Iqbal Park in Srinagar, she found just a handful of Congress workers in a ground that could accommodate tens of thousands. A furious Indira Gandhi now used a compliant press to whip up a storm of protest at alleged irregularities. On 28 May, the *Statesman* led with the story of a *Reign of Terror in Kashmir*.[34] The situation in Kashmir was barely helped by the increasing personal antipathy between Indira Gandhi and Farooq, a dissolute playboy, the 'disco' chief minister as he was called and a quixotic politician who went out of his way to antagonise Delhi. Given Indira's predilection for overthrowing democratically elected state governments, there was in any case a limited likelihood of her refraining from invention in a state so central to her emotional and geopolitical interest.

Farooq, by attending a meeting of opposition leaders organised by N.T. Rama Rao, chief minister of Andhra Pradesh, after his surprise defeat of Congress in the 1983 state elections, was hardly calculating to win over Indira Gandhi. In April 1984, Jagmohan, a loyal Gandhi acolyte, was appointed governor in Kashmir, and three months later, Farooq Abdullah's government was dismissed and he was replaced by his brother-in-law, G.M. Shah. Shortly afterwards, showing that 'the emergency' disaster had not curbed her authoritarian instincts, Indira also dismissed N.T. Rama Rao in Andhra Pradesh. The folly of Indira's actions was soon revealed, when new elections brought Rama Rao sweeping back to power.

In Kashmir the unpopularity of the Shah government, caused by both its illegitimacy and its unprecedented levels of corruption, helped nurture the beginnings of a Kashmiri resistance movement outside the political framework. As the settlement commissioner had noted, 'Holy men from Arabia have spoken to me with contempt of the feeble flame of Islam which burns in Kashmir. . . .'[35] Sufism, with its weak institutional traditions and liberal teachings, was ill-suited to resistance activity. However, as a consequence of Mrs Gandhi's depredations, radical jihadist groups would begin to gain traction among the famously 'peace loving' Kashmiris.

In the Punjab too, Indira Gandhi interfered in the democratic process with equally dire consequences for the future. Indira and Sanjay had sought to limit the power of the Akali Dal party with its Sikh secessionist instincts, by nurturing a young demagogue named Jarnail Singh Bhindranwale, whom they hoped would split the Sikh vote. As Mark Tully and Satish Jacob concluded in their study of *Amritsar, Mrs. Gandhi's Last Battle* (1985), 'It was Indira Gandhi's Congress Party which launched Bhindranwale, and it was Indira Gandhi's government, which allowed him to usurp its role in the Punjab.'[36]

The strategy backfired when Bhindranwale stoked a much more violent Sikh separatist movement, which called for a Sikh state called Khalistan. With the slaughtering of cows and murdering of Hindus and Sikh critics, communal tensions in the Punjab were raised to fever pitch. From July 1982, Bhindranwale took control of the sixteenth-century Golden Temple in Amritsar from where co-ordinated terror attacks were launched across the state; gradually his supporters infiltrated the police and other state organs.

Indira Gandhi, cynically content to enjoy the electoral benefits of the Hindu backlash, which was increasingly important against a background of the growing power of regional-linguistic parties, allowed the Punjab to descend into chaos. When Indira finally determined on military intervention in April 1984, the Golden Temple's fortifications were such that Operation Blue Star launched against Bhindranwale forces cost almost a third of the 1,000 Indian troops sent in to root him out.

Combining rocket and mortar assault with bloody hand-to-hand fighting, Indian forces finally managed to take control of the now half-destroyed Golden Temple. Bhindranwale was slain along with over 1,000 civilians. (The carnage drew parallels with General Dyer's infamous Amritsar massacre of 1919). The sacking of the Golden Temple, an appalling atrocity committed on the most important of the holy sites built by the fifth Sikh guru Arjan Dev (1563–1606), was a catastrophic misjudgement that led directly to Indira Gandhi's own death.

Fearing reprisals, Indira's personal security was stepped up, although she refused to dismiss her Sikh bodyguards. On the morning of 31 October 1984, a day to be devoted to a BBC interview with Peter Ustinov, a meeting with former British Labour Prime Minister James Callaghan and a formal dinner with Princess Anne, Indira Gandhi was gunned down by her bodyguards. Beant Singh shot her five times with his pistol, to be followed by a spray of machine gun fire from Satwant Singh. In Delhi, Sikhs were sought out and butchered. Some 3,000 are thought to have perished while a further 50,000 fled the capital.

It is difficult to be charitable in evaluating Indira's brutally interrupted reign of 18 years. To her credit, she proved herself an able and hard-working populist campaigner, a brilliant garnerer of votes, who was able to sustain the legacy of the Nehru name both to win elections and to maintain control of her party. Also as a political operator, Indira Gandhi was constantly under-rated by her male colleagues, both in opposition and within Congress. In the end she proved herself tougher and more ruthless than all of them. No lesser figure than Kissinger commented that 'She had few peers in the cold blooded calculation of the elements of power.'[37]

However, apart from keeping herself in power, her legacy to India could barely have been worse. To suggest, as former BBC correspondent Mark Tully does, that with Indira, politics came before statesmanship (in the context of Kashmir) glosses over the dire intentions and consequences of her rule. Indira Gandhi went well beyond her father in politicising and subverting the independence of the civil service; she undermined the ethics and democratic voice of parliament; she sought to control the press and corrupt it; she undermined the independence of the judiciary; the democratic authority of state governments was destroyed by her spurious use of 'presidential rule'; cabinet government was entirely subsumed by the wholly unconstitutional devolvement of power to her grotesquely irresponsible son, Sanjay; her military adventurism fully established India's reputation as the bully boy of the sub-continent; for the future, her playing on local religious feelings as a means of garnering votes sowed the seeds of severe communal problems.

Worse than the consequences of her family obsession with Kashmir, which required a defence expenditure of 60 per cent of India's total budget, she furthered a Marxist – Leninist economic agenda that, within a decade of her death, would bring the Indian economy to its knees. The constitution barely survived her attempts to bend it to her authoritarian will. Those who defend Indira, point to her ending of the 'emergency', a crisis of her own making. Even over this event she could not admit her failings. Her paranoid delusions were clearly displayed to journalist Dom Moraes when, in the context of her decision to call elections to end the 'emergency', she told him that 'I had this sense that more and more foreign influences were seeking for excuses to disrupt, perhaps even to destroy, this country.'[38]

Isolated by temperament and upbringing, surrounded by sycophants, Indira clung to authoritarianism because she had neither the intelligence nor the emotional confidence to do otherwise. By the indulgence of her son, Sanjay, a man whose instincts were even more conspicuous in the totalitarian mould than his mother, Indira was fortunate in his death that she did not leave India an even worse legacy. In conclusion Indira Gandhi was a fatally flawed individual, emotionally and intellectually deficient, who, in the supreme arrogance of her inherited 'quasi regal' status, did immense damage to India and the welfare of its people, particularly by the adoption of a hardline Marxist–socialist economic agenda.

30

Kennedy: Vietnam and the Vienna Summit

America—Vietnam: 1954—63

A merica's war in Vietnam has provoked more debate and has been more divisive than any other issue in post-war American history. Costing some 58,000 American lives out of total casualties of 1.5 million, the Vietnam War was fought at a significant human cost. In addition, between 1954 and 1975, America expended some US$ 106 billion on the defence of South Vietnam, a figure many times the aggregate annual GDP of both North and South. Not surprisingly, the origins and nature of this war are critical to the debate. Was the war in South Vietnam simply an indigenous rural uprising against a corrupt Southern dictatorship? This is the claim that was put forward by the North, and which was later taken up by the peace movement in the USA. Also what role did President Kennedy, the iconic figure of post-war liberal America, play in the American engagement in Vietnam? Would he have committed America to a major Asian conflict in the same way as his vice president and successor Lyndon Johnson?

Vietnam is a peculiarly narrow 'S'-shaped country 1,000 miles long, consisting of a narrow coastal plain frequently interspersed with mountainous jungle. At either end the country broadens out into a dumb-bell shape; these contain the Red River Delta in the north and the Mekong Delta in the south. Here the country widens to 300 miles from its narrowest point of 45 miles. Most of the population is squeezed into the narrow, fertile strips of rice paddy, which make up just one-sixth of Vietnam's land mass.

Historically, Vietnam had existed as a homogenous culture if rarely a political entity. In 208 BC, in the Chinese annals of *Nan-yüeh*, the Vietnamese were noted as a people occupying present day North Vietnam (*Tonkin*). Vietnam as an entity had begun as an adjunct to the warlords of Southern China, and was ruled by the Chinese as a province until 939. Only with the decline of the Tang dynasty did a Vietnamese kingdom emerge. Growing strength brought Vietnam into conflict with the Chams who occupied what is now Central Vietnam (*Annam*). Champa was conquered and absorbed in 1069, and there followed a steady southward migration, fed by a growing land-hungry population, which finally ended with the displacement of Cambodians from the Mekong Delta by the end of the eighteenth century.

The normal pattern of migration occurred when population growth in a village forced its younger members to leave to seek new land to support them. Moving further and further south, new settlements were secured, and official recognition sought from the Emperor. He would give the new village a name and send articles of association that would be housed in a communal building and used for public ceremonies. The village was the advance guard of expansion, and retained, right up to the twentieth century, an importance which outstripped national political institutions. Hence, the Vietnamese proverb 'the laws of the Emperor yield to the customs of the village'.[1]

The topography of the country and the logistics of government made political unity difficult to achieve. By 1516, there were three ruling warlord dynasties (the *Nguyễn*, *Mac* and *Trinh* families) competing for power from their territorial bastions. The consolidation of power by the *Nguyễn* along the coastal plain south of the Red River Delta led to the effective partition of Vietnam in the late seventeenth century. This division was formalised by the building of a wall at the 18th parallel, which extended for 11 miles to a height of 18 feet. However, when unification of the country was finally achieved in the late eighteenth century, it was soon brought to an end by French incursions. Curiously, but probably not entirely coincidentally, the seventeenth-century division of the country was almost exactly that faced by America in the aftermath of the 1954 Geneva Conference.

In the aftermath of Geneva, however, there was a lull in the communist attempt to advance southwards. Having secured recognition for the Democratic Republic of Vietnam, Hô Chí Minh and Party General Secretary Trường Chinh (pseudonym meaning 'Long March') pushed forward with radical land reforms to create rural communes. As with collectivisation in Russia, the Great Leap Forward in China, the *Chollima* (flying horse) in North Korea, the results were disastrous.

While the *Việt Minh* had been very successful in co-opting peasants against village headmen in the classic Maoist model, co-operatisation cut across the deeply rooted traditions of Vietnamese village life. From 1954 to 1956, rural unrest was widespread. In Nghe An Province, thousands of peasants were massacred. Although never officially acknowledged, the socialist agricultural experiment in North Vietnam probably cost 100,000 or more lives. Along with rural unrest came brutal purges of perceived enemies.

Võ Nguyên Giáp, minister of defence and hero of the war of liberation against France, was appalled. At the 10th Congress of the Central Committee of North Vietnam's Communist Party, Giáp admitted to a 'terror, which became too widespread'; 'Instead of recognizing education to be essential, we resorted . . . exclusively to . . . disciplinary punishments, expulsion from the Party, executions . . . worse still, torture came to be regarded as a normal practice during party organization'.[2]

The economic catastrophe caused by collectivisation was a catalyst for political change. Its architect, Trường Chinh, was forced to step down as general secretary. Hồ, who occupied the ceremonial post of chairman of the party, reluctantly agreed to take over his post as a 'stop-gap'. However, the new faction emerging within the party consisted of a group of Southern-born party leaders, including Public Security Minister Trần Quốc Hoàn, Lê Dúc Tho and Lê Duẩn, who effectively replaced Trường in 1957 but formally became general secretary in 1960. (Lê Duẩn would replace the deceased Hồ Chí Minh as titular leader in 1969, and remained general secretary of the party until his death in 1986.)

Lê Duẩn was an able organiser, who was noted for his plain-speaking and arrogance. Unlike the Northerners, Hồ, Trường and Giáp, the rival Southern faction was not from the 'gentry scholar' class; more importantly, they favoured a more rapid liberation of the South. Unlike Giáp, who wanted to build up a conventional army in the North with weaponry provided by the Soviets, Lê Duẩn favoured a build-up of guerrilla activity in the South to speed up unification. Following the more peaceful 'line' favoured by the new Soviet leader Khrushchev, at the 9th Plenum in April 1956, Hồ advocated that the party 'should hold aloft the banner of peace'.[3] However, with the sudden promotion of Lê Duẩn at the beginning of 1957, this policy would be quickly reversed.

The Việt Cộng (the Vietnamese Communist guerrilla force set up in the late 1950s to replace the Việt Minh in the South) now launched a campaign of terror in the South. At first, this was aimed at recalcitrant village headmen opposed to the takeover of their villages by the Việt Cộng, but soon this expanded to murder and bombings in Saigon. The Hồ Chí Minh trail was also developed, and units of 50–200 men were sent to the South to support the guerrillas. At the party conference in 1960, Hồ publicly announced the strategy to liberate South Vietnam.

Later that year, Hồ called for the formation of the National Liberation Front of South Vietnam to control the war effort in the South. This was the formal name of the more commonly known Việt Cộng. The Việt Cộng was organised into a variety of forces. Main units were full-time professionals of 2,000 men; regional units were also full-time, but had less training and consisted of 500 man units; finally, village Việt Cộng units were part-time and comprised 10–12 soldiers. All units were shadowed by powerful political officers. Key to the development of forces in the South was the opening up of the Hồ Chí Minh trail through Laos and Cambodia. At first, this rough track was used by units of 50–200 soldiers, but eventually it would become a highway of supply to the Việt Cộng.

In the early 1960s, there were significant overhauls to the operating structure of the Việt Cộng. The relative failure of Lê Duẩn's tactics led to the restoration of Trường Chinh and the Northern-based strategies of Giáp. Finding themselves thwarted by better organised forces, the Việt Cộng was increasingly reinforced by better-trained troops from the North. In addition to combat commanders, the North supplied ordnance technicians, logisticians and communication experts.

Weaponry, which had previously comprised a jumble of Chinese, French, Soviet and American equipment, was also upgraded and standardised; at this point, the Kalashnikov automatic rifle, the AK-47, became the standard *Việt Cộng* firearm. Unit sizes were also increased with the first 10,000-man division being created in 1964. The change wrought a dramatic effect on *Việt Cộng* military productivity in the South. Between 1957 and 1960, there were 2,000 kidnappings and 1,700 assassinations. Thereafter, assassinations carried out by the *Việt Cộng* reached a peak of 2,000 in 1963 alone, while kidnappings in the same year were 7,200. More importantly, military attacks by *Việt Cộng* units increased from negligible numbers before 1960 to over 15,000 per annum by 1963.

The post-Geneva period also saw political changes in South Vietnam. Emperor Bảo Dại, a long-running and far from popular enigma in the Vietnamese political landscape, was dethroned after Prime Minister Ngô Dinh Diệm organised the passage of a motion of dismissal through the National Assembly in April 1955. The transition process was completed by a referendum six months later which won a 98 per cent vote in favour of a republic to be headed by Diệm, who was elevated from prime minister to president. In essence however, the vote, undoubtedly rigged, created a democratic constitution that was little more than a fig leaf for President Diệm's military-backed dictatorship.

Ngô Dinh Diệm had earned a rare reputation for diligence and integrity as a provincial administrator under the French in the 1930s, though his greatest advantages derived from his move to America where he studied at a Catholic seminary in New Jersey. As a devout Catholic, a religion he shared with President Kennedy, he garnered support from that community in the USA. Most importantly, he courted senior American political figures, notably Hubert Humphrey, a Democrat senator from Minnesota. Consequently, his putsch against the Imperial family was treated favourably by an American administration to whom he now turned for support. French links were largely rejected, particularly as their policies now inclined them to treating Hồ Chí Minh as an 'Asian Tito'; (in other words a 'soft' communist friendly to the west).

Diệm quickly sought to establish a much greater control of law and order than his predecessor. In large part, this consisted of crushing the powerful religious cults that had begun to dominate South Vietnam. *Cao Dài* (great religion of the third period of revelation and salvation) was founded by Ngô Văn Chiêu, who held seances to talk with spirits in 1919 and came to believe that Confucius, Buddha, Christ and Mohammed were incarnations of the same spirit. By the 1930s, the sect had 1 million members; *Cao Dài* included Joan of Arc, Victor Hugo, Jefferson and Winston Churchill in its eclectic pantheon of saints.

Meanwhile, *Hoa Hoa* was a pre-war sect that used ancient texts for prophecies and faith healing. The *Binh Xuyen* was a mafia group founded by a river bandit, which came to control drugs and prostitution and much of the police force in Saigon. They were the first group to be purged. Later, Diệm turned on the leaders of the other two sects, and captured and executed their leaders.

Diệm's rule was also marked by remarkable levels of nepotism. His brother Ngô Dinh Nhu established a political vehicle for family rule in the Revolutionary Labour Movement; Nhu's father-in-law became ambassador to the USA; of the other brothers, one became a provincial governor, another became Archbishop of Hué, while a third became ambassador to the United Kingdom.

Most controversially, however, Nhu's wife became the most influential figure in Diệm's court. Usually portrayed as a cross between 'Salome' and 'Lady Macbeth,' she came to symbolise the venal corruption, cruelty and intolerance of the regime. The usually restrained Robert McNamara, Kennedy's secretary for defence, described her as 'bright, forceful, and beautiful, but also diabolical and scheming_a true sorceress'.[4]

Increasingly, Diệm's government alienated powerful factions within Vietnam. In a foretaste of future problems, Diệm's palace was surrounded by three airborne battalions in November 1960. They demanded a broader government, which was only partially conceded. However, Diệm's jealousy of successful officers became an increasing hindrance to operations against *Việt Cộng* insurgency. Lt Colonel John Paul Vann, whose epic life was recorded in Neil Sheehan's *A Bright Shining Lie* (1989), noted that rather than risk a successful engagement, which could arouse Diệm's jealous insecurities, that one senior officer refused to deploy his troops and would only call for artillery or airborne strikes.

Meanwhile in America, Diệm began to lose popular support in face of the suppression of Buddhist interests. When authorities in Hué refused the flying of flags to celebrate Buddha's birthday on 3 June 1963, riots followed in which nine people were killed. Popular unrest spread to Saigon. Here passions were further inflamed by Madame Ngô Dinh Nhu's accusation that the rioters were communist traitors.

On 11 June, a Buddhist monk Thich Quảng Dúc immolated himself in public; the photographs of the burning monk that subsequently appeared in US papers and magazines severely shook America's faith in its Asian ally. From this point, popular American support for Diệm declined rapidly. Popular protest in Saigon continued to mount, and on 21 August, Diệm's brother arrested 30 monks and raided their pagodas in a round up of more than 1,400 supposed activists. On the 23 August, students of Saigon University also took to the streets. By the autumn of 1963, Diệm's enemies comprised a virtual roll-call of interest groups within Vietnamese society: peasants, Buddhists, the religious sects, students, politicians, the media, foreign diplomats and most importantly the military.

When McNamara, President Kennedy's secretary of state for defence, went to Saigon on 23 September and recommended cutbacks in the US defence aid programme, Diệm's generals took this as a sign that America favoured change. This was now increasingly true. However, there were no good alternatives in sight.

The new ambassador to Saigon, Henry Cabot Lodge Jr, who was being advised by Hilsman, the assistant secretary of state for Far Eastern Affairs, reported:

> We must . . . tell key military leaders that the US would find it impossible to continue to support the government of Vietnam militarily and economically unless steps to release the monks are taken immediately which we recognize requires the removal of the Nhus from the scene.[5]

Tacit support for a coup against Diệm was now sought by a cabal of Vietnamese generals. Cabot Lodge strongly advocated that America back this course; in spite of Kennedy's own misgivings and those of General Harkins (commander of US forces in Vietnam), Cabot Lodge was given the go ahead. Diệm's palace was surrounded. Although Diệm and his brother escaped to *Cholon* (the name of Saigon's Chinese district), where they took refuge in the Catholic Church, they gave themselves up the following day, and were picked up by a military personnel carrier to be taken to military headquarters. On the way, the president and his brother were knifed and shot to death. For America, the assassination of Diệm was a significant inflection point in its increasing exposure to Indochina.

However, in the transition briefing between the outgoing Eisenhower administration and the incoming Kennedy team, the main emphasis of talks had not been about Vietnam but Laos. Over five years, the Eisenhower administration had spent US$ 300 million in trying to keep the country pro-Western. Clifford Clark, a transition advisor reported that 'President Eisenhower stated that Laos is the present key to the entire area of South East Asia. If Laos were lost to the Communists, it would bring an unbelievable pressure to bear on Thailand, Cambodia and South Vietnam.'[6] For Kennedy, Laos was the poisoned chalice to be inherited from his predecessor. The president-elect told the journalist Theodore Sorensen, 'Whatever's going to happen in Laos, an American invasion, a Communist victory or whatever, I wish it would happen before we take over and get blamed for it.'[7] However, this was not a problem that Kennedy could avoid; as Kennedy was preparing to take office, the Soviets were airlifting 45 tons of supplies daily to the communist *Pathet Lao* (literally 'Land of Laos'; a guerrilla group equivalent to the *Việt Minh*) who were busy expanding their positions in the *Plaine des Jarres* (a plain covered in 4,000-year-old stone jars from a forgotten Mons-Khmer Dynasty).

As President Eisenhower well understood from his previous incarnation as a general and supreme allied commander in Europe, Laos provided the key to the security of Indochina. South Vietnam's narrow defensive border with North Vietnam could be infiltrated along Laos's long border which straddled the Western end of the Demilitarised Zone established by Geneva. This in effect was the strategic imperative of the Hô Chí Minh trail that wound through Laos, and would later extend to Cambodia, which abutted South Vietnam's south-western flank. According to McNamara, Eisenhower's briefings left a deep impression on the new president.

Indeed, Laos would provide the first Indochina crisis of the Kennedy presidency. After Geneva, Prince Souvanna Phouma had attempted to follow a neutral path between the communist *Pathet Lao*, supported by his half-brother Prince Souphanouvong against the pro-American faction of Prince Boun Oum. However, when Souvanna was ousted by the American-supported Phoui Sananikone, communist sympathiser Prince Souphanouvong managed to escape from detention and joined up with *Pathet Lao* in Northern Laos.

However, in August 1960, Phoui Sananikone's ruling pro-American grouping was removed by a palace coup led by a Paratroop Commander, Kong Le. He supported a return to neutral government under Prince Souvanna. The return of Souvanna was also supported by the Soviet Union which supplied Kong Le with arms. Then, after fierce fighting for control of the capital city, Vientiane, Kong Le was also overthrown. He too threw in his lot with the Communist *Pathet Lao* guerrilla forces, which now protected the jungle passes through which the Hô Chí Minh trail threaded.

In spite of the dire warnings from his predecessor, President Kennedy now committed the fatal error which not only led directly to conflagration of *Việt Cong* activity in South Vietnam, but also catastrophically undermined America's long-term ability to successfully fight communism in Indochina. At the 4 June 1961 Vienna Summit meeting between Soviet leader Nikita Khrushchev and President Kennedy, it was agreed that Laos would be neutral and independent and its leaders chosen by the Laotian people; this was formally agreed in Geneva the following year in July with a joint declaration on the neutrality of Laos. Khrushchev, who had been delighted that Kennedy, a man he viewed as a weak liberal, had narrowly defeated Nixon for the presidency, had no intention of abiding by the joint communiqué on Laotion neutrality. Importantly, the Soviet Union's ally, North Vietnam, unlike America, was not bound even by international law to abide by this agreement. (Kennedy's hope that direct negotiations would restrain Soviet aggression was soon undermined by the building of the Berlin Wall which began just 39 days after the Vienna Summit.)

Thus, Kennedy abandoned the driving tenet of Eisenhower's policy not to yield control of Laos, which held the key to all of Indochina. As America would discover, 'neutrality' for Laos was no bar to North Vietnam's use of Southern Laos as a supply route for soldiers, weapons and supplies, to outflank the Demilitarised Zone at the Vietnamese 17th parallel, and thereby support the *Việt Cộng* along Vietnam's long western flank. The strategic importance of Laos was not lost on France's military nemesis and America's future military protagonist, General Giáp.

After Giáp's reorganisation of the *Việt Cộng* in1960, and the rapid escalation of terrorist and military attacks, there were now serious concerns about the stability of South Vietnam. By 1961, the *Việt Cộng* were estimated to control 58 per cent of the countryside of South Vietnam, and in May 1961 Kennedy sent Vice President Johnson to reconnoiter the situation.

The conclusion of America's policy review was that Diệm needed to implement land reform in order to secure the rural population. However with his main support coming from large landowners, this request was at odds with Diệm's political power base. In a sign of deteriorating security in September 1961, the *Việt Cộng* captured Phuoc Vinh just 89 km North of Saigon; the South Vietnamese army relieved the city the following day, but not before the *Việt Cộng* had carried out a public execution of the provincial chief. In 1961 President Kennedy sent an additional 1,000 troops, (called advisors because of the restrictions imposed by the 1954 Geneva conference). By December 1962 Kennedy had increased the number of advisors to 16,000.

Activity escalated in May 1962 when North Vietnamese forces attacked Laos. Kennedy responded with increased aid to Vietnam, with particular emphasis on improving the logistical and communication abilities of the South Vietnamese army (Army of the Republic of Vietnam, ARVN). In addition, Kennedy increased special forces to 9,000, and authorised them to wear the green beret. With increasing use of helicopters, and the creation of some 2,000 strategic hamlets, McNamara believed that the balance of the conflict was tipping back in America's favour. By now, the US military forces had escalated to 17,000, although their modus operandi was severely restricted. However, the defeat of a combined US–ARVN force in a botched operation raised comment in the US press that America was getting little for its US$ 400 million per annum in aid and the cost of 50 American lives.

In the light of doubts about Diệm's leadership and the sustainability of a credible or desirable political system in South Vietnam, it was somewhat surprising that more focus was not given to the question of whether continued military support for the regime was desirable. Barry Goldwater, senator for Arizona, and presidential candidate on the Republican ticket in 1964, was not alone in raising doubts about the half-hearted American approach. Even Kennedy's advisors were in two minds as to the advisable course to take. McNamara recalls in his account of the period in *In Retrospect, The Tragedy and Lessons of Vietnam* (1995) that P.J. Honey, a Vietnamese language speaker and lecturer at the School of Oriental and African Studies (SOAS) in London, a former strong supporter of Diệm, had now changed his mind; Diệm had deteriorated with age.

The bad news, however, was that Honey rated the chances of finding someone better than Diệm at only 50 per cent. (It is interesting to note that both Mao and Hô thought that Kennedy had blundered in orchestrating Diệm's removal.) With doubts among his advisors and Asian specialists, it is perhaps not surprising that Kennedy's approach to Indochina should have lacked clarity.

It was also unhelpful that some of the best young Asian experts in the State Department, John Paton Davies, John Stewart Service and John Carter had been purged during Senator McCarthy's communist witch hunt of the 1950s. As McNamara admitted, Kennedy 'failed to pull together a divided US government. Confronted with a choice among evils, he remained indecisive for too long'.[8]

Against this background, it is a moot point whether President Kennedy would have let America be further dragged into the quagmire of Indochina. When informed that Diệm had been slain, Kennedy apparently turned white. After all, Kennedy, the devout Catholic, had effectively acquiesced to Diệm's overthrow and subsequent murder. Schlesinger observed that he was 'sombre and shaken,' while Forrestal recalled that the Diệm's death 'shook him personally, bothered him as a moral and religious matter . . . shook his confidence . . . in the kind of advice he was getting about South Vietnam'.[9]

McNamara strongly believed that Kennedy's reactions to Diệm's death, the loss of confidence in the solubility of the South Vietnam regime issue and his record of conciliatory action, as demonstrated by his handling of the Cuban missile crisis, are enough to indicate that Kennedy would not have been drawn further into Vietnam. Some of his advisors had also cautioned on the economic cost. J.K. Galbraith, the renowned liberal economist, warned Kennedy against spending, 'our billions in those distant jungles'.[10] Furthermore, Kennedy doubted, wrongly as it turned out, whether 'the United States would ever receive military support from our SEATO allies'.[11] Internationally, Kennedy had also been counselled on Vietnam by General Charles de Gaulle, the French president that 'You will sink step by step into a bottomless military and political quagmire, however much you spend in men and money.'[12]

On the other hand, Kennedy also appreciated the risks if America abandoned Vietnam. As late as 9 September 1963, in a reaffirmation of 'domino' theory, he told the NBC news anchorman, David Brinkley, that

> China is so large, looms so high just beyond the frontiers, that if South Vietnam went, it would not only give them an improved geographical position for a guerrilla assault on Malaya, but would also give the impression that the wave of the future in Southeast Asia was China and the Communists.[13]

The dilemma facing Kennedy regarding future policy towards Vietnam was coloured by his dismal failure to prevent communist control of Laos. As he told journalist Charles Bartlett, 'We've already given up Laos to the Communists, and if I give up Vietnam I won't really be able to go to the people.'[14] Would Kennedy have risked the humiliation and political consequences of American withdrawal from Indochina when the American public was so fiercely supportive of the fight against world communism? With an issue of such importance, where the calls for action or non-action in Vietnam were so finely balanced, it is impossible to judge in which direction Kennedy would have jumped. The argument is purely academic. Within three weeks of President Diệm's murder, Kennedy himself would be assassinated in Dallas.

Kennedy's life and presidency, with its aura of *Camelot*, has escaped the scrutiny that it deserves. As the historian Conrad Black has observed, 'Jackie [Onassis] and her in-laws successfully peddled the bunk about *Camelot*.'[15] Absurd attention has also been paid to the numerous conspiracy theories that surround his death. Kennedy has been the subject of more legend and less fact than any other modern president.

However, 40 years later, the *Camelot* image is beginning to crack. Increasingly, attention is now paid to his ropey private morals, his relationship with Marilyn Monroe and other tawdry affairs. The role of his father Joe Kennedy, allegedly a prohibition era smuggler, who by some accounts bought the Electoral College votes of Illinois which helped decide his son's closely fought election victory over Richard Nixon, has also come to light. Also, Kennedy has escaped lightly for his role in the murder of President Diệm, an allied head of state; 'We must bear a good deal of responsibility for it,' he lamented, 'the way he was killed . . . made it particularly abhorrent'.[16]

Most importantly however, other than the disastrous 'Bay of Pigs' invasion to overthrow Castro and the subsequent 'Cuban missile crisis, too little focus has been paid to Kennedy's foreign policy particularly with regard to Asia and the catastrophic decision to abandon Laos at the Vienna Summit to communist 'neutrality'; by ignoring President Eisenhower's warnings about the need to safeguard Laos, Kennedy set the pattern for America's disastrous conduct of the war in Indochina.

By treating Vietnam as a discreet entity, by refusing to openly engage with Communist forces for the whole of Indochina including Laos and Cambodia, Kennedy laid down a military strategy whose limited objectives made real the likelihood of failure. From 1959 onwards, North Vietnam used the 'Hô Chí Minh trail' through Laos and Cambodia to control a guerrilla war in South Vietnam aimed at the unification of Vietnam under Communist rule. If blame is to be apportioned for the eventual American tragedy in Indochina, and its loss to communism, then Kennedy must share equal blame with his successor, President Johnson.

31

'The Year of Living Dangerously'

Indonesia: 1950—68

If Sukarno and Hatta can be lauded for their success in creating an independent Indonesian state, their attempts at establishing democracy fell woefully short. By the time that Prime Minister Sastroamidjojo's cabinet resigned in March 1957, there had been 17 governments since 1945. Divisions abounded between and within parties. The Partai Nasional Indonesia (PNI), which Sukarno had founded in 1927, was the natural party of government given Sukarno's almost god-like status. However, the Muslim vote split between the moderate *abangan* PNI, and the strictly Muslim *Santri* Islamic parties including the Masyumi and NU.

The political left was also split between the PKI (Indonesian Communist Party) and the PSI (Socialist Party). Uneasy short-term alliances abetted a culture of patronage and corruption. Neither did poor economic performance help develop political stability. In common with most of the newly liberated Asian economies, Indonesia pursued autarkic socialist economic policies, which stymied economic development.

From 1955, Prime Minister Sastroamidjojo, and a cabinet coalition of PNI, NU and number of smaller Islamic and Indonesian parties, pushed through an even greater 'Indonesianisation' of economic activity through nationalisation of banks, shipping and imports. Corruption was endemic and made the development of business almost impossible. An Indonesian businessman complained, 'Nobody in business can stay honest in this country today . . . you've got to get an import permit from the government. For this you have to pay kickbacks to officials in half a dozen ministries. . . '.[1]

Apart from abysmal economic management by the political parties, the constitution was additionally undermined by the increasing hostility of both the president and the Indonesian army. In 1956, Sukarno was already seeking to undermine parliamentary democracy; he complained to a meeting of youth delegates that 'we are afflicted by the disease of parties which, alas, alas, makes us forever work against one another!. . . Let us bury them, bury them'.[2]

Neither were the antics of Indonesia's early governments appreciated by the increasingly powerful army and their Chief of Staff General Nasution. At the tender age of 31, Nasution had taken over leadership of the army from the liberation military hero General Sudirman after his death in 1950. The army, which viewed itself as central to the liberation movement in spite of its somewhat desultory military performance versus the Dutch, nevertheless awarded itself a major constitutional role in the post-war settlement.

Sapta Marga, a seven-part military oath sworn by all soldiers, propounded the defence of *Pancasila* as a foremost element of its creed. In this context, military intervention could always be justified. In a 1962 speech, Nasution asserted that 'The placement of members of the Armed Forces as functional representatives in the government organs of the Republic of Indonesia is a feature of our state organisation which is unique in the world.'[3]

In the first few years of independence however, the role of the army was muted by its own divisions and the inexperience and lack of confidence of its new young commander. On 17 October 1952, Nasution had to face down a group of disaffected officers who organised a mass civilian protest outside Sukarno's presidential palace to protest the domination of the army by a westernised urban Javanese clique.

By 1955, Nasution, himself a Sumatran and rare non-Javanese among the military elite, was strongly enough embedded within the army to organise a unified military objection to the imposition of a new chief of staff, Colonel Bambang Utojo, by the PNI administration. The fall of Prime Minister Ali's government over this issue marked an important turning point in the relationship of the army to the government. Most importantly, it was only the army that possessed the raw executive power to establish the unitary authority of the state, which Sukarno had so arbitrarily centralised in 1950.

In the initial stages of Indonesia's independence however, the military merely added to the centrifugal forces which prevented political centralisation. Powerful regional commanders had successfully resisted the encroachment of the state bureaucracy on what they regarded as their personal fiefdoms. By 1956, army officers in Sumatra had completely usurped the authority of the state, and within two years defiance had turned into rebellion. Although the rebel forces were defeated by Colonel Achmad Yani, guerrilla action continued until 1961.

In addition to Sumatra, separatist conflicts also developed in Aceh, whose people had never accepted the constitutional settlement imposed by Sukarno and his Javanese elite. It was only after 1955, when Nasution sought to undermine the regional military fiefdoms by rotation of generals and senior officers, that the army became a unifying force in the development of an Indonesian nation.

Moreover, after the abandonment of the post-independence constitution in 1957, and its replacement with 'guided democracy', Sukarno's policies tended to increase the power of the army. Faced with an alarming economic deterioration after the nationalisation policies of his last cabinet, Sukarno sought to re-engage the popular appeal of the fledgling state by railing once more against foreign imperialists. The West Irian issue was a suitable diversion.

The conquest of West Irian, which had remained in Dutch hands after independence, now came to the front of his agenda. Nationalisation of all Dutch assets and expulsion of some 47,000 Dutch people was the typical ploy of a flailing post-colonial state. That this would have long-term deleterious effects on the Indonesian economy was not foreseen. Also, after the nationalisation of Dutch enterprises in 1957, the army took the leading role in the management of plantations, mining, banking and trade. The loyalty of the generals and senior officers was increasingly bought with commercial perquisites.

Unsurprisingly, corruption became rife. Although Nasution, a devout and somewhat ascetic Muslim, tried to reign in his senior officers, notably General Suharto, who was then the commander in Central Java, he was fighting an irresistible tide of greed. John Hughes, a journalist in the early 1960s, also noted that generals, indeed most officials, were so poor that 'There was no point trying to reach these sources at their offices . . . they were all moonlighting at other jobs. . .'.[4] Nevertheless, when 'guided democracy' was abandoned in 1960 in favour of reversion to the 1945 constitution, the balance of power had shifted markedly towards the military.

Before 1958, there were no army representatives in the cabinet; in the first 'restoration' cabinet, a third of ministers were from the military. Also, five army officers were appointed as provincial governors in 1960. Representation of the military was also considerably increased in the People's Representative Council and Provisional People's Consultative Assembly.

However, the army was not the only power group on the rise in the late 1950s. The communist PKI, whose leadership had been wiped out after the Maduran uprising, was resuscitated by Dipa Nusantara Aidit, a forest worker's son and part-time tailor's assistant, and Njoto, who now jointly steered the communist party along a constitutional path to power. They developed a powerful nationwide organisation and infiltrated all of Indonesia's institutions including the military. Aidit was also the first revolutionary to encourage practising Muslims to become Communists, thereby creating an Islamo–Marxist fusion (a radical approach which would later be adopted in the Middle East by many Islamic fundamentalists). Aidit would later boast that 'There are more real Moslems in the Communist Party than in small Moslem Parties.'[5]

From just 8,000 members in 1953, the PKI had swelled to 3 million members by 1963 and an estimated 20 million sympathisers in affiliated organisations; it had become the largest party in Indonesia and the third largest communist party in the world. Most importantly, Aidit, the PKI secretary general, won the ear of Sukarno. The president, who had been a Marxist sympathiser since his early days as a dissident, increasingly warmed to the socialist path and propagated his own ideology as 'NASAKOM', a fusion of Indonesian values with socialism. Aidit also realigned the PKI with Chinese rather than Soviet communism. This fitted well with Sukarno's 'non-aligned' stance which was also embraced by India and China. Along with China, which had fought the American army to a standstill in Korea, these three countries attempted to fuse a common 'non-aligned' axis, whose agenda, as expressed at the Bandung Conference in Indonesia in 1955, was transparently, anti-western and specifically anti-American.

America's popularity was further dented by Sukarno's discovery that the US Clark Airforce Base in the Philippines was being used to support anti-communist rebels in Sumatra and Sulawesi. Although President Kennedy was largely support-ive of Sukarno's forceful annexation of West Irian from the Dutch in 1963, relations with America, albeit Indonesia's largest provider of aid, continued to deteriorate with the onset of war in Vietnam. Sukarno hailed the Vietnamese National Libera-tion Front (NLF) as a model of national revolutionary endeavour, and a PNI leader asserted that

> The Vietnamese have every right to try to unify their country. To speak of aggression from the North is like accusing Indonesia of aggression in West Irian. If anyone is the aggressor in Vietnam, it is the United States'.[6]

The hypocrisy of his utterances against America which had striven unwaver-ingly to support Indonesian self-determination both politically and financially, were made ever more unpalatable by Sukarno's increasingly excoriating rhetoric against American imperialism; this, at the same time as he was seeking to expand Indone-sia at the expense of Malaysia, whose independence from Britain he perversely interpreted as being a continuation of neo-colonialism. In consequence, Sukarno demanded that the secretary general of the United Nations should send a mission to the Malaysian provinces of Sarawak and Sabah to ascertain the wishes of the people.

Also, Sukarno sanctioned guerrilla attacks against British military positions. Above all, Sukarno detested the first Malaysian Prime Minister Tunku Abdul Rah-man, who had presumptuously negotiated independence without deference to In-donesia, in Sukarno's eyes the regional superpower. On 3 May 1965, Sukarno called on 'volunteers' to 'dissolve the puppet state of Malaysia'.[7] Sporadic attacks were launched on the Malay peninsula in August 1965 with dismal results, but broader military campaigns, supported by some factions in the army, including Nasution, were stymied by General Yani and his moderate army faction.

International 'grandstanding' was a poor substitute for substantive policies to improve the welfare of his people. This role as Indonesia's president came a dis-tant second to securing his own power base. Aware that his policies, domestic and international, were constantly enhancing the role of the army, Sukarno sought to play them off against another competitor for power. Sukarno, the supreme pop-ulist, had long appreciated the mass mobilisation abilities of the communists, and above all he was only too willing to abet a counterweight to the growing power of the army.

When Nasution authorised the arrest and interrogation of the PKI leadership in July 1960, Sukarno intervened to secure their release. Two years later, Sukarno successfully moved against Nasution. When the latter moved to become minister of defence, as a means to control all the armed forces, the Chief of Staff of the Air Force Omar Dhani, an ally of Sukarno, refused to serve under an army officer. The ploy, probably arranged by Sukarno, enabled him to insist that all service heads report to him directly.

Nasution, who had resigned his role of chief of staff of the army in favour of General Yani, now found himself sidelined into a defence co-ordinating role with little power. A reorganisation of *Koti* (Supreme Operations Command) in July 1963 also furthered the promotion of Yani at the expense of Nasution. Yani, whose sybaritic lifestyle in the Jakarta social elite made him a more amenable military leader for his similarly notoriously lecherous president, adopted a more moderate accommodative stance towards Sukarno, versus the more hostile anti-Sukarno faction led by Nasution. In spite of the more compliant army chief of staff, the military *Koti* increasingly became the most powerful organ of state in place of the Cabinet.

Although on the issue of Malaysia, the hawkishness of Sukarno and the PKI was largely endorsed by the army factions led by Nasution, which were hostile to Sukarno, the relationship between the army and Sukarno continued to deteriorate in the 1960s, as the president's domestic policies swung further and further to the left. The sudden appropriation of American assets in Indonesia indicated an increasingly hostile line to the USA's growing regional influence.

On the domestic front, the PKI, which had pushed for land reform legislation in 1959–60, determined on a faster implementation against opposition from the PNI and the NU. The PKI promoted squats on government estates, and in some areas land was forcibly seized. In 1964, PKI unions sequestered the estates of the listed British plantation company, Anglo-Indonesian PLC. Faced with an increasing communist threat, the army and its anti-communist allies, started to mobilise counter forces. The army established the Central Organisation of the Indonesian Socialist Employees (SOKSI), comprising largely employees of army-run companies, as a 'worker' counterweight to the PKI unions.

In the press, there grew an increasingly acrimonious debate between the PKI-controlled *Harian Rakjat* newspaper, and *Merdeka* (Freedom), a newspaper owned by the anti-communist ambassador to London, B.M. Diah. Supporters of this latter group established the BPS (The Preservation of Sukarnoism Body), an organisation nominally dedicated to the support of Sukarnoism, as a thinly-veiled anti-communist block.

Sukarno himself, increasingly dependent on PKI support, accused the BPS of wanting to 'kill Sukarno with Sukarnoism',[8] and abolished it on 17 December 1964. Three weeks later, *Merdeka* and ten other anti-communist journals and newspapers had their licenses revoked, forcing them to close. Using their influence, the PKI now called for the removal of Adam Malik, minister of trade, and Chaerul Saleh, minister for industry and mining. The communists also pressed forward attacks on corruption within the army.

Communist activity was brought to a crescendo by the PKI's 45th anniversary celebrations in May 1965, at which Sukarno and Aidit addressed a mass rally; the special guest speaker was North Vietnamese leader Lê Dúc Tho. Sukarno denounced 'Communistophobia at home'.[9] In his Independence Day speech in August 1965, Sukarno proclaimed, 'We are now fostering an anti-imperialist axis . . . the Jakarta-Phnompenh-Hanoi-Peking-Pyongyang Axis.'[10] American policy maker Ewa Pauker concluded that the PKI's 'patient, careful, extremely dextrous' leaders '. . . may well succeed in making Indonesia the Fifteenth Communist State'.[11]

Meanwhile, the army under Yani had developed secret links with the Malay leadership through General Suharto, assured the new Malaysian state of their lack of support for the conflict. Nevertheless, the fake war with Malaysia served a useful purpose in allowing a partial restoration of martial law, which allowed the army to check the growing PKI influence in the government administration. A new regional security system called *Pepelrada* was established in September 1963 with broad emergency powers, which allowed detention of individuals for up to 30 days. These regional organisations reported to General Yani as chief of staff of *Koti*.

While relatively insignificant in scale, the Malaysian conflict increasingly added to the ideological differences between the army and Sukarno. By 1965, Sukarno's public statements were becoming increasingly radical. 'Let us build anti-imperialist economies, genuinely national economies that stand on their feet, mutually assisting each other, and not relying upon the so-called aid of the imperialists. . .'.[12] For the army, a bankrupt state such as Indonesia, which was barely able to pay and equip its troops, was hardly in a position to insult the USA, the major contributor of military and foreign aid.

In anticipation of a final showdown with the army in its quest for total political power, the PKI also sought to penetrate the senior ranks of the army and, for this purpose, set up a special bureau to coordinate infiltration from November 1964. The air force, only formed in 1962, was already implacably hostile to the army, and was therefore a natural ally of the PKI; the Chief of Staff Air Marshall Surjadi Surjadarma was a leftist sympathiser. While the navy under Vice Admiral Eddy Martadinata was close to Nasution and the anti-Sukarno faction of the army, some of the younger naval officers were believed to be closer to the PKI. The police force was also split, but the commander of the Jakarta police, Brigadier General Sawarno Tjokrodiningrat, was seen as a PKI sympathiser.

The most aggressive sign of PKI's strategy to usurp the military came in January 1965, when Aidit proposed to Sukarno the setting up of peasant and worker militia, in addition to the appointment of political commissars (on the Chinese model) within the armed forces. Sukarno later claimed that it was Chinese Foreign Minister Zhou Enlai, at their November 1964 meeting, who had suggested a Fifth Force consisting of 21 million volunteers. Indeed, Sukarno turned to China to supply him with weapons; an air force commander was despatched to Beijing to secure delivery of 100,000 small arms.

Unsurprisingly, the army acted with alarm over the threat to set up a competing armed militia. Nasution protested that 'it is not possible for a force to work if its
commander must be from the PNI with deputies from the religious and Communist parties'.[13] Yani put pressure on Sukarno to back down and on 27 May Sukarno
backtracked and explained that 'What I meant was that all branches of the armed
forces must be committed to the spirit and unity of Nasakom.'[14] As for the 'people's militia', the army parried and then smothered the proposal by accepting that,
in principle, all Indonesians should be armed to defend the fatherland if it came
under attack.

As the summer passed, the Communists raised the political temperature. Communists publicly demanded that 'corruptors, capitalist bureaucrats, pilferers, and
charlatans' should be dragged to the gallows, or 'shot in public'.[15] Their leader,
Aidit, advised, 'The progressive revolutionary people must be ready at any time
to respond with matching actions to barbarous acts'.[16] Joining in with this increasingly violent rhetoric, Sukarno laid into the army in a speech to the Communist University Student's Association, '. . . there were loyal generals, but now
they have become protectors of counter revolutionary elements. These we must
crush'.[17]

Against this background of political uncertainty, the formal economy was also
collapsing. In both 1963 and 1964, budget deficits exceeded the sum of government revenues. For fiscal year ending December 1964, inflation rose by 134 per
cent. Sukarno remained scornful of his foreign critics; he told them, 'I consider
your psychological warfare the barking of a dog. Tens of times you have claimed that
Indonesia under Sukarno would flounder, would collapse, would be destroyed. But
we are immune. You have predicted the Indonesian economy would collapse. But it
did not.'[18] In one sense Sukarno was correct; while the urban economy had effectively collapsed, the agricultural economy, blessed by land of remarkable fertility,
had not yet succumbed to the 'collectivisation' planned by the PKI, and remained
resilient in its primitive subsistence culture.

In addition to Indonesia's economic woes, Sukarno's health was becoming increasingly fragile. On 4 August he vomited and fainted. In a political environment
of extreme tension between the competing political claims of the army and the
PKI, intimation of their president's mortality could only lead to plots for the succession. When a coup finally emerged in the early hours of 1 October 1965, it
could hardly have come as a surprise. An American political scientist recalled that
his 'interview notes and general observations of October 1st reveal not a single
instance of individuals who expressed surprise at the course of events publicly disclosed early that day'.[19]

Forces commanded by Colonel Untung, a former paratrooper who had been
appointed to the command of the presidential guard, stormed the houses of seven
leading generals in the early hours of 1 October. Yani was shot in the back by palace
guards after he turned to change into his uniform when he was told that President

Sukarno required his immediate attendance; the dying general was dragged from the arms of his eleven-year-old son and dumped into a truck. Generals Harjono and Pandjaitan were also killed; the others, Suprapo, Parman and Siswomihardji, were taken to the air force base at Halim. Nasution managed to dash across his garden under fire from the conspirators and leapt over the wall into the neighbouring Iraqi Embassy; the fortunate general escaped with nothing more than a broken ankle. However, his five-year-old daughter Irma was gunned down and would later die of her wounds.

Colonel Untung, along with co-conspirator Major Sujono, was joined at Halim by PKI leader Aidit, and Brigadier General Supardjo, a communist sympathiser who also held a grudge against General Yani for his slow promotion. Sukarno had heard of the coup while staying with his third wife in the south of Jakarta; he then went immediately to the home of his fourth wife in West Jakarta, before proceeding to Halim, where the air force kept a US$ 2 million Lockheed Jet-Star on permanent standby for the president. At Halim, Sukarno also found Omar Dhani, head of the Indonesian air force, a communist sympathiser who had introduced the study of Marxism into the syllabus of the staff college. Dhani had also allowed Halim to be used as a secret base for the training of Communist shock troops.

At Halim, the three captured generals were taken behind the camp's field kitchen; here, in a frenzied attack by communist soldiers, men and women, the generals were tortured, beaten with rifle butts, and shot to pieces before being thrown down a well. One of the women later confessed, 'Someone shouted "Kill the capitalist bureaucrats!" ... Our platoon leader [another woman] gave us razor blades. We slashed at their bodies. Our platoon leader then told them to gouge out their eyes. The women did that ... The Generals cried out in pain.'[20] Meanwhile, assassins were sent out to find General Nasution.

Troops from the Diponegoro division were sent to occupy Merdeka Square, and at 7 am a radio broadcast informed the nation that the arrested members of the Council of Generals were sponsored by the US Central Intelligence Agency, and had actively plotted since the president's illness in August. They were accused of being 'power crazy, neglecting the welfare of their troops, living in luxury over the sufferings of their troops, degrading women and wasting the nation's money'.[21]

The conspirators declared their intention to set up a New Revolutionary Council to be chaired by Colonel Untung. The statement declared that the air force 'has always and will continue to support all progressive-revolutionary movements'.[22] Notwithstanding the apparent evidence of PKI complicity in the coup, Benedict Anderson and Ruth McVey, in a Cornell University paper, published soon afterwards, concluded that the PKI was not involved and argued that the PKI 'had been doing very well by the peaceful road'.[23]

Others have argued that the plot was initiated by Sukarno or his successor, General Suharto. In fact, on the evening of 30 September, General Suharto was visiting his son Tommy in hospital, where he was being treated for scalding from a domestic accident. Colonel Latief, a co-conspirator would later recount that he went to the hospital to tell Suharto that seven generals would be 'brought' before the president; 'I waited for a reaction from [Suharto], to see if he would make a decision or not. But Pak Harto [Suharto] just kept silent, until I took my leave and went home.'[24] It was an account that Suharto denied.

Even if Latief did visit the hospital, there is no reason to suppose that Suharto would have taken much notice of a statement which gave little indication of a coup, particularly in an environment where all kinds of spurious rumours were circulating. Certainly Nasution and the other senior generals would not have supported Suharto if they had suspected his involvement. What is clearly known is that the rebel officers from the Central Javanese Diponegoro Division were communist sympathisers with close affiliation with the PKI leadership. Indeed, there is no evidence to suggest anything other than Lt. Colonel Ismael Saleh's official army account, which concluded that 'The coup, staged to look like an 'internal army affair' was executed by the PKI men in the officer corps.'[25]

However, the coup plotters failed to press home their advantage. The rebel forces sat inactive in central Jakarta. Suharto was woken by a cameraman, Hamid Syamsuddin, who had heard the shooting and had later been informed of the kidnappings; the general dressed into field uniform at 6 am and drove to his office in Merdeka Square. He immediately set about acquiring intelligence as to who was 'friend or foe', and took control of the army. Hearing of Nasution's survival, Suharto kept him in hiding before organising an armoured escort to bring him to KOSTRAD headquarters on the evening of 1 October. Here, the two generals would spend the next three months sleeping in army cots in adjacent offices.

General Suharto, who had fallen out with both Yani and Nasution, was perhaps fortunate to have been left out of the group of seven generals marked by the plotters, but he was generally seen as non-political, and, more importantly, not part of a faction. As the day progressed, Suharto gradually took control of the situation by winning pledges of support from Nasution and other high-ranking officers. When Sukarno, with the backing of Aidit and Untung, sent Supardjo to inform the remaining army senior command that General S. Pranato had been chosen to succeed Yani, General Suharto, rising to his moment of opportunity, courageously dismissed the appointment and refused Pranato permission to go to Halim.

The rebels, who had failed to provide food and water for the troops in the sweltering heat of Merdeka Square, now found the Brawijaya battalion suborned by Suharto at 4 pm by promises of rations. On hearing of this defection, the Diponegoro battalion withdrew to Halim at 6 pm. At 9 pm, Suharto broadcast the army's intention to crush the rebellion.

The outcome was now not in doubt. Having failed to win control of the army's high command, Colonel Untung, with no armour, was defenceless. Government troops advanced on Halim, which was taken over after minor skirmishes at 6.10 am on 2 October. Aidit had already fled to Yogyakarta. Sukarno meanwhile, having realised that things were going badly for the plotters, the so-called September 30th Movement, went with his Japanese wife Dewi to his weekend palace at Bogor.

In spite of President Sukarno's questionable behaviour, and implicit support for the coup, the traditional reverence for leaders remained. However, Sukarno's ultimate authority had been severely damaged. In a tense five-hour meeting with his military commanders on 2 October, General Suharto, already emerging as Sukarno's key adversary, continued to reject the appointment of Pranato until Suharto had been given full command and authority to restore order and security.

Sukarno still denied the involvement of the PKI and the air force; this was a ludicrous pretence, and Sukarno's continued support for the communists within days of the coup rapidly diminished the remaining stock of the president's credibility and respect. Remarkably on 2 October, in spite of the failure of the coup, the Communist newspaper, *Harian Rakjat*, published a glowing testimonial to the September 30th Movement, in which the editorial declared that 'We the people fully comprehend what Lieutenant Colonel Untung has asserted in carrying out his public duty.'[26] Suharto felt secure enough in his position to publicly contradict his president's assurances that the PKI was not involved in the coup. Suharto now imposed a draconian crackdown on the left. All their newspapers were banned. Indeed, the only press now allowed to print were the army-controlled *Angkatan Bersenjata* and the *Berita Yudha*.

Armed Forces Day on 5 October was marked by massive funeral displays for the fallen generals. At a cabinet meeting at Bogor Palace on 6 October, Suharto later noted, 'I felt uneasy in an atmosphere of hearty laughter. I was annoyed to see PKI people there, since I had become convinced that they were certainly connected with the kidnapping and murder of my friends.'[27] Suharto resolved to crush the communists.

Others were already taking revenge into their own hands. At the funeral of Nasution's daughter, six days after the coup attempt, attended by hierarchy of all the armed forces, Admiral Eddy Martadinata gave the order to the leaders of the Moslem student groups to *sikat* (sweep) the Communists. The following day, the PKI headquarters were torched. Army units made no attempt to intervene. By contrast, Muslim students swept by the American Embassy shouting, 'Long live America!'[28], while the offices of the Chinese Commercial Counsel were ransacked.

On 8 October, the editor of *Angkatan Bersenjata* reported that the coup had been planned by PKI leader Aidit. PKI youth demonstrations were fired on. Aidit's house was literally ripped apart. A similar spontaneous uprising against the communists started around the whole country; in Sumatra, General Kemal Idris would later confess that 'I told my men to seize members of the Communist Party before I had any authority to do so.'[29]

Aidit, who had retreated to the communist bastions of Central Java, now called for an uprising of the *Gestapu* groups. (*Gestapu* was coined from the initials of the

September 30th Movement, *Gerakan September Tiga Puluh*). However, with news that Suharto was now firmly in command of Jakarta, the impetus lay firmly with the loyalists. Last stands were made by communist groups in the Central Javan cities of Jogyakarta and Solo, and on the slopes of Mount Merapi.

Gradually, the plot's ringleaders were rounded up. Colonel Latief was shot in the leg after being found taking a bath at his wife's house on 9 October. Colonel Untung tried to pass through the tightening cordon on a bus but was recognised and arrested. Colonels Usman and Suherman were killed in fire-fights around Mount Merapi, while General Supardjo managed to evade capture until 1967. As for Aidit, he was captured in a small *kampong* (village) on the outskirts of Solo on 22 November, and was probably executed within hours, though considerable mystery surrounds his death.

Aidit's close associate in the PKI, Njoto, took refuge in the homes of leftist sympathisers and even presidential palaces. However, his close personal friendship with President Sukarno could not save him. After attending a cabinet meeting on 6 November, he was promptly arrested, taken away and shot.

Suharto, who had by now replaced Pranato as commander of the army, and was also made chief of staff of *Koti*, gave orders for the regional commanders to curb the PKI in any manner they saw fit. Having defeated the hard core of PKI fighters, the army turned to root out communist sympathisers. General Sarwo Edhy, commander of the elite shock troops of the RPKAD para-commandos described how they

> decided to encourage the anti-communist civilians to help with the job. In Solo we gathered together the youth, the nationalist groups, the religious [Moslem] organisations. We gave them two or three days training, then sent them out to kill the communists'.[30]

Over the next three months, Indonesia witnessed widescale purges of PKI supporters. Starting with arrests, operations against the PKI soon turned into mass slaughter. Religious animosities and family vendettas were also played out in the carnage.

Around the great Buddhist temple of Borobudur, near Jogyakarta. The heaviest slaughter of communists and suspected communists took place around the great Buddhist temple of Borobudur; the black-shirted youth (Ansor) of the Nahdatul Ulama (Muslim Teachers Party) were the most active in hacking or shooting their victims to death. Often the massacres were indiscriminate. A disgusted professor at Gadjah Mada University in Jogjakarta recalled that 'The anti-communists certainly had a grudge. But there was no need to kill children, too. In one family, women, children over six, everybody was killed. And they call themselves religious people. But they killed like pigs.'[31]

Heads of communists were spiked and publicly displayed. Children used the wrapped heads of communists as footballs. Bodies were tipped into rivers. Some stretches of river were log jammed with corpses; 'The bodies floated out to the ocean. People refused to eat seafood for a long time.'[32] In the coastal town of Tjirebon, a guillotine was set up and used day after day. In an orgy of killing *Ansor* squads roamed the countryside looking for victims. Often they received official blessing from their Muslim clerics. The bloodiest massacres frequently occurred when the communists attempted to fight back.

Massacres were not confined to Central and Eastern Java. In the now romantic idyll of Bali whose Governor, Sutedja, was a communist sympathiser, it is estimated that between 40,000 and 50,000 men, women and children were butchered. According to one official on the island, 'In many villages, it was a point of honour to have executed communists. A village was ashamed when it had not killed.'[33] Sarwo Edhy would later say that 'In Bali we have to restrain them, make sure they don't go too far.'[34] Yet in Bali, the military authorities trucked 'people from village A to Village B, and vice versa, so that one need not slit one's neighbours throat'.[35]

It is estimated that some 300,000–400,000 people perished within a few months of the attempted PKI coup of October. However, the eventual death toll may have been well over 1 million people if *The Economist* estimate is to be believed. As for the root causes, frenzied bloodlust aside, it is difficult to disagree with the army's justification, 'It was the communists or us. If we hadn't killed them, they would have killed us.'[36] For America, the defeat of the communists was a godsend. Ironically, Indonesia, with little or no help from the USA, dealt the most crushing setback to communism in Asia during the post-war period.

Compared to the well-publicised massacres of the Indian Partition, the cultural revolution and the Cambodian 'Killing Fields', the vast cull of human life in Indonesia in 1966–7 made little impact on western consciousness. The CIA would later conclude in their report on the coup and its aftermath that the anti-PKI massacres in Indonesia ranked with the Soviet purges, Nazi atrocities and the Chinese 'Great Leap Forward' as the least known of the mass murders of the twentieth century. Even the widely lauded Peter Weir film *The Year of Living Dangerously* (1982) (starring Mel Gibson and Sigourney Weaver) only offers the September 30th Movement and its subsequent massacres as a backdrop to a romantic fiction in which the communists are clearly lauded as 'the good guys'.

As for CIA complicity in the massacre, historian Theodore Friend has concluded that this would be a 'monstrously mistaken compliment.'[37] Indeed, he largely agrees with the American ambassador Marshall Green, who recorded in his memoirs that with regard to efforts to defeat communism, 'We rather lucked out in Indonesia . . . it was indeed all rather miraculous'.[38]

Despite the massacre of Sukarno's allies and the fragility of his position, Sukarno refused to abandon his socialist stance. Sukarno, a supremely arrogant man, who had created for himself a mythology of almost divine 'Kingship,' had an unfailing belief in his own ability to tap popular sentiment. He refused the banning of the PKI, and on 21 December he managed to alienate what was left of his support within the armed forces by implying in a speech that the communist 'sacrifices in Indonesia's struggle for freedom were greater than the sacrifices of other parties and groups'.[39]

With the country thrown into chaos by the coup and its aftermath, inflation spiralled out of control. Petrol prices now rose from 4 rupees per litre to 250 rupees, while postal and telephone charges rose by 1,000 per cent and train fares by 400 per cent. Rising popular discontent was channelled towards Sukarno. The new strong man of Indonesian politics, Suharto, was probably wise to ignore, for the moment, the calls of the anti-Sukarno faction led by Nasution, to have President Sukarno removed from office.

In spite of his now tenuous lifeline, Sukarno refused to trim his rhetoric; at a cabinet meeting on 16 January 1966 he declared, 'I will not move a millimeter. . . . I am Sukarno, the Great Leader of the Revolution. As Luther, Martin Luther, said at the Church in Wurtenberg _ here I am, I can do nothing else. . . '.[40] Sukarno, it seems, still believed that he could out-manoeuvre the inexperienced Suharto.

In an atmosphere of popular unrest, undoubtedly stoked by Suharto himself, Sukarno could only turn to the army for protection. There were huge demonstrations outside the presidential palace on 24 February 1966, when Sukarno tried to install a new cabinet. Ministers had to be brought in by helicopter. Outside, the troops fired on and killed students. On 28 February, in an open challenge to the generals, Sukarno declared, 'I am convinced that the majority of the Indonesian people now want to return the Indonesian revolution to its progressive revolutionary foundations. . . . In fact I have repeatedly and openly declared, yes, I am a Marxist. . .'.[41]

In the circumstances, Sukarno could hardly have been surprised when, on 11 March, he was passed a note during a cabinet meeting, informing him that unidentified troops had taken positions in front of the palace. The troops were commanded by a Suharto ally, General Kemal Idris, who had orders to frighten the president and to arrest Foreign Minister Subandrio, if the occasion arose. Fearing a coup, Sukarno fled by helicopter to his palace at Bogor with his close associates Chaerul Saleh and Subandrio; the latter had jumped up so quickly to follow the president that he did not even have time to put on his shoes.

Suharto, who had excused himself attendance at the cabinet meeting because of a sore throat, sent three generals to the president's country residence at Bogor, where an ultimatum was delivered. Effectively, Sukarno threw himself on Suharto's mercy; the outcome was an order for Suharto 'to take all steps considered necessary to ensure security, calm, and stability of the government'.[42] Suharto immediately ordered army units into the streets. Word of Sukarno's surrender spread rapidly. Soldiers on the streets were cheered and mobbed with hugs and flowers. On 12 March Suharto dissolved the PKI. Sukarno's cabinet was disbanded and on 17 March, Subandrio was arrested.

After the purge of Sukarno cronies, Suharto appointed Nasution and other officers hostile to the president to senior posts. Instead of taking advantage of

Suharto's moderate approach to his position, Sukarno continued to openly express his support for socialist ideologies, and for campaigns against colonialism and imperialism.

However, Suharto, who had long favoured an end to hostilities with Malaysia, sent Adam Malik to meet Malaysian Deputy Prime Minister Tun Abdul Razak in Bangkok, where a peace accord was negotiated. In addition, Suharto also pressed for Indonesia's rejoining of the United Nations. Apart from the clear unwinding of Sukarno's policies, in the autumn of 1966, pressure on the president increased further as his former supporters were brought to court.

Former minister for central banking, Jusuf Muda Dalam, was sentenced to death for corruption and for having six wives, which was two more than the number allowed under Islamic law (it is not clear whether the 20 other mistresses he had accrued around the country were taken into account). Dalam's testimony also laid bare President Sukarno's own demands for financial favours for his mistresses. Indonesians were scandalised by the revelations made in court by secretaries, singers and actresses. Subandrio was sentenced to death for his part in the PKI plot against the army. In December, former Air Force Commander Omar Dhani was also put on trial, which further exposed Sukarno's own role in the attempted army coup.

Any lingering popular regard for Sukarno was now destroyed; the spell that he and his legend had cast over the Indonesian people was broken once and for all. Both the populace and the army were suitably aroused. Parliament, which had by now been purged of Sukarno's supporters, met to pass a resolution calling for a new *Majelis Permusyawaratan Rakyat Sementara* (MPRS: Provisional People's Consultative Congress) to depose the president. A special session of the MPRS opened on 8 March 1967 and duly appointed Suharto as acting president. Even then, Suharto not only refused to put Sukarno on trial, but allowed him to use his title as 'president' until May.

It was two months before Sukarno's images were removed from all government offices. Throughout, Suharto had acted with cautious restraint in toppling Indonesia's revolutionary leader. Suharto was only fully confirmed in his role as president in March 1968, while Sukarno remained under house arrest until his death in June 1970.

Sukarno's legacy to the nation was the creation of an Indonesian state, the existence of which was not the inevitable corollary of the collapse of the Dutch Empire in the Indonesian archipelago. Like many of his contemporary nationalist leaders in post-war Asia, Sukarno's ability to rouse the people and articulate the idea of nationhood, however shallowly rooted in the actualities of history, far exceeded his abilities as a ruler.

In H.J. Benda's *Decolonisation in Indonesia* (1965), he concludes:

> ... essentially what we have witnessed is the agonizing, difficult adjustment of Indonesia to its own identity. ... it may be suggested that, substantially, the Java-centric or

really Djakarta-centric-polity is recapturing some of the political facets of the past. . . If it is intensely bureaucratic, cavalierly disdainful of economic rationalism, vengefully repressive of Islamic competition, jealousy assertive vis-à-vis the Outer Islands, and, finally, grandiosely exuberant in foreign affairs, it is in the final analysis only acting out its own logic'.[43]

The tragedy for Indonesia is that Sukarno, the hero of its independence movement, was a corrupt, demagogic dictator with a vastly inflated ego, who abused his position of power to leave behind him a dysfunctional political system dominated by self-serving generals. Furthermore, as a convinced Marxist, he left behind an economy ravaged by the failures of command and control socialism.

32

LBJ and the Vietnam Quagmire

Vietnam: 1963—9

With John F. Kennedy's assassination, his successor, Vice President Lyndon B. Johnson (LBJ), was left to deal with what was fast becoming the thorniest of America's foreign policy issues. Johnson, who had himself been sent to Vietnam by Kennedy earlier in the year, was not unaware of the difficulties inherent in Indochina. On the mess that he inherited, Johnson described it as 'a big juicy worm with a hook right in the middle of it'.[1] However, he shared the basic incorrect premise of his predecessor, that the Soviet Union and China were operating in tandem to achieve global hegemony.

Nevertheless, the death of Kennedy, and his replacement by Johnson, created a hiatus which should have given opportunity for deeper reflection on the strategy being pursued in Vietnam. That President Johnson did not do so was a result not only of his own character, never reflective at the best of times, but also of the grand domestic agenda that was his life's ambition. In addition, Johnson chose to continue to leave the Vietnam conflict largely to the guidance of Secretary of Defence Robert McNamara, who he inherited from President Kennedy.

As had been predicted by some of Kennedy's advisors, the fall of Diem left a vacuum at the heart of the South Vietnamese political system. When the National Intelligence Estimate reported in September 1964 that 'The odds are against the emergence of a stable government capable of effectively prosecuting the war in South Vietnam',[2] it was not reaching a conclusion that was any surprise to the White House. In spite of these misgivings, the Johnson administration never appears to have stood back to seriously consider the possibility of withdrawal from Vietnam. McNamara would later lament this as a lost opportunity.

Yet, any analysis of the seemingly gentle drift into an Asian war, which was to consume virtually the entire American political landscape for the next decade, cannot be made without an understanding of President Johnson's character. The man who bears ultimate responsibility for the catastrophe, which was about to befall America, was one of the most extraordinary individuals ever to lead his country. Sandwiched between the supposed youthful brilliance of Kennedy's 'Camelot' and Nixon's 'Machiavellian' court, one might have expected the 'stand-in' vice president to be somewhat overshadowed; yet Johnson outshines them both in the sheer macabre perversity of his nature.

Born in Stonewall, Texas on 27 August 1908, Lyndon Johnson was a man of vast ego. Humiliated by his father's failures, Johnson was the classic insecure small-town boy intent on finding family redemption through fame and fortune on a larger stage. As a young boy his predilection for power was immediately apparent. He would only play games with other boys if he was voted their leader; otherwise he would go away and sulk. He had a monomaniacal desire to impose his will upon others. A roommate of Johnson's, Fritz Koeniger, described how he behaved when he drove a car without a horn and wanted to overtake the vehicle in front, 'he'd pull right up behind some car and bang the side of his door, just smash it_hard_with his open palm so it sounded like a crash, almost, over and over until they'd pull over'.[3]

The feelings and sensibilities of others were there to be trampled on. At college he would simply grab everyone else's food. Also as a young man he would ingratiate himself with powerful people, while he delighted in humiliating those less powerful. Later, Vice President Hubert Humphrey would be invited to Johnson's Texas ranch and made to wear a cowboy outfit that was vastly too big, so that the president could laugh at him. Humphrey was also forced to shoot deer, which he hated. On one occasion when Johnson stopped his car to relieve a call of nature, he urinated down the leg of a Secret Service officer who protested, 'Mr. President you are urinating on me'; Johnson replied, 'I know I am . . . it's my prerogative.'[4]

Johnson's boastfulness was legendary. At college he would unzip his trousers to display his penis, which he called 'Jumbo'. His habit of publicly displaying his genitals would last a lifetime. He would also speak about his sexual conquests in graphic anatomical detail. Often however, his supposed conquests were pure fantasy. From an early age he was known as an inveterate braggart and liar. Nevertheless, through force of will he invariably chased and won the richest girl in town. His desire for money was only a little less than his craving for power. He would wear the most expensive custom-made suits, shoes and boots. His cufflinks and watch had to be solid gold and he loved to be able to take groups out to expensive nightclubs. Money occasionally caused him trouble. In 1944, Roosevelt had to intervene to prevent him being prosecuted for tax fraud.

To his wife, however, Johnson was invariably mean. In fact, his abusive treatment of 'Lady Bird', born Claudia Alta Taylor, daughter of the richest businessman in Karnack, Texas, became legendary. He would regularly shout orders at her in front of guests. He rarely listened to others. At college in San Marcos, a fellow boarder Horace Richards recalled, '. . . if someone tried to talk _well, he would just ride over you until you stopped. He monopolized the conversation from the time he came in to the time he left'.[5] The vulgarity of his behaviour was unrestrained by normal social codes. Johnson would drink 'highballs' and belch loudly.

Aides were called into the lavatory for discussions; he would shit and fart in front of them.

Though his marriage to 'Lady Bird' was remarkably enduring, she was forced to put up with his endless womanising. Mistresses included his Hispanic secretary and a ranch employee known as 'the Dairy queen'. There were many less formal encounters, however. After losing his presidential nomination campaign in 1960, Johnson took heavily to drink. At night he would drunkenly roar around the hotel until he could find a secretary to take to bed. In womanising, as in all things, he was competitive. Of the famously philandering President Kennedy, he would comment, 'Why, I had more women by accident than he ever had by design.'[6]

In spite of personal characteristics which rarely made him popular, Lyndon Johnson developed a career in which he emerged as a remarkable congressional power broker. Though an intelligent man, his success was not achieved by intellectual finesse. He rarely read anything longer than a magazine article. However, by ferocious industry, the sheer will of his character, cajoling and bullying, he succeeded in becoming a dazzlingly effective manager of the senate in his role, first as Democrat majority leader 1955–61, and later as president.

Johnson would often be seen grasping a fellow congressman's lapel in his left hand, while his right hand would encircle his victim's shoulder, pulling him closer to his face. The unyielding stare coming from his vast head, with its 'elephantine' ears, would extract promises of senatorial support; sometimes they were given just to get away from his overbearing presence. Absolute loyalty was also required of his staff; about one new employee he demanded that 'I want him to kiss my ass in Macy's window at high noon, and tell me it smells of roses. I want his pecker in my pocket.'[7] Neither was he slow in using threats and bribes to get his way. As a young staffer working for Maury Maverick in the 1934 San Antonio elections, Johnson would happily sit in the Plaza Hotel dispensing dollar bills to buy the votes of Mexican-Americans.

When in power, the crudeness of Johnson's bullying manner was juxtaposed against his powerful sense of insecurity. He loathed the thought that he might be considered a Texas hick. Nevertheless he was well aware that his manner of behaviour did not marry well with his radical liberal political stance. Johnson saw enemies and conspiracies everywhere, particularly within his own party. With regard to Democratic Party liberals he was always fearful that his name was 'shit and always has been and always will be. I got their goddamn legislation passed for them, but they gave me no credit'.[8] 'What's the difference between a cannibal and a liberal?', Johnson once joked, 'A cannibal doesn't eat his friends.'[9]

Curiously, Johnson's lack of inner confidence was exacerbated by his unorthodox route to power by way of Kennedy's assassination. Self-doubts about his political legitimacy gnawed at his soul. At moments he displayed complete paranoia. Railing incoherently against his liberal opponents once he declared, 'I am not going to have anything more to do with liberals. . . . They all just follow the communists

line_liberals, intellectuals, communists. . . . I can't trust anyone anymore. I'm going to get rid of everybody who doesn't agree with my policies'.[10] At times Lady
Bird and others worried about his sanity. In the lead up to the decision to send
more troops to Vietnam, Johnson described to his press secretary, Bill Moyers, his
feeling that he was being drawn into a Louisiana swamp 'that's pulling me down'.[11]
He said this while lying in bed with the covers pulled almost over his head.

Inner doubts, however, did nothing to diminish his lust for power; indeed they
may have fed his massive personal ambition. Every position he held was a staging
post for something greater. From an early age he swore that he would be president.
Losing out to Kennedy for the 1960 Democratic nomination was perhaps Johnson's
lowest moment. His loathing of Kennedy and his family knew no bounds. He would
say of Kennedy:

> 'It was the goddamnest thing. . . here was a whippersnapper . . . he never said a word
> of importance in the Senate and he never did a thing. But somehow. . . . He managed
> to create the image of himself as a shining intellectual, a youthful leader who would
> change the face of the country.'[12]

Kennedy's offer to Johnson to be his vice presidential running mate did nothing to diminish Johnson's resentment of the young upstart. Though in finishing
Kennedy's presidential term, LBJ noted some obligation to his rival's legacy, he
was determined 'to put my own stamp on this administration in order to run for
office'.[13] Also in the run-up to the 1964 elections, Johnson delighted in the idea of
refusing to have Bobby Kennedy as his vice presidential running mate, even though
this would have been politically astute. Political bitterness between the two remained a long running sore until Bobby Kennedy, like President Kennedy before
him, was assassinated.

Furthermore, the Kennedy political stance was too tame for Johnson. He declared that 'I am a Roosevelt New Dealer. As a matter of fact, John F. Kennedy
was a little too conservative to suit my taste.'[14] Above all his hero was Roosevelt.
By nature, the 'interventionism' implicit in the New Deal was clearly in sync with
his bullheaded character. Johnson did not merely want to be leader of his country.
He wanted to go down in history as a man who, by the will of his character, could
create a social utopia. Had he but known it, Lyndon Johnson was not so dissimilar
in character and ambition to America's arch enemy Mao Zedong.

Through a massive programme of 'interventionist' legislation Johnson wished
to fundamentally transform American society by abolishing poverty at a stroke.
At Michigan University in 1964, in the run-up to his presidential contest with
Republican Barry Goldwater, Johnson avowed, in a speech which gave a name to
his social welfare programme, that 'In your time we have the opportunity to move
not only towards the rich society and the powerful society, but upward to the Great
Society.'[15]

In spite of the Great Society project, which was the overwhelming ambition of
his life, that would differentiate him from Kennedy and assure his place in history,

President's Johnson's ego would not allow him to admit defeat on Vietnam even though he was aware that deeper engagement in the war might damage his ability to implement his social plans. As Lady Bird later reflected, Vietnam 'wasn't the war he wanted. The one he wanted was on poverty and ignorance and disease and that was worth putting your life into'.[16]

However, after a meeting with Cabot Lodge, Johnson avowed that he was not 'going to let Vietnam go the way of China. I told them to go back and tell those generals in Saigon that Lyndon Johnson intends to stand by our word, but by God, I want something for my money. I want 'em to get off their butts and get out in those jungles and whip hell out of some Communists. And then I want them to leave me alone, because, I got some bigger things to do right here at home'.[17]

Unfortunately for Johnson, events in Vietnam were moving rapidly to undermine his desire to focus on domestic issues. The year 1964 had started badly. In January, the murdered President Diệm's successor, former vice president Nguyễn Ngọc, was deposed in a bloodless coup by General Nguyễn Khành. Added to political instability, the North now launched the *Việt Cộng* into the highest level of insurgency yet experienced by the South. In Saigon itself, the *Việt Cộng* seemed able to plant bombs at will. Such was the level of danger that American officers were ordered to go out in pairs.

North Vietnamese aggression was also evident at sea. On 1 August 1964, the destroyer, *USS Maddox,* was fired on by North Vietnamese torpedo boats, which had attacked outside the 12-mile international limit in the Bay of Tonkin. There were no American casualties, and Johnson decided not to respond. However when a further attack by five North Vietnamese torpedo boats was made on the *USS Maddox* and the *USS C. Turner Joy* on 4 August, retaliatory air strikes were ordered. In the first strike of the air war on North Vietnam, fighter bombers hit four naval bases and an oil depot. Twenty-five torpedo boats were destroyed at a cost of two aircraft shot down. Opinion polls in America were overwhelmingly in favour of President Johnson's aggressive action.

In response to the 'Tonkin Bay' incidents, Johnson demanded of Congress a resolution on 7 August 1964 backing firmness in responding to the threat of communism in Vietnam. In a testament to the wholesale popularity of the Vietnam War in the mid-1960s, it is notable that the resolution was unanimous in the House of Representatives and only suffered two votes against in the Senate. Johnson, the master manipulator of Congress, had given himself 'carte blanche' for the future conduct of the war. However, it is unlikely that many in Congress intended to authorise the president

> without further, full consultation the expansion of US forces in Vietnam from 16,000 to 550,000 men, initiating large-scale combat operations with the risk of an expanded war with China and the Soviet Union, and extending US involvement in Vietnam for many years to come.[18]

Perversely, in spite of the overwhelming support for the war from all sections of American society, Johnson continued to be half-hearted in response to North Vietnamese attacks. When the *Việt Cộng* launched a surprise attack on 2 November 1964 at the American air base at Biên Hòa near Saigon, killing five and wounding 76, Johnson refused the army's request for retaliatory action. Two days later, Johnson won a landslide presidential election victory against Barry Goldwater, the Republican candidate. Showing that his reticence to escalate the war was not simply political expedience, Johnson also refused to retaliate when a *Việt Cộng* attack on the Brink Hotel on Christmas Eve killed two with a further 52 people wounded.

The early months of 1965 brought another severe deterioration in the Vietnamese situation. General Khành, who had been overthrown in 1964 and replaced by a high council headed by Prime Minister Trồn Vằn Huong, was restored to power again by another military coup. In January, civil disturbances followed enlargement of South Vietnam's own military draft. In Hué a library was burnt to the ground. *Việt Cộng* encroachment in the countryside increased. At Binh Giã on the Vietnamese coast near Saigon, the town was occupied by the *Việt Cộng*, who killed six Americans and 177 South Vietnamese.

In response Johnson sent his National Security Advisor, George Bundy, to Vietnam to review the situation. His arrival was greeted by a major *Việt Cộng* attack on a US army compound in the Central Highlands. When Bundy telephoned to recommend bombing retaliation, Johnson finally yielded and 49 bombers were sent to bomb North Vietnamese barracks at Dồng Hói. Three days later on 10 February, 23 American soldiers were killed by a *Việt Cộng* attack on their barracks. On 3 March, Johnson approved the start of 'Operation Rolling Thunder', the name given to the unprecedented and continual bombing campaign aimed at North Vietnam.

Even now the essential timidity of LBJ's approach to war was indicated by the fact that air raids were at first limited to two to four per week using a total of 12 planes each. Sorties would eventually rise from 25,000 in 1965 to 108,000 by 1967. Strategic Air Command (SAC) commander Curtis LeMay famously stated that the North could be 'bombed back into the Stone Age'.[19]

The problem with the effectiveness of bombing the North was that there were so few industrial targets to bomb. To all intents and purposes North Vietnam, as an industrial economy, already was in the Stone Age. The *Việt Cộng*'s weapons were manufactured in China and the Soviet Union, not in North Vietnam. Indeed, the report of the war game Sigma II-64, conducted by the joint chiefs of staff in September 1964, concluded that 'industrial and military bombing would not quickly cause cessation of the insurgency in South Vietnam... might have but minimal effect on the living standard'.[20]

In addition to B-40 bombers, America had also established air superiority through the Phantom F-4 fighter. The MiGs avoided dogfights. It was therefore particularly galling to the US Air Force that, until 1967, LBJ would not allow Vietnamese MiGs to be attacked on the ground. To shoot them down, the Americans would first try to coax MiGs into the air. This was achieved in the most spectacular air battle of the war on 2 January 1966, when MiGs were lured off the ground by 'pretend' bombers only to be faced by faster F-4 Phantoms; led by Colonel Robin Olds of the 8th Tactical Wing, American pilots shot down seven MiGs.

Tactical innovations included the use of helicopters, particularly the Bell UH-1 nicknamed 'Huey' which increasingly became an air gunship armed with machine guns and rockets. In 1965, the 1st Cavalry Division (airmobile) was created. Assembled by the army into air divisions, these helicopter-troop units proved some of the most effective of the war, and were responsible for America's first battle triumph of the war at La Drang Valley. The air cavalry was most famously shown in the seminal 1979 Francis Ford Coppola Vietnam War film, *Apocolypse Now*, starring Marlon Brando, Martin Sheen and Robert Duvall; the latter famously leads his forces into the attack playing *The Ride of the Valkyries* (from Wagner's opera *Die Walküre*) from his 'Huey' helicopter. Other notable technological achievements during the war included experiments with defoliants and herbicides as weapons.

Significant advances in development of transistors made the Vietnam War the first in which electronics played a major part. In 1966 America developed and used the first 'wall eye' glide bombs with a TV camera on their nose. The Vietnam War propelled America along the path of military electronics and was one of the progenitors of California's fast-growing 'high tech' industry. However, as a military operation, Rolling Thunder was fatally flawed, in spite of McNamara's famed statistical tallies of its success.

For 1965, he claimed the sinking of 1,500 boats and barges; 650 railwagons and 800 trucks were destroyed. In 1966, when LBJ finally authorised attacks on Vietnamese industry, virtually all power and cement facilities were destroyed within days. When the US Air Force was allowed to widen the scope of its attacks in 1967, they destroyed most bridges linked to China, all MiG fighter air bases, and laid mines on inland waterways.

However, the North was largely impervious to industrial destruction. North Vietnam's capital city, Hanoi (Hà Nội), and its port of Haiphong (Hăi Phòng) remained inviolate because of LBJ's fears of provoking China; American memories of the Korean War were still fresh. Thus, no bombing was allowed within 30 miles of Hanoi, and ten miles of Haiphong, which was the conduit for more than 85 per cent of all Soviet and Chinese supplies. Combined with the refusal to launch air attacks within 30 miles of the Chinese border and more importantly with the refusal to countenance attacks on the Hô Chí Minh trail in Laos and Cambodia, LBJ's strategy ensured that the *Việt Cộng* in the North and South would always be supplied. The US Air Force's scope for operational activity was so hedged around with exclusions that most of the strategic power of their air superiority was denuded.

Above all, it was Johnson's interference with his generals' strategic preferences that guaranteed the military failings of America in Vietnam. General Westmoreland, who had replaced General Harkins as head of Military Assistance Command, Vietnam (MACV) in 1964, like President Eisenhower before him, could see that

Laos held the key to the defeat of the *Việt Cộng*. In the Central Highlands the North was using the Hồ Chí Minh trail to circumvent the Demilitarised Zone at the 17th Parallel and build up forces that would eventually enable them to cut South Vietnam in two.

Westmoreland wanted to defeat this strategy by extending the American forces in a defensive line across the Demilitarised Zone, and then to extend it across the Laotian panhandle. With five divisions, Westmoreland felt that the North could be held at bay until the South Vietnamese Army was strengthened to a point where it could take over. Johnson's refusal to countenance this plan, and his insistence on the use of the American Army to defend enclaves, ensured the ability of the North to build up the *Việt Cộng* forces in the South and played into the hands of the Mao–Giáp encirclement strategy. Later General William DePuy, commander of the 1st Infantry Division, would conclude that the American forces could not bring the *Việt Cộng* to battle often enough to win a protracted war of attrition.

Search and destroy missions from the protected enclaves were rarely successful. In August 1965, a *Việt Cộng* unit located on the Vân Tường Peninsula was swept by 4,000 marines; the *Việt Cộng* lost 700 men to just 50 marines. But when the marines retreated to their enclaves, the area was simply reoccupied by the *Việt Cộng*. The villages were therefore offered no long-term protection from communist infiltrators, who became deeply entrenched in South Vietnam's most powerful and all-pervasive social unit. 'Almost totally lacking was an appreciation of the political and social dimensions of insurgency and its role in the larger framework of revolutionary war.'[21]

Only slowly did the Johnson administration come to appreciate the importance of the Vietnamese village. In 1966, Robert Komer was appointed to implement the so-called Pacification programme (Civil Operations and Rural Development Support, CORDS), which brought American agricultural expertise to villages in addition to advice on medicine, education, and hygiene. Then, in 1967 McNamara instituted a system of hamlet evaluation that monitored the status of South Vietnam's villages. It was claimed that the number of secure hamlets rose from 4,702 to 5,340 during 1967.

However, like all of McNamara's numerical analyses, they failed to take into account that government statistics always tend to support the success of an incumbent administration. McNamara confused statistics with reality. Mistakenly, the secretary of defence came to the conclusion that the cross-over point in North Vietnam's sustainable losses occurred in April 1967.

Johnson's schizophrenic approach to the fighting of the Vietnam War was further revealed in the method by which he announced his decision to increase troop commitments from 75,000 to 125,000. It was hidden in a press conference laced with talk about the Great Society and appointments to the Supreme Court. Johnson even joked that 'If you have a mother-in-law with only one eye and she has it in the centre of her forehead you don't keep her in the living room.'[22]

Later, when the number of American troops in Vietnam was again doubled, Johnson tried to obscure the fact by making incremental increases of just 15,000 per month. As McNamara would later admit, '. . . the fact that the nation had embarked on a course carrying it into a major war was hidden'.[23] However, it is to McNamara's credit that he did not later pull his punches when it came to self-criticism for the failure of Johnson's policies in Vietnam; 'We failed to draw Congress and the American people into a full and frank discussion and debate of the pros and cons of a large scale US military involvement in South East Asia before we initiated action.'[24]

In addition to camouflaging the extent of military operations in Vietnam, Johnson also curtailed operations that could have ensured victory. Leaving aside the disastrous strategic decision to militarily ignore Laos, Cambodia and the Hô Chí Minh trail, Johnson was always reluctant to fully commit America to the effective prosecution of the war.

In large part this reflected a preference to focus time and resources on his Great Society project; however, there was also the nagging fear that America would be dragged into another conflict with China. The Johnson administration was haunted by the experience of the Korean War. When more aggressive action against enemy targets was recommended by General Earle Wheeler, the chairman of the joint chief of staff, Johnson queried 'Do you think this will involve the Chinese communists and Soviets?' When Wheeler replied, 'No Sir', Johnson, referring to the Chinese attack on the American army in Korea in 1952, countered, 'Are you more sure than MacArthur?'[25]

Unlike Korea, where a unified command was established, and possibly because of MacArthur's 'loose-canon' behaviour during that war, Westmoreland was never given total command of forces in Vietnam, where the South Vietnamese government was allowed to fob off calls for integrated control. In addition, the US air force and navy were independently controlled by the commander of the Pacific forces in Hawaii. Indeed, Westmoreland reported to the naval commander in the Pacific, Admiral Ulysses S. Grant Sharp.

Johnson's catastrophic errors of strategy were further compounded by his refusal to back his generals in their request for a force large enough to get the job done. In spring 1966, President Johnson contrived to send a further 200,000 soldiers to Vietnam in the sure knowledge that this was not enough to win the war. The slow build-up of US forces and their inappropriate deployment merely allowed the enemy time to increase its strength. By 1967, the US army had committed 7 of its 18 divisions to Vietnam, yet Johnson never fully engaged in the fight to win the war.

In addition to Johnson's own failings as a war leader, he was unfortunate to inherit Kennedy's Secretary of Defence Robert McNamara, who shared the new president's left-wing social agenda but, after initially favouring the military buildup, became an increasingly dispirited and reluctant war-maker. Kissinger described

McNamara as 'an unfortunate choice for managing the war . . . above all McNamara did not have his heart in the assignment. He had wanted to relate the awesome power of our nation to humane ends; he had no stomach for an endless war. . . '.[26] Perversely, the conflict frequently became referred to as 'McNamara's War'.

For much of the time McNamara remained obsessed by solving the political and social problems of South Vietnam, rather than focusing on the military solutions to winning the war. In July 1964, he told the Senate Appropriations Committee that 'the primary problem in South Vietnam is not a military problem. The primary problem is a political and economic problem. Unless we can introduce political and economic reform in that country, there is not any possibility of a military solution'.[27] Events would prove him entirely wrong.

When the US army and ARVN showed themselves more than a match for the Việt Cộng, Vietnamese villages, once their security had been guaranteed, much preferred a Southern dictatorship to Northern communism. Contrary to the opinions of the liberal war critics, who took their cues from Ho's propaganda effort, the growth of the Việt Cộng in the South came largely from reinforcements sent down the Hô Chí Minh trail rather than indigenous recruitment.

Not until 15 March 1966 was a US army report commissioned on what it would take to win the war. To the shock of the president, General Johnson (no relation), army chief of staff to Vietnam, reached a conclusion that it would take 500,000 soldiers five years. Although the US troops in Vietnam would eventually exceed this number, President Johnson baulked at the political and economic consequences of this commitment.

Both the president and McNamara endured appalling personal torment every time Westmoreland requested more troops. In September 1965, 35,000 were requested, taking the total up to 210,000. This requirement was revised up to a total of 325,000 by July 1966, but still with no guarantee of eventual success. Yet McNamara, who would later deliver veiled criticism of Westmoreland, never seems to have worked out that with the absence of a Cambodian and Laotian strategy, the North Vietnamese were able to supply the Việt Cộng at will with troops and weaponry down the Hô Chí Minh trail. In 1966 alone, the North Vietnamese funnelled some 60,000 troops into the South, bringing their total forces up to some 300,000. In 1967, infiltration along the Hô Chí Minh trail added a further 90,000 troops.

If Westmoreland's troop requirements were a moving target, it was in large part because the resources of the enemy were continually being augmented in numbers of troops and equipment. Indeed, the Việt Cộng was not some lightly armed insurgency group as was often portrayed in the liberal press. Mortars and howitzers imported from China and the Soviet Union were carried down the Hô Chí Minh trail. Hundreds of thousands of porters carried 105 mm and 120 mm shells. Heavier pieces were taken by mules or buffaloes. Porters would walk up to nine miles of mountain per day. In addition to the armaments of the ground forces, the North had Soviet MiG-17 fighters, which were later added to by MiG-19s and MiG-21s. They also deployed sophisticated surface-to-air missiles (SAMs).

Ultimately, America was ill-equipped to win a war of attrition which the absence of Laos–Cambodia strategy made inevitable, not because it was militarily incapable of doing so, but because the American people could not sustain an appetite for a conflict, which their leaders palpably showed no signs of wanting to win. By contrast, Giáp, within a totalitarian system, had estimated that his losses of nine to every one American were sustainable indefinitely.

For America the war was not sustainable, in terms of numbers of troops, casualties or duration. Both Johnson and McNamara became increasingly despairing of a military solution, but hoped that the North could be drawn into a negotiated peace. How this was going to be achieved without first gaining a decisive military advantage was never explained.

Johnson's numerous bombing pauses merely gave the North confirmation that America did not have the heart to continue to prosecute the war. In February 1967, Johnson rounded on Bobby Kennedy, one of the early espousers of the peace movement, and told him that 'The war will be over this year, and when it is, I'll destroy you and every one of your dove friends. You'll be dead politically within six months.'[28] Just five months later however, Johnson asked despairingly of McNamara, 'Are we going to be able to win this goddamned war?'[29]

Also by 1967, Johnson's Democrat Party was being torn apart by the war. Johnson was appalled by the increasing defamation of his name by the largely liberal and by now pro-peace press. Although Johnson boasted that he treated the columnists as 'whores', in truth he was deeply hurt. The president's lack of candour in the conduct of the war was beginning to rebound disastrously. In August 1967, James Deakin of *St Louis Post-Despatch* wrote, 'the relationship between the president and the Washington press corps has settled into a pattern of chronic disbelief'.[30] The increasing number of US casualties and 'body bags' were also beginning to dispel Johnson's belief that the human cost of Vietnam would be far fewer than the 30,000 Americans killed in the Korean War.

As for McNamara, he was completely shaken when Jackie Kennedy suddenly started to beat him on the chest and demanded, 'do something to stop the war'.[31] Former supporters of the war were also turning hostile. Senator William Fulbright, who had voted for the Tonkin Resolution, started a series of lectures entitled '*The Arrogance of Power*' (1966), in order to attack Johnson's handling of the war. Although the American heartland remained determinedly pro-war to the end, domestic opposition was growing stronger, particularly in California and the East Coast.

Howard Zinn's 1967 publication *The Logic of Withdrawal* was in the vanguard of polemic tracts advocating an end to American involvement in Vietnam. Zinn, Professor of Government at Boston University, was typical of the academic East Coast's opposition to the war on the best-intentioned liberal grounds; 'The best way we can show our concern for both the economic well-being and the political freedom of the Vietnamese is to take the billions in economic aid that have gone for death and turn them to the service of life.'[32]

According to the liberal left America had no moral business intervening in a dispute which was essentially a civil war. As Philippe de Villiers argued in *Histoire du Vietnam 1945–1951*, '. . . the insurrection existed before the communists decided to take part'.[33] The pro-peace campaigners also brought race into the equation after Martin Luther King changed his stance towards the war to a critical one in April 1967. Howard Zinn reported that a black field worker for the Student Non-violent Coordinating Committee told him, 'You know I just saw one of those *Việt Cộng* guerrillas on TV. He was dark-skinned, ragged, poor, and angry. I swear, he looked just like one of us.'[34] Underlying all the liberal objections to the war lay a moral equivalence towards the communist regime in the North and the sundry dictatorships that operated in the South. That there was an overwhelming preference by the Vietnamese population for the southern model, however corrupt, over the communist alternative, was singularly ignored.

On 2 November, Norman Morrison, a Baltimore Quaker, immolated himself to death in front of the Pentagon. The first mass anti-war rallies took to the streets. On 27 November, 40,000 protestors marched in Washington. Indictment for draft avoidance grew rapidly after 1965. Conscientious objection as a percentage of the draft had risen to 8 per cent by 1967, and would eventually rise to 41 per cent by 1971.

Foreign opinion was also swinging steadily against America. In a memo to Johnson in May 1967, McNamara urged that 'There may be a limit beyond which many Americans and much of the world will not permit the USA to go. The picture of the World's greatest superpower killing or seriously injuring 1,000 non-combatants a week, while trying to pound a tiny backward nation into submission on an issue whose merits are hotly disputed, is not a pretty one.'[35]

Diplomatic efforts to initiate peace talks through British Prime Minister Harold Wilson and Soviet Premier Kosygin had fallen through in early 1967. Hopes revived in June through the good offices of Henry Kissinger and his contacts in Paris; a message was relayed through Raymond Aubrac, an old friend of Hồ Chí Minh, who was a godfather to his daughter, to the effect that there would be a bombing ceasefire in return for peace discussions. However in October, North Vietnam refused the overture.

Meanwhile in despair for their hopes of a rapid military victory, Westmoreland again urged deployment of troops in Laos and Cambodia. Failing a positive response to this logical request, the joint chiefs of staff suggested the use of tactical nuclear weapons. On 29 November, President Johnson announced McNamara's election as president of the World Bank; effectively he had sacked his secretary for defence.

The combination of war costs which, by 1968, amounted to US$ 26.5 billion per annum, with the rising expense of the Great Society legislation, was beginning to bankrupt the federal government. Johnson quadrupled education spending to US$ 12 billion by 1967. Welfare and medical expenditure was also rising rapidly. Although gross domestic product rose 39 per cent in the Kennedy-Johnson era, a federal budget deficit of US$ 29 billion was forecast for the fiscal year 1968.

The budget deficit and the long term-spending embedded in the Great Society legislation was to cripple America's economy throughout the 1970s. Of more immediate concern for Johnson, inflation was beginning to rise at the same time that the White House was advocating the need for higher income and corporate taxes. By 1968 therefore, Johnson's policies had brought him to a point where the war had turned into an expensive stalemate. Rising American casualties, a growing popular sense of pointlessness to the war in Asia, combined with emerging strains in the American economy left Johnson's presidency bereft of friends.

Eisenhower had reasoned, as it turned out with complete prescience, 'If Laos is lost to the free world, in the long run we will lose all of South East Asia.'[36] In the aftermath of the Vietnam War, there was a post-hoc reassessment of the strategic need to combat communism, which had been the lynchpin of American foreign policy since the Second World War. McNamara argued that 'like most Americans I saw Communism as monolithic'.[37] Like many commentators from the left and right of the political spectrum, McNamara now argued that the Asian wars were unnecessary because an analysis of South East Asia would have shown that the communist states would have ended up fighting each other.

The basic philosophy of the domino theory, which was barely questioned before the war, was now overthrown completely. 'Looking back on those meetings, it is clear our analysis was nowhere near adequate', he argued.[38] McNamara also alludes to the 'totally incorrect appraisal of the "Chinese threat" to our security that pervaded our thinking'.[39] George Kennan, a long-term opponent of the Vietnamese War, argued at a Senate hearing in February 1966 that the Chinese 'suffered an enormous reverse in Indonesia. . . . That does rather confine any realistic hopes they may have for an expansion of their authority'.[40]

Hindsight is a fine thing, but at the time it was far from clear that China had broken completely or permanently with the Soviet Union. The bankruptcy of the Soviet's socialist economic system is now taken for granted, but as late as the early 1980s, China's analysis was that the Soviet Union, not America, was the growing political power in Asia. Also the break between the communist regimes in Vietnam and Cambodia was in the future.

Even with the benefit of hindsight, it is doubtful whether the people of South Vietnam, Cambodia or Laos would agree that the Vietnam War was not worth fighting; certainly the hundreds of thousands of Vietnamese political prisoners, the Vietnamese boat people and the victims of the Khmer 'Killing Fields' might not agree. Also, the relative success of the South Korean, Taiwanese, Thai and Malaysian economies shows what might have been possible in a 'free' Indochina under the American military and economic umbrella.

As for 'domino theory', Vietnam's neighbours were less sanguine than later liberal American commentators about the need to halt communism. South Korea, Thailand, Taiwan, the Philipinnes, New Zealand and Australia sent troops in support of their American allies. They were not forced to do so; halting communism in Vietnam was in their self-interest.

Their active support belies the notion that 'domino theory' was some abstruse notion dreamt up by policy wonks at the White House. In 1994 Lee Kwan Yew, president of Singapore, and no mean commentator, concluded that the defence of South Vietnam, albeit failed, gave his country ten years in which to prepare against communism. Communist advance in Indochina may not have threatened the USA directly, but it did threaten the cause of a free world for which America had consistently fought since 1939. When McNamara argues that the Vietnam War should not have been fought because '. . . we exaggerated the dangers to the USA of their actions', his analysis is surely wrong in not taking into account the broader issues at stake in the defence of Indochina.[41]

The Vietnam War was worth fighting; but it was not worth fighting badly. The tragedy for both America and more so South Vietnam was that Johnson started his presidency with a clear mandate to go out and win the war. Popular support in the USA was overwhelming. *The Washington Post* and *The New York Times*, the two newspapers eventually most closely associated with the peace movement, were earlier among the fiercest advocates of war. In March 1963, *The New York Times* affirmed that 'the cost of saving Vietnam is large, but the cost of Southeast Asia coming under the domination of Russia and Communist China would be still larger'.[42] Even as late as July 1965, Johnson enjoyed 65 per cent poll support for his Vietnam policies. America also enjoyed the luxury of strong commitment to the war from its allies even though British absence was a blow.

Lyndon Johnson however, focused as he was on his *Great Society* reforms, determined not to be a war president. For Johnson, his utopian ideological preferences would not be deflected by the pragmatism required of high office. Johnson's desire to avoid a long and costly entrapment in Vietnam was reflected in the lack of vigour with which he set about the war. Inevitably this coloured the military strategy that was adopted. A vigorous response to infiltration of South Vietnam along the Hô Chí Minh trail, and a determination to halt communism in Indochina, would have necessitated a willingness to engage communist forces in Laos and Cambodia and hold the line of the 17th parallel agreed at Geneva; a strategy well understood by Eisenhower and later by the American generals who were given the task to fight the war in Vietnam.

Up until 1966, Johnson could probably have taken Congress and the American people with him on a determined plan for all-out victory in Vietnam and

Indochina. While never accepting the requirement for an all-out war to maintain a pro-Western, non-communist Indochina, Johnson was too proud to adopt the logical alternative, which was complete withdrawal. To Cabot Lodge he declared, 'I am not going to lose Vietnam. I am not going to be the president who saw South East Asia go the way China went. . . '.[43]

Too bull-headed to accept the logical alternative to fighting the Vietnam War, which would have been a complete military withdrawal from Vietnam and surrender of Indochina to communism, Johnson ended with the worst possible outcome, a protracted war of attrition that ended with more human and economic cost to the USA, than if he had fought a decisive encounter for the whole of Indochina in the first place.

33

The Trouble with Tigers

Sri Lanka: 1945—94

Sri Lanka's pre-war path to self-government and independence gave little indication of the trouble to come in the post-independence era. Ceylon, as Sri Lanka was known before 1972, had been occupied by the Portuguese in the sixteenth century and the Dutch in the seventeenth century and was ceded to the British at the end of the eighteenth century; it became a crown colony in 1802 and was fully unified under British control after the quelling of an independent Sinhalese state in the highlands around Kandy. In the nineteenth century the economy expanded rapidly, driven by the growth in tea, rubber and coconut plantations. Also constitutional self-determinism moved quietly ahead after the Montagu Declaration in 1917 called for a progressive development towards self-government in the Indian sub-continent.

In imitation of Indian nationalism, a largely Sinhalese Ceylon National Congress was formed in 1919, which represented the largely Buddhist (70 per cent) population of the island. At the same time a Tamil Congress, representing the 15 per cent Tamil population, was also formed. By 1924 Ceylon was represented by a council of 49, of whom just 12 were officials appointed by the British government; for the remainder, elections were carried out with a franchise of 204,997 voters. Apart from the Ceylon Labour Union led by Goonesinha, there were few calls for universal suffrage. Nevertheless, a special commission under Lord Donoughmore would recommend the creation of a board of ministers of which three would be Crown appointed versus seven Ceylonese; in a radical advance Donoughmore would also recommend an increase in the suffrage to include all men over 21 and all women over 30 years of age.

During the Second World War, Ceylon's governor pushed further constitutional change. Full responsibility for government under the Crown in all matters of civil administration was pledged by the Colonial Office in March 1943. The new constitution that followed comprised an upper house with 30 members, of which 15 were chosen by the governor. He also had the power to choose six members of the lower house. It was a pale imitation of Westminster, with the lower house designed to be the centre of power. The new constitution was overwhelmingly accepted by the Ceylonese State Council in November 1945.

In the headlong rush to divest themselves of empire, in the straightened conditions of post-war Britain, the Labour government of Clement Attlee announced Ceylon's independence in February 1947 and scheduled elections for September. Power to amend the constitution was now vested in the House of Representatives, which could achieve changes only with a two-thirds majority. Independence arrived on 4 February 1948 though the country remained a member of the Commonwealth and the governor was simply replaced by a governor general. Membership of the United Nations had to wait however; the Soviet Union vetoed the application on the grounds that Ceylon's independence was a sham.

With the emergence of a moderate United National Party (UNP) as the dominant political party, the newly emerged Ceylon appeared set fair for a stable independent future. The UNP, founded by D.S. Senanayake and including his son Dudley as well as such notables as Sir John Kotelawala, J.R. Jayewardene and S.W.R.D. (Solomon) Bandaranaike, was committed to liberal democracy and the free market; though largely neutral in international affairs, its bias was clearly pro-Western. With a post-war rise in demand leading to a rapid increase in rubber prices and the expansion of the economy, the party appeared to have every chance of political dominance in the manner of India's Congress Party.

This cosy relationship was undone by the defection of S.W.R.D. Bandaranaike in 1951. Solomon Bandaranaike, an Oxford-educated member of the Sinhalese elite, was a leading figure in a group known as the *Sinhala Maha Sabha*; this Buddhist Sinhalese nationalist organisation was his pre-war power base, and in his new party, the Sri Lanka Freedom Party (SLFP), he used a political strategy oriented towards the Buddhist majority. In 1957, the Buddhist nationalist SLFP was able to unseat the ruling UNP led by Prime Minister Sir John Kotelawala, whose pro-Western outlook of the Colombo elite meant little to the rural voters courted by Bandaranaike, who ran his campaign on a 'Sinhala only' slogan.[1] The Buddhists also made much of the fact that the 1956 elections fell on the 2,500th anniversary of the death of Buddha and the supposed landing of Vijaya and his Buddhist followers on the island of Ceylon.

The electoral coalition alliance organised by Bandaranaike crushed the UNP, whose vote fell from 44 per cent to 28 per cent, gaining them just eight of the 95 contested seats in the House of Representatives. Bandaranaike and his SLFP government, with for the first time an all-Sinhalese cabinet, now set out on a path of pro-Sinhalese adjustment and socialist economic development; to this end, in 1957, he appointed a Buddha Sasana (message) Commission.

Two Buddhist centres at Vidyodaya and Vidyalankara became state-funded universites. Also he sought to raise access to education and literacy across the whole population; however, the move towards imposing Sinhalese as the language of education through the Official Language Act was to have a profound effect on the

Tamil community. As the historian G.C. Mendis claimed during an address to the
Royal Asiatic Society on 10 December 1966,

> If the decision of 1944 had been allowed to continue most of the 69% Sinhalese would
> not have considered it necessary to learn Tamil as they had few opportunities for em-
> ployment in the Northern and Eastern provinces.
>
> On the other hand, many Tamils living in the Dry Zone in order to find employ-
> ment in the Sinhalese Wet Zone would have considered it necessary also to learn Sin-
> halese. The Indian Tamils living in the central parts would have found it necessary even
> more. And gradually Sinhalese automatically would have become the main language of
> the country and of the government whatever the situation culturally. . . .[2]

Historically, the British rulers had found the Tamil minority to be by far the
harder working and intellectually dextrous of the two communities, with the result that Tamils dominated education and the civil service. The British had wisely
maintained a policy of language parity between Sinhalese and Tamil; the sudden
reversion to a Sinhalese nationalism, aimed at reducing the proportion of Tamils in
higher education and the civil service, undermined the island's long-held racial and
communal harmony. Under the new quota systems, Tamils would be replaced by
less well-educated and qualified Sinhalese. Bandaranaike stoked the fire that would
eventually lead to religious and ethnic conflagration.

However, Bandaranaike's reforms did not go far enough for the radical Buddhist faction that he had helped to inflame. On the morning of 25 September 1959,
a Buddhist monk, Talduwe Somarama Thero, visited Bandaranaike at his home at
Rosemead Place and, just as the prime minister was paying the formal courtesies
offered to a Buddhist monk, pulled out a pistol and shot Bandaranaike in the stomach at point-blank range. He died the following day.

After a brief interlude, Bandaranaike's wife, Sirimavo (Ratwatte), the daughter
of a landed aristocratic family, was elected to succeed her husband. The inexperienced Sirimavo Bandaranaike would prove a formidable politician, leading the
SFLP for the next 40 years. A thick-set battle axe of a woman, Mrs Bandaranaike
was the original 'iron lady' with a handbag; visitors were warned that things were
not going well if she started to fidget with her bag, opening and shutting it with an
ever-increasing snap.

She proved to be an even stauncher socialist than her husband. Apart from continuing the nationalisation of Ceylon's plantations, Mrs Bandaranaike nationalised
banking and insurance. Bus transport had earlier been nationalised as was cargo
handling in Colombo. Much to the annoyance of America, petroleum companies
were taken over by the Ceylonese government. The Bandaranaikes also set about a
social transformation with the 1958 Paddy Lands Acts seeking to break the traditional links between landowner and tenant. Village headmen, through whom the
British had ruled for over a century, were replaced with transferable officials. Religious diversity and tolerance was further undermined by the state takeover of private Christian denomination schools. Such was the unhappiness with this process

that Roman Catholic elements within the army even launched an attempted coup d'état.

Mrs Bandaranaike managed to hold together her United Left Front alliance until she attempted to take control of Lake House, the largest newspaper group in Ceylon. When 13 members of her own party voted against her, Mrs Bandaranaike called an election in March 1965. Although she narrowly lost to an opposition coalition, the UNP with 66 seats out of 151 had to rely on the SLFP dissidents for support. The result was a government too weak to overthrow Mrs Bandaranaike's religious or economic policies. Socialist economic inertia was now driving up unemployment, as well as causing devaluation and inflation.

The SLFP won back power in the 1970 elections. The increasing problems of a socialist economy were heightened by the First Oil Crisis and a food crisis in 1973. The government's response was yet more socialist. In 1974 the Sri Lankan government set up a monopolistic purchasing agency, the Paddy Marketing Board. However, by setting purchase prices too low, farmers merely withheld their crops which they proceeded to sell on a rapidly developing black market. In its first year of operation, the board collected just 20.5 per cent of the country's crop.

State control of imports was also imposed with the Co-operative Wholesale Establishment being given the right to import all essential commodities; non-essential imports were handled by the State Trading Corporation. Large private companies were also nationalised, including the British Ceylon Corporation and Wellawatta Spinning and Weaving Mills Ltd. Mrs Bandaranaike also passed the Business Undertakings (Acquisitions) Act which enabled the government to take over any enterprise with over 100 employees.

Mrs Bandaranaike's second term of office moved rapidly to create a full-blown socialist command economy. Exchange controls were strictly enforced. Food was increasingly rationed and, as the government finances dwindled, rations for subsidised rice were reduced from two to one pound per week. Sugar was allotted at three quarters of a pound per month. Economic policies became increasingly intrusive. Savings were made compulsory. A ceiling was put on ownership of residential property. There was a flurry of new taxes, including a special tax on car ownership.

Given that Mrs Bandaranaike's policies were Marxist in all but name, it was perhaps surprising that the first challenge to her rule should come not from the Tamils as might have been expected, but from the Sinhalese left. Rohana Wijeweera was a typical lower middle class ideologue, who felt himself excluded from the ruling Sinhalese elite. Born in the coastal fishing village of Kottegoda in southern Sri Lanka, he was brought up a communist by his father and won a scholarship to study medicine in the Soviet Union in 1960. By the time he left Russia, he had become disillusioned with the Soviets and would eventually be barred from re-entry. He was an opinionated, quarrelsome man who proceeded then to fall out with the Chinese branch of the Communist Party that he had made his home. Here too he was expelled.

In 1967 Wijeweera set up the Janatha Vimukthi Peramuna (JVP) in a house in Akmeemana in the Galle district of southern Sri Lanka. The JVP attracted the increasing numbers of young who had been educated by the Bandaranaike reforms, enthused by Sinhalese nationalism, but left bereft of jobs and opportunity by the SLFP's socialist economic policies. 'Save the Motherland from Indian Imperialism' was a core lecture for recruits, and it advocated a unitary Sri Lankan state and deplored the potential influence of neighbouring India on the Tamil population. Wijeweera would later explain that he '. . . began organising classes in Marxism in Colombo, expanding them into the countryside, and . . . [they] then moved into Universities and schools'.[3]

Insurrection began with a grenade and firebomb attack on the US embassy in Colombo on 8 March 1971. Two weeks later, bombs were exploded at Peradeniya University near Kandy. Later searches would reveal caches of bomb-making materials hidden on campus. An acerbic Mrs Bandaranaike complained that 'I cannot understand what the University Administration was doing while the entire campus was systematically turned into a munitions factory.'[4] On 5 April 1971, the JVP and its estimated 100,000 supporters launched an attack on 100 police stations in southern Sri Lanka in an attempted coup d'état. The following day the JVP failed in a plot to kidnap the prime minister. Although the attempted coup was poorly organised, Bandaranaike's government was badly shaken. The rebel's munitions, which were traced as North Korean in origin, resulted in the expulsion of North Korea's Embassy.

On 23 April Mrs Bandaranaike was able to declare that the rebellion was over, the JVP was defeated and '3,188 rebels had surrendered.'[5] Mopping-up operations continued and ended with what General Attygalle estimated was over 16,000 rebels killed or captured. An alarmed government dropped over 500,000 leaflets onto the JVP strongholds; it was entitled 'A Notice to Misguided Youth.' Although the Sinhalese JVP movement became quiescent, it did not disappear. The state of emergency declared by Mrs Bandaranaike was not lifted until February 1977, prior to the elections, in preparation for which all political detainees including Wijeweera were released.

The result of the JVP insurrection was not to liberalise Bandaranaike's economic and political regime, but to make it even more authoritarian in character. Special legislation was passed to take over the Associated Newspaper Group, while criticisms of the Bandaranaike government led to the company being shut down in April 1974. Meanwhile The Times Group also fell to government supporters. Furthermore the Sri Lankan Broadcasting Corporation was increasingly used for propaganda. Public meetings were banned until September 1972, while the main opposition party, the UNP, was closed down for 18 months in 1973–4.

Mrs Bandaranaike also used the emergency to skew employment and promotion in the bureaucracy towards supporters of the SFLP. Meanwhile the left-leaning prime minister, in spite of accepting British helicopters after the emergency as well as Soviet Mig fighters, cut links with the Commonwealth. In 1972, Ceylon was renamed Sri Lanka and the country was declared a republic. Perhaps the most damaging of all her policies, however, was educational 'standardisation', whereby Bandaranaike, perhaps motivated by the Sinhalese uprising of the JVP, sought to bias the education system further in favour of the Buddhist majority.

Mrs Bandaranaike's rule proved catastrophic for her country. By the 1977 elections, the economy had been decimated by a totalitarian control that was Marxist–Leninist in all but name. Civil liberties had also been sharply eroded. More importantly, the Tamil population of the northern Jaffna Peninsula had been completely alienated from the Sri Lankan state. As the historian K.M. de Silva would comment, 'It would be true to say that the UF government sowed the wind and its successor reaped the whirlwind.'[6]

In the short term, national elections ended the SFLP's long-held domination of Sri Lankan politics. The UNP manifesto in 1977 called for a rolling back of Mrs Bandaranaike's autocratic state: 'We will ensure . . . that every citizen, whether he belongs to a majority or minority, racial, religious or caste group, enjoys equal and basic human rights and opportunities.'[7] The UNP leader, Jayewardene, also promised the Tamils 'all possible steps to remedy grievances'.[8] After a landslide victory, Jayewardene sought to re-establish political and social stability with the aim of restoring an economy brutalised by socialism; 'Foreign investors', warned the new prime minister, '. . . would hardly care to come when there are riots and governments are overthrown by bloody coups and not by the ballot'.[9]

Junius Richard Jayewardene (often known in Sri Lanka as JR), a member of the Sinhalese elite, was himself a tall, slim man of aristocratic bearing. A lawyer and son of a former Supreme Court judge, he was by nature arrogant, autocratic and aloof; he also used his government majority to change the constitution to a presidential system and controversially had Mrs Bandaranaike barred from running against him. Also, in a questionably fought referendum, he prolonged the life of parliament by six years. To his credit however, he deregulated state controls and breathed some life back into his country's moribund economy. However, as a young man he had converted from Christianity to Buddhism and was as much a staunch supporter of Sinhalese values as his predecessor.

In the run-up to the 1982 elections, Jayewardene's intentions were clear:

> We are contesting this election to win at a time most favourable to us. We intend to demolish and completely destroy the opposition politically. Roll up the political map of Sri Lanka. You will not need it for another ten years.[10]

Jayewardene easily defeated the SLFP candidate Hector Kobbekaduwa; the SLFP lost its power as a political force when Mrs Bandaranaike was banned from politics and deprived of her civic rights in 1977. She would spend the next 17 years in the political wilderness, fighting to keep control of her Freedom Party and playing off her rivals, notably her own children, her daughter Chandrika and her homosexual son Anura. In the 1982 presidential elections, the rehabilitated terrorist JVP leader Wijeweera also re-emerged to poll over a quarter of a million votes and scored a creditable third place.

However, it was the Tamil question that would dominate Jayewardene's government and that of all of his successors. Tamil issues were long standing and complex. In the Northern Province of Jaffna, the Hindu worshipping Tamils formed the majority of the population, while in the Eastern Province they were equally numerous as the Sinhalese. However, this Hindu population, which formed the ancient Tamil population of Sri Lanka and accounted for just 7 per cent of the population, was supplemented by 'Indian' Tamils (from *Tamil Nadu*, 'Land of the Tamils', an Indian state of 70 million people whose capital is *Chennai*, 'Madras') who had migrated from India in the nineteenth century largely to feed the demand for manual labour needed by the fast-growing Ceylonese plantation industry. They were mainly located in the central and southern plantation regions. Independence left this 'Indian' group bereft of rights, and by 1961 only 10 per cent of the community's applications for citizenship had been processed.

The rights of 'Indian' Tamils were of natural concern to the Indian government in Delhi, and in 1964 Mrs Bandaranaike negotiated a deal whereby 525,000 stateless 'Indian' Tamils would be relocated to India in return for Ceylonese citizenship to be given to 300,000. A remaining 150,000 were not dealt with until 1974, when President Jayewardene agreed to 'share' them with India. As Sir John Kotelawala had warned Nehru when he visited Ceylon in 1939, 'We are certainly not going to keep Indians in employment when our people are unemployed. When it is a question of retrenchment, the Indians have to go.'[11] In spite of these efforts at repatriation, economic decline and fighting over the spoils of land redistribution led to conflicts in these agrarian communities and a spate of Sinhalese–Indian riots after 1977.

The 'Indian' Tamil problems, however, were minor compared to the increasing disillusionment of the northern Ceylonese Tamils. Historically they had been represented by the Tamil Congress and subsequently by its breakaway, the Federal Party. The Ceylon Workers Congress (CWC), formerly the Ceylon Indian Congress, spoke on behalf of the Tamil population. Increasingly this group, re-named the Tamil United Liberation Front (TULF), developed into the main *organisation* of Tamil political aspirations; as the Sinhalese political monopoly hardened, increasingly TULF called for political autonomy if not complete independence. The political, economic and educational bias of policies pursued by the dominant SFLP group of Mr and Mrs Bandaranaike had bred a disillusioned youth, who believed that the constitutional approach could not work. Tamils entering engineering courses fell from almost half of all students in 1969 to just 14.2 per cent in 1975. For the educated Tamil youth, frustration turned to violence.

While the TULF preached non-violence, by the 1970s their Youth Leaguers increasingly refused to follow the 'Gandhian' approach for rectification of their

grievances. In May 1975 the Youth Leaguers reorganised themselves as the Liberation Tigers of Tamil Eelam (LTTE); they would become popularly known as the
Tamil Tigers. The leader that emerged from this group was Velupillai Prabhakaran,
a devout Hindu who claimed to draw his inspiration from the holy 'Mahabharata'
texts. He had originally been an admirer of Gandhi, but his tutor, a Tamil activist V.
Navaratnam, persuaded him that nothing could be achieved through liberal democracy. Prabhakaran reputedly explained, 'I got the feeling we should hit back [at the
Sinhalese] and we should have a separate country.'[12]

He dropped out of school at the age of 16 and formed his own gang. His legend expanded rapidly after he was credited with personally shooting the Mayor
of Jaffna. Ideology, which was not Prabhakaran's strong suit, was provided for
the group by a young Sinhalese Oxford graduate, Anton Balasingham, who cannibalised Marxist-Leninism to produce a Tamil version. However, it was the ruthlessly driven and monomaniacal Prabhakaran who provided charismatic and ruthless leadership. Cadres were brainwashed with Tiger propaganda and sworn to loyalty at a formal acceptance ceremony; graduates were presented with a container
with a cyanide pill for use when captured. Recruits also had to forswear marriage
for five years after joining the Tigers.

Extra-legal activities started with the robbing of banks for funds and the assassination of local politicians and policemen. A heavy-handed military reaction
sparked riots in which 98 Tamils and 30 Sinhalese lost their lives. Tamil Tiger also
began attacks on trains running between Colombo and Jaffna. Although the killings
died down in the immediate aftermath of Sirimavo Bandaranaike's fall from power
in 1977, the failure of the UNP leader Jayewardene to address Tamils' grievances
brought an escalation of Tamil Tiger activity in the early 1980s. The killing of a
UNP candidate in May 1981 was followed by the murder of a policeman and three
others at an election rally on 1 June. Some 100 police officers in Jaffna then went
on a rampage of revenge looting and burning of Tamil property. On 28 July a
police station was attacked, with a police inspector shot dead, three wounded and
guns and uniforms stolen. Unhelpfully an LTTE spokesman now claimed that since
1972 the Tigers had been responsible for '20 policemen killed, together with five
politicians and five informers'.[13]

At the beginning of August a backlash against Tamils had begun in the capital Colombo. By the time that Jayewardene had declared a state of emergency on
17 August, police, who had in many cases ignored or participated in the atrocities,
confirmed that 'seven tamils had been killed, and 196 incidents of arson, 35 of
looting, and 15 of robbery' had been reported.[14] By now the attention of India
was also becoming focussed on events in Sri Lanka; in Madras and the surrounding
state of Tamil Nadu, 12 September brought a one-day sympathy strike.

In the north, the Jaffna Peninsula, with its narrow neck linking the Tamil heartland to the rest of Sri Lanka, had become a virtual 'no-go' area for police, who had
to leave their fortified compounds in convoys of four or five vehicles. In reaction

to the growing Tamil threat, Jayewardene initiated a new police paramilitary force designated as the 60th Special Task Force. A training and interrogation centre was set up at Elephant Pass.

A Prevention of Terrorism Act was also passed which allowed for detainment of terrorist suspects for up to 18 months. Later the sixth constitutional amendment of August 1983 would ban all political parties that advocated separatism. Politicians were required to

> solemnly declare and swear that I will uphold and defend the constitution . . . and that I will not, directly or indirectly, in or outside of Sri Lanka, support, espouse, promote, finance, encourage or advocate the establishment of a separate state within the territory of Sri Lanka.[15]

Politically there would be no concessions. Jayewardene remained adamant that he would maintain a unitary Sri Lankan state; on 11 July 1983 he told the *Daily Telegraph*, 'I am not worried about the opinion of the people . . . . Now we can't think of them. Not about their lives or their opinions of us.'[16] Two weeks later the Tamil insurrection would begin in earnest. On 23 July Tamil Tigers led by Kittu, their regional commander, ambushed a jeep and an army troop carrier outside Jaffna, killing an officer and 14 soldiers. Next day Ceylonese troops went on a brutal rampage against Tamil civilians. The Jaffna events inflamed riots in Colombo with mobs burning cars; people were pulled from cars or doused with petrol before being set alight.

At the high-security prison at Welikade, jailed Sinhalese criminals stormed the wing devoted to Tamil political detainees and butchered 37 of them with clubs and knives. Mob violence erupted throughout the country. A second Welikade massacre occurred on 28 July; this time 15 Tamils were butchered including R. Rajasunharan, secretary general of the Gandhian Society. The police did little to protect the Tamil minority from the rampaging mobs and in many cases joined in the communal assaults.

As the United Nations reported on 19 August, 'The riots had been made worse by government indifference to the fate of the Tamils.'[17] As ever, the civilian population suffered most from the civil war. By the end of 1984, 24,000 Sinhalese had fled from Tamil areas to refugee camps. Two years later more than 80,000 civilians from all communities lived in camps, not including the hundreds of thousands of Tamils who had fled to the Indian state of Tamil Nadu.

Although international pressure now forced President Jayewardene into the so-called Amity Talks with the Tamils, both sides used the 18-month lull to prepare militarily. With just 16,000 troops plus an additional 10,000 reservists, the Sri Lankan government was ill-prepared to fight a guerrilla war. Using the 1947 Defence Agreement, Jayewardene called upon the Thatcher government to provide armaments.

Also the Sri Lankan government employed a channel island company, Eeny-Meeny Ltd. (a military consultancy consisting of former SAS soldiers), which was recruited to train 300 police into a specialist anti-terrorist force (STF) at a training camp near Kandy. Help with counter-terrorism was also sought from the Israelis, and in May 1984, the Sri Lankan Foreign Ministry, somewhat foolishly, announced the setting up of an Israel 'Special Interest Section' stationed within the US Embassy in Colombo. President Reagan too had assured Jayewardene of his support. However, the Israeli–American connection served to alienate Sri Lanka's Muslim population.

By now the Tamil Tigers had become as much a criminal gang as a liberation army. Civilians were forced to contribute funds, while the 'the boys need this car' became a familiar expression to car owners. Even Hindu temples were looted. As a Tamil fighter explained to a *Times* journalist, 'The only way to get a proper donation is by force. Jungle life is not that easy. When you see people living in comfort you expect them to contribute to the cause.'[18]

Increasingly too, the control of the Jaffna Peninsula and districts in the Eastern Province fell under the influence of local war lords and gangs, distinguishing themselves with outlandish hair styles, clothes and names. Fiction mixed strangely with fact; Hollywood films were used as training manuals including *The Lion of the Desert* (1981), a historically accurate film financed by Libya's Colonel Qaddafi, starring Anthony Quinn as Libyan resistance leader, Omar Mukhtar, holding up Italian tanks with mines; Sylvester Stallone in *Rambo* (1985) was also a favourite.

As the insurrection progressed, Tamil Tigers fought for control of their territory against rival organisations such as the Marxist People's Liberation Organisation (PLOTE), the Tamil Eelam Liberation Organisation (TELO) and the anti-TULF, Marxist Eelam People's Revolutionary Liberation Front (EPRLF). The Tigers effectively annihilated TELO with a massacre of 200 people in April-May 1986, while the EPRLF were crushed later that autumn. Even the government STF's Chief Superintendent Nimal de Silva complained about the inter-Tamil atrocities: 'This is butchery', he declared, 'The Tiger are hell-bent on annihilating other groups.'[19] Furthermore TULF, the political arm of the Tigers (a relationship similar to Sinn Fein and the IRA in Ireland), had become largely subservient to the Tamil Tigers.

The ending of the Amity Talks led to renewed violence. Buses became targets for Tamil suicide bombers, while Tiger guerrilla forces massacred Sinhalese farmers. On 18 January 1985 security forces revenged themselves by killing Tamil Catholic priest Father Bastian and eight parishioners in his church at Vankalai; Father Bastian had been targeted for helping to collect and bury 110 Tamil victims of a security force massacre in Eastern Province district of Mannar in the previous month.

In August 1985, President Jayewardene set up a counter-insurgency force of 100 officers and 10,000 troops and in October passed a Mobilisation and Supplementary Forces Act; he was now determined to suppress the Tamil uprising whatever the cost to civilian life. With the arrival of Saladin armoured cars, ten British

Cougar patrol boats, Italian SF 260 aircraft, 30 South African personnel carriers and 20 Bell helicopters from Singapore, Jayewardene could now claim that 'The army is better equipped and trained now, and I expect them to end the guerrilla violence by the end of the year.'[20]

Between 1 March 1985 and 31 January 1986, Amnesty reported that the government had carried out 2,578 killings, 12,105 arrests and 547 disappearances. In addition in March 1986, whole Tamil communities were denied a livelihood by a ban on fishing; with a bankrupted economy, fighting was the only occupation that remained to young men. By 1986 it was estimated that over 70 per cent of Tamil youth were working for one or other of the resistance gangs.

In Jaffna, production of armaments became the principal manufacturing enterprise; Kittu, the Jaffna commander, who carried a monkey on his shoulder and kept a copy of *Che Guevara's memoirs* laid open in his suburban Jaffna villa, boasted to *The Times* war reporter, John Swain, that he had a factory producing 100 grenades and 25 mortars per day. The Tamil uprising had descended to total war. As a TULF leader complained to *The Hindu* newspaper in India, 'our fishermen cannot go fishing, and our cultivators cannot cultivate'.[21]

By now the Indian government was taking an increasingly active interest in proceedings. Operation Liberation, launched by the Sri Lankan government in 1987, threatened to overrun the hapless Tamil population who were on the brink of starvation as the government forces tightened the noose around the Jaffna Peninsula. There were now 135,000 Tamil refugees across the 18-km wide Palk Strait; the government of Tamil Nadu, reacting to popular anger against the Sri Lankan government, offered US$ 3.2 million in aid to the Tamils. On 3 June, the Indian Air Force broke into Sri Lankan airspace to make drops of food and medicine. The threat of an Indian invasion was imminent.

To stave off the seemingly inevitable conflict, President Jayewardene held talks with Rajiv Gandhi and reached agreement on a way forward in July 1987. The India–Lanka Accord provided for an Indian Peace Keeping Force (IPKF) to maintain law and order in return for a surrender of Tamil weapons. According to Gandhi, 'It would be a short sharp exercise and our boys should be back home soon.'[22] The Accord also allowed that India would train Sri Lanka's armed forces and in return would be offered the use of their deep-water ports. With regard to a Tamil future, power would devolve to provincial councils; in the Eastern Province, a referendum would be held to decide whether the province would join the Northern Province or provide its own council.

The spirit of the Accord was short lived. Prabhakaran reluctantly agreed to welcome the IPKF, but a guerrilla army with no guns would have been a force without power; apart from handing over a collection of ancient weapons, the Tamil Tigers kept their arms. Moreover, there were internal clashes with the increasingly dispirited Muslim population and complaints that the IPKF were not intervening to uphold the peace. Within Sri Lanka itself, a rejuvenated SFLP opposed the 'pro-Indian' Accord and organised what turned out to be a violent march on Colombo. Furthermore Jayewardene undermined his promise of northern political autonomy when he refused to accept the first three proposed Tamil candidates for the Northern Council.

However, the event which precipitated the collapse of the Accord was the capture of a group of Tamil leaders and their bodyguards on their way to India to smuggle arms on 5 October 1987. Twelve of the arrested Tamil Tigers committed suicide with their now famous cyanide pill. The response by the LTTE leadership was to order an attack on the north in which more than 200 Sinhalese civilians were butchered. The Sri Lankan government pressed the IPKF to act to restore order; the Indian army, who already had a cause to fire on Tamil Tiger forces in September, now launched an all-out assault on the Jaffna Peninsular.

The first skirmishes were a disaster for India; a 70-strong Sikh force landed at a hockey field located close to the Tiger's Jaffna headquarters and found that they had fallen into a trap. Surrounded, the Sikhs held out till the following day when they ran out of munitions. They then fixed bayonets and charged the Tiger positions; only one Sikh soldier survived. In response, a shocked Indian army rushed Russian-supplied T-72 tanks to Sri Lanka. Although the IPKF would eventually take the city of Jaffna, killing some 607 Tigers in the process, the remaining terrorists simply slipped into jungle retreats.

For the Indians, it was a pyrrhic victory. Tamil civilian casualties were heavy. IPKF had only half defeated the Tigers, while the people they had come to help now hated the Indian invaders. Furthermore opinion back in India had turned hostile to a conflict which had claimed over 1,000 Indian soldiers their lives in the Sri Lankan venture; the Tigers were now claiming to be '. . . frying alive Indian prisoners with necklaces of tires'.[23] What started for Rajiv as a military adventure and a political opportunity to win votes in India's Dravidian south had turned into an electoral liability. For Jayewardene and the UNP too, the position had changed; the Sinhalese were increasingly unhappy at the Indian army occupation, and the SFLP were making political capital over the issue. Jayewardene's Indian gambit had failed; an exhausted and dispirited man, he retired from politics in 1988.

Jayewardene's elected successor, Ranasinghe Premadasa, had served as Jayewardene's prime minister but had been notably cool on the Accord. He was the first leader from outside the Buddhist elite, coming from a humble family background; as such he had proved himself useful to Jayewardene in bringing in the votes of the urban poor with whom he could connect. Unusually Premadasa, who lived a modest unostentatious life, was a free marketeer and believed that the creation of wealth could aid the poor. Premadasa now set about removing the Indian army by first agreeing with the Tamil Tigers that it was in all their interests for them to leave. Under cover of a truce, the Indian army had departed by March 1990.

However, as soon as they were gone, the LTTE established de facto rule over the Northern Province. With the need for political negotiation now dissolved, the political leadership of the Tamils by the TULF was openly challenged; TULF's leader, Amirthalingam, had been murdered by the Tigers in July 1989. The leader of the PLOTE was also assassinated. After March 1990, the Tigers captured some 600 Sinhalese and Tamil police in the Northern Province and had them executed. In the Eastern Province the Tamil Tigers were less successful; after initially attacking the Muslim community, the Sri Lankan army, now 80,000 strong, drove them back to their Jaffna stronghold. Here the Tamil Tigers forced the Sri Lankan army to retreat from their fortified positions at Jaffna Fort.

The Tigers were not the only revolutionary group to plague the last years of the Jayewardene presidency. The India–Lankan Accord spurred a revival in Wijeweera's JVP: the leader and his Politburo began to train their guerrilla cadre in remote jungle locations. As for Wijeweera, he changed his identity, took the name Attanayake, bought land and a bungalow in St. Mary's estate near Kandy and used tea planting as his cover. With an estimated 2,000 activists, Wijeweera inaugurated a reign of terror with a spate of assassinations.

On 2 December 1987 T. Perera, STF police superintendent, was assassinated in his car by a motorbike gunman. Jayewardene condemned the assassination campaign and described the JVP as 'animals with a homicidal nature'.[24] The following day the UNP chairman, Abeywardene, was also killed. Two months later Vijaya Kumaratunga, former heart-throb movie star and the husband of Sirimavo Bandaranaike's daughter Chandrika, was shot in the back and killed outside his home by Lionel Ranasinghe, a former peanut seller who had become a top JVP assassin.

Kumaratunga had been leader of the Sri Lanka Mahajana Party (SLMP) whose main policy was to negotiate a peace with the Tamil Tigers, anathema to the Sinhalese nationalist sentiments of the JVP. Over the next two years the JVP killed an estimated 2,500 people. UNP politicians now hired armed guards, who in effect turned into a paramilitary force. A loose organisation called the Green Tigers was thus formed which worked with police to root out and kill suspect JVP supporters. Atrocities became commonplace on both sides.

Conflict came to a head when the JVP called on Sri Lanka's soldiers to throw down their weapons and desert and also threatened their families if they failed to comply. It was now a fight to the death. For the security forces the breakthrough came with the capture of a Politburo member, which led them to uncovering Wijeweera's whereabouts. He was arrested while shaving at 2 pm on 12 November 1989 in his plantation house. From here he was taken to Colombo and questioned at the headquarters of 'Operation Combine' along with numbers of curious generals and the Deputy Defence Minister General Ranjan Wijeratne. Questioning was concluded at 3.45 am on 13 November. He must have sensed his fate; as he was being taken downstairs, he told one of his captors, 'I am very happy I met you even at the last moment. I may not live any longer. Please convey my message to my wife.'[25]

Wijeweera was then blindfolded and bundled into the back of a green Mitsubishi Pajero SUV. He was taken to Colombo Golf Course where he was shot dead on the 12th hole. Julian West, later a war correspondent with the Sunday Telegraph, who lived in an adjacent villa, recalls being woken by the shot; an account of the slaying is vividly described in her novel *Serpent in Paradise* (2007), which is set in the period of the JVP troubles. Most of the Politburo was rounded up and within months the JVP had been effectively crushed.

Whether President Premadasa ordered the slaying of Wijeweera is unclear. While the JVP problem may have been solved, the Tamil Tigers proved much less tractable. To all intents and purposes, they now controlled the Jaffna Peninsula, and while the Eastern Province had mainly been cleared of Tigers, assassinations continued unabated. The most spectacular of these was achieved by a nail bomb suicide bomber who assassinated Rajiv Gandhi at an Indian election rally in Tamil Nadu. The Tamils are renowned for their acts of revenge; unfortunately for Premadasa, his valet Mohideen befriended a Tamil who got close enough to assassinate the president at his home on 1 May 1993. The blast dismembered Premadasa's body.

His successor Chandrika Kumaratunga, who had fled to England in the immediate aftermath of her husband's assassination, had eventually returned to Sri Lanka where she eclipsed her mother Sirimavo Bandaranaike. After 17 years of UNP rule, Sri Lanka was ready for a change, and Kumaratunga's long-standing desire for peace negotiations with the Tamil Tigers now seemed attractive to an exhausted population. She was elected prime minister as head of a People's Alliance government on 9 August 1994 and later in November won the presidency.

Kumaratunga then created a world first in a democracy by making her mother, Mrs Bandaranaike, prime minister. However, on the intractable issue of the Tamils, Chandrika Kumaratunga also failed. In spite of her conciliatory approach, she was soon rebuffed by the LTTE. Like her predecessor she had to revert to a policy of military containment. However, in contrast to Premadasa, she survived an assassination attempt, though lost vision in one eye, during the Tamil Tiger terrorist assault on her final rally of a presidential campaign on 18 December 1999. The Tamil Tiger troubles, which had been so much created by the racial and economic policies of her parents in the 1950s and 1960s, continued to haunt the entire Sri Lankan political process.

34

Nixon in China

America-China: 1969–71

A Yugoslav fashion show at the Palace of Culture in Warsaw on 3 December 1969 was the unlikely scene of a diplomatic engagement which set in train the most startling geopolitical rapprochement of the twentieth century. At this event, Walter Stoessel, the US ambassador to Poland, button-holed his Chinese counterpart, Lei Yang. This was a terrifying prospect for a Chinese ambassador used to the studied avoidance of US officials; it was only after Lei Yang had been chased down a flight of stairs that Stoessel was able to impress upon the fleeing diplomat the request for serious talks between the USA and China. Zhou Enlai, China's premier, was later to joke with Kissinger that Stoessel's cornering of Lei Yang had almost given their ambassador a heart attack.

The astonishment of the Chinese was not altogether surprising, given the extraordinary degree of isolation between the USA and China in the aftermath of the clash of their armies on the Korean peninsula, where American and Chinese troops had fought to a standstill. As the famous American post-war sinologist John King Fairbank commented, 'From 1950 to 1971 Washington sent more men to the moon than to China. . . '.[1]

Historic relations apart, there were current issues that, at first sight, made any normal discourse between China and America unlikely. The US army's occupation of the southern part of China's historic neighbour and vassal state, Vietnam, ostensibly as a means of holding back the Communist 'dominoes', had held back the possibility of any relationship between these great Asian powers for almost a decade. Meanwhile, America's support for Taiwan was a festering sore with little prospect of solution. What then brought about this astonishing volte-face in American policy towards its supposed mortal enemy, communist China?

In large part, the dramatic shift in American policy can be attributed to President Nixon, who possessed a geopolitical sophistication that his predecessors noticeably lacked. Historian Paul Johnson has posited that 'It was Nixon's Californian orientation which inclined him towards Peking; he saw the Pacific as the world-arena area of the future.'[2] This may certainly have been a factor in Nixon's world view, but it is clear from his career and interests that he always had a keen interest

in international affairs and an intellectual acumen to match. During the years following his defeat by John F. Kennedy in the 1960 presidential elections, Nixon
travelled widely and listened to the counsels of elder statesman.

In 1963, French President Charles de Gaulle had advised Nixon that 'It would
be better for you to recognize China before you are obliged to do so by the growth
of China.'[3] When Nixon, now as head of state himself, visited France again in
1969, De Gaulle again urged, with regard to China, that the USA should not 'leave
them isolated in their rage'.[4] Indeed in 1964, President de Gaulle, in defiance of
America, became the first Western leader to recognise the People's Republic of
China (PRC).

Also, after Nixon's presidential defeat, he took a European vacation and visited Konrad Adenauer, whom Nixon had befriended on the German chancellor's
first visit to America in April 1953. In spite of his passionate hatred of communism, Adenauer, the other great European statesman of the post-war period, also
opined that the USA should seek a rapprochement with China 'as a buffer to Soviet
expansionism'.[5] De Gaulle's belief that national interest would in the long term
win out over ideology was also alluded to by Lee Kuan Yew who told Nixon that
'Mao is painting on a mosaic. Once Mao dies and the rains come, what he has
painted will wash away.'[6]

Nevertheless, against the background of the American relationship with China
over the 1950s and 1960s, Nixon's vision of the future was breathtaking in its
radicalism. Writing in *Foreign Affairs* in 1967, Nixon expressed the opinion that

> taking the long view, we simply cannot afford to leave China forever outside the family
> of nations, there to nurture its fantasies, cherish its hates and threaten its neighbors.
> There is no place on this small planet for a billion of its potentially most able people
> to live in angry isolation.[7]

The peculiarly close historic relationship of the USA to China expressed itself most
forcefully through the 'China lobby' that saw in Taiwan the remnants of 'true'
China. This group, like most of the governmental advisors of the period, saw world
communism as a united block of expansionist countries. American policy after
Korea was to manage a containment of advancing communism in Asia, Europe,
South America and Africa.

Although Nixon's views were clearly those of a minority, both in the Democratic Party and on the right of his own Republican Party, there were threads that
linked the logic of Nixon's policies to the past. President Truman's Secretary of
State Dean Acheson had valiantly laboured and failed to square the improbable circle of Chiang Kai Shek's retreat to 'fortress' Taiwan under American protection,
combined with trying to drive a wedge between the Soviet Union and the newly
established PRC. Even after he failed, he remained convinced that there would
eventually be a Sino-Soviet falling out.

Such diplomatic and ideological subtleties were lost on President Eisenhower
and Acheson's Republican successor, John Foster Dulles, who typified the 'Cold

War warrior' in his depiction of the struggle against communism as God against godlessness; they put their trust in nuclear power with which America was capable of pursuing policies of 'massive retaliation'. Eisenhower was equally clear cut in seeing the Chinese as 'hysterical', 'irrational' and 'fanatical'; given that China was launched on the *Great Leap Forward* during this period, Eisenhower's views in this respect were more accurate than he could possibly have realised. However, in foreign policy, China's leaders were distinctly pragmatic and mirrored Nixon's and Kissinger's beliefs in the importance of 'balance of power'.

By contrast, Acheson before them had eschewed the 'blunderbuss' approach. For him geopolitics was not a moral crusade, but a pragmatic game of balance. In 1954, Acheson wrote to Truman that the balance of power was the best 'international sheriff'. He was the ultimate pragmatist who believed that the pursuit of peace could not be achieved by dogma and ideology. To an audience of military officers at the National War College in December 1949, Acheson asserted that America should 'limit objectives, to our ourselves away from the search for the absolute, to find out what is within our powers. . . . We must respect our opponents'.[8] Indeed, the threads of geopolitical pragmatism were to lead Dean Acheson, a fiercely loyal democrat, becoming an unlikely, but valued advisor to Nixon.

With the very public Soviet-Sino split of 1960, an earlier evaluation of the possibility of a rapprochement with China might have been expected of the Kennedy presidency. Although some of Kennedy's advisors seem to have harboured thoughts in this direction, there was no serious exploration of this possibility. With intelligence reports of the progress of China's nuclear programme, fear of nuclear proliferation increasing became Kennedy's major concern. Glenn Seaborg, chairman of the Atomic Energy Committee, noted Kennedy's remark in February 1962, 'the whole reason for the test ban treaty is related to the Chinese situation. Otherwise, it wouldn't be worth the disruption and fighting with Congress etc'.[9]

Far from being encouraged by the Chinese rift with the Soviets, a rift that Truman's Democrat administration had sought, Kennedy could only see the problems of a world that was moving from the bi-polar 'Cold War' line up, to something much more complex. He even seems to have entertained the idea of a first strike against the PRC nuclear facilities at Lop Nor and Lanzhou. A handwritten note to Averell Harriman, who was in Moscow to negotiate the Limited Test Ban Treaty, is illuminating in this regard: 'You should try to elicit Khrushchev's view of means of limiting or preventing Chinese nuclear development and his willingness either to take Soviet action or to accept US action aimed in this direction.'[10] These instructions give a strong hint that, with Russian backing, Kennedy might have been prepared to authorise a pre-emptive nuclear strike.

President Lyndon Johnson shared Kennedy's vision of a Communist world, which in spite of the Sino-Soviet split, was nevertheless homogeneously bent on an ideological conquest of the world. It is somewhat remarkable that Johnson and his advisers should have blundered into the quagmire of Vietnam without ever seriously questioning whether nationalism could override communist ideological brotherhood. When Vice President Johnson inherited the presidency after Kennedy's assassination, the Sino-Soviet split was three years old and one might have supposed that the development of an antagonistic relationship between the two great communist powers might have cast doubts on the homogeneity of the Communist world.

Even Johnson's Secretary of Defence Robert McNamara failed, by his own admission, to think through the strategies implicit in American involvement in Vietnam. As he stated in his 'mea culpa' of an autobiography, 'We misjudged then _as we have since_ the geopolitical intentions of our adversaries.'[11] Although Johnson's advisors Averell Harriman and Secretary of State Dean Rusk believed in an opening to China, the Texan president was adamant in his hostility. An exchange recorded by Johnson's future press secretary, Bill Moyers, was revealing: 'If we don't do something it'll go under—any day . . . they'll think with Kennedy dead we've lost heart. So they'll think we're yellow and don't mean what we say.' 'Who?' Moyers asked. 'The Chinese. The fellas in the Kremlin. . . . I'm not going to let Vietnam go the way of China.'[12] Yet his obsessive fear that the Chinese would enter the war as they had done in Korea, neither helped him prosecute the war in Vietnam nor nudged him to think creatively about the Chinese relationship.

By the time Nixon was elected president in 1968, even the pro-war politicians realised that the political will to fight a war was evaporating. Earlier in the year, MacNamara, after questioning the geopolitical and military logic of the administration's policies in Vietnam, resigned from Johnson's administration as secretary of defence. Although majority public opinion remained favourable to the war effort, as it did to the end, a clear shift in sentiment was now apparent. The appearance of stalemate at least gave ground to the possibility of rethinking Asian strategy. In this respect, Richard Nixon was the right man at the right time. To his good fortune he also discovered a brilliant National Security advisor Dr Henry Kissinger.

Heinz Alfred Kissinger, later Henry when the family moved to America, was born in 1923 in the village of Leutershausen, 30 miles east of Nuremberg. Kissinger's father Louis was a teacher who, as an orthodox Jew, lost his job when the 1935 Nuremberg Laws forced him out of his government post. After the promptings of his mother Paula, the Kissingers made a timely move to America in August 1938.

After serving with the American army in Europe, where he ended up working in counter intelligence, Kissinger went to Harvard in 1947 to study government and philosophy. In his vigorous intellectual belief in the possibility of 'free will', Kissinger focused admiration towards Metternich and Bismarck, the great nineteenth-century practitioners of power politics. His senior year thesis became legendary, not only for its 383 page length, the longest ever submitted either before or since, but also for its brilliance. He was duly awarded a summa cum laude.

In writing his doctoral dissertation, '*A World Restored: Metternich, Castlereagh and the Problems of Peace 1812–22*' (1957), Kissinger explored how the great statesmen of the period, through application of 'real-politik', had restored order to a

European world thrown into disorder by the French Revolution and the emergence of Napoleon Bonaparte. As an academic background, Kissinger could not have chosen a better subject with which to prepare for a post-revolutionary world in Asia. However, it was a chance meeting with future Kennedy White House favourite, Harvard Professor Arthur Schlesinger Jr, that started him along the road away from academia towards government. Schlesinger asked him to comment on a paper he had written attacking the Eisenhower–Dulles policy of 'massive retaliation'. Schlesinger was so impressed with Kissinger's commentary that he arranged for it to be published in *Foreign Affairs*, and its thesis formed the kernel of the Kennedy administration's 'flexible response' strategy.

It was as a renowned Harvard intellectual and strategy 'wonk' that Kissinger came to Nixon's attention. However, when he was elected, President Nixon had met Kissinger only once; the five-minute meeting took place at the Christmas cocktail party of the recently widowed Clare Booth Luce, whose husband Henry Luce, a leading light of the 'China Lobby', had been the editor and publisher behind *Time* magazine.

Nixon praised Kissinger's book on *Nuclear Weapons and Foreign Policy* (1957); in spite of the shortness of the meeting, a bond had been struck between Nixon, the edgy and aloof politician, and the dazzling and charismatic Harvard intellectual with a heavy German brogue. In spite of his social insecurities and his early difficulties with 'small talk', Kissinger possessed extraordinary talents for the job in hand; intimidating intellect apart, he had an insatiable appetite for work, a relish for detail, and above all the personal charm, humour and ability to flatter, which made him a superb negotiator.

Subsequently, Kissinger became a hate figure to the increasingly powerful 'neocon' right, who viewed him as an extemporiser for dealing with communists, while he has long been demonised by the left for his association with Nixon and the bombing of Cambodia. In fact, while in office, he remained close to the Washington Democrat elite; it indicated a talent for playing all sides that infuriated the ever-mistrustful Nixon. According to Nixon's Chief of Staff Bob Haldeman, '. . . in the evenings, a magical transformation took place. Touching glasses at a party with liberal friends, the belligerent Kissinger would suddenly become a dove–according to the reports that reached Nixon'.[13] The paradox was that the right wing Kissinger was also the outsider Jewish immigrant who, at first, often felt less at home in Republican establishment circles.

Whatever their differences in character, the 'odd couple', as Nixon and Kissinger were described by the latter's biographer Walter Isaacson, shared a passion for foreign affairs and a matching framework for how to set about the task. The first thing that Kissinger and Nixon agreed upon was the need to bypass the elephantine and bureaucratic state department. William Rogers may have been secretary of state under Nixon, but it was the president and his national security advisor who ran foreign policy from the Oval Office. As Nixon later admitted,

'From the outset of my administration I planned to direct foreign policy from the White House.'[14]

By curious chance, Kissinger's role for Nixon came closely to resemble that of his hero Metternich with the Hapsburg Emperor Francis I of Austria. Within the Nixon–Kissinger 'double act', it is interesting to speculate on who performed the greater role. It seems clear that the intellectual drive to change America's relationship with China started with Nixon. Kissinger, who was undoubtedly in tune with the president, was recruited as a precociously talented implementer of Nixon's vision. Both Lord Black, the biographer of Franklin D. Roosevelt and Richard Nixon, and Sir James Goldsmith, who were friendly with both men, gave the balance of intellectual credit for American foreign policy in this period to Nixon. Perhaps this was inevitable in view of Nixon's long-held and 'wonkish' interest in foreign policy and his position as president. However, given Kissinger's phenomenal intellect and already proven innovative approach to defence strategy, he undoubtedly brought intellectual creativity to foreign policy; he also enabled Nixon to wrest foreign policy away from the State Department and to bring it into the White House. Even more importantly, his execution of difficult diplomatic tasks proved quite brilliant.

It is interesting to note the differences in their books; Nixon, always the generalist compared to Kissinger's forensic analysis and bludgeoning logic. However, like all great partnerships, Nixon and Kissinger gave every appearance of being 'joined at the hip', and to attempt to separate out their achievements would miss the point. Their strength lay in their togetherness in strategy, if not in personal relationship. At one point, Nixon's paranoid envy of Kissinger's increasing fame and celebrity status led him to ask Bob Haldeman, the White House chief of staff 'to devise a method of cutting off contact between Kissinger and the press through the White House switchboard'.[15]

On assuming office, Nixon launched a three-pronged international strategy; to achieve detente with the Soviet Union through Strategic Arms Limitation Talks (SALT) and a Non-Proliferation Treaty; to engage in talks with the North Vietnamese, and pursue a policy of 'Vietnamisation' in the South; and lastly, to make conciliatory noises towards China with the hope of drawing them into the broad tent of global security.

This was no easy task. It is hard to envisage that just 30 years ago two of the world's largest countries could find it difficult to find channels of communication. Yet this was the task that faced Nixon and Kissinger. Nixon therefore approached Nikolai Ceauşescu, the Rumanian Communist dictator, to convey a message to the Chinese that the USA was keen to talk. Kissinger was also encouraged by Air Marshall Sher Ali Khan, who briefed Kissinger on his meetings with the Chinese leaders, and informed him that in foreign affairs they were far from being the irrational ideologues often portrayed. Indeed, he characterised their leadership as 'disciplined, pragmatic and reliable'.[16] Subsequent to this meeting, Pakistan's President Yahya Khan was also called upon to channel communications.

If the means by which the Nixon administration approached its task appears somewhat dysfunctional, and its choice of channels bizarre or even dubious, the peculiarities of the situation need to be put in context. Nixon risked the humiliation of a Chinese rebuff; he had to be sure, not only that they would respond to his overtures, but also that they would be willing to discuss the possibility of a relationship in spite of the obvious differences over Vietnam and Taiwan.

A rebuff could have damaged the negotiations with the North Vietnamese at the Paris peace talks, jeopardised attempts at detente with the Soviet Union, and risked alienation of Nixon's relations with Congress and the right wing of his own party that included such staunch anti-communists as Senator Barry Goldwater and Californian Governor Ronald Reagan. Indeed, in order to allay the fears of the right, and to show the Chinese that a conciliatory policy did not necessarily imply weakness, Nixon announced an anti-ballistic missiles (ABM) programme to combat the Chinese nuclear threat: 'The Chinese threat against our population as well as the danger of an accidental attack, cannot be ignored.'[17]

Needless to say that the 'carrot and stick' approach to China opened the possibility of confusion, both within China and the US administration, as to Nixon's real aims. The complex process of communication with China moreover had to be carried out without the knowledge of the State Department for fear that internecine turf wars would disrupt the diplomatic process. Many 'Russia' watchers within the State Department assumed that any approach to China would damage the moves towards detente with the Soviets. By contrast, Kissinger's analysis, which in hindsight proved correct, was that 'the Soviets were more likely to be conciliatory if they feared that we would otherwise seek a rapprochement with Peking'.[18]

At the beginning of Nixon's presidency, China policy was not even discussed at cabinet level. At the National Security Council meeting on 14 August 1969, Nixon startled his colleagues by suggesting that in connection with the skirmishes being reported on the Sino-Soviet borders, it was more likely to be the Soviets who were the aggressors. This was a shock for many who were armed with the memories of the Chinese invasions during the Korean War. At this meeting, Nixon also argued that it would not be in America's interests for the Soviets to defeat China.

At the same time that Nixon was preparing the political argument for a move towards China, the Chinese leadership itself was re-evaluating its foreign policy. As early as 1956, Mao had been startled by the ease with which Khrushchev had repudiated Stalin. Invasions of Hungary and Czechoslovakia had also raised suspicions. Then in 1958, Mao stunned the Soviets by turning down their proposals for military cooperation that had been under consideration since 1955. By 1960, Mao was convinced that the Soviet Union had been usurped by revisionists. Furthermore, Khrushchev attempted to bully China in a way that Stalin would never have contemplated. After returning from Washington via Beijing, First Secretary Khrushchev upbraided the Chinese foreign minister by telling him that 'In military matters, I listen to you as a Marshall. Now within the Party, I am a First Secretary, you are only a Politburo member. You should listen to me.'[19]

When Enver Hoxha, Albania's communist dictator, denounced the Soviet Union, China moved to replace the Soviets as their backers with offers of grain and funds. The rupture was sealed when Khrushchev angrily attacked the Chinese delegation at the Romanian Party Congress. Now the Soviets had a competitor for the leadership of world Communism. This was particularly reflected in an increasing attempt by Mao to build a block of influence in Africa, and between 1960 and 1962 the number of delegations to the African continent doubled. Influence in Asia was also expanded. A 'Treaty of Friendship and Mutual Non-aggression' was signed with Burma in 1960, followed by agreements with Nepal and Cambodia. In the same year, a treaty concerning dual nationality was signed with Indonesia, and relations were improved with Mongolia and Afghanistan. Funding was also provided to Sri Lanka.

The Sino-Soviet split of the 1960s had clearly been a watershed event, but with America increasingly drawn into Indochina, and with Taiwan launching raids on mainland China, they, like the Americans, did not perceive the opportunity for rapprochement. Also quite probably, the Chinese did not think of the Soviet split as permanent. Indeed, when Khrushchev was toppled in a coup in 1964, on the same day that China detonated its first nuclear device, Mao and Zhou Enlai had expected to restore relations.

The nature of their intentions was made evident when Zhou headed a 50-man delegation to celebrate the remembrance of the Bolshevik Revolution in November. However, Brezhnev made it clear that he would perpetuate 'Khrushchevism without Khrushchev'.[20] Far from seeking a rapprochement with Mao, the Soviet Defence Minister Marshall Malinovsky made the ultimate cocktail party gaffe when he remarked to Zhou's colleague He Long, 'We've already got rid of Khrushchev; you ought to follow our example and get rid of Mao Zedong.'[21]

In the second half of the decade, China's concern increased further with the invasion of Czechoslovakia in 1968 and the enunciation of the Brezhnev Doctrine that suggested that Communist states, outside the Soviet Union, should only be entitled to a limited sovereignty. Given that Brezhnev left it unstated whether this should only apply to the states of Eastern Europe, it left open the possibility of application to China. The progress of detente between the Soviet Union and America also threatened complete geopolitical isolation. However, it was the border clashes at the mouth of the Ussuri River in 1969, the same location as the first battle between Russia and China in 1652, which increased the urgency for China to review its foreign policy options.

Historically, much of the Eastern Soviet Empire was disputed. In the late nineteenth century, as the Qing dynasty declined, the Russians had seized vast territories amounting to 650,000 square miles. A Russian foreign minister of the period asserted that 'The absorption by Russia of a considerable portion of the Chinese

Empire is only a matter of time.'[22] The Chinese leadership was not unaware that Russia had been an expansionist empire since the fifteenth century. The Russian Revolution did not appear to change this appetite. In the aftermath of the Bolshevik Revolution, the Soviets reneged on a promise to annul the unequal treaties made by the tsars, and in 1921 they sponsored the Mongolian People's Revolutionary Party, and brought a traditional Chinese satellite within the Russian orbit. By the 1930s, the province of Sinkiang was virtually controlled by the Soviets.

Added to these historic disputes were the memories of Stalin's initial condescension towards Mao and his agrarian-based revolution. For China, the real fear was of Soviet, not American expansionism. Indeed, Nixon's 'Vietnamisation' policy, far from reassuring China, threatened the possibility that as a weakened America withdrew from Asia, the Soviets would replace them. Remarkably, when Kissinger and Zhou Enlai opened up to each other, the Chinese premier encouraged America to sustain its interests in Asia. In the late 1960s, America's Asian Empire was actively welcomed by the Chinese as a bulwark to the Soviet Union.

Throughout the summer of 1969, disputes spread along the Ussuri River. Brezhnev and his Foreign Minister Kosygin became increasing paranoid about the Chinese threat, and forces were increasingly transferred from the Western front to the East. By mid-1973, the Soviets had transferred 1 million soldiers to the Chinese border plus a fleet of 150 ships in the Pacific. Also, 100 ABMs were stationed around Moscow and Leningrad. In the ultimate gesture in 1969, the Soviets, through overtures made to the USA through attachés in Tokyo and Canberra, and later at higher levels, floated the idea of a joint pre-emptive strike on Chinese nuclear facilities.

With the heightened state of conflict between China and the Soviets therefore, the timing of Nixon's presidential victory was highly propitious in regard to his ambition for a Chinese rapprochement. In spite of the many difficulties in communication, it became clear that within a year of Nixon's presidential victory, his secret channels and public utterances were beginning to produce a favourable response. Between November 1969 and June 1970, American diplomats around the world reported ten instances of conversations with their Chinese counterparts. This was in stark contrast to the frosty withdrawals that had been a feature of chance meetings between American and Chinese diplomats since the Korea War. Indeed, it was this that persuaded Nixon and Kissinger to launch American Ambassador Walter Stoessel on his Warsaw charm offensive. The response was immediate, with a Chinese invitation to Stoessel to their embassy followed by an agreement to recommence in earnest the stalled Warsaw negotiations.

If the Chinese were encouraged by the Stoessel encounter, they must have been even more impressed by Nixon's foreign policy report to Congress on 18 February 1970, in which he proposed the 'one and a half war strategy'; Nixon argued:

> ... the nuclear capability of our strategic and theater nuclear forces serves as a deterrent to full-scale Soviet Attack on NATO Europe or Chinese attack on our Asian

allies; the prospects for a coordinated two-front attack on our allies by Russia and China are low because of the risks of nuclear war and the improbabilities of Sino-Soviet co-operation.[23]

Previously, defence spending and strategy had been predicated on a simultaneous attack by both Russia and China. Kissinger successfully argued the illogicality of this former approach, as any such co-ordinated attack would almost inevitably lead to nuclear conflict. Importantly, this change in defence policy signalled to the Chinese that the new American administration understood that China was an independent political entity, not to be treated as part of an amorphous ideological grouping.

Indeed, it was now clear from the Warsaw talks that China's current concerns, contrary to the wisdom of the academic sinologists, were more geopolitical than regional; in other words, the Chinese concerns about the Soviet Union far out-weighed their regional concerns with regard to Vietnam and Taiwan. For the Chinese, this had come into sharper focus as American intentions in South East Asia were more clearly revealed. As Henry Kissinger observed in *The White House Years* (1979), 'The Chinese . . . saw the scale of our effort in Vietnam as disproportionate to any objectives to be achieved, and hence believed its only rational purpose could be to turn Indochina into a springboard for an eventual assault on China'.[24] Thus, when Zhou Enlai understood in early 1970, before most Americans, that the USA was on its way out of Vietnam, the Chinese also began to perceive the possibilities developing out of the Warsaw talks.

At the 136th Warsaw meeting, the possibility of an American government visit to China was finally accepted by the Chinese ambassador. Throughout 1970, positive signals came from both sides. Nixon lifted some trade restrictions. In July, a number of American prisoners were released. Actions were beginning to match words. On October 1st National Day, the American writer Edgar Snow was invited to stand 'side by side with Mao at the review of the annual parade'.[25] Meanwhile, in an interview with *Time* magazine for October, Nixon boldy asserted that 'if there is anything I can do before I die, it is to go to China'.[26]

The thaw in the relations of the two powers now advanced rapidly. After President Khan's visit to China in November 1970, he brought back a handwritten letter from Zhou and Mao; in a regression to nineteenth-century diplomacy, the Pakistan ambassador would not hand over the letter but would only read it out to Nixon and Kissinger at the White House. Another message of invitation was relayed through the good offices of Rumania's President Ceauşescu. The 'China watchers' at the State Department now noted that Soviet leader Leonid Brezhnev had replaced the USA as the great hate figure in the Chinese press.

Most spectacularly however, the developing Sino-American cordiality became public through 'ping pong'. At the 31st World Table Tennis Championship in Nagoya in March 1971, the American player Glenn Cowan befriended the Chinese triple world champion, Chuang Tse-tung, and gave him a tee-shirt. A present was reciprocated the next day, along with an invitation for the whole USA team to

visit China. A week later, a stunned American table tennis team was being welcomed by Zhou in person at the Great Hall of the People. On the same day, the
USA lifted further trade embargoes. The American team was duly invited back to
China. Ping-Pong diplomacy heralded a start to normalisation of relations between
the two countries.

Now finally, after this prolonged period of 'testing the water', a formal invitation to come to China was received once more through the Pakistan channel. Who
would go? Having considered and rejected George Bush (senior), Nelson Rockefeller, Alexander Haig and David Bruce, head of the Paris peace delegation, Nixon
settled on Kissinger. The relatively unknown Henry Kissinger was selected, almost
certainly because he shared with Nixon a complete understanding and intellectual
support for the job at hand. While Kissinger spent the summer swotting up on
Chinese history and culture, an elaborate charade was planned to keep Kissinger's
trip secret.

Firstly, Secretary of State William Rogers, still in the dark over the White
House's Chinese diplomacy, had to be persuaded to overrule the State Department's objections to a Far Eastern tour, planned as camouflage for Kissinger's visit
to Beijing. A trip to the sub-continent ended in Islamabad, where, with the help of
President Khan, Kissinger feigned illness, and supposedly rested up at the presidential guesthouse. In fact, he was flown by a Pakistan International Airlines (PIA)
Boeing to Beijing in the early hours of 9 July 1971, accompanied by three assistants and two astonished secret service agents. The plan went smoothly apart from
Kissinger forgetting his shirts; he was to meet Zhou Enlai with an ill-fitting shirt
borrowed from a colleague that was tagged 'Made in Taiwan'.

Zhou had also left little to chance. The US journalist James Reston, who happened to have been due in Beijing at the same time as Kissinger, was refused permission to fly from Canton to Beijing, and was literally put on a 'slow train'. Less
easy was Korean leader Kim Il Sung, who by previous arrangement also visited
China on 9 July; Zhou spent the day flitting between his incompatible guests, both
in ignorance of the other's presence.

Kissinger found Zhou to be a man of extraordinary intelligence, charm and
skill. He was also delighted to find that 'The Chinese were cold practitioners of
power politics, a far cry from the romantic humanitarians imagined in Western
Intellectual circles.'[27] Kissinger spent seven hours with Zhou on the first day of
this two-day visit, and both sides laid out their positions. This confirmed to each
side that their disagreements over Taiwan and Indochina did not stand in the way
of a geopolitical arrangement, which was aimed at facing down Soviet expansionism. Most importantly, in a conversation that was some 20 years overdue, a senior
American government official was able to explain face to face to the Chinese government that American policy in Asia was not aimed at the overthrow of communist China.

Kissinger returned to Chaklala airport in Pakistan on 11 July, and sent back
the code word 'Eureka' to indicate the success of his mission to Nixon. An ecstatic

Nixon immediately broke security arrangements to demand a full report. Four days later, a co-ordinated world announcement was made with Nixon appearing on television to tell a startled public about Kissinger's secret mission to China, and to herald the president's forthcoming visit. 'The meeting between the leaders of China and the United States is to seek the normalization of relations between the two countries and also to exchange views on questions of concern to the two sides.'[28]

Overnight Kissinger became one of the most famous men on the planet. A grateful Nixon took him to celebrate dinner with crab accompanied by a bottle of Chateau Lafite-Rothschild 1961. As Kissinger had forecast, the Soviets did not react with hostility. Indeed, talks with the Soviets now speeded up, and before Nixon's own visit to Beijing he hosted Soviet Foreign Minister Gromyko in Washington; subsequent to his going to China, Nixon also visited Moscow in May 1972.

If Kissinger's trip to China was pure drama, Nixon's visit was a theatrical spectacular. Such is the power of the image of his visit that it now lies rooted in modern culture, although its most famous expression in the form of the John Adams' opera, *Nixon in China* (1987), in sympathy with liberal historic revision, is hardly flattering to Nixon or Kissinger. Both Mao and Nixon were obsessed by the use of media. Kissinger himself would comment on the '...monomaniacal obsession of the Nixon White House with public relations'.[29] As Nixon descended the steps of his plane when it arrived in Beijing, other passengers were held back by security guards so as to provide a lone pictorial of the president. At the bottom of the steps, Nixon dramatically extended his hand to Zhou in the full knowledge of John Foster Dulles's refusal to shake Zhou's hand at the Geneva Conference in 1954.

Later, at Mao's residence, *The People's Daily* photographed the epic moment when Nixon and Mao greeted each other. Indeed, clasping both his hands Mao greeted him with the jest, 'Our common old friend, Generalissimo Chiang Kai-shek, doesn't approve of this.'[30] For 1,000 years, world leaders, Ghengis Khan among them, had come to pay homage at the court of the 'Middle Kingdom' but Nixon must have been the first to have his every mouthful at every banquet recorded for posterity. To strains of *'America the Beautiful'*, Nixon was forced to drink copious amounts of Mao-Tai in ritual toasting; an experience that may have numbed the president's senses enough to make palatable the excruciatingly boring revolutionary Chinese theatre which followed. At least Nixon did not have to prostrate himself in *kowtow* to Mao, as the British diplomat Lord Macartney had famously refused to do to the Chinese Emperor in 1793.

Behind the scenes, Kissinger and Zhou worked feverishly to produce a joint communiqué that would satisfy both sides. For this purpose, the two negotiators were finely matched. In a remarkable and revolutionary document of its type, both sides itemised the issues on which they could not agree, as well as stating their common ground. Taiwan was the thorniest issue around which the two sides had to find suitable words, but even that was resolved without bitterness in a way that heralded the 'One China' myth that continues to the present day. Taiwan was an obstacle and not the focus of rapprochement. The essence of the discussions and the point of the meetings were 'on the requirements of the balance of power, the international order, and long term trends of world peace'.[31]

Some of the American press acted with hostility to the Shanghai communiqué. The *Detroit Press* screamed, 'They got Taiwan; we got egg rolls' while the *Boston Globe* reported, 'Nixon makes concessions on Taiwan, Pledges pullout'.[32] In reality, the Chinese had been told that America could not renege on its 1954 security pact with Taiwan, and this had been accepted. In general however, the historic significance of the treaty was recognised around the world. For a generation there had been speculation that China would be the instigator of a third world war. This possibility was now averted.

For China, Mao and Zhou had gained a quasi-ally against the Soviets, and with entry to the United Nations also gained at the end of 1971, their country's long period of isolation was now over. For Nixon and Kissinger, they had achieved a transition from the instability that had threatened from the end of 1960 with the development of a Chinese nuclear capability. Also, they had succeeded in rupturing the USA–Soviet Union/Chinese bi-polarity, which had hitherto dominated the post-war era. A tripartite system of global security now pertained, and Kissinger looked forward to a future in which Europe and Japan would add to this balance of forces. In *Diplomacy* (1994), Kissinger noted that '. . . the soaring rhetoric of the Kennedy period had set goals that were beyond America's physical and emotional capacities'.[33] The Nixon-China visit was a logical realisation that America did not have the economic resources to sustain its ambitions for global balance alone.

Apart from this however, America's greatest gain came from the opening up of China to knowledge of the West. The televised visit of the Chinese 'ping pong' team to the USA showed Chinese audiences for the first time that America was not rotting at the core and about to collapse. Quite the opposite; as Kuang-Sheng Liao has observed, 'the more China became aware of her backwardness, the more attractive Westernisation became and leftism, with its anti-foreign bent, lost its appeal'.[34] Anti-American demonstrations in China fell from 260 in 1970 to 16 in 1972 and 0 by 1978. In the long term, the opening up of the country to international communication sounded the death knell of China's socialist economic system. The Nixon-Kissinger rapprochement with China provided their finest hour and their most memorable achievement; it was perhaps the most important geopolitical event of the second half of the twentieth century but not one for which either has received due credit, as their diplomatic triumph came to be overshadowed by the opprobrium of the Vietnam War and by the Watergate scandal.

35

The Night of the Intellectuals

Bangladesh–Pakistan: 1965–73

By 1969 Ayub Khan, by now in poor health after a bout of pneumonia, was a dispirited leader of his country. In spite of a decade of robust economic growth, the Pakistan president, forever damaged by the lost war with India, could claim little credit, other than by his spurning of the allures of socialist command economics. Free market policies pursued by his Finance Minister Shoaib, a World Bank executive, and his successor N.M. Uquali had ensured a significant out-performance of the Pakistan economy vis-à-vis Indian economy; indeed, in spite of the uneven division of assets at Partition, by the end of the 1960s Pakistan's GDP per capita was 30 per cent higher than that of India.

However, Ayub's political enemies merely pointed to the concentration of wealth in a few hands, including his son Gauhar Ayub. Indeed the chief economist at the Pakistan Planning Commission, Dr Mahbub Ul-Haq, estimated that 66 per cent of the entire industrial capital was concentrated in the hands of 22 families; they also controlled 80 per cent of banking and 97 per cent of insurance. After being forced to use the army to maintain calm in the cities, Ayub Khan concluded that his time was up, and resigned on 25 March 1969.

Pakistan's Army Chief, General Mohammed Yahya Khan, stepped into the political vacuum. He immediately declared martial law and abolished the 1962 Constitution. He also proposed elections for a Constituent Assembly to draft a constitution within 120 days, though reserving the right for himself to veto the outcome.

In reality, Yahya Khan largely ignored both the political and bureaucrat classes, handing out the most powerful jobs in government to his military friends. In contrast to the austere Ayub, Yahya Khan was a flamboyant outgoing man with a reputation for hard drinking and womanising. The Nawab of Kalabagh described him as 'a debauch and drunkard'.[1] He once famously failed to appear from his bedroom for a meeting to bid farewell to the visiting Shah of Iran; a tremulous servant asked the president's mistress to enter Yahya Khan's rooms to wake him, where she found a famous Pakistani actress performing fellatio on her country's leader.

Yahya Khan sought to calm the situation in East Pakistan by promising a higher level of government expenditure in Bengal. In the West, he also satisfied a long-standing grievance by restoring the political apparatus of the four provinces of Pakistan and lifting bans on political activity. The new president also accepted Bengalis' demands for 'one man-one vote' and promised elections to be held in 1970.

Newly elected US President Nixon, who had visited Pakistan twice as Eisenhower's vice president, and three times subsequently, again visited the sub-continent in mid-summer 1969. Yahya Khan was a friend, and it was through his good offices that Nixon's offers of talks with the Chinese, at the beginning of 1970, were relayed to Zhou Enlai. Henry Kissinger, Nixon's first-term national security advisor, would eventually take off on a secret flight to Beijing from Pakistan for the talks with Maoist China that would bring about the most dramatic and possibly the most beneficial shift in the geopolitical landscape in the post-war period.

Unfortunately for Yahya Khan, his early attempts to pacify the political situation in Pakistan, had merely papered over the deepening fault lines in the edifice of post-independence Pakistan. National elections held on 7 December 1970, brought a result which the traditional power brokers in West Pakistan must long have feared.

Sheikh Mujib, having been able to unite not only the Awami League but also the whole of Bengal, behind his six-point programme for full regional autonomy for East Pakistan, won 160 out of 162 seats in the East, out of a Pakistan parliamentary total of 300. In theory, Mujib could now form a Pakistan government dominated by his eastern constituency. His programme called for a radically decentralised political structure, with the powers of the centre stripped down to defence, foreign affairs and currency.

It seems likely, however, that even this confederated proposal was a cover for a more radical agenda; Pakistan intelligence managed to bug a meeting in which Mujib declared that 'My aim is to establish Bangladesh: .... Who will challenge me once the elections are over?'[2] Meanwhile in the West, Zulfikar Ali Bhutto's Pakistan People's Party (PPP) won 81 seats out of 140.

The Awami League hardliners now pressed increasingly publicly for full independence for East Pakistan (Bangladesh). The clamour for independence heightened after a dilatory response from Islamabad to the aftermath of a devastating cyclone which destroyed vast swaths of Bengal and drowned an estimated 250,000 people. Mujib continued to press his claims to form a government. He raised fears that if his moderate approach failed, he would be swept away by the hardliners. On 17 April 1971, Mujib asserted that the army 'must come to their senses. Can't they see that I alone can save East Pakistan from Communism? If they make a fight of it, I shall lose the leadership within a few years. Naxalites will take action in my name. They will even carry my picture at first, to gain the confidence of the people. Then, they will take over.'[3]

For Yahya Khan and the Western establishment, the formation of a Mujib administration could see a potentially permanent shift in political power to Bengal, perhaps even the removal of the capital to Dhaka in the East. To many Pakistanis in the West, this was unthinkable. With stupendous arrogance, given the minority position of his party, Bhutto declared that 'No constitution could be framed, nor could any government at the centre be run without my party's co-operation . . . [and he was] not prepared to occupy the opposition benches in the National Assembly.'[4]

A power sharing arrangement with the West, which Yahya Khan proposed to Sheikh Mujib, was naturally spurned. Bhutto also stirred the pot by threatening to boycott the first meeting of the new Parliament slated for 3 March 1971, unless Mujib agreed to a power sharing agreement with West Pakistan and settlement of all constitutional issues. Mujib again refused. Indeed, Mujib countered that he would not attend the new Pakistan Parliament until martial law was abandoned and power transferred to the majority Awami League. Back in Dhaka, Mujib raised the stakes by declaring, 'Our struggle today is a fight for freedom, a fight for independence.'[5] In the meantime, national strikes paralysed East Pakistan.

With the political situation bubbling to a crisis, Yahya Khan went to Dhaka on 15 March 1971 to negotiate a settlement with Mujib but left without success. He was not helped by Bhutto's initial refusal to go to East Bengal to participate in negotiations, and subsequently by his insistence that the PPP be included in any resulting government. Mujib refused to take Bhutto, 'a Trojan horse' into his cabinet.[6] American Ambassador Farland called for a peaceful political settlement between East and West but warned the State Department that military intervention was imminent. In return they advised him that 'We do not believe that we can play a useful role as a middleman or mediator in an essentially Pakistani domestic concern.'[7]

On Pakistan's National Day on 23 March, Awami League supporters took to the streets and raised banners for an independent Bangladesh. Sheikh Mujib and the Awami League leadership meanwhile called for a relationship of 'confederation' with West Pakistan. The proposal was little more than a fig leaf; there can have been little doubt in the West, that 'confederation' would have been a short step to full independence for Bengal. Late on 23 March, Yahya Khan complained to Mujib that 'The whole world was laughing at him.'[8] Yahya Khan was at end of this tether. He finally decided to take decisive and unilateral action. In the early hours of 25 March 1971, he launched 'Operation Searchlight' in East Pakistan. Sheikh Mujib was denounced for treason and arrested. A news blackout and curfew were imposed. In Dhaka, the capital of East Pakistan, foreign journalists were confined to the Intercontinental Hotel.

For weeks, the Pakistan army based in Dhaka had been confined to barracks as the Bengali population ran riot. When 'Operation Searchlight' was launched, it unleashed a premeditated reign of terror of medieval brutality, Later the Hamoodur Rahman Commission would conclude that 'It was as if a ferocious animal having been kept chained and starved was suddenly let loose.'[9]

The Pakistan army swept through Dhaka, slaughtering the leaders of the Awami League and the Bengali 'intelligentsia' in their homes. A lucky few survived. Runa Alam, now a Washington-based financier, was saved because her scientist parents, formerly based in West Pakistan, had guards posted at their home by a Pakistan general who was a friend. The following day, the family, with their baby daughter, managed to find their way to the border to make their escape. The so-called *Night of the Intellectuals*, in which thousands of Bengali Pakistani academics, scientists, teachers, lawyers, students and artists were murdered by their own army, remains one of the most shocking, though least known, of Asia's post-war atrocities. 14 December is still mourned as *Shaheed Buddhijibi Dibosh* (the day of the martyred intellectuals).

The Dhaka intelligentsia was not the only target. The Pakistan army had also turned on Bengal's Hindu and other minority populations; in May an order was issued for the ethnic cleansing of all Hindus. Brigadier Mian Taskeenudin recalled that 'Many junior officers took the law into their own hands to deal with so-called miscreants. . . . The discipline of the Pakistani Army, as was generally understood, had broken down.'[10] While the official Pakistan government report under Hamoodur Rahman concluded that 26,000 were killed, most subsequent estimates have been in the hundreds of thousands though some go as high as 3 million. *The New York Times* concluded that in Dhaka alone some 35,000 people were killed in the opening days of 'Operation Searchlight'. In addition, as many as 200,000 Bengali women are thought to have been raped with reports that some were even kept as sex slaves in the Pakistan army's Dhaka cantonment. Millions of refugees fled across the border to India.

Meanwhile President Nixon and the State Department remained silent. Telegrams from the American consulate, which reported the atrocities in Dhaka from the opening night, were ignored by the White House. On 7 April *The New York Times* complained that 'Washington's persistent silence on recent events in Pakistan is increasingly incomprehensible in light of eye witness evidence that the Pakistan Army has engaged in indiscriminate slaughter.'[11]

However, *The New York Times* was wrong in describing the US government's silence as 'incomprehensible'; it was completely comprehensible to those in the know, such as Ambassador Farland. At the same time as the crisis in East Pakistan crisis was coming to a head, world-changing negotiations to bring about a historic reconciliation between the USA and China were being carried on with Yahya Khan acting as an intermediary. On 27 April, just a month after the Pakistan army's assault on Bengal, Kissinger received the crucial message inviting a secret US envoy to Beijing. American Democrat Party leaders were rightly appalled at Nixon's apparent disregard for human rights in Bangladesh. Revelations that arms exports to Pakistan were continuing brought howls of criticism from Senator Edward Kennedy. On the 3 May, *Time* magazine described Dhaka as 'a city of the dead'.[12]

Nixon did eventually yield to the arms ban, though he refused to suspend aid. However, he exhorted his administration, 'Don't squeeze Yahya at this time.'[13] Indeed, on the 31 August, Nixon wrote a personal note to Yahya Khan, in which he confided:

> ...I want you to know that without your personal assistance the profound break-through in relations between the USA and [Peoples Republic of China] would never have been accomplished. . . . Those who want a more peaceful world in the generations to come will be forever in your debt.[14]

However, Nixon also used his influence with Yahya not to execute Mujib, who had secretly been put on trial for treason.

As Christopher Hitchens polemic work *The Trial of Henry Kissinger* (2001) has shown, some political commentators tend to ignore the moral dilemma faced by the Nixon administration. 'Realpolitik' required hard and sometimes impossible moral choices. Pakistan was an ally in the Cold War against the Soviet Union. In addition by speaking out over Pakistani atrocities, the Nixon administration might have let slip the possibility of reconciliation with China, and the securing of a long-term global peace. In practical terms too, there was little that America could have done to restrain an out of control Pakistan army and the massacres it was perpetrating.

With refugees pouring across the border into India, the international reper-cussions of Yahya's actions now became apparent. Indira Gandhi told the BBC, 'We have no intention of absorbing these people here_ no matter what. I am absolutely clear.'[15] Apart from the refugee issue, for India, the opportunity to weaken Pak-istan was irresistible. Prime Minister Indira Gandhi created the preconditions for this goal by signing a treaty of friendship with the Soviets on 9 August 1971.

Within East Pakistan meanwhile, guerrilla fighters, the *Mukti Bahini*, upped the tempo of resistance to the occupying West Pakistan army. In November, Indira Gandhi finally unleashed the Indian army against East and West Pakistan. At the United Nations, the US Ambassador George Bush (Senior) accused India of being 'the major aggressor'.[16] Although the United Nations Assembly voted 104 to 11 for a ceasefire motion, India's new ally, the Soviet Union, threw down a veto in the UN Security Council.

Pakistan's forces in the East were annihilated, while in the West, the Pakistan army was running short of fuel. Nixon raised the stakes by calling a startled Soviet agriculture minister, Vladimir Matskevich, who happened to be visiting Washing-ton. The message Nixon asked him to relay to Moscow was blunt; '. . . if the Indians continue their military operations, we must inevitably look toward a confrontation between the Soviet Union and the United States. The Soviet Union has a treaty with India; we have one with Pakistan.'[17] China too, while refraining from military ac-tion, began to put pressure on India to bring the war to an end.

Bhutto, now deputy prime minister, addressed the United Nations Security Council again on 15 December, and, in another extravagant performance, denounced France and Britain, while praising China and the USA. Bhutto capped his dramatic display by bursting into tears, tearing up his notes and storming out of the chamber after vowing 'a thousand years of war' with India and declaring that he 'would not be a party to legalizing aggression'.[18]

On the evening of 16 December, Indira Gandhi, having taken some 93,000 Pakistan soldiers as prisoner, volunteered a ceasefire in the conflict now waging in West Pakistan. The East, soon to become Bangladesh, was lost to Pakistan forever, but at least the West was to be saved as an independent nation. For Yahya Khan, the loss of East Pakistan was a disaster. He was shouted at by former support-ers. A pro-West Bengali leader complained that 'Yahya kept drinking while East Pakistan was sinking into the ocean.'[19] The fall of Yahya Khan was inevitable; the rise of Bhutto equally so. Pakistan's post-independence experiment in presidential democracy was over.

So why did constitutional democracy and national unity fail in Pakistan where it appeared to succeed so relatively well in neighbouring India? Inevitably some commentators point to the apparent contradictions inherent in the political doc-trine implicit in Islam. However, Islamic practice in Pakistan was far from doctri-naire. At independence, Jinnah proclaimed to the Pakistani people, '. . . you are free to go to your temples, you are free to go to your mosques or to any other place of worship in this state of Pakistan. You may belong to any religion or caste or creed'.[20] Toleration thus asserted by Pakistan's founders was barely compatible with the doctrines of an Islamic state. Ambivalence was implicit in the preamble to the 1956 Constitution; the document insisted on *Allah's* sovereignty over man but did not clarify whether *Sharia* law would play a part in the legal system.

The tentative place for Islam did not satisfy Pakistan's *Mullahs*. The rapid in-crease in Pakistan's urban population after Partition had brought to political promi-nence a more radical branch of Islam. Historically, the Islam of the countryside had been dominated by moderate Sufis, who chose not to wield political power; how-ever, *Jamaat-e-Islami* (the Islamic Society), founded in 1941 by Maulana Maududi, found a ready audience for a more radical and political brand of Islam in Pakistan's burgeoning cities and small towns.

Indeed, it was street violence led by Maulana that led to a brief period of mar-tial law in 1953, when Governor General Ghulam Muhammad dismissed Prime Minister Nazimuddin and asked General Ayub Khan to restore order. Within the army too, younger officer cadres were more attracted to *Jamaat-e-Islami*, even if the higher echelons remained highly westernised and firmly rooted in the moderniser camp. Nevertheless, taken as a whole, radical Islam never became the mainstream in Pakistan political life; arguably radical groups, at least in the early period of Pak-istan history, played a smaller role in the political life of the nation than in Islamic Malaysia where democratic government quickly took root.

In the opinion of some, the low level of education also made Pakistan unsuit-able for democratic government. By 1990 adult literacy was just 36.4 per cent;

female literacy was just 23 per cent. However, similar levels of illiteracy were also apparent in India. Unlike India though, Pakistan leaders failed to break the feudal structure of social deference. Land reform in Pakistan barely scratched the surface of a redistribution, which could have created an independent agricultural electorate. As it was, the continuation of the *Zamindari* (landlord) system sustained a feudal structure which was antipathetic to democracy.

In terms of democratic deficit, it could also be argued that the Muslim League was significantly more fractured than the Congress Party in India. Fifty-seven per cent of the population of Karachi were refugees in the 1951 census, and accounted for an astonishing 46 per cent of the population of Pakistan in the 12 largest cities. Jinnah's Muslim League was fatally split between these urban refugees (*Muhajirs*), the landed aristocracy and the Bengali Muslim Leaguers.

Yet, for all these socio-political drawbacks to the establishment of democracy in Pakistan, it could equally be argued that India faced far greater difficulties. Indeed, it could be said that the vastly more culturally and linguistically diverse India possessed a far poorer soil for the planting of democratic modes of government.

A much better root cause of the failure of democracy in Pakistan can be found in the bizarre regional structure imposed on Pakistan by the mechanisms of Partition. Jinnah's concept of an independent Pakistan was predicated on a belief that the Muslim population of India would not be allowed full access to their political rights in a democracy dominated by Hindus, and particularly by Nehru's Congress Party. The idea that ties of language and culture might be more binding than Islam was largely ignored. As one Bengali noted, 'The language movement has actually laid the foundation . . . of a truly non-communal and democratic movement in the country.'[21] In setting out on the creation of an independent Pakistan, the country's political founders failed to appreciate that racial and regional discrimination could be an issue equally as divisive as religion.

There seems little doubt that the imposition of Urdu as the national language hastened the divide with East Pakistan (later Bangladesh). Even in West Pakistan, only 8 per cent of the population spoke Urdu compared to 48 per cent Punjabi, 13 per cent Sindhi, 8 per cent Pashto and 3 per cent Baluchi. Liaquat affirmed at the Constituent Assembly meeting in February 1948 that 'It is necessary for a nation to have one language and that language can only be Urdu and no other language.'[22]

Jinnah, himself a poor Urdu speaker, was equally committed to the single language project. However, he was jeered and barracked by Bengali students when he insisted that the state language was going to be Urdu. For the Bengalis, however, the imposition of Urdu was seen as project sought by the political elite in West Pakistan.

When Nazimuddin, prime minister and leader of the Muslim League, continued to assert the primacy of Urdu in January 1952, he stirred riots which ended with the death of three students. However, language was just one of many issues which offended Bengal; despite being the largest province by population with more people than the other four put together, the central government, the Pakistan bureaucracy and the army were based in the West. Bengalis represented just 1 per cent of the three armed forces. Even if Bengali had been nominated as an official language, and the offices of state equally divided between the East and the West, it is arguable whether the 1,000-mile divide between two regions, linked only by an air bridge between Karachi and Dhaka, could ever have been sustainable.

Finally, it must also be allowed that the unresolved issue of Kashmir remained a festering wound at the heart of Pakistan political life, which poisoned relations with India, exaggerated the role of the army in Pakistan society and predisposed its presidents to precipitate military action. For Ayub Khan at least, a promising period of political stability under a presidential constitution and a solid economic performance encouraged by a free market model was dashed to pieces by military adventurism in Kashmir _ a state whose devolvement to India after Partition proved a curse to both India and Pakistan, and undermined the delicate political balance of East and West.

In summary, socio-economic conditions provided a less than ideal platform for the establishment of democracy in post-independence Pakistan. Additionally, Jinnah, the man whose prestige after 1947 was virtually limitless, must take some blame for not moving rapidly to establish a constitutional framework. He was also clearly guilty of failing to recognise that the cultural differences between West Pakistan and Bengal in the East were as great, if not greater than those that divided Muslim from Hindu. Arguably, however, given the peculiar East–West geographic construct of a Pakistan divided in the middle by a hostile India and only connectible by air, the eventual establishment of an independent Bangladesh in East Pakistan was almost inevitable. That factor alone made the establishment of a constitutional democracy that would satisfy East and West Pakistan virtually impossible.

36

Têt Offensive: Lost Victories

America-Vietnam: 1968–75

Having lost the 1960 presidential election to J.F. Kennedy by the narrowest margins, and then been defeated in a 1962 electoral contest for the governorship of California, Nixon's political career, which included his years as vice president to Dwight Eisenhower, appeared to be over. He disappeared into legal work in New York. When he re-emerged as the 1968 presidential candidate, it was one of the most surprising political comebacks in American political history. From a conservative Quaker background in California, Nixon was ideally placed to capture the backlash of America's social conservative majority against the hippie counterculture which, in its leading role in the vociferous and sometimes violent anti-war movement, had become increasingly prominent in the media.

As early as in 1966, Senator Stuart Symington had warned President Johnson that 'Nixon will murder us. He will become the dove of all times. There has never been a man in American public life that could turn so fast on a dime.'[1] Indeed, Nixon promised 'peace with honor' without ever detailing the specifics of how he would deal with the thorny issue of Vietnam. Faced by Nixon's 'secret plan' to end the conflict, his democratic opponent, Hubert Humphrey, was by contrast fatally tainted by the Democrat's running of the war. Nixon won comfortably.

In 1969 he inherited a disastrous foreign policy. America was undermining its economic vitality by spending US$ 26.5 billion per annum by 1968 on an apparently unending conflict that an increasingly large minority of its population, mainly supported by the dominant East and West Coast media, wished to terminate as quickly as possible and regardless of consequences. For Nixon, a former vice president, an astute observer of America's broader interests in the geopolitical battle with the Soviet Union for the control of Asia, a simplistic unilateral withdrawal from Vietnam was not an acceptable option.

By some measures, Nixon's job had been made harder by the launch of the Têt Offensive by the North Vietnamese on 30 January 1968; it started a month-long battle for control of South Vietnam. The battle was prompted by the rise to power of the Soviet faction in the North Vietnamese politburo, led by the southern-born

Lê Duẩn, which, pushed by the Kremlin, wanted an immediate military victory in the South. In a combined attack on 38 cities including Saigon by the southern based Việt Cộng of the National Liberation Front (NFL) and the People's Army of Vietnam (PAVN), the North Vietnamese government hoped to score a decisive victory. The strategy was for the PAVN to launch attacks from the North to tie down the American forces on the border at the 17th parallel while the Việt Cộng attacked the southern cities and lead a general uprising.

Militarily the result of the Tết Offensive was a stunning defeat for the North. Although the progenitor of the strategy behind Tết, General Nguyễn Chin Thanh, had been killed by a B-52 bomb in 1967, his plan devolved to General Giáp. Previously burned by his experience of going head to head with the French at Vinh-Yen, Mao-Khe and Ninh-Binh in 1951, Giáp had warned against direct confrontation with American military might. He was proved correct. After initial gains, the Việt Cộng was decisively defeated. The infrastructure of the Việt Cộng in the South, which had been patiently built up over decades, was smashed. A senior Việt Cộng officer complained that 'First of all, casualties everywhere were very high, very high, and the spirit of the soldiers dropped to a low point.'[2]

Having been forced out of the cities, the Việt Cộng were forced into their underground lairs where their tunnel systems were intensively bombed. B-52 could make craters 12 metres deep, and many hundreds of Việt Cộng fighters were buried alive. Stanley Karnow, an American historian, visited Dr Duong Hoa after the war who 'bluntly denounced the venture [the Tết Offensive] as a grievous miscalculation by the Hanoi hierarchy, which... had wantonly squandered the Southern insurgent movement'.[3]

Perhaps most importantly, there was no general uprising; the war in the South was a counter-insurgency operation and not the civil war suggested by anti-war lobbyists such as the Boston University historian and political scientist Howard Zinn. Contrary to the belief of the Northern leaders, and indeed many Western liberals, the rural Vietnamese, except under duress, did not support communism and its concomitant collective farms. (Indeed, when given a choice in 1954, over a million Vietnamese had walked southwards away from communism and towards freedom – a choice that people had always made in favour of freedom whether in Korea or Eastern Europe.)

Operations by North Vietnam's regular army were equally disastrous. The epicentre of the battle was for the isolated hilly area known as Khe Sanh, which the US army had seized in 1967 and turned into a marine garrison. The site had been cleared of tree cover, a difficult task because the branches and trunks were so full of shrapnel that it was almost impossible for chainsaws to work. Perhaps fortunately for the Americans, General Westmoreland also upgraded the airstrip. In the manner of the battle of Diên Biên Phu, the Vietnamese attacked in waves and Hill 861 at the perimeter of Khe Sanh became a scene of bloody hand-to-hand combat. Here, the stench of the bodies in Vietnam's humid climate became so intense that the defenders had to wear gas masks.

American media became obsessed with the battle. The seminal media figure of the Vietnam era, Walter Cronkite, predicted that 'Khe Sanh could well fall with a terrible loss of American lives, prestige and morale' and that at best America was 'mired in a stalemate'.[4] It was a battle which riveted a nation and occupied some 25–50 per cent of American media coverage while it lasted.

However, unlike Diên Biên Phu where the French had only 200 airplanes, America had 2,000. General Westmoreland was able to keep the troops supplied; airplanes and helicopters managed to deliver over 12,000 tons of supplies to Khe San. Eventually, the First Cavalry Division as well as two battalions of the 1st Marines managed to relieve the besieged fortress. Contrary to media predictions, Khe Sanh was a great victory for America; a few marine regiments had tied down several North Vietnamese army divisions and killed over 5,000 of their troops with many thousands more injured.

However, Khe Sanh was not the main target. For General Giáp, Khe Sanh 'was a diversion, but one to be exploited if we could cause many casualties and win a big victory'.[5] Giáp attacked the historic coastal city of Hué that he hoped to turn into a fortress, from which he could liberate South Vietnam's northernmost provinces. Ten PAVN battalions launched an assault which almost overwhelmed the city's defenders; again there was no anti-American uprising by Hué's citizens. In the suburbs, the population including officials, priests and civilians were massacred; victims included Dr Horst Gunther Krainick, a German paediatrician and his wife and several French priests. One of them, Father Urbain, was buried alive – a typical North Vietnamese punishment. In another shallow grave, the authorities later found Father Bùu Dầng and 300 of his parishioners.

Only determined fighting by the US marines, who managed to relieve the defenders and then bring reinforcements by helicopter to a football pitch that they had managed to secure, enabled them to keep a tenuous hold of the city. It was a close-run battle, but after three weeks, the North Vietnamese army was forced to retreat.

In reality, it was a crushing defeat for the attackers who lost an estimated 40,000 soldiers compared to 4,324 for the Americans, the Army of the Republic of Vietnam (AVRN), Australian and Korean forces combined. General Westmoreland would later surmise that the *Việt Cộng* attacks in the South 'were designed strategically to divert our attention away from the vulnerable Northern provinces...'.[6] Although the fighting's aftermath lasted into 1969, the North Vietnamese had lost the defining battle of the war; also the *Việt Cộng*'s southern infrastructure had been sacrificed for nothing.

For Nixon, the outcome of the Tết Offensive, the defining battle of the military conflict in Vietnam, proved both a blessing and a curse. On the one hand, after Tết, political power swung away from the Southerners in North Vietnam's politburo and back towards the Northerners for whom the building of a strong North Vietnam was a priority. Also, the North's fighting capacity had been decimated both in the regular army and the *Việt Cộng* in the South. *Việt Cộng* officer Trình Dục recalled that during 1968 he had had 'to reorganize my unit three times. . . . Twice, the entire unit was killed. Each time I reorganized, the numbers were smaller. It was almost impossible to get recruits'.[7]

After the battle, the North had rushed 80,000 largely untrained troops into the field; before Têt, 82 per cent of Northern recruits had over six months training; afterwards that figure fell to 40 per cent. It produced a decline in quality which experienced marines such as Lieutenant Colonel Justin Martin were able to notice. In the North, the massive loss of life also had an impact; a university student would later recall, 'Many parents tried to keep their sons out of the army . . . other draftees mutilated themselves or managed to find other ways to fail the physical. People with money were able to pay doctors to disqualify their children.'[8]

The North needed time to recuperate and regroup. General Trần Van Trà noted that after Têt, 'The Military Region Nine Command [Western Nam Bộ] sent a message recommending straightforwardly that the regional Command order an immediate cessation of hostilities, so that we could reorganize the forces. The troops were no longer capable of fighting.'[9] This gave breathing space for Nixon's policy of Vietnamisation, whereby South Vietnam's military capability would be built up so that they could stand up to the Northern armies without US military presence.

Indeed, in April 1970, Nixon was able to announce the withdrawal of 150,000 troops; by 1972, he had been able to reduce American forces in Vietnam from a peak of 500,000 to just 69,000. By contrast, the South Vietnamese army, ARVN, was increased to 1 million troops by 1970; they were equipped with the most modern M-16 rifles, 12,000 M-60 machine guns, 40,000 M-79 grenade launchers and 2,000 heavy mortars and howitzers. In spite of this massive rearmament, by 1972 Nixon had also managed to reduce America's Vietnamese budgetary drain to US$ 3 billion per annum, 89 per cent less than the peak figure under Johnson.

If the victory of American arms in the Têt Offensive provided an opportunity for Nixon's strategy of honourable withdrawal to succeed, it also perversely served to undermine American civilian morale. While the Têt was a significant military victory, as a defensive battle it had appeared to go so badly at first that by the time the battle had been won, it was not clear, until a much later date, even to the American generals, how comprehensively the enemy had been damaged.

Anti-war opponents, both in the media and among the Democratic leadership, were quick to pronounce Têt a military defeat for America; it was a conclusion which surprised and delighted the leadership in Hanoi. The effect on civilian morale of the inaccurate claim of defeat by important sections of American society was devastating. With the benefit of hindsight, General Giáp was able to claim:

> . . . that was our biggest victory; to change the ideas of the United States. The Têt offensive had been directed primarily at the people of South Vietnam, but as it turned out it affected the people of the United States more.[10]

In addition, Nixon's March 1969 decision to bomb the Hô Chí Minh trail in Cambodia as well as Laos, plus his authorisation of ARVN incursions into Laos and Cambodia in April 1970, suggested that Nixon was expanding the American war effort. On 30 April, Nixon's television address told the American nation that he had authorised the invasion of Cambodia and that 'If when the chips are down, the world's most powerful nation acts like a pitiful, helpless giant, the forces of totalitarian and anarchy will threaten free nations and free institutions throughout the world.'[11]

Though the Cambodian strategy made sound strategic sense in its attack on *Việt Cộng* strongholds across the border, and was a logical follow-up to the success of Têt, for America's liberal left however, the appeal to America's broader geopolitical interests and responsibilities, which in their fight against Communism both Democrat and Republican administrations had remained united since the Second World War, fell on stony ground. Nixon was aware of the likely backlash; he warned his daughter, Julie, 'it's possible that the campuses are really going to blow up after this'.[12]

It was a forecast that became truer than he could possibly have feared. Until the election of 1968, Vietnam had been a Democrat war; though the anti-war protest movement had already begun to swell, with the election of a Republican, moreover a perceived right-wing Republican deemed to represent the conservative values both of middle-America and the US military–industrial complex, Democrat protestors now felt less constrained to unleash their full fury. On 15 October 1969, over 1 million Americans participated in the National Moratorium Day.

In Manhattan, Hollywood stars Woody Allen and Shirley Maclaine addressed huge crowds. The young were attracted in droves and included the children of many White House insiders such as Defense Secretary Melvin Laird, Nixon's Chief of Staff H.R. Haldeman, Secretary of Labor George Shultz and future Budget Director Casper Weinberger. Even the wife of Anthony Lake, a senior advisor to Henry Kissinger, and later President Clinton's national security advisor, went on the anti-war rally. A month later, another mass rally was held by a newly organised Mobilisation to End the War (MOBE). Some 250,000 demonstrators congregated on the Washington Mall.

These demonstrations were nothing as compared with the protest movement that gathered pace after the invasion of Cambodia. Although overall American support for the war in Vietnam remained solid until the end, the protest movement in American universities grew to uncontrollable proportions. Across the nation, 536 campuses had to be shut down for periods, while in California Governor Reagan was forced to close the entire state university system.

The movement reached its apogee at Kent State University on 2 May when the Reserve Officers Training Corps (ROTC) building was burnt down. A campus demonstration two days later was met by a group of inexperienced Ohio National Guardsmen, who, when forced to retreat by stone-throwing students, opened fire.

Four students were killed, including two women; two of the dead, Sandra Scheuer and William Schroeder, were not taking part in the demonstration, and were simply walking between classes. For the Nixon administration, in spite of his condemnation of the Ohio National Guard, it was a public relations disaster. Some war supporters were less charitable. J. Edgar Hoover, director of the Federal Bureau of Investigation (FBI), described one of the women killed as 'nothing more than a whore anyway'.[13]

Whatever the circumstances, the Kent State shootings marked a sharp point of deterioration in the public mood, though a simple majority of the public remained supportive. Photography student John Filo's image of Mary Ann Vecchio kneeling over the dead body of fellow student Jeffrey Miller became one of the most used images of the war. Historically in the twentieth century, America had always swung between expansionism and isolationism, particularly when soldiers' lives were lost in far-away conflicts, and the ongoing Vietnamese War was no exception. Ignoring the logic of America's geopolitical obligations, there were always demagogues, who for political advantage or unbendable conviction, were able to whip up a storm of protest against the seemingly endless casualties of the war in Vietnam.

Indeed, Pat Buchanan, a Nixon aide, wrote to the president to warn him that the war 'will now be won or lost on the American Front'.[14] Indeed, the danger for the Nixon strategy 'peace with honor' was that America would lose the will to fight before his plans could come to fruition. Some Americans even supported the *Việt Cộng* if only in the hope that their victory would prove the correctness of their views. David Horowitz, the founder of the New Left and editor of *Ramparts* magazine, acknowledged that 'Those of us who inspired and then led the antiwar movements did not just want to stop the killing as so many veterans of those domestic battles now claim. We wanted the Communists to win.'[15]

The John Filo photograph was not the only image which began to sap America's will to fight. During the Tết Offensive, photo journalist Eddie Adams won a Pulitzer Prize for showing an image of General Nguyễn Ngọc Loan shooting a bullet into the side of the head of a *Việt Cộng* Captain, Nguyễn Van Lém, at point blank range. The story of this horrific execution during the *Việt Cộng* attack on Saigon frequently omits the fact that this *Việt Cộng* soldier was a captured terrorist assassin, who had just murdered the wife and children of one of the general's best friends. Episodes such as these were used unstintingly by Nixon's opponents to undermine his Vietnam strategy. Vietnam became the first television war, and it brought the ghastliness of human conflict into the living room for the first time.

Atrocities did indeed occur on both sides; however, of the combatant nations, only the American public was bombarded with horror in their living rooms. Nevertheless, real atrocities did serve to sap the morale of an American public, which began to doubt the morality of the American cause. During the Tết Offensive, over 400 inhabitants from the village of *My Lai*, aged between 1 and 82, men and women, were herded into ditches and machine-gunned by Lt. William Calley and his platoon, after he had been ordered to clear the area of *Việt Cộng*. Numbers of women were also apparently raped. A greater massacre was only prevented by an American helicopter crew, who landed their gunship between Calley and the villagers and threatened to open fire if the massacre continued.

It was not an isolated episode. In January 1971, the Vietnam Veterans against the War (VVAW) launched an investigation of war atrocities, the so-called Winter Soldier Investigation; some 125 veterans testified. Marine Sergeant Scott Camil was able to offer 'testimony involving burning of villages, calling in of artillery on villages for games, corpsmen killing wounded prisoners, napalm dropped on villages, women being raped, women and children being massacred . . . bodies shoved out of helicopters'.[16]

To support its programme of immediate withdrawal, the anti-war movement was also largely successful in its aim of portraying the American army in Vietnam as racist, full of drugs, prone to fragging its officers, and generally reluctant to fight. It is estimated that there were some 100 officers killed in about 2,000 incidents of 'fragging'; to put this figure in perspective however, it should be remembered that over 2 million Americans served in Vietnam. On a pro-rata basis, the level of 'fragging' was actually higher in the Australian army in Vietnam.

As for the colour issue, after the abolition of 'all black' regiments after their poor performance in the Korean War, regiments were racially mixed. The average rifle unit consisted of 50 per cent black and Hispanic troops, with the white troops being preponderantly from poor backgrounds, particularly from the South. Educated white middle-class children had a number of means of avoiding the draft or securing relatively safe berths. However, it has always been thus; the foot-soldiers of history have always come from the poorer classes. Nevertheless, the unfairness of the draft system led to changes in 1967.

The anti-war lobby also pointed to 'draft dodging' as a measure of the unpopularity of the war in Vietnam; in reality, there were just 50,000 draft dodgers during the war which compared very favourably with the 337,000 in the Second World War. It might also be noted that more than two-thirds of soldiers who served in Vietnam were volunteers compared with just one-third in the Second World War. There is no doubt that, perhaps for the first time in history, narcotics were freely available and the Pentagon itself admitted that 30 per cent of its troops in Vietnam had used heroine. Prostitution, not an unusual phenomenon of war, became rampant with a 'working girl' population in Saigon estimated at 30,000; remarkably, one in four Americans who served in Vietnam contracted venereal disease.

However, there are no foundations in the belief that Americans fought badly even though the 365-day 'tour' for American troops was organisationally disruptive; indeed, in the major battles such as Khe Sanh and Hué, US troops fought with great bravery and distinction. Also, it is interesting to note that in a study carried out in 1980, in spite of the outcome of the war, 71 per cent of veterans were happy that they went to Vietnam and 66 per cent of them averred that they would serve again in the same situation.

Nevertheless, there can be little doubt that the aimlessness and ineptitude of the direction of the war under President Johnson contributed to an undermining of morale. As Nixon began to wind down American ground forces' direct involvement, it must have been difficult to sustain the energy of the troops. Inevitably towards the end of the troop withdrawals, 'last casualty' syndrome became prevalent. As Naval Lt. John Kerry, later a presidential candidate, famously declared, 'How do you ask a man to be the last man to die for a mistake?'[17]

Neither should the brilliance of Soviet and North Vietnamese propaganda be underestimated. Large sections of the American media became convinced by the protestations of Cambodian and Laotian neutrality as they were bombed by the USA. In fact, their neutrality had long since been violated by the North Vietnamese. Many of the anti-war movements believed that Cambodian civilians were being bombed indiscriminately, whereas in reality air strikes were concentrated on the Việt Cộng's supply line along the Hồ Chí Minh trail and other North Vietnamese installations embedded deep in Laos and Cambodia. The bombing of the North was characterised as indiscriminate, but even Malcolm Brown, a New York Times journalist hostile to the Nixon administration, was forced to admit that 'I expected to observe ruins everywhere. But Hanoi and Haiphong are almost completely unscathed, and the surrounding countryside appears to have been barely touched.'[18]

The anti-war movement also swallowed the myth that North Vietnam was attempting to liberate a Southern peasantry oppressed by a brutal dictatorship in what was in essence a civil war against a corrupt elite in Saigon; the reality was that North Vietnam had launched a brutal suppression of its own people when over a million citizens had marched southwards to escape communism after the Geneva Peace accord in 1954. As for the 'David versus Goliath' image portrayed by the North, it was largely overlooked that the Soviet Union and China were providing their allies with over US$ 1 billion of supplies per annum, including the most advanced Soviet weaponry. Above all, America's detractors accepted the Soviet line that its empire, based on a repressive totalitarian model, had a moral equivalence with an American Empire based on the ideals of free trade, democracy and political self-determination.

Whatever the reality of troop morale and the effectiveness of Soviet propaganda, it is clear that America's political caste, and their willingness to conduct the war, was severely undermined by the fierce social divisions that emerged over the conduct of the war. As President Nixon would later tell David Frost, during the course of his famous discourses with the British television interviewer, 'This Nation was torn apart in an ideological way by the War in Vietnam as much as the Civil War tore apart the nation when Lincoln was president.'[19]

Having promised peace as the main plank of his 1968 election, Nixon had to deliver while at the same time committing to withdrawal of troops. This was an almost impossible balancing act. As Henry Kissinger would later recall, 'Withdrawal would become like 'salted peanuts' to the American public; the more troops we withdrew, the more would be expected, leading eventually to demands for total unilateral withdrawal, perhaps within a year [this in fact happened].'[20] At the same time, Nixon and Kissinger would soon discover that, notwithstanding the defeat suffered in the Tết Offensive, bringing the enemy to the negotiation table could not be done without a continued credible American military threat.

From the time of Nixon's election in 1968, it took almost 15 months for Kissinger, through his contacts in Paris, to eventually arrange a first meeting with the North Vietnamese. In a series of three secret meetings between 20 February and 4 April 1970, Kissinger travelled to a military air force base in Germany before being picked up by President Pompidou's private jet to take him to Paris. Even Secretary of State William Rogers was not informed of the Paris meetings. Here, Kissinger met Lê Dúc Tho, a hard-line Marxist–Leninist, who displayed constant paranoia about 'capitalist tricks' while at the same time lecturing and haranguing his American counterpart. Aware of the withdrawal pressures on the Americans, North Vietnam believed that time was on their side. As Lê Dúc Tho suggested to Kissinger, 'Before, there were over a million US and puppet troops, and you failed. How can you succeed when you let the puppet troops do the fighting?'[21]

The negotiations went nowhere, and in October 1970, Nixon, in a public speech, offered a ceasefire and proposed a timetable for withdrawal of American troops. This was immediately rejected by the North Vietnamese representative, Xuan Thuy, in Paris. Faced with the refusal of North Vietnam to come to the table, Nixon inevitably concluded that they would have to be forced to negotiate a peace settlement. In part, this strategy was conducted in an attempt to isolate Vietnam by a diplomatic onslaught of detente with both the Soviet Union and China.

However, this alone could not force North Vietnam to discuss a peace treaty over a war which they felt that they could win if given enough time. Given the withdrawal of American troops, and indeed the success of Operation Phoenix in clearing out *Việt Cộng* resistance in the South, there were no other options to bombing barring an invasion of the North – an unrealistic option given Nixon's peace stance. Indeed, bombing was the only alternative point of pressure that could bring the North to the negotiating table. Between July 1970 and February 1971, the US Air Force carried out 8,000 sorties, a rate of 300 per day.

While bombing helped bring pressure, it did not immediately bring North Vietnam to the table. In fact, North Vietnam had by now had three years to recuperate from the military setback represented by the Tết Offensive. With the South seemingly weakened by the withdrawal of American troops, the North, rearmed by the Soviets, again believed that they could win the war on the ground. In the Easter Offensive on 30 March 1972, three PAVN divisions supported by heavyweight Russian artillery equipment and T-54 tanks crossed the 17th parallel and initially swept aside the South's ARVN forces.

In response, Nixon launched Operation Linebacker, a bombing campaign of which the president boasted, 'the bastards have never been bombed like they're going to be bombed this time'.[22] Up to this point, the administration of both Johnson and Nixon had limited bombing attacks on the North to just 25 miles above the Demilitarised Zone (DMZ). For the first time, Nixon now authorised bombing up to 250 miles north of the DMZ. Smart bombs were used to destroy the Thanh Hóa Bridge, while the mining of Haiphong harbour began to stem the flow of sophisticated Soviet equipment.

In spite of pro-forma Soviet complaints about the escalation of American bombing, the detente summit in Moscow with Brezhnev, Kosygin and Podorny went ahead as planned on 22 May. Indeed, Kissinger had warned the Soviet ambassador, 'Anatol [Dobrynin], we have been warning you for months that if there were an offensive we would take drastic measures to end the war once and for all.'[23] With the failure of North Vietnam's Easter Offensive, the Soviet foreign minister visited Hanoi and told them that it was time to negotiate. Mao also urged them to be more flexible. The Nixon–Kissinger strategy of diplomacy and bombs appeared to be paying off. As Kissinger would later say of the bombing campaigns, '. . . we had to carry the war to North Vietnam; only this could force a conclusion of the war'.[24]

In spite of the resumption of the Paris negotiations, and Nixon's crushing defeat of Democrat challenger George McGovern in the 1972 presidential elections, by December Lê Dúc Tho had fallen back to the familiar tactics of vacillation. The White House, which had unilaterally halted the 'Linebacker' bombing campaign, again decided that it needed a resumption of bombing to bring the North Vietnamese back to serious negotiations. The result was 'Linebacker II' which became better known as the 'Christmas' bombings. Some 1,750 sorties were flown and dropped 40,000 tons on docks and shipyards.

Although some residential areas were also destroyed, the civilian damages and casualties were much less than claimed by the North Vietnamese and their anti-war allies in America. Nixon was accused of being a murderer and behaving like a Nazi. *The Economist* magazine was more sanguine in its analysis when it pointed out that the Hanoi death toll was 'smaller than the number of civilians killed by North Vietnamese artillery bombardment of An Loc in April. . . . this is what makes the denunciation of Mr. Nixon as another Hitler sound so unreal'.[25]

Linebacker II produced a virtually instant result. The North Vietnamese returned to serious negotiation and on 14 January 1973 Kissinger was able to return triumphantly to America with a peace agreement. (Having received a copy of the peace agreement, Lyndon Johnson, who had been so tormented by the war, died on 22 January.) On the following day, President Nixon made a television appearance to announce the Vietnam peace. It was a remarkable triumph of arms and diplomacy, a result which had seemed almost impossible to achieve when he had won the presidency just four years previously. Yet Kissinger would later observe that after Nixon's speech, he found the melancholic president sitting alone and 'brooding' in the Lincoln room: '. . . this man, so lonely in his hour of triumph, so ungenerous in some of his motivations, had navigated our nation through one of the most anguishing periods in its history'.[26] For his efforts at negotiating the peace, Henry Kissinger would be awarded the Nobel Peace Prize, a joint award with Lê Dúc Tho who declined the honour.

Having apparently achieved the 'peace with honor' in Vietnam as well as the restoration of relations with China, the historic first 'moonwalk' by Armstrong and Aldrin in July 1969, and one of the biggest presidential electoral victories in American history (carrying 49 out of 50 states), it might have been expected that Nixon could have spent his second term in quiet contemplation of his domestic and international triumphs. That January 1973 came to be seen as the apogee of his success from which he fell with stunning rapidity, was the result of a series of misfortunes, miscalculations and outright scandalous and illegal conduct by the president and his White House staff.

On 17 June 1972, five burglars had been caught breaking inside the offices of the Democratic National Committee which were housed in the Watergate office complex. The burglars carried sophisticated surveillance equipment and included in their number James McCord Jr, a former CIA operative who was a 'security' employee for the Republican Committee to Re-Elect the president (CRP; though it later came to known as CREEP). In October 1982, *The Washington Post* reporters, Bob Woodward and Carl Bernstein, reported that the FBI's investigations had concluded that Nixon's own staff had authorised the break-in as part of a dirty tricks campaign to re-elect the president; information on the FBI investigation was provided by 'Deep throat', a mysterious informant, who was only identified as Mark Felt, a former associate director of the FBI, on 31 May 2005.

While Nixon had not authorised the break-in, it came to light through the Watergate tapes, recordings of Nixon in the Oval Office, that the president had orchestrated a cover-up. In addition to charges of evasion of taxes, the acceptance of illegal campaign contributions and the Democrat charges that the secret bombing of Cambodia was illegal, the president was now apparently guilty of attempted obstruction of justice. Nixon was hardly helped by the resignation in October 1973 of his Vice President Spiro Agnew for accepting bribes. When it became clear that he had lost the support of his own party, which would have resulted in his almost certain impeachment by Congress, Nixon duly resigned on 9 August 1974.

For both America and South Vietnam, the Watergate affair and its outcome was a catastrophe. In the nature of all post-war treaties with communist states, the Treaty of Paris, which brought an end to the war in Vietnam, was regarded not as a legally binding accord, as was the case in America, but merely as a breathing space in which the North could regroup after it setback in the Spring 1972 Offensive.

As early as 1973, the southern hardliners in North Vietnam's politburo were calling for another 'final' offensive to conquer the South. North Vietnam now began the construction of Corridor 613, a re-worked route for the Hô Chí Minh trail, which unlike the original footpath was a robust-enough highway to accommodate the 10,000 trucks (including the huge Russian Zils with their six-ton capacity and six-wheel drive), hundreds of tanks and a 5,000 km fuel pipeline. By the end of the war, the Hô Chí Minh trail through Laos and Cambodia would resemble an elongated colony consisting of repair workshops, factories, hospitals, staging posts and rest camps; with its many offshoots, the trail would stretch over 20,000 km.

Thus provisioned, on 26 December 1974, General Van Tien Dung was able to begin the artillery bombardment of Vietnam's Phuóc Long Province situated 70 km from Saigon, from within 'neutral' Cambodia. Unsupported by American bombing, there was a collapse in ARVN morale; as North Vietam's politburo leader, Lê Duân, pointed out, '... never have we had military and political conditions so perfect or a strategic advantage so great as we have now'.[27]

The attack on Phuoc Long Province was followed on 9 March by an advance across the central highlands to cut off the ARVN forces defending the 17th parallel. It was a classic flanking operation predicted by Eisenhower as far back as 1959, when he had warned Kennedy that allowing Laos and Cambodia to fall into Communist hands would lead to the loss of all of Indochina; (by the mid-1970s, North Vietnam had an army of 80,000 men permanently stationed in Laos under General Vo Ban). With Saigon pressed from the West, and South Vietnam cut in half, defeat was now inevitable; on 30 April 1975, North Vietnamese tanks entered Hanoi and 'liberated' Saigon.

'Peace with honor' ended with the squalid scenes of American marines fending off civilians as they tried to board the final helicopters leaving from the roof of the US embassy. It was a humiliation that would take many years to shake off. In New York, a crestfallen Henry Kissinger cancelled his tickets to see Noel Coward's play *Present Laughter*; he would note that 'For the first time in the postwar period America abandoned to eventual Communist rule friendly people who had relied on us ... [it] ushered in a period of American humiliation.'[28] If it was a humiliation for the USA, it was a tragedy for the people of Indochina, who, over the succeeding decade, would suffer appalling hardship, cruelty, and death by the depredations of the totalitarian socialist North Vietnamese regime which filled America's shoes.

Subsequently, it became a frequent charge that President Nixon and Kissinger had orchestrated a US withdrawal to allow a decent interval before South Vietnam's inevitable collapse. It was a charge that barely fitted with Kissinger's formidable determination throughout his career to defend America's Asian allies; in his account of *The White House Years* (1979), Henry Kissinger would declare, 'We sought not an interval before a collapse, but a lasting peace with honor.'[29]

The Watergate crisis, ending with the resignation of the president, transformed the landscape in which the Cold War was fought. From mid-1973, Nixon and his Secretary of State Kissinger were denuded of executive power. Congress blocked the bombing of Cambodia where the Hô Chí Minh trail provided the supply lines to

South Vietnam's open flank. Without access to American Air Force support, South Vietnam was laid bare to Giáp's flanking strategies. In addition, the Democrat-controlled Congress also chose in successive years to cut military aid to their allies; it was a shattering blow to their morale. Nixon's policy of Vietnamisation was predicated upon the continued provision of air support and military aid; without it the South Vietnamese government could only wait for the North to gather its forces.

Compounding the sequestration of American aerial and financial support was South Vietnam's economic collapse after the withdrawal of America's 250,000 troops and support staff. By 1968, normal economic activity in Vietnam had all but ceased and the economy had become virtually reliant on providing support services to the fantastically well-provisioned American army. US soldiers could be lifted out of a fire-fight with the *Việt Cộng* and minutes later be eating steak and fries with ice-cold Coca-Cola and ice cream in air-conditioned bases. Sometimes helicopters would arrive in mid-battle with crates of iced beer. Movies were shown 24 hours a day, seven days a week.

The supporting American infrastructure was vast. The US army would eventually leave behind it 2.5 million cubic metres of refrigerated storage, 71 swimming pools, 30 tennis courts, 90 service clubs, 159 basketball courts, two bowling alleys and 357 libraries. Without this vast army, with its spending power of billions of dollars, the Vietnamese economy collapsed after 1972, merely compounding the sense among the South Vietnamese elite and its armed forces that it had been abandoned.

South Vietnam was not aided by an inadequate army. ARVN was badly led. General Westmoreland would later describe the Vietnamese as '. . . good people, hard-working, energetic, the smartest of all the oriental people. The problem with ARVN was the leadership; there were just not enough competent officers'.[30] By contrast, the North Vietnamese Army was led by a military commander widely recognised to be a military genius. Robert McNamara, President Johnson's Secretary of Defence would surmise that 'We underestimated the power of nationalism to motivate a people to fight and die for their beliefs and values.'[31] Nevertheless, Giáp was able command his troops with a ruthless discipline and a disregard for human life that only an authoritarian state could exercise. As General Westmoreland would also point out, with regard to the huge casualties Giáp forces incurred at Khe San, in the US army he would have been instantly dismissed. In the final tally, some 1.1 million *Việt Cộng* and Northern troops perished in the war compared with 58,000 American soldiers.

For former President Nixon, the loss of South Vietnam to the communists was a personal tragedy of Shakespearean proportion. Nixon, without doubt the most sophisticated analyst of America's geopolitical imperatives to hold the presidency in the twentieth century, had achieved by 1973 the apparently impossible task of withdrawing all American ground troops while imposing crushing military defeats on North Vietnam; a peace deal with North Vietnam, now isolated by Nixon's policies of detente with the Communist powers, had also been struck. It seemed a dramatic turnaround from the catastrophic conduct of the war in Indochina by Presidents J.F. Kennedy and Lyndon B. Johnson. South Vietnam's future seemed secure. In spite of an increasingly vociferous anti-war lobby, Nixon nevertheless still managed to carry a majority of the American population in support of his Vietnam policies; the crushing defeat of George McGovern in the 1972 election was ample testament to how thinly supported was the extreme anti-war movement of Zin, Chomsky and portions of the East Coast media establishment.

The subsequent collapse of the South Vietnamese regime has sometimes been blamed on a Democratic-controlled Congress, which withdrew air support and financial backing for South Vietnam, thereby effectively abandoning their former allies to attack from Soviet-backed North Vietnam. Watergate, the First Oil Crisis, recession and the collective sigh of relief that American troops were out of Vietnam after the most bruising and divisive international military campaign combined to sap the energy and resolve of politicians from all parties.

However, in the ultimate analysis, it was Nixon who was the architect of his own downfall and the loss of South Vietnam to communism. In 1950, Nixon, after defeating congresswoman Helen Gahagan Douglas in a senatorial election in which he successfully smeared his opponent as the 'Pink Lady', a left-wing sympathiser, was himself tagged with the epithet 'Tricky Dick' by *The Independent Review*. It was a label which stuck largely because it contained an element of truth. Nixon, an often brooding melancholic figure, was riven by suspicions and paranoia; his deviousness was a reflection of his own personal demons. When he learnt of the origins of the Watergate break-in, he discarded the option of coming clean over the actions of some of his colleagues; by trying to cover up the break-in and having been exposed in his attempt to pervert the course of justice, in one stroke he shredded all personal credibility. The executive power of his presidency evaporated almost instantly. With this collapse came the inability to articulate and pursue the policies that could have saved South Vietnam; whether this would have happened is inevitably a matter of conjecture, but Kissinger's view that 'But for the collapse of executive authority as a result of Watergate, I believe we would have succeeded'[32] demands to be considered seriously.

President Kennedy, like Eisenhower before him, regarded Vietnam as 'the cornerstone of the Free World in Southeast Asia, the keystone to the arch, the finger in the dyke. . . .'[33] The loss of the country to the free world system was a great victory for the Soviet Union in the struggle for global power and an immense setback to America's Asian Empire. Although Lee Kuan Yew, the Singaporean leader, would later say that America's war in Vietnam had given South East Asia a decade's breathing space to prepare for the communist onslaught, at the time the picture seemed far less rosy.

In 1972, Chinese Foreign Minister Zhou Enlai had pleaded with Alexander Haig, then Nixon's deputy assistant to the president for national security affairs, as he was seeing him off at the airport, 'Don't lose in Vietnam; don't withdraw from Southeast Asia.'[34] After the fall of Vietnam to the communists, countries such as Thailand felt abandoned and open to attack, while in China, Zhou Enlai and Mao almost gave up on America as a potential ally against Soviet expansion in Asia. Indeed, it was immensely fortunate for America's Asian Empire that by the end of the Vietnam War, the communist world appeared irrevocably split between the Soviet Union and the People's Republic of China; this alone probably saved further defeats in America's long-running war with the Soviet Union.

37

The Bombing of Cambodia

Cambodia: 1969–73

The post-war history of Cambodia has tended to be neglected by comparison with its larger neighbour Vietnam. The point was well illustrated by William Shawcross's title *Sideshow: Kissinger, Nixon and the Destruction of Cambodia* (1979), which is a poignant account of the collapse of civil government in 1970s Cambodia and its replacement by the genocidal regime of Pol Pot's Khmer Rouge. Yet any military analysis of post-war Indochina demonstrates that through Cambodia lay the path to North Vietnam's defeat of South Vietnam in 1975. Had the South merely had to defend the narrow neck of land some 60 miles wide that constitutes the 17th Parallel, the agreed division between North and South at Geneva in 1954, it is clear that this would have been easily defended, not only by the Americans, but also by the South Vietnamese themselves.

However, it was the fact of Vietnam's long Western borders flanked by Laos in the north and Cambodia in the south, two countries porous to North Vietnamese infiltration, that determined the outcome of a communist-dominated Indochina. Along the so-called Hô Chí Minh trail, which passed through both Cambodia and Laos, the Soviet Union via its agent, the Vietnamese People's Liberation Army (PLA), supplied a guerrilla war in the South with men and arms, which would eventually wear down their opponents.

Indeed it is worth noting that in the late 1950s and early 1960s the geopolitical concerns of US policy-makers, and Presidents Eisenhower and Kennedy, centred on Laos. In March 1961, Kennedy observed that all of South East Asia would be endangered if Laos was lost to communism; yet he promoted the Laos Neutrality Agreement with Soviet leader Krushchev, which, as historian Conrad Black points out, he 'should never have endorsed, and which Hanoi had ignored'.[1] By the late 1960s, Laos was considered largely beyond defence, but as for Cambodia, Kissinger would point out, 'Strategically, Cambodia could not be considered a country separate from Vietnam.'[2] Far from being the 'Sideshow' in North Vietnam's war to unite the South under Communism, Cambodia was in many respects the 'Main show'. That this understanding has never been fully espoused must in large part be explained by the inconvenience it poses to the historical consensus represented by the anti-Vietnam War era historians who have dominated the historiography of this conflict.

Though in 1945 Vietnam's population of 25 million significantly outnumbered Cambodia's population of 8 million and was generally perceived to be the jewel in France's Empire in Indochina, it was Cambodia that had the more illustrious history. Between 802 and 1431, Cambodia was the centre of South East Asia's greatest empire. The 600-year Angkor Empire extended from Indochina through Thailand to both Malaysia and Burma. The might of the Angkorean Period was based on water technology; canals, sluices, dams and irrigation systems elevated Cambodia's economy and enabled the Angkors to enslave their neighbours. However, steady decline had set in from the end of this period, and by the eighteenth century it was clear that Vietnam was in the ascendant; roles were reversed and Cambodia became Vietnam's vassal state.

Cambodia regained full independence from Vietnam only in 1847 after the release of members of the Royal Family who had been held hostage in Hué, the Vietnamese Imperial capital. Independence was short-lived, however. In fighting off the regal claims of an ex-monk Pou Kombo in 1867, King Norodom needed to call on the services of French forces, and from this point Cambodia's independence was severely compromised.

Interest in the region was further heightened by the discovery of Angkor Wat, the great Buddhist temple complex of South East Asia, by the French naturalist Seim Reap. With the collection of taxes coming under French control in 1892, soon followed by the power to appoint King Norodom's advisors, Cambodia had effectively ceased to be independent by 1904, although the colonial period usually dates from the accession of his more compliant half-brother Sisowath, who died in 1927 and was replaced by his son Monivong. The latter's death in 1941 brought to the throne Prince Sihanouk, a young Lycée student. Norodom's great grandson, Sihanouk, had the advantage of unifying the two princely houses on account of his mother being King Monivong's daughter.

Norodom Sihanouk was an intelligent, cultivated man, who became the lynchpin of Cambodian politics for the next 50 years. He was both an inveterate and boastful womaniser and a hard-working administrator, who nevertheless liked to act out his fantasies as a bandleader and film director. In spite of his deviousness as a politician, Sihanouk retained the devotion of his people, but lost the trust of most of those who had dealings with him. With the liberation of Cambodia from the Japanese in 1945, Sihanouk had taken the opportunity to declare independence. However, the French, determined to rebuild an empire and expunge the embarrassment of Vichy France, returned to Phnom Penh in 1946. In characteristic colonial style, the French restored all street names to those of French heroes and renamed the celebratory national holidays. Sihanouk swallowed his pride and remained head of state in name only.

National elections brought the left-leaning Democrats' victory, but in their calls for independence, they were simply ignored by the French. Although the Democrats saw Sihanouk as a French stooge, he was able to negotiate a measure of independence in a treaty of 1949. Two years later, the exiled Nationalist leader Son Ngoc Thanh was allowed to return to Cambodia. By this time, however, it was the new hard left parties that were beginning to take up the running in the fight for independence.

In assembly, the pro-communist left gained in strength as the *Krom Prachaechon* (People's Party). Outside the constitutional structure, a covert Communist Party had for over 20 years existed under the umbrella of the Indochinese Communist Party set up by Hô Chí Minh in 1930. In 1951 this cross-national organisation was disbanded and replaced by the Khmer People's Revolutionary Party. Sihanouk would eventually refer to the radical left as 'Khmer Rouge', a moniker that stuck to the extent that the communists would use it themselves.

Under pressure from the war being fought in Vietnam, Sihanouk skilfully exerted further pressure on France for concessions on independence. French resources had increasingly been drawn to the defence of Vietnam to the extent that by 1953, there were just two French pacification battalions in Cambodia and five battalions of the Royal Khmer Army, out of a total of 237 battalions in Indochina. In that year Sihanouk was granted authority over military and foreign affairs. The Treaty of Geneva in 1954 finally brought real independence for Cambodia. On the back of North Vietnam's hard-fought war with France, culminating in the Battle of Diên Biên Phu, Sihanouk had won independence for his country.

Sihanouk had no intention of being a mere constitutional monarch however. In a mock abdication, he set up his own party, the *Sangkum Reastr Niyum* (the People's Socialist Community). Through a campaign of intimidation of both the press and opposition candidates, Sihanouk, already popular in the countryside, secured 75 per cent of the popular vote and all seats in the assembly. He ruled as chief of state for the next 15 years, with his parents installed as monarchs.

In spite of this apparently secure base, Sihanouk had to navigate a precarious path between left and right. Although tending towards socialism in his beliefs, Sihanouk initially resisted the calls of the far left. In 1963, he launched the anti-left campaign that forced Pol Pot, already a leading figure in the Khmer Rouge, to flee the teaching post that was his cover for revolutionary activity. However, Sihanouk was militarily powerless to block the North Vietnamese army's invasion of Eastern Cambodia to facilitate its supply lines down the Hô Chí Minh trail.

As the North stepped up its pressure to win outright victory in the mid-1960s, Sihanouk conceded further ground to the North Vietnamese Communists, by allowing the stationing of PLA troops in 'sanctuaries' near the Cambodian border with South Vietnam and allowing Soviet supplies, bound for the *Việt Cộng*, to enter via the Cambodian port of Sihanoukville. While proclaiming neutrality, Sihanouk, instead of calling for US help in beating back the communist invaders, entered into a secret treaty with North Vietnam. In effect Sihanouk, only partially under duress, became the Soviet Union's silent partner with North Vietnam in the war against America.

Set against these pressures from the left, Sihanouk's army generals and Cambodia's business magnates were staunchly anti-communist. They bitterly regretted Sihanouk's break with the USA and his government's leftward march, albeit forced by their stronger North Vietnamese neighbour. The loss of American military aid, costing the government some 15 per cent of its budget revenue, formed a major part of this resentment.

In addition, Sihanouk's nationalisation of the banks and the import–export trade alienated the commercial classes, who, along with the generals in Phnom Penh, were deprived of the traditional booty of the Asian ruling classes. Grain traders responded by selling over a quarter of the rice crop to North Vietnam, thus helping them to keep their armies supplied. Sihanouk's response in 1967 was to requisition rice at fixed prices, a policy that cost him support among the agrarian population. There was even an armed uprising in the rice-growing heartland of Battambang. Sihanouk's 'Buddhist-Socialist' policies also produced a deleterious effect among the educated classes. With Sihanouk devoting an extraordinary 20 per cent of his regime's budget to education, he produced a society awash with intelligentsia but one that could not create jobs. The new unemployed educated elite were readily open to left-wing ideology.

Events in 1969 highlighted the idiosyncratic character of Sihanouk's long reign. First, he opened a casino to raise funds for his financially beleaguered government, thus alienating religious elements within the country; the ruin and suicide of a number of prominent people were also noted. Then, later in the year, Sihanouk's obsession with the glamorous world of film led him to sponsor an international film festival in Phnom Penh. Sihanouk's own entry was awarded a special prize in the form of a statuette made of gold provided by the Cambodian National Bank. Such was the eccentricity of his rule that Sihanouk is difficult to define in conventional terms. As Vietnamese historian Nguyễn Khac Vien has concluded, 'At times he was a paternalistic despot, at others a patriotic nationalist, and sometimes he combined both roles.'[3]

The precarious balancing act weaved by Sihanouk for almost 30 years, which had kept Cambodia at the periphery of the conflict in Indochina, was now drawing to a close. Cambodia was about to be brought centre stage. The defeat of the *Việt Cộng* and the PLA in the 1968 Têt Offensive increased the North's reliance on the 'sanctuaries' provided within Cambodia's borders; in effect, North Vietnam expanded its occupation of Cambodia's borderlands.

In addition, the US elections had brought to power President Nixon, a man with a sophisticated approach to geopolitical manoeuvre, whose 'realpolitik' approach to international affairs differed markedly from that of his predecessor

Lyndon Johnson. Nixon had been elected on a pledge to bring the war in Vietnam to an end. However, both he and his National Security Advisor Henry Kissinger believed that successful negotiation could be achieved only through strength. Defeating North Vietnam militarily was the only way to force them to negotiate peace. As soon as he came into office, Nixon demanded a change in strategy with regard to Cambodia; in a memo to Kissinger, he demanded,

> I want a precise report on what the enemy has in Cambodia and what, if anything, we are doing to destroy the build-up there. I think a very definite change of policy toward Cambodia probably should be one of the first orders of business.[4]

This marked a reversion to the Eisenhower view of the strategic importance of Cambodia.

In fact, even President Johnson had been prepared to authorise covert operations by Green Berets, who had been operating in Cambodia under the code name of 'Daniel Boone' since 1967. They operated in two-man teams without uniforms and papers and would accompany local mercenaries on raids. However, on 17 March Kissinger and Nixon raised the stakes by starting a secret bombing campaign against the North Vietnamese 'sanctuaries' on the Cambodian border, which were the lynchpin of North Vietnam's war on the South.

Sensitive to Soviet and Chinese reactions, with whom they were negotiating detente, let alone from the anti-war politicians of both parties, Nixon decided to keep the bombing secret because he feared that Congress would try to veto a move, which on a superficial analysis embroiled the USA in another conflict in Indochina. The bombing strategy was indeed essential in the Nixon and Kissinger attempt to force North Vietnam to the negotiating table by defeating them militarily on the one hand and trying to isolate them diplomatically on the other.

Mistakenly perhaps, they baulked at having to publicly explain that the bombing of Cambodia was not an attack on another sovereign nation but an extension of the war against a covert ally of North Vietnam as part of a geopolitical strategy designed to bring the enemy to the negotiating table; however, given the necessarily clandestine nature of the diplomacy with the Chinese, the Nixon administration's use of subterfuge was perhaps not surprising. Nevertheless, even within the White House, there were dissensions. Secretary of Defense Laird agreed with the policy, but argued that 'It was goddamed stupid to try to keep it secret.'[5]

In a convoluted tactical operation designed to obscure the truth, targets in Cambodia were programmed against pre-planned alternate targets in South Vietnam. Over the next 14 months the secret bombing of Cambodia, comprising some 3,875 sorties with 100,000 tons of bombs, severely damaged the North's ability to make war in South Vietnam. Eventually the secret bombing campaign was exposed when the radio operator Major Hal Knight, who supposedly had been overlooked for promotion and whose job it was to substitute false strike

reports, wrote to Senator William Proxmire of Wisconsin that the American people 'have a right to know how the war has been conducted'.[6] The secret bombing
may have caused serious damage to the North Vietnamese war effort, but its exposure was another blow to the credibility of Nixon and Kissinger with the US
Congress.

However, the bombing had other consequences. To avoid American bombing,
the North Vietnamese army spread deeper into Cambodia. This in turn created
popular alarm within Cambodia and a mass displacement of Cambodians. While
many liberals such as the American socialist historian William Blum (*Killing Hope:
US Military and CIA Interventions Since the Second World War* (1995)) have attributed
this refugee tragedy to the actions of America, Cambodians themselves blamed
North Vietnam and their own government which had abetted the *Việt Cộng* occupation of their country. In early March 1970, there were serious riots against North
Vietnam; in Phnom Penh, the North's embassy and that of the *Việt Cộng* were attacked by 20,000 young Cambodians. Already disenchanted with Sihanouk's economic and foreign policies, the Cambodian establishment began to stir for the removal of his pro-North Vietnamese government.

Sihanouk himself badly misjudged the seriousness of the situation. Taking an
annual vacation in Grasse in the south of France, under the pretext of having medical treatment, Sihanouk underestimated the gravity of the unrest back in Phnom
Penh. Meandering back via planned visits to Russia and China, Sihanouk spent
five days in Moscow, only to be told by Prime Minister Kosygin of Lon Nol's coup
while they were on their way to the airport. A civil servant and cousin of Sihanouk,
Sisowath Sirik Matak, had gone to Prime Minister Lon Nol's house on the evening
of 17 March 1970, threatened him with a gun and made him sign a declaration
supporting the ousting of Sihanouk. Put to the National Assembly, there were
86 to 3 votes in favour of removing Sihanouk as head of state. Even Sihanouk's
own party had had enough. The reluctant Lon Nol duly became Cambodia's new
leader.

The role of the USA in the overthrow of Sihanouk has been hotly disputed.
Sihanouk himself squarely blamed Nixon and Kissinger in a tendentious book called
My War with the CIA (1973). However, as he had by this time decamped to Beijing
and put himself firmly into the Communist camp, Sihanouk's claims need to be
treated with caution. Although the USA would readily acknowledge its support
for Lon Nol, there is scant evidence for an American hand behind the coup. Indeed what is perhaps remarkable is that given Sihanouk's covert alliance with North
Vietnam, America should have been so squeamish about seeking his removal. Although former Saigon CIA analyst Frank Snepp alluded to help that was given to
possible replacements for Sihanouk, including Lon Nol and more specifically Son
Ngoc Thanh, leader of the nationalist Khmer Serei, no evidence of a CIA plot has
come to light.

This was confirmed by William Colby, director of the CIA between 1973 and 1976, who stated that

> Lon Nol may well have been encouraged by the fact that the US was working with Son Ngoc Thanh. I don't know of any specific assurances he was given but the obvious conclusion for him, given the political situation in South Vietnam and Laos, was that he would be given United States Support.[7]

In spite of assertions by some that there was an American plot to topple Sihanouk, there is only evidence of low-key support for some of his possible successors. Given the amount of information that has come out about President Kennedy's authorisation for the overthrow of President Diem in 1963, an event which led to the latter's murder, it seems inconceivable that similar information would not have come into the public domain if Nixon and Kissinger had plotted to oust Sihanouk. There is no evidential reason to disbelieve Henry Kissinger's subsequent protestations of innocence regarding the fall of Sihanouk.

With Lon Nol now in power, the delicate balancing act pursued by Cambodia throughout the post-war period was consigned to history. Sihanouk threw himself behind a Chinese-backed military onslaught on Phnom Penh by the Khmer Rouge and the North Vietnamese army. In response in April 1973, Lon Nol, who had been elevated to the presidency in the previous year, privately called for American help to repel the communist invaders with a request for aid to increase the army from 35,000 to 60,000.

On 14 April, Lon Nol publicly accepted the need for US help: 'because of the gravity of the situation, it is deemed necessary to accept from this moment on all unconditional foreign aid from all sources'.[8] Soon Lon Nol's requirement would grow to 200,000 men. Indeed Cambodia became an increasing recipient of American aid, as President Nixon tried to prevent the overthrow of an ally and a country on whose ability to repulse the Khmer advance would depend the success of his long-term plan for South Vietnam to defend itself.

To add to Nixon's difficulties in negotiating a peace treaty with North Vietnam, it became clear that Cambodia would not be deliverable in terms of inclusion in any settlement between America and North Vietnam. Also further troop withdrawals were planned for 20 April, thus confirming in the mind of Lê Dúc Thọ, North Vietnam's negotiator in Paris, the hopelessness of America's military position. How to remain strong enough to pose a military threat big enough to force the North to the negotiating table, while satisfying Congress's demand for American troop withdrawal from Vietnam, was a constant conundrum for the Nixon White House.

In the face of these problems, the Nixon administration decided on a course of action that was to match the secret bombing of Cambodia for contentiousness. The proposal now mooted was that the South Vietnamese army (ARVN) should launch a ground attack on the *Việt Cộng* sanctuaries in Cambodia. Following the advice of General Westmoreland, who cautioned that these attacks could not be fully effective without US military support, it was planned that American forces would also back up ARVN's invasion of Cambodia.

Not unaware of the impact that this decision would have on public opinion, the various options were weighed at a National Security Council meeting on 22 April. Here a decisive intervention by Spiro Agnew in favour of aggressive military action in the 'Fishhook' and 'Parrot's beak' areas of Cambodia secured a decision to invade. Even within the administration the decision was divisive. From Kissinger's own staff, William Watts, Antony Lake (later National Security advisor to President Clinton) and Roger Morris resigned.

On 30 April, Nixon announced the new military action on television with a famously aggressive speech written by Pat Buchanan, later to become a well-known political pundit on television and then a Republican presidential candidate. Nixon justified the engagement in Cambodia by saying that to take no action against the North Vietnamese 'sanctuaries' would pose unacceptable risks to those American servicemen remaining in Vietnam, after the withdrawal of a further 150,000 troops.

Though the Chinese and Soviets made 'pro-forma' complaints about the violation of Cambodia's neutrality, both of America's geopolitical rivals continued their ongoing talks with barely an interruption. The opposition from within America was considerably rougher. From within the ranks of the liberal press establishment, there was universal condemnation of this perceived expansion of the war. *The New York Times* complained of 'a virtual renunciation of the president's promise of disengagement from South East Asia', while the *Wall Street Journal* asserted that 'Americans want an acceptable exit from Indochina not a deeper engagement.'[9]

On 1 May, a 43,000-strong South Vietnamese force, backed by 31,000 US troops, invaded Cambodia in pursuit of the North Vietnamese army and COSVN (Central Office South Vietnam), their southern headquarters. Back in America, student activity against the war was leading to severe civil unrest. Cambodia lit the fuse. Three days after the invasion of Cambodia, student disruption at Ohio's Kent University led to the call-out of the National Guard, who responded to violence by opening fire and killing four students. The nation was traumatised. Liberal anti-war demonstrations erupted across the nation. So fierce was the noise outside the White House that Kissinger was forced to sleep in the basement.

In spite of the hostility of the press and the apparent popular unrest on the street, opinion polls showed that 'Middle-America' stayed firmly behind the president's policies. However, though Nixon proclaimed the 'thousands of rockets and millions of rounds of ammunition'[10] that American and South Vietnamese forces had found in the *Việt Cộng*'s Cambodian sanctuaries, the American press was not listening. The invasion of Cambodia was seen only as an extension of the war, not as a means of foreshortening American involvement. The Senate, furious at the lack of presidential consultation on the invasion, gave in to the howls of the media. On

30 June 1970, the Senate voted 58 to 37 to pass the Cooper-Church Amendment, which in revised form passed both houses on 22 December and prohibited further military activity in Cambodia. As Kissinger concluded in his memoirs, 'The Senate had voted to give the Communists a free hand in Cambodia even though in the judgement of the Executive branch this doomed South Vietnam.'[11]

Unable to intervene militarily, the Nixon administration could, however, offer money to the beleaguered Cambodian government. Increasingly, Cambodia developed all the symptoms of a welfare junkie. The inflow of dollars, which by 1973 accounted for 95 per cent of government income, distorted all economic activity. Corruption within government and the military was rife. Officers even sold arms and supplies to the Khmer Rouge. Lon Nol's family was reportedly a prime beneficiary of commissions on arms sales. Also, finding soldiers prepared to fight was increasingly difficult. A conscription act in the summer of 1973 led to young men being taken from cinema queues and press-ganged into service. Inevitably, army desertions rose rapidly. Out of 230,000 troops at the beginning of 1974, 8,000 deserted in March alone.

In spite of the increasing levels of US military aid, after 1973, the increasing antipathetic attitude of Congress to the president affected the nature of the support that could be given to America's Cambodian ally. In *No More Vietnams* (1987), Nixon complained that 'Congress had prohibited us from undertaking military operations with ground troops on Cambodian territory .... We therefore chose our only remaining options: We resumed bombing Khmer Rouge positions.'[12] Although the bombing was a successful limiter of Khmer advances on Phnom Penh, it nevertheless helped their recruitment to the cause.

In 1973 *The New York Times* reported a villager who complained that 'The bombers may kill some Communists but they kill everyone else too.'[13] With an estimated 130,000 refugees from the bombing, fertile ground was created for Khmer Rouge recruitment officers, who would take people to see bomb craters. However, support for the Khmer Rouge was not unanimous. Richard Moose and James Lowenstein, staffers to the Senate Foreign Relations Committee that was invariably hostile to President Nixon, reported after a visit to Cambodia that ready popular support existed for Lon Nol. They also noted the Cambodians were 'mystified by the signs of American hesitancy in arming them to defend against an invading force armed by China and the Soviet Union'.[14]

After securing a settlement with North Vietnam in Paris, Nixon's problems in maintaining support for Cambodia increased. At first, American airpower, now diverted to concentrate solely on Cambodia, helped thwart continued advances on Phnom Penh by the Khmer Rouge and their North Vietnamese allies. Again Nixon faced vehement political opposition. The American Civil Liberties Union filed for an injunction against the bombing on the grounds that it was illegal, now that there were no US citizens to protect. In June 1973, both houses voted to end all bombing by the end of June. Refusing to accept that Cambodia should be left to its fate, Nixon vetoed the bill. However, Mike Mansfield, the Democrat majority leader in the Senate, warned that legislative action to stop the bombing would continue by attachments added to other bills 'again and again and again, until the will of the people prevails'.[15]

By now Nixon was being fatally undermined by the developing Watergate scandal, and he reluctantly agreed to a 15 August bombing deadline. Even this failed to assuage the liberal left. Senator Edward Kennedy thought the agreement 'infamous'; Senator Eagleton protested that 'Congress cannot sanction an unconstitutional and illegal endeavour for "just a little while".' Senator Tip O'Neill complained that 'Cambodia is not worth one American life.'[16]

With the president now committed to end the bombing of North Vietnamese 'sanctuaries' and the Khmer Rouge in Cambodia by August, the intervening months were used to expend the maximum possible tonnage against the Khmer Rouge. In the last seven months after the ceasefire with North Vietnam alone, some 257,465 tons were dropped on Cambodia, compared to the total of 160,000 tons dropped on Japan during the whole of the Second World War. However, after August 1973, without American bombing support, let alone ground support operations, Lon Nol's army had neither the leadership nor the training to repel the ferocious Khmer Rouge advance. In the absence of American help, Cambodia was doomed.

In July, President Thieu of South Vietnam warned Nixon: 'Cambodia is a weak country and if Sihanouk were overthrown, or if we encourage his overthrow, it is highly likely the Communists will take over.'[17] The tragedy for Cambodia was that by the time of Sihanouk's downfall in 1970, the USA no longer possessed the self-confidence or will power to engage the advancing communist forces on what was erroneously perceived by Democrats and by many Republicans to be a war separate from the conflict in Vietnam.

Nixon had come to office with a pledge to withdraw American forces from Vietnam. In spite of their geopolitical realism, and their understanding that the war in Cambodia was an integral part of the plan to stem communism in both Vietnam and Indochina as a whole, Nixon and Kissinger were never able to mobilise sufficient support in Congress. Even their bombing of Vietnamese forces located across the Cambodian border was tentative and secret. Not that this assuaged opposition within Congress. In 1974 the House Judiciary Committee proposed impeachment of the president on the grounds of the illegal and 'massive bombing of neutral Cambodia'.[18] Robert Drinan went as far as to observe that Nixon's conduct was 'more shocking and more unbelievable than the conduct of any president in any war in all of American history'.[19]

Remarkably, virtually all the academic establishment placed the blame for the destabilisation and fall of Cambodia squarely on the shoulders of Nixon and Kissinger. In this they took their cue from Sihanouk. 'Lon Nol was nothing without them', asserted Sihanouk, 'and the Khmer Rouge were nothing without Lon Nol. They demoralized Cambodia, they lost all of Indochina to the communists, and they created the Khmer Rouge'.[20] Similarly, William Shawcross blamed Nixon for the destabilisation of Cambodia and concluded, 'Cambodia was not a mistake;

it was a crime.'[21] Yet the evidence clearly demonstrates that it was the North Vietnamese invasion of Cambodia that initiated the destabilization of that country.

The reality was that, unlike America, the North Vietnamese had never been compromised in their disregard for the neutrality of Cambodia. In largely ignoring Laos and Cambodia, Presidents Kennedy and Johnson had forced the US army to fight the North with one arm firmly tied behind its back. By contrast, since 1959, General Giáp, North Vietnam's minister of defence, had made the invasion and control of Cambodia and Laos the fulcrum of the North's military strategy to conquer the South. The tragedy of Cambodia was not that it was bombed by Nixon, but that Presidents Johnson and Kennedy before him had decided not to include the defence of Cambodia as part of the war to save Indochina from communism.

In 1969, starting with the secret bombing, and later through land invasion, Nixon simply responded to the extensive use of Cambodia as a front-line for North Vietnamese operations. Cambodia had always represented a key component of the defence of Indochina from Communism. Eisenhower had recognised this fact; Kennedy recognised the same strategic truths but then chose to ignore them; President Johnson seemingly never fully understood the strategic need to defend the whole of Indochina from communism. In the mid-1960s, Lyndon Johnson might have carried Congressional support for operations to defeat the Vietnamese in Cambodia, but by 1968 it was too late.

Unfortunately for Cambodia and Vietnam, by the time the USA again had a leadership that recognised the umbilical link between these countries, the popular face of American politics was set against any policies that hinted at a deeper entrenchment in Indochina. Even if Nixon and Kissinger had been able to communicate their intentions better, or if the credibility of the presidency, severely damaged during the Johnson presidency, had not been shredded by the Watergate scandal, it is doubtful whether Congress's determination to exit Cambodia could have been thwarted. As Kissinger was to observe in *Years of Upheaval* (1982), 'Our inability to maintain domestic support doomed Cambodia'.[22] It also doomed South Vietnam.

38

Revolution's End: The Deaths of Mao, Zhou Enlai, and Lin Biao

China: 1970—6

At the 9th Chinese Communist Party Congress held in April 1969, Lin Biao appeared to be the hero of the hour. After his surprise call-up to replace Liu Shaoqi in 1966, Lin had dutifully stepped into the position of Mao's successor in waiting. He had loyally followed Mao's twists and turns in policy during the Cultural Revolution, and when the Red Guards had threatened to overthrow the party altogether, his units had ensured its survival. At the 9th Party Congress, Lin was formally named as Mao's successor, and this was written into the new Chinese Communist Party (CCP) constitution.

In addition, Lin's position was hugely enhanced by the increased presence of the People's Liberation Army (PLA) in all the organs of state and party; in 1969, army officers accounted for 52 per cent of the politburo and 62 per cent of the chairmen of revolutionary committees. Also compared to 1956, when the PLA represented 19 per cent of the Central Committee, army personnel amounted to 45 per cent after at the 9th Congress.

Such was his position of military and political power that *The Economist* went as far as to suggest that Lin Biao could become the instigator of another 'World War'. Yet a mere 30 months later, Lin was dead. As he fled China with his family, Lin Biao's plane crashed in the mountains of Mongolia and killed all on board. What caused this remarkable fall from grace? President Nixon, who arrived in China shortly after Lin's demise, was told by Mao that 'a reactionary group [was] opposed to our contact with you . . . the result was they got on an airplane and fled abroad.'[1] However, this was a far from accurate summation of events.

For the purpose of Mao's aim to reinvigorate the party through the Cultural Revolution, his choice of an unwaveringly loyal head of the PLA was astute. In all other respects, Lin Biao was an entirely inappropriate future leader of China. He had risen to prominence as possibly the most successful field officer of the civil war with the *Kuomintang*. When the Communist state was established in 1949, Lin was the third-ranked Marshall in the PLA behind Zhu De and Peng Dehui. As the general in charge of Central Southern China, Lin played little part in the politics of the first decade of the CCP, and only came to prominence when he was appointed to the Party Central Committee on 25 May 1958. With Zhu De in honourable retirement, Lin grasped his opportunity to advance by launching one of the more vicious attacks on Peng Dehui, by then the senior ranking Marshall, at the infamous Lushan Conference in 1959.

As head of the PLA from 1959, Lin further burnished his credentials as a loyal acolyte by launching perhaps the most famous campaign of political indoctrination of the twentieth century. A small breviary of Mao's sayings and writings was packaged in a small red book. Mao's *Little Red Book* was produced in millions and distributed to troops for study at political sessions that took on the fervour of institutionalised religious gatherings. The images of drab-suited PLA soldiers and later the Red Guards, waving their *Little Red Books*, became some of the most lasting images of 1960s China. The PLA became the vanguard of the movement to build Mao's personality cult, a policy that Mao half-heartedly denounced and privately encouraged. Lin also won Mao's favour by such egalitarian measures as abolishing officers' uniforms. The development of China's nuclear capability under his watch also enhanced his position.

However, beneath the surface Lin Biao was a far from stable personality. Severely wounded during the war with Japan, by the 1960s, Lin Biao was not a healthy man. In addition, an addiction to opium in the 1940s seems to have seriously impaired his mental faculties. He developed a paranoid fear of light, air and water. Since he was unable to drink liquids, his wife 'Ye Qun made sure he received liquid by dipping steamed buns in water'[2]; his fear of even the sound of water made it impossible for him to use a toilet. He would urinate and defecate in a bedpan placed on his bed with a quilt draped over his head. Dehydration made him susceptible to 'kidney stones' in his urinary tract, an excruciating condition. Frequently, he would cancel meetings rather than face daylight or open air. He wore his clothes skin-tight, and Mao's doctor Zhisui Li noted that his uniform might have been glued on.

Added to the problems of a neurotic, if not paranoid personality, Lin was surrounded by a court of family members, who intrigued constantly on his behalf. Leading this group was another of the graspingly ambitious and venal wives, who characterised Mao's court. When she was not ministering to Lin in his sick bed, Ye Qun, as head of his personal office and also as head of the General Office of the Military Affairs Committee, controlled not only access to his office but also the flow of documents to his desk. As one of his secretaries would later comment, 'Ye Qun did many things behind Lin Biao's back while holding high his banner'.[3] Such was her incessant nagging that Lin would on occasions banish her for days. In scenes reminiscent of a court farce, Ye Qun would then go running to an amused Mao to ask him to intercede.

Above all, however, Lin Biao was fatally flawed in having almost no political ability other than an unfailing obsequiousness to Mao. Apart from resisting the chaos of the Cultural Revolution within the army and emphasising on occasions the importance of production, Lin acted as Mao's loyal cheerleader. Indeed, so excessive was this trait that it probably irritated Mao more than it flattered him. However, it is clear from the documentation circulated among the senior leadership that he contributed little by way of comment or initiative. What then was the root cause of his downfall?

The official Chinese explanation lay in two parts. First, Lin Biao was accused of political differences with Mao over the nature of the latter's genius. In the new constitutional proposals for which Lin was responsible, it was inserted into the text that Mao had 'inherited, defended and developed Marxism-Leninism with genius, creatively and comprehensively.'[4] Mao demurred and crossed out this piece of arrant nonsense. More importantly perhaps, he refused Lin's assertion that Mao's own position should be written and defined in the constitution as state chairman.

Mao declined this role, which he had given up to Liu Shaoqi in 1959, but Lin's perseverance in trying to persuade Mao to accept this position (apparently on six occasions) was interpreted as an attempt by Lin to grasp this position for himself. This struggle over the state chairmanship came to a head at the 9th Central Committee Plenum meeting from 23 August to 6 September 1970. Mao again refused and snapped that whoever wanted to take on the job should do so. The second part of the explanation lies in Lin's supposed opposition to Zhou and Mao's planned rapprochement with the USA. Although Lin's fatal flight to Russia is sometimes cited as evidence of his Soviet leanings, it is also obvious that he had few alternative destinations.

Altogether, the idea that a combination of Lin's vaunting ambition and his refusal to accept an alliance with America led him to launch a coup d'état seems somewhat far-fetched. Lin had after all tried to refuse Mao's offer to replace Liu Shaoqi in 1966. However, even an unambitious Lin must have been aware of the danger of being the 'No. 2', particularly to a character as unpredictable as Mao. Indeed, written evidence of these thoughts was found in his papers; 'Today he uses sweet words and honeyed talk to those whom he entices, and tomorrow puts them to death for fabricated crimes'.[5]

Lin would also not have been reassured by Mao's suggestion that Lin too should have a successor, particularly when ultra-leftist Zhang Chunqiao was touted as a possibility. Though it is possible that once in power, he might well have been paranoid enough to want to shore up his position with a title that had once belonged to Liu Shaoqi, there seems little evidence that he sought to overthrow Mao. If there was a plot initiated by his 24-year-old son Lin Liguo, deputy head of the combat department of the Air Force, to blow up Mao's train as it returned to Beijing on 8–11 September, it was almost certainly a last-minute plan embarked on when a purge of Lin Biao seemed inevitable.

In looking for the real cause of Lin Biao's fall, the quixotic and paranoid behaviour of Chairman Mao himself again becomes paramount. It could not have
been lost on a man of Mao's finely tuned political antenna that in seeking to control the Cultural Revolution, he had created the 'spectre of Bonapartism'.[6] Having
purged the party of 'capitalist revisionism', he could not have relished the idea that
after his death, his precious revolution would revert to a bureaucratic military dictatorship; after all, that, in the form of the *Kuomintang*, is what Mao had defeated.
If Lin Biao's fears for his future revealed themselves in paranoia over the seemingly
minor issue of the state chairmanship, it seems certain too that Mao was paranoid
about the power that had now been handed to the army.

If Mao was not instinctively fearful of Lin's powerful position as head of the
army, Mao's wife, Jiang Qing, and the ultra-leftists were certainly feeding poison
into Mao's ears. While Jiang and Lin may have been perceived as allies at the beginning of the Cultural Revolution, it was circumstance rather than purpose which
had thrown them together. Lin disliked Jiang and where possible kept her at a distance. On one occasion in February 1967, at a meeting regarding the role of the
Cultural Revolution in the military, an exasperated Lin, who was usually quietly
spoken, shouted at his wife to 'get Jiang Qing out of here'.[7]

Indeed it was Lin's wife, Ye Qun, sensing the potential for danger from the
ultra-leftists, who went out of her way to soothe relations between her husband and
Jiang Qing. After 1969, however, Lin stood squarely in the way of the ultra-left's
possibility of seizing power, and not surprisingly they actively conspired against
him. As for the 'survivors', as Zhou and the other leaders who rode out the Cultural Revolution are sometimes called, it seems unlikely that they did anything to
protect Lin from either Mao or the ultra-left. While Zhou never seems to have
pushed himself as a candidate to take over from Mao, it would have been curious
if he had not been a little jealous of Lin who, in an earlier era, had been his pupil.

However, with the onset of Parkinson's disease, a neurological illness well-
known for producing psychological as well as physical disorder, particularly paranoia, there was clearly no need for logic to play a major part in Mao's wish to
destroy Lin Biao. Autocratic dictators can knock down favourites as quickly as
they build them up. In familiar style, Mao's first target was a loyal acolyte of Lin.
The hapless Chen Boda, the former Mao secretary and left-wing intellectual who,
after the disbandment of the Cultural Revolutionary Group, had jumped on the
Lin bandwagon as his ticket to power, was the first to be purged at the Lushan
Plenum. The warning signs for Lin were clear.

In the autumn of 1970, in a re-run of the precautions taken by Mao before the
Cultural Revolution, the leadership of the Beijing Military Region was reorganised
to secure Mao's 'back garden'. In April 1971, new appointments were made to the
Military Affairs Commission to offset the power of Lin's ally and Head of the Air
Force Wu Faxian. By summer of 1971, Mao was touring Wuhan, Changsha and
Nanchang on a trip clearly designed to bolster support.

Commenting on the Second Plenum, Mao said, 'A certain person was very anxious to become state chairman, to split the Party, and to seize power.'[8] By September 1971, for Lin Biao and his family, clearly aware of Mao's intentions, the prospects looked bleak enough for precipitate action. Having rejected his daughter Doudou's appeals that he should move into honourable retirement like Marshall Zhu De before him, Lin's only choices were to try to raise the standard of revolt in Guangdong, his old stomping ground of South Central, or to flee to Russia. This, it seems, was his chosen and ultimately fatal path.

In the wake of the demolition of Lin Biao and his clan, and the purge of his followers that came in its wake, it seemed that a degree of normalcy might return to the government of China. Zhou, who had loyally carried out the plan to isolate Lin Biao and who also invited and negotiated with Henry Kissinger to bring Nixon to China, now seemed in the ascendant, and in 1972 he went some way in trying to repair the damage of the Cultural Revolution.

Indeed, it was over this period that the 'survivor group', including Zhou, Vice Premier Li Xiannian and former Marshal Zhu De, came to the fore; this softening in Mao's stance, in part a reaction to the Lin Biao episode, brought with it a rehabilitation of many of the 'victims' of the Cultural Revolution. These included former Foreign Minister Chen Yi, whose death in 1972, to the astonishment of his family, was met with Mao's surprise attendance and oration at his funeral. Most importantly however, 'Capitalist Roader No. 2', Deng Xiaoping, who, after the death of Lin Biao, wrote to Mao asking to be rehabilitated in November 1971 and again in August 1972, was allowed to return to the capital and to the court of the 'Emperor'. 'He simply walked in one evening at a reception for Prince Sihanouk'.[9] It was as if he had just come back from a vacation.

Yet Mao was still wedded to the principles of perpetual revolution; he would not allow the pendulum to swing too far back to the pragmatists. Throughout the early 1970s, Mao remained true to his revolutionary ideals and what he perceived to be the successes of the Cultural Revolution. While his personal relations with the ultra-left, particularly his wife, whom he ordered out of the government compound in 1975, remained fraught with tension, he nevertheless continued to espouse their cause.

However, Mao caused astonishment when he hand-picked a 36-year-old junior cadre official from Shanghai to be his successor. Wang Hongwen was a worker's leader in Shanghai, who had emerged as a 'beneficiary' of the Cultural Revolution; representing both youth and workers, he may have appeared to Mao as an acceptable face of the Cultural Revolution.

In May 1973, he was catapulted into the number three position in the politburo. Along with ultra-leftist Zhang Chunqiao and Yao Wenyuan, he was asked to prepare documents for the 10th Party Congress. It soon became clear even to Mao that Wang Hongwen had been massively over-promoted. Apart from his liking for the trappings of power, particularly hunting and fishing, Wang palpably failed to develop a strong independent line that Mao clearly hoped would enable him to manage both the 'survivor–pragmatist' group on the one hand and the ultra-leftists on the other. He rapidly became Jiang Qing's pawn, and when Mao referred, for the first time, to the 'Gang of Four' at a politburo meeting in July 1974, Wang was clearly in her camp along with Zhang Chunqiao and Yao Wenyuan.

In spite of these criticisms of his wife, Mao continued to play off all sides. His energy for intrigue was remarkable in view of his assertion that 'The time for me to report to Marx is nearing every day.'[10] Although Mao's appetite for campaigns was somewhat diminished as his end approached, for the first time Mao seems to have given encouragement to attacks on Zhou Enlai, who had infuriated the ultra-left by his rehabilitation of Deng and the cadres overthrown during the Cultural Revolution. Jiang organised a barrage of intellectual criticism of Lin Biao and Confucius. In particular, the *Analects of Confucius* were quoted to criticise the twelfth-century statesman, the Duke of Zhou. The obvious pun was intended to link criticism of Lin Biao and Zhou Enlai together in what became known as the *pi lin, pi kong* campaign. By now, however, Zhou Enlai was in any case a spent force. Diagnosed with stomach cancer in 1973, Zhou moved out of the government complex on 1 June 1974 and into the Capital Hospital, where he spent the next 18 months.

While the 'work-alcoholic' Zhou continued to operate from his sick bed, his energies were naturally diminished and Mao desperately needed a replacement. In another volte-face, which no doubt reflected his despair at the failure of Wang and the irresponsibility of the ultra-left, Mao turned once more to Deng Xiaoping. On Deng's return to Beijing in 1973, Mao had put him to work with Wang on a tour of the country to produce a report on the state of affairs.

At the beginning of 1974, Zhou devolved the handling of foreign affairs to Deng Xiaoping, who registered a triumph when he was sent to New York to address the General Assembly of the United Nations. On his return to Beijing, no doubt reflecting Mao's view of his trip, Deng was greeted by virtually the entire politburo at the airport. In October 1974, Mao himself proposed that Deng should assume the role of Zhou's deputy, with the title vice premier, and take over the effective day-to-day role as China's chief administrator.

Deng was also reinstalled in all his former positions, including chief of staff of the PLA and vice chairman of the Military Affairs Commission. For a 70-year-old man, Deng launched into his revived career with astonishing vigour. In a whirlwind of conferences and seminars, Deng set the tone for 1975 to be a year of return to pragmatism and stability. In themes that were to become his hallmark in the 1980s, Deng Xiaoping stressed the need for industrial research and investment, the acquisition of foreign technology and importantly the restoration of management power and stable worker relations. He also felt confident enough to argue for the restoration of material incentives. Notwithstanding his heterodox views, Mao supported Deng, while continuing to propagate the leftist agenda which attacked wage differentials and free market symbols such as commodity exchanges.

In hindsight, it is clear that Deng overplayed his hand; he should have bided his time. However, with Mao now visibly in decline, Deng may well have judged that this was the time to move to establish his reputation with the 'survivor–pragmatist' camp. From early 1974 to mid-1975, Mao developed cataracts that prevented him from reading. During this period, all documents were read out to him by his young female companion, Zhang Yufeng.

Also, now beset with Parkinson's disease, Mao's speech was becoming increasingly slurred and virtually incomprehensible to all but a handful of helpers. From his grunts, Zhang would often have to guess at the meaning. Meanwhile, Zhou was also in fast decline. On 8 January, he finally succumbed to cancer. Zhou Enlai, the brilliant, hardworking and dogged bureaucrat, had been the perpetual sidekick to Mao throughout his tyranny. He was a difficult man to judge, not strong enough to replace or overthrow Mao, or to prevent his catastrophic policies, but able nevertheless, at times, to deflect the worst of his cruelties. Deng, who gave the funeral address, later offered the following summary of the life of this indefatigable servant of the Chinese revolution:

> Premier Zhou was a man who worked hard and uncomplainingly all his life . . . survived the 'Cultural Revolution' when we were knocked down . . . able to survive and play the neutralizing role . . . which reduced the losses. He succeeded in protecting quite a number of people.[11]

Mao was not a sentimental man, however. Not once in the months of Zhou's illness did Mao send him a note of comfort or sympathy. Indeed, in his last act of spite and contrariness, Mao supported the increasingly virulent attacks of the ultra-left on both Zhou and Deng. Former tyro of the left Kang Sheng even rose from his sick bed, though he too was dying of cancer, to warn Mao of plots to overthrow the revolution.

In November 1975, when Mao called a politburo notification conference at which Hua Guofeng read out a summary of the chairman's speech that criticised attacks made on the Cultural Revolution, it was clear to everyone that support had been withdrawn from Deng and the 'pragmatists'. Zhou was probably fortunate to die when he did rather than face the humiliating possibility of being purged. Meanwhile Deng, on the day that he was purged for the second time, fled the capital under the protection of elements in the army loyal to him and spent the next nine months in hiding.

In making Hua Guofeng his chosen successor, Mao had pitched his last surprise. Although not in the same league of misjudgments as Lin Biao or Wang Hongwen, Hua Guofeng was still a dud. Apart from coming from Mao's home province of Hunan, where he had been first secretary, he had little to recommend him; even Mao could do little more than describe him as a safe pair of hands. He limply suggested that Hua 'had experience in work at the prefectural and provincial levels, and his performance as Minister of Public Security over the past several years is not bad. Secondly he is loyal and honest. Thirdly he is not stupid.'[12]

Why did Mao fail to appoint a 'leftist' successor? Here one can only surmise that he believed that the appointment of his wife or Zhang Chunqiao might have risked a reaction from the army, which would have swept away the revolution altogether. Perhaps in an ideal world, Mao would have found a man who combined Deng Xiaoping's energy and administrative skills with the revolutionary fervour of the ultra-leftists. However, in Mao's inhuman appetite for the revolutionary perfectibility of man, he was unable to understand that these goals were by their nature incompatible.

The appointment of a political makeweight did not augur well for the future. Mao's death on 9 September 1976 left a vacuum that Hua Guofeng was ill-equipped to fill. While it would be difficult to dispute Mao's genius as a revolutionary, his career as an autocratic leader of his country had ultimately proved a disaster. Apart from an ill-chosen successor, he left behind him a political system in which the army, rather than the constitution, was the final arbiter of power.

In the CPP, Mao left a legacy of corruption and fear; his attempts to purify the party during the Cultural Revolution merely served to create a bitter factional strife, which could be played out only after his death. As for his management of the economy, his utopian logic had ended the lives of tens of millions of peasants in the worst mass starvations of the twentieth century. While advances had been made in industry, largely as a result of the re-unification of China and the restoration of peace, the seeds of bureaucratic ossification of heavy industry, which had characterised all of the post-war command economies, were firmly planted in Maoist China. Some 32 years later, the problems of the state-owned enterprises have yet to be fully resolved.

If Mao Zedong had a positive legacy, it was the ending of the era of 'warlordism' and the reunification of China under strong central rule; he achieved this by a brilliantly conceived and executed revolution. Above all, however, Mao left a Chinese population traumatised by the ruthlessness of his rule and by his quixotic and destructive switches in policy. By the standard of the liberal democracies of the West, Mao had clearly failed to create a system that could provide a better quality of existence for his people; however, even by his own measures he was a failure. Far from leaving a Chinese people changed in its nature by revolutionary purity, Mao left a country disillusioned in the process and purpose of a revolution that had been his life's work. The author of *The Wild Swans* (1992), Jung Chang, records on hearing of Mao's death:

> The news filled me with such euphoria that for an instant I was numb. My ingrained self-censorship immediately started working: I registered the fact that there was an orgy of weeping going on around me, and that I had to come up with a suitable performance .... I swiftly buried my head in her shoulder and heaved appropriately.[13]

39

The Murder of Aquino: The Disgrace of Ferdinand Marcos

Philippines: 1960–86

It would be an understatement to suggest that Ferdinand Marcos had a murky past. In 1939 he was found guilty of murdering Julio Nalundasan, a politician who had defeated Marcos's father to win a Congressional seat in 1935. Somewhat inexplicably, Marcos, by now a young law student who conducted his own appeal, was released from prison without having to serve his ten-year sentence. His saviour, Laurel, was a Supreme Court judge, who was later to become the Philippines pro-Japanese wartime leader. Laurel was apparently impressed by the young Marcos who had graduated top in his bar exams albeit from his prison cell.

Marcos's activities in the war were equally murky. It was later proven by the CIA that his post-war claims to have been an anti-Japanese guerrilla leader were entirely spurious. Given the pedigree of Laurel, who became his sponsor and friend, and the known pro-Japanese leanings of his father, the likelihood of his being an anti-Japanese war hero was always unlikely. However, in view of the wartime double dealing of most of the Filipino elite, of which he was an undoubted member, his political opportunism at least was unexceptional.

Marcos had been born into a minor line of agricultural 'gentry' on 11 September 1917 in the Northern Luzon town of Sarrat. His grandfather, Fructusoso Edralin, the illegitimate son of a Spanish provincial judge, owned a coffee plantation. While his father's family were thus classic Spanish *mestizo* stock, his mother, a teacher and daughter of storekeepers, was a Quetulios; this wealthy merchant family were Chinese *mestizo* from Ilocos Sur.

While Mariano Marcos may have been Marcos's registered father, it was rumoured that his mother, Josefa Edralin, seven years older than her husband, had actually been made pregnant by Ferdinand Chua, a wealthy Chinese businessman from Ilocos. It seems likely that Chua, who became Ferdinand Marcos's godfather, paid off Mariano Marcos, and funded his son's move to Manila and his political career. Inheriting his father's political ambitions, Ferdinand Marcos came to prominence in 1959 when, in a snub to the American-financed 'alliance' ticket, voters preferred the outsider Marcos and his candidates.

Two years later, Marcos declined to run for president, but provided funding and strategic help for Macapagal in his election victory over the incumbent Garcia. An astonishing sum, equivalent to 13 per cent of GDP, was spent on the campaign. Support for Macapagal soon dissipated. An attempt at land redistribution alienated the traditional family elites, while its modest ambition was a disappointment to rural electoral voters. The commercially important Chinese community was alienated by a campaign of forced expulsion of Chinese residents, while American support was undermined by the expulsion of an American businessman, Harry Stonehill.

Nevertheless, Macapagal continued to pursue vigorous anti-communist policies, which, in the light of America's increasing engagement in Vietnam, was the overriding policy desire of successive American administrations. For the 1965 presidential elections, there were no clear ideological divides between the candidates, the incumbent Macapagal and Ferdinand Marcos. For once, America was ambivalent and stood aside.

The 'money game', which was the main post-war determinant of electoral politics, remained the key to success. Apparently it was Imelda Marcos, using a profusion of tears in her pleading, who won the financial backing of the powerful sugar baron Fernando Lopez; he also became Marcos's running mate. Out of a total of 8 million votes cast, Marcos won by a comfortable 600,000 margin.

Standing in Luneta Park, Marcos greeted his supporters with the assurance that he had won a 'mandate for greatness'.[1] In a statement whose irony would wear thin over the next two decades, the new president promised to end 'every form of waste or conspicuous consumption'.[2] However, with some US$ 100 million spent on the election, much of it provided by Marcos and his financial backers, it was not surprising that he and his cronies would need to seek an early payback from their investment.

Marcos used government funds to enable him to take over banks, factories and hotels. Those hostile to Marcos had their assets sequestered and given to his family members. A brother was given stakes in insurance, banking and real estate, while a sister became a significant ship owner. Marcos's mother became a business magnate with interests in tobacco, timber and food processing.

A close business relationship with Marcos also helped Benigno Aquino's cousin, Eduardo Cojuangco, become the richest man in the Philippines; Cojuangco built a virtual monopoly in the Philippines' important coconut industry; acquired control of San Miguel, the country's dominant beer company; and built bottling plants for both Coca-Cola and Pepsi. His eventual wealth was estimated at US$ 4 billion. Marcos also took care to reward his military by turning a blind eye to illegal smuggling and logging. In effect, army generals were given licence to operate as racketeers.

Imelda also immersed herself in the systematic looting of the Philippines. Through her posts as governor of metropolitan Manila, minister of human settlement and chairman of some 23 government agencies and corporations, Imelda controlled huge budgets, patronage and access to decision making. Through her sponsorship, Manila acquired some 11 five-star hotels and a 5,000-seat international convention centre.

In a particularly notorious episode, Benjamin 'Kokoy' Romualdez 'persuaded' Eugenio, the dying proprietor of an electrical company, whose son was being held in prison on conspiracy charges, to hand over his assets to the Marcos family. At Eugenio's funeral in Quezón, Imelda suddenly made an unannounced appearance when armed men brought an ornate chair to the front of the service, from where she presided over ceremonies. Nevertheless, Eugenio Junior languished and died in jail.

If the main aim of the Marcos regime was to make money, the precondition was the acquisition and maintenance of power. On becoming president, Marcos also appointed himself as minister of defence, a post which he held for the next 13 years. He proceeded to secure military allegiance; of the army's 25 most senior officers, some 14 were forced into retirement. They were replaced with loyal cronies from his home region of Ilocos Norte. Most significantly, Marcos's cousin Colonel Fabian Ver started his rise to power by being appointed commander of the Marcos's own Security Command.

The corrupt Marcos regime did little to assuage agrarian support for the continuing communist insurgency. Communist aggression took on a new energy after radical leader Jose Maria Sison left the Soviet-backed PKP (*Partido Komunista ng Philipinas*) in 1968 to form a new Chinese-supported Communist Party of the Philippines (CPP). The CPP developed a military wing, the New People Army (NPA), which was led by the former Huk guerrilla leader Dante Buscayno. Curiously, Buscayno had been introduced to Sison by a rising Liberal Party senator, Benigno Aquino, who was far more left wing in his leanings than the policies espoused by his party.

In spite of growing corruption and political unrest, Marcos was re-elected president in 1969 with a margin of victory which had increased to 2 million votes. By most accounts, the election victory was corruptly purchased to a degree that was exceptional even by Filipino standards. Eduardo Quintero from Leyte, Imelda's home province, would later reveal that she had passed him bribes on 18 occasions.

Such were the financial resources used by Marcos to secure victory that the national budget was effectively depleted. Marcos's victory was followed by increasing questioning of his legitimacy, which came to a head with a 20,000-strong anti-government demonstration by peasants and students in 1970. The following August saw further electoral disruption when grenades were thrown at a Liberal Party rally in Plaza Miranda; six people were killed and 100 injured.

Violence also erupted in the Southern islands where Muslims were massacred by Christian gangs. Marcos, who was later shown by the CIA to have orchestrated the attacks on Muslims, used the unrest to accuse the communists of responsibility. This was a convenient pretext for the suspension of habeas corpus. Aquino, who had increasingly emerged as a likely winning candidate for the 1973 presidential elections, was arrested and charged with participation in the supposed political insurrections. In spite of Marcos's manoeuvring, the Liberals continued to win seats in senatorial elections.

As presidential elections approached, a series of 'supposed' insurgency bombings rocked Manila. Bombs exploded in March, April, May and June. In July, there was an escalation to three terrorist explosions, followed by seven in August and five more in early September. The bombings, now widely presumed to have been organised by Marcos, gave him the excuse he needed to plan the imposition of martial law with General Juan Ponce Enrile.

In spite of the misgivings of the US ambassador Henry Byroade, who attempted to dissuade him from this course, Marcos suspended the constitution on 22 September. In a piece of surreal theatre, Marcos's chief of defence arranged for his own car to be attacked. This pretext for the imposition of martial law was followed by the arrest of Aquino and the leaders of the Liberal Party. Supporters, including journalists, publishers and priests, were also arrested. Tanks occupied the streets. The brilliantly conducted coup saw minimal popular backlash.

Although President Nixon had supposedly been pre-warned of the coup plot, neither the State Department nor the CIA warned off Marcos. Indeed, a Rand Corporation report in November 1972 went as far as to conclude that Marcos had instigated the coup with the tacit approval of an American government, which was keen to safeguard its economic and strategic interests. The American Chamber of Commerce in Manila was quick to announce support for the coup within days.

To sound out the Nixon administration, Alejandro Melchor was sent to Washington, where the coup was welcomed by the Chairman of the Joint Chiefs of Staff, Admiral Thomas Moorer. Equally positive communication was received from long-term Philippines supporter Senator Daniel Inouye of Hawaii; even Democrat chairman of the Senate Foreign Relations Committee, and long-time scourge of President Nixon, Senator William Fulbright, was found to be supportive. In the American press, only *The Washington Post* failed to endorse the coup; by contrast *The New York Times* expressed America's consensus sentiment when it described Marcos as a figure of 'strength in a nation of uncertainty'.[3]

Marcos justified his reversion to martial law after the issue of Proclamation 1081, on the grounds that the Philippines were 'imperilled by the danger of a violent overthrow, insurrection and rebellion'.[4] This was an exaggerated claim. The government's claim that they faced an 8,000-strong NPA rebel force was risible. The American ambassador knew as much and cabled the State Department accordingly. The Rand Corporation would later conclude that NPA forces numbered about 1,000. In the face of the apparent evidence of Marcos's duplicity, why did the Nixon administration yield so passively to the termination of democracy in the Philippines?

With the benefit of hindsight it seems likely that political passivity towards Marcos, evident in both Republicans and Democrats, was caused by the overriding imbroglio of the Vietnamese War. Nixon, Kissinger and Congress were entirely focussed on the issues of negotiating peace with North Vietnam and withdrawal of their forces from the South.

In its conduct of foreign policy, America has, characteristically, only been able to hold one key issue in focus at any one time. In post-war history, nothing dominated the foreign policy agenda of America as much as Vietnam. The Philippines was not only a sideshow, but it was a positively benign sideshow. Marcos was not a perfect ally, but at least he was an ally. Moreover, he represented a political caste, which had consistently faced down communism.

To expect Nixon to set about the undermining of a natural ally, while in the process of disengaging from Vietnam, would have been absurd in the context of the global conflict with communism. Also with hindsight, the full extent of Marcos's depravity is now known, but for the American State Department there was no expectation that martial law was anything more than a temporary interruption in the Philippines' less-than-perfect democratic process.

On a more prosaic level, the USA had invested heavily in the defence of the Philippines. Between 1946 and 1972, the USA spent some US$ 2.52 billion on a security force that had almost doubled in strength, from 37,000 to 62,000. Neither did Marcos's usurpation of power diminish American enthusiasm to fund his government. Military aid to the Philippines in 1973 was tripled. Over the next decade, the Philippines acquired Tiger II fighters, Huey helicopters and C-47 transport planes. The size of the Philippines armed forces was also increased to 200,000.

Marcos was fully aware of the financial value of American support and the increasing strategic importance of the Philippines after the fall of Indochina to the Communists. The lease payments on Clarke Field and Subic Bay amounted to some 3 per cent of the Philippine GDP, and were a key source of government finance. Such was Marcos's confidence in his position that in 1976 he turned down a US$ 1 billion five-year deal for America's use of its key military installations.

However, Marcos was slow to appreciate that the political mood in America during the mid-1970s was changing. The apparent Vietnam debacle, ending with the loss of the whole of Indochina, combined with the Watergate scandal, laid open presidential executive powers to unprecedented scrutiny. The high tide of the CIA's unchecked global activity and influence had now passed. An era of 'accountability' had arrived.

The long war in Vietnam, with its pitiful outcome, had undermined American belief in its force of arms. Militarism was now a dirty word. In 1971, Vice President Agnew told graduates of the Air Force Academy that 'You are facing a world where your efforts, your patriotism, your sacrifice will probably be denigrated.'[5]

Increasing numbers of Americans now questioned their country's international activities. In the USA, membership of Amnesty International grew from just 3,000 in 1974 to 50,000 two years later.

The 'moral' imperative in American foreign policy, which had remained largely inert since the isolation of the 1920s and 1930s, resurfaced, and was a key ingredient in sweeping the unknown outsider, Jimmy Carter, to the White House. By the time Carter had become president, the American Congress had already elevated the role of the coordinator for human rights and humanitarian issues to the rank of an assistant secretary of state with an independent Human Rights Bureau. To this newly important post, Carter appointed Patricia Derian, a radical civil rights activist from Mississippi.

Derian, later nicknamed Pat 'Durian' (after the foul-smelling Asian fruit) by Carlos Romulo, MacArthur's speech writer, applied her domestic human rights positions with crass arrogance in dealing with sovereign nations allied to America in the war with communism. Although Richard Holbrooke, assistant secretary of state for East Asian and Pacific affairs, managed to thwart the impact of the most ludicrous of the international human rights positions adopted by Derian and other liberal Carter appointees, the conditions imposed on the conduct of US foreign policy had seemingly changed forever. Marcos had little awareness of how, in the long term, this would affect his position within the context of America's global strategic considerations.

In the short term, Derian's visit to Manila in 1978 stirred trouble. Attacks on Minister of Defence Enrile were compounded by a shouting match with Marcos, who declared that he would not be a hostage to 'dollar diplomacy'. In general, Derian's provocations around Asia simply served to undermine America's foreign policy objectives, while doing little to progress the cause of human rights.

Meanwhile in the Philippines, legislative elections, which were finally held in 1978, led to a sweeping and fraudulently won victory of Marcos's New Society Party over Aquino's People's Party. Popular sentiment had clearly been with Aquino. Political scientist Carl Land, who went to observe the election at first-hand, noted that

> Neighbourhood rallies for the opposition were packed with members of the working and lower middle classes, who stood for hours to hear the candidates lambaste the regime. Neighbourhood rallies for the government candidates, on the other hand, drew much smaller numbers, mostly children and local riffraff who had been provided with chairs and sandwiches and, in some cases, had been paid to attend.[6]

In parliament (*Batasan*), opposition candidates won a derisory 13 seats. Philippines democracy was of course completely discredited. The absurdity of the result nevertheless had some positive long-term results. A free press was able to deride the *Batasan* as 'an expensive Xerox copying machine',[7] while Senator Salonga noted that 'This election may be a sham, I will say that, but it has awakened the slumbering sense of injustice of the people'.[8]

Much to America's consternation, election victory was followed by the negotiation and signing of a non-aggression pact with Vietnam. Marcos also abolished tax concessions for American companies. However, a complete breakdown in relations was never a realistic option for either side. The spats between America and the Philippines in 1978 were more in the nature of a tiff between friends.

In 1978, US Ambassador Richard Murphy, by warning that a human rights report currently under preparation might prevent aid to the Philippines after it was published, managed to force Marcos's signature to a US$ 500 million deal for military, naval and air bases until 1991; this was half the amount offered by Kissinger a few years earlier.

However the World Bank increased its loan allocations to the Philippines from US$ 317.5 million in 1976 to US$ 536 million in 1978. President Carter's liberal credentials were little burnished by his administration's reversion to 'real politik'. An opposition group including former President Macapagal, four nuns and two bishops published an open letter denouncing Carter's support for Marcos. Nevertheless, the importance of America's Philippine bases soon became apparent when, as a reward for Soviet military help in repelling a Chinese invasion of Vietnam in February 1979, the Vietnamese government gave the Soviet Union a long-term base for their Pacific fleet at Cam Ranh Bay, some 290 km northeast of Saigon.

If the election of President Carter embedded 'political correctness' in the conduct of foreign policy and caused dissension in America's relations with its allies, his defeat to Ronald Reagan brought a return to a more unquestioning approach to America's allies. Jeanne Kirkpatrick, a former Marxist apostate, who became Reagan's foreign policy advisor in his 1980 election campaign and later his ambassador to the United Nations, argued with indubitable logic that America was right to support authoritarian regimes that were hostile to communism, not only because they were allies but also because they retained the possibility of moving towards democracy_ an outcome which was barred to communist states. The 'Kirkpatrick Doctrine,' as it became known, was a forerunner of aggressive pro-democratisation policies of the 'neo-conservative' wing of the Republican Party.

As Elliot Abrams, a Reagan supporter noted, 'where human rights violations were a problem, US interests would take priority'.[9] Predictably, Reagan's State Department was purged of 'liberals'. Derian's replacement at the Human Rights Bureau was Ernest Lefever, a friend of the South African regime, who had publicly called for the removal of human rights legislation.

Marcos's depredations continued unchecked. Although he had lifted martial law on 17 January 1981, Marcos forced through a constitutional amendment which provided six-year presidential terms. He also enshrined the right of the president to dissolve the legislature and to nominate his successor. A plebiscite on these issues achieved a not very credible 80 per cent vote in favour.

Such was the disillusionment with the political process that in the elections planned for June 1983, moderate opposition candidates decided to boycott them.

In a sign of shifting loyalties, even Laurel's son, Senator Salvador Laurel, now joined the opposition to Marcos. Even more seriously for Marcos, Enrile's removal as minister of defence and his replacement by Marcos's cousin and placeman, General Fabian Ver, created a split within the Philippines army and a focal point for military opposition to the regime.

While the first cracks in the Marcos regime were now appearing, the Reagan administration remained trenchant in its support. After the 1983 elections in which Marcos insisted there had been a completely improbable 90–95 per cent turnout, Vice President George Bush (senior) was despatched to Manila to attend the inauguration. Bush congratulated Marcos, saying, 'We love your adherence to democratic principles.'[10]

The degree of Marcos's vote rigging and suppression of the opposition could not have been a mystery to either the Carter or the Reagan administration. Between 1977 and 1985, the Marcos regime made some 21,000 political arrests; rumours of 'disappeared' persons abounded. Furthermore, over this period there were an estimated 2,400 political assassinations, which were mainly extra-judicial murders carried out by Marcos's Special Forces.

In spite of increasing signs of popular unrest, including an anti-government rally of 100,000 office workers, and a shift in business funding to Marcos's political opponents, American support remained steadfast. When Ronald Reagan cancelled a planned visit to the Philippines in 1983, Vice President Bush argued that the USA 'should not cut away from a person who, imperfect though he may be on human rights grounds, has worked with us'.[11]

From this point, however, disillusionment with the Marcos regime began to grow rapidly in US political circles, and even within the Reagan administration. Congress, by refusing to take a monitoring role in the 14 May Philippines Legislative elections, made clear its distaste for President Marcos and its desire to disassociate itself from a corrupt electoral process. Marcos did little to help his cause by his increasingly erratic behaviour, not helped by the degenerative illness *Lupus Erythematosus*, an incurable auto-immune disease, from which he would eventually die; a man in need of constant dialysis and several kidney transplants was not capable of being in full mastery of his faculties, let alone events. When the opposition won as many as 59 out of 183 seats, Marcos, during a CBS interview, explained the opposition success by saying, 'I would presume that our instructions to our people to allow the opposition to win some seats might have been taken too literally.'[12]

Splits with the Reagan administration now grew wider. A report to the State Department by James Nach reported that there was a minor Maoist insurgency in the Philippines, but that it lacked external support. However, in a startling conclusion, he argued that the Marcos regime was so discredited that a backlash might eventually result in a communist takeover. Admiral Crowe, the chairman of the joint chiefs of staff, agreed with Nach. 'Things had to change. Marcos was not making the decisions that had to be made ... and the country was slinging down-hill. So I felt, he had to go.'[13]

Although Indiana Republican Richard Lugar agreed with Crowe, and Secretary of State George Shultz appeared amenable to persuasion, Secretary of Defence Casper Weinberger and CIA Director William Casey remained implacably opposed to ditching Marcos. In spite of America's policy impasse, the Reagan administration took the precaution of looking for an alternative military base in the Pacific region.

US Congressional pressure on the Philippines was also mounting. Senator John Kerry, the Democrat senator for Massachusetts, led a bill which passed 89 to 8 in favour of an amendment to foreign aid for the Philippines, which tied future fund-ing on progress in human rights and democracy. As for the president, he urged re-form on Marcos while avowing continued loyalty. Whatever the doubts about Mar-cos's regime, and the increased pressure from lobbyists and human rights groups in America, there seemed little real threat to his hold on power as long as he was perceived to be a bastion of defence against communism.

However, it was the 1983 murder of Benigno Aquino, which entirely altered the perceptions and was the key event leading to his eventual downfall. Like Mar-cos, Aquino came from the Filipino elite. Born on 27 November 1932, Benigno Aquino was also the son of an aspiring politician, though one who was more suc-cessful than Marcos's own father. Aquino's father, a losing rival for Laurel's post as prime minister under the Japanese, nevertheless became a loyal acolyte to the Japanese occupiers and died while facing 'collaboration' charges after the war. Be-nigno, by all accounts an unexceptional and indolent student, albeit with a fondness for talking, was a typical 'rich kid', who was given a job through family connec-tions on *The Manila Times* at the age of 18. Sent to Korea to cover the war there, he had acquired a certain celebrity status when he returned to go to university.

In spite of a dalliance with Ferdinand Marcos's future wife Imelda, at the age of 21 Aquino married Maria Corazón Cojuangco, the daughter of one of the Philip-pine's richest *mestizo* families and became a part owner of a vast sugar plantation called Hacienda Luisita. From this power base in the region of Tarlac, he became a mayor at the age of 22, and at 35 became the Philippines youngest senator. Apart from sharing the same social background, even girlfriends, as a member of the same fraternity at the University of the Philippines, Marcos and Aquino were more fac-tional rivals than ideological opposites. Although Aquino was more associated with liberal and left-leaning values than Marcos, it would be a mistake to assume that he was either anti-American or pro-Communist.

As a potential political rival to Marcos, Aquino was imprisoned. It was not personal, it was just politics. When Aquino fell ill in prison, Imelda visited him for two hours in hospital. Indeed, in a gesture of affection, Aquino gave her the gold cross that he had worn for the seven years of his imprisonment. Released from prison by Marcos on the grounds of ill-health, but probably because Marcos feared a backlash if he were to die while incarcerated, Aquino happily took up a teaching post at Harvard University at the invitation of Samuel Huntington and subsequently went on to teach at the MIT Centre for International Affairs.

At this institution, Professor Lucian Pye recalled that Aquino used to speak to Marcos on the telephone; he noted, 'I'd leave the office and come back to find Aquino shouting into the phone . . . but they seemed like friends at other times.'[14] Such political positions as Aquino did take can be seen more in terms of the traditional jockeying for position and patronage within the Philippine elite than any expression of a radically different philosophy. Indeed, it is doubtful whether, had he succeeded in acquiring presidentship, he would have proved any less venal than his predecessors.

After his release from prison, Aquino abandoned the hard-line 'popular uprising' approach that had characterised his earlier opposition to Marcos, and embraced a more passive 'Ghandian' vision of resistance. In this spirit, on 21 August 1983, he defied Marcos's banishment to arrive uninvited at Manila airport in the company of his brother-in-law Ken Kashiwahara, an *ABC* reporter, Max Vanzi of *UPI* and Katsuo Ueda of the *Kyodo News Agency*.

On arrival at Manila airport, soldiers bundled Aquino down the stairs leading from the airplane and shot him in the back of the head. Photographs of Aquino's corpse, crumpled on the tarmac in a blood-spattered white suit, flashed around the world. His martyrdom became the focal point of revolt. After the killing, a furious Marcos reportedly rose from his sickbed to throw a glass at his wife. He at least must have realised that the martyrdom of Aquino was a disastrous mistake.

Whether she had a hand in the murder has never been proven. However, on the night of the murder, Imelda made a point of visiting the major hotels in Manila, a means of guaranteeing her maximum social visibility. Was it an act of bravado or the sheer arrogance of power? A visiting English shipping financier John Pike, who witnessed one of her triumphal hotel visits, noted that she was a 'picture of utter corruption . . . bloated into clothes that were too tight . . . smug and arrogant'.[15] It was widely assumed by most people present that she and her supposed lover, General Ver, were responsible. Indeed, it has to be asked how the killing of Aquino could have been carried out without the orders of General Ver, chief of the armed forces of the Philippines.

Aquino's wife Corazón and her coterie of advisors now launched a brilliant propaganda campaign. Wearing only 'yellow', the colour denoting the 'yellow ribbons' hung out to welcome back her ill-fated husband, Cory, as she became known, and the body of her husband were fêted for all the 75-mile journey back to his home province of Tarlac. (This flat sugarcane-producing area of Luzon was owned almost entirely by the Aquino family.) There his body was laid out in the cathedral the day after his killing. The body was seemingly left deliberately untouched after his execution, presumably to create maximum shock and anger among the Filipinos, who queued eight hours to see him.

John Pike, one of the few foreigners to see the body, recalled that his *barong tagalog* (a traditional translucent Filipino shirt made of pineapple or banana fibre) was soaked and bespattered with blood. A hole in his left chin denoted where the bullet fired into the back of his head had exited; traces of dried blood lingered around the mouth, nostrils and eyes of his strangely imploded face. Outside the cathedral, Cory, dressed in black, stayed through the night to greet mourners. After commiserating with the demure and somewhat bewildered widow, John Pike recalled that one of Cory's large retinue sidled up to him to ask whether he was from *The Times of London*. It was already apparent that the grieving widow was to be the centrepiece for an orchestrated opposition to President Marcos. When Aquino's body was brought back to Manila, it was followed by millions in an 18-mile-long cortège; the popular uprising against the Marcos regime had started.

Aquino's death heightened political tensions. When John Pike noted the nervous distraction of a certain female doctor at a dinner party given by 'Peachy' Prieto at Baggio (the hill station for the Manila rich set) the day after Aquino's execution, the hostess, the daughter of a former newspaper baron, whose newspaper had been closed down by Marcos, told him that the doctor had been warned that she was on Marcos's 'death list'; in the intimate world of the Filipino elite there was nothing astonishing in the fact that one of Marcos's generals had revealed details of the death list to 'Peachy'. Naturally there was an assumption by the opponents of Marcos that the assassination of Aquino might be a prelude to a broader ranging liquidation of the regime's opponents.

Notably, the funeral was attended by the US Ambassador Michael Armacost and Cardinal Sin, the archbishop of Manila, who provided a suitable eulogy for the occasion. Armacost, formerly close to President Marcos, returned to the USA as an enemy of his regime, and gave evidence to Congress, which helped corral support for Cory Aquino. In October 1983, Congressman Solarz, an influential long-time Asian lobbyist, called for a 'thorough, independent, and impartial investigation of the Aquino assassination'.[16] The House approved his motion by 413 votes to 3. Although General Ver and 25 others were indicted for the murder of Aquino in January 1985, predictably they were all acquitted by the end of the year.

After the murder of Aquino, the nature of Philippine politics, and more particularly the Marcos regime, came under the full glare of global media interest. The scale of his electoral fraud was fully displayed. Marcos foolishly agreed to do media interviews for which he was inadequately prepared; when newscaster David Brinkley asked Marcos why, in one town, he had won a 13,000 to nothing vote over Aquino, Marcos replied that they were 'probably his relatives'.[17]

In California, the significant Filipino population was scandalised by articles in July 1985 in *The San Jose Mercury*, which exposed the billions that Marcos had stashed in overseas accounts. Revelations of Marcos's vast hidden assets also appeared in *The Washington Post* and *The New York Times*. Furthermore, on 22 January 1986, *The New York Times* also uncovered the fiction of Marcos's anti-Japanese guerrilla career. These stories inevitably percolated back to the Philippines.

To compound Marcos's problems, the corruption and economic mismanagement of his regime, combined with political uncertainties, had led to disastrous economic performance by the mid-1980s. Compared to Marcos's estimated personal wealth of US$ 10 billion, the Philippines had an external debt of some US$ 26 billion with a debt/service ratio in excess of 35 per cent of government revenues.

Meanwhile, much of the population was starving. The United Nations's Food and Agricultural Organisation (FAO) estimated that the average national calorie intake was some 270 calories below the minimum subsistence level of 2,210 calories recommended by the World Bank. Between 1972 and 1978 alone, real wages declined by 30.6 per cent. By 1985, *The Economist* magazine predicted that the 'country's economy may now be locked into a decline that only radical change can keep from ending in complete disaster'.[18]

At the beginning of 1986, opposition to Marcos increasingly took to the streets. A rally at Luneta Park attracted a crowd of 1 million people. The military too began to waver. Enrile, a former military crony of Marcos, had become so fearful of an attempt on his life that he walked everywhere carrying a sub-machine gun and surrounded by a private militia. Now at the denouement of the Marcos regime, Enrile joined forces with his bitter rival Ramos, and took refuge with military supporters at the army base at Camp Aguinaldo.

With the growing chaos, the US 7th Fleet gathered in Manila bay in order to impart a sense of order. Cardinal Sin, calling on the support of Filipino Catholics, encouraged nuns, priests and students to gather at Camp Aguinaldo for an all-night vigil. Some 40,000 Aquino supporters defended the perimeters of the camp as tank forces loyal to Marcos approached. During the stand-off, the USA urged restraint. Aquino supporters sang nationalist songs and handed flowers to the soldiers bearing down on Camp Aguinaldo.

Attack helicopters sent by Marcos to fire on Enrile changed sides when they saw the crowds, and joined the protesters. In the conflict played out in front of the American media, Ramos vowed that the people would overwhelm Marcos. Meanwhile, Marcos insisted on the legality of his position and assured viewers that 'I don't believe that President Reagan would ask me to step down.'[19] He was wrong. A message was passed by Secretary of State George Shultz to the Philippines that Marcos should resign. Paul Laxalt, the Republican senator for Nevada, took on the role of messenger and told Marcos that Reagan was offering him asylum. Marcos did not take the hint immediately, and asked whether Reagan wanted him to resign. Laxalt replied, 'I think you should cut and cut cleanly. I think the time has come.'[20]

Hours later, Marcos and his entourage evacuated Malacanang Palace by helicopter and went to Clark Field, where they boarded a plane for America. Within hours, mobs swept through Malacanang Palace, where they famously discovered Imelda's hoard of shoes; bizarrely her shoe collection would come to symbolise the corruption of the Marcos regime. Cory Aquino, dressed in yellow, was sworn into office as the new president.

While it is possible to paint the entire Marcos episode simply as an example of the poor post-war maladministration of Asia, the problems of the Philippines are in many ways typical of the dilemma which faced successive American governments in dealing with hegemonic allies. As a 1972 Congressional Report noted with respect to both the Philippines and South Korea:

> ... in both countries we appear to be immobilized by our own presence and by commitments which Presidents Park and Marcos are able to use as leverage in obtaining from us what they want ... turning their weakness into assets in dealing with us as patron and protector.[21]

On the one hand, America could stand accused of being too overbearing or imperialist if intervention was too overt, while on the other hand the basic premise of American military presence in Asia was to combat Communism. As President Reagan mused, 'there are things there [the Philippines] ... that do not look good to us from the standpoint ... of democratic rights ... what is the alternative? It is for a large Communist movement to take over the Philippines.'[22]

The problem for the USA was that, in the Philippines, American standards of governance in public life were not imposable because the ideal of 'self-determination' remained a key leitmotif of post-war American foreign policy; a standard Imperial conquest would, in many ways, have been much easier. This meant that to a large extent American presidents had to step back from intervening in many political arrangements that they found distasteful; the only exception to this rule was Communism, a system of government which, unlike the various right-wing autocratic tyrannies of which Marcos's was typical, was demonstrably resistant to democratic change.

With hindsight, some have accused America of being guilty of overestimating the communist threat in the Philippines. However, by their own estimates, certainly exaggerated, the Communist Party of Philippines (CPP) controlled one in five of the country's 42,000 villages and claimed a mass base of about 2 million people with 25,000 active guerrillas. In view of the conflicting evidence as to the threat posed by the communists, it is not perhaps surprising that President Reagan, and many of his closest advisors, maintained their support for Marcos for too long. The delay may have had long-term benefits. Ultimately, the path to a democratic future was one chosen by the populace; in this respect it was probably a better outcome for its future than another political system foisted on the Philippines by the USA.

40

Coups d'Etat: A Way of Life

Thailand: 1958—91

The coup d'état is the most singular characteristic of modern political Thai history. The first coup in Thailand's modern history took place in 1782, and it was 130 years before the next one in 1912. Thereafter, coups arrived in seemingly ever more rapid succession: 1932, June 1933, October 1933, 1947, 1948, 1949, June 1951, November 1951, 1957, 1958, 1971, 1973, 1976, March 1977, October 1977, 1981, 1985, 1989, 1990, 1991 and 2006. Such were the regularity of coups, successful and unsuccessful, that they rarely impacted on daily life.

On one occasion, *The Far East Economic Review* reported that a Bangkok hotel had distributed the following announcement to its guests:

> To All Our Dear Guests, Please be informed that a *light* government revolution is going on this morning. The public is then requested to keep calm and if possible stay out of busy areas until the situation is back to normal. There is nothing to panic. Please just be aware of the situation in case you have to be out of the hotel. Thank you for your kind attention and cooperation. The management.[1]

Indeed it could be argued that coup d'états were a necessary corollary of a non-democratic system of government. Montri Chenvidyakam, a Thai commentator, noted that 'Thai politics is military politics, and as coups, armed forces, and control of key positions in the political structure are necessary for it as elections, political parties, and popular support are for democracy . . . .'[2]

It might readily be deduced that Thai society was not ready for democracy. This was the conclusion that General Sarit reached after the overthrow of the legendary pre-war and post-war leader General Phibun in 1958. Phibun, who had gone through numerous political reincarnations since he was a young student in Paris in the 1920s including a stint as a pre-war fascist clone of Adolf Hitler, had eventually converted to the ideals of democracy in the waning years of his political pre-eminence, after a tour of a booming post-war America and Britain.

By contrast, General Sarit, who, after his removal of Phibun, was forced to go to America for medical treatment of cirrhosis of the liver, came to a diametrically opposite view while he convalesced in England. The transplantation of

European-style institutions into a predominantly feudal Thai culture could not work; Sarit concluded that Thailand worked best with authoritarian government. The case was succinctly put to the US government by the Thai Ambassador Thanat Khoman:

> The fundamental cause of our political instability in the past lies in the sudden trans-plantation of alien institutions onto our soil without proper regard to the circumstances which prevail in our homeland . . . . If we look at our national history, we can see very well that this country works better and prospers under an authority, not a tyrannical authority, but a unifying authority around which all elements of the nation can rally.[3]

In his absence, Sarit's deputy, General Thanom Kittikachorn, took control of the government and oversaw a loss to the Democrats in the March 1958 by-elections. Democratic government was short-lived, however. When Sarit returned to Bangkok in October, he immediately abolished the constitution and decided to rule Thailand through decrees from a 'Revolutionary Council'; 'Democracy' would be exercised by a government which promoted the monarchy and ruled with responsiveness to the wishes of the people.

Management of the economy was centralised under the National Economic Development Board with five-year plans implemented from 1961. The technocrat-style government did not go unrewarded; in the ten years between 1959 and 1969, Thailand's real GNP rose by 8.6 per cent per annum. However, political stability, indicated by a 13-year period after 1958 without a coup attempt, combined with the economic benefits that accrued from America's military build-up in Indochina were probably the greatest contributors to Thailand's emerging prosperity.

War brought to Bangkok the modern Asian detritus of bars, coffee shops and massage parlours. Demand for urban labour exploded and absorbed the excess of an agricultural population that was expanding rapidly. A Thai population that had numbered just 14.4 million in 1937 had grown to 26.3 million by 1960, and was 44.3 million 20 years later. Even by 1980, however, the agricultural population still represented 90 per cent of the total.

Sarit himself did not live to see the benefits of his regressive approach to Thailand's constitutional problems. By 1963, he had killed himself by his consumption of brandy, a bottle of which was nearly always in his possession. As a totalitarian ruler, Sarit possessed many of the qualities that marked so many of Asia's post-war leaders. Like Suharto and Mao, he indulged his excessive libido with prolific numbers of mistresses.

At the time of his death, the low estimates were that he kept 50 mistresses; the high estimates were as many as 80. His sexual greed was matched by his financial rapaciousness. The creation of his financial fortune was based on control of the booming post-war opiate drug trade of the Golden Triangle; later in his life, he secured a monopoly on rice gunny sacks, which was particularly lucrative in an economy where rice was both the major commodity and the country's largest export. He also left some 8,000 acres of land, and his untimely death led to a sordid public squabble for assets by his first and second wives.

The succession followed without drama to General Thanom, who proved a worthy if not charismatic successor. His deputy prime minister and also minister for the interior, General Praphas Charusathian, married off his daughter to Thanom's son. A tight familial clique now ruled Thailand for the next decade.

In the 1960s, the key issues turned from Thailand's constitutional and political future to the national security problems posed by the expansion of the communist threat in South East Asia. For Sarit, Laos had been Thailand's main foreign policy problem. Not only was his cousin General Phoumi Nosavan head of the right-wing faction in Laos, but more importantly the advance of the communist *Pathet Lao* threatened to destabilise Thailand's eastern border. With the post-war fall to communism of China and Burma, its northern and western neighbours, Thailand was acutely sensitive to the advance of communism in Indochina on its eastern flank.

Disappointed by the toothless rhetoric of SEATO, both Sarit and the USA moved closer together on their security interests, and in the wake of the Laotian crisis of the early 1960s, Thailand, through the Rusk–Thanat agreement, secured an open-ended American commitment to its defence. As US involvement in Indochina deepened, the defence relationship with Thailand gathered in importance. By 1968, the USA had stationed some 600 aircraft including B52s at Tapao from where bombing, reconnaissance and secret commando operations were launched. Thailand was far from passive in its role as America's ally. Thanom sent air force and naval detachments to fight in South Vietnam, and by 1969 some 11,000 troops (14 per cent of the Thai army) were stationed there.

The Thai government's fear of communism was not groundless; for them 'communist domino theory' was all too real. As communists took hold of North Vietnam and Laos, the Communist Party, suppressed by Phibun, started to revive its fortunes with help from cadres trained in neighbouring countries, including China. By 1967, communist guerrillas were operating in the provinces of Chiang Rai and Nan. In 1968, attacks spread to Loei, Phitsanulok and Phetchabun. Communism within the Malay community of Southern Thailand also flared back to life. For both the US and the Thai government, the possibility that Thailand would be the next 'domino' to fall to communism was a genuine fear.

Close attachment to the USA came with a cost, however; international pressure for political change was also increasingly matched by the popular mood. In 1968, Thanom yielded to the demands for change by reintroducing a two-chamber legislature closely modelled on the 1932 Constitution. The Upper Chamber was to be appointed. Although elections in February 1969 produced a majority for the government party in the Lower House, the military came under increasing pressure as the Asian economy turned down after President Nixon started the withdrawal of American military resources from Indochina.

The devaluation of the dollar, after Nixon's disengagement from Bretton Woods, also undermined an economy which was further damaged by the First Oil Crisis. Fearing that opposition parties would take control of the Lower House and stir increasing popular resentment, Thanom staged a military coup against his own government, banned political parties and cracked down on press freedom.

However, popular unrest did not abate as the economic crisis deepened. Thanom and Praphas were approaching military retirement age, while the only likely successor, Thanom's son, did not offer the prospect of a change of government. Massive demonstrations, orchestrated by student militants, disrupted Bangkok in October 1973 and provoked violent clashes with the police. The military took a decisive stand by its refusal to intervene on Thanom's behalf, and, when King Bhumibol, intrinsically a supporter of Thanom, agreed to meet a student delegation and subsequently refused to publicly back the government, both Thanom and Praphas were forced into exile. Bhumibol's public intervention was crucial:

> Today is a day of great sorrow, the most grievous in the history of our Thai nation . . . .
> I call on all sides and all people to eliminate the causes of violence . . . in order that our
> country can return to normalcy as soon as possible.[4]

The era of the military junta was over.

The president of the King's Privy Council, Dr Sanya Dharmasakti, became the new prime minister, and he ushered in a single-chamber constitution to be fully elected in January 1975. With no clear majority, a government of Democrats led by Seni Pramoj and supported by left-wing parties lasted just two weeks. In its place, Seni Pramoj's brother, Kukrit Pramoj, a leader of the Social Action Party, formed a new coalition of 17 parties of the left and right.

However, the return to democracy merely added to the instability created by the end of America's participation in the Vietnamese War and by the continued onslaught of the North on the now isolated South Vietnamese army. In May 1974, US forces in Thailand were cut from 50,000 to 34,000. Feeling increasingly isolated, the Thai government even courted a resumption of diplomatic relations with China now that they had turned against their former Soviet and Vietnamese allies.

In desperation, the new Thai government even sought to treat with Hanoi and curried favour with Russia by recognising Rumania and Czechoslovakia. As former Foreign Minister Thanat Khoman explained:

> The present government is committed to following a policy of equidistance_ the US,
> Soviet Union, China, Japan, Western and Eastern Europe . . . . It was not my personal
> feelings, but the resolution of the American Congress banning US forces from taking
> part in overseas operations. If they can't perform military duties why are they here? As
> tourists? It doesn't make sense . . . . Executive commitments are completely meaning-
> less if Congress is not willing to go ahead. What are promises if we are unsure of the
> position of the [American] legislative branch? If the US Congress was to pass a reso-
> lution tomorrow that if Thailand were attacked the US would join Thailand's defence,

I would be the first to advocate that American forces remain. At present, however,
they are a liability.[5]

In March 1976, the Thai government announced that US military activity in Thailand must end.

In the West, the political isolation of Thailand was one of the least remarked
upon international repercussions of America's withdrawal from Indochina, caused
by the defenestration of the Republican presidencies of both Nixon and Ford.
The passing of the War Powers Act, and the hostility of the Democrat-controlled
Congress to any further commitments to South East Asia, appeared to tie the hands
of the American presidency with regard to the defence of their Asian hegemony.
The low point in the hitherto umbilical relationship with the Thai government
came at the end of 1975, when the Democrat majority leader in the Senate, Mike
Mansfield, called for an end to economic aid to Thailand. Even Henry Kissinger
omitted Thailand from the list of America's essential defence commitments.

Suddenly cut adrift from American support, which had anchored Thailand's
post-war stability, repressed social and political divisions soon came to the surface.
Thailand was fractured by powerful paramilitary groups, supporting left- and right-
wing philosophies. Both the New Force movement and Village Scout movement
sought to expose and terrorise communist sympathisers. Meanwhile, in Bangkok,
militant left-wing students became increasingly violent. In 1976, there was a dramatic increase in political assassinations.

The explosive political atmosphere was not helped by the return of the exiled
former dictator, General Thanom. Following the Thai mythology of the Prince-
Penitent, Thanom now returned to Thailand to live as a Buddhist monk at the
Royal Temple of Wat Boworniwes, and was accorded a warm welcome from both
the political right and the Royal family.

The radical student body was incensed. Thammasat University students hung
Crown Prince Vajiralongkorn in effigy. The response from an army-controlled radio station was an exhortation to kill students and communists. On 6 October
1976, Thammasat University was attacked by paramilitary groups with the active
co-operation of the police. Students were beaten, lynched or burned alive. With a
descent into civil unrest, the army once again intervened to suspend the constitution. However, they backed off a resumption of a military junta-style government,
and the Military Administrative Council appointed Thanin Kraivichien, a former
high court justice, as prime minister.

Contrary to expectations, Thanin proved far more authoritarian than the military regimes that had gone before him. He purged the bureaucracy and educational
establishments of left-wing sympathisers, and imposed a rigid control of unions
and the press. In the bureaucracy, anti-communist indoctrination classes became
mandatory. Many fled to join the Communist guerrillas operating in the hill states,
including a former governor of the central bank, the Bank of Thailand, and the
Rector of Thammasat University.

Thanin was himself dismissed as prime minister by the military in October 1977, to be replaced by General Kriangsak Chomanand, who promised elections under a new constitution in 1979. The purges of the left were brought to a halt and exiles were encouraged to return from the hills. After the ensuing elections, Kriangsak formed a government, but he was forced to resign under pressure from the army's new commander in chief, General Prem Tinsulanonda, he was forced to resign. Prem, a close friend of the King, who had had an effective career in counter-insurgency, became Thailand's new prime minister, leading a coalition of Democrats and the Social Action Party.

The emergence of Prem as a strong leader could not have come at a more pro-pitious moment. The fall of Thailand's eastern neighbour Cambodia to the Khmer brand of communism was barely welcome news for the Thai government, even though the Khmers appeared to pose little immediate external military threat.

However, the finely honed and Soviet-equipped Vietnamese army was a differ-ent matter. Thai foreign policy appeared to have muted this danger after a charm offensive was rewarded with Vietnamese 'overfly' rights at the beginning of 1978. However, the overthrow of the Khmer regime in December 1979 by the Soviet–Vietnamese alliance suddenly posed a very real military threat to Thailand.

Soviet occupation of a Vietnamese air base at Cam Ranh Bay brought Mig 23s and TU-16 bombers, and appeared to offer a credible threat to America's post-war Asian hegemony. In addition to the military threat, Thailand was also inundated with refugees. By 1983, Thailand had to support some 157,807 refugees including 74,955 Laotions, 71,976 Cambodians and 10,876 Vietnamese. In addition, there were 200,000 Cambodians in camps along the border.

Suddenly, relations with the USA were upgraded. Even President Carter and the Democrats were now alerted to the new dangers of Soviet expansion; Secretary of State Cyrus Vance noted that 'the fighting in Kampuchea poses an increasingly serious danger to the security of the region. . . '.[6]

The 'U Thant-Dean Rusk' Communiqué was revived. The sale of 12 F-16s to Thailand was authorised, as well as 'surface to surface' Harpoon missiles. Ameri-can aid to Thailand increased by 300 per cent to US$ 119.5 million in 1978, fol-lowed by another huge jump to US$ 420 million in 1979; Prem also sought and received help from Vietnam's new adversary, China. Thus came about the weird, if not repugnant, alliance of Thailand, China and President Jimmy Carter's Ameri-can administration with the genocidal Pol Pot Regime in Cambodia; in this ultimate 'realpolitic' alliance of convenience, Carter had come a long way from his much heralded 'moral' foreign policy with which he came to power. Western-backed Khmer Rouge forces, stationed along the Thai borders, now operated against the puppet Vietnamese government of Semring in Phnom Penh. Even newly elected Prime Minister Thatcher was a willing supporter of this unholy alliance; rarely can the imperatives of the geopolitical battle against Soviet expansion have required conjunction with such unsavoury bedfellows.

There followed perhaps the most important coup attempt in post-war Thai history. In 1981, General Sant Chitpatima, leading a cadre of young officers, seized government offices and the all-important radio station in Bangkok. The so-called April Fools Day Rebellion appeared to have won.

However, King Bhumibol now staged his finest moment. The King and General Prem fled Bangkok and defiantly raised the Thai Royal Standard at the military base at Khorat; from the radio station there, Queen Sirikit was chosen to go on air to call for defiance of the rebels. The rally to arms behind the King demonstrated the affection in which the monarch was now held; by 3 April the rebellion was over. General Prem retook the capital without loss of life.

In this episode, King Bhumibol Adulyadej emerged as perhaps the most outstanding monarch of any country in the twentieth century. His reputation was not easily earned. When he returned from Europe in 1950, Thailand had been without a resident monarch for almost 20 years. Since the overthrow of the monarchic system of government in 1932, the role of a constitutional monarch had never been established. From the start, however, Bhumibol earned a high reputation for integrity.

In sharp contrast to monarchies in many other countries, the King engaged in more than a self-indulgent lifestyle and ceremonial activities. Using the law degree acquired in Switzerland, he sat as a Bangkok district judge. Bhumibol also travelled extensively throughout his kingdom using his privy purse to open medical facilities for the poor (his father had been a qualified doctor).

In addition, he developed a dazzling array of personal skills. Bhumibol became a successful jazz musician and sometimes played on radio stations. His compositions became widely performed and he would become a member of the Vienna Institute of Music and Arts. He became a skilled artist, translator and writer; a 2002 published novel, *The Story of Thong Daeng* about his dog, Khun Thong Daeng (meaning 'copper'), became a best seller. Bhumibol also patented a number of rainmaking devices. The last of these was for a 'super-sandwich' for which patent was granted in June 2003; this process involves the seeding of warm and cool clouds at different altitudes to produce rain.

From the beginning, Bhumibol demonstrated political bravery. In 1952, he refused to preside over ceremonies for a new constitution implemented by Phibun, and showed himself to be almost as hostile to military dictatorship as he was to communism. Indeed, he remained firm in his belief that it was the military overthrow of the monarchy in the 1930s that lay at the root of Thailand's political instability. In 1982, Bhumibol reflected that his uncle King Prajadhipok 'would have set up a real democracy in a few years instead of the [Promoter's] government that was not well devised, not well studied. We still have the effects of it'.[7]

In spite of his contempt for the military and political castes, which he believed to be responsible for Thailand's miseries, Bhumbol played his role with impeccable balance. He never overstepped the mark with Thailand's rulers in such a way as to risk the overthrow of the monarchy, while he managed never to be seen as either cravenly supportive or a hostage to his governments.

His 'impartial' philosophy of kingship was robustly thought out and vigorously implemented. In a January 1980 BBC documentary *Soul of the Nation*, Bhumibol asserted that

> It's quite normal that people should use the king. He's there to be used . . . But the way of using depends on us also, that we are doing things that are good for the country, for the people, and [that] we don't have any secrets . . . ordinary people must look up to somebody who is impartial. And if one wants to destroy somebody who is impartial, well, one destroys one's self.[8]

Most importantly, when he intervened in the political arena, it was to curb excesses of the right and left. Bhumibol managed to disassociate himself from Phibun and his era, and though he supported the military duumvirate of Thanom and Praphas, when popular opposition to their rule reached a crescendo, he actively sided with the students to call time on their junta. From the time of the 'April Fool's Day' Coup of 1981, it became fully recognised that the King was the political arbiter of last resort. In spite of Thailand's problems with communist insurgency, and the economic downturn that followed in the wake of the Second Oil Crisis, Prem's standing had been immeasurably strengthened by his stance with the King at Khorat; his power was further enhanced by the victory of his parties in the general election of April 1983.

Another military coup took place in 1985, but was treated with scant seriousness by an urban population which carried on with their normal working day. A radio announcement at 7.30 am informed the public that 'The Revolutionary Party, which comprises the military, police, and civilian parties, has seized national sovereignty as of 6.00 am on September 9th 1985, and the situation is firmly under the control of the Revolutionary Party.'[9] Although the coup resulted in the death of numbers of civilians when tanks opened fire, the rebellion was easily overcome. Without the support of the King, it stood very little chance of success.

Prem had wanted to stand down as early as 1983, but was persuaded to stay on until July 1988, when Bhumibol celebrated being Thailand's longest serving monarch. General Prem enjoyed a graceful retirement and the unique distinction of being Thailand's only post-war ruler to leave office with his reputation higher than when he started. He achieved this in spite of the continued corruption of the army and the political caste, particularly in logging, construction and port management. Nevertheless, the Thailand he handed over to his successor was finally emerging as a fast-growing developing economy now capable of attracting foreign investment.

In spite of Thailand's vastly improved economic performance and the stability brought by General Prem and King Bhumibol, the military remained determinedly wedded to the belief in their right to wield ultimate political power. As so often in Thai history, Prem's successor was a military officer with a distinguished service record; Chatichai Choonhavan fitted this model perfectly. During the war, he fought in both the Shan States and Indochina. Politically he was ideally placed. His father, Phin Choonhavan, had been General Phibun's field commander.

Also, the Choonhavan family headed the Soi Rajakru clan, which came to prominence with its business and political alliance with General Sarit. As a Western diplomat observed:

> There is a strong sense of being born to rule in the Thai establishment and anyone outside that close circle of kinship and school ties is looked upon literally as a communist agent, the mob, or disloyal to the King and the nation's religion.[10]

Although his family connections led to the effective exile of Chatichai on foreign office postings after the successful coup which replaced Sarit, he was brought back by Thanom in 1972. There followed an incident which guaranteed him popular esteem and fame. In December 1973, the Palestinian terrorist organisation 'Black September' stormed the Israeli Embassy in Bangkok and took six Israeli hostages. In an act of exceptional bravery, Chatichai exchanged himself for the hostages. His career in politics was now set.

On 24 July 1988, Chatichai's Chart Thai Party won 88 seats versus 52 for the Democrats and 49 for Social Action. Smaller grouping included Rassadorn with 20 seats; United Democrats with 5; and Palang Dharma, led by a former Bangkok governor, with 14 seats. After the traditional horse-trading, Chatichai formed a coalition government. As *The Far East Economic Review* noted on 18 August, 'Little regard was given to competence or qualifications in choosing the Cabinet. Instead, influential personalities and wealthy party sponsors were named to several important posts. Among them were some veteran politicians with controversial past records.'[11]

A strike at the Electricity Generating Authority led Chatichai to mobilise the army. Although the collapse of the strike ended the immediate problem, a far more serious military crisis emerged a year later. In March 1990, General Chavalit Yongchaiyudh, an acolyte of Prem, stepped down as army commander in chief, and, in traditional lockstep, became minister of defence.

Three months later, General Chavalit was forced out of the Cabinet by its civilian members because of charges of corruption; a ludicrous excuse to sack a cabinet member in light of the complete knowledge that all Thai senior military officers and politicians entered their profession to make money. However, by the end of the 1980s, even the Chatichai government was beginning to be troubled by Thailand's deforestation, which had filled the personal coffers of the generals and politicians. To replenish the pecuniary void, Thailand's corrupt establishment just turned its attention to logging the Shan States of Burma.

The festering discontent of the army, based on the fear that their corrupt privileges would be purloined by civilian politicians, erupted into open rebellion in February 1991. On 23 February, Chatichai was arrested at Don Muang Airport, as he was about to board a plane to Chiang Mai to meet King Bhumibol in order to present his nomination for the post of deputy secretary of defence. Army leaders Suchinda and Sunthorn abolished the 1978 constitution, but tried to soften their move by promising new elections within six months. Anand Panyarachun was appointed as an interim prime minister on 2 March 1991. It was a return to political instability in a country in which the only political constant remained the King.

Indeed, the monarch's singular success as an impartial arbiter had by now become part of the coup process. The conundrum of Thai politics was well understood and described by Richard Nation in *the Far East Economic Review* in 1976, when he concluded that

> the art of the successful coup in Thailand today is considerably more refined than earlier and requires every bit as much tact and finesse as running a parliamentary government. The necessary elements require not only the balance of force in the army, but also the legitimacy and unity of Supreme Command, the approval of the King and support from some of the new figures of national stature with credible political following.[12]

Normally, political systems in most post-war Asian countries provided a veneer to extreme political instability beneath the surface. In Thailand's case the reverse was true; extreme systemic political instability hid what was generally a stable, social and political order.

41

Zulfikar Ali Bhutto and General Mohammed Zia ul-Haq

Pakistan: 1973–88

B orn of a wealthy Bombay family, Zulfikar Ali Bhutto was educated at the city's Cathedral High School. From a mansion on wealthy Carmichael Road, he lived the dissolute life of Bombay's young social elite. The legendary Indian actress Nargis Dutt described the young Bhutto as 'very charming and likeable but always reeking of gin and perfume ... Bhutto, as I know him, was a feudal landlord with princely pleasures, drinks, shikar and dancing with a new girl every night'.[1] He was then afforded an expensive international education at the University of Southern California in 1947, followed by Berkeley in June 1949, where he took an honours degree in political science in 1950. He then proceeded to Oxford. Here he studied law, which was duly followed by a call to the bar at Lincoln's Inn in 1953. Like Jinnah and Iskander Mirza before him, Bhutto was a Shia Muslim in a country which was overwhelmingly Sunni.

When he returned to Pakistan, he taught constitutional law at Sindh Muslim College and was invited to join a delegation to the United Nations in 1957. From this early break, Bhutto soon threw himself into politics and within five years was rewarded by becoming commerce minister in Iskander Mirza's cabinet in 1958. Later as a member of Ayub Khan's cabinet, he was still its youngest minister, and by 1963 he had been elevated to the major post of foreign minister. It was a massive over-promotion for a man of moderate intellectual ability with a hugely inflated ego and belief in his own infallibility.

While his hawkish policies, including his assurances that China would stage a border war to keep Indian forces pinned down, were a prime cause of Ayub Khan's ill-fated plan to invade India over the Kashmir issue, he nevertheless managed to emerge as a popular hero. Polished and urbane in manner, Bhutto was also given to dramatic public displays of emotion. A widely reported theatrical episode at the United Nations, followed by his posturing display of discontent with the peace with India agreed at the Treaty of Tashkent, burnished his popularity back home and laid the foundations for the Pakistan People's Party (PPP), which he set up on 30 November 1967.

Again the disastrous 1971 civil war between East and West Pakistan, which Bhutto and the PPP had been so instrumental in causing and which brought about a crushing defeat by the Indian army and the creation of an independent East Pakistan (Bangladesh), did nothing to impede Bhutto's rise to power. Bhutto had reportedly told Yahya before the war that 'East Pakistan is no problem. We have to kill 20,000 people there and all will be well.'[2] Like many utopian leaders of his epoch, Bhutto was nonchalantly ruthless and careless of mass slaughter. He shared the common disdain for Pakistan's majority population, the Bengalis. Following the war, Pakistan President Yahya Khan was forced to step down after a coup by young officers, and the presidential system of democracy fell with him.

Far from sharing the opprobrium for the failed military adventure in East Pakistan, Bhutto's star rose as he postured yet again at the United Nations as a steadfast nationalist determined to restore his country's honour. In a speech televised in Pakistan he stormed out of a UN Security Council meeting, having torn a Polish peace proposal to shreds and vowed to fight a 'thousand years of war' with India.[3] The performance guaranteed him the presidency, when he returned to Rawalpindi. Throughout his career, Bhutto skilfully shifted the blame for his failures onto others. Describing the art of politics, Bhutto insisted that 'a politician must have fairly light and fairly flexible fingers, to insinuate them under the bird and take away the eggs, one by one, without the bird realizing it'.[4] He was an altogether brilliant populist politician, who became best known for his slogan 'Roti, Kapra, Makan' (bread, clothes, shelter).[5]

With the removal of political rivalry from the East Pakistani Awami League after it became independent Bangladesh, Bhutto's PPP had the field to itself. In 1972 his first task was to bring about peace with India and restore Pakistan's eroded borders. At the peace talks with Indira Gandhi, he persuaded her, without informing his colleagues, that he would accept the status quo on Kashmir: in return India would give back the 5,139 square miles that its army had seized from Pakistan during the war. However, Bhutto rightly calculated that it was too soon for him to be seen to accept the independence of Bangladesh, with the result that his soldiers remained in Indian captivity.

Following the reform of the constitution in 1973, which abolished Pakistan's presidential system, the National Assembly completed the formality of electing Bhutto as prime minister on 12 August 1973. The constitutional changes were designed to promote strong parliamentary democracy. The role of chief of the army was assigned to a non-uniformed officer, who now officially usurped the leading military post previously occupied by the commander-in-chief of the army.

First indications were that the youthful rabble-rouser had morphed into a more mature politician in prime ministerial office. In February 1974 Bhutto formally recognised the independent state of Bangladesh. Even the American State Department, which had from the early 1960s spotted his demagogic tendencies, now noted that he 'displayed an air of confidence and maturity', clearly designed to build the public image of Pakistan as a reliable friend of the USA.[6] However, in reality, Bhutto immediately set about reducing Pakistan's dependence on the USA and moved foreign policy towards a 'non-aligned' status. Ideologically he moved to merge Islam with socialism; it was a political strategy which echoed that of Sukarno in Indonesia.

At this point, with an overwhelming majority in the National Assembly, Bhutto's powers were virtually unlimited. He did not use them wisely. Bhutto introduced a sweeping programme of socialist nationalisation, which included not only banks and major industrial enterprises including steel, chemicals, cement and energy, but also small agricultural businesses; in July 1976 the government took control of several thousand wheat-milling, rice-husking and cotton-ginning units. The policy was economically disastrous; one Karachi businessman admitted that

> Before they took over our plants, I went to the ten best people in the organization, and set each of them up in business, stripping my company of its most important machine tools and people. The Pakistan government got a shell, and they have never been able to make a profit.[7]

Included in the nationalisation programme was a foundry business started by the father of Nawaz Sharif; this future prime minister and main rival to Bhutto's daughter Benazir would never forgive this injustice. Sharif's father was forced to move to the Middle East to restart his life. Predictably there was a flight of Pakistan émigrés and capital. Until this point Pakistan's free market policies had at least allowed Pakistan's economy to outpace its much larger socialistic neighbour, India. Blighted by socialist uncompetitiveness and corruption, the relative outperformance of Pakistan now began to falter. Meanwhile civil servants were stripped of their constitutional guarantees of job tenure. The civil service structure inherited from the British was swept away and replaced with a District Management Group. The policy led to a collapse in the quality of governance in Pakistan.

More importantly, from the point of view of his political survival, Bhutto's economic policies eventually alienated the key middle-class constituency both in the cities and in the countryside. His pre-election promise to decentralise government was broken almost immediately when he dismissed the government of Baluchistan on 12 February. In sympathy the government of the North-West Frontier Province also resigned. The result according to historian Lawrence Ziring was 'another Pakistani Civil War, and another one that Bhutto had provoked'.[8]

Political leaders in Pakistan ignored the centrifugal forces of tribalism at their peril; as tribal chief Nawab Akbar Bugti Khan pointed out, 'I have been a Baloch for several centuries, I have been a Muslim for 1,400 years. I have been a Pakistani for just over fifty.'[9] Ignoring the lessons of East Pakistan, Bhutto rejected the demands for more regional autonomy, claiming that federation was ridiculous 'for a country that wants to count for something in the world'.[10]

Bhutto also passed an amendment which gave executive power to ban any political party operating in a manner prejudicial to the sovereignty or integrity of the country. The subsequent banning of Pakistan's main opposition party, the National Awami League, was a clear indication that Bhutto intended to lead his country towards a one-party socialist state. Opposition rallies were broken up by violent mobs, often with the encouragement of the police.

In the short term he was unassailable. However within four years, in spite of his 'leftist' leanings, he managed to alienate intellectuals, students and trade unionists; by the elections of 1977 he was deeply unpopular, which was manifested in extensive street violence. The March elections of that year brought divisions to a head. A landslide victory for Bhutto, with 155 seats won out of 200, was patently rigged. The reported 80 per cent official turnout was implausibly high. The opposition Pakistan National Alliance (PNA) supporters took to the streets. Bhutto called in his Chief of the Army Staff Mohammed Zia ul-Haq to impose martial law in Karachi, Islamabad and Lahore.

The military intervention brought to the fore the incongruous, caricature figure of General Zia. With his black, slicked-down hair, with its central parting, combined with a 'handlebar' moustache, he looked like a Hollywood villain from the era of silent movies. In 1975, Zia, a devout Muslim, apparently a man without guile or political ambition, had been leapfrogged by Bhutto over six other generals to take the post of Chief of Army Staff.

In addition to falling out with his electorate, Bhutto also managed to alienate Pakistan's long-term ally, the USA. When President Carter banned the export of tear gas to Pakistan on human rights grounds, he touched paranoid nerves that were never far from the surface of Bhutto's fragile psyche. Typically, Bhutto overreacted. In a highly charged speech to the National Assembly on 28 April 1977, the Pakistan prime minister accused the USA of financing 'a vast, colossal, huge international conspiracy'[11]; he also alleged that Pakistan was being punished for supporting the Palestinian cause against Israel. It was a performance designed to deflect from the failure of his domestic policies.

Responding to Bhutto's rabble-rousing rhetoric, wholly unsupported by the facts, Cyrus Vance sent a sharply worded message which nevertheless left room for conciliation. Bhutto responded with arch duplicity. The American chargé d'affaires in Islamabad would later recall that

> Bhutto, being a real political rogue and rascal, went out in an open jeep around Rawalpindi and had all his supporters out in the streets and he was waving this letter from Secretary Vance, saying that the Americans had apologized to him. Of course, it wasn't at all, and then we got the Department to release the text.[12]

Bad blood between the supposed allies was further created by Carter's decision to withdraw an offer to sell 110 A-7 attack aircrafts. Bhutto, unable to accept that he was the author of his own misfortunes, told the Saudis that the USA was responsible for his political problems in Pakistan.

In response to continued civil unrest, the undermining of civil institutions by Bhutto and perhaps reflecting an exasperation at the fall-out with America, whose support was essential for the Pakistan army, Zia launched a coup d'état code-named 'Operation Fair Play'. Leaders of all the political parties were put under house arrest. Bhutto was moved to the government rest house at Murree Hill Station. Bhutto, who had an unfailing belief in his own destiny and importance, used to say that 'the Himalayas would weep the day I relinquish my office'.[13] Not only did the Himalayas not weep, but neither did the Pakistan people.

After his detainment, the deposed prime minister was telephoned by Zia, who told him, 'I'm sorry Sir, I had to do it . . . but in ninety days I'll hold new elections. You'll be elected Prime Minister again, of course, Sir, and I'll be saluting you.'[14] Zia's call more probably reflected naivety than disingenuousness. Zia would not be the only Pakistani general to find that seizing power was easier than giving it away.

Bhutto's response to arrest soon reminded General Zia of life's brutal realities. Aside from publicly lambasting Zia for his actions, the prime minister also reminded Zia that the penalty for treason under the 1973 constitution was execution. It was a typically reckless outburst. Zia must have felt the chill of the hangman's noose, when, after Bhutto's release, the prime minister was enthusiastically welcomed back to Karachi by his supporters.

Bhutto set about planning for new elections called for 18 October. Zia and his generals could only be alarmed that the outcome might be favourable for the PPP; their fate at the hands of a bitter and vengeful Bhutto could easily be imagined. On 3 September, Bhutto was arrested again and this time charged for the murder of a rival Punjabi politician, who had been ambushed and gunned down. Elections were postponed indefinitely.

Albeit the de facto head of state, Zia only reluctantly accepted the presidency a year later in September 1978. By then Bhutto had been found guilty of murder in a Lahore court and was sentenced to death. The conviction was appealed to the High Court, and appeals for clemency were made by world leaders including President Carter. For four days from 18 December 1978, Bhutto argued his own defence and asked, 'not for mercy or clemency but justice'.[15]

The turning-away of calls for clemency from the Pope, Kurt Waldheim (the general secretary of the United Nations), the Soviets, the Saudis and France was perhaps not surprising; declining appeals from America, Pakistan's major ally and financial benefactor, was another matter. However, President Carter's failure to come to the aid of the Shah of Iran, who fell to the radical Islamic revolution of Ayatollah Khomenei, sharply diminished America's sway over the action of General Zia. Calls for clemency from the USA could now be spurned with impunity.

Having lost his High Court appeal in February 1979 by just one vote, Bhutto was hanged at 2.04 am, three hours ahead of schedule, on 4 April. On receiving confirmation of Bhutto's death, General Zia turned to his generals and said, 'The bastard's dead.'[16] The American Ambassador Hummel could only reflect, '. . . if I had been in Zia's shoes I would not have wanted a live Bhutto in some prison from which he could escape at any time or be sprung'.[17] The execution of Bhutto may have been regretted by the Western powers, but his demise was barely mourned. Sir Morrice James, who had been the British High Commissioner to Pakistan in the mid-1960s, thought of Bhutto as 'a Lucifer, a flawed angel'.[18]

The execution of Bhutto, against the wishes of President Carter, did not endear Zia to Washington. Worse was to follow. False rumours of the seizure of the Grand Mosque in Mecca by the USA and Israel led to a mob attack on the American Embassy in Islamabad. On the roof of the embassy a US marine was shot dead, 80 cars were wrecked and their petrol used to set fire to buildings. The government was slow to intervene. A staff member of the National Security Council meetings described relations between the two countries as 'about as bad as with any country in the world, except perhaps Albania and North Korea'.[19]

Meanwhile in Pakistan, Zia, a devout Muslim since childhood, embarked on a policy of Islamisation while doing little to reverse the socialist economic policies of Bhutto. Although Finance Minister Mohammed Khan Junejo introduced deregulatory policies including lifting of controls on small firms, he was sacked after one year, and the improved short-term economic performance of Pakistan was largely attributable to a rapid growth in domestic and external debt which rose to 80 per cent of GDP. Defence expenditure rose at an unsustainable 9.2 per cent per annum. Corruption, which had become endemic within the socialist state apparatus created by Bhutto, now moved increasingly into the army. Here control of the drug trade through Afghanistan and Pakistan became a major contributor to the private wealth of generals.

For the first time since independence, Zia introduced discrimination against non-Muslims. Decorated Fighter Pilot Cecil Chaudhry, a Christian who was refused a staff officer appointment by Zia, even though it had been approved by the Air Board, confirmed that 'Before the Zia era a Christian did make it to the number two post in the Air Force. But after the Zia era no non-Muslim was able to make it even to Group Captain. It was the same in the army.'[20] For Zia, Islam was the rock on which Pakistan itself was built. 'Take Islam out of Pakistan and make it a secular state,' he claimed, and 'it would collapse'.[21]

Under Zia, radical Islam prospered in all spheres of life, from the army to the encouragement of radical Madrassa schools; it is estimated that some 12,000 of these mosque schools were created during his rule. Of these, the Deobandi schools sometimes gave military training and became centres for radical indoctrination and literature advocating sectarian violence. Many of these schools were financed by Saudi Arabia and its Wahabi version of Sunnism. Zia also allowed the *Tablighi Jamaat* (an Islamic missionary society) to conduct their missions within the army. Islamic studies were introduced at the Staff College at Quetta, where one lecturer, Colonel Abdul Qayyum, insisted that education should not be used just to produce soldiers, engineers and doctors but 'Muslim soldiers, Muslim engineers, Muslim doctors, Muslim officers and Muslim men'.[22] In addition, he was openly supportive of the Jamaat-i-Islam Party.

In May 1980 Zia created a Federal Shariah Court and appointed *ulemas* (Muslim scholars) as judges. After 1982, *ulemas* also sat on the Shariah Appellate Bench of the Supreme Court. Koranic punishments were also introduced. Adulterous women could be given 100 lashes with a cane or even stoned. Even raped women could be treated as adulterers. Beatings and even amputations could also be given for crimes such as perjury or blasphemy.

In November 1984 Zia offered a referendum to gauge the popular support for his Islamisation policies; the government announced that 98 per cent of people on a 62 per cent turnout voted in favour. The facts were disputed by the opposition, which estimated that the poll turnout was just 10 per cent. In 1985 Zia felt secure enough to try to normalise Pakistan's constitutional arrangements by offering a National Assembly election for the first time since he had pulled national elections in 1977.

However, political parties were banned. Nevertheless in a plebiscite which recorded a 52 per cent turnout, five out of nine of Zia's cabinet were defeated. Subsequently in choosing a little-known Sindhi politician, Mohammed Khan Junejo, as prime minister, Zia had hoped for a compliant ally, a wish that would eventually be disappointed. Nevertheless, when he ended eight years of martial law on 31 December 1985, Zia took the precaution of passing the eighth amendment to the 1973 constitution, which passed ultimate power of veto to the president, thus reversing the paramountcy of parliament introduced by Bhutto.

However, it was the ISI (Directorate for Inter-Services Intelligence) which would bring the last major political crisis of General Zia's presidency. On 10 April 1988, a munitions worker at Ojiri Camp dropped a defective mortar shell; he not only blew himself up, but with him went US$ 120 million worth of ordnance. Islamabad and Rawalpindi were inadvertently bombarded. With the death of over 100 people and some 1,100 injured, Prime Minister Junejo sought to avoid political opprobrium by passing blame for the disaster to Akhtar Rahman, chairman of the Joint Chief of Staff, who was also head of the ISI. In a conflict with the army, there could be only one winner. The eighth amendment was used to sack Prime Minister Junejo. Zia put himself forward as the new prime minister and called for National Assembly elections in November 1988.

Before the elections took place, Zia was killed on 17 August when his C-130 transport plane, returning to Islamabad from Bahawalpur, where the president observed an American Abrams M-1 tank in action, inexplicably crashed. On board with Zia, American Brigadier General Herbert Wasson and 30 others were all killed. In a joint investigation by Americans and Pakistanis, it was concluded by the former that there had been a mechanical failure, while Pakistanis suspected sabotage.

With Zia's demise, the path to restoration of democracy lay invitingly open; with elections already slated within three months of Zia's death, party politics could resume. Both Ghulam Ishaq Khan, president of the Senate, who became Pakistan's president by dint of the provisions of the 1973 constitution, and the army declined to interfere in the restoration of democracy to Pakistan.

42

Pol Pot: Deconstructionism and Genocide

Cambodia: 1973–79

The genocide carried out by the Khmer Rouge in Cambodia between 1975 and 1979 is closely associated with its eponymous leader 'Pol Pot', the revolutionary name adopted by the young Saloth Sâr. He was born on 19 May 1925 in a house on stilts above a river downstream of Kompong Thom, a typical Cambodian settlement. His father was a wealthy peasant who owned 50 acres of rice-paddy and six buffaloes. However, Pol Pot was destined never to work in the fields. His cousin had been a palace dancer, who subsequently became one of King Monivong's wives. Pol Pot's older sister, Roeung, also became a consort to the king. His family thus favoured, he was drawn into the royal circle and became a frequent visitor to the Royal Palace. The adolescent Pol Pot would even be pleasured in the king's harem.

Through these connections, Pol Pot was sent to be educated for a year at a Royal Monastery and then attended an elite Catholic school, Lycée Sisowath. Here among the 120 students, he became the closest friend of Lon Non, whose elder brother Lon Nol would later become Cambodia's head of state and be defeated by Pol Pot's Khmer Rouge Army. After failing his *brevet* exam at Lycée, along with his friend Lon Non, Pol Pot, unlike his richer friend, was forced to go to Technical School in the northern suburbs of Phnom Penh. As for his character, a fellow student Mey Mann would recall, 'He never said very much. He just had that smile of his. He liked to joke, he had a slightly mischievous way about him. And there was never the least hint of what was to come'.[1]

At Technical School, he finally passed his *brevet* and was given a scholarship to study radio engineering in Paris; at that point he was one of only 250 Cambodian students to have been sent overseas for education since the turn of the century. Sharing the same passage to France, Mey Mann remembered that they worried about the cold weather in Paris and the food but 'Politics never came up. Not once. It was just a great adventure.'[2]

Yet these would be the most formative years for the 26-year-old Pol Pot. In Paris he entered the École Française de Radioélectricité, where one of King Monivong's nephews, Prince Sisowath Somonopong, was also studying; the Prince took care of him, found him lodgings and introduced him to friends. The liberal mentor of the 'Paris Group', or what Prince Norodom Sihanouk would call the 'super-intellectuals', was Keng Vannsak, a nephew of a Cambodian princess, who studied at the prestigious École Normale Supérieure at St. Cloud, followed by the School of Oriental and African Studies (SOAS) in London. However, at first, Pol Pot's group of friends was not politically radical.

In his first summer, he joined an 'international labour brigade' going to build motorways outside Zagreb in Yugoslavia. Yet his conversion to communism was not immediate. The following summer, his friends, including Ieng Sary, went to Berlin for a 15-day 'World Youth Festival for Peace', which was a communist front organisation, while Pol Pot went back to Yugoslavia on a camping holiday. Nevertheless, through the introduction of friends, he subsequently joined a cell of the secret group known as the *Cercle Marxiste*. For the time being, he remained a follower rather than a leader. Here, he would meet his circle of friends and co-revolutionaries, later coming to be known as the 'Paris Group', who were to dominate both his life and the fortunes of his country.

Increasingly however, it was the lessons of the French Revolution rather than Marx and his emphasis on the urban proletariat which fascinated Pol Pot. Influenced by the Russian anarchist Prince Pëtr Kropotkin and his book *The Great French Revolution* (1909), the 'Paris Group' turned its focus to the French Revolution. A combination of bourgeois intellectuals and peasants had together overthrown the ancien régime; 'The Revolution was prepared and made by two great movements. One was the current of ideas . . . which came from the bourgeoisie. The other, the current of action, came from the popular masses_ the peasants and labourers. . . .'[3]

Robespierre, the leader of the Montagnards in the French Revolution, and the implacable butcher of the Guillotine, was particularly admired. One of the Paris Group members would later recall, 'Robespierre's personality impressed me . . . he was incorruptible and intransigent . . . you must always be on the side of the absolute_ no middle way, no compromise. . . .'[4] Pol Pot wrote with florid hyperbole that monarchy was 'as foul as a putrefying sore'.[5]

Pol Pot and Ieng Sary now formed the core of the 'Paris Group'. Linking these latter two in Paris were the Khieu sisters: Thirith, who married Ieng Sary, and Ponnary, who later married Pol Pot. Further members of this group who were to become Khmer leaders included Hou Youn, Khieu Samphân and Hu Nim. While these latter three flourished academically, and would return to Cambodia to appointments at the Faculties of Law and Economics at Phnom Penh University, Pol Pot, described by a contemporary as a young man of average ability but with a clear desire for power and short-cut means of getting to the top, returned to Cambodia in 1953 having flunked his courses three years in succession.

The quiet, charming, intellectually limited Pol Pot may not have garnered academic achievement, but his assignation to the Phnom Penh branch of the Communist Party would have its advantages. Working diligently within the party organisation, he eventually assumed command when, in 1962, Communist Party Secretary Tou Samouth was arrested by security police, tortured and murdered while looking for medicine for a sick child. Prince Sihanouk asserted that it was Pol Pot who had ordered the murder, but it seems more likely to have been done by General Lon Nol, the defence minister, to whose house Tou Samouth was reportedly brought before being buried on wasteland. The murder followed a crackdown on dissidents launched by Sihanouk after a supposed plot to kill him at the beginning of the year; in February, the left wing *Pracheachon* newspaper was closed down after it complained, 'our staff are under day and night surveillance by armed police with cameras and binoculars'.[6] The shut-down of radical groups conveniently preceded the elections set for June.

In 1967, Pol Pot studied in Beijing and was a first-hand witness of the Cultural Revolution. He was to remain a staunch supporter of Chairman Mao, whom he eulogised with a funeral oration after his death in 1976. In 1970, after the toppling of the Marxist-leaning Prince Sihanouk and his replacement by the right-wing Lon Nol, Pol Pot and his group, including his wife Ieng Sary, and Son Sen, fled the capital to spend the next five years orchestrating a peasant-based Khmer Rouge uprising that would eventually overthrow not only the Lon Nol government, but also Cambodia's entire social order.

In spite of Pol Pot's protestations of support for Mao, it is clear that the peculiar hallmarks of the Khmer Rouge regime were far from being Maoist. Mao's peasant revolution occupied the countryside, and then developed the revolution from an urban base. However the Cultural Revolution, which epitomised Mao's belief in the need for perpetual revolution, was driven by urban workers, students and a radical sect within the Communist Party leadership, which was actively pushed forward by Mao himself.

The roots of Pol Pot's ideas for the radical de-urbanisation of Cambodia were evident even in the early years of the Paris Group. In *'La Paysannerie du Cambodge'*, Hou Youn's doctoral thesis at the Sorbonne, his analysis displayed a regressive economic analysis quite at odds with the determinist underpinnings of orthodox Marxist–Leninism; Hou Youn argued that 'The commercial system, the selling and exchanging of agricultural production in our country, suppresses production and squeezes the rural areas dry and tasteless, permanently maintaining them in poverty. What we habitually call "cities" or "market towns" are pumps which drain away the vitality of the rural area.'[7]

Similarly, while lecturing at Phnom Penh University, Khieu Samphân espoused equally radical views advocating 'the need to start the new society from zero, basing it on the peasant masses. They are pure,' he asserted, 'Everything in the old society must go. We must return to nature, based on the peasantry.'[8] In the simplistic expression of one Khmer cadre, 'People are good. Cities are evil. This is why we shall do away with the cities.'[9]

Even though neither orthodox Marxist–Leninism nor the models of the Cultural Revolution were the benchmark for the Khmer revolution, 'Maoism proved a useful ideological tool, for it stresses the capacity of human willpower to triumph over material conditions and so reverse historical trends.'[10] The self-belief of the 'Paris Group' in their ability to effect an immediate transformation of their country to a socialist utopia displayed a limitless hubris. Pol Pot equated his achievements to Alexander the Great, Napoleon and Hitler – though he believed he had exceeded them all.

When the communist Khmer Rouge troops finally overcame the stubborn year-long defence of Phnom Penh on 17 April 1975, they walked into a city whose numbers had been swelled by hundreds of thousands of war refugees. Under virtual siege for months, the populace was close to starvation in spite of an American airlift of thousands of tons of supplies. Before the fall of Phnom Penh, Sydney Schanberg of *The New York Times* reported that '. . . some have swollen bellies. Some are shrunken. A 10 year old girl has dehydrated to the size of a 4 year old. . . . all have dysentery'.[11] United States Agency for International Development (USAID), in a report on Cambodia in April 1975, suggested that 'if ever a country needed to beat its swords into ploughshares in a race to save itself from hunger, it is Cambodia'.[12] Rice output fell from 3.8 million tons in 1973 to just 655,000 tons in 1974.

Meanwhile, journalists reported that 'for the privileged elite the good life of tennis, nightclubs, expensive French meals, and opulent, brandy drenched dinner parties went on almost to the end . . .'.[13] On 6 April, at the American Embassy, Ambassador Dean entertained the few remaining journalists and served his finest wine declaring that he did not want it to fall into the hands of the Communists.

Desultory last-minute attempts at negotiation saw the US Ambassador to Beijing George Bush (senior) being requested by Henry Kissinger to seek another meeting with the Chinese leadership on 11 April. However, the bid to bring Prince Sihanouk back to Phnom Penh to replace Lon Nol, who had been forced to resign on 1 April, was far too late. Sihanouk, well aware that the Khmer Rouge was now certain of total victory, denounced the American initiative. At 6 am on the following day, Ambassador Dean prepared for the final evacuation of staff from Phnom Penh; as American diplomatic and military staff departed at 9 am, in the company of acting President Saukam Khoy, a Khmer mortar round killed a bystander watching the departing helicopters.

With the exception of Lon Nol's brother, Prime Minister Sisowath Sirik Matak, and most policemen and army officers who were summarily executed, most of Phnom Penh's population regarded the arrival of the Khmer Rouge with relief, even joy. In places, the young soldiers, drably dressed in khaki uniform, were greeted by cheering crowds. The behaviour of the conquerors soon shattered the initial euphoria. Journalist Dith Pran recalled that they looked as though they were from 'a different world . . . They never smiled at all. They didn't even look like

Cambodians'.[14] Indeed, they were peasants from Cambodia's furthest hinterlands who 'had never seen money, they didn't even know what a car was'.[15] They drank water from toilet bowls thinking they were wells. The tires of abandoned vehicles were cut up to make sandals.

Within hours, relief turned to alarm as the entire population was ordered to leave the city. A Khmer Rouge cadre told Father Ponchaud, a Catholic mission-ary, that 'The City is bad because there is money in the city. People can be re-formed but not cities. By sweating to clear the land, sowing and harvesting crops, men will learn the real value of things.'[16] Some Khmer units, those not affiliated to the dominant 'Paris Group' faction of Pol Pot, denied the 'exodus' rumours and tried to reassure people that everything would soon return to normal or that they would be allowed to return in a few days. One refugee recalled the use of a ruse: 'The American imperialists will bomb the hospital_you must evacuate immediately.'[17]

It was a shambolic exercise; moving 2.5 million people out of a city at a few hours notice could hardly have been otherwise. The roads out of Phnom Penh were so jammed there was barely room to walk. The heat in April, Cambodia's hottest month, was sweltering; the main body of the city's population took five days to cover eight miles. Those in private cars and trucks were ordered to abandon them; treasured consumer good such as televisions, fans, fridges, sofas, sewing machines and so on were left scattered by the roadside. With no further need for money, it was used to light fires. For some, it was too much. A new Peugeot car was driven down a riverbank into the flowing current, 'There were people inside. A man in the driver's seat, a woman beside him and children looking out the back with their hands pressed against the windows . . . nobody got out . . . a rich family committing suicide.'[18]

Pol Pot wrote later that the evacuation was 'an extraordinary measure . . . that,' he boasted, 'one does not find in the revolution of any other country'.[19] 'Agricul-ture', he declared, 'is the key to both nation building and to national defence'.[20] An autarkic socialist model state was planned. In his doctoral thesis at the Sorbonne in 1959, Khieu Samphân had written, 'International integration is the root cause of the under-development of the Khmer economy'.[21] Pol Pot aimed to expand the nation's agriculture in order to accumulate capital to fund a modern industrial economy within 15–20 years. His aim was to run fast to compete with Vietnam. At first, this would be achieved by manpower and later by mechanisation. He also aimed to double or triple the population of Cambodia from 7 million to 15–20 mil-lion as rapidly as possible.

De-urbanisation and reversion to an agricultural society were not absurd ideas to some contemporaneous western 'experts'; An American aid expert, Joel Charney, who was head of Oxfam in South East Asia, declared that Pol Pot's rural development plans, 'were they found in a consultant's report, would win the approval of a wide cross-section of the [Western] development community'.[22]

In Europe, Pol Pot's 'empty the city' and rural retreat policies found favour with some 'Greens' including leading British environmentalist and founder of the *The Ecologist* magazine 'Teddy' Goldsmith (author of *The Great U turn: De-Industrialising Society*, 1988).

Within days, the city of Phnom Penh was deserted. A French woman, Laurence Picq, who was married to one of Ieng Sary's foreign office staff, arrived from Beijing in October 1975 and described the impression of 'an empty planet'; there was 'Not a soul, not a dog, not a bird, not even a flower.'[23] Libraries, museums and monuments were destroyed; the Cambodian National Bank was blown up as was the Catholic Cathedral. Buddhism was banned. The process of urban destruction was repeated in every city and town in Cambodia. 'A whole nation was kidnapped and besieged from within.'[24]

As the urban population was herded on foot to new settlements in jungle clearings, a new social order was imposed. From now on, the city dwellers would be categorised as 'New' people. In Democratic Kampuchea, there would be three classes: *penh sith*, people with full rights, (mostly Khmer cadres); *triem*, candidates for full rights referred to as 'ancients' or 'base' people, who were the indigenous peasant population; and *bannheur*, those with no rights, usually called 'new' people, who were urban dwellers. From the start, it was made clear that the *bannheur* ('new' people) were expendable. They were told, 'Keeping you is no profit; losing you is no loss.'[25] The Khmer cadres, who oversaw the urban exodus, were mainly peasant teenagers. Many had been taken from their parents and indoctrinated in special schools with simplistic slogans learnt by rote; they were also taught to practice sadism on animals.

The process of urban dispersal was almost immediately catastrophic in terms of human life. Weakened by malnutrition and the exertions of a forced march, many of the *bannheur* fell by the wayside from illness or exhaustion. 'We must have passed the body of a child every 200 yards', recalled one survivor.[26] Also, the old who could not keep up dropped by the roadside, where they stayed until death caught up with them; the lucky were put out of their misery by the Khmer Rouge, who shot or clubbed them to death.

The hospitals had also been evacuated and the sick were forced into the exodus. Father Ponchaud recalled that of these

> The strongest dragged themselves pitifully along, others were carried by friends, some lying on beds pushed by their families with their plasma and IV drips bumping alongside. I shall never forget one cripple who had neither hands nor feet, writhing along the ground like a severed worm.[27]

The immediate evacuation of the city was estimated to have cost 20,000 lives within days; it was a mere taste of what was to follow. Those who fled to the South West soon faced a cholera epidemic, which flared up within two weeks of the evacuation. An estimated 100,000 people perished from cholera in the South West alone.

For those who survived the initial exodus, many found that in the beginning food at least was plentiful. After the privations of besieged Phnom Penh, this at least must have been a relief. However, hopes were short-lived. A refugee recalled, 'In 1975, we all ate rice until October, and then only gruel (*baba*). In 1976, we had rice until July, and in 1977, rice until February. In 1978, we had no rice at all, only gruel.'[28]

All reminiscences of the survivors revolve around the scramble for food. Without inventiveness, death was inevitable. In his epic account *Stay Alive My Son* (1988), Pin Yathay, a former qualified engineer in the Ministry of Public Works, sold belongings to get extra rations from a black market which was often run by the cadres themselves. Khmer guards would fail to report the dead and continued to garner their food rations. Possessions would be bartered. A good watch could fetch 60–80 cans of rice.

On one occasion, Pin Yathay bought two chickens for $200, which provided a 'feast' for 14. More routinely, frogs were sought for grilling; even a toad was eaten though its toxic flesh had gut-wrenching consequences. Another survivor Pen Boun recalled, 'to survive we were obliged to eat rats, grasshoppers, lizards, toads, centipedes, earth worms . . . '[29]; the former state pharmacist would also find leaves, snails and crabs to supplement four ounces of rice per person as reward for 10–13 hours of forced agricultural labour.

Foraging did not guarantee survival, however. As Pen Boun goes on to record, 'The population of the village of Ta Amp was about 4,000 when we arrived, but by the time we were liberated, it was reduced to about 1,000.'[30] Herded into communes and periodically moved to new settlements, often separating family members, people lost all sense of individuality or humanity. Dith Munty recalled bitterly:

> We were ill fed, clad in rags and reduced to slavery. Human rights were trampled underfoot, the right to eat with one's family and free marriage were replaced by 'eat in Common' and forced marriage by groups of 30 to 50 to 60 couples each time . . . .[31]

Meals at home were not allowed. Eating implements were confiscated. Watery rice gruel was served by central canteens. Normal human contact ended in this new world. Leaving aside the abolition of money, post, telegraph and telephone, it became dangerous to express opinions or display emotions. Pith Yathay chided his son for whistling a pre-revolutionary song, 'He should have learned by now not to show any sign of happiness.'[32] A visiting Yugoslav television crew observed that the only smile in Cambodia was on the face of Pol Pot; music, singing and dancing were noticeably absent; 'There was no singing to be heard, nor did we see any folk dancing.'[33]

Not everyone died of malaria or malnutrition, however. Democratic Kampuchea, as it incongruously became known, developed all the familiar tools and methodologies of a totalitarian state. At Tuol Sleng high school in the suburbs of

Phnom Penh, a *Santebal* (special branch) operation was set up to 'interview' enemies of the state. Here, a weedy maths teacher, Kang Kek Iew who went by the
revolutionary name of 'Duch', recruited young cadre members, nearly all between
the ages of 17 and 21, to interrogate, extract confessions, torture and kill thousands of prisoners.

At the beginning, the inmates were officers of the former regime, but increasingly the cells were filled with the victims of Pol Pot's purges of his own cadres.
This included Hu Nim, a former 'Paris Group' intellectual, who was deemed to be
too close to the Chinese Cultural Revolution. As one interrogator reported, 'We
whipped him four or five times to break his stand, before taking him to be stuffed
with water.'[34] Also purged were the regional or zonal commanders; unlike the
'Paris Group', their brand of communism was often of the *Issarak*, post-war communist organisation that had worked closely with the *Việt Minh* and the *Việt Cộng*.
In particular, the East Zone, under So Phim, had worked closely with the North
Vietnamese in the management of the Hồ Chí Minh trail and the 'sanctuaries' that
lined the borderland with South Vietnam.

The Paris Group's attacks on large segments of the population were not simply class-based or aimed at purging potential political rivals. There was also a concerted aim to annihilate certain racial groups. While the population of Cambodia
was 80 per cent Cambodian, the population of towns and cities contained large
numbers of Chinese and Vietnamese. In the countryside there were also Thais,
Laotians and Islamic Chams. These populations suffered disproportionately from
ethnic cleansing.

The Vietnamese, who increasingly came to be seen as a regional rival for power
in Indochina, became a particular target for liquidation. In 1978, the Khmer leadership published the *Black Paper*, which was Pol Pot's version of Cambodia's history, particularly in its relationship with Vietnam; in this he declared that 'The
Kampuchea's people are perfectly aware of the Vietnamese treacherous acts, sub-
terfuges and hypocrisy. They have always seethed with a deep rancour.'[35]

Cambodian attempts to purge the Vietnamese population were marked by exceptional brutality. A description of an attack on a Vietnamese village is particularly
gruesome:

> ...a fleeing child was caught by a soldier who cut off his leg and threw him into
> the flames ...[Mrs Trong Thi Rot] was disembowelled and had a seven-month foe-
> tus placed on her chest .... All eight persons in Nguyen Thi Nganh's house were
> disembowelled. The killers then took out her five-month-old foetus, then cut off her
> breasts and chopped her body in three parts. Her two year old boy was torn in two
> and dumped in a well.[36]

As for Islamic Chams, their language was suppressed and the Khmers forced
them to eat pork. Out of an estimated 250,000 Chams, some 90,000 lost their lives
in the four years after 1975. Random slaughter of foreigners was also recorded.

In April 1976, in the province of Southern Kandal, the Khmer arrested 57 Arabs, Pakistanis and Indians, including 40 women and children; the prisoners were sent to Tuol Seng for liquidation.

Apart from the targeted racial genocide practised by the Khmer Rouge, the inhumanity of the system was perhaps best expressed by the random acts of brutality and terror carried out by low level cadres. Unlike Princess Savethong Sisowath Monipang, who survived the war by feigning stupidity and hiding her aristocratic roots, her husband, a doctor, was shot for being an intellectual.

This group was particularly hard hit. Between 1968 and 1979, the number of lecturers and professors fell from 725 to 50, while the number of teachers fell from 21,311 to 2,793. Of the 1,000 intellectuals and experts who returned to Cambodia in 1975, with the idealistic expectation of being able to help their country, only 85 survived. Thiounn Chhum, who was plucked from a rice field in August 1978 and told to reorganise the finances of Democratic Kampuchea, was a lucky but rare exception to the massacre.

Execution was not always as clinical as a firing squad or a bullet to the head. Denise Affonco recalled following guards who had arrested a 'New' person for some trifling offence:

> Butcher Ta Sok, a big knife in his hand, made a long incision in the abdomen of the miserable victim, who screamed with pain like a wild beast ... groped for his liver which he cut out and started to cook in a frying pan already heated by Ta Chea .... [37]

She also recalled a group of 40 men, women and children buried alive at the same time. Others were simply worked to death or died of casual brutality or neglect. In the construction of grand irrigation schemes, often hopelessly engineered, workers sometimes had to stand in ditches in water up to their necks for a whole day. Unseen leeches grew to vast proportions on their bodies, and it was not unknown for them to penetrate workers' anuses, never to reappear.

By the time of the overthrow of Pol Pot's regime, it is estimated that some 2.5–3 million people out of a total population of 7 million had lost their lives to the Khmer Rouge. The extent of the slaughter was not unknown to the regime. 'Although a million lives have been wasted,' Pol Pot told a group of cadres in 1977, 'our party does not feel sorry. Our party needs to be strong.'[38] There were regional variations to the slaughter. The north west region suffered disproportionately high losses probably because the Khmer cadres here were young and heavily radicalised. Also, in this traditionally fertile area, food requisitions were highest.

By contrast, the East, under the control of older, more experienced and less radical cadres, fared somewhat better. Also 'Ancients' were more likely to have survived than the urban 'New' people, against whom the odds of survival were heavily stacked. The losses suffered by Phnom Penh families defy belief. Pin Yathay was the only known survivor of the exodus of his 17 family members to the countryside, including his wife and children. Similarly, Princess Monipang was the lone survivor of her 24 family members. In *Journey to Cambodia* (1981), Honda Katuiti's survey of survivors, he noted that from a large extended family sent to Battambang in 1975, only two survived. Regional variations were also observed. Two groups of families with 182 members suffered just four deaths in the Eastern Zone, but 70 deaths after their transfer to Battambang and other places. However, many 'New' families simply disappeared without trace.

Within a year of overthrowing Lon Nol, the Khmer regime proclaimed that they had leapfrogged other socialist countries to number one position in the communist hierarchy in terms of the level of 'socialism' achieved. China, which they ranked second, was now 4–10 years behind. Vietnam was ranked seventh. Although the secret CPK magazine, *Tung Padevat*, declared that class warfare needed to continue in the countryside, it boasted that 'the bourgeoisie have nowhere to go. They have become satellite to the worker–peasant power . . . their classes have already collapsed . . .'.[39]

While it is important to acknowledge the Marxist–Leninist, albeit unorthodox, origins of the Khmer revolution, some attention must also be paid to its peculiar French roots. By 1975, the older generation of post-war communists, who had been happy to fight side by side with their North Vietnamese comrades, had been displaced in the leadership by a group, whose revolutionary and intellectual processes had been formed almost entirely in Paris. By 1979, the 'Paris Group' had, through a series of purges, effectively wiped out the older generation of Communists. It is not without significance, therefore, that aspects of the Paris Group's revolutionary thinking mirrored so closely the dominant French philosophies of post-war France.

In their belief that they could mould Cambodia in any form they wished, the 'Paris Group' developed a political creed based on a perversion of the philosophical proposition of Jean-Paul Sartre that the world was man's existential creation. In other words, the world did not create man; man created the world. In his simplistic interpretation of the philosophic approach of Kant and Heidegger, Jean-Paul Sartre laid out visions that were excitingly attractive to young radicals; if man could impose upon the world what he willed, there were no constraints.

The 'deconstructionism' of Roland Barthes, Michel Foucault and Jacques Derrida embellished this world without constraints, and filtered into revolutionary thought. Frantz Fanon, author of *The Wretched Earth* (1963), advocated that '. . . to tell the truth, the proof of success lies in a whole structure being changed from the bottom up . . .'.[40] The idea that Cambodia should completely sever its links with the capitalist world was also encouraged by the analysis of French Marxist theorist Samir Amin, who proposed that 'In the undeveloped countries the traditional economic system has been gradually destroyed by its integration into the world capitalist system.'[41]

The influence of French philosophic and revolutionary concepts can be seen in the Paris Group's belief that 'man' could effect an instant transformation of society. In his doctoral thesis for the Sorbonne in 1959, Khieu Samphân had called for self-conscious autonomous development to change Cambodian society. Later, the Khmer leadership also emphasised the sui generis nature of the revolution. Pol Pot, who relied heavily on North Vietnamese and Chinese support in his defeat of Lon Nol, claimed quite falsely that the Khmer Rouge had won 'without any foreign connection or involvement'.[42] Reportedly, Pol Pot told his followers that 'everything should be done on the basis of self reliance, independence and mastery. The Khmers should do everything on their own'.[43] Like Kim Il Sung's philosophy of *Juche* (self-reliance) in North Korea, much admired by the 'Paris Group', the Khmer leadership placed significant emphasis on its self-reliance and its individual destiny. Their suspicion of Vietnamese desire for hegemony in Indochina was perhaps not surprising, but China too was treated with suspicion.

When Zhou Enlai died in January 1976, a foreign ministry official warned that 'We must beware of China. It is true that we owe her a great deal, and it is a great country. But she wants to make us a satellite.'[44] Mau Khem Nuon, who was assigned to lecture returning Cambodian intellectuals on the nature of the Khmer revolution, stressed that Democratic Kampuchea had to have 'independence mastery' and could not rely on China.

The hubris of the Khmer leadership is encapsulated in a story told by Prince Sihanouk about a meeting in Beijing between Zhou Enlai and Khieu Samphân and Madame Ieng Sary:

> The great Chinese statesmen counselled the Khmer Rouge leaders: 'Don't follow the bad example of our "Great Leap Forward". Take things slowly . . . by way of response to this splendid and moving piece of almost fatherly advice, Khieu Samphân and Ieng Thirith just smiled an incredulous and superior smile.'[45]

The Khmer leadership was impervious to advice. Like the 'Great Leap Forward' in China, the Khmer leadership fostered absurd plans for a tripling of rice output in four years. As Australian historian Ben Kiernan concluded, 'Economically the country had become one, "gigantic workshop" of indentured agrarian labour.'[46]

Fortunately for the people who survived the four-year reign of terror initiated in 1975, the Khmer Rouge regime was short-lived. Goaded by the increasingly bellicose language of Pol Pot, and the very real attacks on the Vietnamese populations of Cambodia and the cross-border raids and incursions within Vietnam itself, the Vietnamese stirred themselves to yet another military expedition. The Khmer Rouge was no match for the vastly more experienced, better equipped and battled hardened troops of the Vietnamese army. In a short campaign, the Khmer Rouge were expelled from Phnom Penh and forced to retreat to north eastern enclaves on the Thai borders. The peasants, who had supported the Khmer Rouge in their bid to topple Lon Nol, were equally supportive of their demise. There were few 'New' people left to join them in their delight.

In 1979, Pol Pot and Ieng Sary fled to Beijing where Pol Pot reportedly told Deng Xiaoping that their mistake had been to follow the line of the Cultural Revolution and the Gang of Four. It is unlikely that the pragmatic Deng would have been impressed. However, with Vietnam now an ally of the Soviet Union, China could not abandon a partner in fighting the growth of a powerful military opponent on its southern border.

In spite of China's disdain for Pol Pot's ideology, Deng Xiaoping would keep the Khmer Rouge alive for its geopolitical possibilities. However, the horror of the Khmer Rouge genocide was ended; so too was Pol Pot's dream of recreating a socialist version of the great empire of the Angkors. The Khmer Rouge experiment, which, in terms of the proportion of population murdered, engineered the most brutal genocidal episode of the twentieth century, was the construct of a group of Parisian intellectuals who believed that social order could be taken from the 'laboratory' of philosophical proposition and imposed by 'pure will' without any constraints of culture, religion, law or economics. The 'Killing Fields', as they have become known in Cambodia, have now become a tourist attraction and a cruel example of the follies of utopian socialism.

PART IV

Communism in Retreat

43

The Gang of Four

China: 1976—9

The death of Zhou Enlai in January 1976, and the purge of Deng Xiaoping the following month, seemed to clear the political field for Mao's wife, Jiang Qing, and the ultra-leftists. They immediately leapt at the opportunity to denigrate Zhou's memory in the press and to push forward with their agenda. In the Shanghai magazine, *Gang Wenhui*, the ultra-left editors were encouraged to attack Zhou's memory and he was duly described as a 'Capitalist Roader'. The discipline that Deng had begun to instill in the administration of Chinese government immediately fell by the wayside.

At this point, however, there were extraordinary popular uprisings in favour of Zhou Enlai. Millions had crowded his funeral procession; the laying of wreaths and memorials culminated with an assembly of 2 million demonstrators on Sunday 4 April. Criticisms of Zhou were met by riots in Nanking. In Beijing, ostensibly as part of the public mourning for Zhou, wall posters began to appear, which attacked Jiang and the ultra-left. Even Mao was criticised. Eventually, the mayor of Beijing intervened and authorised the police, with the assistance of Hua Guofeng, Mao's chosen successor, and the Public Security Bureau, to crack down on the wave of protestors in Tiananmen Square.

However, the clearing of wreaths and memorials provoked a violent backlash in which police vans were attacked and a police station set alight. After these violent clashes, protestors were arrested and imprisoned. In a temporary alignment with Hua in the confrontation of popular unrest, the 'Gang of Four' ignored these signs of unpopularity and pressed on with their push for power.

The mass reaction to the death of Zhou was more than just an outpouring of grief; it was also a coded message of support for the man perceived as his protégé, Deng Xiaoping. However, Deng had disappeared; contrary to the 'Gang's' belief that he was in hiding in his home province of Sechuan, Deng went secretly to Canton under the escort of a politburo member, General Xu Shiyou. In effect, Deng had gone underground. He travelled across the country 'incognito' in a blanked-out paddy wagon moving from one hiding place to another and arranging clandestine meetings with supporters. Deng was under no illusion about the nature of the struggle to come after Mao's death, and his exhortations to the PLA generals loyal to him were quite plain; 'Either we accept the fate of being slaughtered . . . or we should struggle against them [the Gang of Four] as long as there is still any life in our body.'[1]

With the aging Mao now virtually incoherent, Jiang and her supporters attacked Hua Guofeng, who, along with the 'survivor' group's Li Xiannian and Ye Jianying, seemed to be the only barrier to absolute power. The court squabbled as the fast-fading dictator sank into incoherence in his final months. Any restraint that they may have felt was immediately swept away when Mao died on 9 September 1976 at ten minutes past midnight at the age of 83. Jiang shocked many by her coolness at Mao's death and her disinterest in his funeral arrangements; at meetings after his death, she appeared far more concerned with the expulsion of Deng Xiaoping from the Communist Party. An even more obvious sign of tension surfaced after Mao's death. In the Great Hall where Mao was laid in state, Jiang Qing's arrival occasioned a cat fight with Mao's cousin; to the amusement of the party leadership, Jiang's wig flew off in the melee and revealed a completely bald head.

Meanwhile in the government compound, Mao's young protégé, Wang Hongwen, set up headquarters and issued instructions for provincial governments to report to him. Although the militia was being prepared for action in the ultra-left stronghold of Shanghai, the 'Gang' members themselves stayed in Beijing to orchestrate the battle for power.

At a politburo meeting on 29 September, Jiang, with the support of Zhang Chunqiao, pressed for resolution of her future role. Aggressive public speeches and the usual press coverage followed. Fearing that the Gang of Four was planning a coup, politburo member Ye Jianying, one of the 'survivor group', went into hiding. On 5 October, Hua Guofeng called the 'survivor group' leaders including Ye Jianying and Li Xiannian to a conference at the PLA headquarters in the western hills outside of Beijing. This cabal decided that it was time to pre-empt the 'Gang of Four', and sent Wang Dongxing, head of Unit 8341, the elite bodyguard unit of the party leadership, to arrest Jiang and her three confederates on 6 October.

There was no resistance. An uprising in Shanghai failed to materialise. As for the vast bulk of the Chinese population, there was barely restrained rejoicing. Even Jiang's own maid spat at her employer when she was arrested. The vileness of her character had done little to win her any friends in the party leadership. President Nixon described her as:

> tough, humorless, totally unfeminine, the ideal prototype of the sexless, fanatical Chinese woman . . . I have never met a more cold, graceless person. . . . She was so intense that beads of perspiration appeared on her hands and forehead. Her first comment was typical of her abrasive, belligerent attitude: 'Why did you not come to China before now?'[2]

However, in the end, it was not Jiang's personality that doomed the Gang of Four; simply they had vastly overestimated their strength. While Mao was alive, they were protected; the gang had been his instrument for maintaining the momentum of revolutionary activity that lay at the core of his personal quest. Even Mao must have suspected that the Gang enjoyed little popularity. When Mao had sent Deng and 'Gang' member Wang Hongwen on a joint tour of China, he asked them both on their return what would happen after his death. Wang flattered Mao that the people would sustain his revolutionary philosophy, while Deng told him that the power of the regional military commanders would return the country to 'Warlordism'. Mao believed Deng, with the result that a system of military rotation was implemented.

By the end, Mao did not exude much confidence in the permanence of his achievements. In his first meeting with Mao, Nixon flattered him by saying, 'The Chairman's writings moved a nation and have changed the world.' Mao replied, 'I have not been able to change it. I have only been able to change a few places in the vicinity of Peking.'[3] Indeed, it is a testament to the blinkered ideology of the Gang members that they could not understand the inherent conservatism of human nature, the fact of which the ageing Mao had become only too gloomily aware.

The harshness of the ultra-left philosophy was hardly conducive to popularity; in its fundamentalist doctrine, the gang believed that without revolutionary purity, material advancements were not worth having. Jiang affirmed that 'we would rather have socialist weeds than capitalist crops'.[4] As for using foreign technology to assist economic growth, this was anathema; she referred to this as 'sniffing foreigners' farts and calling them sweet.'[5]

Most importantly however, the philosophy of the ultra-left failed to attract any of the powerful groups that could have made a difference in their battle for power. The army had never succumbed to revolutionary fervour. Even Lin Biao, Mao's faithful lieutenant during the Cultural Revolution, drew the line at economic disruption and disorder within the ranks of the PLA. By their nature, soldiers are drawn to order and discipline, and the gang's agenda of constant revolution with its intimation of chaos was never likely to appeal.

The security apparatus also remained immune to the suasion of the ultra-left. But what about the Red Guard which had been such a potent force during the Cultural Revolution? Surely they were a powerful constituency available to the Gang? However, evidence shows that far from creating a generation of revolutionary heroes, the Cultural Revolution, after the initial frenzies, produced disillusionment and disaffection. Even within the party structures, the Gang of Four enjoyed only limited support.

Mao's Cultural Revolution had sought a total ethical transformation of the Chinese population with the destruction of 'the four "olds"_old ideas, old customs, old culture, old habits.'[6] However, as Mao well understood, the ability of the Communist Party to achieve this transformation was fatally undermined by the middle class's access to higher education. China, which had invented civil service examinations some 1,300 years earlier, exalted scholarship. As historian Robert Taylor concludes in *China's Intellectual Dilemma: Politics and University Enrolment 1949–78*

(1981), 'By 1965 it had become clear to Mao Zedong and his supporters that the only way in which the Liust (Liu Shaoqi) subversion of the Party's educational philosophy could be prevented was by the closure of the Universities and institutes....'[7] Indeed, the Cultural Revolution could in part be interpreted as Mao's strategy to destroy Lui Shaoqi, his putative successor.

In sending the Red Guards out to the countryside in 1968, Mao expected to achieve an interchangeability of the roles of teachers, workers and students. It is clear from contemporary accounts that this policy failed utterly. In *Son of Revolution* (1984), Judith Shapiro outlined the career of her husband, Liang Heng, as Red Guard (two years), peasant (two years) and factory worker (four years). The desolation of Liang Heng's existence was excruciating, starting from the point when it was 'discovered' that his father was a rightist and he was forced publicly to disown him.

At the age of 13, he was forced to stand guard over a famous pianist, Liu Shi-Kun. After hours of silence when the pianist asked for water, Liang Heng recalled:

> I didn't know what to do. A revolutionary shouldn't give water to his enemy, but I couldn't just stand there with water in the thermos only a few feet away. But what if someone saw me? ... I quickly poured a cup from the thermos ... as he drank it down I said fiercely, 'You can't tell anyone about this or next time I won't give you anything at all.'[8]

Eventually, Liang Heng was able to return to Changsha to resume an education, but the constant terror of his situation had left him devoid of all feelings. As life gradually returned to normal, that void was not replenished with love of revolution but with a deep-seated hatred of all that Maoism stood for. 'By experiencing disaster my generation did learn one terribly important thing_the danger that lies in blind obedience.'[9]

Similarly, Jung Chang recalls in the autobiograhical *Wild Swans* (1992) that when she was about to be sent on her Cultural Revolution exodus with her middle school to Sichuan Province:

> An official had come from Ningnan to talk to us, and he had described the subtropical climate (of Sichuan) with its high blue sky, huge red hibiscus flowers, foot-long bananas, and the Golden Sand River____ the upper part of the Yangtze____ shining in the bright sun, rippled by gentle breezes.[10]

In Sichuan, the harsh reality of living next to a pig-stye soon became apparent to Chang and her classmates.

Furthermore, the urban Red Guards soon learned the truth of the Great Leap Forward and its economic, moral and humanitarian disaster in the countryside. Another former Red Guard recalled that for the peasants:

> Times had been better ... even under the *Kuomintang*, when a man could work, save some money, invest it, and improve himself ... they also preferred Liu Shaoqi to Mao because they identified Liu with private plots ... in ten short days, my world had been challenged by the reality of peasant life and attitudes.[11]

Far from creating a cadre of ultra-leftists, the effect of the Cultural Revolution was to produce a bitter, disaffected generation who returned to their cities often after 6–10 years in exile. Their families and communities had been flung to the far winds, and they returned to cities denuded of community, cultural or spiritual life. A Belgian 'orientalist' art dealer, married to a school teacher, recalled in his account, *Ombres Chinoises* (1976), that Beijing had become a murdered town, and a disfigured ghost of what was once one of the most beautiful cities in the world.

Although from 1970, after a four-year hiatus, there had been a new class of university student admitted, entrance remained limited. Also, students were selected according to class rather than academic ability. The curriculum had been entirely politicised by the few teachers who had survived the Cultural Revolution. Books, of course, had been burnt in the Red Guard bonfires and were in short supply.

At the trial of the Gang of Four, they were accused of purging 142,000 teachers from the Ministry of Education. In addition, 53,000 scientists were removed. The death of Mao, some ten years after the start of the Cultural Revolution, thus coincided with the growth of popular revulsion and disillusionment with the individuals and institutions responsible for the depredations of the Cultural Revolution.

Acts of barbarity produce calibrated responses. Just as the brutal utopian fervour of the Paris Commune during the French Revolution gave way to the hedonism of the Directory, as the repressive totalitarianism of the Brezhnev era was replaced by the anarchic licence and ostentatious materialism of the Yeltsin years, so the Cultural Revolution paved the way for the creation of conditions which made possible the market-oriented reforms of the Deng Xiaoping era. The sad truth for Mao and the 'Gang of Four' is that their ultra-leftist policies had given rise to revulsion by the older generation of revolutionairies, the 'Survivor Group', and a complete disaffection with the Cultural Revolution by the Chinese populace. When Mao died in 1976, Maoism died with him.

While the death of revolutionary fervour lay at the heart of the downfall of the Gang of Four in the autumn of 1976, it is probable that, through the ineptitude of their plotting and failure to secure military backing, they would have failed anyway. On the surface, Hua Guofeng was the apparent winner from the death of Mao; in reality, he was fatally undermined by the demise of Maoism.

On 7 October, in the immediate aftermath of the arrest of the Gang of Four, Hua's chairmanship of the party and of the Military Affairs Commission was confirmed. Plodding bureaucrat that he was, Hua could not understand that post-Mao, the Chinese world had fundamentally changed. Supposedly Mao had told him in April 1976, 'with you in charge I am at ease'.[12] Hua's legitimacy was hung on the trust that Mao had placed in him, not realising that with the changing mood this was now a liability rather than an attribute.

In setting out his stall as leader, Hua reaffirmed the importance of the Cultural Revolution, described the Tiananmen Memorial incident as counter-revolutionary and attacked 'Deng' and the so-called 'rightists'. Hua used the press to puff up his image, and posters were commissioned to show Mao and Hua side by side. In February 1977, *The People's Daily*, mouthing the policies of the new leader, declared that henceforth the government would 'unswervingly adhere to *whatever* instructions Chairman Mao had issued'.[13]

In the aftermath of Mao and their fortunate escape from the Gang of Four, the followers of the formulaic Maoist dogmas were disparagingly referred to as the *whateverists*; regurgitation of the failed policies of the past 30 years was not what the party or the Chinese people wanted to hear. With the economy faltering, not helped by the July earthquake that had decimated Tangshan and caused the deaths of 220,000 people, Hua Guofeng was pressured to bring Deng back to the centre of public life.

Notably, it was an old revolutionary Chen Yun who led the call for Deng's rehabilitation. After negotiations carried out by Wang Dongxing, Deng was restored at the July 1977 Plenum, and at the 11th Congress in August he returned as the third-ranking member of the Politburo Standing Committee, after Hua and Ye Jianying. By this stage, Deng Xiaoping's support for Hua was largely nominal. Although at the Congress, Deng dutifully mouthed revolutionary platitudes, his taking up of the slogan, 'Seek truth from facts',[14] gave a clear signal to those used to the coded language of the era that Deng was advocating a return to the path of pragmatic development.

Over the next 12 months, Deng used his restoration to mobilise opinion in the Chinese press. In May 1978, Deng Xiaoping published an article entitled 'Practice Is the Sole Criterion for Testing the Truth', which appeared in *The People's Daily* and the *Liberation Army News*. Continuing the work begun in exile, Deng also won over regional military commanders and officials. By December 1978, Deng's push for change had become overwhelming.

At the 3rd Plenum of the Central Committee, Deng's ascendancy was confirmed by the posthumous exoneration of Peng Dehuai, the Chinese military hero of the Korean War who had stood up against Mao's Great Leap Forward policies at Lushan. Those purged during the Tiananmen Memorial demonstrations were also rehabilitated. The rise of Deng was also confirmed by the promotion of his supporters to the politburo, including Hu Yaobang, Deng Yingzhao and Wang Zhen. The highest profile lobbyist for Deng Xiaoping, party veteran Chen Yun, was promoted to the Standing Committee. Although for drama, the plenum did not match Khrushchev's denunciation of Stalin, Maoist philosophy had been forcefully renounced. Although Hua nominally continued to hold his offices of state, Maoism was now dead; the era of Deng Xiaoping had begun.

44

The End of the Tyrants

Korea: 1979–2001

The sudden demise of President Park at the hands of an assassin left no obvious candidates for succession. Neither were there constitutional means of replacing the fallen president. As a temporary measure, Prime Minister Choi Kyu Hah became the acting president, but reflecting the popular desire for more open government, Choi, a career diplomat and bureaucrat, not a politician, issued a statement on 10 November 1979 that the constitution would be amended 'to promote democracy'.[1]

However, with no political mandate or military support base, Choi was stranded. In the absence of formal solutions, a power struggle within the military provided the mechanism by which President Park was replaced. Some seven weeks after the death of Park, a two-star General, Chun Doo Hwan, who was head of the Defence Security Command, made the decisive bid for power. Supported by officers of the 11th Graduating class of the Korea Military Academy, with links to the Taegu area of North Kyongsang, Chun arrested Chung Seung-Hwa, who was the most senior army officer in the Republic of Korea.

Chun's first approach to the former regime's opponents was conciliatory. Some 600 dissidents including Kim Dae Jung were liberated. In March 1980, the universities were reopened. However, these measures had little calming effect on the perennial student opposition to authority. Mass student demonstrations provoked a new roundup of opposition leaders including Kim Young Sam and Kim Dae Jung.

Subsequently, a popular uprising in Kwangju, the capital of South Cholla Province, forced a withdrawal of Korean paratroopers from the city. Chun's reaction was both speedy and ruthless. On the following day, troops were withdrawn from the United Nations force with the permission of their American commander, and Chun launched a savage assault on Kwangju with a high loss of life among the rebels. *Asia Watch* reported:

> . . . beating, stabbing, and mutilating of unarmed civilians, including children, young girls and aged grandmothers. They forced both men and women to strip naked, made others lie flat on the ground and kicked them. Several sources tell of soldiers stabbing or cutting off the breasts of naked girls; one murdered student was found disemboweled,

another with an X carved in his back. About twenty high school girls were reported killed at Central High School. The paratroopers carried out searches in side streets, fired randomly into the crowds, carted off the bodies in trucks and piled them in the bus terminal. They even took the wounded out of hospitals.[2]

In succeeding decades, this brutal episode would become the leitmotif of student hostility towards the USA, which, under the 'moralistic' presidency of Jimmy Carter, was accused of sponsoring the reign of terror in Kwangju.

On the same day, Chun dismissed his civilian cabinet and replaced it with a 25-member Special Committee for National Security Measures. His usurpation of power was completed by his election to a seven-year presidential term by the Electoral College set up by its predecessor, the National Conference for Unification. Martial law was also imposed with a midnight to 4 am curfew throughout the country; it provided an amusing game of 'curfew busting' for visiting foreigners and tourists, and illegal drinking dens prospered. Authoritarian control, aimed principally at students, even stretched to a ban on long hair.

The American position on Chun's usurpation of power was not made public by a Carter administration committed to a 'moral' foreign policy. However, the Carter administration's support for the continuation of military rule was nonetheless real in spite of it never being made explicit. Richard C. Holbrooke, then assistant secretary of state for East Asian and Pacific Affairs, described the pro-democracy demonstrators as 'a relative handful of Christian extreme dissidents'.[3]

On 22 May, President Carter's government formally approved the South Korean army's use of force to retake the city of Kwangju. Following the Kwangju uprisings, opposition leader Kim Dae Jung was tried for sedition, found guilty and sentenced to death. Only the intervention of the governments of the USA and Japan persuaded President Chun to commute the death sentence. From attempted liberal beginnings, Chun had by now fully reverted to the style of authoritarian rule adopted by General Park.

It was hardly coincidental that the period of unrest, which started before the death of Park, coincided with the painful contraction of the economy, which took place as a result of the Second Oil Crisis. Korea's highly leveraged industrial concerns took the brunt of the rapid rise in oil prices. In response, Chun's government sought to relax the country's centralised economic management, while forcing through mergers and rationalisation in steel, chemicals and shipbuilding.

Energy conservation was imposed with draconian force. Neon advertising hoardings were banned and streetlights were turned off, leaving the city of Seoul eerily dark at night; elevators were decommissioned, forcing executives to climb up and down the stairwells of the newly constructed high-rise office buildings; one in every two light bulbs were removed.

In response to international criticisms of Korea's centralised control of the economy, Chun's government asked the Asia Development Bank for advice on how to liberalise the capital markets; a team from the Sovereign Advisory Department of the London-based investment bank, Samuel Montagu & Co., was sent to compile a report which included a 'road map' to capital market deregulation.

By the time this project was completed, a strong recovery in the Korean economy allowed the government to row back on its earlier deregulating intentions. Nevertheless in 1985, a commitment was made to open up the capital markets to foreign investment and to allow up to 50 per cent foreign ownership of publicly listed Korean companies by 1990. In broad terms, however, Chun maintained most elements of the authoritarian nexus that had enabled the economy to thrive under General Park. As a Korean corporate executive was reported saying in *The Far Eastern Economic Review* article in July 1984, 'It is in our own selfish interest to have a strong government that controls students and labor so that everything will blossom and grow and we can continue to make profits.'[4]

In international relations, Chun continued the bridge-building polices of his predecessors. In August 1981, President Chun declared that 'Japan is an ally. . . . The time has come when we should forget the unfortunate history of the past.'[5] Relations with China were also increasingly relaxed as commercial interests began to take precedence over former conflicts. Under Deng Xiaoping, the new China was also open to improvement in relations. China's foreign minister wryly noted on 25 January 1981 that 'The door of China–Korea relations is obviously closed at present, but it is in the state of not being locked.'[6]

In May 1982, financial scandals emerged involving Chun and his relations. Predictably new waves of protest were sparked. Kim Young Sam, already under house arrest, went on hunger strike to further encourage the popular mood. As for Kim Dae Jung, from August 1983, he became increasingly active in stirring opposition from exile in the USA.

In June of the following year, the two Kims jointly promoted a consultative committee for the promotion of democracy. The outcome of this process was the creation of a new opposition party, the New Korea Democratic Party (NKDP), which was formed in time to fight National Assembly elections in February 1985, where it took 101 out of 299 seats.

As for Chun, the increasingly discredited president was by now seen as a 'lame duck'. From April 1986, Chun engaged with the opposition in negotiations for a future constitution to be agreed by all parties. The attempt at conciliation was doomed to failure. However, when Chun broke off negotiations and ordered that the presidential elections would be decided by the Electoral College, student demonstrations erupted once again.

Moreover, it was clear that unrest was not confined alone to the student bodies which traditionally took the front line in opposition to the government. Chun's position further deteriorated with revelations that student leaders had been imprisoned and beaten. Chun's hardline position was tacitly supported by the US government. However, on 22 June 1987, Chun was forced to reopen constitutional negotiations, and a week later full political rights were restored to Kim Dae Jung.

For the opposition, the personal rivalry between Kim Dae Jung and Kim Young Sam now proved decisive in Korea's future direction. Apart from the rivalry between these two long-standing figures, Chun's opponents were also hostile to the pre-1979 opposition. An attempt to unify the opposition was made with the Re-unification Democratic Party, which was launched on 1 May 1987. However, the degree of uneasy compromise was apparent in the decision to make Kim Young Sam leader and Kim Dae Jung as unofficial co-leader.

Nevertheless, with mounting popular unrest against a self-perpetuating government, Roh Tae Woo, Chun's candidate for presidential succession, was forced to placate his opponents. On 29 June 1987, Roh issued a 'Declaration of Democratisation and Reforms' to pre-empt the opposition and place himself in a favourable electoral light. Chun would later explain that

> In view of the mounting demand for a direct presidential election, accepting such a demand would be the most popular move. I concluded that Candidate Roh should announce an acceptance of a direct election as his own decision . . . I told him that his acceptance of a direct election would make him a hero.[7]

The patched-up alliance between Kim Young Sam and Kim Dae Jung could not sustain itself when both politically ambitious candidates were presented with the opportunity of running for the presidency in the direct elections now promised. In October, Kim Dae Jung made the split official by launching his own party and announcing himself as a candidate for the presidency.

The failure of the opposition to unite played decisively into the hands of the establishment candidate, Roh Tae Woo, a government insider in both the Park and Chun regimes. Indeed, Roh had succeeded Chun in five successive posts. Both men were also members of the *Hanahoe* (group of one), a clandestine group that operated within the army. In the three-way contest that ensued on 16 December, Roh won 36.6 per cent of the vote versus 28 per cent for Kim Young Sam and 27 per cent for Kim Dae Jung. With no second round of voting, Roh was confirmed as president with a five-year mandate.

Noticeably after Roh was forced to loosen labour regulation, trade unions managed to extract unprecedented wage settlements, which rose by some 15 per cent during his administration. Roh also relaxed restrictions on contact with North Korea. In February 1989, the group chairman of Hyundai was allowed to visit North Korea and even made an agreement to develop a tourist resort, though permission for this was later rescinded.

From the popular vote in the National Assembly elections in April 1988, it was clear that there was a growing disconnect from the system that had brought political stability and rising living standards, with the increased desire on the part of the electorate for political accountability. Roh's Democratic Justice Party won just 25 per cent of the vote and a minority of 125 seats out of 299. Sensing the mood of change, just three months later, 300 judges issued public statements demanding the return of their full independence lost under General Park's regime. Roh yielded to the pressure by appointing an independent chief justice, and effectively ended presidential control of the judiciary.

In spite of liberalisation, some aspects of the Roh presidency did not change. Roh's call for a 'clean and honest society' was patent humbug. For greed and corruption, his presidency was without parallel in the post-war era. The corrupt nexus between politicians and Korea's dominant *Chaebol* (business conglomerate) remained firmly in place.

The growing institutional hostility to the old regime soon became clear. At the end of 1988, the National Assembly called hearings, which presented overwhelming evidence of widespread corruption during President Chun's administration. Investigations ended with indictments of 47 of Chun's relations and colleagues. The result was that Chun was forced to give US$ 14 million to the government while he himself retreated into exile, taking the extraordinary step of removing himself to Paekdam-sa Temple in Kwangwon Province. To add to the woes of Roh and the ruling establishment, the Korean economy, impacted by the fall in US demand, following the stock market crash in the autumn of 1987, also slowed dramatically. Again, students were the focus of unrest. At Dongeui University in Pusan, seven students were killed by riot police.

For forthcoming elections, however, the opposition were still weakened by their division. In local elections at Youngdungp'o, a neighbourhood in the south of Seoul, Kim Dae Jung's party scored 30 per cent of the vote compared to 18.8 per cent for Kim Young Sam. The outcome represented not only a crushing blow to Kim Young Sam's morale, but also an opportunity for the governing elite.

Roh concluded that it would be better to co-opt Kim Young Sam into the ruling elite, and thereby obviate the likelihood of an outright loss to the opposition. Kim Young Sam thereby concluded a cynical alliance giving the Democratic Liberal Party (DLP) a majority of 219 out of 299 seats; as part of the pact, Roh agreed to support Kim Young Sam as the presidential candidate for 1992.

Although Kim Young Sam and the DLP proceeded to lose some 70 seats in the 1992 National Assembly elections, through his pact with the government, he put himself in a stronger position than would otherwise have been the case. For his part, Roh's presidency conceded, albeit reluctantly at times, considerable powers to other branches of the constitution. Perhaps most importantly he managed to ward off further military intervention in the political process, and thereby enabled the possibility of a peaceful transition of power from one elected president to another for the first time in the history of the Republic of Korea.

In December 1992, the presidential elections were contested by the DLP's Kim Young Sam, Kim Dae Jung and the 76-year-old Chung Ju Yung, founder and patriarch of Korea's most powerful *Chaebol* (Hyundai). By switching sides from the opposition to the DLP, Kim Young Sam inherited all the electoral advantages traditionally enjoyed in Korea by the incumbent, while Kim Dae Jung's home base of Cholla was also less populous than his long-time adversary. As for Chung, his candidacy may well have had a spoiling effect on the opposition vote. Kim Young Sam won the presidency with 42 per cent of the vote compared to 34 per cent and 16 per cent for Kim Dae Jung and Chung, respectively.

At his inauguration, Kim declared that the two major themes of his presidency would be anti-corruption and financial restructuring. As part of the anti-corruption drive, Kim insisted that he and all his ministers and senior bureaucrats would produce public statements of their financial assets. Fifth Republic insiders, who were known for their financial greed, were also targeted, including the mayor of Seoul and the speaker of the National Assembly.

Three months after his election, Kim felt secure enough in his position vis-à-vis the army to replace the army chief of staff and the commander of the Defence Security Command. Also, the Agency for National Security Planning, the new name given to the discredited Korean Central Intelligence Agency (KCIA), was instructed to reduce its domestic surveillance. In a measure designed to express the increasing openness of the Republic of Korea, streets around the presidential 'Blue House' were opened for public access.

The most radical step taken to eliminate fraud and corruption was Kim's banning of the 'fake name' account system, whereby it was estimated that up to 20 per cent of bank accounts were falsely registered to enable tax evasion and corrupt payments. A radical overhaul of the Korean financial sector was also promised. By the end of his first year in office, Kim's popularity in opinion polls stood at record levels for a Korean president.

After a quick start in 1993, Kim's reform agenda stalled. The president was unable to unlock the relationships which bonded the country's banks to the *Chaebol* system. Kim, devoid of a sharp intellect, was a former opposition leader whose policies historically had been constructed with the sole aim of attaining power; he was wholly unqualified to solve the structural problems facing his country.

Popular support for the president fell when trade union strikes, at Hyundai and at the Korean National Railways, were broken. A poor showing for the DLP at regional elections in 1995 showed Kim the need to demonstrate a more radical face. In a sop to the populist sentiment, Kim authorised further judicial attacks on his predecessors. Both Chun and Roh were manacled and imprisoned and paraded humiliatingly in front of the TV cameras. Charged with corruption, mutiny and treason, Chun was sentenced to death and Roh to a long prison sentence. It was the restorative that Kim's presidency needed. In April 1996 elections, Kim won 139 out of 199 seats.

Restoration of Kim's popularity proved short-lived. With supreme irony, Kim, his family and associates became completely enmeshed in the scandal surrounding Hanbo Iron and Steel Company at the start of 1997. The company, some US$ 5 billion in debt, had used political influence to sustain loans that staved off the company's bankruptcy. The ensuing collapse of the Korean stock market, and the economic crash it triggered, caused Kim to leave office humiliatingly mired in financial scandal and economic failure.

In the succeeding election between Lee Hoi Chang for the DLP and Kim Dae Jung, the perennial challenger and now ageing opposition leader finally claimed the prize of the presidency with 40.2 per cent of the vote compared to 39.7 per cent for Lee. As with Kim Young Sam before him, Kim Dae Jung's victory was enabled by a curious alliance, this time with the rump of the Conservative Party under Jong Pil, a prime minister under the presidency of Park in 1974 when Kim Dae Jung had been captured and almost assassinated by the Korean CIA.

The new president faced enormous challenges. Korea faced a rapidly rising trade deficit as demand for exports collapsed; economic collapse exposed the disastrous levels of leverage in corporate Korea and the 'Crony capitalist' financial system, which had extended loans to corporations simply as political favours. As *The Far Eastern Economic Review* had noted in the early 1980s, 'Virtually the whole economy has fallen under the domination of . . . [the] Chaebol . . . they have literally left no stone unturned in their expansion and control of domestic industries and markets.'[8]

The whole banking sector faced collapse. The economy was bailed out to the tune of US$ 57 billion by the IMF on 21 November 1997. Conditional reforms including restructuring of the corporate and financial sectors combined with tight monetary and fiscal policies, liberalisation of labour markets and lifting of restrictions on foreign investment. Unemployment rose from just 2 per cent to over 8 per cent; the economy itself contracted by 8.5 per cent.

Resistance to the changes was immense with vested interests occupying every nook and cranny of Korea's economic structure. Although foreign companies took advantage of the situation to make speculative investments in the newly open environment, the obstacles to change were formidable. Even Wilbur Ross, the brilliant 'vulture' financier, then an employee of NM Rothschild & Sons, who would later rescue the American steel industry through his assemblage of unwanted assets in the International Steel Group Inc., could not prize open the Korean system in spite of its desperate need for capital and expertise.

The major *Chaebols* too were recalcitrant in trying to reach the targets imposed by Kim Dae Jung's administration of reducing leverage from 500 per cent to 200 per cent. The process was too onerous for some; Daewoo, one of the four big and the most aggressively expansionist of the *Chaebol*, slipped into liquidation.

Though some assets were sold and others restructured, the *Chaebol* played for time; as the economy started to recover, 'reform fatigue' at first stalled and then blocked change. In the meantime, the *Chaebol* still found the finance to begin heavy investment in new growth areas; Samsung Electronics targeted 'liquid crystal displays' (LCDs) with heavy investment, which laid the foundation for their current global domination of that industry.

Opposition to Kim now came from Lee Hoi Chang, who used the DLP to form the Grand National Party (GNP). However, in the National Assembly elections in April 2000, Kim won a narrow victory with 140 seats versus 133 for the GNP. Three months after his electoral victory, Kim orchestrated an historic summit meeting with the North Korean leader Kim Jong Il; a further enhancement to Kim Dae Jung's popularity came with the award of the Nobel Peace Prize for his efforts in bringing peace to the Korean peninsula.

However, Kim Dae Jung too, like his predecessor, suffered a humiliating fall from grace when it was disclosed that his son was guilty of receiving 'cash for favours', the traditional and seemingly endemic vice of all Korean politicians. In spite of his tarnished reputation, the Kim Dae Jung era brought political economic normalcy to South Korean politics and further consolidated the constitutional stability of the country.

45

Dr Mahathir: The Acerbic Autocrat

Malaysia: 1981–2003

Born in a *kampung* (village) in the northern state of Kedah in July 1925, Mahathir bin Mohamad was to become Malaysia's longest serving prime minister and the man who came to define its modern history. Though through his father's side he could trace his origins to Kerala in southern India, he regarded himself as truly Malay, a son of the soil (*bumiputra* or *bumi*); indeed, he came to represent the extreme view of Malay nationalism.

However, his first career was medicine not politics. In 1953 he graduated from King Edward VII Medical College in Singapore and took his first job working for the Malayan government as a medical officer. Perhaps his Indian blood gave him a drive and energy which were wholly atypical of the normal Malay. Musa Hitam would later complain that it was 'humanly impossible to go at the pace he's [Mahathir] kept going'.[1] He had a ferocious attention to detail and would constantly jot down his observations in a notebook, even being known to comment on the condition of airport latrines. Such was his lavatorial obsession that Mahathir invented an Islamic toilet. 'Low Brow' was always Mahathir's preferred taste; he was not a great reader, although he had a predilection for popular fiction writers such as Sidney Sheldon and Tom Clancy.

He had taken an active political interest from the age of 21 when he joined the United Malays National Organisation (UMNO) at inception in 1946. However, his political career gathered pace relatively slowly. After an internal party dispute, he decided not to stand for election in 1959 in spite of his position as chairman of the Political Committee. Representative office did not arrive until Malaysia's third elections in 1964 when he was elected member for Kota Setar South. Even then his political path did not run smoothly as he lost out to the Pan-Malaysian Islamic Party (PAS) in 1969 after declaring that he did not require any of the Chinese vote to win re-election.

His extreme pro-*bumi* views did not endear him to the racial harmony policies pursued by Tunku Abdul Rahman after independence. After the race riots of 13 May 1969, Dr Mahathir was dumped by UMNO's Supreme Council and later thrown out of the party altogether; his crime was an open letter to Tunku in which he criticised Malaysia's first prime minister for being too close to the Chinese and causing the Malays '. . . to run amok, killing those they hate because you have given them [the Chinese] too much face'.[2] This setback was to prove the making of Mahathir. While barred from politics, he wrote *The Malay Dilemma* (1970) in which he lamented the genetic and hereditary deficiencies of the indigenous Malay people and argued that their lack of economic progress, the reason for the 1969 race riots, would have to be compensated for by pro-active economic discrimination.

The book was banned by Tunku, but the intellectual core of the argument provided the basis for the establishment of NEP (New Economic Policy) by Tunku's successor, Tun Abdul Razak. Mahathir was allowed to rejoin UMNO in 1972 and immediately re-emerged as a leading party figure, being appointed a senator in 1973. He relinquished this post in 1974 to fight to regain a parliamentary seat, and he was returned unopposed; appointed as minister of education, he also became one of the three vice presidents of UMNO. Further advancement came with his appointment by Prime Minister Tun Hussein Onn as deputy prime minister in 1978 and as minister of trade and industry. Finally, albeit the most junior of the candidates in a three-way battle with Ghafar Baba and Tengku Razaleigh, Mahathir won out to become prime minister after Onn's resignation for health reasons in 1981.

Having achieved the highest office in Malaysia, Mahathir retained a steely grip on power for the next 22 years. Both individuals and institutions that barred his path were brushed aside. The Malaysian monarchy was an early target. Royal assent, which hitherto held a power of veto over legislation, was removed; now the King, in Malaysia's rotating monarchy, could hold up a government bill only for 30 days. Also, the Gomez affair provided Mahathir with the opportunity to remove the legal immunity enjoyed by the royal families. (The Sultan of Johore attacked a school hockey coach, Gomez, with a hockey stick after the sultan's son was dropped from the team. When the police took no action, Gomez went to the press.)

Within UMNO, Mahathir sought to eliminate his competitors and possible successors. He was a natural bully and, when challenged, would seek to crush opponents. A former Welfare Minister Shahrir Abdul Samad commented that Dr Mahathir 'will not think of negotiating his way out of a problem the way his predecessors, with their legal backgrounds, would have done. The medical situation is to cut out the cancer'.[3] In 1984, Mahathir pitched Musa Hitam against Tengku Razaleigh Hamza for the vice presidency of UMNO; Musa won 59 per cent of the vote, which allowed Mahathir to purge his long-time rival Razaleigh.

Being Mahathir's deputy was never an easy position to fill, however. In 1986 Mahathir replaced Musa Hitam as deputy prime minister with Ghafar Baba. The aggrieved Musa Hitam now joined forces with Razaleigh to launch a bid for the vice presidency and presidency of UMNO, respectively. It was a bitter contest for control. Mathathir cleverly used the radical young politician, Anwar Ibrahim, immensely popular with the rural muslim vote, to swing the election his way. In a closely fought election, the 1,500 delegates gave Mahathir a 43-vote margin of victory against Razaleigh, and Ghafar Baba a 41-vote win over Musa Hitam. Mahathir purged all remaining opponents within UMNO and used his victory to centralise power and awarded himself the Ministries of Home Affairs and Justice.

Mahathir also had a limited belief in constitutional democracy. He believed in the supreme power of parliament and rejected the independence of the judiciary. 'Democracy has a distressing tendency to get out of control . . .', Mahathir asserted and '. . . has come to mean individual rights. . . . The individual hasn't the right to do what he likes if it hurts the majority'.[4] When his orders, from the Ministry of Home Affairs, to cancel the work permits of two of *The Asian Wall Street Journal* correspondents were revoked by an appeal to the High Court, Mahathir was apoplectic. However, appeals by the retired Lord President Mohamed Suffian Hashim and by former Prime Minister Tunku to observe the independence of the judiciary were firmly rebuffed.

From his ministerial post as justice minister, Mahathir was able to put pressure on the judiciary to throw out a complaint of vote tampering in the June 1987 election, which was brought by 11 UMNO members. Nevertheless, in the High Court, Justice Harun Hashim declared that UMNO had been in breach of the 1966 Societies Act. Mahathir simply ignored the judgement. When the case was taken to the Supreme Court, Mahathir engineered the dismissal of the Lord President, Supreme Court Justice Salleh Abas. Furthermore, five Supreme Court judges were expelled by Mahathir when they allowed Salleh's writ of injunction against the tribunal of impeachment, which had been set up to try Salleh. A revised constitution was now promulgated, which increased the powers of the president. In one blow, Mahathir had destroyed the independence of the judiciary on which Malaysia's legal profession had long prided itself.

In addition, Mahathir silenced opposition in the press by shutting down newspapers, *The Star, Sin Chew Jit Poh* and the weekly *Watan* in 1987, as well as ordering the detention of 106 people on a variety of spurious charges. Mahathir had long been an opponent of press freedom. As a cabinet minister in 1974 he had sponsored media controls. In 1981 Mahathir took the trouble to write an article for *The New Straits Times* in which he argued that 'journalists often distorted news for self serving and nefarious objectives'.[5]

Control of domestic press became increasingly apparent after Mahathir became prime minister. It was a repression that he justified to ASEAN journalists in 1985: '. . . freedom too can corrupt and absolute freedom can corrupt absolutely . . . so long as the press is conscious of itself being a potential threat to democracy . . . then democratic governments have the duty to put it right'.[6] Clearly unaware of *1984*, George Orwell's famed 1949 novel about totalitarianism, Mahathir further tightened media controls in 1984 by the passing of an amendment to the 1972 Official Secrets Act; this was used against *The Far East Economic Review*. In addition, the Printing Press Publications Act and the Control of Imported Publications Act were used to suppress *The Asian Wall Street Journal*, *The Far East Economic Review*, *Time* and *Asiaweek*.

However, Mahathir did not just throttle the press by legislation and closing its presses; by the end of his first decade in power, the government, through Pernas, the state holding company, owned 12 newspapers and three television channels. Press censorship became particularly draconian when corruption was exposed. In 1986 *The Wall Street Journal* was banned from Malaysia for reporting details of a share swap transaction involving his Finance Minister Daim Zainuddin. Daim, who was from the same *kampong* (village) as Mahathir, remained the key financial figure behind the prime minister's regime even when he left the Ministry of Finance. Not for the last time, Mahathir declaimed against a Zionist conspiracy and vowed 'to take action against anybody whose thinking was not in line with the majority view'.[7]

The blaming of Jews was one of the covers for a racially oriented economic policy designed to transfer the wealth of the Malay Chinese to the *bumiputra* under the mantle of NEP. Throughout Mahathir's leadership, the nation's wealth was systematically stripped for the favoured coterie around the prime minister. Thus, when privatisation took place in the Malaysian Airline Systems in 1985, some 40 per cent ended in the hands of its Chairman Tajudin Ramli, who was widely believed to have been funded by UMNO.

By 1990 poor and middle class Malays were beginning to realise that NEP was not advancing their economic prosperity because they lacked the political contacts and party affiliations of the elite beneficiaries. As for the Chinese community, they increasingly felt that the objectives of NEP had been met and objected to the continued 'race tax', with which they felt burdened. From the 1990s the Chinese voted with their feet, as emigration rates started to rise.

Where Mahathir tried to direct the economy, his efforts were usually disastrous. HICOM (Heavy Industries Corporation of Malaysia) was used to finance a 70 per cent stake in the Proton motor-manufacturing company with a 30 per cent stake held by Mitsubishi. It was an abysmal venture, which failed to make money even with the protection provided by huge duties on imported vehicles. The Proton was a poorly designed and engineered product which was unable to break into the US market and became something of a joke in the United Kingdom. In 1988, Proton achieved sales of just 24,000 compared to the budgeted figure of 90,000. Eventually Mahathir would be forced to approve the replacement of Proton Malay management with Japanese staff. Far from being a flagship project, Proton turned into a saga of government ineptitude.

Also Renong, a front company for UMNO, was awarded government contracts including the building of a new bridge between Malaysia and Singapore, as well as being included in the Sabah electricity privatisation. When Renong ran into financial difficulty in 1997, it was allegedly bailed out to the tune of RM2.4 billion, supposedly with money taken out of the Employees Provident Fund. It was not the only disaster inspired by government investment. HICOM's investments in Kedah Cement and Perwaja Steel also had to be bailed out. Perwaja Steel was developed with a new technology, which used subsidised offshore gas to convert imported iron ore into sponge iron; the untested process was completely unable to produce a workable product and over US$ 1 billion had to be written off.

A further US$ 200 million was lost when the Malaysian government tried to support the price of tin; speculators simply sold against them. Other dubious investments included the 1,483-feet-high Petronas Twin Towers, a vanity project to show that Malaysia could fund the world's tallest building. (The Petronas Towers, containing the highest McDonald's outlet in the world, were equal first tallest buildings in the world when they were built in 1998, until the Taipei 101 building in Taiwan superseded them in 2004.)

In northern Sumatra it was suspected that corrupt local officials and politicians turned a blind eye to the illegal land clearances that were created by the deliberate burning of rain forests. In 1997, 30 fires broke out in Sumatra in one week. In the early autumn, Malaysian schools had to be closed and 25,000 people had to be treated for respiratory illnesses. Meanwhile activists who sought to defend the rights of the jungle tribal peoples were attacked. Bruno Manser, a Swiss activist, living with the Penans tribe in Sarawak, was castigated by the Malaysian government for encouraging

> . . . the Penans to take the law into their own hands and to use poison darts, bows, arrows and *parangs* [knives] . . . . What right have you to condemn them to primitive life forever . . . stop being arrogant and thinking that it is white man's burden to decide the fate of the peoples of the world.[8]

Under Mahathir, corruption scandals, many of which were suspected to reach into the upper echelons of UMNO, were swept under the carpet. When the Hong Kong property company Carrian collapsed, it became clear that Bank Bumiputra's Hong Kong branch was largely responsible for financing George Tan's speculative adventure; loans had risen far above the bank's statutory reserve requirement. The implication was that authority must have been given in Kuala Lumpur. Tengku Razaleigh, then finance minister, who was responsible for the Central Bank, Bank Negara and through that the government-owned Bank Bumiputra, denied any responsibility for lending policy.

It was surely no coincidence that Mahathir chose this moment to pass a new Official Secrets Act; this helped to shut out whatever light of truth that might have emerged from the Carrian episode. Where the 'consultancy fees' paid by Carrian to Bumiputra Malaysia Finance (BMF), a Bank Bumiputra subsidiary, ended up was never made public.

The only executive of BMF to be convicted was an official extradited from London. The fact that the Malaysian government White Paper, finally released in

January 1986, eschewed the casting of any blame suggested that the fraud fell close
to the prime minister's inner circle. Ultimately Mahathir would use Petronas, the
state oil company, to cover the US$ 1.2 billion losses. He failed to learn the lesson
of government-owned banks. In 1993, Bank Negara itself recorded an astonishing
RM12.8 billion of losses on the currency exchanges.

Dr Mahathir proved as argumentative in conducting his country's international
relations as he was in domestic affairs. Perhaps not surprisingly, his first target was
Malaysia's former colonial master Great Britain. After the Thatcher government
raised tuition fees for 15,500 students studying in Britain, Mahathir introduced a
'buy British last' policy. He also refused to attend the Commonwealth Heads of
Government meetings in 1981 and 1983. In 1985 Mahathir said of these meetings
that they 'should admit that it really cannot contribute towards the solving of the
problems faced by its members'.[9]

Nevertheless, after the Falklands War, Mahathir developed a respect for Mrs
Thatcher and relations between the two countries improved. In 1989, the quixotic
Mahathir was happy enough to host the Heads of Commonwealth Meetings in
Kuala Lumpur. For the most part, however, Mahathir pursued a 'look East' policy.
Sometimes the bias inflicted self-harm; in choosing a construction company for the
Penang Bridge project, Mahathir chose Hyundai of Korea rather than a lower bid
from France.

Although Mahathir continued the NEP policies of rebalancing *Bumi* economic
interests versus the Chinese population, in reality it was foreign investment that
was forced out. Although the *Bumi* share of Malaysian stock market capitalisation
rose by 2.4 per cent to 20.6 per cent in the 25 years to 1995, the Chinese share also
rose from 27.2 per cent to 40.9 per cent; it was almost entirely foreign investment
that was forced out of the market, with a fall in their share of Malaysia's stock
market from 63.4 per cent to 27.7 per cent.

Spats with Lee Kuan Yew in Singapore were frequent. Bridges, railway links,
water supply and so forth were all subject to disputes. However, nothing aroused
his fury more than Lee Kuan Yew's comments to *The Straits Times* on 17 September 1998, when he characterised the main theme running through his memoirs
as 'the fight against Malay extremism'.[10] Mahathir also conducted a war of words
with Australian Prime Minister Paul Keating, who described the Malaysian prime
minister as 'recalcitrant' for not attending the 1993 APEC (Asia-Pacific Economic
Co-operation) meeting.

However, Mahathir, who did not regard the 'white'-run countries of Australia
and New Zealand as part of Asia, wanted to place political emphasis on the East
Asia Economic Group (EAEG) from which these two were excluded. Furthermore, when Singapore and France proposed a biennial summit between Asia and
the European Union, Mahathir made sure that ASEM excluded Australia and New
Zealand. Mahathir remained implacably hostile to Western interests and after the
first Gulf War became increasingly vocal in his attacks on America and the power

of the United Nations Security Council:

> ...the UN presents a shattered image with a threadbare moral authority .... The
> victors of 1945 have clung tenaciously to the levers of power. They control the high
> ground, exercising influence and power as nakedly as when they were colonial powers.
> Only the masks have changed.[11]

However, the defining battle of Mahathir's prime ministership was with Anwar
Ibrahim, his chosen successor. Anwar, the youthful intellectual Muslim leader, was
the most popular Malay politician; his star quality had proven a vital vote winner
for UMNO and Mahathir. In 1993, when Mahathir dropped his deputy Ghafar
Baba and replaced him with Anwar, it seemed that the prime minister had found
his successor. In September 1995 Mahathir declared, 'I give the party to Anwar.
Anwar is my heir apparent. He will take over from me.'[12] The role of heir apparent
to Mahathir was notoriously dangerous, however, and Anwar started to make a
number of crucial mistakes.

Either out of a sense of integrity for which he was renowned or perhaps because of a desire to hasten his own elevation to the prime ministership, Anwar
criticised Petronas's financial bailout of Mahathir's son Mirzan. Mahathir responded
vigorously by declaring that Petronas's decision was entirely commercial. Few believed him. In *Time* magazine, Chandra Muzaffar argued that for Anwar, it was
the 'biggest mistake of his career'.[13] Ensuing revelations of government contracts
awarded to the friends or family of Mahathir's administration were swiftly followed
by the removal of the chief editors of Malaysia's two most prominent newspapers,
Utasan Malaysia and *Berita Harian*.

Other events conspired to divide the former allies. When UMNO youth leader
Rahim Tamby Chik was charged with engaging in sex with an underage girl in
1994, Anwar pressed for his resignation and noted that moral corruption tended
to rise with economic euphoria. By contrast, Dr Mahathir maintained his support
for Rahim. It was now becoming clear that competing political and economic factions were coalescing around the prime minister and Anwar. Meanwhile Finance
Minister, Daim Zainuddin, whom *Asiaweek* rated as more powerful than Anwar,
clashed with Anwar over the financial rewards of privatisation and infrastructure
projects. In the Bakun Dam project, Daim's associates were preferred to Anwar
and his backers. After his fall from grace, Anwar would affirm that Mahathir and
his family had 'siphoned off billions'.[14]

In spite of the disagreements, Mahathir and Anwar at least maintained the fa-
cade of unity. At the UMNO General Assembly meeting in 1995, Anwar told his
colleagues that 'If I am asked to go back to university, I am not sure there is a
university which can provide training as good as you have given me.'[15] In spite of
widespread rumours of a rift, in 1997, Mahathir in turn told Anwar that his succession was assured, though he added the barbed remark that Anwar was sometimes panicky about timing. Within UMNO meanwhile, Anwar supporters were

growing more powerful; Mahathir may well have feared a putsch and decided to act before he was pushed.

On 2 September Mahathir, having failed to persuade him to resign, sacked Anwar Ibrahim as both deputy prime minister and finance minister. Anwar was also expelled from UMNO by the Supreme Council. It was a ruthless purge. Mahathir took over the Ministry of Finance portfolio and left the post of deputy vacant. Mahathir would later say that what he wanted as a deputy was 'an exact replica of myself'.[16] Anwar now plotted a general rebellion within UMNO, and at the General Assembly in 1998, Mahathir's government was denounced for corruption and nepotism by Datuk Zahid, UMNO's new youth leader. Forewarned of the plot, the government orchestrated media publication of economic favours that had been granted to Anwar's followers. Accusations were also made against him of homosexual encounters and witnesses were procured, probably through bribery and threats.

Meanwhile Mahathir unravelled Anwar's pro-IMF programme in the wake of the Asian financial crisis, made Daim minister for special functions and imposed capital controls to thwart the currency speculators whom he accused of being part of an international Zionist-Imperialist plot. 'Colonial control of land by military strength can no longer be accepted by societies worldwide ...', declaimed Mahathir, '... control through currency trading has similar effects'.[17]

Formal charges were made against Anwar, and after he made a nationwide speaking tour, winning large audiences, the Malaysian government engineered his arrest. Not satisfied with a six-year sentence for corruption, the police now charged Anwar with sodomy. Famously, the imprisoned Anwar was severely beaten up by the Malaysian Police Chief Rahim Noor. Although the treatment of Anwar aroused enormous domestic and international condemnation, Mahathir had a commanding control of his party and the nation's electoral machine. Although Mahathir's share of the popular vote fell from 65 per cent to 56.6 per cent, he still won 148 out of 193 seats.

Although the Malaysian army had never sought a political role since independence, Mahathir took no chance with this traditional source of power. The prime minister's brother-in-law, Major General Hashim Mohammed Ali, was appointed to the command of the Malaysian peninsula and later became Chief of Staff. Also with the deteriorating relationship with the Chinese community, which under Mahathir increasingly felt its second-class status, Mahathir also sought to bulk up the popular vote by stretching out a hand to the Islamic community. Anwar had built this constituency for him with the setting up of the Islamic Development Foundation and the Islamic Bank in 1984 and the Islamic Insurance Company in 1985. Anwar also founded the Institute of Policy Development for the training of student leaders, junior managers and public servants.

It is hard not to disagree with the *Aliran* monthly in September 1998, when it commented, 'Let us not be naïve. Anwar is not your innocent bystander.... He is a seasoned political *gajah* [elephant/big figure] who played for the highest stakes in the political game, and lost.'[18] Anwar Ibrahim was not simply the religious intellectual and author of *The Asian Renaissance* (1996); he was the darling of the international community and a friend of World Bank President James Wolfensohn and UN Secretary General Kofi Annan. His 'martyrdom' should not obscure us from the fact that he was a politician intent on gaining power within Mahathir's UMNO framework.

This system was inherently corrupt; the orchestration of economic benefits to supporters was an integral part of the path to power. Mahathir, with his loyal henchman Diem, proved himself a master of this game. It was a path which undermined the original integrity of the constitution. Even former Prime Minister Tunku railed against UMNO's abuse of power as 'improper and irregular . . . to amass wealth at the expense of other business ventures'.[19]

The justification for Mahathir's perversion of the Malay constitution into a dictatorial fiefdom was twofold. First, he refused to accept the Western interpretation of democracy, believing, and frequently stating, that it did not suit Malay culture and religion. In an address to Trinity College, Oxford, in 1985, Mahathir proclaimed that 'Many authoritarian governments have been elected by the will of the people who want strong no-nonsense administration.'[20] What Mahathir perhaps misunderstood about Western democracy was that at its base lay more than the right to vote and the protection of civil liberties; the right to own property without fear of appropriation by the state, flagrantly violated by Mahathir's government with regard to the Chinese community, is an even more inherent right of a citizen in a democracy.

The effective looting of the state by UMNO for the benefit of its members and supporters, albeit modest by the standards of Indonesia's ruling family, not only struck at the root of Malaysia's democratic credentials but over time also impoverished Malaysian people. Mahathir's defence of his authoritarian style was self-pleading for government by kleptocracy. The fact that Malaysia did not suffer the same level of political theft experienced by Indonesia under Suharto, and indeed appeared to perform successfully over the Mahathir period, should not blind observers to the implicit corruption of his constitutional dictatorship.

At independence in 1957, Malaysia was one of the most stable and wealthy of Asia's economies. Although by 1995 Malaysia had achieved a GDP per capita of US$ 9,400, a country of comparable size, Taiwan, achieved a growth in GDP per capita from US$ 170 in 1962 (ranking it with the Congo and Somalia) to over US$ 25,000 by 1995. With every comparable advantage, Malaysia underperformed, a fact which in large part can be attributed to the corruption of the UMNO monopoly of power, to wasteful government-directed investment and to the barriers put up to foreign direct investment. Mahathir's burnished reputation is barely deserved; he was a racial bigot who throughout his career displayed monomaniac tendencies which served to leave his countrymen much poorer than they should have been.

46

Suharto: Rule of the Kleptocrats

Indonesia: 1965—98

Suharto's origins were far removed from the bourgeois revolutionaries that characterised Sukarno and his clique. Suharto was born on 8 June 1921 in the tiny hamlet of Kemusuk, some 15 km from Yogyakarta in Central Java. His father was a minor local official responsible for irrigation. However, he came from a broken family; his parents divorced just five weeks after he was born. He was then brought up by a great aunt and returned to his mother's house only at the age of four, after she remarried.

Although his upbringing was set against the constant feuding and struggles of his parents, early accounts suggest that he was a good student and a robust soccer player. However, having managed to get a position in a village bank, he subsequently lost his job and had to work as a labourer until joining up with the Royal Netherlands East Indies Army. His first military act was hardly distinguished. He deserted. This may well have been preferable to surrender to the Japanese in March 1942, after which some 30,000 Indonesian troops are thought to have died in the appalling conditions of captivity.

Suharto then joined the police force and developed a good relationship with his Japanese commanders, who recommended him for *Peta*, their nationalist military force. *Peta* was to become the revolutionary army that would fight for independence from the Dutch after the war. During the post-war struggles, Suharto's military career took off when he became a major responsible for activity in the Yogyakarta region.

After independence, Suharto was given a command in Sumatra and Kalimantan where, like most other generals, he sought to maximise the commercial advantages of his position. Illegal smuggling of rubber to Malaysia, with which Indonesia was technically at war, brought Suharto his first fortune; he even persuaded his brother to give up school teaching to run his commercial activities in liaison with Chinese businessmen. Such was the embedded nature of smuggling and corruption within Indonesia's revolutionary army that a furious foreign minister even resorted to waving wads of Singaporean customs forms in front of unrepentant generals.

Even in an army renowned for corrupt practice, it is notable that the post-independence commander in chief, General Nasution, would single out Suharto for special reprimand for his commercial practices. Fortunately for Suharto, a successful campaign against the Dutch in West Irian, Holland's last remaining colonial outpost, brought him the reward of a top post in Java as the commander of the General Reserve, which was reconstituted as the *Kostrad* (Army Strategic Central Reserve) in 1963. By this point, Suharto was in a group of just eight major generals in the army, of whom Army Chief Yani, now the commander in chief, was one. However, Suharto remained largely detached from the two largest military factions dominated by Yani and Nasution.

The slaughter of seven generals including Yani, in the abortive PKI (Communist Party) coup of 1966, therefore opened the way for Suharto's climb to power. First, he had to deal with General Nasution. Indonesia's post-war army chief, whose power Sukarno had filleted by promoting him to the armed forces' co-ordinating role, was keen to re-establish his political fortunes. General Sumitro later reflected that 'the senior officers of the time had hoped that General Naustion would move forward to replace Bung Karno [Sukarno]'.[1]

However, Suharto secured for himself leadership of *Kopkamtib* (operations command to restore security and order) and managed to deflect Nasution's attempt to gain appointment to the vacant vice presidency, which might well have put him in line to succeed the now tottering Sukarno. Nasution was sidelined into a powerless civilian position as chairman of the MPRS. Meanwhile, the decimation of leading army figures gave Suharto a virtually free hand in replacing them with loyal acolytes. Also, the Diponegoro Division, which was used by the conspirators, was purged of its leading officers. The air force, whose leadership was implicated in the coup against the army, was quickly brought under control.

Otherwise however, Suharto sought to consolidate his position with characteristic caution. Regional commanders supportive of Sukarno were eased out. Guile was preferred to brute force; Major General Adjie, the commander in Siliwangi, was quietly sent to London in 1966 to be the new ambassador. Until 1969, the communist-leaning navy continued to criticise the new government through its weekly newspaper *El Bahar*, which was edited by a nephew of Sukarno, Navy Secretary Commodore Puguh. However, in 1969, Suharto sent the head of the navy to Moscow as an ambassador and replaced him with a friend, Admiral Sudomo, who had been a colleague during the West Irian campaign.

Having achieved the goal of neutering ideological opposition within the armed forces, Suharto took the opportunity to curtail the operational independence of the various arms of the services and bring them all under his direct control. The military nature of the Suharto regime became yet clearer when appointments to civilian posts also began to be made by the military. The democratic fig leaf was laid ever barer by a new law promulgated to allocate one-third of seats in the MPR to the army.

Neither did Suharto ignore management of the electoral system. Parties were banned from having permanent organisations and could operate only within a limited time frame prior to elections. In essence, Suharto aimed to abolish party politics, which he believed were responsible for much of the instability of the post-independence period. On a visit to Lampung in June 1968, he urged the people 'to leave behind the political and religious controversies in the interests of achieving national stability, which is an absolute condition for carrying out development'.[2] Suharto's New Order rejected the whole notion of political opposition as being lacking in national spirit.

However, from an early stage, Suharto flagged his intention of maintaining the national philosophy of 'Pancasila' adopted by his predecessor during Indonesia's early independence. It was clear that adaptations would be necessary. Speaking to the Interim People's Representative Council on 16 August 1967, Suharho asserted:

> The corruption of Pancasila and the 1945 Constitution during the Old Order period had deep and far-reaching consequences; it in fact destroyed the lifeblood of the nation and state. Pancasila was corrupted with the birth of Nasakom, a concept that attempted to combine communism with the implementation of Pancasila. . . . we fell for the strategy of the Indonesian Communist Party, which accepted Pancasila only as a tool to be used for seizing power in the framework of international communism.[3]

In rejecting the Communist Party, Suharto rejected all parties. Under the leadership of an old military friend Ali Murtopo, Suharto developed an administrative body known as Sebkar-Golkar (the Joint Secretariat of Functional Groups), which had been set up by Sukarno in 1964 as his own party machine. It did not present a political programme as such, but simply co-opted government workers to its membership; perversely, given Suharto's hatred of Communism, Sebkar-Golkar became like the Chinese communist party which existed with the sole function to support the status quo of the state. In spite of its shallow roots, GOLKAR, as it became known, swept to an overwhelming victory with 62.8 per cent of the vote and 236 seats in the DPR at the elections of 5 July 1971.

The main opposition Muslim NU grouping captured just over 18 per cent of the vote; its continued survival as a party was largely dependent on accommodation with the regime's policies. Pious Muslims, such as former Vice President Mohammed Hatta, were indeed prevented by Suharto from founding a modern Islamic party based on the former *Masjumi* power base. Although Islamic followers were expanding rapidly in Indonesia, there appeared to be little push for separate political representation; Nurcholish Madjid, head of the Indonesian Students Association, described the attitude of Muslims as 'Islam yes, Islamic parties no!'[4] For most of his reign, at least until his popularity began to fail, Suharto marginalised Islam, preferring to rely on the advice of Christians, traditional Javanese like himself or Chinese businessmen.

GOLKAR's growth as the ubiquitous party of state was such that by 1988 there were some 26 million card-holding members, of whom 9 million were officer cadres, who were tasked with bringing in at least six votes each at elections. Above all, Suharto aimed to create a party so entrenched in the social fabric of Indonesia that there would be no way back for communism. For Suharto, this was a real fear. In March 1969, he asserted that 'if you study the doctrine and tactics of the PKI ... [you realise that] that party will keep on launching illegal movements to try to come back to life'.[5]

Within a centrally controlled military state, Indonesia increasingly developed the repressive qualities familiar to totalitarian regimes. Success in the suppression of the PKI was later followed by a similarly brutal crackdown on crime. Although reported crimes had fallen dramatically from 325,760 in 1962 to 223,768 in 1982, the Army Chief General Murdani ordered *Operation Petrus* to crack down on urban crime.

Supplied with names by police informers, criminals were forced to register and carry identification cards; those who refused were hunted down at night by specially trained army death squads. Criminals were arbitrarily picked up in four-wheel drive vehicles or jeeps and taken to quiet areas to be shot in the back of the head. As a deterrent, bodies would be dumped in rivers or outside cinemas. While a July 1983 poll showed overwhelming support for *Operation Petrus*, international observers were appalled. Amnesty International reported that 'one individual claims to have witnessed the dumping of 200 *gali-gali* [criminals] from prisons throughout Java on one day in May'.[6]

General Murdani, who modernised the army and moved it away from its revolutionary roots, developed the *Bais ABRI* (the Armed Forces Strategic Intelligence Agency) as the most important security organ. In addition, Suharto abolished the Central Intelligence Board, which had been headed by Subandrio, and replaced it with *Bakin* (the State Intelligence Coordinating Body). Among other things, this body developed detailed instruction manuals for treatment of suspected state enemies; in one section, officers were advised to 'Avoid taking photographs showing torture ... of someone being given electric shocks, stripped naked and so on.'[7]

Much of the work of the security apparatus was to keep in check the incipient freedom movements that sporadically burst into life in Aceh (*Aceh Merdeka*, the Free Aceh Movement), West Irian (Free Papua Movement) and Timor (the *Fretilin*, the Timorese Liberation Army). A Timorese, who had worked with Indonesian intelligence, reported that *Fretilin* suspects 'were tortured by hitting them with a blunt instrument, by jabbing lighted cigarettes in their faces around the mouth, or by giving them electric shocks, sometimes on the genitals'.[8] In 1974, Amnesty claimed that Indonesia held some 55,000 political prisoners.

The illiberal nature of Indonesia's government was frequently commented on by *Asia Watch*. In 1988, it observed that 'The Indonesian press is governed by an extreme regime of liberal restraint, the press organs operate under the pervasive threat of closure,' and two years later *Asia Watch* concluded that 'Freedom of expression . . . remains severely curtailed.'[9] Liberal constitutional concepts were entirely alien to Indonesia's nature. As one of Suharto's main legal advisors noted in his doctoral thesis, '. . . the drafter of the 1945 Constitution, through the drafting committee chairman Supomo, was quite firm that the 1945 constitution does not follow the separation of powers theory'.[10]

The Far East Economic Review was equally direct in its criticism of Suharto's illiberal regime: 'The Press acknowledges a number of topics as strictly taboo. These include Suharto's family, questions of ethnicity, race and religion, and the activities of separatist movements—such as those in Aceh, Irian Jaya and East Timor. . . .'[11] The 1966 Press Act effectively suppressed all objective reporting of the government and its activities; only when the demise of Suharto seemed certain did the floodgates open to criticism in the Indonesian press.

In the aftermath of the attempted PKI coup, and its resulting economic disruption, inflation soared to 1,500 per cent in 1966. Probably more by luck than judgement, Suharto's retention of Sukarno as a nominal presence probably helped deflect much of the opprobrium for the disastrous economic conditions which, after 20 years of Sukarno, had left Indonesia even poorer than India. That was about to change. Undoubtedly, political stability, however dearly bought in terms of human rights, was a great boon to economic activity. The removal of the PKI, and the new military government's fierce anti-communist stance, also favoured business investment particularly from overseas.

Above all, however, Indonesia benefited almost immediately from a flood of foreign aid. Foreign Minister Adam Malik recalled that, as his first task, '[he] was instructed by President Suharto to tackle the problem of overseas assistance for Indonesian economic development.'[12] Whereas previously the USA and Japan had provided Indonesia with aid, more in hope than expectation that the country would escape the communist's grasp, the fall of Sukarno and the emergence of a right-wing military dictatorship was a boon which America seized with open purses.

After their expulsion by Sukarno, the International Monetary Fund (IMF) was invited back to Indonesia, and it immediately produced credits of US$ 300 million from donor countries and a further US$ 200 million in the following year. The importance of Indonesia as a bulwark to communism should not be understated; McNamara, after leaving his post as President Johnson's secretary of state for defence to become head of the World Bank, made Jakarta his first overseas trip in his new post. Not surprisingly, the combination of aid and stability brought an end to the period of seven years, between 1960 and 1967, in which the Indonesian economy had grown by just 2 per cent per annum; a disastrous performance relative to a population that was growing at more than 3 per cent per annum.

However, it was oil, not aid or stability, which was the main contributor to the 5 per cent real GDP growth rate that Indonesia achieved between 1971 and 1997. The First Oil Crisis brought a vast windfall to an Indonesian economy, which was barely above subsistence level. Foreign investment flows increased from just US$ 222 million by 1971 to US$ 1 billion in 1973.

Exports of US$ 595 million in 1967 increased to US$ 4.67 billion. Also, the government's revenues rose by 500 per cent. In the Second Oil Crisis in 1979, oil and gas earnings would rise as high as US$ 19 billion. Indeed, between 1974 and 1988, oil and foreign aid combined never accounted for less than 55 per cent of government revenues, of which aid was between 5 per cent and 15 per cent. In the 1980s, the percentage of oil and aid increased to over 70 per cent of government revenues.

With peace, political stability, international goodwill and foreign aid, combined with the windfall of an oil price boom, which increased from less than a dollar a barrel in the 1960s to well over US$ 30 in the early 1980s, Indonesia was presented with a platform from which it could have joined the ranks of the 'newly industrialised' countries. With fewer advantages in terms of natural resources, the military regimes in Korea and Taiwan were pointing the way forward to achieving robust economic development.

However, while these two countries found a means of balancing political corruption inherent in most totalitarian states, with a rapid and sustainable economic advance based on high levels of domestic capital formation, foreign direct investment (FDI) and export of manufactured products to the eager consumer markets of the USA, Indonesia palpably failed to use its oil windfall to create the conditions for industrial development. The reasons for this lie principally in the systematic looting of the national economy by Suharto, his family and his cronies.

In Indonesia, it is a popular joke that while their first president, Sukarno, was mad for sex, their second president was mad for money. Yet on the face of it, Suharto was an unlikely figure of greed. Unlike Yani and his clique, he did not indulge in the life of the flashy mistresses and five star hotels, which was the normal habitat of Indonesia's new rich.

His wife, Ibu Tien, was both fat and ugly. Yet he would dutifully return most days to eat lunch with her. He was devoted to her and to his children; perhaps mindful of his own unhappy upbringing, his family was central to his life. While his own tastes were modest in terms of his own home, its furnishings and the pursuit of pleasure, he was unable to resist the indulgence of his wife and children. Perversely, in 1970, he launched a scathing attack on some of his own generals for the material wealth and profligacy being displayed by their children. Yet Suharto's own family would become legendary for excess.

His eldest daughter Tutut (Siti Hardiyanti Rukmana), born in 1949, took financial cuts on government procurements ranging from F16 fighters to contracts for the construction of a Jakarta subway. By the mid-1990s, her personal wealth was estimated at some US$ 2 billion. Meanwhile, Bambang built up an interest in some 140 companies including the Jakarta Grand Hyatt Hotel; his stakes, such as his 60 per cent interest in Indonesia's state satellite company, often cost him nothing. In Suharto's Indonesia, access to influence was everything.

Siti Hediati Herijadi, otherwise Titiek, born in 1959, owned the Plaza Senayan, Jakarta's elite shopping mall for Western luxury brands. This was one of her 80 business interests. Son Sigit Harjojudanto, born in 1951, owned 17.5 per cent of the Liem-controlled Bank of Central Asia and reputedly had a net worth of some US$ 450 million.

The youngest sibling Siti Hutami Endang, born in 1964, developed interests in telecom, property and trading companies but was a relative pauper with an estimated net worth of a mere US$ 100 million. Suharto's younger brother also owned interests in food oils, chicken processing and fertilisers. The next generation also joined the family business. Sigit's son Ari Sigit, born in 1972, was allegedly behind the peddling of 'ecstasy' in Jakarta, as well as more conventionally 'acquiring' a monopoly selling fertiliser pellets.

However, it was 'Tommy', born in 1962 as Hutomo Mandala Putra, who became the legendary playboy son and a bye-word for filial indulgence and corruption. Like Indira Gandhi's son Sanjay, Tommy was an unsavoury hooligan with an obsession for fast cars. While it is not surprising for a playboy son of a dictator to drive Lamborghini sports cars, Tommy went one better by buying the company.

Like Sanjay too, Tommy was interested in flying and was involved with Sempati Air; he also imported liquefied gas; owned toll roads; and acquired interests in timber, wood manufacturing, sugar and palm oil plantations, gas exploration, fertiliser production, construction, advertising and media. Famously, he was granted a monopoly on the importation of cloves, which is the ubiquitous ingredient of Indonesia's favourite *Kretek* cigarettes.

But it was monopoly rights to the tax-free importation of Korean Kia motor cars under the guise of a sham Indonesian manufacturing enterprise, which undercut Hyundai Motor (who were in local manufacture with Bambang), that became an international scandal and marked out Tommy for rapacious greed even within his own family. At the apex of the children's commercial activity stood their mother, who collected money through her so-called charitable foundations known as *yayasan*. Though she can hardly be described as a moral paragon, after Ibu Tien's death in April 1996, any vestiges of restraint on her children's activities were swept away.

Suharto himself was not left out of the financial dealing, though he employed a fig leaf of discretion by directing operations through his business cronies, Liem Sioe Liong and Bob Hassan. Rake-offs on virtually all aspects of the economy were sieved through Suharto's own *yayasan*.

By the mid-1990s, the Suharto family wealth, much of it allegedly held offshore in Switzerland and other black money havens, was estimated by the CIA at US$ 20 billion. However, some private estimates put the figures five times higher. By the time of his fall in 1997, Suharto's family, with shareholding interests in some 1,250 companies, was almost certainly the world's richest. The president would lamely declare that 'There are people who say that I am rich; indeed I am rich, but only as the Chairman of the Foundations.'[13]

Suharto's business cronies prospered in tandem. Liem became Indonesia's richest banker and industrialist, whose conglomerate empire had a turnover of US$ 9 billion representing some 5 per cent of GDP. Through his company Apkindo, Bob Hassan was the leading figure in Indonesia's vast timber industry and became closely associated with the 'Asian smogs' produced by destruction of the Indonesian rainforests in the 1990s.

Another Suharto associate, Prajogo Pangestu, was awarded concessions on 5.5 million hectares of forest. His slash and burn activities were held responsible by many for the forest fires which raged for several years from 1997 and which created the pall of smoke that stretched over large parts of the Indonesian archipelago and much of South East Asia. It was later estimated that the 'Asian smogs' caused tens of thousands of respiratory-related deaths. Such was Prajogo's wealth that when Bank Duta, a Suharto-owned bank, lost US$ 420 million in currency speculation, he chipped in US$ 220 million to bail it out.

In 1970, the head of Pertamina boasted of his personal wealth in an interview with *Time* magazine, 'I'm big in tobacco exports, drugstores, a textile factory, rubber estates and have interests in six or seven companies.'[14] Taking its cue from the top, graft in Indonesia became institutionalised at all levels of the military–civilian bureaucracy.

As Bernard Crouch, the leading historian of modern Indonesia, has noted:

> As in the patrimonial states of traditional Java, where officials obtained their income from benefices rather than salaries, army officers were expected to make the most of their appointments in the bureaucracy and other government agencies which were often seen as rewards for earlier loyalty.[15]

Perhaps the most infamous of Suharto's cronies, Technology Minister Dr Ir Bucharuddin Habibie had a doctorate in aeronautical engineering at the Technische Hoschschule in Aachen. He then became a vice president at Messerschmitt-Bolkow-Blohm, before returning to Indonesia as Suharto's technology advisor. The dysfunctional nature of the Indonesian government was such that Habibie was able to authorise the purchase of 39 East German warships for the navy, in the teeth of fierce opposition from both the navy and the minister of defence.

Naturally, there was speculation as to the size of the 'commissions' paid on the US$ 1.2 billion refurbishment contract. In 1991, Habibie was excused from the payment of tax. Also, in 1994, Suharto diverted funds intended for reforestation into Habibie's aircraft projects. In spite of these advantages, Habibie's aerospace projects never advanced beyond the 'low-tech' assembly of small aircraft. By 1997, such was the notoriety of the aerospace project that the IMF made its closure one of the conditions for their emergency funds, even though Habibie himself was by then Indonesia's vice president.

At the heart of the culture of graft lay Pertamina, the state-owned oil company, which had forcibly acquired Royal Dutch Shell's properties in 1965. Under

Suharto's direction, Pertamina tied up joint ventures with Mobil in October 1968, and then with other oil majors. Oil production rose from 174 million barrels in 1966 to 476 million barrels in 1975, enabling Pertamina to become a cash cow for heavy industrial investments in steel, petrochemicals and fertilisers.

More importantly, money was siphoned from Pertamina to fund the Indonesian army; in *Angkatan Bersenjata*, the forces newspaper, an editorial on 4 March 1970 admitted that the government's military budget and non-official funding sources were almost equal. Pertamina was the main source of funds, although contributions were also sourced from *Bulog* (National Logistics Board), which monopolised trading in essential commodities such as rice.

Less successfully, the army sponsored an early entry into the commercial world with PT Berdikari, a limited liability company whose sole purpose was to raise funds for the army leadership. Through PT Berdikari, set up by Bank Dharm Ekonomi, the army controlled monopolies such as sole dealership of imported Mercedes Benz, already the car of choice for Indonesia's 'Kleptocracy'. Corruption did not necessarily guarantee viability; under the leadership of Brigadier General Suhardiman, a Yani acolyte, the bank collapsed in 1968.

Not surprisingly, Pertamina, Indonesia's greatest corporate cash cow, was dogged by scandal; its head, Ibnu Sutowo, was distinguished by a career in which General Nasution had suspended him from his staff group for corrupt financial practice. This did not prevent Sutowo, then a colonel, from being promoted to the rank of lieutenant general under Suharto. For Indonesia's new president, Ibnu Sutowo was without doubt perfectly qualified to run Indonesia's national oil company.

From 1968, Suharto would demand funds from Pertamina; such was the increase in Pertamina's short-term debt that an alerted IMF had to take action to intervene with Suharto, but without success. By 1975, Pertamina's total debts amounted to twice Indonesia's foreign currency reserves. Indeed, in spite of the explosive rise in the global oil price in the 1970s, Pertamina was brought to financial collapse in 1976 with cumulative debts of US$ 10 billion.

Government procurement was organised through the state secretariat by another Suharto ally, General Sudharmono. Within this organisation, Sudharmono created an agency known as 'Team 10', which was set up to manage 'commissions' on all government contracts and to provide equity participations for the Suharto family and the president's own slush fund known as *Bantuan Presiden*.

The legacy of corruption in the judiciary, inherited from Sukarno, continued unabated with his successor. The state of Indonesia's legal institutions was summed up by the American State Department in 1997:

> Judges are civil servants employed by the executive branch, which controls their assignments, pay and promotion . . . corruption is a common feature of the legal system and the payment of bribes can influence prosecution, conviction and sentencing in civil and criminal cases.[16]

Judges who failed to toe the line were simply seconded to godforsaken regional circuits where they were left to rot. Sops to Western notions of liberal democracy, such as the 1981 Code of Criminal Procedure, introduced defendants' rights; in practice, the codes were simply ignored. Without an effective independent judiciary, even a National Human Rights Commission, appointed to investigate the notorious massacre of Timorese at Dili in 1991, was powerless to bring those responsible to account.

In spite of the monolithic and apparently totalitarian nature of the Suharto regime, Indonesian government in the Suharto period was not without its politics; however, it was the 'court' politics of a feudal monarchy rather than anything recognisably modern. Political action took the form of jockeying for position within the military elite. The nature of this political intrigue was revealed in 1973, when military rivals prevented Ali Murtopo, the architect of GOLKAR, from becoming the organisation's first chairman.

The power struggle between him and General Sumitro, the commander of the *Kopkamtib*, was eventually decided by the dismissal of Sumitro. In a reaction against American influence, particularly its economic system, Murtopo set up a Centre for Strategic and International Studies, which took aim at the technocrats who had usurped economic management since Suharto's assumption of power. The strategy, which was aimed at shifting economic power and advantage towards the 'financial' generals, was also supported by the *Merdeka* (Liberty) newspaper and the weekly *Ekspres*, both owned by the former Minister of Information, B.H. Diah.

Whatever the shifting sands within his inner court, the ultimate arbiter of Suharto's fate, as with his predecessor, was the army. As long as it was loyal, he was untouchable. General Murdani, who had served under Suharto in West Papua, was a Murtopo protégé, who was brought back to Jakarta to head up the security forces in 1974. However, Murdani, who eventually rose to become commander in chief of ABRI (Armed Forces of the Republic of Indonesia) in 1983, and was particularly responsible for modernisation of the army and for moving it away from its revolutionary roots, increasingly sided with the military against the 'financial' generals. The result was that Murdani, the professional soldier, came into conflict with Suharto.

Suharto's rift with the army came to head in 1988, when Murdani called for the president to restrain his children. Although Suharto replaced Murdani with a more pliable figure, he thereafter failed to command the wholehearted support of the military generals. Other less powerful military critics of Suharto's New Order were more harshly dealt with. Lt. General Hartono Dharsono, who was a constant critic of the corruption of the army's financial clique, was removed to diplomatic posts first in Bangkok and then in Phnom Penh. Although he was later made secretary general to ASEAN, Suharto eventually removed him from all posts. He was charged with subversion and given a ten-year jail sentence.

Murdani, who had been removed to the less powerful post of minister of defence, nevertheless continued to manoeuvre against Suharto and the ruling clique. By the early 1990s, in an atmosphere reminiscent of the last years of Sukarno, Murdani and the ABRI began to jockey for position in the succession.

At the beginning of 1993, ABRI, in defiance of the convention that the president could choose his own successor, nominated former commander in chief Try Sutrisno for the vice presidency. Though this plan failed, numbers of senior officers supported the December campaign of Megawati Sukarnoputri (President Sukarno's daughter) to become leader of the opposition PDI (*Partai Demoskrasi Indonesia Perjuangen*, Indonesia Democratic Party Struggle). Eventually, the opposition PDI, whose creation Suharto's New Order had endorsed in 1973, began to throw off the shackles imposed by GOLKAR.

Similarly, the Muslim political voice began to grow. Sukarno had also created PPP (*Partai Persuatuan Penbangunan*, the United Development Party) as a puppet opposition party out of a jumble of Islamic groupings; however, the charismatic Abdurrahman Wahid, otherwise known as Gus Dur, withdrew the NU (*Nahdlatul Ulama*) from the PPP in 1984, and gradually built up his organisation into the most powerful Islamic voice in Indonesia.

With a membership of 135 million, Gus Dur's NU provided a powerful chorus to leading figures such as Megawati and Murdani, who were calling for greater democracy. Such was the growing power of the pro-democracy groups, inside and outside the army, that Suharto increasingly sought support from an anti-Chinese Islamic group, the Muhammadiyah, which claimed 28 million members. Within the army too, Suharto tried to create a new support base by identifying with the Islamic 'Green' faction led by his son-in-law, Prabowo.

As opposition to the government grew, attempts to destabilise opposition parties became ever more desperate. In 1994, the chairman of GOLKAR, by now Suharto's daughter Tutut, attempted to overthrow Gus Dur's leadership of NU in an election which he narrowly won by 174 votes to 142.

More successful was the government-organised coup to unseat Megawati from the leadership of the PDI, at its national Congress at Medan in June 1996. It was a pyrrhic victory, however, as it simply served to stoke the fires of popular resentment and unrest. Megawati and her followers now joined ranks with the PPP and demonstrated under their umbrella. In spite of the possibility of subversion charges, which carried with it the threat of death penalty, the opposition grew more daring. Just before the DPR (*Dewan Parwakilan Rakyat*, lower house of legislature) elections in March 1997, the PPP publicly denounced the structure of the DPR. As always in Indonesia, it was the student body on the streets which led the public demand for change.

International events were also conspiring to undermine Suharto in the 1990s. The communist threat of the PKI was now ancient history; the fall of the Soviet Union and Deng Xiaoping's free market reforms in China had eased global tensions. US fears that Indonesia might fall to communism had eased at the same time that America, particularly under Bill Clinton's leadership, was increasingly insistent that its allies and trading partners should improve on their human rights record.

The takeover of East Timor in 1976, and its subsequent absorption into Indonesia, followed by the increasing suppression of the indigenous population, had dissipated whatever residues of gratitude America felt for a president who had dealt a major blow to the communist domination of Asia. Neither did Suharto's return to the 'anti-colonial' rhetoric of his predecessor, to justify his annexation of East Timor, endear him to his allies in the West; 'For two hundred years we have been separated by the wall erected by colonial governments . . . The people of East Timor will unite with their blood brothers in the unitary state of the Republic of Indonesia.'[17]

For Indonesia, the sanctity of the post-revolution unitary state was paramount to the country's security. The ever present fear was that if one province, such as Aceh, Ambon, Situbondo, or Ketapang, escaped the roost, the centrifugal forces of Indonesia's diverse ethnicity would split the country asunder. Major General Sudrajat, in a panel discussion on the subject, presented the army's historic view quite clearly: 'The danger is that federalism will lead our nation to disintegrate along ethnic lines', he asserted, 'so we are talking about something far more serious than the secession of a couple of provinces. . . . Our country consists of 260 ethnic groups . . . if we were to move to a federation, where would we start?'[18]

Also, overseas, there had been sporadic leakage of the information about the scale of corruption in the Suharto government. In 1975, the death of Haji Thahir, effectively the chief of staff to Lieutenant General Sutowo, the head of Pertamina, brought about a bitter family squabble over Singaporean bank accounts, which alone revealed some US$ 80 million in assets. These facts naturally leaked back to Indonesia where they became a catalyst for student unrest.

Also, such was the World Bank's damning indictment of the corruption and mismanagement of the economy that the Indonesian government refused to accept the report. When David Jenkins, an Australian investigative reporter, uncovered the expansive corruption of President Suharto in a series of articles in 1986, relations with Australia were sorely tested; their reporters were barred from Indonesia during Ronald Reagan's visit in 1986.

However, the articles, which were reprinted in America in such eminent publications as *The New York Times*, *The Washington Post* and *The International Herald Tribune*, merely confirmed what had already been widely rumoured. For years, Western businessmen in Asia agreed that Indonesia was uniquely corrupt, and when the Hong Kong-based Political and Economic Risk Consultancy Limited reported that Indonesia was 'the most corrupt country in Asia',[19] it was no more than the statement of the obvious.

Of even greater international significance in Suharto's downfall was the unravelling of the credit-fuelled boom that Asia had experienced in the mid-1990s. Starting with the seemingly innocuous collapse of Hanbo Iron and Steel Company

in South Korea in January 1997, currency fears began to undermine Asian countries in an unstoppable domino effect. In August, Indonesia was forced to de-link
from the US dollar and the rupiah collapsed in value to 6,000 to the dollar. By
October, Indonesia was calling on the IMF for a US$ 43 billion rescue package.
Economic management descended into chaos. A budget of ludicrous optimism,
announced on 6 January 1998, brought panic buying and a further collapse of the
rupiah to 10,000 to the dollar. By 22 January, the rupiah had fallen to 17,000.

The IMF insisted on terms of extreme humiliation for Suharto: funding of
Tommy's Timor motor project was to stop; the Habibie aerospace projects were
to be suspended. Sukarno, in a metaphor of crushed hubris, signed the IMF agreement with the imposing figure of the IMF's Managing Director Michel Camdessus
towering over him. Walter Mondale, the losing 1984 Democrat presidential candidate, whom President Clinton had sent to Jakarta to persuade Suharto to accept
the IMF terms, told the embattled Indonesian leader that life would be better in six
months. Suharto replied, 'I don't have six months . . . there will be a revolution.'[20]

As unrest grew, Suharto circled the wagons in a last ditch attempt to stay in
power. He became increasingly reliant on his clique of cronies; on 14 March 1998,
Tutut organised a new cabinet which included Bob Hassan and Habibie, now vice
president. To counter the increasing influence of the anti-Suharto Red and White
factions in ABRI, General Wiranto was moved to the Ministry of Defence, while
Subagyo Hadi Siswoyo from the pro-Suharto Green faction was appointed new
commander in chief of the army.

Fearing the worst, Suharto also rapidly promoted his ambitious son-in-law,
Prabowo (also the leader of the Green faction), to the rank of major general and
to the command of *Kostrad* (Army Strategic Reserve Command), Jakarta's security
forces. The promotion of the hard-line Prabowo aroused strong popular feelings.
This combined with fuel and bus ticket price increases, ignited what was already an
incendiary atmosphere. Jakarta erupted into riots after the murder of six students
in campus by students loyal to Prabowo. Chinese shopkeepers were attacked and
murdered. The billionaire Chinese industrialist Liem had his house burnt out.

In the ensuing riots, the death toll rose to an estimated 1,000 people. A desperate populace, now racked by rapidly rising inflation and unemployment, took to
looting and burning shopping malls. Increasingly armoured cars and tanks roamed
the streets to maintain a semblance of order. Yet when students entered the parliamentary buildings, General Wiranto offered them protection.

Finally, in May 1998, ABRI's generals, both current and retired, demanded the
resignation of Suharto. The MPR was petitioned, and even that body's chairman,
Harmoko, a former Suharto loyalist, called for the president's resignation. On 19
May 1998, Suharto announced that he would not participate in the presidential
elections slated for the following year. A reform committee and cabinet were also
promised. The seeming delaying tactics merely infuriated the Jakarta mob, which
again took to the streets.

Two days later, former vice presidents Sutrisno, Sudharmono and Umar Wirahadikusumah begged Suharto to resign. Later that evening of 20 May, General Waranto would finally deliver the coup de grace on Suharto's increasingly tortured reign. Suharto agreed to resign in return for protection for his family. At 11 pm, Vice President Habibie was informed that he would assume the presidency the following day. Would Suharto wriggle out of his commitment? At midnight, the US Secretary of State Madeleine Albright broadcast a statement calling for his resignation. The next morning, on 21 May at 9 am, Suharto read out a statement in which he resigned and apologised for his 'mistakes and shortcomings'.[21]

Loathed throughout the country and treated with contempt by the IMF and the international money markets, Habibie was never likely to be more than a make-weight president. Nevertheless, faced with little choice, he despatched the remnants of Suharto's faction. Habibie resisted Prabowo's demand to be made commander-in-chief of the army and transferred him instead from Jakarta to the calm backwaters of the military college at Magelang. Prabowo's allies in the army were similarly purged. Hassan and Tutut were removed from the cabinet. With the last remaining members of his coterie removed, Suharto and his clan had no way back. The rule of the kleptomaniacs was over.

47

Rogue State

North Korea: 1980–2005

At the 6th Party Congress in 1980, Kim Il Sung's son, Kim Jong Il, the so-called Dear Leader, was nominated as his father's successor. From that date, Kim Jong Il was promoted in state propaganda to a level only just below the Great Leader himself. Increasingly the regime became a 'duumvirate'. The elevation of the Dear Leader did not lead to changes in policy. Indeed, in 1982 Kim Jong Il published *On the Juche Idea*, a further recycling of the North Korean ideology of self-reliance.

Three years later, the Foreign Languages Publishing House in Korea published Choe In Su's nauseous hagiography of Kim Jong Il's life, *The People's Leader*, which reached the conclusion that

> As long as dear Comrade Kim Jong Il, the great thinker and theoretician, outstanding genius of leadership, boundlessly benevolent teacher of the people, and the great man of the century, stands at the head of the Worker's Party of Korea and of the revolution, the Korean people will be crowned with lasting victory and glory and will enjoy eternal prosperity and happiness.[1]

Yet, in the decade of Kim Jong Il's elevation, Korea became decreasingly relevant on the world stage; in the West, Reagan and Thatcher had set about revitalising the Anglo-Saxon economies; Asian countries too, impressed by the transformations of South Korea and Taiwan, were beginning to liberalise their economies and welcome foreign investment, while North Korea's closest neighbour and ally, China, was quietly abandoning socialism as Deng Xiaoping set his country on a capitalist path. Expatriate Chinese capital was returning to China and beginning to transform its economy. As Erik Cornell, the Ambassador who opened the Swedish Embassy in 1975 noted, 'Little did we then realize that in the future, from a Pyongyang horizon, we would come to realize that we were back in the West when we crossed the *Jalu River* and returned to China.'[2]

The foreign businessmen from Europe and Japan, who had flooded into the capital, Pyongyang, in the 1970s, looking to sell products with their own government's credit, had long since ceased to visit. Even the COMECON countries abandoned their erstwhile ally, Korea. As for the 'non-aligned' states, they had effectively shunned the North Koreans at their conference in Colombo in 1976 because of their increasingly strident and bellicose anti-imperialist language. Here too the ideology of self-reliance, *Juche*, was rejected; as Kenyan minister Tom Mboya noted at a pan-African conference, 'I accept the slogan of self reliance. The man in the bush has always been self-reliant and that is the reason why he is still in the bush.'[3]

By any standards, by the 1980s, North Korea's isolation from the world was extraordinary. Diplomats from Indonesia would have to fly to Pyongyang via Moscow. Food and essential equipment were flown in from Helsinki. As North Korea delinked itself from the world, even senior government representatives developed absurd concepts of standard behaviour. Erik Cornell recalled that when he informed officials that 'I had no right at all to give orders to Swedish businessmen, the North Koreans doubled up with laughter. . . .'[4]

Increasingly, North Korea became a looking-glass world in which everyday life simply parted company with normal realities. An expensive underground transport system had been built in Pyongyang, yet vast multi-lane roads built through the centre of the capital remained deserted apart from the occasional horse and cart or the black Mercedes-Benz 500SL cars, which ferried apparatchiks around the city. At Nampo, near Pyongyang, a visiting Western financier was astonished to see a port devoid of ships or cargo for export or import, with the exception of 30 black Mercedes-Benz 500 SL destined for North Korea's elite socialist apparatchiks. The capital city proffered bizarrely empty streets devoid of traffic but pavements packed with workers. For reasons that could not be ascertained, there appeared to be no bicycles in the city.

Products arbitrarily bought overseas by state authorities were imported into North Korea and gifted to deserving members of the Workers Party of Korea. Japanese televisions and radios had their country of origin removed and replaced by plaques inscribed as 'Gifts of the Benevolent Great Leader.' Other products were offered to designated cadres through state stores. Miss-pricing was commonplace. Cars were priced by distributors according to size, and a Polish ambassador gleefully purchased a Porsche for US$ 4,000; cost accounting simply did not exist. Everyday consumer goods, let alone luxuries, were not available to ordinary workers. Shops ceased to exist. Food and other products were distributed at factories. As a city without shops, Pyongyang presented the visitor with a strangely faceless experience.

However, the capital itself boasted half a dozen 'Five Star' hotels, a fact proudly announced by the government's official guides. All but one of these was purely 'Potemkin' in functionality, with lobby staff employed by the government to disguise the fact that the hotels had no guests. What was more difficult to hide was that the country was devoid of electricity. Walking at night in Pyonyang, with a total absence of street or building lighting, was a curious experience for the foreign visitor; even in winter, the offices of senior politicians and bureacrats were icy cold.

To improve the quality of life for its citizens, North Korea's leadership came up with eccentric innovations. For the rare drivers on the largely empty streets of Pyongyang, a 'blue' light was added to traffic lights. The city was proud of its four-colour traffic lights, but increasingly these had to be switched off to save electricity and were replaced by female 'traffic directors' supposedly picked for their beauty by the Dear Leader, Kim Jong II. To improve the productivity of the fishing indus-try, the Great Leader ordered peculiar modifications to the fleet; '. . . you must put engines in your boats so that you can go further out to sea! Now it can take four days to the fishing grounds, and four back again. Put a tractor engine in the boats, that's easy'.[5]

In spite of such 'labour saving' initiatives, life for the average North Korean was one of unending drudgery. All but the highest ranks of the bureaucracy were required to work one day a week as manual labourers; two hours a day had to be devoted to the study of the works of the Great Leader. Four 'free' days a year were allowed on the Leader's birthday, State Founding Day, Labour Day and Party Founding Day; a fifth was added to celebrate the Dear Leader's birthday. Apart from the regimentation of daily life, freedom of movement for ordinary citizens was almost completely curtailed.

Erik Cornell's history of *North Korea under Communism* (2002) is entirely sus-tained by anecdotes detailing the absurdity of life in Pyongyang. Naturally, the North Korean security services played a major role. Cornell recalls the embar-rassment of a maid serving dinner at the embassy:

> . . . a sudden crackling noise emanated from under her skirts as she was serving dinner _
> it sounded like someone trying to tune into a station on an old fashioned radio. She
> abruptly stopped serving and rushed back into the kitchen _ evidently the tape recorder
> was malfunctioning.[6]

Life in Pyongyang was sometimes amusing only in hindsight. Opening nights of films were far from exciting events. Describing an excruciatingly boring wartime drama about the Great Leader, Cornell wrote that

> . . . as the music of the heavens grew to a crescendo, a figure could be seen coming
> out of the forest, lit up from behind by the rays of the sun which finally formed a halo
> around the person's head. When we could eventually discern that it was the Leader's
> mother, all the Koreans present stood up and joined together in a chorus of cheers,
> while jumping up and down in front of their seats and clapping their hands with their
> arms stretched up over their heads.[7]

The musical film, *The Song of Paradise*, included such catchy numbers as *'My Juche Country'*; *'Under the Fatherly Leader's Loving Care'*; *'We shall boast of our Paradise before the Whole World'*; *'The Leader's Theses on Socialist Agriculture bear rich fruit'* and *'We shall remain faithful to the Great Leader.'*

Personality cult was developed to an extraordinary degree. Even gifts to the Great Leader were displayed at vast expense in a one kilometre long, marble-lined tunnel dug into a mountainside to the north of Pyongyang. Here, in the many rooms leading off this Orwellian passageway and culminating in a vast circular hall, was displayed the miserable detritus that constitutes official present giving. When a visiting English banker, on arriving in the so-called 'Great Hall', spotted the particularly ghastly present, a glass ball on a plinth, that he had himself conveyed to Kim II Sung, his tour guide burst into tears of joy. In North Korea, there appeared to be none of the cynicism towards the regime that characterised other communist countries before their fall. 'Brainwashing', which was inculcated into the education system from childhood, was highly effective.

Even by Soviet or Maoist standards, the democratic charade played out in the North Korean parliament was extraordinary. Conducted over three days, twice a year, the 529 assembly members were called to a theatre-like auditorium; on stage, Kim II Sung would sit alone at a desk with the 33 Standing Committee members of the Supreme People's Assembly massed behind him. Ministers read prepared statements extolling successes and, with oleaginous praise, attributed huge achievements to the Great Leader. From behind his desk Kim II Sung would dispense occasional comments, rather like a father reading through his child's school report. The assembly was treated as nothing more than a rubber stamp, which dovetailed neatly with Kim II Sung's explicitly stated belief that the concept of 'equality before the law' was simply a bourgeois lie.

In view of his disregard for the rule of law within North Korea, it was perhaps not surprising that there should be a flagrant disregard for legal norms outside of the country. North Korean embassies became well known for using their exemptions on alcohol and tobacco to engage in racketeering in these commodities. In Copenhagen, Oslo and Stockholm, this activity also extended to drug dealing; likewise in Japan, where North Korean diplomatic staff were regularly engaged in criminal activity.

In spite of the increasingly bizarre character of the North Korean regime, the country nevertheless attracted a bandwagon of international supporters. In a selection of favourable international articles published in 1981 with the title *Kim II Sung, The Brilliant Banner of Juche*, French journalist Jean Barre compared North Korea favourably with the West:

> I explained to my colleagues, incredulous at first, then ever more interested, that the Korean working people pay no taxes, that they are provided with decent dwelling houses free of rent, and that almost all charges are borne by the state. . . . In the capitalist countries a minority of the ruling classes live in luxury, while the majority of the urban and rural proletariat lead a hard and miserable life. . . .[8]

Barre was in no doubt who was responsible for the improved life enjoyed by the North Koreans after 'the US and its satellites . . . had destroyed everything. . . . This prosperity in my opinion, is attributable to the sustained leadership of Marshal Kim Il Sung, the greatest statesman of our time . . . '.[9]

Visits by British Labour Party Members of Parliament, William Wilson, Dennis Canavan and Ted Fletcher also gave credence to the regime. William Wilson noted that North Korea 'confronts US Armed Forces . . . and across the water is Japan . . . in such a situation as this it is easy to understand why Korea has adopted the "Juche" philosophy . . . Independence and self sufficiency must be the byword of any country in the position that Korea is in'.[10]

Despite the vast discrepancies already evident in the economic performance of North and South Korea, Wilson was typically laudatory of the achievements of the North, declaring that 'Korea's greatest asset is in its leader Kim Il Sung.'[11] In his peon of praise for the North, Wilson concludes that

> The American troops should go home. I do not believe the American troops are in Korea for the protection of Korea . . . it was a great and unforgettable experience that we had in the Democratic People's Republic of Korea. If Kim Il Sung invited us to go again, I do not think we shall want asking twice.[12]

Notwithstanding plaudits from British socialists, by the end of the 1980s, North Korea had become an irrelevance. In spite of lavish facilities built to host the Olympic Games, Kim Il Sung was shocked to find both China and the Soviet Union in support of the games taking place in the South. When Gorbachev called an East Asian meeting with both Koreas, it was quickly seen as an attempt to lure the South Koreans into providing investment for the development of Siberia; the northerners were sidelined as it was clear that ' "North Korea" was not only of no interest as a collaborator, rather, it was seen as a liability with its demands for ideological solidarity, on top of its bad record of debt repayments and its importunate delivery requirements.'[13]

The economic disparities between North and South Korea had become only too evident to allies and enemies alike. Although by the 1980s, Korea had ceased to produce budgets or economic statistics, itself a sure indication of failure, it was clear that the economy was faltering, and becoming increasingly reliant on Soviet subsidies even to be able to feed its own people. By contrast, the South was experiencing rapid economic growth, and in 1990 reported a GDP per capita of US$ 5,559 compared to an estimate of below US$ 1,000 in the North. In spite of North Korea's stuttering economic performance, the army, in a manner typical of post-war communist countries, continued to absorb increasing amounts of the nation's economic resources.

The repressive nature of North Korean life was clearly hidden from public view. Yet, sudden and unexplained disappearances of senior members of the government were not missed by the small body of foreign residents. Also, the occasional escapee would attest to the existence of prison camps for large numbers of political dissidents; summary execution of dissidents and purges of party members were also frequent.

If the North Korean economy stagnated, or suffered a moderate decline in the 1980s, worse was to come. The start of the new decade ushered in a catastrophic decline in the North Korean economy. With the collapse of the Soviet Union, the political will to sustain Kim Il Sung evaporated. Imports of subsidised Soviet oil fell from 400,000 tons in 1990 to just 100,000 in 1991. The result was widespread industrial dislocation; more significantly, without fuel to operate farm equipment, agricultural productivity also collapsed, with the result that food self-sufficiency fell to just 60 per cent. It is estimated that in the five years to 1995, real GDP declined by at least 20 per cent. In that year it is thought that between 500,000 and 1 million people died of hunger. North Koreans fled to the Chinese border with many dying en route; others were executed for making the attempt to leave North Korea to find food.

Following a 1998 survey, which concluded that some 63 per cent of North Korean children were undernourished, United Nations agencies, including the World Food Program (WFP), the Food and Agricultural Organisation (FAO), the United Nations International Children's Emergency Fund (UNICEF) and the World Health Organisation (WHO), rushed to intervene; by 2000, international aid was providing 40 per cent of North Korea's food requirements. Food was not received with gratitude. An editorial in *Rodong Sinmun* pointed out that ' "The Imperialists" aid is a tool of aggression . . . a dangerous toxin which brings about poverty, famine and death, not prosperity.'[14]

Faced with the collapse of the North Korean economy, factions within the army and the ruling elite manoeuvred for a change in economic policy. In the autumn of 1993, at the invitation of the North Korean government, foreign economists were invited to go to Pyongyang to address a committee of the Standing Committee on the subject of 'capitalism'. This bizarre request necessitated a journey to Beijing, where a day was spent acquiring visas for North Korea, making it a two-day journey to get to Pyongyang from Hong Kong.

An uninterrupted two-hour presentation to an assembly of generals and bureaucrats was followed by questions; the first of these was, 'What is a convertible preference share?' Leaving aside the strangely arcane nature of this question, which clearly ignored the major issues raised by the presentation, the North Korean General was asked how, given the absence of any capital market in Pyongyang, he had ever heard of 'convertible preference shares'? The answer was both brief and illuminating: 'We watch CNN.'[15]

It was apparent that the North Korean leadership had privileged access to Western news sources, and was fully aware of the gulf in living standards that had opened up with the West. The visit to Pyongyang ended with the signing of heads of agreement on future co-operation; negotiations with the North Korean government entered the realms of the surreal when their negotiators offered to name a new zoo in Rajin-Sonbong after the visiting economist; a further sweetener was that a statue of the visitor's company chairman could be built, even larger than those of Kim Il Sung, and in any material. An invitation followed to attend Kim Il Sung's next birthday party.

The major result of this 'mini' opening to market forces was the creation of a free trade zone at Rajin-Sonbong where the borders of Russia, China and North Korea all meet. The head of Rajin-Sonbong Free Economic and Trade Zone, went as far as to say that 'socialist markets have disappeared' and 'there is only a capitalist world market'; 'This plan', he asserted, 'is a temporary bridge to connect our economy'.[16]

In addition to the creation of a free trade zone, liberalisation also paved the way for the start-up of North Korea's only privately owned bank, involving a joint venture between Peregrine, a Hong Kong-based investment bank and a North Korean government enterprise. The bank, subsequently owned by Paul Pheby, a British financial entrepreneur based in Hong Kong, operated profitably for more than a decade. However, these marginal free market developments had little effect on the broader structural impediments to the overall economic performance of the North Korean economy.

Evidently, the pro-reform faction did not win out in the struggle for power; the sponsor of the western financiers and economist's visit in 1993, suddenly disappeared without explanation two years later and was presumed to have been purged and probably executed. It was likely that the sudden death of Kim Il Sung in 1994 precipitated a power struggle within the North Korean hierarchy. During an apparent hiatus of several years, Kim Jong Il remained invisible, either for a period of mourning, but more likely as he sought to establish his own power base. He certainly retained his father's paranoia for personal safety, preferring to travel to Moscow by train, supposedly loaded with his favourite epicurean foods, rather than risk flying.

Like his father, Kim Jong Il rarely ventured away from North Korea. He has remained little known, apart from his love of food (including sushi regularly flown from Japan) and a reputed playboy lifestyle in his youth. In visual appearance, he was notable for his penchant for platform shoes to boost his diminutive height; his 'bouffant' hairstyle and garish tunic suits gave him the appearance of a miniature, pot-bellied, Elvis Presley impersonator. Reputedly, he was even more demanding of loyalty than his father and had a fastidious attention to the minutiae of government.

By the late 1980s, North Korea had ceased to be a serious military threat to the South. Indeed, ten years earlier, President Carter had seriously contemplated withdrawal of American forces from the Korean peninsula. With both China and Russia now under the leadership of free market reformers, and geopolitically inclined to eschew Cold War confrontations of the type favoured by Kim Il Sung and his son, North Korea found itself completely isolated.

Moreover, by its adoption of catastrophic socialist command economy structures, North Korea had undermined its ability to fight a conventional war. Without fuel, it was now inconceivable that Kim Il Sung could sustain the logistics for pro-tracted military engagement. Though a surprise attack could cause damage to the South, victory was now impossible and the most likely outcome would be to bring down the North's hereditary dictatorship.

However, in 1989, US satellite pictures revealed the existence of a North Ko-rean nuclear reprocessing plant. With the realisation that North Korea's barmy dic-tatorship had the capability of producing nuclear-weapon-grade plutonium from spent fuel rods, international interest in North Korea was suddenly reawakened. With technology almost certainly acquired from Dr Khan, the entrepreneurial founder of Pakistan's nuclear programme, North Korea was well on its way to producing nuclear weapons; this in spite of the fact that, under Soviet pressure, Kim Il Sung had signed the Non-Proliferation Treaty in 1985. In 1990, America duly accused North Korea of pursuing a secret weapons programme; the dispute ended temporarily following high-level talks between North and South Korea. As a result, President George Bush (senior) withdrew tactical nuclear weapons from the Korean peninsular.

In return, the North responded by ratifying the Safeguards Agreement to the Non-Proliferation Treaty, which it had refused to do in 1985. Subsequently, the United Nations affiliate, the International Atomic Energy Agency (IAEA), was able to conduct six inspections of the North Korean facilities between May 1992 and January 1993. In this new spirit of compromise, 'Team Spirit' war games, carried out between American and South Korean forces, were cancelled in 1992.

However, given Kim's flagrant disregard for the 'bourgeois' notion of law, there was scant chance that international agreements would be honoured. In Febru-ary 1992, American intelligence uncovered two undeclared North Korean nuclear facilities. The CIA now averred that Kim Il Sung had nuclear weapons. Kim Il Sung's response was to cancel IAEA inspections; in addition North Korea was put on military alert, and she withdrew from the Nuclear Non-Proliferation Treaty. The threat of North Korea becoming a nuclear power was also something that in-coming President Clinton 'was determined to avoid'.[17] When he threatened eco-nomic sanctions against North Korea at a time of dire economic performance, North Korea again caved in to pressure and IAEA officials were allowed back into the country to inspect the original seven sites.

Reconciliation was short-lived. Inspectors soon arrived at an impasse with the North over access during the inspection process. President Clinton now sought United Nations support for economic sanctions. President Clinton also increased American forces in South Korea, and shipped Patriot air defence missiles to the peninsula. Clinton's Defence Secretary William Perry even seemed to threaten a pre-emptive nuclear strike against North Korea, when he refused to rule this out as one of the American options.

In June 1994, former President Carter was invited to North Korea where, with President Clinton's blessing, he brokered a peace deal; a freeze on the nuclear programme in return for talks. Although negotiations in Geneva conducted by Warren Christopher and Ambassador Gallucci were set back for a month following the sudden death of Kim Il Sung in July, seven months later a deal was reached whereby the USA would fund the construction of light water reactors and guarantee 500,000 tons of heavy oil per annum.

Trade, investment and diplomatic relations would naturally follow. By finding long-term solutions to North Korea's power problems in exchange for a full surrender of its nuclear weapons programme, including dismantling of existing facilities and export of some 8,000 fuel rods, President Clinton sought to bring an end to the nuclear threat. He appeared to have succeeded. Nevertheless, North Korea's missile testing continued to be a concern. However, in 1998, Kim Jong Il suspended missile tests and in May, President Clinton sent a letter to Kim Jong Il which proposed a 'road map' to normalisation of relations, and a broad range of assistance in return for permanent abandonment of nuclear and missile ambitions.

In trying to reach a permanent solution, Secretary of State Madeleine Albright became the first high-level government visitor to North Korea, and almost persuaded President Clinton to follow, convinced that his trip could conclude an agreement. However, as Clinton records in his memoir *My Life* (2004):

> Although I wanted to take the next step, I simply couldn't risk being halfway around the world when we were so close to peace in the Middle East, especially after Arafat had assured me that he was eager for an agreement and had implored me not to go.[18]

For President Clinton, and probably for any American president, an Israel–Palestinian settlement would always be the more important prize for posterity.

The Clinton presidency ended with North Korean issues still hanging. In fact, after President Clinton left office, it became clear to the new administration that former President Clinton, like President Bush (senior) before him, had been duped by the Kim regime. In 1998, Kim Jong Il authorised a programme to produce highly enriched uranium in a laboratory. With no settlement reached on a missile programme, Clinton had merely delayed, not thwarted, North Korea's intention to become a nuclear power. Not surprisingly, given the failed experience of bilateral negotiations with the North Koreans, the incoming President George W. Bush decided that a multilateral approach was preferable. Given that the problem of a North Korea with nukes was more pressing for South Korea, China, the Soviet Union and Japan than for itself, the Bush administration decided that it would only negotiate in partnership with these countries.

China, in particular, which viewed North Korea as a 'client state', was probably correctly seen as the country with the greatest leverage on North Korean behaviour. Nevertheless, President George W. Bush himself made his position crystal clear. Using the phrase scripted for him by political analyst and historian David Frum, President Bush linked North Korea with Iraq and Iran as part of a global 'Axis of evil.' This speech, which most succinctly enshrined President Bush's foreign policy after 9/11 was the template that continued to guide American policy towards North Korea.

On returning to Hong Kong from Pyongyang (via Beijing), a western economist was interviewed by an intelligence officer and reported that, in his view, North Korea did not have the logistical capability to fight a conventional war. However, before embarking on a conflict with North Korea, it was also noted that the Americans 'might like to ask China first'.[19] That indeed was the issue for the USA. North Korea itself might not be a formidable enemy; even its nuclear capability could be relatively easily targeted; however, any military action against Kim Jong Il's regime would be considered an attack on China's sphere of influence and therefore on China itself. The Korean War, in which over 1 million Chinese soldiers lost their lives, including Mao's own son, remained fresh in the memory of China's political elite. However frustrated by Kim Jong Il's behaviour it could not be expected that China would agree to any significant ratchetting up of pressure on its long time confederate. Negotiations with threats of economic sanctions therefore remained the only practicable path for American foreign policy.

However, the scope for internal change in North Korea was limited. As Secretary of State Madeleine Albright recalled in her memoir *Madam Secretary*:

> Seeing average North Koreans on the streets, I was tempted to imagine budding Thomas Jeffersons [or Kim Dae Jungs] striding by; nursing their thirst for freedom, waiting only for an opening to express their desire for democratic rule. This was, however, surely a fantasy: Most North Koreans entered government-run nurseries at the age of three months. The tots I met at the World Food Program were as well drilled as any army drum and bugle corps ... most likely they were so preoccupied with survival that they didn't spend much time questioning what they had no reason to believe they could change. It was clear they had little accurate knowledge of the outside world.[20]

Perversely, the vast United Nations programmes to feed the North Koreans has sustained a regime which, in its continued pursuit of nuclear capability, has threatened the lives of hundreds of millions of Japanese, Chinese, Russians and Koreans. Constrained from attacking Kim Jong Il's rogue state by his country's 'satellite' relationship with China and prevented by global humanitarian concerns from starving it into submission, America and the United Nations' attempts to resolve the long term security problems posed by North Korea escaped the best efforts of Presidents Bush (senior), Clinton and George W. Bush; the threat created by North Korea remained intractable and it seemed that only changes in the country's domestic political landscape would be likely to alter its destabilising influence in the region.

48

Bloodlust and Revenge

Bangladesh: 1971–96

In emerging as a fledging nation in 1971, Bangladesh (formerly East Pakistan) had to endure perhaps the bloodiest civil war of the post-war era. It is estimated that over three million people died in the conflict between East and West Pakistan. Its educated intellectual elite had been decimated by the slaughter of the professional classes in what came to be known as 'the Night of the Intellectuals'; in addition over 200,000 women had been raped by Western Pakistani soldiers and over 250,000 people had been made homeless in refugee camps across the border in India. Many of its most able people found themselves interned in the West. Furthermore, East Pakistan's infrastructure of roads and railways had been destroyed. This then was the situation faced by the iconic leader of Bangladesh's fight for freedom, Sheikh Mujibur Rahman (more usually known as Sheikh Mujib or *Bangabandhu*, friend of Bengal), when, on 10 January 1972, he returned from captivity, via London and Delhi, to be greeted by rapturous crowds in Dhaka.

Even for the most able of leaders, the restoration of Bangladesh would have been a daunting task. For Mujib, a charismatic revolutionary leader but a woefully inadequate ruler, it was a task for which he was hopelessly ill-suited. Within two days of returning to Bangladesh, he stepped down as president to become prime minister of a unicameral parliament, the prime minister being chosen by the president but with the approval of parliament. The four tenets of Sheikh Mujib, known as *Mujibad*, were nationalism, socialism, secularism and democracy. Mujib displayed his communal tolerance by including two Hindus in his first cabinet. However, his governmental appointments, strongly laced with nepotism, gave a lead which soon characterised his government. Both his nephew Sheikh Fazlul Haq and brother-in-law Abdur Rab Serniabat were given lucrative posts. Throughout the government at every level, appointments were made as rewards for loyalty and as the means to make money. It was a legacy that still plagues the governance of Bangladesh.

This highly selective process also discriminated against those Bangladeshis, many of them the most able of their country, who were interned in the West during and after the war. This was particularly true of the army; repatriated soldiers from

West Pakistan, who made up half of the 55,000-strong army, were discriminated against by a prime minister who gave preference to members of the *Mukti Bahini* (freedom fighters), many of whom, amateur guerrilla fighters, felt that they were owed position and favour. Like many of Asia's successful revolutionary armies, they also believed that they had a legitimate stake in their country's governance.

In addition to the selective organisation of the army, Mujib managed to alienate even this organisation by the creation of a highly personalised guard, the *Jatiyo Rakhi Bahini* (National Security Force). The 10,000-strong force was made to take a personal oath of loyalty to Mujib; it was also rewarded with special privileges, equipment and supplies. It was characteristic of the favouritism endemic in Mujib's style of government, which alienated all strands of society and the regular army in particular.

Nevertheless, independence euphoria guaranteed a landslide election victory for Mujib in the nation's first elections in 1973. The Awami League won 73.2 per cent of the vote and 292 out of 300 seats. In addition to the conventional constituencies, there were 15 indirectly elected women's seats. The pro-Moscow faction of the Awami League won 8 per cent of the vote while the pro-Beijing faction won 5 per cent; the *Jatiya Samajtantrik Dal* (JSD, the far-left scientific socialism party) won 6.5 per cent of the vote.

Mujib's popularity sank with remarkable rapidity. Having alienated the army, Mujib now proceeded to antagonise most other groups in Bangladeshi society. After a spate of attacks on corrupt rural Awami League officials, Mujib declared a state of emergency on 28 December 1974. The power of the judiciary was reduced while press freedom was limited. A month later, Bangladesh's democratic government was in effect abolished. Mujib amended the constitution to create a presidential system and awarded himself a five-year term. Opposition parties were banned though some leftist parties were allowed to join BAKSAL (people's, peasant's and worker's party), which was Mujib's creation for a single-party state. President Abu Sayeed Chowdhury resigned in anticipation of these changes, while General Osmany, former head of the *Mukti Bahini*, and many others quit their parliamentary seats.

Mujib also launched what he termed a 'second revolution' to ensure democracy for the *sarboharas* (have nots). Appropriation of companies owned by West Pakistanis and their placement in the hands of corrupt favourites, combined with nationalisation of all major corporations led to an exodus of Bangladesh's already thin entrepreneurial class, while doing nothing to alleviate urban poverty. However, in a largely agricultural economy, mass protest was caused by Mujib's plans to introduce socialist rural collectives in direct imitation of the Soviet Union and China.

Mujib's socialist dictatorship was short-lived. On 15 August 1975, four army majors, who resented Mujib's 'private army' (the *Rakhi Bahini*) and the abolition of political parties, organised a coup d'état. Mujib's private residence was stormed and 27 members of the household including Mujib, women and children were gunned down. His house remains untouched to this day, with the blood and bone from the victims still spattering the walls. However, few in Dhaka seemed to have mourned his passing. He was survived by two daughters who escaped death by dint of being on a tour of Germany.

The scope of the coup remained limited with its main aim being the removal of Mujib. After the expulsion from office of the three senior BAKSAL politicians, the senior remaining figure, Mushtaque Ahmed, took over leadership of the government with the four majors occupying his residence. Mushtaque was western leaning and a moderate within the framework of BAKSAL politics. Although ten of Mujib's cabinet remained, they planned a return to parliamentary democracy; political activity was to be recommenced in August 1976 with a general election in February 1977. BAKSAL and the state provision of a single party would be abolished.

Perhaps most importantly, Major General Ziaur Rahman (Zia) was appointed army chief of staff. It was Zia at the start of the civil war, who had declared himself head of government on 26 March 1971, when he had launched 'Voice of Independent Bangladesh' from Chittagong where his freedom fighters had gained control; in the opening broadcast, he had announced:

> I, Major Ziaur Rahman, at the direction of *Bangobondhu* Mujibur Rahman, hereby declare that the independent People's Republic of Bangladesh has been established. At his direction, I have taken command as the temporary Head of the Republic. In the name of Sheikh Mujibur Rahman, I call upon all Bengalis to rise against the attack by the West Pakistani Army. We shall fight to the last to free our Motherland. By the grace of Allah, victory is ours. Joy Bangla'.[1]

By this act, it was later thought that Mujib was jealous of Zia and believed that the young officer had overstepped his authority, with the result that he had been overlooked as the obvious choice as chief of staff of the army.

However, there was natural discontent within the senior echelons of the army to being governed by a group of junior army majors. Some five months after the overthrow of Mujib, on 4 Nov, Brigadier Khalid Musharraf launched another coup which forced Mushtaque's resignation in favour of Chief Justice Abu Sadat Muhammad Sayem. General Zia was replaced by Brigadier Musharraf. On the day after the coup, the three BAKSAL leaders, who had been removed from office, were assassinated.

Musharraf's coup lasted all of three days. Soldiers within the Dhaka cantonment with affiliations to the far-left JSD party revolted against the Musharraf regime on 6 November. The following day, Musharraf was killed in a gun fight. Not surprising perhaps, Mushtaque, who had been removed by Musharraf, was too frightened to resume the presidency, even on a temporary basis, and he advocated that Chief Justice Sayem continue in the role to which the former coup had elevated him. Sayem now became Chief Martial Law Administrator (CMLA); the heads of the armed services were also appointed as deputy CMLAs with all ministerial positions divided between them. The deputies included General Zia, who, it seems, was very reluctantly persuaded to return to the post of chief of staff of the army.

The JSD now sought to leverage the position that the coup had brought. Their political prisoners were released and they advocated the implementation of a system of political commissars at all levels of the military command structure. Zia quickly put an end to this renewed threat from the left. JSD's leaders were re-arrested and in July 1976 its military head, the former freedom fighter Colonel Abu Taher, and progenitor of Zia's political advance, was hanged for inciting rebellion.

In what was effectively a collegiate dictatorship, Zia nevertheless emerged as its charismatic leader. He was a distinguished soldier. He had won numerous bravery awards during the Indo-Pakistan War of 1965 and had subsequently become a teacher at the Pakistan Military Academy. After returning from a course in West Germany, Zia was posted to Chittagong with the rank of major, as second in command of the 8th East Bengal Regiment, where he became a leading figure in the War of Liberation.

With the ministries of home affairs and finance within his allotted portfolio, he commanded Bangladesh's key ministries including, importantly, the police and intelligence. He travelled around the country with relentless energy and built a broad base of popularity by his imposition of law and order. By promoting on merit and ending Mujib's brand of favouritism, he may have antagonised some of the more poorly trained freedom fighters, but overall he developed a reputation for fairness and, in contrast to Mujib, a respect for law. Mujib's elite presidential guard was also merged into the regular army structure.

Stability did not come quickly. In April 1976, the majors responsible for the murder of Mujib joined with Air Vice Marshal Muhammad Ghulam Tawab in an attempted coup. Tawab was exiled. His job was difficult to fill. Tawab's replacement was killed within six months while the next incumbent, Air Vice Marshal A.G. Mahmud, was sacked in December 1978. Also, the armed services decision, in November 1976, to postpone elections, caused the nominal head of government, Chief Justice Sayem, to resign. General Zia, with the support of his service colleagues, now declared himself the new president of Bangladesh. Mushtaque, head of the Democratic League, also protested the delay in the election schedule and several of his colleagues were arrested. The following year, Mushtaque was charged with corruption during his brief tenure of office and was duly imprisoned.

Zia introduced a 19-point programme, whose main emphasis was to focus on increasing the productivity of the rural areas. In a referendum for his programme, there was an 85.5 per cent turnout of whom almost 99 per cent voted for the popular president. Zia also made a number of adjustments to the constitution; the first move was made towards recognising the central position of Islam in Bangladesh with the phrase *Bismiliah-ir-Rahmanir Rahim* (In the name of Allah, the Benificent, the merciful); in Article 25(2), a provision was inserted that the state should endeavour to consolidate, preserve and strengthen fraternal relations among Muslim countries based on Islamic solidarity. Zia also modified the constitution's socialist stance.

In spite of the changes introduced by Zia, instability within the military continued. On 30 September 1977, a mutiny broke out in Bogra; although it was quickly put down with just three people killed, another mutiny occurred in Dhaka in October. Dhaka Radio was briefly captured, and in a battle for Dhaka airport, numbers of officers were shot dead. However, an attack on Zia's own residence was successfully beaten back.

To support his programme, Zia launched a political party on 1 September 1978, the Bangladesh Nationalist Party (BNP), with himself at its head. Restrictions were also lifted on political activity in time for elections in February 1979. The BNP won a convincing majority with 207 seats out of 300, though vote rigging was widely suspected. The main opposition came from an alliance led by General Osmany that mainly comprised the Awami League. With the first session of parliament on 1 April, martial law was lifted. One of the first acts of parliament introduced by Zia was an Indemnity Bill to confer immunity on the majors, Dalim, Rashid and Faruk, who had killed Sheikh Mujib; they were also given positions in the Ministry of Foreign Affairs from where they were posted overseas. It was probably the leniency of this policy that caused Mujib's daughter to imply in later years that Zia was somehow linked and responsible for her father's assassination.

Although Zia is normally described as yet another of Bangladesh's post-war dictators, it seems likely that he was trying to stabilise the constitutional direction of the country and move towards democratic norms. How successful this would have been remains uncertain, though Zia remained a popular figure; unfortunately, on an inspection visit to Chittagong, his rule was cut short when he was assassinated by a group of soldiers led by Major General Muhammad Manzur. Manzur, a former freedom fighter, was commander of the army in Chittagong, and was due to be posted to a desk job in Dhaka; apparently, he was also disappointed to be passed over as chief of staff of the army, a job which had gone to General Ershad. However, the army remained loyal to Ershad, and Manzur was cornered and killed. In the trial of army officers that followed, many were found guilty of treason and hanged.

After the killing of Zia, Vice President Sattar became acting president and also called for a presidential election in 180 days as demanded by the constitution. Sattar won 65.5 per cent of the votes versus 26 per cent for Kamal Hossain who stood for the Awami League, which was now led by one of Mujib's surviving daughters, Sheikh Hasina Wajid. Sattar chose a politician Mirza Nurul Huda as his vice president, a move which seemingly cut the political link of the army with the Bangladeshi presidency. This was not acceptable to Lt. General Ershad, who demanded an institutional role for the army in the operation of government. Facing what appeared to be the threat of a coup, Sattar yielded to agreeing a National

Security Council on which three civilians would be represented alongside three service chiefs.

The Council was not enough for the ambitious Ershad, who deposed the government on 24 March 1982 and declared martial law. On 27 March, Ershad appointed Abul Fazal Muhammad Ahsanuddin Chowdhury as the country's new president; meanwhile, Ershad gave himself the title of 'President of the Council of Ministers', in effect an executive prime minister. Ershad was correctly seen by Bangladeshis as driven by overriding personal ambition; 'At this critical juncture of the country,' he declared, 'the patriotic armed forces had to respond to the call of the people by taking this extreme measure, for the nation had no other alternative'.[2] It was a hollow argument for his destruction of the constitution, little fortified by a personality which lacked the charisma of General Zia.

Unlike Zia's period of rule, the prisons began to fill again with political prisoners. Ershad also dismantled the village government structure implemented by Zia, seeing it as a support structure for the BNP. In its place, he created a sub-district system called *upazilla,* which he set up as a power structure to support his own party, the *Jana Dal* (People's Party), which later became the *Jatiya Party* (National Party). Ershad also decentralised the court system from Dhaka and advocated a move towards Shariah law with Arabic becoming part of the basic educational curriculum. The proposals made in December 1982 provoked demonstrations, which led to the arrest of General Zia's widow, Begum Khaleda Zia.

In between battling opposition parties, Sheikh Hasina's Awami League and Begum Zia's BNP, and the popular protests they led in a constant series of *hartal* (general strikes), Ershad carried out a far-reaching economic reconstruction. Enterprises, which had usually been turned loss-making or bankrupted by the state, were restored to their owners, and public enterprises were auctioned. Banks and financial companies were also liberated from their government yoke. Privatisation was not a policy which endeared him to the left or the trade unions, but he laid a foundation for an improvement in Bangladesh's economic performance.

Ershad finally gave in to the call for democracy from the widow, Begum Zia, and the bereaved daughter, Sheikh Hasina. Political activity was authorised again from 1 January 1986. However, Ershad's attempt to draw the opposition groups into parliamentary elections, thus legitimising his government, was initially met with refusal by both women. However, Hasina could no longer resist the temptation of power, and agreed to participate in a parliamentary election set for 7 May 1986.

However, in the first session of Parliament on 9 July 1986, Hasina and the Awami League boycotted the parliament. To further burnish his credentials as a would-be democrat, Ershad resigned as chief of army staff on 28 August 1986 and put himself up for election to the presidency on October 15. Begum Zia resolutely refused to participate while the indecisive Hasina agreed and then changed her mind. The result was a contest of Ershad against non-entities; though Ershad won 83.6 per cent of the vote, it was estimated that as little as 20 per cent of the population voted.

Dhaka now became locked in a popular struggle for control which later became known as the 'Siege of Dhaka'; by the end of 1987, Ershad's two female opponents had brought the city to a standstill. He was forced to declare a state of emergency and dissolve parliament on 6 December. New parliamentary elections were set for 3 March 1988. Believing that they now had Ershad on the run, both the BNP and the Awami League boycotted an election which brought Eshad 252 seats out of 300 for his *Jatiya Party*. Further unrest was brought by a constitutional amendment, which declared Islam to be the state religion. It was not a happy year, with 1988 seeing the worst floods on record causing thousands of deaths and creating an estimated 25 million homeless.

In July 1989, Ershad further attempted to pacify the opposition by imposing a limit of two terms on the presidency. However, by 1990, popular demonstrations in Dhaka were again on the verge of bringing the country to collapse. Begum Zia and Hasina agreed on one point alone, which was the removal of Ershad; that apart, they were wrapped in mutual loathing.

On 27 November 1990, Ershad declared the third state of emergency of his rule; however, with mounting unrest, Ershad's generals informed him that he could no longer count on their support if he could not bring peace to the streets. Although Ershad offered a new round of parliamentary and presidential elections in June 1991, his offer was swiftly declined. Ershad had no choice but to resign on 4 December. Collectively the opposition parties agreed on the nomination of Chief Justice Shababuddin Ahmed as acting president. In a vengeful act characteristic of Bengali politics, Ershad and his wife were arrested a week after his resignation.

Parliamentary elections run in March 1991 were contested around the personalities of the leaders of the BNP and the Awami League. The main subtext of Sheikh Hasina's campaign as head of the Awami League was to achieve revenge for her father by bringing his assassins to trial. This apart, the main differentiation with the BNP campaign was Hasina's call for a return to a parliamentary system – curiously, the one which her father had abolished on his way to creating a one-party dictatorship.

For the BNP, Begum Zia referred little to her murdered husband and focussed on a pragmatic nationalist approach with an expressed desire to continue the privatisation policies of Ershad. The electoral distribution favoured the BNP: with 31 per cent of the popular vote, they won 140 out of 300 seats, while the Awami League, with just 0.4 per cent less of the popular vote, won just 88 seats; even with Ershad in prison, his *Jatiya* Party won 35 seats. The closeness of the vote persuaded Begum Zia that she might be wise to agree to Hasina's wish to revert to a parliamentary system. In a rare spirit of co-operation, the two leaders set up a Joint Select Committee to agree the required constitutional amendment bills which needed their joint vote to achieve a two-thirds majority. With the change in the constitution, Begum Zia became prime minister on 6 August 1991.

The first crisis faced by Begum Zia was a devasting cyclone which swept in from the Bay of Bengal with 20 feet high waves killing an estimated 138,000 people, causing US$ 2.5 billion worth of damage and leaving 10 million people homeless (albeit smaller than the 1970 cyclone which killed an estimated 500,000 people). Much to the annoyance of the opposition, United States Marines, on their way back from victory over Saddam Hussein in the 'Desert Storm' campaign, were diverted to provide help in dealing with the catastrophe.

Begum Zia also pushed forward Bangladesh's economic revitalisation by pursuing radical deregulation and internationalisation policies. The government lifted some restrictions on foreign exchange and initiated tax exemptions for exporters. New foreign direct investment laws for the first time allowed 100 per cent ownership of Bangladeshi companies by foreign investors. Perhaps most importantly, the capital markets were deregulated allowing for the first time a foreign investment bank, Peregrine Securities, to open a business in the country and initiate a transformation of the country's stock market and its ability to raise risk capital.

Peregrine Bangladesh, led by Runa Alam, a repatriate and fortunate child survivor of the infamous massacre of the intellectuals by Pakistan's army in the War of Liberation, also began to help Bangladesh market itself internationally as an opportunity for foreign direct investment. By abandoning the United Nations approach of selling itself as a 'basket case' to garner international aid, Bangladesh, for the first time, began to show itself as a business opportunity. It was an approach that looked to the Asian model. Begum Zia's administration was a key turning point in the abandonment of socialistic economic policy, which had dominated Bangladesh since independence. For a woman who had been a quiet housewife prior to the death of her husband, Begum Zia's transformation of attitudes in Bangladesh was a remarkable achievement. At last, Bangladesh began to unravel a future from its bloody start as an independent nation, and enter the modern age.

49

Cory Aquino and the Rocky Path to Democracy

Philippines: 1986–2000

As a political figure, Corazón Aquino was a dramatic and essential symbol of the Filipino desire for democracy and freedom from tyranny; as a leader she was little better than a twittering housewife. After the murder of her husband, 'Cory' naturally became the figurehead of resistance to Marcos. Problems with her lack of intellectual ability and political aptitude soon became apparent. As de facto leader of the Filipino opposition, she accepted an interview with *The New York Times* and was faced with questions from hard-bitten hacks, A.M. Rosenthal, Seth Mydans and Warren Hoge. Her performance was completely inept. After the meeting, Hoge noted that 'Abe [Rosenthal] and I were pretty much stunned . . . both of us walked out of there thinking we could not remember talking to a public figure more naïve about the responsibilities and abuses of power.'[1]

Her muddled answers regarding her attitude to communism and the future of the US military bases displayed particular stupidity. On his return to the USA, Abe Rosenthal went to a White House dinner, where he informed President Reagan that Cory Aquino was an 'empty-headed housewife [with] no positions.'[2]

Such was the alarm among her American friends that they hurriedly hired the Democrat's public relations firm, DH Sawyer & Associates. They constructed a script which aligned her political views with those that were acceptable to the broad spectrum of American political opinion: hostility to communism and continued support for the US military bases. In other words they did enough to prevent America taking an 'over-my-dead-body' position on the fall of Marcos and his replacement by Corazón Aquino. However, the augers for a productive Aquino presidency were not good.

Though frequently described as a 'revolution' in the international media, the fall of Marcos heralded a return to the oligopolistic rule of the landed families. Amando Doronila, a columnist and chairman of the editorial board of *The Manila Chronicle*, described the Aquino revolution as a 're-feudalisation,' in which 'the return to political warlordism or tribal politics dominated by the family dynasties foreshadows the reassertion of the oligarchical tendencies in Philippine politics'; furthermore the revolution had 'no ideological motivation to change the social and power structure; it merely sought to change rulers without restructuring society'.[3]

While it was a blessing that Cory Aquino did not implement any ideological programme to restructure Philippine society, which was the bane of so many post-war Asian economies, she was wholly unprepared and incapable of managing a government that could transform her backward country. Not reverting to a socialist command economy was perhaps the major, and not unimportant, achievement of her administration. However, for Cory the restoration of democracy was her central task and the only one of which she was capable.

Cory Aquino's first act was to appoint a constitutional commission with 48 delegates. They produced a 100-page draft constitution which was closely modelled on that of 1935. It included a bill of rights and, importantly for the Philippines, economic future, emphasised the rights to ownership of private property under law, which Marcos had done so much to undermine. In light of the corruption of the judicial system, 15 new justices were elevated to the bench.

Aquino also appointed a 'Presidential Commission for Good Government'. Although its supposed task was to track down the monies purloined by Marcos and his cronies, the commission proved spectacularly unequal to the challenge, and only US$ 160 million of the suspected billions was ever returned. Courts appeared reluctant to pursue the Marcos family with any vigour. Indeed in 2001, Amy Marcos, breezed into her law class in London to announce that they had just won back US$ 800 million. However, government ministries were purged of known Marcos cronies, and local government was similarly cleaned up. In the vacuum thus created, there followed an unseemly scramble to control patronage by Laurel's Unido Party and Pimentel's Laban.

In a broad attempt at national reconciliation, Aquino released 500 political prisoners. As a result, the communist NPA agreed to a ceasefire. The Moro National Liberation Front in Mindanao also accepted a truce. With regard to the army, Aquino took the opportunity presented by Marcos's flight to carry out a wide-reaching purge; 24 out of 36 generals were retired.

Meanwhile the 'heroes' of the recent revolution, Enrile and Ramos, resumed their bitter competition. Enrile found himself increasingly isolated, not just for the riches that he had accumulated as a former Marcos crony, but because Aquino increasingly relied on the support of Ramos. In spite of the changes, Aquino's relationship with the army remained uneasy. Predictably a probe into army graft was unpopular, as was Aquino's appointment of left-wing advisers including 'Bobbit' Sanchez, who became labour minister, and Joker Arroyo.

July 1986 saw the first of many coup attempts. Marcos's vice presidential candidate in the 1986 elections, Arturo Tolentino, with a few hundred troops, seized the Manila Hotel and proclaimed his presidency. The coup turned into a bloodless farce when the troops ended their revolt after three days and, as a punishment, were made to do press-ups before being sent back to barracks.

More seriously, Enrile became a hostile presence when he criticised Aquino's presidency and was replaced by General Rafael Ileto. After Aquino's 'honeymoon' period, agricultural unrest also surfaced on 22 January, when the Farmer's Movement of the Philippines led a march to Malacanang Palace. When the ensuing demonstration turned violent, some 19 people were killed and 100 wounded. Although the plebiscite for the new constitution was passed overwhelmingly, the prospects for stability were marred by the fact that the army, the major potential source of instability and a significant loser in the fall of Marcos, voted against it. With the demise of a strongly centralised military regime, local insurgency and 'warlordism' tended to re-emerge.

A growing number of assassinations, including that of American Colonel James Rowe, an insurgency advisor, were a sign of growing social and political chaos. A second more serious coup was attempted by Colonel Gregorio Honasan, who led the Philippine Military Academy in an attack on the presidential palace; the assault, repelled by the presidential guard, cost 53 lives. Aquino's son was also injured. Finally recognising that she was in a fight for survival, Aquino dumped her remaining left-wing advisors including Joker Arroyo. The military was purged again, and a 60 per cent pay rise for the army was used to palliate simmering discontent.

Aquino's softer approach had little impact. Another revolt took place on 1 December 1989, led by 3,000 elite Filipino troops, including the Scout Rangers. Eight days of fighting ensued. While refusing actively to intervene, President Bush (senior) showed America's hand by using American Air Force jets to patrol the skies above Manila.

Honasan was again behind the coup, which was probably financed by former Marcos associate, billionaire Eduardo Cojuangco, who was also Cory's relation. In April 1990, there was yet another cull of 40 army officers including 20 generals. Yet Honasan, apparently protected by the military, remained at large and was able to conduct television interviews with CNN and others. Overseas, Vice President Salvador Laurel, smelling the possibility of personal advancement, greeted the coup attempt as an act of 'democracy in its fullest and complete sense'[4] and made it clear that he was prepared to serve as prime minister under a military government.

Cory's attempt to re-establish her own credibility backfired when she arrested Enrile in February 1990. Having been comfortably secured in especially prepared rooms at a military base, the Supreme Court released him on just US$ 3,500 bail. The charges of rebellion and murder were a ham-fisted attempt to remove the threat of Enrile as an alternative political power. Once freed, he proclaimed his innocence from trumped-up charges and ironically likened his persecution to that of Benigno Aquino. A final coup attempt against Aquino took place on 6 October 1990 when a former bodyguard to Marcos, Colonel Alexander Noble, declared independence for Mindanao, another example of 'Opera bouffe',[5] as *The Economist* described Filipino public life.

In spite of the chaotic progress of Cory's government, the mere removal of Marcos unleashed a powerful economic rebound. Real GDP grew by 5.9 per cent in 1987 and a further 9 per cent in 1988. However, the economy fell by 3 per cent in 1989, and it became apparent that there were serious structural impediments to growth, in particular the lack of electric power.

President Marcos's decision to build a nuclear power project, in a volcanically susceptible area, meant that an effectively mothballed plant was costing the insolvent Filipino government US$ 355,000 per day. Economic management was amateur. For a visiting financier, a richly furnished Central Bank, whose reception sported a sign reading *'Leave handguns at reception'*[6], was unable to furnish monthly external capital flow figures until a secretary appeared with a mechanical adding machine; the financier, while waiting for the sums to be completed, was however rewarded by the governor of the Central Bank of the Philippines with a feast of sandwiches and snacks while he waited. Fortunately, the IMF was only too willing to provide generous help to the post-Marcos government.

With a largely agrarian population growing at close to 3 per cent per annum, and a Manila population of 10 million out of a 65 million Filipino population by the early 1990s, most international agencies saw land reform as critical. The lack of land reform, in a country where most estates were owned by absentee landlords, had long been highlighted as a root cause of social and economic malaise. Solita Monsod, the minister of economic planning, was tasked with setting out a sweeping agrarian reform package.

However, the Comprehensive Agrarian Reform Law of 1988 watered down a proposal for forced distribution of 11.1 million hectares. This was reduced to 3.5 million hectares, while beneficiaries were reduced from 3 million to 2 million farmers. However, with a price tag of US$ 70 billion over 10 years, even these reduced targets were wholly unrealistic. Perhaps fortunately for the Philippines, the programme was delayed by disputes, court hearings and scandals; little land ended up being transferred.

Far more important to the future prosperity of the Philippines was the setting of conditions for foreign capital investment. In this respect, political instability and a failure to address the structural impediments to investment, including basic infrastructure, were not helpful. Coup d'états eviscerated the tourist industry on which the Philippine economy was highly dependent, while companies such as Sony were forced to delay projected capital projects. The Philippines' most successful export was people. Indeed, remittances from the extensive Filipino diaspora became a vital crutch to the economy.

Aquino's relations with the USA remained frosty. Reagan was not unnaturally suspicious of the left-leaning Filipino leader. The failure of Reagan to make a stop in the Philippines, after a visit to Sukarno in Indonesia, was rightly interpreted as a snub. In spite of anti-American feelings, on the part of both Filipinos and their president, Aquino's need for American support was pressing. In October 1988, the government had reached an interim agreement with the USA on the continued lease of Clark Field, Subic Bay and the Crow Valley Range Complex, which allowed a 300-square-mile bombing run; the provisional fee agreed was some US$ 480 million per annum, against a previous price of US$ 180 million, though considerably less than the asked for US$ 1.2 billion. Not only was this a considerable income source for the government, but, with the US armed forces being the second largest employer in the Philippines, America's Pacific bases accounted for some 3 per cent of GDP. However, taking petty revenge, Cory Aquino delayed negotiations and snubbed Secretary of Defence Dick Cheney, by refusing to meet him during an Asian tour in February 1990.

The delay was costly. The massive eruption of Mount Pinatubo wiped out Clark Field and rendered Crow Valley useless. At the same time as US forces were being forced to evacuate, the collapsing Soviet Empire suggested that the enemy bases at Cam Ranh Bay and Da Nang might not be sustainable. The needs of the US Pacific Basin defence were now up for reassessment.

A new offer of US$ 203 million for the Philippines Subic Bay was now viewed as a humiliation. In the Philippines Senate, the projected new treaty was voted down. Aquino's brother-in-law described it as a 'vote for a truly sovereign and independent Filipino nation . . . a vote to end a political adolescence tied to the purse-strings of America, a crippling dependence'.[7] Albeit unhappy at the outcome, America prepared a complete withdrawal of its forces; for the first time in nearly 100 years, the Philippines would be free of American forces on its soil; for the first time in 350 years, there would be no foreign army stationed in the Philippines.

With Aquino having used up the credit gained from the overthrow of President Marcos, she wisely decided to bow out of her office, her main contribution to Philippines politics having been the not inconsiderable achievement of passing over intact a democratic political system and a free market economy. In reality however, little had changed from the failed post-war period. As Cardinal Sin complained of Aquino's term in office, 'the old politics has come back to dismay us all_ the positioning for power, the corruption, the grandstanding, the influence peddling, the petty bickering.'[8]

The spotlight on corruption even turned its attention to Aquino's Commission for Good Government. While Cory herself remained clean, her brother-in-law was accused of gaining from Marcos's sequestered assets, and her own brother and his wife were also accused of using their connections to take control of gambling interests.

In 1992, some 17,205 electoral posts came up for election including the presidency, 24 senators, 73 governors and 200 Congressmen. Some of the major figures from the Philippines' darker past re-emerged to hold themselves up for re-election. Eduardo Cojuangco, the country's leading business tycoon, having re-gained control of the major brewing company, San Miguel, made a presidential bid; Enrile put himself forward for the senate; Vice President Salvador Laurel ran for the old 'right wing' Nationalist Party.

An anti-corruption judge and former government minister, Miriam Defen-sor Santiago, stood on a populist anti-corruption ticket. Jovita Salonga, a political prisoner under Marcos, headed the Liberal Party, with Pimental as his vice presi-dential candidate. Ramon Mitra became leader of the Liberal Democratic Party having defeated General Fidel Ramos. Ramos immediately formed his own party, Lakas. Most bizarrely, Imelda Marcos returned from exile in a hired Boeing 747 and declared that in spite of her 'impoverishment', she would stand for president as head of a newly established Truth and Beauty Party. From this smorgasbord of candidates, General Ramos, who had staunchly supported Aquino, both in oppo-sition and throughout her government, was a convincing winner with 24 per cent of the presidential vote. The relatively unknown Miriam Santiago was runner-up. However, former film actor Senator Joseph Estrada, who ran as vice presidential candidate on the Cojuangco ticket, won the vice presidential race.

Ramos was sworn into office on 30 June 1992. Perhaps the most competent and successful of the Philippines' post-war presidents, Ramos was known for being a steady and moderate figure. He was from a typical 'Ilustrado' family. His father was a Congressman in 1946, who would later become foreign minister, while his sister Leticia Ramos Shahani became a senator and head of the Foreign Affairs Committee.

Fidel Ramos himself was educated with the Philippine military elite and was sent to West Point. He became chief of the Philippine Constabulary before Marcos's declaration of martial law. In the closely knit world of the Filipino elite, he was un-usual for being a protestant. Typical of the family-dominated world of Filipino pol-itics however, he could lay claim to being a second cousin of Marcos. Nevertheless, he maintained a reputation for incorruptibility.

Ramos inherited serious economic problems dating from the Marcos era, which Cory Aquino not only had been unable to solve, but had also exacerbated. Shortage of power was crippling the Philippines. 'Brown outs' – interruptions to electricity provision – would often last for 10 hours at a stretch. The country became dependant on noisy diesel generator sets. Ramos took the difficult but ap-propriate decision to abandon the disastrous US$ 2.2 billion Westinghouse nuclear project. He then proved his liberal economic credentials by lifting currency con-trols and creating attractive conditions for foreign direct investment, a move which would enable a rapid development of power generation facilities.

Perhaps most importantly for the economy and future of the Philippines, he created a climate of political stability. Unlike Cory, Ramos commanded respect as a leader; the vacillations, petty squabbles and ineptitude of the Cory presidency were put aside. Essentially he also commanded the respect of the army. Soon after taking office, Lee Kuan Yew of Singapore told Ramos that 'what a country needs to develop is discipline rather than democracy . . . the exuberance of democracy leads to undisciplined and disorderly conditions which are inimical to development'.[9]

There were limits to what Ramos could do about democracy, but he nevertheless took a firm and pragmatic approach to solving the Philippines' political instability. Ramos's call on Congress to lift a 35-year ban on the Communist Party was not interpreted as a move towards a left-wing social and economic agenda. The extreme left's justification for military activity was further undermined in August 1992, by the arrest of the Maoist New People's Army (NPA) commander Romulo Kintanar and his wife, while they were undergoing plastic surgery, for purposes of disguise. Ramos, a man of the moderate right, was equally successful in bringing the rebellious extreme right to heel. On 23 December the serial leader of right-wing coup attempts, Honasan, was forced to sign a ceasefire on behalf of his paramilitary supporters.

Although Ramos's six-year term ended with the taint of corruption, the repercussions of the Asian Economic Crisis and suspicions about his ambition to extend his presidency by amending the constitution to allow for a second term, he nevertheless bowed to popular protest and left office in 1998 as perhaps the most successful of the Philippines' post-war presidents. Importantly his presidency brought a degree of normalcy to the political system and the Philippine economy.

50

Deng Xiaoping: 'Capitalist Roader No. 2'

China: 1974–96

When Deng Xiaoping arrived in New York in April 1974 as part of the Chinese delegation to the United Nations General Assembly, Henry Kissinger ignored him. The official head of the delegation was Foreign Minister Qiao Guanhua, and it was assumed that Deng's interests were primarily economic. In his memoir, *Years of Renewal* (1999), Dr Kissinger recalls that a week after his arrival he invited Deng to dinner with his delegation only to discover the shocking truth, that, not only was Deng 'the real head of the Chinese delegation', but that 'far from having been restored to ease Zhou's burden, Deng's assignment was, in fact, to replace him'.[1]

Deng did not immediately impress. He stuck closely to the specifics of Mao's brief and appeared almost as if he were on a 'training mission'. As Kissinger concludes, 'none of us considered Deng as a major, much less a seminal, figure'.[2] In this case, first appearances were deceptive. In the history of the twentieth century, there are few individuals who have contributed more to the material welfare of their country than Deng Xiaoping; Mao may have been a great revolutionary but it was Deng who was China's great modern nation builder.

Yet as the introduction to Henry Kissinger implies, Deng was not an obvious figure. Compared to Mao, little is known about his life, and his character remains somewhat of a mystery. Born in 1904, Deng's family had been village elders in Northern Sichuan since the eighteenth century. His father, with just 13 acres of land, was a landowner respectable enough to be on friendly terms with Yang Sen, one of Sichuan's three warlords. Deng's father suffered a macabre death in 1940, when, returning from pilgrimage, he was set upon and decapitated; his body was also chopped in half.

By then, Deng was already a 'Long Marcher', and a rising revolutionary figure. Deng Xiaoping had been taken to France by his uncle in 1920, and there, like many immigrants before him, including Zhou Enlai, Hồ Chí Minh and Pol Pot, became interested in revolutionary ideology. As well as working as a labourer for Creusot Iron and Steel and then at a Renault Auto Plant, Deng met Zhou Enlai, who was living in Paris, and even shared his apartment.

At just over 5 feet in height, Deng would not have been anybody's idea of a military hero. However, it was as a military commissar in the Taihang region during the Civil War against the nationalists that Deng came to prominence. After serving as a regional military commissar in South West China, where he had built a formidable reputation as an administrator in the post-war period, Deng was relocated to Beijing on Mao's orders in 1952. Such was Mao's regard for Deng's abilities that he was almost unique in being fast tracked to the upper echelons of the party in the early 1950s. In 1954, he was promoted to secretary general of the party and among the leadership ranked behind only Liu Shaoqi and Zhou Enlai. At this period, there can be little doubt that Deng Xiaoping shared the ideological vision of his mentor.

When Mao went to Moscow in November 1957 for the 40th anniversary of the Bolshevik Revolution, Deng was charged with leading the delegation responsible for ideological issues and was ferocious in his attack on the Soviet line. When Russia's renowned theoretician, Suslov, was put to flight over the construction of a *Unity Manifesto*, Mao's delight with the feisty Deng led him to boast extravagantly to Khrushchev about the virtues of his 'little' general. Throughout his career, Mao would appreciate and use Deng's management skills as well as his forthright intelligence. 'Deng is a rare and talented man,' Mao once remarked, 'he finds solutions. He deals with difficult problems responsibly'.[3] It was Mao's personal regard for Deng that almost certainly spared him death during the Cultural Revolution.

Deng's daughter described him as laconic, good hearted and a lover of food and football. He was also somewhat introverted. Above all, he remained optimistic in the face of adversity. This latter quality must have come in useful after being twice purged by Mao. Less well known is that Deng was also imprisoned and tortured during an internecine battle within the Communist Party in 1933. The political attack was led by Li Weihan. It is a curiosity that when Deng's wife, Jin Wiying, then divorced him to marry Li Weihan, Deng appeared not to bear him any grudge. In later years, he continued to work amicably with Li, and he even took up Li's son as his protégé. This extreme example of Deng's forbearance shows him in marked contrast to Mao; Deng's rule was marked by a lack of the arbitrary personal cruelty that became such a feature of Mao's regime. Apart from his hatred of Jiang Qing and the extremists of the left, Deng, in spite of a sometimes quick and caustic tongue, enjoyed cordial and easy relations with his senior colleagues.

After the death in childbirth of his first wife, and divorce from the second, Deng's next attempt was unusually successful. Rare among the leadership, he became a devoted husband and family man and was constantly photographed among them. Also he lived modestly. He disliked the government compound of Zhongnanhai, where 'Deng had never forgiven the Central Garrison for not protecting him during the Cultural Revolution'[4] and chose to live in a modest residence where his chief luxury was a large conference room, which doubled as a home cinema.

Mao may have liked classical poetry, but Deng Xiaoping preferred 'shoot-em-up' Hollywood action movies such as *Rambo: First Blood Part II* (1982), starring Sylvester Stallone. Other pastimes included bridge, which he played regularly with his senior colleagues including Hu Yaobang. Deng's modesty also extended to his position as leader. He refused to take on senior titles, and unlike Mao and Hua Guofeng, he ordered that his picture should not be displayed in public. Statues too were forbidden. Neither did he give himself honorific titles such as 'wise leader' or 'great leader'. Again unlike Mao, there is no evidence that Deng's supreme power led to an intellectual or moral degeneration.

Although he came to power at the advanced age of 73, the tiny figure of Deng imparted energy, intelligence and power. Philosopher, Dr Simon May, formerly an advisor to former British Prime Minister Edward Heath in the early 1980s, and a member of the cabinets of European commissioners Christopher Tugendhat and Jacques Delors, met Deng Xiaoping on two occasions and described him as a 'compelling presence' when he entered a room. With foreigners he also developed a laconic wit. In 1986, he thanked Queen Elizabeth of England for coming such a long way to see an 'old Chinese man'.[5]

On coming to America in January 1979, Deng's wit and charm conquered all before him. When discussing China's 'Most Favoured Nation' trade access to US markets with American political leaders, he drew laughter when he commented on the Jackson–Vanik amendment that denied status to countries that did not permit free emigration. 'This is no problem to us. But do you really want 10 million Chinese?'[6]

On the same visit, Jimmy Carter took Deng to the Kennedy Centre Opera House to listen to American music and watch the Harlem Globetrotters. Deng went on stage and charmed audience and performers in such a way that Walter Mondale admitted, 'It is a good thing you're not an American citizen, because you'd be elected to any office you sought.'[7] Also the TV projection of the diminutive, beaming Deng Xiaoping, wearing a cowboy hat at a Texan barbecue, was guaranteed to endear him to an American audience. In effect, Deng reconnected China with that special relationship enjoyed with the USA, which had existed before the Second World War.

Deng Xiaoping's performance for the Americans was not without stratagem. Normalisation of relations with the USA lay at the heart of his plans for China's future. Although there can be seen here some continuity with the process initiated between Nixon–Kissinger and Mao–Zhou Enlai at the time of the Shanghai Communiqué, there were in fact substantial differences of intention on the part of China's new leader. Mao's differences with the Soviet Union were ideological in that he disdained Stalin's successors for pursuing an anti-revolutionary 'revisionist' line; this was also entwined with fears that the Soviet Union might wish to exercise a degree of sovereign control over China, as expressed in the Brezhnev Doctrine. By contrast, Deng was more pragmatist than 'revisionist', and had been painted as such with the epithet 'Capitalist Roader No. 2', at the time of his purge during the Cultural Revolution. In 1979, Deng's hostility to the Soviets was both geopolitical and ideological but the underpinnings of his rapprochement with America were economic.

In the immediate aftermath of Mao's death, Hua had pursued a policy of hostility to the Soviets but had done little to advance the process of normalisation with the USA. America too had been impeded in its development of the Chinese relationship by the 'Watergate' years that brought Nixon's resignation from office, and which was followed by a truncated single-term Ford administration. President Carter's first attempt to reinvigorate relations with China was a complete failure. Secretary of State Cyrus Vance visited China on 21 August 1977, only to be greeted with a lukewarm reception. At the obligatory banquet not a single politburo member attended. Hua Guofeng was abrupt on the issue of Taiwan: 'Taiwan province is China's sacred province. We are determined to liberate Taiwan. When and how is entirely an internal affair of China, which brooks no foreign interference whatsoever.'[8] In part, the failure was due to Vance's own lukewarm attitude to China, but Hua, with his stiff Maoist orthodoxy, was also not best suited to engaging the USA.

Carter's second attempt was more successful. Washington let it be known that the USA was willing to accede to China's demand that Taiwan should cease to be recognised diplomatically. Also, National Security Advisor Brzezinski, who visited China in May 78, wholly endorsed the Nixon–Kissinger rapprochement strategy. Brzezinski declared that the USA shared China's resolve to 'resist the efforts of any nation which seeks to establish global or regional hegemony . . . neither of us dispatches international marauders who masquerade as non-aligned to advance big power ambitions'.[9] His hosts described the visit as 'two steps forward'. Although less heralded than the Nixon-Kissinger Shanghai Communiqué, which dramatically announced to the world the rapprochement with communist China, President Carter's development of the China relationship was a triumph for which he has received little credit.

The success must in part have come from the re-emergence and strengthening hand of Deng who, a few months after Brzezinski's visit, let it be known that he wished to visit the USA. With just a few hours notice given to Taiwan, Carter announced 'normalisation' of relations with China on 15 December. Diplomatic relations commenced on 1 January 1979, and Deng arrived for his celebrated visit at the end of the month. Deng's hand is evident in the speed at which the 'normalisation' process was accomplished and, although it was another year before Hua was completely sidelined, Deng clearly arrived in the USA as China's leader in waiting.

Deng's ambitions with regard to 'normalisation' were clearly geopolitical and when he spoke at President Carter's White House dinner reception, he took the opportunity for lavish swipes at the Soviets, much to his host's discomfort. As early as his meetings with Kissinger in 1974, he had expressed concern at America's geopolitical overextension; Deng described it as having 'ten fleas under ten fingers'.[10] He told the Yugoslav ambassador that 'The Americans are Bastards . . . But they are honest bastards. The Russians are also liars.'[11] In 1979, fear of Soviet encirclement in Asia was still uppermost in his thoughts. Eisenhower's concern of the 1950s that 'What is now the back door may become the front door' would similarly describe Deng's own fears, particularly with regard to Vietnam, which the Soviets had wooed with a military alliance signed in November 1978.[12] However, there was another element to his wooing of America and one that tends to be understated. Deng wanted American technology and investment. In the pantomime of government foreign visits, as much as their words, leaders send signals by their actions and visits. Deng took time to go to a Ford auto plant, a Hughes tool company and the Johnson Space Center. Agreements were signed on science and technology as well as cultural and consular exchanges. It was the economic sphere that lay at the heart of Deng's plans for China's future.

For Deng, the whole point of socialism was to increase people's living standards. His practice of communism was not of the utopian genre; for him, it was simply the practical means by which one could raise production and eliminate poverty. This was a long way from the utopian purity demanded by Mao. Deng would have understood the cynicism of the peasant who said 'In socialism all is well, even if there is nothing to eat.'[13] Deng's version of socialism was different; as he explained to the premier of Czechoslovakia in 1987 'To build socialism it is necessary to develop the productive forces. Poverty is not socialism.'[14]

However for Deng, unadulterated 'capitalism' was not an alternative for China because he believed that it could only enrich a small minority. Perhaps reflecting his French education, his approach to economics was of the European-style mercantilist, or 'fixed cake' approach to economic prosperity. In April 1987, he told a visiting Spanish socialist:

> The problem we have to solve is how to enable our one billion people to cast off poverty and become prosperous. If we adopted the capitalist system in China, probably fewer than 10% of the population would be enriched, while over 90% would remain in a permanent state of poverty.[15]

Deng's methods, having grown out of the hard school of military necessity during his years with the 129th Division in the Civil War, were practical not theoretical. He loathed the theocratic purity of material relativism, which led Jiang Qing and the ultra-left to declare that the student who left his exam papers blank was a hero of the revolution. To Deng this was foolish nonsense. Hard work, hierarchy, management, competence, skill and reward were concepts that he sought to reintroduce into Chinese society.

After the catastrophe of the Great Leap Forward, Deng, along with Liu Shaoqi, Chen Yun, Zhou and other leaders, had sought to bring about a pragmatic approach to economic management. At the end of June 1962, Deng was reported as saying at the Central Committee Secretariat, 'It doesn't matter if a cat is black or white, as long as it catches the mouse it is a good cat.'[16] The old Sichuanese 'Cat' saying became permanently associated with Deng's pragmatic brand of economic reform.

588 EMPIRES AT WAR

For Deng, the USA was just such a 'cat'. Indeed, American–Chinese trade grew rapidly from US$ 1.189 billion in 1978 to US$ 13.5 billion in 1988. Exports to the USA grew from a miniscule US$ 600,000 in 1979 to US$ 25.7 billion in 1992. Trade with America's ally Japan also increased rapidly with Chinese imports, particularly of machine tools and manufacturing equipment, growing from US$ 3.6 billion in 1979 to US$ 12.0 billion in 1992.

From small beginnings, the rate of foreign investment in China also began to grow. By 1983, there were 188 foreign equity investments and 1,047 contractual joint ventures, and US$ 2.3 billion of foreign capital had been brought into China out of US$ 6.6 billion committed. Even the White House began to take note. Ronald Reagan recalled that in March 1984 'Treasury Secretary [Regan] had come back from a trip to Beijing with an intriguing report: The People's Republic of China was moving slowly but surely toward acceptance of a free enterprise market, and inviting investment by foreign capitalists.'[17]

Landmark deals included the Great Wall Hotel in Beijing, the incorporation of the Beijing Jeep Company and an oil project funded by Atlantic Richfield. By the early 1990s, inward foreign investment commitments to China were running at more than US$ 30 billion per annum.

While Deng's 'open door' policy to America and the capitalist world was an important plank in his transformation of China, it was his domestic reforms that enabled the country to profit from his international strategies. To the four modernisations, of agriculture, industry, science and technology, were added a fifth goal, namely defence. These goals were written into the party constitution at the 11th Congress in 1977, and then into the state constitution at the Fifth National People's Congress in 1978. When asked by Japanese Prime Minister Masayoshi Ohira, 'What is the aim of your four modernizations?'[18] Deng's answer was characteristically to the point. China had to quadruple China's GNP to US$ 1 trillion by the year 2000. Likewise, per capita income had to rise to US$ 1,000.

Agriculture was the first part of the economy to be addressed. It was no secret that the commune system much beloved by Mao and the ultra-left had been an abject failure. As Standing Committee member Li Xiannian told a foreign visitor, 'Under collectivization the peasants simply downed tools and turned their bottoms to the sun.'[19] Harking back to the much criticised experiments in 'household responsibility' in Anhui Province in the early 1960s, Deng introduced a semi-privatised production system, and by 1984 it covered 98 per cent of the country. At first, assignment of land was short term, but later 15-year leases were offered. In 1987, sale of land usage rights was also permitted. Growth in the agricultural sector was spectacular, with a 49 per cent aggregate rise in production between 1978 and 1984.

An industrial responsibility system was also introduced in 1978, whereby profits could be retained for bonuses and investment. 6,600 companies had been moved to this system by 1980, and all state companies were transferred by 1982.

Managers were also incentivised with four-year contracts that could be renewed depending on performance. The introduction of corporate taxation at 55 per cent in 1983 was an innovation that enabled managers to plan investment.

Also, Deng sought to produce efficiencies of scale by the amalgamation of some 42,000 enterprises between 1982 and 1985. However, it was the green light to private enterprise that did most to develop an economic growth rate unparalleled in Chinese history. While the improvements in the state-owned sector enjoyed mixed success, private-owned businesses grew dramatically. Their number rose from just 100,000 in 1978 to 17 million in 1985.

In addition to the measures to deregulate the economy, Deng also sponsored the drive to develop special economic zones (SEZs) after they were suggested at the Central Work Conference in April 1979. At first, these were set up in Guangdong and Fujian provinces adjacent to Hong Kong and Taiwan. By 1984, there were 5 SEZs, and after touring these regions he authorised the setting up of a further 14. With special tax incentives and employment regulations, the SEZs were set up to act as magnets to foreign investment, particularly from the industrialists of China's Asian diaspora. In spite of the high levels of corruption that came to light in these areas, they succeeded spectacularly in attracting Chinese expatriate capital investment.

Gradual experiments in deregulation of prices also began the process of bringing rationality to spending and investment. Fixed capital formation grew at a staggering 42.8 per cent in 1985, and throughout the decade capital investment was exceptionally high even by the standards of the other fast-growing Asian economies. As early as 1983, foreign exchange reserves reached US$ 20 billion exceeding those of the United Kingdom. More importantly, from Deng's point of view living standards rose rapidly. Consumer items such as washing machines, refrigerators and televisions now flooded the country. Consumption of foods rarely eaten in the average diet, such as chicken, rose rapidly. Sale of cooking oils also increased at a double-digit rate throughout the decade. The famines, which had characterised 2,000 years of Chinese history, were brought to an end. For many Chinese, alleviation of this fear alone was the ultimate luxury.

In the 1980s, economic success became self-fulfilling but frequently led to excessive expectations from investors and consumers alike. Investment booms were followed by dramatic crashes. De-control of prices was highly productive for farmers but brought inflation difficulties for urban workers. The path from a command economy system to what Deng described as 'market socialism' was fraught with difficulties. Enthusiasm for money making transformed Chinese culture. Businessmen were the new heroes. Remarkably, the autobiography of Lee Iacocca, the charismatic chairman of Chrysler, became a best-selling book in China in 1987. However, dealings with foreign investors were complicated by the lack of a common commercial language. State bureaucrats brought up on 'quotas and output targets', did not commonly understand concepts such as 'profit', 'return on capital' or 'depreciation'. The enthusiasm for change often rode ahead of the expertise required to achieve it.

A British investor on an exploratory visit to Shanghai to research the opening of Chinese capital markets in 1988, was hosted to a banquet by the deputy mayor of Shanghai, where he was loaded with heavy bundles of computer printouts listing local state-owned companies 'for sale'. These loss-making 'no hopers' were as unappetising as the furry brown sea slugs offered for dinner. However, for the visiting businessman, there was no doubting the infectious appetite for entrepreneurial activity that permeated all walks of life. As a Beijing law graduate doing a doctorate at Nuffield College Oxford noted, after the appalling experience of communism, 'there are no real communists in China. You can only find them at Oxford and Cambridge'.[20] The Chinese student had been shocked to end up arguing the capitalist cause against his socialist Oxford tutors.

Through the process of change it has to be asked: Did Deng really continue to believe in socialism? Or was socialism, as Kissinger describes it, a formal liturgy that allowed Deng to abandon all the rest? Evidence is hard to produce. Above all, Deng was a pragmatist as displayed in one of his favourite sayings, 'Cross the river by feeling the stones.'[21] What is clear, however, is that Deng, the hard-line Marxist follower of Mao of the early post-war period, was clearly showing signs of change in the early 1960s, as the leadership set about implementing reforms to correct the damage done by the 'Great Leap Forward'.

The scale of this human tragedy, which by some estimates cost 40 million lives, and which was caused by the forced introduction of the commune collective system of agriculture, must have had an enormous impact on the feelings and beliefs of all but the most hard hearted of revolutionaries. Deng, the tender-hearted family man, was unlikely to have been unmoved by this calamity. It is noticeable that among the first people to be rehabilitated by Deng, albeit posthumously, was Peng Dehuai, who had dared to confront Mao with the failure of the Great Leap in 1958.

Deng's pragmatism towards the socialism versus capitalism issue was well illustrated by how he viewed the people of Hong Kong. In June 1984, he commented:

> The qualifications for a patriot are respect for the Chinese nation, sincere support for the motherland's resumption of sovereignty over Hong Kong and a desire not to impair Hong Kong's prosperity and stability. Those who meet those requirements are patriots, whether they believe in capitalism or feudalism or even slavery. We don't demand that they be in favour of China's socialist system; we only ask them to love the motherland and Hong Kong.[22]

Later in the year, Deng himself reflected on the fact that a little bit of capitalism wouldn't do China any harm. The Chinese press was equally relaxed. On 7 December 1984, *The People's Daily* reported that 'since Marx has already been dead for 101 years . . . some of his assumptions are not necessarily appropriate'.[23] Later in the same month, *The New York Times* quoted a Chinese official as saying that 'most people today don't care whether something is capitalist or socialist. They just want to live their lives to improve. The details are for the theoreticians'.[24]

By the late 1980s, Deng, through his overseas travel, his meetings with foreign leaders, and above all from having seen the enormous benefits to accrue to those regions that had adopted the culture of enterprise, must have lost much of his faith in socialist economics. However, the Chinese Communist Party was a brand, and he was well aware of its importance in a political sense even if the socialist economic ingredients were being adapted or abandoned.

Whatever Deng may have felt about socialist economics, he was always aware that he had to balance the new with the prejudices of the revolutionary old guard. It was probably this factor and the legitimacy of the communist regime, which above all prevented him from a public and wholesale abandonment of socialism. Notably, however, in June 1988, Deng Xiaoping strongly recommended to the President of Mozambique 'not to practice socialism'.[25]

Whatever Deng's core beliefs, through the pragmatic application of non-socialist policies, he achieved a dramatic change not only in the material quality of life of the vast bulk of the Chinese population but also brought China back into the compass of the leading nations. With a real GDP growth rate of almost 10 per cent per annum throughout the 1980s, China emerged as the giant among the world's developing economies. By 1994, the value of output produced by the private sector accounted for 50 per cent of GDP compared to less than 20 per cent a decade earlier.

About 1.2 billion Chinese people, for the first time in their history, had been truly dragged into the global trading system, and China now ranked as a world power in its own right. Extrapolating trends of economic development, western futurologists now predicted that China would become the great world power of the twenty-first century. Such is the legacy of Deng's leadership and its dramatic effect on the future possibilities of the Chinese people, that by any calculation he would rank as one of the great statesmen of this or any era. It is somewhat ironic therefore that, balanced against these achievements, he is now better known by most in the West as the architect of the Tiananmen Square Massacre.

51

Benazir and Sharif: Rise and Fall of the Demagogues

Pakistan: 1988–99

After the execution for murder of Zulfikar Ali Bhutto and the mysterious airplane crash of his nemesis, General Zia, the door was opened to a new generation of political combatants. A fiercely contested election between Benazir Bhutto, a Sindi, who had inherited her father's leadership of the Pakistan People's Party (PPP), and Nawaz Sharif, a Punjabi businessman and leader of the Sharif Islamic Alliance, whose father had suffered at the hands of Ali Bhutto's nationalisation policy, ended with a narrow victory for Benazir. Pakistan's military, naturally fearful of the possibility that Benazir would seek revenge for her father's execution, was persuaded by the USA to allow her to become prime minister. Nevertheless, it was a three-sided marriage; her power was in effect shared with the chief of staff of the army, and the Pakistan president, vested with the power of Zia's 8th Amendment to exercise a veto over government.

Benazir was educated by her father in the West, where she went to Harvard in the early 1970s. It was a pampered upbringing. Their indulgent father bought all the clothes for the children, Benazir and Murtaza, at Saks Fifth Avenue, where their measurements were kept on file. In New York, she had the pick of her father's vast collection of first editions. Her father, obsessed like many post-war Asian leaders with Napoleon, read to her tales of his exploits from the age of just six.

At Radcliffe college she became a feminist, memorising passages of Kate Millett's *Sexual Politics* (1970), and marched against the war in Vietnam; she would later tell Mary Anne Weaver, 'I felt very strongly about it . . . I was Asian, and Asian blood was being spilled.'[1] During the war with East Pakistan, later to be Bangladesh, Benazir temporarily left Radcliffe (Harvard) and worked for her father in New York as he wrestled to get United Nations backing for the Pakistan cause. While she was there she met George Bush (senior), who was then the US ambassador at the United Nations. When they were introduced, he told her, 'My son [George W. Bush] is up at Harvard too. Call me if you need anything.'[2] She did need something. When they met again 16 years later, Benazir asked the now President Bush (senior) for 60 F-16 fighter jets.

The experience in New York whetted her political appetite. This was clear on her arrival to study at Oxford, where she soon immersed herself in Oxford Union politics, a launch pad for many British political careers, becoming its first Asian president. In the first of her many disputed elections, she won her union presidency after a re-run election caused by her complaints of illegal canvassing by her opponent. The new leader of the opposition Conservative Party, Margaret Thatcher, who had met her father, invited Benazir to tea and they subsequently became friends. Benazir admired Thatcher's 'political conviction': 'She doesn't test the wind. She goes where she wants to go. I admire her single-mindedness . . . she's got tremendous courage.'[3]

She returned to Pakistan after graduation, and after her father's execution came to prominence as his natural successor. Held for a long period in prison and then under house arrest, she was allowed to return to England in 1984. Here she remained leader in exile of the PPP, until the death of Zia enabled her to make a dramatic and highly charged return to Pakistan to contest the November 1988 elections.

As Pakistan's president, Benazir Bhutto had her first meeting with President George Bush (senior) at the funeral of Emperor Hirohito in February 1989. An invitation was extended to her to visit the USA in June. The youthful 35-year-old Benazir, with her dramatic looks and exotic garb, wowed the staid corridors of Washington's political institutions, and was excitedly received as she addressed a joint session of Congress.

However, she soon disappointed the liberal community, which had probably expected too much of her. Dr Hamida Khurho, an Oxford-educated friend of the Bhutto family reflected that

> People were expecting a liberal, Western-educated woman with forward-looking programs . . . but the first thing she did was to shroud herself in a *chador* [traditional Pakistani gown] . . . [began] praying incessantly at saints' tombs, the most superstitious part of Islam . . . she could have been a reformer, but she wasn't; she did nothing for women, which she could have done.[4]

Whatever her faults as a leader, she did however understand that her own liberal instincts would not have won her votes in socially conservative Pakistan. More importantly, back home her star waned rapidly, not because she was a liberal or a bad vote winner, but because she was a hopeless administrator who failed to introduce a single item of noteworthy legislation. More damaging still, her recently acquired husband, Asif Ali Zardari, soon gained a reputation for avarice and corruption.

When Benazir broke the tacit agreement not to interfere in military appointments and when she moved, and failed, to replace the Chairman of the Joint Chief of Staff Admiral Iftikhar Ahmed Sirohey, relations with the army deteriorated rapidly. Increasingly, Army Chief of Staff Aslam Beg and President Ghulam Ishaq became her confirmed enemies. (A largely Punjabi army was inherently hostile to the Sindi-based Bhuttos; in 1972, the army comprised just 2.2 per cent Sindis and they had no representatives at senior officer level.) A phoney war ended on 6 August 1990 with the dismissal of Benazir by the president using his 8th Amendment veto.

Her interior minister, General Babar, who had also served her father, would later complain about the entrenched elite that

> The ISI, the Army, and the president had been running the show for so long that they simply didn't want to give up. They got so carried away with all these fundamentalist movements across the Islamic world. They thought that once they got Afghanistan they'd go across to the Soviet Central Asia Republics and into Kashmir.[5]

The dismissal of Benazir from office ushered in a decade of political instability as sequences of election and dismissals gave power either to Benazir or her long-time political opponent Nawaz Sharif. Elected to office for the first time in November 1990, Sharif had fought his campaign calling for an end to corruption. In spite of this and his generally pro-business economic strategies, there was little apparent change to the corruption endemic in Pakistan business and politics.

Loans from state-owned banks were reportedly directed to industrialists who financed political campaigns. Licenses, frequently monopolies, were similarly awarded. Indeed Pakistani cricketer turned politician, Imran Khan, a constant critic of political corruption in his country, complained that any businessman who backed a political party was looking for at least a ten times return on investment. As for Benazir's spouse by arranged marriage, Asif Ali Zadari, who she appointed as Minister for Investments, he came to be known as 'Mr Ten per cent'[6] for the rate of commission he was alleged to have taken from transactions.

On 18 April 1993, President Ghulam Ishaq Khan, goaded into action by Sharif's attempt to trim his powers, again used the 8th Amendment to remove Sharif and dissolve the National Assembly. The president was briefly overruled and Sharif restored to power by the Supreme Court on 26 May 1993. To end this running constitutional battle, the army finally intervened and Sharif was again removed from power on 18 July. He was replaced by Moin Qureshi, a retired World Bank vice president, who was charged with running an interim administration.

For the first time in 20 years, Pakistan had a leader concerned with the economic welfare of its people. After the socialism of Bhutto, the Islamisation of Zia and the rapacious demagoguery of Benazir and Sharif, Pakistan reverted to a period of 'disinterested' government. Qureshi pushed through anti-corruption measures and economic reforms. Borrowers of more than US$ 35,000, who had defaulted on loans, were publicly listed and shamed; both Benazir and Sharif were publicly humiliated by their inclusion. Qureshi also introduced income tax on the previously untouchable 'feudal' landlords. The rupee was devalued, and the central bank was given autonomy to set interest rates. In just three months, the country's foreign exchange reserves rose from just US$ 180 million to US$ 448 million.

For the long-suffering citizens of Pakistan, this welcome lacuna proved all too brief as National Assembly elections on 6 October 1993, the third such in five years, brought Benazir back to power. It might have been expected that Benazir would have learnt from her past mistakes. She did not. Her husband, Zardari, became reputedly even more rapacious in his financial procurements; 'Mr Ten Per Cent' became known as 'Mr Twenty Per Cent'.

A Geneva magistrate, Daniel Devaud, would later claim to have found a number of their British Virgin Island Companies with Swiss bank accounts amounting to US$ 13 million and a Swiss safe deposit box containing a U$ 175,000 necklace. Much of this money was thought to have come from 'kickbacks' from SGS-Cotecna, a Swiss-based company that was hired by Benazir's government to improve customs collection on imports. (This was the same company that later won a contract in the Iraqi 'oil-for-food' scandal and employed the United Nations secretary general's son, Kojo Annan, for 'consultancy' services.)

Benazir and Zadari would eventually be found guilty of money laundering by a Swiss court on 6 August 2003. When questioned on this subject by Eric Margolis, a *Toronto Sun* reporter, Benazir, using the diversionary tactics for which her father was famous, responded that 'I've never had a bank account in Switzerland since 1984. Why would the Swiss do this to me? Maybe the Swiss are trying to divert attention from the Holocaust Gold scandal.'[7] Ownership of a large mansion was uncovered in the south of England, part of overseas assets which by some accusations amounted to US$1.5bn. Trials for corruption eventually fizzled out. (Zardari would later be accused of murder and dealing in heroin; the charges would never be proven, though his eventual release from prison in 2004 was thought to have been done largely for reasons of political expediency). More importantly Benazir did little to burnish the Pakistan economy and merely added to Pakistan's already ruinous external debt burden.

Her reputation was further damaged when Murtaza Bhutto, an increasingly strident critic of his sister, was gunned down at a police blockade in Karachi on 20 September 1996; a killing, believed by some to have involved Benazir's husband, who apparently loathed his brother-in-law. Now tainted with suspicions of fratricide, Benazir also sought to tamper with the independence of the judiciary. After the prime minister refused to abide by court orders which limited her ability to sack and nominate judges, Pakistan's new president, Leghari, a former Benazir ally, followed the path of his predecessor by dismissing Benazir and dissolving the National Assembly on 5 November 1996. Popular support for Benazir had withered to such a degree that there was barely a murmur of discontent at her removal.

With yet another failure in Pakistan's democracy, the army yet again considered the possibility of deferring elections until the economic and political problems created by Benazir could be resolved; the relative success of the short-lived Qureshi government must have given the army pause for thought. However, the Clinton administration pushed for speedy elections. In an interview with Pakistan's *Friday Times*, the American ambassador, Thomas Simons Jnr, asserted that, 'The answer for bad democracy is more democracy.'[8]

More democracy arrived on 4 February 1997, with a landslide victory for Sharif which most observers saw as more of a vote against Benazir than a vote for the new prime minister. With a huge majority in the National Assembly, Sharif moved rapidly to abolish the 'veto' embedded in the 8th Amendment and hence the power of the president to dismiss him.

On 14 August 1997, Pakistan celebrated its 50th anniversary; its muted celebration by Sharif's government and the population at large reflected the universal understanding that constitutionally, Pakistan's record was nothing less than pitiful. To *The New York Times*, Sharif put a brave face on the anniversary:

> In 50 years we've had our ups and downs like any other nation in the world. We've been off track, but we're on track now . . . of course, the enemies of Pakistan try to present it as a failed state. But it's not a failed state.[9]

It was hardly a ringing endorsement.

Sharif continued to destroy all obstacles to his personal enjoyment of power. Rather than addressing Pakistan's appalling economic and social problems, Sharif focused his political energies on destroying democratic constraints. In a dispute with Chief Justice Sajjad Ali Shah over the appointment of judges, Sharif won out and forced his retirement. A now powerless President Leghari registered his disapproval by resigning.

The army, for once led by a 'non-interventionist', General Karamat, refused to act. Sharif brought Pakistan into further disrepute by cancelling American electricity generation deals which had been negotiated and signed during Benazir's prime ministership. At a stroke, Sharif destroyed Pakistan's ability to attract private international finance for infrastructure projects. Also, during the foreign exchange crisis of 1998, when Sharif froze all foreign currency bank accounts, the Pakistani government effectively looted billions of dollars from personal accounts.

Sharif's alleged personal corruption was counter-pointed by populist policies such as the 'own-your own taxicab scheme', which proved ruinously expensive to the already overloaded budget. Sharif also sought to reduce the scale of the army by unorthodox methods. He told a colleague that his plan was to induct 100,000 soldiers into the Water and Power Development Authority and the Pakistan Railways. At the same time, making peace with India would reduce the scale of the army's commitments. Cutting the army budget was a dangerous tactic for any elected politician in post-independence Pakistan, where the army was both powerful and ravenous for ever more funding. On one occasion, when asked by a news conference whether she intended to cut the defence budget, Benazir replied, 'Not unless we want the army to take over again.'[10]

It did at first seem that Sharif would make some progress in restoring relations with India. In February 1999, Sharif hosted a visit from Indian prime minister, Vajpayee, at which the resumption of bus services between India and Pakistan was celebrated. Two months later, India's BJP government lost a confidence ballot by a single vote. Vajpayee remained as head of a caretaker government until autumn elections. Restoration of good relations was put on hold.

In spite of the apparently improving picture of Indo–Pakistan relations, the Pakistan army crossed the Line of Control which divided Pakistan and Indian-controlled Kashmir. The point of contention was a remote mountain position, some 17,000 feet high, with commanding views and within artillery range of the Indian-controlled town of Kargil. The heights also controlled the only road linking Srinagar and Ladakh. The strategy was to bombard Kargil and the roads connecting it to India and thus cut off Indian control of the province of Ladakh.

Politically Sharif sought to distance himself from what he described as insurgents beyond his control. This was palpably not true; the Indian army later found Pakistani markings on captured weapons and insignia of the Gilgit Scouts. Both of Pakistan's key allies, China and the USA, refused to support Sharif. Much to the chagrin of most Pakistanis, Prime Minister Sharif had to back down from his previous statements. The Pakistani troops were eventually dislodged from their artillery positions by heroic Indian troops who managed to scale the formidable Kargil heights while under fire, before assaulting enemy positions and dislodging Pakistani forces. However, the denouement only served to further embitter relations between the prime minister and the army as Sharif sought to blame Army Chief General Musharraf for the debacle. For Sharif it was a dangerous strategy. He had already removed Musharraf's predecessor, General Karamat, and the army were sensitive to its position. As historian Ian Talbot has pointed out, 'The only institution to survive Pakistan's first half century was the Pakistan Army.'[11] The threat of a coup was now widely anticipated.

In the event, it was Sharif who moved first against General Musharraf, who was both chairman of the joint chiefs and chief of the army staff. While returning on a Pakistan International Airlines (PIA) flight from Sri Lanka on 12 October 1999, Sharif's government announced that he had been sacked. Furthermore, his plane was ordered to divert out of the country, even though it did not have enough fuel to reach another destination. From the air, Musharraf managed to contact his key supporters who sent forces to occupy the airfield; with characteristic ineptitude, Sharif had failed to guard the air flight traffic control facilities.

Musharraf landed in Karachi, where he was eventually coaxed off the airplane once he had been assured that the airport was secure. Not surprisingly, Musharraf chose to interpret Sharif's actions as an assassination attempt. Within the space of half an hour, Musharraf went from being the object of an assassination attempt to becoming the fourth post-independence military leader of his country. Though the Clinton administration was opposed to this development, in the circumstances, there was little that could be done. For the time being at least, rule by the demagogues, Benazir and Sharif, was over.

By 1997, popular disillusionment with the political process was such that voter turnout had fallen to just 35.1 per cent. Over its first half century, the Pakistan political system completely failed to deliver material advances to its people. Although life expectancy increased from 43 in 1960 to 60 in 1997, thanks to the increased global availability of antibiotics and other basic medicines, Pakistani daily calorie intake remained one of the lowest in the world, ranking below Burkina Faso. By 1990, expenditure on health care was just 1.8 per cent of the government budget, with the result that for most citizens there was no state provision of medical care. City infrastructure in Pakistan had effectively collapsed under the weight of urban migration. With a population growth rate in excess of 2.2 per cent, Pakistan's population of 174 million was expected to increase to more than 250 million in 20 years.

To add to Pakistan's difficulties, the Pakistan economy descended into shambles during the 'demagogue era'. In the 1960s, the pro-business policies of General Mohammed Ayub had achieved 8–16 per cent growth in manufacturing per annum, albeit from a low base. Zulfikar Ali Bhutto's nationalisation of banks and insurance companies and ten other basic industries reversed the positive trends within the economy. Before Bhutto came to power, Pakistan, in spite of the bankrupt state into which it was born, had accumulated just US$ 3 billion of external debt by 1970.

In the next 20 years, Bhutto and his successors compounded the problems inherent in state socialism by rapidly increasing the country's external debt to over US$ 25 billion, an enormous figure compared to government revenues of just US$ 12 billion in 2003. Much of the money spent is still unaccounted for. With just 2.5 telephones per 100 people, the country can only be described as chronically backward. In 2003, average income per capita of US$ 2,100, on a purchasing power parity basis, was some 30 per cent lower than India, a reversal of the situation in the 1960s.

In 1944, Jinnah had stated that 'no nation can rise to the height of glory unless your women are side by side with you'.[12] Yet by the end of the demagogue era, few countries had a female population so poorly educated and oppressed, and where 'honour' killing of young girls was so widespread. A national education system effectively collapsed, and literacy rates of 54 per cent (66 per cent for men versus 42 per cent for women) were well below those of neighbouring India (70.2 per cent for men versus 48.3 per cent for women). Not surprisingly, thousands of Wahabi, mainly Saudi financed religious schools (*madrassas*) filled the educational vacuum. At the end of 2002, almost 2 million students were estimated to being educated in some 10,000–13,000 unregistered *madrassas*.

With the loss of East Pakistan (Bangladesh), it might have been anticipated that Pakistan would become easier to rule. Democratic organs had almost inevitably

foundered in a country divided by culture and a thousand miles of Indian territory. Surely the new compact Pakistan, formerly West Pakistan, should have
flourished as a functioning democracy. However, formidable regional problems
remained. The most populous states of the Punjab and Sind had to co-opt the
independent-minded smaller states of Balochistan and the Pathan's North West
Frontier Province. There were also the Federally Administered Tribal Areas and
administration of the disputed areas of Jammu and Kashmir controlled by the Pakistan army.

To add further to the political mix, the Mohajirs (Muslim refugees who had
come to Pakistan at Partition) increasingly demanded their own political entity
and national identity from the early 1980s. At its high point, the Mohajir Qaumi
Movement (MQM) led by a former student leader, Altaf Hussain, won 13 out of
15 seats in Karachi in 1988.

Like many liberation movements, the MQM became a militant, quasi-gangster
organisation that effectively controlled the city. The army would eventually un-
cover torture cells, where the MQM used an electric drill on knees and elbows.
Murders reached a peak of 1,586 in 1995 alone. At a British High Commission
reception in Islamabad in 1999, an MQM senator, Nasreen Jaleel, complained that
'When I walk into a room like this all these people see the word terrorist written
all over my forehead.'[13] Although the numbers of murders had declined by the end
of the decade, the role of the army was essential in restoring some semblance of
civic order to Karachi.

In addition to the MQM problem, tensions were also apparent between the
Sind and Punjab. The Punjab-dominated army was always suspicious of Sindi politicians, and the mutual suspicions were heightened by Zia's sacking of 1,746 Sindi
bureaucrats and also by the 'judicial' murder of Zulfikar Ali Bhutto. In 1981, the
Movement for Restoration of Democracy in Sind was started, and resulted in
the deployment of 45,000 troops to quell street violence; hundreds were killed
in the civil unrest.

Yet for all of Pakistan's diversity, this country, approximate in size to California,
presented far fewer ethnic and religious problems to the operation of democracy
than neighbouring India. Neither was the construction of Pakistan's institutions to
blame for the country's problems. In truth, Pakistan was unfortunate in having political leaders over the last three decades of the century, Zulfikar Ali Bhutto, his
daughter Benazir and Nawaz Sharif, who were contemptuous of the key democratic right to own property under law, who tried to manipulate the constitution
to guarantee effective one-party rule, and who showed scant regard for the core
institutions of state. Pakistan's failure was the result of catastrophic governance.
By 1999, few Pakistanis were sorry to see the rule of the demagogues brought to
a close.

52

The Narcotic State

Burma: 1948–2005

From the first day of its independent existence, 4 January 1948, Burma was a failed state. U Nu, who inherited the leadership of the AFPFL (the League), after the assassination of Aung San six months earlier, had been Aung San's senior at university, but had been bypassed by his protégé both during and after the war. While Aung had grasped the possibility of portraying himself as a liberating military hero, however dubious the reality of that claim, Nu, the quiet intellectual, had been forced into the background. Most importantly, by dint of his leadership qualities, Aung had grasped power because he won the backing of dedicated troops. Nu lacked both the charisma of his predecessor and the means to enforce his will.

Almost immediately the independence settlement began to unravel. The communists, whom, for reasons of internecine rivalry rather than ideology, Aung had expelled from the League, openly rebelled within weeks of independence. By the end of the year, more than 15,000 partisans were participating in violent insurrection against the government. Nu's attempt to neutralise the insurrection by promoting 'leftist unity' was a dismal failure. The Communist Party of Burma (CPB), increasingly able to rely on support from China after their victory over the Kuomintang, remained one of the many armed 'tribes' that consistently harassed the Burmese government. Only in 1988, when China withdrew its support from the CPB, did the communist threat finally come to rest.

The CPB was the least of Burma's problems. The tribal minorities, whom Britain, advised by Lord Mountbatten, had so shamefully abandoned, had never accepted the constitutional settlement that Aung and Prime Minister Attlee had stitched up in London at the beginning of 1947. The new League regime, like its nineteenth-century monarchic predecessors, wanted nothing less than the traditional Burman suzerainty over the tribal states. For the purpose of imposing Burman supremacy, General Ne Win, (later Chairman of the Revolutionary Council and Prime Minister), set about recruiting *Sitwundan* (Burman regional militias); in effect, this was a political paramilitary force, whose role was to terrorise the tribal minorities. When the murder of prominent Karenni nationalists went unpunished, insurrection followed, which included the defection of Karen units in the Burmese army. At the end of 1948, *Sitwundan* committed a landmark atrocity when they threw grenades into Karen churches during Christmas services.

Karen rebels were now joined by a Kachin rifles battalion and detachments of Paus and Mons. Meanwhile, the Burmese army was in disarray following the resignation of the Karen commander in chief and many of the tribal officers, who comprised the heart of Burma's military forces. In the assault that the Karen National Defence Organisation (KNDO) now launched on Rangoon, the city was only saved by the reinforcement of the Burma army from the British government in Delhi, which rushed troops to defend the fledgling state.

Rangoon was ultimately defended by PVO paramilitary units loyal to the government, combined with a Burma army Gurkhas unit and sundry Burmese irregular troops. However, the factor which most probably saved the regime was the disunity of the tribal minority forces. Constantly changing alliances and fractures within the tribal groups had long been a feature of Burmese politics. Indeed, with hundreds of different clans and dialects even within the same tribes, unity was almost impossible to achieve.

While Burma rose to become the world's largest narcotic state, forming the raison d'etre for the country's importance, normal politics was reduced to a sideshow. Prime Minister Nu, battered by the intractable problems posed by the tribal minorities, failed to honour the pledges for equal treatment that Aung San had made at Panglong. Government posts were increasingly reserved for Burmans, while Buddhism became de facto the national religion. Meanwhile, the army, under Ne Win's leadership, was increasingly 'Burmanised'.

The military also assumed a larger role in Burmese society by appropriating key economic and commercial roles. In 1951, the Defence Services Institute (DSI) started an army personnel store in Rangoon with a 600,000 Kyat loan provided by U Nu. By exempting merchandise from excise taxes and customs duties, the store proved extremely successful and enabled the state to purchase the loyalty of its troops, who could also resell products to supplement income. Eighteen more stores followed.

Following the DSI's lead, the army also embarked on other commercial projects including an international trading house. As the Burmese army grew in stature, so too did its sense of political importance; as in Indonesia and Thailand, the army increasingly saw itself as the guardian of Burma's values. At an army conference at Meiktila in 1958, a speaker declared:

> ... What we dread most is that unscrupulous politicians and deceitful Communist rebels and their allies may take advantage of ... inadequacies in the Constitution and bring about in the country gangster political movements, syndicalism, anarchism and a totalitarian regime.[1]

Ironically, the army itself soon filled the role thus described.

Given Burma's chronic political instability, the possibility of a military coup was always high. Indeed, as early as 1951, the CIA had reported that there was a

> ...struggle for control of the armed forces between the government and the army Commander-in-Chief, General Ne Win. For some time government leaders have been attempting to undermine Ne Win's dominant personal position within the army ... there is a continuing possibility that Ne Win might attempt a military coup, which could lead to protracted violence.'[2]

In 1956, the tribals had managed to co-ordinate their political activity to the degree that they had formed the National United Front (NUF of racial minorities), and in the elections of that year they won 36.9 per cent of the vote and 48 seats in the General Assembly. Two years later, the ruling AFPFL League split into two factions divided by the issue of the tribal minorities. The 'Cleans' led by the Nu-favoured alliance with the NUF in order to reach a lasting settlement with the minorities, while the 'Stables' led by Kyaw Nyein and Ba Swe favoured a strong unitary Burma.

However, when the 'Cleans' government of Nu offered separate state status to the Arakan and Mon tribes, the Chins immediately demanded their own independence. The downward spiral into anarchy was cut short when Nu was 'persuaded' by colonels Maung Maung and Aung Gyi to appoint a caretaker government led by the Army Chief Ne Win. The military immediately drafted 134 high-ranking officers into government departments. The mirage of a civilian constitutional settlement had soon dissipated.

In 1959 the civil war restarted, with the Karens, Karennis, Mons and Chins forming a military alliance with the CPB. This was followed by an uprising of the Shans in 1960 and the Kachins in 1961. Although in February 1960, there was a brief return to parliamentary government under Nu, notable mainly for Nu's constitutional amendment making Buddhism the state religion, Ne Win brought Burma's second limited experiment in democracy to an end on 2 March 1962. After watching a visiting troupe of Chinese ballet dancers, Ne Win had Nu arrested at his home at 2 am; his 17-year-old son was gunned down during the operation, while Sao Shwe Thaike, Burma's first president, was taken away and executed. Five other ministers were imprisoned.

Ne Win, an unstable psychotic, was a tyrant in the classic mould. A womaniser and drinker, Ne Win was also addicted to fortune telling. He was obsessed by fears of his own untimely death. Supposedly he once shot his mirror image as a means of escaping a similar fate. With echoes of *Macbeth's* 'Burnham Wood', he cut down *go go* trees because he feared that the expression 'cut down the go go trees', meaning to commit suicide, was a sign of his own fate. In the 1970s, in order to protect himself from a political attack from the right, he ordered that cars should no longer drive on the left.

From 1962, Ne Win ruled by decree through a Revolutionary Council; in theory, the 1947 constitution was simply in a state of suspension, but unlike the brief 'caretaker' period, Ne Win did not present himself before the parliament. However, in 1974, Burma's independence constitution was abolished and replaced by one which simply confirmed Ne Win's military totalitarian rule. Although the Burmese government was at war with the CPB, Ne Win now imposed an extreme socialist system on Burma.

Advised by Ba Nyein, a Marxist who had founded the Burma Workers and Peasants Party, Ne Win nationalised all shops in 1963. Aye Saung, formerly a student activist, recalled that soldiers would appear outside shops 'with green signboards, bearing the words 'People's Shop No. (-).'³ 'For the next few days, the soldiers stayed in the shop. They seemed to be making a list of the goods. After a week, there was nothing on the shelves, and the shop closed down.'⁴ In addition, Ne Win, in spite of his far from puritan lifestyle, also banned racing, beauty contests and dancing. An already impoverished economy collapsed completely. When students marched against the government, Ne Win had them gunned down in a ruthless slaughter. The Student's Union was then dynamited; unsurprisingly, students fled to the hills and joined the flourishing resistance movements.

The removal of civilian government and all opposition allowed the military to begin the systematic rape of Burma's economic resources. The army's General Trading Company became the monopoly importer of coal supplies to Burma Railways and other government agencies. The military also dominated the transport industries, including buses, trucking and shipping; even the 'pedacabs' were financed by army officers. Banking was a natural extension of these activities; the army confiscated all banks in Burma including those that were foreign-owned. Newspapers were also nationalised, giving government control of all media outlets. Not surprisingly, in the ten years to 1973, the numbers of government employees leapt from 368,000 to 623,529.

The DSI also diversified from its 'military only' general stores to take over Burma Hotels Limited, the owner of the legendary Strand Hotel. Other business activities included the Rangoon Electric Works and the Continental Trading House, which owned fisheries, poultry farms and fuel distribution companies. Most property, including Rangoon's lavish colonial villas, ended up in the hands of senior army officers, while property speculation was backed by government funds. Journalist U Thaung complained that 'A powerful military officer could build as many rent-guaranteed houses as he wanted without investing much at all.'⁵

Over time, military greed became uncontrollable; eventually all trading companies were confiscated along with Burma Oil Company and Anglo-Burma Mines Company. By 1973 the government also owned 814 private schools, 132 factories (including Unilever's operations), 182 cinemas and 24 shipping companies. Private property, except that owned by the military, was effectively abolished when Ne Win declared that 'one unfinished business which mocks our declaration that . . . we will not permit the exploitation of man by man . . . it concerns the continued extraction of tenancy rent by the landlords'.[6] Naturally, in Ne Win's autarkic world foreign investment was also effectively banned.

As Burma's civil war raged between the League and the tribal states after 1948, the civil war in China was coming to a decisive conclusion with the victory of Mao's army's over the *Kuomintang* (KMT) and the flight of Chiang Kai Shek to Formosa. In the West of China, the remnants of the *Kuomintang* armies under Chen Wei Chen and Ting Tsuo Shou decided to fight on and regrouped across the border in the hill tracts that divided the two countries. The Burma-based *Kuomintang* also recruited local mercenary groups from among the tribal populations. Famously, one of these militia leaders was a young Shan aristocrat called Olive Yang, who had been educated at the exclusive Guardian Angels Convent at Lashio; she went under the unflattering sobriquet of 'Miss Hairy Legs'. One of Olive's lieutenants, Lo Hsing Han, whose elder brother was a chief inspector of police in Kokang, was to become one of Burma's wealthiest drug barons.

The *Kuomintang* forces moved to Mong Hsat, where they occupied the air base that the American forces had built to supply the wartime Special Operations Executive (SOE) Unit 136. From Bangkok, they were supplied by General Clair Chennault of 'Flying Tigers' fame, a friend of Chiang, who, after the war, set up Civil Air Transport flying C-46s and C-47s. Also, with the Americans now increasingly concerned with the spread of communism, the CIA became only too anxious to finance the *Kuomintang's* renegrade band of troops. Robert North, an OSS veteran who headed The Far East Film Company in Bangkok, distributed anti-communist propaganda films for the CIA and acted as a financial conduit to the *Kuomintang*.

For the USA, a fiercely anti-communist army on the borders of China which could also keep communism at bay in Burma was well worth supporting. The CIA-backed conflict lasted over a decade until January 1961, when the *Kuomintang* base at Mong Pa Liao was overrun by a co-ordinated attack by three divisions of China's People's Revolutionary Army and the Burmese army.

However, the *Kuomintang* was not financed by the CIA alone. In a 1967 interview, *Kuomintang's* General Duan observed that 'In these mountains the only money is opium.'[7] The Trans-Salween Highlands, occupied by the Kuomintang, was an area ideal for the cultivation of high-grade poppies. The highlands had long been a centre for growing poppies and small-scale production of opium. During the Second World War, Merrill's Marauders had used it as currency to pay informers. However, as Yunnanese farmers fled Mao's regime, and started to massively expand cultivation, the *Kuomintang* developed a highly lucrative narcotics industry.

Manufactories were built close to the Mong Hsat air base, from where heroin was easily shipped to Bangkok, which soon became the world's greatest drugs entrepot. From an estimated opium yield of just 30 tons in 1948, the output of the region grew to 2,560 tons by 1996; an increase of 8,533 per cent. Given that a standard 1.6 kg packet of raw opium could be sold for $1,000 at 1989 prices, the industry was not only significant in scale but was also by far the largest business in Burma. It is curious to reflect that an area of the world, whose drug industry would become a key target of the US Drug Enforcement Agency (DEA), owed its origins and rapid growth to the logistical and financial support of the American army and CIA.

The *Kuomintang* was not alone in wanting to exploit the lucrative opium trade. Ne Win became the key figure in the development of the industry. After taking command of the army, the *Sitwundan* declined in importance, but was revived in 1955 as the *Pyu Saw Hti*. From this group in the early 1960s, Ne Win created a further paramilitary entity known as the *Ka Kwe Yei* (meaning defence affairs); by using this force to control road transport, Ne Win was able to muscle in on the wealth generated by narcotics. In effect, the Burmese government went into joint venture with the drug barons. Also, as a Shan analyst explained, Ne Win's nationalisation of economic resources 'delivered the economy into the hands of the opium traffickers. As such, opium became the only viable crop and medium of exchange'.[8]

When drug baron Lo Hsing Han was arrested in Bangkok, he was extradited to Rangoon where he was offered a pardon by Ne Win. Indeed, the Burmese government helped him recruit an army, with the explicit aim of providing a counterbalance to the CPB (Communist Party of Burma), which had also entered the drug industry to finance its continuing civil war.

The extent to which the Communist Party had become 'just another gang' was well illustrated in the career of Moh Heng, a drug baron, who had joined the CPB in the 1950s, and later left to establish his own Shan State Communist Party. Another drug baron, Ma Xuefu, a Yunnanese exile from Mao's China, became a successful opium merchant who eventually moved to Bangkok in 1964 to run a number of legitimate businesses including the June Hotel. Perversely, this hotel became a popular haunt of American Peace Corps volunteers in the 1960s. Meanwhile, Ma Xuefu's Cha Mon Tea Company became an ideal front for the international trading of heroin. He was also connected to the triads and to General Li, a former *Kuomintang* general, who had become a powerful drugs warlord and rival to Khun Sa.

Khun Sa, meaning 'Prince Prosperous', became internationally the most famous of the drug barons; born Zhang Qifu, he was a man of Shan origin. He originally recruited his own army to fight against the *Kuomintang*, and then negotiated *Ka Kwe Vei* (Defence Affairs Force) status with Ne Win's government. His accommodation with the Burmese government enabled him to build the first morphine factory in Rangoon at Vingngun.

As for the *Kuomintang*, Khun Sa concluded a truce with them whereby he paid fees, that is protection, for safe transit of mule trains, sometimes a mile long, which came down from the highlands. Refusal to pay *Kuomintang* transit fees in 1967 led to one of the most famous episodes of the Golden Triangle narcotic history. The *Kuomintang* ambushed a convoy that had been consigned to General Ouane, the commander in chief of the Laotian army; fearing the loss of his valuable cargo of raw opium, Ouane ordered the Laotian air force to bomb the *Kuomintang* forces and then sent in his own troops to carry off the prize.

Later, Khun Sa formally agreed a deal with Burmese General Aye San on 7 March 1984 at the garrison town of Mong Ton, whereby Khun Sa would be allowed 'free trade in opium and its derivatives if he undertook to use his troops trained for jungle warfare, against the minorities' insurgent groups and the communist guerrillas'.[9]

The rapid growth of the narcotics industry in the Golden Triangle increasingly brought Burma to the attention of the US government. Ne Win, in effect a communist, but at war with the Chinese backed CPB, may have seemed the leader of a state with which America could do business. However, the complex mesh of competing narcotics cartels masquerading as political movements defied easy analysis, and until the early 1990s it was assumed that Ne Win was actually fighting narcotics.

It was Senator Jesse Helms who finally informed the Senate Foreign Relations Committee of the truth of Ne Win's complicity in the drug trade. Indeed, in 1986, the Reagan administration had supplied Ne Win's regime with Bell 205 helicopters, Thrust aircraft, pilot training and chemical agent 2,4-D. While the equipment was indeed used to spray opium fields, Ne Win targeted only those that were controlled by rival gangs. Furthermore, the highly toxic chemical sprays, banned in the USA, polluted rivers and drinking supplies. Ne Win's use of Burma's military to support narcotic activities was not limited to aerial bombardment of competitors. The army was also instructed to cut down coffee and tea plantations and other 'legal' crops to force the expansion of poppy cultivation.

Any concessions wrought by the US government from Ne Win were short-lived, as he was easily capable of outwitting American monitors. In 1988, the Burmese government reinforced its local defence forces, now called *Pyithu Sit*, to further its political and commercial objectives. Indeed, its renewed activities may have added to the pressure which ultimately brought about the collapse of the CPB (Communist Party of Burma) in 1989. The CPB, whose support from China had terminated in August 1988, following a border treaty with Burma, increasingly became an anachronism as money-making from narcotics had largely replaced its political functions.

The coup de grâce for the CPB came from an internal revolt by Commander Peng Kya Shen and the ethnic minorities, who rebelled against Burman leadership. The Wa mutineers captured the party headquarters and central armoury at Panghsang on the Yunnan border, and proceeded to smash portraits of Marx, Engels, Lenin, Stalin and Mao; 'They have cheated the people of the Wa region,' the mutineers declared, 'and through their lies and propaganda have dragged us into their sham revolution.'[10]

While some 300 ageing communist leaders and their families escaped to China, the troops split into resistance groups including the Myanmar National Democratic Alliance Army, and the United Wa State Army. Other former communist officers and their troops were won over by the drug baron Lo Hsing Han.

The demise of the CPB allowed an even faster expansion of the narcotics trade. *Pyithu Sit*'s partners in the drug traffic to Rangoon comprised an increasingly disparate range of groups, including the Burma National Defence Alliance Army, the Myanmar National Solidarity Party, the National Democratic Army, the Kachin Defence Army, the Pau National Organisation, the Palaung State Liberation Front and the Shan State National People's Liberation Organisation.

The collapse of the CPB, in theory a victory for the USA, was a disaster with regard to the exploitation of the narcotic wealth of the Golden Triangle. The CPB at its peak had controlled some 80 per cent of the poppy fields, and party policy had been to limit production. The party administrators would take a 20 per cent 'protection' tax on output, and opium was stockpiled at local offices before communist officials of the 'Trade Department' sold it to Chinese traders.

Increasingly, top officials used the opium trade to provide for their families. However, after a rat infestation decimated crops in the region under their control, the CPB distributed famine relief in the form of 1,600 kg of opium. Nevertheless, the official attitude to the narcotics trade continued to be ambivalent. As late as 1985, the CPB launched a 'rectification' campaign aimed at curbing the private trading of opium. Indeed, this was one of the perverse outcomes of the opium industry in Burma's 'Golden Triangle'; 'Paradoxically, the area controlled by the orthodox Marxist–Leninists of the CPB, became a haven for free trade in then socialist Burma.'[11] However, with the fall of the CPB, the suppressed juices of free market activity were unleashed with even greater force. In the four years after the collapse of the CPB, Burma's opium output is estimated to have doubled.

However, it was Khun Sa who remained king of the jungle. From 1987, he rapidly expanded his empire along the Shan and Thai borders. As a military force, he now commanded troops and weaponry to match those of the neighbouring countries. By 1995, his narcotics operations supported an army of 12,000, including defectors from the now defunct CPB; his high-tech arsenal even acquired SAM-7 missiles.

Even when nominally detained by a Burmese government, seemingly doing the bidding of the West, Khun Sa managed his narcotics group from a luxurious, 'prison' compound outside Rangoon, where he occupied himself during his confinement with a harem of four young wives. Khun Sa's children managed the day-to-day activities of the cartel in the highlands, including a complex that has been described as a 'mini-Las Vegas', where opium exchanges were made in return for gold bars.

Of the seven family owned opium refineries around Homong, two were managed by Tin Oo, a well-connected general in the Burmese army. However, much of the financing of these industrial operations probably came from shadowy Chinese business syndicates in Hong Kong, Bangkok and Taiwan. Meanwhile, marketing of the cartel's heroin was done in Chiang Mai in Northern Thailand by Ma Zhengwen, a Chinese Muslim from Yunan who fronted the I-Chin Mining Company. Also, Khun Sa's son, Sam Seun, controlled the family's jade operations in Kachin.

Khun Sa's daughter acted as the group financial controller for a business empire which also included gambling interests in Mergui.

In 1991, the US Drug Enforcement Agency described Burma in their annual report as 'the world's largest producer of heroin',[12] a product for which America provided over half the market. As the threat of communism declined with the fall of the Soviet Union, the threat posed by narcotics rose in the pecking order of America's global problems.

A preventative crop substitution programme financed by the United Nations had also been a naive, even farcical, failure. Embarrassingly, the United Nations placed an important centre for their International Drug Control Programme outside Rangoon, close to the main criminal laboratories for manufacture of methamphetamines. Their expensively funded expatriate employees probably mingled socially with the crime gangs' specialist chemists imported from Europe. United Nation's incompetence was grotesquely displayed in April 1997, when a museum of 'drug suppression' was opened at Mong La by drug baron Lin Mingxian, a former Communist warlord; the ceremony was attended by government officials, diplomats from Rangoon and United Nations' dignitaries.

In June 1994, the US Deputy Assistant Secretary of State for East Asian and Pacific Affairs Thomas Hubbard told the House of Representatives sub-committee on Asian and Pacific Affairs that 'it is unlikely that the heroin trade can be curtailed without fundamental political change in Burma'.[13] A despairing American embassy in Rangoon came to the conclusion that 'export of opiates alone appear to be worth as much as all legal exports', and that the government, 'makes no perceptible effort to bar investments funded by the production or export of narcotics'.[14] America could no longer tolerate the threat posed by a renegade state integrated with a global narcotics mafia. From this point, America became increasingly hostile towards Burma.

It was estimated that in 1995 Burma, with 2,300 tons, produced almost double the opium of its nearest rival Afghanistan with 1,250 tons; far behind these two stood Laos with 200 tons and Pakistan with 180 tons. Not only had Burma increased volumes dramatically, but purity levels of its retail product had also improved from 7 per cent in 1981 to 26.6 per cent in 1991 and 39.7 per cent in 1995. Higher purity product increased addiction as it allowed non-injectable use and raised the number of users exponentially; it also avoided the risk of HIV and prolonged the lives of customers. However, greater purities brought a higher risk of overdosing; in the USA, hospital emergency episodes for addicts increased from 42,000 per annum in 1989 to 64,000 per annum in 1994 out of a population of 600,000 addicts.

In 1996, Pao Yochang, head of the United Wa State Army, East Asia's largest heroin trafficking organisation, was openly photographed shaking hands with U Ko Lay, the mayor of Rangoon, in the journal *New Light of Myanmar*. Narcotics trafficker Lo Hsing Han was chairman of Kokang Import Export Co., which was the largest shareholder of Asia World Group with some US$ 200 million invested in hotel projects in Burma including the Traders Hotel, the Shangri-La and the Equatorial in Rangoon and the Sedona in Mandalay; associated investments included a Tiger Beer plant, a paper mill, textiles, palm oil plantations and construction.

Lo Hsing Han, who acted as an agent after an amnesty with the government in 1980, had rapidly built up his operations on the ruins of the CPB infrastructure. By the early 1990s, such was his military power working with the Peng brothers, who ran the Myanmar National Democratic Army, that it was reckoned that he could even 'outgun' Khun Sa. The wealthy Lo family also invested in Rangoon's container port facilities, and operated the highway between Lashio and the Chinese border. Similarly, it was Khun Sa's money that built the new highway between Rangoon and Mandalay.

A despairing Secretary of State Warren Christopher noted that '. . . the threat its [Burma's] heroin trade poses to our nations is growing. Major drug traffickers receive government contracts and launder money in state banks. The warlord, Khun Sa, remains unpunished . . . '.[15] Eventually in 1998, President Clinton banned investment in Burma having complained in the previous autumn that

> the role of drugs in Burma's economic and political life and the regime's refusal to honour it own pledge to move to multi-party democracy are really two sides of the same coin, for both represent the absence of the rule of law.[16]

However, the growing US hostility towards Burma was as much related to geopolitics as drugs.

Rangoon's relationship with China was also changing. The demise of the CPB removed any lingering reason for China and Burma not to resume the traditional 'client state' relationship between the two countries. China, newly invigorated by Deng Xiaoping's free market reforms, was now strong enough to perform as ringmaster to its 'client states'. In 1990, Rangoon began to import arms from China, including F7 jets, gunboats, tanks, missiles, radar and personnel carriers. In the ten years from August 1988, cross-border trade with Burma rose from US$ 15 million to US$ 800 million per annum. Investment from China came to dominate parts of the economy. In effect, Mandalay became a Chinese-owned city with its bars and hotels financed by the drug trade; even construction gangs used Chinese labour. The relationship with China became central to Burma's prosperity in the post Ne Win era. General Than Shwe, chairman of SLORC, described China as 'the Myanmar people's most trusted friend'.[17]

For ASEAN and the West, the threat was more than the drugs now swamping America and Europe. China could now count on a strategic port of supply on the Indian Ocean – a vital toehold in the expansion of China's geopolitical reach. Reportedly, in 1994 the Indian navy detained a Chinese survey ship with electronic monitoring equipment. ASEAN's response was to adopt a policy of 'constructive engagement'.

Narcotics remained the primary focus of Western interest in Burma to a degree that allowed SLORC (State Restoration Law and Order Council) to conduct
ethnic cleansing of the minorities at will. In 1992, for the second time in 30 years,
the Muslim Rohingyas of Arakan were brutally assaulted; with their mosques and
villages destroyed, some 250,000 fled across the border into Bangladesh. It was
a pattern of assault on the tribal minorities that was to re-occur throughout Ne
Win's dictatorship.

The 'soft' approach favoured by Burma's neighbours did not satisfy the more
aggressive hard-line stance favoured by the Clinton administration. When Secretary of State Madaleine Albright (Warren Christopher's successor) protested
against the admission of Burma to ASEAN, the Malaysian foreign minister commented, 'I can't help if she is uncomfortable.'[18] The development of the Burmese
economy by China also posed an increasing threat to Thailand. The Thai army
which had a tradition of operating pursuits across Burma's border was suddenly
barred from entry in 1995; increasingly America's long-standing ally Thailand,
whose army was less 'battle hardened' than Burma's, looked isolated within the
region.

The intractable political problem of the tribal minorities, which Earl
Mountbatten and the British government had inexcusably ducked in the post-war
settlement, was the root cause of the development of a warlord culture financed
by the international narcotics industry. Denied the normal routes of political and
social development by the Burmese government's refusal to countenance devolved
government, the tribal states were driven to finance their military survival by ever-
greater resort to the drugs trade.

Ultimately, what started as drug financed tribal political resistance movements
to the tyranny of the Burman centralisers were subsumed by criminal culture. At
a certain point, political overtures from the Burmese government ceased to have
any meaning. As the US State Department noted in 1999, 'Cease-fire agreements
with ethnic insurgent groups dependant on the narcotics trade involve an implicit
tolerance of continued involvement in narcotics for varying periods of time.'[19]

International agencies, riddled with ineptitude, failed to stem the rise of
Burma's narcotics culture. The US policy itself was far from blameless for the
creation of a gangsters' haven, whose tentacles of power now had global reach.
Apart from the US government's ineffectual efforts to stem American consumer
demand for narcotics, successive administrations could never decide whether its
priority was to fight communism or the narcotics industry.

In the 1950s, Harry Anslinger, chief of the US Federal Bureau of Narcotics was
convinced that the flood of Yunnanese opium into America was a communist plot.
Given that Chairman Mao had banned the production of opium in China and that
the warlords in the borderlands that divide China, Burma, Thailand and Laos were
beyond China's control, it seems likely that Anslinger's information was, like most
US intelligence in the area, faulty. Given Burma's patchwork of tribal minorities

and their myriad factions, clan loyalties and paramilitary gangs in the horseshoe of impenetrable hills and jungle that surround the Burman plains, accurate intelligence was virtually impossible.

Even the US strategy itself was deeply fissured in its objectives. The geopolitical need to contain communism led to the financing and military supply of *Kuomintang* forces still loyal to Taiwan and committed to the overthrow of Mao's regime in China. The unintended consequence of the CIA's support for the *Kuomintang* remnants operating within Burma's borders was to finance a military group which internationalised the production and marketing of narcotics through triad networks worldwide.

Likewise in their dealing with the Burmese government, the USA could never decide whether to try to work with them or not. In the late 1980s, undercover agent Michael Levine quit his post at the DEA complaining, 'we gave up the drug war in favour of a war against communism. In fact, we made a conscious choice . . . the war on drugs is a fraud'.[20]

In addition, there were always business and lobby groups for whom the opportunity to do business in Burma outweighed any moral issues. In 1993, Lester Wolff, a well-known human rights activist, cast aside his moral scruples to accept employment as a PR lobbyist for Burma's generals, wishing to 'help improve relations between our peoples and our governments . . . to better the understanding of the views and policies of the Union of Myanmar in the United States'.[21]

China too pursued a deeply ambiguous policy towards the regime in Burma. By the 1970s, Chinese government became deeply alarmed at the growing addiction problem in Yunan Province; although the explosive growth of the narcotics industry was targeted largely at the USA and to a lesser extent, European markets, there was also seepage into the tribal communities and neighbouring Chinese provinces. Also, the growth of Chinese gangster groups, particularly among the outcast Muslim communities of Western China, presented a security challenge to the authority of the state.

Thus, China, like the USA, flip-flopped in its relationship with Burma. By the mid-1980s, the Chinese government was encouraging the leadership of the CPB to go into retirement in China, but it was only after the Wa-led coup, which effectively terminated the CPB as an operational force in Burma, that relations with China were able to be established on a favourable footing. For China, the geopolitical prize of restoring Burma as a loyal satrap nation, with an opening onto the Indian Ocean, was too great a prize to worry about the ethics of the 'Narcotic' state built by Ne Win.

Most importantly from a Western viewpoint, Burma's geopolitical importance to China meant that a solution to the problem of the incarcerated Aung San, her country's democratically elected leader, remained intractable. Even Burma's membership of ASEAN failed to reign in the country's role as one of the world's pre-eminent rogue states.

53

Rajiv Gandhi: The Reluctant Pilot

India: 1984—9

Rajiv Gandhi lived the invisible life of one of Delhi's upper middle class urban professionals. Displaying the dilution of Nehru's intellectual stock, already evident in his mother, Indira, and not furthered by her marriage to Feroze Gandhi, who flunked his degree at the London School of Economics, Rajiv Gandhi was an unexceptional pupil of the Doon School in Dehradun. This imitation English public school westernised Rajiv to the extent that, in later life, even his Hindi was suspect.

Mark Tully, the long-serving BBC correspondent in Delhi, noted that 'Once, when I was interviewing him [Rajiv], he heard me speak to a cameraman in Hindi and said, 'You speak Hindi very well.' I replied, 'Not really . . . I wish I spoke better.' He laughed and said, 'I wish I did too.'[1] From the Doon School, Indira engineered a place for him at Cambridge where he did little work, played around and eventually met his future wife, Sonia Maino, who was learning English at a language school in the town. Having failed to take a degree at Cambridge, his mother procured a place for him at Imperial College, London, where it was felt that a degree in engineering would be more to his taste. Rajiv failed here too.

Returning to Delhi, Rajiv learnt to fly at the Safdarjung Flying School in New Delhi and eventually settled into the secure, if somewhat pedestrian, life of a co-pilot for Indian Airlines. Rajiv's interests reflected the comfortable lifestyle of his milieu. He liked cars, computers and gadgets. Like his brother, Sanjay, he read technology magazines. His tastes were largely western. He wore 'designer' jeans and Gucci shoes. He had a Cartier watch. With his Italian wife, he was a frequent diner at the Casa Medici restaurant in the Taj Hotel. He loved popular music, though possibly not as much as his hi-fi system that was reputedly one of the best in the country.

Commenting on Rajiv and his contemporary, the Chief Minister of Kashmir Farooq Abdullah, Tavleen Singh in *Kashmir: A Tragedy of Errors* (1996) observed that 'both married middle-class European women who would ideally have been happiest living in the heart of suburbia in some European city, watching television in the evening surrounded by their families'.[2] Indeed Rajiv was a quiet, respectable, professional 'family man'; in summary he was amiable, unassertive, meticulous, slow paced, private and dull.

However, he had the Gandhi name. After Sanjay killed himself flying over Delhi, Rajiv was gradually drawn into the family business – the running of India. Within nine months, Rajiv had given up his flying career and was brought into Indira Gandhi's *durbar* (court). He explained, 'The way I look at it is that Mummy has to be helped somehow.'[3] Within two years, he was general secretary of Congress (I). It does not seem to have occurred to Rajiv that the alternative to nepotism was that his mother might have drawn on the political experience of leaders within her party and ministerial cabinet; hoiking her remaining son out of a pilot's seat into government was not the only option available to Indira Gandhi.

However unassuming in character, Rajiv nevertheless, like his grandfather, mother and brother, had an unfailing sense of his own 'noblesse'. Thus, when his mother was assassinated in 1984, Rajiv, an immature novice in the ways of Indian politics, let alone the arts of statesmanship, had no hesitations in accepting the leadership of Congress (I). As Rajiv was reported saying, 'Congress is to politics what the *Ganges* [River] is to our culture_ the mainstream.'[4]; he might also have added that Congress without a Gandhi to lead it was hardly a party at all.

In spite of Rajiv Gandhi's patent lack of credentials to be a leader of his country, by intellect, character or training, his early years of power were characterised by heady success. First, the elections held in the wake of his mother's death brought out a vast sympathy vote for Rajiv. The December 1984 poll brought a Congress tally of 401 seats out of 495 in the *Lok Sabha* (lower house), a majority which dwarfed even Nehru's haul of 371 seats in 1957. Helped by his youthful good looks, open countenance and reputation as a 'Mr Clean', Rajiv appeared as a breath of fresh air in Indian politics. His opening speeches also indicated that a new approach to Indian political and economic leadership was in the offing.

Addressing the Indian people a day after he had scattered his mother's ashes from a plane above the Himalayas, Rajiv suggested that 'Private industry should acquire the strength competition provides by reducing costs and absorbing new technology. Both public and private sectors should venture into new fields and develop indigenous technology.'[5]

Rajiv retained for himself the ministerial portfolios for science and technology, electronics, space and civil aviation and set out an agenda which included bringing drinking water to the villages (20 per cent did not have this facility), education via satellite communication and television for all. Reflecting his own geeky interests, Rajiv wanted 'a computer in every school by the 21st Century'.[6] However, in India, there was a need for even the most basic of technologies; many villages could not afford blackboards or chalk, let alone teachers and computers. Rajiv also wanted to improve health by introducing a programme of immunisation. He urged the use of science to improve yields in cattle and to develop alternative sources of cooking oils, which were largely imported.

Rajiv wowed the press by running his life from two Toshiba laptop computers and by making his office staff computer literate. To advise on the advancement of Indian technology, Rajiv also brought back from America a successful technology engineer, Sam Pitroda, who had sold his telephone switching systems business to Rockwell International. This seemed an appropriate choice in a country where 800 million people shared just 5 million telephones and where it could take five years and copious bribery to acquire a telephone connection.

In Rajiv's India, technology would banish poverty. It was a utopian vision symptomatic of the family into which he had been born. In an address to Indian scientists, Rajiv instructed that 'the litmus test for any scientific activity in India is how far it helps to remove poverty'.[7] Underlying Rajiv's programme was a genuine, albeit naive desire to modernise India and eliminate the poverty that was the globally renowned characteristic of Indian life. In addressing the US Congress in Washington, Rajiv announced that

> India is an old country, but a young nation and like the young everywhere, we are impatient. I am young, and I too have a dream. I dream of an India strong, independent, self-reliant and in the forefront, in front rank of the nations of the world in the service of mankind.[8]

For the world's press, Rajiv was too good to be true; 'Gandhi is off to an amazingly fast start',[9] enthused *Newsweek*. For 18 months after his election, he milked adulatory reviews both internationally and domestically.

However, his dreams and aspirations lacked substance. Like Nehru and Indira Gandhi before him, Rajiv lacked the intellectual ability or interest to work out why India's economy had failed to liberate its people from grinding poverty. Even though Energy Minister Vasant Sathe wrote an article suggesting that the whole concept of the public sector might have been a mistake, an article presumably written with Rajiv's acquiescence, Rajiv never made serious efforts to dismantle the bureaucratic socialist state.

Of India's 220 state-owned industries, less than half made a profit; yet apart from a state-owned scooter factory, none of these were restructured, let alone returned to the private sector. The result was chronic industrial and economic underperformance. In India, 125,000 workers produced less steel than 14,000 in South Korea. The underdevelopment of the telecommunications industry was not caused by a shortage of either telephones or demand, but by the incurable incompetence of a monopolistic state bureaucracy. 'Speed' money had to be paid for every bureaucratic 'chop' to fall on sheaves of forms and applications demanded by the state, whether for telephones, government manufacturing licences or even access to power provision by the state electricity boards. However, 'speed' in the context of Indian state bureaucracies was a question of 'stop or go', not 'fast or slow'.

Rajiv also clung to the notion that India could develop entirely through 'self-reliance', an economic fallacy he shared with North Korea's Kim Il Sung. Although Rajiv's government gave licences to favoured Indian companies for the manufacture and assembly of foreign consumer products, notably 'white goods' such as washing machines, TVs, etc., foreign multinational investment was disallowed. Regulations introduced by Indira Gandhi preventing foreign companies owning more than 50 per cent of an Indian company had led to the withdrawal of IBM and Coca Cola among other multinational corporations from the Indian economy in 1977.

The result was that both state-owned industries and 'screwdriver' assembly plants manufactured products that, in the global market place, were sub-standard. With years of experience of piloting airline customers back to India, Rajiv should have noticed that returning Indian passengers were awash with foreign-imported consumer products, for which there was a thriving black market in the major cities of Bombay and Delhi. For sophisticated Delhi inhabitants such as Rajiv, the brand of a product was much less important than avoidance of one stamped with 'Made in India'.

Sadly for India, much of its industrial output could only be sold in that other huge market for sub-standard goods, the Soviet Union. Addressing the Indian engineering industry, Rajiv made the accurate observation that 'we are selling to a captive market, we are selling to a market which is not responsive to quality. We are selling really in an absolute seller's market.'[10] In spite of this admonition to Indian industrialists, Rajiv seemed entirely unaware that India's industrial backwardness was almost entirely the result of an autarkic economic edifice of which his family had been the architects. Indeed he remained in thrall to the 'Bombay Club' of Indian industrialists who were vehemently opposed to deregulation and foreign investment.

Contrary to Mark Tully's comments in *No Full Stops* (1991) that 'Socialism had become unfashionable in the West, so it was no surprise that Rajiv had attempted to wriggle out of its grip',[11] Rajiv made little or no attempt to adopt the supply-side reforms pioneered by Ronald Reagan and Margaret Thatcher, which were beginning to power the recoveries of the Ango-Saxon economies from the mid-1980s.

Eventually, it was not the economic failings of Rajiv's government that were to prick the bubble of his popularity honeymoon. From 1986, 'Mr Clean' found himself spattered with 'dirt' from the most serious corruption scandal to have hit India since independence. In part the problems stemmed from Rajiv's punctilious minister of finance who, apart from raising his reputation by controlling inflation and improving revenue collection, also garnered plaudits for his vigorous pursuit of corrupt businessmen. As Girilal Jain, editor of *The Times of India*, described him, 'Mr. V.P. Singh has seen himself in the role of a Savonarola who would burn down

Rome rather than allow "Sin" to prosper. The vengeance with which he went after the tallest man in Indian industry as Finance Minister spoke for itself.'[12]

Singh had shocked the corporate establishment by the arrest of leading industrialist Lalit Mohan Thapar for illegal holdings of foreign currency. In October 1986 he went further by publishing a blacklist of companies with customs and excise arrears. However, when it was disclosed that V.P. Singh was employing an American detective agency, the Fairfax Group, to investigate Indian businessmen, including Rajiv's close friend, the wildly popular movie star Amitabh Bachchan, Singh was shifted to the Ministry of Defence. Three months later V.P. Singh was expelled from the party, after he pursued the recipients of an illegal 7 per cent commission believed to have been paid on two submarines purchased from Howaldt Deutsche Werke. The Delhi political world, and more importantly the Indian public, drew the conclusion that Rajiv had yielded to pressure from his corrupt industrialist friends.

While this episode tarnished Rajiv's image, it was a report by a Swedish radio station in 1987 that bribes had been paid by the Swedish defence company Bofors to secure a US$ 1.3 billion artillery contract, which was to mire his government in the most damaging and long-running corruption scandal. A few days before this revelation, Arun Singh had reiterated Rajiv's 'no middlemen' policy for defence contracts. Furthermore the contract had been negotiated and awarded while Rajiv himself held the defence portfolio prior to relinquishing it to V.P. Singh.

As the scandal unfolded, the Swedish government confirmed that a payment of 32 million krona (US$ 5 million) had been made to the Swiss bank accounts of a company called Pitco (later named Moresco), which were linked to the Hinduja family. However, The Hindu newspaper confirmed that bribes, as much as 10–14 per cent of the value of the contract, had been paid out. While Rajiv forcefully denied any knowledge of wrongdoing, in addition to denying having received any of the kickback himself, his credibility was seriously undermined.

Further damage was caused by the attempts to cover up the crime. In September 1989, former Army Chief General Sundarji denied Rajiv's parliamentary assertion that the combined services had not wanted the cancellation of the Bofors contract after the discovery of the Swedish bribe. A month later, the editor of The Hindu complained that the government was threatening to stop advertising in the newspaper if their investigations into the Bofors story continued. The comptroller and auditor general report on Bofors sealed a damning indictment of the government.

Although Rajiv's long-time colleague and deputy in the Ministry of Defence, Arun Singh, resigned, the main casualty of Bofors was the prime minister's reputation as 'Mr Clean'. While the recipients of Bofors money have never been revealed, it has been postulated that Sanjay, before his death, may well have instituted a system of automatically reaping commissions for all defence contracts, including those for Harrier jump jets, Westland G-30s and the Mirage 2000 fighter. With

Rajiv's vast parliamentary majority, there was little that the opposition could do. However, the resignation of virtually the whole of the opposition in *Lok Sabha*, at the suggestion of N.T. Rama Rao, provided a national publicity coup to highlight the Bofors scandal.

In other areas too the positive start to Rajiv's government evaporated. In spite of his mother's execution at the hands of Sikh extremists, Rajiv held out a moderating hand to Punjab. While insisting that 'The Sikhs are as much a part of India as any other community',[13] Rajiv entered negotiations with the Sikh moderate Sant Longowal, leader of the *Akali Dal* (Immortal Party). In a settlement announced in July 1985, Rajiv offered the Punjab the exclusive use of the city of Chandigarh as state capital and a commission to increase water rights to the Punjab.

However, within a month of making the accord, Longowal was shot dead by a Sikh extremist. Further violence continued with the blowing up of an Air India Boeing 747 over Ireland while on a flight from Toronto to Delhi. Also a bomb exploded in baggage for a Bombay-bound Air India plane in Tokyo and an assassination attempt was made on Rajiv.

There was a further escalation of violence in 1986 within the Punjab; General Arun Kumar Vaidya, formerly army chief of staff at the time of Operation Bluestar at the Golden Temple, was murdered. The tense situation was further impaired by the imposition of presidential rule in April 1987. Those of a cynical bent, in other words all of Delhi's political journalists, saw this manoeuvre as a shameless Hindu vote-winning ploy just five weeks before elections in the neighbouring state of Haryana.

Rajiv's craven regard for the Hindu vote was best shown by the fact that he failed to implement the two main provisos of the accord with Longowal. In addition, only one of the 3,870 Sikhs' murders in Delhi, in the aftermath of Indira Gandhi's assassination, had been resolved by end of Rajiv's term of office. As Akali Dal MP Balwant Singh Ramoowalia pointed out in July 1989, 'Now people have lost faith in the Prime Minister and the situation has become so dangerous that no Akali leader is willing to show the sort of courage and initiative that Sant Longowal showed.'[14]

Rajiv regained some credibility for his government when Operation Black Thunder starved out Sikh terrorists, who had again occupied the Golden Temple. The lack of casualties, combined with revulsion at the actions of the Sikh terrorists, gave scope for Rajiv to make ground for achieving peace in the Punjab. However, Rajiv again aroused local hostilities by passing the 59th constitutional amendment in Lok Sabha, which allowed the prime minister to call for a state of emergency on the grounds of 'internal disturbance'. With echoes of Indira's tyranny during 'the Emergency', the Sikhs saw this as legislation directly aimed at the Punjab. The opportunity to reconcile the Punjab problem was now ended.

Meanwhile in Assam, Rajiv missed the chance to halt the student unrest, which had brought six years of fighting over the issue of Bangladeshi immigration rights.

A policy of expulsions and disenfranchisements had been agreed with the young Assamese leaders within a year of Rajiv taking office. Once again Rajiv failed to implement agreements with communal leaders.

Thereafter the local Assam Gana Parishad Party swept Congress aside in the state elections of 1985, making Assam the fifth state to be ruled by a regional party rather than a national one and the eighth state in all to be lost to Congress control. Rajiv compounded his mistakes in Assam by giving spurious grounds for postponing *Lok Sabha* elections in the state in 1989. In spite of Rajiv's sweeping *Lok Sabha* victory in the national elections of 1985, he was unable to do anything to reverse the continued state-by-state decline of Congress as a national party in the face of regional challengers.

However, Rajiv's failures in the Punjab and Assam were of minor consequence compared to the problems that he inflamed in Kashmir and Sri Lanka. In November 1986 Farooq Abdullah was persuaded to return to Kashmir as chief minister by an agreement that would see power sharing between his own Kashmir National Conference Party and Congress. In response, Congress's chief minister in Kashmir, Mufti Mohammed Sayed, predicted that Congress would be wiped out in the state and immediately resigned to join the Janata Dal party. As Tavleen Singh pointed out, the merging of the main parties in Kashmir created 'a vacuum in the opposition, it would mean political suicide for both parties'.[15] In exchange for the short-term attractions of power, Farooq had bartered away the roots of his popularity which lay in his defence of Kashmir rights in defiance of Congress.

Into the vacuum stepped the extremist fundamentalist Islamic party, the Jamaat-e-Islami, which as part of the Muslim United Front (MUF) reaped the electoral position formerly occupied by the Kashmiri National Conference. Farooq's position was further eroded after the state elections of March 1987, by the blatant ballot rigging carried out by the National Conference with Congress's connivance. Following the arrest of some 600 young MUF workers, young men now poured over the borders to Pakistan to be trained and armed by Muslim fundamentalists. Their eventual return to Kashmir would presage a change from that state's traditionally moderate Sufi form of Islam to an increasingly radicalised Islamic fundamentalism.

When Rajiv came to power, the Tamil issue in Sri Lanka was also becoming increasingly violent; the Tamil Tigers, the revolutionary group seeking independence for the Hindu worshipping Tamils, were seeking to wrest effective independent control of the northwest of the country from Sri Lanka's Buddhist majority. Indira Gandhi, with an eye to the Tamil vote in Tamil Nadu, had turned a blind eye to the training and funding of Tamil fighters from the mainland. Political expediency also guided Rajiv. In response to Rajiv's offer of help to resolve the dispute, Sri Lanka's President Jayewardene responded, 'The only help we need is for you to stop exporting terrorism to Sri Lanka by training Tamil guerrillas.'[16]

Jayewardene had few options however. Sri Lanka, with 15 million inhabitants, was dwarfed by its neighbour, and both the USA and the Britain declined to become involved in what they saw as a regional dispute outside the scope of their geopolitical interests. When Rajiv protested about food shortages in Jaffna, the Tamil stronghold being surrounded by the Sri Lankan army, Jayewardene had to either parley with the Indian government or risk invasion, as happened in East Pakistan in that country's civil war.

However, after two years of sporadic peace talks starting in 1985, Rajiv unilaterally invaded Sri Lankan airspace with five Antonov-32 supply planes and escorting Mirage fighters, so as to provide relief to Jaffna. Jayewardene was forced to admit that 'The Sri Lankan government had no means of resisting India's unilateral action physically, nor will it be able to do so in the future.'[17] A peace accord was later signed in July 1987, which restored Tamil as an official language, promised a referendum and agreed the release of Tamil political prisoners. More importantly, Jayewardene accepted an Indian peace-keeping force, which, at its peak, numbered 70,000 men. In effect, Rajiv had usurped Sri Lankan sovereignty.

In practice the arrangement soon fell apart. The Sri Lankan Tamils took Rajiv's money but did not surrender their weapons. After Indian forces imprisoned 12 Tamil Tigers, who then committed suicide, all basis of trust between the Tamils and the occupying Indian forces broke down. Velupillai Prabhakaran, the terrorist leader of the Tamil Tigers, now ended the ceasefire and organised attacks on Indian patrols.

Meanwhile the Buddhist Sinhalese were equally furious with Jayewardene for yielding to the Indians, and the Sri Lankan president was fortunate to escape an assassination attempt. With the open hostility of the Tamils, whom they had originally come to help, the Indian army became bogged down in a battle of attrition. According to the New York-based journalist Ved Mehta, 'The Tamil Tigers blamed Rajiv of undermining their near revolution in Sri Lanka, and they also claimed that as a consequence of his intervention their cause has suffered an international eclipse.'[18]

Out of sight of the world's gaze, a violent conflict now unfolded. As Mervyn de Silva, the editor of *The Lanka Guardian*, wrote in *The Far East Economic Review* in August 1989, 'There are more soldiers in Sri Lanka than Vietnamese troops in Cambodia or Syrian forces in Lebanon. Yet, no voices are raised in august assemblies, no resolutions passed. Not many tears are shed over Sri Lanka's killing fields.'[19] Rajiv's expansionist policies did not go unnoticed in Delhi however; *The Illustrated Indian Weekly* asked whether India was emerging as the bully boy of the subcontinent. Rajiv also turned his attention to Nepal, where that government had angered India by the purchase of weapons from China, even though this was allowed under the Peace and Friendship Treaty signed by Rajiv's grandfather, Nehru. Withdrawal of Indian's rights to property and employment also raised concerns in

Delhi notwithstanding the Indian government's own draconian prohibitions on foreign ownership of land in India. Rajiv simply imposed trade tariffs on land-locked Nepal and denied it access to oil. *The Economist* was led to conclude that India was 'trying to turn Nepal into a vassal state'.[20]

Despite the coercive nature of India's foreign policy and the build-up of India's military strength through acquisition of nuclear-powered submarines from the Soviet Union, the former Falkland's war aircraft carrier *HMS Hermes* from Britain and the domestic development of short- and medium-range missiles, Rajiv continued Nehru's practice of issuing pious homilies on peaceful non-alignment.

In December 1985, Rajiv posited the lofty thought that 'Empires have come and gone, conquest has been succeeded by liberation. What has endured is the abiding non-violence of Buddha, Jesus and Mahatma Gandhi.'[21] In spite of his recent military purchases and his ready use of Indian military power, Rajiv also declared that 'we defend ourselves not with weapons but with words . . . by building public opinion against war'.[22] At a banquet held for Rajiv in Washington, he informed his hosts that 'We are for complete nuclear disarmament, dismantling weapons, and the destruction of stock piles.'[23] He optimistically asked for this 'to take place as soon as possible'.[24]

Rajiv was unable to comprehend that in the competing ideological expansion of the Soviet Union and America in the post-war era, Mutually Assured Destruction (MAD) was the best guarantor of peace between the rival superpowers. Instead he maintained throughout his life a blind faith in the great international institutions. In spite of overwhelming evidence of corruption and malfeasance at UNESCO, Rajiv was furious at Ronald Reagan's withdrawal from this body.

Neither was his faith in the Non-Aligned Movement in the least bit diminished by the 29 conflicts between its 100 members between 1961 and 1989. Noticeably however, in spite of Rajiv's assertion that 'We have no intentions to produce a nuclear weapon',[25] he continued to refuse signature of the Non-Proliferation Treaty, although India had exploded a nuclear device in Rajasthan as far back as 1974.

Not surprisingly, Rajiv was an inveterate attendee of worthy international conferences. In spite of his government's development of delivery systems for nuclear devices, Rajiv hypocritically preached nuclear disarmament at the United Nations General Assembly, a body he was to address on three occasions during his five years in power. He attended a Commonwealth meeting in Nassau in 1985, plus mini-Commonwealth summits in London (1986) and Vancouver (1987), to discuss South Africa. He chaired the Non-Aligned Movement in Harare in 1986 and attended its forum in Belgrade in 1989. In addition he went to Dhaka, Bangalore and Islamabad for annual meetings of the newly formed SAARC (South Asian Association for Regional Cooperation).

While Rajiv was always quite at home in the attenuated world of international symposia, he found the humdrum world of economic management, domestic and particularly communal politics much more difficult to cope with. When the wife of a well-off Madhya Pradesh Muslim lawyer forced her ex-husband through the courts to pay a monthly maintenance, he refused, on the grounds that it was in contravention of Sharia law. Rajiv, eager to court the Indian Muslim vote, foolishly passed the Muslim Women's Bill. Predictably there was a backlash from the Hindu community, furious at a system which allowed separate communal laws. Rajiv, like Nehru and Indira Gandhi before him, baulked at the introduction of the common civil code, which the framers of the Indian constitution had originally envisaged.

Worse still for the future of communal relations in India, Rajiv attempted to balance his blatant attempt to buy off the Muslim vote, by seeking to woo the Hindu vote by his actions at the Muslim mosque at Ayodhya. The Moghul Emperor Babar had halted in the town in 1528 and had decided to build a mosque on the supposed site of the Hindu god Ram's birthplace. Until 1949 both religions had used the site, with the Muslims inside the mosque and the Hindus worshipping at the shrine on the outside.

Communal tensions arose only after 1949, when Hindus broke into the mosque to leave Hindu statues inside. Thereafter the mosque at Ayodhya became the focal point of the growing Hindu nationalism that had awakened in India during the 1980s. Encouraged in part by the first-time national airing of television dramas based on the *Ramayana* and the *Mahabharata*, and by constant use of communal tactics to produce votes for the Nehru dynasty, increasing numbers of Indians wished the government to affirm that India was a Hindu state.

Faced with the growing electoral threat of the BJP (Bharatiya Janata Party) to his Hindu vote, Rajiv used the state television monopoly, Doordarshan, to televise the unlocking and opening of the Ayodhya mosque to Hindus. Notably Rajiv launched his 1989 election campaign from Faizabad near Ayodhya. The blatant use of the 'Hindu card' was to have catastrophic consequences for race relations in India over the succeeding decade. Rajiv's decision to allow Hindu worship in the mosque at Ayodhya created a major political issue out of a minor one. As Mark Tully has commented, Rajiv 'behaved as though religious sentiment was just another factor to be manipulated for political purposes'.[26]

The mystery is how Rajiv, starting out with such a wellspring of popular support, ended by miscalculating so disastrously on so many issues of domestic policy. Tully has argued that Rajiv did not understand that with politics in India there was the 'need to make yourself available to as many people as possible and the need to gather information from as many sources as possible'.[27]

Like his mother, Rajiv undermined cabinet government through his reliance on a small cotery of westernised friends, including his former airline pilot colleague Satish Sharma. Sharma, whom Rajiv would later have to defend regarding questions as to how he could afford his imported marble swimming pool, was not the type of advisor who could keep Rajiv abreast of what was happening on the ground. Eventually, Rajiv would turn back to his mother's chief advisor R.K. Dhawan, now rehabilitated from corruption scandals of his own, to provide him with a conduit to his own party. However Rajiv, comfortable with New Delhi's 'haute bourgeoisie', never felt at home with the rough characters who represented Congress in the Lok Sabha. Unlike Indira, who developed an encyclopaedic knowledge of her Congressmen and their individual motivations, Rajiv would always be a stranger to his own party.

In one respect however, Rajiv's attitude to Congress exactly mirrored that of his mother. The party belonged to the Gandhi family. When Congress Party state ministers overstepped the line with regard to their loyalty to the Gandhi family, Rajiv was as swift at summary removal as his mother. Between 1980 and 1989, Rajiv and his mother ousted nine Congress Party chief ministers from the 12 major states in which Congress (I) held power. So lobotomised had Congress become that after Rajiv's death, the leadership of the party was immediately offered to his Italian wife Sonia (albeit a naturalised Indian since 1983). When asked about Sonia's acceptance of the post, a party spokesman assured journalists that 'There is no question of her refusing. She is a party member, and the decision will be communicated to her in due course.'[28]

In 1989 Rajiv went to the polls. The credibility of his government, worn down by the accusations of corruption inspired by Bofors and other scandals, was shattered and the Congress Party succumbed to the loss of its huge parliamentary majority. While Congress (I) with 193 seats remained the largest single party, Janata Dal, with 141 seats, led by Rajiv's former minister V.P. Singh, was able to form a government with the tacit support of the BJP, which won 88 seats; meanwhile the Communists and other leftists mustered 51 seats.

V.P. Singh, also from Allahabad in Uttar Pradesh, was more a man of the people despite his princely connections and his education at the Doon School. However, this did not prevent his government from being short-lived. Controversy over Singh's decision to implement the 1980 Mandal Commission report on the 'Backward Castes', which provided them with a 27 per cent increase in their allocation of government jobs, in addition to the 22 per cent already reserved for 'scheduled' castes and tribes, stirred a violent backlash in northern India. Seventy-five young men died of self-immolation. The affirmative action programme for the 'Backward Castes' split the National Front Alliance.

After an 18-month break from power, Rajiv once again launched himself into an electoral campaign. Well aware that the election was going better than his humiliation of 1989, on the last day of voting he flew down to the insignificant town Sriperumbudur in Tamil Nadu, where he was to give his final election speech. A young Tamil girl from Sri Lanka stepped forward to present Rajiv with a bouquet, and, as she did so, she triggered a package of half a kilogram of RDX explosive embedded with 2-mm steel pellets, which was strapped to her waist. Rajiv Gandhi, aged 51, died instantly. The assassination was probably copied from either Frederick Forsythe's thriller novel *The Negotiator* (1989), later a film (1998;

starring Samuel L. Jackson and Kevin Spacey) or from the Hollywood film *The Delta Force* (1986; starring Lee Marvin and Chuck Norris).

Not surprisingly perhaps, Rajiv had reaped the revenge exacted by sufferers of one of his many overbearing international political stratagems. In many respects Rajiv was the most likeable of the Gandhi dynasty and many of his instincts, particularly in respect of the need to dismantle India's command economy, were correct. However, he was flawed in intellect and character and lacking in experience to carry out the demanding job of ruling India; ultimately his life ended on a macabre, tragic note. He was the third member of the Nehru dynasty to have failed to advance the material welfare of the Indian people.

54

The Tiananmen Square Massacre

China: 1987-9

In the autumn of 1978, as the final negotiations for normalisation of relations with the USA were being conducted by Deng Xiaoping, he was also manoeuvring to complete the encirclement and destruction of Mao's chosen successor, Hua Guofeng. Beginning in November, at the work conference in advance of a Central Committee meeting, Deng's allies began to prepare the ground for his attack on the policies of the past. Then on 13 December 1978, Deng gave a speech that launched a full-blooded assault on the Maoist legacy. With a barely veiled attack on the cult of Mao and his 'Little Red book', he urged that dogma and book worship had to end. A re-evaluation of the Cultural Revolution was called for. In addition, Deng lamented the state of the economy and demanded a new strategy.

Beijing was electrified. As word spread of the direction of the work conference in its criticism of Hua, young office and factory workers started to agitate for more freedom. Big character posters criticising Mao were put up on Democracy Wall. Students joined in with sit-ins and strikes. Flattered and encouraged by the evidence of popular support, Deng gave free reign to his street supporters. To the American columnist Robert Novak he asserted 'The writing of big-character posters is permitted by our constitution. We have no right to negate or criticize the masses for promoting democracy . . . the masses should be allowed to vent their grievances.'[1]

However, it was both the great strength and paradox of Deng Xiaoping that while he promoted economic liberalisation on the one hand, he remained a staunch authoritarian of the hard-left socialist school on the other. In *China Today*, he asserted in a March speech, 'we can never dispense with the leadership by the party and extol the spontaneity of the masses'.[2] Whenever street protests led beyond criticism to challenging the legitimacy of the party and its rule, Deng clamped down. In his speech in March 1979, Deng laid out the four authoritarian principles from which he never wavered: '1. We must keep to the socialist road 2. We must uphold the dictatorship of the proletariat 3. We must uphold the leadership of the communist party 4. We must uphold Marxism and Leninism and Mao Zedong thought.'[3]

Deng's path was clear if somewhat contradictory to Western ears; he believed in radical reform of government and party and a pragmatic approach to economic development, but not at the cost or indeed risk of undermining the central role of the party in the government of China. By the end of March, Deng was complaining that 'certain bad elements have raised sundry demands that cannot be met at present or are altogether unreasonable'.[4] On 2 April, Deng authorised a crackdown on student and worker unrest. Wei Jingsheng, the prominent liberal editor of the magazine *Exploration*, who had attacked Deng's betrayal of the people with the accusation that Deng had only worn the 'mask of protector of democracy',[5] was arrested and, after his trial in October, was sentenced to 15 years in prison.

Was this mere expediency to keep onside the 'old guard' revolutionaries such as Li Xiannian and Chun Yen on whose support he relied? The answer is almost certainly not. It is tempting to believe that Deng was some social democrat reformer held back by the practicalities of party politics. In fact, however, there can be no doubt that Deng, in the political arena, was a hardline communist. As Dr Simon May, who was present at wide-ranging discussions with Deng in the early 1980s, has asserted, 'he was a passionate Communist . . . it was not merely a "formal liturgy"'.[6] In February 1980, Deng authorised the removal of Article 45 which gave the constitutional right to free speech. Both public debate and the right to put up big-character posters were banned.

Such has been the success of Deng's economic policies that the skill with which he manoeuvred politically, without which economic progress would have been stymied, can easily be overlooked. To ensure progress, Deng had to ditch Hua and the Maoist plodders. By March 1980, Deng's takeover was complete with the removal from the politburo of Hua Guofeng's key supporters, Wang Dongxing and Wu De. In August 1980, Hua was forced out as premier, and a year later the now crushed Hua also resigned as chairman of the Central Committee and chairman of the Military Affairs Commission (MAC). However, Deng could not dump Mao entirely in the manner in which Khrushchev attempted to dispose of Stalin's legacy. In August 1980, Deng was quite adamant when he told the Italian journalist Oriana Fallaci that 'we will adhere to Mao Zedong thought. We will not do to Chairman Mao what Khrushchev did to Stalin'.[7]

In China, the legacy of Mao was like the combined legacy of Marx, Lenin and Stalin in the Soviet Union. To completely renounce Mao would have undermined both the credibility and the legitimacy of the party. The trial of the Gang of Four was an important part of this ideological navigation process; starting in November 1980, and lasting for three months, ten leaders were prosecuted. Only Jiang defended herself; this was done along the well-worn lines of the 'just following orders' variety. However, her language was on occasion robust, as with her assertion, 'I was Chairman Mao's dog.'[8] Nevertheless the result proved highly useful to Deng. The conclusion of the trial served to undermine those 'beneficiaries' of the Cultural Revolution, placemen such as Hua Guofeng and justify its victims such as

Deng Xiaoping. Leaving aside the events of the Cultural Revolution and the Great Leap Forward, however, Deng's rewriting of Chinese history still left central space for Mao the great socialist revolutionary.

Such was the success of Deng's combination of political authoritarianism and economic liberalism that it was a grateful and enthusiastic crowd that gathered at the 1 October annual revolution rally in Tiananmen Square, in 1984. Students, a group that had four years earlier demonstrated for greater freedoms, now displayed a greeting banner *Ni hao Xiaoping* (Hello Xiaoping); a jokey informality which would have been inconceivable in the Mao era. However, the first wave of Deng's economic recovery was beginning to run its course. Not for the last time boom would bring problems of inflation, increasing evidence of corruption and difficult choices as to the direction of future policy.

The leadership was shocked by the revelation of a vast illegal import operation being conducted by high-ranking bureaucrats on the island of Hainan, from where luxury foreign goods were being sold to customers throughout China. The illegal diversion of foreign currency amounted to US$ 600 million for the purchase of an estimated 90,000 motor cars, 120,000 motorbikes and 250,000 video recorders in a 15-month period from January 1984. Corruption was a problem almost inevitable in the public–private economy being developed by Deng.

With remarkable prescience, a Chinese dissident student accurately predicted the problem in 1984:

> When there is not enough to go round, the market regulated enterprises will use all kinds of methods including bribery to get hold of energy resources and raw materials destined for large enterprises under the state plan. The income of the staff and workers in the large enterprises, which are subject to guidance planning will not be as high as those working in market regulated enterprises, . . . in order to bribe the units to open wide their back doors. This kind of unhealthy practice will increase and, if it does not attract notice, will become ever more prevalent . . . economic crime will increase by leaps and bounds.[9]

Corruption and an official inflation rate, which at 9 per cent was probably only half the real level, brought out sharp divisions in policy that had been developing since the early 1980s. The year 1985 saw urban violence for the first time in six years. Crime and lawlessness were also on the increase. At the party conference in September Chen Yun, the veteran economic administrator and most prominent of the elders who had pushed for Deng's rehabilitation in 1976, now came out strongly in favour of a halt to further liberalisation. At this point, Deng's sympathies lay strongly with the liberalising faction including his putative successor, Party Secretary Hu Yaobang. In 1986, Hu Yaobang pushed for an even more aggressive reform including wide-ranging price decontrol. In a May Day speech Hu Qili, a supporter of Hu Yaobang, called for Marxist concepts which 'experience had already proved to be outmoded or not entirely correct', to be abandoned.[10]

The autumn saw widespread student unrest. Fang Lizhi, an astrophysicist and vice president of the Chinese University, argued vociferously for 'human rights' and democratic accountability. On 18 November, Fang addressed the students at Tongji University, 'I am here to tell you that the socialist movement, from Marx and Lenin to Stalin and Mao Zedong, has been a failure.... I think that complete Westernisation is the only way to modernize.'[11] As unrest spread Deng once again spoke up against the political ramifications of liberalisation; 'We must not imitate the West, and no liberalization should be allowed.'[12] After the public burning of *The Beijing Daily* on 6 January, Deng felt compelled to move. At the 16 January meeting of the politburo, Deng backed the hardliners and called for Hu Yaobang to resign.

The schizophrenic nature of Deng's policies soon showed in the moderation of public attacks allowed on Hu Yaobang so as not to put off foreign investors, and the appointment of a reluctant Zhao Ziyang as his successor. Zhao Ziyang, whose own flagship area of reform was 'urban regeneration', was also a moderniser. Like Hu Yaobang, he sought political as well as economic reform. 'Different groups of people may have different interests and views,' he noted, and 'they too need opportunities and channels for the exchange of ideas'.[13] In these ideas, it is clear that Zhao Ziyang, like Hu Yaobang before him, had the support of Deng. Evidently Deng was not against political reform per se; he believed that the party needed to reform itself by removing the 'status quo' bureaucrats and politicians of the Maoist era who opposed change. However, political reform was unacceptable to Deng when it transgressed on the legitimacy of the party as sole authoritarian ruler of China.

From the moment of Deng's rehabilitation, he had tried to withdraw to the background of Chinese politics. Apart from the chairmanship of the MAC (Military Affairs Committee), he held none of the high offices of party or state, preferring to operate through his chosen successors Hu Yaobang and then Zhao Ziyang. Deng now tried to further distance himself from active politics, and along with other party veterans, such as Chen Yun and Peng Zhen, he stood down from the politburo in October 1987. However, such was his overwhelming prestige and position within the party, and significantly in the army, that he was unchallenged in staying on as chairman of the MAC. Even when he stepped down from this position in 1989, Deng remained China's paramount leader.

The other veterans were also difficult to dislodge entirely. Chen remained chairman of the Central Advisory Commission, and Yang Shangkun became permanent vice chairman of the MAC. Furthermore as *The Tiananmen Papers* (2001) indicate, despite Deng's 'retirement', by a secret resolution of the Standing Committee, Deng was given the power of veto over any decision of China's nominal leaders. Although the mechanics of this deal might have been secret, it was an 'open' fact that Deng Xiaoping was the real ruler and ultimate source of all power in China. Certainly throughout the 1980s and beyond, the experience of high-level visitors to China was that the basic premise of Deng's supremacy was never a matter of doubt.

In spite of Hu Yaobang's fall, the Chinese economy continued to grow rapidly with agricultural output expanding by 4.7 per cent in 1987 and industrial output by 16.5 per cent in the same year. However, the crackdown on corruption that had followed Hu Yaobang's downfall also fell into abeyance. Inflation, particularly food price inflation, continued as the major bane of existence for most urbanites. In 1987, a survey of 2,300 city dwellers from 33 cities showed that two-thirds of the urban population believed that their real incomes were falling. It is clear that withdrawal of agricultural food subsidies as a result of price decontrol hit city dwellers hardest. Given that expenditure on food accounted for between 40 per cent and 60 per cent of disposable income for most Chinese urbanites, it is easy to understand why food price inflation was the foremost social problem.

Urban unrest was further fuelled by plans to privatise housing and decontrol rents. Consolidation of state enterprises was also leading to the layoff of workers, particularly part-time workers who had recently migrated from the countryside. Urban unemployment was rising rapidly, bringing with it increasing signs of social stress including begging, vagrancy and crime. In spite of the problems of dislocation caused by rampant economic growth, in May 1988, Deng exhorted Zhao Ziyang to speed up the reform process; he announced that 'We now have the requirements to risk comprehensive wage and price reforms.'[14]

Yet annual inflation, which by some estimates had reached 25–40 per cent, was already explosive and rumours of further reform led to panic buying of some commodities. A backlash from the left and the veterans was not long in coming. Premier Li Peng, backed by the veteran old guard, sought to reign in Zhao Ziyang. In August 1988, he was duly removed from economic decision taking. Provincial autonomy on borrowing and investment was pulled back to central government; a move that seriously discomfited regional governments, as a visiting economist noted at a meeting with the deputy mayor and government officials in Shanghai in autumn 1988. Also by December, prices controls were reintroduced in 36 categories.

In spite of these attempts to temper the effects of reform on the urban population, unrest swept the cities in the first months of 1989. The now traditional grievances of inflation, corruption and nepotism of the party leadership came to the fore. In the universities, calls also came for human rights and democracy. Fang Lizhi, in an open letter to Deng Xiaoping, asked for the release of Wei Jingsheng, the leading dissident of the 1979 unrest. In the universities, democratic clubs and debating groups sprang up. Street demonstrations followed.

Just as the death of Zhou Enlai had brought spontaneous street demonstrations in Tiananmen Square in 1976, so now the death of Hu Yaobang of a heart attack on 15 April 1989 launched Beijing's students into a frenzy of activity. Tiananmen

Square in Beijing, where the Chinese people had, throughout Imperial history, traditionally brought their grievances to the Gate of Heavenly Peace, once again proved to be the focus of protest. On the 17 April, students marched on Tiananmen Square and laid a wreath to Hu Yaobang at the base of the monument to heroes. A petition was presented to members of the National People's Congress at the Great Hall of the People. The petition demanded clearance of Hu Yaobang's name, an end to anti-liberalisation purges, publication of the assets of political leaders and those of their relatives, freedom of speech including a liberated press and lifting of restrictions on street demonstrations. Added to this potpourri of demands were the self-serving requests for increased educational funding and increased salaries for teachers and intellectuals.

Events moved rapidly towards a complete shutdown of central Beijing as students occupied Tiananmen Square. On 22 April, 100,000 students marched in orderly ranks to attend Hu Yaobang's funeral at the Great Hall, where Zhao Ziyang delivered a traditional oration which was unstinting in its praise. Although Deng attended, Chen Yun and a number of the 'old guard' pointedly stayed away. The municipal authorities allowed the students to stay overnight in Tiananmen Square, and they were not to vacate it until the night of the now infamous 'Massacre' on 4 June.

In the midst of the crisis, Zhao Ziyang made the fatal error of leaving the country for a state visit to North Korea. Taking advantage of his absence, the hardliners called a meeting of the politburo on 24 April at which they overwhelmed the liberal opposition, who had thus far pursued a soft approach to the students. The next day Li Peng and Yang Shangkun won Deng's approval for a tougher approach. He hoped that a strongly worded editorial in *The People's Daily* on 26 April headed, *'Clearly raise the banner of opposition to the turmoil'*,[15] would calm the situation. However, much to Deng's chagrin, the people's hero had now turned villain and his words merely inflamed the Beijing populace. On 27 April, waves of students, cheered on by bystanders, broke through police lines to reach Tiananmen Square.

The stand-off continued, but after several weeks, with student enthusiasm beginning to wane, it might have been expected that the student protests would fizzle out. However, a long-planned visit by Soviet First Secretary Gorbachev began on 15 May. In hindsight, it might have been the less humiliating choice for the Chinese government to have postponed his visit. The students and populace of Beijing now feted Gorbachev, the hero of 'perestroika' and 'glasnost'. The logic of this support for a man, whose views on economics were much more conventionally socialist and hardline than those of Deng, was somewhat perverse. However, if the intention was to embarrass the Chinese leadership, the students certainly succeeded.

With Tiananmen Square now impassable, much of the schedule of Gorbachev's state visit had to be reorganised. Raisa Gorbachev's plans to lay a wreath at the hero's monument were cancelled entirely. As he was driven in a circuitous route to a meeting with Deng Xiaoping, a baffled Gorbachev muttered, 'Who the hell is in charge here?'[16]

Emboldened by their apparent success, the students now moved to more extreme forms of protest with publication of a daily newspaper and the start of a hunger strike. A declaration of the hunger strike was posted with colourful if somewhat cloying prose:

> In this bright, sunny month of May, we have begun a hunger strike. During the glorious days of our youth, we have no choice but to abandon the beauty of life. Yet how reluctant, how unwilling we are! The nation is in crisis___beset by rampant inflation, illegal dealings by profiteering officials, abuses of power, corrupt bureaucrats, the flight of good people to other countries, and the deterioration of law and order. Compatriots, fellow countrymen who cherish morality, please hear our voices.[17]

A further symbolic gesture of defiance was initiated with the construction of a 30-feet-high plaster representation of the Statue of Liberty, which stood eye to eye with an edifice topped by Mao. If the more extremist approach was beginning to alarm some of the moderate students and their professors, others were venturing even further in their attack on the state. Yan Jiaqi, a member of the Chinese Academy of Social Sciences, helped draft 'The 17th May Proclamation', which asserted that Deng was a dictator and that the current government of China could not 'be accepted as the government of the Republic'.[18]

After months of student and popular unrest, the occupation of Tiananmen Square by the students was now beginning to spiral out of control. The setting up of an independent trade union, the Beijing Autonomous Workers Federation, gave ominous signs of a disintegration of government authority in the cities. After a month of demonstrations, the police force was near exhaustion. For the survivors of the Cultural Revolution, Deng included, who had endured the cruelty of the student Red Guards, the outlook must have appeared terrifying.

Within the ruling elite, the battle lines were now starkly drawn. Of the five members of the Standing Committee, only Zhao Ziyang and Hu Qili advocated dialogue with the students, while Yao Yilin and Li Peng insisted that the time had come to impose martial law. With Qiao Shi, responsible for law and order and security, abstaining from the vote on 16 May, the decision was tied. However, whatever the vote, the final decision would have been taken to Deng and the elders.

There can have been little doubt as to the outcome. Though Deng had always pushed forward liberal successors, his attitude to student uprisings in 1979 and again in 1986 was also consistent; criticism was fine only up to the point where it threatened the integrity of party and state. What is perhaps surprising is Deng's forbearance in allowing the Tiananmen situation to continue for so long, particularly as he had well-developed fears for the stability of the party, in light of the popular uprisings that had successfully thrown off communist governments in Poland and Hungary. In part, Deng too may have wished not to be involved in the decisions of government as, by this time, he was seeking to stay in the background. However

Deng finally decided that the popular unrest, manifested by the student demonstrations in Tiananmen Square, would have to be brought to an end.

In defeat, a shattered Zhao Ziyang visited the students in Tiananmen Square on 19 May and apologised for having come 'too late'. He was never seen in public life again. On the morning of 20 May, Li Peng decreed the imposition of martial law and banned marches and demonstrations. Yet even now the situation was unclear. The population of Beijing was aroused and would not be quieted. On 21 May, 1 million people demonstrated against martial law. Students with motorbikes formed the 'Flying Tigers' to monitor troop movements around the city. In the suburbs, citizens began to assemble barricades. Meanwhile, many elements in the army were opposed to moving against the people. To shore up support, Deng Xiaoping flew to Wuhan to meet the regional commanders and get their backing for martial law. The last and most reluctant appears to have been the commander of the Beijing region.

Meanwhile, the delay was creating a public relations nightmare for Deng and the Chinese regime. As *Typhoon Brenda* struck Hong Kong, its citizens, locked indoors, sat glued to their TVs watching CNN, until two Chinese bureaucrats arrived to pull the plug on its Chinese transmissions. On Saturday 27 May, 150 entertainers in Hong Kong held a 12-hour pop concert during which they raised US$ 1.5 million for the students. This was in addition to the US$ 3 million in donations raised since April. Commentators speculated as to whether the army, which had gained hugely from Deng's economic liberalisation, might turn on the hardliners and Li Peng in particular.

The BBC, fronted by the redoubtable Kate Adie, along with all the American television networks, ignoring the benefits which might be brought by the pro-western market deregulation of the Chinese economy, delivered an unambiguously pro-student interpretation of events. Yet there was confusion, ambiguity and thuggery too within the ranks of students and their supporters. The moderates, including leaders Wu'er Kaixi and Wang Dan, wanted to end the occupation of Tiananmen Square on 30 May; however, Chai Ling and the radicals overruled them. In a bizarre display of ideological confusion, Chai Ling and his followers wished to stay to the end with their purloined machine gun and rifles and to stage a rendition of the 'Internationale', the anthem of international communism.

In spite of this, Tiananmen's Chinese students have been curiously mythologised as peace-loving democrats; however, a few years earlier, black African students at Beijing University had had to be protected by the army from being attacked, even killed, by Chinese students who accused them of bringing AIDS into China. The idea that Western liberal values ran deep in the veins of Chinese students, any more than it did in the population at large, was clearly misguided. Those who had suffered at the hands of Mao's fervent student disciples during the Cultural Revolution could give ample testament to the potential for irrational violence among crowds of young ideologues.

The first column of soldiers was sent at the run towards Tiananmen Square in the early hours of 3 June. Strangely, they were unarmed and without senior officers. Exhausted, they were blocked at the Beijing Hotel to the east of the Square. Possibly, these were units of the locally stationed 38th Army which was reportedly pro-student. Later that evening heavily armed troops with tanks of the 27th Army, commanded by Yang Shangkun's nephew Yang Chien Hua, moved into Beijing and converged from different directions on Tiananmen Square. Probably reluctant troops were ordered to attack on pain of court martial and possible death by firing squad. Heavy fighting in the suburbs and later in the streets around Tiananmen Square occurred between 10.30 pm and 2.30 am, and it was during this period that most lives are thought to have been lost. Protestors fighting with rocks and Molotov cocktails were gunned down. In some cases, pockets of troops and their armoured carriers were surrounded and set on fire. Escaping tank crews were beaten and, in some instances, set on fire or disemboweled.

Once surrounded, moderate student leaders in Tiananmen Square negotiated a truce that allowed the protestors to file out of the southern corner of the Square, after a democratic voice vote in favour. The uprising in Beijing and other urban centres was over. A week later the roundup of dissident students would begin; many would be brutally incarcerated or indeed executed. Many others, however, had already flown the country. 'Operation Yellow Bird', financed by Hong Kong businessmen, spirited many student leaders out of China.

The 'Tiananmen Square Massacre' (otherwise known as the '4th June Incident') led to an estimated 3,000 deaths including those of soldiers; the bulk of the casualties were thought to be discontented white-collar workers most affected by food price inflation. Student deaths might have been as few as 50. Whatever the facts of this most disputed of historic events, it was a landmark in how the West saw China. For most westerners, the mass media coverage leading up to the events of 3 June was the first glimpse that most people had seen of China, albeit from the comfort of their living rooms. The cuddly image of Deng in a cowboy hat, being feted in America, was completely swept away. China now became a pariah state.

By unfortunate timing the day after the Tiananmen Square 'showdown', a British 'China watcher' was slated to give a speech in San Francisco to a conference of American financial executives on 'The Prospects for Foreign Investment in China'; the speech was hastily rewritten to take account of the 'Tiananmen Square Massacre'. When the 'China watcher' suggested in his presentation that the cause of Chinese unrest was the rapid pace of economic deregulation and its resulting chain of inflation, and moreover that over time the events of 'Tiananmen' would come to be seen as a minor hiccup in the capitalistic development of the Chinese economy, he was greeted frostily. This was not the message being delivered by the American news media or the BBC. Yet within three years, American direct investment into China was breaking new records.

It was a reflection of western media's liberal bias that Deng Xiaoping, who, through the rapid deregulation and economic development of the Chinese economy, had striven to create a society which could not repeat the humanitarian catastophies of the Great Leap Forward, and the Cultural Revolution, in which tens of millions of Chinese perished, came to symbolise the heavy hand of authoritarian brutality. By contrast, Mao continued to enjoy iconic status in the West even after the brutal excesses of the Cultural Revolution and his earlier perpetration of the Great Leap Forward, the greatest mass starvation of the twentieth century, in which tens of millions of Chinese perished.

This is not to say that Deng and the Chinese leadership emerge with much credit from the events of summer 1989. The popular discontent, seen in Chinese cities from 1985 onwards and culminating in the Tiananmen Square massacre, was a testament to the corruption and bureaucratic sloth of the ruling Communist Party. Single-party governments, with their monopolistic control of power and economic resources, are by their nature sclerotic.

The failure of the municipal authorities of Beijing to effect control of the Tiananmen situation was itself indicative of the ineptitude of the ruling bureaucracy. For a supposedly totalitarian regime, the reaction of the authorities to the effective closing of the heart of the capital city by students bordered on the permissive. As Deng himself observed on 18 May, 'What other country in the world would watch more than a month of marches and demonstrations in its capital and do nothing about it?'[19]

However successful Deng's reforms to that point, China remained a backward and largely ineptly managed society. Also, in spite of Deng's intention to effect a retirement and bring on a younger generation of leaders, the Chinese constitution remained dysfunctional. The aura of Deng's personality and his lifelong development of personal and ideological relationships were such that he ended up being as all-powerful as Mao. In addition, his retention of the post of chairman of the MAC was also indicative of his unique authority with the army and of that institution's immense power as arbiter of last resort. The Tiananmen Square uprising highlighted divisions in the Chinese leadership that could not be resolved through the mechanism of constitution and law. In the end the crisis served to show that, like Mao, Deng was an emperor in all but name.

The students too were not blameless for the bloodshed that ensued from their occupation of Tiananmen Square. By rejecting moderate counsel, by bringing the public and civic life of the nation to a grinding halt, they ultimately backed their rulers into a corner, from which the only possible response was the use of force to restore order. Neither did their increasingly diffuse and strident demands make possible a coherent government response to criticisms that did indeed have much validity.

Lastly, their ideological and political muddle and lack of historic context prevented the students from appreciating the immense economic benefits that Deng's rule had brought and would bring to China. By pushing too far the students damaged the cause of political reform, and were fortunate not to derail the process of economic liberalisation. Although city dwellers suffered a high degree of dislocation from these deregulatory economic reforms, the vast majority of Chinese people lived in the countryside, and they were the clear short-term beneficiaries of Deng's modernisation programme.

Noticeably there was little if any support for the urban protestors in the countryside, which remained either apathetic or hostile to the 'townies' who appeared to threaten the disorder and chaos, from which most Chinese were only too happy to have escaped under Deng's leadership. As a rural cadre in Guiyang commented at the end of 1990, 'People here want stability, they don't understand what the students were talking about.'[20]

Most contemporary foreign commentators hugely overstated the importance of the Tiananmen episode; in the end, the established political order was not overthrown and the programme of economic reform was barely disrupted. The course of modernisation for China laid out by Deng after 1978 remained intact. It is perhaps the greatest irony of the 'Tiananmen Square Massacre' that Deng and the Chinese leadership should have attracted international opprobrium for their inept handling of urban discontent resulting from deregulatory policies designed to imitate western capitalist endeavour.

Importantly President Bush (senior), a former ambassador to China, understood well that to withdraw most favoured nation (MFN) trading status or other sanctions would not serve the advancement of economic development, Chinese freedoms or, as Secretary of State, George Baker put it, 'the need to safeguard the underlying strategic relations to the fullest extent'.[21] Bush ignored the torrent of abuse from liberal sections of the media. Writing in the *New York Times*, A.M. Rosenthal lamented that 'at a moment of passion in the story of democracy, [Bush] has been pale and thin'.[22] In his memoirs, President Bush (senior) concluded that 'While angry rhetoric might be temporarily satisfying to some, I believed it would deeply hurt our efforts in the long run.'[23] Thus far history would appear to have supported his analysis. As former President Nixon noted with great prescience in 1994, 'Today China's economic power makes US lectures about human rights imprudent. Within a decade it will make them irrelevant. Within two decades it will make them laughable.'[24]

However, the urban uprising did lay bare the dichotomy inherent in Deng Xiaoping's policy of economic liberalisation combined with social and political authoritarianism. Yet what better alternative did Deng Xiaoping have? In Russia, the collapse of the Communist Party and the anarchic grab for assets and power by freebooting mafias and business oligarchs showed what could also have happened in China. While clearly anti-democratic in a western sense, Deng's policies personified the mood of the Chinese people in their desire for stability, national identity and economic progress. As a Cantonese businessman commented in 1985, 'As long as we have the freedom to make money, the right to vote is not so important.'[25]

Deng was not simply a political authoritarian because he was a communist keen to keep power. He genuinely believed that a more liberal political regime would damage China's possibilities for material advance. Particularly when juxtaposed against the chaotic post-communist experience of Russia, history has not yet demonstrated, in terms of the material welfare of the Chinese people, that Deng's strategy of political authoritarianism and economic liberalism was mistaken. Indeed, under President Vladimir Putin, Russia appears to have changed course and, in curtailing democratic processes and freedoms, has arguably copied the successful authoritarian, market-economic path charted by Deng Xiaoping in China.

55

Property Crash and the Lost Decade

Japan: 1990–2000

In 1987, *Business Week* noted that

> As American Business has ample reason to know, when the Japanese home in on a new market, they aim at the bull's eye. In three short years, guided by strategic planning that subordinates quick profits to long-term market growth, four major Japanese firms, Nomura, Daiwa, Nikko and Yamaichi, are well on their way to becoming major players in US financial markets.[1]

Just as Japan's export-led manufacturers in areas as diverse as motor cars, consumer electronics and machine tools had barrelled their way into a dominant position within the US economy, so America feared that a similar onslaught from Japan's financial sector was now inevitable. Even the American State Department coined the phrase 'Japan Inc.'.

In some cases, American financial companies appeared to buckle under the Japanese onslaught. New York-based Salomon Brothers brought in the head of their Japanese office, a former British bureaucrat, Derek Maugham, to run their company. Goldman Sachs, the premier global investment partnership of the 1980s and 1990s sold 20 per cent of their business to Sumitomo Bank, the most aggressive of the Japanese commercial banks. Meanwhile as the historian Albert Aletzhauser showed in his sensational account of the rise of the *House of Nomura* (1990), Nomura Securities appeared to be on track to become the world's leading investment bank. Yet the transfer of global financial power to Japan was illusory; by 1987, Japan was embarked on one of the greatest speculative financial 'bubbles' of the twentieth century. It was a boom that would mask a sharp decline in Japan's economic growth potential and would end with the greatest financial collapse since the Wall Street Crash of 1929; it would herald a period of economic stagnation which turned into Japan's 'lost decade'.

Japan's stock market crash was spectacular. Having reached a peak of 38,916 on 31 December 1989, the Nikkei Index fell by 48 per cent over the next nine months to 1 October. At its peak, the Japanese stock market represented 43 per cent of the entire market capitalisation of all the world's stock markets, a ratio that had risen from just 10 per cent a decade earlier. Paper losses in the stock market were three times more than all outstanding Third World debt. Institutional losses were spectacular, but for individuals the losses were more immediately painful. The Japanese individual investors, who had bought the virtually monopolistic and 'blue-chip' Nippon Telephone and Telegraph (NTT) when it was privatised at a price equivalent to a 250 times multiple of price to earnings, lost 80 per cent of their investment.

The stock market boom had been prompted by a spectacular growth in financial liquidity within the Japanese financial system in the wake of the Plaza Accord of 1985. Signed at the Plaza Hotel in New York, the participating central banks of the G5 economies (the USA, Britain, France, Japan and West Germany) pledged US$ 10 billion to help drive down the value of the US dollar, particularly against the main export currencies of the yen and the deutsche mark. This was a belated response by the Reagan administration and his then Treasury Secretary James Baker and Finance Minister Takeshita, to try to unravel the US trade deficit which had reached 3.5 per cent of gross domestic product (GDP). This was largely attributed to Japan's export of consumer and capital goods, an onslaught which reached its apogee with Japan recording a current account surplus equivalent to 4.3 per cent of its GDP in 1986.

In fact, by the time that co-ordinated G5 intervention arrived, the dollar had already started to depreciate. The combination of central bank intervention in the money markets and an easing of Japanese monetary policy, which saw the discount rate reduced from 5 per cent to 2.5 per cent between January 1986 and February 1987, produced a liquidity 'bubble', which inflated an already strong stock market. Excess liquidity was further spurred by a Japanese economy which 'slowed' to 2.6 per cent GDP growth in 1986 under the impact of a higher yen, which adversely impacted the export-led economy. At the same time, the dollar began its decline from a peak of ¥ 239 to the US$ in 1985 to ¥85 in 1994.

The resulting explosion of Japanese financial liquidity, which the Plaza Accord inaugurated, fed first into financial assets and then even more importantly into property. For the entire post-war period, property had been the investment of choice for Japanese investors. Arcane property laws which restricted the development of urban centres created a perpetual shortage of both office space and residential accommodation. With a rapid post-war rise in Japan's population, caused largely by an astonishing 30-year increase in life expectancy between 1947 and 1997, property had provided consistently high returns. Preference for property now turned into a mania.

With the discount rate down to 2.5 per cent, companies could raise money at virtually negative rates of interest. By launching dollar Eurobonds with warrants (long-dated options) attached, Japanese corporations could swap the proceeds back in yen. The Eurobond launches were accompanied by the formulaic ritual of a lunchtime banquet for investors, usually held at the Savoy Hotel on the Strand in London, followed by the offering of 'goody bags' to the attendees, usually analysts and fund managers. The funds thus raised financed the greatest property investment binge of the twentieth century. By 1990, speculation had reached such a pitch that new office development started in that year alone was equivalent to 11 per cent of total Japanese office building stock. In Ginza, the price of land rose to US$ 60,000 per square metre.

Speculation was not confined to the office market. On the stock market, as property prices rocketed, companies were re-rated based on the value of their historic land holdings. If these were in city centres, particularly Tokyo, the impact on share price could be spectacular. When it leaked into the market that Ishikawajima-Harima Heavy Industries, a major manufacturer of nuclear turbines, ships and heavy electrical equipment, owned huge tracts of land in the dock areas adjacent to Japan's financial business district, the company's share price rose by 1,000 per cent in a little over a year.

Residential speculation did not lag behind. New apartments were bid up to extraordinary valuations many times the price per square foot of comparable cities such as London and New York. Nothing better illustrated the absurdity of the property price boom than the explosion in golf course construction and development. Between 1989 and 1991, Japan saw the building of 160 new golf courses, an addition of almost 10 per cent to the stock of 1,700 golf courses in Japan; more remarkably, there were a further 1,200 golf courses in the construction or planning stage.

Membership prices spiralled and became an investment asset in their own right. It was a market which ended up being serviced by more than 70 golf membership brokerage companies. Single membership prices for the more sought-after clubs rose as high as US$ 2 million; it was a speculation which, in its absurdity, matched the great Dutch Tulip Bubble of the early seventeenth century. At its peak, the value of golf course memberships in Japan exceeded US$ 200 billion, more than the GDP of most countries. As asset prices rose, so did the borrowing that could be made against increased land and property values. Speculation became a self-feeding monster.

In addition to the excesses apparent in Japan, individuals and corporations went on an international spending binge. Mitsubishi Trust bought the world-famous landmark Rockefeller Centre in New York; it launched a mania for trophy assets. In 1990, Cosmo World, a modest-sized developer, paid US$ 830 million for the Pebble Beach Resort located on the sought-after coastline around Carmel, south of San Francisco; two years later, it was sold at a loss of US$ 320 million. Similarly, the Daiichi Real Estate Company put the New York Tiffany Building up for sale five years after paying a record US$ 959 per square foot in 1986. For a time, Japanese investors became the largest buyer of property in California and virtually monopolised real estate investment in Hawaii. The boom in overseas property acquisition was followed by the Japanese bankers, who, by the end of 1991, owned 24.5 per cent of all of California's bank assets. Media trophies were also acquired. Matsushita bought MCA while Sony purchased Columbia Pictures.

The asset 'bubble', into which Japan now entered, was not simply a result of the easy money policies adopted by Satohishi Sumita and the Bank of Japan in the wake of the Plaza Accord. The much-vaunted ministry of finance (MOF) was institutionally corrupt. Unlike MITI which, contrary to its reputation in the West, had only a weak control over the manufacturing sector, the MOF ruled banking and financial services with an iron fist. Whereas in the manufacturing sector Japanese companies benefited from the 'free-for-all' of domestic competition, while in the finance sector competition was severely curtailed.

The differences were most marked in the productivity performance of the two parts of the economy. Whereas total factor productivity in the manufacturing sector more than doubled between 1960 and 1980, productivity in the non-manufacturing sector advanced by only 3 per cent. It was a problem which afflicted all those sectors sensitive to political funding and control such as agriculture, construction and finance. Thus, agricultural productivity fell by 26 per cent compared to a 47 per cent rise in Japanese manufacturing sector, while over the same period Japanese productivity in the construction sector fell by 24 per cent. In financial industries productivity simply stagnated.

Since the war, the MOF and the Bank of Japan had been gradually increasing their power over the financial markets. Between 1960 and 1972, MOF's banking regulations increased from 656 pages to 1297 pages. In 1962, Japanese tax law was changed to favour trust banks and insurance companies over mutual funds which helped to solidify the *keiretsu* (interlocking shareholding) system. Between 1960 and 1973 the proportion of equity controlled by these financial institutions increased from 23.2 per cent to 33.9 per cent.

Also pension fund asset allocation was severely controlled by the MOF, with large allocations being given to government bonds and other liquid instruments versus equities, which until the early 1990s were limited to 10 per cent assets. Unlike America, where pension funds, mutual funds and corporate raiders, using innovative financial techniques, enabled a dramatic restructuring of its corporate sector during the Reagan presidency, corporate Japan simply ossified. The beneficiaries of this system were the political and bureaucratic caste, the former from political funding and the latter from the generous system of *amakudari* (the method of rewarding a bureaucrat with a lucrative job on retirement, literally translated as 'descent from heaven'), which provided plum sinecures in the insurance companies and trust banks.

Under pressure from America, the necessary process of restructuring the financial sector, begun with deregulation of interest rates, merely contributed to the financial bubble. Rather than compensating for reduced profits by lowering deposit rates or increasing lending margins, banks sought to retain market share at the expense of profits. They achieved this with no apparent pain. Stock gains filled the gap, and by March 1990, these amounted to 42 per cent of banking profits. While banks became more dependent on stock gains, their subsidised borrowers could invest in the stock market. It was a delightful virtuous circle while the bull market lasted.

Also the Bank for International Settlements (BIS) in Basel, the body that overseas the rules governing settlements between banks', allowed Japanese banks to fudge their 8 per cent minimum capital ratio allowance by counting 45 per cent of Japanese banks' stock market unrealised gains towards their capital. By 1989, Japan's entire banking structure and its solvency had become dependent on the continuation of the bull market in equities. It was a fault line that would prove catastrophic when the bull market ended.

As equity markets started to collapse at the beginning of 1990, the effect on the Japanese banks balance sheets was instantaneous. Weaker institutions were the first affected. Between March and September 1990, the number of Japanese regional banks that could meet their BIS capital adequacy target of 8 per cent fell from 50 to 4. Within 18 months, however, even larger institutions were in trouble. By mid-1991, an estimated 30 banks with assets of ¥2.6 billion (US$ 22 billion) were teetering on the edge of financial failure.

By contrast, the Insurance Fund set up in 1971 to cover depositor losses in case of bank failure had deposits of just ¥455 million. Frequently, losses on property were hidden within subsidiaries of the financial institutions, which were not required to produce consolidated year-end accounts. These so-called *Jusen* (special housing loan companies), subsidiaries of the financial institutions set up in the 1970s to focus on consumer lending, had moved aggressively into property lending in the late 1980s. An audit carried out in 1995 by MOF revealed that 74 per cent of *Jusen* loans were irrecoverable.

With the stock market collapse, Japan's virtuous circle became a self-feeding spiral of decline. Property became almost instantly unsaleable. Although the National Land Agency reported residential property prices as rising by 2.7 per cent in the year to July 1991, this figure did not reflect a complete collapse in actual reported transactions. The reality was that bids were being made for property at discounts of between 30 per cent and 50 per cent of official prices. The rush to unload property had begun. Financial institutions, however, could not offload property without undermining their balance sheets; assets were now carefully shuffled to non-visible entities to prevent the horrific truth from emerging.

For individuals, the problems of unloading assets were compounded by the scale of inheritance taxes which made the offloading of historically owned assets an unfeasible way of reducing borrowings that had been taken out against property. An environment of easy credit soon became one of no credit. For individuals who had taken out long-term mortgages (sometimes 100 years or so-called three-generation mortgages), the future looked bleak and whole families faced technical bankruptcy. Inevitably consumer demand also collapsed.

As is the case with all financial crashes, stories of corruption, criminality or excess soon emerged. The arrest of a 61-year-old Osaka spinster, Nui Onoue, for obtaining loans using fake certificates of deposit, provided an outstanding example of banking laxity; this owner of two Osaka restaurants managed to borrow ¥240 billion (US$ 2 billion), which she used to become one of the most famous stock market speculators. Every evening, stockbrokers would swarm to her restaurant to ensure they received market orders and many would stay to hear 'midnight rites' performed, which supposedly divined the stock market.

The stock market 'bubble' also drew gangsters into the mêlée. Susumu Ishii, on taking over as head of Inagawa-Kai (Japan's second largest gangster organisation), decided to modernise his organisation by downgrading drugs, prostitution and extortion and increasing activities in finance, property and golf. Ishii borrowed ¥36 billion (US$ 250 million) from Nomura Securities and Nikko Securities to operate an illegal 'cornering' of the stock of Tokyu Corporation (a major railroad and property group) and Honshu Paper. The contact with Tabuchi, the president of Nomura, was made through a *Sokaiya* (the name given to stock market extortionists who refrained from creating havoc at corporate annual general meetings in return for fees). In addition, as property prices rose, so did the practice of *jiage* (whereby gangsters evicted owners from their properties by threats thus enabling them to build blocks of land for redevelopment).

Apart from the securities companies, Japan's most blue-chip financial institution Sumitomo Bank also became embroiled in a financial scandal when its chairman, Isoda, allowed a gangster, a specialist in *jiage*, to be appointed to the board of Itoman & Co., a listed trading company based in Osaka. The gangster was a front man for Ho Yong Chung, an Osaka-based gangster of Korean origin, who systematically looted Itoman by increasing the company's loans by 85 per cent between March and September 1990 to carry out a series of fraudulent loans and purchases. After an MOF inquiry, Sumitomo's chairman, Isoda, was forced to resign. Foreign financial institutions also became unwittingly embroiled in gangster connections. *Inagwa-kai* paid a US$ 250,000 fee to Prescott Bush and Company (brother of President Bush senior) for an introduction, which led to the purchase of a 38 per cent stake in Asset Management International Financing and Settlement.

The *Yakuza* (gangsters) thus became institutionalised in the mechanism of the 'bubble economy'. As Robert Delfs concluded in an article for *The Far East Asia Economic Review*, the growth of the *Yakuza* influence reflected 'an underlying trait in Japanese society _ the tendency to resort to personal and extra legal ways of solving problems when institutional methods fail'.[2]

When the head of a foreign financial institution sacked one of his managers for physically attacking another employee, he was visited by the senior lawyer of one of Tokyo's main *Yakuza* gangs. The lawyer, impeccably dressed in a steely grey suit, requested an outlandish figure of compensation for the sacked employee, who happened to be the son of a high-ranking gangster; it was an offer that he could not refuse. An attempt by the financier to negotiate down the compensation package was met with howls of anguish from his fellow Japanese directors; he spent the next month of negotiation checking the underside of his car each morning and evening.

Such was the institutionalisation of gangsters within Japanese culture that their conferences became important media events. At one such meeting for a grand dinner at the New Otani Hotel in Tokyo, streams of gangsters with shiny suits, black shirts and white ties were televised as they arrived in their black Mercedes Benz 500 SL or Cadillacs, the cars of choice for the *Yakuza*. Gangsters were so much a part of the fabric of Japanese society that their numbers were statistically presented by the government each year down to the last digit. To combat the *Yakuza* problems, the Japanese government enacted a law in 1992, which made it illegal to belong to the *Yamaguchi-gumi* and six other gangs.

Apart from the increasing involvement with *Yakuza* gangs, Japanese financial institutions also engaged in illegal stock manipulation through the operation of *Eiygyo Tokkin* accounts, whereby favoured customers were guaranteed returns from the stock market. Favoured customers included the largest institutional accounts, including the *Yakuza*, which the big four securities companies eventually confessed to paying ¥65 billion (US$ 500 million).

In a society where the small-fry investors were suffering crippling losses, *tokkin* accounts turned into one the bear market's most sensational scandals. The president of Nomura Securities, Yoshihisa Tabuchi, was forced to resign when it was disclosed that the company had tried to deduct losses from the *tokkin* accounts as 'business payments'. Subsequently, Nomura's chairman (by coincidence also called Tabuchi) was also forced to resign as well as relinquish his post as vice president of the *Nippon Keidanren* (Japan Business Federation). It was an indication of the endemic corruption of the system that both Tabuchis kept their offices and salaries at Nomura. There could not have been a bigger contrast with America, where a few weeks after the Tabuchi downfall, John Gutfreund, a brilliant 38-year veteran and chief executive of Salomon Brothers, was unceremoniously ejected from the company without recompense and made to take responsibility for his company's relatively minor trading infringements.

In the 1990s, solutions to Japan's financial crash and its aftermath were slow to emerge. Although government provided funding of ¥60 trillion (US$ 50 billion) to protect the depositors of failed banks, the MOF, tarnished by its responsibility for the crash and mired in corruption scandals of its own, was unable or unwilling to exact the tough measures on the financial institutions with which, for reasons of *amakudari*, it was umbilically linked. As late as March 1998, non-performing loans at the top 19 banks (including the Long-Term Credit Bank (LTCB) and Nippon Credit Bank, which were later nationalised) amounted to ¥57 trillion, a sum equivalent to 15.7 per cent of all outstanding loans and representing 18 per cent of GDP.

In 1995, some five years after the crash, the government set up two 'bad' loan disposal agencies: Resolution and Collection Bank and the Housing Loan Administration. In another shuffle of the deckchairs, these institutions would later be consolidated into the Resolution and Collection Organisation. Although the government co-ordinated bad loans into the Resolution and Collection Organisation (modelled on the American Resolution Trust Corp which sorted out the 1980s savings and loan crisis in the USA), the Japanese government failed to operate it with any success.

Whereas, in America, the Resolution Trust had cleared property assets to market, thus putting assets back to work in the economy. Japan's Resolution and Collection Organisation merely sat on its hands; to expose the real fall in the price of Japanese real estate assets would have harmed powerful vested financial interests. Indeed, the failure to clear to market was one of the main reasons for the continued stagnation of the Japanese economy throughout the 1990s.

With Japan's export-driven economy having run out of steam, the country needed to look to its domestic economy to provide growth. However, the service sectors remained stuck with arcane laws which prevented productivity growth. In a decade in which countries such as the USA and Britain spawned dominant retail giants such as Wal-Mart and Tesco, in Japan 55 per cent of retail sales remained under the control of some 1.5 million 'mom and pop' stores. In 1974, the Liberal Democratic Party (LDP), attempting to protect some of its core constituents, the small business community, passed the Large Scale Retail Store Law which limited shops to 5,382 square feet; this was just 10 per cent of the size of the smallest K-Mart in the USA. Furthermore, local ordinances required retailers to obtain approval for a new supermarket from all the shopkeepers within a 300 m radius.

Although the Japanese population had risen rapidly after the Second World War on the back of rising life expectancy, from the 1950s population birth rates plummeted and a rapid population ageing took place with inevitable consequences for economic growth. Apart from the 600,000 Koreans shipped to Japan before the war, post-war Japan remained a remarkably racially homogeneous society compared to the USA; though this was useful for social stability, it contributed to the stagnation of the economy in the 1990s. In 1990, immigrants represented just 0.9 per cent of the population. However, by 2010 it was estimated that the population over the age of 60 would exceed the population below the age of 20. At the same time, Japan's population is expected to peak.

With Japan no longer able to count on a rapidly rising population and export growth to drive economic activity, the easy path to growth had ended by the 1990s. Also the traditionally long working hours associated with Japan's era of success had begun to erode by the end of the 1980s. Average working hours per annum per worker fell from 2,239 hours in 1970 to 1,891 hours in 1997; in spite of the fact that hours worked per capita still remained 10 per cent more than Germany and most European economies, Japan's advantages had diminished. 'The success of the Japanese economy will increasingly depend on hard won productivity gains, responses to a declining supply of labour and its ability to maintain high rates of return to capital.'[3]

Japan's 'bubble' economy also hid structural problems in the Japanese corporate sector. In an increasingly globalised economy, Japan's traditional seniority wage and promotion system, a legacy of wartime controls introduced in September 1939 which had helped reduce wage costs in the post-war period, now served to undermine productivity.

Ossification of Japanese corporations was reflected in an increasingly profitless fight for market share. In a period of high growth, easy credit and high leverage, the woeful return on capital of Japanese corporations could be disguised. By comparison during the corporate renaissance inspired by President Reagan's supply-side reforms of the American economy in the early 1980s, achievement of high return on capital and shareholder return had become a mantra.

Also, in the post-war period, Japanese corporations failed to set aside adequate funds for retirees when their workforce was young. Pension underfunding increasingly came to haunt the corporate sector as workforces aged at the same time as productivity was beginning to stagnate. In the 1990s, the older Japanese companies were forced to begin to set aside pension provisions out of profits and cash flow for worker retirements and redundancies.

After the crash, these weaknesses became increasingly highlighted. A global recession, collapse of Japanese consumer demand and a curtailment of credit brought about a long period of profit stagnation. Corporate borrowing, seemingly cost free, which had risen inexorably during the bubble, was now a millstone in a period of low profits and declining asset prices. In Japan's prolonged deflation which saw a decline in the retail price index throughout the 1990s, even low-interest rate loans were burdensome, and de-leveraging became the new trend. However, business rationalisation was made difficult partly because of the lifetime employment system and partly because of weak shareholder power to demand better return on capital because of the power of the *keiretsu* (share crossholding) system. The pace of corporate restructuring proved desperately slow. Some six years after the crash, Yamaichi Securities, once Japan's largest securities company, was forced into liquidation. Hokkaido Takushoku Bank went to the wall in the same year.

Japanese political response to the new economic environment was even tardier. The nexus of vested interests (bureaucracy, politicians and big business) which had done so much to create a stable business environment in the post-war period was ill-adapted to change. Apart from voting ever-bigger 'Keynesian' public works spending, which had the effect of sustaining the economy and preventing a deflation turning into a depression, the political–bureaucratic caste remained paralysed. The public works programme might have staved off depression and kept alive the construction sector, the main source of political contributions (where 90 per cent of companies were estimated to be technically insolvent), but at a high cost to long-term government indebtedness.

Otherwise measures to restructure the Japanese economy did not begin to emerge for five years or more after the crash. Prime Minister Hashimoto announced plans for deregulation of brokerage commissions in November 1996. The central bank was made independent of MOF in February 1998, and later in the year, Prime Minister Obuchi finally tackled the banking system by passing a bill in October 1998 to provide for an injection of public funds in return for the government receiving preference shares.

The MOF, whose draconian control of the finance sector had been one of the main causes of the 'bubble' economy, was reorganised with its powers significantly diminished. However, the semi-monopolistic position of the Japanese post office which dominated the country's savings industry, and which was a repository of intractable vested interest, remained inviolate to change.

The social consequences of Japan's stagnation were dire. Racked by corruption scandals, Japan's political and business class gave a sorry example of leadership; the post-war acceptance of authority began to break down. 'Salary-men', the workaholic backbone of Japan's post-war economic boom, were increasingly prone to depression and suicides became commonplace. Little advance had been made by the female workforce. In spite of the Equal Employment Opportunity Law of 1986, women still earned an average of 50 per cent less than men compared to a 25 per cent differential in the USA. Increasingly, women and many new graduates now preferred to work for foreign companies where they would be better treated and rewarded.

Commentators also noted the growth of a dispirited youth. In 1997, juvenile crime alone rose by 20 per cent and broad crime rates soared during the decade. Schoolgirl prostitution, where girls swapped sex for Louis Vuitton handbags, became symptomatic of the decline in Japan's moral backbone. *Ijime* (school bullying) became a major social issue after Kiyoteru Okochi, a 13-year-old junior high school student, committed suicide; apart from the usual schoolyard bullying, breaking his bicycle and general harassment, he had been forced to bring money to his tormentors every day – an extortion which eventually totalled over US$ 10,000. Subsequently, the widespread problem of *Ijime* became a national media obsession.

Scandals, which in the aftermath of the stock market crash, had particularly afflicted financial companies, spread to the manufacturing sector. Bridgestone Tire Company experienced a product disaster with a defective tyre sold through its American Firestone arm in 2000. Mitsubishi Motors was also found to have covered up manufacturing defects, while Snow Brand, a leading dairy company, was exposed for recycling milk sent back from stores. Japan's legendary name for quality started to be eroded. Their formerly highly reputed management culture also began to be questioned, particularly after Renault's purchase of a controlling stake in the moribund Nissan Motor, which was turned around by the cost cutting and rationalisation techniques of the Franco-Lebanese executive Carl Ghosn.

Only towards the end of the decade did Japanese corporations begin to adopt the culture, albeit sporadically, of 'return on equity' and 'shareholder value'. This was aided by the increasing arrival of American hedge fund managers, private equity funds and 'merger and acquisition' executives. It was only in 2002 that NM

Rothschild & Co. and Mitsui & Co. launched Japan's first leverage buyout fund; a financially driven technique for extracting corporate value, which Kohlberg Kravis & Roberts (KKR) and Forstmann Little had pioneered in America in the later 1970s.

However, overall it was a bleak decade at the end of which *The Japan Times* concluded in its New Year editorial

> The last ten years have been a dismal experience. In the economic sphere Japan has degenerated from the pinnacle of world success to a fumbling giant; the art of governance is in shambles; and the nation has seen the rise of a moral vacuum as classrooms have turned into battlefields and teenagers sell their bodies in the name of subsidized friendship.[4]

If the 1990s were a disaster for Japan's economy, bringing with it a perceived social disintegration, the stock market crash of 1990 also brought a long overdue wake-up call for an LDP that had become complacent and corrupt after its long monopoly of power. The 1980s had seen easy election victories for the LDP in the Japanese Diet. In 1980, the party won 284 seats out of 500 (47.9 per cent of vote), followed by 250 seats in 1983 (45.7 per cent of vote) and 300 seats in 1986 (49.4 per cent).

Yet, even before the 1990 crash, LDP support started to slide as corruption scandals began to swirl around its leaders. When Noboru Takeshita, known as *senkyo no kamisama* (god of elections) and leader of a 113 strong faction, was forced to step down as prime minister in May 1989, just a month after his secretary committed suicide, his popularity rating had fallen to a record low of 3.9 per cent. For the LDP as a whole, polls showed support of just 27 per cent of voters, just 1 per cent ahead of the Japan Socialist Party.

Predictably, the LDP performed badly in the 1989 elections as voters punished the ruling party for the Recruit Cosmos scandal which had forced Takeshita's resignation. (Recruit was a human resources company which before listing its subsidiary Cosmos, offered shares to a large number of politicians who benefited from the skyrocketing share price.) Nevertheless the LDP managed to cling to power and Toshiki Kaifu was made prime minister with the Takeshita–Ozawa faction pulling the purse strings. Kaifu was inevitably a weak, makeshift leader. Despite the broadly demanded calls for *seiji kaikaku* (political reform), vested interest with the LDP proved far too hard for Kaifu to overcome. The prime ministership of his successor, the hardly inspiring veteran Kiichi Miyazawa, was swamped by the *Sagawa Kyubin* affair.

In 1992, it was revealed that *Sagawa Kyubin* had funnelled billions of yen in payments to some 200 politicians. Shin Kanemaru, formerly the right-hand man of Kakuei Tanaka, and vice president of the LDP, who had inherited leadership of the Takeshita faction, was also shown to have accumulated a vast fortune from payoffs by construction and telecom companies, as well as having links with senior *Yakuza* figures. He was forced to resign from the Diet.

There now followed a factional power struggle which Ichiro Ozawa, Kanemaru's protégé with strong links to the construction industry and its funding, lost to Ryutaro Hashimoto and Keizo Obuchi; Ozawa, a reputedly haughty, scheming politician with neo-nationalist sympathies, who had been tainted by his connection to Kanemaru, now split the LDP and with 35 mainly younger LDP members joined up with a former faction member Hata Tsutomu to form the Renewal Party calling for the restructuring of Japan's political system.

It was a bold personal transformation by Ozawa who more than any other Japanese politician had the 'image of a politician adept at operating in the smoke-filled back rooms and geisha houses of the Japanese political world'.[5] Ten other LDP members also split away to form *Sakigake* (the Harbinger Party). The new parties immediately called for reform and voted with the opposition in a motion of no confidence in 1993. Miyazawa dissolved the house and called for elections in July which brought an end to 48 years of continuous LDP rule.

Though they remained the largest party with 39.5 per cent of the popular vote and 223 Diet seats, the LDP was crushed in the great urban metropolises of Tokyo–Yokohama and Osaka–Kobe; a coalition of opposition parties now formed a government under the leadership of Prime Minister Morihiro Hosokawa, leader of *Nihon Shinto* (New Japan Party) which had been formed in 1992. Although the Social Democratic Party of Japan (SDPJ) lost half of its representation, it remained the largest of the eight coalition partners. Meanwhile, Ozawa's Renewal Party achieved a remarkable first-time performance winning 55 seats from its 69 candidates; by backing a coalition government, Ozawa hoped to steal away more power hungry members from the LDP.

However, with the socialist SDPJ blocking any increase in consumption tax to reduce burgeoning government deficits and remaining protective of civil service union employees, it was clear that reform would be muted. Although a start was made with deregulation of rice imports, the introduction of single-member constituencies and outlawing of corporate donations to politicians, it was a minimal agenda; the introduction of state funding of parties, a means supposedly of weaning away politicians from their corporate funding links, was stymied by the funds allocated which would only cover 3 per cent of a politician's annual outgoings. A corruption scandal now re-emerged with the revelation that Hosokawa too was linked to *Sagawa Kyubin*, and he was forced to make a sudden resignation. It dealt a shattering blow to the credibility of the new parties and their pretensions to be seen as 'clean hand' reformers.

The fall of Hosokawa brought about the conjunction of three opposition parties into a new parliamentary association; the Renewal Party, the Japan New Party and the Democratic Social Party joined forces to create a new grouping called *Kaishin* (renovation). Led by Ozawa's frontman Tsutomu Hata, a new governing coalition was formed. Hata, who had a reputation as a clean if somewhat dull politician, was known as 'Mister Spare, as in spare tire, always available if needed but rarely used.'[6] However, the SPDJ were furious that they had not been consulted about the formation of *Kaishin*; their chairman denounced, 'the formation suddenly of a new *Kaiha* [faction or grouping] just before the formation of a cabinet is a violation of trust within the coalition government'.[7] Then the socialist SPDJ stormed out of the government, leaving Hata with a minority administration. It lasted two months and was brought down by a classic piece of political chicanery.

The LDP, its instincts for power still intact, agreed a Faustian pact whereby they joined with the SPDJ and backed its leader Tomiichi Murayama as the new prime minister. His administration, formed in June 1994, was the first socialist government to lead the country since the prime ministership of Katayama Tetsu in 1947–8. Prime Minister Murayama promptly abandoned virtually all the tenets that had defined his socialist party since its inception. The existence of the Self-Defence Forces (SDF) was accepted, as was the security treaty with the USA; the socialists now claimed that the SDF was 'legal . . . although not constitutional'.[8] The socialists also approved of closer ties with South Korea and the party ceased to criticise visits to the Yasukuni Shrine or pursue its historic campaign against the performance of the national anthem in schools accompanied by the raising of the nation's flag. The SDPJ also supported a rise in the consumption tax to 5 per cent.

Meanwhile, Ozawa turned the *Kaishin* grouping into a new party to be called *Shinshinto* (New Frontier Party) including the former Renewal, *Komeito* and the Democrats plus 22 members of Hosokawa's New Japan Party; the maverick and ambitious Ozawa, who took over as the new party's chairman and financial comptroller, looked to the new party to revolutionise Japan in the manner of the strong leaders who had led the Meiji Restoration.

However, it was an opposition party of convenience and hardly one of conviction. Ozawa, a neo-nationalist, sometimes compared to Margaret Thatcher, an iconic figure to Japanese politicians in the early 1990s, was barely compatible with the pacifist leaning Hosokawa and the former 'Buddhist'-influenced *Komeito* Party. Ozawa, still preferring to remain in the background, pushed forward former Prime Minister Kaifu to be its leader; Kaifu had resigned from the LDP after failing to block the Murayama cabinet. Kaifu's leadership was short-lived and he would be replaced by Ozawa.

In the governing alliance meanwhile, the socialist prime minister, Murayama, ran into trouble as he was forced to take responsibility for the slow government response to the devastating Kobe earthquake, which killed 5,478 people and destroyed 277,000 homes. He was also blamed for the security lapses which led to the terrorist millennial Buddhist–Hindu sect, *Aum Shinrikyo* (Supreme Truth), attack on three underground trains using sarin gas. Four *Aum* terrorists, using sharpened umbrellas, had punctured bags containing the sarin liquid, whose odourless gas rapidly attacks muscles and nerves; apart from killing 12 passengers, a further 5,500 people were made seriously ill as a result of the attack.

It would later transpire that police had botched investigations into an earlier attack using sarin gas which had killed nine people in Matsumoto City in 1994.

Murayama, after abandoning long-standing socialist policies towards the USA, was also embarrassed by the rape of a Japanese schoolgirl by an American soldier on Okinawa. In the midst of these upsets, governorship elections in Tokyo and Osaka shocked the political system by rejecting the political parties in favour of maverick independents. In April 1995, *The Far East Economic Review* described the upset in an article headed *'Bring on the Clowns'*.[9] Polls now showed that 80 per cent of the population distrusted politicians and that 60 per cent of the electorate was now 'floating'. It was an appropriate response from a disgruntled electorate furious at the political vacuum which had paralysed their economically stagnant country. After resigning as prime minister in January 1996, SPDJ leader, Murayama, was replaced by LDP faction leader Ryutaro Hashimoto.

Elections held in October 1996 produced a surprisingly good result for the LDP, with the party increasing its seats from 211 to 239. Furthermore, of the new single-member constituencies, the LDP won 169 seats versus 96 for Ozawa's New Frontier Party. The result confirmed not only the historical election strength of the LDP vote gathering machine but also the relative weakness of the opposition in co-ordinating funding and building a rival electoral organisation.

Overall New Frontier's representation fell from 160 to 156 Diet seats. If the result was disappointing for New Frontier, it was a disaster for the SDPJ, who were made to pay for their collaboration with the LDP; they won just 4 single-member seats and 15 seats overall. By contrast, the Democratic Party won 52 seats and the Japan Communist Party won 26 seats. As the *Anatomy of the 1996 Lower House Election* concluded, 'it was impossible to sweep away deep-rooted habits among voters backing individual candidates rather than parties . . .'.[10] Expectations that the introduction of single-member constituencies would promote British-style political debate and a movement towards a two-party system proved woefully misguided. The *Anatomy* concluded that 'neither policy debate as the core of the party-based electioneering nor campaigning in which a leader's image played an important role . . . materialised scarcely at all'.[11]

The relative electoral failure of New Frontier now led to its break-up. Some members defected back to the LDP, enabling it to re-establish a parliamentary majority. The ever-inventive Ozawa decided to dissolve New Frontier and replaced it with the Liberal Party, a party name that had disappeared with the merger of the Liberals and Democrats in the 1950s. Ozawa also sought an LDP alliance; it was a miscalculation which saw further defections to the Democrat Party without gaining him the support of the LDP Prime Minister Hashimoto, who no longer needed Ozawa's votes.

However, Hashimoto's administration was also short-lived. High-profile bankruptcies and continuing poor economic performance served to undermine his position and he stepped down in July 1998 after a poor showing by the LDP in the Upper House elections. He was succeeded as LDP president and as prime minister by Keizo Obuchi on 30 July 1998. Obuchi spoke like a reformer; he compared the composition of the Diet as being like the old Soviet Union, full of sons of politicians, bureaucrats and former union officials. He also surprised the nation by appointing a 37-year-old woman, Noda Seiko, to the cabinet.

It was hardly a reform package, however, and its thin veneer was soon demonstrated by the appointment of Miyazawa, a former failure both as finance minister and as prime minister, to another term at MOF. As for Obuchi himself, like most Japanese politicians, he lacked charisma and came to be derided as the man who had 'as much pizzas as a cold pizza'.[12] If the LDP lacked direction, so did the leading opposition group in spite of its leader, Naoto Kan, advocating that the Democratic Party had to be 'the party of Thatcher and Blair'.[13]

When the Democratic Party ditched Naoto Kan for Hatoyama Yukio, grandson of a former prime minister, opposition to the LDP within the Diet increased and under pressure from former prime ministers, and now 'king-makers', Nakasone and Takeshita, Obuchi was persuaded to bring Ozawa's Liberals into the cabinet. Included in the deal was an agreement to reduce the size of the House of Representatives to 450 (from 500) and cut the number of ministries by two. When factions within the LDP were unhappy with the new arrangements, Obuchi brought the *Komeito* into the ruling coalition.

In the Diet elections in June 2000, the LDP won a 233 majority of seats in the revised 450-seat House of Representatives. A completely shattered opposition saw the Democrats as the chief opposition with only 10 per cent of the popular vote. After a decade of political chaos, dominated by factional horse-trading and opposition manoeuvring, against the backdrop of a moribund economy, the LDP had emerged more powerful than ever. It was hardly an outcome that its performance in office deserved; however, the LDP's electoral re-emergence demonstrated the strength of its party machine and the intellectual bankruptcy of the opposition parties.

It was also in part a reflection of the cultural political norms unique to Japan amongst the world's leading democracies. As Gerald Curtis points out in *The Logic of Japanese Politics* (1999):

> For many people, the act of voting was not so much an exercise of individual political choice as much as an expression of solidarity with the community or a way to return a favor [*giri*] incurred to someone who was involved in the election campaign.[14]

For international observers, the re-emergence of the LDP from the lost decade was hardly a cause of rejoicing; the Japanese people and their political leaders appeared to have buried their heads in the sand and avoided giving any mandate for economic reform that the 'lost decade' should have demanded.

56

Narasimha Rao and the Quiet Revolution

India: 1990–2003

When Stephen Sackur, on the BBC World's *Hardtalk* programme in October 2005, asked the brilliant lawyer turned economist and finance minister P.V. Chidambaram why he appeared to have abandoned his socialist beliefs, the Indian politician bluntly replied, '. . . socialist means do not deliver. We tried that for 30 years'.[1] Nehru, who after independence had started out down a moderate left-wing Fabian path in the manner advocated by his friends at the London School of Economics, had turned to an increasingly nationalist hardline socialism; his daughter, Indira Gandhi, merely ratcheted Indian politics even further to the left by increasing the government's grip on the key sectors of the economy including banking, insurance, transport, oil and heavy industry. Furthermore with the effective ejection of foreign-owned companies, India became a closed semi-Sovietic economy. Although in the 1980s she and her son Rajiv made some minor adjustments to business tax rates and made other encouragements to private sector business, India remained stalled with what became known as the 'Hindu growth rate'.

For most of the post-war period, growth barely exceeded the burgeoning rate of increase in the Indian population. In the 45 post-war years to 1990, the population of India grew by over half a billion people, more than the combined population of Europe. For India's population, the opportunity costs attributable to command socialism were staggering. It has been estimated that the failure of India to follow the free market model of many of the Asian countries led to a protracted agrarian and humanitarian catastrophe, which cost as many, if not more lives than Mao's 'Great Leap' forward (estimated 30 million dead), albeit over a longer period.

Amartya Sen, a Harvard economist, calculated that had Indian mortality rates just matched those of China, deaths per year would have been 4 million less per annum by the 1980s. This meant that the death toll of the great famine caused by the 'Great Leap Forward' was replicated every eight years in India. Nehru and Indira Gandhi, to whom this tragedy is directly attributable, are not usually associated with the mass murderers of modern history, such as Hitler, Stalin and Mao, but arguably they belong to that undesirable Pantheon.

In the countryside a growing population found itself unable to eke out even subsistence living, and famine was commonplace. Those who escaped to the cities found lodging in unofficial encampments which became the most populous and squalid slums on the planet. (The notorious Soweto slums of Johannesburg are luxurious compared to their counterparts in Bombay and Calcutta; much to the embarrassment and annoyance of many Indians, the desperate condition of the Bombay slums, as well as child-trafficking, were widely viewed in Danny Boyle's Oscar winning film *Slumdog Millionaire* (2008). Water and sanitation were constant problems, and the country was a laboratory for deadly diseases including plague, smallpox, polio, typhoid, dysentery, dengue fever and the greatest killer of them all, malaria. Outbreaks of viral malaria, which could cause death within 24 hours, killed tens of thousands even in the 1990s. An outbreak of plague in the wealthy diamond city of Surat created a national panic. In Bombay, lepers roamed the streets as beggars.

Life expectancy was short. In 1990s India, even a middle class 60-year-old was an ancient compared to his Western counterpart who might be considering global travel or adventure holidays. For the majority of the Indian population, life was brutal and short. In Bombay in 1993, a foreign banker employed a 28-year-old cook who had already been in domestic service for 15 years. At the age of 13 she had left her village near Mangalore in southwest India, where she lived in a mud floored hut with her mother and sister, and had travelled alone by train to Bombay.

Only speaking the Mangalore dialect of Marialum, barely a word of Hindi, she had gone from house to house asking for work. Eventually happening upon a servant also from Mangalore, she had been taken into work as the fifth chamber maid of the wife of a wealthy property owner; in this position her main duty was to pluck by hand the pubic hairs of her mistress. Working her way up from the bottom, she had graduated to the kitchen and eventually secured work with foreigners, always a plum position because of their relatively humane treatment of employees by comparison with rich Indians. Perversely many of India's wealthy were devout socialists, who deplored the bidding away of their servants and employees by foreign incomers in the 1990s.

Because the cook was one of the tens of millions of 'unregistered' people born in the countryside, she had had to bribe officials to get registration papers to make her an official person. This was symptomatic of a bureaucracy and political system riddled with corruption. The poor were excluded by expense from this bureaucratic world and lived on the borderlines of official existence. The cook from Mangalore, for example, eventually saved enough money to own an apartment in Bombay on 'non-registered' land with no access to mains water.

When an English executive imported his belongings into India, which he was allowed to do free of tax, he was visited by customs officers who demanded import tax on his small wine cellar, which they now claimed was taxable at 500 per cent. Faced by a US$ 40,000 tax bill, the executive decided to have his cellar shipped back to England, only to be told that this was not allowed and that the wine would be confiscated. The result of negotiations was an US\$ 8,000 cash bribe. It was generally thought that the head of customs in Bombay raked in annual income in the millions; however, the head of customs in Rajasthan, who controlled the trafficking of opium, was supposed to be many times richer.

Rent control and draconian laws on development meant that the great cities could not house their poor, provide offices for incoming businesses or house incoming foreign businessmen. The lack of supply meant that property prices per square meter in Bombay were multiples of London and Tokyo.

It took one foreign executive six months to find suitable accommodation; in a beautiful but completely dilapidated Edwardian waterfront property adjacent to the 'Five Star' Taj Hotel, an apartment became available to rent notwithstanding the fact that it was being operated as a brothel and drug den owned by a former inspector of police. The rooms, divided into cubicles, were gutted by up to 50 workmen at a time, using tools that would not have been out of place in the nineteenth century. Even with bribes, there was a 6 to 12 month wait for a new telephone number from the state telephone company, and evenings for the foreign executive were spent fielding telephone calls for prostitutes.

The police inspector, who had reputedly acquired his lucrative post by dint of providing girls to the chief minister of Maharashtra to whom he had been bodyguard, also allegedly took protection money from the numerous bordellos and drug dens operating in the area. In the short walk between his apartment and the Taj Hotel, the executive would daily be offered exotic services; child prostitution was a commonplace. More horrifying still, young children were bought and deliberately mutilated at birth by 'beggar masters'; they would patrol the streets around the best hotels seeking charity from foreign tourists. Here they jostled for custom with 'spider-men' who, with their backs bent double by polio, walked on hands and legs or with skateboard men, legless torsos, who sped through the traffic propelled only by their hands.

Rent control did little to help the poor. Inhabitants of buildings stayed put, handing their apartments and their increasingly derisory rents to their offspring. Landlords unable to afford repairs from their rents left buildings to rot. In effect, after independence, the owners of property had their assets sequestered by government, hardly a recipe for encouraging property development or housing for the growing urban masses. Rent control and building restrictions alone were estimated to have cost India 2 per cent per annum real GDP economic growth since independence.

The result on people's lives was invidious. Multimillion dollar apartment buildings looked like dilapidated government tenement blocks; driving from the airport, the city gave every impression of being a massive rotting hulk. Even the rich threw their household waste out of the window. Housing of any sort was a luxury however. In the squalid streets, the poorer workers would sleep rough on the pavements in lines, for which they would have to pay protection to the local beat policemen.

Around Bombay, the poor would do their ablutions at dawn and dusk on the beaches or railway lines, which at sunset offered a vast array of squatting buttocks. Women would do their ablutions at night in dark corners. Every year homeless women would die from cobra bites as they squatted in the gloom. In spite of this, conditions in the countryside were worse, and the great cities suffered a never-ending stream of migration, which merely exacerbated the problem of urban squalor.

> . . . the whole orchestra typical of the Indian city. A never ending procession of buses, cars, trucks, taxicabs, three-wheelers, motorcycles, bicycle rickshaws, bicycles and a great many carts and push trolleys laden with vegetables passed before their eyes. Shops and beggars occupied all the footpaths. Pedestrians overflowed onto the main road, causing frequent traffic jams. Here and there on the pavement, astrologers sat with their holy books. Some of them had cages of *mainas* — small birds believed to be the medium through which God conveyed His messages regarding the future of humans. . . .[2]

It was a mediaeval world fascinating to the tourist but hiding an excruciating mass of human deprivation and suffering.

Life was cheap in India. A foreign visitor remembered being in Bombay, the capital of Maharashtra, when more than 10,000 people were killed by an earthquake in the provincial town of Latur. During the course of a day of meetings, not a single Indian raised or discussed a subject that in Europe would have been the focal point of conversation and concern. Asked about the apparent indifference, an Indian executive told the foreign visitor that such tragedies were normal and that death, even on such a large scale, did not cause the same shock as in the West.

Indian politicians liked to proclaim their country as the world's largest democracy; in reality it had merely become the world's largest demagoguery. Votes of the majority rural poor, half of whom were illiterate, were bought by land distribution, which often embedded inefficient small-scale agriculture, and by free electricity and subsidised credit; sometimes they were simply bought for cash. Nehru and Indira Gandhi and her children, who all lived far beyond any income that their political salaries could have afforded them, may have abused their powers, but they were the least offenders compared to the chief ministers of Indian states. As Prime Minister Narasimha Rao would later note of the political system, 'Power became a game, a source of entertainment, like the fights between gladiators in the Roman Empire or cockfights and bullfights in mediaeval Indian principalities. . . . The people figured nowhere.'[3]

In the state of Tamil Nadu (where the capital city *Madras* was renamed *Chennai*), the movie industry was so powerful, with an output in the Tamil language which exceeded even that of Bollywood, that it produced a succession of screen stars turned politicians, whose corruption became legendary throughout India. Chief

Minister Jayalalitha, after a career as an actress, became best known for a wedding thrown for a favourite which reputedly cost US$ 30 million and used so many lights that it caused power shortages throughout the state; purportedly no industrial investment could pass Jayalalitha's purview without a political contribution of 10 per cent of the value of the project. Ultimately the costs of the corrupt 'licence raj' were borne by an Indian population which suffered shoddy, overpriced goods. Only the middle classes such as Rajiv Gandhi, the airline pilot, were able to go overseas and bring back electronic goods that worked. In the early 1990s, the carousels at baggage arrival in Bombay would be overflowing with 'brown goods' boxes.

While the corrupt politicians could be and sometimes were thrown out of office, the judiciary was largely irremovable. Possessing the vestiges of a British-based judicial system, English speaking and sporting the paraphernalia of wigs and gowns, the system lacked the one essential prerequisite of a democracy, namely honesty. In criminal cases, police and judges could be bought; sons of the rich even bought themselves out of murder charges.

For the economy it was equally disastrous. Wealthy industrialists could pay to have their rival's business plans held up in the courts. Foreign investment, particularly in infrastructure, became stymied by legal action. Thus, in an infamous episode, Enron's US$ 250 million private power plant at Dabhol became legally blocked. At the end of the 1990s, two brilliant expatriate Indian professors of science and robotics at Carnegie Mellon University, Dr Raj Reddy and Dr V.S. Arunachalam, had developed a business plan to light up an optical fibre network already laid around India by the military and saw their prospective business, IUNET, for which funding was readily available at the end of the 1990s, fizzle out in vexatious court action. A world leading fibre network, which would have boosted the Indian knowledge industries particularly in software and outsourcing, was thereby denied to the country.

Such was the depravity of the socialist economy bequeathed by Nehru and his family some 40 years after independence. Superficially a democracy, India, by its policies of economic autarky, had sunk into a state of global irrelevance; Nehru's Congress Party had created a world of Dickensian, if not mediaeval, squalor. Finally in 1991 the country began to be rescued by a combination of indigenous and exogenous crises and by one of the world's least known and most unlikely revolutionaries, Narasimha Rao.

Rao was born to a poor Brahmin family on 28 June 1921 in a village in the southern state of Andhra Pradesh where his native language was Telugu. He studied at Osmania University and at Bombay and Nagpur. He graduated with a master's degree in law. He also became a brilliant linguist speaking Urdu, Marathi, Hindi, Telugu and English fluently; in addition he learnt 12 other languages including French and Spanish. Rao was active in the independence movement and served in cabinets under Nehru and Indira Gandhi. Between 1971 and 1973 he was also chief minister of Andhra Pradesh in the capital city of Hyderabad. He remained an Indira loyalist during the Congress split in 1969 and during the emergency (1974–7), for which he was rewarded with major cabinet posts including home affairs, defence and foreign affairs.

Effectively retired from front-line politics in the early 1990s, Rao was brought back to the centre by Congress Party 'kingmakers' as a makeshift leader after the assassination of Rajiv Gandhi and elections in 1991. As he concludes in his autobiographical fiction *The Insider* (1998), the protagonist central figure Anand

> who had decided to retire from active politics and declined to contest the Lok Sabha [lower house] elections, was called upon to shoulder the Prime Minister's task _ suddenly, unexpectedly, in an extraordinary turn of events. A new phase of his life had begun.[4]

Rao was appointed to lead a minority Congress-led government and served a full five-year term in office in that capacity. Importantly, he oversaw a radical transformation of the nature of the Indian economy and laid the foundations for India's emergence as a major world economic power by the end of the twentieth century.

On becoming prime minister, Rao faced an unprecedented economic crisis. The Soviet Union was on the point of collapse and with it a communist economy which was India's main trading partner. The long period of quasi-communistic rule and pro-Soviet alliance by Nehru and Indira Gandhi had created an economy whose industrial products could only be traded with that other sub-standard producer, the Soviet Union. Theirs was a virtually hermetically sealed world occupying a parallel universe of industrial and consumer products, which could not have competed in a global free market. With the collapse of the Soviet Union and its Eastern European satellites and rapidly falling demand for Indian goods at the start of the 1990s, India's industrial economy was catastrophically compromised. To compound the problem, international demand also collapsed, bringing recession in America and Europe.

Finally the onset of the First Gulf War, with President George Bush's decision, backed by a United Nations mandate, to expel Saddam Hussein from Kuwait, which he had invaded on 2 August 1991, dramatically cut remittances from Indian workers in the Middle East. With international reserves down to just a few months, India faced a drastic balance of payments crisis. Rao, who became prime minister in June 1991, undertook a 100-day package of economic reforms. Little noticed by most international commentators and press, it was a revolutionary programme, which fundamentally transformed India's economic performance and began the long process of improving the living standards of its people.

The men chosen by Rao to transform the Indian economy were two brilliant technocrats, Manmohan Singh, who was made finance minister, and P. Chidambaram, minister for commerce. Singh, born in Gah in West Punjab on 26 September 1932, was seemingly a career academic. After gaining a master's degree from Punjab University, Singh went to St. John's College, Cambridge, where he took an undergraduate degree in 1957, winning the Adam Smith Prize while he was there. In 1962 he took a doctorate from Nuffield College, Oxford, and thereafter pursued an academic career in India. However, he was gradually drawn into the political world and became governor of the Reserve Bank of India in 1982, in which post he served for three years. He entered politics with the Indian National Congress, though only in the upper house.

Meanwhile P. Chidambaram, born on 16 September 1945, a Tamil politician from Madras, was both a successful lawyer and a Harvard MBA. Originally a leftist Congress supporter who had risen to prominence under Rajiv Gandhi, he had become convinced of the futility of socialist economics and a firm believer in free market reform and deregulation.

The reform package was far reaching. Perhaps its most important aspect was the ending of economic autarky; foreign companies were now encouraged to become 100 per cent owners of corporations in India. International corporations such as Coca Cola and Unilever, which had retreated from the Indian market 20 years earlier, began to return. In addition, state monopolies such as television, airlines and telecommunications were thrown open to competition. Around these two central ministerial figures were also a group of 'young turks', such as Jairam Ramesh (now India's Environment Minister), who, in the wake of India's foreign exchange crisis, pushed through a paradigm shift in the direction of India's economic management.

Also the impact of foreign-owned TV stations was dramatic. The breaking of *Doordarshan*'s state-owned TV monopoly, with its monotonous diet of Sovietic-style leader worship, brought to a startled audience the delights of modern broadcasting. It not only opened up the government to media criticism, but also opened the eyes of the Indian middle classes as to how far below the rest of Asia the Nehru dynasty's far left economic policies had deposited them. Media deregulation brought a seismic shift, not only in consumer expectations but also in the political and economic methods by which they were achievable.

Fixed-line telephony was deregulated but, more importantly, licences were auctioned for digital mobile, bringing an influx of modern technology and investment. With one bound, India developed a mobile telephone system, which was a generation ahead of the analogue mobile systems in the USA. The globalisation of telecommunications and transport also enabled Indian companies to seek new international markets in the development of service industries. With an educated low-cost English-speaking population, Western companies soon found that they could reduce costs by putting corporate back-office functions into India.

America's General Electric led the way, followed by a host of imitators. American medical practitioners would have their taped records transcribed overnight in India. This subsequently spawned a rapidly growing outsourcing industry, whereby companies could reduce specific back-office costs such as 'call centres' by relocation to the fast-developing technology centres in Bangalore, India's 'silicon valley',

New Delhi and Hyderabad. British Airways became an early pioneer in the relocation of its back-office systems to India.

Towards the end of the 1990s, fears of the so-called millennium bug also
proved a boon to India's knowledge industries. The software capacity to deal with
the scale of the problem in the West did not exist, and international businesses
increasingly hired companies such as Infosys, Satyam Systems and Tata Systems
to solve their problems. Having gained international credibility with the quality of
their work, Bangalore-based software companies grew rapidly. With a vast army of
well-educated English-speaking graduates, other Indian industries also prospered.
The business of 'generic' pharmaceutical products, once dominated by Italian
producers, now shifted to India, where the key cost of science graduates could
be sharply diminished. As a result, companies such as Ranbaxy Laboratories Ltd.
became world leaders in this field.

Finance was also transformed with the arrival of the investment banking herd.
Jardine Fleming, a typical early entrant in new markets, created a dramatic market
presence in Bombay under the leadership of Mark Bullough, who soon become an
influential figure in the corridors of power in New Delhi. Other investment banks
followed: Barings, Peregrine, Crédit Lyonnais, Goldman Sachs, Salomon, CSFB
and James Capel (HSBC). Between them they transformed the professionalism of
the capital markets, dragged Indian financial companies into modern techniques
and brought new methods of raising money for Indian corporations.

As in America, they became aspirational companies for the best business graduates and soon became the leading recruiters from Ahmedabad Institute of Management, the leading Indian business school. Stock broking, corporate finance, derivatives, bond trading, privatisation and venture capital all became the new common
currency of the business and financial press. It was a radical departure from the
culture of state financing through government-controlled banks. Although privatisation of banks and insurance remained sensitive issues, the socialist consensus was
well and truly smashed. By the end of the decade, even communist-controlled Bengal with its ancient capital of Calcutta was seeking to attract foreign investment.

The impact of Rao's reforms on economic growth was soon apparent. In the
decade after 1994, the Indian economy achieved real GDP growth of 6.8 per cent,
making it one of the world's fastest-growing countries. Given the scale of the unofficial sectors of the economy, unrecorded by government statistics, it is probable
that real growth even exceeded these figures. Meanwhile by comparison with the
foreign exchange crisis faced by Rao in 1991, India's reserves had risen to US$ 145
billion by 2005.

India's economy never suffered the complete collapse faced by the Soviet Union.
Though in the post-war period the Indian National Congress adopted economic
policies that were largely Sovietic in nature, small businesses largely escaped while
larger ones could at least operate, albeit within the limitations of a closed economy; socialism never penetrated as deeply in India as the Communist Party did in

the Soviet Union. Also, India never had a runaway military – industrial complex absorbing an increasing percentage of GDP; Nehru and Indira Gandhi, for all their faults, only sought regional hegemony, not global ideological conquest.

Nevertheless the combination of Sovietic economic policies, a corrupt bureaucracy and a political system tending to demagoguery produced a sclerotic society and a political caste, which became venal, corrupt and indifferent to the fate of its citizens. It would be difficult to argue that India delivered more for its citizens than the government of the Soviet Union, which at least provided its citizens with a comprehensive health and education system. Narasimha Rao, a sickly retiree, albeit under the duress of economic crisis, rescued his country from the socialist tyranny imposed by Nehru and his heirs; he is perhaps the most unsung hero of the latter half of the twentieth century, having achieved almost as much for the economic liberation of his country as Deng Xiaoping in China.

57

The Savaging of the Tiger Economies

Asia: 1996—8

Between 1955 and 1999, the average rate of GNP growth in South Korea was 9 per cent per annum. It was an economic performance closely matched by Hong Kong, Singapore and Taiwan. Slightly lower down the scale, Thailand and Malaysia achieved growth of 7.5 per cent and 7 per cent respectively between 1966 and 1999. Even the poorest of the region's performers, Indonesia and the Philippines, achieved real GDP growth of 6.5 per cent and 4 per cent respectively in the post-war period. In an epoch in which the global economy achieved rates of economic growth unprecedented in world history, the economic performance of 'free' Asia, as distinct from socialist Asia, was remarkable. As Toyoo Gyohten, Japan's vice president for international affairs at the Ministry of Finance, would later reflect, 'It is fair to say that because of the very rapid growth, Asia eliminated very fundamental problems of poverty.'[1]

By the early 1990s, the idea was rapidly gaining ground that the future lay with Asia; President Clinton even based his global strategy on this perception. While Japan had been laid low by a stock market and property crash, the 1980s boom of the Reagan–Thatcher era had come to an end with a recession in America and Europe, and the Soviet Union and its satellite economies had collapsed, Asia's 'Tiger' economies seemed impervious to the chaos around them.

The exceptional post-war performance of the Asian economies was no miracle; it was a direct consequence of a number of readily explicable phenomena. Pax Americana, the protective umbrella thrown over 'free' Asia by American hegemony, established an era of relative peace and stability from which economies could prosper. Those countries that performed the best – Korea, Taiwan, Hong Kong and Singapore – also, by different means, channelled savings and investment into export-led industries, which were able to take advantage of America's open markets.

Given the low labour input costs, the combination of the booming American consumer market and Asia's price competitiveness provided an open goal for export-led growth. Increasing globalisation, served by better and cheaper global transport and telecommunications, merely served to expand the opportunities for cost reduction; in America, where the Reagan economic revolution had fed the in-vestor demand for ever-increasing returns on capital and shareholder performance, the desire for outsourcing to cheaper labour markets further fed the flight of jobs and investments to Asia.

In addition to the increasing globalisation of industrial activity, from the 1980s there was a spectacular rise in global financial activity. In 1983, there were just two foreign portfolio managers based in Tokyo; by the end of the decade there were dozens. In Hong Kong the growth in the number of commercial bank branches had exploded after deregulation in 1975, but the real transformation came with 'Big bang' in London, which brought the American investment banks to London, and began a global expansion that quickly took them to Hong Kong, Singapore and Tokyo, the three centres which established themselves as financial leaders in Asia in the 1980s.

In their wake, the portfolio investment of pension funds and mutual funds followed. By the early 1990s, Asian markets could show exceptional investment returns, which were largely uncorrelated with the US stock market. For the rapidly expanding pension fund consultants (William M. Mercer, Callan, Frank Russell, Watson Wyatt, Wilshire etc.), it appeared an ideal opportunity to recommend asset diversification. Asian portfolio investment, as a subset of 'Global Emerg-ing Markets', became the hottest new area for the young bucks of the invest-ment world. From their Hong Kong base, Asian investment companies spread their wings throughout the region, opening offices in economies previously untouched by Wall Street.

By 1990, net inflows of foreign portfolio investment in emerging markets to-talled US\$ 3.2 billion in 1990, and had risen to US\$ 48.5 billion in 1995. Sales of bonds by developing economies were even more spectacular, rising from just US\$ 100 million in 1991 to US\$ 53.8 billion by 1997. Having been badly stung by Latin America in the 1980s, commercial banks were relatively late to the party. However, in 1994 they lent US\$ 8.9 billion, a figure which had jumped to US\$ 41.1 billion in 1997. Meanwhile, a further source of capital inflow into Asia, for-eign direct investment (FDI) by overseas corporations and individuals, also grew spectacularly from US\$ 23.7 billion in 1991 to US\$ 120.4 billion in 1997.

These private flows of money to Asia represented an extraordinary shift from the 1950s and 1960s, when the governments of developed economies directed more than 50 per cent of all investment capital flows to the emerging or undevel-oped economies. As Professor Jeffrey Winters has observed:

> In 1995, private capital accounted for three-fourths of all investment resources deliv-ered to the developing world. Portfolio investment rose to fifty percent of total net capital flows to developing economies by 1996 from just two percent in 1987. And three quarters of this staggering sum is in the hands of fewer than one hundred emerg-ing market fund managers.[2]

Suddenly in the eyes of private investors worldwide, Asia became 'de-risked'. Yield premiums over US treasury rates fell dramatically in the immediate aftermath of the Mexican crisis; even in markets such as Thailand and Indonesia, secondary markets yields fell to as low as 1 per cent above US Treasury Bonds. For Asian companies starved of funds in the post-war period, the opportunity to gorge on foreign credit was too good to be true.

Hong Kong, which was the epicentre of Asia's credit expansion, also spawned a new market in corporate bonds, the market which had been pioneered by Mike Milken at Drexel Burnham Lambert in the USA in the 1980s. In Asia, the market was built up by Peregrine Investments Holdings, an upstart investment bank founded by Philip Tose and Francis Leung in 1988; this maverick outfit, far-sighted in its view that China was in the process of becoming a major free market economy, had grown rapidly as a raiser of funds for emerging Chinese corporations.

By helping CITIC Hong Kong [Holdings] Ltd. acquire a shell company with a listing in Hong Kong, Peregrine also promoted the rapid growth of the so-called *Red Chip* market, which did so much to announce China's arrival on the global business stage. In 1994, Philip Tose, who had by now developed Peregrine into one of the most admired and fastest growing companies in Asia (even becoming a case study at Harvard Business School), filched a team from Lehman Brothers to set up a bond department at Peregrine, and under the leadership of Andre Lee, an executive of Korean–French Canadian descent, the company established a commanding lead in the issue and sale of Asian corporate debt. On the back of this business, Peregrine's balance sheet had grown to US$ 5.3 billion dollars by 1997, some six times its capital base.

Although the avalanche of capital investment sustained nominal economic growth among the 'Tiger' economies, beneath the surface all was not well. Paul Krugman, a professor of economics at Stanford University, pointed to the problem as early as 1994, when in an article entitled '*The Myth of Asia's Miracle*' in *Foreign Affairs* magazine, he wrote that 'Sustained output in a nation's per capita income can only occur if there is a rise in output per unit of input.'[3] The problem that he identified was that although investment capital in Asia was growing rapidly, the use to which it was being put was questionable. By 1994, returns on investment in Asia were falling, a fact that was becoming increasingly clear from stagnating stock market performance after 1993.

Already by the early 1990s, the export growth of the leading ASEAN nations was falling; Thailand, Indonesia, Malaysia and the Philippines had enjoyed 15 per cent annualised growth in exports between 1978 and 1989, but this had fallen to 4 per cent by 1990–1. As the economists Borestein and Lee noted, Asia's economic performance was becoming increasingly 'sustained by higher and higher levels of investment even in the face of declining productivity of capital and almost vanishing corporate profitability'.[4]

The first cracks in the Asian economy appeared in Thailand. While the country had every appearance of stability, with a 15-year track record of strong economic performance, stable inflation and a currency pegged to the US dollar, the hidden reality was less attractive. Thai companies, finding that they could borrow dollars at lower rates than the Thai baht, went on a speculative borrowing and investment spree which went, not on productive capacity, but on the building of luxury hotels and speculative office developments. Jeffrey Sachs, director of the Harvard Institute for International Development, compared Thailand's trauma to the 1995 Mexican crisis, 'Thailand's 1997 crisis has the same hallmarks: overvaluation of the real exchange rate coupled with booming bank lending, heavily directed at real estate.'[5]

Money was channelled by Chinese-controlled banks with their corrupt political connections. As MIT economist Rudiger Dornbusch observed, 'In Thailand, every politician owns a bank and every bank owns two politicians.'[6] The opening up of foreign bank lending through the Bangkok International Banking Facility (BIBF) merely exacerbated the problem of excess credit; lending was encouraged by government hints that banking licences would be awarded dependent on the volume of lending by foreign banks. Between 1993 and 1996, Thai external debt, mostly dollar-denominated short-term debt, rose from US$ 45.8 billion to US$ 88.6 billion.

The first attacks on Thailand's fixed dollar parity began towards the end of 1996. The first signs of stress in the corporate sector began to emerge when a real estate company, Somprasing Land, defaulted on a Eurobond issue. Unbeknownst to the market, the governor of Thailand's Central Bank was spending US$ 25 billion in currency reserves on trying to maintain the Thai baht currency parity with the dollar. Amnuay Viravan, finance minister in General Chavalit Yongchaiyudh's weak coalition government, fatefully asked, 'Why do I have to learn from the Mexican crisis? It's an entirely different story in this part of the world.'[7]; a week after his resignation on 25 June 1997, the Central Bank could no long sustain its financial support for the Thai baht and was forced to float the currency; the baht did not float, it sank.

Weighed down with an increasing level of US dollar debt, the collapse of the baht sparked widespread corporate default, which further increased financial panic. The International Monetary Fund (IMF) was called in to orchestrate the biggest government bail-out since the Mexican crisis, and on 14 August the Chavalit government agreed to a drastic restructuring programme in return for a US$ 17.2 billion emergency credit.

The Thai crisis set off a wave of stock market selling by foreign investors. In addition, speculators attacked the other fixed-parity currencies of Asia. As the pressure rose in neighbouring Malaysia, Prime Minister Dr Mahathir launched into a ferocious attack on foreigners; the Jewish hedge fund operator George Soros and his Quantum Fund came in for particular abuse and he was branded a 'criminal' and a 'moron'. In October, Mahathir declared, 'We are Muslims and the Jews are not happy to see Muslims progress. We may suspect that they have an agenda but we do not want to accuse them ... We cannot make wild accusations ... they will twist our arm.'[8] Ignoring the fact that foreign investors had bought Malaysian assets in the first place, Mahathir accused them of racism for selling them.

In reality, the hedge funds and other foreign investors were merely exposing the fault lines in the corrupt oligopoly of economic and political power, which had so diminished the economic performance of the Asian economies in the early 1990s. In spite of the benefits that had accrued to the Malaysian economy from free trade and foreign capital, Mahathir denounced currency trading as 'unnecessary, unproductive and immoral. It should be stopped. It should be made illegal. We don't need currency trading. We need to buy money only when we want to finance real trade'.[9] It was a typical politician's response to try to deflect blame from poorly conceived economic policies; British Prime Minister John Major had also ranted feebly against speculators at the door of No. 10 Downing Street, when his flawed attempt to maintain parity with the European Exchange Rate Mechanism (ERM) was being destroyed by the currency markets in 1992.

Rather than dealing with the rampant corruption within the Malaysian financial system, Mahathir's answer was to revert to a closed economy of capital controls and fixed exchange rates. To an audience of students in Japan, Mahathir declaimed that 'having lost their globe-girding colonies, the Europeans now want to continue their dominance through dictating the terms of trade, the systems of government and the whole value-system of the world including human rights and environment protection'.[10]

Neither was Japan spared the blowback of the emerging systemic Asian financial crisis. The reversal of the decade-long yen appreciation in 1995 saw a rising dollar which harmed the export competitiveness of the 'dollar linked' Asian economies, while boosting Japanese exporters. Meanwhile, the Japanese government remained stubbornly resistant to domestic structural reform. Already weak Japanese financial markets were badly hit by declining Western confidence in Asia throughout the autumn of 1997. On 3 November, Sanyo Securities, a second-tier Japanese brokerage business, which had gambled on building the world's largest trading floor at the end of the 1980s 'bubble' economy, filed for bankruptcy. Three weeks later, a sobbing Shohei Nozawa, President of Yamaichi Securities, one of Japan's oldest brokerage companies and one of the 'Big Four', announced the company's insolvency to a shocked phalanx of reporters.

Japan's financial shock was a mere ripple compared to the tsunami which now swept through the much more exposed Korean economy. Financial deregulation in the Korean market in the early 1990s had led to a boom in the setting up of investment banks, which now flooded the economy with credit. Total external debt in Korea had swelled from US$ 54.4 billion in 1994 to US$ 78.4 billion in 1995 and US$ 160.7 billion in 1996. More importantly, short-term debt had increased from US$ 14 billion to US$ 73 billion in just two years; by 1997, short-term debt amounted to 47 per cent of the whole.

The Korean *chaebol* (conglomerate) system which, through the corrupt nexus of banks and politicians, had channelled capital towards large-scale capital investment projects throughout the post-war period, at the expense of small to medium size enterprises, continued to commandeer this massive expansion of credit. As the economist Sherman Robinson warned in 1994, the banking system was increasingly vulnerable to the corrupt allocation of capital which was 'a central plank in the patronage networks that sustain political power and cement networks of support'.[11]

Rather than seek out new areas for investment, the *chaebol* cannibalised each other's territory by copycat investment which merely served to reduce the Korean economy's already poor return on capital. In 1996, the largest motor manufacturer, Hyundai, only produced 27.9 cars per employee per annum compared to the 44.7 per employee that Toyota had achieved as far back as 1974. Even after Korea's third largest car maker, Kia Motors, had gone bankrupt, Samsung (the country's second largest *chaebol*) invested US$ 2.5 billion in a new motor manufacturing venture of which only US$ 123 million came from its own funds.

As a result of the *Chaebol* system, which had worked well in the immediate post-war era, the economy had become highly concentrated in areas such as steel, construction, shipbuilding, motor manufacture and electronics. With its narrow industrial concentration and corporate leverage up to 500 per cent of capital, the Korean economy was dangerously exposed to any downturn. In the second half of 1996, a collapse in semiconductor prices, which accounted for 25 per cent of Korea's exports, was largely responsible for an increase in Korea's current account deficit from 2 per cent in 1995 to 4.9 per cent in 1996.

As with Thailand, the first cracks in the corporate sector began to show up early in 1997. In January, Hanbo Steel collapsed with US$ 7 billion in debt. The head of the company, Chung Tae Soo, had gambled 5,000 billion won on a new steel mill in a company with only 300 billion won in shareholder's funds. For a company with a net cash flow of just 60 billion won, it was being vastly over-funded. It soon became apparent that this funding was made available by Korea First Bank through the influence and kickbacks of Kim Hyun Chul, the son of the Korean president. Ironically, President Kim Young Sam had come to power on an 'anti-corruption' ticket.

It was not coincidental that Hanbo had been generally credited with financing President Kim's election campaign in 1992. The Hanbo scandal was followed by the collapse of 5 out of Korea's 30 *chaebols*, including Sammi, Jinro, Haitai, New Core and Kia. By mid-summer, the downward pressure on the Korean won, combined with capital flight and a rapidly collapsing economy, was putting unbearable pressure on an economy overleveraged on short-term dollar debt. By November, the country was close to default and required a US$ 57 billion rescue package from the IMF on 3 December, a record figure that dwarfed the US$ 18 billion provided to Mexico in February 1995.

In spite of the scale of the Korea bail-out, the biggest national disaster of the Asian financial crash was still to come. Under President Suharto, Indonesia had become recognised as the most corrupt country in Asia. In *Lords of the Rim: The Invisible Empire of the Overseas Chinese* (1995), his picaresque account of the Pacific Basin countries, Sterling Seagrove wrote:

> Instead of the Chinese controlling the economy and the army providing protection in return for kickbacks, as they do in Thailand, in Indonesia the army controls all commerce while the Chinese run it for them in return for kickbacks.[12]

Throughout 1997, the Indonesian rupiah had, in common with other Asian currencies, been under constant downward pressure and another IMF bail-out was looming.

A bad situation turned to catastrophe when it was revealed on 2 January 1988 that Peregrine, the leading Hong Kong-based investment bank, had committed one-third of its capital to a US$ 260 million bridging loan to Steady Safe, a Jakarta-based taxi company, whose main surety was its link to President Suharto's daughter Tutut. The Indonesian rupiah fell from 17,000 to 27,000 to the US dollar within a few days, leaving the currency 80 per cent down on the levels of a year previously. Riots and looting now broke out in the streets. The reckless issuance of 'junk' bond financings by Peregrine's bond team to weak Indonesian corporations, without the knowledge of the experienced head of Peregrine's Indonesian investment bank, was at best foolhardy. Steady Safe folded and brought with it the demise of Peregrine, which unlike New York investment banks did not have a Federal Reserve to come to its rescue with injections of liquidity. When Peregrine's credit lines were pulled by their Japanese bankers, they had nowhere else to turn for funds. Hong Kong's Hang Seng Stock Exchange Index also collapsed.

On 15 January, Michel Camdessus, the managing director of the IMF arrived at Indonesia's presidential palace and, famously, with arms folded in what was interpreted by the media as a deliberate humiliation, stood over President Suharto as he signed an agreement to restructure the economy in return for a financial rescue package. With some US$ 120 billion of debt (including derivatives), the Indonesian economy was in a parlous condition.

The IMF strictures on bank closures, and reduction of government spending, merely added to the economic contraction that was already under way. In 1998, the Indonesian economy contracted by almost 15 per cent; it was an economic performance, which for atrociousness, was only matched by Korea (-14 per cent); the next worst performance of any of the Asian economies was Thailand whose GDP fell by 8 per cent. In July 1998, the World Bank report concluded that, 'No country in recent history, let alone one the size of Indonesia, has ever suffered such a dramatic reversal of fortune . . . words alone cannot describe the numbing shock that has been afflicted on this country of 200m people. . . .'[13]

The severity of the collapse of the Indonesian economy proved to be the fulcrum of debate about whether the IMF had itself exacerbated the crisis. In some quarters, the contracts which the IMF had forced on the defaulting Asian countries were described as being taken from the 1980's Latin debt crisis textbook, where countries were forced to swallow a diet of government fiscal retrenchment.

Joseph Stiglitz, senior economist at the World Bank, argued that the IMF's 'ideological' prescription for higher interest rates was likely to increase economic strains and precipitate even higher levels of capital flight. Camdessus, a former French socialist bureaucrat, was seen by many as hopelessly unqualified to deal with what was essentially a market crisis. Trent Lott, Republican Senate leader announced, 'I'd like to get rid of the head of the IMF. He's a socialist from France.'[14] *Newsweek* echoed the popular American view that he was a 'colourless bean counter'.[15]

Camdessus also had an intellectual run-in with Steve Hanke, an economist from John Hopkins University, who had helped establish 'currency boards' in countries as far-ranging as Argentina, Bulgaria, Lithuania and Bosnia. While a currency board might well have served Indonesia, Camdessus refused to countenance an IMF loan if President Suharto chose that option; for the IMF the rescue of 'Suharto Inc.' was not a politically acceptable option whatever the damage to the Indonesian economy.

The spat between rival economists and institutions was symptomatic of the diversity of explanations for this unprecedented regional crisis. For Mahathir the problem was excessive liberalisation combined with what he believed was a malevolent western conspiracy orchestrated by Jewish financiers. Curiously, Mahathir's nemesis, George Soros, largely agreed with Mahathir about the irresponsibility of financial markets was concerned; Soros, whose hedge fund was single-handedly, though erroneously, blamed by some for Britain's expulsion from the ERM in 1992, was to become an increasingly hostile critic of financial markets, which he claimed, '.... resented any kind of government interference, but they hold a belief that, if conditions get rough, the authorities will step in'.[16]

IMF Chief Michel Camdessus felt that the Asian crisis was ascribable to the new problems caused by the corrupt government–private nexus:

> Maybe because we were working too hard monitoring and putting public affairs back in order, policies facilitating complacency in the private sector appeared in the shadows as the public sector was being straightened out. They either went unnoticed or were tolerated in the booming environment that ruled over this region for such a long time ... we witnessed the collapse of economics based on too much credit and not enough shareholder funds and direct investment.[17]

Paul Krugman pointed the finger at Asia's poor record in using capital expenditure, a similar problem to Japan's economy in the 'bubble' era, while Professor

Jeffrey Winters blamed the sheep-herd mentality of largely British and American fund managers. Others blamed 'crony' capitalism, the system whereby politicians corruptly channelled lending towards themselves and their friends. In 1998, Richard Holbrooke (the future US ambassador to the United Nations) reflected on a lack of openness:

> The Asian economies that have entered the mainstream of the global economy, and those closed countries that have entered it_ Korea, Taiwan, China, the four Tigers, Japan_ cannot have it both ways. They can't go to the markets to borrow money and then say we won't show you our books . . . .'[18]

Kim Dae Jung, who was elected president of Korea, just as the Korean economy was collapsing, believed that the Asian crisis reflected a lack of democracy: 'I think Asia's economic crisis stems mainly from a lack of democracy', he told *Time* magazine in March 1998. Political immaturity was also blamed by Kavi Chongkittavorn who wrote:

> Before the financial meltdown in July, most Thais thought politics were a separate entity from economics. . . . So long as the economy continued to grow, they were complacent and willing to ignore official corruption that puts the interests of politicians before interests of the country.[19]

Unsurprisingly, North Korea's great leader saw the Asian collapse as the inevitable death knell of capitalism.

For the World Bank, the problems lay in the lack of structural maturity of the emerging economies. It noted in 1997:

> The world's financial markets are rapidly integrating into a single global marketplace . . . if they have adequate institutions and sound policies, developing countries may proceed smoothly along the road to financial integration and gain the considerable benefits that integration can bring. Most of them, however, lack the prerequisites for a smooth journey, and some may be so ill-prepared that they lose more than they gain from financial integration.[20]

For Harvard economist Jeffrey Sachs, the crash of the Asian Tigers was just another financial crash, part of the normal flux of capitalist endeavour. He thought that the Asian crash was largely a financial panic of the non-governmental market sector and that the IMF attack on fiscal expenditure and its demand for higher interest rates was therefore inappropriately targeted. In June 1998, Sachs claimed in *The New York Times* that 'The IMF had become the Typhoid Mary of emerging markets, spreading recession in country after country.'[21]

In large part, it is difficult not to agree with Sachs' view that financial crashes and economic downturns are the normal adjusting mechanism, which re-allocates resources, both labour and capital, at the end of economic upturns where over expansion of credit and investment are usual. In Asia, between 1996 and 1998 however, credit excess, a normal characteristic of the final throes of a business cycle, was carried to extreme lengths. As John Maynard Keynes pointed out in his *General Theory of Employment, Interest and Money* (1936), 'speculators may do no harm as bubbles on a steady stream of enterprise. But the position is serious.... When the capital development of a country becomes the by-product of the activities of a casino ....'[22]

The reasons for Asia's abnormally overblown credit cycle were not that Asia's capital markets had deregulated too fast, but that they had done so too little. In Indonesia, Korea, Thailand and Malaysia, capital markets had been selectively opened to foreign capital without the concomitant breaking of the nexus between politics and capital allocation by the financial sector. In essence, private fixed capital formation (in other words, investment in plant and equipment) in these Asian countries was being directed by government with the same lack of regard for financial return as socialist command economy systems.

It is an often misunderstood fact that in the post-war period the socialist economies of Eastern Europe achieved a higher rate of growth in fixed capital formation than the West; however, it is productivity of capital, both labour and financial, which is the key determinant of economic growth. Asian countries, with their 'directed credit' systems, followed the economic rule that governments, monopolistic producers of services without the competitive requirement to produce economic rates of return, are profligate investors of money. In this respect, the Asian economies, with their corrupt government–private nexus, between 1994 and 1998, failed utterly, just as Japan had failed in the late 1980s.

In hindsight, it was fortunate for Asia that for the most part market mechanisms did eventually work. Although the short-term economic consequences were dire, there were significant longer-term benefits to the Asian crash. The pace of opening up Asian markets to foreign competition in the financial sector increased, while improved regulatory frameworks were put in place. Although not eradicated, the political–financial links, which had done so much to precipitate the Asian crisis, were severely weakened; voters also became more alert to political corruption.

With regard to Asian corporations, Michael Porter, the Harvard Business School guru, had noted that Asian 'companies don't have strategies. They do deals'.[23] Also, as a result of political corruption, Asian companies also tended to be 'license gathering' structures. Perhaps most importantly, in the aftermath of the Asian crash, companies began to change their strategic priorities, looking less at market share and scale and more at return on capital.

The Asian crash also heralded a new wave of young Asian managers, trained in American business schools, who eschewed Asia's traditional management methods; in many cases, it was the returning children of Asian industrialists who began the rebuilding process. While many commentators questioned the future viability of the Asian economies, in truth the preconditions for strong economic performance remained; high rates of saving and private fixed capital formation, low government expenditure as a proportion of GDP, growing populations and a young population age structure. Ultimately, the Asian financial crash was a cathartic experience which, in spite of the short-term devastation it inflicted, set the stage for the next Asian advance.

The Asian crash marked another significant change. The 'Chinese' economies of Hong Kong and Taiwan were only lightly scathed by the financial crash, while China with its closed capital markets remained impervious to the whole experience. It was an important turning point. Economist and noted Goldman Sachs Asian expert, Dr Ken Courtis, observed that 'China's additional competitiveness was at the heart of the process that unleashed the crisis in Southeast Asia'.[24] Indeed, China's share of OECD exports had risen to 16 per cent in 1995 from just 8.5 per cent at the beginning of the decade. By comparison, the share of the four major ASEAN countries had increased by just 2 per cent to 23 per cent over the same period. Up until 1997, few would have questioned Japan's economic leadership in Asia, but afterwards it was increasingly China that was perceived as Asia's economic superpower.

58

A Bungled Surrender

Hong Kong: 1980–7

The brilliance of Hong Kong's post-war success story was all the more remarkable for the fact that communist China sat like an elephant in the colony's front garden. For the most part, Hong Kong behaved in the post-war period as if China was not there, but at the back of the city's consciousness, it was well understood that the 'elephant' would not go away. The roots of the problem lay in the origins of Hong Kong's secession to Britain. After the First Opium War, caused by British insistence on being able to sell opium to China against her government's wishes, the Treaty of Nanking in 1842 ceded the island of Hong Kong to Britain. The Second Opium War produced further humiliation for the Chinese Emperor, and at the Convention of Peking, the Kowloon Peninsula (the mainland area facing Hong Kong) and the island of Lantau were also ceded to Britain in perpetuity. A final insult, as the Chinese viewed these incursions, took place in July 1898, when China was forced to grant a 99-year lease to the 'New Territories', a sizeable tract of mainland China adjacent to Hong Kong.

For China these were 'unequal treaties' forced upon it in the nineteenth century by the imperialist British, other European powers and the USA. Whatever the legalities, after the war the Chinese, both the *Kuomintang* and Mao's communists, regarded Hong Kong as an inseparable part of China; if the ceding of Hong Kong could be achieved because of Britain's superior power, it could be reversed when China itself had become more powerful than Britain.

However, in the immediate aftermath of the Second World War, it was not in the interests of either the *Kuomintang* or the communists to seek to redress the balance. Even after Mao's defeat of Chiang Kai Shek and the latter's retreat to the island of Formosa (Taiwan), the return of Hong Kong was not on the agenda; Mao had much bigger tasks to hand and made it clear that the return of Hong Kong was not a priority, though he was concerned that the Chinese people should 'not be treated as inferior to others in the matter of taxation' and that they should have 'a voice in the government'.[1] Some, probably unwisely, would interpret this remark as demonstrating that Mao was not intrinsically hostile to democracy.

Nevertheless, the issue of the 'New Territories' lease, due to expire on 30 June 1997, hung over the long-term future of the colony. Without the New Territories, from where the Crown Colony drew its water supply and electricity, not to mention its basic foodstuffs, it was questionable whether the Hong Kong Island and the Kowloon Peninsula could survive. The unanswered question, indeed the question that successive governors were loath to ask for fear of the answer and the effect it might have on Hong Kong's confidence, was_what would happen in 1997? Would China reclaim the New Territories when the 99 year lease expired or would the Chinese government, in light of the success that Britain had made of Hong Kong and its indisputable value as a trading entrepôt for China itself, grant an extension to the Crown Colony leases?

Some took the view that it was simply a matter of time before Hong Kong was delivered back to China. Governor David Trench (1964–71) opined that Britain 'should look for a suitable opportunity to negotiate our withdrawal from China, as soon as a more moderate regime emerges there. . . '.[2] Meanwhile his predecessor, Sir Robert Black (1958–64) thought that it was better not to mention the elephant on the front lawn; he believed it was 'vital for Hong Kong's stability that there should be no official or authorized pronouncement on Hong Kong's future until and unless this became clearly unavoidable'.[3]

In the booming 1970s, Governor Murray MacLehose (1971–81) followed Sir Robert Black's line that it was better to say nothing. However, like an itching scab, by 1979 MacLehose was unable to resist the idea of scratching at the subject of Hong Kong's future; using a visit to Beijing in 1979, and with the blessing of British Foreign Secretary David Owen, MacLehose raised the subject of the New Territories lease with Deng Xiaoping. Although the Chinese Ministry of Foreign Affairs advised against this course of action, MacLehose chose to ignore them. It was a mistake. Though Deng Xiaoping was still in the throes of consolidating his position in China as their new supreme leader, he responded to MacLehose with devastating clarity:

> It has been our consistent view that the People's Republic of China has sovereignty over Hong Kong . . . . However, we will treat Hong Kong as a special region. For a considerable length of time, Hong Kong may practice its capitalist system while we practice our socialist system.[4]

Deng was equally unyielding about the leases; they would not be renewed and China would recover Hong Kong. MacLehose's weak hand had been unequivocally called. On returning to Hong Kong, MacLehose covered up the directness of the Chinese leaders by obfuscation. 'You know the long-standing Chinese position on Hong Kong, that it is part of China and a problem to be solved when the time is ripe', but he went on to emphasise the importance '. . . the Chinese leaders attach to the value of Hong Kong, to the contribution that it could make to the modernisation programmes. . . '.[5]

By raising the subject of Hong Kong, MacLehose merely alerted Deng to the Hong Kong issue and raised its profile with China's new leader. Deng's close colleague Liao Chengzhi was appointed director of the Hong Kong and Macao Affairs Office, and at a CCP meeting in March 1981, it was decided that Hong Kong (not just the leases) would be recovered in 1997. Nevertheless, Deng had by this stage come to fully understand Hong Kong's value to China as a conduit for the modernisation which he craved. Deng adopted the unique policy position that came to be defined by the epithet 'one country, two systems'. It was a policy that would be applied to both Hong Kong and Taiwan; it was a radical approach, which swept to one side the objections of those Chinese leaders who feared that this approach risked undermining socialism in China. It was a typical example of Deng's famed pragmatism.

With Hong Kong now in play, it was deemed necessary that the new British prime minister, the Conservative leader Mrs Margaret Thatcher, should go to Beijing to broach a deal with the Chinese leadership. She was fresh from her crushing military victory over Argentina in her recovery of the Falklands Islands. In her autobiography *The Downing Street Years* (1993), Mrs Thatcher would recall that 'this was, if anything, a drawback. . . . The Chinese leaders were out to demonstrate that the Falklands was no precedent for dealing with the Colony.'[6] The prime minister had been loath to concede that Hong Kong a Island, British sovereign territory since 1842, should be ceded to a foreign power. However Hong Kong, unlike the Falklands or indeed the island of Gibraltar (off the Spanish coast), was entirely dependent on mainland China; furthermore, unlike the Falklands, it was not defendable.

Those who attacked Mrs Thatcher for not defending Hong Kong's sovereignty either ignored or did not understand China's overwhelming economic and military might; some 30 years previously, a much weaker and less well equipped Chinese army had inflicted a crushing defeat on an American army in North Korea. The British fallback position was therefore pitched realistically to 'exchange sovereignty over the island of Hong Kong in return for continued British administration of the entire colony well into the future'.[7]

However, in meetings with Chinese Premier Zhao Ziyang, it was clear that the issue of the return of Hong Kong, territories and island, was not negotiable; the people of Hong Kong were Chinese and had to be returned to China. However, in her meeting with Deng Xiaoping, who took exception to Thatcher's manner and reputedly referred to her as that 'stinking woman', it became clear that China valued the continued success of Hong Kong and would seek to maintain its prosperity. Deng now delivered an ultimatum. It outlined a 12-point policy which allowed Britain two years in which to negotiate a handover agreement; failure to achieve that would result in China announcing a unilateral agreement. That Hong Kong Island was sovereign British territory was entirely ignored by the Chinese.

Leaking of the 12-point paper to the Hong Kong media created instant panic. The clearest barometer of how much confidence the Hong Kong Chinese placed in

PRC trusteeship of Hong Kong was the 25 per cent fall in the stock market within ten days of Mrs Thatcher leaving China. The Hong Kong dollar also fell by 12 per cent in value. News of Hong Kong's future set off a stampede of Hong Kong Chinese executives going overseas to qualify for Australian or Canadian passports, or indeed passports for any country other than Hong Kong. Brochures for exotic destinations littered the dealing desks of Hong Kong's financial companies. The mood in Hong Kong was one of gloomy resignation.

Early negotiations proved difficult as the British side tried to avoid the Chinese demand for the British to renounce sovereignty over Hong Kong. Thatcher finally broke the deadlock by writing to Zhao saying that she 'would be prepared to recommend to parliament that sovereignty over the whole of Hong Kong should revert to China'.[8] China also refused to accept that the new governor, Sir Edward Youde, should represent Hong Kong and would only deal with him as part of the British delegation, thus showing that the talks were being held 'government to government'. The former British ambassador to Beijing, Sir Percy Craddock, was retained post-retirement age to conduct negotiations for the British government.

In yet another fallback position, the British government now tried to negotiate for the retention of an administrative role after 1997. This proposal too met with blunt rejection. PRC negotiator, Zhou Nan, categorically stated that China was determined to recover sovereignty and administrative control over Hong Kong. The perceived impasse, in effect another holding position in the long British retreat, created a second wave of panic in Hong Kong. People stocked up on essential supplies as the Hong Kong dollar slid to 9.5 to the US dollar in September 1983, compared to 5.9 to the US dollar in the previous year. (The Hong Kong currency panic of that autumn was solved in October 1983, largely through the promptings of an English economist, John Greenwood, whose proposal for the monetary operation of a US dollar peg at HK$ 7.80 to the US dollar was taken up by Finance Secretary Sir John Bremridge.)

Relations between the negotiating parties deteriorated further as the PRC leadership, completely unable to fathom the workings of the free market in currencies and shares, blamed the Hong Kong financial panic on British manipulation. The Chinese could not understand that Britain could not stop investors taking their money out of Hong Kong; when Deng had suggested to Mrs Thatcher that the British government should stop this happening, she had been forced to 'explain that as soon as you stop money going out you effectively end the prospect of new money coming in'.[9] In spite of Mrs Thatcher's economics lesson, Britain was again forced to retreat as they grudgingly had to accept complete de-linkage of Britain from Hong Kong in 1997.

The next complication that arose was Deng's wish to form a joint commission to supervise the handover. It was a pragmatic idea but served to install a new fear in Hong Kong that the PRC would immediately become the colony's shadow government; this was not the intention. In the end a less-threatening Sino-British

Joint Liaison Group (JLG) was established, and it was made clear that this was a consultative committee and not an executive institution. Foreign Secretary Sir Geoffrey Howe concluded the agreement in July 1984, though the final drafting and ratification took until May 1985.

In the famed 'Joint Declaration' (Joint Declaration of the Government of the United Kingdom of Great Britain and Northern Ireland and the Government of the People's Republic of China on the Question of Hong Kong), the PRC committed itself to the establishment of 'a Hong Kong "Special Administration Region" (SAR) upon resuming the exercise of sovereignty over Hong Kong'.[10] The PRC also guaranteed 'a high degree of autonomy, except in foreign and defence affairs', and the Joint Declaration stated that 'laws currently in force in Hong Kong would remain basically unchanged'. Hong Kong's British governor would be replaced by a chief executive who would be appointed 'on the basis of the results of elections or consultations to be held locally'.[11]

Hong Kong would also enjoy freedom of religious worship, freedom of speech and publication, private property, inheritance and protection of foreign investment. The city would become a free port and a separate customs territory; it would be subject to neither Chinese taxes nor requisitions of its financial reserves. It was planned to give Chinese passports to Hong Kong citizens though these would be separate from those issued by the mainland PRC. The 'Basic Law' enacted on the principles set out in the Joint Declaration would remain unchanged for 50 years. It was a remarkable document which displayed in full Deng Xiaoping's pragmatic approach to China's revitalisation.

In hindsight it is clear that Deng's approach was no smokescreen, but in the mid-1980s it was much less certain that the PRC, just seven years after the death of Mao, would follow through with the Joint Declaration. After all, Britain had no means of enforcing compliance. Having yielded Hong Kong's sovereignty, Britain would have to accept the PRC's impending mandate whatever it brought and its interpretation of the Joint Declaration. Although the Crown Colony system was to be replaced by a government, which would also comprise a 'legislature ... constituted by elections', the PRC would inevitably hold a veto to the changes proposed by Britain. The limits to PRC power were now only the degree to which Britain was seen as an 'honest' and competent manager of Hong Kong and the perceived will of the Hong Kong people themselves.

Since the ditching of the 'Young Plan' in the immediate post-war period, Hong Kong had been ruled as a benign autocracy within the Crown Colony system. Thereafter Hong Kong's governors had followed the line expounded by Sir Robert Black, who told the Colonial Office that there was 'emphatically no emotional popular support for democracy'.[12] It was also argued that the PRC would not support any move towards democracy, which might be seen as leading the colony down the path of independence. In essence the British attitude was neatly summed up by Lord Kadoorie, major shareholder of the Peninsula Hotel group and CLP

Holdings Ltd. (formerly China Light and Power), who advocated that Hong Kong 'was one big business which must have a good management and a well chosen board of Directors'.[13]

The moves that the British colonial administration now made towards democratisation inevitably aroused suspicion in the PRC. Two months before the publication of the Joint Declaration, the Hong Kong government published a consultative green paper outlining a concept of political reform and with unseemly haste published a white paper proposal just a month later, setting out provisions for 24 elected members out of a 56-member Legislative Council (LEGCO).

The PRC was probably correct in supposing that Britain's sudden introduction of democracy was a means of tilting the balance of the Joint Declaration back in Britain's favour. The proposals were vehemently denounced by Xu Jiatun, the PRC Central Committee member and representative in Hong Kong. Deng was not prepared to see democracy in Hong Kong dance to this new British tune. Again Britain was forced to climb down and agree to the deferment of any political reform until the 'Basic Law' had been negotiated and fully promulgated.

In return for agreeing to this deferral, Britain would be allowed input in the political settlement. The LEGCO elections, slated for 1995, would be organised under a system agreed by both sides, so that it would continue to serve unchanged after the handover in 1997; this came to be known as the 'through-train' arrangement. With yet another hurdle apparently overcome, a Basic Law Drafting Committee (BLDC) now set about its task. It was a difficult balancing act between finding a democratic path acceptable to the PRC and one that would also satisfy the increasing democratic ambitions of the Hong Kong populace. However, when the convenor of the BLDC committee on 'PRC [People's Republic of China]-SAR [Special Administrative Region] relations' came out in favour on no democracy until the holding of a referendum in 2011, the public mood was severely shaken, particularly as the media had concluded that 'democracy' was one of the goals permitted by the Joint Declaration.

The Hong Kong Chinese population, which had woken up to the idea of democracy only after the Thatcher visit in September 1982, had nevertheless remained largely ambivalent about its virtues. However, the 'Tiananmen Square' episode, with its perceived brutal suppression of an incipient democracy movement, now tipped the Hong Kong Chinese into a more fervent appreciation of democracy's benefits. In Hong Kong, some 500,000 people (out of a population of 6 million) marched in sympathy with the Tiananmen Square demonstrators. An October 1989 poll would show that over 70 per cent of the Hong Kong population had no confidence in the PRC honouring its pledges after the 1997 takeover.

After Tiananmen Square, there was no doubt as to the popular desire for democracy in Hong Kong. By contrast the PRC was shaken by democracy's dangers, and within the leadership, even the advisability of the 'one country, two systems' philosophy was questioned. In addition, the PRC's confidence was further undermined by the collapse of the Soviet Union. The result was a tightening of the PRC's control of the Basic Law-drafting process and the addition of provisions to enhance PRC control over the Hong Kong Special Administrative Region (SAR).

Nevertheless the Basic Law, under Deng's direction, remained true to 'one country, two systems', and it was promulgated under Article 31 of the PRC constitution of 1982, which permitted the Chinese state to 'establish Special Administration Regions' when necessary. The remarkable flexibility of Deng's arrangement was best indicated by the inherent contradictions that were allowed between the PRC constitution and the Basic Law. Whereas Article 5 of the PRC constitution states that 'the state upholds the uniformity and dignity of the socialist legal system . . . no law or administrative or local rules and regulations shall contravene the constitution',[14] Hong Kong Basic Law Article 4 asserts that 'the socialist system and policies shall not be practised in the Hong Kong Special Administration Region'.[15] In essence the PRC was happy to remain flexible with regard to the Basic Law as long as it possessed ultimate control. The Basic Law was to all intents and purposes a Chinese recreation of the British Crown Colony system.

Although the Tiananmen Square Massacre had generated considerable hostility towards the PRC amongst the Hong Kong Chinese population, they were soon to learn that the support of Britain had defined limits. In the face of the possibility of the 'Armageddon Scenario', in which the PRC would renege on everything, increasing calls came for Britain to confer full citizenship to 3.25 million Hong Kong citizens. Howls of protest at the prospect of a flood of Chinese immigrants into the Britain were led by leading Conservative Party politician Norman Tebbit. Eventually just 50,000 British citizenships were awarded, and the Hong Kong populace was left in no doubt as to how far British loyalty stretched.

In spite of the difficulties faced by both sides, a compromise solution was reached for achieving democratic accountability within LEGCO. There would be 18 elected seats (out of 60) for 1991 LEGCO elections, 20 for 1997 (now under the Chinese SAR), 24 for 1999 and 30 for 2003. In addition, in an attempt to restore confidence to the Hong Kong people, a bill of rights was introduced 'to incorporate provisions of the International Covenant on Civil and Political Rights as applied to Hong Kong. . .'.[16] Nevertheless, the first LEGCO election proved a disaster for pro-PRC candidates, as the pro-democracy parties won 58 per cent of the vote and 15 of 18 seats, including the 12 won by the United Democrats led by the pro-democracy reformers Martin Lee and Sezto Wah.

The perceived defeat for the PRC was further exacerbated by the row with Hong Kong's Governor Wilson over his Port and Airport Development Strategy (PADS), announced in October 1989. The choosing the option of a very expensive new airport at Check Lap Kok, which eventually cost US$20 billion, aroused PRC suspicions that PADS was a device to prevent the PRC getting their hands on Hong Kong's extensive financial reserves; in other words it suggested that the PRC leadership could not be trusted.

Also the new airport project required huge borrowing. Like watching an elderly relative splurge the family inheritance, the PRC naturally doubted British motives. The deadlock was only broken when the PRC, keen to break their diplomatic isolation, agreed to the airport as long as John Major, who had replaced the deposed Mrs Thatcher as Conservative Party leader and prime minister, visited Beijing in September 1991.

Thus far it could be argued that the British, given their weak hand, had handled the Hong Kong handover with considerable aplomb. Furthermore, the assorted British diplomats and mandarins who had run the Crown Colony since the war, both in the capacity of governors and financial secretaries, had performed remarkably in transforming a wrecked wartime economy under Japanese rule into a model of capitalist endeavour and wealth creation, which had benefited a largely grateful Chinese population.

In spite of this record of success, the new British Prime Minister John Major now decided that he was dissatisfied with the conduct of British policy in Hong Kong. John Major, who had been plucked from relative obscurity by a cabal of Conservative Party grandees to succeed Mrs Thatcher, after a successful party putsch against her, was seen as a man in the 'C2 Social Class' and therefore perfectly equipped to lead Britain's increasingly meritocratic and classless society.

The formidable Mrs Thatcher would have been a difficult act to follow for even the strongest of men. Prime Minister John Major was unable to control his party and proved to be a leader largely bereft of ideas as to how and where to lead the party after the radical free market transformation of the British economy carried out by his predecessor; he was not helped by a complacent party used to power and riven by bitterness over the ousting of Mrs Thatcher. The Conservative Party was also genuinely divided on the issue of further economic and constitutional integration into the European Union.

Major was a grey man, a little Englander who liked warm beer and cricket, ridiculed by cartoonists who often portrayed him with his underpants worn outside his trousers, a metaphor for his weak leadership. Most importantly however, John Major, a former British-based personnel manager at Standard Chartered Bank, was a politician with little international, let alone Asian, experience. Major now decided to overthrow post-war tradition by appointing a 'professional' politician instead of a mandarin to be Hong Kong's last governor; he apparently believed that a politician with guile would be able to deal more successfully with the 'wily' Chinese.

It was a disastrous miscalculation. The Chinese were immediately alerted to the political appointment and, ever sensitive, indeed paranoid over the nuances of position, naturally suspected that Britain was pulling a final trick before the handover. If Major's decision to discard the 'Hong Kong team' of former bureaucrats was a poor one, his choice of governor was worse. Christopher Patten (now Lord Patten of Barnes and chancellor of Oxford University) was regarded as a highly intelligent individual who had worked his way up the Tory Party hierarchy, starting in the party back offices after leaving Oxford and eventually becoming head of research before becoming MP for the Bath constituency. He was social, affable, articulate, urbane and ambitious. As an experienced political strategist, he was chosen by John Major to lead his Conservative Party leadership campaign.

Unfortunately for Patten, in spite of a Conservative Party victory under John Major in the 1991 elections, he lost his parliamentary seat in Bath; instead of being rewarded with the position of foreign minister, which he was widely tipped to get in the wake of a Conservative Party election victory, Prime Minister Major, in a display of nineteenth-century patronage, offered him the consolation prize of the governorship of Hong Kong, a job for which he was grossly underqualified. This should not necessarily have been a disadvantage. As a close friend of John Major and Foreign Secretary Douglas Hurd, Patten enjoyed far greater political access and privilege than any of his 'mandarin' predecessors, who were quietly shuffled into retirement. Unlike his predecessors however, who had seen governorship in Hong Kong as a last job before retirement and the award of honours, Patten, thwarted in his Conservative Party ambitions, saw the Hong Kong job as a stepping stone in his political career.

Unlike his forebears he arrived in Hong Kong to much media fanfare with his photogenic family of young girls. In contrast to Wilson and Craddock, Patten lacked any experience of Asia. A media-savvy politician was a new experience for Hong Kong, and unlike his predecessors, he set out to woo his new constituency in the classic manner of a British politician. In this Patten succeeded brilliantly at first and achieved the unique distinction of becoming the only governor of Hong Kong to acquire a nickname, 'Fat Pang' – a reference to his slightly corpulent figure.

In October 1992, Patten, ignoring the Craddock view that democratisation had been taken as far as was practicable under the Joint Declaration and Basic Law, announced a political reform agenda to an expectant LEGCO and waiting Hong Kong populace. His recommendations included a divorce of the Executive Committee (EXCO) from the LEGCO; he would give up his position as president of LEGCO and submit himself to questions as the chief executive of EXCO. In addition, voting age would be reduced from 21 to 18, the number of voted seats on LEGCO would be increased to 20, constituencies would be made single seat while corporate voting would be replaced with individual voting in the 21 functional constituencies. Functional seats would be increased by nine, a change which was needed to enable the LEGCO of 1995 to dovetail with the arrangements laid down by the Basic Law.

More power would also be devolved to the District Boards, who would now be charged with election of 10 LEGCO members. Overall it was a modest and intelligent plan. However, deploying his professional political skills, he oversold it to the Hong Kong populace and the world media as a major step forward in democratisation. *Fat Pang*'s popularity soared. In reality Patten's scheme, if implemented in its entirety, would still only return a third of LEGCO's members by direct vote.

For the PRC government, Patten's populist programme was simply proof of Britain's strategy to undermine the Chinese government prior to the handover. Douglas Hurd, the patrician British foreign minister, as out of his depth as Christopher Patten in his understanding of the Chinese position, grandly declared that 'The days of negotiation with Peking over the heads of Hong Kong were in the past.'[17] Understandably perhaps the Chinese overreacted. PRC representative Zhou Nan fulminated that the British mistakenly believed that 'after the dissolution of the Soviet Union, China would also face the same kind of changes' and wanted to 'use proxies installed with their help to extend British colonial rule, turn Hong Kong into a semi-independent political entity, and unrealistically wish to influence political developments in China'.[18]

The Chinese reaction may have been somewhat hysterical, but it was a fair indication of how badly Patten had mismanaged the relationship with China. As Sir Percy Craddock despairingly observed, 'the reforms and the manner of their promulgation represented a 180 degree turn in British policy on co-operation and convergence. . . '.[19] Perhaps Patten's cardinal error was the failure to visit the PRC leadership in Beijing as soon as he arrived in Hong Kong. Given that there were just five years to handover, it was the least courtesy that could have been expected of the new governor. Neither were relations between the two countries helped by Patten's poor personal relationship with Zhou Nan.

However Patten, the consummate politician, chose to ignore the fact that anything done in Britain's remaining five years of 'trusteeship' was *de facto*, if not *de jure*, done at PRC sufferance. Forcing the Chinese government to have to publicly state their reasons for objecting to his proposals may have been a clever political game in a democracy, but was guaranteed to backfire in dealing with the PRC. For the PRC too, the idea of being lectured on democracy by a politician from a country that had done nothing to implement democratic reform in the Crown Colony until it became clear that it would revert to China, appeared to be the height of hypocrisy.

Having nailed his agenda so publicly in the Hong Kong media, Patten, when he visited Beijing in October, was in a difficult position. The PRC, for reasons of face, could not back down from the position of resentment which they had assumed, and neither could Patten. However, having backed the PRC into a corner, there could be only one winner. The PRC whirled their propaganda machine into a torrent of invective against Patten and isolated him from any future direct contact with the Chinese government. At this point a more internationally adroit British prime minister might have realised his mistake and replaced Patten.

However, Patten was close to his political masters and, moreover, had skilfully played the global media to promote himself as a hero of western democratic values.

For the future of Hong Kong and its people, it was a pointless display; however, for Patten's ego, vanity and future career, it was brilliantly opportunist in the use of a western media still wearing 'Tiananmen Square Massacre goggles', which failed to look beyond the emotive issues of the student uprising of 1989 to the continuing deregulation of the Chinese economy and its society.

Within the British parliament, Patten's personal PR was masterly; a Hong Kong-based financial executive noted the shock on the faces of MPs Winston Spencer-Churchill and Virginia Bottomley, when it was explained to them what a failure Patten had been as governor. Only politicians familiar with the region, such as Edward Heath, knew that Patten's governorship had been a disaster. Eventually Patten was able to parley his media success in Hong Kong into being appointed by Tony Blair as European Commissioner for External Affairs; notably, throughout his tenure at the European Commission, Patten was quiescent on the lack of democratic accountability of this executive arm of the European government; this was a curious omission given that when he arrived in Hong Kong he had pompously declared that 'I owe it to the community to make my own position plain. I have spent my entire career engaged in a political system based on representative democracy. It would be surprising if that had not marked me.'[20]

Although the PRC resumed its negotiations with the British government, overtly not with Patten, the process stumbled wearyingly through 17 rounds of talks. Because of the need to hold local elections, the British need for a settlement was pressing. Eventually, a frustrated and resentful Governor Patten unilaterally passed his 1992 proposals into law in June 1994 through LEGCO.

It seems that Patten believed that the PRC would not dare to unravel his reforms. It was another in a long litany of mistakes. The PRC terminated all talks with Britain; the 'through-train' concept was dead. In its place the Chinese now started to build what came to be termed the 'new kitchen' and set up a Preliminary Working Committee (PWC) for the Hong Kong SAR. Once the Patten reforms were legislated by LEGCO, Jiang Zemin ordered the PWC to 'rely on our own resources as the basis and staunchly follow the directive of upholding our interest to ensure the stable transition. . . '.[21]

In the 1995 elections, the pro-PRC candidates won just 16 out of 60 candidates, with the result that the Chinese government decided not to have new elections in 1997 but to appoint their own LEGCO. Qian Qichen had been appointed to chair a preparatory committee in January 1996 with the task of establishing a selection committee for the first government of the Hong Kong SAR. Nevertheless, China was not oblivious to public opinion, and 33 of the existing 60 elected LEGCO members were offered positions in the PRC's provisional LEGCO; even four pro-democracy members from the Association for Democracy and People's Livelihood were included. Also in December 1996, Tung Chee-Hwa, a Hong Kong Chinese shipping magnate with long business connections to the PRC, was appointed as chief executive of SAR to take over from Governor Patten on 1 July

1997. The PRC's 'new kitchen' would be completed without any input from Hong Kong's last colonial governor.

Britain's last major colonial asset was seen off in appropriate pomp and splendour, with the lowering of the flag at Government House on 30 June 1997. There were 4,000 invited guests from around the globe including Charles, Prince of Wales; Prime Minister Tony Blair; Foreign Minister Robin Cook; Christopher Patten and British Armed Forces Chief of Staff Sir Charles Guthrie.

The PRC relished the occasion. In Beijing, the Chinese held a vast street party and celebrated the 'greatest occasion for a public celebration since the founding of the PRC in 1949'.[22] For China it was a moment to savour a reversal of 150 years of humiliation. Accordingly, the PRC delegation to Hong Kong included Jiang Zemin, Premier Li Peng, General Zhang Wannian, chairman of the Central Military Commission and Tung Chee-Hwa.

In the pouring rain a PRC flag and an SAR flag were raised together. The SAR flag was smaller and was raised at half the speed of the PRC flag; it was symbolic of 'one country two systems', but that did not mean that they would be 'equal systems'. Across the border in Shenzhen the new LEGCO had already passed the Reunification Bill, which included 13 measures which effectively wiped out Patten's reforms.

The appointment of Christopher Patten as Hong Kong's last governor was not disastrous to the life and safety of the colony's citizens, as was the case with the appointment of Lord Mountbatten as India's last governor. However, Patten's populist policies raised unrealistic and unachievable expectations within the Hong Kong population. Although Patten won international acclaim by his 'Democratic' posturing, and significantly enhanced his own career, his popularity plummeted in Hong Kong when it became clear that his personal agenda was more important than that of the people he was meant to represent. The Hong Kong population itself became sharply fissured on the issue of democracy, and Patten, by his actions, created a mood of depressed anxiety, which did nothing to help investment or consumer and business confidence. Neither did he assuage the chronic housing crisis in Hong Kong, which was the major social issue of his governorship. He also sullied British relations with China at a time when commercial opportunities for international companies were growing rapidly.

The result of Patten's policies was that Hong Kong's SAR began life with no democratic content at all; it is inconceivable that this would have been the outcome had Prime Minister John Major left the proven British 'mandarins' in charge. For the Chinese, the Patten episode was largely irrelevant; the future of Hong Kong in 1997 was decided the moment that MacLehose raised it with Deng Xiaoping in 1979.

Ever pragmatic, the Chinese welcomed Patten back to China when he later became Europe's External Affairs Commissioner; the PRC's dealing with Patten over Hong Kong was not personal; it was simply a matter of restoring China's historic

border and exercising their full rights to sovereignty. Their subsequent stewardship has shown that the PRC was just as concerned to preserve the entrepreneurial
strengths of Hong Kong as the former colony's own citizens. For Hong Kong, the
story of benign and efficient post-war colonial management thus ended with a bun-
gled surrender, but not an outcome that would irretrievably jeopardise its future
prosperity. Fortunately by the time that British politicians became involved in Hong
Kong's management, its wealth and long-term success were already assured.

59

One China or Two?

Taiwan: 1947–2005

In 1936, Mao Zedong outlined the basis of China's future foreign policy: 'It is the immediate task of China to regain all our lost territories, not merely to defend our sovereignty below the Great Wall. This means that Manchuria must be regained.'[1] Clearly, Japan's occupation of Manchuria was the immediate focus of policy, but Mao also laid down long-term markers for the future. He expanded further on the theme by saying:

> We do not, however, include Korea, formerly a Chinese colony, but when we have established the independence of the lost territories of China and if the Koreans wish to break free from the chains of Japan's imperialism, we will extend to them our enthusiastic help. The same thing applies to Formosa. . . .'[2]

By implication, in Mao's mind, Formosa would enjoy the same future status as North Korea – independent, but a client state of China. However, at the Great Powers meeting in Cairo in 1941, it was decided that Formosa would revert to China after the defeat of the Japanese. Indeed, at the San Francisco Peace Treaty, concluded with America in 1951, Japan gave up all rights to Formosa and the Pescadores Islands, without the treaty indicating to which country sovereignty had passed. Whatever Mao's original thinking on the subject, and the international legal niceties, the retreat of the Chinese nationalist government to Taiwan guaranteed that the island would be treated as a future territory to be retrieved by the People's Republic of China (PRC).

With the Nixon–Kissinger rapprochement with China, the PRC had prised open the possibility that one day their relationship with America could be such that it would become more important to the USA than the long-term defence of Taiwan (the Republic of China: ROC). However, both sides recognised that this would take time and any long-term solution went unspecified. In the meantime, Nixon gave assurances that 'Our dialogue with the PRC (will) not be at the expense of our friends. . . . With the Republic of China, we shall maintain our friendship, our diplomatic ties, and our defence commitment.'[3]

At the heart of the mutual understanding between the USA and China lay the idea that the PRC and the ROC were parts of 'One China'. Stability lay in this agreement; the PRC could maintain the fiction that Taiwan was part of China, and wait, confident that, over time, economic power and weight of arms would force Taiwan into acceptance of Chinese sovereignty.

In 1978, reunification with Taiwan was written into the constitution, while in 1982 Deng Xiaoping told the Communist Party's National Congress that one of the three main tasks for the 1980s was 'to strive for reunification and particularly for the return of Taiwan to the motherland...'.[4] However, Deng was famously realistic about planning for the long term.

For Taiwan the problems were much greater. The threat that America could withdraw its military protection was a real fear; while, in a classical definition of superior offensive power using a 3:1 advantage, the PRC would need to be able to land a force of 900,000 troops to defeat Taiwan's 300,000-strong army, the realities after the early 1980s were that the PRC had nuclear weapons, while the ROC depended on the USA for their theoretic deterrent.

Also, any security the Taiwanese leadership may have felt it derived from its powerful economic performance, and Taiwan's growing commercial importance to America, was catastrophically undermined at the end of the 1970s. On 1 January 1979, President Carter announced that 'the United States ... recognises the People's Republic of China [PRC] as the sole legal government of China'.[5]

Although the Carter–Vance plan, a reversion to 'realpolitik' by the Democrat president, was the logical conclusion to Nixon's Shanghai Communiqué, the shocked reaction within Taiwan was even greater than the rapprochement negotiated some six years earlier between Henry Kissinger and Zhou Enlai. The Taiwanese foreign minister responded by asserting that America's policy would

> jeopardize the security of the 16 million Chinese on Taiwan, but would also violate the lofty ideals upon which the American nation was built and the moral principles emphasized by the Carter administration and thus erode the credibility of the United States among the free peoples the world over.[6]

To Taiwan's alarm moreover, the initiative had come from President Carter, who sent his National Security Advisor Zbigniew Brzezinski as his emissary to China to negotiate a stronger relationship with the PRC. Ominously for Taiwan, Carter also cancelled an agreement to sell them F-4 fighter jets. James Shen, the ROC ambassador in Washington, complained bitterly that he

> could not detect even the slightest hint of regret by Holbrooke [Assistant Secretary of State for East Asian and Pacific Affairs] that the US Government had willfully violated one of the basic principles of diplomacy: good faith and mutual respect. The United States had treated some of her enemies with greater consideration.[7]

Republicans were equally incensed; Senator Barry Goldwater condemned the decision as 'one of the most cowardly acts ever performed by a president of the United States'; Senator Robert Dole described it as 'a slap in the face to our staunchest friend and ally, the Republic of China on Taiwan, and to Congress.... Who will be our ally if we are so willing to dump our allies?'[8]

The agreement was followed by Deng Xiaoping's goodwill visit to Washington where he showed himself to be the emerging leader of his nation. Democrats at least had fewer qualms about abandoning their erstwhile allies; Senator Edward Kennedy welcomed 'a new era of cooperation between two great societies whose people have been isolated from one another for so many years'.[9]

Despite this setback for the Nationalist government in Taiwan, Carter was not unaware of America's moral obligation to its long-term ally. Although the ROC now had to close its US embassy, soon to be followed by most of Taiwan's embassies worldwide, a representative office was maintained, and Carter ordered his administration to carry on all relationships as before. Support for Taiwan furthermore was codified in a Congressional bill that became the Taiwan Relations Act passed on 16 March 1979. In effect therefore, America both declared the Communists to be the 'sole legal government of China', while at the same time pledging military support and undying friendship with the ROC, in effect the illegal self-proclaimed government of China.

According to Senator Muskie, the Taiwan Relations Act legislation was 'For the purposes of US domestic law,' an arrangement that viewed Taiwan, 'as a country, absent the official status'.[10] The PRC was not a little miffed that their breakthrough relationship with the USA was not quite as all-embracing as it had originally hoped. The irate PRC Foreign Minister Min Huang Hua sent for the American Ambassador Leonard Woodcock and warned him that the legislation was 'unacceptable to the Chinese government . . . great harm will be done to the new relationship that has just been established between China and the United States'.[11] But the new relationship was too important. In the end, the PRC leadership simply had to swallow hard.

They were not the only ones who had to swallow an unpalatable truth. Ronald Reagan, the Republican candidate for the presidency, was appalled that Taiwan, America's staunchest ally against communism, had been, in his eyes, betrayed. After defeating Carter in the 1980 presidential elections, Reagan pointedly invited both the general secretary of the *Kuomintang* and the governor of Taiwan Province to his inauguration.

Yet, even Reagan came to recognise that the Soviets represented the larger threat; in spite of his sympathies towards the Taiwanese cause, the president realised that the splitting of communist China from the Soviet Union was too large a prize to give away. Nevertheless, Reagan pushed for a limited revival of arms sales to Taiwan. At the same time, Secretary of State Alexander Haig, an ardent backer of the new China relationship, pushed for an extension of the relationship with the PRC by supplying arms. China became only the second communist country after Yugoslavia to be upgraded in accordance with the US Arms Export Control Act from Category P (Hostile Communist) to Category V (Friendly non-aligned).

In spite of the improved relations with the USA, the friendship was far from perfect. It was sometimes difficult for leaders of communist China to comprehend that the branches of the US government did not always speak with one voice. While the executive supported the 'One China' principle, the US Congress managed to pass a resolution offering support to the Taiwan independence movement.

Congress was also outspoken in its views on Chinese human rights; persecution of intellectuals, limitations on free speech and the authoritarian nature of the birth control programme all came under attack. The sale of China's HY-2 *Hai Ying* (sea eagles) anti-ship cruise missiles, commonly known as Silkworm, to the Middle East was also criticised. On the other side, China was furious at the invitation to the Dalai Lama to speak to Congress, which gave him an opportunity to press for Tibetan independence. Delays in implementation of the lifting of certain technology restrictions in trade with China also infuriated the PRC leadership.

America's honeymoon relationship with the PRC was not destined to last. Contrary to communist China's analysis at the beginning of the 1980s, which saw the Soviet Union as being in the ascendant in the global power rivalry with the USA, within a decade it was apparent that the USA was triumphant and the Soviet Union in collapse.

In a speech in Vladivostok on 28 July 1986, Soviet General Secretary Mikhail Gorbachev signalled a major shift in the previously confrontational relationship with China, with whom relations had broken down in the early 1960s; he expressed a desire to enter into talks with China to resolve outstanding differences, including border disputes on the Amur River and Chenpao Island. A concrete expression of this reduction in tension took place in February 1989, when the Soviet Foreign Minister Eduard Shevardnadze, later president of Georgia, announced cut-backs of 200,000 troops on the Eastern border.

A first full summit between the two great eastern powers took place in Beijing on 15 May 1989, just as the 'Tiananmen Square' episode was reaching its climax. Indeed, the Tiananmen denouement, resulting in a swathe of moral outrage from the 'Free World', merely had the effect of pushing the Soviets and the PRC closer together. For China, the threat of US hegemony was now greater than that of the Soviet Union. In Taiwan, the renewed shift towards Chinese suspicion of America could only be welcomed. America also took note of China's rapprochement with the Soviets. No better indication of the rebalancing of the Taiwan–American relationship can be shown than the decision by President Bush (senior) on 2 September 1992 to sell them F-16s.

Within Taiwan however, there were also changes threatening the delicate balance of the country's relationship with the PRC. Chiang Ching Kuo's gradual liberalisation of Taiwan's political system, which began in 1972 as his father was ailing, began to undermine the 'One China' principle, the curious concept accepted by China, Taiwan and America, which bound both the PRC and the ROC in their fragile stability.

Chiang Ching Kuo was born in 1910 and served a stiff apprenticeship in Russia from the age of 16 until he was 27. He served in the Russian army, worked as an apprentice in an electrical plant, on a collective farm and in a heavy machinery plant in the Urals. It was here he met and married his Russian wife Sofanina. Having lived through collectivisation, and the Stalinist purges that accompanied it, both of them returned to China as convinced anti-communists.

In 1939, he became a commissioner in South Kiangsi province and was apparently unusual among *Kuomintang* administrators for his suppression of opium, gambling and prostitution. After joining the evacuation to Taiwan, Chiang organised the new intelligence services, served as a military commissar and was appointed by his father to head a 'Nazi'-style Youth Corps. From 1965, he served as minister of defence, and then became premier in 1972.

Although Chiang later became converted to the cause of democracy, he was a man formed in the dictatorial mould of his father. Obsessed with personal privacy, Chiang forced Henry Liu, who wrote an unauthorised biography of the Taiwanese leader, to flee the island. On 15 October 1984, Liu was shot dead in a suspected contract killing at his home in California. The murder investigation implicated both a Taiwan crime syndicate known as the Bamboo Union and the Taiwanese security services. Chiang's son Chiang Hsiao Wu was also allegedly involved, and was sent to Singapore to represent Taiwan in order to keep him out of the public eye. A furious Reagan administration even threatened to cut off arms supply.

In spite of this background, Chiang Ching Kuo became a devoted if cautious convert to democracy. Somewhat unfairly, in a 1983 interview with *Der Spiegal*, Chiang Ching Kuo was informed that 'Never before in modern history has there been a country as long under martial law as Taiwan.'[12] In fact, martial law was more actually a 'state of mind' reflecting the peculiar nature of Taiwan's 'Cold War' with the mainland; there was no curfew or troops on the streets.

Also, democratic reforms were already in process. Apart from the first elections held in 1972, in the same year, Chiang secretly encouraged a group of professors and students at National Taiwan University to form a discussion group advocating political liberalisation; the government allowed this group's magazine *The University* to circulate freely. The 1970s saw the development of an opposition movement known as *Tangwai* (literally 'outside the party'), which comprised Taiwanese factions and indeed some prominent mainlander politicians.

Martial law was an early target. The opposition protested that 'Martial law is not supposed to be used to deal with every type of possible crisis and then become a permanent institution. . . . In democratic nations, martial law is only a temporary provision.'[13] In 1977, the regime's opponents struck up enough courage to form the Tangwei Campaign Assistance Corps, which became a *de facto* party although its members went out of their way not to portray it as such. Eventually, the Democratic Progressive Party (DPP) would grow out of this organisation.

Perversely, it was the decision by President Carter and his Secretary of State Cyrus Vance to formalise diplomatic relations with China and cease formal diplomatic recognition of the ROC (Taiwan), which postponed the development of democracy in Taiwan. Elections planned for 1978 were delayed for a year after the 'Carter' shock, but in 1979 an opposition grouping prepared itself for elections for the first time. In the event, an opposition rally on 10 December 1979 turned into a riot; a panicked government arrested opposition leaders, and in the following year 47 opposition politicians were found guilty of political crimes by a military court and were jailed. Shi Ming The, the general manager of the opposition *Formosa* Magazine, having recently completed a 15 year jail term for promoting an opposition movement, was now given a life sentence.

However, democratic reform was delayed, not abandoned. In 1983, Chiang Ching Kuo conceded that 'No political party can maintain its advantage forever if it does not reflect public opinion and meet the people's demands.'[14] Nevertheless, Chiang did not want to move too far ahead of his party. It was against a background of considerable internal opposition that a process of democratisation was formally authorised in October 1986 at a meeting of the *Kuomintang*'s Third Central Committee. On 5 October Chiang argued that 'The times have changed, events have changed, trends have changed. In response to these changes, the ruling party must adopt new ways to meet this democratic revolution and link up with this historical trend.'[15]

Public scepticism continued. However, in a meeting with Katherine Graham of the *Washington Post* on 7 October 1986, Chiang Ching Kuo confirmed in unambiguous terms that martial law would be lifted and the formation of political parties allowed. Then, in National Assembly elections in 1986, the opposition DPP, having foresworn to uphold the constitution and disassociate itself from any affiliate advocating violence, won 35.2 per cent of the vote and some 22 per cent of seats. The reasons for Chiang's late conversion to democracy remain unknown. As *The Asian Wall Street Journal* reported in November 1987, 'The reason for the democratic turn is a mystery. . . . Mr. Chiang is in no hurry to shed light on these events. He hasn't written about his life and has declined to cooperate with biographers.'[16]

Although Chiang set the path to democratic reform, his very existence was itself a barrier to the development of true democracy. He perhaps realised this, and was determined that there would be no more 'family' succession to the presidency. When Chiang died on 13 January 1988, he was succeeded by his vice president, Lee Teng Hui.

The end of the Chiang family lineage might have been a radical step, but perhaps the succession of Lee Teng Hui, a local 'non-mainlander', was possibly even more significant. Also for the first time he appointed a cabinet that was made up by a majority of *indigenous* Taiwanese. After a 'National Affairs Conference' in 1990, which laid the groundwork for a radical reworking of Taiwan's political system, the 'old' mainland deputies in all chambers were finally forced into retirement. Nevertheless, in concession to the 'mainland' factions, Lee chose as his deputy, Hau Peitsun, a *Kuomintang* general.

True democratic electoral contests now became the norm. At local and mayoral elections in 1989, the DPP polled 37.59 per cent of votes and won 28.6 per cent of seats. In 1993, the DPP increased their share of the vote to 40 per cent, while the *Kuomintang* vote fell from 53.5 per cent to just 47.5 per cent; nevertheless, this share still enabled them to win 61.9 per cent of seats. In National Assembly elections however, the *Kuomintang* vote held stronger.

A 71.2 per cent share of the vote in 1991 garnered 79.6 per cent of seats. By the early 1990s, it was clear that democracy in Taiwan had arrived, however imperfect some of its features. Aside from the *Kuomintang's* institutional strength with over 2 million party members, they also possessed overwhelming power in the media. The two largest selling newspapers, the *United Daily News,* and *The China Times* were owned by *Kuomintang* Central Committee members. Election budgets were also disproportionate. In 1994, the *Kuomintang* budget was fifty times larger than that of the DPP.

Financial issues aside, the DPP was also deeply divided between the larger 'Formosa' faction, and the 'New Tide', which took a more radical stance in its desire for full independence from China. The opposition to the government was also contested by the Justice Alliance and the Taiwan Welfare State Alliance. Aside from the inherent disadvantages faced by the opposition parties was the fact that many Taiwanese, particularly the middle classes who were estimated at 2.5 million by 1985, did not want to rock a system which had brought them stunning prosperity, and therefore voted for the *Kuomintang*, not out of political or communal sympathy, but out of economic rationalism.

Unsurprisingly, Taiwan's economic performance and its unrestrained capitalistic endeavour were not major issues separating the political parties. Between 1952 and 1991, real GNP in the Taiwanese economy grew by a remarkable 8.7 per cent per annum with a peak performance of 11.4 per cent in 1976. Agriculture as a percentage of GDP fell from 36 per cent in 1952 to 7 per cent in 1985. A largely agrarian post-war society had been transformed into the consummate Asian 'tiger' economy.

With some 706,500 companies in 1983, Taiwan achieved the distinction of having more companies per capita than any other country in the world. Taiwan also gained the lesser distinction of becoming the counterfeit capital of Asia. Taiwan accumulated increasingly vast trade imbalances. In 1987, US imports per capita from Taiwan represented some US$ 200, versus just US$ 10 per capita for exports. For software alone it was estimated that Taiwan accounted for 90 per cent of the global counterfeit market. There is no better example than Taiwan of how America's 'free market' economic umbrella, which allowed its allies virtually unrestrained access to its markets, brought prosperity to its Asian hegemony in the post-war era.

Taiwan was not just affluent; it was becoming one of the world's most educated countries. In 1990, some 34.1 per cent of 20–24 year-old Taiwanese were
at university compared to just 23.5 per cent in the United Kingdom. The economic success of Taiwan also showcased the abysmal failure of socialist economics
as practiced in China; Taiwan's progress made a deep impression on the later PRC
leadership. As President Lee remarked, 'In recent years, the economic miracle
in Taiwan created by the Republic of China has forced the communist leaders in
China to raise the slogan, "learning economics from Taiwan."'[17] If Deng Xiaoping
was the architect of China's development of a modern capitalistic economy, it was
also true that Taiwan was the most important model and inspiration.

However, if by the 1990s Taiwan and China were drawing together in terms of
their economic systems, their political relations were beginning to founder, paradoxically over the issue of 'One China'. In Taiwan, there was increasing belief
in certain quarters of the opposition that with the civil war and the role of the
mainlanders beginning to recede into the distance, there was a need to address
Taiwan's 'de facto' existence as an independent country. As the moderate DPP
leader Chang Chun Hong pointed out, 'An independent Taiwan is a very good idea,
and it is the final solution to Taiwan's political problems. But the *Kuomintang*, together with Communist China, is making the term a terrible concept to the people
of Taiwan.'[18] While the moderate *Kuomintang* factions wanted to move cautiously
towards this position, the New Tide Party wanted an immediate declaration of
independence.

Ultimately, it could be argued that China too could, over time, move towards
the Taiwan political model in the way that it has done economically. As President
Lee pointed out with regard to China's future, 'When economic reform has developed to a certain stage, political reform will inevitably be encouraged. It will not
be just superficial reform of political institutions, but reform that moves towards
real liberal democracy.'[19]

Deng Xiaoping had also set China upon a gradualist path to reunification; as
early as October 1974, he expressed the view that China should take a peaceful and
little-by-little approach to the problem. In 1981, Deng's government announced
that Taiwan would be able to enjoy 'a high degree of autonomy as a special administrative region'.[20] Given a continuation of the moderate gradualist philosophies
of leaders like Lee, Deng and their successors, there remained the prospect of a
peaceful political union, which could be accomplished over time.

However, the *Kuomintang* position, which 'de facto' accepted that the Communist Party in China was there to stay, did not address the immediate political
reality that the majority of Taiwanese did not consider themselves Chinese. In the
monthly magazine *Yuanjian* (Global Views Monthly), a poll revealed that just 32
per cent of Taiwanese considered themselves to be Chinese. Taiwanese outside of
their country were even more trenchant in their preferences; some 89 per cent of
Taiwanese residents in the USA favoured independence.

If that political sentiment ever translated into an immediate call for independence, and its subsequent implementation, there seems little doubt that given China's overwhelming foreign policy objective for reunification with Taiwan, a declaration of war would be almost immediate. As the official American position for both Republicans and Democrats has been that Taiwan was an ally to be defended from attack, the very real possibility existed of an armed conflict between America and China, the world's two largest economies. As China's economic power increased, there remained a risk that pressure would increasingly be brought to bear on Taiwan. As early as 1972, Lee Kuan Yew forewarned that 'It is certain that China will extend its power in South East Asia.'[21]

While China remains focused on raising the living standard of its vast population, the issue of Taiwan remained muted, but it was not inconceivable that in the event of China's economic growth stalling, the Communist Party could revert to international rhetoric over Taiwan to divert its citizens from domestic problems. Meanwhile, the White House, under the presidency of either party has been working towards the goal described by political commentator, William Kristol of helping 'bring about the peaceful transformation of Beijing's dictatorship into a democracy like Taipei's'.[22] This remains an uncertain project however, particularly as 'non-democratic' China now comprehensively outperforms the western democracies. The issues of 'one China or two' therefore are not simply arcane concepts, but represent perhaps the greatest current fault-line in the peaceful global co-existence of Asia's two superpowers.

60

Nukes and Mullahs

Pakistan: 1973–2005

From its birth, the USA viewed Pakistan as one of the cornerstones of its containment of the Soviet Union. By contrast, Pakistan saw the USA as the natural guarantor of its survival against India. The possibility that India, a vastly larger country, could force a reunification of the sub-continent was never far from the minds of Pakistan's rulers. Alliance with America was not a natural relationship. America's commitment to Israel always meant that Pakistan's rulers, in deciding their international allegiances, had to suppress their Islamic sympathies towards the Palestinians. America, meanwhile, was forced to yield its democratic preferences as it did business with successions of military regimes.

Also, whereas the US government had been able to bring political and economic pressure to bear on countries such as Argentina, Brazil, South Korea and Taiwan not to develop nuclear weapons, with Pakistan they failed. For future global security, this failure was compounded in importance by the rise of a militant Islamic socialism committed to the overthrow of western civilisation. Unwittingly, and with the benefit of hindsight, America's support for Pakistan helped cultivate conditions which aided the growth of Islamic fundamentalism.

Both India and Pakistan had refused to sign the 1968 Nuclear Non-proliferation Treaty, thus leaving open the possibility that they would seek to develop nuclear weapons. However, it was not until 1972 that Zulfikar Ali Bhutto ordered Pakistan scientists to develop a nuclear capability in the Punjabi city of Multan. When two years later, on 18 May 1974, Bhutto heard of India's successful testing of a nuclear device, he was appalled, though publicly he would only describe it as 'a fateful development'.[1]

America soon made it clear that Pakistan should not follow in India's footsteps. Peter Constable, the State Department director responsible for Pakistan, warned them not to follow, '... the politically risky and costly development of nuclear explosives'.[2] President Ford and Secretary of State Henry Kissinger continued the pressure with offers of 110 A-7 attack bombers on the one hand and threats that a Democrat victory in the upcoming presidential elections might bring a less favourable administration.

Whatever the US protestations, Pakistani efforts to produce a bomb were being advanced by a Pakistani metallurgist, Abdul Qadeer Khan; he took information that had been gained working in the Netherlands to begin development of the ultracentrifuge uranium enrichment process, which lay at the heart of the nuclear process. With Khan at its head, the Pakistani nuclear effort also sought help elsewhere.

French Prime Minister Jacques Chirac foolishly approved the sale of a uranium reprocessing plant to Pakistan. The Pakistan government's intentions were clearly flagged when, after Chirac was sacked by President Giscard D'Estaing, the French government changed its mind on the sale of reprocessing plant and offered a 'co-processing' plant instead, which only produces fuel rods usable in nuclear reactors. In February 1978, Zia rejected this alternative; Andre Jacomet, a French nuclear expert, was not the only person to conclude that Pakistan's real motivations in seeking a nuclear reactor were to access bomb-making technology.

In a backlash against the Watergate scandal and the Nixon–Ford administrations, in November 1977, American voters duly elected an 'ethical' Democrat, President Carter, who was committed to a humanitarian approach to foreign policy. Relations with first Bhutto, and then a fiercely Islamic General Zia, not surprisingly, were strained. When Carter visited India in January 1978, Pakistan was omitted from the schedule. In a rare suspension of Pakistan relations, President Carter also cut off economic aid as retaliation for the suspected nuclear programme.

In spite of concrete intelligence of the Pakistan bomb-making project, Zia refused to admit it. On September 1979, he told *The New York Times*, 'Pakistan is not making a bomb. Pakistan is not in a position to make a bomb and has no intention of making a bomb.'[3] The Pakistan president's statement did not tally with the hypersensitivity displayed by the defence establishment towards their nuclear facility at Kahuta. While driving near Kahuta, the French ambassador to Pakistan was stopped at a roadblock and severely beaten by security forces.

However, the true nature of the real interests which bound Pakistan to America were put into sudden and stark relief by the Soviet invasion of Afghanistan on Christmas Eve 1979. The geopolitical necessities of dealing with the Soviet invasion of Afghanistan put paid to American pressure on Zia to abandon his nuclear weapons programme. Improvement in relations between the two countries was instantaneous.

The Carter administration, whose muted response to the communist coup which had toppled President Sardar Mohammed Daoud in Kabul nine months earlier, may well have encouraged the aggressive Soviet intervention in Afghan politics, immediately reaffirmed the bilateral security agreement, which the USA and Pakistan had initiated in 1959. The Soviet invasion awoke echoes of the nineteenth-century 'Great Game', in which Great Britain had feared Russia's intentions as regards India; this time it would be America that would take up the challenge of thwarting Russia on the northern peripheries of the sub-continent.

Accepting the opprobrium of India as the price of military aid for Pakistan, President Carter increased money and supplies and authorised the sale of F-16 bombers. At the initial stages America, like the Soviets in their support for the North Vietnamese at the start of the war for control of Indochina, was keen not to be seen as an active participant. The CIA funded acquisition of Soviet stock weaponry, much of it from Soviet ordnance factories in Egypt, or old British Lee Enfield rifles, rather than risk American equipment. The CIA, which, rather than the Pentagon, became the main conduit for America's covert military involvement in Afghanistan, funnelled its military aid through Pakistan's Inter-Services Intelligence Directorate (ISI).

On 3 October 1980, Zia was welcomed to the White House by President Carter. Carter's conversion to the world of 'realpolitik' was cut short with the election of Ronald Reagan, thus denying Carter a second term as president, this staunchest of 'Cold War warriors' was sure to further improve relations with Pakistan. The new American administration immediately offered an 800 per cent increase in military support for Pakistan with a five-year US$ 3.2 billion package. Unlike Carter's shilly-shallying support for its allies, Reagan was determined to show clear and determined support for those countries prepared to stand up against Soviet expansion. As Nicholas Veliotes, under secretary of state for the Near East and South Asia, made clear, it was now American policy 'to give Pakistan confidence in our commitment to its security and provide us reciprocal benefits in terms of our regional interests'.[4]

The relief of the Pakistan government to the change in American foreign policy *away* from the high-minded utopianism of Jimmy Carter, was palpable; as Foreign Minister Shahi pointed out, 'The previous Carter administration offer did not carry for us credibility in a US–Pakistan relationship commensurate . . . [with] what we considered to be the magnitude of the threat.'[5] For Zia, the new Reagan administration had one further major benefit over that of Carter; it was not interested in lecturing its allies on human rights and democratic deficiencies. When General Arif told Secretary of State Alexander Haig that 'We would not like to hear from you the type of government we should have', Haig replied, 'General, your internal situation is your problem.'[6]

In the conduct of its covert war against the Soviets in Afghanistan, Pakistan also started to receive help from an unlikely source. A notorious Houston socialite and chat show hostess, Joanne Herring, became an unlikely but staunch cheerleader for the *Mujahedin* and a film she brought back from Afghanistan, during the shooting of which she was fired on by Soviet gunships, brought powerful support in Washington for the Afghan cause. Helpfully, her young lover, Charlie Wilson, a former naval officer and a hard-drinking, womanising Texas Congressman, was a member of the House Appropriations Sub-committee on Defence; he pushed through a dramatic increase in covert funding for the *Mujahedin* with particular emphasis on anti-helicopter weaponry; this bizarre story was made into a film, *Charlie Wilson's War* (2007), starring Tom Hanks and Julia Roberts.

The build-up of this operation received staunch support from William Casey, Reagan's appointee as head of the CIA. Casey was a Wall Street banker who had held senior economist posts under Presidents Nixon and Ford and, more relevantly, was a veteran of the OSS. Casey instructed his office in Islamabad 'to grow the war'.[7]

Thus, the USA, combined with matching funding from Saudi Arabia, increased covert spending on supporting the *Mujahedin* from US\$ 60 million in 1981 to US\$ 400 million in 1984, and then to US\$ 600 million in 1986. So as not to flag direct American involvement in the Afghan war, Soviet ordnance was purchased in Egypt, Eastern Europe and China and was shipped to Karachi, then transported overland to Ojiri Camp near Rawalpindi–Islamabad airport, where it was sorted into small lots by the ISI and trucked to *Mujahedin* collection points in the borderlands of Peshawar. Here some 40 separate guerrilla groups were supplied.

Casey's operations were notably successful and, by mid-1984, the CIA was convinced that the war in Afghanistan had become un-winnable for the Soviets. As the British had discovered to their cost in the 19th Century, the Afghans were fearsome fighters; the CIA's head of station noted that 'the Afghans were bloodthirsty and cruel fighters who simply refused to give up'.[8]

Unlike the war against Soviet-backed guerrillas in Nicaragua, Congressional approval for the conduct of covert operations in Afghanistan was never called into question. The CIA, with just two full-time operatives in Pakistan, was inevitably largely reliant on the ISI who, echoing Zia's own conservative Islamic views, gave overwhelmingly disproportionate support to the fundamentalist Afghan factions, Osama Bin Laden included, who wanted to recreate Afghanistan as a 'pure' Islamic state. Perversely, one of ISI's most favoured groups was led by Gulbuddin Hekmatyar, who was on record as a virulent opponent of the USA. For the CIA, it was a marriage of convenience. As the CIA's head of station asserted, 'They were all . . . basically fundamentalist. There were no Thomas Jeffersons on a white horse among the Afghan resistance leaders.'[9]

Meanwhile, the Soviet conflict was drawing to a conclusion. This was not immediately apparent when Gorbachev became general secretary of the Communist Party in 1985. The Soviet Union's youthful new leader intensified the Soviet military effort in Afghanistan. Soviet success with increasing use of the formidable MI-24 Hind helicopter gunship gave the new leadership cause for hope. The MI-24, one of the ugliest flying machines ever designed, was known as the 'Krocodil' by the so-called Soviet 'Hooligans' who flew with them and as 'Satan's Chariots' by the *Mujahedin*.

In response to this threat, President Reagan, ignoring Pentagon warnings that sophisticated lightweight land-to-air guided missiles called 'Stingers' could end up in the hands of terrorists (which they eventually did in the first Chechen War against Russia in the 1990s), decided to release them to the *Mujahedin*. The first Stinger success against a 'Krocodil' took place in September 1986 and had an immediate impact on the battlefield. By 1989, some 333 'Krocodils' had been lost.

As for Gorbachev, his doubts about the war first became apparent as early as 26 February 1986, at the 27th Congress of the Soviet Communist Party, when he described Afghanistan as 'a bleeding wound'.[10] Eighteen months later, Soviet Foreign Minister Eduard Shevardnadze (later to become president of independent Georgia) privately advised Secretary of State Shultz that the Soviets would leave Afghanistan within a year.

For Zia, the Pakistani military leadership and the ISI, the impending defeat of the Soviets gave implicit possibility to the long-held dream that Afghanistan could become a de facto client to Islamabad. America was largely complicit with this aim. With the defeat of the Soviets in Afghanistan, the Reagan administration largely regarded victory as an important box ticked in the war being waged to end Soviet expansion, and another nail driven into the very existence of the 'Evil Empire'.

The Reagan administration would have been shocked had they been able to see in hindsight that the ruins of Soviet imperialism in Afghanistan would help spawn America's next global enemy. As the leading ideologue and mentor of the Arabic jihadists fighting with the Mujahedin would explain in his book *Defending the Land of the Muslims is Each Man's Most Important Duty*:

> This duty does not end with victory in Afghanistan; jihad will remain an individual obligation until all the lands that were Muslim are returned to us so that Islam will reign again: before us lie Palestine, Bohara, Lebanon, Chad, Eritrea, Somalia, the Philippines, Burma, Southern Yemen, Tashkent and Andalusia.[11]

By contrast, as Michael Armacost, an Asian expert at the State Department, would point out, 'The United States was not much interested in the internal Afghan setup and did not have the capacity to understand this.'[12]

With the war in Afghanistan clearly turned in America's favour by 1984, it was no coincidence that the issue of the Pakistani nuclear weapons programme, held in abeyance since 1979, re-emerged on the US government's agenda. President Reagan now cautioned Zia not to enrich uranium beyond the 5 per cent level, above which it was possible to use it to produce a bomb. With Reagan, Zia was evasive, but to Senator Daniel Moynihan he asserted that, with regard to making a nuclear weapon, 'We are nowhere near it. We have no intentions of making such a weapon. We renounce making such a weapon.'[13]

When the CIA produced a design blueprint of the Pakistan bomb and detailed satellite photographs of the Kahuta facility, Zia merely commented, 'Maybe it is a goat shed.'[14] Munir Ahmad Khan, the chairman of the Pakistan Atomic

Energy Commission, would later add that American pressure made no impact on the Pakistan nuclear programme. Indeed, Zia and his government rightly calculated that his country's short-term importance as an ally against communism far outweighed American concerns about Pakistan's nuclear intentions. With regard to preventing nuclear proliferation in the sub-continent, America's policies were hopelessly compromised.

It was only a matter of time before Pakistan's nuclear programme, the subject of years of phoney dispute with America, would become official. In January 1987, Dr A.Q. Khan confirmed to a visiting Indian journalist what the world had known for a long time, which was that Pakistan had a nuclear capacity. Ominously, Khan was also quoted in a British paper, *The Observer*, saying, 'The word "peaceful" associated with a nuclear programme is humbug'[15]; Zia was naturally furious.

However, Khan's disclosure now forced Zia to acknowledge the reality of Pakistan's nuclear programme. He told a visiting *Time* magazine reporter in February 1987 that he could write that Pakistan could build a bomb whenever it wished. It could hardly have surprised anyone when, in July 1987, a Canadian Pakistani was apprehended for trying to export 'maraging' steel to Pakistan; this specialised nickel infused steel, twice as hard as stainless steel and 35 per cent harder than titanium alloys, is used in golf clubs (not known as a major industry in Pakistan) and atomic bomb casings and centrifuges.

With the Afghan war drawing to a close following withdrawal of Soviet forces, and signs of impending collapse in the Soviet Empire, it is clear with the benefit of hindsight that the American administrations of Presidents Reagan and George Bush (senior), and later Bill Clinton, failed to grasp the implications of the post-war settlement of the region. By contrast, the Pakistan government seized the opportunity presented by the vacuum in American policy. Although Foreign Minister Yaqub Khan thought that the ascendant *Mujahedin* would be unlikely to be pro-Pakistan after they had finally taken Kabul, the head of ISI, Lt General Hamid Gul, had a strong preference for Hekmatyar and other fundamentalists. Inadvertently, America continued to provide financial support for fundamentalist Afghan groups who viewed their benefactor as the 'Great Satan'. Richard Armitage, assistant secretary of defence under George Bush (senior), and later a deputy secretary of state under George W. Bush, admitted that 'We drifted too long in 1989 and failed to understand the independent role that the ISI was playing.'[16]

Just as the Soviet–Afghan war had boosted Pakistan–American relations, so its ending brought a new coolness in its wake. President Bush's deputy National Security Council advisor was frostily received by President Ghulam Ishaq, while Chief of the Army Staff Aslam Beg was 'accusatory and confrontational'.[17] Pakistan's nuclear programme again emerged as a main bogey of contention. CIA intelligence now indicated that uranium cores had been machined; Pakistan denied the charge. In addition, the Bush (senior) administration was waking up to the maverick role being played by the ISI, with clear indications that they were also sponsoring fundamentalist insurgents in an increasingly violence-riven Kashmir. In spite of the deterioration of relations, the Pakistan government did not believe that the Bush administration would implement the Pressler Amendment sanctions, passed during the Reagan presidency, which allowed for cutting off aid to Pakistan if the country was found to have developed an atom bomb.

The Pakistan government was therefore stunned when the US$ 564 million economic and military aid programme, promised for 1991, was indefinitely frozen. Caught in the ban were the long-promised F-16s. It was a devastating blow to the Pakistan military. Not surprisingly, the Pakistani government and population believed that their country had been cynically exploited during the Soviet–Afghan war, and that they had been summarily abandoned once their usefulness to America's geopolitical cause had passed. Nevertheless, the Sharif government hoped that the USA would soon relent. However, at a meeting with under secretary of state for security affairs, President Ghulam and Sharif were told, 'We can't change our policies. You have to change yours.'[18]

In September 1991, the USA and the Soviet Union agreed to stop supplying weaponry to their respective agents in Afghanistan. If the Soviets thought that this would help preserve their puppet President Najibullah, they were mistaken; however, Gorbachev could barely have conceived that it would be the break-up of the Soviet Union itself, after a failed coup d'etat by his generals, which would precipitate the final victory of the *Mujahedin*. In April 1992, Najibullah's Interior Ministry changed sides, thus allowing the *Mujahedin* entry into Kabul. The Pakistan government, through the ISI, could now seek to exercise a 'client state' control over its now fundamentalist neighbour.

Ignoring the long-term implication of this development, America's main interest in Pakistan continued to be the latent nuclear threat. Fears about the construction of the bomb now turned to issues of delivery systems. Pakistan had failed to develop its own missiles, but the CIA discovered at the beginning of 1991 that China was providing M-11 missiles.

For the Americans, though it was disputed by the Chinese, this put the Chinese government in breach of the Missile Technology Control Regime (MTCR); this agreement put a 300 km/500 kg limit on missiles for export. Bush (senior) deferred the decision on sanctions to his successor Bill Clinton, who defeated him in the December 1992 elections. The issue of the 'Chinese connection' would also re-emerge in 1995 when the CIA concluded that some 5,000 ring magnets, essential in the construction of high-speed centrifuges for uranium enrichment, had been sold to Pakistan.

Pakistan's relations with the new Clinton regime in Washington started poorly. Secretary of State Warren Christopher somewhat bizarrely coupled Pakistan with Burma as a problem state. Moreover, the ISI's involvement in terrorism in Kashmir caused the new administration to put Pakistan on the terrorism watch list. Though Sharif attempted a crackdown on terrorists in response to the American pressure, insurgent groups, who had been amply trained and funded by the USA and the Saudis during the decade-long Afghan–Soviet war, simply moved across the border. These Islamic radicals also intensified their efforts against India. In a trend that would become clearer over the next decade, the insurgents no longer saw themselves restricted to any one theatre of operation; increasingly, Muslim fundamentalists could draw on a fungible stock of terrorists to act in Afghanistan, Kashmir or wherever.

In tandem with the alarming growth in fundamentalist insurgency that the USA had unwittingly financed in the 1980s, drug trafficking from Afghanistan and the North West Frontier Province was also growing. By the early 1990s, 20 per cent of drugs sold in the USA were being produced in the North West Frontier Province. Though it is hard to calculate, at least some of the money gained from this source is likely to have helped fund insurgency groups. Action to curb this traffic was practically non-existent. The Pakistan Narcotics Control Board even had its phones disconnected, because it could no longer pay its bills.

By the end of Bill Clinton's first year in office, his administration had moved to a more pragmatic policy towards Pakistan. Essentially, Washington now realised that it was too late to prevent Pakistan getting nuclear weapons, or to persuade them to give them up; the new strategy was to press for a freeze in the nuclear weapons race with India and to press for independent verification. Neither India nor Pakistan reacted positively to these suggestions. Benazir Bhutto told Deputy Secretary of State Strobe Talbott, 'If we are unilaterally pressed for the capping, it will be discriminatory and Pakistan will not agree to it.'[19]

Nevertheless, there was some thaw in the relationship with America during the first Clinton administration. In particular, the Pakistan army enjoyed excellent relations with its American counterpart. Goodwill was provided by the sending of 6,000 Pakistani troops to Somalia, and a further 3,000 to Bosnia on peacekeeping operations. Later in February 1995, the Pakistan government also won a lot of credit for inviting US officers to join them on a raid, which produced the arrest of Ramzi Yusul, one of the Islamic terrorists believed to have masterminded the 'first' fundamentalist plot to blow up the World Trade Centre on 26 February 1993.

The result of better relations was some easing of the Pressler sanctions on aid to Pakistan. President Clinton also chose to ignore the fact that Benazir Bhutto was shown to have lied during her visit to Washington in 1995, when she told the administration that Pakistan had not resumed production of weapons-grade uranium, that is, above 5 per cent enrichment. Even when it was demonstrated that Benazir was noticeably soft on drug barons (her husband Asif Ali Zardari was later accused of being involved in laundering drug money), Clinton still waived sanctions on the grounds that it would not serve the public interest. Perhaps not surprisingly, given Clinton's undistinguished record in dealing with Pakistan, Benazir Bhutto failed to achieve even a single entry in the former president's autobiography, *My Life* (2004).

The Pakistan government now made a fateful decision regarding its choice of friendly agents in Afghanistan. The ISI, with the support of Benazir's Interior

Minister Naseerullah Babar, formerly a confidant of her father, wanted to support a government consisting largely of Pashtuns, who had been educated in the *madrassas* (Islamic religious schools of an increasingly fundamentalist bent) of Baluchistan. These fighters known collectively as the *Taliban* won a switch of financial and political support from Pakistan, which had previously been enjoyed by the *Mujahedin* commander, Hekmatyar.

Following the puritanical rules of the *Deobandi* sect of Sunni Islam, the *Taliban* brought a new strain to the long-drawn-out civil conflict in Afghanistan. American Afghan expert, Barnett Rubin, described them as 'fire and brimstone, backwoods preachers with an AK-47'.[20] Its regimented disciples proved more than a match for the fiercely regional *Mujahedin* warlords. One of the strategic aims of Pakistan's new alliance was to pursue Benazir's vision of overland trade links to Central Asia. To promote this concept, Babar, the minister of the interior, led a convoy of trucks to Turkmenistan, passing through Heart and Kandahar. US Ambassador John Monjo, who joined this curious expedition, was astonished at the ability of the *Taliban* to face down the normal requests for money by the *Mujahedin*.

Yet, Kabul itself remained under the control of the official government of President Burhanuddin Rabbani supported by the *Tajiks*, the northern tribes of Afghanistan, under their leader Ahmad Shah Massoud, the 'Lion of Panjshir', a leading anti-Soviet warlord. Pakistan's relations with Rabbani, also a *Tajik*, suffered after he established a relationship with India. Not surprisingly, the Pakistan government favoured the *Pashtun*, Pakistani-educated *Taliban*.

On 11 September 1996, the *Taliban* took Jalalabad and two weeks later they entered Kabul. Rabbani and Massoud withdrew to the North. Massoud would later become leader of the Northern Alliance that continued to fight the *Taliban*, until he was killed by suicide bombers posing as Belgian cameramen on 9 September 2001, just two days before the infamous 9/11 attack on the World Trade Centre in New York. Many believe that the assassination was ordered by Osama Bin Laden as a favour to his *Taliban* protectors.

As for the USA, the *Taliban* victory was at first viewed if anything positively, seen as it was through the prism of Pakistan preference. The Clinton administration was also probably influenced by Unocal, the American oil company, which was negotiating with the *Taliban* for protection of a pipeline that they wanted to build through Afghanistan. Indeed, Unocal executives at the company's head office in Sugarland, Texas, met with a *Taliban* delegation at the end of 1997; this was followed by a State Department meeting with the *Taliban*'s minister of mines. These visits had taken place, notwithstanding Secretary of State Madeleine Albright's denunciation of the *Taliban*'s human rights record in the previous month.

Toni Marshall and Tom Carter of *The Washington Times* complained that women's rights, which were defended in public vis-à-vis the *Taliban*, were being discarded in favour of the commercial interests of American energy companies. However, during President Clinton's second term in office, his administration's attitude towards Afghanistan started to shift. This may in part have resulted from a clearer focus after the election campaign against Bob Dole, or more likely a change in personnel; the ambassador to India, Thomas Pickering, was appointed under secretary of state for political affairs, while Karl Inderfurth replaced Raphael as assistant secretary of state for South Asia.

The importance of the non-proliferation issue to the USA was now to be de-emphasised. The new team was increasingly dissatisfied with what it saw as the linkage between the ISI, and its support for the *Taliban* with fundamentalist insurgency into Kashmir; General Hamid Gul, former head of ISI, and the man most often associated with the pro-*Taliban* faction within the Pakistan military would later go as far as to suggest that the 9/11 attack on the World Trade Centre was a Zionist conspiracy. If the ISI could use the *Taliban* to topple the Soviet regime in Kabul, why not use it to destabilise the Indian occupation of Kashmir too? This thought must have occurred to all parties, including the Indian government in New Delhi.

Alarmingly for America, signs of a hardline Islamist opposition to American culture and values were also beginning to emerge within Pakistan itself. The *Taliban* now appeared to be infecting groups within Pakistan. A fundamental group called for the arrest and trial in Pakistan of Michael Jackson and Madonna as 'the torch-bearers of American society, their cultural and social values . . . that are destroying humanity. They are ruining the lives of thousands of Muslims and leading them to destruction, away from their religions, ethics and morality'.[21] It was a harbinger of the increasing disaffection of the Pakistan people with the USA, and it began to raise the possibility in the mind of Western politicians that the 'nuclear'-armed government of Pakistan could fall to a populist jihadist electoral shift or a broadly based uprising.

For America, the possibility of a major conflagration on the sub-continent became increasingly real; America's attitude to the *Taliban* increasingly hardened though the Clinton administration would never have considered an active strategy of regime change in Afghanistan. That would have to wait until the '9/11' assault on the World Trade Centre, when the Pentagon and White House began to question all previous assumptions about the risks posed by the *Taliban* government in Afghanistan, and the fundamentalist terrorists which it nurtured and supported. For the Islamic radicals, who for several decades, had been increasing in strength worldwide, albeit largely beneath the radar of international political consciousness, Al Qaeda's attack on America was a wake-up call for a new broad-ranging assault on the perceived economic and cultural dominance of the West. As the Hamas weekly, *Al-Risala*, noted on 13 September 2001, 'Allah has answered all our prayers.'[22] A new ideological battle to defeat America's global hegemony had begun.

PART V

End of America's Asian Empire

61

Asia Redux

Asia: 1990—2010

The collapse of the Soviet Bloc in 1989 and the subsequent formal dissolution of its empire in 1991 effectively ended the Cold War. The remains of the Soviet Union's bid to become the hegemonic power in Asia were left in tatters. Unable to afford its Pacific Ocean fleet, Russia's ships rotted in the harbours of Vladivostok. The former Soviet naval base at Cam Ranh Bay in Vietnam was finally abandoned in July 2002.

For Asia's emerged and emerging nations, there was relief from the fear of communism; perhaps less observed, there was also liberation from American influence. The foreign policy of these nations immediately began to respond to the new freedoms by taking a more independent track. Yet with one eye on the emerging power of China and the possibility that the Chinese might become the new 'bully boy' in the Asian neighbourhood, it was always unlikely that there would any abrupt repudiations of the American relationship; a balanced and opportunistic neutrality would appear to be the most likely medium-term policy for most Asian nations.

In general, the ending of the Cold War enabled Asia's nations to begin to normalise their political development. With the notable exceptions of North Korea and Burma, which remained in the Marxist–Leninist dark ages, Asia advanced rapidly down the track of free market economics with countries such as Vietnam and Cambodia emerging as the region's new 'Tiger' economies.

Also apart from Pakistan, Asia began to lose the larger-than-life characters and brutal political dramas that characterised its development in the post-war period. Like post-war Europe, economics, wealth distribution, trade, health, education and environment became the normal chaff of Asian politics. Collectively the region emerged as not only the largest GDP region of the world (the USA included), but also the fastest growing.

China

The rise of Jiang Zemin to power was unexpected. Born in Anhui province in 1926, Jiang earned a degree in electrical engineering from Shanghai Jiaotong University after the war and then trained at the Stalin Automobile Works in Moscow in the 1950s. He continued his auto career at Changchun First Automobile before transferring to work in Shanghai's government. Rising to become a member of the Central Committee of the Communist Party, he was appointed minister of electronic industries in 1983. Two years later he became the mayor of Shanghai and then the party chief.

From this position of relative obscurity he was plucked to become China's new leader as general secretary of the Communist Party in 1989. In effect he was the choice of Deng Xiaoping, who dismissed his predecessor, Zhao Ziyang, for being too weak in dealing with the students occupying Tiananmen Square in the events leading up to the famed 'Massacre' or '4th June incident'. By contrast, Jiang had been forceful in dealing with unrest in Shanghai, and he may also have been chosen as a compromise candidate over better known and more obvious leaders such as Li Ruihuan and Premier Li Peng.

Well known as a fervent advocate of the economic reform programme of Deng Xiaoping, Jiang was a perfect choice as a moderniser who nevertheless was strongly resistant to political liberalism. While his political aura and prestige meant that Deng continued his non-official role of supreme leader until his death in 1997, Jiang Zemin was able to use this period of protection to consolidate his position within the party. Although Jiang has been much criticised for his political conservatism and his failure to root out corruption within the Communist Party, it is difficult to argue with a record which saw the Chinese economy achieve an average real growth in GDP of 9 per cent per annum over the 12 years of his leadership.

By the time he completed the hand of power with the passing of the chairmanship of the Central Military Commission of the PRC to Hu Jintao in 2005, China had risen to become not only the largest exporter to the USA but also the world's major manufacturing economy. Jiang Zemin's understanding of the symbiotic relationship with the USA was underlined by his conciliatory foreign policy. When President Clinton, unable to get UN support, bombed Serbia under the auspices of NATO in 1999 and accidentally destroyed the Chinese Embassy in Belgrade, killing a number of Chinese diplomats in the process, Jiang Zemin merely went through pro-forma gestures of protest.

Also with regard to Taiwan, Jiang Zemin helped foster increased commercial relationships while ignoring the threats of some Taiwanese politicians to sever the China connection and declare unilateral independence. For Jiang Zemin and indeed his successor, Hu Jintao, foreign policy has largely been subsumed to making China the world's economic powerhouse. As Jiang Zemin explained in the early 1990s:

> History had shown that the current international competition was based on a nation's comprehensive economic and scientific strength. For China this meant that the planned growth rate of six per cent was insufficient to catch up with the leading nations of the West. The rate had to be adjusted upwards, to at least nine or ten percent.[1]

In achieving this economic transformation, in effect China has become a commercial partner to the USA in a manner envisaged by President Truman and

Secretary of State Dean Acheson after the Second World War; by doing so however, China has also become America's main competitor for political hegemony in Asia.

However, with the exception of the 'Taiwan' factor, there is no reason to believe that China and the USA should be unable to sustain a harmonious geopolitical relationship; as Zheng Bijian, a Chinese political strategist and academic, has pointed out with regard to the development of East Asia, '. . . it would not be in China's interest to exclude the United States. . . . In fact, Beijing wants Washington to play a positive role in the region's security as well as economic affairs'.[2] Thus far America has accepted this position at face value.

Taiwan

The issue of 'independence' remained the focal point of Taiwan politics. Perversely for the last 20 years, both the *Kuomintang* President Lee Teng Hui (1988–2000) and his successor Chen Shui Bian (2000–8) from the Democratic Progress Party supported the idea of Taiwanese independence and the abandonment of the convenient fiction of 'One China', which allowed the People's Republic of China to claim theoretic sovereignty over its former province.

Chen Shui Bian's position took sophistry on the 'independence' issue to new levels, promising not to declare Taiwanese independence as long as China did not threaten military attack on the island state; also, Chen maintained the stance of the Democratic Progress Party that Taiwan (the Republic of China: ROC) was already de facto an independent nation and therefore had no need to declare its independence.

The reality, as all Taiwanese leaders have recognised, is that China would in all likelihood launch a military assault on Taiwan if the ROC declared independence. America, whose unwaveringly avowed policy since President Truman has been the defence of its ally Taiwan, has consistently put pressure on the ROC's presidents to tone down rhetoric on the issue of independence. On this subject President George W. Bush was even more publicly vehement than his predecessors. For Taiwanese leaders the fear must be that the USA would not ride to their rescue if they declared unilateral independence from China.

Nevertheless, Taiwan remains the finely balanced issue on which the continuance of peaceful relations between the USA and China now rests. As Denny Roy has concluded in *Taiwan: A Political History* (2003), 'The United States and China face the prospect of a war over Taiwan that neither side wants. China is committed to attack Taiwan under certain circumstances, while the United States is committed to defend Taiwan under certain circumstances.'[3] In this respect, the further opening of trade, investment and travel arrangements with the mainland by Kuomintang President Ma Ying-jeou (elected in May 2008), who has vowed a policy of no reunification, no independence and no war, has come as a huge relief to all observers of China–Taiwan relations.

Meanwhile, aggressively free market economic policies have remained a constant. With a GDP per capita of US$ 15,500 (ranked 35th in the world), Taiwan remains one of Asia's most productive and rapidly growing economies.

Japan

The new century began almost as badly as the last had ended. Prime Minister Obuchi, having launched one of 13 economic rescue plans since the slump of 1990, saw the Japanese economy limp into the twenty-first century. However, the 62-year-old Obuchi suffered a massive heart attack on 1 April 2000 and died one month later.

His successor Yoshiro Mori managed the unenviable record of becoming the most gaffe-prone prime minister in living memory. At Obuchi's funeral, he failed to bow and clap in the traditional manner required of the Japanese funeral rite; given that even the frequently derided President George W. Bush had managed this task with aplomb, Mori was ridiculed in the Japanese press. Most notoriously however, when informed that the USS Greeneville, while practising an emergency surface drill, had sunk a Japanese fishing boat and killed nine students and teachers, Mori continued to play his round of golf. Meanwhile at a meeting with Shinto leaders, Mori managed to scandalise liberal Japan when he affirmed Japan's position as the nation of the Gods with the Emperor at its centre. Nothing could demonstrate more clearly the long-term ramifications of General MacArthur's cover-up of Emperor Hirohito's war guilt during the Tokyo War Crimes Trial as well as the deeply ingrained 'Emperor–God' myth propagated by the Japanese Imperial court propagandists in the early 1920s.

Mori's embarrassing premiership lasted barely one year, and on 26 April 2001, he was replaced by Junichiro Koizumi whose five-year premiership brought the long-awaited turnaround in the Japanese economy. In large part, the recovery was autonomous with the long deflation, brought about by the property slump of the early 1990s, coming to an end. However, there is little doubt that Koizumi's financial reforms, particularly the dramatic reduction of Japanese banks' Non-Performing Loans ratio which allowed them to start lending more aggressively, contributed to a rebound in the stock market and property prices.

Koizumi himself exuded a new period of optimism. As a long-haired maverick within the LDP, a divorcee and proclaimed 'reform' politician, he marked a break with the grey men who had dominated Japan's post-war political life. In April 2001, he promised to 'change the LDP, change Japan'[4] and quickly set about his task with a new-look reforming cabinet.

He was a politician who realised that the LDP had to move away from the rural redoubts, whose over-weighted voting power had allowed the party a virtual political monopoly for half a century. Koizumi, a graduate from Tokyo's fashionable Keio University, was the perfect figure to court the urban vote showing his cultural diversity, if not quirkiness, by his reverence for Elvis Presley on the one hand and

Wagner and Sibelius on the other. It was an identification that could have come from the pages of Haruki Murakami, the totemic novelist whose books so perfectly capture the *zeitgeist* of Japan's modern urban generation.

Koizumi's reformist style was not without substance. He took on vested rural interests within his own party by attacking the antiquated state-controlled management and investment policies of the Japanese Post Office. Having failed to force through the privatisation of the post office, Koizumi sacked his LDP rebels and called a general election on the post office issue and surprised everyone by achieving a landslide victory. Post office privatisation followed. It was a significant reform issue, but more importantly it showed that it was possible for a forceful charismatic politician to triumph over the stodgy conservatism of LDP factional politics.

Also by changing the name of the *Japan Self Defence Agency* to the *Japanese Ministry of Defence*, Koizumi indicated that the cowering passivity of post-war Japan in international politics should be brought to an end. The change was not merely symbolic. Koizumi also broke the mould by sending Japanese soldiers to support Americans in Iraq, the first overseas deployment of Japanese soldiers since the Second World War.

However, the effects of the institutional cover-up of Emperor Hirohito's war crimes orchestrated by General MacArthur in the post-war period are still evident; the failure to confront Hirohito's past meant that Japan never fully faced its recent history – in particular the genocide committed in Northern China and the brutal enslavement of the peoples of Asia. As recently as October 2008, General Toshio Tamogami, Japan's air chief of staff, declared in an historical essay that 'We need to realise that many Asian countries take a positive view of the Great East Asia War.... It is certainly a false accusation to say that our country was an aggressor nation.'[5] The backlash from shocked Asian governments and their citizens was predictable.

However, Koizumi's successors failed to build on his impetus for change and the collapse of the economy after the 2007–2009 Global Credit Crisis brought the LDP's greatest electoral catastrophe in the 30th August lower house elections. The Democratic Party of Japan (DPJ), led by Yukio Hatoyama, won a landslide victory with more than 300 seats out of 480. This result will probably be seen as the ultimate vindication of Ichiro Ozawa's 15 year long attempt to create a credible two party system in Japan. Whether the DPJ will bring much needed deregulation of Japan's economic and social structures or push through a more nationalist agenda long advocated by Ozawa's *'Blueprint for a New Japan'* (1993), including the development of an independent nuclear deterrent, remains to be seen.

South Korea

Roh Moo-Hyun won a landslide victory as the candidate of the ruling Millennium Democratic Party in 2003 and was sworn into office as president on 14 May 2004. A noted human rights lawyer with a record of support for anti-authoritarian causes,

Roh continued his predecessor's liberal foreign policy agenda. However, the 'sunshine policy' with its opening up to North Korea, which had brought Kim Dae Jung the Nobel Peace Prize, came under increasing scrutiny and criticism as their northern siblings launched series of missile and nuclear tests.

Roh, seen as anti-American, also drew criticism from his support base for his sending of troops to Iraq. However, it was an action which did little to smooth the strained relations with the USA, which strongly disapproved of the economic support given to North Korea; President George W. Bush could only view this policy as undermining the international efforts to bring Kim Jong Il to the negotiating table on nuclear weapons.

In reaction to Roh's policies, the 2007 presidential elections were won by the leader of the Grand National Party, Lee Myung-Bak, who ran a campaign demanding better relations with the USA, a tougher line with North Korea, and more pro-market policies including further deregulation and encouragement of foreign investment. Nevertheless, South Korea's 'underperforming economy' achieved 4.9 per cent real GDP growth in 2007. Notwithstanding the global recession which started in 2008, the South Korean economy, with the world's highest broadband penetration and most computer-literate society, continues to look well placed to advance upwards in the rankings of wealthy nations.

North Korea

In December 1995, the Korean Peninsula Energy Development Organisation (KEDO) agreed to provide North Korea with power through a South Korean-designed light water reactor. On an interim basis the agreement also provided North Korea with fuel oil, though because of declining coal extraction, one North Korean expert noted pessimistically that even with this subsidy North Korea would 'need additional energy if it is to retain its estimated 1991 level of electrical consumption'.[6] The quid pro quo was that North Korea would suspend production of uranium and its nuclear weapons programme. KEDO, whose sponsors also included the USA and Japan, hoped that the deal would bring long-term stabilisation to relations with North Korea.

However, with renewed scrutiny of North Korean activities after the '9/11' attack on the World Trade Centre, it was becoming increasingly evident from intelligence that North Korea, part of President George W. Bush's 'axis of evil', was reneging on its agreements. In October 2002, North Korean officials, when presented with incontrovertible evidence, admitted that there was a clandestine programme to produce weapons-grade uranium.

While South Korea continued its 'sunshine' policy, relations with the West froze. On 9 October 2006, North Korea announced its first detonation of a nuclear device. However, a further switch in North Korean policy took place in 2007 when under six-party talks (USA, China, Russia, Japan, South Korea and North Korea) the North Koreans suddenly agreed to suspend and then dismantle its nuclear programme in return for fuel aid and political concessions, notably from the USA. Adding to a litany of broken agreements, North Korea failed to meet a December 2007 deadline to make full disclosure.

Although North Korea's destruction of a cooling tower at its Yongbyon nuclear facility on 27 June 2008 brought hope that the country would retreat from its nuclear weapons ambitions, the mysterious rogue state, with its unpredictable leader Kim Jong Il, remained a thorn in the side of all the major nations who, for once, were united in their desire to relieve North Korea of its nuclear capability. In the meantime, North Korea's decrepit Marxist–Leninist economy remained entirely dependent on foreign food aid to feed its people.

In 2009, Kim Jong Il, following a long illness possibly involving a heart attack, launched a long-range missile test which flew over Japan; in the West it was seen as a means of shoring up the image of an ailing dictator prior to 'mock' elections which extended his rule. However, the test indicated the development of technologies that could transport a nuclear warhead to the shores of the USA, and brought a barrage of international protest. In a response which has typified his dealings with the West, Kim responded by throwing out all international nuclear observers and shutting down the '6 party talks'. Though Kim Jong Il undoubtedly knows that an opening to the free world is required to change North Korea's dire economic course, the problem remains that 'the North wants change without regime change'.[7] Following the visit of former President Bill Clinton to North Korea, a condition for the release of two American journalists, the North's policies switched again to a positive track. Direct negotiations have begun yet again with South Korea.

Thailand

In 1991 Thailand experienced its 17th coup d'état since the Second World War. Apart from a 13-year gap between 1958 and 1971, coups had come along at least every four years. After 1991 Thailand appeared to have reverted to normal political and economic development; even the Asian crash and economic crisis of 1997 went by without military intervention.

Normalisation seemed even further entrenched when relatively cleanly fought 2001 elections brought an election victory for the *Thai Rak Thai* Party (TRT: Thais love Thailand Party). The party founded in 1998 by Thaksin Shinawatra, a mobile phone entrepreneur and billionaire, came to power on a moderately populist economic agenda, which promised reform of health and education. Universal health care was subsequently introduced and education restructured to allow better access for the poor. (Access to health care increased from 76 per cent to 96 per cent of the population.) In addition, Prime Minister Thaksin forced through a privatisation programme and encouraged foreign investment. It was a clearly thought through programme of economic reform and marked a distinct switch from the personality-driven platforms of political predecessors from the traditional ruling elite.

However, Thaksin, a former policeman from a poor background, was an outsider whose support from the largely rural north and centre of Thailand ranged him against the military, political and urban elite. Accusations of bribery, corruption, nepotism and tax fraud reflected the fears of a political establishment which increasingly felt excluded from the corridors of power and influence.

Internationally he also attracted opprobrium for his ruthless suppression of Muslim insurgency in Thailand's southern province; (Thailand, like many countries in Asia and the West, was subject to terrorist actions after '9/11' by radical Islamic groups). In particular, the storming of Krue Se Mosque and the massacre of 84 Muslim protesters by the army at Tak Bai brought Thaksin torrents of criticism from international human rights groups.

Nevertheless, Thaksin's distinctive and directed programmes of reform won him a landslide electoral victory in 2005, with 374 seats out of 500. It was an election noted as the least corrupt in Thai history. However, it was an alarming result for the Bangkok political establishment.

The clearest opportunity for attack on Thaksin came with his sale of his family mobile telephone business, Shin Corporation. Criticism came in two parts: first that the US$ 1.88 billion proceeds of the sale were tax free, albeit this was in line with rules on disposal of listed shares; and second that this supposedly strategic national asset was sold to a foreign owner, Temasek Holdings, the sovereign fund managed by the Singapore government.

In response, the People's Alliance for Democracy (PAD) attempted to bring life in Bangkok to a halt as it organised mass protest rallies against the prime minister. The revolt of the urban bourgeoisie and Bangkok establishment created a political crisis which forced Thaksin to dissolve parliament on 24 February 2006. In elections called for 2 April, the PAD, fearing another crushing electoral defeat at the hands of the still immensely popular Thaksin, decided to boycott the poll. The result was a massive 462-seat victory for TRT, a result which was then challenged in protracted constitutional proceedings in the courts.

Taking advantage of the political chaos, the Thai military, using the specious title *Council for National Security*, launched a bloodless coup which took control of government while Thaksin was attending a United Nations meeting in New York. TRT was abolished and its leading politicians banned from participation in politics, while Thaksin was ordered to return to Thailand to face corruption charges. Meanwhile his assets in Thailand were seized. The new military junta meanwhile sparked a financial market crisis by its cack-handed introduction of rules designed to deter foreign investors.

The junta, having promised new elections within 12 months, redesigned the constitution, reducing the number of parliamentary seats to 480, part elected by constituency and part by voter proportion. The attempt to gerrymander the constitution failed disastrously. TRT supporters switched to the People's Power Party (PPP) and swept to victory against the 'anti-Thaksin' Democrat Party with 233 seats against 165. On 28 January 2008, the outspoken 72-year-old Samak

Sundaravej was voted in as prime minister with a 310-seat coalition and immediately vowed, 'I have to bring [Thaksin] back to the limelight. We will use the
same policies.'[8]

With the formation of a coalition government with minor parties, it now
seemed likely that Thaksin would be allowed to return from his international
exile. However, apparently under pressure from his wife, he foreswore future
participation in politics. Instead, while in exile, Thaksin briefly devoted his energies to buying Manchester City Football Club and hired the former England
manager, Sven-Göran Eriksson, to run his team. It remained to be seen whether
Thaksin would remain the political power behind the scenes of Thai politics or
whether, under pressure of verdicts of corruption against him and his wife, he
would remain an exile. However, the establishment pressure on Thaksin and his
supporters continued unabated. His brother-in-law, Somchai Wongsarat, became
prime minister after his predecessor, Samak Sundaravej, was forced to resign from
office after a Constitutional Court found him in breach of Article 267 of the constitution of Thailand by dint of hosting two cookery shows on television while holding
the post of prime minister.

There now appeared to be an insoluble split in the country between the PAD,
supported by the largely urban establishment and military-backed elite, which has
traditionally enjoyed the spoils of office, and the rurally supported PPP. Indeed
the PAD, by its November 2008 occupation of Bangkok Airport, appeared to be
prepared to sacrifice Thailand's economy to prevent the elected government of
the PPP remaining in power. Neither the army nor the police appeared willing
or able to support the increasingly isolated incumbent Prime Minister Wongsarat.
Wongsarat too fell foul of the courts when the Constitutional Court banned him
from politics for five years for electoral fraud; his party was banned, though it
seems likely to reformulate under a new name. Continued political chaos seems
inevitable, given the inability of political parties to accept electoral defeat. Unfortunately, the political stability once offered by King Bhumibol has also waned with
his age and health and the lack of a clear or viable succession.

In spite of the slightly barmy 'opera bouffe' nature of Thai politics, and the
coup d'états which were a normal part of the Thai political process, the impact
on the country's economic performance was minimal. Real GDP growth in 2007
was 4.5 per cent. However growth declined to 2.75 per cent in 2008 and reflecting the joint effects of the global credit crunch, the PAD airport occupation,
and the PPP disruption of an ASEAN meeting scheduled to be held in Bangkok,
the short-term outlook remains bleak and the longer-term outlook increasingly
uncertain.

Malaysia

In 2002, the irascible Dr Mahathir tearfully announced his retirement to a shocked
UMNO assembly; his party, denuded of all opposition during his 22 years of

authoritarian rule, cravenly begged him to stay on for a further 18 months. He duly accepted. In his last month in office he continued in the abrasive manner in which he had ruled. Australia was verbally attacked along with President George W. Bush, whom he accused of being a liar; East Timor was hectored on the perils of democracy, and he continued his anti-Semitic rants against the global power of the Jews. Furthermore, he promised that he would continue 'to say nasty things about other countries'[9] after his retirement on 31 October.

His legacy has been and will be much debated. Although income per capita rose from US$ 2,320 per capita to US$ 8,920 during his 22 years in power, and the Malaysian economy continues to sustain a high level of growth, arguably a less corrupt and communally biased economic policy would have produced a much richer society comparable with neighbouring Singapore. Furthermore, there is little doubt that his rule, particularly the crushing of an independent judiciary and a free press, and the monopolisation of economic perks for party supporters served to undermine the normal checks and balances within a democratic constitution. For a man who constantly criticised western democracy, it is unlikely that he was unduly worried by the slide towards single-party constitutional dictatorship which he effectively imposed on his country.

Mahathir was succeeded by his long-time deputy Abdullah Badawi, a man chosen for his weak political following within UMNO. Nevertheless, the mild-spoken and likeable Badawi, in spite of counterblasts off-stage by his predecessor, won a comfortable victory in the 2004 elections. However, there have subsequently been no indications that he has fulfilled his election promise to eradicate corruption from within the UMNO ruling elite. Indeed Prime Minister Badawi, after a disastrous electoral performance in 2008, in which he lost the party's customary two-thirds majority, has been subjected to intense criticism from the irrepressible Dr Mahathir. The government in hand with the judiciary also renewed its charges of sodomy against Anwar, who reemerged as the most popular and articulate of the opposition leaders. Criticism of widespread corruption and Chinese anger at the systemic favouritism to Malays began to undermine the racial compact sustained by Mahathir and his predecessors.

In April 2009, Badawi stepped down to be replaced as prime minister by his deputy Najib Tun Razak, the son of Malaysia's second prime minister. In response to criticisms, Najib set about deregulating financial companies to foreign investment and also abolished the 30 per cent *bumiputra* (indigenous Malay) requirement for certain industries. However, given the degree to which Najib is beholden to a racial compact which has been inherently corrupt, and to party power brokers who have benefitted from a generational monopoly of power, it remains to be seen if the new prime minister can halt UMNO's relative electoral decline and continue its grip on power.

Singapore

Singapore entered the new century as boringly successful as it ended the last; there can be no greater compliment to a government that has, since the retirement of Lee Kuan Yew, the towering founder and figurehead of this island nation, continued the entirely professional management of an economy that has produced a GDP per capita of US$ 37,000 (some three times higher than neighbouring Malaysia). The country is ranked the 17th wealthiest per capita in the world.

The main problem now facing Singapore is that the high cost of labour makes the economy vulnerable to the relocation of fixed capital assets by the multinational corporations that originally brought jobs and investment to Singapore. Thus far Singapore has been able to move up the value curve by improvements in education and a switch to fast-growing service industries, but a feature of the country's highly paid mandarin politicians is that they constantly look ahead to new challenges and problems. In his 2001 National Day Rally, Prime Minister Goh reflected on the need to attract talented foreigners to Singapore: '. . . if we do not top up our talent pool from outside, in ten years time, many of our high-value jobs we do now will migrate to China and elsewhere . . . .'[10] Thus far there has been no sign that the government is not capable of dealing with the future challenges created by Singapore's economic success.

With an astonishing US$ 222 million in reserves, the city state of Singapore is both rich and prudent, and its management of national assets has made Temasek Holdings one of the world's most admired sovereign funds. Its Chief Executive Ho Ching is married to Singapore's third and current Prime Minister Lee Hsien Loong, the son of the country's founder Lee Kuan Yew. (The 80-year-old Lee Kuan Yew remains a senior minister and controls the Government Investment Corporation (GIC), which manages the country's foreign reserves.)

Lee Hsien Loong's qualifications for high office were far more than birth. He was awarded a first-class degree in mathematics from Trinity College, Cambridge, and then gained a master's in public administration from Harvard. There followed military training at Fort Leavenworth and a military career until the age of 32, when he entered government. After spells at the Ministry of Trade and Industry, and then as minister of defence, chairman of the Monetary Authority of Singapore, minister of finance and deputy prime minister, he became prime minister in succession to Goh Chok Tong in August 2004.

Although *The Economist* has carped that 'The authorities are not yet ready to allow Singaporeans complete freedom to chew gum . . .'[11], and the international press has, over the years, produced litanies of minor complaints at the lack of civic freedoms, it is difficult to argue with the spectacular success of Singapore in advancing the educational, health and material prospects of its citizens.

The Philippines

The forcing from office of Joseph Estrada, who had been elected to office in 1998, was a sign of the increasing maturity of the Philippine political system. Although his impeachment trial had to be aborted when 11 senators refused to open the envelope supposedly containing proof of his corruption, he eventually yielded to popular pressure on the streets and left office in January 2001. In May, he was arrested and charged with 'plunder'.

Estrada was replaced by his former deputy Gloria Macapagal-Arroyo. The daughter of the president who had lost his office to President Marcos in the 1960s, Gloria Arroyo was an experienced politician who had worked in the administration of Corazón Aquino. Appointed secretary of the Ministry of Social Welfare and Development as well as deputy president to Estrada, she resigned her positions to join in the popular calls for his removal from office. Macapagal-Arroyo replaced Estrada in 2001 and ruled well enough to secure re-election in June 2004. In 2003 she had forcefully put down an attempted military coup which occupied a hotel and shopping mall in Makati City in Manila.

After her election victory in 2004, the president soon became embroiled in charges of electoral corruption. Later in 2006, Brigadier General Danilo Lim was arrested for plotting a coup d'état. In November, during his trial with supposed co-conspirators, he and others walked out of their trial and seized the second floor of Manila's Peninsula Hotel. The farcical rebellion came to an end when an army armoured personnel carrier dramatically smashed into the hotel's lobby. Within days a Makati court dismissed all charges against the so-called conspirators.

In spite of the sometimes comedic spectacle of the Filipino domestic politics, economic performance, averaging over 4.5 per cent real GDP growth under the presidency of Macapagal-Arroyo, has exceeded that of any of her recent predecessors.

Indonesia

After the withdrawal of Suharto's successor, President Habibie, from the presidential contest in October 1999, a close presidential contest resulted in victory for Abdurrahman Wahid who garnered 373 votes to Megawati's 313. After street riots in support of Megawati Sukarnoputri, daughter of President Sukarno, Indonesia's founding first president, she was appointed vice president. It was a necessary compromise in the febrile atmosphere of Indonesian politics that followed the toppling of President Suharto after the 1997 Asian economic crisis.

President Wahid (often known as *Gus Dur*) had proved a successful gatherer of moderate Muslim political influence in the coalition of Muslim groupings known as *Nahdlatul Ulama* (NU). In the aftermath of Suharto's resignation, Wahid decided to form a more conventional political party as a competitor to GOLKAR, the ruling state party that had been developed by Suharto. The thus formed PKB (the National Awakening Party), albeit dominated by former NU members, was declared a secular organisation open to all. Curiously it would be with the support of GOLKAR, anxious to keep Megawati from the presidency, which would enable the *Gus Dur*, PKB leader, to win enough votes for the presidency.

As president however, Wahid, with many accusations of corruption against him, proved an unmitigated disaster, managing to alienate all sections of the political elite as well as popular support. His cabinet turned against him, and on 23 July 2001 the MPR instigated impeachment proceedings. With the army also bringing pressure to bear, Wahid resigned and flew to America for medical treatment on 25 July.

Wahid was replaced in office by Megawati, who somewhat bizarrely withdrew from day-to-day activity in government, seeing her role as largely symbolic; in her quasi-absence the military regained much of the power that it had temporarily lost with the fall of Suharto. Although she contested the 2004 elections, Megawati fought an inept campaign which was badly undermined by her lack of leadership in the office of the presidency. After her defeat, she slipped quietly back into private anonymity, not even acknowledging, let alone attending, the inauguration of her successor.

Former General Susilo Bambang Yudhoyono was sworn into office on 20 October 2004. Susilo, as he was known in Indonesia, was a career officer who had been destined for high command since graduating top of his class at the Indonesian Army Academy in 1973. He served in a wide range of military capacities, even spending a year in Bosnia-Herzegovina as the chief military observer for the United Nations Peacekeeping Force. Having been appointed to President Wahid's first cabinet as minister of energy and mines, General Susilo was moved within a year to the key role of minister for politics and security. In this latter post he was required to mediate between Wahid and former President Suharto and to organise the removal of the army from Indonesian political life. In both tasks he was stymied by the developing crisis of Wahid's own presidency.

Ultimately, General Susilo gained a probably undeserved reputation for political liberalism when he refused to implement a state of emergency demanded by Wahid to shore up his crumbling rule. The dismissal of General Susilo sounded the death knell of Wahid's presidency and the trigger to the motion for his impeachment.

This event was to play out in almost identical fashion while serving under President Megawati. Here too as minister for politics and security, he eventually refused to attend her cabinet and resigned his position while calling a press conference to announce his candidacy for president. The fairly run elections, which saw a turnout of 80 per cent of registered voters, was a victory for Susilo and the democratic process. As *The Economist* observed on 18 September 2004, 'Less than a decade ago, democratic elections in Indonesia were nothing but a pipe-dream. Now they are becoming routine.'[12]

General Susilo's presidency was marked by series of natural disasters including the Asian Tsunami which devastated Aceh Province; the eruption of Mount

Merapi, a major earthquake in Yogyakarta, and a further tsunami in West Java. In addition, Indonesia was badly affected by the deadly bird flu. Government responses to these disasters were much criticised, and General Susilo received his fair share of popular opprobrium. On the positive side, rising oil and commodity prices, and a return of foreign investment, helped Indonesia to achieve a more than 5.5 per cent per annum growth in real GDP since his election.

Reflecting this improved performance, Susilo's ruling Democrat Party won 148 seats in the 9 April 2009 elections, comfortably ahead of GOLKAR (108) and Megawati's PDIP (93). On 8 July 2009 incumbent President Susilo won a landslide victory in the Presidential elections.

Burma

The continued incarceration under house arrest of popular Burmese leader Aung San continues to dominate international perceptions of this once-prosperous British colony. Prime minister elect Aung San has been detained since her National League for Democracy Party won a governing mandate in 1990's assembly elections. The Sakharov and Nobel Prizes awarded to her have been scant compensation for people whose country has experienced one of the world's most regressive governments.

Burma remains under the governance of a military dictatorship which operates a de facto Marxist–Leninist regime where in effect most of the country's productive assets are owned or controlled by the army. Wealth where it exists comes mainly from Burma's only flourishing free market industry – narcotics – though much of this business too is in the hands of the military. The most recent popular revolt against Burma's military tyranny, led by Burma's Buddhist monks in 2007, was brutally crushed. Burma's long-suffering people are now among the poorest in the world, and in Asia, the country's inept management and impoverished outlook is only matched by North Korea.

2009 saw the arrest, trial, guilty verdict and 18 month sentence for Aung San Suu Kyi for allowing a cranky American to swim across a lake and stay in her residence. Though it has been widely speculated that this show trial was done to exclude her from participation in forthcoming elections, her treatment by the Burmese government has done nothing to enhance the reputation of the regime whose future, in any case, remains secure as long it remains within the Chinese orbit of influence.

India

Having initiated the dramatic shift to a market economy under the unlikely leadership of Prime Minister Narasimha Rao, the Congress Party, without a Gandhi at the helm, fell into a period of factional strife. Electoral decline was furthered by the rise of strong regional and ethnic parties. By contrast the rising BJP, a pro-business and Hindu nationalist party, appeared focussed and more in tune with the desire for a new beginning for India that emerged in the early 1990s. Following two

weak coalition governments in 1996 and 1998, in which the BJP-dominated National Democratic Alliance (NDA) was brought down by its partners, the BJP, with
a record 183 seats in the October 1999 elections, at last won a strong governing
mandate.

India now embarked on its second wave of concerted pro-market reforms.
Prime Minister Atal Bihari Vajpayee and his Finance Minister Yashwant Sinha pushed
through a major privatisation programme combined with further deregulation of
rules on foreign ownership and investment. An open-sky policy brought a boom
in airline investment and capacity. Furthermore, the BJP copied the spectacular
success of Deng Xiaoping's Special Economic Zones, which had done so much to
encourage foreign direct investment and technology transfer in China.

Internationally the BJP also focussed on economics. A South Asia Free Trade
Agreement was signed with Pakistan, Nepal, Bangladesh and Sri Lanka in 2004;
before this, a historic reconciliation was achieved with Pakistan by the Lahore Declaration, which committed India to peace with its northern neighbour. In 1999
Vajpayee himself rode the inaugural Delhi–Lahore bus. Although a 2002 summit
with President Musharraf failed, the feeling emerged that, in spite of Islamic terrorist attempts to unsettle the relationship, the rapprochement between the two
countries was unlikely to be reversed.

With India now launched on the track of spectacular real GDP growth, it was
assumed that Vajpayee would easily win the 2004 elections. However, the BJP's
'India shining' slogan failed to take account of the fact that India's largely rural population had not yet felt any benefit from the country's economic take-off. As Robert
Stern wrote in *Changing India* (2003), improvements in living standards were not
taking place 'among the poor. It is taking place in its expanding middle classes'.[13]
Although the Indian Planning Commission noted that the number of people living
below the poverty line had decreased from 36 per cent to 27 per cent in the ten
years to 1999–2000, that still left a staggering 270 million in this group. Also, the
BJP's political fortunes sank spectacularly in states where it had allied itself with
unpopular ruling parties such as the AIADMK (All India Anna Dravida Munnetra
Kazhagam) in Tamil Nadu and the TDP (Telugu Desam Party) in Andhra Pradesh.

Congress's shock victory at the head of the United Progressive Alliance brought
to the fore perhaps the most unlikely Asian leader of post-war history. Born in the
small Italian town of Lusiana, which, nestling in the foothills of the Southern Alps,
lies some 50 km north from Vicenza, Sonia Gandhi's (née *Edvige Antonia Albina
Maino*) family moved to Orbassano near Milan where her father developed a small
building contracting business. However, in 1964 they were not wealthy enough to
entirely fund her move to Cambridge to study English at the Bell Language School
and, when Rajiv Gandhi, studying at Trinity College, Cambridge, wooed her, she
was still earning her keep by waitressing.

They married in 1969 and Sonia then lived the life of a wealthy suburban wife
of an Indian Airlines pilot. With Rajiv she was catapulted into Indian politics after
the murder of Indira Gandhi and again after the assassination of her husband; she

was left with two young children and became the effective holder of the Gandhi-Congress Party franchise. Elected to the presidency of Congress in 1998, after the 2004 elections she found herself in the remarkable position of being an Italian-born prime minister elect of India.

Although not the first foreign-born female president of Congress (an honour which went to the Clapham, London-born English woman Annie Besant in 1917), Sonia Gandhi was nevertheless the first foreigner to hold real power. It was an astonishing and, to some and possibly most of all to her, a terrifying prospect.

However, in a move of unusual perspicacity and good judgement, Sonia Gandhi took the remarkable decision to step back from the prime ministerial role; perhaps realising that winning votes was a different skill to managing her adopted country, Sonia offered the prime ministership to Manmohan Singh, the Sikh technocrat finance minister who had so effectively transformed India into a market economy under Narasimha Rao in 1991. Also with the appointment of the intellectually brilliant P. V. Chidambaram as finance minister, India now had a formidable pro-market team driving economic regeneration. Entrepreneurs and investors breathed a collective sigh of relief and have since driven the Indian economy to new heights of growth and emergent prosperity. On Sonia's part it was a masterstroke. It can only be imagined where India would place in the world had Nehru, Indira Gandhi and Rajiv Gandhi, all brilliant vote gatherers, appointed pro-market technocrats to govern the country.

To the relief of international investors and Indian business alike, in the 2009 Lok Sabha elections Congress Party increased its representation to 206 seats and with its partners in the UPA (United Progressive Alliance) set about forming a virtually unchanged government.

Pakistan

While post-war India has gone from strength to strength, Pakistan, its Partition sibling, has remained mired in difficulty. While the usurpation of government by General Musharraf brought a welcome return to technocratic management of the economy and a marked improvement in its performance, international events served to undermine the new president. In the aftermath of Al-Qaeda's attack on the World Trade Centre on 11 September 2001, Pakistan moved to the frontline in the 'war on terror' announced by President George W. Bush.

Although Musharraf proved a loyal American ally in the fight against radical Islamic terrorist groups including Al-Qaeda's protectors, the Taliban, who governed Afghanistan until they were toppled by Afghan warlords financed by America, the retreat of the Taliban and Al-Qaeda, including it is assumed Osama Bin Laden, to the mountainous and inaccessible tribal borderlands of Pakistan created a long-term problem for the new Pakistan leadership.

In spite of the billions of US dollars poured into the Pakistan military, not only did the Pakistan army make no headway in rooting Taliban out of their borders, but the Taliban themselves, having regrouped in the Pakistan borders, made a strong military comeback in southern Afghanistan. Many in Congress asked with increasing stridency what exactly America was receiving from Musharraf for its capacious military subsidies?

The result of the Taliban comeback has been that the British, French and American armies, as part of the NATO force in Afghanistan, have by some accounts, since 2005, been involved in some of the heaviest and most prolonged military actions seen since the Second World War. From an increasingly fractious and now dominant Democratic Party in the US Congress, the attacks on Musharraf, a man easily portrayed as a stooge and proxy of President George W. Bush, increased markedly. Furthermore, military action by the Pakistan army against the Taliban in the tribal areas wrought havoc with displacement of the indigenous population; in the short term at least the results of this policy have been to radicalise the local population and bring about a wave of suicide bombing to urban Pakistan for the first time.

Neither did Musharraf help his own cause by his constant delays to the reintroduction of democracy which undermined his pleas that his military coup was intended to restore democracy to Pakistan. Moreover, although the economy undoubtedly improved, it was also true that the key beneficiary was the Pakistan Army, which has assumed an even more pivotal role in the financial and economic control of the country. Perhaps not surprisingly, given the records of Benazir and Sharif, Musharraf displayed an obvious contempt for the political caste which ran Pakistan after Partition and placed all his trust in military colleagues. Rumours of corruption, one of the long-term banes of Pakistani political life, remained widespread.

Musharraf's growing unpopularity was given focus by his undermining of the independence of the judiciary by his sacking of Chief Judge Iftikhar Muhammad Chaudhry on 9 March 2007. Waves of popular protest led by Pakistan's lawyers soon followed. Although both Benazir and Sharif, as former prime ministers, had themselves been accused of tampering with the judiciary, they launched into a popular if hypocritical defence of the democratic virtues of an independent judiciary.

To make his situation worse, Musharraf's violent suppression of the radical clerics inside the Lal Masjid Mosque alienated large swathes of even the more moderate 'Islamist' element of the population. With the risk that Musharraf might be toppled, with unknown quantities to fill his shoes, and facing increasing opprobrium for its support for a ruler seen in the western media as increasingly dictatorial, the US department began to look to a solution which would show that Pakistan was moving back towards democracy.

The strategy focused on Pakistan People's Party leader Benazir Bhutto. Benazir, a highly capable schmoozer with the western media and the political elite in Washington and London, put herself forward as the secular and anti-terrorist candidate capable of challenging the Taliban.

Ever the opportunist, Benazir believed her moment had come to make a triumphal re-entry into Pakistan politics; for a weakened Musharraf, forced to give up his post as chief of army staff in order to run for president, Benazir was the only alternative given that Nawaz Sharif, still leader of the Pakistan Muslim League, was the man loathed for having almost killed Musharraf in his attempt to remove him from military command. For the State Department, it was hoped that a Benazir–Musharraf alliance would improve Pakistan's performance in the fight against Muslim extremism while burnishing the Bush presidency's pro-democratic credentials.

The somewhat optimistic plan seemed to be on track before a second attempt on Benazir's life, since her return to Pakistan, succeeded in killing her. Benazir, another of the sub-continent's charismatic harvester of votes, had just finished a political rally when, ignoring the advice of her security advisers, she stood up through the sun roof of her SUV and presented herself as a target to a radical Islamic assassin. It was a tragic death. However, given Benazir's abysmal record of performance in office and her poor history of co-habitation with the Pakistan army, it seems doubtful whether she could have been a solution to Pakistan's long-term problems.

The feudal nature of Pakistan's politics was displayed in her political will, in which she bequeathed her party jointly to her husband Zardari, a man formerly known as 'Mr. 10 per cent' because of his alleged corruption, and her 19-year-old son Bilawal Bhutto-Zardari, a carefree student at Christchurch College, Oxford. At the press conference at which Benazir's son's distinctly un-democratic political inheritance was announced, Bilawal aggressively declared, without a trace of irony, that with regard to his mother's assassination, 'Democracy is the best revenge.'[14]

Within months of the two opposition parties to Musharraf winning the postponed parliamentary election and vowing to form a coalition government, Zardari had fallen out with Sharif. However, they later reached an accommodation to seek the impeachment of President Musharraf and forced him to resign. It was the ultimate revenge of the demagogues; not surprising, Zardari and Sharif soon fell out, and it was Zardari who became Pakistan's new prime minister and was left to face an effective civil war against the Taliban in the border territories, increasing waves of terrorist bombing, both within Pakistan and outside, notably the Mumbai Massacre of 26 November 2008, as well as a collapsing economy. Although in 2009 the Pakistan government finally took action to repel the Taliban, which had advanced down the Swatte valley to within 100 km of the capital, bizarrely the Pakistan Army continued to assert that India remained the greater threat to the country.

Bangladesh

Prime Minister Khaleda Zia, leader of the Bangladesh Nationalist Party (BNP), resigned her third term of office on 27 October 2006. Chaos ensued. A fight for the control of the appointment of chief advisor to the caretaker government was fought out on the streets between supporters of the BNP and the Awami League, led by its long-term leader Sheikh Hasina. Zia's broadly pro-business government had collapsed in a torrent of accusations of corruption. Subsequently in March and April 2007, both of Prime Minister Khaleda Zia's sons were arrested.

With Bangladesh's two warring women leaders having failed to agree, a neutral caretaker, Chief Advisor, President Iajuddin Ahmed, was forced to step in and assume this mantle himself. The notoriously obstinate Sheikh Hasina continued to claim that the electoral process had taken an unconstitutional path and that the system was biased against the Awami League. In effect Sheikh Hasina boycotted future elections.

After a year of bewildering legal process in which the exile of Zia and Hasina was mooted, on 11 January 2007 an exasperated President Iajuddin resigned as chief advisor while admitting that his caretaker government and the electoral commission had failed to produce conditions conducive for the holding of elections. As Professor Craig Baxter observed of Bangladesh's two long-serving party leaders after the 1996 elections, 'Chances for stability would be enhanced if the opposition's respect for the government and the government's respect for the opposition – so clearly missing in the previous parliament – were to develop with the new administration.'[15] Unfortunately, over the ensuing decade, the mutual distrust and detestation of these two embittered women seemed to have deteriorated even further. As political commentator Mizanur Rahman Shelly noted in *The Independent* (Dhaka) on 24 October 1995, the Bangladeshi 'predicament is the impractical stubbornness of their leaders to come to terms as to how a civil society should resolve its problems in a civilized manner'.[16]

While remaining president, Iajuddin appointed Fakhruddin Ahmed as chief advisor, and supported by the army, his government attempted to crack down on political corruption while organising conditions for an electoral poll by the end of 2008. In the meantime the army restricted press freedom, and both leaders of the main political parties continued to face legal proceedings. In spite of these difficulties the electoral poll took place with Sheikh Hasina and her Awami League campaigning on the promise of 'Digital Bangladesh', winning a landslide victory over her long-standing BNP opponent, Begum Zia.

Sri Lanka

Dealing with the Marxist–Leninist Tamil Tigers (the LTTE) remained the single largest issue dominating Sri Lankan political life. In December 2001, President Chandrika Bandaranaike Kumaratunga was forced to 'cohabit' with Prime Minister Ranil Wickremasinghe after his UNP defeated the president's People's Alliance.

In February 2002, Wickremasinghe negotiated a 'permanent' ceasefire with the Tamil Tigers and agreed to conduct peace talks in Norway. However, on 4 November 2003, using the justification that the UNP was yielding too much to the Tamil Tigers, President Kumaratunga suspended parliament while her prime minister was visiting America and unilaterally deployed the Sri Lankan army.

New elections were called and President Kumaratunga joined forces with the leftist JVP (*Janatha Vimukthi Peramuna*; People's Liberation Front); the resulting 25-party coalition, the UPFA (United People's Freedom Alliance) won elections held on 2 April 2004 and formed a government with Mahinda Rajapaksa as prime minister. When the Supreme Court rejected Kumaratunga's bid to extend her constitutional term after 25 November 2005, she was replaced by Rajapaksa, who won the ensuing presidential election. The extremely violent conflict with the Tamil Tigers continued unabated. However, after peace negotiations again broke down in 2006, President Rajapaksa launched an aggressive military campaign which by the spring of 2009 appears to have resulted in the complete defeat of the Tamil Tigers and re-capture of all the territory under their control.

To the undoubted relief of the government the infamous leader of the Tamil Tigers, Velupillai Prabhakaran, while fleeing in an ambulance, was killed in one of the final engagements of the conflict.

Vietnam

With a population of 85 million people, Vietnam has emerged over the last 20 years as Asia's newest tiger economy with a real GDP growth rate of 8.2 per cent in 2006, expected to be exceeded in the year ending 2007. Like China, the Vietnam government retained a single-party and autocratic governmental system while pursuing increasingly pro-market reforms, including land privatisation and the development of capital markets.

When *Doi Moi* (literally 'renovation'), an equivalent to the Soviet Union's *perestroika*, was started in 1986, Saigon's central squares were still usurped for volley ball games rather than being used for non-existent traffic. Under the dead weight of Marxist–Leninism, Vietnam's economy had ground to a halt, and its government adopted even more aggressive policies to encourage foreign direct investment after the dissolution of its Soviet sponsor in the early 1990s.

Most importantly, Vietnam's young population appears to have left behind the legacy of war and embraced the free market. As Ho Si Khoach, a professor of history at Hô Chí Minh University, concluded about his students in almost wistful manner, 'We looked ahead to war. They look ahead to peace.... They don't want to study the subjects we did – history, philosophy, poetry. The majors they're choosing now are business, economics, English language, computer sciences.'[17] As a mark of its arrival in the global economy, Vietnam was granted entry into the World Trade Organisation in November 2006.

Cambodia

Reacting to the collapse of socialism in the Soviet Union on 17 October 1990 the ruling Kampuchean People's Revolutionary Party held a Congress and officially abandoned Marxist–Leninism. The name of the party was changed there and then to the Cambodian People's Party (CPP), and they committed themselves also to the development of a free market economy and liberal democracy. They immediately threw themselves on the mercy of the United Nations whose first members of the Advance Mission (UNAMIC) arrived three weeks later. For the UN it was a new and daunting task. As UN Secretary General Pérez de Cuéllar remarked, it 'will probably be the biggest and most complex [mission] in the history of the United Nations'.[18]

Under the auspices of the United Nations and copious amounts of aid from the USA and Europe, a new constitution was promulgated in 1993, which was a parliamentary system headed by a symbolic constitutional monarch. King Norodom Sihamoni was elected to office by a nine-man throne council after the surprise abdication of King Norodom Sihanouk in 2004.

Cambodia's Prime Minister Hun Sen has effectively ruled the country since 1985 when it was still under Vietnamese military occupation. Since 1993, he has ruled as leader of the CPP, though because of the peculiarities of the constitution which do not allow a party to rule alone with less than two-thirds of parliamentary seats, he has for most of this period ruled in partnership with the royalist FUNCINPEC (Front Uni National pour un Cambodge Indépendant, Neutre, Pacifique, et Coopératif) led by Prince Norodom Ranariddh. The only exception to this coalition was a military coup in 1997 by troops loyal to Hun Sen, after which Prince Ranariddh was removed from office. This bloody spat was patched up after July 2003 elections in which Hun Sen again won most seats but failed to secure a two-thirds majority.

Like its neighbours Vietnam and Laos, from the early 1990s Cambodia moved down a free market track, though it became notorious for the dominance in its economy of political corruption and the operation of mafia gangs. Inevitably the economy was held back by the protracted war against remnants of the Khmer Rouge, and it was only in 1999 that the country experienced its first year of peace in 30 years. Nevertheless, from a dauntingly low base, the Cambodian economy achieved a real GDP growth rate in excess of 8 per cent in 2007, and it is expected that it will participate in the market-led regeneration of Indochina in the decade ahead.

Remarkably, it was only in 2007 that the arrest and prosecution began of those Khmer leaders who were responsible for the 'killing fields' by which name the genocide of Cambodians in the mid-1970s is best known. Arrestees included Kang Kek lew (Aka *Duch*), the head of the notorious Tuol Sleng prison, from which few of its inmates ever emerged, and Khieu Samphan, a close friend and confidante of Pol Pot and Nuon Chea, second in command to Pol Pot during the period of his rule between 1975 and 1979. Although *Duch* has been put on trial, it remains an open question whether most of the accused will live long enough to stand trial or, like their leader Pol Pot (who died in 1998), will die of natural causes before conviction and punishment are handed out.

62

From Cold War to End of Empire

America-Asia: 1945–2010

> If America were to become a dropout in assuming the responsibility for defending
> peace and freedom in the world ... the rest of the world would live in terror....
> (President Nixon)[1]

President Roosevelt envisaged a post-war world in which his wartime allies including the Soviet Union would participate in a global federation, ultimately realised
in the United Nations, which would maintain global peace and security. It was
a dream that, for Roosevelt's successor Harry Truman, would be dashed by Soviet expansionism and their perpetuation of an autarkic socialist trading system.
In response, America had to abandon its utopian vision of the post-war world.
In its place, the USA created its own defensive empire based on military alliances
with other liberal democracies, and nations which accepted a market-oriented economic system. It became a bi-polar world. Now, some 60 years later, with America
triumphant in the Cold War against its adversary, the Soviet Union, and with the
rebalancing of global economic power, a new world order has begun to emerge.

'To Serve and Not to Dominate the World'

The path to a system of global governance was signposted in a key address made
in Chicago on 5 October 1937. Here, President Franklin D. Roosevelt (FDR) first
signalled that he had come to the conclusion that American isolationism, which had
characterised American foreign policy since the First World War, was no longer
intellectually tenable. 'The peace, the freedom, and the security of 90% of the
world is being jeopardised by the remaining 10% who are threatening a breakdown
of all international order and law. . . ,' he declared, '. . . The moral consciousness of
the world . . . must be aroused to the cardinal necessity of honouring the sanctity
of treaties, of respecting the rights and liberties of others and of putting an end to
acts of international aggression'.[2]

From this point onwards, Roosevelt set America on course to prepare for a
global conflict in which he felt that his country would have to participate. In effect,
Roosevelt was seeking to expand the scope of the Monroe Doctrine, which at its

inception in 1823 had proclaimed America's right to intervene to protect South American countries from European hegemony. But now the Monroe Doctrine would embrace the whole world in its defence against Nazi and Japanese aggression. It was a turning point of immense importance, which dictated the course of American foreign policy for the second half of the twentieth century; notably every president since Roosevelt's Chicago speech has followed the path of 'global responsibility'.

In 1937, Roosevelt had predicted to H.G. Wells, author of *War of the Worlds* (1898), that a new world war would break out in 1941. In December 1937, America would get a foretaste of what was to come when the gunboat *USS Panay*, anchored on the Yangtze River was sunk by Japanese bombers. In an hour-long attack, two oil tankers belonging to Standard Oil were also sunk. Although in this instance Japan apologised and paid US$ 2 million in compensation, the aggressive intent of this emerging Asian power was clear.

Roosevelt did not just look eastwards for threats; his main preoccupation was the threat from Europe. In March 1939, FDR organised an exercise for the US's Pacific fleet, including a passage through the Panama Canal, which was clearly intended as an exercise for the defence of America from an invasion launched from Europe. The role envisaged for America by FDR was not lost on Germany's Nazi elite; Adolf Hitler, in his speech of 28 April 1939, in which he revoked the non-aggression pact with Poland, concluded with remarks aimed squarely at the American president:

> Mr. Roosevelt, I fully understand that the vastness of your nation and the immense wealth of your country allow you to feel responsible for the history of the world and the history of all nations. I, Sir, am placed in a much more modest and smaller sphere.[3]

Hitler was correct. Roosevelt did now feel responsible for 'all nations'; America, FDR realised, was the global giant and there was no getting around this fact. If Americans wished to live in a peaceful world, they would have to organise it.

> As early as 1922 British Conservative Party leader had admitted that Britain no longer had the resources to police the world. By contrast Roosevelt declared in December 1940, the United States was the 'great arsenal of democracy' against 'a gang of outlaws'.[4]

The creation of a post-war world would be imbued with all of America's values; a world without empires, with national self-determinism, democracy, free trade and a world policed by a confederation of allies.

Roosevelt's utopian vision was endorsed by President Harry Truman; in his first speech to Congress on 16 April 1945, he asserted that 'The responsibility of a great state is to serve and not to dominate the world.'[5] Like Roosevelt, Truman believed that a collective of the victorious powers would oversee a benign new world order. It was a somewhat naive hope.

The propensity to issue international moral lectures became a feature of post-war American foreign policy. President Roosevelt, and many of his successors, showed a peculiar lack of self-knowledge; not only was America an Imperial nation, possessed of its own empire, but in seeking to destroy the empires of others while at the same time imposing a confederated global governance, America could only succeed in expanding its own global hegemony. This proved most true of Asia where the political vacuum created by the economic chaos of the post-war period, and the departure of the European Empires, was even greater than that of Europe.

The Soviet Dynamic

The optimistic global political vision of Roosevelt inherited by his successor Harry Truman was soon dispelled. The United Nations (a term first used by Roosevelt) was established on 24 October 1945 by 51 nations with a permanent Security Council comprising the USA, the Soviet Union, China, Britain and France. It soon became stymied by the reversion of the Soviet Union to the promotion of global revolution. The wartime alliance, which the Americans believed would follow through in the post-war period to the extent that the US Bureau of Foreign and Domestic Commerce and American companies were eagerly preparing for a trade boom with the Soviets, was simply one of convenience for Stalin. In the event, the trade boom never materialised.

Far from being a partner in building a stable post-war future, the Soviet Union was now an implacable enemy. The problem as Robert Conquest pointed out in *Reflections on a Ravaged Century* (1999) was that in the Union of Soviet Socialist Republics (USSR), any socialist utopian ideals or 'any real connection with proletarian interest has long since evaporated'.[6] It was a development which was perhaps most brilliantly portrayed in George Orwell's satirical novel, *Animal Farm* (1945). The Soviet Union had become the most cynical of power structures. The Jewish journalist and playwright Isaak Babel told a friend that 'Today a man only talks freely to his wife_ at night, with the blankets pulled over his head.'[7]

Sadly he failed to take his own advice. In 1938, in a conversation which was later reported to the police and led to his execution, Babel opined that 'Soviet power is only sustained by ideology. Without that it would be over in ten years.'[8] The Soviet Union, bereft of moral or economic virtue, could only maintain its vitality by instilling in its people the constant threat of foreign attack. Xan Smiley, a foreign correspondent, observed in *The Daily Telegraph* on 14 December 1987 that Russians were stupefied when told that Britain and America had given up compulsory National Military Service; 'They always look at me in disbelief. Everything here is mentally geared up for war. Readiness for war against capitalism is part of the education.'[9] Soviets were bred for perpetual hostility towards the West.

Alexander Solzhenitsyn, author of *One Day in the Life of Ivan Denisovich* (1962) and *The Gulag Archipelago* (1973–8), also recognised that the Soviet socialist system was so corrupt, venal and pointless that it could not brook any self-examination; by necessity, 'The primitive refusal to compromise is elevated into a theoretical principle and is regarded as the pinnacle of orthodoxy.'[10] To sustain a system bereft of any internal logic, the Soviet Union ended with the exercise of power reaching 'transcendental heights' of arbitrariness.[11]

Here was an enemy totally incomprehensible to the American political elite. Though even within America, a country not unfamiliar with utopian sects, Marxist–Leninism did make some inroads; as George Kennan, former consular analyst in Moscow, to whom would fall the task of waking the Truman administration to the Soviet threat, would recall in his *Memoirs 1950–1963* (1972), 'The penetration of the American governmental services by members or agents [conscious or otherwise] of the American communist party in the late 1930s was not a figment of the imagination of the hysterical right-wingers of a later decade.'[12] Senator Eugene McCarthy's unsavoury demagogic witch hunt to 'out' American communists merely served to undermine those who genuinely sought to combat Soviet propaganda and influence.

The death of Stalin did not change Soviet expansionist ambitions. Khrushchev may have engaged in detente with the West, but this was little more than a deception to allow him to undertake a much more aggressive policy of communist expansion in the Third World. As Khrushchev's biographer, William Taubman, has noted in *Khrushchev, The Man and His Era* (2003), 'By barnstorming abroad, by smothering foreign statesmen with personal attention, by breaking through distrust with his own energy and tenacity, he would woo the West while at the same time undermining it.'[13] Khrushchev, a heavy drinker of Russian vodka, would, in private, spew venom against the West. The apogee of his duplicitous international strategy of detente was the binding of President Kennedy to 'neutrality' for Laos at their Vienna Summit on 4 June 1961; overshadowed at the time by the issue of 'Berlin' and other matters, it was a disastrous mistake by Kennedy, which ultimately led to America's loss of Indochina to Soviet domination.

The root cause of Soviet hostility did not simply lie in Deputy Foreign Minister Maxim Litvinov's assertion that '. . . conflict between the Communist and capitalist world was inevitable'.[14] His troops having spied the relative wealth of even Poland and the Balkans, let alone Germany, compared with the abysmal conditions of the Soviet Union, Stalin had no choice but to retreat behind ideological barriers.

Boris Pasternak, author of the seminal post-war novel *Doctor Zhivago* (1957), felt that after the war there was a 'presage of freedom in the air'.[15] He was to be cruelly disappointed. As far as maintaining the Soviet power structure, Stalin and Khrushchev and their successors were right to be paranoid in sustaining an inflexible front; as soon as Gorbachev publicly put a mirror up to the Soviet system, it crumbled within years. Isaak Babel's forecast that without a sustained belief in its ideology, the Soviet Union would collapse, did ultimately prove correct.

America's Post-War Asian Empire

For the Truman administration, the revelation of the Soviet Union's true nature changed the direction of the post-war political settlement. Given the Soviet veto and later the communist Chinese veto, the original point of the United Nations as conceived by the USA was now void; it could no longer be viewed as a 'confederation' of responsible nations dedicated to the rule of law and global co-operation.

As for allies, Britain, as noted by observers on both sides of the Atlantic, was now a 'busted flush' and it could no longer serve as a near-equal partner in holding back the communist menace in Europe, let alone Asia; as early as 13 August 1945, Lord Keynes had written a memo stating, 'our external policies are very far from being adjusted to impending realities'.[16]

Keynes projected a cumulative net deficit of £1.25 billion over the three years from 1946 to 1948 and that was being optimistic; 'The conclusion is inescapable,' wrote Keynes, 'that there is no source from which we can raise sufficient funds to enable us to live and spend on the scale we contemplate except the United States.'[17]

The means by which America would now have to seek a stable world order had to change. They would have to lead a federation of subordinate allies; the express purpose of these new structures would be to fend off the expansion of the Soviet Empire. In 1949, the North Atlantic Treaty Organisation (NATO) was signed with European allies and formed the bastion of anti-Soviet defence in Europe. Although President De Gaulle seemingly pulled out of NATO in a theatrical flourish in 1958, France remained only semi-detached with protocols for how it would reintegrate its forces if required. Like Britain, France also developed an independent nuclear deterrent. However, as Robert Kagan has pointed out in *Power and Paradise* (2003), 'France's Force de Frappe was largely symbolic and did not relieve dependence on the US.'[18]

In Asia, America also had to re-evaluate FDR's attitude to the European Empires. With the fall of China to Marxist–Leninism, America was left bereft of heavyweight allies in Asia, as it had been by the incapacity of Britain in Europe. While America was able to leave relatively minor engagements such as the defeat of communism in Malaysia to Britain, in Vietnam America gave massive support to France in their efforts to stem Hô Chí Minh's communist onslaught from the North. By the time of the French debacle at Diên Biên Phu, the USA was providing some 80 per cent of France's military costs in Indochina.

By contrast to the US government's hostility to French Empire in the immediate aftermath of the Second World War, when in Algeria in 1957 Senator J.F. Kennedy had given a speech of encouragement to anti-French nationalists, he was slapped down by a furious President Eisenhower and his Secretary of State John Foster Dulles. Dean Acheson also rounded on Kennedy's 'foolish words that wound . . . a dispirited ally'.[19] In order to beef up the defence of Asian countries,

America sought to create in SEATO an Asian replica of NATO. However, these economies were too weak and too preoccupied with their own political development to be reliable pillars of support.

In reality, America had to rely on ad hoc alliances of sympathetic allies to confront the dangers of communist expansion. Although the Korean War was dressed up as a United Nations effort, after the fortunate absence of the Soviet Union, which had temporarily withdrawn from the organisation, it was in effect an American war, first against a Soviet-equipped North Korean army and second against the Chinese People's Liberation Army. In Japan, America needed to change course by encouraging the revitalisation of a country whose industrial power it had originally intended to dismantle; Japan would be built up to become the main economic bulwark to communist advance in Asia.

Indeed before the end of the Second World War, America had realised that the envisaged international political structure alone could not guarantee global security. American analysis of the inter-war years had concluded that global financial instability, after the collapse of the Gold Standard and the protectionism that ensued, was the major cause of the 'Great Depression' and the political instability that followed.

As Cordell Hull, US secretary of state from 1933 to 1944, commented, 'When nations cannot get what they need by the normal processes of trade, they will continue to resort to the use of force.'[20] As early as 1943, Dean Acheson told a Congressional Committee that the post-war world required 'an arrangement which has the effect of increasing production in the world of consumption and employment, and reducing the barriers of trade and doing away with discrimination'.[21]

America was uniquely placed to ensure a smooth recovery path to global economic growth; in 1945, America, with just 5 per cent of the world population, accounted for over half of its Gross Domestic Product (GDP). The Bretton Woods agreement pegged global currencies to the dollar, giving it a quasi-Gold Standard status, which ensured international financial stability in the arduous recovery phase of the global economy after the Second World War.

In addition, stabilising institutions, such as the International Monetary Fund (IMF) and the World Bank, were underwritten by American economic power. The USA subscribed one-third of the US$ 9.1 billion capital for the International Bank for Reconstruction and Development (the World Bank). However, post-war economic reconstruction was mainly dependent on free trade, with the anchor being America's open market to foreign goods. By allowing the virtual pillage of its own markets by foreign goods, America bank-rolled the start up of Asian manufacturing. In addition, 'American capital' not only 'underwrote a staggering array of new technologies' but 'promoted their broad distribution around the world'.[22] Apart from funding the Marshall Plan in Europe, the USA was also a consistent donor of economic and military aid in Asia. As well as providing financial capital, the USA encouraged technology transfer to its trading partners.

In hindsight, it is easy to underestimate the scale of the task which America undertook in Asia. It was a region so poor that in 1946, the great South African leader, Jan Smuts, thought it was a continent almost inevitably lost to communism; 'The prospect of Asia', he wrote, 'is a pitiable one from the human point of view'.[23]

America did not shirk the economic challenge. Recipients of American aid included China (pre-revolution), Pakistan, India, Bangladesh, Sri Lanka, Thailand, Indonesia, Cambodia, Laos, South Vietnam, Korea, Taiwan and Japan. It was this combination of American financial munificence and the post-war Bretton Woods economic structure that would first rebuild Japan and later the whole of Asia. As President Truman concluded about the economic choices facing America after the Second World War:

> We are the giant of the economic world. Whether we like it or not, the future pattern of economic relations depends on us. The world is waiting and watching to see what we will do. The choice is ours. We can lead the nations to economic peace or we can plunge them into economic war.[24]

Although the political and economic structures created by America after the Second World War could not be described as altruistic, given American politicians' natural desire to further the economic goals of its own citizens, America demanded remarkably little from the countries within its embrace. Unlike that other expansionist democracy from a bygone age, fifth-century Athens, which converted the Delian League _ constructed to confront the threat of Persia to the Greek states _ into the Athenian Empire, America did not force its allies to pay annual 'tributes' for their protection. (Only when it had become as wealthy as America, did some arm twisting take place for Japan's government to contribute to wars such as the first gulf conflict in 1991; even then the amount was a pittance compared to the costs borne by the USA.)

Allies such as Thailand, Taiwan, Korea and Australia sent sizeable armies in support of American forces in Vietnam (as they had done before during the Korean War); it was a choice that was freely made. However, when military support was refused by allies, it was not followed by invasion, the toppling of Asian governments or the withdrawal of American aid.

Leaving aside vanquished Japan, with a few well-known exceptions, such as the assassination of President Diệm in South Vietnam, America intervened surprisingly little in the direction of domestic political development and almost never after the Watergate debacle of the early 1970s. Even when the CIA did try to control events in Asian countries, particularly in the immediate post-war period, they achieved very mixed success. In general, America only attempted intervention in domestic politics when there was a very real risk that a country would fall to communism. Otherwise, as President Nixon told Eric Sevareid of CBS news in January 1971, 'We recognized the right of any country to have internal policies and an internal government different from what we might approve of. What we were interested in was their policy toward us in the foreign policy field.'[25]

What is clear from the analysis of political developments in Asian nations after the Second World War is that America was almost always consistent in its championing of political self-determinism. President Lyndon Johnson declared:

> To any in Southeast Asia who ask our help in defending their freedom, we shall give it. In that region there is nothing we covet, nothing we seek_ no territory, no military position, no political ambition. Our one desire_ our one determination_ is that the people of Southeast Asia be left in peace to work out their own destinies in their own way.[26]

This was a sentiment that could have been expressed by any post-war American president.

Unlike past empires, including its own nineteenth-century conquest of the American continent, the USA did not seek to colonise Asia. The American Empire in Asia after 1945 was built on commerce and trade, not on territorial conquest. Although American administrations consistently sought advantageous opportunities for its corporations, they never made the right to trade on equal terms a prerequisite of its defensive umbrella; trade terms with Asian countries were invariably skewed against the USA.

Even when Asian competition threatened the future of the Detroit motor industry, a symbol of American economic power, America refused to buckle to demands to restrict free trade; as President Reagan would later comment, 'I believed that once we started down the road to protectionism, there would be no way back, no way of telling where it would end.'[27]

Indeed, America sustained an Asian trading system which was largely lopsided in favour of Asian countries, whether in terms of trade barriers or enforcement of technology patents. American presidents could always justify imbalances on the broader grounds that the prosperity of Asian nations and their contribution to global stability was in the long-term interest of the USA. In other words, as Robert Kagan noted in *Paradise and Power* (2004), 'The United States is a behemoth with a conscience.'[28]

The Damning of America

In spite of the apparent beneficence and 'light touch' of the American Empire, hostility to the USA has sometimes been almost as apparent among its beneficiaries as its enemies. In part, this has been driven by envy; in the Second World War, American servicemen in Britain were frequently referred to as 'overpaid, over-sexed and over here', a line attributed to the English comedian Tommy Trinder. America's wealth and power has, since the war, been as much envied as Britain's had been before the First World War.

For some Europeans, the end of the American economic power could not come soon enough. In 1991, Helmut Schmidt, the former socialist German chancellor (1974–82) mistaking the significance of a recession in the USA, declared categorically that 'Mrs. Thatcher is an awful woman and Ronald Reagan is very stupid. The Anglo-Saxon system is finished.'[29] As has already been noted, some elements within the European Union have always wanted to build Europe as a global political rival to the USA. In Japan and Asia, America's apparent omnipotence and the presence of its military and naval bases at Okinawa (Japan), Yokosuka (Japan), Osan (South Korea) and Subic Bay (the Philippines) inevitably led to resentment and the feeling that national sovereignty was being undermined.

Asian students who flocked to McDonalds in their Levi jeans to drink Coca-Cola and discuss James Dean movies often provided the most vociferous and hostile voices to these military manifestations of American power. Throughout Asia, anti-Americanism within the university systems was also a reflection of the growing influence of socialist utopianism, which became prevalent amongst the academic elite in the post-war period.

The Soviet Union, by adopting the iconographic methods of the Tsarist Russian Orthodox Church, had developed a brilliant state propaganda system to propagate Marxist–Leninism after the Russian Revolution. When it turned to international projection of its ideology, the Soviet Union was constantly able to out-manoeuvre western governments, whose liberal democratic values could easily be turned against them. In the international sphere, the Soviet Union spent unstintingly on propaganda aimed at undermining the West's resistance. The Soviet politburo was quite open in this strategy. In *The Foreign Policy of the Soviet Union* (1975), Andrei Gromyko, foreign minister under Brezhnev, asserted that 'The Communist Party subordinates all its theoretical and practical activity in the sphere of foreign relations to the task of strengthening the position of socialism, and the interests of further developing and deepening the world revolutionary process.'[30] It was not a strategy calculated for the pragmatic advance of Soviet interests. Later, Alexander Belonogov, former Soviet ambassador to the United Nations suggested that 'the hyper-ideologization of foreign policy in the past often strongly prevented us from discerning where our interests lay in the international arena'.[31]

Detente was not designed as a means of developing peaceful economic and political coexistence with the West; it was part of a broader strategic plan to deflect international suspicions of the Soviet Union. 'In conditions of slackened international tension, the pointer of the political barometer moves left', Brezhnev told a conference of European and communist parties at Karlovy Vary in Czechoslovakia on 24 April 1967; 'Our party', he continued, 'has always warned that in the ideological field there can be no peaceful existence, just as there can be no class peace between the proletariat and the bourgeoisie'.[32]

The Soviet Union successfully infiltrated Western and Asian media organisations to spread its message. German and French media organisations were well known to be full of journalists on the Soviet payroll. They were rarely 'outed'. However, in France in 1980, the journalist Pierre-Charles Pathe and his Soviet handlers, who worked at UNESCO, were convicted. Throughout Asia, journalists could be bought at much lower cost; in India, it was thought that as many as 100 journalists were on the Soviet payroll. The Soviet Union invested US$ 100 million alone in the anti-neutron bomb campaign in Europe.

Politicians were also won over either by direct funding or organised junkets to the Soviet Union in which they were 'Potemkined'. These propaganda campaigns also proved very successful in painting Western leaders as 'dangerous'. Remarkably, in spite of the invasion of Afghanistan by the Soviet Union in 1979, in that year, an analysis of American newspapers showed that the word 'bellicose' was linked with Ronald Reagan 211 times, Margaret Thatcher 41 times and Leonid Brezhnev just 5 times.

In reality, American politicians, far from being consistently bellicose, were preoccupied with the concept of restraint. American presidents were all too aware of the dangers of America's extraordinary power; in his farewell address, President Eisenhower, often portrayed as the archetype of the American geopolitical 'hawk', warned against the '... conjunction of an immense military establishment and large arms industry. ... In the councils of government, we must guard against the acquisition of unwarranted influence, whether sought or unsought, by the military–industrial complex'.[33] From the moment when the USA developed the atom bomb, the issue of restraint had been high up the agenda of American governments.

Perhaps the most successful Soviet propaganda strategy, however, was the inculcation of the idea of 'moral equivalence'; thus to take the most extreme example, America's attempt to defend South Vietnam was deemed to be an immoral act even though it was North Vietnam that was invading the South. Perversely America, which never attempted to invade or conquer North Vietnam, was painted as the aggressor nation.

The Vietnamese and Korean wars were portrayed by American critics as the aggression of a superpower against the 'people'. Yet in both these countries, where people were given the choice between the Marxist–Leninism state to the North or its alternative in the South, millions walked towards freedom. The exodus from these Marxist–Leninist states would have been greater in both cases if Hồ Chí Minh and Kim Il Sung had not closed the borders and imposed regimes of brutal repression to prevent further disaffection.

Noam Chomsky in *American Power* (1967) compared the USA in Vietnam to the Nazis in Poland. He also propagated the myth put about by North Vietnamese and Soviet propaganda, not only that USA was the aggressor but also that in the Vietnam War a sophisticated American industrial society attacked an agricultural society without modern weaponry, 'We can hardly avoid asking ourselves to what extent the American people bear responsibility for the savage American assault on a largely rural population in Vietnam....'[34] In reality, North Vietnamese forces and the *Việt Cộng* were provided with the latest Soviet equipment, not just rifles, machine guns and mortars but also tanks, heavy artillery and the most up-to-date warplanes.

The fact that the USA was fighting a proxy war with the Soviet Union in Vietnam is still ignored by some. During his presidential candidacy in 2004, when Senator John Kerry, himself a Vietnam veteran, was asked by CNN why he had advocated withdrawal from Vietnam (but not from Iraq), he answered by means of justification that the Vietnam War was a 'civil war'. Leaving aside the degree to which the Iraq War could be described as a civil war after the American conquest in 2003, Kerry's answer implicitly denied the obvious fact that America was at war with the Soviet Union in Vietnam; whatever his views of the appropriateness of American Cold War strategy in Asia, to describe the Vietnam War as simply a 'civil war' was patently absurd.

Soviet propaganda filled American campuses from the mid-1960s onwards and helped to create a student mindset that was hostile to its own government. Howard Zinn would note with pride that during the last 'anti-war teach-in' at Brandeis University in 1975, a student ran down the aisle with the news that 'Saigon has fallen, The War is over; . . . the auditorium exploded in cheers.'[35] Even the moderate anti-war camp in America adopted a posture of anti-US militarism as if America was the invader of South Vietnam rather than its defender against communist attack. The young Bill Clinton, a Rhodes scholar, far removed from the later president who, providing the main air attack forces for NATO, bombed Serbia into submission, wrote to his local Reserve Officers' Training Corps (ROTC) to tell them that the leaders of his generation found themselves 'loving their country but hating their military'.[36]

The future President Clinton's opposition to the war was based on the arguments of his 'home town' hero, the Arkansas Senator William Fulbright, who in his book, *The Arrogance of Power* (1966), argued against the war on the grounds that America could not understand the complexities of Vietnamese politics and that communism was not itself monolithic but riven by nationalist rivalries. Fulbright was the longest serving Chairman of the Senate Foreign Relations Committee (1945–74) and a well-informed commentator, who gave a rational critique of American policy in Vietnam. In particular, he warned against military action by great powers acting with aggressive 'moralism'. Like most of his contemporaries however, Fulbright, who had become disillusioned with the war having at first supported it, did not understand that America's greatest miscalculation in Vietnam was the failure to grasp the military significance of Cambodia and Laos. As *Empires at War* has argued, it was the failure of presidents Kennedy and Johnson to adopt a coherent military strategy for the defence of the whole of Indochina, that sapped America's political will for the conflict.

The delight in the US defeat by certain sections of American society came as no surprise to an American public that had seen Hollywood celebrities such as Jane Fonda rooting for the enemy. After a visit to Hanoi in 1972, Jane Fonda had declared that President Nixon would '. . . never be able to turn Vietnam, north and south, into a neo-colony of the United States by bombing, invading, by attacking in any way'.[37] As Henry Kissinger concludes in his memoirs, 'The total collapse of non-communist Indochina, which three American administrations had striven to prevent in the name of national security and honour, was, for this group, nothing less than a desirable national catharsis.'[38]

'Moral equivalence' was the method by which America's fiercest post-war critics, such as Noam Chomsky and Howard Zinn in America, and John Pilger and Harold Pinter in Britain, could blind themselves to the nature of the foes that the USA was trying to oppose. Thus, Noam Chomsky could make the breath-taking claim that in the post-war era in Asia, 'The US essentially reconstructed the co-prosperity sphere of Japanese fascism though now as a component of the US-dominated global order'[39] – an assertion which completely ignored America's record in bringing freedom, democracy and prosperity to Asia. The contrast to Japan's Asian slave colonies could not have been starker. Leaving aside the ex-treme left, even relatively moderate liberal commentators such as the respected English historian Arnold Toynbee noted that 'The president . . . to the ears of peo-ples who have suffered from Western domination in the past, his voice sounds like the Kaiser's and like Hitler.'[40]

In part American party politics also played a significant role in the damn-ing of America. Vietnam was in essence a Democrat war initiated by President J.F. Kennedy and massively broadened in scale by his Democrat successor Lyndon Johnson. As soon as Richard Nixon became president, it became politically expe-dient for the Democrats to portray Vietnam as a Republican war. Nixon was not helped by the fact that, at the same time that he was reducing the scale of America's commitment to the war, he nevertheless had to expand the net of military opera-tions to Cambodia and Laos in order to fight a strategically intelligent war against North Vietnam in a way that would force them to sign a peace treaty.

As historian Conrad Black has pointed out, 'Nixon should have known the Democrats well enough to know that they would wait the minimum period nec-essary before declaring Vietnam to be Nixon's war and then undercutting him at every opportunity.'[41] (Political opportunism during the Cold War was not con-fined to the Democrats; Dwight Eisenhower and the Republicans had been equally exploitative of an unpopular war in Korea to enable a landslide defeat of Demo-crat presidential nominee Adlai Stevenson in 1952.) Tactics that were cynical but not unexpected in the context of the US party system nevertheless, with regard to Vietnam, did a large amount of the Soviet's propaganda for them. It can be counted a failure of Nixon that while he was locked into tactics of secrecy in the operation of his international diplomacy, he failed to counter the Democrat charges. Neither did it help that his plan to extricate America from Vietnam with honour took far longer than he had bargained for.

In many cases, the internal criticism of American foreign policy was also a thinly veiled attack on America's free market economic system. Chomsky con-cluded that 'It is reasonably clear that unless the commercial and industrial system comes under some sort of popular democratic control, political democracy will be a sham and state power will continue to serve inhuman ends.'[42]

For many anti-Americans, the solution to its economic and political dominance has been not only to seek an illusory economic 'third way' but also an attempt to co-opt the USA into a 'world government' in which sovereign nations would be suborned to multinational institutions. Former head of the European Commission, Romano Prodi, claimed that European multilateral government

> ...has a role to play in world 'governance'....the rule of law has replaced the crude interplay of power ... power politics have lost their influence ... by making a success of integration we are demonstrating to the world that it is possible to create a method for peace.[43]

Indeed, 'world government' is a Kantian model much admired by European politicians, who realise that Europe itself lacks credible military power to back its foreign policy. As Metternich had once declared, diplomacy without an army is like music without an orchestra. Because of its weak military capability, Europe, the richest grouping of nations on the planet, is nevertheless a political pygmy on the global stage. Ignoring the reality that it was the USA, a sovereign nation, that created the conditions for post-war peace and prosperity, European leaders, when in disagreement with the USA, have been in the forefront of efforts to bind the American leviathan to international legal codes and agreements. It is thus somewhat of a paradox that subsequent to the collapse of the Soviet Empire, it has been the European Union which has been the largest beneficiary in terms of the eastward expansion of its hegemony.

Perversely, it was the USA which laid the foundations of this international legal system. In the heady utopian days which followed the Second World War, the USA pulled lawyers from all over the world to man War Crimes Tribunals at Nuremberg and Tokyo. It was a natural corollary of America's desire for a United Nations to act as a global governing federation that international law should be one of its main components; the organisation still describes itself as a 'global association of governments facilitating cooperation in *international law*, international security, economic development, and social equity'.[44] Codification of international law was also set in train after the Second World War by the creation of the International Law Commission.

The result has sometimes proven inimical to America's interests. The constraints of 'realpolitik' and the exercise of global power have sometimes brought the USA into conflict with the desire of other nations to expand the scope of international law. By contrast, European nations, bereft of real international power, have tended to support those legal scholars who claim that international law has now developed to a level that makes it not only independent but also superior to sovereign law. It is not surprising that, given its overwhelmingly important post-war role as the only capable global enforcer in the 'free world' and its historic belief in law as an instrument of democracy, America has largely continued to define international law as a construct which only derives legitimacy through sovereignty. However, the American government too has frequently used arguments of 'international law' when this has been convenient.

It has become a familiar mantra of the USA's political opponents, when America is in conflict with their interests, that the USA is acting 'illegally', an accusation frequently made about America's defence of South Vietnam. American bombing of *Việt Cộng* base camps and the Hồ Chí Minh trail in Laos and Cambodia was judged by many observers to be an 'illegal' attack on sovereign nations, even though those same critics never applied the same criteria to North Vietnam's military occupation of Cambodia, Laos and South Vietnam. The development of international law thus came to be an effective 'one way' propaganda stick with which opponents could beat America.

Reagan and Thatcher: Anglo-Saxon Revival

By the end of the 1970s, the moral high ground that America appeared to have inherited after the Second World War had been sharply eroded; to many eyes, including those of the Deng Xiaoping's China, America was not only losing the military battle for command of Asia but, under the withering fire of Soviet propaganda, was also losing the battle for 'hearts and minds'.

It seemed hardly possible that in just over a decade, the Soviet Union would not only be defeated in the Cold War and then lose its Eastern European and Asian Empires, but would disintegrate altogether. That this was achieved was in part due to the towering figures of President Ronald Reagan and Prime Minister Margaret Thatcher _ two highly articulate politicians who attacked Soviet propaganda head on.

In the aftermath of the loss of Vietnam and the Watergate scandal, the USA underwent a lengthy period of introspection, which enabled the 'moralistic' Jimmy Carter to defeat the incumbent Gerald Ford, who succeeded to the presidency after Nixon's resignation. In his memoirs, *Keeping Faith: Memoirs of a President* (1982), President Carter would recall:

> I was deeply troubled by the lies our people had been told; our exclusion from the shaping of American political and military policy in Vietnam, Cambodia, Chile, and other countries; and other embarrassing activities of our government, such as the CIA's role in plotting murder and other crimes.[45]

It was a self-criticism that could have been crafted by the Soviets. In an election address to the University of Notre Dame on 22 May 1977, Carter called for '... a new foreign policy based on constant decency in it values and an optimism in our historical vision'.[46] Zbigniew Brzezinski, President Carter's national security advisor averred that 'by emphasising human rights America could again make itself the carrier of human hope, the wave of the future ... restore America's political appeal to the Third World'.[47]

For Asian nations however, the Carter emphasis on human rights in American foreign policy was a sign of weakness not strength. While the Soviet Union appeared to be getting stronger, America's allies were becoming increasingly demoralised; in 1978, former British Prime Minister Harold Macmillan wrote, 'Things are as bad as they could be, and they are getting worse. The Europeans have to deal with the weakest American Administration in my lifetime.'[48] Although President Carter would, later in his term of office, begin the rebuilding of the American military and adopt a more traditional defence of America's interests, overall his presidency was the nadir of post-war American power and influence.

However, Carter's was a pessimistic message that a still youthful and vigorous USA would not accept twice. In the 1980's presidential race, Ronald Reagan, a masterful public performer, reminded the American people that the Soviets were the 'bad guys'; it was an upbeat message which began to reaffirm American belief in its own moral certainties and the superiority of its political and economic culture.

Rather than denigrating American values and culture, Reagan turned his guns on the abhorrent nature of the Soviet system. He recalled in 1989 that he was

> amazed that our national leaders had not philosophically and intellectually taken on the principles of Marxist–Leninism. We were always too worried we would offend the Soviets if we struck at anything so basic. Well, so what? Marxist–Leninism thought is an empty cupboard. Everyone knew it by the 1980s, but no one was saying it.[49]

'In foreign policy issues as in other matters,' Treasury Secretary Donald Regan noted of the president, 'he [Ronald Reagan] proceeded on the basis of his instincts and a few fundamental convictions: democracy supported by a market economy resulted in a better life for people everywhere than did Marxist–Leninism or other forms of totalitarianism based on planned economies'.[50] He reaffirmed the liberal Whig tradition that advocated the advance of western civilisation.

Reagan took the message to the enemy. In China, he extolled the virtues of free speech and the market economy and quoted from the Declaration of Independence, 'We believe in the dignity of each man, woman and child. Our entire system is founded on an appreciation of the special genius of each individual, and of his special right to make his own decisions and lead his own life';[51] while in Moscow, he lauded the openness of America compared to Russia when he recalled:

> a letter from a man [who] said you can go to live in France, but you cannot become a Frenchman; you can go to Germany, you cannot become a German_ or a Turk, or a Greek or whatever. But anyone, from any corner of the world, can come to live in America and become an American.[52]

At the Palace of Westminster, in a speech to the British Parliament on 8 June 1982, Reagan reaffirmed the Anglo-Saxon values and the sense of mission in America's battle with the Soviet Union, 'the Evil Empire' as he so famously called it.

> Historians looking back at our time will note the consistent restraint and peaceful intentions of the West. They will note it was the democracies who refused to use the

threat of their nuclear monopoly in the forties and fifties for territorial gains. Had that nuclear monopoly been in the hands of the Communist World, the map of Europe_ indeed, the world_ would look very different today.[53]

In President Reagan, the West found a champion who could more than match Soviet propaganda. At the same time British Prime Minister Thatcher, who became a close confidante and ally of Reagan, delivered equally strident and morally assertive statements on the superiority of Western and particularly Anglo-Saxon values.

Moreover, Reagan was not prepared to repeat the humiliations of the past; in April 1985, Reagan reminded journalists on the 10th anniversary of the fall of Saigon that

> We signed the peace accords . . . and we made a pledge to [Saigon]. And when the North Vietnamese did violate the agreement and the blitz started . . . and then the administration in Washington asked the Congress for the appropriations to keep our word, the Congress refused. We broke our pledge. . . .'[54]

Reagan backed up his vigorous stance against the Soviet Empire by calling for a dramatic US$ 1.5 billion increase in defence expenditure from 1981 including a range of new defence programmes such as the prodigiously expensive 'star wars' nuclear shield initiative, known as the Strategic Defence Initiative (SDI). Strobe Talbott later described it as 'the ultimate example of advertising an imaginary product'.[55] Yet it was a terrifying gauntlet thrown down to an increasingly bankrupt Soviet Union. In spite of Reagan's aggressive rhetoric, his presidency was peculiarly notable for its minimal military activity.

Indeed it was Great Britain's defeat of Argentina's military dictators in the Falklands War, under the leadership of Mrs Thatcher, that provided a turning point in Soviet and Asian perception of the West's rekindled determination to defend its civilisation and values, which during the 1970s had been written off as corrupt and in decline. As Alexander Haig pointed out in *Caveat* (1984):

> The Falklands crisis was the most useful and timely reminder of the true character of the West in many years. Indeed, Britain's actions in the Falklands may have marked a historic turning point in what has been a long and dangerous night of Western passivity.[56]

Collapse of the 'Evil' Empire

The USA did not fully regain its potent military image until the 1991 First Gulf War when, at the rapid and successful conclusion of Operation Desert Storm, President Bush (senior) was able to declare, 'By God, we've kicked the Vietnam syndrome once and for all.'[57]

But by this stage the Soviet Empire had already collapsed. As well as the intellectual revitalisation of the western mission, victory was brought about by the reinvigoration of the Anglo-Saxon market economic system by Reagan and

Thatcher; this coincided with the disastrous Soviet invasion of Afghanistan, which overstretched an economy, already ravaged by socialist central planning.

In the 20 years to 1990, it was estimated that Soviet GDP fell by at least 25 per cent; by that time the military–industrial complex of the Soviet Union was absorbing more than 40 per cent of the nation's resources. In 1991, a year which began in Kuwait with the American destruction of Iraq's army was followed in August by the Soviet army's attempted coup against Gorbachev in August 1991, and ended with liquidation of the Soviet Union.

On 8 December, the presidents of Russia, Ukraine and Belarus signed the Belavezha Accords which formally dissolved the union and established the Commonwealth of Independent States in its place; on Christmas Day, President Gorbachev resigned his presidency of the USSR and yielded power to Boris Yeltsin, and on the following day, 26 December, the senior government body, the Supreme Soviet, dissolved itself. It was perhaps less well understood that this date also marked the high tide of American Empire.

Although after the dissolution of the Soviet Union, some commentators, particular among the neo-conservative hawks, saw in China another enemy for America to combat. They were wrong; the reality was that China too had been vanquished. After Mao, Secretary of State Alexander Haig observed that the Chinese leadership had become 'weary of impractical theory and revolutionary religiosity. . . '.[58] In March 1984, Ronald Reagan noted that 'Treasury Secretary [Regan] had come back from a trip to Beijing with an intriguing report: The People's Republic of China was moving slowly but surely toward acceptance of a free enterprise market, and inviting investment from foreign capitalists.'[59] To these acute observers, including President George Bush (senior) who had spent a year as ambassador in Beijing, it was already clear by the late 1980s that China was being co-opted into the American trading world envisaged in the post-war 'confederated' system.

Even after the Tiananmen Square episode in 1989, President Bush (senior), ignoring the extreme measures urged by some neo-cons and indeed liberals, issued no more than formulaic protests against China. Notably, Bush did not withdraw China's most favoured nation (MFN) status. (China had been granted MFN status after the restoration of full diplomatic relations in 1979, but because of the Jackson–Vanik amendment, it was made subject to annual review depending on 'human rights'.) President Bush (senior) realised that it was far more important for America's long-term interest to embrace China's emerging free market economy and draw it into the global trading system.

As former President Ronald Reagan pointed out:

> . . . there were people in their government trying slowly to increase democracy and freedom in China, and the student's revolt, as courageous as it was, might in the long run have made it more difficult for them to carry out what they were trying to do.[60]

The determination to stand by trade commitments to China in spite of the Tiananmen Square episode is a legacy for which President Bush (senior) has rarely been given due credit. President Bill Clinton continued Bush's 'soft' approach to China when in 1994 he cut the link between 'human rights' and the annual granting of MFN status; 'We are far more likely to have human rights advances when it is not under the cloud of the annual question of MFN review.'[61]

Indeed, China had moved far further down the track of democratic development than many of Washington's hawks were prepared to admit. The foundations of democracy in the West were based on the development of property rights enshrined in *Magna Carta*; America's own revolution in the War of Independence was also started in the name of property rights not democracy as defined by universal franchise, which came much later. In this respect, China, which by the early 1980s, under Deng Xiaoping's guidance, had moved to allow individuals to own property under law, made the first crucial step along the path of free market development and democracy.

Deng, who had visited the USA in 1979, told an Asian leader, 'If I were born again China might have a market economy today.'[62] Subsequently, civil rights have advanced substantially and China has also allowed a limited experiment in franchise in Hong Kong. It is now a commonplace that China is a major component of a global world trading system, which was one of the keys to America's post-war Asian strategy; indeed, the value of China's exports to the USA now exceed those of Japan. To a large degree, China has largely fulfilled the role envisaged for it by Roosevelt and Truman in the 1940s.

In summary, the reinvigoration of the Anglo-Saxon economies and their determination to confront the Soviet Union head on was an important component of American victory in the Cold War. However, it was above all the implosion of an ossified socialist command economy system in Russia, China and indeed India, which presaged the collapse of Soviet hegemonic ambitions. By the end of the 1980s, those who ran these Communist Bloc countries no longer believed in the ideologies that had sustained them. The war of empires in the post-war world was ultimately as much lost by the Soviet Union as it was won by the USA.

Peace Dividend: Global Expansion of American Values

With the Cold War won, George Bush (senior) lost the presidency during a recession in which his opponent, Bill Clinton, had canvassed on the domestic economy, with his campaign team reminding itself that 'it's the economy, stupid';[63] Clinton, whose administration benefited from a sparkling autonomous economic recovery enabled by the supply-side reforms of the Reagan years, now found itself bereft of purpose. 'Foreign policy is not what I came here to do,'[64] he reportedly complained after the first three months of his presidency.

Yet geopolitics provided President Clinton with the most scope for creativity; in part this reflected the structure of the American constitution which gives the presidency much greater executive powers in foreign affairs than domestic policy, but in part it was also because Clinton was faced with a barrage of international policy issues. Clinton was the first elected post-war president to face a world without having to face a hostile Soviet Union. Now the problem was a collapsing Russian economy which nevertheless had a nuclear arsenal. Also without the Cold War, foreign policy was a blank page. At first Clinton struggled to fill it; having set out to be a 'domestic' president, Clinton fell back on the foreign policy advice of Anthony Lake, a former Kissinger aide who became Clinton's national security advisor, to sustain his presidency; Clinton, a highly intelligent and articulate politician, now proffered a muscular and interventionist foreign policy which, laced with 'Wilsonian' moralism, sought to contain rogue states and 'enlarge' American cultural and economic presence.

The Clinton administration, in an earlier form of George W. Bush's 'Axis of evil', identified five rogue 'Backlash States' (Iraq, Iran, Libya, North Korea and Cuba) and noted their pursuit of gaining access to 'weapons of mass destruction' (WMD); although Clinton discussed the possibility of invading Iraq with Newt Gingrich, Republican House leader (who told him that there was no Congressional support for this), he ultimately plumped for a policy of vigorous containment, which included constant aerial bombardment of Saddam Hussein's suspect facilities. In addition, he ordered air strikes against Baghdad after Saddam Hussein's attempted assassination of former President George Bush in June 1993. Later, President Clinton authorised the bombing of supposed terror camps in Afghanistan and the destruction of a pharmaceutical plant in Khartoum, Sudan, in response to the suspected Osama Bin Laden attacks on the US embassies in Kenya and Tanzania on 7 August 1998.

In his paper *Confronting Backlash States* (1994), Lake outlined an aggressive American foreign policy which sought '. . . to neutralize, contain, and, through selective pressure, perhaps eventually transform these backlash states . . . into constructive members of the international community'.[65] Apart from the almost continuous bombing of Iraq, Clinton's two most active policies were his bombing of Serbia and subsequent invasion of Kosovo, both done without United Nation's approval, and his attempt to bribe North Korea to give up uranium enrichment and its development of nuclear weapons. However, for Clinton 'Enlargement' became the keynote word for the new American foreign policy, which was in essence a reversion to America's traditional policy of commercial expansion, a policy which its detractors described as economic imperialism. Clinton, increasingly concerned with national competitiveness, created the National Economic Council with the aim of promoting exports and elevated the status of the Commerce Department which was put under Ron Brown.

Also, adopting the strategy advocated by White House Advisor Robert Zoellick, Clinton focussed his economic 'Engagement and Enlargement' strategy on the 'Big Emerging Markets' (BEM). The BEM strategy, which was a refinement of his predecessor's Asian strategy, focussed on China and India in particular and was a recognition that the weight of global economic power was moving towards Asia. As Under Secretary of State for Commerce and International Trade Jeffrey Garten noted, 'We are entering an era when foreign policy and national security will increasingly revolve around our commercial interests, and when economic diplomacy will be essential to resolving the great issues of our time.'[66]

In effect, Clinton returned America to the 'utopian' path on which it had set out after the Second World War. With the defeat of the Soviet Empire, and the capitalist transformation of China, there were no perceived enemies. America could now return to a 'confederated' approach to global rule which it had envisioned with the establishment of the United Nations, and a global free trade system within which American enterprise could flourish. As President Clinton's intervention in Serbia and Iraq indicated, this did not mean that America would abstain from an active interventionist foreign policy.

Through 'Engagement and Enlargement', President Clinton sought to embed American commercial and cultural power across the globe. It was a strategy of expansion, with its emphasis on trade and wealth creation, which was entirely consistent with American history. However, it was not empire building in the classic meaning of the word. The expansion of American cultural and commercial interest implied neither political nor territorial domination. Even the 'anti-Vietnam War' Bill Clinton rushed to the defence of American intentions when Communist Party leader Lê Khà Phiêu, during a historic visit to Hô Chí Minh City in November 2000, urged him to repudiate the US imperialism in Vietnam; 'I told the leader in no uncertain terms that while I had disagreed with our Vietnamese policy, those who had pursued it were not imperialists or colonialists, but good people who believed that they were fighting communism.'[67]

Beginning of the End of America's Empire

The clash of empires, between the USA and the Soviet Union, which characterised the post-war era, and which had its more dramatic conflicts in the battle for control of Asia, ended with more of a whimper than a defining military conflict. The Soviet Empire collapsed on the anvil of a reinvigorated Anglo-Saxon belief in its moral and economic purpose, the failure of the socialist planned economy system and a war in Afghanistan on the outer fringes of Asia, which taxed Soviet economic capacity beyond endurance.

Meanwhile China, the Soviet Union's former ally, driven to despair by the inept economic and social experimentations of Mao, was brought from the edge of chaos towards a market-based economy by the pragmatic Deng Xiaoping. The Cold War had produced an unquestionable winner; the USA had become what many termed the world's only 'global superpower', though in reality America merely returned itself to the position of global supremacy that it had established as early as 1918. (In fact, even before the start of World War I, America was producing double the iron and steel output of the UK and Germany combined.)

The Al Qaeda attack on the World Trade Centre in 2001 and the sharp divisions that have emerged over President George W. Bush's decision to invade Afghanistan and Iraq have obscured the fact that since 1990, the world has largely moved towards the collective responsibility system envisioned by Roosevelt. America and the emerging great powers (Europe, China, India and Russia) all have Muslim populations, a minority of whom represent a terrorist threat; however, given the combined economic and military resources of these great powers, the threats of Al Qaeda and associated groups represent an uncomfortable but relatively minor disturbance to world order compared to the post-war threat posed by the now discredited Marxist–Leninism states. More importantly, all of the world's major power blocks share a vested interest in containing the threat of Muslim terrorism.

For the long term, it is perhaps more important to observe that China, Russia, India and Europe all supported United Nations resolutions aimed at limiting Iraq's access to WMD; the great powers also appear united in their wish to deprive both Iran's and North Korea's access to offensive nuclear capability.

With economic growth within the structure of an increasingly global free market in goods and services, for the time being at least, the issues that unite the world's most powerful nations are far greater than the issues that divide them. It is a trend towards ideological convergence that was identified by Francis Fukuyama in his seminal book, *The End of History* (1992).

It is interesting to note that today the defining issues that now divide nations revolve around climate change, carbon emissions, agricultural subsidies, competition for scarce resources and trade liberalisation. The ideological divisions of the Cold War have all but disappeared; even in Europe the semi-autarkic, *Colbertist* economic system sometimes championed by France in the post-war period now seems largely discredited. With the end of the era of post-war political leaders such as Mitterrand, Chirac and Helmut Kohl, the emergence of President Sarkozy in France and Chancellor Merkel in Germany has heralded a generational change towards a less parochial and more pro-American stance. The election of the liberal and highly articulate Barack Obama as president of the USA seems likely to encourage this trend. As Martin Walker recalled almost regretfully in *The New Yorker*:

> Now the age of geopolitics has given way to the age of what might be called geo-economics. The New virility symbols are exports and productivity and growth rates and the great international encounters are the trade pacts of the economic superpowers.[68]

In defeating the Soviet Union, America also set in train the dissolution of its own Asian Empire. As this book has argued, America's post-war hegemony was not held together by force alone, but by the common interest in contesting the expansion of the Marxist–Leninism states, the Soviet Union and China. In proclaiming, as President Reagan did, that '. . . freedom is not the sole prerogative of a lucky few, but the inalienable and universal right of all human beings',[69] America could not conceivably have sustained an empire after its battles with the Soviet Union and Maoist China were won.

The binding power of American Empire was the economic and financial structure including aid, which President Truman and his successors established in the post-war period under Bretton Woods. The World Bank and the IMF were the organs of this American Empire. However, the move by Asian countries towards models of liberal democracy, now largely complete, was mainly autonomous and not imposed. The combination of the retreat of Marxist–Leninism to marginal areas such as North Korea, Burma, and Nepal, and the rapid economic rise of the Asian nations, have loosened the bonds that tied Asia to the USA.

This was almost immediately apparent in Japan after 1991, where a United Nations voting record that had almost always been with the USA veered to an independent track. The change in mood was anticipated in the publication of an essay *'The Japan That Can Say No'* (1989) written by Akio Morita (founder of Sony) and Shintaro Ishihara (novelist, playwright and maverick politician who became governor of Tokyo in 1999), which advocated that 'Japan should provide for its own defences and follow its own strategic interests.'[70] It was a view to which all the Asian nations, because of their rising wealth, could increasingly subscribe.

There are now signs in America's 'sub-prime' credit crisis of 2007–09 that the post-war growth of US consumption, Asian imports and its financing by dollar debt have reached their limits; in effect this has been the mechanism, formed at Bretton Woods, by which America's commercial and political hegemony of Asia has been sustained. The seemingly unshakeable dollar which, since Bretton Woods, has formed the economic backbone of America's domination of Asia, may never regain its former role. The noted Asian economic strategist Christopher Wood (author of CLSA's strategy news report *Greed and Fear*) predicted from the outset that the American credit crisis could mark 'the final death throes of the US dollar paper standard'.[71] Also George Soros, the renowned financial speculator and economic commentator, has cogently argued that the 60-year super-boom in credit will end America's global economic and political power which will in turn shift to the creditor nations of Asia. It is nevertheless worth pointing out that one of the perverse effects of the global credit crisis, in the short term at least, was to precipitate a flight to the US dollar even though American institutions were the cause of the financial panic.

The use of the US dollar as the world's reserve currency may take some time to die. While it was clear to a UN commission comprising Joseph Stiglitz, the former

World Bank chief economist, that the Bretton Woods system, which created a global reserve currency based on the US dollar and enabled Americans to finance consumption from the savings of those countries which sell goods to America, is not a sustainable model, there remains limited appetite for change. This 'Vendor' finance system, which has built vast pools of dollar savings outside of America, means that the US Federal Reserve never has full control over its monetary system. Meanwhile, global savers are financing the US deficit at minimal interest cost. The size of the capital and trade imbalances between America and Asia were certainly contributory factors in the unusually deep global recession which started at the end of 2008.

In spite of the scale of the crisis, the Chinese proposal for the creation of a new world reserve currency was strongly rejected by Tim Geithner, President Obama's treasury secretary. However, Russia, China, India, Brazil and the Middle-Eastern petro-states have started a bandwagon of support for looking at ways to reduce the omniscience of the US dollar. Even IMF Chairman Dominique Strauss-Kahn has indicated that such discussions are 'legitimate'. A long-term move away from the use of the US dollar as the world's dominant reserve currency now seems certain.

As every year passes, America's weight of economic power relative to Asia diminishes. After the war, American Gross Domestic Product (GDP) represented over half of global GDP; by contrast, as measured on a purchasing power parity basis in 2004, the combined GDP of Asia's ten largest economies was US$ 19.6 trillion versus US$ 12.37 trillion for the USA and US$ 12.18 trillion for the European Union. Asia will soon exceed the combined GDP of America and Europe. With China, India and most Asian countries currently achieving annual GDP growth some two to three times greater than the USA, it is clear that the economic gap between Asia and the USA will grow rapidly.

Given that the population of Asia's ten largest economies is 3.22 billion (of which China and India account for 1.3 billion and 1.1 billion, respectively) compared to just 295 million in the USA and 456 million in Europe, it is not difficult to imagine, as long as these Asian countries continue to pursue a free market model, that the region will soon dominate global economic activity. As Samuel P. Huntington noted in *Clash of Civilisations* (1996), 'Power is shifting from the long predominant West to non-Western civilizations.'[72] Although this shift in economic power has not been sudden and in real GDP terms has been in process since the 1950s, it is only now that the geopolitical impact is being recognised.

At current growth rates, Chinese aggregate GDP (on a purchasing power parity basis) will exceed that of America within 20 years, while aggregate Indian GDP can be expected to overtake America within 50 years. Far from being part of an American hegemony, Japan, China, India and the smaller 'tiger' economies have already become fierce competitors to America; in particular, as Chinese commercial power expands, its regional influence, particularly in the Asian countries with a large Chinese diaspora, is increasingly challenging that of America.

The 2007–9 American credit crisis should not lead observers to dismiss America's future influence in Asia entirely; the US economy has been written off before and it would be a mistake to underestimate America's powers of recovery. Unlike Europe, Americans and their leaders have an unflagging belief in capitalist endeavour. Both Republicans and Democrats are largely resistant to the moral arguments offered for high taxation. Also, with regard to global influence, America remains the only country in the world able to project its military power on a global scale.

Nevertheless, the financial crisis in the USA, with the humiliating semi-nationalisation of some of its financial institutions and auto-manufacturers, has almost certainly speeded up the diminution of American hegemony in Asia. With the seemingly unstoppable relative decline of the US economy, it could also be argued that the world is moving towards the five power blocks (America, Russia, China, Europe and India) envisioned by Henry Kissinger in *Diplomacy* (1994). What is evident from current economic trends is that America, often described as the world's only superpower, will, most likely over the next 50 years, become only a great power among many. The age of America's global dominance, which, in reality, spanned almost the entire twentieth century, will come to an end in the twenty-first century.

Empires in Renewed Conflict?

Arguably, the convergence of the world's power blocks towards free market economics and their joint interest in controlling nuclear proliferation and the spread of Islamic fundamentalism brought a new stability to the world order. However, some problematic ideological and competitive divisions remain.

After a brief flirtation with democracy under President Yeltsin, Russia increasingly reverted to non-democratic authoritarianism. In spite of universal suffrage, Russia, under President Vladimir Putin, leader of an effective oligarchy of former KGB associates, retracted most of the features that characterise a democracy: the media was brought under government control, the political independence of provinces was curtailed, opposition parties and their political leaders were harassed and Chechnya, which tried to re-establish its historic independence, was crushed with its capital city, Grozny, all but obliterated by heavy bombing and shelling.

Many opponents of the Russian government were gunned down or otherwise died mysteriously. One of the best known, Anna Politkovskaya, the fearless journalist and author of *The Dirty War* (2003) and *Putin's Russia* (2004), was shot dead in her apartment elevator. The poisoning of a naturalised British citizen, Alexander Litvinenko, a KGB 'whistleblower', by polonium-210, a rare chemical element, 97 per cent of whose global production is Russian, suggested the strong possibility of state involvement in his murder. Meanwhile, with attacks on the assets of foreign companies such as BP p.l.c, even the right to own 'property under law' came into question.

Also, the Russian judiciary appeared to revert to its historic role as an arm of the state executive. Nevertheless, it could be argued that more economic and institutional progress has been made by Russia under the new authoritarian regime than under President Yeltsin, when the democratic state was dominated by the anarchic commercial warlordism of the 'business oligarchs'. In addition, it should be noted that Putin's Russia has not abolished capitalism though it has rowed back on liberal economics with regard to national control of natural resources and key industries. (Given the semi-nationalisation of key parts of the American and British financial system, credible criticism of Putin on this point, however justified, is going to be rendered virtually impossible for the foreseeable future.)

As evidenced by computer attacks on Estonia (where the evidence points to Russian involvement), the military occupation of Georgia and the increasing pressure on the Ukraine not to join NATO, a re-emergent, authoritarian Russia, buoyed by oil revenues (at least until mid-2008), appeared keen to not allow any further erosion of its regional hegemony. However, the costs of aggressive military behaviour in an integrated world economy soon became clear; even the limited military invasion of Georgia brought about immediate collapse in the Russian stock market and significant capital flight.

Annoyance with the West was perhaps understandable. At Russia's expense, 'democratic' Europe has been the most aggressively expansionist of the power blocks over the last decade. With American military power at its back, the European Union used the collapse of the Soviet Union to add Poland, Estonia, Latvia, Lithuania, Bulgaria, Rumania, Hungary, the Czech Republic, Slovakia and Slovenia to its regional hegemony. In all likelihood, other former communist Balkan states such as Croatia, Serbia and Bosnia-Herzigovina will also be added to the European Union. By the standards of any age, this would be called empire building.

Although the European Union would no doubt deny any charge of imperialism on the grounds that expansion was not achieved with force of arms, it was nevertheless made possible by America's victory in the Cold War. Also, the implicit defensive umbrella of NATO, with its American military capability, was one of the major perceived benefits of European absorption for the former 'Eastern Bloc' countries. European Union expansion has in a very real sense been achieved militarily, even though it was achieved with relatively little military input of its own. It would be naive to think that the Russian government and its proud people could look upon this loss of empire and regional influence to the European Union with anything but unhappiness; when Russia re-emerged with considerable economic success, the fact that it sought some redress of its loss of regional hegemony should have surprised no one.

The European Union clearly took advantage of its economic strength and military alliance with the USA in the 1990s to expand its empire; unlike the post-war

American Empire in Asia, the eastward expansion of the European Union, post-Cold War, has been structured *de facto* and *de jure* as an expanded part of its constitutional framework. The European Union's political smugness vis-à-vis Russia on account of its democratic credentials must also have rung hollow in the ears of its former Cold War adversaries; in spite of the accretion of the bulk of Europe's executive power since its inception, the European Commission and its president, who are appointed solely by political patronage, have noticeably failed to introduce any form of franchise to prove their democratic accountability. In addition, the failure of European governments (with the notable exception of Ireland) to offer their citizens a referendum on the Lisbon Treaty, a virtual repeat of the European Constitution, which was resoundly defeated by referendum in many of the countries that held one, represents a dismal failure of democratic intent.

Against this background, the question now being asked is whether a new Cold War is emerging? *The Return of History and the End of Dreams* (2008) by Robert Kagan and *The New Cold War* (2008) by Edward Lucas both argue that the American, European and the Asian democracies are facing new ideological battles for supremacy with Russia and China. Whether these battles augur a new Cold War or suggest a return to regional competition between power blocks is open to debate and indeed semantic definition. However, as none of the world's new empires are pushing for a return to socialist, autarkic, command economy systems, it seems unlikely that any new conflicts will take on the all-embracing antipathies of the past. It would be absurd to believe that ideological plans for global conquest, as was the case with Marxist–Leninism, will be revived by Russia. It should be remembered that 'command socialism' now only remains the preserve of a number of 'outlier' regimes such as North Korea, Burma and Cuba and a global jihadist movement to which all the world's major power blocks are implacably opposed.

Competition between empires need not necessarily mean conflict. China, in particular, has demonstrated that free market economic development is not incompatible with authoritarian government. Also, China has shown over the last 30 years that there is no reason why a developing free market economy controlled by an authoritarian political system cannot coexist with the liberal democracies of the USA, Europe, India, Japan and most of Asia. In historic perspective, the recent tensions in the Ukraine and Georgia may turn out to be little more than the adjustment of new borders between the power blocks. What is clear is that neither America nor the European Union, both of which encouraged Georgia's pro-western, anti-Russian stance, have any intention of backing up their support with military intervention.

Furthermore, the progress of the former military dictatorships of Asia, such as Korea and Taiwan, has demonstrated that economic liberalism, as it develops an economically and politically sophisticated populous, has had a tendency to push governments towards democratic norms. Even China, since Deng Xiaoping's assumption of power in the 1980s, has smoothed some of its authoritarian edges;

new communication and information technologies as well as greater freedom to travel have increased the demand and access to media and ideas which would be difficult for the Chinese state to fully control even if it wanted to. Since the reforms introduced by Deng Xiaoping in the early 1980s, China has also become a nation of property owners. A new property law, promulgated on 1 October 2007, for the first time gave private property equal status in law and protection to publicly owned property. It should not be forgotten that modern Anglo-Saxon democracy had its roots in property rights, which came a long time in advance of universal suffrage. Therefore, it is not inconceivable that both China and Russia, when they achieve a critical mass of middle-class property owners, may, over time, revert more towards the liberal western model of political development.

Conclusions

The post-war achievements of the American Empire in Asia have been extraordinary. Liberal democracy and market economics have become the mainstream doctrines of national development worldwide; all of the major nations, even Russia and China at least with regard to economics, subscribe in large degree to their tenets. These ideologies were not imposed on Asia in the totalitarian manner of Marxist–Leninism. Contrary to popular myth, the influence of the CIA on the political self-development in Asia was at best marginal. As Tim Weiner has concluded in *Legacy of Ashes: The History of the CIA*, 'The fictional CIA, the one that lives in novels and movies, is omnipotent. The myth of a golden age was of the CIA's own making . . . .'[73] Bretton Woods, not the CIA, was America's weapon of choice in the Cold War. In reality, it was largely through a process of political self-determinism and individual choice through the ballot box that the concepts of free trade and liberal democracy gained increasing traction throughout Asia; arguably, the belief in capitalism is now more vigorous in Asia than in Europe.

America may have provided a security blanket and open access to its consumer markets, but as the narrative of Asian countries covered by this book makes clear, liberal political and economic development was largely autonomous. As the experience of North Korea, North Vietnam and indeed Berlin and Eastern Europe has shown, when given the choice, individuals march with their feet towards liberty and capitalism.

The widespread acceptance of liberal democracy and free market economics in the latter part of the twentieth century is a far cry from the 19 democracies that emerged from the Second World War, where socialism held sway even in many of these countries. In the aftermath of this conflict, socialism appeared to offer many participants in the democratic process the alternative and possibly dominant path to future global economic and political development. In most of Europe, even the conservative parties, until the arrival of Mrs Thatcher as prime minister in Great Britain in 1979, adhered to the socialist consensus that certain of a nation's key industries should be run by the state. Even by 1974, only 39, or one in four countries, could be described as democratic. By the end of the millennium this figure had leapt to 117. By the end of the twentieth century, in the crucible of geopolitical competition, liberal democracy and American capitalism had proved crushingly victorious. America's victory was neither inevitable nor was it to easy to come by; it had to be fought for. It was a victory made possible by the reinterpretation of American foreign policy and its objectives by the two great twentieth-century Democrat presidents, Franklin D. Roosevelt and his successor Harry Truman. The latter, in his setting out the course of American policy at the start of the Cold War, proved an adept, pragmatic and courageous leader; as a somewhat innocuous sounding and looking Mid-Westerner, a former habidasher from Kansas City, Harry Truman was also one of the unlikeliest politicians to end up fronting the western response to the Soviet threat.

He also surrounded himself with such outstanding advisors, namely, General George Marshall, Dean Acheson, Averell Harriman, George Kennan, John McCloy, Robert Lovett and Charles Bohlen, that the historian Paul Johnson has described them as 'probably the finest group of American leaders since the Founding Fathers'.[74] From the experience of the two world wars, President Truman, like Roosevelt before him, realised that American security could not be guaranteed by passive isolationism. Truman was aware that if America did not actively fill power vacuums left by states in decline, particularly within the Asian sphere, then the Soviet Union with its powerful 'universal' ideology, inimical to the US long-term economic and security interests, might fill the void. Ultimately in the fighting of the Cold War, it should also not be forgotten that it was overwhelmingly American fighting men who paid with their lives to achieve the freedom which much of the world now takes for granted.

All American presidents, both Democrat and Republican, have since followed the foreign policy precepts and accepted the responsibilities set out by Roosevelt and Truman. The result was the creation of an American hegemony over most of Asia. However, by taking up the challenge that their overwhelming post-war economic and military strength demanded, America not only served its own interests but also saved large swathes of the world from the impoverishing tyranny of communism.

This ascendancy has not always made America popular; however, it would be salutary for America's critics to imagine a post-war world in which the American people had rejected the global vision of presidents Franklin Roosevelt and Harry Truman, and left Asia to be absorbed by the Marxist–Leninism ideologies of Stalin and Mao and their respective successors.

Bertrand Russell, the great British philosopher and pacifist, had written despairingly after the Second World War that America had the ability to 'establish a world empire by means of an atom bomb'[75]; the fact that America chose not to do so was an extraordinary testament to its moral character and virtues. The USA even refrained from conventional attacks to disable other states on the verge of acquiring nuclear weapons. In 1963, William Foster, President Kennedy's director of arms control and disarmament, urged that 'an anonymous airplane . . . go over there, take out the Chinese facilities . . . rather than face the threat of a China with nuclear weapons'.[76] In a pattern of restraint characteristic of all post-war presidents, Kennedy demurred from the exercise of the full weight of America's military power.

As Henry Kissinger observed, 'No empire has avoided the road to Caesarism unless, like the British Empire, it devolved its power before this process could develop . . . a deliberate quest for hegemony is the surest way to destroy the values that made the United States great.'[77] America's post-war Asian Empire was a hegemony built for mutual security and economic advancement, not a conquest for unilateral benefit or perpetual political domination.

American power did not lead to 'Caesarism'; having renounced territorial or colonial expansion in the first decade of the twentieth century, America sustained its belief in the right to political self-determinism of individual nation states even when, as after the Second World War, it possessed overwhelming economic and military power, not to mention its unique nuclear capability. After the Second World War, the USA, with its nuclear weaponry, had the capability to achieve absolute world power and spurned it.

Moreover, after expending vast resources, human and capital on the defeat of the Soviet Empire, the USA immediately started the process of helping to re-build Russia, for 45 years its bitter 'Cold War' enemy. Thus, President Clinton championed a US$ 2.5 billion Congressional aid programme for the former Soviet economies. The American government gave no thought to punishment. Neither was it altruistic; American governments since independence have always sought to enrich their own citizens through industry and commerce. With the continued US support of free market mechanisms, this endeavour has also enriched Asia.

The clash of empires, between economic liberalism on the one side and autarkic totalitarianism on the other, was played out in its most dramatic episodes in post-war Asia. The region, the world's most populous, which started the post-war period in grinding poverty, emerged, through America's free trade umbrella, by the end of the century as its fastest growing.

With the defeat of the Soviet Empire, the need for America's Asian Empire, indeed the raison d'etre for its existence and the glue of 'mutual security' that kept it together, has started to weaken. The rapid growth and increasing economic strength of the Asian economies has also served to nurture the unbundling process; a process which the US government may not like, but which it has not tried to reverse using force. The 2007–09 credit crisis which, at least in the short term, appears to have crushed the financial power of Wall Street, may also serve to bring the demise of Bretton Woods with its US dollar reserve currency system on which so much of America's post-war Asian hegemony has rested.

The speed of the 'unbundling' process in America's Asian Empire may also depend on the extent to which China begins to exert 'non-benign' regional power in the wake of its gathering economic might. A non-democratic China flexing its regional muscles might serve to extend America's hegemony as the smaller Asian countries could continue to choose American protection over that offered by China. More likely, many countries will prefer a balancing act by appeasing both sides. However, if, as Ross Terrill predicts in the conclusion to his book *The New Chinese Empire* (2004), 'China will produce a modern democratic state',[78] then the requirement for any vestiges of American hegemony may disappear altogether, although modern history provides ample evidence that even a democracy can behave as a bully. However China develops, the extinction of all traces of American hegemony in Asia is unlikely to be a short-term outcome.

America's central role in achieving the current global geopolitical stability was well put by President Ronald Reagan, the most articulate post-war exponent of American values. In a letter to the Soviet Union's leader Leonid Brezhnev, he wrote:

> When the Second World War ended, the United States had the only undamaged industrial power in the world. Our military might was at its peak_ and we alone had ultimate weapons; the nuclear weapon, with unquestionable ability to deliver it anywhere in the world. If we had sought world domination then, who could have opposed us? But the United States followed a different course_ one unique in all the history of mankind. We used our power and wealth to rebuild the war-ravaged economies of the world, including those nations who had been our enemies.[79]

No part of the world more clearly reflects the transforming effects of this strategy than Asia.

For the USA, the building of one of the world's most successful empires in the first 233 years of its history was a considerable achievement, but perhaps the greater accomplishment of the American people was to shield Asia, indeed the world, from communism after the Second World War, make its liberal democratic and economic values globally dominant, and its own empire increasingly redundant.

Notes

1. American Empire and Its Competitors

1. Toqueville, Alexis de, *Democracy in America* (Chicago: University of Chicago Press, 2002) p.267
2. Johnson, Paul, *A History of the American People* (New York: Harper Collins, 1997) p.998
3. Williams, E.N., *The Ancient Regime in Europe: Government & Society in the Major States 1648–1789* (London: The Bodley Head, 1970) p.3
4. *Ibid.*, p.3
5. Kissinger, Henry, *Diplomacy* (New York: Touchstone, 1994) p.20
6. Williams, *The Ancient Regime in Europe*, p.4
7. Harvey, Robert, *Liberators, Latin America's Struggle for Independence 1810–1830* (London: John Murray, 2000) p.3
8. *Ibid.*, p.249
9. Tuchman, Barbara, *The First Salute: A View of the American Revolution* (New York: Ballentine Books, 1988) p.42
10. Williams, *The Ancient Regime in Europe*, pp.4–5
11. *Ibid.*, p.14
12. Johnson, *A History of the American People*, p.139
13. Williams, *The Ancient Regime in Europe*, p.496
14. Tuchman, *The First Salute*, p.298
15. Harvey, *Liberators*, p.23
16. *Gone With the Wind* [1938 Film], opening scene
17. *Gone With the Wind* [1938 Film], last scene
18. Morison, Samuel, Henry Steele Commager and William E. Leutchenburg, *The Growth of the American Republic*, Vol 1 (London: Oxford University Press, 6th edition, 1969) p.230
19. Johnson, *A History of the American People*, p.216
20. *Ibid.*, p.257
21. *Ibid.*, p.266
22. Hague, William, *William Pitt the Younger* (London: Harper Collins, 2004) p.240
23. Harvey, *Liberators*, p.248
24. Morison, Commager and Leutchenburg, *The Growth of the American Republic*, Vol 1, p.411
25. Johnson, *A History of the American People*, p.379
26. *Ibid.*, p.379
27. Brands, H.W., *The Age of Gold* (London: Heinemann, 2005) p.30
28. *Ibid.*, p.450
29. Johnson, *A History of the American People*, p.278
30. *Ibid.*, p.280
31. Morison, Commager and Leutchenburg, *The Growth of the American Republic*, Vol 1, p.440
32. Brown, Dee, *Bury My Heart at Wounded Knee* (New York: Henry Holt & Co., 1970) p.90
33. *Ibid.*, p.67
34. Billington, R.A., *Westward Expansion: A History of the American Frontier* (New York: Experienced Books, 2nd edition, 1960) p.156

35. Brands, *The Age of Gold*, p.193
36. *Ibid.*, p.43
37. *Dodge City Times*, July 1877
38. Lumis, Trevor, *Pacific Paradises* (Melbourne: Pluto Press, 2005) p.170
39. *Ibid.*, p.175
40. *Ibid.*, p.175
41. Morison, Commager and Leutchenburg, *The Growth of the American Republic*, Vol 2, p.238
42. Lumis, *Pacific Paradises*, p.194
43. Morison, Commager and Leutchenburg, *The Growth of the American Republic*, Vol 2, p.241
44. *Ibid.*, p.242
45. Haines, Gerald and J. Samuel Walker (eds), *American Foreign Relations: A Historiographical Review* (London, Frances Pinter, 1981) p.49
46. *Ibid.*, p.133
47. Chomsky, Noam, *Deterring Democracy* (New York: Hill and Wang, 1992) p.124
48. Meade, Walter Russell, and Richard C. Leone (eds), *Special Providence* (New York, Alfred A. Knopf, 2002) p.106
49. *Ibid.*, p.115
50. Chomsky, *Deterring Democracy*, p.117
51. Morison, Commager and Leutchenburg, *The Growth of the American Republic*, Vol 2, p.313
52. Caro, Robert, *Master of the Senate: The Years of Lyndon Johnson* (New York: Alfred A. Knopf, 2002) p.36
53. *Ibid.*, p.36
54. *Ibid.*, p.36
55. Landes, David S., *The Unbound Prometheus* (Cambridge: Cambridge University Press, 1972) p.326
56. Williams, *The Ancient Regime in Europe*, p.498
57. Morison, Commager and Leutchenburg, *The Growth of the American Republic*, Vol 2, pp.257–8
58. *Ibid.*, p.316
59. Crockatt, Richard, *The Fifty Years Wars: United States and the Soviet Union in World Politics 1941–1991* (New York: Routledge, 1995) p.21
60. Kissinger, Henry, *Diplomacy*, p.24
61. Macmillan, Margaret, *Peacemakers: The Paris Conference of 1919 and its attempts to End War* (London: John Murray, 2002) p.17
62. *Ibid.*, p.240
63. Morison, Commager and Leutchenburg, *The Growth of the American Republic*, p.549
64. Crockatt, *The Fifty Years Wars*, p.22
65. Kissinger, *Diplomacy*, p.244
66. Macmillan, *Peacemakers*, p.17
67. Kissinger, *Diplomacy*, p.244
68. Macmillan, *Peacemakers*, p.17
69. *Ibid.*, p.19
70. *Ibid.*, p.325
71. Brendon, Piers, *The Dark Valley: A Panorama of the 1930s* (London: Jonathan Cape, 2000) p.178
72. Macmilan, *Peacemakers*, p.320
73. Barnett, Corelli, *The Collapse of British Power* (London: Pan Books, 2002) p.346

74. Smuts, *Jan Christian Smuts* (London, Cassell & Co., 2002) p. 360
75. Morison, Commager and Leutchenburg, *The Growth of the American Republic*, p.623
76. Madariaga, *Ivan the Terrible* (Yale University Press, 2005) p.95
77. Crockatt, *The Fifty Years Wars*, p.25
78. Maclean, Fitzroy, *Portrait of the Soviet Union* (London: Weidenfeld & Nicolson, 1987) p.37
79. Crockatt, *The Fifty Years Wars*, p.29
80. *Ibid.*, p.29
81. *Ibid.*, p.31
82. Mclain, James, *Japan, A Modern History* (New York: W.W. Norton & Co., 2002) p.294
83. *Ibid.*, p.296
84. *Ibid.*, p.296
85. Macmillan, *Peacemakers*, p.321
86. *Ibid.*, p.326
87. Macmillan, *Peacemakers*, p.321
88. Barnett, *The Collapse of British Power*, p.250
89. Macmillan, *Peacemakers*, p.55
90. *Ibid.*, p.340
91. *Ibid.*, p.343
92. Barnet, *The Collapse of British Power*, p.253
93. *Ibid.*, p.253
94. Chomsky, Noam, *American Power* (New York: The New Press, 1967) p.205
95. Brendon, *The Dark Valley*, p.176
96. *Ibid.*, p.187
97. Macmillan, *Peacemakers*, p.349
98. Morison, Commager and Leutchenburg, *The Growth of the American Republic*, p.623
99. *Ibid.*, p.623
100. *Ibid.*, p.544
101. Macmillan, *Peacemakers*, p.321
102. Crockatt, *The Fifty Years Wars*, p.44
103. Black, Conrad, *Franklin Delano Roosevelt* (London: Weidenfeld & Nicolson, 2003) p.683
104. *Ibid.*, p.679
105. *Ibid.*, p.683
106. Crockatt, *The Fifty Years Wars*, p.50
107. *Ibid.*, p.37
108. Kaplan, Amy and Donald E. Pease, *The Cultures of United States Imperialism* (Durham, Duke University Press, 1993) p.3
109. Ferguson, Niall, *Empire: How Britain Made the Modern World* (London: Allen Lane, 2002) p.370
110. Chomsky, *American Power*, p.207
111. Ward-Perkins, Bryan, *The Fall of Rome, and the End of Civilization* (New York: Oxford University Press, 2005) p.176
112. *Ibid.*, p.176
113. Haines and Walker (eds), *American Foreign Relations*, p.18
114. Kissinger, *Diplomacy*, p.238
115. Porter, Bernard, *Empire and Superempire,* (Newhaven, CT and London: Yale University Press, 2006) p.65
116. Kissinger, *Diplomacy*, p.239

117. *Ibid.*, p.238

118. *Ibid.*, p.238

119. Haines and Walker (eds), *American Foreign Relations*, p.66

120. Crockatt, *The Fifty Years Wars*, p.34

121. Adler, Selig, *The Isolationist Impulse: Its Twentieth Century Reaction* (New York, Abelard-Schuman Ltd., 1957) p.142

122. Meade, Russell and Leone, *Special Providence*, p.127

2. Potsdam, Hiroshima and the Atom Bomb

1. Rhodes, Richard, *The Making of the Atom Bomb* (New York: Touchstone, 1998) p.714

2. *Ibid.*, p.714

3. *Ibid.*, p.711

4. Regan, Donald T., *For the Recor* (London: Hutchinson, 1998) p.120

5. McCullough, David, *Truman* (New York: Simon & Schuster, 1992) p.456

6. *Ibid.*, p.412

7. *Ibid.*, p.447

8. Rhodes, *The Making of the Atom Bomb*, p.697

9. *Ibid.*, p.698

10. Ambrose and Brinkley (eds), *American Foreign Policy since 1938* (New York: Penguin, 8th revised edition, 1997) p.47

11. Chace, James, *Acheson, The Secretary of State who Created the American World* (New York: Simon & Schuster, 1998) p.120

12. McCullough, *Truman,* p.443

13. *Ibid.*, p.439

14. Bix, *Hirohito and the Making of Modern Japan* (New York: Harper Collins, 2001) p.513

15. *Ibid.*, p.509

16. Bix, *Hirohito and the Making of Modern Japan*, p.509

17. Bailey, Paul J., *Postwar Japan, 1945 to the Present* (Oxford: Blackwell Publishers, 1996) p.24

18. McCullough, *Truman,* p.413

19. *Ibid.*, p.459

20. Bix, *Hirohito and the Making of Modern Japan,* p.517

21. Behr, Edward, *Hirohito* (London: Hamish Hamilton, 1989) p.393

22. Storry, Richard, *A History of Modern Japan* (Harmondsworth: Penguin Books, 1990) p.233

23. McCullough, *Truman*, p.460

24. Bailey, *Postwar Japan*, p.21

25. Behr, *Hirohito*, p.377

3. Mao and the Chinese Revolution

1. Chang, Iris, *The Rape of Nanking: The Forgotten Holocaust of World War II* (New York: Basic Books, 2002) p.216

2. Salisbury, Harrison E., *The New Emperors: China in the Era of Deng and Mao* (London: Harper Collins, 1992) p.15

3. *Ibid.*, p.26

4. Kurnow, Stanley, *Mao and China* (London: John Murray, 1996) p.29

5. *Ibid.*, p.31

6. Becker, Jasper, *Hungry Ghosts: China's Secret Famine* (London: John Murray, 1996) p.28

7. Teiwes, Frederick C., 'The Establishment and Consolidation of the New Regime', in Mac-Farquhar, Roderick (ed.), *The Politics of China: The Eras of Mao and Deng* (New York: Cambridge University Press, 2nd edition, 1993) p.20

8. Johnson, Chalmers, *Revolutionary Change* (Boston: Little, Brown and Company, 1966) p.149

9. Becker, *Hungry Ghosts*, p.31

10. Crook, David and Isabel, *Ten Mile Inn, Revolution in a Chinese Village* (London: Routledge & Kegan Paul, 1959) p.62

11. Fairbank, John King, *The Great Chinese Revolution: 1800–1985* (New York: Harper and Row, 1986, and London: Windus, 1987) p.267

12. *Ibid.*, p.267

13. Evans, Richard, *Deng Xiaoping and the Making of Modern China* (London: Hamish Hamilton, 1993) p.113

14. McCullough, *Truman*, p.744

15. Crook, *Ten Mile Inn*, p.34

16. Mackerras, Colin, *East Asia*, p.236

17. Teiwes, Frederick C., *The Politics of China, Politics and Purges in China: Rectification and the Decline of Party Norms, 1950–55* (New York: M.E. Sharpe, 1979) p.12

4. Emperor Hirohito and the Tokyo War Crimes Trial

1. Behr, Edward, *Hirohito, Behind the Myth* (London: Hamish Hamilton, 1989) p.361

2. Bix, *Hirohito and the Making of Modern Japan* (New York: Harper Collins, 2001) p.519

3. Behr, *Hirohito*, p.365

4. Bix, *Hirohito and the Making of Modern Japan*, pp.534–5

5. Dower, *Embracing Defeat: Japan in the Wake of WWII* (New York: The New Press, 1999), p.35

6. Bix, *Hirohito and the Making of Modern Japan*, pp.7–8

7. *Ibid.*, p.29

8. Dower, *Embracing Defeat*, p.335

9. Bix, *Hirohito and the Making of Modern Japan*, p.267

10. *Ibid.*, p.372

11. *Ibid.*, p.374

12. Behr, *Hirohito*, p.145

13. Dower, *Embracing Defeat*, p.284

14. *Ibid.*, pp.282–3

15. *Ibid.*, p.280

16. *Ibid.*, p.281

17. Bix, *Hirohito and the Making of Modern Japan*, p.585

18. *Ibid.*, p.567

19. Dower, *Embracing Defeat*, p.287

20. *Ibid.*, p.289

21. Behr, *Hirohito*, p.3

22. Bix, *Hirohito and the Making of Modern Japan*, p.3

23. *Ibid.*, p.3

24. *Ibid.*, p.585

25. Dower, *Embracing Defeat*, pp.323–4

26. Behr, *Hirohito*, p.409

27. *Ibid.*, p.414

28. Bix, *Hirohito and the Making of Modern Japan*, p.610

29. *Ibid.*, p.610

30. Dower, *Embracing Defeat*, p.451

31. Eiji, Takemai, *The Allied Occupation of Japan* (London: Continuum International Publishing Group Ltd., 2002) p.45

32. Dower, *Embracing Defeat*, p.305

33. *Ibid.*, p.305

34. *Ibid.*, p.378

5. Mahatma Gandhi: Passive Aggression

1. Arnold, David, *Gandhi, Profiles in Power* (Harlow: England, Pearson Educational Ltd., 2001) p.38

2. Roberts, Andrew, *Emminent Churchillians* (London: Weidenfeld & Nicolson, 1994) p.83

3. Wolpert, Stanley, *Gandhi's Passion, The Life and Legacy of Mahatma Gandhi* (New Delhi: Oxford University Press, 2001) p.25

4. Arnold, *Gandhi*, p.218

5. Richards, Glyn, *The Philosophy of Gandhi* (London: Curzon Press Ltd., 2001) p.41

6. Moon, Penderel, *The British Conquest and Dominion of India* (London: Gerald Duckworth & Co., 1989) p.1120

7. Dobbs-Higginson, Michael S., *Asia Pacific: Its Role in the New World Disorder* (London: Heinemann, 1994) p.183

8. Wolpert, *Gandhi's Passion*, p.75

9. *Ibid.*, p.122

10. *Ibid.*, p.73

11. *Ibid.*, p.85

12. Richards, *The Philosophy of Gandhi*, p.12

13. *Ibid.*, p.122

14. Wopert, *Gandhi's Passion*, p.113

15. *Ibid.*, p.118

16. Richards, *The Philosophy of Gandhi*, p.122

17. Nehru, Jawaharlal, *Autobiography* (London: John Lane, The Bodley Head, 1936) p.525

18. Wolpert, *Gandhi's Passion*, p.143

19. *Ibid.*, p.150

20. *Ibid.*, p.151

21. Gilbert, Martin, *Churchill, A Life* (London: Heinemann, 1991) p.507

22. Kissinger, Henry, *Does America Need a Foreign Policy?* (New York: Simon & Schuster, 2001) p.156

23. Barnett, Correlli, *The Collapse of British Power* (London: Pan Books, 2002) p.146

24. *Ibid.*, p.134

25. Brown, Judith M., *Modern India: The Origins of Asian Democracy* (New Haven: Yale University Press, 2003) p.329

26. Young, Robert, J.C., *Postcolonialism: A Historical Introduction* (Oxford and Malden, MA: Blackwell Publishers Ltd., 2001) p.331

27. Arnold, *Gandhi*, p.6

6. 'An Iron Curtain Has Descended'

1. Ferguson, Niall, *Empire: How Britain made the Modern World* (London: Allen Lane, 2002) p.370

2. Alonzo L. Hamby, *A Life of Harry S. Truman: Man of the People* (New York and Oxford: Oxford University Press, 1995) p.270
3. *Ibid.*, p.331
4. Conquest, Robert, *Reflections on a Ravaged Century* (New York: John Murray, 1999) p.154
5. LaFeber, Walter (ed), *The Origins of the Cold War* (New York: John Wiley & Sons Inc., 1971) p.138
6. *Ibid.*, p.138
7. Ambrose, Stephen E. and Douglas G. Brinkley, *Rise to Globalism: American Foreign Policy since 1938* (New York: Penguin, 8th revised edition, 1997) p.58
8. Hamby, *A Life of Harry S. Truman*, p.391
9. Kennan, George F., *The Cloud of Danger* (Boston and Toronto: Atlantic Little-Brown Books, 1977) 'The Long Telegram', pp.547–59
10. *Ibid.*, pp.547–59
11. *Ibid.*
12. *Ibid.*
13. *Ibid.*
14. *Ibid.*
15. LaFeber (ed), *The Origins of the Cold War*, p.154
16. *Ibid.*, p.154
17. *Ibid.*, p.154
18. McCormick, Thomas J., *America's Half Century: United States Foreign Policy in the Cold War and After* (Baltimore: Johns Hopkins University Press, 2nd edition, 1995) p.72
19. LaFeber (ed), *The Origins of the Cold War*, p.156
20. Kissinger, Henry, *Does America Need a Foreign Policy?* (New York: Simon & Schuster, 2001) p.32
21. Senarclens, Pierre de, *From Yalta to the Iron Curtain: The Great Powers and the Origins of the Cold War* (Oxford: Berg Publishers, 1995) p.89
22. Ambrose and Brinkley, *Rise to Globalism*, pp.110–11
23. *Ibid.*, p.111
24. Goold-Adams, Richard, *The Time of Power: A Reappraisal of John Foster Dulles* (London: Weidenfeld & Nicolson, 1962) p.51
25. Caro, Robert, *Master of the Senate: The Years of Lyndon Johnson* (New York: Alfred A. Knopf, 2002) p.542
26. *Ibid.*, p.546
27. Hersh, Seymour M., *The Dark Side of Camelot* (New York: Little, Brown and Company, 1997) p.441
28. Ambrose and Brinkley, *Rise to Globalism*, p.132
29. *Ibid.*, p.169
30. Ambrose, Steven E., *Eisenhower, Soldier and President* (London: Pocket Books, 2003) p.390
31. Hamby, *A Life of Harry S. Truman*, p.536
32. *Ibid.*, p.537
33. Conquest, *Reflections on a Ravaged Century*, p.152

7. Stalin, Mao and Truman: Post-War Alliances

1. Volkogonov, Dimitri, *Stalin* (London and New York: Weidenfeld & Nicolson, 1991) p.538
2. Kissinger, Henry, *The White House Years* (London: Weidenfeld & Nicolson, 1979) p.1054
3. Chace, James, *Acheson, The Secretary of State who Created the American World* (New York: Simon & Schuster, 1998) p.219

4. Kennan, George F., *The Cloud of Danger* (Boston and Toronto: Atlantic Little-Brown Books, 1997) p.18

5. Kennan, George F., *Memoirs 1950–1963* (New York: Pantheon Books, 1983) p.221

6. *Ibid.*, p.28

7. *Ibid.*, pp.43–4

8. Chace, James, *Acheson*, p.224

9. Kissinger, *The White House Years*, p.479

10. Kissinger, Henry, *Diplomacy* (New York: Touchstone, 1994) p.479

8. Chiang Kai Shek and the Flight to Taiwan

1. Fenby, Jonathan, *Genearlissimo: Chiang Kai-Shek and the China He Lost* (London: The Free Press, 2003) p.68

2. *Ibid.*, p.85

3. *Ibid.*, p.11

4. *Ibid.*, p.13

5. *Ibid.*, p.165

6. *Ibid.*, p.387

7. *Ibid.*, p.170

8. *Ibid.*, p.411

9. *Ibid.*, p.373

10. *Ibid.*, p.425

11. *Ibid.*, p.398

12. *Ibid.*, p.425

13. *Ibid.*, p.412

14. *Ibid.*, p.419

15. *Ibid.*, p.453

16. *Ibid.*, p.453

17. *Ibid.*, p.454

18. *Ibid.*, p.460

19. Roy, Denny, *Taiwan: A Political History* (Ithaca, NY: Cornell University Press, 2003) p.56

20. *Ibid.*, p.61

21. *Ibid.*, p.62

22. Philips, Steven, *'Between Assimilation and Independence, Taiwanese Political Aspirations under Nationalist Chinese Rule, 1945–1948'*, Murray A. Rubinstein (ed), *Taiwan: A New History* (New York: M.E. Sharpe Inc., 2007) p.283

23. *Ibid.*, p.72

24. Philips, *'Between Assimilation and Independence'*, p.295

25. Douglas Mendel, *The Politics of Formosan Nationalism* (Berkley: University of California Press, 1970) p.145

9. MacArthur, Yoshida and the American Occupation of Japan

1. McClain, James, *Japan: A Modern History* (New York: W.W. Norton & Co., 2002) p.523

2. Manchester, William, *American Caesar: Douglas MacArthur 1880–1964* (Boston: Little, Brown and Company, 1978) p.466

3. Dower, John, *Embracing Defeat; Japan in the Wake of WWII* (New York: The New Press, 1999) p.41

4. Dower, *Embracing Defeat*, p.291

5. Manchester, *American Caesar*, p.36

6. *Ibid.*, p.48

7. McClain, *Japan*, p.525

8. Dower, *Embracing Defeat*, p.79

9. Manchester, *American Caesar*, p.470

10. Keenan, George, *Memoirs 1925–1950* (New York: Pantheon Books, 1967) p.384

11. *Ibid.*, p.384

12. To the author, 1973

13. McClain, *Japan*, p.533

14. Dower, *Embracing Defeat*, p.126

15. *Ibid.*, p.156

16. *Ibid.*, p.77

17. McClain, *Japan*, p.540

18. Dower, *Embracing Defeat*, p.378

19. *Ibid.*, p.360

20. Manchester, *American Caesar*, p.500

21. Dower, *Embracing Defeat*, p.71

22. Eiji, Takemai, *The Allied Occupation of Japan* (London: Continuum International Publishing Group Ltd., 2002) p.278

23. Sims, Richard, *Japanese Political History since the Meiji Restoration, 1868–2000* (London: Hurst & Co., 2001) p.46

24. Eiji, *The Allied Occupation of Japan*, p.482

25. McClain, *Japan*, p.551

26. Beasley, W.G., *The Rise of Modern Japan II* (London: Phoenix, 2001) p.228

27. Harvey, Robert, *American Shogun, MacArthur, Hirohito and the American Duel with Japan* (London: John Murray, 2006) p.199

28. Manchester, *American Caesar*, p.470

10. Hô Chí Minh and the Battle of Diên Biên Phu

1. McAlister, John T. Jr, *Vietnam: The Origins of Revolution* (New York: Princeton University Alfred Knopf Centre for International Studies, 1969) p.193

2. *Ibid.*, p.192

3. *Ibid.*, p.162

4. *Ibid.*, p.219

5. Duiker, William J., *Ho Chi Minh* (New York: Hyperion, 2000) p.45

6. McAlister, *Vietnam*, p.52

7. Shaplen, Robert, *The Lost Revolution: Vietnam 1945–1965* (London: Andre Deutsch, 1966) p.36

8. *Ibid.*, p.37

9. *Ibid.*, p.49

10. Duiker, *Ho Chi Minh*, p.570

11. Pike, Douglas, *Vietcong: The Organisation and Techniques of the National Liberation Front of South Vietnam* (Boston: MIT Press, 1966) p.36

12. Windrow, Martin, *The Last Valley: Dien Bien Phu and the French Defeat of Vietnam* (London: Weidenfeld & Nicolson, 2004) p.135

13. Shaplen, *The Lost Revolution*, p.33

14. *Ibid.*, p.35

15. Reischauer, Edwin O., *Beyond Vietnam, The United States and Asia* (New York: Alfred A. Knopf, 1968) p.21

16. Lacouture, Jean, *De Gaulle, The Rebel 1890–1944* (New York: W.W. Norton and Co., 1993) p.338

17. Shaplen, *The Lost Revolution*, p.31

18. McAlister, *Vietnam*, p.275

19. *Ibid.*, p.38

20. *Ibid.*, p.275

21. *Ibid.*, p.277

22. *Ibid.*, p.281

23. *Ibid.*, p.288

24. Shaplen, *The Lost Revolution*, p.43

25. Trager, Frank N., *Why Vietnam?* (New York: Praeger, 1966) p.75

26. Shaplen, *The Lost Revolution,* p.79

27. Windrow, *The Last Valley*, p.179

28. *Ibid.*, p.205

29. Shaplen, *The Lost Revolution*, p.93

30. Windrow, *The Last Valley*, p.348

31. *Ibid.*, pp.425–6

32. Kennan, George, *The Cloud of Danger* (Boston and Toronto: Atlantic Little-Brown Books, 1977) p.59

33. Brendon, Piers, *Ike: His Life and Times* (London: Secker and Warburg, 1987) p.286

34. Ambrose, Stephen E., *Eisenhower: Soldier and President* (London, Pocket Books, 2003) p.373

35. *Ibid.*, p.374

36. Brendon, *Ike*, p.290

37. Trager, *Why Vietnam?*, p.84

38. *Ibid.*, p.95

39. Brendon, *Ike*, p.288

40. Kennan, *The Cloud of Danger*, p.60

41. Lacouture, *De Gaulle*, p.281

11. General Phibun: National Socialist Dictator

1. Wright, Joseph J., *A History of Modern Thailand* (Thailand: Asia Books, p.1991) p.50

2. *Ibid.*, p.50

3. Stowe, Judith A., *Siam becomes Thailand* (Honolulu: University of Hawaii Press, 1991) p.220

4. Dhiravegin, Likhit, *Democracy: The Evolution of the Thai Political System* (Singapore: Times Academic Press, 1992) p.115

5. Wright, *A History of Modern Thailand*, p.185

6. *Ibid.*, p.50

7. Stowe, *Siam becomes Thailand*, p.38

8. Wyatt, David K., *Thailand: A Short History* (New Haven, CT: Yale University Press, 1982) p.249

9. Wright, *A History of Modern Thailand*, p.101

10. *Ibid.*, p.121

11. Cooper, Donald F., *Thailand: Dictatorship or Democracy?* (London: Minerva Press, 1995) p.14

Notes   767

12. *Ibid.*, p.21
13. Stowe, *Siam becomes Thailand*, p.313
14. Wright, *A History of Modern Thailand*, p.164
15. *Ibid.*, p.186
16. Wyatt, *Thailand: A Short History*, p.279
17. Cooper, *Thailand: Dictatorship or Democracy?*, p.174
18. *Ibid.*, p.139
19. *Ibid.*, p.139
20. *Ibid.*, p.148
21. Cooper, *Thailand: Dictatorship or Democracy?*, p.149
22. Dhiravegin, *Democracy*, p.140

12. From Independence to Dependency

1. *Nationmaster.com, Encyclopedia, Manuel L. Quezon*, p.1
2. Blitz, Amy, *The Contested State* (Oxford: Rowman & Littlefield, 2000) p.67
3. Steinberg, David Joel, *The Philippines* (Boulder, CO: Westview Press, 1994) p.25
4. *Ibid.*, p.107
5. Celoza, Albert F., *Ferdinand Marcos and the Philippines* (Westport, CT: Praeger Publishers, 1997) p.7
6. Shalom, Stephen Rosskamm, *The United States and the Philippines* (Philadelphia: Institute for Human Issues, 1981) p.5
7. *Ibid.*, p.7
8. Blitz, *The Contested State*, p.5
9. *Ibid.*, p.74
10. *Ibid.*, p.76
11. Hamiliton-Paterson, James, *America's Boy: The Marcoses and the Philippines* (London: Granta Books, 1998) p.107
12. Blitz, *The Contested State*, p.77
13. *Ibid.*, p.82
14. *Ibid.*, p.83
15. *Ibid.*, p.88
16. *Ibid.*, p.88
17. *Ibid.*, p.87
18. Hamiliton-Paterson, *America's Boy*, p.160
19. Shalom, *The United States and the Philippines*, p.41
20. *Ibid.*, p.92
21. Hamiliton-Paterson, *America's Boy*, p.178
22. Shalom, *The United States and the Philippines*, p.40

13. Lord Mountbatten and the Partition of India

1. Arnold, David, *Gandhi, Profiles in Power* (Harlow: England, Pearson Educational Ltd., 2001) p.208
2. Wolpert, Stanley, *A New History of India* (New York: Oxford University Press, 1997) p.333
3. *Ibid.*, p.333
4. Wolpert, Stanley, *Gandhi's Passion: The Life and Legacy of Mahatma Gandhi* (Delhi: Oxford University Press, 2001) p.213
5. Wolpert, *A New History of India*, p.329

6. Moon, Penderel, *The British Conquest and Dominion of India* (London: Gerald Duckworth & Co., 1989) p.1087

7. *Ibid.*, p.1087

8. Lall, Arthur, *The Emergence of Modern India* (New York: Columbia University Press, 1981) p.51

9. *Ibid.*, p.89

10. Wolpert, *A New History of India*, p.334

11. *Ibid.*, p.20

12. Lall, *The Emergence of Modern India*, p.86

13. Wolpert, *A New History of India*, p.325

14. *Ibid.*, p.326

15. *Ibid.*, p.329

16. Menon, V.P., *The Transfer of Power in India* (New Delhi: Orient Longman, 1957) p.141

17. Moon, *The British Conquest and Dominion of India*, p.17

18. Datta, S.K. and Rajeev Sharma, *Pakistan: From Jinnah to Jehad* (New Delhi: UBS Publishers, 2002) p.25

19. Wolpert, *A New History of India*, p.343

20. Datta and Sharma, *Pakistan*, p.25

21. Lall, *The Emergence of Modern India*, p.103

22. Menon, *The Transfer of Power in India*, p.216

23. Roberts, Andrew, *Eminent Churchillians* (London: Weidenfeld & Nicolson, 1991) p.63

24. *Ibid.*, p.71

25. Von Tunzelmann, Alex, *Indian Summer: The Secret History of the End of Empire*, p.131

26. Roberts, *Eminent Churchillians*, p.125

27. Zeigler, Philip, *Mountbatten* (London: Guild, 1985) p.354

28. Roberts, *Eminent Churchillians,* p.81

29. *Ibid.*, p.133

30. *Ibid.*, p.82

31. Datta and Sharma, *Pakistan*, p.60

32. *Ibid.*, p.85

33. Edwardes, Michael, *Nehru: A Political Biography* (London: Allen Lane, Penguin, 1991) p.210

34. *Ibid.*, p.211

35. Roberts, *Eminent Churchillians*, p.113

36. *Ibid.*, p.113

37. *Ibid.*, p.114

38. *Ibid.*, p.113

39. *Ibid.*, p.114

40. *Ibid.*, p.114

41. Keay, John, *Sowing the Wind: The Seeds of Conflict in the Middle East* (London: John Murray, 2003) p.508

42. Gopal, Sarvepalli, *Jawaharlal Nehru: A Biography, Volume One: 1889–1947* (London: Jonathan Cape, 2005) p.342

43. *Ibid.*, p.357

44. Lall, *The Emergence of Modern India*, p.106

45. Menon, *The Transfer of Power in India*, p.435

46. Roberts, *Eminent Churchillians*, p.129

47. Lall, *The Emergence of Modern India*, p.51

14. Origins of the Korean War

1. Fehrenbach, T.R., *This Kind of War* (Dulles, VA: Brassey's, 2nd edition, 1963) p.12
2. Sandler, Victor, *The Korean War, No Victor, No Vanquished* (London: UCL Press, 1999) p.20
3. Gunther, John, *The Riddle of MacArthur* (London: Hamish Hamilton, 1951) p.163
4. *Ibid.*, p.163
5. *Ibid.*, p.163
6. *Ibid.*, p.164
7. Sandler, Victor, *The Korean War,* p.40
8. *Ibid.*, p.41
9. Mackerras, Colin, *Eastern Asia* (Melbourne: Longman Australia, 1992) p.290
10. Hobsbawm, Eric, *Age of Extremes* (London: Penguin, 1994) p.434
11. Kissinger, Henry, *Diplomacy* (New York: Touchstone, 1994) p.474
12. Gunther, *The Riddle of MacArthur*, p.168
13. *Ibid.*, p.172
14. Fehrenbach, *This Kind of War,* p.5
15. Volkogonov, Dmitri, *Stalin* (London and New York: Weidenfeld & Nicolson, 1991) p.540

15. Aung San: Revolutionary and Turncoat

1. Tucker, Shelby, *Burma: The Curse of Independence* (London: Pluto Press, 2001) p.78
2. Aung San Suu Kyi, *Freedom from Fear* (New York: Penguin, 1995) p.8
3. *Ibid.*, p.11
4. *Ibid.*, p.12
5. *Ibid.*, p.57
6. Wintle, Justin, *Perfect Hostage: Aung San Suu Kyi, Burma and the Generals* (London: Arrow, 2007) p.104
7. Tucker, *Burma,* p.116
8. Lintner, Bernil, *Burma in Revolt* (Thailand: Silkworm Books, 1999) p.70
9. Tucker, *Burma,* p.56
10. Aung San, *Freedom from Fear*, p.15
11. Tucker, *Burma,* p.65
12. *Ibid.*, p.58
13. Callahan, Mary P., *'Making Enemies: War and State Building in Burma'* (Cambridge, MA: World Peace Foundation, 1998) p.54
14. Von Tunzelmann, Alex, *Indian Summer, The Secret History of the End of Empire* (London: Simon & Schuster, 2007) p.134
15. *Ibid.*, p.134
16. Tucker, *Burma,* p.15
17. *Ibid.*, p.62
18. *Ibid.*, pp.134–5
19. *Ibid.*, p.16
20. Wintle, *Perfect Hostage*, p.137
21. *Ibid.*, p.114
22. *Ibid.*, p.120
23. *Ibid.*, p.120
24. Lintner, *Burma in Revolt*, p.79
25. Tucker, *Burma,* p.122
26. Callahan, 'Making Enemies', Rotberg (ed), *Prospects for a Democratic Future*, p.59

27. Gravers, Mikail, *Nationalism as Political Paranoia in Burma* (Richmond: Nordic Institute of Asian Studies, Curzon, 1999) p.72

28. Tucker, *Burma*, p.137

29. *Ibid.*, p.137

30. Callahan, 'Making Enemies', Rotberg (ed) *Prospects for a Democratic Future*, p.54

31. Tucker, *Burma*, p.155

32. Von Tunzelmann, *Indian Summer*, p.136

33. *Ibid.*, p.136

34. Callahan, 'Making Enemies', Rotberg (ed), *Prospects for a Democratic Future*, p.52

16. Sukarno: The Founding Father

1. Hughes, John, *The End of Sukarno, A Coup That Misfired: A Purge That Ran Wild* (Singapore, Archipelago Press, 2002) p.60

2. Feith, Herbert and Lance Castles (eds), *Indonesian Political Thinking, 1945–1965* (Ithaca, NY: Cornell University Press, 1970) p.47

3. *Ibid.*, p.30

4. Jon M. Reinhardt, *Foreign Policy and National Integration: The Case of Indonesia* (New Haven: Yale University South East Asian Studies, 1971) p.18

5. Leo Suryadinata, *Interpreting Indonesian Politics* (Hong Kong: Times Academic Press, 1998) p.74

6. Feith and Castles (eds), *Indonesian Political Thinking*, p.47

7. Weinstein, Franklin B., *Indonesian Foreign Policy and the Dilemma of Dependence* (Ithaca, Cornell University Press, 1976) p.59

8. Feith and Castles (eds), *Indonesian Political Thinking*, p.32

9. Lee, Oey Hong, *War and Diplomacy in Indonesia 1945–50* (Townsville, QLD: Australia, James Cook University of North Queensland, 1981) p.118

10. *Ibid.*, p.127

11. Friend, Theodore, *Indonesian Destinies* (Cambridge, MA: The Belknap Press of Harvard, University Press, 2003) p.36

12. Lee, *War and Diplomacy in Indonesia*, p.186

13. Friend, *Indonesian Destinies*, p.37

14. Lee, *War and Diplomacy in Indonesia*, p.189

15. *Ibid.*, p.251

17. Independence and the Racial Contract

1. Shome, Anthony S.K., *Malay Political Leadership* (London: Routledge Curzon, 2002) p.38

2. Case, William, *Elites and Regimes in Malaysia* (Clayton: Monash Asia Institute, 1996) p.53

3. *Ibid.*, p.72

4. Shome, *Malay Political Leadership*, p.44

5. Sodhy, Pamela, *The US–Malaysian Nexus* (Kuala Lumpur: Institute of Strategic and International Studies, 1991) p.39

6. Shennan, Margaret, *Out in the Midday Sun, The British in Malaysia 1880–1960* (London: John Murray, 2000) p.307

7. Sodhy, *The US–Malaysian Nexus*, p.30

8. *Ibid.*, p.28

9. Shome, *Malay Political Leadership*, p.51

10. Shennan, *Out in the Midday Sun*, p.302

11. Sodhy, *The US–Malaysian Nexus*, p.57
12. Shennan, *Out in the Midday Sun*, p.302
13. Shome, *Malay Political Leadership*, p.59
14. Shennan, *Out in the Midday Sun*, p.339
15. Case, *Elites and Regimes in Malaysia*, p.103
16. *Ibid.*, p.96
17. Sodhy, *The US–Malaysian Nexus*, p.70
18. *Ibid.*, p.116
19. Shennan, *Out in the Midday Sun*, p.19
20. Sodhy, *The US–Malaysian Nexus*, p.146
21. Shome, *Malay Political Leadership*, p.82
22. *Ibid.*, p.82
23. *Ibid.*, p.86
24. Sodhy, *The US–Malaysian Nexus*, p.150

18. Lee Kuan Yew: Pocket Giant

1. Yew, Lee Kuan, *The Singapore Story* (Singapore: Prentice Hall, 1999) p.52
2. *Ibid.*, p.52
3. *Ibid.*, p.53
4. *Ibid.*, p.54
5. *Ibid.*, p.74
6. Huff, E.G., *Economic Growth of Singapore: Trade and Development in the 20th Century* (Cambridge: Cambridge University Press, 1997) p.294
7. Lee, *The Singapore Story*, p.233
8. *Ibid.*, p.319
9. *Ibid.*, p.341
10. *Ibid.*, p.398
11. *Ibid.*, p.398
12. *Ibid.*, p.553
13. *Ibid.*, p.554
14. *Ibid.*, p.559
15. *Ibid.*, p.606
16. *Ibid.*, p.566
17. *Ibid.*, p.566
18. *Ibid.*, p.606
19. *Ibid.*, p.569
20. *Ibid.*, p.569
21. *Ibid.*, p.611
22. *Ibid.*, p.614
23. *Ibid.*, p.615
24. Hilley, John, *Malaysia: Mahathirism, Hegemony and the New Opposition* (Basingstoke: Palgrave, 2001) p.34
25. Lee, *The Singapore Story*, p.41
26. *Ibid.*, p.42
27. *Ibid.*, p.442
28. *Ibid.*, p.443
29. *Ibid.*, p.657

30. *Ibid.*, p.660
31. Nixon, Richard, *Leaders* (New York: Buccaneer Books, 1994) p.310
32. Leifer, Michael, *Singapore's Foreign Policy, Coping with Vulnerability* (New York: Routledge, 2000) p.12
33. Nixon, *Leaders*, p.312

19. Capitalist Redoubt

1. Tsang, Steve, *Hong Kong, A Modern History* (London: I.B.Tauris, 2004) p.124
2. *Ibid.*, p.125
3. *Ibid.*, p.126
4. *Ibid.*, p.131
5. *Ibid.*, p.141
6. *Ibid.*, p.143
7. *Ibid.*, p.147
8. Walsh, Frank, *A History of Hong Kong* (London: Harper Collins, 1997), p.461
9. *Ibid.*, p.437
10. Tsang, *Hong Kong*, p.148
11. *Ibid.*, p.151
12. *Ibid.*, p.153
13. Walsh, *A History of Hong Kong*, p.447
14. Tucker, Nancy Bernkopk, *Taiwan, Hong Kong and the United States 1945–1992* (New York: Twaine, 1994) p.214
15. *Ibid.*, p.211
16. Walsh, *A History of Hong Kong*, p.439
17. Tsang, *Hong Kong*, p.159
18. Chang, Jung and Jon Halliday, *Mao, The Unknown Story* (London: Jonathan Cape, 2005) p.591
19. Walsh, *A History of Hong Kong*, p.452
20. Tsang, *Hong Kong*, p.165
21. Patten, Christopher, *East and West* (London: Macmillan, 1998) p.19
22. Tsang, *Hong Kong*, p.168
23. Walsh, *A History of Hong Kong*, p.461
24. Tsang, *Hong Kong*, p.171
25. Walsh, *A History of Hong Kong*, p.461
26. *Ibid.*, p.462
27. Tsang, *Hong Kong*, p.205

20. The Korean War

1. Leckie, Robert, *Conflict, The History of the Korean War* (New York: G.P. Putnam Sons, 1962) p.37
2. Hastings, Max, *The Korean War* (London: Michael Joseph, 1987) p.44
3. McCullough, David, *Truman* (New York: Simon & Schuster, 1992) p.776
4. Hastings, *The Korean War*, p.56
5. *Ibid.*, p.56
6. *Ibid.*, p.75
7. *Ibid.*, p.59
8. Leckie, *Conflict*, p.56

9. Hastings, *The Korean War*, p.110
10. *Ibid.*, p.112
11. *Ibid.*, p.91
12. Leckie, *Conflict*, p.133
13. Hastings, *The Korean War*, p.150
14. *Ibid.*, p.130
15. *Ibid.*, p.194
16. *Ibid.*, p.150
17. *Ibid.*, p.194
18. Leckie, *Conflict*, p.221
19. Hastings, *The Korean War*, p.208
20. McCullough, *Truman*, p.854
21. Hastings, *The Korean War*, p.245
22. Lee, Steven Hugh, *The Korean War* (Harlow: England, Pearson Education, 2001) p.69
23. Hastings, *The Korean War*, p.407

21. The Great Leap Forward

1. Hong Ying, *Daughter of the River* (London: Bloomsbury, 1997) p.35
2. Li, Zhisui, *The Private Life of Chairman Mao* (London: Chatto & Windus, 1994) p.125
3. Fenby, Jonathan, *The Penguin History of Modern China, The Fall and Rise of a Great Power, 1850–2008* (London: Allen Lane, 2008) p.401
4. Li, *The Private Life of Chairman Mao*, p.277
5. Gao, Anhua, *To the Edge of the Sky* (Bergenfield, NJ: Overlook Press, 2003) p.66
6. Zheng, Shiping, *Party v. State in Post 1949 China* (Cambridge: Cambridge University Press, 1997) pp.81–2
7. *Ibid.*, p.85
8. Teiwes, Frederick C., *Politics and Purges in China: Rectification and the Decline of Party Norms, 1950–55* (New York: M.E. Sharpe, 1979) p.218
9. Domenach, Jean Luc, *The Origins of the Great Leap Forward* (Boulder, CO: Westview Press, 1995) p.166

22. Dictatorship and Prosperity

1. Jo, Yung-Hwan (ed), *Taiwan's Future, Arizona State University* (Hong Kong: Union Research Institute for Arizona State University, 1974) p.146
2. Bianco, Lucien, *Origins of the Chinese Revolution 1915–1949* (Stanford, CA: Stanford University Press, 1971) p.13
3. Roy, Denny, *Taiwan: A Political History* (Ithaca, NY: Cornell University Press, 2003) p.90
4. Bullard, Monte R., *The Soldier and the Citizen, The Role of the Military in Taiwan's Development* (Armonk: M.E. Sharpe, 1997) p.46
5. *Ibid.*, p.67
6. *Ibid.*, p.193
7. *Ibid.*, p.144
8. *Ibid.*, p.144
9. *Ibid.*, p.139
10. Fu, Jen-Kun, *Taiwan and the Geopolitics of the Asian–American Dilemma* (New York: Praeger, 1992) p.14

11. *Ibid.*, p.38
12. *Ibid.*, pp.40–1
13. Jo, Yung-Hwan (ed), *Taiwan's Future,* p.190
14. Fu, *Taiwan and the Geopolitics of the Asian–American Dilemma*, p.49
15. Roy, *Taiwan*, p.131

23. Nehru: The Fashioning of a Legend

1. Wolpert, Stanley, *Nehru: A Tryst with Destiny* (New York: Oxford University Press, 1997) p.351
2. Frank, Katherine, *Indira Gandhi: The Life of Indira Nehru Gandhi* (London: Harper Collins, 2001) p.134
3. Nixon, Richard, *Leaders* (New York: Buccaneer Books, 1994) p.270
4. Frank, *Indira Gandhi*, p.58
5. Edwardes, Michael, *Nehru: A Political Biography* (London: Allen Lane, Penguin, 1971) p.248
6. Oldenburg, Philip (ed), *India Briefing: Staying the Course* (Armonk, NY: M.E. Sharpe, 1995) p.150
7. *Ibid.*, p.131
8. Menon, V.P., *The Transfer of Power to India* (New Delhi: Orient Longman, 1957) p.416
9. *Ibid.*, p.129
10. Gopal, Sarvepalli, *Jawaharlal Nehru: A Biography, Volume One: 1889–1947* (London: Jonathan Cape, 1979) p.42
11. *Ibid.*, p.121
12. Edwardes, *Nehru*, p.269
13. Young, Robert J.C., *Postcolonialism* (Oxford and Malden, MA: Blackwell Publishers Ltd., 2001) p.191
14. Edwardes, *Nehru*, p.274
15. Gopal, Sarvepelli, *Jawaharlal Nehru: A Biography, Volume Two, 1947–1956* (New Delhi: Oxford University Press, 1984) p.59
16. Kissinger, Speech in India, New Delhi, 1994
17. Chace, James, *Acheson: The Secretary of State who Created the American World* (New York: Simon & Schuster, 1998) p.292
18. Brendon, Piers, *Ike: The Life and Times of Dwight Eisenhower* (London: Secker & Warburg, 1987) p.377
19. Frank, *Indira Gandhi*, p.263
20. Dallek, Robert, *Flawed Giant: Lyndon Johnson 1960–1973* (New York: Oxford University Press, 1998) p.14
21. Wolpert, Stanley, *Nehru: A Tryst with Destiny*, p.116
22. Brown, Judith, *Nehru: A Political Life* (New Haven: Yale University Press, 2003) p.325
23. Oldenburg (ed), *India Briefing*, p.1

24. Jinnah and Pakistan's Failed Constitution

1. Datta, S.K. and Rajeev Sharma, *Pakistan: From Jinnah to Jehad* (New Delhi: UBS Publishers, 2002) p.33
2. *Ibid.*, p.39
3. *Ibid.*, p.69
4. *Ibid.*, p.7
5. *Ibid.*, p.7

6. Collins, Larry and Dominic Lapierre, *Freedom at Midnight: The Epic Drama of India's Struggle for Independence* (New York: Harper Collins, 1997) p.285

7. Harrison, Selig S., Paul H. Kreisberg and Dennis Kux (eds), *India & Pakistan: The First Fifty Years* (Cambridge: Cambridge University Press, 1999) p.7

8. *Ibid.*, p.20

9. Ziring, Lawrence, *Pakistan: At the Crosscurrent of History* (Oxford: One World Publications, 2003) p.74

10. Jaffrelot, Christophe (ed), *A History of Pakistan and its Origins* (London: Anthem Press, 2004) p.62

11. Datta and Sharma, *Pakistan*, p.55

12. *Ibid.*, p.26

13. Harrison, Kreisberg and Kux (eds), *India & Pakistan*, p.3

14. *Ibid.*, p.83

15. Afzal, M. Raique, *Pakistan: History and Politics, 1947–1971* (Karachi: Oxford University Press, 2001) p.137

16. Harrison, Kreisberg and Kux (eds), *India & Pakistan*, p.100

17. Datta and Sharma, *Pakistan*, p.93

18. Harrison, Kreisberg and Kux (eds) *India & Pakistan*, p.111

19. Talbot, Ian, *Pakistan: A Modern History* (London: C. Hurst & Co., 2005) p.170

20. Harrison, Kreisberg and Kux (eds), *India & Pakistan*, p.133

21. *Ibid.*, p.148

22. *Ibid.*, p.154

23. Harrison, Kreisberg and Kux (eds), *India & Pakistan*, p.157

24. Cohen, Philip, *The Idea of Pakistan* (Washington, DC: Brookings Institution Press, 2004) p.52

25. Harrison, Kreisberg and Kux (eds), *India & Pakistan*, p.163

26. *Ibid.*, p.168

27. *Ibid.*, p.388

25. Fall of Rhee and Park's 'Economic Miracle'

1. Kim, Se-Jin, *The Politics of Military Revolution in Korea* (Columbia, SC: The University of South Carolina Press, 1971) p.93

2. *Ibid.*, p.94

3. Koo, Youngnok and Dae-sook Suh (eds), *Korea and the United States* (Honolulu: University of Hawaii Press, 1984) p.98

4. Han, Sung-joo, *Continuity and Change in Korean–American Relations* (Seoul: Asiatic Research Center, Korea University, 1982) p.147

5. Kim, *The Politics of Military Revolution in Korea*, p.120

6. Han, *Continuity and Change in Korean–American Relations*, p.129

7. Koo and Suh (eds), *Korea and the United States*, p.208

8. Kim, *The Politics of Military Revolution in Korea*, p.35

26. Kim Il Sung: The 'Great Leader'

1. Han, Sung-Joo, *Continuity and Change in Korean–American Relations* (Seoul: Asiatic Research Center, Korea University, 1982) p.80

2. Buzo, Adrian, *The Making of Modern Korea* (New York: Routledge, 2002) p.96

3. Yang, Sung Chul, *The North and South Korean Political Systems* (Elizabeth, NJ: Hollym International Corp, 1999) p.379
4. Koo, Youngnok Koo and Dae-sook Suh (eds), *Korea and the United States* (Honolulu: University of Hawaii Press, 1984) p.178
5. Buzo, *The Making of Modern Korea*, p.98
6. Han, *Continuity and Change in Korean–American Relations*, p.81
7. Yang, *The North and South Korean Political Systems*, p.277
8. Zagoria, Donald S. and Young Kun Kim, *North Korea and the Major Powers*, p.27
9. Kim Il Sung, *The Brilliant Banner of Juche*, B.C.Gupta (Pyongyang, North Korea: Foreign Languages Publishing House, 1981) pp.130–31
10. Buzo, *The Making of Modern Korea*, p.124
11. *Ibid.*, p.124
12. Zagoria and Kim, *North Korea and the Major Powers*, p.31
13. Brands, William J. (ed), *The Two Koreas in East Asian Affairs* (New York: New York University Press, 1976) p.73
14. Han, *Continuity and Change in Korean–American Relations*, p.99
15. Zagoria and Kim, *North Korea and the Major Powers*, p.36
16. Koo and Suh (eds), *Korea and the United States*, p.164

27. The Todai Oligarchs

1. McClain, James L., *Japan: A Modern History* (New York: W.W. Norton & Co., 2002) p.571
2. Blomstrom, Magnus, Byron Gangnes and Sumner La Croix (eds), *Japan's New Economy: Continuity and Change in the Twenty-First Century* (New York: Oxford University Press, 2001) p.31
3. Ramseyer Mark J. and Frances McCall Rosenbluth, *Japan's Political Marketplace, MITI and the Japanese Economic Miracle* (Cambridge, MA: Harvard University Press, 1993) p.101
4. *Ibid.*, p.24
5. Hrebenar, Ronald J., *The Japanese Party System* (Boulder, CO: Westview Press, 1992) p.10
6. *Ibid.*, p.10
7. *Ibid.*, p.184
8. *Ibid.*, p.122
9. *Ibid.*, p.153
10. McClain, *Japan: A Modern History*, p.579
11. Ramseyer and McCall Rosenbluth, *Japan's Political Market Place*, p.121
12. Yoshibumi, Wakamiya, *The Postwar Conservative View of Asia* (Tokyo: LTCB International Library Foundation, 1999) p.12
13. *Ibid.*, p.13
14. *Ibid.*, p.14
15. *Ibid.*, pp.20–1
16. *Ibid.*, p.79
17. Edstrom, Bert, *Japan's Evolving Foreign Policy Doctrine* (London: Macmillan Press Ltd., 1999) p.84
18. *Ibid.*, p.148
19. Sims, Richard, *Japanese Political History since the Meiji Restoration, 1868–2000* (London: Hurst & Co., 2001) p.287
20. *Ibid.*, p.11

28. The Cultural Revolution

1. Li, Zhisui, *The Private Life of Chairman Mao* (London: Chatto & Windus, 1994) p.489
2. Chen, Da, *Colours of the Mountain*, p.8
3. Li, *The Private Life of Chairman Mao*, p.480
4. Salisbury, Harrison E., *China in the Era of Mao and Deng* (London: Harper Collins, 1992) p.183
5. MacFarquhar, Roderick, *The Origins of the Cultural Revolution, Vol III: The Coming of the Cataclysm, 1961–1966* (New York: Columbia University Press, 1993) p.333
6. *Ibid.*, p.333
7. *Ibid.*, p.169
8. Mozingo, David, *The Chinese Army and the Communist State: State and Society in Contemporary China* (Ithaca, NY: Cornell University Press, 1993) p.100
9. MacFarquhar, *The Origins of the Cultural Revolution*, p.169
10. *Ibid.*, p.277
11. Li, *The Private Life of Chairman Mao*, p.440
12. Lawrence, Alan, *China under Communism* (New York: Routledge, 1998) p.71
13. Li, *The Private Life of Chairman Mao*, p.364
14. *Ibid.*, p.443
15. Teiwes, Federick C., *The Establishment and Consolidation of the New Regime, 1949–57* (Cambridge: University of Cambridge Press, 1967) p.21
16. Harry Harding, 'The Chinese State in Crisis', in MacFarquhar, Roderick (ed), *The Politics of China: The Eras of Mao and Deng* (New York: Cambridge University Press, 2nd edition, 1993) p.170
17. *Ibid.*, p.223
18. *Ibid.*, p.234

29. Indira Gandhi: A Study in Nepotism

1. Moraes, Dom, *Mrs. Gandhi* (London: Jonathan Cape, 1970) p.157
2. Frank, Katherine, *Indira Gandhi: The Life of Indira Nehru Gandhi* (London: Harper Collins, 2001) p.171
3. Bhatia, Krishnan, *Indira: A Biography of Prime Minister Gandhi* (London: Angus & Robertson Ltd., 1974) p.272
4. Nixon, Richard, *Leaders* (New York: Buccaneer Books, 1994) p.286
5. Lall, Arthur, *The Emergence of Modern India* (New York: Columbia University Press, 1981) p.170
6. Frank, *Indira Gandhi*, p.297
7. Bhatia, *Indira*, p.221
8. Frank, Katherine, *Indira Gandhi*, p.302
9. Dixit, J.N., *My South Block Years, Memoirs of a Foreign Secretary* (New Delhi: UBS Publishers, 1996) p.37
10. Fishlock, Trevor, *Gandhi's Children* (London: Harper Collins, 2001) p.81
11. Moraes, *Mrs. Gandhi*, p.137
12. Frank, *Indira Gandhi*, p.335
13. *Ibid.*, p.336
14. Bhatia, *Indira*, p.253
15. *Ibid.*, p.240

16. Frank, *Indira Gandhi*, p.339

17. *Ibid.*, p.340

18. *Ibid.*, p.347

19. Bhatia, *Indira*, p.204

20. *Ibid.*, p.261

21. Lall, *The Emergence of Modern India*, p.194

22. Frank, *Indira Gandhi*, p.374

23. Lall, *The Emergence of Modern India*, p.206

24. Frank, *Indira Gandhi*, p.379

25. *Ibid.*, p.380

26. *Ibid.*, p.409

27. *Ibid.*, p.411

28. Mrs Thatcher to the Author at RAC

29. Fishlock, *Gandhi's Children*, p.90

30. Frank, *Indira Gandhi*, p.441

31. *Ibid.*, p.450

32. Singh, Tavleen, *Kashmir: A Tragedy of Errors* (New Delhi: Penguin Books, 1996) p.242

33. *Ibid.*, p.35

34. *Ibid.*, p.39

35. *Ibid.*, p.8

36. Tully, Mark and Satish Jacob, *Amritsar: Mrs. Ganhi's Last Battle* (London: Jonathan Cape, 1985) p.219

37. Fishlock, *Gandhi's Children*, p.86

38. Moraes, *Mrs. Gandhi*, p.264

30. Kennedy: Vietnam and the Vienna Summit

1. McAlister, John T., *Vietnam: The Origins of the Revolution* (New York: Princeton University Alfred A. Knopf Center for International Studies, 1969) p.32

2. Trager, Frank N., *Why Vietnam?* (New York: Praeger, 1966) pp.154–5

3. *Ibid.*, p.494

4. McNamara, *In Retrospect: The Tragedy and Lessons of Vietnam* (Westminster, MD: Times Books, 1995) p.42

5. *Ibid.*, p.53

6. *Ibid.*, p.35

7. Sorensen, Theodore C., *Kennedy* (New York: Smithmark Publishers, 1995) p.640

8. McNamara, *In Retrospect*, p.70

9. *Ibid.*, p.84

10. Dallek, Robert, *Flawed Giant; Lyndon Johnson 1960–1973* (New York: Oxford University Press, 1998) p.18

11. McNamara, *In Retrospect*, p.39

12. McCormick, Thomas J., *America's Half Century* (Baltimore: John Hopkins University Press, 2nd edition, 1995) p.150

13. McNamara, *In Retrospect*, p.64

14. Hersh, Seymour, M., *The Dark Side of Camelot* (New York: Little, Brown & Co., 1997) p.418

15. Black, Conrad, *Richard Milhous Nixon: The Invincible Quest* (London: Quercus, 2007) p.456

16. Weiner, Tim, *Legacy of Ashes: The History of the CIA* (London: Allen Lane, 2007) p.210

31. 'The Year of Living Dangerously'

1. Hughes, John, *The End of Sukarno: A Coup That Misfired, A Purge That Ran Wild* (Singapore: Archipelago Press, 2004) p.101

2. David Bourchier and Vedi R. Hadiz (eds), *Indonesian Politics and Society* (London: Routledge, Curzon, 2003) p.5

3. Castles, Lance and Herbert Feith (eds), *Indonesian Political Thinking, 1945–1965* (Ithaca, NY: Cornell University Press, 1970) p.430

4. Hughes, *The End of Sukarno*, p.9

5. *Ibid.*, p.91

6. Weinstein, Franklin B., *Indonesian Foreign Policy and the Dilemma of Dependence* (Ithaca, NY: Cornell University Press, 1976) p.139

7. Crouch, Harold, *The Army and Politics in Indonesia* (Ithaca, NY: Cornell University Press, 1970) p.67

8. *Ibid.*, p.66

9. *Ibid.*, p.68

10. *Ibid.*, p.67

11. *Ibid.*, p.68

12. Weinstein, *Indonesian Foreign Policy*, p.32

13. Crouch, *The Army and Politics in Indonesia*, p.38

14. *Ibid.*, p.89

15. Hughes, *The End of Sukarno*, p.24

16. *Ibid.*, p.24

17. *Ibid.*, p.24

18. *Ibid.*, p.99

19. Crouch, *The Army and Politics in Indonesia*, p.96

20. Hughes, *The End of Sukarno*, p.56

21. Crouch, *The Army and Politics in Indonesia*, p.97

22. *Ibid.*, p.98

23. *Ibid.*, p.103

24. Elson, R.E., *Suharto: A Political Biography* (Cambridge: Cambridge University Press, 2001) p.115

25. Crouch, *The Army and Politics in Indonesia*, p.112

26. Hughes, *The End of Sukarno*, p.86

27. Elson, *Suharto*, p.35

28. Hughes, *The End of Sukarno*, p.145

29. *Ibid.*, p.153

30. *Ibid.*, p.163

31. *Ibid.*, p.167

32. Friends, Theodore, *Indonesian Destinies* (Cambridge, MA: The Belknap Press of Harvard University Press, 2003) p.110

33. Hughes, *The End of Sukarno*, p.190

34. *Ibid.*, p.190

35. Friend, *Indonesian Destinies*, p.115

36. Hughes, *The End of Sukarno*, p.198

37. Friend, *Indonesian Destinies*, p119

38. *Ibid.*, p.119

39. Crouch, *The Army and Politics in Indonesia*, p.164

40. *Ibid.*, p.167

41. *Ibid.*, p.168

42. Bourchier and Hadiz (eds), *Indonesian Politics and Society*, p.32

43. Reinhardt, Jon M., *Foreign Policy and National Integration: The Case of Indonesia* (New Haven: Yale University South East Asia Studies, 1971) p.10

32. LBJ and the Vietnam Quagmire

1. McNamara, Robert S., *In Retrospect: The Tragedy and Lessons of Vietnam* (Westminster, MD: Times Books, 1995) p.101

2. *Ibid.*, p.154

3. Caro, Robert, *Means of Ascent* (New York: Vintage Books, 1990) p.126

4. Dallek, Robert, *Flawed Giant: Lyndon Johnson 1960–1973* (New York, Oxford University Press, 1998) p.186

5. Caro, *Means of Ascent*, p.154

6. Dallek, *Flawed Giant*, p.408

7. Johnson, Paul, *A History of the American People* (New York, Harper Collins, 1997) p.277

8. Dallek, *Flawed Giant*, p.123

9. *Ibid.*, p.124

10. *Ibid.*, p.281

11. *Ibid.*, p.282

12. *Ibid.*, p.7

13. *Ibid.*, p.61

14. *Ibid.*, p.61

15. Johnson, *A History of the American People*, p.729

16. Dallek, *Flawed Giant*, p.249

17. *Ibid.*, p.100

18. McNamara, *In Retrospect*, p.17

19. Johnson, *A History of the American People*, p.735

20. McNamara, *In Retrospect*, p.153

21. Matloff, Maurice (ed), *American Military History* (New York: Combined Books, 1996) p.281

22. Dallek, *Flawed Giant*, p.277

23. McNamara, *In Retrospect*, p.206

24. *Ibid.*, p.322

25. Dallek, *Flawed Giant*, p.373

26. Kissinger, Henry, *The White House Years* (London, Weidenfeld & Nicolson, 1979) p.298

27. McNamara, *In Retrospect*, p.110

28. McNamara, *In Retrospect*, p.260

29. *Ibid.*, p.283

30. Johnson, *A History of the American People*, p.740

31. McNamara, *In Retrospect*, p.258

32. Zinn, Howard, *Vietnam: The Logic of Withdrawal* (Boston: Beacon Press, 1989) p.113

33. *Ibid.*, p.98

34. *Ibid.*, p.19

35. McNamara, *In Retrospect*, p.269

36. *Ibid.*, p.36

37. *Ibid.*, p.30

38. *Ibid.*, p.39

39. *Ibid.*, p.219
40. *Ibid.*, p.215
41. *Ibid.*, p.321
42. Johnson, *A History of the American People*, p.737
43. Dallek, *Flawed Giant*, p.99

33. The Trouble with Tigers

1. Bullion, Alan J., *India, Sri Lanka and the Tamil Crisis 1976–1994* (London and New York: Pinter, 1995) p.18
2. *Asia Times*, 1 December 2001
3. O'Balance, Edgar, *The Cyanide War: Tamil Insurrection in Sri Lanka* (London: Brassey's UK, 1989) p.7
4. *Ibid.*, p.8
5. *Ibid.*, p.9
6. Bullion, *India, Sri Lanka and the Tamil Crisis*, p.24
7. *Ibid.*, p.25
8. *Ibid.*, p.25
9. *Ibid.*, p.27
10. *Ibid.*, p.30
11. *Ibid.*, p.46
12. O'Balance, *The Cyanide War*, p.13
13. *Ibid.*, p.18
14. *Ibid.*, p.18
15. Bullion, *India, Sri Lanka and the Tamil Crisis*, p.32
16. *Ibid.*, p.31
17. O'Balance, *The Cyanide War*, p.21
18. *Ibid.*, p.52
19. *Ibid.*, p.97
20. *Ibid.*, p.55
21. *Ibid.*, p.59
22. Bullion, *India, Sri Lanka and the Tamil Crisis*, p.122
23. O'Balance, *The Cyanide War*, p.106
24. *Ibid.*, p.122

34. Nixon in China

1. Fairbank, John King, *China Watch* (Cambridge, MA: Harvard University Press, 1987) p.125
2. Johnson, Paul, *Modern Times* (New York: Harper Collins, 1997) p.684
3. Nixon, Richard, *Leaders* (New York: Buccaneer Books, 1994) p.74
4. *Ibid.*, p.74
5. *Ibid.*, p.160
6. Nixon, Richard, *The Real War* (London: Sidgwick & Jackson, 1980) p.141
7. *Ibid.*, p.318
8. McCullough, David, *Truman* (New York: Simon & Schuster, 1992) p.756
9. Freedman, Lawrence, *Kennedy's War: Berlin, Cuba, Laos and Vietnam* (New York and Oxford: Oxford University Press, 2000) p.259
10. *Ibid.*, p.272

11. McNamara, Robert S., *In Retrospect: The Tragedy and Lessons of Vietnam* (Westminster, MD: Times Books, 1995) p.321

12. Dallek, *Flawed Giant: Lyndon Johnson: 1960–1973* (New York: Oxford University Press, 1998) p.100

13. Isaacson, Walter, *Henry Kissinger: A Biography* (New York, Touchstone, 1992) p.191

14. *Ibid.*, p.151

15. Black, Conrad, *Richard Milhouse Nixon: The Invincible Quest* (London: Quercus, 2007)

16. Isaacson, *Henry Kissinger,* p.181

17. *Ibid.*, p.13

18. *Ibid.*, p.13

19. Goldstein, Steven M., *Chinese Foreign Policy Relations, Nationalism and Internationalism: Sino-Soviet* (New York: Oxford University Press, 1994) p.247

20. MacFarquhar, Roderick, *The Origins of the Cultural Revolution, Vol III: The Coming of the Cataclysm, 1961–1966* (New York: Columbia University Press, 1997) p.416

21. *Ibid.*, p.365

22. Nixon, *The Real War* (London: Sidgwick & Jackson, 1980) p.57

23. Kissinger, Henry, *The White House Years* (London: Weidenfeld & Nicolson, 1979) p.222

24. *Ibid.*, p.685

25. *Ibid.*, p.699

26. *Ibid.*, p.699

27. *Ibid.*, p.747

28. *Ibid.*, p.760

29. *Ibid.*, p.769

30. *Ibid.*, p.1062

31. *Ibid.*, p.1074

32. *Ibid.*, p.1092

33. Kissinger, *Diplomacy* (New York, Touchstone, 1994) p.622

34. Liao, Kuang-Sheng, *Antiforeignism and Modernization in China 1860 to 1980* (Hong Kong: Chinese University of Hong Kong, 1984) p.217

35. The Night of the Intellectuals

1. Datta, S.K. and Rajeev Sharma, *Pakistan: From Jinnah to Jehad* (New Delhi: UBS Publishers, 2002) p.97

2. Bennett-Jones, Owen, *Pakistan: Eye of the Storm* (New Haven, CT: Yale University Press) pp.160–1

3. Afzal, M. Rafique, *Pakistan History and Politics 1947–1971* (Karachi: Oxford University Press, 2001) p.404

4. Bennett-Jones, *Pakistan History and Politics,* p.163

5. Jaffrelot, Christophe (ed), *A History of Pakistan and Its Origins* (London: Anthem Press, 2004) p.55

6. Rose, Leo and Richard Sisson, *War and Secession: Pakistan, India, and the Creation of Bangladesh* (Berkley, CA: University of California Press, 1990) p.130

7. Harrison, Selig S., Paul H. Kreisberg and Dennis Kux (eds), *India & Pakistan: The First Fifty Years* (Cambridge: Cambridge University Press, 1999) p.186

8. Rose and Sisson, *War and Secession,* p.130

9. Bennett-Jones, *Pakistan,* p.167

10. *Ibid.*, p.170

11. Harrison, Kreisberg and Kux (eds), *India & Pakistan*, p.187
12. Datta and Sharma, *Pakistan*, p.148
13. Harrison, Kreisberg and Kux (eds), *India & Pakistan*, p.190
14. *Ibid.*, p.105
15. Datta and Sharma, *Pakistan*, p.146
16. Harrison, Kreisberg and Kux (eds), *India & Pakistan*, p.200
17. *Ibid.*, p.201
18. *Ibid.*, p.204
19. Datta and Sharma, *Pakistan*, p.140
20. Harrison, Kreisberg and Kux (eds), *India & Pakistan*, p.134
21. Jaffrelot (ed), *A History of Pakistan and its Origins*, p.58
22. Talbot, Ian, *Pakistan: A Modern History* (London: C. Hurst & Co., 2005) p.26

36. Têt Offensive: Lost Victories

1. Buzzanco, Robert, *Masters of War: Military Dissent and Politics in the Vietnam Era* (Cambridge: Cambridge University Press, 1996) p.102
2. Woodruff, Mark, *Unheralded Victory: Who Won the Vietnam War?* (London: Harper Collins, 1999) pp.49–50
3. *Ibid.*, p.57
4. *Ibid.*, p.133
5. Macdonald, Peter G., *Giap: The Victor in Vietnam* (London: The Fourth Estate, 1993) p.290
6. 'What did the North Vietnamese Hope to Gain with Their 1968 Tet Offensive?', *Perspectives* magazine, February 1963, pp.62–70
7. Woodruff, *Unheralded Victory*, p.58
8. *Ibid.*, p.185
9. *Ibid.*, p.186
10. Macdonald, *Giap*, p.269
11. Buzzanco, *Masters of War*, p.106
12. *Ibid.*, p.106
13. *Ibid.*, p.107
14. *Ibid.*, p.111
15. Woodruff, *Unheralded Victory*, p.225
16. Buzzanco, *Masters of War,* p.116
17. *Ibid.*, p.114
18. Woodruff, *Unheralded Victory*, p.206
19. Frost, David, *I Gave Them a Sword: Frost on Nixon* (London: Macmillan, 1978) p.295
20. Kissinger, Henry, *The White House Years* (London: Weidenfeld & Nicolson, 1979) p.284
21. *Ibid.*, p.444
22. Woodruff, *Unheralded Victory*, p.174
23. Kissinger, *The White House Years*, p.1117
24. *Ibid.*, p.1113
25. *Ibid.*, p.1454
26. *Ibid.*, p.1476
27. Buzzanco, *Masters of War*, p.128
28. Isaacson, *Kissinger*, p.647
29. Kissinger, *The White House Years*, p.1470

30. Macdonald, *Giap*, p.308

31. McNamara, *In Retrospect*, p.322

32. Kissinger, *The White House Years*, p.147

33. Trager, Frank N., *Why Vietnam?* (New York: Praeger, 1966) p.123

34. Haig, Alexander M., *Caveat* (London: Weidenfeld & Nicolson, 1984) p.202

37. The Bombing of Cambodia

1. Black, Conrad, *Richard Milhous Nixon: The Invincible Quest* (London: Quercus, 2007) p.475

2. *Ibid.*, p.486

3. Burchett, Wilfred, *The China, Cambodia, Vietnam Triangle* (Chicago: Vanguard Books, 1982) p.49

4. Isaacson, Walter, *Henry Kissinger: A Biography* (New York: Touchstone, 1992) p.171

5. *Ibid.*, p.179

6. Shawcross, William, *Sideshow: Kissinger, Nixon and the Destruction of Cambodia* (London: Andre Deutsche, 1979) p.287

7. *Ibid.*, p.122

8. Kissinger, *The White House Years* (London, Weidenfeld & Nicolson, 1992) p.472

9. *Ibid.*, p.510

10. Black, *Richard Milhous Nixon*, p.674

11. Kissinger, *The White House Years*, p.513

12. Nixon, Richard, *The Real War* (London: Sidgwick & Jackson, 1980) p.175

13. Kiernan, Ben, *The Pol Pot Regime: Race, Power, and Genocide in Cambodia under the Khmer Rouge 1975–9* (New Haven, CT and London: Yale University Press, 1996) p.21

14. Kissinger, *The White House Years*, p.519

15. Shawcross, *Sideshow*, p.284

16. *Ibid.*, p.285

17. Kissinger, *The White House Years*, p.459

18. *Ibid.*, p.249

19. Isaacson, *Henry Kissinger*, p.273

20. Shawcross, *Sideshow*, p.396

21. Brady, Christopher, *United States Foreign Policy towards Cambodia, 1972–92* (Basingstoke: Macmillan Press Ltd., 1999) p.355

38. Revolution's End: The Deaths of Mao, Zhou Enlai, Lin Biao

1. Sun, Warren and Frederick C. Teiwes, *The Tragedy of Lin Bao: Riding the Tiger During the Cultural Revolution 1966–1971* (Honolulu: University of Hawaii Press, 1996) p.123

2. Li, Zhisui, *The Private Life of Chairman Mao* (London: Chatto & Windus, 1994) p.454

3. Sun and Teiwes, *The Tragedy of Lin Bao*, p.15

4. *Ibid.*, p.109

5. MacFarquhar, Roderick, *The Succession to Mao and the End of Maoism, 1969–82* (Cambridge: Cambridge University Press, 1993) p.258

6. *Ibid.*, p.255

7. Sun and Teiwes, *The Tragedy of Lin Biao*, p.53

8. MacFarquhar, *The Succession to Mao*, p.270

9. Salisbury, Harrison E., *The New Emperors: China in the Era of Deng and Mao* (London: Harper Collins, 1992) p.327

10. *Ibid.*, p.342

11. MacFarquhar, *The Succession to Mao*, p.297

12. Lawrence, Alan, *China under Communism* (New York: Routledge, 1998) p.96

13. Chang, Yung, *The Wild Swans* (New York: Knopf Publishing, 1992) p.658

39. The Murder of Aquino: The Disgrace of Ferdinand Marcos

1. Blitz, Amy, *The Contested State* (Oxford: Rowman & Littlefield, 2000) p.103

2. *Ibid.*, p.103

3. *Ibid.*, p.12

4. *Ibid.*, p.18

5. Frum, David, *How We Got Here: The 70's: The Decade That Brought You Modern Life — For Better or Worse* (New York: Basic Books, 2000) p.86

6. Celoza, Albert F., *Ferdinand Marcos and the Philippines* (Westport CT: Praeger Publishers, 1997) p.64

7. *Ibid.*, p.65

8. *Ibid.*, p.66

9. Blitz, *The Contested State*, p.140

10. Edel, Wilbur, *The Reagan Presidency: An Actor's Finest Performance* (New York, Hippocrene Books, 1982) p.186

11. Blitz, *The Contested State*, p.160

12. *Ibid.*, p.18

13. *Ibid.*, p.163

14. *Ibid.*, p.137

15. John A. Pike to the author

16. Blitz, *The Contested State*, p.161

17. *Ibid.*, p.176

18. Steinberg, David Joel (ed), *In Search of Southeast Asia* (Sydney: Allen & Unwin, 2nd edition, 1987) p.134

19. Blitz, *The Contested State*, p.180

20. Hamilton-Paterson, James, *America's Boy: The Marcoses and the Philippines* (London, Granta Books, 1998) p.392

21. Celoza, *Ferdinand Marcos*, p.164

22. *Ibid.*, p.164

40. Coups d'Etat: A Way of Life

1. Wright, Joseph J., *A History of Modern Thailand* (Thailand: Asia Books, 1991) p.284

2. *Ibid.*, p.267

3. Wyatt, David K., *Thailand: A short History* (New Haven, CT: Yale University Press, 1982) p.280

4. Wright, *A History of Modern Thailand*, p.210

5. Jackson, Karl D. and Wiwat Mungkandi Jackson (eds), *United States–Thailand Relations* (Berkley: University of California Institute of East Asian Studies, 1986) p.165

6. *Ibid.*, p.233

7. Wright, *A History of Modern Thailand*, p.185

8. *Ibid.*, p.195

9. *Ibid.*, p.283

10. *Ibid.*, p.39

11. Cooper, Donald F., *Thailand: Dictatorship or Democracy?* (London: Minerva Press, 1995) p.330
12. Wright, *A History of Modern Thailand*, p.246

41. Zulfikar Ali Bhutto and General Mohammed Zia ul-Haq

1. Datta, S.K. and Rajeev Sharma, *Pakistan: From Jinnah to Jehad* (New Delhi: UBS Publishers, 2002) p.100
2. *Ibid.*, p.106
3. *Ibid.*, p.112
4. *Ibid.*, p.108
5. Cohen, Stephen P., *Emerging Power* (Washington, DC: Brookings Institute, 2004) p.79
6. Harrison, Selig S., Paul H. Kreisberg and Dennis Kux (eds), *India & Pakistan: The First Fifty Years* (Cambridge: Cambridge University Press, 1999) p.210
7. Cohen, *Emerging Power*, p.82
8. Ziring, Lawrence, *Pakistan: At the Crosscurrent of History* (Oxford, One World Publications, 2002) p.142
9. Bennett-Jones, Owen, *Pakistan: Eye of the Storm* (New Haven, CT: Yale University Press, 2002) p.109
10. *Ibid.*, p.110
11. Harrison, Kreisberg and Kux (eds), *India & Pakistan*, p.230
12. *Ibid.*, p.230
13. *Ibid.*, p.133
14. *Ibid.*, p.233
15. *Ibid.*, p.237
16. Weaver, Mary Anne, *Pakistan: In the Shadow of Jihad and Afghanistan* (New York: Farrar, Straus and Giroux, 1997) p.167
17. Harrison, Kreisberg and Kux (eds), *India & Pakistan*, p.238
18. *Ibid.*, p.238
19. *Ibid.*, p.245
20. Bennett-Jones, *Pakistan*, p.254
21. Datta and Sharma, *Pakistan*, p.173
22. Cohen, *Emerging Power*, p.15

42. Pol Pot: Deconstructionism and Genocide

1. Short, Philip, *Pol Pot: The History of a Nightmare* (London: John Murray, 2004) p.44
2. *Ibid.*, p.46
3. *Ibid.*, p.70
4. *Ibid.*, p.73
5. *Ibid.*, p.79
6. *Ibid.*, p.140
7. Burchett, Wilfred, *The China, Cambodia Vietnam Triangle* (Chicago: Vanguard Books, 1981) p.51
8. *Ibid.*, p.56
9. Jackson, Karl D., *Cambodia 1975–78: Rendezvous with Death* (Princeton, NJ: Princeton University Press, 1989) p.182
10. Kiernan, Ben, *The Pol Pot Regime: Race, Power, and Genocide in Cambodia under the Khmer Rouge 1975–79* (London: John Murray, 2004) p.27

11. Shawcross, William, *Sideshow: Kissinger, Nixon and the Destruction of Cambodia* (London: Andre Deutsche, 1979) p.349

12. United States Agency for International Development, April 1975 Report on Cambodia

13. Shawcross, *Sideshow*, p.317

14. Short, *Pol Pot*, p.268

15. *Ibid.*, p.269

16. *Ibid.*, p.270

17. Jackson, *Cambodia 1975–78*, p.182

18. Short, *Pol Pot*, p.279

19. *Ibid.*, p.288

20. *Ibid.*, p.288

21. *Ibid.*, p.289

22. *Ibid.*, p.290

23. Kiernan, *The Pol Pot Regime*, p.148

24. *Ibid.*, p.8

25. Chandler, David, *The Tragedy of Cambodia* (New Haven: Yale University Press, 1991) p.17

26. Kiernan, *The Pol Pot Regime*, p.183

27. Short, *Pol Pot*, p.273

28. Chandler, *The Tragedy of Cambodia*, p.302

29. Burchett, *The China, Cambodia Vietnam Triangle*, p.82

30. *Ibid.*, p.82

31. *Ibid.*, p.96

32. Yathay, Pin, *Stay Alive My Son* (London: Bloomsbury, 1987) p.81

33. Chandler, *The Tragedy of Cambodia*, p.304

34. Kiernan, *The Pol Pot Regime*, p.352

35. Burchett, Wilfred, *The China, Cambodia Vietnam Triangle*, p.68

36. Shawcross, *Sideshow*, p.385

37. Burchett, *The China, Cambodia Vietnam Triangle*, p.88

38. Shawcross, *Sideshow*, p.382

39. Kiernan, *The Pol Pot Regime*, pp.96–7

40. Jackson, *Cambodia*, p.247

41. *Ibid.*, p.245

42. Kiernan, *The Pol Pot Regime*, p.102

43. *Ibid.*, p.12

44. *Ibid.*, p.135

45. Jackson, *Cambodia*, p.31

46. Kiernan, *The Pol Pot Regime*, p.164

43. The Gang of Four

1. MacFarquhar, Roderick, *The Succession to Mao and the End of Maoism, 1969–82* (Cambridge: Cambridge University Press, 1993) p.306

2. Nixon, Richard, *Leaders* (New York: Buccaneer Books, 1994) pp.242–3

3. Kissinger, Henry, *The White House Years* (London: Weidenfeld & Nicolson, 1979) p.1063

4. Chang, Yung, *The Wild Swans* (New York: Knopf Publishing Group, 1992) p.618

5. *Ibid.*, p.618

6. Walsh, Frank, *A History of Hong Kong* (London: Harper Collins, 1997) p.467

7. Fairbank, John, King, *China Watch* (Cambridge, MA: Harvard University Press, 1987) p.163

8. *Ibid.*, p.179

9. *Ibid.*, p.176

10. Chang, *The Wild Swans*, p.508

11. Harding, Harry, 'The Chinese State in Crisis', in MacFarquhar, Roderick (ed), *The Politics of China: The Eras of Mao and Deng* (New York: Cambridge University Press, 1993) p.246

12. Terrill, Ross, *The New Chinese Empire* (New York: Basic Books, 2004) p.133

13. Lawrence, Alan, *China under Communism* (New York: Routledge, 1998) p.99

14. Evans, Richard, *Deng Xiaoping and the Making of Modern China* (London: Hamish Hamilton, 1993) p.226

44. The End of the Tyrants

1. Oh, John Kie-Chiang, *Korean Politics* (Ithaca, NY and London: Cornell University Press, 1999) p.75

2. Hart-Landsberg, Martin, *Korea: Division, Reunification, and US Foreign Policy* (New York: Monthly Review Press, 1989) p.190

3. *Ibid.*, p.191

4. *Ibid.*, p.193

5. Byung-joon Ahn, 'The US in Korea–Japanese Relations', Han, Sung-Joo (ed), *Continuity and Change in Korean–American Relations* (Seoul: Asiatic Research Center, 1982) p.145

6. Byung-joon Ahn, 'The US in Korea–Japanese Relations', p.137

7. Oh, *Korean Politics*, p.94

8. Hart-Landsberg, *Korea*, p.187

45. Dr Mahathir: The Acerbic Autocrat

1. Shome, Anthony S.K., *Malay Political Leadership* (London: Routledge Curzon, 2002) p.199

2. Munro-Kua, Anne, *Authoritarianism and Populism in Malaysia* (New York: St. Martins Press, 1996) p.56

3. Shome, *Malay Political Leadership*, p.132

4. *Ibid.*, p.153

5. *Ibid.*, p.158

6. *Ibid.*, p.158

7. *Ibid.*, p.159

8. Mauzy, Diane K. and R.S. Milne, *Malaysian Politics under Mahathir* (London: Routledge, 1999) p.118

9. *Ibid.*, p.123

10. Shome, *Malay Political Leadership*, p.180

11. Mauzy and Milne, *Malaysian Politics under Mahathir*, p.125

12. Shome, *Malay Political Leadership*, p.148

13. *Ibid.*, p.150

14. Hilley, John, *Malaysia: Mahathirism, Hegemony and the New Opposition* (Basingstoke: Palgrave, 2001) p.107

15. Milne and Mauzy, *Malaysian Politics under Mahathir*, p.150

16. Hilley, *Malaysia*, p.107

17. Shome, *Malay Political Leadership*, p.174

18. Hilley, *Malaysia*, p.152

19. Munro-Kua, *Authoritarianism and Populism in Malaysia,* p.110

20. Milne and Mauzy, *Malaysian Politics under Mahathir*, p.181

46. Suharto: A Study in Kleptocracy

1. Elson, R.E., *Suharto: A Political Biography* (Cambridge: Cambridge University Press, 2001) p.142

2. *Ibid.*, p.175

3. Bourchier, David and Vedi R. Hadiz (eds), *Indonesian Politics and Society* (London: Routledge Curzon, 2003) p.37

4. *Ibid.*, p.88

5. Elson, *Suharto*, p.176

6. Bourchier and Hadiz (eds), *Indonesian Politics*, p.187

7. Tanter, Richard, Mark Sheldon and Stephen R. Shalom, *Bitter Flower, Sweet Flowers: East Timor, Indonesia and the World Community* (Oxford: Rowman and Littlefield, 2001) p.246

8. Ibid., p.247

9. Kingsbury, Damien, *The Politics of Indonesia* (New York: Oxford University Press, 2005) p.155

10. Bourchier and Hadiz (eds), *Indonesian Politics*, p.237

11. Kingsbury, *The Politics of Indonesia*, p.156

12. Elson, *Suharto*, p.150

13. *Ibid.*, p.17

14. Crouch, Harold, *The Army and Politics in Indonesia* (Ithaca, NY: Cornell University Press, 1978) p.287

15. *Ibid.*, p.285

16. Kingsbury, *The Politics of Indonesia*, p.194

17. Elson, *Suharto*, p.213

18. Bourchier and Hadiz (eds), *Indonesian Politics*, p.272

19. *Jakarta Post*, 31 March 1977

20. Elson, *Suharto*, p.288

21. *Ibid.*, p.293

47. Rogue State

1. Su, Choe, *The People's Leader* (Pyongyang: Foreign Languages Publishing House, 1985) p.379

2. Cornell, Erik, *North Korea under Communism: Report of an Envoy to Paradise* (London: Routledge, 2002) p.10

3. *Ibid.*, p.45

4. *Ibid.*, p.22

5. *Ibid.*, p.49

6. *Ibid.*, p.18

7. *Ibid.*, p.29

8. Jean Barre, 'There's Nothing Impossible to the Koreans', in *Kim Il Sung, The Brilliant Banner of Juche* (Pyongyang: Foreign Languages Publishing House, 1981) p.171

9. *Ibid.*, p.171

10. William Wilson, 'A British MP's Visit to Korea', in *Kim Il Sung, The Brilliant Banner of Juche* (Pyongyang: Foreign Languages Publishing House, 1981) p.157

11. *Ibid.*, p.157

12. *Ibid.*, p.159

13. Cornell, *North Korea under Communism*, p.103

14. French, Paul, *North Korea: The Paranoid Peninsula, A Modern History* (New York: Palgrave Macmillan, 2005) p.124

15. North Korean general to the author, Autumn 1993, Pyongyang, North Korea

16. Hart-Landsberg, Martin, *Korea: Division, Reunification, and US Foreign Policy* (New York: Monthly Review Press, 1989) p.155

17. Clinton, Bill, *My Life* (New York: Alfred A. Knopf, 2004) p.561

18. *Ibid.*, p.938

19. Author to intelligence officer, Autumn 1993, Ritz-Carlton, Hong Kong

20. Albright, Madeline, *Madam Secretary* (London: Macmillan, 2003) p.468

48. Bloodlust and Revenge

1. Baxter, Craig, *Bangladesh: From a Nation to a State* (Boulder, CO: Westview Press, 1997) p.86

2. *Ibid.*, p.108

49. Cory Aquino and the Rocky Path to Democracy

1. Amy Blitz, *The Contested State* (Oxford: Rowman & Littlefield, 2000) p.172

2. *Ibid*, p.173

3. Steinberg, David Joel, *The Philippines* (Boulder, CO, Westview Press, 1994) pp.151–2

4. *Ibid.*, p.164

5. Steinberg, David, *The Philippines*, p.184

6. As seen by the author at Central Bank in Manila in 1987

7. Steinberg, *The Philippines*, p.180

8. *Ibid.*, p.190

9. *Ibid.*, p.202

50. Deng Xiaoping: 'Capitalist Roader No. 2'

1. Kissinger, Henry, *Years of Renewal* (London: Weidenfeld & Nicolson, 1999) p.163

2. *Ibid.*, p.164

3. Goodman, David S.G., *Deng Xiaoping and the Chinese Revolution* (London and New York: Routledge, 1994) p.117

4. Li, Zhisui, *The Private Life of Chairman Mao* (London: Chatto & Windus, 1994) p.636

5. Evans, Richard, *Deng Xiaoping and the Making of Modern China* (London: Hamish Hamilton, 1993) p.263

6. Hsu, C.Y., *China Without Mao, The Search for a New Order* (New York: Oxford University Press, 2nd edition, 1990) p.72

7. *Ibid.*, p.72

8. *Ibid.*, p.59

9. *Ibid.*, p.60

10. Kissinger, *Years of Renewal*, p.164

11. Terrill, Ross, *The New Chinese Empire* (New York: Basic Books, 2004) p.261

12. Brendon, Piers, *Ike, The Life and Times of Dwight Eisenhower* (London: Secker & Warburg, 1987) p.285

13. Domenach, Jean Luc, *The Origins of the Great Leap Forward* (Boulder, CO: Westview Press, 1995) p.58

14. Evans, *Deng Xiaoping and the Making of Modern China*, p.121
15. *Ibid.*, p.280
16. MacFarquhar, Roderick, *Origins of the Cultural Revolution, Vol III: The Coming Cataclysm, 1961–66* (New York: Columbia University Press, 1993) p.223
17. Reagan, Ronald, *An American Life* (London: Hutchison, 1990) p.369
18. Hsu, C.Y., *The Rise of Modern China* (New York: Oxford University Press, 2000) p.841
19. Evans, *Deng Xiaoping and the Making of Modern China*, p.250
20. Chinese graduate to the author 1989
21. Fishman, Ted C., *China Inc.* (London: Simon & Schuster Ltd., 2005) p.67
22. Evans, *Deng Xiaoping and the Making of Modern China*, p.270
23. Baum, Richard, *Reform and Reaction in Post Mao China: The Road to Tiananmen* (New York: Routledge, 1991) p.371
24. *Ibid.*, p.371
25. Hsu, *The Rise of Modern China*, p.901

51. Benazir and Sharif: Rise and Fall of the Demagogues

1. Weaver, Mary Anne, *Pakistan, In the Shadow of Jihad and Afghanistan* (New York: Farrar, Straus and Giroux, 1997) p.182
2. *Ibid.*, p.184
3. *Ibid.*, p.184
4. *Ibid.*, p.193
5. *Ibid.*, p.205
6. Talbot, Ian, *Pakistan, A Modern History* (London, C. Hurst & Co., 2005) p.293
7. Margolis, Eric, 7 October 1999
8. Harrison, Selig S., Paul H. Kreisberg and Dennis Kux (eds), *India & Pakistan: The First Fifty Years* (Cambridge: Cambridge University Press, 1999) p.339
9. *Ibid.*, p.340
10. Bennett-Jones, Owen, *Pakistan: Eye of the Storm* (New York, CT: Yale University Press, 2002) p.237
11. Talbot, *Pakistan*, p.253
12. Harrison, Kreisberg and Kux (eds), *India & Pakistan*, p.144
13. Bennett-Jones, *Pakistan*, p.127

52. The Narcotic State

1. Tucker, Shelby, *Burma: The Curse of Independence* (London: Pluto Press, 2001) p.187
2. Lintner, Bernil, *Burma in Revolt* (Thailand: Silkworm Books, 1999) p.157
3. *Ibid.*, p.221
4. *Ibid.*, p.221
5. Tucker, *Burma*, p.189
6. *Ibid.*, p.26
7. Lintner, *Burma in Revolt*, p.236
8. *Ibid.*, p.233
9. *Ibid.*, p.235
10. *Ibid.*, p.364
11. *Ibid.*, p.362
12. Tucker, *Burma*, p.178
13. *Ibid.*, p.178

14. Lintner, *Burma in Revolt*, p.167

15. *Ibid.*, p.180

16. Tucker, *Burma*, p.179

17. Ott, Martin C., *Burma: A Strategic Perspective* (Washington: National Defence University, Institute For National Strategy Studies, 1996) p.73

18. Ott, *Burma*, p.76

19. Fink, Christiana, *Living Silence* (New York: Zed Books, 2001) p.239

20. Lintner, *Burma in Revolt*, p.417

21. *Ibid.*, p.419

53. Rajiv Gandhi: The Reluctant Pilot

1. Tully, Mark, *No Full Stops* (New York: Penguin, 1991) p.332

2. Singh, Tavleen, *Kashmir: A Tragedy of Errors* (New York: Penguin Books, 1996) p.97

3. Fishlock, Trevor, *Gandhi's Children* (Madison: University of Wisconsin Press, 1983) p.91

4. Nugent, Nicholas, *Rajiv Gandhi: Son of a Dynasty* (London: BBC Books, 1990) p.60

5. *Ibid.*, p.60

6. Mehta, Ved, *Rajiv Gandhi and Rama's Kingdom* (New Haven: Yale University Press, 1994) p.81

7. *Ibid.*, p.62

8. Varma, Srikanta, *A Portrait of Rajiv Gandhi* (London: Arnold-Heinemann, 1985) p.159

9. Aluwahia, B.K., *Rajiv Gandhi* (New Delhi: Cosmo Books, 1985) p.55

10. *Ibid.*, p.61

11. Tully, *No Full Stops*, p.333

12. Healy, Kathleen, *Rajiv Gandhi: The years of power* (New Delhi: Vikas Publishing House, 1989) p.186

13. Nugent, *Rajiv Gandhi*, p.91

14. Healy, *Rajiv Gandhi*, p.102

15. Singh, *Kashmir*, p.97

16. Nugent, *Rajiv Gandhi*, p.111

17. *Ibid.*, p.117

18. Mehta, *Rajiv Gandhi*, p.152

19. Nugent, *Rajiv Gandhi*, p.119

20. *Ibid.*, p.126

21. Healy, *Rajiv Gandhi*, p.299

22. *Ibid.*, p.33

23. *Ibid.*, p.33

24. Healy, *Rajiv Gandhi*, p.33

25. *Ibid.*, p.34

26. Tully, *No Full Stops*, p.334

27. *Ibid.*, p.335

28. Healy, *Rajiv Gandhi*, p.153

54. The Tiananmen Square Massacre

1. MacFarquhar, Roderick (ed), *The Politics of China: The Eras of Mao and Deng* (New York: Cambridge University Press, 2nd edition, 1993) p.23

2. Evans, Richard, *Deng Xiaoping and the Making of Modern China* (London: Hamish Hamilton, 1993) p.235

3. *Ibid.*, p.234
4. MacFarquhar (ed), *The Politics of China*, p.234
5. MacFarquhar, Roderick, *The Succession to Mao and the End of Maoism,* 1969–82 (Cambridge: Cambridge University Press, 1993) p.326
6. Dr Simon May to the author
7. Goodman, David S.G., *Deng Xiaoping and the Chinese Revolution* (London & New York: Routledge, 1994) p.122
8. Evans, *Deng Xiaoping and the Making of Modern China*, p.241
9. MacFarquhar (ed), *The Politics of China*, p.369
10. Evans, *Deng Xiao Ping and the Making of Modern China*, p.278
11. MacFarquhar (ed), *The Politics of China*, p.394
12. *Ibid.*, p.280
13. *Ibid.*, p.413
14. *Ibid.*, p.425
15. *People's Daily*, 26 April 1989
16. Greene, John Robert, *The Presidency of George Bush* (Laurence: University Press of Kansas, 2000) p.93
17. Link, Perry and Andrew J. Nathan (eds), *The Tiananmen Papers* (New York: Public Affairs, 2001) p.155
18. Mackerras, Colin, Pradeep Taneja and Graham Young, *China since 1978* (Melbourne: Longman, 2nd edition, 1998) p.41
19. Link and Nathan (eds), *The Tiananmen Papers*, p.204
20. Mackerras, Colin, *Eastern Asia* (Melbourne: Longman Australia, 1992) p.46
21. Greene, *The Presidency of George Bush*, p.94
22. *Ibid.*, p.94
23. *Ibid.*, p.94
24. Huntington, Samuel P., *The Clash of Civilizations and the Remaking of World Order* (New York: Simon & Schuster, 1996) p.195
25. Chinese businessman to the author, Canton, China, 1983

55. Property Crash and the Lost Decade

1. Blomstrom, Magnus, Byron Gangnes and Sumner La Croix (eds), *Japan's New Economy: Continuity and Change in the Twenty-First Century* (New York: Oxford University Press, 2001) p.31
2. Wood, Christopher, *The Japanese Economic Collapse* (London: Sidgwick & Jackson, 1992) p.133
3. Blomstrom, Gangnes and La Croix (eds), *Japan's New Economy*, p.72
4. Mclain, James L., *Japan: A Modern History* (New York: W.W. Norton & Co., 2002) p.629
5. Curtis, Gerald L., *The Logic of Japanese Politics: Leaders, Institutions, and the Limits of Change* (New York: Columbia University Press, 1999) p.89
6. *Ibid.*, p.181
7. *Ibid.*, p.182
8. Bouissou, Jean-Marie, *Japan: The Burden of Success* (London: Hurst & Company, 2002) p.288
9. *Ibid.*, p.291
10. Sims, Richard, *Japanese Political History since the Meiji Restoration* (London: Hurst & Company, 2001) p.352
11. *Ibid.*, p.353

12. Bouissou, *Japan*, p.298
13. Curtis, *The Logic of Japanese Politics*, p.194
14. *Ibid.*, p.222

56. Narasimha Rao and the Quiet Revolution

1. *Hardtalk* interview of Shri P. Chidambaram with Stephen Sackur, 19 October 2005
2. Narasimha Rao, P.V., *The Insider* (New Delhi: Viking, 1999) p.557
3. *Ibid.*, p.538
4. *Ibid.*, p.833

57. The Savaging of the Tiger Economies

1. Riès, Philippe and Peter Starr, *Asia Storm: The Economic Crisis Examined* (Boston: Tuttle Publishing, 2000) p.12
2. *Ibid.*, p.15
3. *Ibid.*, pp.12–13
4. Noble, Gregory W. and John Ravenhill (eds), *The Asian Financial Crisis and the Architecture of Global Finance* (New York: Cambridge University Press, 2000) p.90
5. Mallet, Victor, *The Trouble with Tigers; The Rise and Fall of South East Asia* (London: Harper Collins, 1999) p.146
6. Riès and Starr, *Asia Storm*, p.58
7. *Ibid.*, p.51
8. *Ibid.*, p.66
9. *Ibid.*, p.68
10. Mallet, *The Trouble with Tigers*, p.50
11. Noble and Ravenhill (eds), *The Asian Financial Crisis*, p.126
12. Riès and Starr, *Asia Storm*, p.144
13. Noble and Ravenhill (eds), *The Asian Financial Crisis*, p.215
14. Riès and Starr, *Asia Storm*, p.226
15. *Ibid.*, p.219
16. *Ibid.*, p.120
17. Noble and Ravenhill (eds), *The Asian Financial Crisis*, p.54
18. Riès and Starr, *Asia Storm*, p.215
19. *Ibid.*, p.193
20. *Ibid.*, p.62
21. Noble and Ravenhill, *The Asian Financial Crisis*, p.52
22. Riès and Starr, *Asia Storm*, p.69
23. Mallet, Victor, *The Trouble with Tigers: The Rise and Fall of South East Asia*, p.160
24. Riès and Starr, *Asia Storm*, p.172

58. A Bungled Surrender

1. Tsang, Steve, *A Modern History of Hong Kong* (London: I.B.Tauris, 2004) p.206
2. *Ibid.*, p.211
3. *Ibid.*, p.211
4. Tsang, *A Modern History of Hong Kong*, p.214
5. *Ibid.*, p.215
6. Thatcher, Margaret, *The Downing Street Years* (New York: Harper Collins, 2003) p.259

7. *Ibid.*, p.259
8. Tsang, *A Modern History of Hong Kong*, p.221
9. Thatcher, *The Downing Street Years*, p.262
10. Tsang, *A Modern History of Asia*, p.226
11. *Ibid.*, p.226
12. *Ibid.*, p.206
13. Walsh, Frank, *A History of Hong Kong*, p.546
14. Tsang, *A Modern History of Hong Kong*, p.243
15. *Ibid.*, p.244
16. *Ibid.*, p.250
17. Walsh, Frank, *A History of Hong Kong*, p.549
18. Tsang, *A Modern History of Hong Kong*, p.260
19. Walsh, *A History of Hong Kong*, p.549
20. *Ibid.*, p.546
21. Tsang, *A Modern History of Hong Kong*, p.264
22. *Ibid.*, p.269

59. One China or Two?

1. Jo, Yung-Hwan (ed), *Taiwan's Future* (Hong Kong: Union Research Institute for Arizona State University, 1974) p.182
2. *Ibid.*, p.182
3. Jo (ed), *Taiwan's Future*, p.100
4. Fu, Jen-Kun, *Taiwan and the Geopolitics of the Asian–American Dilemma* (New York: Praeger, 1992) p.56
5. *Ibid.*, p.54
6. Leng, Shao-chuan (ed), *Chiang Ching-Kuo's Leadership in the Development of the Republic on Taiwan* (Lanham, MD: University Press of America, 1993) p.146
7. Jen-Kun Fu, *Taiwan and the Geopolitics of the Asian–American Dilemma*, p.67
8. *Ibid.*, p.69
9. *Ibid.*, p.70
10. *Ibid.*, p.72
11. *Ibid.*, p.73
12. Leng (ed), *Chiang Ching-Kuo's Leadership*, p.35
13. Roy, Denny, *Taiwan: A Political History* (Ithaca, NY: Cornell University Press, 2003) p.158
14. *Ibid.*, p.153
15. *Ibid.*, p.173
16. Leng (ed), *Chiang Ching-Kuo's Leadership*, p.34
17. Wu, Jaushieh Joseph, *Taiwan's Democratisation* (Hong Kong: Oxford University Press, 1995) p.144
18. *Ibid.*, p.151
19. *Ibid.*, p.6
20. Evans, Richard, *Deng Xiaoping and the Making of Modern China* (London: Hamish Hamilton, 1993) p.337
21. Terrill, Ross, *The New Chinese Empire* (New York: Basic Books, 2004) p.253
22. *Ibid.*, p.337

60. Nukes and Mullahs

1. Kux, Dennis, *Disenchanted Allies: The United States and Pakistan 1947 to 2000* (Baltimore: Johns Hopkins University Press, 2001)
2. *Ibid.*, p.219
3. *Ibid.*, pp.239–40
4. *Ibid.*, p.257
5. *Ibid.*, p.258
6. *Ibid.*, p.257
7. *Ibid.*, p.261
8. *Ibid.*, p.273
9. *Ibid.*, p.275
10. Griffiths, John. C., *Afghanistan: A History of Conflict* (London: André Deutsch, 2001) p.183
11. Burke, Jason, *Al Qaeda: The True Story of Radical Islam* (London: Penguin, 2004) p.73
12. Kux, *Disenchanted Allies*, p.287
13. *Ibid.*, p.289
14. *Ibid.*, p.279
15. *Ibid.*, p.284
16. *Ibid.*, p.299
17. *Ibid.*, p.306
18. *Ibid.*, p.314
19. *Ibid.*, p.327
20. *Ibid.*, p.336
21. Pillar, Paul, *Terrorism and US Foreign Policy* (Washington: The Brookings Institution, 2001) p.64
22. Lewis, Bernard, *Holy War and Unholy Terror: The Crisis of Islam* (London: Weidenfeld & Nicolson) p.121

61. Asia Redux

1. Marti, Michael E., *China and the Legacy of Deng Xiaoping* (Dulles, VA: Brassey's Inc., 2002) p.1856
2. Zheng, Bijan, *Foreign Affairs: 'China's Peaceful Rise to Great Power Status'* (Cambridge: Cambridge University Press, 1997) p.24
3. Roy, Denny, *Taiwan: A Political History* (Ithaca, NY: Cornell University Press, 2003) p.242
4. *The Economist*, 25 December 2004
5. BBC News, 31 October 2008
6. Noland, Marcus, 'Why North Korea will Muddle Through', *Foreign Affairs*, July/August 1997, p.109
7. French, Paul, *North Korea: The Paranoid Peninsula, A Modern History* (New York: Palgrave Macmillan, 2005) pp.288–9
8. *Associated Press*, 28 January 2008
9. *The Economist*, 1 November 2003
10. Peebles, Gavin and Peter Wilson, *Economic Growth and Development in Singapore* (Cheltenham, UK: Edward Elgar, 2002) p.264
11. *The Economist*, 24 July 2004
12. *The Economist*, 18 September 2004
13. Stern, Robert W., *Changing India* (New York: Cambridge University Press, 2003) p.6
14. BBC News, Radio 4, 30 December 2007

15. Baxter, Craig, *Bangladesh: From a Nation to a State* (Boulder, CO: Westview Press, 1997) p.126
16. *Ibid.*, p.161
17. Lamb, David, *Vietnam Now* (New York: Public Affairs, 2002) p.71
18. Gottesman, Evan, *Cambodia: After the Khmer Rouge* (New Haven: Yale University Press, 2002) p.344

62. From Cold War to End of Empire

1. Melanson, Richard A., *American Foreign Policy since the Vietnam War: The Search for Consensus from Nixon to Clinton* (Armonk, NY: M.E. Sharpe, 3rd edition, 2000) p.47
2. Black, Conrad, *Franklin Delano Roosevelt* (London: Weidenfeld & Nicolson, 2002) p.425
3. *Ibid.*, p.518
4. Ferguson, Niall, *Empire: How Britain made the Modern World* (London: Allen Lane, 2002) p.370
5. McCullough, David, *Truman* (New York: Simon & Schuster 1992)
6. Conquest, Robert, *Reflections on a Ravaged Century* (New York: John Murray, 1999) p.113
7. *Ibid.*, p.111
8. *Ibid.*, p.112
9. *Ibid.*, p.162
10. *Ibid.*, p.112
11. *Ibid.*, p.109
12. *Ibid.*, p.151
13. Taubman, William, *Krushchev: The Man and his Era* (London: The Free Press, 2003) p.348
14. Conquest, *Reflections on a Ravaged Century*, p.154
15. *Ibid.*, p.156
16. Barnett, Corelli, *Lost Victory* (London: Pan Books, 2003) p.28
17. *Ibid.*, p.41
18. Kagan, Robert, *Power and Paradise* (New York: Alfred A. Knopf, 2003) p.17
19. Mahoney, Richard D., *JFK: Ordeal in Africa* (New York: Oxford University Press, 1983) p.20
20. McCormick, Thomas J., *America's Half Century: United States Foreign Policy in the Cold War and After* (Baltimore: John Hopkins University Press, 2nd edition, 1995) p.51
21. *Ibid.*, p.52
22. Kissinger, Henry, *Does America need a Foreign Policy?* (New York: Simon & Schuster, 2001) p.211
23. Smuts, J.C., *Jan Christian Smuts* (London: Cassell & Co. Ltd., 1952) p.508
24. McCormick, *America's Half Century*, p.72
25. Melanson, *American Foreign Policy since the Vietnam War*, p.73
26. Kissinger, *Does America Need a Foreign Policy?* p.247
27. Reagan, Ronald, *An American Life* (London: Hutchinson, 1990) p.241
28. Kagan, *Power and Paradise*, p.41
29. Helmut Schmidt to the author and colleagues, Goring Hotel, London, 1991
30. Conquest, *Reflections on a Ravaged Century*, p.169
31. Ouimet, Mathew, *The Rise and Fall of the Brezhnev Doctrine in Soviet Foreign Policy* (Chapel Hill, NC: The University of North Carolina Press, 2003) p.4
32. *Ibid.*, p.169

33. Ambrose, Stephen E. and Douglas Brinkley, *Rise to Globalism: American Foreign Policy since 1938* (New York: Penguin, 1997) p.169

34. Chomsky, Noam, *American Power and the New Mandarins* (New York: The New Press, 1967), foreword, p.v

35. *Ibid.*, p.ix

36. Zinn, Howard, in Chomsky, Noam, *American Power and The New Mandarins* (New York: The New Press, 1967) foreword, p.viii

37. Transcript from US Congress House Committee on Internal Security Areas, HR 16742, 19–25 September 1972, p.7

38. Frum, David, *How We Got Here: The 70's: The Decade That Brought You Modern Life – For Better or Worse* (New York: Basic Books, 2000) p.305

39. Chomsky, *American Power*, p.262

40. *Ibid.*, p.403

41. Black, Conrad, *Richard Milhous Nixon: The Invincible Quest* (London: Quercus, 2007) p.570

42. Chomsky, *American Power*, p.403

43. Kagan, *Power and Paradise*, p.60

44. United Nations Charter

45. Carter, Jimmy, *Keeping Faith: Memoirs of a President* (Fayetteville, AR: University of Arkansas Press, 1995) p.147

46. *Ibid.*, p.147

47. Melanson, *American Foreign Policy since the Vietnam War*, p.99

48. Lasky, Victor, *Jimmy Carter: The Man and the Myth* (New York: Richard Marek Publishers, 1989) p.382

49. Cannon, Lou, *President Reagan* (New York: Public Affairs, 2000) p.273

50. Regan, Donald T., *For the Record: From Wall Street to Washington* (London: Hutchinson, 1988) p.295

51. Cannon, *President Reagan,* p.404

52. *Ibid.*, p.404

53. Noonan, Peggy, *When Character was King: A Story of Ronald Reagan* (New York: Penguin, 2002) p.203

54. Melanson, *American Foreign Policy since the Vietnam War*, p.151

55. McCormick, *America's Half Century*, p.229

56. Haig, Alexander M., *Caveat* (London: Weidenfeld & Nicolson, 1984) p.298

57. Melanson, *American Foreign Policy since the Vietnam War*, p.224

58. Haig, *Caveat*, p.195

59. Reagan, *An American Life*, p.369

60. *Ibid.*, p.373

61. Washington Council on International Trade, 4 November 1997

62. Haig, *Caveat*, p.196

63. Blumenthal, Sidney, *The Clinton Wars* (London: Viking, 2003) p.120

64. Melanson, *American Foreign Policy since the Vietnam War*, p.47

65. Lake, Anthony, *Confronting Backlash States* (Executive Office of the President, 1994) p.45

66. Melanson, *American Foreign Policy since the Vietnam War*, p.272

67. Clinton, *My Life*, p.930

68. Ambrose and Brinkley, *Rise to Globalism*, p.407

69. Melanson, *American Foreign Policy since the Vietnam War*, p.314

70. McCormick, *America's Half Century*, p.251

71. Wood, Christopher, *Greed and Fear*, to the author, October 2007

72. Huntington, Samuel P., *The Clash of Civilizations and the Remaking of World Order* (New York: Simon & Schuster, 1996) p.29

73. Weiner, Tim, *Legacy of Ashes: The History of the CIA* (London: Allen & Lane, 2007) p.513

74. Johnson, Paul, *A History of the American People* (New York: Harper Collins, 1997) p.830

75. Moynahan, Brian, *Claws of the Bear: The History of the Red Army from the Revolution to the Present* (New York: Houghton Mifflin, 1989) p.243

76. Hersh, Seymour, M., *The Dark Side of Camelot* (New York: Little, Brown and Company, 1997) p.441

77. Kissinger, *Does America Need a Foreign Policy?*, p.287

78. Terrill, Ross, *The New Chinese Empire* (New York: Basic Books, 2004) p.342

79. Reagan, *An American Life*, p.273

Bibliography

America

Albright, Madeline, *Madam Secretary* (London: Macmillan, 2003)

Ambrose, Stephen E. and Douglas Brinkley, *American Foreign Policy since 1938* (New York: Penguin, 8th revised edition, 1997)

Black, Conrad, *Franklin Delano Roosevelt* (London: Weidenfeld & Nicolson, 2003)

Black, Conrad, *Richard Milhous Nixon: The Invincible Quest* (London: Quercus, 2007)

Blumenthal, Sidney, *The Clinton Wars* (London: Viking, 2003)

Boyer, Paul S. (ed), *The Oxford Companion to the United States History* (New York: Oxford University Press, 2001)

Boyer, Paul S. (ed), *Reagan as President* (Chicago: Ivan R. Dee, 1990)

Brendon, Piers, *Ike: The Life and Times of Dwight Eisenhower* (London: Secker & Warburg, 1987)

Brands, H.W., *The United States in the World: A History of American Foreign Policy* (Boston: Houghton Mifflin, 1994)

Brookhiser, Richard, *Alexander Hamilton: American* (New York: The Free Press, 1999)

Brown, Dee, *Bury My Heart at Wounded Knee* (New York: Henry Holt & Co., 1970)

Bush, George W., State Visit Speech, Banqueting Hall (November 2003)

Cannon, Lou, *President Reagan* (New York: Public Affairs, 2000)

Caro, Robert A., *Master of the Senate: The Years of Lyndon Johnson* (New York: Alfred A. Knopf, 2002)

Caro, Robert A., *Means of Ascent: The Years of Lyndon Johnson* (New York: Vintage Books, 1990)

Caro, Robert A., *The Path to Power: The Years of Lyndon Johnson* (New York: Vintage Books, 1990)

Carter, Jimmy, *Keeping Faith: Memoirs of a President* (Fayetteville, AR: University of Arkansas Press, 1995)

Chace, James, *Acheson: The Secretary of State Who Created the American World* (New York: Simon & Schuster, 1998)

Chomsky, Noam, *American Power and the New Mandarins* (New York: The New Press, 1967, 2002)

Clarke, Jonathan and Stefan Halper, *America Alone: The Neo-Conservatives and the Global Order* (New York: Cambridge University Press, 2004)

Clinton, Bill, *My Life* (New York: Alfred A. Knopf, 2004)

Commager, Henry Steele, William E. Leuchtenburg and Samuel Eliot Morison, *The Growth of the American Republic*, Volumes I & II (London: Oxford University Press, 6th edition, 1969)

Dallek, Robert, *Flawed Giant: Lyndon Johnson 1960–1973* (New York: Oxford University Press, 1998)

Dallek, Robert, *Ronald Reagan: The Politics of Symbolism* (Cambridge, MA: Harvard University Press, 1999)

D'Este, Carlo, *Eisenhower: Allied Supreme Commander* (London: Weidenfeld & Nicolson, 2002)

De Tocqueville, Alexis, *Democracy in America* (Chicago: University of Chicago Press, 2002)

Edel, Wilbur, *The Reagan Presidency: An Actor's Finest Performance* (New York: Hippocrene Books, 1992)

Fleming, Thomas, *The Louisiana Purchase* (Hoboken, NJ: John Wiley & Sons Inc., 2003)

Freedman, Lawrence, *Kennedy's Wars: Berlin, Cuba, Laos and Vietnam* (New York and Oxford: Oxford University Press, 2000)

Friedman, Thomas, *The Lexus and the Olive Tree* (London: Harper Collins, 1999)

Friedman, Thomas, *The World is Flat: A Brief History of the Globalised World in the 21st Century* (London: Allen Lane, 2005)

Frost, David, *I Gave Them a Sword: Frost on Nixon* (London: Macmillan, 1978)

Frost, David, *Frost / Nixon* (London: Macmillan, 2007)

Frum, David, *An End to Evil* (New York: Random House, 2003)

Frum, David, *The Right Man: The Surprise Presidency of George W. Bush* (New York: Random House, 2003)

Frum, David, *How We Got Here: The 70's: The Decade That Brought You Modern Life – For Better or Worse* (New York: Basic Books, 2000)

Goldberg, Robert Alan, *Barry Goldwater* (New Haven: Yale University Press, 1995)

Goold-Adams, Richard, *The Time of Power: A Reappraisal of John Foster Dulles* (London: Weidenfeld & Nicolson, 1962)

Greene, John Robert, *The Presidency of George Bush* (Lawrence: University Press of Kansas, 2000)

Griffiths, John. C., *Afghanistan, A History of Conflict* (London: André Deutsch, 2001)

Gunther, John, *The Riddle of MacArthur: Japan, Korea, and the Far East* (London: Hamish Hamilton, 1951)

Haig, Alexander M., *Caveat* (London: Weidenfeld & Nicolson, 1984)

Haines, Gerald K. and J. Samuel Walker (eds), *American Foreign Relations: A Historiographical Review* (London: Frances Pinter Ltd., 1981)

Hamby, Alonzo L., *Man of the People: A Life of Harry S. Truman* (New York and Oxford: Oxford University Press, 1995)

Harvey, Robert, *American Shogun, MacArthur, Hirohito and the American Duel with Japan* (London: John Murray, 2006)

Hersh, Seymour M., *The Dark Side of Camelot* (New York: Little, Brown and Company, 1997)

Hitchens, Christopher, *The Trial of Henry Kissinger* (New York: Verso Press, 2001)

Isaacson, Walter, *Benjamin Franklin: An American Life* (New York: Simon & Schuster, 2003)

Kaplan, Amy and Donald E. Pease, *Cultures of United States Imperialism* (Durham: Duke University Press, 1993)

Kennan, George F., *The Cloud of Danger* (Boston and Toronto: Atlantic Little-Brown Books, 1977)

Kennan, George F., *Memoirs 1925–1950* (New York: Pantheon Books, 1967)

Kennan, George F., *Memoirs 1950–1963* (London: Hutchinson & Co. Ltd., 1973)

Kissinger, Henry, *Does America Need a Foreign Policy?* (New York: Simon & Schuster, 2001)

Kissinger, Henry, *The White House Years* (London: Weidenfeld & Nicolson, 1979)

Kissinger, Henry, *Years of Renewal* (London: Weidenfeld & Nicolson, 1999)

Kissinger, Henry, *Years of Upheaval* (London: Weidenfeld & Nicolson, 1982)

Kupchan, Charles A., *The End of the American Era: U.S. Foreign Policy and the Geopolitics of the Twenty-First Century* (New York: Alfred A. Knopf, 2002)

Lake, Anthony, *Confronting Backlash States* (Washington: Executive Office of the President, 1994)

Larson, Arthur, *Eisenhower: The President Nobody Knew* (New York: Charles Scribner's Sons, 1968)

Lasky, Victor, *Jimmy Carter: The Man and the Myth* (New York: Richard Marek Publishers, 1989)

Leone, Richard C. and Walter Russel Meade, *Special Providence: American Foreign Policy and How It Changed the World* (New York: Alfred A. Knopf, 2002)

MacArthur, Douglas, *Reminiscences* (London: Heinemann, 1964)

Mahoney, Richard D., *JFK: Ordeal in Africa* (New York: Oxford University Press, 1983)

Manchester, William, *American Caesar: Douglas MacArthur 1880–1964* (Boston: Little, Brown and Company, 1978)

Mason, Robert, *Chickenhawk* (London: Corgi, 1984)

Matloff, Maurice (ed), *American Military History* (New York: Combined Books, 1996)

Matusow, Allen J., *Nixon's Economy* (Lawrence: University Press of Kansas, 1998)

McCormick, Thomas J., *America's Half Century: United States Foreign Policy in the Cold War and After* (Baltimore: Johns Hopkins University Press, 2nd edition, 1995)

McCullough, David, *Truman* (New York: Simon & Schuster, 1992)

Melanson, Richard A., *American Foreign Policy Since the Vietnam War: The Search for Consensus from Nixon to Clinton* (Armonk, NY: M.E. Sharpe, 3rd edition, 2000)

Nixon, Richard, *The Memoirs of Richard Nixon* (London: Book Club Associates, 1978)

Nofi, Albert A., *The Spanish American War, 1898* (Pennsylvania: Combined Books, 1996)

Noonan, Peggy, *When Character was King: A Story of Ronald Reagan* (New York: Penguin, 2002)

Pillar, Paul, *Terrorism and US Foreign Policy* (Washington: The Brooking Institution, 2001)

Reagan, Ronald, *An American Life* (London: Hutchinson, 1990)

Regan, Donald T., *For the Record: From Wall Street to Washington* (London: Hutchinson, 1988)

Renwick, Robin, *America and Britain in Peace and War* (London: Macmillan Press, 1996)

Renwick, Robin, *Fighting with Allies* (London: Macmillan Press, 1996)

Russet, Bruce M., *No Clear and Present Danger: A Skeptical View of the US Entry into World War II* (New York: Harper Torchbooks, 1972)

Sixsmith, E.K.G., *Eisenhower* (Pennsylvania: Combined Publishing, 1973)

Sorensen, Theodore C., *Kennedy* (New York: Harper & Row, 1965)

Soros, George, *The Bubble of American Supremacy* (London: Weidenfeld & Nicolson, 2004)

Summers, Anthony, *The Arrogance of Power: The Secret World of Richard Nixon* (London: Phoenix Press, 2001)

Tuchman, Barbara, *The First Salute: A View of the American Revolution* (New York: Ballantine Books, 1988)

Walker, Martin, *Makers of the American Century* (London: Vintage, 2001)

Weiner, Tim, *Legacy of Ashes: The History of the CIA* (London: Allen Lane, 2007)

Burma

Aung San, Suu Kyi, *Freedom From Fear* (New York: Penguin, 1995)

Fink, Christiana, *Living Silence* (New York: Zed Books, 2001)

Furgusson, Bernard, *Beyond the Chindwin* (London: Collins, 1962)

Gravers, Mikail, *Nationalism as Political Paranoia in Burma* (Richmond: Nordic Institute of Asian Studies, Curzon, 1999)

Lintner, Bertil, *Burma in Revolt* (Thailand: Silkworm Books, 1999)

Lyman, Robert, *Slim, Master of War: Burma and the Birth of Modern Warfare* (London: Constable, 2004)

Maung, Mya, *Totalitarianism in Burma* (New York: Paragon House, 1992)

Ott, Martin C., *Burma: A Strategic Perspective* (Washington: National Defence University, Institute For National Strategy Studies, 1996)

Rotberg, Robert I. (ed), *Burma: Prospects for a Democratic Future* (Cambridge, MA: World Peace Foundation, 1998)

Taylor, Robert H. (ed), *Burma: Political Economy under Military Rule* (London: Hurst & Co., 2001)

Taylor, Robert H., *The State in Burma* (London: C. Hurst & Co., 1987)

Thompson, Julian, *War in Burma 1942–1945* (London: Pan Books, 2002)

Tucker, Shelby, *Burma: The Curse of Independence* (London: Pluto Press, 2001)

Webster, Donovan, *The Burma Road* (London: Macmillan, 2003)

Wintle, Justin, *Perfect Hostage: Aung San Suu Kyi, Burma and the Generals* (London: Arrow, 2007)

Cambodia

Brady, Christopher, *United States Foreign Policy Towards Cambodia 1972–92* (Basingstoke: Macmillan Press Ltd., 1999)

Butchett, Wilfred, *The China Cambodia Vietnam Triangle* (Chicago: Vanguard Books, 1981)

Chandler, David, *A History of Cambodia* (Boulder, CO: Westview Press, 2000)

Chandler, David, *The Tragedy of Cambodian History* (New Haven: Yale University Press, 1991)

Gottesman, Evan, *Cambodia: After the Khmer Rouge* (New Haven: Yale University Press, 2002)

Haas, Michael, *Cambodia: Pol Pot and the United States, The Faustian Pact* (New York: Praeger Publishers, 1991)

Jackson, Karl D., *Cambodia 1975–78: Rendezvous with Death* (Princeton, NJ: Princeton University Press, 1989)

Kiernan, Ben, *The Pol Pot Regime: Race, Power, and Genocide in Cambodia Under the Khmer Rouge 1975–79* (New Haven, CT and London: Yale University Press, 1996)

Shawcross, William, *Sideshow: Kissinger, Nixon and the Destruction of Cambodia* (London: Andre Deutsche, 1979)

Sheehan, Neil, *A Bright Shining Lie* (New York: Vintage Books, 1989)

Short, Philip, *Pol Pot: The History of a Nightmare* (London: John Murray, 2004)

Sihanouk, Prince Norodom, *War and Hope: The Case for Cambodia* (London: Sidgwick & Jackson, 1980)

Vickery, Michael, *Cambodia 1975–1982* (Sydney: George Allen and Unwin, 1984)

Yathay, Pin, *Stay Alive My Son* (London: Bloomsbury, 1987)

China

Abramowitz, Morton and Richard Moorsteen, *Remaking China Policy: U.S.–China Relations and Government Decision Making* (Cambridge, MA: Harvard University Press, 1971)

Becker, Jasper, *Hungry Ghosts: China's Secret Famine* (London: John Murray, 1996)

Benewick, Robert and Paul Wingrove (eds), *Reforming the Revolution* (London: Macmillan Education, 1988)

Bianco, Lucien, *Origins of the Chinese Revolution* (Stanford, CA: Stanford University Press, 1971)

Bloodworth, Dennis, *An Eye for the Dragon* (New York; Farrar Straus & Giroux, 1970)

Breslin, Shaun, *Mao* (Harlow: Pearson Education Ltd., 1998)

Chang, Jung and Jon Halliday, *Mao, The Unknown Story* (London: Jonathan Cape, 2005)

Chang, Jung, *Wild Swans: Three Daughters of China* (New York: Knopf Publishing Group, 1992)

Chang, Iris, *The Rape of Nanking: The Forgotten Holocaust of World War II* (New York: Basic Books, 2002)

Chen, Da, *Colours of the Mountain* (New York: Anchor Books, 2001)

Craddock, Percy, *Experiences of China* (London: John Murray, 1999)

Crook, David and Isabel Crook, *Revolution in a Chinese Village: Ten Mile Inn* (London: Routledge & Kegan Paul, 1959)

Domenach, Jean Luc, *The Origins of the Great Leap Forward* (Boulder, CO: Westview Press, 1995)

Edmonds, Richard Louis (ed), *The People's Republic of China After 50 Years* (New York: Oxford University Press, 1999)

Elleman, Bruce A., *Modern Chinese Welfare 1975–1989* (New York: Routledge, 2001)

Evans, Richard, *Deng Xiaoping and the Making of Modern China* (London: Hamish Hamilton, 1993)

Fairbank, John King, *China Watch* (Cambridge, MA: Harvard University Press, 1987)

Fairbank, John King, *The Great Chinese Revolution: 1800–1985* (New York: Harper and Row, 1986, and London: Windus, 1987)

Fenby, Jonathan, *The Penguin History of Modern China, The Fall and Rise of a Great Power, 1850–2008* (London: Allen Lane, 2008)

Fishman, Ted C., *China Inc.* (New York: Simon and Schuster, 2005)

Gao, Anhua, *To the Edge of the Sky* (Bergenfield, NJ: Overlook Press, 2003)

Goldstein, Steven M., *Chinese Foreign Policy Relations, Nationalism and Internationalism: Sino-Soviet* (New York: Oxford University Press, 1994)

Goodman, David S.G., *Deng Xiaoping and the Chinese Revolution: A Political Biography* (London and New York: Routledge, 1994)

Granqvist, Hans, *The Red Guard: A Report of Mao's Revolution* (London: Pall Mall Press, 1967)

Gutmann, Ethan, *Losing the New China: A Story of American Commerce, Desire and Betrayal* (San Francisco: Encounter Books, 2004)

Harding, Harry, 'The Chinese State in Crisis', in MacFarquhar, Roderick (ed), *The Politics of China: The Eras of Mao and Deng* (New York: Cambridge University Press, 1993)

Hessler, Peter, *River Town: Two Years on the Yangtze* (London: John Murray, 2001)

Hsu, Immanuel C.Y., *China Without Mao: The Search for a New Order* (New York: Oxford University Press, 2nd edition, 1990)

Hsu, Immanuel C.Y., *The Rise of Modern China* (New York: Oxford University Press, 2000)

Johnson, Chalmers, *Revolutionary Change* (Boston: Little, Brown and Company, 1966)

Karnow, Stanley, *Mao and China* (London: John Murray, 1996)

Lam, Willy Wo-Lap, *The Era of Jiang Zemin* (Singapore: Simon and Schuster (Asia), 1999)

Lawrence, Alan, *China under Communism* (New York: Routledge, 1998)

Li, Zhisui, *The Private Life of Chairman Mao* (London: Chatto & Windus, 1994)

Liao, Kuang-Sheng, *Antiforeignism and Modernization in China 1860 to 1980* (Hong Kong: Chinese University of Hong Kong, 1984)

Link, Perry and Andrew J. Nathan (eds), *The Tiananmen Papers* (New York: Public Affairs, 2001)

MacFarquhar, Roderick, *The Origins of the Cultural Revolution, Vol. I: Contradictions among the People, 1956–1957* (London: Oxford University Press, 1974)

MacFarquhar, Roderick, *The Origins of the Cultural Revolution, Vol. II: The Great Leap Forward, 1958–1960* (London: Oxford University Press, 1983)

MacFarquhar, Roderick, *The Origins of the Cultural Revolution, Vol. III: The Coming of the Cataclysm, 1961–1966* (New York: Columbia University Press, 1997)

MacFarquhar, Roderick (ed), *The Politics of China: The Eras of Mao and Deng* (New York: Cambridge University Press, 2nd edition, 1993)

MacFarquhar, Roderick, *The Succession to Mao and the End of Maoism, 1969–82* (Cambridge: Cambridge University Press, 1993)

Mackerras, Colin, Pradeep Taneja and Graham Young, *China since 1978* (Melbourne: Longman, 2nd edition, 1998)

Marti, Michael E., *China and the Legacy of Deng Xiaoping* (Dulles, VA: Brassey's Inc., 2002)

Miles, James, *The Legacy of Tiananmen: China in Disarray* (Ann Arbor, MI: The University of Michigan Press, 1997)

Mozingo, David, *The Chinese Army and the Communist State: State and Society in Contemporary China* (Ithaca, NY: Cornell University Press, 1983)

Roberti, Mark, *The Fall of Hong Kong* (New York: John Wiley & Sons Inc., 1994)

Robinson, Thomas W. and David Shambaugh (eds), *Chinese Foreign Policy* (Oxford: Clarendon Paperbacks, 1994)

Salisbury, Harrison E., *The New Emperors: China in the Era of Deng and Mao* (London: Harper Collins, 1992)

Sargeant, Harriet, *Shanghai: Collision Point of Cultures 1918–1939* (New York: Crown Publishing, 1991)

Schell, Orville, *Mandate of Heaven* (New York: Simon and Schuster, 1994)

Short, Philip, *The Dragon and the Bear* (London: Hodder & Stoughton, 1976)

Short, Philip, *Mao: A Life* (London: Hodder & Stoughton, 1999)

Spence, Jonathan D., *The Search for Modern China* (London: Hutchinson, 1990)

Sun, Warren and Frederick C. Teiwes, *The Tragedy of Lin Bao: Riding the Tiger during the Cultural Revolution 1966–1971* (Honolulu: University of Hawaii Press, 1996)

Suyin, Han, *Eldest Son: Zhou Enlai and the Making of Modern China, 1898–1976* (London: Jonathan Cape, 1994)

Teiwes, Frederick C., *Politics and Purges in China: Rectification and the Decline of Party Norms, 1950–1955* (New York: M.E. Sharpe, 1979)

Van Kemenade, Willem, *China, Hong Kong, Taiwan Inc.* (London: Abacus, 1997)

White, Gordon, *Riding the Tiger: The Politics of Economic Reform in Post-Mao China* (London: Macmillan, 1993)

Whiting, Allen S., *China Crosses the Yalu: The Decision to Enter the Korean War* (Stanford, CA: Stanford University Press, 1960)

Woetzel, Jonathan R., *Capitalist China: Strategies for a Revolutionized Economy* (Singapore: John Wiley & Sons (Asia), 2003)

Xingjian, Gao, *Soul Mountain* (London: Flamingo, 2001)

Xizhe, Peng and Guo Zhigang (eds), *The Changing Population of China* (Oxford: Blackwell Publishers, 2000)

Yang, Benjamin, *Deng* (Armonk, NY: M.E. Sharpe Inc., 1998)

Ying, Hong, *Daughter of the River* (London: Bloomsbury, 1997)

Zheng, Shiping, *The Institutional Dilemma: Party vs. State in Post-1949 China* (Cambridge: Cambridge University Press, 1997)

General

Adler, Selig, *The Isolationist Impulse: Its Twentieth Century Reaction* (New York: Abelard-Schuman Ltd., 1957)

Ambrose, Stephen E. and Douglas G. Brinkley, *Rise to Globalism: American Foreign Policy since 1938* (New York: Penguin, 1997)

Ambrose, Steven E., *Eisenhower, Soldier and President* (London, Pocket Books, 2003)

Asher, Robert E. and Edward S. Mason, *The World Bank since Bretton Woods* (Washington, DC: The Brooking Institution, 1973)

Atkinson, Dan and Larry Elliott, *The Age of Insecurity* (London: Verso, 1998)

Barnett, Correlli, *The Collapse of British Power* (London: Pan Books, 2002)

Barnett, Correlli, *The Lost Victory* (London: Pan Books, 2002)

Barnett, Correlli, *The Verdict of Peace* (London: Pan Books, 2002)

Baxter, Craig, Charles H. Kennedy, Yogendra Malik and Robert C. Oberst, *Government and Politics in South Asia* (Boulder, CO: Westview Press, 5th edition, 2002)

Beinin, Joel and Joe Stork (eds), *Political Islam: Essay for Middle East Report* (London: I.B. Tauris, 1998)

Berger, Mark T. and Douglas A. Borer (eds), *The Rise of East Asia: Critical Versions of the Pacific Century* (London: Routledge, 1997)

Billington, R.A., *Westward Expansion: A History of the American Frontier* (New York: Experienced Books, 2nd edition, 1960)

Blackwell, Robert D. and F. Stephen Larrabee (eds), *Conventional Arms Control and East West Security* (Oxford: Clarendon Press, 1989)

Bragg, Melvin, *The Adventure of English: The Biography of a Language* (London: Hodder & Stoughton, 2003)

Brandon, Piers, *The Dark Valley: A Panorama of the 1930s* (London: Jonathan Cape, 2000)

Brands, H.W., *The Age of Gold* (London: Heinemann, 2005)

Brown, Judith M., *Modern Asia: The Origins of Asian Democracy* (New York and Oxford: Oxford University Press, 1994)

Chomsky, Noam, *Deterring Democracy* (New York: Hill and Wang, 1992)

Christie, Clive J., *A Modern History of South East Asia: Decolonisation, Nationalism and Separatism* (London and New York: I.B. Tauris, 1996)

Cohen, Stephen P., *Emerging Power* (Washington, DC: The Brookings Institution Press, 2001)

Conquest, Robert, *Reflections on a Ravaged Century* (New York: John Murray, 1999)

Cooper, Robert, *The Breaking of Nations: Order and Chaos in the Twenty First Century* (London: Atlantic Books, 2003)

Cotterell, Arthur, *East Asia: From Chinese Predominance to the Rise of the Pacific Rim* (London: Pimlico, 2002)

Crockatt, Richard, *The Fifty Years Wars: The United States and the Soviet Union in World Politics 1941–1991* (New York: Routledge, 1995)

De Senarclens, Pierre, *From Yalta to the Iron Curtain: The Great Powers and the Origins of the Cold War* (Oxford: Berg Publishers, 1995)

Dobbs-Higginson, Michael S., *Asia Pacific: Its Role in the New World Disorder* (London: Heinemann, 1994)

Ferguson, Niall, *Empire: How Britain Made the Modern World* (London: Allen Lane, 2002)

Ferguson, Niall, *Colossus: The Rise and Fall of the American Empire* (London: Allen Lane, 2005)

Ferguson, Niall, *The War of the World* (London: Allen Lane, 2006) p.525

Friedberg, Aaron L., *The Weary Titan* (Princeton, NJ: Princeton University Press, 1988)

Friedman, Norman, *The Fifty Year War: Conflict and Strategy in the Cold War* (Annapolis, MD: Naval Institute Press, 2003)

Fukuyama, Francis, *The End of History and the Last Man* (London: Penguin Books, 1992)

Gibson, Arrell Morgan with John Whitehead, *Yankees in Paradise: The Pacific Basin Frontier* (Albuquerque: University of New Mexico Press, 1993)

Gilbert, Martin, *Churchill: A Life* (London: Heinemann, 1991)

Goldstein, Steven M., *The Asian Financial Crisis: Causes, Cures, and Systemic Implications* (New York: Societies & Associations, 1998)

Goldstein, Steven M., 'Nationalism and Internationalism: Sino-Soviet Relations', in Robinson and Shambaugh (eds), *Chinese Foreign Policy: Theory and Practice* (Oxford: Clarendon Press, 1994)

Griffiths, John C., *Afghanistan: A History of Conflict* (London: André Deutsch, 2001)

Hague, William, *William Pitt the Younger* (London: Harper Collins, 2004)

Harvey, Robert, *Liberators: Latin America's Struggle for Independence 1810–1830* (London: John Murray, 2000)

Hiro, Dilip, *Between Marx and Muhammad* (London: Harper Collins, 1995)

Hobsbawm, Eric, *The Age of Extremes: A History of the World 1914–1991* (London: Penguin, 1994)

Hopkirk, Peter, *The Great Game* (London: John Murray, 1990)

Huntington, Samuel P., *The Clash of Civilizations and the Remaking of the World Order* (New York: Simon & Schuster, 1996)

Hurst, David, *On Westernism: An Ideology's Bid for World Dominion* (Reading: G. Hartley & Co. 2003)

Johnson, Chalmers, *The Sorrows of Empire: Militarism, Secrecy and the End of the Republic* (London: Verso, 2004)

Johnson, Paul, *Modern Times* (London: Weidenfeld & Nicholson, 1983)

Judd, Denis, *The Lion and the Tiger: The Rise and Fall of the British Raj* (Oxford and New York: Oxford University Press, 2004)

Kagan, Robert, *The Return of History and the End of Dreams* (New York: Alfred A. Knopf, 2008)

Kagan, Robert, *Power and Paradise* (New York: Alfred A. Knopf, 2003)

Keay, John, *Last Post: The End of Empire in the Far East* (London: John Murray, 1997)

Keay, John, *Sowing the Wind: The Seeds of Conflict in the Middle East* (London: John Murray, 2003)

Keegan, John, *Intelligence in War* (London: Pimlico, 2004)

Kepel, Gilles, *Jihad: The Trial of Political Islam* (London: I.B. Tauris, 2002)

Kissinger, Henry, *Diplomacy* (New York: Touchstone, 1994)

Kynaston, David, *The City of London, Vol. III: Illusions of Gold 1914–1945* (London: Chatto & Windus, 1999)

LaFeber, Walter (ed), *The Origins of the Cold War 1941–1947* (New York: John Wiley & Sons Inc., 1971)

Landes, David S., *The Unbound Prometheus: Technological Change and Industrial Revolution in Western Europe from 1957 to the Present* (Cambridge: Cambridge University Press, 1972)

Landes, David S., *The Wealth and Poverty of Nations* (London: Little, Brown & Company, 1998)

Lee, Steven Hugh, *Outposts of Empire: Korea, Vietnam and the Origins of the Cold War in Asia, 1949–1954* (Liverpool: Liverpool University Press, 1995)

Lewis, Bernard, *Holy War and Unholy Terror: The Crisis of Islam* (London: Weidenfeld & Nicolson, 2003)

Lewis, Bernard, *The Middle East: 2000 Years of History from the Rise of Christianity to the Present Day* (London: Phoenix Giant, 1998)

Lloyd, T.O., *The British Empire, 1558–1995* (Oxford: Oxford University Press, 1996)

Lucas, Edward, *The New Cold War* (London: Bloomsbury, 2008)

Lumis, Trevor, *Pacific Paradises: The Discovery of Tahiti & Hawaii* (Melbourne: Pluto Press Australia, 2005)

Mackerras, Colin, *Eastern Asia* (Melbourne: Longman Australia, 1992)

Macmillan, Margaret, *Peacemakers: The Paris Conference of 1919 and Its Attempt to End War* (London: John Murray, 2002)

Mallet, Victor, *The Trouble with Tigers: The Rise and Fall of South East Asia* (London: Harper Collins, 1999)

Marlay, Ross and Clark D. Neher, *The Winds of Change: Democracy and Development in South East Asia* (Boulder, CO: Westview Press, 1995)

Nixon, Richard, *The Real War* (London: Sidgwick & Jackson, 1980)

Nixon, Richard, *Leaders* (New York: Buccaneer Books, 1994)

Noble, Gregory W. and John Ravenhill (eds), *The Asian Financial Crisis and the Architecture of Global Finance* (New York: Cambridge University Press, 2000)

Ohmae, Kenichi, *The End of the Nation State* (New York: Harper Collins, 2004)

Pipes, Richard, *Property and Freedom* (New York: Alfred A. Knopf, 1999)

Potter, Bernard, *Empire and Superempire: Britain, America and the World* (New Haven, CT and London: Yale University Press, 2006)

Rasanayagam, Angelo, *Afghanistan: A Modern History* (London: I.B.Tauris, 2003)

Riès, Philip and Peter Starr, *Asian Storm: The Economic Crisis Examined* (Boston: Tuttle Publishing, 2000)

Roberts, Andrew, *Eminent Churchillians* (London: Weidenfeld & Nicolson, 1994)

Rozman, Gilbert (ed), *The East Asian Region: Confucian Heritage and its Modern Adaptation* (Princeton: Princeton University Press, 1991)

Schlesinger, Arthur M., *The Vital Center: The Politics of Freedom* (London: Andre Deutsch, 1970)

Schweizer, Peter and Caspar Weinberger, *The Next War* (Washington, DC: Regnery Publishing, 1998)

Sharma, Shalendra D., *Crisis, Reform and Recovery: The Asian Financial Crisis* (Manchester: Manchester University Press, 2003)

Skidelsky, Robert, *John Maynard Keynes: Fighting for Britain 1937–1946* (London: Macmillan, 2000)

Smuts, J.C., *Jan Christian Smuts* (London: Cassell & Co. Ltd., 1952)

Spencer, Metta (ed), *Separatism, Democracy, and Disintegration* (Lanham, MD, Boulder, CO, New York and Oxford: Rowman & Littlefield, 1998)

Spurr, Russell, *Enter the Dragon* (London: Sidgwick & Jackson, 1989)

Steinberg, David Joel (ed), *In Search of Southeast Asia* (Sydney: Allen and Unwin, 2nd edition, 1987)

Thatcher, Margaret, *The Downing Street Years* (New York: Harper Collins, 2003)

Tusa, Ann and John, *The Nuremberg Trial* (London: Macmillan, 1981)

Von Tunzelmann, Alex, *Indian Summer, The Secret History of the End of Empire* (London: Simon & Schuster UK Ltd., 2007) p.134

Ward-Perkins, Bryan, *The Fall of Rome and the End of Civilization* (New York: Oxford University Press, 2005)

Williams, E.N., *The Ancient Regime in Europe: Government & Society in the Major States 1648–1789* (London: The Bodley Head, 1970)

Winchester, Simon, *Pacific Rising: The Emergence of a New World Culture* (New York: Prentice Hall, 1991)

Woolley, Benjamin, *Savage Kingdom: Virginia and the Founding of English America* (New York: Harper Collins, 2007)

Young, Robert J.C., *Postcolonialism: An Historical Introduction* (Oxford and Malden, MA: Blackwell Publishers Ltd., 2001)

Zeigler, Philip, *Mountbatten* (London: Guild, 1985)

Hong Kong

Morris, Jan, *Hong Kong: Epilogue to Empire* (London: Viking, 1988)

Patten, Christopher, *East and West* (London: Macmillan, 1998)

Roberti, Mark, *The Fall of Hong Kong: China's Triumph & Britain's Betrayal* (New York: John Wiley & Sons Ltd., 1994)

Tsang, Steve, *A Modern History of Hong Kong* (London: I.B.Tauris, 2004)

Welsh, Frank, *A History of Hong Kong* (London: Harper Collins, 1997)

Yahuda, Michael, *Hong Kong: China's Challenge* (London: Routledge, 1996)

India

Adams, Jad and Philip Whitehead, *The Dynasty: The Nehru–Gandhi Story* (London: Penguin Books, 1997)

Ahluwalia, BK, *Rajiv Gandhi* (New Delhi: Cosmo Books, 1985)

Akbar, M.J., *Nehru: The Making of India* (London: Viking, 1988)

Arnold, David, *Gandhi: Profiles in Power* (Harlow, England: Pearson Education Ltd., 2001)

Bhargava, G.S., *Morarji Desai* (New Delhi: Indian Book Company, 1977)

Bhatia, Krishnan, *Indira: A Biography of Prime Minister Gandhi* (London: Angus & Robertson Ltd., 1974)

Bose, Sumantra, *Kashmir: Roots to Conflict, Paths to Peace* (Cambridge: Harvard University Press, 2003)

Brown, Judith M., *Nehru: A Political Life* (New Haven: Yale University Press, 2003)

Brown, Judith M. (ed), *Modern India: The Origins of Asian Democracy* (New Delhi and New York: Oxford University Press, 2nd edition, 1994)

Brunton, Paul, *In Search of Secret India* (Bombay: B.I. Publications, 1970)

Collins, Larry and Dominic Lapierre, *Freedom at Midnight: The Epic Drama of India's Struggle for Independence* (New York: Harper Collins, 1997)

Dalal, Ramesh, *Rajiv Gandhi's Assassination* (New Delhi: UBS Publishers, 2001)

Das, M.N., *The Political Philosophy of Jawaharlal Nehru* (London: George Allen & Unwin, 1961)

Desai, Meghnad, 'Economic Reform: Stalled by Politics?' in Oldenburg (ed), *India Briefing: Staying the Course* (Armonk, NY: M.E. Sharpe, 1995)

Devi, Maharani Gayatri, *A Princess Remembers: The Memoirs of the Maharani of Jaipur* (New Delhi: Rupa & Co., 1995)

Dixit, J.N., *My South Block Years: Memoirs of a Foreign Secretary* (New Delhi: UBS Publishers, 1996)

Edwardes, Michael, *Nehru: A Political Biography* (London: Allen Lane, Penguin, 1971)

Fishlock, Trevor, *Gandhi's Children* (Madison: University of Wisconsin Press, 1983)

Frank, Katherine, *Indira Gandhi: The Life of Indira Nehru Gandhi* (London: Harper Collins, 2001)

Gandhi, M.K., *An Autobiography, or The Story of My Experiments with Truth* (London: Penguin Books, 2001)

Ganguly, Sumit, *Conflict Unending: India–Pakistan Tensions Since 1947* (New York: Columbia University Press, 2001)

Gopal, Sarvepalli, *Jawaharlal Nehru* (London: Jonathan Cape, 1975)

Gopal, Sarvepalli, *Jawaharlal Nehru: A Biography, Volume One, 1889–1947* (Delhi: Oxford University Press, 1975)

Gopal, Sarvepalli, *Jawaharlal Nehru: A Biography, Volume Two, 1947–1956* (London: Jonathan Cape, 1979)

Gopal, Sarvepalli, *Jawaharlal Nehru: A Biography, Volume Three, 1956–1964* (Delhi: Oxford University Press, 1984)

Goshi, Suniti Kumar, *India and The Raj, 1919–1947, Glory, Shame and Bondage* (Bombay: Research Unit for Political Economy, 1995)

Harrison, Selig S., Paul H. Kreisberg and Dennis Kux (eds), *India & Pakistan: The First Fifty Years* (Cambridge: Cambridge University Press, 1999)

Healy, Kathleen, *Rajiv Gandhi: The Years of Power* (New Delhi: Vikas Publishing House, 1989)

Hough, Richard, *Mountbatten: Hero of Our Time* (London: Weidenfeld & Nicolson, 1980)

Jacob, Satish and Mark Tully, *Amritsar: Mrs. Gandhi's Last Battle* (London: Jonathan Cape, 1985)

Jenkins, Rob, *Democratic Politics and Economic Reform in India* (Cambridge: Cambridge University Press, 1999)

Keay, John, *India: A History* (London: Harper Collins, 2000)

Khilnani, Sunil, *The Idea of India* (London: Penguin Books, 1998)

Kumar, Ramesh, *Congress and Congressism in Indian Politics* (New Delhi: Deep & Deep Publications, 1994)

Lall, Arthur, *The Emergence of Modern India* (New York: Columbia University Press, 1981)

Manor, James, 'India's Chief Ministers and the Problem of Governability', in Oldenburg (ed), *India Briefing: Staying the Course* (Cambridge: Cambridge University Press, 1997)

Masani, Zareer, *Indira Gandhi: A Biography* (London: Hamish Hamilton, 1975)

Mehta, Ved, *Rajiv Gandhi and Rama's Kingdom* (New Haven: Yale University Press, 1994)

Menon, V.P., *The Transfer of Power in India* (New Delhi: Orient Longman, 1957)

Moon, Sir Penderel, *The British Conquest and Dominion of India* (London: Gerald Duckworth & Co., 1989)

Moraes, Dom, *Mrs. Gandhi* (London: Jonathan Cape, 1980)

Naqvi, Saeed, *The Last Brahmin Prime Minister* (Delhi: Har-Anand, 1996)

Nugent, Nicholas, *Rajiv Gandhi: Son of a Dynasty* (London: BBC Books, 1990)

Nehru, Jawaharlal, *Autobiography* (London: John Lane, The Bodley Head, 1936)

Oldenburg, Philip (ed), *India Briefing: Staying the Course* (Armonk, NY: M.E. Sharpe, 1995)

Ramesh, Jairam, Kautilya. *Toady: Jairam Ramesh on a Globalizing India* (Delhi: India Rearch Press, 2002)

Rao, Narasimha P.V., *The Insider* (New Delhi: Viking, 1999)

Reddy, Narendra, P.V., *Narasimha Rao: Years of Power* (New Delhi: Har-Anand Publications, 1993)

Richards, Glyn, *The Philosophy of Gandhi* (London: Curzon Press Ltd., 1991)

Schofield, Victoria, *Kashmir in Conflict* (New York: I.B.Tauris, 2003)

Shurmer-Smith, Pamela, *India: Globalisation and Change* (New York: Oxford University Press, 2000)

Singh, Patwant, *India and the Future of Asia* (London: Faber and Faber, 1966)

Singh, Patwant, *The Sikhs* (London: John Murray, 1999)

Singh, Tavleen, *Kashmir: A Tragedy of Errors* (New Delhi: Penguin Books, 1996)

Stern, Robert W., *Changing India* (New York: Cambridge University Press, 2003)

Talbot, Ian, *India & Pakistan: Inventing the Nation* (London: Arnold Publication, 2000)

Tidrick, Kathryn, *Gandhi: A Political and Spiritual Life* (London and New York: I.B.Tauris, 2006)

Tully, Mark, *No Full Stops in India* (New York: Penguin, 1991)

Varma, Srikanta, *A Portrait of Rajiv Gandhi* (London: Arnold-Heinemann, 1985)

Venkateswaran, R.J., *Reforming Indian Economy: The Narasimha Rao and Manmohan Singh Era* (New Delhi: Vikas Publishing House, 1996)

Von Tunzelmann, Alex, *Indian Summer: The Secret History of the End of Empire* (New York: Simon & Schuster, 2007)

Williams, Donovan and E. Daniel Potts (eds), *Essays in Indian History, in Honour of C.C. Davies* (London: Asia Publishing, 1973)

Wolpert, Stanley, *A New History of India* (New York: Oxford University Press, 1997)

Wolpert, Stanley, *Gandhi's Passion: The Life and Legacy of Mahatma Gandhi* (Delhi: Oxford University Press, 2001)

Wolpert, Stanley, *Nehru: A Tryst with Destiny* (New York: Oxford University Press, 1996)

Wood, John R., 'On the Periphery But in the Thick of it; Some Recent Indian Political Crises Viewed from Gujerat' in Oldenburg (ed), *India Briefing: Staying the Path* (Armonk, NY: M.E. Sharpe, 1995)

Ziegler, Philip, *Mountbatten* (New York: Alfred A. Knopf, 1985)

Indonesia

Bourchier, David and Vedi R. Hadiz (eds), *Indonesian Politics and Society* (London: Routledge Curzon, 2003)

Burdiman, Arief (ed), *Reformasi: Crisis and Change in Indonesia* (Clayton, Australia: Monash Asia Institute, 1999)

Burdiman, Arief (ed), *State and Civil Society in Indonesia* (Clayton, Australia: Monash University, 1990)

Castles, Lance and Herbert Feith (eds), *Indonesian Political Thinking, 1945–1965* (Ithaca, NY: Cornell University Press, 1970)

Crouch, Harold, *The Army and Politics in Indonesia* (Ithaca, NY: Cornell University Press, 1978)

Elson, R.E., *Suharto: A Political Biography* (Cambridge: Cambridge University Press, 2001)

Forrester, Geoff and R.J. May (eds), *The Fall of Suharto* (Bathurst, New South Wales: Crawford House Publishing, 1998)

Friends, Theodore, *Indonesian Destinies* (Cambridge, MA: The Belknap Press of Harvard University Press, 2003)

Hughes, John, *The End of Sukarno: A Coup that Misfired, A Purge that Ran Wild* (Singapore: Archipelago Press, 2002)

Kingsbury, Damien, *The Politics of Indonesia* (New York: Oxford University Press, 2005)

Lee, Oey Hong, *War and Diplomacy in Indonesia 1945–50* (Townsville, QLD, Australia: James Cook University of North Queensland, 1981)

Manning, Chris and Peter Van Dierman (eds), *Indonesia in Transition: Social Aspects of Reformasi and Crisis* (London: Zed Books, 2000)

Paris, Jonathan and Adam Schwarz (eds), *The Politics of Post-Suharto Indonesia* (New York: Council of Foreign Relations Press, 1999)

Ramage, Douglas, *Politics in Indonesia: Democracy, Islam and the Ideology of Tolerance* (New York: Routledge, 1995)

Reinhardt, Jon M., *Foreign Policy and National Integration: The Case of Indonesia* (New Haven: Yale University South East Asia Studies, 1971)

Ricklefs, M.C., *A History of Modern Indonesia* (London: Macmillan Education, 1981)

Suryadinata, Leo, *Interpreting Indonesian Politics* (Hong Kong: Times Academic Press, 1998)

Weinstein, Franklin B., *Indonesian Foreign Policy and the Dilemma of Dependence* (Ithaca, NY: Cornell University Press, 1976)

Japan

Akamatsu, Paul, *Meiji 1968: Revolution and Counter-Revolution in Japan* (Boston: George Allen and Unwin Ltd., 1972)

Agawa, Hiroyuki, *The Reluctant Admiral: Yamato and the Imperial Navy* (Tokyo: Kodansha International Ltd., 1979)

Aletzhauser, Albert, *The House of Nomura: The Rise to Power of the World's Most Powerful Company* (London: Bloomsbury Publishing, 1990)

Amyx, Jennifer, *Japan's Financial Crisis: Institutional Rigidity and Reluctant Change* (Princeton, NJ: Princeton University Press, 2004)

Bailey, Paul J., *Postwar Japan: 1945 to the Present* (Oxford: Blackwell Publishers, 1996)

Barenblatt, Daniel, *A Plague Upon Humanity: The Secret Genocide of Axis Japan's Germ Warfare Operation* (Oxford: Souvenir Press, 2004)

Beasley, W.G., *The Rise of Modern Japan II* (London: Phoenix, 2001)

Beasley, W.G. (ed), *Modern Japan: Aspects of History, Literature and Society* (London: George Allen and Unwin, 1975)

Behr, Edward, *Hirohito: Behind the Myth* (London: Hamish Hamilton, 1989)

Bix, Herbert P., *Hirohito and the Making of Modern Japan* (New York: Harper Collins, 2001)

Blomstrom, Magnus, Byron Gangnes and Sumner La Croix (eds), *Japan's New Economy: Continuity and Change in the Twenty-First Century* (New York: Oxford University Press, 2001)

Bouissou, Jean-Marie, *Japan: The Burden of Success* (London: Hurst & Company, 2002)

Brackman, Arnold C., *The Other Nuremburg: The Untold Story of Tokyo War Crimes Trials* (New York: William Morrow & Co, 1987)

Buckley, Roger and William Horsley, *Nippon New Superpower: Japan since 1945* (London: BBC Books, 1990)

Calder, Kent E., *Crisis and Compensation: Public Policy and Political Stability in Japan* (Princeton, NJ: Princeton University Press, 1988)

Cortazzi, Hugh (ed), *Japan Experiences: Fifty Years, One Hundred Views; Post War Japan Through British Eyes* (Folkestone: Japan Library, 2001)

Curtis, Gerald L., *The Logic of Japanese Politics: Leaders, Institutions, and the Limits of Change* (New York: Columbia University Press, 1999)

Davies, Gavan, *Prisoners of the Japanese* (New York: William Morrow & Co., 1994)

Dower, John, *Embracing Defeat: Japan in the Wake of WWII* (New York: The New Press, 1999)

Dower, John and Richard Sims, *Japan in Peace and War: Japanese Political History since the Meiji Renovation 1868–2000* (London: Hurst & Company Ltd., 2001)

Dower, John, *Japan in War and Peace* (London: Harper Collins, 1993)

Edgerton, Robert B., *Warriors of the Rising Sun: A History of the Japanese Military* (New York: W.W. Norton & Co., 1997)

Edstrom, Bert, *Japan's Evolving Foreign Policy Doctrine* (London: Macmillan Press Ltd., 1999)

Eiji, Takemai, *The Allied Occupation of Japan* (London: Continuum International Publishing Group Ltd., 2002)

Emmott, Bill, *The Sun Also Sets: Why Japan Will Not Be Number One* (London: Simon and Schuster, 1989)

Erdstrom, Bert, *Japan's Evolving Foreign Policy Doctrine* (London: Macmillan Press Ltd., 1999)

Giffard, Sydney, *Japan: Among the Powers 1880–1990* (New York and London: Yale University Press, 1994)

Hellmann, Donald C. and John H. Malkin (eds), *Sharing World Leadership? A New Era for America & Japan* (Washington, DC: American Enterprise Institute for Public Policy Research, 1989)

Holland, Harrison M., *Japan Challenges America* (Boulder, CO: Westview Press, 1992)

Hrebenar, Ronald J., *The Japanese Party System* (Boulder, CO: Westview Press, 1992)

Huber, Thomas M., *The Revolutionary Origins of Modern Japan* (Stanford, CA: Stanford University Press, 1981)

Irokawa, Daikichi, *The Age of Hirohito: In Search of Modern Japan* (New York: The Free Press, 1995)

Jane, Fred T., *The Imperial Japanese Navy* (London: Conway Maritime Press, 1984)

Johnson, Chalmers, *MITI and the Japanese Miracle: The Growth of Industrial Policy 1925–1975* (Stanford, CA: Stanford University Press, 1982)

Kawashima, Yutaka, *Japanese Foreign Policy at the Crossroads: Challenges and Options for the Twenty-First Century* (Washington, DC: The Brookings Institution, 2003)

Kishimoto, Koichi, *Politics in Modern Japan* (Tokyo: Japan Echo Inc., 4th edition, 1997)

Kunio, Yoshihara, *Japanese Economic Development* (New York: Oxford University Press, 1994)

Lifton, Robert Jay, *Death in Life: Survivors of Hiroshima* (New York: Random House, 1967)

Matsumoto, Koji, *The Rise of the Japanese Corporate System* (London: Kegan Paul International, 1994)

McClain, James L., *Japan: A Modern History* (New York: W.W. Norton & Co., 2002)

Mosley, Leonard, *Hirohito: Emperor of Japan* (London: Weidenfeld & Nicolson, 1966)

Nagatsuka, R., *I Was a Kamikaze* (London: Abelard Schuman Ltd., 1973)

Nakamura, Takafusa, *A Showa History of Japan, 1926–1989* (Tokyo: University of Tokyo Press, 1998)

Nakamura, Takafusa, *The Postwar Japanese Economy* (Tokyo: University of Tokyo Press, 1995)

Ramseyer, J. Mark and Frances McCall Rosenbluth, *Japan's Political Marketplace* (Cambridge, MA: Harvard University Press, 1993)

Ratcliffe, C. Tait and Thomas R. Zengage, *The Japanese Century: Challenge and Response* (Hong Kong: Longman, 1988)

Reading, Brian, *Japan: The Coming Collapse* (London: Weidenfeld & Nicolson, 1992)

Rhodes, Richard, *The Making of the Atom Bomb* (New York: Touchstone, 1998)

Roberts, John G., *Mitsui: Three Centuries of Japanese Business* (New York: Weatherhill, 2nd edition, 1989)

Sansom, George, *A History of Japan, 1334–1615* (Stanford, CA: Stanford University Press, 1987)

Sansom, George, *A History of Japan, 1615–1867* (Stanford, CA: Stanford University Press, 1987)

Seagrave, Sterling, *The Yamato Dynasty* (London: Bantam Press, 1999)

Sims, Richard, *Japanese Political History since the Meiji Restoration, 1868–2000* (London: Hurst & Co., 2001)

Steven, Rob, *Japan's New Imperialism* (New York: M.E. Sharpe Inc., 1990)

Storry, Richard, *A History of Modern Japan* (Harmondsworth: Penguin Books, 1990)

Tasker, Peter, *Inside Japan: Wealth, Work and Power in the New Japanese Empire* (London: Penguin Books, 1987)

Vogel, Steven K. (ed), *US Japan Relations in a Changing World* (Washington, DC: The Brookings Institution, 2002)

Weston, Mark, *Giants of Japan* (New York: Kodansha International, 1999)

Williams, David, *Japan: Beyond the End of History* (London: Routledge, 1994)

Wood, Christopher, *The Bubble Economy* (New York: The Atlantic Monthly Press, 1992)

Wood, Christopher, *The Japanese Economic Collapse* (London: Sidgwick & Jackson, 1992)

Woronoff, Jon, *Japan as Anything but Number One* (London: Macmillan, 1996)

Yoshibumi, Wakamiya, *The Postwar Conservative View of Asia* [*Sengo Honshu no Ajia Kan*] (Tokyo: LTCB International Library Foundation, 1999)

Korea (North and South)

Barnds, William J., and Young Kun Kim (eds), *The Two Koreas in East Asian Affairs* (New York: New York University Press, 1976)

Breen, Michael, *Kim Jong Il: North Korea's Dear Leader* (Singapore: John Wiley & Sons, 2004)

Buzo, Adrian, *The Making of Modern Korea* (New York: Routledge, 2002)

Catchpole, Brian, *The Korean War* (London: Constable & Robinson, 2000)

Cornell, Erik, *North Korea under Communism: Report of an Envoy to Paradise* (London: Routledge Curzon, 2002)

Dae-Sook, Suh, *Kim II Sung: The North Korean Leader* (New York: Columbia University Press, 1988)

Eberstadt, Nicholas and Richard J. Ellings (eds), *Korea's Future and the Great Powers* (Seattle: University of Washington Press, 2001)

Fehrenbach, T. R., *This Kind of War* (Dulles, VA: Brassey's, 2nd edition, 1963)

French, Paul, *North Korea: The Paranoid Peninsula, A Modern History* (New York: Palgrave Macmillan, 2005)

Griffin, W.E.B., *Retreat Hell!* (New York: G.P. Putnam Sons, 2005)

Han, Sung-joo, *Continuity and Change in Korean–American Relations* (Seoul: Asiatic Research Center, Korea University, 1982)

Hart-Landsberg, Martin, *Korea: Division, Reunification, and US Foreign Policy* (New York: Monthly Review Press, 1989)

Hastings, Max, *The Korean War* (London: Michael Joseph, 1987)

Hickey, Michael, *The Korean War: The West Confronts Communism, 1950–1953* (London: John Murray, 1999)

Kim II Sung, The Brilliant Banner of Juche (Pyongyang: Foreign Languages Publishing House, 1981)

Kim, Se-Jin, *The Politics of Military Revolution in Korea* (Columbia, SC: The University of South Carolina Press, 1971)

Koo, Youngnok and Dae-sook Suh (eds), *Korea and the United States* (Honolulu: University of Hawaii Press, 1984)

Leckie, Robert, *Conflict: The History of the Korean War* (New York: Da Capo Press, 1996)

Leckie, Robert, *The History of the Korean War 1950–1953* (New York: G.P. Putnam Sons, 1962)

Lee, Steven Hugh, *The Korean War* (Harlow, England: Pearson Education, 2001)

Lowe, Peter, *The Origins of the Korean War* (London: Longman, 2nd edition, 1997)

Martin, Bradley K., *Under the Loving Care of the Fatherly Leader: North Korea and the Kim Dynasty* (New York: Thomas Dunne Books, 2004)

Oberdorfer, Don, *The Two Koreas* (London: Warner Books, 1999)

Oh, John Kie-Chiang, *Korean Politics* (Ithaca, NY and London: Cornell University Press, 1999)

Owen, Joseph R., *Colder Than Hell: A Marine Rifle Company at Chosin* (New York: Ivy Books, 1997)

Sandler, Stanley, *The Korean War: No Victors, No Vanquished* (London: UCL Press, 1999)

Srivastava, M.P., *The Korean Conflict* (New Delhi: Prentice Hall of India Private Ltd., 1982)

Stueck, William, *The Korean War: An International History* (Princeton, NJ: Princeton University Press, 1995)

Su, Choe In, *Kim Jong II: The People's Leader* (Pyongyang: Foreign Languages Publishing House, 1985)

Yang, Sung Chul, *The North and South Korean Political Systems* (Elizabeth, NJ: Hollym International Corp, 1999)

Laos

Evans, Grant, *A Short History of Laos: The Land in Between* (Crows Nest, Australia: Allen & Unwin, 2002)

Pakistan and Bangladesh

Afzal, M. Rafique, *Pakistan History and Politics 1947–1971* (Karachi: Oxford University Press, 2001)

Baxter, Craig, *Bangladesh: From a Nation to a State* (Boulder, CO: Westview Press, 1997)

Bennett-Jones, Owen, *Pakistan: Eye of the Storm* (New Haven, CT: Yale University Press, 2002)

Bhutto, Benazir, *Daughter of the East: Benazir Bhutto* (London: Hamish Hamilton, 1989)

Cohen, Stephen Philip, *The Idea of Pakistan* (Washington, DC: Brookings Institution Press, 2004)

Datta, S.K. and Rajeev Sharma, *Pakistan: From Jinnah to Jehad* (New Delhi: UBS Publishers, 2002)

Jaffrelot, Christophe (ed), *A History of Pakistan and Its Origins* (London: Anthem Press, 2004)

Jahan, Rounaq (ed), *Bangladesh: Promise and Performance* (London: Zed Books Ltd., 1996)

Jalal, Ayesha, *The Sole Spokesman: Jinnah, The Muslim League and the Demand for Pakistan* (Cambridge: Cambridge University Press, 1985)

Kux, Dennis, *Disenchanted Allies: The United States and Pakistan 1947 to 2000* (Baltimore: Johns Hopkins University Press, 2001)

Niazi, A.A.K., *The Betrayal of East Pakistan* (Karachi: Oxford University Press, 2001)

Rose, Leo E., and Richard Sisson, *War and Secession: Pakistan, India, and the Creation of Bangladesh* (Berkeley, CA: University of California Press, 1990)

Scholfield, Victoria, *Kashmir in Conflict: India, Pakistan and the Unending War* (New York: I.B.Tauris, 2003)

Talbot, Ian, *Pakistan, A Modern History* (London: C. Hurst & Co., 2005)

Tinker, Hugh, *India and Pakistan: A Short Political Guide* (London: Pall Mall Press, 1962)

Weaver, Mary Anne, *Pakistan: In the Shadow of Jihad and Afghanistan* (New York: Farrar, Straus and Giroux, 1997)

Wells, Ian Bryant, *Jinnah: Ambassador of the Hindu–Muslim Unity* (London: Seagull Books, 2005)

Zaheer, Hasan, *The Separation of East Pakistan: The Rise of Bengali Muslim Nationalism* (Karachi: Oxford University Press, 1994)

Ziring, Lawrence, *Pakistan: At the Crosscurrent of History* (Oxford: One World Publications, 2003)

Philippines

Blitz, Amy, *The Contested State* (Oxford: Rowman & Littlefield, 2000)

Celoza, Albert F., *Ferdinand Marcos and the Philippines* (Westport, CT: Praeger Publishers, 1997)

Guerrero, Eileen and Robert H. Rose, *Corazon Aquino and the Brushfire Revolution* (Baton Rouge: Louisiana State University Press, 1995)

Hamilton-Paterson, James, *America's Boy: The Marcoses and the Philippines* (London: Granta Books, 1998)

Shalom, Stephen Rosskamm, *The United States and the Philippines* (Philadelphia: Institute for Human Issues, 1981)

Steinberg, David Joel, *The Philippines* (Boulder, CO: Westview Press, 1994)

Singapore and Malaysia

Andaya, Barbara Watson and Leonard Y. Andaya, *A History of Malaysia* (London: Palgrave Macmillan, 2nd edition, 2001)

Case, William, *Elites and Regimes in Malaysia* (Clayton: Monash Asia Institute, 1996)

Hilley, John, *Malaysia: Mahathirism, Hegemony and the New Opposition* (Basingstoke: Palgrave, 2001)

Hooker, Virginia Matheson, *A Short History of Malaysia: Linking East and West* (Crows Nest, Australia: Allen & Unwin, 2003)

Huff, W.G., *The Economic Growth of Singapore* (Cambridge: Cambridge University Press, 1994)

Leifer, Michael, *Singapore's Foreign Policy* (New York: Routledge, 2000)

Mauzy, Diane K. and R.S. Milne, *Malaysian Politics under Mahathir* (London: Routledge, 1999)

Mauzy, Diane K. and R.S. Milne, *Singapore Politics under the People's Action Party* (London: Routledge, 2002)

Munro-Kua, Anne, *Authoritarianism and Populism in Malaysia* (New York: St. Martin's Press, 1996)

Peebles, Gavin and Peter Wilson, *Economic Growth and Development in Singapore* (Cheltenham, UK: Edward Elgar, 2002)

Shennan, Margaret, *Out in the Midday Sun: The British in Malaysia 1880–1960* (London: John Murray, 2000)

Shome, S.K., *Malay Political Leadership* (London: Routledge Curzon, 2002)

Short, Anthony, *The Communist Insurrection in Malaya 1948–1960* (London: Frederick Muller Ltd., 1975)

Smith, Colin, *Singapore Burning: Heroism and Surrender in World War II* (London: Viking, 2005)

Sodhy, Pamela, *The US–Malaysian Nexus* (Kuala Lumpur: Institute of Strategic and International Studies, 1991)

Yew, Lee Kuan, *From Third to First, The Singapore Story: 1965–2000, The Memoirs of Lee Kuan Yew* (Singapore: Singapore Press Holdings, 2000)

Soviet Union

Breslauer, George W., *Gorbachev and Yeltsin as Leaders* (Cambridge: Cambridge University Press, 2001)

Hosking, Geoffrey, *Russia: People & Empire 1552–1917* (London: Harper Collins, 1997)

Kotkin, Stephen, *Armageddon Averted: The Soviet Collapse 1970–2000* (Oxford: Oxford University Press, 2001)

Maclean, Fitzroy, *Portrait of the Soviet Union* (London: Weidenfeld & Nicolson, 1987)

McFaul, Michael, *Russia's Unfinished Revolution* (Ithaca, NY: Cornell University Press, 2001)

Moynahan, Brian, *Claws of the Bear: The History of the Red Army from the Revolution to the Present* (New York: Houghton Mifflin, 1989)

Ouimet, Matthew J., *The Rise and Fall of the Brezhnev Doctrine in Soviet Foreign Policy* (Chapel Hill, NC: The University of North Carolina Press, 2003)

Schapiro, Leonard, *The Communist Party of the Soviet Union* (New York: Random House, 1960)

Service, Robert, *Russia: Experiment with a People* (Cambridge: Harvard University Press, 2003)

Taubman, William, *Krushchev: The Man and His Era* (London: The Free Press, 2003)

Volkogonov, Dmitri, *Political Leaders from Lenin to Gorbachev* (London: Harper Collins, 1998)

Volkogonov, Dmitri, *Stalin* (London and New York: Weidenfeld & Nicolson, 1991)

Sri Lanka

Bullion, Alan J., *India, Sri Lanka and the Tamil Crisis 1976–1994* (London and New York: Pinter, 1995)

De Silva, Chandra Richard, *Sri Lanka: A History* (New Delhi: Vikas Publishing House, 1997)

O'Balance, Edgar, *The Cyanide War: Tamil Insurrection in Sri Lanka* (London: Brassey's, 1989)

Stewart, Pamela J. and Andrew Strathern, *Violence: Theory and Ethnography* (New York and London: Continuum, 2002)

Tambiah, S.J., *Sri Lanka: Ethnic Fratricide and the Dismantling of Democracy* (Chicago, IL: The University of Chicago Press, 1986)

Taiwan

Fenby, Jonathan, *Generalissimo: Chiang Kai-Shek and the China He Lost* (London: The Free Press, 2003)

Fu, Jen-kun, *Taiwan and the Geopolitics of the Asian–American Dilemma* (New York: Praeger, 1992)

Jo, Yung-Hwan (ed), *Taiwan's Future* (Hong Kong: Union Research Institute for Arizona State University, 1974)

Leng, Shao-Chuan (ed), *Chiang Ching-Kuo's Leadership in the Development of the Republic of China on Taiwan* (Lanham, MD: University Press of America, 1993)

Mendel, Douglas, *The Politics of Formosan Nationalism* (Berkley: University of California Press, 1970)

Philips, Steven, *Between Assimilation and Independence, Taiwanese Nationalist Aspirations under Nationalist Chinese Rule, 1945–1948* (Stanford: Stanford University Press, 2003)

Roy, Denny, *Taiwan: A Political History* (Ithaca, NY: Cornell University Press, 2003)

Taylor, Jay, *The Generalissimo's Son: Chiang Ching-Kuo and the Revolutions in China and Taiwan* (Cambridge, MA: Harvard University Press, 2000)

Tucker, Nancy Bernkopk, *Taiwan, Hong Kong and the United States 1945–1992* (New York: Twayne, 1994)

Wu, Jaushieh Joseph, *Taiwan's Democratisation* (Hong Kong: Oxford University Press, 1995)

Thailand

Bullard, Monte R., *The Soldier and the Citizen: The Role of the Military in Thailand's Development* (Armonk, NY: M.E. Sharpe, 1997)

Cooper, Donald F., *Thailand: Dictatorship or Democracy?* (London: Minerva Press, 1995)

Dhiravegin, Likhit, *Democracy: The Evolution of the Thai Political System* (Singapore: Times Academic Press, 1992)

Jakson, Karl D. and Wiwat Mungkadi (eds), *United States–Thailand Relations* (Berkeley: University of California Institute of East Asian Studies, 1986)

Stowe, Judith A., *Siam Becomes Thailand* (Honolulu: University of Hawaii Press, 1991)

Wright, Joseph J. Jr, *A History of Modern Thailand* (Thailand: Asia Books, 1991)

Wyatt, David K., *Thailand: A Short History* (New Haven, CT: Yale University Press, 1982)

Vietnam

Brendon, Piers, *Ike: His Life and Times* (London: Secker & Warburg, 1987)

Buzzanco, Robert, *Masters of War: Military Dissent and Politics in the Vietnam Era* (Cambridge: Cambridge University Press, 1996)

Burchett, Wilfred, *The China, Cambodia, Vietnam Triangle* (London: Vanguard Books, 1982)

Chanoff, David and Doan Van Toai, *Vietnam: A Portrait of its People at War* (London: I.B.Tauris, 1996)

Duiker, William J., *Ho Chi Minh* (New York: Hyperion, 2000)

Haynsworth, H.C. and J. Edward Lee, *Nixon, Ford and the Abandonment of South Vietnam* (Jefferson, NC: McFarland & Co, 2002)

Hitchens, Christopher, *The Trial of Henry Kissinger* (New York: Verso Press, 2001)

Isaacson, Walter, *Henry Kissinger: A Biography* (New York: Touchstone, 1992)

Kennan, George F., *Memoirs 1950–1963* (London: Hutchinson & Co, 1973)

Kimball, Jeffrey, *Nixon's Vietnam War* (Lawrence, KS: University Press of Kansas, 2000)

Kissinger, Henry, *The White House* Years (London: Weidenfeld & Nicolson, 1979)

Lacouture, Jean, *De Gaulle: The Rebel 1890–1944* (New York: W.W. Norton and Co., 1993)

Lamb, David, *Vietnam Now* (New York: Public Affairs, 2002)

Macdonald, Peter G., *Giap: The Victor in Vietnam* (London: The Fourth Estate, 1993)

McAlister Jr., John T., *Vietnam: The Origins of Revolution* (New York: Princeton University Alfred A. Knopf Center for International Studies, 1969)

McNamara, Robert S., *In Retrospect: The Tragedy and Lessons of Vietnam* (Westminster, MD: Times Books, 1995)

Nalty, Bernard C., *The Vietnam War* (Smithmark, NY: Salamander Books, 1996)

Nixon, Richard, *No More Vietnams* (Seattle: Comet, 1986)

Pike, Douglas, *Vietcong: The Organisation and Techniques of the National Liberation Front of South Vietnam* (Boston: MIT Press, 1966)

Quinn-Judge, Sophie, *Ho Chi Minh: The Missing Years* (London: Hurst & Co., 2003)

Reischauer, Edwin O., *Beyond Vietnam: The United States and Asia* (New York: Alfred A. Knopf, 1968)

SarDesai, D.R., *Vietnam: Past and Present* (Boulder, CO: Westview Press, 4th edition, 2005)

Shaplen, Robert, *The Lost Revolution: Vietnam 1945–1965* (London: Andre Deutsch, 1966)

Sheehan, Neil, *A Bright Shining Lie: John Paul Vann and America in Vietnam* (London: Jonathan Cape, 1989)

Trager, Frank N., *Why Vietnam?* (New York: Praeger, 1966)

Windrow, Martin, *The Last Valley: Dien Bien Phu and the French Defeat in Vietnam* (London: Weidenfeld & Nicolson, 2004)

Wintle, Justin, *Romancing Vietnam: Inside the Boat Country* (London: Viking, 1991)

Woodruff, Mark W., *Unheralded Victory: Who Won the Vietnam War?* (London: Harper Collins, 1999)

Zinn, Howard, *Vietnam: The Logic of Withdrawal* (Boston: Beacon Press, 1989)

Index